LONDON
POCKET STREET ATLAS

T0318129

CONTENTS

Reference Page	1
Key to Map Pages	2-3
Large Scale Map Pages	4-27
Map Pages	28-125
Underground Railway Map	126-127
Congestion Charging Zone Map	128-129
Congestion Charging Information	130
Index to Streets, etc	131-350

EDITION 12   2023

Published by Geographers' A-Z Map Company Limited
An imprint of HarperCollins Publishers
Westerhill Road
Bishopbriggs
Glasgow
G64 2QT

www.az.co.uk
a-z.maps@harpercollins.co.uk

HarperCollinsPublishers
Macken House, 39/40 Mayor Street Upper, Dublin 1, D01 C9W8, Ireland

12th edition 2023

© Collins Bartholomew Ltd 2023

This product uses map data licenced from Ordnance Survey
© Crown copyright and database rights 2022 OS AC0000808974

AZ, A-Z and AtoZ are registered trademarks of Geographers' A-Z Map
Company Limited

A catalogue record for this book is available from the British Library.

ISBN 978-0-00-858177-0

10 9 8 7 6 5 4

Printed in India

REFERENCE

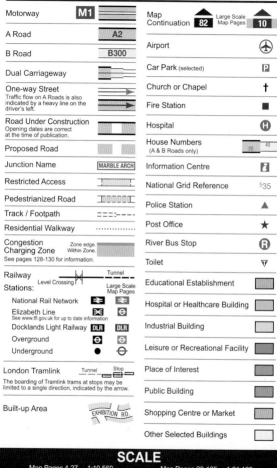

Motorway	M1
A Road	A2
B Road	B300
Dual Carriageway	
One-way Street Traffic flow on A Roads is also indicated by a heavy line on the driver's left.	
Road Under Construction Opening dates are correct at the time of publication.	
Proposed Road	
Junction Name	MARBLE ARCH
Restricted Access	
Pedestrianized Road	
Track / Footpath	
Residential Walkway	
Congestion Charging Zone See pages 128-130 for information.	Zone edge. Within Zone.

Railway   Level Crossing   Tunnel

Stations: Large Scale Map Pages

National Rail Network		
Elizabeth Line See www.tfl.gov.uk for up to date information		
Docklands Light Railway	DLR	DLR
Overground		
Underground		

London Tramlink   Tunnel   Stop

The boarding of Tramlink trams at stops may be limited to a single direction, indicated by the arrow.

Built-up Area   EXHIBITION RD.

Map Continuation	82 Large Scale Map Pages 10
Airport	✈
Car Park (selected)	P
Church or Chapel	†
Fire Station	■
Hospital	H
House Numbers (A & B Roads only)	20 40
Information Centre	i
National Grid Reference	535
Police Station	▲
Post Office	★
River Bus Stop	R
Toilet	▽
Educational Establishment	
Hospital or Healthcare Building	
Industrial Building	
Leisure or Recreational Facility	
Place of Interest	
Public Building	
Shopping Centre or Market	
Other Selected Buildings	

SCALE

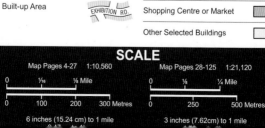

Map Pages 4-27   1:10,560

0	1/16	1/8 Mile
0	100 200	300 Metres

6 inches (15.24 cm) to 1 mile

Map Pages 28-125   1:21,120

0	1/8	1/4 Mile
0	250	500 Metres

3 inches (7.62cm) to 1 mile

KEY TO MAP PAGES

2

Muswell Hill
A504
Kingsbury
A41
Hendon
Hornsey
A1
A4140
Golders Green
Highgate

| 28 | 29 | 30 | 31 | 32 | 33 | 34 |

Neasden
Cricklewood
Hampstead

| 42 | 43 | 44 | 45 | 46 | 47 | 48 |

Willesden
Kilburn
Camden Town

Maida Vale
Marylebone
Finsbury

| 56 | 57 | 58 | 59 | 60 | 61 | 62 |

A406
A40
Notting Hill
Paddington
LARGE S

Acton
Kensington
Mayfair
SECTION

| 70 | 71 | 72 | 73 | 74 | 75 | 76 |

Shepherd's Bush
Hammersmith
Westminster

Kew
A4
Chiswick
Chelsea

| 84 | 85 | 86 | 87 | 88 | 89 | 90 |

Barnes
Fulham
Battersea
Stockwell

A205
Clapham

| 98 | 99 | 100 | 101 | 102 | 103 | 104 |

Putney
Wandsworth

A205
Roehampton

| 112 | 113 | 114 | 115 | 116 | 117 | 118 |

Wimbledon
Streatham

A308
A3
A24
A216
A23

Mitcham

SCALE

0   1   2 Miles

0   1   2   3 Kilometres

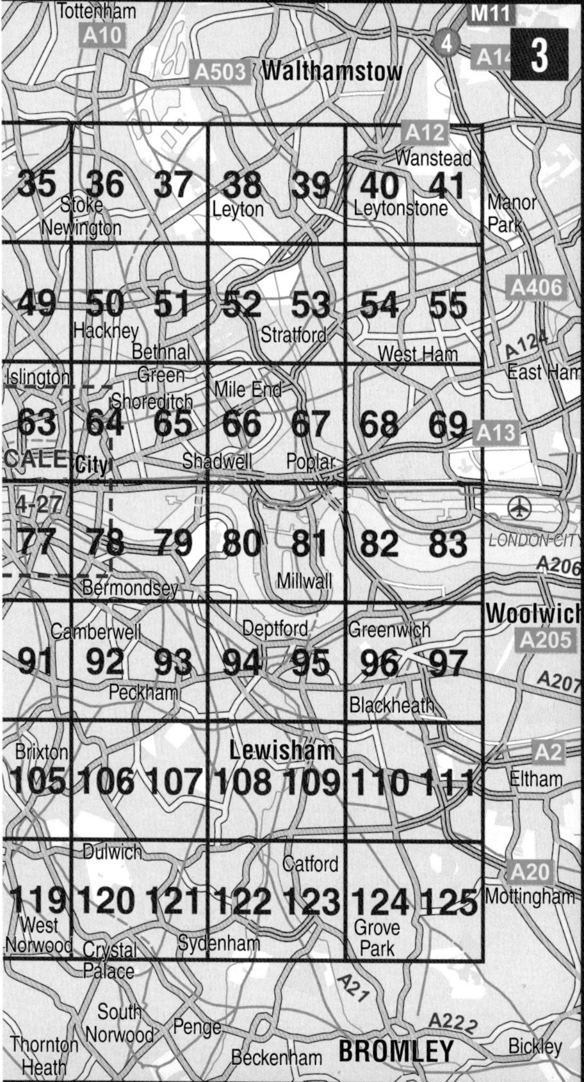

Tottenham
A10
A503 **Walthamstow**

A12
Wanstead
35 36 37 38 39 40 41
Stoke
Newington
Leyton
Leytonstone
Manor
Park

A406
49 50 51 52 53 54 55
Hackney
Bethnal
Green
Stratford
West Ham
A124
East Ham
Islington
Shoreditch
Mile End
63 64 65 66 67 68 69
CALE
City
Shadwell
Poplar
A13

4-27
77 78 79 80 81 82 83
Bermondsey
Millwall
LONDON CITY
A206

Camberwell
Deptford
Greenwich
Woolwich
91 92 93 94 95 96 97
Peckham
Blackheath
A205
A207

Brixton
Lewisham
105 106 107 108 109 110 111
Eltham
A2

Dulwich
Catford
119 120 121 122 123 124 125 Mottingham
West
Norwood
Crystal
Palace
Sydenham
Grove
Park
A20

South
Thornton Norwood
Heath
Penge
Beckenham
A21
A222
BROMLEY
Bickley

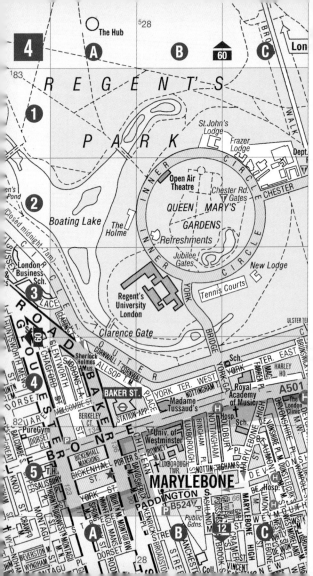

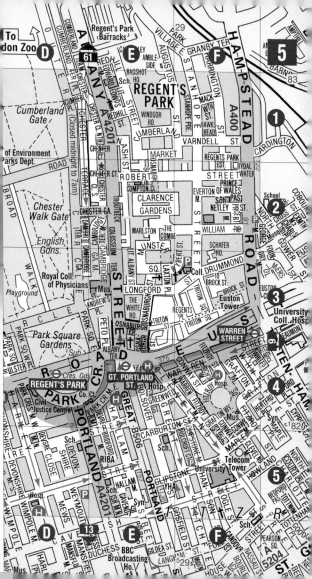

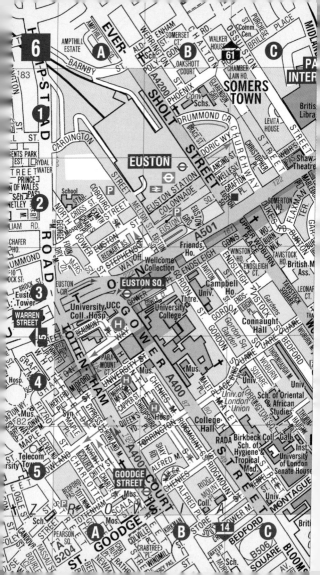

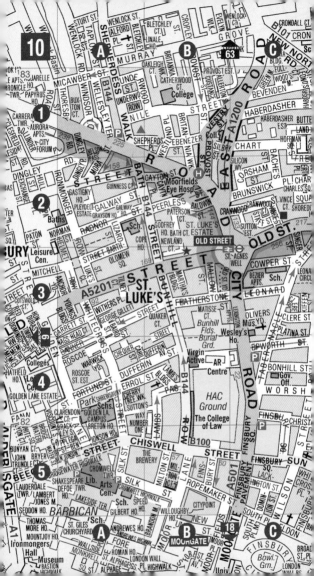

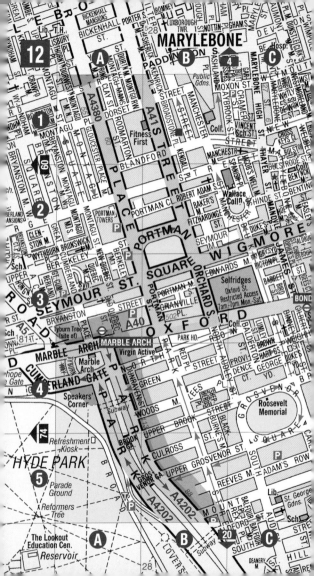

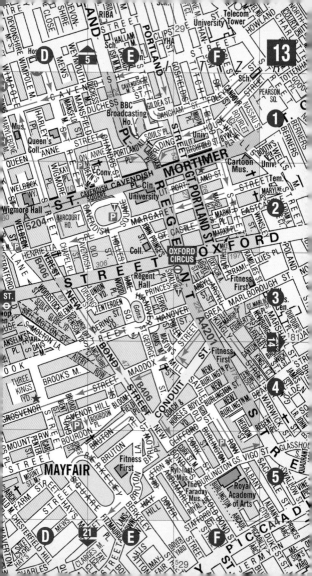

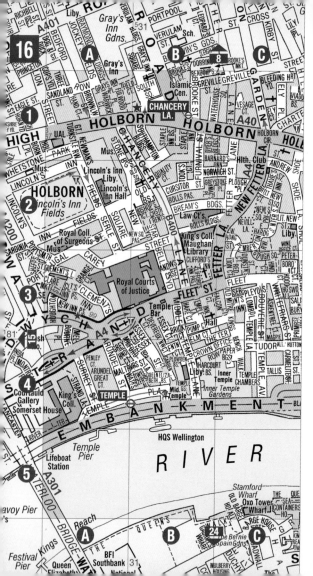

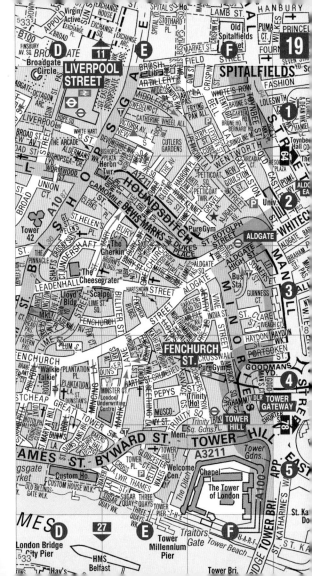

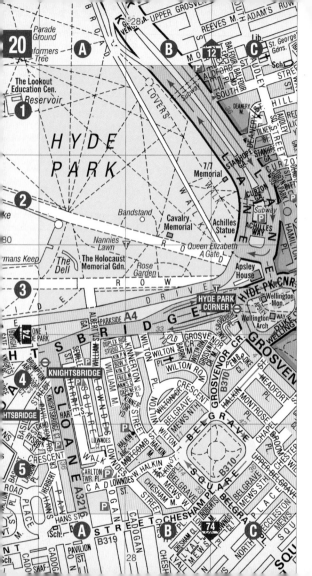

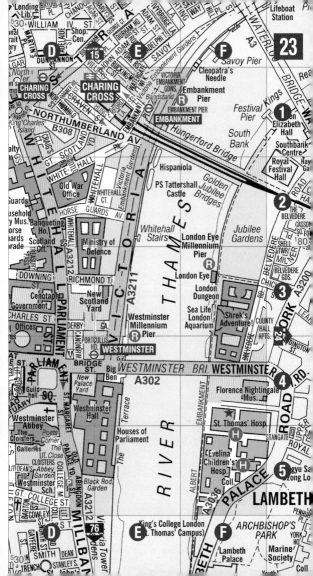

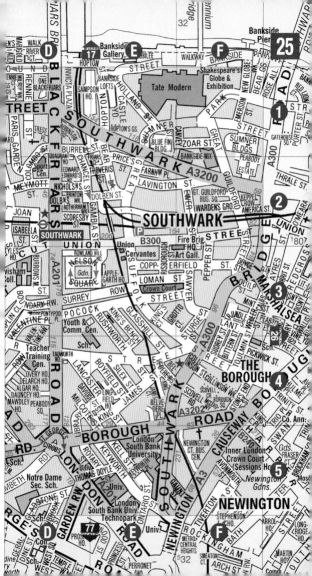

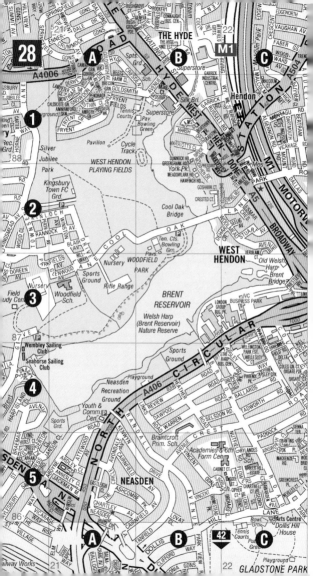

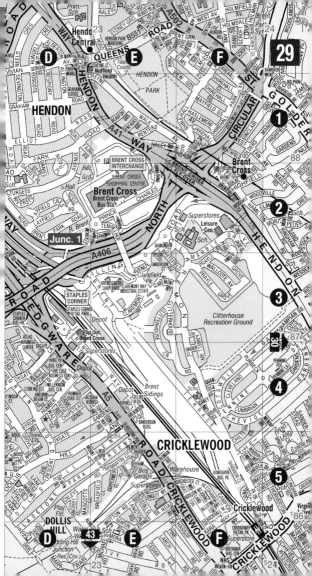

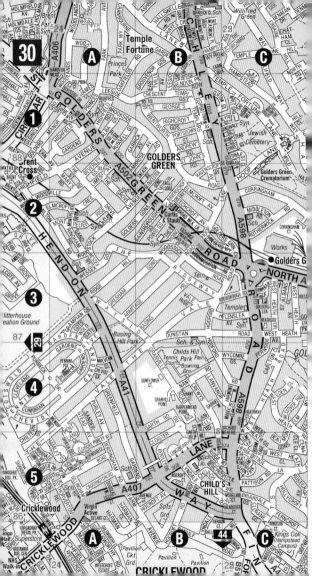

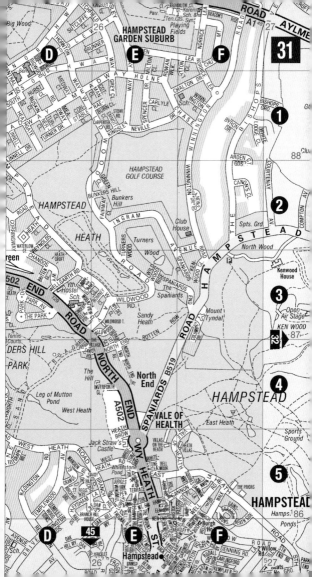

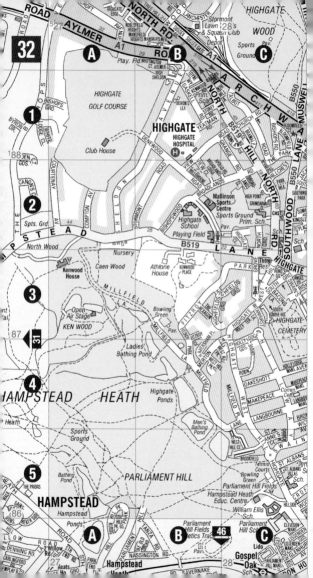

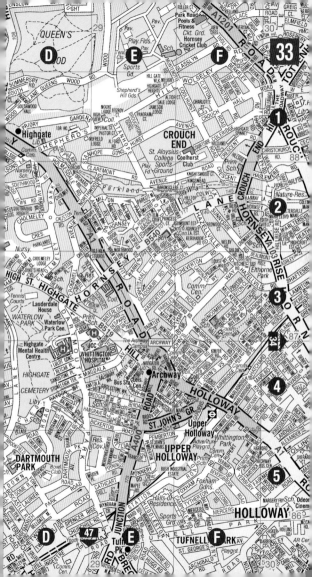

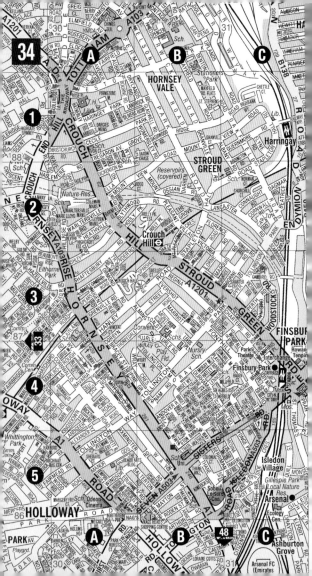

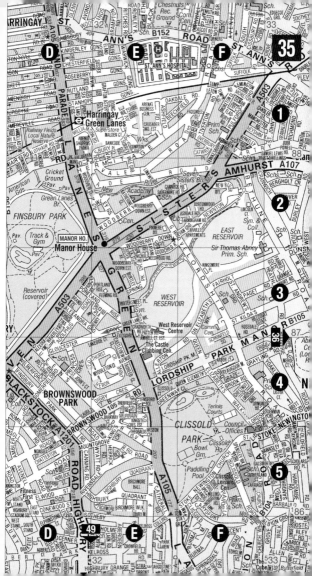

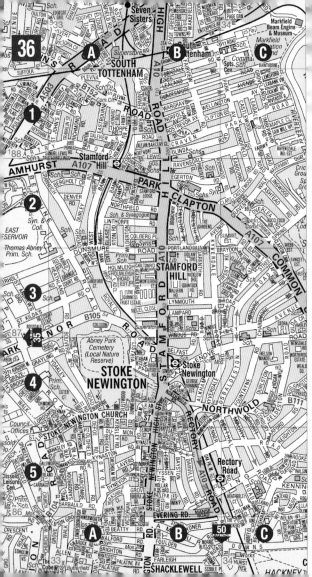

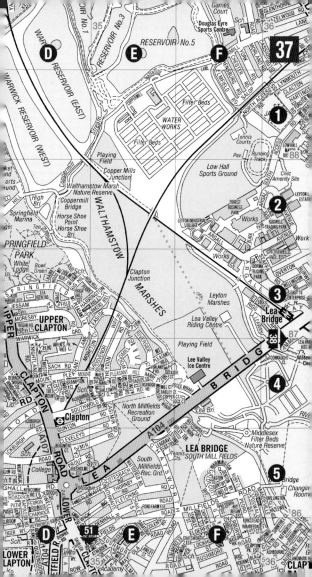

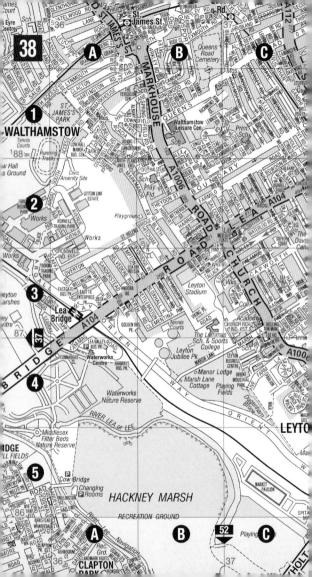

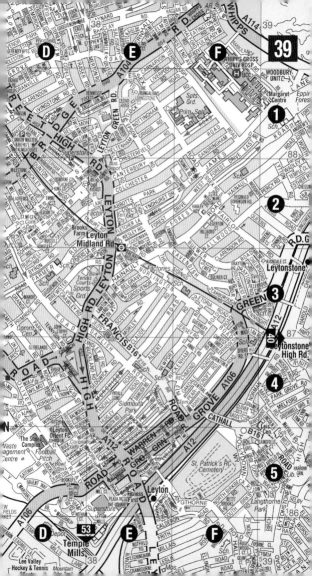

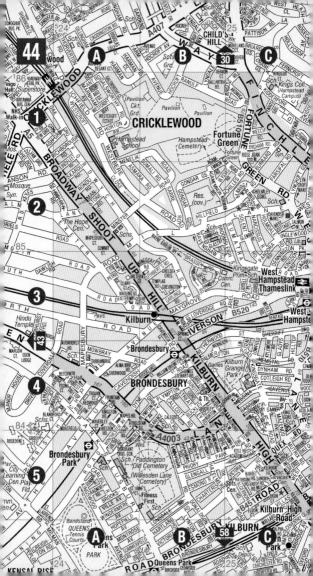

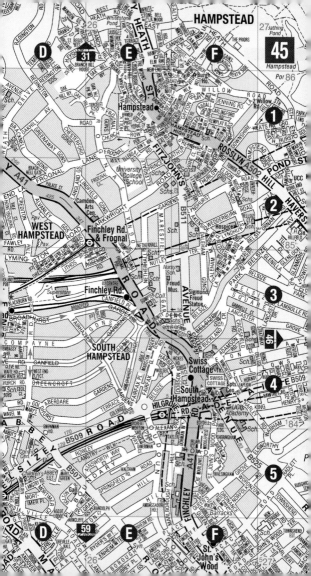

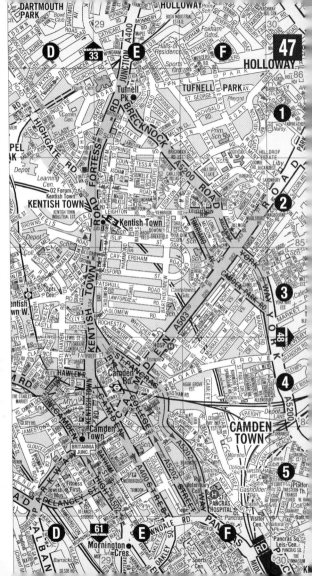

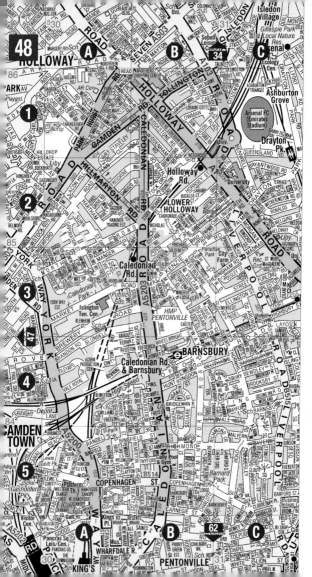

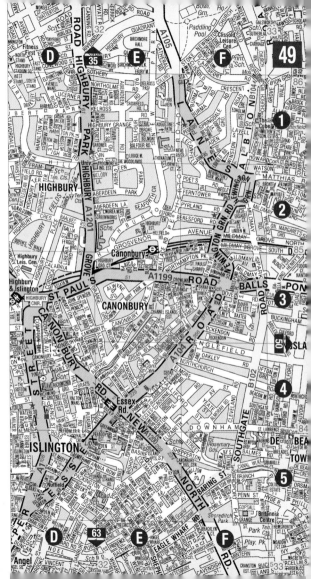

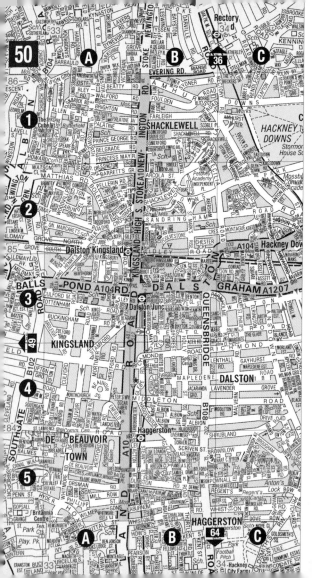

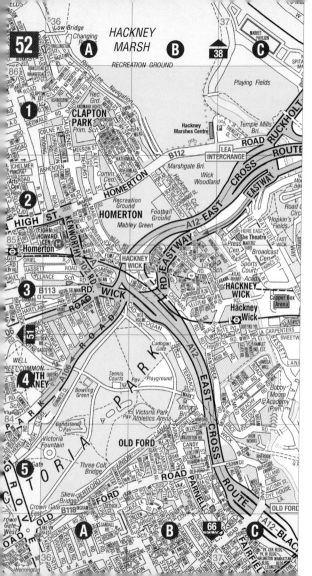

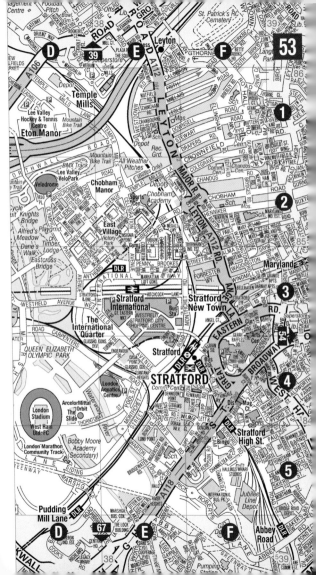

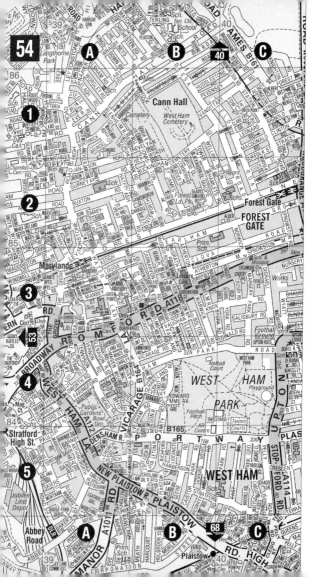

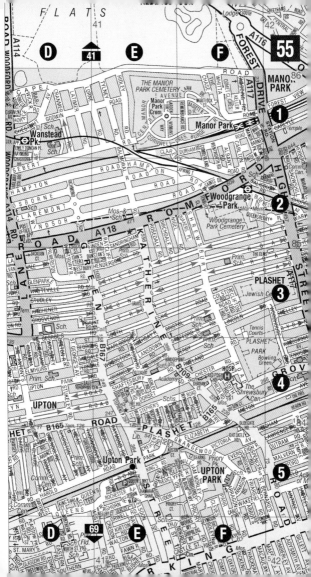

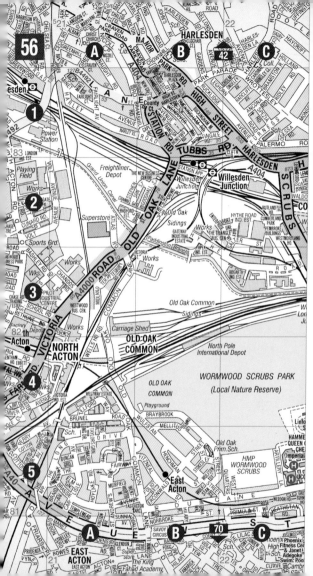

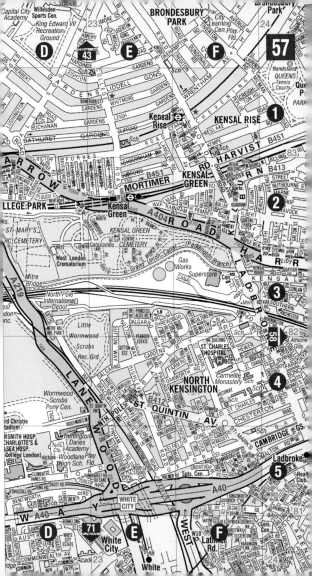

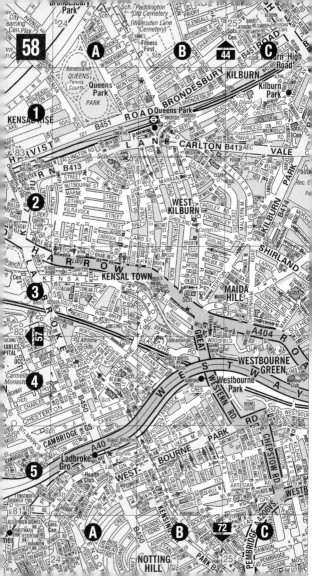

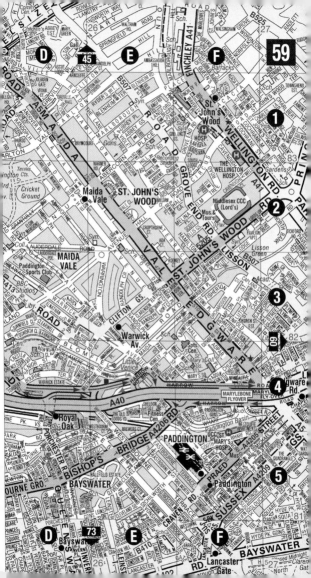

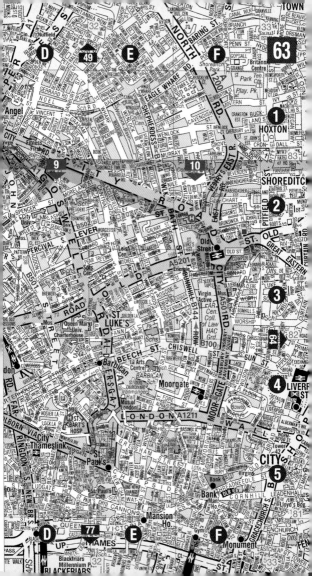

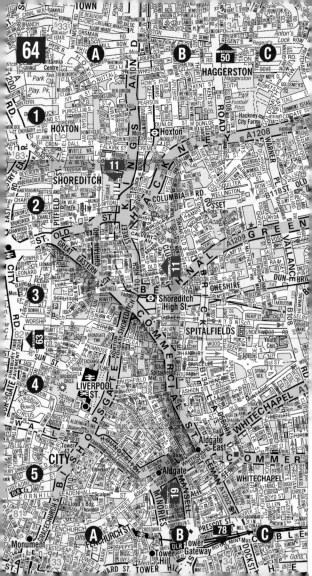

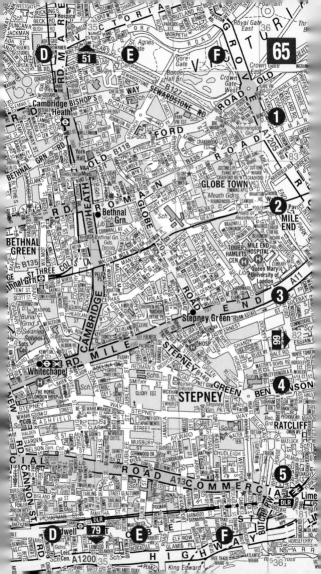

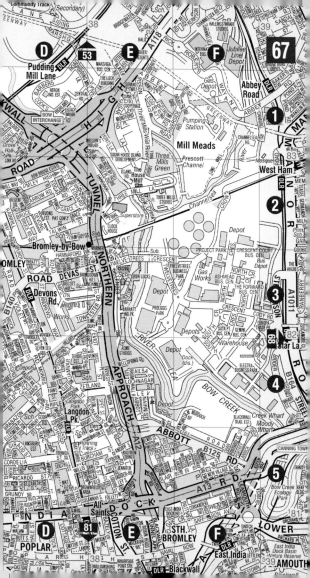

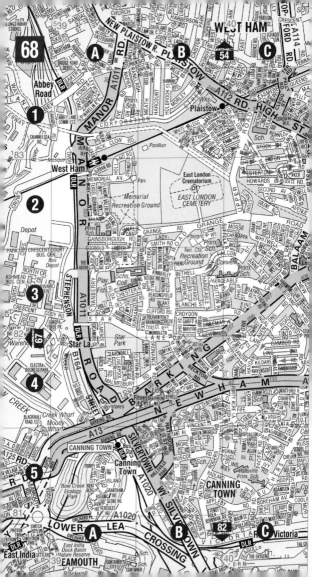

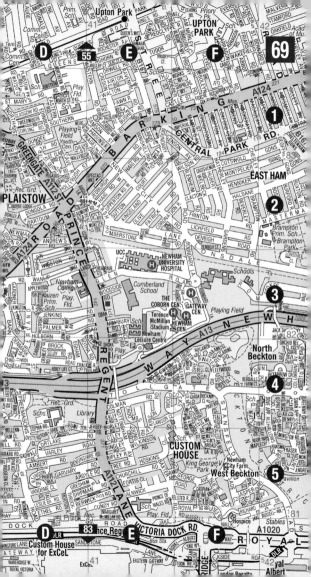

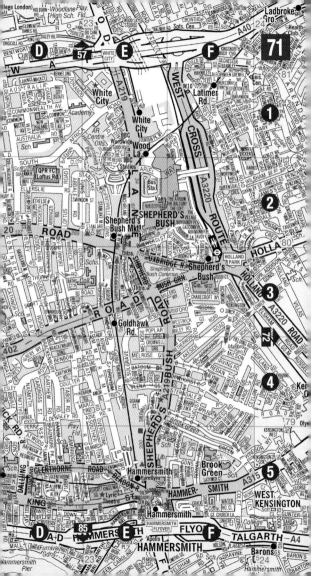

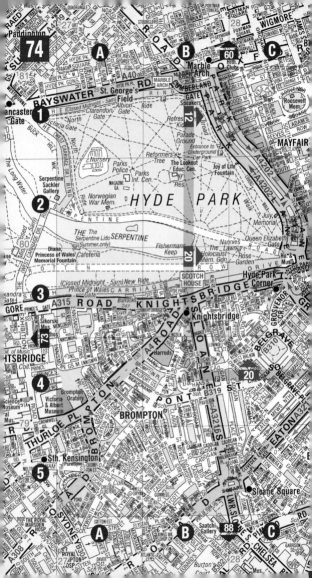

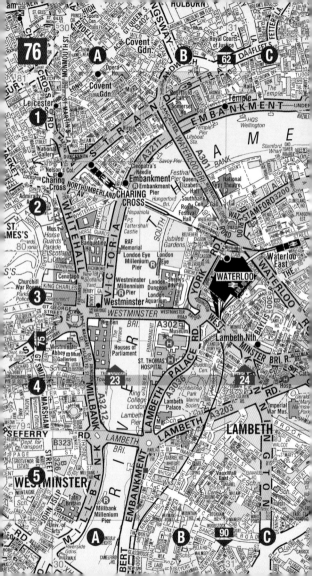

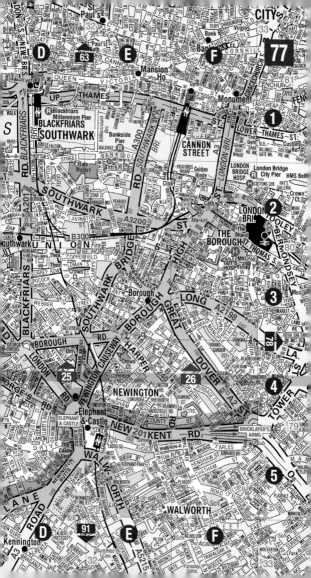

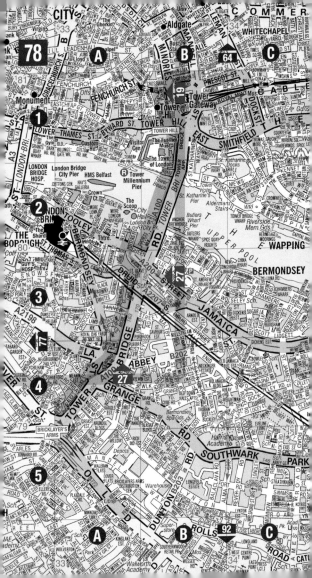

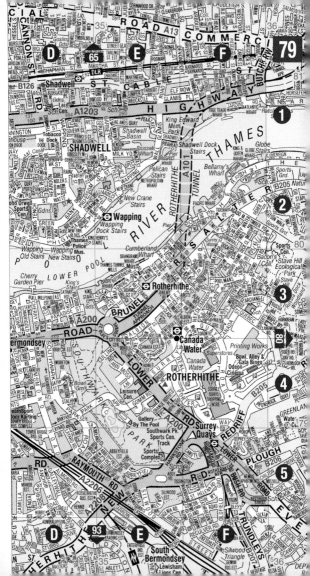

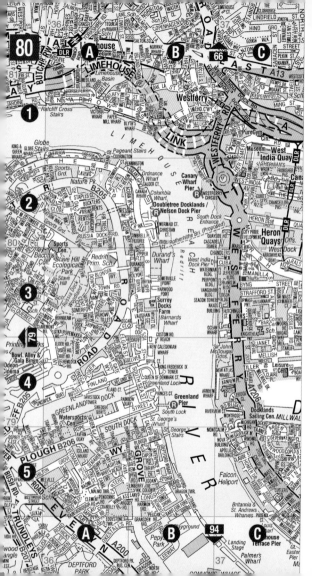

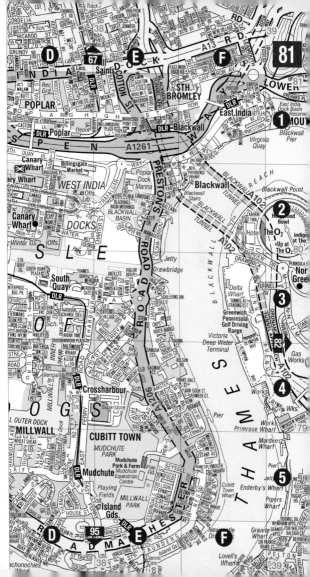

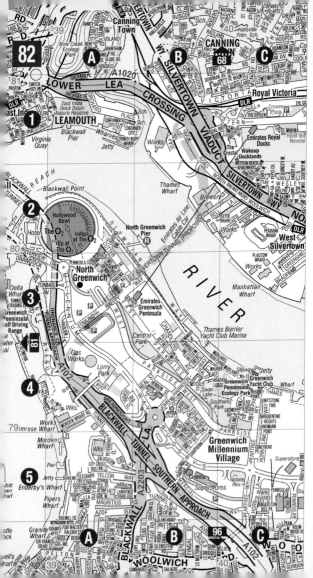

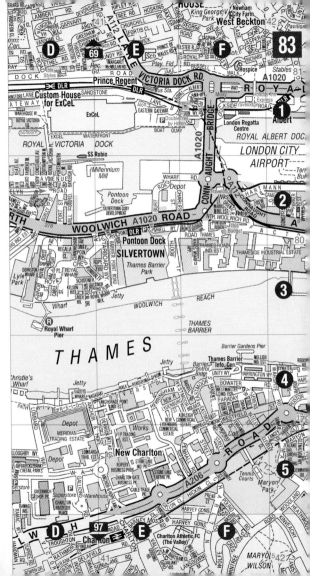

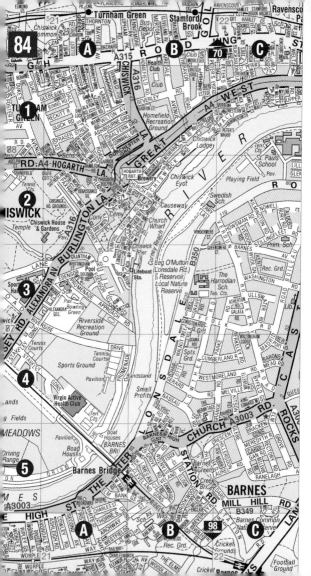

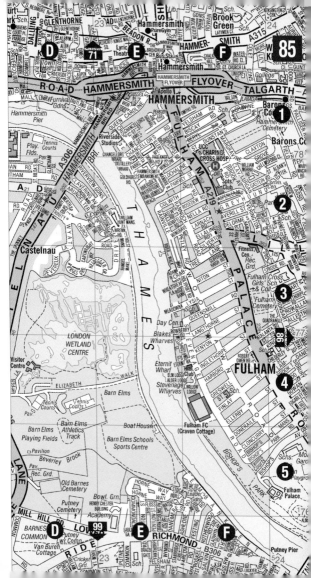

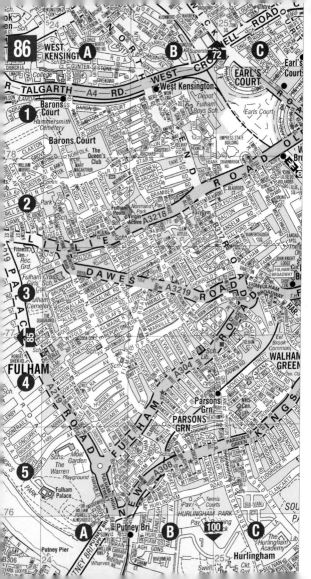

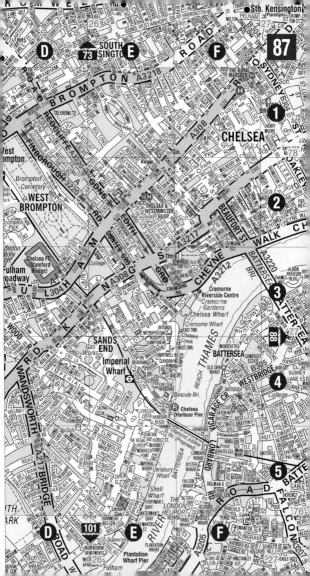

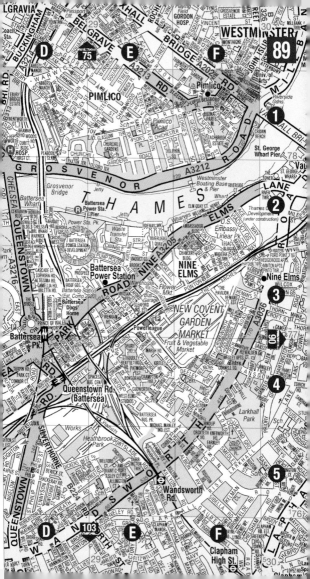

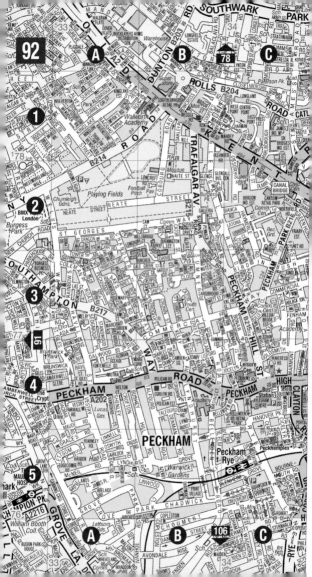

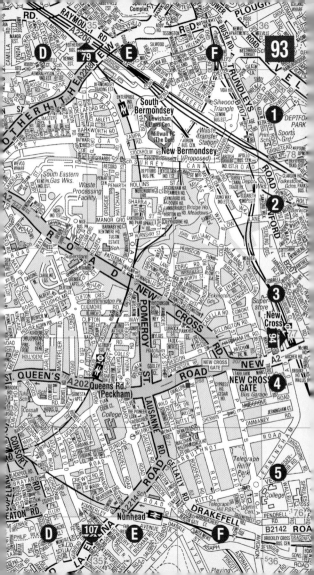

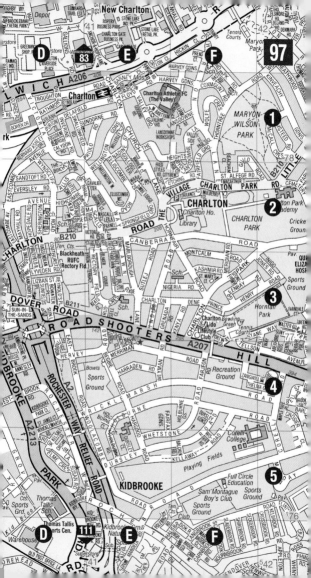

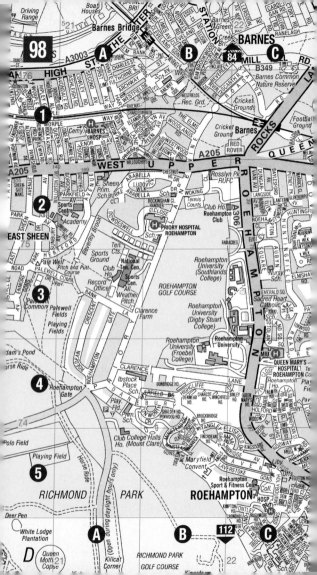

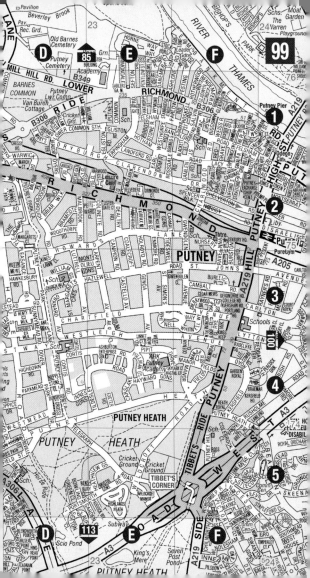

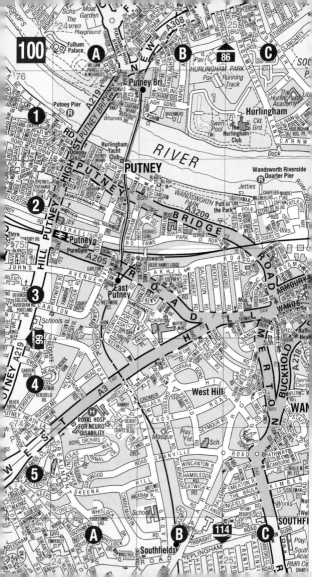

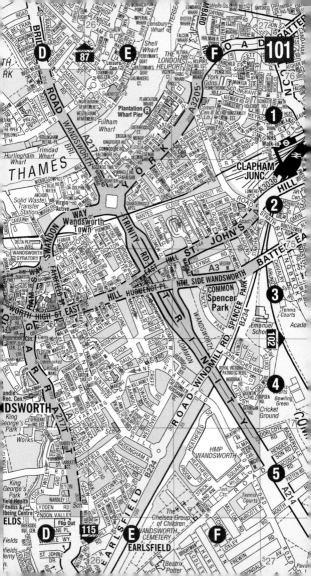

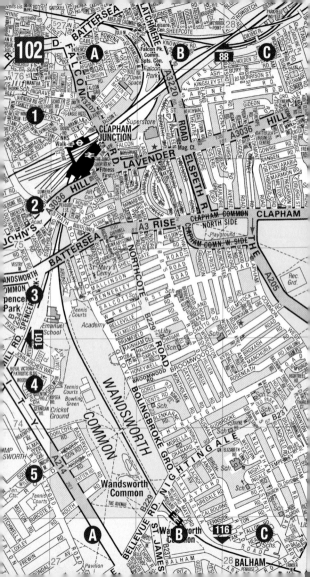

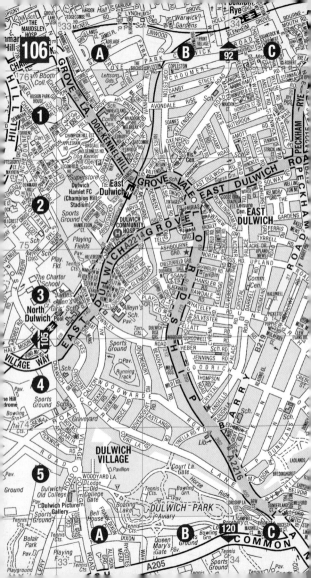

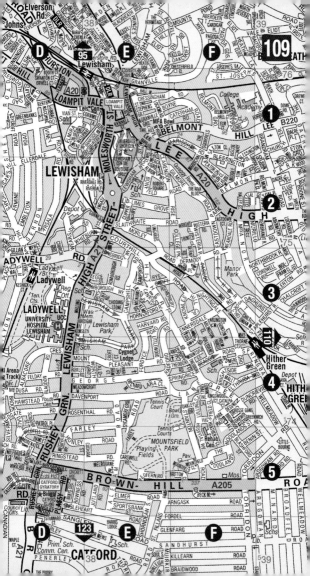

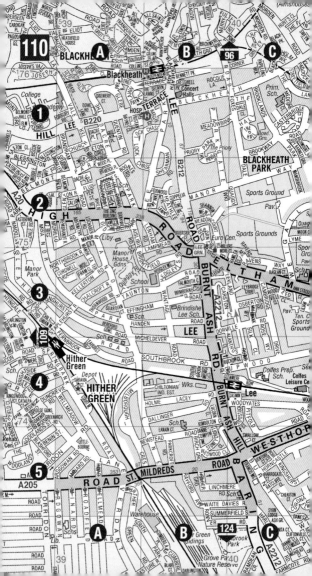

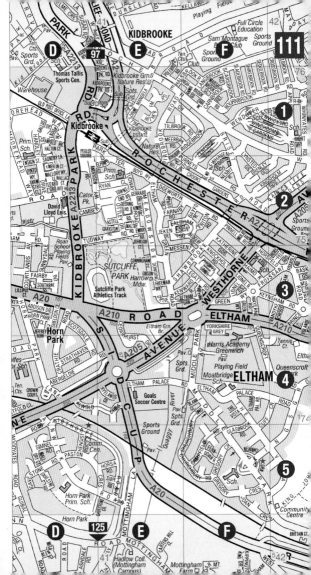

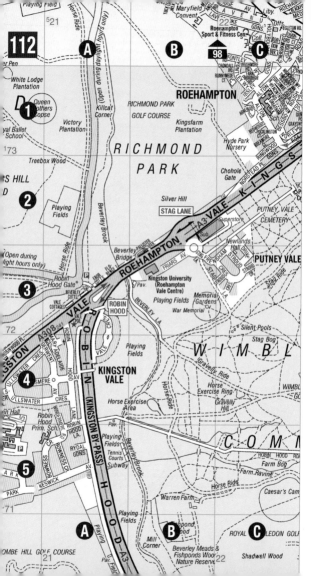

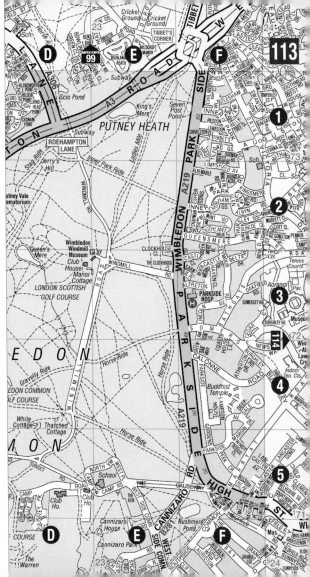

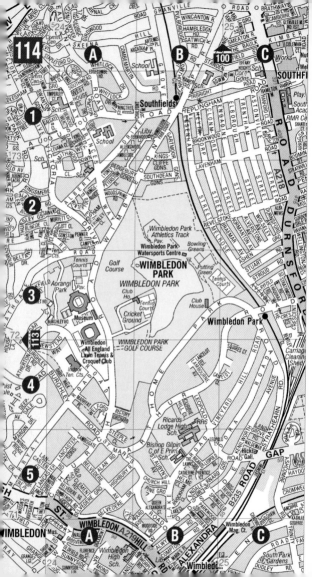

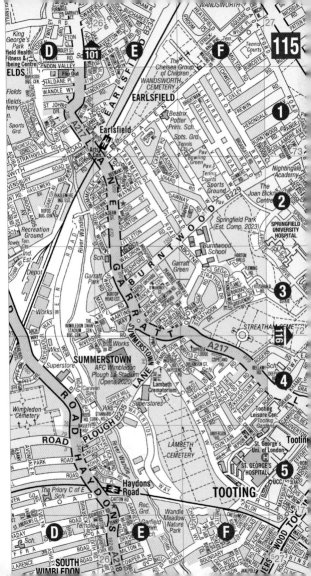

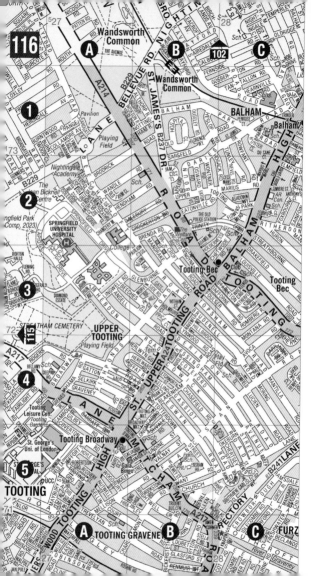

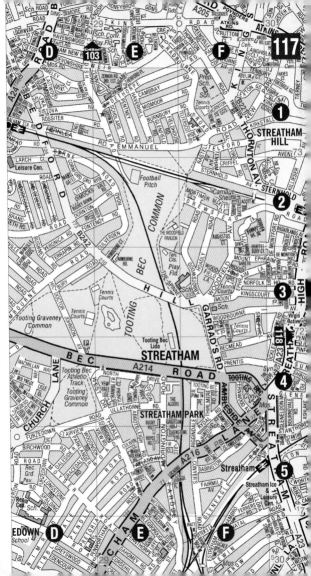

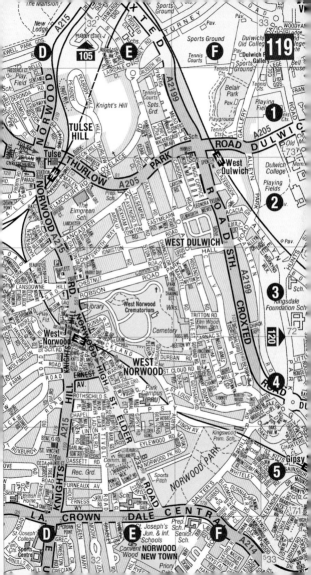

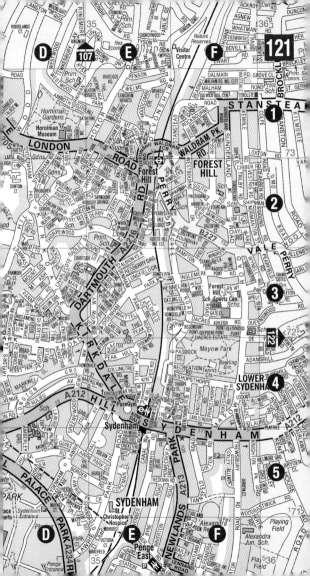

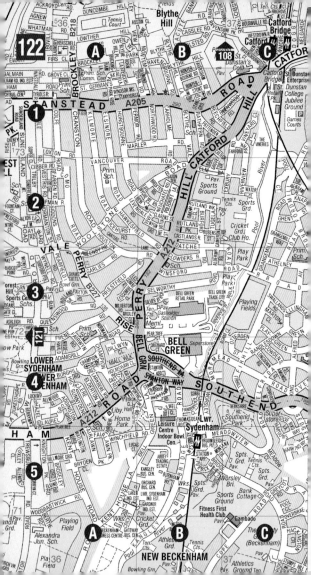

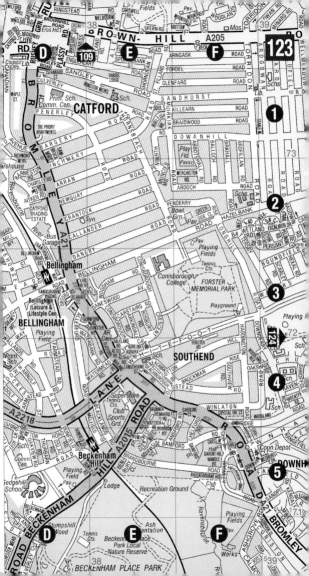

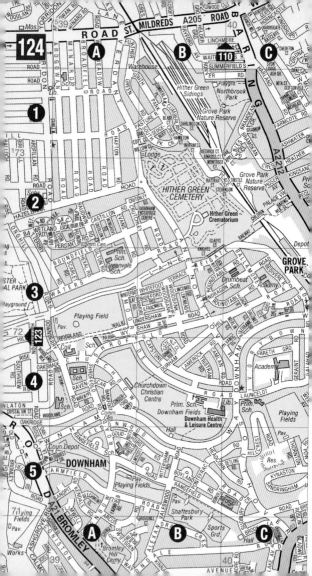

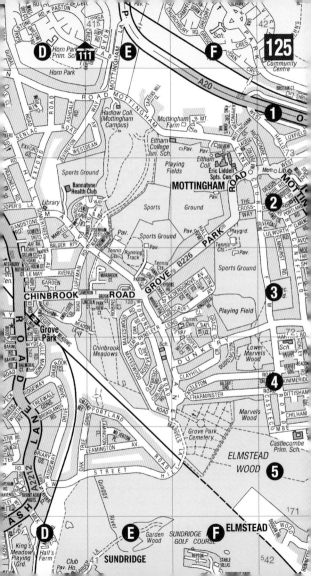

Correct at time of going to print. For the latest information see

MAYOR OF LONDON

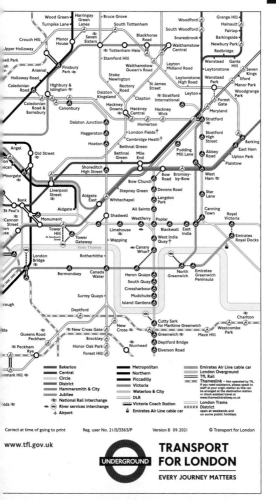

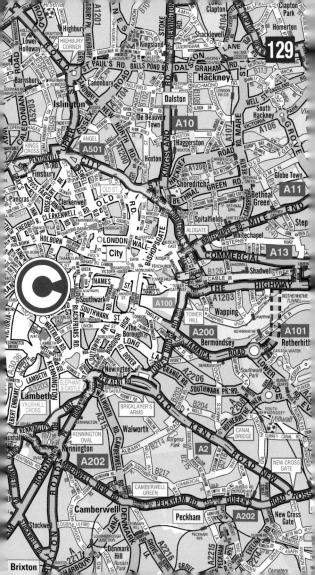

Congestion Charging Zone

- The daily charge applies Monday to Friday, 7.00am to 6.00pm, 12.00pm to 6.00pm Saturday and Sunday, and bank holidays. No charge between Christmas Day and New Year's Day bank holiday (inclusive)

- Payment of the daily charge allows you to drive in, around, leave and re-enter the charging zone as many times as required on the same day.

- Payment can be made in advance, or on the day of travel, or by midnight of the third day after travel. Payment after the day of travel will incur an increased cost.

- You can pay using Auto Pay (registration required), online, or using the official TfL App.

- Some vehicle types and classes are exempt, and some classes of road users can apply for a discount scheme.

- Penalty charge for non-payment of the daily charge by midnight on the third day after the day of travel.

This information is correct at the time of publication.

Visit www.tfl.gov.uk/modes/driving for more information on London's driving zones.

INDEX

Including Streets, Places & Areas, Industrial Estates,
Selected Flats & Walkways, Junction Names
and Selected Places of Interest.

HOW TO USE THIS INDEX

1. Each street name is followed by its Postcode District and then by its map reference;
   e.g. **Abbeville Rd.** SW4.....4E **103** is in the SW4 Postcode District and is to be found in square
   4E on page **103**. The page number is shown in bold type.

2. A strict alphabetical order is followed in which Av., Rd., etc. (though abbreviated) are read in full
   and as part of the street name; e.g. **Alder M.** appears after **Aldermans Wlk.** but before **Aldermoor Rd.**

3. Features that cannot be shown on the mapping appear in the index with the thoroughfare to which
   they are connected shown in brackets; e.g. **Aftab Ter.** E1.....3D **65** (off Tent St.)

4. Addresses that are in more than one part are referred to as not continuous.

5. Places and areas are shown in the index in BLUE TYPE and the map reference is to the actual
   map square in which the town centre or area is located, not to the place name shown on the map;
   e.g. BARNES.....5B **84**

6. An example of a selected place of interest is **Adelphi Theatre**.....5E **15**

7. Junction names are shown in the index in **BOLD CAPITAL TYPE**; e.g. **ANGEL**.....1C **62**

8. Map references for entries that appear on large scale pages **4–27** are shown first, with small scale
   map references shown in brackets; e.g. **Abbey St.** SE1.....5E **27** (4A **78**)

GENERAL ABBREVIATIONS

All. : Alley
Apts. : Apartments
App. : Approach
Arc. : Arcade
Av. : Avenue
Bk. : Back
Blvd. : Boulevard
Bri. : Bridge
B'way. : Broadway
Bldg. : Building
Bldgs. : Buildings
Bus. : Business
C'way. : Causeway
Cen. : Centre
Chu. : Church
Circ. : Circle
Cir. : Circus
Cl. : Close
Coll. : College
Comn. : Common
Cnr. : Corner
Cott. : Cottage
Cotts. : Cottages
Ct. : Court
Ctyd. : Courtyard
Cres. : Crescent
Cft. : Croft
Dpt. : Depot
Dr. : Drive
E. : East

Emb. : Embankment
Ent. : Enterprise
Est. : Estate
Fld. : Field
Flds. : Fields
Gdn. : Garden
Gdns. : Gardens
Gth. : Garth
Ga. : Gate
Gt. : Great
Grn. : Green
Gro. : Grove
Hgts. : Heights
Ho. : House
Ho's. : Houses
Ind. : Industrial
Info. : Information
Junc. : Junction
La. : Lane
Lit. : Little
Lwr. : Lower
Mnr. : Manor
Mans. : Mansions
Mkt. : Market
Mdw. : Meadow
Mdws. : Meadows
M. : Mews
Mt. : Mount
Mus. : Museum
Nth. : North

No. : Number
Pal. : Palace
Pde. : Parade
Pk. : Park
Pas. : Passage
Pav. : Pavilion
Pl. : Place
Pct. : Precinct
Prom. : Promenade
Quad. : Quadrant
Ri. : Rise
Rd. : Road
Rdbt. : Roundabout
Shop. : Shopping
Sth. : South
Sq. : Square
Sta. : Station
St. : Street
Ter. : Terrace
Twr. : Tower
Trad. : Trading
Up. : Upper
Va. : Vale
Vw. : View
Vs. : Villas
Vis. : Visitors
Wlk. : Walk
W. : West
Yd. : Yard

2 Temple Place ...... **4B 16 (1C 76)**
.... *(off Temple Pl.)*
2 Willow Rd. 1A 46
7 July Memorial 2C 20 (2C 74)
10 Brock St. NW1...... 3F 5 (3E 61)
.... *(off Triton Sq.)*
18 Stafford Terrace 4C 72
.... *(off Stafford Ter.)*
60 St Martins La. WC2...............
.... 4D 15 (1A 76)
.... *(off St Martin's La.)*
198 Contemporary Arts
& Learning........................ 4D 105
.... *(off Railton Rd.)*
201 Bishopsgate
EC2....................... 5E 11 (4A 64)
.... *(off Bishopsgate)*

A

Abady Ho. SW1...........................5F 75
.... *(off Page St.)*
Abberley M. SW4.............. 1D 103
Abbess Cl. SW2................ 1D 119
Abbeville M. SW4................ 2F 103
Abbeville Rd. SW4.............. 4E 103
Abbey Cl. E5....................... 1C 50
Abbey Cl. SW8...................... 4F 89
Abbey Ct. NW8...................... 1E 59
.... *(off Abbey Rd.)*
Abbey Ct. SE17..................... 1E 91
.... *(off Macleod St.)*
Abbey Ct. SE6..................... 4C 108
Abbey Dr. SW17.................. 5C 116
Abbey Est. NW8................... 5D 45
Abbeyfield Est. SE16...........5E 79
Abbeyfield Rd. SE16...........5E 79
.... *(not continuous)*
Abbey Gdns. NW8.................1E 59
Abbey Gdns. SE16............... 5C 78
Abbey Gdns. SW1...5D 23 (4A 76)
.... *(off Great College St.)*
Abbey Gdns. W6.................. 2A 86
Abbey Ho. E15..................... 1A 68
.... *(off Baker's Row)*
Abbey Ho. NW8...................... 1E 59
Abbey Ho. .... *(off Garden Rd.)*
Abbey La. E15....................... 1E 67
Abbey La. Commercial Est.
E15... 1A 68
Abbey Life Ct. E16.............. 4D 69
Abbey Lodge NW8............... 2A 60
.... *(off Park Rd.)*
Abbey Mansion M. SE24....3D 105
Abbey M. E17..................... 1C 38
Abbey Orchard St.
SW1........................ 5B 22 (4F 75)
Abbey Orchard St. Est.
SW1........................ 5C 22 (4F 75)
.... *(not continuous)*
Abbey Rd. E15..................... 1F 67
Abbey Rd. NW6.................. 4D 45
Abbey Rd. NW8.................... 5E 45
Abbey Rd. Apts. NW8...........1E 59
.... *(off Abbey Rd.)*
Abbey Road Station (DLR)....1A 68
Abbey St. E13.................... 3D 68
Abbey St. SE1........ 5E 27 (4A 78)
Abbey St. SE16................... 3A 78
Abbey Trad. Est. SE26...... 5B 122
Abbot Ct. SW8.................... 3A 90
.... *(off Hartington Rd.)*

Abbot Ho. E14.......................1D 81
.... *(off Smythe St.)*
Abbotsbury NW1.....................4F 47
.... *(off Camley St.)*
Abbotsbury Cl. E15...............1E 67
Abbotsbury Cl. W14............. 3A 72
Abbotsbury Ho. W14............. 3A 72
Abbotsbury M. SE15...........1E 107
Abbotsbury Rd. W14............ 3A 72
Abbots Ct. W8...................... 3D 73
.... *(off Thackeray St.)*
Abbotshade Rd. SE16..........2F 79
Abbotshall Rd. SE6............1F 123
Abbot's Ho. W14.................... 4B 72
.... *(off St Mary Abbot's Ter.)*
Abbots La. SE1....... 2E 27 (2A 78)
Abbotsleigh Rd. SW16.......4E 117
Abbots Mnr. SW1................. 5D 75
.... *(not continuous)*
Abbots Pk. SW2.................. 1C 118
Abbot's Pl. NW6.................. 5D 45
Abbot's Rd. E6....................... 5F 55
Abbots Ter. N8........................ 1A 34
Abbotstone Rd. SW15.......... 1E 99
Abbot St. E8....................... 3B 50
Abbots Wlk. W8.................... 4D 73
Abbotswell Rd. SE4............. 3B 108
Abbotswood Rd. SE22.......2A 106
Abbotswood Rd. SW16.........3F 117
Abbott Rd. E14...................... 4E 67
.... *(not continuous)*
Abbotts Cl. N1...................... 3E 49
Abbotts Ho. SW1...................1F 89
.... *(off Aylesford St.)*
Abbotts Pk. Rd. E10............. 2E 39
Abbott's Wharf E14............5C 66
.... *(off Stainsby Pl.)*

Abbotts Wharf Moorings
E14...5C 66
.... *(off Stainsby Rd.)*
Abchurch La. EC4...... 4C 18 (1F 77)
Abchurch Yd. EC4...... 4B 18 (1F 77)
Abdale Rd. W12..................... 2D 71
Abel Ho. SE11....................... 2C 90
.... *(off Kennington Rd.)*
Aberavon Rd. E3.................. 2A 66
Abercorn Cl. NW8.................. 2E 59
Abercorn Cotts. NW8........... 2E 59
.... *(off Abercorn Pl.)*
Abercorn Mans. NW8...........1E 59
.... *(off Abercorn Pl.)*
Abercorn Pl. NW8.................. 2E 59
Abercorn Wlk. NW8.............. 2E 59
Abercorn Way SE1............... 1C 92
Abercrombie Rd. E20...........2D 53
Abercrombie St. SW11........ 5A 88
Aberdale Ct. SE16................. 3F 79
.... *(off Garter Way)*
Aberdare Gdns. NW6........... 4D 45
Aberdeen Ct. W9................... 3F 59
.... *(off Maida Vale)*
Aberdeen La. N5................... 2E 49
Aberdeen Mans.
WC1........................... 3D 7 (3A 62)
.... *(off Kenton St.)*
Aberdeen Pk. N5.................. 2E 49
Aberdeen Pl. NW8................ 3F 59
Aberdeen Rd. N5.................. 1E 49
Aberdeen Rd. NW10............. 2B 42
Aberdeen Sq. E14................ 2B 80
Aberdeen Ter. SE3............... 5F 95
Aberdeen Wharf E1..............2D 79
.... *(off Wapping High St.)*
Aberdour St. SE1.................. 5A 78

Aberfeldy Ho. SE5................ 3D 91
.... *(not continuous)*
Aberfeldy St. E14.................... 4E 67
.... *(not continuous)*
Aberford Gdns. SE18............4F 97
Abergeldie Rd. SE12........... 4D 111
Abernethy Ho. EC1... 1F 17 (4E 63)
.... *(off Bartholomew Cl.)*
Abernethy Rd. SE13............. 2A 110
Abersham Rd. E8.................. 2B 50
Abid M. SE15......................... 5C 92
Ability Pl. E14...................... 3D 81
Ability Plaza E8................... 4B 50
.... *(off Kensington Village)*
Ability Towers EC1... 1F 9 (2E 63)
.... *(off Macclesfield St.)*
Abingdon W14......................... 5B 72
.... *(off Kensington Village)*
Abingdon Cl. NW1.................... 3F 47
Abingdon Cl. SE1................... 5B 78
.... *(off Bushwood Dr.)*
Abingdon Ct. W8.................... 4C 72
.... *(off Abingdon Vs.)*
Abingdon Gdns. W8................ 4C 72
Abingdon Ho. E2....... 3F 11 (3B 64)
.... *(off Boundary St.)*
Abingdon Lodge W8.............. 4C 72
Abingdon Mans. W8.............. 4C 72
.... *(off Pater St.)*
Abingdon Rd. W8................... 4C 72
Abingdon St. SW1...5D 23 (4A 76)
Abingdon Vs. W8.................... 4C 72
Abinger Gro. SE8.................. 2B 94
Abinger Ho. SE1......... 4B 26 (3F 77)
.... *(off Gt. Dover St.)*
Abinger M. W9........................ 3D 58
Abinger Rd. W4.................... 4A 70
Ablett St. SE16..................... 1E 93
Abney Gdns. N16.................. 4B 36
Abney Pk. Cemetery Local
Nature Reserve 4A 36
Abney Pk. Ter. N16............... 4B 36
.... *(off Cazenove Rd.)*
Aborfield NW5........................2E 47
Aboyne Rd. NW10................. 5A 28
Aboyne Rd. SW17..................3F 115
Abyssinia Cl. SW11............. 2A 102
Abyssinia Ct. N8................... 1B 34
Abyssinia Rd. SW11............. 2A 102
Acacia Bus. Cen. E11.......... 5A 40
Acacia Cl. SE8...................... 5A 80
Acacia Gdns. NW8................1F 59
Acacia Gro. SE21.................2F 119
Acacia Pl. NW8......................1F 59
Acacia Rd. E11..................... 4A 40
Acacia Rd. E17..................... 1A 38
Acacia Rd. NW8....................1F 59
Acacia Wlk. SW10................. 3E 87
.... *(off Tadema Rd.)*
Academy, The SW8............... 2D 90
Academy Apts. E8................. 2D 51
.... *(off Dalston La.)*
Academy Bldgs. N1.1D 11 (2A 64)
.... *(off Fanshaw St.)*
Academy Ct. E2..................... 2E 65
.... *(off Kirkwall Pl.)*
Academy Gdns. NW6............5C 44
Academy Gdns. W8............... 3C 72
Academy Ho. E3.................... 4D 67
.... *(off Violet Rd.)*
Acanthus Dr. SE1.................. 1C 92
Acanthus Rd. SW11............. 1C 102
Accommodation Rd. NW11..3B 30
Acer Rd. E8........................... 4B 50
Ace Way SW11.......................2F 89

Acfold Rd. SW6 .... 4D 87
Achilles Cl. SE1 .... 1C 92
Achilles Ho. E2. .... 1D 65
.... (off Old Bethnal Grn. Rd.)
Achilles Rd. NW6 .... 2C 44
Achilles Statue 2C 20 (2C 74)
Achilles St. SE14. .... 3A 94
Achilles Way W1 ...1C 20 (2C 74)
Acklam Rd. W10 .... 4A 58
.... (not continuous)
Ackmar Rd. SW6. .... 4C 86
Ackroyd Dr. E3. .... 4B 66
Ackroyd Rd. SE23. .... 5F 107
Acland Ct. SW16 .... 5A 118
Acland Cres. SE5 .... 1F 105
Acland Ho. SW9 .... 4B 90
Acland Rd. NW2. .... 3D 43
Acme Studios
   E14: Lon Gillender St. 4E 67
Acme Studios
   E14: Lon Leven Rd. 4E 67
.... (off Leven Rd.)
Acol Ct. NW6 .... 4C 44
Acol Rd. NW6 .... 4C 44
Acorn Ct. E3 .... 1C 66
.... (off Morville St.)
Acorn Gdns. W3 .... 4A 56
Acorn Pde. SE15 .... 3D 93
Acorn Production Cen. N7 .....4A 48
Acorn Wlk. SE16 .... 2A 80
Acorn Way SE23 .... 3F 121
Acre Ct. SE22. .... 2C 106
Acre La. SW2. .... 2A 104
Acre Rd. SW19 .... 5F 115
Acris St. SW18 .... 3E 101
Acton Apts. N1 .... 5F 49
.... (off Branch Pl.)
Acton Ho. E8 .... 5B 50
.... (off Lee St.)
Acton M. E8 .... 5B 50
Acton Pk. Est. W3 .... 3A 70
Acton St. WC1 .....2F 7 (2B 62)
Acton Va. Ind. Pk. W3. .... 3B 70
Acuba Ho. SW18 .... 2D 115
Ada Ct. N1 .... 5E 49
.... (off Packington St.)
Ada Ct. W9 .... 2E 59
Ada Gdns. E14. .... 5F 67
Ada Gdns. E15. .... 5B 54
Adagio Point SE8 .... 2D 95
.... (off Copperas St.)
Ada Ho. E2. .... 5C 50
.... (off Ada Pl.)
Adair Ho. SW3 .... 2A 88
.... (off Oakley St.)
Adair Rd. W10. .... 3A 58
Adair Twr. W10 .... 3A 58
.... (off Appleford Rd.)
Ada Kennedy Ct. SE10. ....3E 95
.... (off Greenwich Sth. St.)
Adam & Eve Ct.
   W1. ....2A 14 (5E 61)
.... (off Oxford St.)
Adam & Eve M. W8 .... 4C 72
Ada Maria Ct. E1 .... 5D 65
.... (off James Voller Way)
Adam Cl. SE6 .... 4B 122
Adam Ct. SE11 .... 5D 77
.... (off Opal St.)
Adam Ct. SW7 .... 5E 73
.... (off Gloucester Rd.)
Adamfields NW3 .... 4F 45
.... (off Adamson Rd.)
Adams Ct. E17 .... 1A 38
Adams Ct. EC2 .....2C 18 (5A 64)
Adams Gdns. Est. SE16 ....3E 79

Adams Ho. E14. .... 5F 67
.... (off Aberfeldy St.)
Adams M. SW17 .... 2B 116
Adamson Rd. E16 .... 5C 68
Adamson Rd. NW3 .... 4F 45
Adams Pl. E14. .... 2D 81
.... (off The Nth. Colonnade)
Adams Pl. N7 .... 2B 48
Adamsrill Rd. SE26 .... 4F 121
Adam's Row W1 .....5C 12 (1C 74)
Adams Ter. E3. .... 2C 66
.... (off Rainhill Way)
Adam St. WC2. .....5E 15 (1A 76)
Adam Wlk. SW6 .... 3E 85
Adana SE13. .... 5E 95
Ada Pl. E2. .... 5C 50
Adare Wlk. SW16 .... 3B 118
Ada Rd. SE5 .... 3A 92
Adastral Ho. WC1. ....5F 7 (4B 62)
.... (off Harpur St.)
Ada St. E8 .... 5D 51
Adderley Gro. SW11 .... 3C 102
Adderley St. E14. .... 5E 67
Addey Ho. SE8. .... 3B 94
Addington Gro. SE26 .... 4A 122
Addington Ho. SW9. .... 5B 90
.... (off Stockwell Rd.)
Addington Lofts SE5. .... 3E 91
.... (off Bethwin Rd.)
Addington Rd. E16. .... 3A 68
Addington Rd. E3. .... 2C 66
Addington Rd. N4 .... 1C 34
Addington Sq. SE5 .... 2F 91
.... (not continuous)
Addington St. SE11 .....4A 24 (3B 76)
Addis Ho. E1. .... 4E 65
.... (off Lindley St.)
Addisland Ct. W14 .... 3A 72
.... (off Holland Vs. Rd.)
Addison Av. W11. .... 2A 72
Addison Bri. Pl. W14. .... 5B 72
Addison Ct. NW6. .... 5C 44
.... (off Brondesbury Rd.)
Addison Cres. W14 .... 4A 72
.... (not continuous)
Addison Dr. SE12. .... 3D 111
Addison Gdns. W14 .... 4F 71
Addison Gro. W4. .... 4A 70
Addison Ho. NW8. .... 2F 59
.... (off Grove End Rd.)
Addison Pk. Mans. W14 ....4F 71
.... (off Richmond Way)
Addison Pl. W11. .... 2A 72
Addison Rd. E11. .... 1C 40
Addison Rd. W14 .... 3A 72
Addle Hill EC4 .....3E 17 (5D 63)
Addlestone Ho. W10 .... 4E 57
.... (off Sutton Way)
Addle St. EC2 .....1A 18 (5E 63)
Addy Ho. SE16. .... 5E 79
Adela Ho. W6. .... 1E 85
.... (off Queen Caroline St.)
Adelaide Av. SE4. .... 2B 108
Adelaide Cl. SW9 .... 2C 104
Adelaide Community Gdn. 4B 46
.... (off Adelaide Rd.)
Adelaide Ct. E9 .... 2A 52
.... (off Kenworthy Rd.)
Adelaide Ct. NW8 .... 1E 59
.... (off Abbey Rd.)
Adelaide Gro. W12 .... 2C 70
Adelaide Ho. E15. .... 1B 68
Adelaide Ho. SE5 .... 5A 92
Adelaide Ho. W11 .... 5B 58
.... (off Portobello Rd.)

Adelaide Rd. E10 .... 5D 39
Adelaide Rd. NW3. .... 4F 45
Adelaide Rd. SW18 .... 3C 100
Adelaide St. WC2 .....5D 15 (1A 76)
.... (not continuous)
Adela St. W10 .... 3A 58
Adelina Gro. E1 .... 4E 65
Adelina M. SW12 .... 1F 117
Adeline Pl. E1. .... 4E 65
.... (off Adelina Gro.)
Adeline Pl. WC1 .....1C 14 (4F 61)
Adelphi Ct. E8 .... 4B 50
.... (off Celandine Dr.)
Adelphi Ct. SE16 .... 3F 79
.... (off Garter Way)
Adelphi Ct. W4 .... 2A 84
Adelphi Ter. WC2 .....5E 15 (1A 76)
Adelphi Theatre 5E 15 (1A 76)
.... (off Strand)
Adeney Cl. W6. .... 2F 85
Aden Gro. N16. .... 1F 49
Adenmore Rd. SE6. .... 5C 108
Aden Ter. N16. .... 1F 49
Adeyfield Ho. EC1 .....2C 10 (2F 63)
.... (off Cranwood St.)
Adie Rd. W6 .... 4E 71
Adine Rd. E13 .... 3D 69
Adler St. E1 .... 5C 64
Adley St. E5. .... 2A 52
Admiral Ct. SE5. .... 4A 92
.... (off Havil St.)
Admiral Ct. SW10. .... 4E 87
.... (off Admiral Sq.)
Admiral Ct. W1. .....1B 12 (4C 60)
.... (off Blandford St.)
Admiral Ho. SW1. .... 5E 75
.... (off Willow Pl.)
Admiral Hyson Ind. Est.
   SE16. .... 1D 93
Admiral M. W10 .... 3F 57
Admiral Pl. SE16. .... 2A 80
Admirals Ct. SE1. .....2F 27 (2B 78)
.... (off Horselydown La.)
Admiral's Ga. SE10. .... 4D 95
Admiral Sq. SW10. .... 4E 87
Admiral's Twr. SE10. .... 2D 95
.... (off Dowells St.)
Admiral Wlk. SE8. .... 5C 94
Admirals Wlk. NW3. .... 5E 31
Admirals Way E14. .... 3C 80
Admiralty & Commercial Court
   .... 2B 16 (5C 62)
Admiralty Arch London
   .... 1C 22 (2F 75)
Admiralty Av. E16 .... 3D 83
Admiralty Cl. SE8. .... 3C 94
Admiralty Ho. E1 .... 1C 78
.... (off Vaughan Way)
Admiral Wlk. W9 .... 4C 58
Adolf St. SE6 .... 4D 123
Adolphus Rd. N4 .... 4D 35
Adolphus St. SE8 .... 3B 94
Adpar St. W2 .... 4F 59
Adrian Av. NW2 .... 3D 29
Adrian Boult Ho. E2 .... 2D 65
.... (off Mansford St.)
Adrian Ho. E15. .... 4F 53
.... (off Jupp Rd.)
Adrian Ho. N1. .... 5B 48
.... (off Barnsbury Est.)
Adrian Ho. SW8 .... 3A 90
.... (off Wyvil Rd.)
Adrian M. SW10 .... 2D 87
Adriatic Apts. E16. .... 1C 82
.... (off Western Gateway)

Adriatic Bldg. E14 .... 1A **80**
.................................(off Horseferry Rd.)
Adriatic Ho. E1 ....3F **65**
.....................................(off Ernest St.)
Adron Ho. SE16 ....5E **79**
...............................(off Millender Wlk.)
Adstock Ho. N1 ....4D **49**
....................................(off The Sutton Est.)
Advance Rd. SE27 ....4E **119**
Adventurers Ct. E14 ....1F **81**
...................................(off Newport Av.)
Adys Lawn NW2 ....3D **43**
Ady's Rd. SE15 ....1B **106**
Aegean Apts. E16 ....1C **82**
..................................(off Western Gateway)
Aegon Ho. E14 ....4D **81**
....(off Lanark Sq.)
AFC Wimbledon Plough La.
  Stadium 4E **115**
Affleck St. N1 ....1A **8** (1B **62**)
Afghan Rd. SW11 ....5A **88**
Afsil Ho. EC1 ....1C **16** (4C **62**)
...................................(off Viaduct Bldgs.)
Aftab Ter. E1 ....3D **65**
....(off Tent St.)
Agamemnon Rd. NW6 ....1B **44**
Agar Gro. NW1 ....4E **47**
Agar Gro. Est. NW1 ....4F **47**
Agar Pl. NW1 ....4E **47**
Agar St. WC2 ....5D **15** (1A **76**)
Agate Cl. E16 ....5F **69**
Agate Rd. W6 ....4E **71**
Agatha Cl. E1 ....2D **79**
Agave Rd. NW2 ....1E **43**
Agdon St. EC1 ....3D **9** (3D **63**)
Age Exchange 1B **110**
..................................(off Blackheath Village)
Agincourt Rd. NW3 ....1B **46**
Agnes George Wlk. E16 .... 2F **83**
Agnes Ho. W11 ....1F **71**
..................................(off St Ann's Rd.)
Agnes Rd. W3 ....2B **70**
Agnes St. E14 ....5B **66**
Agnew Rd. SE23 ....5F **107**
Agricola Ct. E3 ....5B **52**
..................................(off Parnell Rd.)
Ahoy, The Cen. 1C **94**
...................................(off Stretton Mans.)
Aigburth Mans. SW9 ....3C **90**
...................................(off Mowll St.)
Aileen Wlk. E15 ....4B **54**
Ailsa St. E14 ....4E **67**
Ainger M. NW3 ....4B **46**
..................................(off Ainger Rd.)
Ainger Rd. NW3 ....4B **46**
Ainsdale NW1 ....1F **5** (1E **61**)
..................................(off Harrington St.)
Ainsdale Dr. SE1 ....1C **92**
Ainsley St. E2 ....2D **65**
Ainslie Wlk. SW12 ....5D **103**
Ainsty Est. SE16 ....3F **79**
Ainsty St. SE16 ....3E **79**
Ainsworth Cl. NW2 ....5C **28**
Ainsworth Ct. SE15 ....5A **92**
Ainsworth Rd. NW10 ....2D **57**
..................................(off Plough Cl.)
Ainsworth Ho. NW8 ....5D **45**
...............................(off Ainsworth Way)
Ainsworth Ho. W10 ....2A **58**
..................................(off Kilburn La.)
Ainsworth Rd. E9 ....4E **51**
Ainsworth Way NW8 ....4E **45**
Aintree Av. E6 ....5F **55**
Aintree Est. SW6 ....3A **86**
Aintree St. SW6 ....3A **86**

Aird Ho. SE1 ....5F **25** (4E **77**)
..................................(off Rockingham St.)
Airdrie Cl. N1 ....4B **48**
Airedale Av. W4 ....5B **70**
Airedale Av. Sth. W4 ....1B **84**
Airedale Rd. SW12 ....5B **102**
Airlie Gdns. W8 ....2C **72**
Air St. W1 ....5A **14** (1E **75**)
Aisgill Av. W14 ....1B **86**
..................................(not continuous)
Aislibie Rd. SE12 ....2A **110**
Aiten Pl. W6 ....5C **70**
Aithan Ho. E14 ....5B **66**
..................................(off Copenhagen Pl.)
Aitken Cl. E8 ....5C **50**
Aitken Rd. SE6 ....2D **123**
Ajax Ho. E2 ....1D **65**
..................................(off Old Bethnal Grn. Rd.)
Ajax Rd. NW6 ....1B **44**
Akbar Ho. E14 ....5D **81**
..................................(off Cahir St.)
Akehurst St. SW15 ....4C **98**
Akenside Rd. NW3 ....2F **45**
Akerman Rd. SW9 ....5D **91**
Akintaro Ho. SE8 ....2B **94**
..................................(off Alverton St.)
Alamaro Lodge SE10 ....4B **82**
..................................(off Teal St.)
Alameda Pl. E3 ....1D **67**
Alan Coren Cl. NW2 ....1E **43**
Aland Ct. SE16 ....4A **80**
Alan Hocken Way E15 ....1A **68**
Alan Preece Ct. NW6 ....4F **43**
Alanthus Cl. SE12 ....4C **110**
Alaska Apts. E16 ....1C **82**
..................................(off Western Gateway)
Alaska Bldg. SE13 ....4D **95**
..................................(off Deal's Gateway)
Alaska Bldgs. SE1 ....4B **78**
Alaska St. SE1 ....2B **24** (2C **76**)
Alastor Ho. E14 ....4E **81**
..................................(off Strattondale Rd.)
Albacore Cres. SE13 ....4D **109**
Alba Gdns. NW11 ....1A **30**
Alba M. SW18 ....2C **114**
Alba Highwalk
  EC2 ....1A **18** (4E **63**)
..................................(off Wood St.)
Albany W1 ....5F **13** (1E **75**)
Albany, The 3C **94**
Albany Ct. E1 ....5C **64**
..................................(off Plumber's Row)
Albany Ct. E10 ....2C **38**
Albany Ct. NW10 ....2D **57**
..................................(off Trenmar Gdns.)
Albany Ct. NW8 ....1F **59**
..................................(off Abbey Rd.)
Albany Ctyd. W1 ....5A **14** (1E **75**)
Albany Mans. SW11 ....3A **88**
Albany M. BR1: Broml 5C **124**
Albany M. N1 ....4C **48**
Albany M. SE5 ....2E **91**
Albany Rd. E10 ....2C **38**
Albany Rd. E12 ....1F **55**
Albany Rd. E17 ....1A **38**
Albany Rd. N4 ....1C **34**
Albany Rd. SE5 ....3F **91**
Albany Rd. SW19 ....5D **115**
Albany St. NW1 ....1D **5** (1D **61**)
Albany Ter. NW1 ....4E **5** (3D **61**)
..................................(off Marylebone Rd.)
Albany Works E3 ....5A **52**
..................................(off Gunmakers La.)
Alba Pl. W11 ....5B **58**

Albatross Way SE16 ....3F **79**
Albemarle SW19 ....2F **113**
Albemarle Ho. SE8 ....5B **80**
Albemarle St. W1 ......5E **13** (1D **75**)
Albemarle Wlk. SW9 ....1C **104**
Albemarle Way
  EC1 ....4D **9** (3D **63**)
Alberta Est. SE17 ....1D **91**
..................................(off Alberta St.)
Alberta St. SE17 ....1D **91**
Albert Av. SW8 ....3B **90**
Albert Barnes Ho. SE1 ....4E **77**
..................................(off New Kent Rd.)
Albert Bigg Point E15 ....1E **67**
..................................(off Godfrey St.)
ALBERT BRI. 2A 88
Albert Bri. Rd. SW11 ....3A **88**
Albert Carr Gdns. SW16 .... 5A **118**
Albert Cl. E9 ....5D **51**
Albert Cotts. E1 ....4C **64**
..................................(off Deal St.)
Albert Ct. E7 ....1C **54**
Albert Ct. SW7 ....4F **73**
Albert Ct. Ga. SW1 ....3B **74**
..................................(off Knightsbridge)
Albert Dr. SW19 ....2A **114**
Albert Emb.
  SE1: Lon Kennington La. 1A **90**
Albert Emb. SE1: Lon Lambeth
  Pal. Rd. 5F **23** (4B **76**)
Albert Gdns. E1 ....5F **65**
Albert Ga. SW1 ....3A **20** (3B **74**)
Albert Gray Ho. SW10 ....3F **87**
..................................(off Worlds End Est.)
Albert Hall Mans. SW7 ....3F **73**
Albert Mans. SW11 ....4B **88**
..................................(off Albert Bri. Rd.)
Albert Memorial London 3F **73**
Albert M. E14 ....5B **66**
..................................(off Northey St.)
Albert M. N4 ....3B **34**
Albert M. SE4 ....2A **108**
Albert M. W8 ....4E **73**
Albert Pal. Mans. SW11 ....4D **89**
..................................(off Lurline Gdns.)
Albert Pl. W8 ....4D **73**
Albert Rd. E10 ....4E **39**
Albert Rd. E16 ....2F **83**
Albert Rd. E17 ....1C **38**
Albert Rd. N15 ....1A **36**
Albert Rd. N4 ....3B **34**
Albert Rd. NW6 ....1B **58**
Alberts Ct. NW1 ....3A **60**
..................................(off Palgrave Gdns.)
Albert Sq. E15 ....2A **54**
Albert Sq. SW8 ....3B **90**
Albert Starr Ho. SE8 ....5F **79**
..................................(off Haddonfield)
Albert St. NW1 ....5D **47**
Albert Studios SW11 ....4B **88**
Albert Ter. NW1 ....5C **46**
Albert Ter. W6 ....1C **84**
..................................(off Beavor La.)
Albert Ter. M. NW1 ....5C **46**
Albert Way SE15 ....3D **93**
Albert Westcott Ho. SE17 ....1D **91**
Albery Ct. E8 ....4B **50**
..................................(off Middleton Rd.)
Albion Av. SW8 ....5F **89**
Albion Bldgs. N1 ....1A **62**
..................................(off Albion Yd.)
Albion Cl. W2 ....1A **74**
Albion Ct. SE10 ....5A **82**
..................................(off Azof St.)

Albion Ct. W6 ....5D 71
..............(off Albion Dr.)
Albion Dr. E8 ....4B 50
Albion Est. SE16 ....3F 79
Albion Gdns. W6 ....5D 71
Albion Ga. W2 ....1A 74
..............(off Albion St.)
Albion Gro. N16 ....5A 50
Albion Ho. N18 ....3C 94
..............(off Watsons St.)
Albion M. N1 ....5C 48
Albion M. NW6 ....4B 44
Albion M. W2 ....1A 74
Albion M. W6 ....5D 71
Albion Pde. N16 ....1F 49
Albion Pl. EC1 ...5D 9 (4D 63)
Albion Pl. EC2 ....1C 18 (4F 63)
Albion Pl. W6 ....5D 71
Albion Riverside Bldg.
SW11 ....3A 88
Albion Rd. N16 ....1F 49
Albion Sq. E8 ....4B 50
..............(not continuous)
Albion St. SE16 ....3E 79
Albion St. W2 ....5A 60
Albion Ter. E8 ....4B 50
Albion Vs. Rd. SE26 ....3E 121
Albion Wlk. N1 ...1E 7 (1A 62)
..............(off York Way)
Albion Way E6 ....5F 55
Albion Way EC1 ..1F 17 (4E 63)
Albion Way SE13 ....2E 109
Albion Yd. E1 ....4D 65
Albion Yd. N1 ....1A 62
Albion Ho. SW18 ....4D 101
..............(off Neville Gill Cl.)
Albrighton Rd. SE22 ....1A 106
Albury Ct. SE8 ....2C 94
..............(off Albury St.)
Albury Ho. SE1 ....4E 25 (3D 77)
..............(off Boyfield St.)
Albury M. E12 ....4E 41
Albury St. SE8 ....2C 94
Albyn Rd. SE8 ....4C 94
Alcester Cres. E5 ....4D 37
Alconbury Rd. E5 ....4C 36
Aldam Pl. N16 ....4B 36
Aldbourne Rd. W12 ....2B 70
Aldbridge St. SE17 ....1A 92
Aldburgh M. W1 ...2C 12 (5C 60)
Aldbury Ho. SW3 ....5A 74
..............(off Cale St.)
Aldebert Ter. SW8 ....3A 90
Aldeburgh Cl. E5 ....4D 37
Aldeburgh Pl. SE10 ....5C 82
..............(off Aldeburgh St.)
Aldeburgh St. SE10 ....1C 96
Alden Av. E15 ....2B 68
Aldenham Ho. NW1 ..1A 6 (1E 61)
..............(off Aldenham St.)
Aldenham St. NW1 ..1A 6 (1E 61)
Alden Ho. E8 ....5D 51
..............(off Duncan Rd.)
Aldensley Rd. W6 ....4D 71
Alderbrook Rd. SW12 ....4D 103
Alderbury Rd. SW13 ....2C 84
Alder Cl. SE15 ....2B 92
Alder Cl. E7 ....2C 54
Alder Gro. NW2 ....4C 28
Alder Ho. E3 ....5B 52
..............(off Hornbeam Sq.)
Alder Ho. NW3 ....3B 46
Alder Ho. SE15 ....2B 92
Alder Ho. SE4 ....1C 108

Alder Lodge SW6 ....4E 85
Aldermanbury EC2 ....2A 18 (5E 63)
Aldermanbury Sq.
EC2 ....1A 18 (4E 63)
Aldermans Ho. E9 ....2A 52
..............(off Ward La.)
Aldermans Wlk. EC2.1D 19 (4A 64)
Alder M. N19 ....4E 33
Aldermoor Rd. SE6 ....3B 122
Alderney Ct. SE10 ....2F 95
..............(off Trafalgar Rd.)
Alderney Ho. N1 ....3E 49
..............(off Arran Wlk.)
Alderney M. SE1 ...5B 26 (4F 77)
Alderney Rd. E1 ....3F 65
Alderney St. SW1 ....5D 75
Alders, The SW16 ....4E 117
ALDERSBROOK 4D 41
Aldersbrook Rd. E11 ....4D 41
Aldersbrook Rd. E12 ....4D 41
Alders Cl. E11 ....4D 41
Aldersford Cl. SE4 ....3F 107
Aldersgate Ct. EC1 ...1F 17 (4E 63)
Aldersgate St. EC1 ...5F 9 (4E 63)
Aldersgrove Av. SE9 ....3F 125
Aldershot Rd. NW6 ....5B 44
Alderson St. W10 ....3A 58
Alderton Cl. NW10 ....5A 28
Alderton Cres. NW4 ....1D 29
Alderton Rd. SE24 ....1E 105
Alderton Way NW4 ....1D 29
Alderville Rd. SW6 ....5B 86
Alderwick Ct. N7 ....3B 48
..............(off Cornelia St.)
Aldford Ho. W1 ......1B 20 (2C 74)
..............(off Park St.)
Aldford St. W1 ......1B 20 (2C 74)
Aldgate E1 ....2F 19 (5B 64)
..............(off Whitechapel High St.)
ALDGATE 2F 19 (5B 64)
..............(off Aldgate High St.)
Aldgate EC3 ....3E 19 (5B 64)
Aldgate Av. E1 ....2F 19 (5B 64)
Aldgate Barrs E1 ....2F 19 (5B 64)
..............(off Whitechapel High St.)
Aldgate Bus Station .3F 19 (5B 64)
Aldgate East Station
(Underground) 2F 19 (5B 64)
Aldgate High St.
EC3 ....3F 19 (5B 64)
Aldgate Pl. E1 ....5B 64
Aldgate Sq. EC3 ....3F 19 (5B 64)
Aldgate Station (Underground)
........................2F 19 (5B 64)
Aldgate Twr. E1 .....2F 19 (5B 64)
Aldham Ho. SE4 ....5B 94
..............(off Malpas Rd.)
Aldine Ct. W12 ....3E 71
..............(off Aldine St.)
Aldine Pl. W12 ....3E 71
Aldine St. W12 ....3E 71
Aldington Ct. E8 ....4C 50
..............(off London Flds. W. Side)
Aldington Rd. SE18 ....4F 83
Aldis M. SW17 ....5A 116
Aldis St. SW17 ....5A 116
Aldred Rd. NW6 ....2C 44
Aldren Rd. SW17 ....3E 115
Aldrich Ter. SW18 ....2E 115
Aldrick Ho. N1 ....5B 48
..............(off Barnsbury Est.)
Aldridge Ct. W11 ....4B 58
..............(off Aldridge Rd. Vs.)
Aldridge Rd. Vs. W11 ....4B 58

Aldrington Rd. SW16 ....5E 117
Aldsworth Cl. W9 ....3D 59
Aldworth Gro. SE13 ....4E 109
Aldworth Rd. E15 ....4A 54
Aldwych WC2 ....3F 15 (5B 62)
Aldwych Bldgs.
WC2 ....2E 15 (5A 62)
..............(off Parker M.)
Aldwych Ct. E8 ....4B 50
..............(off Middleton Rd.)
Aldwych Theatre......3F 15 (5B 62)
..............(off Aldwych)
Aldwyn Ho. SW8 ....3A 90
..............(off Davidson Gdns.)
Alestan Beck Rd. E16 ....5F 69
Alexa Ct. W8 ....5C 72
Alexander Av. NW10 ....4D 43
Alexander Evans M.
SE23 ....2F 121
Alexander Fleming Laboratory
Mus. 5F 59
Alexander Ho. E14 ....4C 80
..............(off Tiller Rd.)
Alexander Ho. SE15 ....5D 93
..............(off Godman Rd.)
Alexander M. W2 ....5D 59
Alexander Pl. SW7 ....5A 74
Alexander Rd. N19 ....5A 34
Alexander Sq. SW3 ....5A 74
Alexander St. W2 ....5C 58
Alexander Studios SW11 ...2F 101
..............(off Haydon Way)
Alexandra Av. SW11 ....4C 88
Alexandra Av. W4 ....3A 84
Alexandra Cl. SE8 ....2B 94
Alexandra Cotts. SE14 ....4B 94
Alexandra Ct. SE5 ....2E 91
..............(off Urlwin St.)
Alexandra Ct. SW7 ....4E 73
..............(off Queen's Ga.)
Alexandra Ct. W2 ....1D 73
..............(off Moscow Rd.)
Alexandra Ct. W9 ....3E 59
..............(off Maida Vale)
Alexandra Cres.
BR1: Broml 5B 124
Alexandra Dr. SE19 ....5A 120
Alexandra Gdns. W4 ....3A 84
Alexandra Gro. N4 ....3D 35
Alexandra Ho. E16 ....2D 83
..............(off Wesley Av.)
Alexandra Ho. W6 ....1E 85
..............(off Queen Caroline St.)
Alexandra Mans. SW3 ....2F 87
..............(off King's Rd.)
Alexandra Mans. W12 ....2E 71
..............(off Stanlake Rd.)
Alexandra M. N4 ....4D 35
Alexandra M. SW19 ....5B 114
Alexandra Pl. NW8 ....5E 45
Alexandra Rd. E10 ....5E 39
Alexandra Rd. E17 ....1B 38
Alexandra Rd. NW8 ....5E 45
Alexandra Rd. SE26 ....5F 121
Alexandra Rd. SW14 ....1A 98
Alexandra Rd. SW19 ....5B 114
Alexandra Rd. W4 ....3A 70
Alexandra St. E16 ....4C 68
Alexandra St. SE14 ....3A 94
Alexandra Ter. E14 ....1D 95
..............(off Westferry Rd.)
Alexandra Wlk. SE19 ....5A 120
Alexandra Wharf E2 ....5D 51
..............(off Darwen Pl.)

Alexandra Yd. E9 ....5F 51
Alexandria Apts. SE17 ....5A 78
...................................(off Townsend St.)
Alexia Sq. E14............................4D 81
Alexis St. SE16..........................5C 78
Alfearn Rd E5............................5E 51
Alford Ct. N1 ....1A 10 (1E 63)
...........................(off Shepherdess Wlk.)
Alford Ho. N6.............................1E 33
Alford Pl. N1 ....1A 10 (1E 63)
Alfreda St. SW11......................4D 89
Alfred Cl. SE16..........................5D 79
...................................(off Bombay St.)
Alfred Dickens Ho. E16.........5B 68
...................................(off Hallsville St.)
Alfred Ho. E9.............................2A 52
...................................(off Homerton Rd.)
Alfred M. W1 ....5B 6 (4F 61)
Alfred Nunn Ho. NW10..........5B 42
Alfred Pl. WC1...............5B 6 (4F 61)
Alfred Rd. E15...........................2B 54
Alfred Rd. W2............................4C 58
Alfred Salter Ho. SE1 ....5B 78
...................................(off Fort Rd.)
Alfred St. E3..............................2B 66
Alfreton Cl. SW19....................3F 113
Alfriston Rd. SW11..................3B 102
Algar Ho. SE1 ....4D 25 (3D 77)
...................................(off Webber Row)
Algarve Rd. SW18...................1D 115
Algernon Rd. NW4....................1C 28
Algernon Rd. NW6....................5C 44
Algernon Rd. SE13..................2D 109
Algiers Rd. SE13.....................2C 108
Alice Gilliatt Ct. W14................2B 86
...................................(off Star Rd.)
Alice La. E3................................5B 52
Alice Owen Technology Cen.
EC1...............................1D 9 (2D 63)
...................................(off Goswell Rd.)
Alice Shepherd Ho. E14.........3E 81
...................................(off Manchester Rd.)
Alice St. SE1..............5D 27 (4A 78)
...................................(not continuous)
Alice Thompson Cl. SE12......2E 125
Alice Walker Cl. SE24.............2D 105
Alie St. E1 ....3F 19 (5B 64)
Aliwal M. SW11.......................2A 102
Aliwal Rd. SW11......................2A 102
Alkerden Rd. W4.......................1A 84
Alkham Rd. N16........................4B 36
Allan Barclay Cl. N15...............1B 36
Allanson Ct. E10.......................4C 38
...................................(off Leyton Grange Est.)
Allard Gdns. SW4...................3F 103
Allardyce St. SW4..................2B 104
Allcroft Rd. NW5......................2C 46
Allenby Rd. SE23.....................3A 122
Allen Ct. E17.............................1C 38
...................................(off Yunus Khan Cl.)
Allendale Cl. SE26..................1F 121
Allendale Cl. SE5....................5F 91
Allen Edwards Dr. SW8..........4A 90
Allenford Ho. SW15.................4B 98
...................................(off Tunworth Cres.)
Allen Ho. W8.............................4C 72
...................................(off Allen St.)
Allen Mans. W8.........................4C 72
...................................(off Allen Rd.)
Allen Rd. E3...............................1B 66
Allen Rd. N16.............................1A 50
Allensbury Pl. NW1.................4F 47
Allen St. W8..............................4C 72
Allenswood SW19...................1A 114
Allerford Ho. E6 ....6D 123

Allerton Ho. N1............1B 10 (2F 63)
...................................(off Provost St.)
Allerton Rd. N16........................4E 35
Allerton St. N1............1B 10 (2F 63)
Allerton Wlk. N7.........................4B 34
Aliestree Rd. SW6....................3A 86
Alleyn Cres. SE21...................2F 119
Alleyn Ho. SE1.........5C 26 (4F 77)
...................................(off Burbage Cl.)
Alleyn Pk. SE21.......................2F 119
Alleyn Rd. SE21........................3F 119
Allfarthing La. SW18...............4D 101
Allgood St. E2...........................1B 64
Allhallows La. EC4 ....5B 18 (1F 77)
Allhallows Rd. E6......................4F 69
Alliance Rd. E13.......................4E 69
Allied Ct. N1...............................4A 50
...................................(off Enfield Rd.)
Allied Ind. Est. W3...................3A 70
Allied Way W3...........................3A 70
Allingham M. N1.......................1E 63
...................................(off Allingham St.)
Allingham Rd. SW4..................4F 103
Allingham M. N1........................1E 63
Allington Cl. SW19...................5F 113
Allington Ct. SW8.....................5E 89
Allington Rd. NW4...................1D 29
Allington Rd. W10....................2A 58
Allington St. SW1 ....5E 21 (4D 75)
Allison Cl. SE10........................4E 95
Allison Gro. SE21.................1A 120
Alliston Ho. E2..........................2B 64
...................................(off Gibraltar Wlk.)
Allitsen Rd. NW8......................1A 60
All Nations Ho. E8...................4D 51
...................................(off Martello St.)
Allnutt Way SW4......................3F 103
Alloa Rd. SE8............................1F 93
Allom Ho. W11..........................1A 72
...................................(off Clarendon Rd.)
Allotment Way NW2..................5F 29
Alloway Rd. E3..........................2A 66
Alloy Ho. SE14.........................2B 94
...................................(off Moulding La.)
Allport Ho. SE5........................1F 105
...................................(off Champion Pk.)
Allport M. E1.............................3E 65
...................................(off Hayfield Pas.)
All Saints Cl. SW8...................4A 90
All Saints Cl. E1.......................1E 79
...................................(off Johnson St.)
All Saints Ct. SW11................3D 89
...................................(off Prince of Wales Dr.)
All Saints Dr. SE3....................5A 96
...................................(not continuous)
All Saints Ho. W11...................4B 58
...................................(off All Saints Rd.)
All Saints Pas. SW18..............3C 100
All Saints Rd. W11...................4B 58
All Saints Russian Orthodox
Cathedral.................................3A 74
All Saints Station (DLR)......1D 81
All Saints Wlk. SE15...............3B 92
Allsop Pl. NW1 ....4A 4 (3B 60)
All Souls Av. NW10..................1D 57
All Souls' Pl. W1 ....1E 13 (4D 61)
Alluvium Ct. SE1 ......5D 27 (4A 78)
...................................(off Long La.)
Allwood Cl. SE26.....................4F 121
Alma Birk Ho. NW6..................4A 44
Almack Rd. E5...........................1E 51
Alma Gro. SE1..........................5B 78
Alma Pl. NW10.........................2D 57

Alma Rd. SW18.........................2E 101
Alma Sq. NW8..........................1E 59
Alma St. E15.............................3F 53
Alma St. NW5...........................3D 47
Alma Ter. E8..............................5B 52
...................................(off Beale Rd.)
Alma Ter. SW18......................5F 101
Alma Ter. W8.............................4C 72
Almeida St. N1..........................5D 49
Almeida Theatre.......................5D 49
...................................(off Almeida St.)
Almeric Rd. SW11...................2B 102
Almington St. N4......................3B 34
Almond Cl. SE15......................5C 92
Almond Ho. E15.......................2A 68
...................................(off Teasel Way)
Almond Rd. SE16.....................5D 79
Almorah Rd. N1........................4F 49
Alnwick Rd. E16.......................5E 69
Alnwick Rd. SE12.....................4D 111
Alperton St. W10......................3B 58
Alphabet M. SW9.....................4C 90
Alphabet Sq. E3.......................4C 66
Alpha Cl. NW1..........................3A 60
Alpha Gro. E14.........................2C 80
Alpha Ho. NW6.........................1C 58
Alpha Ho. NW8.........................3A 60
...................................(off Ashbridge St.)
Alpha Ho. SW4........................2B 104
Alpha Pl. NW6..........................1C 58
Alpha Pl. SW3..........................2A 88
Alpha Rd. SE14........................4B 94
Alpha St. SE15.........................5C 92
Alpine Gro. E9..........................4E 51
Alpine Rd. E10..........................4D 39
Alpine Rd. SE16.......................1F 93
Airic Av. NW10.........................4A 42
Alroy Rd. N4..............................2C 34
Alsace Rd. SE17......................1A 92
Alscot Rd. SE1.........................5B 78
Alscot Way SE1.......................5A 78
Alston Rd. SW17.....................4F 115
Altab Ali Pk...............................5C 64
...................................(off Adler St.)
Altenburg Gdns. SW11..........2B 102
Althea St. SW6.........................5D 87
Althorpe M. SW11....................4F 87
Althorp Rd. SW17....................1B 116
Altima Ct. SE22........................2C 106
...................................(off E. Dulwich Gro.)
Altior Ct. N6...............................1E 33
Altissima Ho. SW11................3D 89
Altitude Point E1......................5C 64
...................................(off Alie St.)
Altius Apts. E3..........................1C 66
...................................(off Wick La.)
Altius Wlk. E20.........................3E 53
Alton Ho. E3..............................2D 67
...................................(off Bromley High St.)
Alton Rd. SW15.......................1C 112
Alton St. E14.............................4D 67
Altura Twr. SW11.....................5F 87
Altus Ho. SE6...........................4E 123
Aluna Ct. SE15.........................1E 107
Alvanley Gdns. NW6...............2D 45
Alverstone Av. SW19..............2C 114
Alverstone Ho. SE11...............2C 90
Alverstone Rd. NW2................4E 43
Alverton St. SE8.......................1B 94
...................................(not continuous)
Alvey St. SE17..........................1A 92
Alvington Cres. E8...................2B 50
Alwold Cres. SE12...................4D 111
Alwyne La. N1...........................4D 49
Alwyne Pl. N1...........................3E 49

Alwyne Rd. N1 ....4E 49
Alwyne Rd. SW19...........5B 114
Alwyne Sq. N1 ....3E 49
Alwyne Vs. N1 ....4D 49
Alyth Gdns. NW11 .... 1C 30
Alzette Ho. E2:..........................1F 65
......................................(off Mace St.)
Amazon St. E1...................5C 64
Ambassador Bldg. SW11.....2F 89
Ambassador Ho. NW8.........5E 45
Ambassador's Ct.
SW1......................2A 22 (2E 75)
........................(off St James's Pal.)
Ambassadors Ct. E8 ....4B 50
....(off Holly St.)
Ambassador Sq. E14 ....5D 81
Ambassadors Theatre
..............................3C 14 (1F 75)
....(off West St.)
Amber Ct. E15....................5E 53
....(off Warton Rd.)
Amber Ct. N7......................3C 48
....(off Bride St.)
Amber Ct. SW17.................4C 116
..................................(off Brudenell Rd.)
Ambergate St. SE17.........1D 91
Amberley Gro. SE26.........5D 121
Amberley Rd. E10 ....2C 38
Amberley Rd. W9 ....4C 58
Amber Way W3 ....3A 70
Amber Wharf E2 ....5B 50
....(off Nursery La.)
Amberley Gro. SE26.........5D 121
Ambleside Cl. SE12 ....3D 125
Ambleside Mdws. SE12.....3D 125
Ambleside Rd. SE12 ....3D 125
Ambler Rd. N4....................5D 35
Ambleside BR1: Broml 5F 123
Ambleside NW1.......1E 5 (1D 61)
....(off Augustus St.)
Ambleside SW19................1A 114
Ambleside Av. SW16..........4F 117
Ambleside Cl. E10...............2D 39
Ambleside Cl. E9.................2E 51
Ambleside Gdns. SW16 .....5F 117
Ambleside Point SE15........3E 93
....(off Tustin Est.)
Ambleside Rd. NW10..........4B 42
Ambrosden Av. SW1 ....5A 22 (4E 75)
Ambrose Av. NW11 ....2A 30
Ambrose Ho. E14 ....4C 66
....(off Selsey St.)
Ambrose M. SW11 ....5B 88
Ambrose St. SE16 ....5D 79
Ambrose Wlk. E3 ....1C 66
Ambulance Rd. E11 ....1F 39
Amelia Ho. E14..................5A 68
....(off Lyell St.)
Amelia Ho. W6 ....1F 85
...................................(off Queen Caroline St.)
Amelia Mans. E20 ....3D 53
....(off Olympic Pk. Av.)
Amelia St. SE17 ....1E 91
Amen Cnr. EC4 ....3E 17 (5D 63)
Amen Cnr. SW17 ....5B 116
Amen Ct. EC4 ....2E 17 (5D 63)
American International University
in London, The, Kensington
Campus, Ansdell Street.....4D 73
....(off Ansdell St.)
American International University
in London, The, Kensington
Campus, St Albans Grove....4D 73

American International University
in London, The, Kensington
Campus, Young Street 3D 73
American University of London,
The...................................5B 34
America Sq. EC3........4F 19 (1B 78)
America St. SE1.........2F 25 (2E 77)
Amerland Rd. SW18..........3B 100
Amersham Gro. SE14.........3B 94
Amersham Rd. SE14 ....4B 94
Amersham Va. SE14 ....3B 94
Amery Gdns. NW10............5E 43
Amery Ho. SE17 ....1A 92
....(off Kinglake St.)
Amesbury Av. SW2 ....2A 118
Amesbury Twr. SW8............5E 89
Ames Cotts. E14 ....4A 66
....(off Maroon St.)
Ames Ho. E2:..........................1F 65
....(off Mace St.)
Amethyst Rd. E15...............1F 53
Amherst Ho. SE16 ....3F 79
....(off Wolfe Cres.)
Amhurst Pde. N16...............2B 36
....(off Amhurst Pk.)
Amhurst Pk. N16 ....2F 35
Amhurst Pas. E8 ....1C 50
Amhurst Rd. E8..................2D 51
Amhurst Rd. N16 ....1C 50
Amhurst Ter. E8 ....1C 50
Amias Ho. EC1 ....3F 9 (3E 63)
....(off Central St.)
Amiel St. E1 ....3E 65
Amies St. SW11 ....1B 102
Amigo Ho. SE1 ....5C 24 (4C 76)
....(off Morley St.)
Amina Way SW16................4C 78
Amisha St. SE1 ....5F 27 (4B 78)
....(off Grange Rd.)
Amity Rd. E15 ....4B 54
Ammanford Grn. NW9.......1A 28
Ammonite Ho. E15..............4B 54
Amner Rd. SW11 ....4C 102
Amor Rd. W6.......................4E 71
Amory Ho. N1 ....5B 48
....(off Barnsbury Est.)
Amott Rd. SE15..................1C 106
Amoy Pl. E14......................1C 80
.....................................(not continuous)
Ampthill Est. NW1........1A 6 (1E 61)
Ampthill Sq. NW1........1A 6 (1E 61)
Ampton Pl. WC1 ....2F 7 (2B 62)
Ampton St. WC1 ....2F 7 (2B 62)
Amroth Cl. SE23.................1D 121
Amroth Grn. NW9...............1A 28
Amstel Ct. SE15 ....3B 92
Amsterdam Rd. E14............4E 81
Amundsen Ct. E14 ....1C 94
....(off Napier Av.)
Amwell Ct. Est. N4..............4E 35
Amwell Ho. WC1 ....1B 8 (2C 62)
.....................................(off Cruikshank St.)
Amwell St. EC1 ....1B 8 (2C 62)
Amyruth Rd. SE4 ....3C 108
Anatola Rd. N19..................4E 33
Anayah Apts. SE8 ....1F 93
....(off Trundleys Rd.)
Anchor SW18 ....2D 101
Anchorage Cl. SW19..........5C 114
Anchorage Ho. E14.............1F 81
....(off Clove Cres.)
Anchorage Point E14..........3B 80
....(off Cuba St.)
Anchorage Point Ind. Est.
SE7.....................................4E 83

Anchor & Hope La. SE7 ....4D 83
Anchor Brewhouse
SE1...................... 2F 27 (2B 78)
Anchor Ct. SW1.................... 5F 75
.....................................(off Vauxhall Bri. Rd.)
Anchor Ho.
E16: Lon Barking Rd............ 4B 68
....(off Barking Rd.)
Anchor Ho.
E16: Lon Prince Regent La.5E 69
...................................(off Prince Regent La.)
Anchor Ho. EC1 ....3F 9 (3E 63)
....(off Old St.)
Anchor Ho. SW10..................2F 87
....(off Cremorne Est.)
Anchor Iron Wharf SE10.....1F 95
Anchor M. N1 ....3A 50
Anchor M. SW12 ....4D 103
Anchor Retail Pk.
Stepney Green....................3E 65
Anchor St. SE16 ....5D 79
Anchor Ter. E1 ....3E 65
Anchor Ter. SE1 ....1A 26 (2E 77)
.....................................(off Southwark Bri. Rd.)
Anchor Wharf E3................4D 67
....(off Yeo St.)
Anchor Yd. EC1 ......3A 10 (3E 63)
Ancill Cl. W6......................2A 86
Ancona Rd. NW10 ....1C 56
Andalus Rd. SW9 ....1A 104
Anderson Cl. W3.................5A 56
Anderson Ct. NW2..............5E 29
Anderson Ho. E14...............1E 81
....(off Woolmore St.)
Anderson Ho. SW17...........5F 115
Anderson Rd. E9.................3F 51
Anderson Rd. SE3 ....2D 111
Anderson Sq. N1.................5D 49
....(off Gaskin St.)
Anderson St. SW3...............1B 88
Anderton Cl. SE5................1F 105
Andora Ct. NW6..................4A 44
.....................................(off Brondesbury Pk.)
Andora Ho. E10..................3A 38
Andover Av. E16 ....5F 69
Andover Ct. E2 ....3D 65
.....................................(off Thee Colts La.)
Andover Pl. NW6.................1D 59
Andover Rd. N7...................4B 34
Andoversford Ct. SE15 ......2A 92
....(off Bibury Cl.)
Andover Ter. W6..................5D 71
....(off Raynham Rd.)
Andre St. E8 ....2C 50
Andrew Ct. SE23................2F 121
Andrewes Gdns. E6 ....5F 69
Andrewes Highwalk
EC2.......................... 1A 18 (4E 63)
....(off Fore St.)
Andrewes Ho. EC2 .. 1A 18 (4E 63)
....(off Fore St.)
Andrew Gibb Memorial, The4B 96
Andrew Pl. SW8 ....3F 89
Andrew Reed Ho. SW18.....5A 100
....(off Linstead Way)
Andrews Crosse
WC2..........................3B 16 (5C 62)
.....................................(off Chancery La.)
Andrews Ho. NW3...............4B 46
....(off Fellows Rd.)
Andrew's Rd. E8 ....5D 51
Andrew St. E14 ....5E 67
Andrews Wlk. SE17 ....2D 91
Anerley Hill SE19 ....5B 120
Anerley St. SW11 ....5B 88

Aneurin Bevan Ct. NW2 ......4D **29**
Anfield Cl. SW12 ....5E **103**
ANGEL 1C **8** (1C **62**)
Angela Carter Cl. SW9 ......1C **104**
Angela Davies Ind. Est.
SE24 ....2D **105**
Angela Hooper Pl.
SW1 ....5A **22** (4E **75**)
................................(off Victoria St.)
Angel Bldg. N1 ....1C **8** (1C **62**)
Angel Ct. E15 ....3F **53**
Angel Ct. EC2 ....2C **18** (5F **63**)
Angel Ct. SW1 ....2A **22** (2E **75**)
Angel Ga. EC1 ....1E **9** (2D **63**)
....................................(not continuous)
Angel Ho. E3 ....2C **66**
................................(off Campbell Rd.)
Angelica Ho. E3 ....5B **52**
................................(off Sycamore Av.)
Angelina Ho. SE15 ....4C **92**
................................(off Goldsmith Rd.)
Angelis Apts. N1 ....1E **9** (1D **63**)
................................(off Graham St.)
Angel La. E15 ....3F **53**
Angel La. EC4 ....5B **18** (1F **77**)
Angell Pk. Gdns. SW9 ....1C **104**
Angell Rd. SW9 ....1C **104**
ANGELL TOWN 4C **90**
Angell Town Est. SW9 ....5C **90**
Angel M. E1 ....1D **79**
Angel M. N1 ....1C **62**
Angel M. SW15 ....5C **98**
Angel Pl. SE1 ....3B **26** (3F **77**)
Angel Sq. EC1 ....1D **63**
Angel Station (Underground)
....1C **62**
Angel St. EC1 ....2F **17** (5E **63**)
Angel Wlk. W6 ....5E **71**
Angel Wharf N1 ....1E **63**
Angel Yd. N6 ....3C **32**
Angerstein Bus. Pk.
SE10 ....5C **82**
Angerstein La. SE3 ....4B **96**
Anglebury W2 ....5C **58**
................................(off Talbot Rd.)
Angler's La. NW5 ....3D **47**
Anglesea Ter. W6 ....4D **71**
................................(off Wellesley Av.)
Anglesea Ho. E14 ....5C **66**
................................(off Lindfield St.)
Angles Rd. SW16 ....4A **118**
Anglia Ho. E14 ....5A **66**
................................(off Salmon La.)
Anglian Rd. E11 ....5F **39**
Anglo Rd. E3 ....1B **66**
Angrave Ct. E8 ....5B **50**
................................(off Scriven St.)
Angrave Pas. E8 ....5B **50**
Angus Ho. SW2 ....5F **103**
Angus Rd. E13 ....2E **69**
Angus St. SE14 ....3A **94**
Anhalt Rd. SW11 ....3A **88**
Anley Rd. W14 ....3F **71**
Annabel Cl. E14 ....5D **67**
Anna Cl. E8 ....5B **50**
Annandale Rd. SE10 ....2B **96**
Annandale Rd. W4 ....1A **84**
Anna Neagle Cl. E7 ....1C **54**
Anne Compton M. SE12 .....5B **110**
Anne Goodman Ho. E1 ....5E **65**
................................(off Jubilee St.)
Anne Matthews Ct. E14 ....4C **66**
................................(off Selsey St.)
Annes Ct. NW1 ....3A **60**
................................(off Palgrave Gdns.)

Annesley Apts. E3 ....4C **66**
................................(off Gresham Pl.)
Annesley Cl. NW10 ....5A **28**
Annesley Ho. SW9 ....4C **90**
Annesley Rd. SE3 ....4D **97**
Annesmere Gdns. SE3 ....1F **111**
Anne St. E13 ....3C **68**
Annette Cres. N1 ....4E **49**
Annette Rd. N7 ....5B **34**
................................(not continuous)
Annexe Mkt. E1 ....5F **11** (4B **64**)
................................(off Spital Sq.)
Annie Besant Cl. E3 ....5B **52**
Anning St. EC2 ....3E **11** (3A **64**)
Annis Rd. E9 ....3A **52**
Ann La. SW10 ....2F **87**
Ann Moss Way SE16 ....4E **79**
Ann's Cl. SW1 ....4A **20** (3B **74**)
................................(off Kinnerton St.)
Ann's Pl. E1 ....1F **19** (4B **64**)
................................(off Wentworth St.)
Ann St. N1 ....5E **49**
Ann Stroud Ct. SE12 ....3C **110**
Ansar Gdns. E17 ....1B **38**
Ansdell Rd. SE15 ....5E **93**
Ansdell St. W8 ....4D **73**
Ansdell Ter. W8 ....4D **73**
Ansell Ho. E1 ....4E **65**
................................(off Mile End Rd.)
Ansell Rd. SW17 ....3A **116**
Anselm Rd. SW6 ....2C **86**
Ansford Rd. BR1: Brom! 5E **123**
Ansleigh Pl. W11 ....1F **71**
Anson Ho. E1 ....3A **66**
................................(off Shandy St.)
Anson Ho. SW1 ....2E **89**
................................(off Churchill Gdns.)
Anson Rd. N7 ....1E **47**
Anson Rd. NW2 ....1D **43**
Anstey Ho. E9 ....5E **51**
................................(off Templecombe Rd.)
Anstey Rd. SE15 ....1C **106**
Anstice Cl. W4 ....3A **84**
Antenor Ho. E2 ....1D **65**
................................(off Old Bethnal Grn. Rd.)
Anthems Way E20 ....2D **53**
Anthony Cope Ct.
N1 ....1C **10** (2F **63**)
................................(off Chart St.)
Anthony Ho. W3 ....3A **70**
Anthony Ho. NW8 ....3A **60**
................................(off Ashbridge St.)
Anthony St. E1 ....5D **65**
Antigua M. E13 ....2D **69**
Antigua Wlk. SE19 ....5F **119**
Antila Cl. E1 ....3F **11** (3A **64**)
................................(off Sclater St.)
Antilles Bay E14 ....3E **81**
Antill Rd. E3 ....2A **66**
Antill Rd. N15 ....5F **25**
Antill Ter. E1 ....5F **65**
Antoinette M. NW2 ....3C **42**
Antoine Hgts.
SE1 ....4D **27** (3A **78**)
................................(off City Wlk.)
Anton St. E8 ....2C **50**
Antony Ho. SE16 ....5E **79**
................................(off Raymouth Rd.)
Antrim Gro. NW3 ....3B **46**
Antrim Mans. NW3 ....3B **46**
Antrim Rd. NW3 ....3B **46**
Apelles St. SE18 ....4F **97**
Apex Ho. E1 ....3F **11** (3B **64**)
................................(off Bacon St.)
Apex Ind. Est. NW10 ....3B **56**

Aphrodite Ct. E14 ....5C **80**
................................(off Homer Dr.)
Aphrodite Ct. E15 ....5E **53**
................................(off Warton Rd.)
Apollo Bldg. E14 ....5C **80**
Apollo Bus. Cen. SE8 ....1F **93**
Apollo Ct. E1 ....1C **78**
................................(off Thomas More St.)
Apollo Ct. E15 ....5E **53**
................................(off High St.)
Apollo Ct. SW9 ....4C **90**
................................(off Southey Rd.)
Apollo Ho. E2 ....1D **65**
Apollo Ho. E3 ....1C **66**
................................(off Garrison Rd.)
Apollo Ho. N6 ....2B **32**
Apollo Ho. SW10 ....3F **87**
................................(off Milman's St.)
Apollo Pl. E11 ....5B **40**
Apollo Pl. SW10 ....3F **87**
Apollo Theatre Piccadilly
............................4B **14** (1F **75**)
................................(off Shaftesbury Av.)
Apollo Victoria Theatre 4E **75**
................................(off Wilton Rd.)
Apostles, The SE23 ....2F **121**
................................(off Church Ri.)
Apothecary St. EC4 ...3D **17** (5D **63**)
Appach Rd. SW2 ....3C **104**
Appian Ct. E3 ....1B **66**
................................(off Parnell Rd.)
Apple Blossom Ct.
SW8 ....3F **89**
................................(off Pascal St.)
Appleby Cl. N15 ....1F **35**
Appleby Ct. SE6 ....4C **108**
Appleby Rd. E16 ....5B **68**
Appleby Rd. E8 ....4C **50**
Appleby St. E2 ....1B **64**
Appledore Cl. SW17 ....2B **116**
Appleford Ho. W10 ....3A **58**
................................(off Bosworth Rd.)
Appleford Rd. W10 ....3A **58**
Applegarth Ho.
SE1 ....3E **25** (3D **77**)
................................(off Nelson Sq.)
Applegarth Rd. SE15 ....3C **92**
................................(off Bird in Bush Rd.)
Applegarth Rd. W14 ....4F **71**
Applegate Ho. E20 ....2E **53**
................................(off Victory Pde.)
Apple Rd. E11 ....5A **40**
Appleshaw Ho. SE5 ....1A **106**
Appleton Rd. SE9 ....1F **111**
Apple Tree Yd. E1 ....2F **65**
................................(off Longnor Rd.)
Apple Tree Yd. SW1 ...1A **22** (2E **75**)
Applewood Cl. NW2 ....5D **29**
Applewood Dr. E13 ....3D **69**
Appold St. EC2 ....5D **11** (4A **64**)
Apprentice Way E5 ....1D **51**
Approach, The NW4 ....1F **29**
Approach, The W3 ....5A **56**
Approach Cl. N16 ....1A **50**
Approach Rd. E2 ....1E **65**
April Ct. E2 ....1C **64**
................................(off Teale St.)
April Glen SE23 ....3F **121**
April St. E8 ....1B **50**
Apsley, The Cen. NW2 ....4C **28**
Apsley Ho. E1 ....4E **65**
................................(off Stepney Way)
Apsley Ho. NW8 ....1F **59**
................................(off Finchley Rd.)

Apsley Ho. SW15 .... 4C 98
............................(off Holford Way)
Apsley House 3C 20 (3C 74)
Apsley Way NW2 .... 4C 28
Apsley Way W1 .... 3C 20 (3C 74)
............................(not continuous)
Aquarelle Ho. EC1 .... 1F 9 (2E 63)
Aquarius Bus. Pk.
  NW2 .... 3C 28
............................(off Priestley Way)
Aquarius Golf Course 4E 107
Aqua Vista Sq. E3 .... 4C 66
............................(off Bow Comn. La.)
Aquila St. NW8 .... 1F 59
Aquinas St. SE1 .... 2C 24 (2C 76)
Arabella Ct. NW8 .... 1E 59
............................(off Marlborough Pl.)
Arabella Dr. SW15 .... 2A 98
Arabella St. SE16 .... 4C 78
Arabian Ho. E1 .... 3A 66
............................(off Ernest St.)
Arabin Rd. SE4 .... 2A 108
Aragon Ct. SE11 .... 1C 90
............................(off Hotspur St.)
Aragon Ho. E16 .... 2C 82
............................(off Capulet M.)
Aragon Twr. SE8 .... 5B 80
Aral Ho. E1 .... 3F 65
............................(off Ernest St.)
Aran Lodge NW6 .... 4C 44
............................(off Woodchurch Rd.)
Aran M. N7 .... 4C 48
............................(off St Clements Cl.)
Arapiles Ho. E14 .... 5F 67
............................(off Blair St.)
Arbery Rd. E3 .... 2A 66
Arbon Ct. N1 .... 5E 49
............................(off Linton St.)
Arbor Ct. N16 .... 4F 35
Arboretum Ct. N1 .... 3F 49
............................(off Dove Rd.)
Arborfield Cl. SW2 .... 1B 118
Arborfield Ho. E14 .... 1C 80
............................(off E. India Dock Rd.)
Arbor Ho. SE14 .... 2B 94
Arbot Ho. SE10 .... 5A 82
............................(off Manilla Wlk.)
Arbour Ho. E1 .... 5F 65
............................(off Arbour Sq.)
Arbour Sq. E1 .... 5F 65
Arbury Ter. SE26 .... 3C 120
Arbuthnot Rd. SE14 .... 5F 93
Arbutus St. E8 .... 5B 50
Arcade, The E20 .... 3E 53
............................(within Westfield Shop. Cen.)
Arcade, The EC2 .... 1D 19 (4A 64)
............................(off Liverpool St.)
Arcade, The N7 .... 1A 48
............................(off Macready Pl.)
Arcadia Ct. E1 .... 2F 19 (5B 64)
............................(off Old Castle St.)
Arcadian Pl. SW18 .... 5B 100
Arcadia St. E14 .... 5C 66
ArcelorMittal Orbit 4D 53
AR Cen. 2A 66
............................(off Rhondda Gro.)
AR Cen. 4D 11 (3A 64)
............................(off Worship St.)
Archangel St. SE16 .... 3F 79
Archbishop's Pl. SW2 .... 5B 104
Archdale Cl. W12 .... 2D 71
Archdale Ho. SE1 ......5D 27 (4A 78)
............................(off Long La.)
Archdale Rd. SE22 .... 3B 106
Archel Rd. W14 .... 2B 86

Archer Apts. N1 .... 1A 64
............................(off Fern Cl.)
Archer Ho. N1 .... 5A 50
............................(off Whitmore Est.)
Archer Ho. SE14 .... 4A 94
Archer Ho. SW11 .... 4F 87
Archer Ho. W11 .... 1B 72
............................(off Westbourne Gro.)
Archer M. SW9 .... 4A 104
Archers Lodge SE16 .... 1C 92
............................(off Culloden Cl.)
Archer Sq. SE14 .... 2A 94
Archer St. W1 .... 4B 14 (1F 75)
Archery Cl. W2 .... 5A 60
Archery Flds. Ho.
  WC1 .... 1A 8 (2C 62)
............................(off Wharton St.)
Archery Steps W2 .... 1A 74
............................(off St George's Flds.)
Arches, The SW8 .... 2A 90
Arches, The E16 .... 3A 68
Arches, The NW1 .... 4D 47
Arches, The SE8 .... 2A 94
Arches, The SW8 .... 3F 89
Arches, The
  WC2 .... 1E 23 (2A 76)
............................(off Villiers St.)
Arches La. SW11 .... 2D 89
Archibald M. W1 ....5C 12 (1D 75)
Archibald Rd. N7 .... 1F 47
Archibald St. E3 .... 2C 66
Archie St. SE1 ....4E 27 (3A 78)
Arc Ho. SE1 .... 4F 27 (3B 78)
............................(off Tanner St.)
Arch St. SE1 .... 5F 25 (4E 77)
ARCHWAY 4E 33
Archway Bus. Cen. N19 .... 5F 33
Archway Bus Station 4E 33
Archway Cl. SW19 .... 3D 115
Archway Cl. W10 .... 4F 57
Archway Leisure Cen. 4E 33
Archway Mall N19 .... 4E 33
Archway M. SW15 .... 2A 100
............................(off Putney Bri. Rd.)
Archway Rd. N19 .... 3E 33
Archway Rd. N6 .... 1C 32
Archway St. SW13 .... 1A 98
Arcola St. E8 .... 2B 50
Arcola Theatre 2B 50
Arctic St. NW5 .... 2D 47
Arcus Rd. BR1: Broml 5A 124
Ardbeg Rd. SE24 .... 3F 105
Arden Ct. Gdns. N2 .... 1F 31
Arden Cres. E14 .... 5C 80
Arden Est. N1 .... 1A 64
Arden Ho. N1 .... 1D 11 (1A 64)
............................(off Arden Est.)
Arden Ho. SE11 .... 5B 76
............................(off Black Prince Rd.)
Arden Ho. SE13 .... 1D 109
............................(off Thurston Rd.)
Arden Ho. SW9 .... 5A 90
............................(off Grantham Rd.)
Ardent Ho. E3 .... 1A 66
............................(off Roman Rd.)
Ardfillan Rd. SE6 .... 1F 123
Ardgowan Rd. SE6 .... 5A 110
Ardilaun Rd. N5 .... 1E 49
Ardleigh Rd. N1 .... 3A 50
Ardley Cl. NW10 .... 5A 28
Ardley Cl. SE6 .... 3A 122
Ardlui Rd. SE27 .... 2E 119
Ardmere Rd. SE13 .... 4F 109

Ardoch Rd. SE6 .... 2F 123
Ardshiel Cl. SW15 .... 1F 99
Ardwell Rd. SW2 .... 2A 118
Ardwick Rd. NW2 .... 1C 44
Arena Bus. Cen. N4 .... 1E 35
Arena Ho. E3 .... 1C 66
............................(off Lefevre Wlk.)
Arena Shop. Pk. 1D 35
Arena Twr. E14 .... 3D 81
Ares Ct. E14 .... 5C 80
............................(off Homer Dr.)
Arethusa Ho. E14 .... 5C 80
............................(off Cahir St.)
Argall Av. E10 .... 2F 37
Argall Way E10 .... 3F 37
Argent Ct. E14 .... 4C 66
............................(off Thomas Rd.)
Argenton Twr. SW18 .... 4D 101
............................(off Mapleton Cres.)
Argo Apts. E16 .... 5B 68
............................(off Sylvia Pankhurst St.)
Argo Bus. Cen. NW6 .... 2C 58
Argon M. SW6 .... 3C 86
Argon Ct. SW9 .... 4C 90
............................(off Caldwell St.)
Argos Ho. E2 .... 1D 65
............................(off Old Bethnal Grn. Rd.)
Argosy Ho. SE8 .... 5A 80
Argyle Ho. E14 .... 4E 81
Argyle Pl. W6 .... 5D 71
Argyle Rd. E1 .... 3F 65
Argyle Rd. E15 .... 1A 54
Argyle Rd. E16 .... 5D 69
Argyle Sq. WC1 .... 1E 7 (2A 62)
............................(not continuous)
Argyle St. WC1 .... 1D 7 (2A 62)
Argyle Wlk. WC1 ...... 2D 7 (2A 62)
Argyle Way SE16 .... 1C 92
Argyll Cl. SW9 .... 1B 104
Argyll Ct. SW2 .... 5A 104
............................(off New Pk. Rd.)
Argyll Mans. SW3 .... 2F 87
Argyll Mans. W14 .... 5A 72
............................(off Hammersmith Rd.)
Argyll Rd. W8 .... 3C 72
Argyll St. W1 .... 3F 13 (5E 61)
Argyll Ter. SW19 .... 5F 99
Arica Ho. SE16 .... 4D 79
............................(off Slippers Pl.)
Arica Rd. SE4 .... 2A 108
Ariel Apts. E16 .... 5C 68
Ariel Ct. SE11 .... 5D 77
Ariel Ho. E1 .... 1C 78
............................(off Vaughan Way)
Ariel Rd. NW6 .... 3C 44
Ariel Way W12 .... 2E 71
Aristotle Rd. SW4 .... 1F 103
Arizona Bldg. SE13 .... 4D 95
............................(off Deal's Gateway)
Ark, The W6 .... 1F 85
............................(off Talgarth Rd.)
Arkindale Rd. SE6 .... 3E 123
Arkley Cres. E17 .... 1B 38
Arkley Rd. E17 .... 1B 38
Arklow Ho. SE17 .... 2F 91
Arklow Rd. SE14 .... 2B 94
Arkwright Rd. NW3 .... 2E 45
Arlesey Cl. SW15 .... 3A 100
Arlesford Rd. SW9 .... 1A 104
Arlidge Ho. EC1 .... 5C 8 (4C 62)
............................(off Kirby St.)
Arlingford Rd. SW2 .... 3C 104
Arlington Av. N1 .... 1E 63
Arlington Bldg. E3 .... 1C 66
Arlington Cl. SE13 .... 3F 109

Arlington Ho. EC1......1C **8** (2C **62**)
...................(off Arlington Way)
Arlington Ho. SE8...............2B **94**
...................(off Evelyn St.)
Arlington Ho. SW1...1F **21** (2E **75**)
Arlington Ho. W12...............2D **71**
...................(off Tunis Rd.)
Arlington Lodge SW2.......2B **104**
Arlington Rd. SE13...........3F **109**
Arlington Pl. SE10.............3E **95**
Arlington Rd. NW1.............5D **47**
Arlington Sq. N1...................5E **49**
Arlington St. SW1...1F **21** (2E **75**)
Arlington Way EC1....1C **8** (2C **62**)
Armada Ct. SE8...................2C **94**
Armadale Rd. SW6.............3C **86**
Armada St. SE8...................2C **94**
Armagh Rd. E3...................5B **52**
Arments Ct. SE5...................2F **91**
...................(off Albany Rd.)
Arminger Rd. W12..............2D **71**
Armitage Ho. NW1..............4A **60**
...................(off Lisson Gro.)
Armitage Rd. NW11............3A **30**
Armitage Ho. SE10.............1B **96**
Armour Cl. N7.......................3B **48**
Armoury, The........................1A **46**
...................(off Pond St.)
Armoury Ho. E3..................5A **52**
...................(off Gunmakers La.)
Armoury Ho. SE8................5D **95**
Armoury Way SW18...........3C **100**
Armsby Ho. E1.....................4E **65**
...................(off Stepney Way)
Armstrong Cl. SE3.............2D **111**
Armstrong Ho. E14.............5A **66**
...................(off Commercial Rd.)
Armstrong Rd. NW10.........4A **42**
Armstrong Rd. SW7............4F **73**
Armstrong Rd. W3..............2B **70**
Arnal Cres. SW18...............5A **100**
Arncliffe NW6.......................1D **59**
Arndale Wlk. SW18............3D **101**
Arne Ho. SE11.....................1B **90**
...................(off Tyers St.)
Arne St. WC2.............3E **15** (5A **62**)
Arne Wlk. SE3......................3C **97**
Arneway St. SW1.................4F **75**
Arnewood Cl. SW15...........1C **112**
Arngask Rd. SE6...............5F **109**
Arnhem Pl. E14....................4C **80**
Arnhem Way SE22..............3A **106**
Arnhem Wharf E14..............4B **80**
Arnold Cir. E2.........2F **11** (2B **64**)
Arnold Est. SE1......4F **27** (3B **78**)
...................(not continuous)
Arnold Ho. SE17..................1D **91**
...................(off Doddington Gro.)
Arnold Ho. SE3...................3E **97**
...................(off Shooters Hill Rd.)
Arnold Mans. W14..............2B **86**
...................(off Queen's Club Gdns.)
Arnold Rd. E3......................2C **66**
Arnot Ho. SE5.....................3E **91**
...................(off Comber Gro.)
Arnott Cl. W4......................5A **70**
Arnould Av. SE5.................2F **105**
Arnside Ho. SE17.................2F **91**
...................(off Arnside St.)
Arnside St. SE17..................2F **91**
Arnulf St. SE6.....................4D **123**
Arnulls Rd. SW16..............5D **119**
Arodene Rd. SW2................4B **104**
Arora Twr. SE10...................2F **81**
Arragon Ho. E8....................5F **55**

Aragon Rd. SW18..............1C **114**
Arran Ct. NW10...................5A **28**
Arran Dr. E12.......................3F **41**
Arran Ho. E14......................2E **81**
...................(off Raleana Rd.)
Arran Rd. SE6.....................2D **123**
Arran Wlk. N1.......................4E **49**
Arrival Sq. E1.......................1C **78**
Arrol Ho. SE1...........5A **26** (4E **77**)
Arrow Ct. SW5.....................5C **72**
...................(off W. Cromwell Rd.)
Arrowhead Quay E14...........3C **80**
Arrow Ho. N1.......................5A **50**
...................(off Wilmer Gdns.)
Arrow Rd. E3........................2D **67**
Arrows Ho. SE15.................3E **93**
...................(off Clifton Way)
Arrowsmith Ho. SE11...........1B **90**
...................(off Tyers St.)
Arsenal FC............................1C **48**
Arsenal Station (Underground)
....5C **34**
Arta Ho. E1...........................5E **65**
...................(off Devonport St.)
Artbrand Ho. SE1.....4D **27** (3A **78**)
...................(off Leathermarket St.)
Artemis Ct. E14...................5C **80**
...................(off Homer Dr.)
Artemis Pl. SW18................5B **100**
Artesian Cl. NW10..............4A **42**
Artesian Ho. SE1.................4B **78**
...................(off Grange Rd.)
Artesian Rd. W2..................5C **58**
Artesian Wlk. E11...............5A **40**
Arthaus Apts. E8.................3D **51**
...................(off Richmond Rd.)
Arthingworth St. E15...........5A **54**
Arthouse Crouch End.........1A **34**
Arthurdon Rd. SE4..............3C **108**
Arthur Henderson Ho. SW6...5B **86**
...................(off Fulham Rd.)
Arthur Horsley Wlk. E7.......2B **54**
...................(off Tower Hamlets Rd.)
Arthur Ho. N1.......................5A **50**
...................(off Halcomb St.)
Arthur Lovell Ct. E14..........5B **66**
...................(off Lovat Cl.)
Arthur Newton Ho. SW11...1F **101**
...................(off Winstanley Est.)
Arthur Rd. N7......................1B **48**
Arthur Rd. SW19................5B **114**
Arthur St. EC4........4C **18** (1F **77**)
Arthur Wade Ho. E2...1F **11** (2B **64**)
...................(off Baroness Rd.)
Artichoke Hill E1..................1D **79**
Artichoke M. SE5.................4F **91**
...................(off Artichoke Pl.)
Artichoke Pl. SE5................4F **91**
Artillery, The Bldg.
E1.........................1E **19** (4A **64**)
...................(off Artillery La.)
Artillery Ho. E15..................3A **54**
Artillery Ho. E3....................5A **52**
...................(off Barge La.)
Artillery La. E1........1E **19** (4A **64**)
Artillery Mans. SW1..5B **22** (4F **75**)
...................(off Victoria St.)

Artillery Pas. E1.......1E **19** (4A **64**)
...................(off Artillery La.)
Artillery Pl. SW1......5B **22** (4F **75**)
Artillery Row SW1....5A **22** (4E **75**)
Artisan Ct. E8......................3C **50**
Artisan M. NW10.................2F **57**
...................(off Warfield Rd.)
Artisan Quarter NW10.........2F **57**
...................(off Wellington Rd.)
Artizan St. E1............2E **19** (5B **64**)
...................(off Harrow Pl.)
Arts La. SE16...........5F **27** (4B **78**)
Arts Sq. E1..........................3A **66**
Arts Theatre Covent Garden
.....................................4D **15** (1A **76**)
...................(off Gt. Newport St.)
Arundel Bldgs. SE1.............4A **78**
Arundel Cl. E15...................1A **54**
Arundel Cl. SW11...............3A **102**
Arundel Cl. SE16................1D **93**
...................(off Verney Rd.)
Arundel Ct. SW13...............2D **85**
...................(off Arundel Ter.)
Arundel Ct. SW3..................1A **88**
...................(off Jubilee Pl.)
Arundel Ct. W11...................1B **72**
...................(off Arundel Gdns.)
Arundel Gdns. W11..............1B **72**
Arundel Gt. Ct. WC2.....4A **16** (1B **76**)
Arundel Gro. N16.................2C **50**
Arundel Mans. SW6.............4B **86**
...................(off Kelvedon Rd.)
Arundel Pl. N1......................3C **48**
Arundel Sq. N7....................3C **48**
Arundel St. WC2.......4A **16** (1B **76**)
Arundel Ter. SW13...............2D **85**
Arvon Rd. N5........................2C **48**
...................(not continuous)
Asbridge Ct. W6..................4D **71**
...................(off Dalling Rd.)
Ascalon Ho. SW8................3E **89**
...................(off Thessaly Rd.)
Ascalon St. SW8..................3E **89**
Ascensis Twr. SW18...........2E **101**
Ascham St. NW5.................2E **47**
Ascot Ct. NW8.....................2F **59**
...................(off Grove End Rd.)
Ascot Ho. NW1.........1E **5** (2D **61**)
...................(off Redhill St.)
Ascot Ho. W9.......................3C **58**
...................(off Harrow Rd.)
Ascot Lodge NW6................5D **45**
Ascot Rd. N15.....................1F **35**
Ashanti M. SE17..................2E **51**
Ash Av. SE17......................5E **77**
Ashbee Ho. E2.....................2E **65**
...................(off Portman Pl.)
Ashbourne Ct. E5................1A **52**
Ashbourne Gro. SE22........2B **106**
Ashbourne Gro. W4.............1A **84**
Ashbridge Rd. E11..............2A **40**
Ashbridge St. NW8..............3A **60**
Ashbrook Rd. N19...............3F **33**
Ashburn Gdns. SW7............5E **73**
Ashburnham Gro. SE10.......3D **95**
Ashburnham Mans. SE10....3E **87**
...................(off Ashburnham Rd.)
Ashburnham M. SW1..........5F **75**
...................(off Regency St.)
Ashburnham Pl. SE10.........3D **95**
Ashburnham Retreat SE10...3D **95**
Ashburnham Rd. NW10.......2E **57**
Ashburnham Rd. SW10.......3E **87**
Ashburnham Twr. SW10......3E **87**
...................(off Worlds End Est.)

Ashburn Pl. SW7.....................5E 73
Ashburn Ent. Cen.
　SW15....................................4E 99
ASHBURTON GROVE.............1C 48
Ashburton Ho. SW9................3B 58
　.................................(off Fernhead Rd.)
Ashburton Pl. W1......1E 21 (2D 75)
Ashburton Rd. E16.................5C 68
Ashburton Ter. E13................1C 68
Ashburton Triangle N5..........1C 48
Ashbury Pl. SW19.................5E 115
Ashbury Rd. SW11...............1B 102
Ashby Ct. NW8........................3F 59
　.......................................(off Pollitt Dr.)
Ashby Gro. N1........................4E 49
　....................................(not continuous)
Ashby Ho. N1..........................4E 49
　......................................(off Essex Rd.)
Ashby Ho. SW9......................5D 91
Ashby M. SE4.........................5B 94
Ashby M. SW2.......................3A 104
　...................................(off Prague Pl.)
Ashby Rd. SE4........................5B 94
Ashbys Ct. E3.........................1B 66
　.................................(off Centurion La.)
Ashby St. EC1...............2E 9 (2D 63)
Aschurch Gro. W12...............4C 70
Aschurch Pk. Vs. W12...........4C 70
Aschurch Ter. W12................4C 70
Ashcombe Ho. E3....................2D 67
　.......................................(off Bruce Rd.)
Ashcombe Pk. NW2.................5A 28
Ashcombe Rd. SW19............5C 114
Ashcombe St. SW6................5D 87
Ashcroft Ho. SW8...................4E 89
　.................................(off Wadhurst Rd.)
Ashcroft Sq. W6.....................5E 71
Ashdale Ho. N4.......................2F 35
Ashdale Rd. SE12.................1D 125
Ashdene SE15.........................3D 93
Ashdon Rd. NW10...................5B 42
Ashdown Cres. NW5................2C 46
Ashdown Wlk. E14..................5C 80
Ashdown Way SW17..............2C 116
Ashenden Rd. E5.....................2A 52
Ashen Gro. SW19..................3C 114
Ashentree Ct. EC4......3C 16 (5C 62)
　.................................(off Whitefriars St.)
Asher Way E1..........................1C 78
Ashfield Ct. SW9....................5A 90
　.................................(off Clapham Rd.)
Ashfield Ho. W14....................1B 86
　.........................(off W. Cromwell Rd.)
Ashfield Rd. N4......................1E 35
Ashfield Rd. W3......................2B 70
Ashfield St. E1........................4D 65
　....................................(not continuous)
Ashfield Yd. E1........................4E 65
Ashford Cl. E17.......................1B 38
Ashford Ct. NW2.....................1F 43
Ashford Ho. SE8.....................2B 94
Ashford Pas. NW2...................1F 43
Ashford Rd. NW2....................1F 43
Ashford St. N1..............1D 11 (2A 64)
Ash Gro. E8.............................5D 51
　....................................(not continuous)
Ash Gro. SW12.......................1F 43
Ash Gro. SE12.......................1C 124
Ashgrove Ct. W9.....................4C 58
　.................................(off Elmfield Way)
Ashgrove Ho. SW1..................1F 89
　...................................(off Lindsay Sq.)
Ashgrove Rd. BR1: Bromi....5F 123
Ash Ho. E14............................3E 81
　...............................(off E. Ferry Rd.)

Ash Ho. SE1............................5B 78
　.............................(off Longfield Est.)
Ash Ho. W10...........................3A 58
　.................................(off Heather Wlk.)
Ashington Ho. E1....................3D 65
　....................................(off Barnsley St.)
Ashington Rd. SW6................5B 86
Ashlake Rd. SW16................4A 118
Ashland Pl. W1...........5B 4 (4C 60)
Ashleigh Commercial Est.
　SE7......................................4E 83
Ashleigh M. SE15...................1B 106
　.................................(off Oglander Rd.)
Ashleigh Point SE23...........3F 121
Ashleigh Rd. SW14................1A 98
Ashley Ct. E3..........................2E 67
　.................................(off Bolinder Way)
Ashley Ct. SW9........................5B 90
　.................................(off Morpeth Ter.)
Ashley Cres. SW11.................1C 102
Ashley Gdns.
　SW1.....................5A 22 (4E 75)
　....................................(not continuous)
Ashley Pl. SW1.........5F 21 (4E 75)
　....................................(not continuous)
Ashley Rd. E7.........................4E 55
Ashley Rd. N19.......................3A 34
Ashley Rd. SW19....................5D 115
Ashlin Rd. E15.........................1F 53
Ashlone Rd. SW15..................1E 99
Ashmead Bus. Cen. E16........3F 67
Ashmead Ho. E9......................2A 52
　.................................(off Homerton Rd.)
Ashmead M. SE8....................5C 94
Ashmead Rd. SE8...................5C 94
Ashmere Gro. SW2................2A 104
Ash M. NW5............................2E 47
Ashmill St. NW1......................4A 60
Ashmole Pl. SW8....................2B 90
Ashmole St. SW8....................2B 90
Ashmore NW1.........................4F 47
　.......................................(off Agar Gro.)
Ashmore Cl. SE15..................3B 92
Ashmore Ho. W14...................4A 72
　......................................(off Russell Rd.)
Ashmore Rd. W9.....................1B 58
Ashmount Est. N19.................2F 33
Ashmount Rd. N19..................2E 33
Ashness Rd. SW11................3B 102
Ashpark Ho. E14....................5B 66
　.................................(off Norbiton Rd.)
Ash Rd. E15............................2A 54
Ashtead Rd. E5........................2C 36
Ashton Hgts. SE23................1E 121
Ashton Ho. SE11.....................1D 91
　.................................(off Cottington St.)
Ashton Ho. SW9......................3C 90
Ashton Reach SE16................5A 80
Ashton Rd. E15.......................2F 53
Ashton St. E14........................1E 81
Ash Tree Ho. SE5....................3E 91
　.......................................(off Pitman St.)
Ashurst Gdns. SW2................1C 118
Ashvale Ct. E3.........................1C 66
　.................................(off Matilda Gdns.)
Ashvale Rd. SW17..................5B 116
Ashview Apts. N4....................2E 35
　.................................(off Katherine Cl.)
Ashville Rd. E11......................4F 39
Ashwater Rd. SE12................1C 124
Ashwin St. E8..........................3B 50
Ashworth Cl. SE5....................5F 91
Ashworth Mans. W9................2D 59
　...................................(off Elgin Av.)
Ashworth Rd. W9....................2D 59

Aske Ho. N1...............1D 11 (2A 64)
　.................................(off Fanshaw St.)
Asker Ho. N7...........................1A 48
Aske St. N1................1D 11 (2A 64)
Askew, The Bldg.
　EC1..........................1F 17 (4E 63)
　.........................(off Bartholomew Cl.)
Askew Cres. W12....................3B 70
Askew Rd. W12.......................3B 70
Askham Ct. W12......................2C 70
Askham Rd. W12.....................2C 70
Askill Dr. SW15.......................3A 100
Asland Rd. E15........................5A 54
Aslett St. SW18......................5D 101
Asman Ho. N1..........................1D 63
　.................................(off Colebrooke St.)
Asmara Rd. NW2.....................2A 44
Asmuns Hill NW11..................1C 30
Asmuns Pl. NW11....................1B 30
Asolando Dr. SE17..................5E 77
Aspect Ct. E14........................3E 81
　.................................(off Manchester St.)
Aspect Ct. SW6.......................5E 87
Aspen Cl. N19..........................4E 33
Aspen Gdns. W6......................1D 85
Aspen Ho. E15.........................2A 68
　...................................(off Teasel Way)
Aspen Ho. SE15......................2E 93
　.................................(off Sharratt St.)
Aspenlea Rd. W6.....................2F 85
Aspen Lodge W8......................4D 73
　.....................................(off Abbots Wlk.)
Aspen Way E14.......................1D 81
Aspern Gro. NW3....................2A 46
Aspinall Rd. SE4......................1F 107
　....................................(not continuous)
Aspinden Rd. SE16................5D 79
Aspland Gro. E8......................3D 51
　.................................(off Amhurst Rd.)
Aspley Ho. SW18....................3D 101
Asquith Ho. SW1.....................4F 75
　.......................................(off Monck St.)
Assam St. E1...........................5C 64
　.................................(off White Church La.)
Assata M. N1...........................3D 49
Assembly Ho. SE14................2B 94
　.......................................(off Arklow Rd.)
Assembly Apts. SE15..............4E 93
　.......................................(off York Gro.)
Assembly Pas. E1...................4E 65
Astbury Bus. Pk.
　SE15....................................4E 93
Astbury Ho. SE11....................4C 76
　.................................(off Lambeth Wlk.)
Astbury Rd. SE15....................4E 93
Astell Ho. E14.........................5A 68
　.......................................(off Lyell St.)
Astell Ho. SW3.......................1A 88
　.......................................(off Astell St.)
Astell Rd. SE3.........................2E 111
Astell St. SW3........................1A 88
Aster Ct. E5.............................4E 37
　.................................(off Woodmill Rd.)
Asterid Hgts. E20....................2E 53
　.................................(off Liberty Bri. Rd.)
Aster Pl. E9.............................4E 51
　.................................(off Frampton Pk. Rd.)
Aste St. E14............................3E 81
Astey's Row N1.......................4E 49
Astle St. SW11........................5C 88
Astley Av. NW2.......................2E 43
Astley Ho. SE1........................1B 92
　.................................(off Rowcross St.)
Astley Ho. SW13.....................2D 85
　.....................................(off Wyatt Dr.)

Astley Ho. W2............................4C 58
..........................(off Furnival St.)
Aston Ho. EC4..........1B 16 (4C 62)
..........................(off Furnival St.)
Aston Ho. SW8...............................4F 89
Aston Ho. W11............................1B 72
..........................(off Westbourne Gro.)
Aston M. W10...............................2F 57
Aston St. E14...............................4A 66
Aston Ter. SW12.......................4D 103
Astonville St. SW18.................1C 114
Aston Webb Ho.
SE1...................2D 27 (2A 78)
..........................(off Tooley St.)
Astor Coll. W1..........5A 6 (4E 61)
..........................(off Charlotte St.)
Astor Ct. E16.................................5E 69
..........................(off Ripley Rd.)
Astor Ct. SW6.................................3E 87
..........................(off Maynard Cl.)
Astoria Ct. E8.................................4B 50
..........................(off Queensbridge Rd.)
Astoria Mans. SW16..................3A 118
Astoria Wlk. SW9....................1C 104
Astra Ho. E3.................................2B 66
..........................(off Alfred St.)
Astra Ho. SE14..............................2B 94
..........................(off Arklow Rd.)
Astral Ho. E1.............1E 19 (4A 64)
..........................(off Middlesex St.)
Astral Ho. SE6...........................4E 123
Astrop M. W6.................................4E 71
Astrop Ter. W6...............................3E 71
Astwood M. SW7.........................5E 73
Asylum Rd. SE15.........................3D 93
Atalanta St. SW6...........................3F 85
Atelier Ct. SE8.................................3C 94
..........................(off Watson's St.)
Atelier Ct. Central E14...........4E 67
..........................(off Leven Rd.)
Atelier Ct. Nth. E14...............4E 67
..........................(off Leven Rd.)
Atelier Ct. Sth. E14...............4E 67
..........................(off Leven Rd.)
Atheldene Rd. SW18.........1D 115
Athelney St. SE6.......................3C 122
Athelstane Gro. E3....................1B 66
Athelstane M. N4...........................3C 34
Athelstan Gdns. NW6...............4A 44
Athelstan Ho. E9.........................2B 52
..........................(off Homerton Rd.)
Athena Ct. SE1..........4D 27 (4A 78)
..........................(off City Wlk.)
Athenaeum Ct. N5........................1E 49
Athene Pl. EC4.........2C 16 (5C 62)
..........................(off Thavie's Inn)
Athenia Ho. E14...........................5F 67
..........................(off Blair St.)
Athenlay Rd. SE15....................3F 107
Athens Gdns. W9...........................3C 58
..........................(off Harrow Rd.)
Atherden Rd. E5...........................1E 51
Atherfold Rd. SW9..................1A 104
Atherstone Ct. W2........................4D 59
..........................(off Delamere Ter.)
Atherstone M. SW7....................5E 73
Atherton Dr. SW19..................4F 113
Atherton Leisure Cen.............3B 54
Atherton M. E7.............................3B 54
Atherton Rd. E7.............................3B 54
Atherton Rd. SW13....................3C 84
Atherton St. SW11......................5A 88
Athlone Cl. E5.................................2D 51
Athlone Ho. E1...............................5E 65
..........................(off Sidney St.)

Athlone Pl. W10............................4A 58
Athlone Rd. SW2........................5B 104
Athlone St. NW5.........................3C 46
Atholl Ho. W9.................................2E 59
..........................(off Maida Vale)
Athol Sq. E14.................................5E 67
Atkin Bldg. WC1.........5A 8 (4B 62)
..........................(off Raymond Bldgs.)
Atkins Ct. E3.................................5B 52
..........................(off Willow Tree Cl.)
Atkins Lodge W8...........................3C 72
..........................(off Thornwood Gdns.)
Atkinson Ct. E10...........................2D 39
..........................(off Kings Cl.)
Atkinson Ho. E13...........................3B 68
..........................(off Sutton Rd.)
Atkinson Ho. E2............................1C 64
..........................(off Pritchards Rd.)
Atkinson Ho. SE17.......................5F 77
..........................(off Catesby St.)
Atkinson Ho. SW11...................4C 88
..........................(off Austin Rd.)
Atkinson Morley Av. SW17.3F 115
Atkinson Rd. E16...........................4E 69
Atkins Rd. E10...............................1D 39
Atkins Rd. SW12........................5E 103
Atkins Sq. E8.................................2D 51
..........................(off Deal's Gateway)
Atlanta Bldg. SE13....................4D 95
..........................(off Deal's Gateway)
Atlanta Ho. SE16...........................4A 80
..........................(off Brunswick Quay)
Atlantic Apts. E16......................1C 82
..........................(off Seagull La.)
Atlantic Bldg. E15........................2F 53
..........................(off Property Row)
Atlantic Ct. E14.............................1F 81
..........................(off Jamestown Way)
Atlantic Ct. SW3...........................1B 88
Atlantic M. SW9...........................2C 104
Atlantic Wharf E1.........................1F 79
..........................(off Jardine Rd.)
Atlas Bus. Cen. NW2..................3D 29
Atlas Gdns. SE7...........................5E 83
Atlas M. E8.....................................3B 50
Atlas M. N7.....................................3B 48
Atlas M. SE13...............................2F 109
Atlas Rd. E13.................................1C 68
Atlas Rd. NW10...........................2A 56
Atlas Wharf E9.............................3C 52
Atney Rd. SW15...........................2A 100
Atrium, The W12...........................2F 71
Atrium Apts. N1............................5F 49
..........................(off Felton St.)
Atrium Hgts. SE8.........................2D 95
..........................(off Creekside)
Atrium Ho. SE8.............................3B 94
Atterbury Rd. N4...........................1C 34
Atterbury St. SW1.......................5A 76
Attewood Av. NW10..................5A 28
Attilburgh Ho. SE1.......5F 27 (4B 78)
..........................(off St Saviour's Est.)
Attleborough Ct. SE23............2D 120
Attneave St. WC1.........2B 8 (2C 62)
Attock M. E17...............................1D 39
Attwood La. SE10.........................5A 82
Atunbi Ct. NW1.............................4E 47
..........................(off Farrier St.)
Atwater Cl. SW2.........................1C 118
Atwell Cl. E10...............................1D 39
Atwell Rd. SE15.............................5C 92
Atwood Ho. W14...........................5B 72
..........................(off Beckford Cl.)
Atwood Rd. W6.............................5D 71
Aube Ho. SE6...............................4E 123
Aubers Ridge Ct. E3....................1B 66
..........................(off Festubert Pl.)

Aubert Ct. N5.................................1D 49
Aubert Pk. N5.................................1D 49
Aubert Rd. N5.................................1D 49
Aubrey Beardsley Ho. SW1....5E 75
..........................(off Vauxhall Bri. Rd.)
Aubrey Mans. NW1...................4A 60
..........................(off Lisson St.)
Aubrey Moore Point E15.......1E 67
..........................(off Abbey La.)
Aubrey Pl. NW8.............................1E 59
Aubrey Rd. N8.................................1A 34
Aubrey Rd. W8...............................2B 72
Aubrey Wlk. W8.............................2B 72
Auburn Cl. SE14...........................3A 94
Aubyn Hill SE27.........................4E 119
Aubyn Sq. SW15...........................3C 98
Auckland Hill SE27...................4E 119
Auckland Ho. W12.......................1D 71
..........................(off White City Est.)
Auckland Rd. E10.........................5D 39
Auckland Rd. SW11..................2A 102
Auckland St. SE11........................1B 90
Auden Pl. NW1...............................5C 46
Audley Cl. SW11..........................1C 102
Audley Dr. E16...............................2D 83
Audley Rd. NW4............................1C 28
Audley Sq. W1.....1D 20 (2C 74)
Audrey St. E2.................................1C 64
Augers La. N1.................................4C 48
Augusta La. N1..............................4C 48
Augusta St. E14...........................5D 67
Augustine Bell Twr. E3.............1C 66
..........................(off Pancras Way)
Augustine Rd. W14.......................4F 71
Augustus Bldg. E1.......................5D 65
..........................(off Tarling St.)
Augustus Cl. W12.........................3D 71
Augustus Ct. SE1...........................5A 78
..........................(off Old Kent Rd.)
Augustus Ct. SW16...................2F 117
Augustus Ho. NW1......1E 5 (1D 61)
..........................(off Augustus St.)
Augustus Rd. SW19..................1F 113
Augustus St. NW1......1E 5 (1D 61)
Aulay Ho. SE16.............................4B 78
Aulton Pl. SE11.............................1C 90
Aura Ct. SE15.................................2D 107
Aurelia Ho. E20.............................2E 53
..........................(off Sunrise Cl.)
Auriga M. N1.................................2F 49
Auriol Ho. W12..............................2D 71
..........................(off Ellerslie Rd.)
Auriol Mans. W14.........................5A 72
..........................(off Edith Rd.)
Auriol Rd. W14...............................5A 72
Aurora Apts. EC1.......1F 9 (2E 63)
..........................(off Bollinder Pl.)
Aurora Apts. SW18......................3C 100
..........................(off Buckhold Rd.)
Aurora Bldg. E14...........................2E 81
..........................(off Blackwall Way)
Aurora Bldg., The
N1.......................1C 10 (2F 63)
..........................(off East Rd.)
Aurora Gdns..................................2D 89
Aurora Ho. E14.............................5D 67
..........................(off Kerbey St.)
Aurora Ho. S6..............................4E 123
Aurora Point SE8...........................5B 80
..........................(off Grove St.)
Austen Ho. NW6...........................2C 58
..........................(off Cambridge Rd.)
Austen Ho. SW17........................3F 115
..........................(off St George's Gro.)
Austin Cl. SE23...........................5A 108

Austin Ct. E6 ....5E **55**
Austin Ct. SE15 ....1C **106**
.............................(off Peckham Rye)
Austin Friars EC2 ...2C **18** (5F **63**)
Austin Friars Sq. EC2 2C **18** (5F **63**)
.............................(off Austin Friars)
Austin Ho. SE14 ....3B **94**
.............................(off Achilles St.)
Austin Rd. SW11 ....4C **88**
Austin St. E2 ....2F **11** (2B **64**)
Austin Ter. SE1 ....5C **24** (4C **76**)
.............................(off Morley St.)
Australian War Memorial
.............................3C **20** (3C **74**)
Australia Rd. W12 ....1D **71**
Austral St. SE11 ....5D **77**
Autumn Cl. SW19 ....5E **115**
Autumn Gro. BR1: Broml 5D **125**
Autumn St. E3 ....5C **52**
Avalon Cl. SE8 ....2A **124**
Avalon Rd. SW6 ....4D **87**
Avantgarde Pl. E1 ....3F **11** (3B **64**)
.............................(off Sclater St.)
Avantgarde Twr. E1..3F **11** (3B **64**)
.............................(off Sclater St.)
Avarn Rd. SW17 ....5B **116**
Avebury Ct. N1 ....5F **49**
.............................(off Imber St.)
Avebury Ct. SE16 ....5E **79**
.............................(off Debnams Rd.)
Avebury Rd. E11 ....3F **39**
Avebury St. N1 ....5F **49**
Aveline St. SE11 ....1C **90**
Ave Maria La. EC4 ......3E **17** (5D **63**)
Avenell Mans. N5 ....1D **49**
Avenell Rd. N5 ....5D **35**
Avenfield Ho. W1 .....1A **10** (2B **74**)
.............................(off Park La.)
Avening Rd. SW18 ....5C **100**
Avening Ter. SW18 ....5C **100**
Avenir Ho. E15 ....3F **53**
.............................(off Forrester Way)
Avenons Rd. E13 ....3C **68**
Avenue, The E11 ....1D **41**
Avenue, The E3 ....3D **67**
.............................(off Devas St.)
Avenue, The EC2 ......2E **19** (5A **64**)
Avenue, The NW6 ....5F **43**
Avenue, The SE10 ....3F **95**
Avenue, The SW18 ....5A **102**
Avenue, The SW4 ....2C **102**
Avenue, The W4 ....4A **70**
Avenue Cl. NW8 ....5A **46**
.............................(not continuous)
Avenue Cl. NW2 ....5B **30**
Avenue Cl. SW3 ....5B **74**
.............................(off Draycott Av.)
Avenue Gdns. SW14 ....1A **98**
Avenue Ho. NW10 ....1D **57**
.............................(off All Souls Av.)
Avenue Ho. NW6 ....4A **44**
.............................(off The Avenue)
Avenue Ho. NW8 ....1A **60**
.............................(off Allitsen Rd.)
Avenue Lodge NW8 ....4F **45**
.............................(off Avenue Rd.)
Avenue Mans. NW3 ....2D **45**
.............................(off Finchley Rd.)
Avenue Pk. Rd. SE27 ....2D **119**
Avenue Rd. E7 ....1D **55**
Avenue Rd. N15 ....1F **35**
Avenue Rd. N6 ....2E **33**
Avenue Rd. NW10 ....1B **56**
Avenue Rd. NW3 ....4F **45**
Avenue Rd. NW8 ....4F **45**

Avenue Studios SW3 ....5F **73**
.............................(off Sydney Cl.)
Averill St. W6 ....2F **85**
Avershaw Ho. SW15 ....3F **99**
Avery Farm Row SW1 ....5C **74**
Avery Row W1 ....4D **13** (1D **75**)
Avery Wlk. SW11 ....1C **102**
Aviary Cl. E16 ....4B **68**
Avigdor M. N16 ....4F **35**
Avignon Rd. SE4 ....1F **107**
Avington Ct. SE1 ....5A **78**
.............................(off Old Kent Rd.)
Avis Sq. E1 ....5F **65**
Avoca Rd. SW17 ....4C **116**
Avocet Cl. SE1 ....1C **92**
Avon Ct. SW15 ....3A **100**
Avon Ct. W9 ....4C **58**
.............................(off Elmfield Way)
Avondale Av. NW2 ....5A **28**
Avondale Ct. E11 ....3A **40**
Avondale Ct. E16 ....4A **68**
Avondale Cres. IG4: Ilf 1F **41**
Avondale Ho. SE1 ....1C **92**
.............................(off Avondale Sq.)
Avondale Mans. SW6 ....4B **86**
.............................(off Rostrevor Rd.)
Avondale Pk. Gdns. W11 ....1A **72**
Avondale Pk. Rd. W11 ....1A **72**
Avondale Pavement SE1 ....1C **92**
Avondale Ri. SE15 ....1B **106**
Avondale Rd. E16 ....4A **68**
Avondale Rd. E17 ....2C **38**
Avondale Rd. N15 ....1D **35**
Avondale Rd. SW14 ....1A **98**
Avondale Rd. SW19 ....5D **115**
Avondale Sq. SE1 ....1C **92**
Avongrove Ct. EC1 ...1A **10** (2E **63**)
.............................(off Bollinder Pl.)
Avon Ho. W14 ....5B **72**
.............................(off Kensington Village)
Avon Ho. W8 ....4C **72**
.............................(off Allen St.)
Avonhurst Ho. NW2 ....4A **44**
Avonley Rd. SE14 ....3E **93**
Avonmore Gdns. W14 ....5B **72**
Avonmore Mans. W14 ....5A **72**
.............................(off Avonmore Rd.)
Avonmore Pl. W14 ....5A **72**
.............................(off Avonmore Rd.)
Avonmouth Apts. SW11 ....2A **102**
.............................(off Monarch Sq.)
Avonmouth St.
........................SE1 ......5F **25** (4E **77**)
Avon Rd. SE4 ....1C **108**
Avro Cl. E9 ....2A **52**
.............................(off Mabley St.)
Avro Ho. SW8 ....3D **89**
.............................(off Havelock Ter.)
Axio Way E3 ....4C **66**
Axis Apts. E1 ....3F **11** (3B **64**)
.............................(off Sclater St.)
Axis Ct. SE10 ....2A **96**
.............................(off Woodland Cres.)
Axis Ct. SE16 ....3C **78**
.............................(off East La.)
Axis Ho. SE13 ....2E **109**
.............................(off Lewisham High St.)
Axminster Rd. N7 ....5A **34**
Aybrook St. W1 ....1B **12** (4C **60**)
Aycliffe Ho. SE17 ....2F **91**
.............................(off Portland St.)
Aycliffe Rd. W12 ....2C **70**
Ayerst Ct. E10 ....2E **39**
Aylesbury Cl. E7 ....3B **54**

Aylesbury Ho. SE15 ....2C **92**
.............................(off Friary Est.)
Aylesbury Rd. SE17 ....1F **91**
Aylesbury St. EC1 ....4D **9** (3D **63**)
Aylesford Ho. SE1 ....4C **26** (3F **77**)
.............................(off Long La.)
Aylesford St. SW1 ....1F **89**
Aylestone Av. NW6 ....4F **43**
Aylmer Ct. N2 ....1B **32**
Aylmer Ho. SE10 ....1F **95**
Aylmer Pde. N2 ....1B **32**
Aylmer Rd. E11 ....3B **40**
Aylmer Rd. N2 ....1A **32**
Aylmer Rd. W12 ....3B **70**
Aylton Est. SE16 ....3E **79**
Aylward Rd. SE23 ....2F **121**
Aylward St.
........................E1: Lon Jamaica St. 5E **65**
Aylward St.
........................E1: Lon Jubilee St. 5E **65**
Aylwin Est. SE1 ....5E **27** (4A **78**)
Aynhoe Mans. W14 ....5F **71**
.............................(off Aynhoe Rd.)
Aynhoe Rd. W14 ....5F **71**
Ayres Cl. E13 ....2C **68**
Ayres St. SE1 ....3A **26** (3E **77**)
Ayrsome Rd. N16 ....5A **36**
Ayrton Gould Ho. E2 ....2F **65**
.............................(off Roman Rd.)
Ayrton Rd. SW7 ....4F **73**
Aysgarth Rd. SE21 ....5A **106**
Ayston Ho. SE16 ....5F **79**
.............................(off Plough Way)
Aytoun Pl. SW9 ....5B **90**
Aytoun Rd. SW9 ....5B **90**
Azalea Ho. SE14 ....3B **94**
.............................(off Achilles St.)
Azania M. NW5 ....3D **47**
Azenby Rd. SE15 ....5B **92**
Azof St. SE10 ....5A **82**
Azov Ho. E1 ....3A **66**
.............................(off Commodore St.)
Azura Ct. E15 ....5E **53**
.............................(off Warton Rd.)
Azure Bldg. E15 ....4F **53**
.............................(off Gt. Eastern Rd.)
Azure Ho. E2 ....2C **64**
.............................(off Buckfast St.)

Baalbec Rd. N5 ....2D **49**
Babbage Ct. SE17 ....2D **91**
.............................(off Cook's Rd.)
Babbage Point SE10 ....2D **95**
.............................(off Norman Rd.)
Babell Ho. N1 ....3D **49**
.............................(off Canonbury Rd.)
Babington Ct. WC1....5E **7** (4A **62**)
.............................(off Orde Hall St.)
Babington Ho.
........................SE1 ......3A **26** (3F **77**)
.............................(off Disney St.)
Babington Rd. SW16 ....5F **117**
Babmaes St. SW1 ....5B **14** (1F **75**)
Bache's St. N1 ....1C **10** (2F **63**)
Back All. EC3 ....3E **19** (5A **64**)
.............................(off Lloyd's Av.)
Back Church La. E1 ....5C **64**
Back Hill EC1 ....4B **8** (3C **62**)
Backhouse Pl. SE17 ....5A **78**
Back La. N8 ....1A **34**
Back La. NW3 ....1E **45**
Back Rd. E11 ....1A **40**
Bacon Gro. SE1 ....4B **78**

Bacon's College Sports Cen.

....2A 80
Bacons La. N6.....................................3C 32
Bacon St. E1.......................3F 11 (3B 64)
Bacton St. E2......................................3B 64
Bacton NW5..2C 46
Bacton St. E2......................................2C 65
Baddesley Ho. SE11................1B 90
......................................(off Jonathan St.)
Baden Pl. SE1........3B 26 (3F 77)
Baden Powell Ho. SE........5E 73
....(off Queen's La.)
Bader Way SW15....................4C 98
Badger Cl. NW2....................................5E 29
Badminton M. E16.................................2C 82
Badminton Rd. SW12.............4C 102
Badric Cl. SW11....................................5F 87
Badsworth Rd. SE5................4E 91
Baffin Way E14....................................2E 81
Bagley's La. SW6..................4D 87
Bagley Wlk. N1.....................................5F 47
Bagnigge Ho. WC1......2B 8 (2C 62)
....(off Margery St.)
Bagshot Ho. NW1.........1E 5 (2D 61)
....(off Redhill St.)
Bagshot St. SE17....................1A 92
Bahram Ct. E2......................................3D 65
....(off Three Colts La.)
Baildon E1..1E 65
....(off Cyprus St.)
Baildon St. SE8....................................3B 94
Bailey Cotts. E14................4A 66
....(off Maroon St.)
Bailey Ho. E3..2D 67
....(off Talwin St.)
Bailey Ho. SW10.................3D 87
....(off Coleridge Gdns.)
Bailey M. SW2......................................3C 104
Bailey Pl. N16......................................2A 50
Bailey St. SE26....................5F 121
Baileys Ho. SW11...............3F 89
....(off Charles Clowes Wl.k)
Bailey St. SE8.......................................5A 80
Bailey Twr. E14...................................1D 79
Bainbridge Ct. SE10.............4C 82
....(off Rennie Street)
Bainbridge St. WC1..2C 14 (5F 61)
Baird Cl. E10..3C 38
Baird Gdns. SE19.................4A 120
Baird Ho. W12......................................1D 71
....(off White City Est.)
Baird St. EC1........................3A 10 (3E 63)
Baizdon Rd. SE3....................5A 96
Baker Ho. E3...2D 67
....(off Bromley High St.)
Baker Ho. WC1.......................4E 7 (3A 62)
....(off Colonnade)
Baker Pas. NW10.................5A 42
Baker Rd. NW10....................5A 42
Bakers Av. E17....................................1D 39
Baker's Fld. N7.....................................1F 47
Bakers Hall Ct.

EC3....................5D 19 (1A 78)
....(off Harp La.)
Bakers Hill E5.......................................3E 37
Bakers La. N6.......................................1B 32
Baker's M. W1..........2B 12 (5C 60)
Bakers Pas. NW3.................1E 45
....(off Heath St.)
Baker's Rents E2....1F 11 (2B 64)
Baker's Row E15.................1A 68
Baker's Row EC1........4B 8 (3C 62)
Baker St. NW1......................4A 4 (3B 60)
Baker St. W1...........4A 4 (4B 60)
BAKER STREET................4A 4 (4B 60)

Baker Street Station

(Underground)..........4A 4 (3B 60)
Baker's Yd. EC1....................4B 8 (3C 62)
....(off Bakers Rd.)
Bakery Cl. SW9....................................3B 90
Bakery Pl. SW11..................2B 102
Bakery St. SE16....................5F 27 (4B 78)
Balaam Leisure Cen............3C 68
Balaam St. E13....................................3C 68
Balaclava Rd. SE1................5B 78
Bala Grn. NW9.....................................1A 28
....(off Ruthin Cl.)
Balboa Ct. E14....................................4A 66
....(off Pechora Way)
Balchen Rd. SE3..................5F 97
Balchier Rd. SE22................4D 107
Balcombe Ho. NW1.............3A 60
....(off Taunton Pl.)
Balcombe St. NW1...............3B 60
Balcony, The W12................2F 71
Balcorne St. E9.....................................4E 51
Balder Ri. SE12...................2D 125
Balderton Flats

W1.........................3C 12 (5C 60)
....(off Balderton St.)
Balderton St. W1..................3C 12 (5C 60)
Baldock St. E3.......................................1D 67
Baldrey Ho. SE10.................1B 96
....(off Blackwall La.)
Baldwin Cres. SE5................4E 91
Baldwin Ho. SW2.................1C 118
Baldwin St. SW11................4C 102
Baldwins Gdns. EC1......5B 8 (4C 62)
Baldwin St. EC1..................2B 10 (2F 63)
Baldwin Ter. N1....................1E 63
Balearic Apts. E16................1C 82
....(off Western Gateway)
Bale Rd. E1...4A 66
Balfern Gro. W4....................1A 84
Balfern St. SW11..................5A 88
Balfe St. N1...1A 62
Balfour Ho. W10..................4C 88
....(off Forfar Rd.)
Balfour Ho. W10..................4F 57
....(off St Charles Sq.)
Balfour M. W1.........1C 20 (2C 74)
Balfour Pl. SW15.................2D 99
Balfour Pl. W1.........5C 12 (1C 74)
Balfour Rd. N5......................................1E 49
Balfour St. SE17...................5F 77
Balfron Twr. E14...................5E 67
Balgove Ct. NW10................3D 43
....(off Eden Gro.)
BALHAM..............................1C 116
Balham Gro. SW12...............5C 102
Balham High Rd. SW12.......1C 116
Balham High Rd. SW17.......3C 116
Balham Hill SW12.................5D 103
Balham Leisure Cen............2D 117
Balham New Rd. SW12.......5D 103
Balham Pk. Rd. SW12.........1B 116
Balham Station (Rail &

Underground).................1D 117
Balham Sta. Rd. SW12.......1D 117
Balin Ho. SE1........3B 26 (3F 77)
....(off Long La.)
Balladier Wlk. E14...............4D 67
Ballamore Rd. BR1: Broml....3C 124
Ballance Rd. E9.....................3F 51
Ballantine St. SW18.............2E 101
Ballantrae Ho. NW2............1B 44
Ballard Ho. SE10..................2D 95
....(off Thames St.)
Ballards Rd. NW2.................4C 28
Ballast Quay SE10................1F 95

Ballater Rd. SW2..............2A 104
Ball Ct. EC3............................3C 18 (5F 63)
....(off Birchin La.)
Balletica Apts. WC2..3K 15 (5A 62)
....(off Long Acre)
Ballina St. SE23...................5F 107
Ballin Ct. E14.......................................3E 81
....(off Stewart St.)
Ballingdon Rd. SW11...........4C 102
Ballinger Point E3.................2D 67
....(off Bromley High St.)
Balliol Rd. W10....................................5E 57
Balloch Rd. SE6...................1F 123
Ballogie Av. NW10...............1A 42
Ballow Cl. SE5......................................3A 92
Balls Pond Pl. N1................................3F 49
Balls Pond Rd. N1...............................3F 49
Balman Ho. SE16.................5F 79
....(off Rotherhithe New Rd.)
Balmer Rd. E3..1B 66
Balmes Rd. N1......................................5F 49
Balmoral Apts. W2.............4A 60
....(off Praed St.)
Balmoral Cl. SW15...............4F 99
Balmoral Ct. NW8................1F 59
....(off Queen's Ter.)
Balmoral Ct. SE12...............4D 125
Balmoral Ct. SE16................2F 79
....(off King & Queen Wharf)
Balmoral Ct. SE17................1F 91
....(off Merrow St.)
Balmoral Ct. SE27................4E 119
Balmoral Ho. E14.................4D 81
....(off Lanark Sq.)
Balmoral Ho. E16.................2D 83
....(off Keats Av.)
Balmoral Ho. SE1.....2E 27 (2B 78)
....(off Duchess Wlk.)
Balmoral Ho. W14...............5A 72
....(off Windsor Way)
Balmoral M. W12.................4B 70
Balmoral Rd. E10.................4D 39
Balmoral Rd. E7....................1E 55
Balmoral Rd. NW2...............3D 43
Balmore Cl. E14...................5E 67
Balmore St. N19...................4D 33
Balmuir Gdns. SW15...........2E 99
Balnacraig Av. NW10...........1A 42
Balniel Ga. SW1...................1F 89
Balsam Ho. E14....................1D 81
....(off E. India Dock Rd.)
Baltic Apts. E16....................1C 82
....(off Western Gateway)
Baltic Ct. E1..2E 79
....(off Clave St.)
Baltic Cl. SE16......................................3F 79
Baltic Ho. SE5......................................5E 91
Baltic Pl. N1..5A 50
Baltic St. E. EC1.......4F 9 (3E 63)
Baltic St. W. EC1......4F 9 (3E 63)
Baltimore Ct. SW1...............5F 75
....(off Vauxhall Bri. Rd.)
Baltimore Ho. SE11..............5C 76
....(off Hotspur St.)
Baltimore Ho. SW18............1E 101
Baltimore Wharf E14............4D 81
Balvaird Pl. SW1..................1F 89
Balvernie Gro. SW18...........5B 100
Balvernie M. SW18...............5C 100
Bamber Rd. SE15.................4B 92
Bamboo Ct. E5......................................4E 37
....(off Woodmill Rd.)
Bamborough Gdns. W12.....3E 71
Bamford Rd. BR1: Broml....5E 123
Bampton Rd. SE23...............3F 121

Banbury Ct. WC2......4D 15 (1A 76)
..................................(off Long Acre)
Banbury Rd. E9.........................4F 51
Banbury Rd. E9.........................4F 51
Banbury St. SW11..................5A 88
Banchory Rd. SE3...................3D 97
Bancroft Ct. SW8....................3A 90
..........................(off Allen Edwards Dr.)
Bancroft Ho. E1..........................3E 65
..................................(off Cephas St.)
Bancroft Rd. E1.........................2E 65
Banfield Rd. SE15..................1D 107
Bangalore St. SW15...............1E 99
Bangla Ho. E8........................5B 50
..................................(off Clarissa St.)
Banim St. W6...........................5D 71
Banister Ho. E9........................2F 51
Banister Ho. SW8...................4E 89
..............................(off Wadhurst Rd.)
Banister Ho. W10....................2A 58
..............................(off Bruckner St.)
Banister Ho. NW6....................4D 45
Banister Ho. W10....................2F 57
Bank, The N6..........................3D 33
Bank End SE1.............1A 26 (2E 77)
Bankfoot Rd. BR1: Broml 4A 124
Bankhurst Rd. SE6................5B 108
Bank La. SW15.........................3A 98
Bank of England Mus.
...............................3B 18 (5F 63)
..........................(off Bartholomew La.)
Bank of England Sports Cen.
....3A 98
Banks Ho. SE1...........5F 25 (4E 77)
..............................(off Rockingham St.)
Bankside SE1............5F 17 (1E 77)
..............................(not continuous)
Bankside Av. SE13.................1E 109
Bankside Gallery.....5E 17 (1D 77)
Bankside Lofts SE1... 1E 25 (2D 77)
..................................(off Hopton St.)
Bankside Pier (River Bus &
Tours).........................5F 17 (1E 77)
Bankside Pl. N4........................1E 35
Bankside Way SE19..............5A 120
Bank Station (Underground &
DLR).......................3B 18 (5F 63)
Bank St. E14............................2D 81
Bankton Rd. SW2.................2C 104
Bankwell Rd. SE13................2A 110
Bannatyne Health Club Grove
Park...................................2D 125
Bannatyne Health Club Maida
Vale.....................................1D 59
..............................(off Greville Rd.)
Bannatyne Health Club Russell
Square.........................3C 6 (3F 61)
..................................(off Woburn Pl.)
Banner Ct. SE16.......................5E 79
..........................(off Rotherhithe New Rd.)
Banner Ho. EC1.........4A 10 (3E 63)
..................................(off Roscoe St.)
Bannerman Ho. SW8...............2B 90
Banner St. EC1..........4A 10 (3E 63)
Banning St. SE10....................1A 96
Bannister Cl. SW2.................1C 118
Bannister Ho. SE14.................2F 93
..........................(off John Williams Cl.)
Bannon Ct. SW6......................4D 87
..................................(off Michael Rd.)
Banqueting House
..........................2D 23 (2A 76)
Banstead Ct. W12.....................1B 70
Banstead St. SE15.................1E 107
Banting Ho. NW2....................5C 28

Bantock Ho. W10.....................2A 58
..................................(off Third Av.)
Bantry Ho. E1..........................3F 65
..................................(off Ernest St.)
Bantry St. SE5.........................3F 91
Banyan Ct. E16.......................2D 83
..................................(off Regalia Close)
Banyard Rd. SE16...................4D 79
Baptist Gdns. NW5.................3C 46
Baquba SE13............................5D 95
Barandon Rd. W11..................1F 71
..................................(off Grenfell Rd.)
Barandon Wlk. W11................1F 71
Barbanel Ho. E1......................3E 65
..................................(off Cephas St.)
Barbara Brosnan Ct. NW8 .....1F 59
Barbara Castle Cl. SW6.........2B 86
Barbauld Rd. N16...................5A 36
Barber Beaumont Ho. E1.......2F 65
..................................(off Bancroft Rd.)
Barberry Ct. E15.....................3A 54
Barbers All. E13......................2D 69
Barbers Rd. E15......................1D 67
Barbican EC2..............5A 10 (4E 63)
..................................(off Silk St.)
Barbican Art Gallery
..............................5A 10 (4E 63)
Barbican Arts Cen......5A 10 (4E 63)
Barbican Cinema 1 Silk St.
..............................5A 10 (4E 63)
..............................(within Arts. Cen.)
Barbican Cinema 2 & 3
Whitecross St........5A 10 (4E 63)
..............................(off Whitecross St.)
Barbican Station (Underground)
..............................5E 9 (4E 63)
Barbican Theatre London
..............................5A 10 (4E 63)
..............................(within Arts Cen.)
Barb M. W6..............................4E 71
Barbon Cl. WC1..........5E 7 (4B 62)
Barchard St. SW18.................3D 67
Barchester St. E14.................4D 67
Barclay Cl. SW6......................3C 86
Barclay Ho. E9.........................4E 51
..................................(off Well St.)
Barclay Path E17.....................1E 39
Barclay Rd. E11.......................3B 40
Barclay Rd. E13.......................3E 69
Barclay Rd. E17.......................1E 39
Barclay Rd. SW6.....................3C 86
Barcombe Av. SW2...............2A 118
Bardell Ho. SE1.......................3C 78
..................................(off Parkers Row)
Bardolph Rd. N7.......................1A 48
Bard Rd. W10...........................1F 71
Bardsey Pl. E1.........................3E 65
Bardsey Wlk. N1......................3E 49
..........................(off Douglas Rd. Nth.)
Bardsley Ho. SE10..................2E 95
..............................(off Bardsley La.)
Bardsley La. SE10...................2E 95
Barents Ho. E1.........................3F 65
..........................(off White Horse La.)
Barfett St. W10........................3B 58
Barfield Rd. E11.......................3B 40
Barfleur La. SE8......................5B 80
Barford Ho. E3.........................1B 66
..................................(off Tredegar Rd.)
Barford St. N1..........................5C 48
Barforth Rd. SE15.................1D 107
Barge Ho. St. SE1......1C 24 (2C 76)
Barge La. E3............................5A 52
Bargery Rd. SE6....................1D 123
Barge Wlk. SE10......................4B 82

Bargrove Cres. SE6...............2B 122
Barham Ho. SE17....................1A 92
..............................(off Kinglake Est.)
Baring Cl. SE12......................2C 124
Baring Ct. N1..........................5F 49
..................................(off Baring St.)
Baring Ho. E14.........................5C 66
..................................(off Canton St.)
Baring Rd. SE12.....................5C 110
Baring St. N1...........................5F 49
Baritone Ct. E15......................5B 54
..................................(off Church St.)
Barker Dr. NW1........................4E 47
Barker Ho. SE17......................5A 78
..................................(off Congreve St.)
Barker M. SW4.......................2D 103
Barker Ho. SW4......................2E 87
Barker Wlk. SW16..................3F 117
Barkham Ter. SE1.....5C 24 (4C 76)
..................................(off Lambeth Rd.)
Barking Rd. E13.......................3C 68
Barking Rd. E16......................4A 68
Barking Rd. E6.........................1F 69
Barkis Ho. W11........................2F 71
Bark Pl. W2..............................1D 73
Barkston Gdns. SW5..............5D 73
Barkway Ct. N4........................4E 35
Barkwith Ho. SE14..................2F 93
..........................(off Cold Blow La.)
Barkworth Rd. SE16...............1D 93
Barlborough St. SE14.............3F 93
Barlby Gdns. W10...................3F 57
Barlby Rd. W10........................4E 57
Barleycorn Way E14..............1B 80
..................................(not continuous)
Barley Cl. S...............................4E 37
Barley Shotts Bus. Pk. W10...4B 58
Barley Wlk. SW18..................3D 101
Barling NW1.............................3D 47
Barlow Dr. SE18........................1E 97
Barlow Ho. N1......1B 10 (1F 63)
..................................(off Provost Est.)
Barlow Ho. SE16.....................5D 79
..................................(off Rennie Est.)
Barlow Ho. W11.......................1A 72
..................................(off Walmer Rd.)
Barlow Pl. W1..............5E 13 (1D 75)
Barlow Rd. NW6......................3B 44
Barlow St. SE17.......................5F 77
Barmeston Rd. SE6...............2D 123
Barmouth Rd. SW18...............4E 101
Barnabas Ho. EC1.....2F 9 (2E 63)
..................................(off King Sq.)
Barnabas Lodge SW8............4A 90
..............................(off Guildford Rd.)
Barnabas Rd. E9.....................2F 51
Barnaby Ct. SE16....................3C 78
..........................(off Scott Lidgett Cres.)
Barnaby Ho. E2.......................2E 93
Barnaby Pl. SW7.....................5F 73
..............................(off Old Brompton Rd.)
Barnard Gro. E15.....................4B 54
Barnard Ho. E2.........................2D 65
..................................(off Ellsworth St.)
Barnard Lodge W9..................4C 58
..................................(off Admiral Wlk.)
Barnard M. SW11...................2A 102
Barnardo Gdns. E1..................1F 79
Barnardo St. E1........................5F 65
Barnard Rd. SW11.................2A 102
Barnards Ho. SE16..................3B 80
..................................(off Wyatt Cl.)
Barnard's Inn EC1..... 1B 16 (5C 62)
..................................(off Fetter La.)

Barnbrough NW1 ....5E **47**
(off Camden St.)
Barnby Sq. E15 ....5A **54**
Barnby St. E15 ....5A **54**
Barnby St. NW1 .....1A **6** (1E **61**)
Barn Cl. NW5 ....2F **47**
(off Torriano Av.)
Barn Elms Athletics Track....5D **85**
Barn Elms Pk. SW15 ....1E **99**
BARNES 5B **84**
Barnes Av. SW13 ....3C **84**
BARNES BRI. 5A **84**
Barnes Bridge Station (Rail)
....5B **84**
Barnes Cl. E12 ....1F **55**
Barnes Common Nature Reserve
....1C **98**
Barnes Ct. E16 ....4E **69**
Barnes Ct. N1 ....4C **48**
Barnes High St. SW13 ....5B **84**
BARNES HOSPITAL 1A **98**
Barnes Ho. E2 ....1E **65**
(off Wadeson St.)
Barnes Ho. NW1 ....4D **47**
(off Camden St.)
Barnes Ho. SE14 ....2F **93**
(off John Williams Cl.)
Barnes Station (Rail) 1C **98**
Barnes St. E14 ....5A **66**
Barnes Ter. SE8 ....1B **94**
Barnet Gro. E2 ....2C **64**
Barnett St. E1 ....5D **65**
Barney Cl. SE7 ....1E **97**
Barn Fld. NW3 ....2B **46**
Barnfield Cl. N4 ....2A **34**
Barnfield Cl. SW17 ....3F **115**
Barnfield Pl. E14 ....5C **80**
Barnham St. SE1 ....3E **27** (3A **78**)
BARNSBURY 4B **48**
Barnsbury Est. N1 ....5B **48**
(not continuous)
Barnsbury Gro. N7 ....4B **48**
Barnsbury Ho. SW4 ....4F **103**
Barnsbury Pk. N1 ....4C **48**
Barnsbury Rd. N1 ....1C **62**
Barnsbury Sq. N1 ....4C **48**
Barnsbury St. N1 ....4C **48**
Barnsbury Ter. N1 ....4B **48**
Barnsdale Av. E14 ....5D **81**
Barnsdale Rd. W9 ....3B **58**
Barnsley St. E1 ....3D **65**
Barnstaple Ho. SE10 ....3D **95**
(off Devonshire Dr.)
Barnstaple Ho. SE12 ....3B **110**
(off Taunton Rd.)
Barnstaple La. SE13 ....2E **109**
Barnston Wlk. N1 ....5E **49**
(off Popham St.)
Barn St. N16 ....4A **36**
Barnwell Ho. SE5 ....4A **92**
(off St Giles Rd.)
Barnwell Rd. SW2 ....3C **104**
Barnwood Cl. W9 ....3D **59**
Baron Cl. N1 ....1C **62**
Baroness Rd. E2 ....2F **11** (2B **64**)
Baronsclere Ct. N6 ....2E **33**
BARONS COURT 1A **86**
Baron's Ct. Rd. W14 ....1A **86**
Barons Court Station
(Underground) 1A **86**
Barons Court Theatre 1A **86**
(off Comeragh Rd.)
Barons Keep W14 ....1A **86**
Barons Lodge E14 ....5F **81**
(off Manchester Rd.)

Baronsmead Rd. SW13 ......4C **84**
Baron's Pl. SE1 .....4C **24** (3C **76**)
Baron St. N1 ....1C **62**
Baron Wlk.
E16: Lon Canning Town.....4B **68**
Baroque Gdns. SE8 ....5A **80**
(off Grand Canal Av.)
Barque M. SE8 ....2C **94**
Barquentine Hgts. SE10.....4C **82**
Barratt Ho. N1 ....4D **49**
(off Sable St.)
Barratt Ind. Pk. E3 ....3E **67**
Barret Ho. NW6 ....5C **44**
Barret Ho. SW9 ....1B **104**
(off Benedict Rd.)
Barrett Cl. SW9 ....3F **91**
(off Dobson Wlk.)
Barrett Ho. SE17 ....1E **91**
(off Browning St.)
Barrett's Gro. N16 ....2A **50**
Barrett St. W1 .....3C **12** (5C **60**)
Barrhill Rd. SW2 ....2A **118**
Barriedale SE14 ....5A **94**
Barrie St. W2 ....1F **73**
Barrie Ho. NW8 ....5A **46**
(off St Edmund's Ter.)
Barrie Ho. W2 ....1E **73**
(off Lancaster Ga.)
Barrier App. SE7 ....4F **83**
Barrier Point Rd. E16.........2E **83**
Barringer Sq. SW17 ....4C **116**
Barrington Cl. NW5 ....2C **46**
Barrington Ct. SW4 ....5A **90**
Barrington Rd. SW9 ....1D **105**
Barrow Ct. SE6 ....1B **124**
(off Cumberland Pl.)
Barrow Hill Est. NW8 ....1A **60**
(off Barrow Hill Rd.)
Barrow Hill Rd. NW8 ....1A **60**
Barrow Store Ct.
SE1 ....5D **27** (4A **78**)
(off Decima St.)
Barry Av. N15 ....1B **36**
Barry Blandford Way E3.....3D **67**
Barry Ho. SE16 ....5D **79**
(off Rennie Est.)
Barry Pde. SE22 ....3C **106**
Barry Rd. SE22 ....4C **106**
Barset Rd. SE15 ....1E **107**
(not continuous)
Barston Rd. SE27 ....3E **119**
Barstow Cres. SW2 ....1B **118**
Barter St. WC1 .....1E **15** (4A **62**)
Bartholomew Cl.
EC1 ....1E **17** (4E **63**)
(not continuous)
Bartholomew Cl. SW18......2E **101**
Bartholomew Ct. E14.........1F **81**
(off Newport Av.)
Bartholomew Ct.
EC1 ....1A **10** (3E **63**)
(off Old St.)
Bartholomew Ho. W10.......3A **58**
(off Appleford Rd.)
Bartholomew La.
EC2 ....2C **18** (5F **63**)
Bartholomew Pl. EC1 1F **17** (4E **63**)
(off Bartholomew Cl.)
Bartholomew Rd. NW5.......3E **47**
Bartholomew Sq. E1 ....3D **65**
Bartholomew Sq.
EC1 ....2A **10** (2E **63**)
Bartholomew St. SE1 ....4F **77**
Bartholomew Vs. NW5.......3E **47**
Bartle Rd. W11 ....5A **58**

Bartlett Cl. E14 ....5C **66**
Bartlett Ct. EC4 .....2C **16** (5C **62**)
Bartlett M. E14 ....1D **95**
Bartletts Pas. EC4 ..2C **16** (5C **62**)
(off Fetter La.)
Bartok Ho. W11 ....2B **72**
(off Lansdowne Wlk.)
Barton Cl. E9 ....2F **51**
Barton Cl. SE15 ....1D **107**
Barton Ct. W14 ....1A **86**
(off Baron's Ct. Rd.)
Barton Ho. E3 ....2D **67**
(off Bow Rd.)
Barton Ho. N1 ....4D **49**
(off Sable St.)
Barton Ho. SW6 ....1D **101**
(off Wandsworth Bri. Rd.)
Barton M. E14 ....3D **81**
Barton M. SW19 ....5E **115**
Barton Rd. W14 ....1A **86**
Barton St. SW1 .....5D **23** (4A **76**)
Bartonway NW8 ....5F **45**
(off Queen's Ter.)
Bartram Rd. SE4 ....3A **108**
Bartrip St. E9 ....3B **52**
Barts & The London School
of Medicine & Dentistry
Whitechapel Campus 4D **65**
(off Turner St.)
Barville Cl. SE4 ....2A **108**
Barwell Ho. E2 ....3C **64**
(off Menotti St.)
Barwick Rd. E7 ....1D **55**
Bascombe St. SW2 ....4C **104**
Baseline Bus. Studios W11 ...1F **71**
(off Barandon Wlk.)
Basevi Way SE8 ....2D **95**
Bashley Rd. NW10 ....3A **56**
Basildon Ct. W1......5C **4** (4C **60**)
(off Devonshire Rd.)
Basil Gdns. SE27 ....5E **119**
Basil Ho. E1 ....5C **64**
(off Henriques St.)
Basil Ho. SW8 ....3A **90**
(off Wyvil Rd.)
Basilica M. SW12 ....4C **102**
Basilica E3 ....1B **66**
Basil Mans. SW3 ....4A **20** (3B **74**)
(off Basil St.)
Basil St. SW3 ....5A **20** (4B **74**)
Basin App. E14 ....5A **66**
Basing Ct. SE15 ....4B **92**
Basingdon Way SE5...........2F **105**
Basinghall Av. EC2 ..1B **18** (5F **63**)
Basinghall St. EC2...1A **18** (5F **63**)
Basing Hill NW11 ....3B **30**
Basing Ho. Yd. E2 ...1E **11** (2A **64**)
Basing Pl. E2.........1E **11** (2A **64**)
Basing St. W11 ....5B **58**
Basin Mill Apts. E2 ....5B **50**
(off Laburnum St.)
Basire St. N1 ....5E **49**
Baskerville Gdns. NW10 ....1A **42**
Baskerville Rd. SW18 ....5A **102**
Basket Gdns. SE9 ....3F **111**
Baslow Wlk. E5 ....1F **51**
Basnett Rd. SW11 ....1C **102**
Basque Ct. SE16 ....3F **79**
(off Garter Way)
Bassano St. SE22 ....3B **106**
Bass Cl. E15 ....5B **54**
(off Plaistow Rd.)
Bassein Pk. Rd. W12 ....3B **70**
Bassett Ho. SW19 ....5D **115**

Bassett La. E20.........................4C 52
Bassett Rd. W10.......................5F 57
Bassett St. NW5........................3C 46
Bassingbourn Ho. N1................4C 48
..............................(off The Sutton Est.)
Bassingham Rd. SW18...........5E 101
Bassishaw Highwalk
EC2...........................1B 18 (4F 63)
..............................(off London Wall)
Bass M. SE22.............................2C 106
Basswood Cl. SE15...................1D 107
Basterfield Ho. EC1... 4F 9 (3E 63)
..............................(off Golden La. Est.)
Bastion Highwalk
EC2...........................1A 18 (4E 63)
..............................(off London Wall)
Bastion Ho. EC2.......1A 18 (4E 63)
..............................(off London Wall)
Bastwick St. EC1.....3E 9 (3E 63)
Basuto Rd. SW6.........................4C 86
Batavia Ho. SE14.....................3A 94
..............................(off Batavia Rd.)
Batavia M. SE14........................3A 94
Batavia Rd. SE14......................3A 94
Batchelor St. N1.......................5C 48
Bateman Ho. SE17....................2D 91
..............................(off Otto St.)
Bateman M. SW4......................4F 103
Bateman's Bldgs.
W1..........................3B 14 (5F 61)
..............................(off Bateman St.)
Bateman's Row
EC2..........................3E 11 (3A 64)
Bateman St. W1........3B 14 (5F 61)
Bate St. E14..............................1B 80
Bath Cl. SE15.............................3D 93
Bath Ct. EC1: Lon St Luke's Est.
..............................2B 10 (2F 63)
..............................(off St Luke's Est.)
Bath Ct. EC1: Lon Warner St.
..............................4B 8 (3C 62)
..............................(off Warner St.)
Bath Ct. SE26...........................3C 120
..............................(off Droitwich Cl.)
Bathgate Ho. SW9...................4D 91
..............................(off Lothian Rd.)
Bathgate Rd. SW19.................3F 113
Bath Gro. E2..............................1C 64
..............................(off Horatio St.)
Bath Ho. E2................................3C 64
..............................(off Ramsey St.)
Bath Ho. SE1............5A 26 (4E 77)
..............................(off Bath Ter.)
Bath Pl. EC2...............2D 11 (2A 64)
Bath Pl. W6................................1E 85
..............................(off Peabody Est.)
Bath Rd. E7................................3F 55
Bath Rd. W4...............................5A 70
Baths Ct. W12............................3D 71
Bath St. EC1...............2A 10 (2E 63)
Bath Ter. SE1.............5F 25 (4E 77)
Bathurst Gdns. NW10..............1D 57
Bathurst Ho. W12.....................1D 71
..............................(off White City Est.)
Bathurst M. W2.........................5F 59
Bathurst St. W2........................1F 73
Batley Pl. N16............................5B 36
Batley Rd. N16............................5B 36
Batman Cl. W12........................2D 71
Batoum Gdns. W6....................4E 71
Batsford Ho. SW19..................4D 115
..............................(off Durnsford Rd.)
Batson Ho. E1.............................5C 64
..............................(off Fairclough St.)
Batson St. W12..........................3C 70

Battenberg Wlk. SE19.............5A 120
Batten Cotts. E14.....................4A 66
..............................(off Maroon St.)
Batten Ho. SW4.........................3E 103
Batten Ho. W10.........................2A 58
..............................(off Third Av.)
Batten St. SW11.......................1A 102
Battersby Rd. SE6....................2F 123
BATTERSEA..................................4C 88
Battersea Arts Cen...................1B 102
..............................(off Lavender Hill)
BATTERSEA BRI............................3F 87
Battersea Bri. Rd. SW11......3A 88
Battersea Bus. Cen.
SW11........................1C 102
Battersea Bus. Pk. SW8.......4E 89
Battersea Church Rd.
SW11.........................4F 87
Battersea Dogs' Home...........3D 89
Battersea Evolution.................3C 88
Battersea High St. SW11.......4F 87
Battersea Pk.......................(not continuous)
Battersea Pk.................................3B 88
BATTERSEA PK.............................3C 88
Battersea Pk. Children's Zoo
..............................3C 88
Battersea Pk. Millennium
Arena........................3C 88
Battersea Pk. Rd. SW11......5A 88
Battersea Pk. Rd. SW8.........4D 89
Battersea Park Station
(Rail)........................3D 89
Battersea Power Sta.
Development SW11.........2D 89
Battersea Power Station Pier
(River Bus)..................2E 89
Battersea Ri. SW11...............3A 102
Battersea Roof Gdns.
SW11........................3D 89
Battersea Sports Cen...........1F 101
Battersea Sq. SW11...............4F 87
Battersea Station
(Underground)...............3E 89
Battishill St. N1......................4D 49
Battlebridge Ct. N1...............1A 62
..............................(off Wharfdale St.)
Battle Bri. La.
SE1..........................2D 27 (2A 78)
Battle Cl. SW19.......................5E 115
Battledean Rd. N5..................2D 49
Battle Ho. SE15........................2C 92
..............................(off Haymerle Rd.)
Batty St. E1...............................5C 64
Batwa Ho. SE16.......................1D 93
Baudwin Rd. SE6....................2A 124
Baulk, The SW18.....................5C 100
Bavaria Rd. N19......................4A 34
Bavent Rd. SE5........................5E 91
Bawdale Rd. SE22..................3B 106
Bawley Ter. E15.......................5F 53
..............................(off Rick Roberts Way)
Bawtree Rd. SE14...................3A 94
Baxendale St. E2.....................2C 64
Baxter Ho. E3...........................2D 67
..............................(off Bromley High St.)
Baxter Rd. E16.........................5E 69
Baxter Rd. N1...........................3F 49
Baxter Wlk. SW16...................2F 117
Bay Ct. E1.................................3F 65
..............................(off Frimley Way)
Bayer Ho. EC1.........4F 9 (3E 63)
..............................(off Golden La. Est.)
Bayes Cl. SE26.........................5E 121
Bayes Ct. NW3..........................4B 46
..............................(off Primrose Hill Rd.)

Bayes Ho. N1.............................4C 48
..............................(off Augustas La.)
Bayfield Ho. SE4......................2F 107
..............................(off Coston Wlk.)
Bayfield Rd. SE9......................2F 111
Bayford M. E8...........................4D 51
..............................(off Bayford St.)
Bayford Rd. NW10...................2F 57
Bayford St. E8...........................4D 51
Bayford St. Bus. Cen. E8.....4D 51
..............................(off Sidworth St.)
Bayham Pl. NW1.......................5E 47
Bayham Rd. W4........................4A 70
Bayham St. NW1......................5E 47
Bay Ho. SE16.............................4A 80
Bayley St. WC1.........1B 14 (4F 61)
..............................(off Horn Link Way)
Baylis Hgts. SE10....................5C 82
Baylis Rd. SE1..........4B 24 (3C 76)
Baynard Ho. EC4.....4E 17 (1D 77)
..............................(off Queen Victoria St.)
Baynes M. NW3........................3F 45
Baynes St. NW1........................4E 47
Bayonne Rd. W6.......................2A 86
Baysixty6 Skate Pk................4B 58
..............................(off Acklam Rd.)
Bayston Rd. N16.......................5B 36
BAYSWATER...................................1E 73
Bayswater Rd. W2...................1D 73
Bayswater Station
(Underground)...............1D 73
Baythorne Ho. E16..................5B 68
..............................(off Turner St.)
Baythorne St. E3......................4B 66
Bayton Ct. E8............................4C 50
..............................(off Lansdowne Dr.)
Baytree Ct. SW2.......................2B 104
Bay Tree Ho. EC1.....4B 8 (3C 62)
..............................(off Baker's Row)
Baytree M. SE17.......................5F 77
Baytree Rd. SW2......................2B 104
Bazalgette Ho. NW8................3F 59
..............................(off Orchardson St.)
Bazalgette Wlk.
EC4..........................4C 16 (1C 76)
Bazeley Ho. SE1.......4D 25 (3D 77)
..............................(off Library St.)
Bazely St. E14..........................1E 81
BBC Broadcasting House
..............................1E 13 (4D 61)
BBC Maida Vale Studios.......3D 59
..............................(off Delaware Rd.)
BBC Studios...............................2E 71
BBC Worldwide..........................1E 71
BDA Dental Mus........1D 13 (4D 61)
Beacham Cl. SE7......................1F 97
Beachborough Rd.
BR1: Broml................................4E 123
Beachcroft Rd. E11..................5A 40
Beachcroft Way N19................3F 33
Beach Ho. SW5..........................1C 86
..............................(off Philbeach Gdns.)
Beachy Rd. E3...........................4C 52
Beacon Bingo Cricklewood....1F 43
Beacon Ga. SE4.........................1F 107
Beacon Hill N7...........................2A 48
Beacon Ho. E14........................1D 95
..............................(off Burrells Wharf Sq.)
Beacon Ho. SE5........................3A 92
..............................(off Southampton Way)
Beacon Point SE10..................2D 95
..............................(off Dowells St.)
Beacon Rd. SE13......................4F 109
Beaconsfield WC1....1F 15 (4B 62)
..............................(off Red Lion St.)

Beaconsfield Cl. SE3 .... 2C **96**
Beaconsfield Rd. E10 .... 4E **39**
Beaconsfield Rd. E16 .... 3B **68**
Beaconsfield Rd. E17 .... 1B **38**
Beaconsfield Rd. NW10 ..... 3B **42**
Beaconsfield Rd. SE17 ...... 1F **91**
Beaconsfield Rd. SE3 .... 3B **96**
Beaconsfield Rd. SW9 .... 2F **125**
Beaconsfield St. N1 .... 5A **48**
Beaconsfield Ter. Rd.
  W14 .... 4A **72**
Beaconsfield Wlk.
  SW6: Lon Parsons Green .. 4B **86**
Beacontree Rd. E11 .... 3B **40**
Beadman Pl. SE27 .... 4D **119**
Beadman St. SE27 .... 4D **119**
Beadnell Ct. E1 .... 1C **78**
  .... (off Cable St.)
Beadnell Rd. SE23 .... 1F **121**
Beadon Rd. W6 .... 5E **71**
Beak St. W1 .... 4A **14** (1E **75**)
Beale Pl. E3 .... 1B **66**
Beale Rd. E3 .... 5B **52**
Beaminster Ho. SW8 .... 3B **90**
  .... (off Dorset Rd.)
Beamish Ho. SE16 .... 5D **79**
  .... (off Rennie Est.)
Beanacre Cl. E9 .... 3B **52**
Bear All. EC4 .... 2D **17** (5D **63**)
Beardell St. SE19 .... 5B **120**
Beardsfield E13 .... 1C **68**
Bear Gdns. SE1 .... 1F **25** (2E **77**)
Bear La. SE1 .... 1E **25** (2D **77**)
Bear Pit Apts. SE1 ... 1F **25** (2E **77**)
  .... (off New Globe Wlk.)
Bearstead Ri. SE4 .... 3B **108**
Bear St. WC2 .... 4C **14** (1F **75**)
Beaton Cl. SE15 .... 4B **92**
Beatrice Cl. E13 .... 3C **68**
Beatrice Ho. W6 .... 1E **85**
  .... (off Queen Caroline St.)
Beatrice Pl. SW19 .... 5F **99**
Beatrice Pl. W8 .... 4D **73**
Beatrice Rd. E17 .... 1C **38**
Beatrice Rd. N4 .... 2C **34**
Beatrice Rd. SE1 .... 5C **78**
Beatrice Webb Ho. E3 .... 1A **66**
  .... (off Chisenhale St.)
Beatrix Apts. E3 .... 3B **66**
  .... (off English St.)
Beatrix Ho. SW5 .... 1D **87**
  .... (off Old Brompton Rd.)
Beatson Wlk. SE16 .... 2A **80**
  .... (not continuous)
Beattie Ho. SW8 .... 4E **89**
Beatty Ho. E14 .... 3C **80**
  .... (off Admirals Way)
Beatty Ho. SW1 .... 1E **89**
  .... (off Dolphin Sq.)
Beatty Rd. N16 .... 1A **50**
Beatty St. NW1 .... 1E **61**
Beauchamp Pl. SW3 .... 4A **74**
Beauchamp Rd. E7 .... 4D **55**
Beauchamp Rd. SW11 ... 2A **102**
Beauchamp St.
  EC1 .... 1B **16** (4C **62**)
Beauchamp Ter. SW15 ...... 1D **99**
Beauclerc Rd. W6 .... 4D **71**
Beauclerk Ho. SW16 .... 3A **118**
Beaufort Cl. SW15 .... 5D **99**
Beaufort Ct. E14 .... 3C **80**
  .... (off Admirals Way)
Beaufort Ct. SW6 .... 2C **86**
Beaufort Gdns. E1 .... 1F **65**
Beaufort Gdns. NW4 .... 1E **29**

Beaufort Gdns. SW3 .... 4A **74**
Beaufort Ho. E16 .... 2D **83**
  .... (off Fairfax M.)
Beaufort Ho. SW1 .... 1F **89**
  .... (off Aylesford St.)
Beaufort Ho. SW3 .... 2F **87**
  .... (off Beaufort St.)
Beaufort Mans. SW3 .... 2F **87**
Beaufort M. SW6 .... 2B **86**
Beaufort St. SW3 .... 2F **87**
Beaufort Ter. E14 .... 1E **95**
  .... (off Ferry St.)
Beaufoy Ho. SE27 .... 3D **119**
Beaufoy Ho. SW8 .... 3B **90**
  .... (off Rita Rd.)
Beaufoy Wlk. SE11 .... 5B **76**
Beaulieu Av. E16 .... 2D **83**
Beaulieu Av. SE26 .... 4D **121**
Beaulieu Cl. SE5 .... 1F **105**
Beaulieu Lodge SE14 .... 4F **81**
  .... (off Schooner Cl.)
Beaumanor Mans. W2 ...... 1D **73**
  .... (off Queensway)
Beaumaris Grn. NW9 .... 1A **28**
Beaumont W14 .... 5B **72**
  .... (off Kensington Village)
Beaumont Av. W14 .... 1B **86**
Beaumont Bldgs.
  WC2 .... 3E **15** (5A **62**)
  .... (off Martlett Ct.)
Beaumont Ct. E1 .... 2F **65**
Beaumont Ct. E5 .... 5D **37**
Beaumont Ct. NW1 .... 5F **47**
Beaumont Ct. W1 ...... 5C **4** (4C **60**)
  .... (off Beaumont St.)
Beaumont Cres. W14 .... 1B **86**
Beaumont Gdns. NW3 .... 5C **30**
Beaumont Gro. E1 .... 3F **65**
Beaumont Ho. E10 .... 2D **39**
  .... (off Skelton's La.)
Beaumont Ho. W9 .... 2B **58**
  .... (off Fernhead Rd.)
Beaumont Lodge E8 .... 3C **50**
  .... (off Greenwood Rd.)
Beaumont M. NW5 .... 2F **47**
  .... (off Charlton King's Rd.)
Beaumont M. W1 ...... 5C **4** (4C **60**)
Beaumont Pl. W1 ...... 3A **6** (3E **61**)
Beaumont Ri. N19 .... 3F **33**
Beaumont Rd. E10 .... 2D **39**
  .... (not continuous)
Beaumont Rd. E13 .... 2D **69**
Beaumont Sq. SW19 .... 5A **100**
Beaumont Sq. E1 .... 4F **65**
Beaumont St. W1 ..... 5C **4** (4C **60**)
Beaumont Ter. SE13 .... 5A **110**
  .... (off Wellmeadow Rd.)
Beaumont Wlk. NW3 .... 4B **46**
  .... (off Ferdinand St.)
Beauvale NW1 .... 4C **46**
  .... (off Ferdinand St.)
Beauval Rd. SE22 .... 4B **106**
Beaux Arts Bldg., The N7 ... 5A **34**
Beavor La. W6 .... 1C **84**
  .... (off Beavor La.)
Beavor La. W6 .... 1C **84**
Beccles St. E14 .... 5B **66**
Bechervaise Ct. E10 .... 3D **39**
  .... (off Leyton Grange Est.)
Bechtel Ho. W6 .... 5F **71**
  .... (off Hammersmith Rd.)
Beck Cl. SE13 .... 4D **95**
Beckenham Bus. Cen.
  BR3: Beck 5A **122**
Beckenham Hill Est.
  BR3: Beck 5D **123**

Beckenham Hill Rd.
  BR3: Beck 5D **123**
Beckenham Hill Rd.
  SE6 .... 5E **123**
Beckenham Hill Station (Rail)
  .... 5E **123**
Beckenham Place Pk. SE6 5E **123**
Beckers, The N16 .... 1C **50**
Becket Ho. E16 .... 2D **83**
  .... (off Constable Av.)
Becket Ho. SE1 ..... 4B **26** (3F **77**)
  .... (off Tabard St.)
Becket Ho. WC1 ...... 2E **7** (2B **62**)
  .... (off Westking Pl.)
Becket St. SE1 ...... 5B **26** (4F **77**)
Beckett Cl. NW10 .... 3A **42**
Beckett Cl. SW16 .... 2F **117**
Beckett Ho. E1 .... 4E **65**
  .... (off Jubilee St.)
Beckett Ho. SW9 .... 5A **90**
Beckfoot NW1 .... 1A **6** (1E **61**)
  .... (off Ampthill Est.)
Beckford Cl. W14 .... 5B **72**
Beckford Ho. N16 .... 2A **50**
Beckford Pl. SE17 .... 1E **91**
Beckham Ho. SE11 .... 5B **76**
  .... (off Gilbert Rd.)
Beckley Ho. E3 .... 3B **66**
  .... (off Hamlets Way)
Becklow Gdns. W12 .... 3C **70**
  .... (off Becklow Rd.)
Becklow M. W12 .... 3C **70**
  .... (off Becklow Rd.)
Becklow Rd. W12 .... 3B **70**
Beck Rd. E8 .... 5D **51**
Beck Sq. E10 .... 3A **38**
Beckton Rd. E16 .... 4B **68**
Beckway St. SE17 .... 5A **78**
  .... (not continuous)
Beckwith Ho. E2 .... 1D **65**
  .... (off Wadeson St.)
Beckwith Rd. SE24 .... 3F **105**
Beclands Rd. SW17 .... 5C **116**
Becmead Av. SW16 .... 4F **117**
Becondale Rd. SE19 .... 5A **120**
Becquerel Ct. SE10 .... 4B **82**
  .... (off West Parkside)
Bective Pl. SW15 .... 2B **100**
Bective Rd. E7 .... 1C **54**
Bective Rd. SW15 .... 2B **100**
Bedale St. SE1 ...... 2B **26** (2F **77**)
Beddalls Farm Ct. E6 .... 4F **69**
Bedefield WC1 .... 2E **7** (2A **62**)
Bede Ho. SE14 .... 4B **94**
  .... (off Clare Rd.)
Bede Sq. E3 .... 3B **66**
  .... (off Joseph St.)
Bedford Av. WC1 ..... 1C **14** (4F **61**)
Bedfordbury WC2 ..... 4D **15** (1A **76**)
  .... (not continuous)
Bedford Cl. W4 .... 2A **84**
Bedford Cnr. W4 .... 5A **70**
  .... (off South Pde.)
Bedford Ct. WC2 .... 5D **15** (1A **76**)
Bedford Ct. Mans.
  WC1 .... 1C **14** (4F **61**)
  .... (off Bedford Av.)
Bedford Gdns. W8 .... 2C **72**
Bedford Gdns. Ho. W8 .... 2C **72**
  .... (off Bedford Gdns.)
Bedford Hill SW12 .... 1D **117**
Bedford Hill SW16 .... 3E **117**
Bedford Ho. SW4 .... 2A **104**
  .... (off Solon New Rd. Est.)

Bedford M. SE6 .... 2D 123
Bedford Pk. Cnr. W4 .... 5A 70
Bedford Pk. Mans. W4 .... 5A 70
Bedford Pas. SW6 .... 3A 86
.......................(off Dawes Rd.)
Bedford Pas. W1 .... 5A 6 (4E 61)
Bedford Pl. WC1 .... 5D 7 (4A 62)
Bedford Rd. N8 .... 1F 33
Bedford Rd. SW4 .... 2A 104
Bedford Rd. W4 .... 4A 70
Bedford Row SE1 ...... 5A 26 (4E 77)
Bedford Row WC1 .... 5A 8 (4B 62)
Bedford Sq. WC1 .... 1B 14 (4F 61)
Bedford St. WC2 .... 4D 15 (1A 76)
Bedford Ter. SW2 .... 3A 104
Bedford Way WC1 ...... 4C 6 (3F 61)
Bedgebury Gdns. SW19 ...... 2A 114
Bedgebury Rd. SE9 .... 2F 111
Bedivere Rd. BR1: Broml 3C 124
Bedlam M. SE11 .... 5C 76
.................(off Walnut Tree Wlk.)
Bedmond Ho. SW3 .... 1A 88
.........................(off Cale St.)
Bedser Cl. SE11 .... 2B 90
Bedwell Ho. SW9 .... 5C 90
Beeby Rd. E16 .... 4D 69
Beech Av. W3 .... 2A 70
Beech Cl. SE8 .... 2C 94
Beech Cl. SW15 .... 5C 98
Beech Cl. SW19 .... 5E 113
Beech Ct. W9 .... 4C 58
......................(off Elmfield Way)
Beech Cres. Cl. N5 .... 1D 49
Beechcroft Av. NW11 .... 2B 30
Beechcroft Cl. SW16 .... 5B 118
Beechcroft Rd. NW11 .... 2B 30
...................(off Beechcroft Av.)
Beechcroft Rd. SW17 .... 2A 116
Beechdale Rd. SW2 .... 4B 104
Beechdene SE15 .... 4D 93
.....................(off Carlton Gro.)
Beechen Pl. SE23 .... 2F 121
Beeches Rd. SW17 .... 3A 116
Beechey Rd. E1 .... 2D 79
......................(off Watts St.)
Beechfield Rd. N4 .... 1E 35
Beechfield Rd. SE6 .... 1B 122
Beech Gdns. EC2 .... 5F 9 (4E 63)
......................(off Beech St.)
Beech Ho. SE16 .... 3E 79
......................(off Ainsty Est.)
Beechmont Cl.
   BR1: Broml 5A 124
Beechmore Rd. SW11 .... 4B 88
Beecholme Est. E5 .... 5D 37
Beech St. EC2 .... 5F 9 (4E 63)
Beech Tree Cl. N1 .... 4C 48
Beechwood Gro. W3 .... 1A 70
Beechwood Ho. E2 .... 1C 64
......................(off Teale St.)
Beechwood Pl. SE10 .... 4E 95
Beechwood Rd. E8 .... 3B 50
Beechwoods Ct. SE19 .... 5B 120
Beechworth NW6 .... 4A 44
Beechworth Cl. NW3 .... 4C 30
Beecroft La. SE4 .... 3A 108
Beecroft M. SE4 .... 3A 108
Beecroft Rd. SE4 .... 3A 108
Beefeater Distillery 1C 90
Beehive Cl. E8 .... 4B 50
Beehive Pl. SW9 .... 1C 104
Beemans Row SW18 .... 2E 115
Beeston Cl. E8 .... 2C 50
Beeston Ho. SE1 .... 5B 26 (4F 77)
......................(off Burbage Cl.)

Beeston Pl. SW1 ...... 5E 21 (4D 75)
Beethoven St. W10 .... 2A 58
Beeton Way SE27 .... 4F 119
Begbie Rd. SE3 .... 4E 97
Begonia Wlk. W12 .... 5B 56
Beirach Moshe Sq. E5 .... 4D 37
Beira St. SW12 .... 5D 103
Bekesbourne St. E14 .... 5A 66
Beldanes Lodge NW10 .... 4C 42
Belfast Rd. N16 .... 4B 36
Belfont Wlk. N7 .... 1A 48
.......................(not continuous)
Belford Ho. E8 .... 5B 50
Belford Rd. SE15 .... 5E 93
Belfry Cl. SE16 .... 1D 93
Belgrade Rd. N16 .... 1A 50
Belgrave Cl. E13 .... 3E 69
Belgrave Ct. E14 .... 1B 80
.......................(off Westferry Cir.)
Belgrave Ct. E2 .... 1D 65
.......................(off Temple St.)
Belgrave Ct. SW8 .... 3E 89
.......................(off Ascalon St.)
Belgrave Gdns. NW8 .... 5D 45
Belgrave Hgts. E11 .... 3C 40
Belgrave Ho. SW9 .... 3C 90
Belgrave Mans. NW8 .... 5D 45
Belgrave M. Nth.
   SW1 .... 4B 20 (3C 74)
Belgrave M. Sth.
   SW1 .... 5C 20 (4C 74)
Belgrave M. W.
   SW1 .... 5B 20 (4C 74)
Belgrave Pl. SW1 ...... 5C 20 (4C 74)
Belgrave Rd. E10 .... 3E 39
Belgrave Rd. E11 .... 4C 40
Belgrave Rd. E13 .... 3E 69
Belgrave Rd. E17 .... 1C 38
Belgrave Rd. SW1 .... 5D 75
Belgrave Rd. SW13 .... 3B 84
Belgrave Sq. SW1 ...... 5B 20 (4C 74)
Belgrave St. E1 .... 5E 65
Belgrave Yd. SW1 ...... 5D 21 (4D 75)
.......................(off Lwr. Belgrave St.)
BELGRAVIA 5C 20 (4C 74)
Belgravia Ct. SW1 .... 4D 75
.......................(off Ebury St.)
Belgravia Gdns.
   BR1: Broml 5A 124
Belgravia Ho. SW1 .... 5B 20 (4C 74)
.......................(off Halkin Pl.)
Belgravia Ho. SW4 .... 4F 103
Belgravia Workshops N19 ...... 4A 34
.....................(off Marlborough Rd.)
Belgrove St. WC1 ...... 1E 7 (2A 62)
Belham Wlk. SE5 .... 4F 91
Belinda Rd. SW9 .... 1D 105
Belitha Vs. N1 .... 4B 48
Bella Best Ho. SW1 .... 1D 89
.......................(off Westmoreland Ter.)
Bellamy Cl. E14 .... 3C 80
Bellamy Cl. W14 .... 1B 86
Bellamy Ho. SW17 .... 4F 115
Bellamy's Ct. SE16 .... 2F 79
.......................(off Abbotshade Rd.)
Bellamy St. SW12 .... 5D 103
Bellasis Av. SW2 .... 2A 118
Bell Dr. SW18 .... 5A 100
Bellefields Rd. SW9 .... 1B 104
Bellenden Rd. SE15 .... 4B 92
Bellenden Rd. Retail Pk. 4C 92
Belleville Ho. SE10 .... 3D 95
.......................(off Norman Rd.)
Belleville Rd. SW11 .... 3A 102

Bellevue Pde. SW17 .... 1B 116
Bellevue Pl. E1 .... 3E 65
Bellevue Rd. SW13 .... 5C 84
Bellevue Rd. SW17 .... 1A 116
Bellew St. SW17 .... 3E 115
Bellfield Cl. SE3 .... 3D 97
Bellflower Cl. E6 .... 4F 69
Bell Gdns. E10 .... 3C 38
.......................(off Church Rd.)
Bellgate M. NW5 .... 1D 47
BELL GREEN 4B 122
Bell Grn. SE26 .... 4B 122
Bell Grn. La. SE26 .... 5B 122
Bell Grn. Retail Pk. 3B 122
Bell Grn. Trade City SE6 ...... 3B 122
Bellhaven E15 .... 3F 53
Bell Ho. SE10 .... 2E 95
.......................(off Haddo St.)
Bellina M. NW5 .... 1D 47
BELLINGHAM 3D 123
Bellingham Grn. SE6 .... 3C 122
Bellingham Grn. Pk. 3C 122
.......................(off Bellingham Green)
Bellingham Leisure & Lifestyle
   Cen. 3D 123
Bellingham Rd. SE6 .... 3D 123
Bellingham Station (Rail) 3D 123
Bellingham Trad. Est. SE6 .... 3D 123
Bell Inn Yd. EC3 .... 3C 18 (5F 63)
Bell La. E1 .... 1F 19 (4B 64)
Bell La. E16 .... 2C 82
Bellmaker Ct. E3 .... 4C 66
Bell Mdw. SE19 .... 5A 120
Bell Moor NW3 .... 5E 31
Bello Cl. SE24 .... 5D 105
Bellot Gdns. SE10 .... 1A 96
.......................(off Bellot St.)
Bellot St. SE10 .... 1A 96
Bells All. SW6 .... 5C 86
Bellscroft Ct. NW3 .... 2F 45
Bell St. NW1 .... 4A 60
Bell St. SE18 .... 4F 97
Belltrees Gro. SW16 .... 5B 118
Bellwether La. SW18 .... 3D 101
.......................(off Ryland Blvd.)
Bell Wharf La. EC4 ...... 5A 18 (1E 77)
Bellwood Rd. SE15 .... 2F 107
Bell Yd. WC2 .... 3B 16 (5C 62)
Bell Yd. M. SE1 .... 4E 27 (3A 78)
Belmont Cl. SW4 .... 1E 103
Belmont Ct. N5 .... 1E 49
Belmont Ct. NW11 .... 1B 30
Belmont Gro. SE13 .... 1F 109
Belmont Hall Ct. SE13 .... 1F 109
Belmont Hill SE13 .... 1F 109
Belmont M. SW19 .... 2F 113
Belmont Pde. NW11 .... 1B 30
Belmont Pk. SE13 .... 2F 109
Belmont Pk. Cl. SE13 .... 2A 110
Belmont Pk. Rd. E10 .... 1D 39
Belmont Rd. SW4 .... 1E 103
Belmont St. NW1 .... 4C 46
Belmore Ho. N7 .... 2F 47
Belmore La. N7 .... 2F 47
Belmore St. SW8 .... 4F 89
Beloe Cl. SW15 .... 2C 98
Belsham St. E9 .... 3E 51
Belsize Av. NW3 .... 3F 45
Belsize Ct. Garages NW3 ...... 2F 45
.......................(off Belsize La.)
Belsize Cres. NW3 .... 2F 45
Belsize Gro. NW3 .... 3A 46
Belsize La. NW3 .... 3F 45
Belsize M. NW3 .... 3F 45
Belsize Pk. NW3 .... 3F 45

Belsize Pk. Gdns. NW3 ....3F 45
Belsize Pk. M. NW3 ....3F 45
Belsize Park Station
(Underground) 2A 46
Belsize Pl. NW3 ....2F 45
Belsize Rd. NW6 ....5D 45
Belsize Sq. NW3 ....3F 45
Belsize Ter. NW3 ....3F 45
Beltane Dr. SW19 ....3F 113
Belthorn Cres. SW12 ......5E 103
Belton Rd. E11 ....1A 54
Belton Rd. E7 ....4D 55
Belton Rd. NW2 ....3C 42
Belton Way E3 ....4C 66
Beltran Rd. SW6 ....5D 87
Belvedere, The
SE1 ....2A 24 (2B 76)
Belvedere, The SW10 ....4E 87
.... (off Chelsea Harbour)
Belvedere Av. SW19 ......5A 114
Belvedere Bldgs.
SE1 ....4E 25 (3D 77)
Belvedere Ct. N1 ....5A 50
.... (off De Beauvoir Cres.)
Belvedere Ct. NW2 ....3F 43
.... (off Willesden La.)
Belvedere Ct. SW15 ....2E 99
Belvedere Dr. SW19 ....5A 114
Belvedere Gdns. SE1 .3A 24 (3B 76)
Belvedere Gro. SW19 ......5A 114
Belvedere M. SE15 ....1E 107
Belvedere M. SE3 ....3D 97
Belvedere Pl. SE1 .....4E 25 (3D 77)
Belvedere Pl. SW2 ....2B 104
Belvedere Rd. E10 ....3A 38
Belvedere Rd.
SE1 ....3F 23 (3B 76)
Belvedere Row Apts. W12 ......1E 71
.... (off Fountain Park Way)
Belvedere Sq. SW19 ....5A 114
Belvoir Ho. SW1 ....5E 75
Belvoir Rd. SE22 ....5C 106
Belz Ter. E5 ....2C 36
Bembridge Cl. NW6 ....4A 44
Bembridge Ho. SE8 ....5B 80
.... (off Longshore)
Bembridge Ho. SW18 ....4D 101
.... (off Iron Mill Rd.)
Bemersyde Point E13 ....2D 69
.... (off Dongola Rd. W.)
Bemerton Est. N1 ....4A 48
Bemerton St. N1 ....5B 48
Bemish Rd. SW15 ....1F 99
Benbow Ct. W6 ....4E 71
.... (off Benbow Rd.)
Benbow Ho. SE8 ....2C 94
.... (off Benbow St.)
Benbow M. E3 ....2B 66
.... (off Tredegar Sq.)
Benbow Rd. W6 ....4D 71
Benbow St. SE8 ....2C 94
Benbury Cl. BR1: Broml 5E 123
Bence Ho. SE8 ....5A 80
.... (off Rainsborough Av.)
Bendall Ho. NW1 ....4A 60
.... (off Penfold St.)
Bendall M. NW1 ....4A 60
.... (off Bell St.)
Bendemeer Rd. SW15 ....1F 99
Benden Ho. SE13 ....3E 109
.... (off Monument Gdns.)
Bendon Valley SW18 ....5D 100
Benedict Rd. SW9 ....1B 104
Benenden Ho. SE17 ....1A 92
.... (off Mina Rd.)

Ben Ezra Ct. SE17 ....5E 77
.... (off Asolando Dr.)
Benfleet Ct. E8 ....5B 50
Bengal Ct. EC3 ....3C 18 (5F 63)
.... (off Birchin La.)
Bengeworth Rd. SE5 ....1E 105
Benham Cl. SW11 ....1F 101
Benham Ho. SW10 ....3D 87
.... (off Coleridge Gdns.)
Benham's Pl. NW3 ....1E 45
Benhill Rd. SE5 ....3F 91
Benhurst Ct. SW16 ....5C 118
Benhurst La. SW16 ....5C 118
Benin Ho. WC1 .....1F 15 (4B 62)
.... (off Procter St.)
Benin St. SE13 ....5F 109
Benjamin Cl. E8 ....5C 50
Benjamin Franklin House
.................................1D 23 (2A 76)
.... (off Craven St.)
Benjamin M. SW12 ....5E 103
Benjamin St. EC1 ......5D 9 (4D 63)
Benjamin Truman Ct. E1 ......3C 64
Ben Jonson Ct. N1 ....1A 64
Ben Jonson Ho.
EC2 ....5A 10 (4E 63)
.... (off Beech St.)
Ben Jonson Pl.
EC2 ....5A 10 (4E 63)
.... (off Beech St.)
Ben Jonson Rd. E1 ....4F 65
Benkart M. SW15 ....4C 98
Benledi Rd. E14 ....5F 67
Bennelong Cl. W12 ....1D 71
Bennerley Rd. SW11 ....3A 102
Bennet M. N19 ....5F 33
Bennet's Hill EC4 .....4E 17 (1E 77)
Bennet St. SW1 ......1F 21 (2E 75)
Bennett Ct. N7 ....5B 34
Bennett Gro. SE13 ....4D 95
Bennett Ho. SW1 ....5F 75
.... (off Page St.)
Bennett Pk. SE3 ....1B 110
Bennett Rd. E13 ....3E 69
Bennett Rd. N16 ....1A 50
Bennett Rd. SW9 ....5C 90
Bennett St. W4 ....2A 84
Bennett's Yd. SW1 ....5C 22 (4F 75)
Benn St. E9 ....3A 52
Bensbury Cl. SW15 ....5D 99
Ben Smith Way SE16 ....4C 78
Benson Av. E6 ....1E 69
Benson Ct. SW8 ....4A 90
.... (off Hartington Rd.)
Benson Ho. E2 ....3F 11 (3B 64)
.... (off Ligonier St.)
Benson Ho. SE1 ....2C 24 (2C 76)
.... (off Hatfields)
Benson Ho. W14 ....5B 72
.... (off Radnor Ter.)
Benson Quay E1 ....1E 79
Benson Rd. SE23 ....1E 121
Bentfield Gdns. SE9 ....3F 125
Benthal Rd. N16 ....4C 36
Bentham Ct. N1 ....4E 49
.... (off Ecclesbourne Rd.)
Bentham Ho. SE1 ....5B 26 (4F 77)
.... (off Falmouth Rd.)
Bentham Rd. E9 ....3F 51
Bentinck Cl. NW8 ....1A 60
Bentinck Ho. SW1 ...5C 22 (4F 75)
.... (off Monck St.)
Bentinck Ho. W12 ....1D 71
.... (off White City Est.)

Bentinck Mans. W1 ..2C 12 (5C 60)
.... (off Bentinck St.)
Bentinck M. W1 ......2C 12 (5C 60)
Bentinck St. W1 ......2C 12 (5C 60)
Bentley Cl. SW19 ....3C 114
Bentley Ct. SE13 ....2E 109
.... (off Whitburn Rd.)
Bentley Dr. NW2 ....5B 30
Bentley Ho. E3 ....3C 66
.... (off Wellington Way)
Bentley Ho. SE5 ....4A 92
.... (off Peckham Rd.)
Bentley Rd. N1 ....3A 50
Bentons La. SE27 ....4E 119
Benton's Ri. SE27 ....5F 119
Bentworth Ct. E2 ....3C 64
.... (off Granby St.)
Bentworth Rd. W12 ....5D 57
Ben Uri Gallery 5D 45
Benville Ho. SW8 ....3B 90
.... (off Dorset Rd.)
Benwell Rd. N7 ....1C 48
Benwick Cl. SE16 ....5D 79
Benworth St. E3 ....2B 66
Benyon Ct. N1 ....5A 50
.... (off De Beauvoir Est.)
Benyon Ho. EC1 ....1C 8 (2C 62)
.... (off Myddelton Pas.)
Benyon Rd. N1 ....5F 49
Benyon Wharf E8 ....5A 50
.... (off Kingsland Rd.)
Berberis Ho. E3 ....4C 66
.... (off Gale St.)
Berber Pde. SE18 ....4F 97
Berber Pl. E14 ....1C 80
Berber Rd. SW11 ....3B 102
Berebinder Ho. E3 ....1B 66
.... (off Tredegar Rd.)
Beregaria Ct. SE11 ....2C 90
.... (off Kennington Pk. Rd.)
Berenger Twr. SW10 ....3F 87
.... (off Worlds End Est.)
Berenger Wlk. SW10 ....3F 87
.... (off Worlds End Est.)
Berens Rd. NW10 ....2F 57
Beresford Ct. E9 ....2A 52
.... (off Mabley St.)
Beresford Rd. N5 ....2F 49
Beresford Ter. N5 ....2E 49
Berestede Rd. W6 ....1B 84
Bere St. E1 ....1F 79
Bergen Ho. SE5 ....5E 91
.... (off Carew St.)
Bergen Sq. SE16 ....4A 80
Berger Ct. E3 ....2E 67
.... (off Bolinder Way)
Berger Rd. E9 ....3F 51
Berghem M. W14 ....4F 71
Bergholt Cres. N16 ....2A 36
Bergholt M. NW1 ....4F 47
Berglen Ct. E14 ....5A 66
Bering Sq. E14 ....1C 94
Bering Wlk. E16 ....5F 69
Berisford M. SW18 ....4E 101
Berkeley Ct. NW1 .....4A 4 (3B 60)
.... (off Marylebone Rd.)
Berkeley Ct. NW10 ....1A 42
Berkeley Ct. NW11 ....2B 30
.... (off Ravenscroft Av.)
Berkeley Gdns. W8 ....2C 72
Berkeley Ho. E3 ....2C 66
.... (off Wellington Way)
Berkeley Ho. SE8 ....1B 94
.... (off Grove St.)
Berkeley M. W1 ....2A 12 (5B 60)

Berkeley Rd. E12 .... 2F **55**
Berkeley Rd. N15 .... 1F **35**
Berkeley Rd. N8 .... 1F **33**
Berkeley Rd. SW13 .... 4C **84**
Berkeley Sq. W1 .... 5E **13** (1D **75**)
Berkeley St. W1 .... 5E **13** (1D **75**)
Berkeley Twr. E14 .... 2B **80**
.... (off Westferry Cir.)
Berkeley Wlk. N7 .... 4B **34**
.... (off Durham Rd.)
Berkley Gro. NW1 .... 4C **46**
Berkley Rd. NW1 .... 4B **46**
Berkshire Ho. SE6 .... 4C **122**
Berkshire Rd. E9 .... 3B **52**
Berlin Ter. E15 .... 2A **54**
Bermans Way NW10 .... 1A **42**
BERMONDSEY 3F **27** (3C **78**)
Bermondsey Exchange
  SE1 .... 4E **27** (4A **78**)
.... (off Bermondsey St.)
Bermondsey Spa Gdns.
  .... 5F **27** (4B **78**)
Bermondsey Sq.
  SE1 .... 5E **27** (4A **78**)
Bermondsey Station
  (Underground) 4C **78**
Bermondsey St.
  SE1 .... 2D **27** (2A **78**)
Bermondsey Trad. Est.
  SE16 .... 1E **93**
Bermondsey Wall E.
  SE16 .... 3C **78**
Bermondsey Wall W.
  SE16 .... 3C **78**
Bermuda Way E1 .... 4A **66**
.... (off Dongola Rd.)
Bernard Angell Ho. SE10 ..... 2F **95**
.... (off Trafalgar Rd.)
Bernard Ashley Dr. SE7 ...... 1D **97**
Bernard Cassidy St. E16 ...... 4B **68**
Bernard Gdns. SW19 .... 5B **114**
Bernard Hegarty Lodge
  E8 .... 4C **50**
.... (off Lansdowne Dr.)
Bernard Ho. E1 .... 1F **19** (4B **64**)
.... (off Toynbee St.)
Bernard Mans. WC1 ..... 4D **7** (3A **62**)
.... (off Bernard St.)
Bernard Myers Ho. SE5 .... 3A **92**
.... (off Havil St.)
Bernard Rd. N15 .... 1B **36**
Bernard Shaw Ct. NW1 .... 4E **47**
.... (off St Pancras Way)
Bernard Shaw Ho. NW10 ..... 5A **42**
.... (off Knatchbull Rd.)
Bernard St. WC1 ...... 4D **7** (3A **62**)
Bernard Sunley Ho. SW9 ..... 3C **90**
.... (off Sth. Island Pl.)
Bernays Gro. SW9 .... 2B **104**
Berners Ho. N1 .... 1C **62**
.... (off Barnsbury Est.)
Berners M. W1 .... 1A **14** (4E **61**)
Berners Pl. W1 .... 2A **14** (5E **61**)
Berners Rd. N1 .... 5D **49**
Berners St. W1 .... 1A **14** (4E **61**)
Berner Ter. E1 .... 5C **64**
.... (off Fairclough St.)
Bernhard Baron Ho. E1 .... 5C **64**
.... (off Henriques St.)
Bernhardt Cres. NW8 .... 3A **60**
Berridge M. NW6 .... 2C **44**
Berridge Rd. SE19 .... 5F **119**
Berriman Rd. N7 .... 5B **34**
Berrington Ho. W2 .... 1C **72**
.... (off Herrington Rd.)

Berry Cotts. E14 .... 5A **66**
.... (off Maroon St.)
Berryfield Rd. SE17 .... 1D **91**
Berry Ho. E1 .... 3D **65**
.... (off Headlam St.)
Berry Ho. SW11 .... 5B **88**
.... (off Culvert Rd.)
Berry La. SE21 .... 4F **119**
Berryman's La. SE26 .... 4F **121**
Berry Pl. EC1 .... 2E **9** (2D **63**)
Berryside Apts. N4 .... 3E **35**
.... (off Swan La.)
Berry St. EC1 .... 3E **9** (3D **63**)
Bertal Rd. SW17 .... 4F **115**
Berthon St. SE8 .... 3C **94**
Bertie Rd. NW10 .... 3C **42**
Bertie Rd. SE26 .... 5F **121**
Bertram Rd. NW4 .... 1C **28**
Bertram St. N19 .... 4D **33**
Bertrand Ho. E16 .... 5D **68**
.... (off Russell Rd.)
Bertrand Ho. SW16 .... 3A **118**
.... (off Leigham Av.)
Bertrand St. SE13 .... 1D **109**
Berwick Ct. SE1 .... 4A **26** (3E **77**)
.... (off Swan St.)
Berwick Rd. E16 .... 5D **69**
Berwick St. W1 .... 2A **14** (5E **61**)
Berwyn Rd. SE24 .... 1D **119**
Beryl Rd. W6 .... 1F **85**
Besant Cl. NW2 .... 5A **30**
Besant Ct. N1 .... 2F **49**
Besant Ho. NW8 .... 5E **45**
.... (off Boundary Rd.)
Besant Pl. SE22 .... 2B **106**
Besant Rd. NW2 .... 1A **44**
Besant Wlk. N7 .... 4B **34**
Besford Ho. E2 .... 1C **64**
.... (off Pritchard's Rd.)
Bessborough Gdns. SW1 ..... 1F **89**
Bessborough Pl. SW1 .... 1F **89**
Bessborough St. SW15 ...... 1C **112**
Bessborough St. SW1 .... 1F **89**
Bessemer Ct. NW1 .... 4E **47**
.... (off Rochester Sq.)
Bessemer Pk. Ind. Est.
  SE24 .... 2D **105**
Bessemer Pl. SE10 .... 4B **82**
Bessemer Rd. SE5 .... 5E **91**
Bessingham Wlk. SE4 .... 2F **107**
.... (off Aldersford Cl.)
Besson St. SE14 .... 4E **93**
Bessy St. E2 .... 2E **65**
Bestwood St. SE8 .... 5F **79**
Beswick M. NW6 .... 3D **45**
Beta Pl. SW4 .... 2B **104**
Bethel Cl. NW4 .... 1F **29**
Bethell Av. E16 .... 3B **68**
Bethersden Ho. SE17 .... 1A **92**
.... (off Kinglake Est.)
Bethlehem Ho. E14 .... 1B **80**
.... (off Limehouse C'way.)
BETHNAL GREEN 2D **65**
Bethnal Green Cen. for Sports
  & Performing Arts 2B **64**
Bethnal Grn. Rd. E1 ..3F **11** (3B **64**)
Bethnal Grn. Rd. E2 ..3F **11** (3B **64**)
Bethnal Green Station
  (Overground) 3D **65**
Bethnal Green Station
  (Underground) 2E **65**
Bethune Rd. N16 .... 2F **35**
Bethune Rd. NW10 .... 3A **56**
Bethwin Rd. SE5 .... 3D **91**
Betjeman M. N5 .... 1E **49**

Betsham Ho. SE1 ...... 3B **26** (3F **77**)
.... (off Newcomen St.)
Better Gym East Village 3E **53**
Better Gym Greenwich 3A **82**
Betterton Ho. WC2 ....3E **15** (5A **62**)
.... (off Betterton St.)
Betterton St. WC2 .....3D **15** (5A **62**)
Bettons Pk. E15 .... 5A **54**
Bettridge Rd. SW6 .... 5B **86**
Betts Ho. E1 .... 1D **79**
.... (off Betts St.)
Betts M. E17 .... 1B **38**
Betts Rd. E16 .... 1D **83**
Betts St. E1 .... 1D **79**
Betty Brooks Ho. E11 ....5F **39**
Betty May Gray Ho. E14 ......5E **81**
.... (off Pier St.)
Beulah Hill SE19 .... 5D **119**
Bevan Ct. E3 .... 1C **66**
.... (off Tredegar Rd.)
Bevan Ho. N1 .... 5A **50**
.... (off Halcomb St.)
Bevan Ho. WC1 .... 5E **7** (4A **62**)
.... (off Boswell St.)
Bevan M. W12 .... 3C **70**
Bevans Ho. SW18 .... 2E **101**
.... (off Eltringham St.)
Bevan St. N1 .... 5E **49**
Bev Callender Cl. SW8 .... 1D **103**
Bevenden St. N1 ...... 1C **10** (2F **63**)
Beveridge M. E1 .... 4E **65**
Beveridge Rd. NW10 .... 4A **42**
Beverley Cl. SW11 .... 2F **101**
Beverley Cl. SW13 .... 5C **84**
Beverley Cotts. SW15 .... 3A **112**
Beverley Ct. NW6 .... 4E **45**
.... (off Fairfax Rd.)
Beverley Ct. SE4 .... 1B **108**
.... (not continuous)
Beverley Gdns. NW11 .... 2A **30**
Beverley Gdns. SW13 .... 1B **98**
Beverley Ho. BR1: Broml 5F **123**
.... (off Brangbourne Rd.)
Beverley La. SW15 .... 3B **112**
Beverley Meads & Fishponds
  Wood Nature Reserve 5B **112**
Beverley Path SW13 .... 5B **84**
Beverley Rd. E6 .... 2F **69**
Beverley Rd. SW13 .... 1B **98**
Beverley Rd. W4 .... 1B **84**
Beversbrook Rd. N19 ....5F **33**
Beverstone M. W1 .... 5A **60**
Beverstone Rd. SW2 .... 3B **104**
Beverston M. W1 ..... 1A **12** (4B **60**)
.... (off Up. Montagu St.)
Bevill Allen Cl. SW17 .... 5B **116**
Bevin Cl. SE16 .... 2A **80**
Bevin Ct. WC1 .... 1A **8** (2B **62**)
Bevington Path
  SE1 .... 4F **27** (3B **78**)
.... (off Tanner St.)
Bevington Rd. W10 .... 4A **58**
Bevington St. SE16 .... 3C **78**
Bevin Ho. E2 .... 2E **65**
.... (off Butler St.)
Bevin Ho. E3 .... 2C **66**
.... (off Alfred St.)
Bevin Sq. SW17 .... 3B **116**
Bevin Way WC1 .... 1B **8** (1C **62**)
Bevis Marks EC3 ...... 2E **19** (5A **64**)
Bew Ct. SE22 .... 5C **106**
Bewdley St. N1 .... 4C **48**
Bewick M. SE15 .... 3D **93**
Bewick St. SW8 .... 5D **89**
Bewley Ho. E1 .... 1D **79**
.... (off Bewley St.)

Bewley St. E1................1E 79
Bewlys Rd. SE27.........5D 119
Bexhill Rd. SE4..............4B 108
Bexhill Wlk. E15.............5A 54
Bexley Ho. SE4..............2A 108
Bezier Apts. EC2.....3C 10 (3F 63)
BFI Southbank......1A 24 (2B 76)
..................(off Waterloo Rd.)
Bianca Ho. N1....1D 11 (1A 64)
...................(off Crondall St.)
Bianca Rd. SE15.............2C 92
Bibury Cl. SE15..............2A 92
.......................(not continuous)
Bickels Yd. SE1....4E 27 (3A 78)
Bickenhall Mans.
   W1................5A 4 (4B 60)
..................(off Bickenhall St.)
Bickenhall St. W1.....5A 4 (4B 60)
Bickerton Rd. N19.........4E 33
Bickley Rd. E10..............2D 39
Bickley St. SW17..........5A 116
Bicknell Ho. E1.............5C 64
........................(off Ellen St.)
Bicknell Rd. SE5..........1E 105
Bicycle M. SW4.............1F 103
Bidborough St. WC1....2D 7 (2A 62)
Biddenham Ho. SE16......5F 79
.....................(off Plough Way)
Bidder St. E16..............4A 68
.......................(not continuous)
Biddesden Ho. SW3........5B 74
...................(off Cadogan St.)
Biddestone Rd. N7.........1B 48
Biddulph Mans. W9........2D 59
.......................(off Elgin Av.)
Biddulph Rd. W9............2D 59
Bideford Rd. BR1: Broml...3B 124
Bidwell St. SE15............4D 93
Big Ben...........4E 23 (3A 76)
Biggerstaff Rd. E15........5E 53
Biggerstaff St. N4..........4C 34
Biggs Row SW15............1F 99
Biggs Sq. E9..................3B 52
Big Hill E5....................3D 37
Bigland St. E1.................5D 65
Bignold Rd. E7...............1C 54
Bigwood Ct. NW11.........1D 31
Bigwood Rd. NW11........1D 31
Bilberry Ho. E3..............4C 66
.......................(off Watts Gro.)
Billingford Cl. SE4.........2F 107
Billing Ho. E1................5F 65
.......................(off Bower St.)
Billinghurst Way SE10....4C 82
Billingley W3.................4C 84
.......................(off Pratt St.)
Billing Pl. SW10.............3D 87
Billing Rd. SW10............3D 87
Billingsgate Market........2D 81
Billing St. SW10.............3D 87
Billington Rd. SE14........3A 94
Billiter St. EC3......3E 19 (5A 64)
Billson St. E14...............5E 81
Bill Voisey Ct. E14..........5A 66
.......................(off Repton St.)
Bilsby Gro. SE9.............4F 125
Bilton Towers W1...3A 12 (5B 60)
..............(off Gt. Cumberland Pl.)
Bina Gdns. SW5.............5E 73
Binbrook Ho. W10..........4E 57
.....................(off Sutton Way)
Binden Rd. W12.............4B 70
Binfield Rd. SW4............4A 90
Binfield St. N1................5A 48
.......................(not continuous)

Bingham Ct. N1..............4D 49
.....................(off Halton Rd.)
Bingham Pl. W1.....4B 4 (4C 60)
Bingham Rd. N1.............3F 49
Bingley Rd. E16.............5E 69
Binley Ho. SW15............4C 98
Binnacle Ho. E1.............2D 79
.................(off Cobblestone Sq.)
Binney St. W1.......3C 12 (5C 60)
Binnie Ho. SE1......5F 25 (4E 77)
.......................(off Bath Ter.)
Binns Rd. W4.................1A 84
Binns Ter. W4.................1A 84
Bioko Ct. E1...................4A 66
.......................(off Ocean Est.)
Bircham Path SE4..........2F 107
..................(off Aldersford Cl.)
Birch Cl. E16.................4A 68
Birch Cl. N19.................4E 33
Birch Cl. SE15...............5C 92
Birchdale Rd. E7.............2E 55
Birchdown Ho. E3...........2D 67
.....................(off Rainhill Way)
Birchfield St. E14...........1C 80
Birch Gro. E11................1A 54
Birch Gro. SE12.............5B 110
Birch Ho. SE14..............4B 94
Birch Ho. SW2...............4C 104
Birch Ho. W10................3A 58
.......................(off Droop St.)
Birchington Ct. NW6.......5D 45
Birchington Ho. E5.........2D 51
Birchington Rd. N8.........1F 33
Birchington Rd. NW6......5C 44
Birchin La. EC3......3C 18 (5F 63)
Birchlands Av. SW12.......5B 102
Birchmere Lodge SE16....1D 93
..................(off Sherwood Gdns.)
Birchmere Row SE3........5B 96
Birchmere Hall N5..........5E 35
Birchmere Wlk. N5.........5E 35
.......................(not continuous)
Birchside Apts. NW6.......1B 58
Birch Va. Ct. NW8...........3F 59
.......................(off Pollitt Dr.)
Birchwood Apts. N4........2E 35
..................(off Woodberry Gro.)
Birchwood Dr. NW3........5D 31
Birchwood Rd. SW17.....5D 117
Birdbrook Ho. N1............4E 49
.....................(off Popham Rd.)
Birdbrook Rd. SE3.........2E 111
Birdcage Wlk. SW1....4F 21 (3E 75)
Birdhurst Rd. SW18.......3E 101
Bird in Bush BMX Track....3D 93
................(off Bird in Bush Rd.)
Bird in Bush Rd. SE15.....3C 92
Bird in Hand M. SE23......2E 121
................(off Bird-in-Hand Pas.)
Bird in Hand Pas. SE23...2E 121
Bird in Hand Yd. NW3......1E 45
Birdsall Ho. SE5.............1A 106
Birdsfield La. E3.............3B 52
Bird St. W1..........3C 12 (5C 60)
Birdwood Av. SE13.........4F 109
Birkbeck Hill SE21........1D 119
Birkbeck M. E8...............2B 50
Birkbeck Pl. SE21..........2E 119
Birkbeck Rd. E8..............2B 50

Birkbeck Rd. SW19........5D 115
Birkbeck St. E2...............2D 65
Birkdale Cl. SE16............1D 93
Birkdale Ho. E14.............5B 80
.....................(off Keymer Pl.)
Birkenhead St.
   WC1.................1E 7 (2A 62)
Birkhall Rd. SE6.............1F 123
Birkwood Cl. SW12........5F 103
Birley Lodge NW8............1F 59
.....................(off Acacia Rd.)
Birley St. SW11..............5C 88
Birnam Rd. N4................4B 34
Birrell Ho. SW9...............5B 90
..................(off Stockwell Rd.)
Birse Cres. NW10...........5A 28
Birtwhistle Ho. E3...........5B 52
.......................(off Parnell Rd.)
Biscay Ho. E1..................3F 65
..................(off Mile End Rd.)
Biscay Rd. W6..................1F 85
Biscayne Av. E14.............2F 81
Biscott Ho. E3..................3D 67
Biscoe Way SE13..........1F 109
Bisham Gdns. N6.............3C 32
Bishop King's Rd. W14.....5A 72
Bishop's Av. E13.............5D 55
Bishop's Av. SW6............5F 85
Bishops Av., The N2.........2F 31
Bishop's Bri. Rd. W2.........5D 59
Bishop's Cl. N19...............5E 33
Bishop's Ct. EC4....2D 17 (5D 63)
.......................(off Old Bailey)
Bishop's Ct. WC2....2B 16 (5C 62)
.......................(off Star Yd.)
Bishops Ct. W2................5D 59
..................(off Bishop's Bri. Rd.)
Bishopsdale Ho. NW6......5C 44
.....................(off Kilburn Vale)
Bishopsgate EC2....2D 19 (5A 64)
Bishopsgate Arc.
   EC2................1E 19 (4A 64)
..................(off Bishopsgate)
Bishopsgate Churchyard
   EC2................1E 19 (4A 64)
..................(off Bishopsgate)
Bishopsgate Institute & Libraries
   ....1E 19 (4A 64)
..................(off Bishopsgate)
Bishopsgate Plaza
   EC2................1E 19 (5A 64)
..................(off Bishopsgate)
Bishops Gro. N2..............1A 32
Bishops Ho. SW8.............3A 90
..................(off Sth. Lambeth Rd.)
Bishop's Mans. SW6........5F 85
Bishops Mead SE5...........3E 91
..................(off Camberwell Rd.)
Bishop's Pk. Rd. SW6.......5F 85
Bishop's Rd. SW11..........3A 88
Bishops Rd. N6................1C 32
Bishop's Rd. SW6............4A 86
Bishop's Ter. SE11...........5C 76
Bishopsthorpe Rd. SE26...4F 121
Bishop St. N1..................5E 49
Bishop's Way E2..............1D 65
Bishops Wharf Ho. SW11...3A 88
.....................(off Parkgate Rd.)
Bishops Wood Almshouses
   E5.......................1D 51
..................(off Lwr. Clapton Rd.)
Bishopswood Rd. N6........2B 32
Bishop Way NW10...........4A 42
Bishop Wilfred Wood Cl.
   SE15..........................5C 92

Bishop Wilfred Wood Ct.
E13 ....1E 69
.........................(off Pragel St.)
Bissagos Ct. E1 ....4A 66
Bissextile Ho. SE13 ....5D 95
Bisson Rd. E15 ....1E 67
Bittern Ct. SE8 ....2C 94
Bittern Ho. SE1 ...... 4F 25 (3E 77)
Bittern St. SE1 .... 4F 25 (3E 77)
Blackall St. EC2 ....3D 11 (3A 64)
Blackbird Yd. E2 ....2B 64
Black Boy La. N15 ....1E 35
Black Bull Yd. EC1 ....5B 8 (4C 62)
.........................(off Hatton Wall)
Blackburne's M.
W1 ....4B 12 (1C 74)
Blackburn Rd. NW6 ....3D 45
Blackett Apts. E3 ....3B 66
.........................(off Hamlets Way)
Blackett St. SW15 ....1F 99
Blackford's Path SW15 ....5C 98
Blackfriars Bri. EC4 ....4D 17 (1D 77)
Blackfriars Ct. EC4 .....4D 17 (1D 77)
.........................(off New Bri. St.)
Black Friars La. EC4 3D 17 (5D 63)
.........................(not continuous)
*Blackfriars Millennium Pier
(River Bus)* 4E 17 (1D 77)
Blackfriars Pas. EC4 ..4D 17 (1D 77)
Blackfriars Rd. SE1 ..1D 25 (3D 77)
*Blackfriars Station (Rail &
Underground)* 4D 17 (1D 77)
Blackfriars Underpass
EC4 ....4C 16 (1C 76)
BLACKHEATH 5B 96
Blackheath Av. SE10 ....3F 95
**BLACKHEATH BMI HOSPITAL,
THE** 1B 110
**BLACKHEATH BMI HOSPITAL
(OUTPATIENT DEPARTMENT),
THE** 1B 110
Blackheath Bus. Cen. SE10..4E 95
Blackheath Bus. Est. SE10 ..4E 95
.........................(off Blackheath Hill)
Blackheath Concert Halls. 1B 110
Blackheath Gro. SE3 ....5B 96
Blackheath Hill SE10 ......4E 95
Blackheath Pk. SE3 ....1B 110
BLACKHEATH PK. 1C 110
Blackheath Ri. SE13 ....5E 95
.........................(not continuous)
Blackheath Rd. SE10 ....4D 95
Blackheath RUFC 3D 97
Blackheath Station (Rail) ..1B 110
Blackheath Va. SE3 ....5A 96
BLACKHEATH VALE 5B 96
Blackheath Village SE3 ...5B 96
Black Horse La. SE1 ...5C 26 (4F 77)
Blackhorse Rd. SE8 ....2A 94
Blacklands Rd. SE6 ....4E 123
Blacklands Ter. SW3 ....5B 74
Black Lion La. W6 ....5C 70
Black Lion M. W6 ....5C 70
Blackmans Yd. E2 ....5C 64
Blackmore Ho. N1 ....5B 48
.........................(off Barnsbury Est.)
Black Path E10 ....2A 38
Blackpool Rd. SE15 ....5D 93
Black Prince Rd. SE1 ....5B 76
Black Prince Rd. SE11 .....5B 76
Blackshaw Rd. SW17 ....4E 115
Blacksmiths Ho. E14 ....5F 67
.........................(off Valencia Cl.)

Blacks Rd. W6 ....1E 85
Blackstock M. N4 ....4D 35
Blackstock Rd. N4 ....4D 35
Blackstock Rd. N5 ....5D 35
Blackstone Est. E8 ....4C 50
Blackstone Ho. SW1 ....1E 89
.........................(off Churchill Gdns.)
Blackstone Ho. NW2 ....2E 43
Black Swan Yd. SE1 3D 27 (3A 78)
Blackthorn Av. N7 ....3C 48
Blackthorn Ct. E15 ....1F 53
.........................(off Hall Rd.)
Blackthorne Ct. SE15 ....3B 92
.........................(off Cator St.)
Blackthorn Ho. SE16 ....3A 80
.........................(off Blondin Way)
Blackthorn St. E3 ....3C 66
Blacktree M. SW9 ....1C 104
BLACKWALL 2E 81
Blackwall Basin Moorings ...2E 81
Blackwall La. SE10 ....1A 96
Blackwall Station (DLR) 1E 81
Blackwall Trad. Est. E14 ....4F 67
BLACKWALL TUNNEL 2F 81
Blackwall Tunnel App. E14 ..1E 81
Blackwall Tunnel Northern App.
E3 ....1C 66
Blackwall Tunnel Southern App.
SE10 ....4A 82
Blackwall Way E14 ....2E 81
Blackwater Cl. E7 ....1B 54
Blackwater Ho. NW8 ....4F 59
.........................(off Church St.)
Blackwater St. SE22 ....3B 106
Blackwell Cl. E5 ....1F 51
Blackwell Ho. SW4 ....4F 103
Blackwood Ho. E1 ....1D 65
.........................(off Collingwood St.)
Blackwood St. SE17 ....1F 91
Blade M. SW15 ....2B 100
Bladen Ho. E1 ....5F 65
.........................(off Dunelm St.)
Blades Ct. SW15 ....2B 100
Blades Ct. W6 ....1D 85
.........................(off Lower Mall)
Blades Ho. SE11 ....2C 90
.........................(off Kennington Oval)
Bladon Ct. SW16 ....5A 118
Blagdon Rd. SE13 ....4D 109
Blagrove Rd. W10 ....4A 58
Blair Av. NW9 ....2A 28
Blair Cl. N1 ....3E 49
Blair Ct. NW8 ....5F 45
Blair Ct. SE6 ....1B 124
Blairderry Rd. SW2 ....2A 118
Blairgowrie Ct. E14 ....5F 67
.........................(off Blair St.)
Blair Ho. SW9 ....5B 90
Blair St. E14 ....5E 67
Blake Cl. W10 ....4E 57
Blake Ct. NW6 ....2C 58
.........................(off Malvern Rd.)
Blake Ct. SE16 ....1D 93
.........................(off Stubbs Dr.)
Blake Gdns. SW6 ....4D 87
Blake Hall Cres. E11 ....3C 40
Blake Hall Rd. E11 ....2C 40
Blake Ho. E14 ....3C 80
.........................(off Admirals Way)
Blake Ho. SE1 ....5B 24 (4C 76)
Blake Ho. SE8 ....2C 94
.........................(off New King St.)
Blakemore Gdns. SW13 ....2D 85
Blakemore Rd. SW16 ......3A 118
Blakeney Cl. E8 ....2C 50

Blakeney Cl. NW1 ....4F 47
Blakenham Rd. SW17 .....4B 116
Blaker Cl. SE7 ....3E 97
.........................(not continuous)
Blake Rd. E16 ....3B 68
Blaker Rd. E15 ....1E 67
Blake's Rd. SE15 ....3A 92
Blake Twr. EC2 .....5F 9 (4E 63)
.........................(off Fann St.)
Blanchard Way E8 ....3C 50
Blanch Cl. SE15 ....3E 93
Blanchedowne SE5 ....2F 105
Blanche St. E16 ....3B 68
Blandfield Rd. SW12 ....5C 102
Blandford Ct. N1 ....4A 50
.........................(off St Peter's Way)
Blandford Ct. NW6 ....4F 43
Blandford Ho. SW8 ....3B 90
.........................(off Richborne Ter.)
Blandford Rd. W4 ....4A 70
Blandford Sq. NW1 ....3A 60
Blandford St. W1 ...1A 12 (5B 60)
Bland Ho. SE11 ....1B 90
.........................(off Vauxhall St.)
Bland St. SE9 ....2F 111
Blann Cl. SE9 ....4F 111
Blantyre St. SW10 ....3F 87
Blantyre Twr. SW10 ....3F 87
.........................(off Worlds End St.)
Blantyre Wlk. SW10 ....3F 87
.........................(off Worlds End Est.)
Blashford NW3 ....4B 46
.........................(off Adelaide Rd.)
Blashford St. SE13 ....5F 109
Blashill Ct. E14 ....1E 81
.........................(off Bullivant St.)
Blasker Wlk. E14 ....1D 95
Blaven Path E16 ....3B 68
Blaxland Ho. W12 ....1D 71
.........................(off White City Est.)
Blazer Ct. NW8 ....2F 59
.........................(off St John's Wood Rd.)
Blechynden Ho. W10 ....5F 57
.........................(off Kingsdown Cl.)
Blechynden St. W10 ....1F 71
Bledlow Cl. NW8 ....3F 59
Bleeding Heart Yd.
EC1 ....1C 16 (4C 62)
.........................(off Greville St.)
Blegborough Rd. SW16 .....5E 117
Blemundsbury WC1 ...5F 7 (4B 62)
.........................(off Dombey St.)
Blendon Row SE17 ....5F 77
.........................(off Orb St.)
Blendworth Point SW15 ...1D 113
Blenheim Cl. N19 ....4A 34
Blenheim Cl. SE10 ....1C 96
.........................(off Denham St.)
Blenheim Cl. SE16 ....2E 79
.........................(off King & Queen Wharf)
Blenheim Cres. W11 ....1A 72
Blenheim Gdns. NW2 ....3E 43
Blenheim Gdns. SW2 ......4B 104
Blenheim Gro. SE15 ....5C 92
Blenheim Ho. E16 ....2D 83
.........................(off Constable Av.)
Blenheim Ho. SW3 ....1A 88
.........................(off Kings Rd.)
Blenheim Pas. NW8 ....1E 59
Blenheim Rd. E15 ....1A 54
Blenheim Rd. E6 ....2F 69
Blenheim Rd. NW8 ....1E 59
Blenheim Rd. W4 ....4A 70

Blenheim St. W1 ....3D 13 (5D 61)
Blenheim Ter. NW8 ....1E 59
Blenheim Twr. SE14 ....3A 94
................(off Batavia Rd.)
Blenkarne Rd. SW11 ....4B 102
Blessington Cl. SE13 ....1F 109
Blessington Rd. SE13 ....1F 109
Bletchley Cl. N1 ......1B 10 (1F 63)
................(off Bletchley St.)
Bletchley St. N1 ......1A 10 (1F 63)
Bletsoe Wlk. N1 ....1E 63
Blick Ho. SE16.....................4E 79
................(off Neptune St.)
Blincoe Cl. SW19.............2F 113
Bliss Cres. SE13.................5D 95
Blissett St. SE10 ....4E 95
Bliss M. W10 ....2A 58
Blisworth Ho. E2 ....5C 50
................(off Whiston Rd.)
Blithehale Ct. E2 ....2D 65
................(off Withan St.)
Blithfield St. W8 ....4D 73
Block Wharf E14 ....3C 80
................(off Cuba St.)
Bloemfontein Av. W12 ....2D 71
Bloemfontein Rd. W12 ....1D 71
Bloemfontein Way W12 ....2D 71
Blomfield Ct. W9 ....3E 59
................(off Maida Vale)
Blomfield Mans. W12 ....2E 71
................(off Stanlake Rd.)
Blomfield Rd. W9.................4D 59
Blomfield St. EC2 ...1C 18 (4F 63)
Blomfield Vs. W2 ....4D 59
Blondel St. SW11 ....5C 88
Blondin St. E3 ....1C 66
Blondin Way SE16..............3A 80
Bloomberg Arc.
EC4......................3A 18 (5F 63)
Bloomberg Ct. SW1..............5F 75
................(off Vauxhall Bri. Rd.)
Bloomburg St. SW1..............5F 75
Bloomfield Ct. E10 ....5D 39
................(off Brisbane Rd.)
Bloomfield Ct. N6.................1C 32
Bloomfield Ho. E1 ....4C 64
................(off Old Montague St.)
Bloomfield Pl. W1 ......4E 13 (1D 75)
................(off Bourdon St.)
Bloomfield Rd. N6.................1C 32
Bloomfield Ter. SW1 ....1C 88
Bloom Gro. SE27...............3D 119
Bloomhall Rd. SE19 ....5F 119
Bloom Ho. E3 ....1D 67
................(off Alameda Pl.)
Bloom Pk. Rd. SW6..............3B 86
BLOOMSBURY 4C 6 (4A 62)
Bloomsbury Ct. WC1 1E 15 (4A 62)
................(off Barter St.)
Bloomsbury Ho. SW4...........4F 103
Bloomsbury Pl. SW18 ....3E 101
Bloomsbury Pl. WC1....1E 15 (4A 62)
Bloomsbury Sq. WC1...1E 15 (4A 62)
Bloomsbury St. WC1 ...1C 14 (4F 61)
Bloomsbury Theatre ...3B 6 (3F 61)
................(off Gordon St.)
Bloomsbury Way
WC1.......................1D 15 (4A 62)
Blore Cl. SW8 ....4F 89
Blore Ct. W1 ....3B 14 (5F 61)
................(off Berwick St.)
Blore Ho. SW10 ....3D 87
................(off Coleridge Gdns.)
Blossom Ct. SE15..............3B 92
................(off All Saints Walk)
Blossom St. E1 ....4E 11 (3A 64)
Blount St. E14 ....5A 66
Bloxam Gdns. SE9 ....3F 111
Bloxhall Rd. E10..................1B 38
Blucher Rd. SE5...................3E 91
Blue Anchor La. SE16..........5C 78
Blue Anchor Yd. E1 ....1C 78
Blue Ball Yd. SW1 ...2F 21 (2E 75)
Bluebell Apts. NW4 ....4E 35
................(off Swan La.)
Bluebell Av. E12..................2F 55
Bluebell Cl. E9.....................5E 51
Bluebell Cl. SE26...............4B 120
Bluebell Ho. SE16 ....3A 80
................(off Bondin Way)
Blue Boar All. EC3....2F 19 (5B 64)
................(off Aldgate High St.)
Blue Bldg. SE10 ....1B 96
................(off Glenforth St.)
Blue Ct. N1 ....5F 49
................(off Sherborne St.)
Blue Elephant Theatre.........3E 91
................(off Bethwin Rd.)
Blue Fin Bldg. SE1 ..1E 25 (2D 77)
................(off Summer St.)
Bluegate M. E1 ....1D 79
Blue Lion Pl. SE1......5D 27 (4A 78)
Blueprint Apts. SW12 ....5D 103
................(off Balham Gro.)
Blues St. E8..........................3B 50
Blue Water SW18..............2D 101
Blundell Cl. E8.....................2C 50
Blundell St. N7 ....4A 48
Blunden Ct. SW6.................3C 86
................(off Farm La.)
Blurton Rd. E5......................1E 51
Blyth Cl. E14........................5F 81
Blythe Cl. SE6......................5B 108
Blythe Hill SE6 ....5B 108
Blythe Hill La. SE6 ....5B 108
Blythe Hill Pl. SE23 ....5A 108
Blythe Ho. SE11 ....2C 90
Blythe M. W14.....................4F 71
Blythendale Ho. E2 ....1C 64
................(off Mansford St.)
Blythe Rd. W14....................4F 71
Blythe St. E2 ....2D 65
Blytheswood Pl. SW16......4B 118
Blythe Va. SE6.....................1B 122
Blyth Hill Pl. SE23 ....5A 108
Blyth Rd. E17 ....2B 38
................(off Brockley Pk.)
Blyth's Wharf E14 ....1A 80
Blythwood Rd. N4 ....2A 34
BMI CITY MEDICAL...2D 19 (5A 64)
................(off St. Helen's Pl.)
BMX Track London, The 2F 91
Boades M. NW3...................1F 45
Boadicea St. N1...................5B 48
Boardwalk Pl. E14 ....2E 81
Boarley Ho. SE17 ....5A 78
................(off Massinger St.)
Boateman Wlk. SE5 ....5C 90
................(off Peckford Pl.)
Boathouse, The E14.............5C 66
Boathouse Cen., The
W10...................................(off Canal Cl.)
Boathouse Wlk. SE15 ....3B 92
................(not continuous)
Boat La. E2 ....5B 50
Boat Lifter Way SE16...........5A 80
Boat Quay E16 ....1E 83
Boatyard Apts. E14 ....1D 95

Bob Anker Cl. E13...............2C 68
Bobbin Cl. SW4 ....1E 103
Bob Marley Way SE24 ....2C 104
Bocking St. E8 ....5D 51
Boddicott Cl. SW19.............2A 114
Boddington Ho. SE14..........4E 93
................(off Pomeroy St.)
Boddington Ho. SW13........2D 85
................(off Wyatt Dr.)
Bodeney Ho. SE5.................4A 92
................(off Peckham Rd.)
Boden Ho. E1.......................4C 64
................(off Woodseer St.)
Bodington Ct. W12..............3F 71
Bodley Mnr. Way SW2 ....5C 104
Bodley Way SE17...............5E 77
Bodmin St. SW18...............1C 114
Bodney Rd. E8.....................2D 51
Bogart Ct. E14.....................1C 80
................(off Premiere Pl.)
Bohemia Pl. E8.....................3E 51
Bohn Rd. E1 ....4A 66
Boileau Rd. SW13 ....3C 84
Boisseau Ho. E1..................4E 65
................(off Stepney Way)
Bolanachi Bldg. SE16 ....4B 78
Bolander Gro. SW6..............2C 86
Bolden St. SE8 ....5D 95
Boldero Pl. NW8 ....3A 60
................(off Gateforth St.)
Boleyn Ho. E16.....................2C 82
................(off Southey M.)
Boleyn Rd. E6......................1F 69
Boleyn Rd. E7......................4C 54
Boleyn Rd. N16....................2A 50
Bolina Rd. SE16 ....1E 93
Bolinder Way E3 ....2C 67
Bolingbroke Gro. SW11 .....2A 102
Bolingbroke Rd. W14...........4F 71
Bolingbroke Wlk. SW11.......4F 87
Bollinder Pl. EC1 .....1F 9 (2E 63)
Bolney Ga. SW7 ....3A 74
Bolney St. SW8...................3B 90
Bolsover St. W1 ....4E 5 (3D 61)
Bolt Ct. EC4 ....3C 16 (5C 62)
Bolt Ho. N1 ....5A 50
................(off Phillipp St.)
Bolton Cres. SE11 ....3C 90
Bolton Cres. SE5 ....3D 91
Bolton Gdns. NW10.............1F 57
Bolton Gdns. SW5 ....1D 87
Bolton Gdns. M. SW10........1D 87
Bolton Ho. SE10 ....1A 96
................(off Trafalgar Rd.)
Bolton Ho. SE11 ....5D 77
................(off George Mathers Rd.)
Bolton Pl. NW8 ....5D 45
................(off Bolton Rd.)
Bolton Rd. E15.....................3B 54
Bolton Rd. NW10.................5A 42
Bolton Rd. NW8 ....5D 45
Boltons, The SW10..............1D 87
Boltons Ct. SW5 ....1D 87
................(off Old Brompton Rd.)
Boltons Pl. SW5 ....1E 87
Bolton St. W1 ....1E 21 (2D 75)
Bolton Studios SW10..........1E 87
Bolton Wlk. N7 ....4B 34
................(off Durham Rd.)
Bombay Ct. SE16 ....3E 79
................(off St Marychurch St.)
Bombay St. SE16 ....5D 79
Bomore Rd. W11 ....1A 72
Bonar Rd. SE15....................3C 92
Bonchurch Rd. W10.............4A 58

Bond Ct. EC4 .... 3B **18** (1F **77**)
Bond Ho. NW6 .... 1B **58**
.... (off Rupert Rd.)
Bond Ho. SE14 .... 3A **94**
.... (off Goodwood Rd.)
Bonding Yd. Wlk. SE16 ...... 4A **80**
Bond St. E15 .... 2A **54**
Bond St. W4 .... 5A **70**
Bond Street Station (Underground
& Crossrail) 3C **12** (5D **61**)
Bondway SW8 .... 2A **90**
Bonfield St. SE13 .... 2E **109**
Bonham Ho. W11 .... 2B **72**
.... (off Boyne Ter. M.)
Bonham Rd. SW2 .... 3B **104**
Bonheur Rd. W4 .... 3A **70**
Bonhill St. EC2 .... 4C **10** (3F **63**)
Bonita M. SE4 .... 1F **107**
Bon Marche M.
SE27 .... 4A **120**
Bonner Rd. E2 .... 1E **65**
Bonner St. E2 .... 1E **65**
Bonnet St. E16 .... 3D **83**
Bonneville Gdns. SW4 ...... 4E **103**
Bonnington Ho. N1 .... 1B **62**
Bonnington Sq. SW8 .... 2B **90**
Bonny St. NW1 .... 4E **47**
Bonsor Ho. SW8 .... 4E **89**
Bonsor St. SE5 .... 3A **92**
Bonville Rd. BR1: Broml 5B **124**
Bookbinders Ct. E1 .... 3D **65**
.... (off Cudworth St.)
Booker Cl. E14 .... 4B **66**
Book Ho. N1 .... 1F **9** (1E **63**)
Boones Rd. SE13 .... 2A **110**
Boone St. SE13 .... 2A **110**
Boord St. SE10 .... 4A **82**
Boothby Rd. N19 .... 4F **33**
Booth Cl. E9 .... 5D **51**
Booth Cl. SE13 .... 1D **109**
Booth La. EC4 .... 4F **17** (1E **77**)
.... (off Baynard St.)
Booth Rd. E16 .... 3E **83**
Booth's Pl. W1 ...... 1A **14** (4E **61**)
Boot St. N1 .... 2D **11** (2A **64**)
Bordeaux Ho. E15 .... 2A **54**
.... (off Luxemburg M.)
Border Cres. SE26 .... 5D **121**
Border Rd. SE26 .... 5D **121**
Bordon Wlk. SW15 .... 5C **98**
Boreas Wlk. N1 ...... 1E **9** (1D **63**)
.... (off Nelson Pl.)
Boreham Av. E16 .... 5C **68**
Boreham Cl. E11 .... 3E **39**
Boreman Ho. SE10 .... 2E **95**
.... (off Thames St.)
Borland Rd. SE15 .... 2E **107**
Borneo St. SW15 .... 1E **99**
BOROUGH, THE 3B **26** (3F **77**)
Borough High St.
SE1 .... 4A **26** (3E **77**)
Borough Mkt. SE1 .... 2B **26** (2F **77**)
.... (off Borough High St.)
Borough Rd. SE1 ...... 4E **25** (4D **77**)
Borough Sq. SE1 ...... 4F **25** (3E **77**)
.... (off McCoid Way)
Borough Station (Underground)
.... 3A **26** (3E **77**)
Borrett Cl. SE17 .... 1E **91**
Borrodaile Rd. SW18 .... 4D **101**
Borrowdale NW1 ...... 2F **5** (2E **61**)
.... (off Robert St.)
Borthwick M. E15 .... 1A **54**
Borthwick Rd. E15 .... 1A **54**

Borthwick Rd. NW9 .... 1B **28**
Borthwick St. SE8 .... 1C **94**
Bosbury Rd. SE6 .... 3E **123**
Boscastle Rd. NW5 .... 5D **33**
Boscobel Ho. E8 .... 3D **51**
Boscobel Pl. SW1 .... 5C **74**
Boscobel St. NW8 .... 3F **59**
Boscombe Av. E10 .... 2C **39**
Boscombe Cl. E5 .... 2A **52**
Boscombe Rd. W12 .... 2C **70**
Boss Ho. SE1 .... 3F **27** (3B **78**)
.... (off Boss St.)
Boss St. SE1 .... 3F **27** (3B **78**)
Boston Gdns. W4 .... 2A **84**
Boston M. SW5 .... 5D **73**
.... (off Collingham Rd.)
Boston Pl. NW1 .... 3B **60**
Boston Rd. E17 .... 1C **38**
Boston Rd. E6 .... 2F **69**
Bosun Cl. E14 .... 3C **80**
Boswell Ct. W14 .... 4F **71**
.... (off Blythe Rd.)
Boswell Ho. WC1 .... 5E **7** (4A **62**)
.... (off Boswell St.)
Boswell St. WC1 .... 5E **7** (4A **62**)
Bosworth Ho. W10 .... 3A **58**
.... (off Bosworth Rd.)
Bosworth Rd. W10 .... 3A **58**
Botanic Sq. E14 .... 5A **68**
Botha Rd. E13 .... 4D **69**
Bothwell Cl. E16 .... 4B **68**
Bothwell St. W6 .... 2F **85**
Botolph All. EC3 ...... 4D **19** (1A **78**)
.... (off Botolph La.)
Botolph La. EC3 ...... 5D **19** (1A **78**)
Botts M. W2 .... 5C **58**
Boughton Ho. SE1 .. 3B **26** (3F **77**)
.... (off Tennis St.)
Boulcott St. E1 .... 5F **65**
Boulevard, The SW17 .... 2C **116**
Boulevard, The SW18 .... 2D **101**
Boulevard, The SW6 .... 4E **87**
Boulevard Walkway E1 ...... 5C **64**
Boulogne Ho. SE1 .... 5F **27** (4B **78**)
.... (off St Saviour's Est.)
Boulter Ho. SE14 .... 4E **93**
.... (off Kender St.)
Boundaries Rd. SW12 ...... 2B **116**
Boundary Av. E17 .... 2B **38**
Boundary Ho. SE5 .... 3E **91**
Boundary Rd. W11 .... 2F **71**
.... (off Queensdale Cres.)
Boundary La. E13 .... 2F **69**
Boundary La. SE17 .... 2E **91**
Boundary Pas. E2 .... 3F **11** (3B **64**)
Boundary Rd. E13 .... 1E **69**
Boundary Rd. E17 .... 2B **38**
Boundary Rd. NW8 .... 5D **45**
Boundary Rd. SW19 .... 5F **115**
Boundary Row SE1 .. 3D **25** (3D **77**)
Boundary St. E2 ...... 2F **11** (2B **64**)
Boundfield Rd. SE6 .... 3A **124**
Bourbon Ho. SE6 .... 5E **123**
Bourbon La. W12 .... 2F **71**
Bourbon Rd. SW9 .... 4C **90**
Bourchier St. W1 .... 4B **14** (1F **75**)
Bourdon Pl. W1 ...... 4E **13** (1D **75**)
Bourdon St. W1 ...... 4E **13** (1D **75**)
Bourke Cl. NW10 .... 3A **42**
Bourke Cl. SW4 .... 4A **104**
Bourlet Cl. W1 ...... 1F **13** (4E **61**)
Bournbrook Rd. SE3 .... 1F **111**
Bourne Cl. E11 .... 1C **40**

Bourne Est. EC1 ...... 5B **8** (4C **62**)
Bourne M. W1 .... 2C **12** (5C **61**)
Bournemouth Rd. SE15 ...... 5C **92**
Bourne Pl. W4 .... 1A **84**
Bourne Rd. E7 .... 5B **40**
Bourne Rd. N8 .... 1A **34**
Bournes Ho. N15 .... 1A **36**
.... (off Chisley Rd.)
Bourneside Gdns. SE6 ...... 5E **123**
Bournes Gdns. SE6 .... 5C **74**
Bourne Ter. W2 .... 4D **59**
Bournevale Rd. SW16 ...... 4A **118**
Bournville Rd. SE6 .... 5C **108**
Bousfield Rd. SE14 .... 5F **93**
Boutflower Rd. SW11 .... 2A **102**
Boutique Hall SE13 .... 2E **109**
Bouton Pl. N1 .... 4D **49**
.... (off Waterloo Ter.)
Bouverie M. N16 .... 4A **36**
Bouverie Pl. W2 .... 5F **59**
Bouverie Rd. N16 .... 4A **36**
Bouverie St. EC4 .... 3C **16** (5C **62**)
Boveney Cl. SE23 .... 4F **107**
Boveney Rd. SE23 .... 5F **107**
Bovet St. E1 .... 4A **66**
.... (off Ocean Est.)
Bovill Rd. SE23 .... 5F **107**
Bovingdon Cl. N19 .... 4E **33**
Bovingdon Rd. SW6 .... 4D **87**
Bovril Cl. SW6 .... 3D **87**
.... (off Fulham Rd.)
BOW 2B **66**
Bowater Cl. SW2 .... 4A **104**
Bowater Ho. EC1 ...... 4F **9** (3E **63**)
.... (off Golden La.)
Bowater Pl. SE3 .... 3D **97**
Bowater Rd. SE18 .... 4B **83**
Bow Bell Twr. E3 .... 5C **52**
.... (off Pancras Way)
Bow Brook, The E2 .... 2D **67**
.... (off Mace St.)
Bow Church Station (DLR)
.... 2C **66**
Bow Churchyard
EC4 .... 3A **18** (5E **63**)
.... (off Bow La.)
BOW COMMON 4C **66**
Bow Comn. La. E3 .... 3B **66**
Bow Creek Ecology Pk. 5A **68**
Bowden Ho. E3 .... 2D **67**
.... (off Rainhill Way)
Bowden St. SE11 .... 1C **90**
Bowditch SE8 .... 5B **80**
Bowdon Rd. E17 .... 2C **38**
Bowen Ct. SE16 .... 5E **79**
.... (off Debnams Rd.)
Bowen Dr. SE21 .... 3A **120**
Bowen Dr. SE7 .... 1D **97**
Bowen St. E14 .... 5D **67**
Bower Av. SE10 .... 4A **96**
Bowerdean St. SW6 .... 4D **87**
Bowerman Av. SE14 .... 2A **94**
Bowerman N. N19 .... 4F **33**
.... (off St John's Way)
Bower St. E1 .... 5F **65**
Bowery Apts. W12 .... 1E **71**
.... (off Fountain Park Way)
Bowes-Lyon Hall E16 .... 2C **82**
.... (off Wesley Av.)
Bowes Rd. W3 .... 1A **70**
Bowes Exchange E3 .... 4D **67**
.... (off Yeo St.)

Bow Fair E3................1C **66**
............(off Fairfield Rd.)
Bowfell Rd. W6................2E **85**
Bowhill Ct. SW9................3C **90**
Bow Ho. N1................5A **50**
............(off Wilmer Gdns.)
Bowie Cl. SW4................5F **103**
BOW INTERCHANGE................1D **67**
Bowland Rd. SW4................2F **103**
Bowland Yd. SW1 ...4A **20** (3B **74**)
............(off Kinnerton St.)
Bow La. EC4................3A **18** (5E **63**)
Bowlby Ho. SE4................2F **107**
............(off Frendsbury Rd.)
Bowl Ct. EC2................4E **11** (3A **64**)
Bowles Rd. SE1................2C **92**
Bowley Cl. SE19................5B **120**
Bowley Ho. SE16................4C **78**
Bowley La. SE19................5B **120**
Bowline Ct. SE10................5A **82**
Bowling Grn. Cl. SW15...5D **99**
Bowling Grn. Ho. SW10 ...3F **87**
............(off Riley St.)
Bowling Grn. La.
    EC1................3C **8** (3C **62**)
Bowling Grn. Pl.
    SE1................3B **26** (3F **77**)
Bowling Grn. Sq. SW12....1C **116**
Bowling Grn. St. SE11 ...2C **90**
Bowling Grn. Wlk.
    N1................1D **11** (2A **64**)
Bow Locks E3................3E **67**
Bowman Av. E16................1B **82**
Bowman Ho. N1................5A **50**
............(off Nuttall St.)
Bowman M. SW18 ...1B **114**
Bowman's Bldgs. NW1 ...4A **60**
............(off Penfold Pl.)
Bowmans Lea SE23...5E **107**
Bowman's M. E1................5C **64**
Bowman's M. N7................5A **34**
Bowman's Pl. N7................5A **34**
Bowmore Wlk. NW1............4F **47**
Bowness Cl. E8................3B **50**
............(off Beechwood Rd.)
Bowness Cres. SW15...5A **112**
Bowness Ho. SE15................3E **93**
............(off Hillbeck Cl.)
Bowness Rd. SE6................5D **109**
Bowood Rd. SW11................3C **102**
Bow River Village E3 ...1E **67**
............(off Global App.)
Bow Rd. E3................2B **66**
Bow Road Station (Underground)
    ....2C **66**
Bowry Ho. E14................4B **66**
............(off Wallwood St.)
Bowsprit Apts. SE8................3D **95**
Bowsprit Point E14................4D **80**
............(off Westferry Rd.)
Bow St. E15................2A **54**
Bow St. WC2................3E **15** (5A **62**)
Bowstring Plaza E3................2B **66**
............(off St Clements Av.)
Bow Triangle Bus. Cen.
    E3................3C **66**
............(not continuous)
Bowyer Ho. N1................5A **50**
............(off Whitmore Est.)
Bowyer Pl. SE5................3E **91**
Bowyer Plaza E3................2B **66**
............(off St Clements Av.)
Bowyer St. SE5................3E **91**
Boxall Rd. SE21................4A **106**
Boxley St. E16................2D **83**

Boxmoor Ho. E2................5C **50**
............(off Whiston Rd.)
Boxmoor Ho. W11................2F **71**
............(off Queensdale Cres.)
Box Tree Ho. SE8................2A **94**
Boxworth Gro. N1................5B **48**
Boyce Ho. SW16................5E **117**
Boyce Ho. W10................2B **58**
............(off Bruckner St.)
Boyce Way E13................3C **68**
Boydell Ct. NW8................4F **45**
............(not continuous)
Boyd Rd. SW19................5F **115**
Boyd St. E1................5C **64**
Boyd Way SE3................2E **111**
Boyfield St. SE1 ...4E **25** (3D **77**)
Boyland Rd. BR1: Broml....5B **124**
Boyle St. W1................4F **13** (1E **75**)
Boyne Rd. SE13................1E **109**
Boyne Ter. M. W11................2B **72**
Boyson Rd. SE17................2E **91**
............(not continuous)
Boyson Wlk. SE17................2F **91**
Boyton Cl. E1................3E **65**
Boyton Ho. NW8................1F **59**
............(off Wellington Rd.)
Brabant Ct. EC3 ...4D **19** (1A **78**)
............(off Philpot La.)
Brabazon Ct. SW1................1F **89**
............(off Moreton St.)
Brabazon St. E14................5D **67**
Brabner Ho. E2................2C **64**
............(off Wellington Row)
Brabourne Cl. SE19................5A **120**
Brabourn Gro. SE15................5E **93**
Bracer Ho. N1................1A **64**
............(off Whitmore Est.)
Bracewell Rd. W10................4E **57**
Bracey M. N4................4A **34**
Bracey St. N4................4A **34**
Bracken Av. SW12................4C **102**
Brackenbury N4................3C **34**
............(off Osborne Rd.)
Brackenbury Gdns. W6...4D **71**
Brackenbury Rd. W6................4D **71**
Brackenfield Cl. E5................5D **37**
Bracken Gdns. SW13...5C **84**
Bracken Ho. E3................4C **66**
............(off Devons Rd.)
Brackley Av. SE15................1E **107**
Brackley Ct. NW8................3F **59**
............(off Pollitt Dr.)
Brackley Rd. W4................1A **84**
Brackley St. EC1 ...4A **10** (3E **63**)
Brackley Ter. W4................1A **84**
Bracklyn Ct. N1................1F **63**
............(not continuous)
Bracklyn St. N1................1F **63**
Bracknell Gdns. NW3....1D **45**
Bracknell Ga. NW3................2D **45**
Bracknell Way NW3................1D **45**
Bradbeer Ho. E2................2E **65**
............(off Cornwall Av.)
Bradbourne St. SW6................5C **86**
Bradbury M. N16................2A **50**
Bradbury St. N16................2A **50**
Bradbury Ho. NW8................1D **59**
............(off Hamilton Ter.)
Braddyll St. SE10................1A **96**
Bradenham Cl. SE17................2F **91**
Braden St. W9................2D **59**
Bradfield Ct. NW1................4D **47**
............(off Hawley Rd.)
Bradfield Rd. E16................3C **82**
Bradford Cl. SE26................4D **121**

Bradford Ho. W14................4F **71**
............(off Spring Va. Ter.)
Bradford Rd. W3................3A **70**
Bradgate Rd. SE6................4D **109**
Brading Cres. E11................4D **41**
Brading Rd. SW2................5B **104**
Brading Ter. W12................4C **70**
Bradiston Rd. W9................2B **58**
Bradley Cl. N7................3A **48**
Bradley Ho. E3................2D **67**
............(off Bromley High St.)
Bradley Ho. SE16................5E **79**
............(off Raymouth Rd.)
Bradley M. SW17................1B **116**
Bradley Rd. SE19................5E **119**
Bradley Rd. SW4................4F **103**
Bradley's Cl. N1................1C **62**
Bradman Ho. NW8................2E **59**
............(off Abercorn Pl.)
Bradmead SW8................3D **89**
Bradmore Pk. Rd. W6...5D **71**
Bradshaw Cl. SW19................5C **114**
Bradshaw Cotts. E14................5A **66**
............(off Repton St.)
Bradstock Ho. E9................4F **51**
Bradstock Rd. E9................3F **51**
Brad St. SE1 ...2C **24** (2C **76**)
Bradwell Ho. NW6................5D **45**
............(off Mortimer Cres.)
Bradwell St. E1................2F **65**
Brady Ho. SW8................4E **89**
............(off Corunna Rd.)
Brady St. E1................3D **65**
Braemar SW15................4F **99**
Braemar Av. NW10................5A **28**
Braemar Av. SW18................2C **114**
Braemar Av. SW19................2C **114**
Braemar Cl. SE16................1D **93**
............(off Masters Dr.)
Braemar Ho. SE6................1B **124**
............(off Cumberland Pl.)
Braemar Ho. W9................2E **59**
............(off Maida Vale)
Braemar Mans. SW7................4D **73**
............(off Cornwall Gdns.)
Braemar Rd. E13................3B **68**
Braemar Rd. N15................1A **36**
Braeside BR3: Beck................5C **122**
Braes St. N1................4D **49**
Braganza St. SE17................1D **91**
Braham St. E2................3D **65**
............(off Three Colts La.)
Braham Ho. SE11................1B **90**
Braham St. E1 ...3F **19** (5B **64**)
Braham St. Pk................2F **19** (5B **64**)
............(off Half Moon Pas.)
Braid Av. W3................5A **56**
Braidwood Pas. EC1...5F **9** (4E **63**)
............(off Aldersgate St.)
Braidwood Rd. SE6................1F **123**
Braidwood St. SE1 ...2D **27** (2A **78**)
Brailey Ho. E10................3A **40**
Brailsford Rd. SW2................3C **104**
Braintree Ho. E1................3E **65**
............(off Malcolm Rd.)
Braintree St. E2................2E **65**
Braithwaite Ho. E15................3F **53**
............(off Forrester Way)
Braithwaite Ho. EC1 ...3B **10** (3D **63**)
............(off Bunhill Row)
Braithwaite St. E1...4F **11** (3B **64**)
Braithwaite Twr. W2................4F **59**
............(off Hall Pl.)
Bramah Grn. SW9................4C **90**
............(off Eythorne Rd.)

Bramah Ho. SW1.................1D 89
Bramah Rd. SW9................4C 90
Bramalea Cl. N6...................1C 32
Bramall Cl. E15...................2B 54
Bramall Ct. N7.....................3B 48
................(off Watkinson Rd.)
Bramber WC1...........2D 7 (2A 62)
................(off Cromer St.)
Bramber Ct. W14...................2B 86
................(off Bramber Rd.)
Bramber Rd. W14..................2B 86
Bramble Gdns. W12...............1B 70
Bramble Ho. E3.....................4C 66
................(off Devons Rd.)
Brambles, The SW19.............5B 114
................(off Woodside)
Brambling Ct. SE8.................2B 94
................(off Abinger Gro.)
Bramcote Gro. SE16..............1E 93
Bramcote Rd. SW15..............2D 99
Bramdean Cres. SE12...........1C 124
Bramdean Gdns. SE12..........1C 124
Bramerton NW6....................4F 43
................(off Willesden La.)
Bramerton St. SW3...............2A 88
Bramfield Ct. N4...................4E 35
................(off Queen's Dr.)
Bramfield Rd. SW11.............4A 102
Bramford Rd. SW18..............2E 101
Bramham Gdns. SW5............1D 87
Bramhope La. SE7................2D 97
Bramlands Cl. SW11.............1A 102
Bramley Cres. SW8...............3F 89
Bramley Ho. SW15................4B 98
................(off Tunworth Cres.)
Bramley Ho. W10..................5F 57
Bramley Rd. W10..................5F 57
Brampton WC1...........1F 15 (4B 62)
................(off Red Lion Sq.)
Brampton Cl. E5...................4D 37
Brampton Ho. SE16...............3E 79
................(off Albatross Way)
Brampton Rd. E6...................2F 69
Brampton Rd. N15................1E 35
Bramshaw Rd. E9.................3F 51
Bramshill Gdns. NW5............5D 33
Bramshill Rd. NW10..............1B 56
Bramshot Av. SE7.................2C 96
Bramshurst NW8...................5D 45
................(off Abbey Rd.)
Bramston Rd. NW10..............1C 56
Bramston Rd. SW17..............3E 115
Bramwell Ho. SE1.....5A 26 (4E 77)
Bramwell Ho. SW1.................1E 89
................(off Churchill Gdns.)
Bramwell M. N1....................5B 48
Bramwell Way E16................2E 83
Brancaster Ho. E1................2F 65
................(off Moody St.)
Brancaster Rd. SW16............3A 118
Branch Hill NW3...................5E 31
Branch Hill Ho. NW3..............5D 31
Branch Pl. N1......................5F 49
Branch Rd. E14...................1A 80
Branch St. SE15...................3A 92
Brand Cl. N4........................3D 35
Brandlehow Rd. SW15...........2B 100
Brandon Ct. E16...................3B 68
Brandon Est. SE17................2D 91
Brandon Ho. BR3: Beck.........5D 123
................(off Beckenham Hill Rd.)
Brandon Mans. W14..............2A 86
................(off Queen's Club Gdns.)
Brandon M. EC2.......1B 18 (4F 63)
................(off Moor La.)

Brandon M. SE17..................5E 77
Brandon Rd. N7....................4A 48
Brandon St. SE17.................5E 77
................(not continuous)
Brandram M. SE13...............2A 110
................(off Brandram Rd.)
Brandram Rd. SE13..............1A 110
Brandrams Wharf SE16.........3E 79
Brandreth Rd. SW17.............2D 117
Brands Ho. NW6...................5B 44
................(off Lincoln M.)
Brand St. SE10....................3E 95
Brangbourne Rd.
 BR1: Broml.......................5E 123
Brangton Rd. SE11...............1B 90
Brangwyn Ct. W14................4A 72
................(off Blythe Rd.)
Branksea St. SW6.................3A 86
Branksome Ho. SW8..............3B 90
................(off Meadow Rd.)
Branksome Rd. SW2..............3A 104
Branscombe NW1..................5E 47
................(off Plender St.)
Branscombe St. SE13...........1D 109
Bransdale Cl. NW6................5C 44
Brantwood Ho. SE5...............3E 91
................(off Wyndam Est.)
Brantwood Rd. SE24.............3E 105
Braque Bldg. SE1.....2F 25 (2E 77)
................(off Union St.)
Brasenose Dr. SW13..............2E 85
Brassett Point E15................5A 54
................(off Abbey Rd.)
Brassey Ho. E14...................5D 81
................(off Cahir St.)
Brassey Rd. NW6..................3B 44
Brassey Sq. SW11.................1C 102
Brassie Av. W3.....................5A 56
Brass Talley All. SE16............3F 79
Brasted Cl. SE26..................4E 121
Brathay NW1............1A 6 (1E 61)
................(off Ampthill Est.)
Brathway Rd. SW18...............5C 100
Bratley St. E1......................3C 64
Bravington Pl. W9................3B 58
Bravington Rd. W9................1B 58
Bravingtons Wlk. N1...1E 7 (1A 62)
................(off York Way)
Brawne Ho. SE17..................2D 91
................(off Brandon Est.)
Braxfield Rd. SE4.................2A 108
Braxted Pk. SW16.................5B 118
Bray NW3.............................4A 46
Brayards Rd. SE15................5D 93
Brayards Rd. Est. SE15.........5D 93
................(off Caulfield Rd.)
Braybrook St. W12...............4B 56
Brayburne Av. SW4...............5E 89
Bray Ct. E2..........................2F 65
................(off Meath Cres.)
Bray Ct. SW16.....................5A 118
Bray Cres. SE16...................3F 79
Braydon Rd. N16..................3C 36
Bray Dr. E16.........................1B 82
Brayfield Ter. N1..................4C 48
Brayford Sq. E1...................5E 65
Bray Pas. E16......................1C 82
Bray Pl. SW3.......................5B 74
Brays Gdns. SE13................4E 109
Brays Gdns. SE6..................5D 109
Bread St. EC4.........3A 18 (5E 63)
................(not continuous)
Breakspears M. SE4.............5B 94
Breakspears Rd. SE4............2B 108
................(not continuous)

Breakwell Ct. W10.................3A 58
................(off Wornington Rd.)
Breamore Cl. SW15...............1C 112
Breamore Ho. SE15..............3C 92
................(off Friary Est.)
Bream's Bldgs. EC4..2B 16 (5C 62)
Bream St. E3........................4C 52
Breamwater Gdns. SW15.......2D 99
Brechin Pl. SW7....................5E 73
Brecknock Rd. N19................1E 47
Brecknock Rd. N7.................2F 47
Brecknock Rd. Est. N19.........1E 47
Brecon Grn. NW9..................1A 28
Brecon Ho. E3......................1B 66
................(off Ordell Rd.)
Brecon Ho. W2.....................5E 59
................(off Hallfield Est.)
Brecon M. N7.......................2F 47
Brecon Rd. W6.....................2A 86
Bredel Ho. E14....................4C 66
................(off St Paul's Way)
Bredgar SE13......................3D 109
Bredgar Rd. N19..................4E 33
Bredhurst Cl. SE20...............5E 121
Bredinghurst SE22...............5C 106
Bredin Ho. SW10..................3D 87
................(off Coleridge Gdns.)
Breer St. SW6.....................1D 101
Breezer's Ct. E1...................1C 78
................(off The Highway)
Breezer's Hill E1...................1C 78
Bremner Rd. SW7..................4E 73
Brenchley Gdns. SE23..........4E 107
Brenda Rd. SW17..................2B 116
Brendon Av. NW10................1A 42
Brendon Ho. W1...................5A 60
Brendon Gdns. SE9...............2F 111
Brenley Ho. SE1......1B 26 (3F 77)
................(off Tennis St.)
Brennand Ct. N19..................5E 33
Brent Ct. NW11....................2F 29
BRENT CROSS.......................2E 29
Brent Cross Bus Station........2E 29
Brent Cross Fly-Over NW4.....2F 29
Brent Cross Gdns. NW4.........1F 29
BRENT CROSS INTERCHANGE...1E 29
Brent Cross Station
 (Underground)....................2F 29
Brentfield Gdns. NW2............2F 29
Brent Grn. NW4....................1E 29
Brent Ho. E9........................3E 51
................(off Brenthouse Rd.)
Brenthouse Rd. E9................4E 51
Brenthurst Rd. NW10.............3B 42
Brentmead Pl. NW11.............1F 29
Brent Mus.............................3D 43
Brent New Ent. Cen. NW10....3B 42
BRENT OLDER PEOPLE DAY
 HOSPITAL...........................5C 42
Brenton St. E14....................5A 66
Brenton Ct. E9......................2A 52
................(off Mabley St.)
Brent Pk. Ind. Est. NW10.......2D 29
Brent Pk. Rd. NW4................2D 29
Brent Reservoir.....................3B 28
Brent Rd. E16.......................5C 68
Brent Sth. Shop. Pk..............3E 29
Brent Ter. NW2.....................3E 29
Brent Trad. Cen. NW10.........2A 42
Brent Vw. Rd. NW9................1C 28
Brentwood Ho. SE18.............3F 97
................(off Portway Gdns.)
Brentwood Lodge NW4..........1F 29
................(off Holmdale Gdns.)

Bressenden Pl.
SW1.....................5E **21** (4D 75)
Bresslaw Ct. E3.......................4B 66
.................................(off Wager St.)
Breton Highwalk
EC2.......................5A **10** (4E 63)
.................................(off Golden La.)
Breton Ho. EC2.......5A **10** (4E 63)
.................................(off Golden La.)
Breton Ho. SE1.......5F **27** (4B 78)
.................................(off St Saviour's Est.)
Brett Cl. N16............................4A 36
Brettell St. SE17.......................1F 91
Brett Ho. Cl. SW15................5F 99
Brettinghurst SE1.....................1C 92
.................................(off Avondale Sq.)
Brett Pas. E8...........................2D 51
Brett Rd. E8.............................2D 51
Brewers Bldgs. EC1...1D **9** (2D 63)
.................................(off Rawstorne St.)
Brewers Ct. W2.......................4E 59
Brewer's Grn.
SW1.......................5B **22** (4F 75)
.................................(off Buckingham Ga.)
Brewer's Hall Gdn.
EC2.......................1A **18** (4E 63)
.................................(off Aldermanbury Sq.)
Brewers La. E20......................2D 53
Brewer St. W1..........4A **14** (1E 75)
Brewery, The EC2....5A **10** (4E 63)
Brewery Ind. Est., The
N1.......................1D **10** (1E 63)
.................................(off Wenlock Rd.)
Brewery Rd. N7........................4A 48
Brewery Sq. EC1.......3E **9** (3D 63)
Brewery Sq. SE1.......2F **27** (3B 78)
.................................(off Horselydown La.)
Brewhouse La. E1.....................2D 79
Brewhouse La. SW15.........1A 100
Brewhouse Wlk. SE16...........2A 80
Brewhouse Yd. EC1 ...3D **9** (3D 63)
Brewster Gdns. W10................4E 57
Brewster Ho. E14.....................1B 80
.................................(off Three Colt St.)
Brewster Ho. SE1.....................5B 78
.................................(off Dunton Rd.)
Brewster Rd. E10......................3D 39
Breyer Group Stadium, The...5D 39
.................................(shown as Leyton Orient FC)
Briant Ho. SE1.........5A **24** (4B 76)
.................................(off Hercules Rd.)
Briant St. SE14.........................4F 93
Briar Ct. E3...............................1C 66
.................................(off Morville St.)
Briar Ct. SW15.........................2D 99
Briardale Gdns. NW3................5C 30
Briar Rd. NW2...........................1E 43
Briar Wlk. SW15.......................2D 99
Briar Wlk. W10.........................3A 58
Briarwood Rd. SW4..............3F 103
Briary Cl. NW3..........................4A 46
Briary Ct. E16...........................5B 68
Briary Gdns. BR1: Broml...5D 125
Brickbarn Cl. SW10..............3E 87
.................................(off King's Barn)
Brick Ct. EC4.........3B **16** (5C 62)
Brickfield Cl. E9.......................3E 51
Brickfield Ho. N1....................5A 50
.................................(off Hertford Rd.)
Brickfield Rd. E3.....................3D 67
Brickfield Rd. SW19..............4D 115
Brickfield Rd. SW4................4F 103
.................................(off Parkfield Rd.)
Brick Kiln One SE13............1E 109
.................................(off Station Rd.)

Brick Kiln Two SE13............1E 109
.................................(off Station Rd.)
Brick La. E1.............................3B 64
Brick La. E2.............2F **11** (2B 64)
Brick Lane Music Hall...........2F 83
BRICKLAYER'S ARMS..........5F 77
Bricklayers Arms Distribution
Cen. SE1.............................5A 78
.................................(not continuous)
Bricklayers St. SE11..............5C 76
Brick St. W1............2D **21** (2D 75)
Brickwood Cl. SE26...............3D 121
Brideale Cl. SE15....................2B 92
Bride Cl. EC4.........3D **17** (5D 63)
.................................(off Bride La.)
Bride La. EC4..........3D **17** (5D 63)
Bridel M. N1............................5D 49
.................................(off Colebrook Row)
Brides M. N7...........................3B 48
Brides Pl. N1...........................4A 50
Bride St. N7.............................3B 48
Bridewain St. SE1...5F **27** (4B 78)
Bridewell Pl. E1.......................2D 79
Bridewell Pl. EC4....3D **17** (5D 63)
Bridford M. W1.........5E **5** (4D 61)
Bridge, The SW11....................3D 89
Bridge App. NW1.....................4C 46
Bridge Av. W6...........................5E 71
Bridge Av. Mans. W6...............1E 85
.................................(off Bridge Av.)
Bridge Cl. W10.........................5F 57
Bridge Ct. E10..........................3B 38
Bridge Ct. E14.........................1F 81
.................................(off Newport Av.)
Bridgefield Ho. W2..................5D 59
.................................(off Queensway)
Bridgefoot SE1........................1A 90
Bridge Gdns. N16....................1F 49
Bridge Ho. E9...........................3F 51
.................................(off Shepherds La.)
Bridge Ho. NW10.....................1F 57
.................................(off Chamberlayne Rd.)
Bridge Ho. NW3.......................4C 46
.................................(off Adelaide Rd.)
Bridge Ho. SE4......................2B 108
Bridge Ho. SW1.......................1D 89
.................................(off Ebury Bri.)
Bridgehouse Ct.
SE1.......................3D **25** (3D 77)
.................................(off Blackfriars Rd.)
Bridge Ho. Quay E14..............2E 81
Bridgeland Rd. E16..................1C 82
Bridge La. SW11.....................4A 88
Bridge Leisure Cen., The...4B 122
Bridgeman Ho. E9....................4E 51
.................................(off Frampton Pk. Rd.)
Bridgeman Ho. W14................5B 72
.................................(off Radnor Ter.)
Bridgeman Rd. N1...................1B 48
Bridgeman St. NW8.................1A 60
Bridge Mdws. SE14.................2F 93
Bridge M. NW10......................3A 42
Bridgemount M. N4..................2B 34
Bridgend Rd. SW18................2E 101
Bridgen Ho. E1........................5D 65
.................................(off Nelson St.)
Bridgepark SW18....................3C 100
Bridge Pl. SW1........................5D 75
Bridgepoint Lofts E7................4E 55
Bridgepoint Pl. N6...................3E 33
.................................(off Hornsey La.)
Bridgeport Pl. E1.....................2C 78
Bridge Rd. E11.........................1F 39
Bridge Rd. E15.........................4F 53
Bridge Rd. E17.........................2B 38

Bridge Rd. NW10......................3A 42
Bridge Rd. Dpt. E15..............5A 54
Bridges Ct. Rd. SW11............1F 101
Bridges Ho. SE5.......................3F 91
.................................(off Elmington Est.)
Bridgeside Lodge N1...............1E 63
.................................(off Wharf Rd.)
Bridges Pl. SW6.......................4B 86
Bridge St. SW1........4D **23** (3A 76)
Bridges Wharf SW11..............1F 101
Bridge Ter. E15........................4F 53
Bridge Theatre..........2F **27** (2B 78)
.................................(off Tower Bri. Rd.)
Bridgetown Cl. SE19.............5A 120
Bridge Vw. W6..........................1E 85
Bridge Vw. Ct. SE1...5E **27** (4A 78)
.................................(off Grange Rd.)
Bridge Wlk. SE8.......................2D 95
.................................(off Copperas St.)
Bridgewalk Hgts.
SE1.......................3C **26** (3F 77)
.................................(off Weston St.)
Bridgewater Highwalk
EC2.......................5F **9** (4E 63)
.................................(off Beech St.)
Bridgewater Ho. E14..............5A 68
.................................(off Lookout Lane)
Bridgewater Rd. E15...............5E 53
Bridgewater Sq. EC2...5F **9** (4E 63)
Bridgewater St. EC2...5F **9** (4E 63)
Bridge Way NW11....................1B 30
Bridgeway St. NW1..................1E 61
Bridge Wharf E2......................1F 65
Bridge Wharf N1......................1B 62
.................................(off Calshot St.)
Bridge Yd. SE1.........1C **26** (2F 77)
Bridgford St. SW18................3E 115
Bridgnorth Ho. SE15..............2C 92
.................................(off Friary Est.)
Bridgwater Ho. W2..................5E 59
.................................(off Hallfield Est.)
Bridle La. W1..........4A **14** (1E 75)
Bridle M. E1.............................5A 64
Bridport SE17..........................1F 91
Bridport Ho. N1........................5F 49
.................................(off Bridport Pl.)
Bridport Pl. N1.........................5F 49
.................................(not continuous)
Bridport Ter. SW8...................4F 89
.................................(off Deeley Rd.)
Bridstow Pl. W2.......................5C 58
Brief St. SE5............................4D 91
Brierfield NW1.........................5E 47
.................................(off Arlington Rd.)
Brierley Rd. E11.......................1F 53
Brierley Rd. SW12.................2E 117
Brierly Gdns. E2......................1E 65
Brigade St. SE3.......................5B 96
.................................(off Tranquil Va.)
Briggeford Cl. E5.....................4C 36
Briggs Ho. E2...........................2B 64
.................................(off Chambord St.)
Brightfield Rd. SE12..............3A 110
Brightling Rd. SE4..................4B 108
Brightlingsea Pl. E14...............1B 80
Brightman Rd. SW18..............1F 115
Brighton Av. E17......................1B 38
Brighton Bldgs.
SE1.......................5D **27** (4A 78)
.................................(off Tower Bri. Rd.)
Brighton Gro. SE14.................4A 94
Brighton Ho. SE5.....................4F 91
.................................(off Camberwell Grn.)
Brighton Rd. N16.....................1A 50

Brighton Ter. SW9...........2B **104**
Brightside Rd. SE13.........4F **109**
Bright St. E14....................4D **67**
Brightwell Ct. N7.............2B **48**
..................*(off Mackenzie Rd.)*
Brightwell Cres. SW17....5B **116**
Brig M. SE8.......................2C **94**
Brigstock Ho. SE5.............5E **91**
Brill Pl. NW1.............1C **6** (1F **61**)
Brimsdown Ho. E3............3D **67**
Brimstone Ho. E15...........4A **54**
..................*(off Victoria St.)*
Brindley Ho. W2.................4C **58**
..................*(off Alfred Rd.)*
Brindley St. SE14..............4B **94**
Brindley Way BR1: Broml...5C **124**
Brine Ho. E3......................1A **66**
..................*(off St Stephen's Rd.)*
Brinklow Ho. W2...............4D **59**
..................*(off Torquay St.)*
Brinkworth Way E9...........3B **52**
Brinsley Ho. E1..................5E **65**
..................*(off Tarling St.)*
Brinton Wlk. SE1......2D **25** (2D **77**)
..................*(off Nicholson St.)*
Brion Pl. E14.....................4E **67**
Brisbane Ho. W12.............1D **71**
..................*(off White City Est.)*
Brisbane Rd. E10...............4D **39**
Brisbane St. SE5................3F **91**
Briscoe Cl. E11..................4B **40**
Briscoe Rd. SW19..............5F **115**
Briset Rd. SE9...................1F **111**
Briset St. EC1..........4D **9** (3D **63**)
Briset Way N7...................4B **34**
Bristol Gdns. SW15............5E **99**
Bristol Gdns. W9................3D **59**
Bristol Ho. SE11................4C **76**
..................*(off Lambeth Wlk.)*
Bristol Ho. WC1........1E **15** (4A **62**)
..................*(off Southampton Row)*
Bristol M. W9....................3D **59**
Bristol Rd. E7....................3E **55**
Bristol Wlk. NW6...............1C **58**
..................*(off Alpha Pl.)*
Briston Gro. N8.................1A **34**
Bristow Ct. E8...................5D **51**
..................*(off Triangle Rd.)*
Bristowe Cl. SW2...............4C **104**
Bristow Rd. SE19...............5A **120**
Britannia Bldg. N1...1B **10** (2F **63**)
..................*(off Ebenezer St.)*
Britannia Bus. Cen. NW2....1F **43**
Britannia Cl. SW4..............2F **103**
Britannia Ga. E16..............2C **82**
BRITANNIA JUNC.................5D **47**
Britannia Leisure Cen........5F **49**
Britannia Rd. E14...............5C **80**
Britannia Rd. SW6..............3D **87**
Britannia Row N1...............5D **49**
Britannia St. WC1......1F **7** (2B **62**)
Britannia Wlk. N1....1B **10** (1F **63**)
..................(not continuous)
Britannia Way SW6............3D **87**
..................*(off Britannia Rd.)*
Britannic Highwalk
EC2..................1B **18** (4F **63**)
..................*(off Moor La.)*
British Gro. W4.................1B **84**
British Gro. Nth. W4...........1B **84**
British Gro. Pas. W4..........1B **84**
British Gro. Sth. W4..........1B **84**
British Library............1C **6** (2F **61**)

British Mus. 1C **14** (4A **62**)
British St. E3.....................2B **66**
British Telecom Cen.
2F **17** (5E **63**)
..................*(off Newgate St.)*
British Wharf Ind. Est.
SE14...............................1F **93**
Britley Ho. E14.................5B **66**
..................*(off Copenhagen Pl.)*
Brittain Ct. SE9.................1F **125**
Brittany Point SE11...........5C **76**
..................*(off Lollard Street)*
Britten Cl. NW11................3D **31**
Britten Ct. E15..................1F **67**
Britten Ho. SW3................1A **88**
..................*(off Britten St.)*
Britten St. SW3.................1A **88**
Britten Theatre...................4F **73**
..................*(off Prince Consort Rd.)*
Brittidge Rd. NW10...........4A **42**
Britton Cl. SE6..................5F **109**
Britton St. EC1.......4D **9** (3D **63**)
BRIXTON........................2B **104**
Brixton Hill SW2................5A **104**
Brixton Hill Cl. SW2...........3B **104**
Brixton Hill Pl. SW2...........5A **104**
Brixton Oval SW2..............2C **104**
Brixton Recreation Cen.....1C **104**
..................*(off Brixton Sta. Rd.)*
Brixton Rd. SW11..............2C **90**
Brixton Rd. SW9................2C **104**
**Brixton Station (Rail &
Underground)**...................2C **104**
Brixton Sta. Rd. SW2.........1C **104**
Brixton Water La. SW2.......3B **104**
Broadash Cl. SW16............3C **118**
Broadbent Cl. N6..............3D **33**
Broadbent St. W1......4D **13** (1D **75**)
Broadbridge Cl. SE3..........3C **96**
Broad Comn. Est. N16........3C **36**
..................*(off Osbaldeston Rd.)*
Broad Ct. WC2.........3E **15** (5A **62**)
Broadfield NW6.................3D **45**
Broadfield Cl. NW2............2E **29**
Broadfield La. NW1............4A **48**
Broadfield Rd. SE6............5A **110**
Broadfields Way NW10......2B **42**
Broadford Ho. E1...............3A **66**
..................*(off Commodore St.)*
Broadgate EC2.........1C **18** (4A **64**)
..................*(off Broadgate Circ.)*
Broadgate Circ.
EC2.................1D **19** (4A **64**)
Broadgate Plaza
EC2..................5E **11** (4A **64**)
Broadgate Rd. E16............5F **69**
Broadgates Ct. SE11.........1C **90**
..................*(off Cleaver St.)*
Broadgates Rd. SW18........1F **115**
Broadgate Twr. EC2...4E **11** (3A **64**)
Broadhead Apts. E3...........2B **66**
..................*(off St Clements Av.)*
Broadhinton Rd. SW4........1D **103**
Broadhurst Cl. NW6...........3E **45**
Broadhurst Gdns. NW6.......3D **45**
Broadlands Av. SW16.........2A **118**
Broadlands Cl. N6..............2C **32**
Broadlands Cl. SW16.........2A **118**
Broadlands Lodge N6.........2B **32**
Broadlands Rd.
BR1: Broml....................4D **125**
Broadlands Rd. N6............2B **32**
Broad La. EC2........5D **11** (4A **64**)
Bradley St. NW8................4F **59**
Broadley Ter. NW1.............3A **60**

Broadmayne SE17.............1F **91**
..................*(off Portland St.)*
Broadmead SE6................3C **122**
Broadmead W14...............5A **72**
Broadoak Ct. SW9............1C **104**
..................*(off Gresham Rd.)*
Broadoak Ho. NW6............5D **45**
..................*(off Mortimer Cres.)*
Broad Pas. W3..................2B **70**
Broad Sanctuary
SW1................4C **22** (3F **75**)
..................*(off Agar Gro.)*
Broadstone NW1...............4F **47**
Broadstone Ho. SW8..........3B **90**
..................*(off Dorset Rd.)*
Broad St. Av. EC2...1D **19** (4A **64**)
Broad St. Pl. EC2......1C **18** (4F **63**)
..................*(off Blomfield St.)*
Broadview Pl. E5.................3E **37**
Broad Wlk.
W1: Lon Hyde Pk...1B **20** (1B **74**)
Broad Wlk.
NW1: Lon Regent's Pk.
.....................................1C **4** (5C **46**)
Broad Wlk. SE3.................5E **97**
Broad Wlk., The W8..........2D **73**
Broadwalk Ct. W8..............2C **72**
..................*(off Palace Gdns. Ter.)*
Broadwalk Ho. EC2...4D **11** (3A **64**)
..................*(off Appold St.)*
Broadwalk Ho. SW7............3E **73**
..................*(off Hyde Pk. Ga.)*
Broad Wlk. La. NW11..........2B **30**
Broadwall SE1........1C **24** (2C **76**)
Broadwater Rd. SW17........4A **116**
Broadway E15....................4F **53**
Broadway SW1.........4B **22** (4F **75**)
Broadway, The N8..............1A **34**
Broadway, The SW13..........5A **84**
Broadway Arc. W6.............5E **71**
..................*(off Hammersmith B'way.)*
B'way. Chambers W6.........5E **71**
..................*(off Hammersmith B'way.)*
Broadway Ho. BR1: Broml...5F **123**
..................*(off Bromley Rd.)*
Broadway Ho. E8................5D **51**
..................*(off Ada St.)*
Broadway Mans. SW6.........3C **86**
..................*(off Fulham Rd.)*
Broadway Mkt. E8...............5D **51**
..................(not continuous)
Broadway Mkt. SW17.........4B **116**
Broadway Mkt. M. E8..........5C **50**
Broadway M. E5.................2B **36**
Broadway Pde. N8.............1A **34**
Broadway Retail Pk...........1F **43**
Broadway Theatre Catford, The
.....................................5D **109**
Broadway Wlk. E14.............1C **80**
Broadwell Pde. NW6..........3D **45**
..................*(off Broadhurst Gdns.)*
Broadwick St. W1...3A **14** (1E **75**)
Broadwood Ter. W8............5B **72**
Broad Yd. EC1.........4D **9** (3D **63**)
Brocas Cl. NW3.................4A **46**
Brockbridge Ho. SW15........4B **98**
Brocket Ho. SW8................5F **89**
Brockham Cl. SW19...........5B **114**
Brockham Dr. SW2............5B **104**
Brockham Ho. NW1............5E **47**
..................*(off Bayham Pl.)*
Brockham Ho. SW2............5B **104**
..................*(off Brockham Dr.)*

Brockham St. SE1 ....5A **26** (4E **77**)
Brockill Cres. SE4 ....2A 108
Brocklebank Ho. SW18......5E 101
Brocklebank Rd. SE7 ....5D 83
Brocklebank Rd. SW18.......5E 101
Brockhurst St. SE14 ....3F **93**
BROCKLEY...............................2F **93**
Brockley Cross SE4 ....1A **108**
Brockley Cross Bus. Cen.
  SE4..2A **108**
Brockley Footpath SE15....1E **107**
  (not continuous)
Brockley Gdns. SE4 ....5B **94**
Brockley Gro. SE4 ....3B **108**
Brockley Hall Rd. SE4.......3A **108**
Brockley Jack Theatre ...3A **108**
Brockley M. SE4................3A **108**
Brockley Pk. SE23 ....5A **108**
Brockley Ri. SE23 ....1A **122**
Brockley Rd. SE4 ....1B **108**
Brockley Station (Rail &
  Overground)..........................1A **108**
Brockley Vw. SE23..........5A **108**
Brockley Way SE4 ....3A **108**
Brockman Ri. BR1: Broml 4F **123**
Brockmer Ho. E1 ....1D **79**
  (off Crowder St.)
Brock Pl. E3 ....3D **67**
Brock Rd. E13...................4D **69**
Brock St. NW1.......3F **5** (3E **61**)
  (off Triton Sq.)
Brock St. SE15.................1E **107**
Brockway Cl. E11 ....4A **40**
Brockweir E2 ....1E **65**
  (off Cyprus St.)
Brockwell Ct. SW2 ....3C **104**
Brockwell Ho. SE11 ....2B **90**
  (off Vauxhall St.)
Brockwell Pk...................4D **105**
Brockwell Pk. Gdns.
  SE24..5C **104**
Brockwell Pk. Lido..........4D **105**
Brockwell Pk. Row SW2....5C **104**
Brockwell Pas. SE24.........4D **105**
Brodia Rd. N16................5A **36**
Brodick Ho. E3 ....1B **66**
  (off Saxon Rd.)
Brodie Ho. SE1 ....1B **92**
  (off Cooper's Rd.)
Brodie St. SE1 ....1B **92**
Brodlove La. E1 ....1F **79**
Brodrick Rd. SW17 ....2A **116**
Brody Ho. E1 ......1F **19** (4B **64**)
  (off Strype St.)
Broken Wharf EC4 ....4F **17** (1E **77**)
Brokesley St. E3 ....2B **66**
Broke Wlk. E8 ....5B **50**
Bromar Rd. SE5................1A **106**
Bromehead St. E1 ....5E **65**
Bromell's Rd. SW4............2E **103**
Bromfelde Rd. SW4.........1F **103**
Bromfelde Wlk. SW4.........5F **89**
Bromfield Ct. SE16..........4C **78**
  (off Ben Smith Way)
Bromfield St. N1 ....5C **48**
Bromhead St. E1 ....5E **65**
  (off Jubilee St.)
Bromleigh Ct. SE23..........2C **120**
Bromleigh Ho. SE1....5F **27** (4B **78**)
  (off St Saviour's Est.)
BROMLEY....................................2D **67**
Bromley-by-Bow Station
  (Underground)..........................2D **67**
Bromley Hall Rd. E14.......4E **67**
Bromley High St. E3.........2D **67**

Bromley Hill BR1: Broml....5A **124**
Bromley Pl. W1 ....5F **5** (4E **61**)
Bromley Rd. BR1: Broml....4F **123**
Bromley Rd. E10..............1D **39**
Bromley Rd. SE6............10 **123**
Bromley St. E1 ....4F **65**
BROMPTON..................................4A **74**
Brompton Arc.
  SW3.......................4A **20** (3B **74**)
  (off Brompton Rd.)
Brompton Cemetery 2D **87**
Brompton Cotts. SW10 ......2E **87**
  (off Hollywood Rd.)
Brompton Pk. Cres. SW6....2D **87**
Brompton Pl. SW3............4A **74**
Brompton Rd. SW1 ...4A **20** (3B **74**)
Brompton Rd. SW3 ....5A **74**
Brompton Sq. SW3...........4A **74**
Brompton Vs. SW6............2C **86**
  (off Lillie Rd.)
Bromwich Av. N6...............4C **32**
Bromwich Av. W3.............1A **70**
Bromyard Ho. SE15..........3D **93**
  (off Commercial Way)
Bromyard Ho. W3.............2B **70**
Bron Ct. NW6....................5C **44**
BRONDESBURY.............................4B **44**
Brondesbury Ct. NW2 ......3F **43**
Brondesbury M. NW6.......4C **44**
BRONDESBURY PK.......................5E **43**
Brondesbury Pk. NW2......3E **43**
Brondesbury Pk. NW6......4E **43**
Brondesbury Pk. Mans.
  NW6..5A **44**
  (off Salusbury Rd.)
Brondesbury Park Station
  (Overground)..........................5A **44**
Brondesbury Rd. NW6 ...1B **58**
Brondesbury Station
  (Overground)..........................4B **44**
Brondesbury Vs. NW6.......1B **58**
Bronsart Rd. SW6 ....3A **86**
Bronte Cl. E7 ....1C **54**
Bronte Ct. W14.................5A **72**
  (off Girdler's Rd.)
Bronte Ho. N16.................2A **50**
Bronte Ho. SW17 ....3F **115**
  (off Grosvenor Way)
Bronte Ho. SW4..............5E **103**
Bronti Cl. SE17................1E **91**
Bronwen Ct. NW8.............2F **59**
  (off Grove End Rd.)
Bronze St. SE8 ....3C **94**
Bronze Wlk. W12 ....1F **71**
Brookbank Rd. SE13.........1C **108**
Brook Cl. SW17 ....2C **116**
Brook Cl. E11...................5A **40**
Brook Ct. EC4..........4B **18** (1F **77**)
  (off Laurence Pountney La.)
Brook Ct. E15...................3E **125**
Brookdale Rd.
  SE6: Lon Catford B'way. ...5D **109**
Brookdale Rd.
  SE6: Lon Medusa Rd. 4D **109**
Brook Dr. SE11................4C **76**
Brooke Ct. W10...............1A **58**
Brooke Ho. SE14 ....4A **94**
Brookehowse Rd. SE6......2C **122**
Brooke Rd. E5...................5C **36**
Brooke Rd. N16................5B **36**
Brooke's Ct. EC1.....1B **16** (4C **62**)
Brooke's Mkt. EC1....5B **8** (4C **62**)
  (off Dorrington St.)

Brooke St. EC1.....1B **16** (4C **62**)
Brookfield N6....................5C **32**
Brookfield Pk. NW5...........5D **33**
Brookfield Rd. E9..............3A **52**
Brookfield Rd. W4...........1A **70**
Brook Gdns. SW13...........1B **98**
Brook Ga. W1...........5A **12** (1B **74**)
BROOK GREEN............................5F **71**
Brook Grn. W6...................4F **71**
Brook Grn. Flats W14 ....4F **71**
  (off Dunsany Rd.)
Brook Ho. E1 ....1C **78**
  (off Fletcher St.)
Brook Ho. W6..................5E **71**
  (off Shepherd's Bush Rd.)
Brook Ho's. NW1..............1E **61**
  (off Cranleigh St.)
Brooking Rd. E7 ....2C **54**
Brooklands Av. SW19 ......2D **115**
Brooklands Ct. NW6..........4B **44**
Brooklands Pk. SE3 ....1C **110**
Brooklands Pas. SW8 ......4F **89**
Brook La. BR1: Broml.......5C **124**
Brook La. SE3 ....5D **97**
Brook Lodge NW11 ....1F **29**
  (off Nth. Circular Rd.)
Brooklyn Ct. W12..............2E **71**
  (off Frithville Gdns.)
Brookman Ho. E3 ....1B **66**
  (off Mostyn Gro.)
Brookmarsh Ind. Est.
  SE10..3D **95**
Brook M. Nth. W2 ....1E **73**
Brookmill Rd. SE8.............4C **94**
Brook Rd. NW2.................4B **28**
Brooks Apts. E3 ....4C **66**
  (off Geoff Cade Way)
Brooksbank Ho. E9............3E **51**
  (off Retreat Pl.)
Brooksbank St. E9.............3E **51**
Brooksby Ho. N1...............4C **48**
  (off Liverpool Rd.)
Brooksby M. N1 ....4C **48**
Brooksby St. N1 ....4C **48**
Brooksby's Wlk. E9 ....2F **51**
Brooks Ct. SW11...............3E **89**
Brooks Farm......................2D **39**
Brookside Rd. N19............4E **33**
Brookside Rd. NW11.........1A **30**
Brooks Lodge N1 ....1A **64**
Brook's M. W1.......4D **13** (1D **75**)
Brook Sq. SE18 ....4F **97**
Brooks Rd. E13.................5C **54**
Brook St. W1.........4C **12** (1D **75**)
Brook St. W2.....................1F **73**
Brooksville Av. NW6..........5A **44**
Brookview Rd. SW16.......5E **117**
Brookville Rd. SW6............3B **86**
Brookway SE3...................1C **110**
Brookwood Av. SW13.......5B **84**
Brookwood Ho. SE1....4E **25** (3D **77**)
  (off Webber St.)
Brookwood Rd. SW18......1B **114**
Broome Way SE5..............3F **91**
Broomfield E17..................2B **38**
Broomfield NW1................4C **46**
  (off Ferdinand St.)
Broomfield Ho. SE17........5A **78**
  (off Massinger St.)
Broomfield St. E14............4C **66**
Broomgrove Rd. SW9.......5B **90**
Broomhill Rd. SW18.........3C **100**
Broomhouse La. SW6........5C **86**
Broomhouse Rd. SW6.......5C **86**
Broomsleigh Bus. Pk. SE26 ...5B **122**

Broomsleigh St. NW6.............. 2B 44
Broomwood Rd. SW11....... 4B 102
Broseley Gro. SE26 .... 5A 122
Brougham Rd. E8 .... 5C 50
Brougham St. SW11............ 5B 88
Brough Cl. SW8 .... 3A 90
Broughton Dr. SW9.............. 2C 104
Broughton Gdns. N6 ....1E 33
Broughton Rd. SW6 .... 5D 87
Broughton Rd. App. SW6.... 5D 87
Broughton St. SW8 .... 5C 88
Broughton St. Ind. Est.
            SW11 .... 5C 88
Browne Ho. SE8 .... 3C 94
            .... (off Deptford Chu. St.)
Brownfield Est. E14............. 5D 67
Brownfield St. E14............... 5D 67
Brown Hart Gdns.
            W1 ....4C 12 (1C 74)
Brownhill Rd. SE6 .... 5D 109
Browning Apts. E3............... 3B 66
            .... (off Hamlets Way)
Browning Cl. W9................... 3E 59
Browning Ct. W14................. 2B 86
            .... (off Turneville Rd.)
Browning Ho. N16................ 1A 50
            .... (off Shakspeare Wlk.)
Browning Ho. SE14 .... 4A 94
            .... (off Loring Rd.)
Browning Ho. W12................ 5E 57
            .... (off Wood La.)
Browning M. W1..1C 12 (4D 61)
Browning Rd. E11................. 2B 40
Browning St. SE17............... 1E 91
Brownlow Ho. SE16............. 3C 78
            .... (off George Row)
Brownlow M. WC1 ...3A 8 (3E 62)
Brownlow Rd. E7 .... 1C 54
Brownlow Rd. E8 .... 5B 50
Brownlow Rd. NW10 .... 4A 42
Brownlow St. WC1 ...1A 16 (4B 62)
Brown's Bldgs. EC3... 3E 19 (5A 64)
Browns La. NW5 .... 2D 47
Brown St. W1 .... 5B 60
BROWNSWOOD PK. 4D 35
Brownswood Rd. N4............. 5D 35
Broxash Rd. SW11 .... 4C 102
Broxbourne Ho. E3............... 3D 67
            .... (off Empson St.)
Broxbourne Rd. E7............... 5C 40
Broxholme Ho. SW6 .... 4D 87
            .... (off Harwood Rd.)
Broxholm Rd. SE27 .... 3C 118
Broxted Rd. SE6.................. 2B 122
Broxwood Way NW8 .... 5A 46
Bruce Cl. W10 .... 4F 57
Bruce Hall M. SW17 .... 4C 116
Bruce Ho. W10 .... 4F 57
Bruce Rd. E3 .... 2D 67
Bruce Rd. NW10 .... 4A 42
Bruckner St. W10................. 2A 58
Brudenell Rd. SW17 .... 3B 116
Bruford Ct. SE8 .... 2C 94
Bruges Pl. NW1 .... 4E 47
            .... (off Randolph St.)
Brune Ho. E1 .... 1F 19 (4B 64)
            .... (off Bell La.)
Brunel Gallery 5C 6 (4F 61)
Brunel Bldg. W2 .... 4F 59
            .... (off Nth. Wharf Rd.)
Brunel Ct. SE16.................... 3E 79
            .... (off Canon Beck Rd.)
Brunel Ct. SW13.................... 5B 84
            .... (off Westfields Av.)
Brunel Est. W2 .... 4C 58

Brunel Ho. E14..................... 1D 95
            .... (off Ship Yd.)
Brunel Ho. SW10 .... 3F 87
            .... (off Cheyne Rd.)
Brunel M. W10 .... 2F 57
Brunel Mus. 3E 79
Brunel Rd. E17 .... 1A 38
Brunel Rd. SE16................... 3E 79
Brunel Rd. W3...................... 4A 56
Brunel Rd. E16 .... 5B 68
Brune St. E1 .... 1F 19 (4B 64)
Brunlees Ho. SE1 .... 5F 25 (4E 77)
            .... (off Bath Ter.)
Brunner Cl. NW11 .... 1D 31
Brunner Ho. SE6................... 4E 123
Brunner Rd. E17 .... 1A 38
Brunswick Cl. Est.
            EC1...................... 2D 9 (2D 63)
Brunswick Ct. EC1 .... 2D 9 (2D 63)
            .... (off Tompion St.)
Brunswick Ct. SE1 ... 4E 27 (3A 78)
Brunswick Ct. SW1 .... 5F 75
            .... (off Regency St.)
Brunswick Flats W11 .... 5C 58
            .... (off Westbourne Gro.)
Brunswick Gdns. W8 .... 2C 72
Brunswick Ho. E2 .... 1B 64
            .... (off Thurtle Rd.)
Brunswick Ho. SE16 .... 4A 80
            .... (off Brunswick Quay)
Brunswick Ho. W6 .... 1E 85
            .... (off Parrs Way)
Brunswick Mans.
            WC1................... 3E 7 (3A 62)
            .... (off Handel St.)
Brunswick M. SW16 ....5F 117
Brunswick M. W1 ...2A 12 (5B 60)
Brunswick Pl. N1 .... 2C 10 (2F 63)
Brunswick Pl. NW1 ...4C 4 (3C 60)
            .... (not continuous)
Brunswick Quay SE16.......... 4F 79
Brunswick Rd. E10 .... 3E 39
Brunswick Rd. E14............... 5E 67
Brunswick Sq. WC1 ... 3E 7 (3A 62)
            .... (not continuous)
Brunswick Vs. SE5 .... 4A 92
Brunton Pl. E14................... 5A 66
Brushfield St. E1 ..... 5E 11 (4A 64)
Brushwood Cl. E14............... 4D 67
Brussels Rd. SW11 .... 2F 101
Bruton La. W1 ....5E 13 (1D 75)
Bruton Pl. W1 ....5E 13 (1D 75)
Bruton St. W1 ....5D 13 (1D 75)
Brutus Ct. SE11.................... 5D 77
            .... (off Kennington La.)
Bryan Av. NW10 .... 4D 43
Bryan Ho. NW10 .... 4D 43
Bryan Ho. SE16 .... 3B 80
Bryan Rd. SE16 .... 3B 80
Bryan's All. SW6 .... 5D 87
Bryanston M. E. W1 ..1A 12 (4B 60)
Bryanston M. W. W1 ..1A 12 (4B 60)
Bryanston Pl. W1 .... 4B 60
Bryanston Sq. W1 ..1A 12 (5B 60)
Bryanston St. W1 ..3A 12 (5B 60)
Bryan St. N1......................... 5B 48
Bryant Ct. E2........................ 5B 50
            .... (off Whiston Rd.)

Bryant Ho. E3 .... 1C 66
            .... (off Thomas Fyre Dr.)
Bryant St. E15....................... 4F 53
Bryant St. E2......................... 5B 50
Bryantwood Rd. N7.............. 2C 48
Bryce Ho. SE14 .... 2F 93
            .... (off John Williams Cl.)
Brydale Ho. SE16................. 5F 79
            .... (off Rotherhithe New Rd.)
Bryden Cl. SE26 .... 5A 122
Brydges Pl. WC2 ....5D 15 (1A 76)
Brydges Rd. E15 .... 2F 53
Brydon Wlk. N1 .... 5A 48
Bryer Ct. EC2.......... 5F 9 (4E 63)
            .... (off Bridgewater Sq.)
Bryett Rd. N7........................ 5A 34
Bryher Ct. SE11................... 1C 90
            .... (off Sancroft St.)
Brymay Cl. E3 .... 1C 66
Brymcourt W9 .... 1D 59
Brynmaer Rd. SW11............ 4B 88
Bryony Rd. W12 .... 1C 70
Bubbling Well Sq. SW18... 3D 101
            .... (off Ryland Blvd.)
Buccleugh Ho. E5 .... 2C 36
Buchanan Ct. SE16............. 5F 79
            .... (off Worgan St.)
Buchanan Gdns. NW10 .... 1D 57
Buchan Rd. SE15 .... 1E 107
Bucharest Rd. SW18........... 5E 101
Buckden Cl. SE12 .... 4C 110
Buckfast St. E2 .... 2C 64
Buck Hill Wlk. W2 .... 1F 73
Buckhold Rd. SW18 .... 4C 100
Buckhurst Ho. N7................. 2F 47
Buckhurst St. E1 .... 3D 65
Buckhurst St. E2 .... 3D 65
Buckingham Arc.
            WC2....................5D 15 (1A 76)
            .... (off Strand)
Buckingham Chambers
            SW1 ....5E 75
            .... (off Greencoat Pl.)
Buckingham Ct. W11 .... 1C 72
            .... (off Kensington Pk. Rd.)
Buckingham Ga.
            SW1 ....4F 21 (4E 75)
Buckingham La. SE23 .... 5A 108
Buckingham Mans. NW6.... 2D 45
            .... (off West End La.)
Buckingham M. N1 .... 3A 50
Buckingham M. NW10......... 1B 56
Buckingham M.
            SW1 .... 5F 21 (4E 75)
            .... (off Stafford Pl.)
Buckingham Palace
            .... 4E 21 (3D 75)
Buckingham Pal. Rd. SW1... 5D 75
Buckingham Pl. SW1 5F 21 (4E 75)
Buckingham Rd. E10 .... 5D 39
Buckingham Rd. E15 .... 2B 54
Buckingham Rd. N1.............. 3A 50
Buckingham Rd. N1.............. 1B 56
Buckingham St.
            WC2................... 1E 23 (1A 76)
Buckland Ct. N1.................... 1A 64
            .... (off St John's Est.)
Buckland Cres. NW3............. 4F 45
Buckland Ho. N1 .... 1D 89
            .... (part of Abbots Mnr.)
Buckland Rd. E10 .... 4E 39
Buckland St. N1.................... 1F 63
Bucklebury NW1 ..... 3F 5 (3E 61)
            .... (off Stanhope St.)
Buckler Ct. N7...................... 2B 48

Bucklers All. SW6 .... 2B 86
Bucklersbury EC4 ...... 3B 18 (5F 63)
Bucklersbury Pas.
EC4 .... 3B 18 (5F 63)
Buckle St. E1. .... 5B 64
Buckley Cl. SE23 .... 5D 107
Buckley Ct. NW6 .... 4B 44
Buckley Ct. SE1 .... 4B 78
Buckley Ho. W14. .... 3A 72
.... (off Holland Pk. Av.)
Buckley Rd. NW6 .... 4B 44
Buckmaster Cl. SW9. .... 1C 104
Buckmaster Ho. N7. .... 1B 48
Buckmaster Rd. SW11. ...... 2A 102
Bucknall St. WC2....2C 14 (5A 62)
Bucknell Cl. SW2 .... 2B 104
Buckner Rd. SW2 .... 2B 104
Bucknill Ho. SW1 .... 1D 89
.... (off Ebury Bri. Rd.)
Buckridge Ho. EC1....5B 8 (4C 62)
.... (off Portpool La.)
Buckshead Ho. W2 .... 4C 58
.... (off Gt. Western Rd.)
Buckstone Cl. SE23 .... 4E 107
Buck St. NW1 .... 4D 47
Buckters Rents SE16 .... 2A 80
Buckthorne Rd. SE4 .... 3A 108
Buckthorn Ho. E15............ 2A 68
.... (off Manor Rd.)
Bude Cl. E17.................... 1B 38
Budleigh Ho. SE15 .... 3C 92
.... (off Bird in Bush Rd.)
Buer Rd. SW6.................... 5A 86
Bugsby's Way SE10 .... 5B 82
Bugsby's Way SE7............ 5C 82
Buick Ho. E3.................... 3C 66
.... (off Wellington Way)
Bulbarrow NW8................ 5D 45
.... (off Abbey Rd.)
Bulinga St. SW1 .... 5A 76
.... (off John Islip St.)
Bullace Row SE5.............. 4F 91
Bullard's Pl. E2................ 2F 65
Bulleid Way SW1.............. 5D 75
Bullen Ho. E1.................... 3D 65
.... (off Collingwood St.)
Bullen St. SW11 .... 5A 88
Buller Cl. SE15 .... 3C 92
Buller Rd. NW10................ 2F 57
Bullfinch Ho. NW9............ 1B 28
.... (off Perryfield Way)
Bullingham Mans. W8 ...... 3C 72
.... (off Pitt St.)
Bull Inn Ct. WC2.... 5E 15 (1A 76)
.... (off Strand)
Bullivant St. E14................ 1E 81
Bull Rd. E15.................... 1B 68
Bulls Gdns. SW3 .... 5A 74
Bulls Head Pas.
EC3.................... 3D 19 (5A 64)
.... (off Lime St. Pas.)
Bull Yd. SE15.................... 4C 92
Bulmer M. W11 .... 1C 72
Bulmer Pl. W11 .... 2C 72
Bulstrode Pl. W1.... 1C 12 (4C 60)
Bulstrode St. W1....2C 12 (5C 60)
Bulwark Ct. E14 .... 5E 81
.... (off Parkside Sq.)
Bulwer Ct. E11..................3F 39
Bulwer Ct. Rd. E11............3F 39
Bulwer Rd. E11 .... 2F 39
Bulwer St. W12..................2E 71
Bunbury Ho. SE15.............. 3C 92
.... (off Fenham Rd.)

Bungalows, The E10..........1E 39
Bunhill Row EC1 .... 3B 10 (3F 63)
Bunhouse Pl. SW1 .... 1C 88
Bunkers Hill NW11............ 2E 31
Bunning Way N7 .... 4A 48
Bunsen Ho. E3.................. 1A 66
.... (off Grove Rd.)
Bunsen St. E3 .... 1A 66
Bunwell Ho. E3.................. 3B 66
.... (off William Whiffin Sq.)
Bunyan Ct. EC2 .... 5F 9 (4E 63)
.... (off Fann St.)
Buonaparte M. SW1............ 1F 89
Burbage Cl. SE1 ....5B 26 (4F 77)
Burbage Ho. N1.................. 5F 49
.... (off Poole St.)
Burbage Ho. SE14............ 2F 93
.... (off Samuel Cl.)
Burbage Rd. SE21............ 5F 105
Burbage Rd. SE24............ 4E 105
Burcham St. E14................ 5D 67
Burchell Ho. SE11............ 1B 90
.... (off Jonathan St.)
Burchell Rd. E10................ 3D 39
Burchell Rd. SE15............ 4D 93
Burcher Gale Gro. SE15.... 3B 92
Burcote Rd. SW18............ 5F 101
Burden Ho. SW8................ 3A 90
.... (off Thorncroft St.)
Burden Way E11................ 4D 41
Burder Cl. N1 .... 3A 50
Burder Rd. N1 .... 3A 50
Burdett M. NW3................ 3F 45
Burdett M. W2.................. 5D 59
Burdett Rd. E14................ 4B 66
Burdett Rd. E3.................. 3A 66
Burfield Cl. SW17............ 4F 115
Burford Cl. E15 .... 5F 53
Burford Rd. E6.................. 2F 69
Burford Rd. E15................ 2B 122
Burford Rd. SE6................ 2F 123
Burford Wlk. SW6.............. 3E 87
.... (off Cam Rd.)
Burges Gro. SW13............ 3D 85
Burgess Bus. Pk. SE5........3F 91
Burgess Ct. SE6 .... 5C 108
Burgess Hill NW2.............. 1C 44
Burgess Ho. SE5 .... 3E 91
.... (off Bethwin Rd.)
Burgess Lofts SE5............ 3E 91
.... (off Bethwin Rd.)
Burgess Pk. 2F 91
Burgess Rd. E15 .... 1A 54
Burgess St. E14................ 4C 66
Burge St. SE1 .... 5C 26 (4F 77)
Burgh House 1F 45
Burghill Rd. SE26............ 4A 122
Burghley Hall Cl. SW19.... 1A 114
Burghley Ho. SW19.......... 3A 114
Burghley Pas. E11 .... 3A 40
.... (off Burghley Rd.)
Burghley Rd. E11 .... 3A 40
Burghley Rd. NW5............ 1D 47
Burghley Rd. SW19.......... 4F 113
Burghley Twr. W3.............. 1B 70
Burgh St. N1.................... 1D 63
Burgon St. EC4....3E 17 (5D 63)
Burgos Gro. SE10 .... 4D 95
Burgoyne Rd. N4.............. 1D 35
Burgoyne Rd. SW9.......... 1B 104
Burgundy Ho. E20 .... 2E 53
.... (off Liberty Bri. Rd.)
Burgundy Pl. W12............ 2F 71
Burke Cl. SW15................ 2A 98
Burke Lodge E13.............. 2D 69

Burke St. E16.................... 4B 68
.... (not continuous)
Burland Rd. SW11............ 3B 102
Burleigh Ho. SW3..............2F 87
.... (off Beaufort St.)
Burleigh Ho. W10.............. 4A 58
.... (off St Charles Sq.)
Burleigh Ho. WC1....2E 7 (2B 62)
.... (off Westking Pl.)
Burleigh Pl. SW15............ 3F 99
Burleigh St. WC2....4E 15 (1B 76)
Burleigh Wlk. SE6............ 1E 123
Burley Ho. E1.................... 5F 65
.... (off Chudleigh St.)
Burley Rd. E16.................. 5E 69
Burlington Arc.
W1.................... 5F 13 (1E 75)
Burlington Cl. W9.............. 3C 58
Burlington Cnr. NW1..........4E 47
.... (off Camden Rd.)
Burlington Ct. E1 .... 1C 78
.... (off Cable St.)
Burlington Gdns. SW6 ...... 5A 86
Burlington Gdns.
W1.................... 5F 13 (1E 75)
Burlington Ho. N15............ 1F 35
.... (off Tewkesbury Rd.)
Burlington Ho. SE16..........3F 79
.... (off Province Dr.)
Burlington M. SW15.......... 3B 100
Burlington Pl. SW6............ 5A 86
Burlington Rd. SW6.......... 5A 86
Burma N16........................ 1F 49
Burma Rd. N16.................. 1F 49
Burmarsh NW5.................. 3C 46
Burma Ter. SE19.............. 5A 120
Burmester Rd. SW17........ 3E 115
Burnaby St. SW10............ 3E 87
Burnand Ho. W14..............4F 71
.... (off Redan St.)
Burnbury Rd. SW12.......... 1E 117
Burne Jones Ho. W14...... 5A 72
Burnell Bldg. NW2............4E 29
Burnell Ho. E20 .... 2D 53
.... (off Peloton Av.)
Burnelli Bldg. SW11.......... 3D 89
.... (off Sopwith Way)
Burnell Wlk. SE1 .... 1B 92
.... (off Cadet Dr.)
Burness Cl. N7.................. 3B 48
Burne St. NW1.................. 4A 60
Burnett Cl. E9.................... 2E 51
Burnett Ho. SE13.............. 5E 95
.... (off Lewisham Hill)
Burney St. SE10................ 3E 95
Burnfoot Av. SW6.............. 4A 86
Burnham NW3.................. 4A 46
Burnham Cl. SE1 .... 5B 78
Burnham Ct. NW6..............4E 45
.... (off Fairhazel Gdns.)
Burnham Ct. W2................ 1D 73
.... (off Moscow Rd.)
Burnham Est. E2................ 2E 65
.... (off Burnham St.)
Burnham St. E2 .... 2E 65
Burnham Way SE26.......... 5B 122
Burnhill Cl. SE15.............. 3D 93
Burnhill Ho. EC1 ....2F 9 (2E 63)
.... (off Norman St.)
Burnley Rd. NW10............ 2B 42
Burnley Rd. SW9.............. 5B 90
Burnsall St. SW3.............. 1A 88
Burns Cl. SW19................ 5F 115
Burns Ho. E2.................... 2E 65
.... (off Cornwall Av.)

Burns Ho. SE17 ....1D 91
...............(off Doddington Gro.)
Burnside Cl. SE16 ....2F 79
Burns Rd. NW10 ....5B 42
Burns Rd. SW11 ....5B 88
Burnt Ash Hgts.
  BR1: Broml 5D 125
Burnt Ash Hill SE12 ....4B 110
Burnt Ash Rd. SE12 ....3B 110
Burnthwaite M. SW6 ....3C 86
...............(off Burnthwaite Rd.)
Burnthwaite Rd. SW6 ....3B 86
Burnt Oak Apts. E16 ....5C 68
...............(off Pacific Rd.)
Burntwood Cl. SW18 ....1A 116
Burntwood Grange Rd.
  SW18 ....1F 115
Burntwood La. SW17 ....3E 115
Burntwood Vw. SE19 ....5B 120
Buross St. E1 ....5D 65
Burrage Ct. SE16 ....5F 79
...............(off Worgan St.)
Burrard Ho. E2 ....1E 65
...............(off Bishop's Way)
Burrard Rd. E16 ....5D 69
Burrard Rd. NW6 ....2C 44
Burr Cl. E1 ....2C 78
Burrell St. SE1 ....1D 25 (2D 77)
Burrells Wharf Sq.
  E14 ....1D 95
Burrell Towers E10 ....2C 38
Burrhill Ct. SE16 ....4F 79
...............(off Worgan St.)
Burroughs Cotts. E14 ....4A 66
...............(off Halley St.)
Burrow Ho. SW9 ....5C 90
...............(off Stockwell Pk. Rd.)
Burrow Rd. SE22 ....2A 106
Burrows M. SE1 ....3D 25 (3D 77)
Burrows Rd. NW10 ....2E 57
Burrow Wlk. SE21 ....5E 105
Burr Rd. SW18 ....1C 114
Bursar St. SE1 ....2D 27 (2A 78)
Burslem St. E1 ....5C 64
Burstock Rd. SW15 ....2A 100
Burston Rd. SW15 ....3F 99
Burston Vs. SW15 ....3F 99
...............(off St John's Av.)
Burtley Cl. N4 ....3E 35
Burton Bank N1 ....4F 49
...............(off Yeate St.)
Burton Ct. SW3 ....1B 88
...............(off Franklin's Row)
Burton Gro. SE17 ....1F 91
Burton Ho. SE16 ....3D 79
...............(off Cherry Gdn. St.)
Burton La. SW9 ....5C 90
...............(not continuous)
Burton M. SW1 ....5C 74
Burton Pl. WC1 ....2C 6 (2F 61)
Burton Ridge Ct. E3 ....1B 66
...............(off Festubert Pl.)
Burton Rd.
  SW9: Lon Akerman Rd... ....5D 91
Burton Rd.
  SW9: Lon Evesham Wlk... .....5C 90
Burton Rd. NW6 ....4B 44
Burtons Ct. E15 ....4F 53
Burton St. WC1 ....2C 6 (2F 61)
Burtonwood Ho. N4 ....2F 35
Burtop Rd. Est. SW17 ....3E 115
Burt Rd. E16 ....2F 83
Burtt Ho. N1 ....1D 11 (2A 64)
...............(off Aske St.)
Burtwell La. SE27 ....4F 119

Burwash Ho. SE1 ....4C 26 (3F 77)
...............(off Kipling Est.)
Burwell Cl. E1 ....5D 65
Burwell Rd. E10 ....3A 38
Burwell Wlk. E3 ....3C 66
Burwood Pl. W2 ....5A 60
Bury Cl. SE16 ....2F 79
Bury Ct. EC3 ....2E 19 (5A 64)
Buryfield Ct. SE8 ....5F 79
...............(off Lower Rd.)
Bury Pl. WC1 ....1D 15 (4A 62)
Bury St. EC3 ....3E 19 (5A 64)
Bury St. SW1 ....1A 22 (2E 75)
Bury Wlk. SW3 ....5A 74
Busbridge Ho. E14 ....4C 66
...............(off Brabazon St.)
Busby Ho. SW16 ....4E 117
Busby M. NW5 ....3F 47
Busby Pl. NW5 ....3F 47
Bushaby Cl. SE1 ....5D 27 (4A 78)
Bushberry Rd. E9 ....3A 52
Bush Cotts. SW18 ....3C 100
Bush Ct. W12 ....3F 71
Bushell Cl. SW2 ....2B 118
Bushell St. E1 ....2C 78
Bushey Down SE12 ....2D 117
Bushey Hill Rd. SE5 ....4A 92
Bushey Rd. E13 ....1E 69
Bushey Rd. N15 ....1A 36
Bush Ind. Est. N19 ....5E 33
Bush La. EC4 ....4B 18 (1F 77)
Bushnell Rd. SW17 ....2D 117
Bush Rd. E11 ....2B 40
Bush Rd. E8 ....5D 51
Bush Rd. SE8 ....5F 79
Bush Theatre 3E 71
Bushwood E11 ....2B 40
Bushwood Dr. SE1 ....5B 78
Buspace Studios W10 ....3A 58
...............(off Conlan St.)
Butcher Row E14 ....1F 79
Butchers Rd. E16 ....5C 68
Bute Gdns. W6 ....5F 71
Bute St. SW7 ....5F 73
Butfield Ho. E9 ....3E 51
...............(off Stevens Av.)
Butler Ct. SW11 ....4A 88
...............(off Hyde La.)
Butler Ho. E14 ....5B 66
...............(off Burdett St.)
Butler Ho. E2 ....2E 65
...............(off Bacton St.)
Butler Ho. E3 ....4B 66
...............(off Geoffrey Chaucer Way)
Butler Ho. SW9 ....4D 91
...............(off Lothian Rd.)
Butler Pl. SW1 ....5B 22 (4F 75)
Butler Rd. NW10 ....4B 42
Butlers & Colonial Wharf
  SE1 ....3F 27 (3B 78)
...............(off Shad Thames)
Butlers Ct. E3 ....1A 66
Butlers Wharf SE1 ...1F 27 (2B 78)
Butlers Wharf W.
  SE1 ....2F 27 (2B 78)
...............(off Shad Thames)
Butley Ct. E3 ....1A 66
...............(off Ford St.)
Butterfield Cl. SE16 ....3D 79
Butterfields E17 ....1E 39
Butterfly Apts. SW11 ....2A 102
...............(off Comyn Rd.)
Butterfly Wlk. SE5 ....4F 91
...............(off Denmark Hill)

Buttermere NW1 ....1E 5 (2D 61)
...............(off Augustus St.)
Buttermere Cl. E15 ....1F 53
Buttermere Cl. SE1 ....5B 78
Buttermere Cl. NW8 ....5F 45
...............(off Boundary Rd.)
Buttermere Dr. SW15 ....3A 100
Buttermere Ho. E3 ....2B 66
...............(off Mile End Rd.)
Buttermere Wlk. E8 ....3B 50
Butterwick W6 ....5F 71
Butterworth Ter. SE17 ....1E 91
...............(off Sutherland Wlk.)
Buttesland St. N1 ....1C 10 (2F 63)
Butts Rd. BR1: Broml 5A 124
Buxhall Cres. E9 ....3B 52
Buxted Rd. E8 ....4B 50
Buxted Rd. SE22 ....2A 106
Buxton Cl. E11 ....2B 40
Buxton Ct. N1 ....1A 10 (2E 63)
...............(off Thoresby St.)
Buxton M. SW4 ....5F 89
Buxton Rd. E15 ....2A 54
Buxton Rd. E6 ....2F 69
Buxton Rd. N19 ....3F 33
Buxton Rd. NW2 ....3D 43
Buxton Rd. SW14 ....1A 98
Buxton St. E1 ....3B 64
Buzz Bingo Stratford 5F 53
Byam St. SW6 ....5E 87
Byards Ct. SE16 ....5F 79
...............(off Worgan St.)
Byas Ho. E3 ....2B 66
...............(off Benworth St.)
Bye, The W3 ....5A 56
Byelands Cl. SE16 ....3F 79
Byfeld Gdns. SW13 ....4C 84
Byfield Cl. SE16 ....3B 80
Byford Cl. E15 ....4A 54
Bygrove St. E14 ....5D 67
...............(not continuous)
Byne Rd. SE26 ....5E 121
Byng Pl. WC1 ....4B 6 (3F 61)
Byng St. E14 ....3C 80
Byrne Rd. SW12 ....1D 117
Byron Av. E12 ....3F 55
Byron Cl. E8 ....5C 50
Byron Cl. SE26 ....4A 122
Byron Cl. SW16 ....5A 118
Byron Ct. NW6 ....4E 45
...............(off Fairfax Rd.)
Byron Ct. SE22 ....1C 120
Byron Ct. SW3 ....5A 74
...............(off Elystan St.)
Byron Ct. W9 ....3C 58
...............(off Lanhill Rd.)
Byron Ct. WC1 ....3F 7 (3B 62)
...............(off Mecklenburgh Sq.)
Byron Dr. N2 ....1F 31
Byron M. NW3 ....1A 46
Byron M. W9 ....3C 58
Byron Rd. E10 ....3D 39
Byron Rd. NW2 ....4D 29
Byron St. E14 ....5E 67
Byron Ter. SE7 ....3E 97
Bythorn St. SW9 ....1B 104
Byton Rd. SW17 ....5B 116
Byward St. EC3 ....5D 19 (1A 78)
Bywater Ho. SE18 ....4F 83
Bywater Pl. SE16 ....2A 80
Bywater St. SW3 ....1B 88
Bywell Pl. E16 ....4B 83
Bywell Pl. W1 ....1F 13 (4E 61)
...............(off Wells St.)
Byworth Wlk. N19 ....3A 34

C

Cabanel Pl. SE11 .... 5C 76
Cabbell St. NW1 .... 4A 60
Cabinet Ct. NW2 .... 5B 28
Cable Car 3B 82
Cable Ct. SE16 .... 5A 82
.................................(off Rope St.)
Cable Ho. WC1 ..... 1B 8 (2C 62)
.........................(off Gt. Percy St.)
Cable Pl. SE10 .... 4E 95
Cable St. E1 .... 1C 78
Cable St. E16 .... 3D 83
Cable Trade Pk. SE7 .... 5E 83
Cable Wlk. SE10 .... 5A 82
Cabot Ct. SE16 .... 5F 79
.............................(off Worgan St.)
Cabot Hall 2C 80
Cabot Sq. E14 .... 2C 80
Cabot Way E6 .... 5F 55
Cabrail Ct. E14 .... 4A 66
.........................(off Aston Street)
Cab Rd. SE1 .... 2A 24 (3C 76)
.............................(off West Rd.)
Cabul Rd. SW11 .... 5A 88
Caci Ho. W14 .... 5B 72
.....................(off Kensington Village)
Cactus Cl. SE15 .... 5A 94
Cactus Wlk. W12 .... 5B 56
Cadbury Way SE16 .... 4B 78
Caddington Rd. NW2 .... 5A 30
Cadell Cl. E2 .... 1B 64
Cade Rd. SE10 .... 4F 95
Cader Rd. SW18 .... 4E 101
Cadet Dr. SE1 .... 5B 78
Cadiz St. SE17 .... 1E 91
Cadley Ter. SE23 .... 2E 121
Cadman Cl. SW9 .... 3D 91
Cadmium Sq. E2 .... 2F 65
.............................(off Palmer's Rd.)
Cadmore Ho. N1 .... 4D 49
.........................(off The Sutton Est.)
Cadmus Cl. SW4 .... 1F 103
Cadmus Ct. SE16 .... 5A 80
.........................(off Seafarer Way)
Cadmus Ct. SW9 .... 4C 90
.............................(off Southey Rd.)
Cadnam Lodge E14 .... 4E 81
.............................(off Schooner Cl.)
Cadnam Point SW15 .... 1D 113
Cadogan Cl. E9 .... 4B 52
Cadogan Ct. E9 .... 4B 52
.............................(off Cadogan Ter.)
Cadogan Ct. SW3 .... 5B 74
.............................(off Draycott Av.)
Cadogan Ct. Gdns. SW1 ...... 5C 74
.............................(off D'Oyley St.)
Cadogan Gdns. SW3 .... 5B 74
Cadogan Gdns. SW1 .... 5B 74
Cadogan Hall 5C 74
.............................(off Sloane Ter.)
Cadogan Ho. SW3 .... 2B 87
.............................(off Beaufort St.)
Cadogan La.
SW1 .... 5B 20 (4C 74)
Cadogan Mans. SW3 .... 5B 74
.............................(off Cadogan Gdns.)
Cadogan Pier (River Bus)
.... 2A 88
Cadogan Pl. SW1 ...5A 20 (4B 74)
Cadogan Sq. SW1 ...5A 20 (4B 74)
Cadogan St. SW3 .... 5B 74
Cadogan Ter. E9 .... 3B 52
Cadoxton Av. N15 .... 1B 36

Cadwal Apts. N1 .... 4A 48
.........................(off Caledonian Rd.)
Caedmon Rd. N7 .... 1B 48
Caernarvon Ho. E16 .... 2D 83
.............................(off Audley Dr.)
Caernarvon Ho. W2 .... 5E 59
.............................(off Hallfield Est.)
Caesar Ct. E2 .... 1F 65
.............................(off Palmer's Rd.)
Cahill St. EC1 .... 4A 10 (3E 63)
Cahir St. E14 .... 5D 81
Caird St. W10 .... 2A 58
Cairncross M. N8 .... 1A 34
Cairnfield Av. NW2 .... 5A 28
Cairns Rd. SW11 .... 3A 102
Caisson Moor Ct. E3 .... 3E 67
.............................(off Navigation Rd.)
Caister Ho. N7 .... 3B 48
Caistor Ho. E15 .... 5B 54
.............................(off Caistor Pk. Rd.)
Caistor M. SW12 .... 5D 103
Caistor Pk. Rd. E15 .... 5B 54
Caistor Rd. SW12 .... 5D 103
Caithness Ho. N1 .... 5B 48
.............................(off Twyford St.)
Caithness Rd. W14 .... 4F 71
Calabria Rd. N5 .... 3D 49
Calais Ga. SE5 .... 4D 91
Calais St. SE5 .... 4D 91
Calbourne Rd. SW12 .... 5B 102
Calcott Ct. W14 .... 4A 72
.............................(off Blythe Rd.)
Calcott Wlk. SE9 .... 4F 125
Calcraft Ho. E2 .... 1E 65
.............................(off Bonner Rd.)
Caldecot Rd. SE5 .... 5E 91
Caldecott Way E5 .... 5F 37
Calder Ct. SE16 .... 2B 80
Calderon Ho. NW8 .... 1A 60
.............................(off Townshend Est.)
Calderon Pl. W10 .... 4E 57
Calderon Rd. E11 .... 1E 53
Caldervale Rd. SW4 .... 3F 103
Caldew St. SE5 .... 3F 91
Caldicote Grn. NW9 .... 1A 28
Caldwell Ho. SW13 .... 3E 85
.............................(off Trinity Chu. Rd.)
Caldwell St. SW9 .... 3B 90
Caldy Wlk. N1 .... 4E 49
Caleb St. SE1 .... 3A 26 (3E 77)
Caledonia Ho. E14 .... 5A 66
.............................(off Salmon La.)
Caledonian Point SE10 ...... 2D 95
.............................(off Norman Rd.)
Caledonian Rd. N1 ...1E 7 (1A 62)
Caledonian Rd. N7 .... 1B 48
Caledonian Road & Barnsbury
Station (Overground) 4B 48
Caledonian Road Station
(Underground) 3B 48
Caledonian Sq. NW1 .... 3F 47
Caledonian Wharf E14 ...... 5F 81
Cale St. SW3 .... 1A 88
Caletock Way SE10 .... 1B 96
Calgarth NW1 ...... 1A 6 (1E 61)
.............................(off Ampthill Est.)
Calgary Ct. SE16 .... 3E 79
.............................(off Canada Est.)
Calia Ho. E20 .... 2E 53
.............................(off Anthems Way)
Caliban Twr. N1 .... 1A 64
.............................(off Arden Est.)
Calico Ct. SE16 .... 4C 78
.............................(off Marine St.)

Calico Ho. E20 .... 3E 53
.............................(off Mirabelle Gdns.)
Calico Ho. EC4 .... 3A 18 (5E 63)
.............................(off Well Ct.)
Calico Ho. SE1 ...... 4D 27 (3A 78)
.............................(off Long La.)
Calico Row SW11 .... 1E 101
Calidore Cl. SW2 .... 4B 104
California Bldg. SE13 .... 4D 95
.............................(off Deal's Gateway)
Callaby Ter. N1 .... 3F 49
Callaghan Cl. SE13 .... 2A 110
Callahan Cotts. E1 .... 4E 65
.............................(off Lindley St.)
Callander Rd. SE6 .... 2D 123
Callard Cl. W2 .... 3F 59
Callcott Ct. NW6 .... 4B 44
Callcott Rd. NW6 .... 4B 44
Callcott St. W8 .... 2C 72
Callendar Rd. SW7 .... 4F 73
Callingham Cl. E14 .... 4B 66
Callisons Pl. SE10 .... 1A 96
Callis Rd. E17 .... 1B 38
Calliston Ct. E16 .... 4C 68
.............................(off Hammersley Rd.)
Callow St. SW3 .... 2F 87
Cally Pool & Gym 5B 48
Calmont Rd. BR1: Broml 5F 123
Calonne Rd. SW19 .... 4F 113
Calshot Ho. N1 .... 1B 62
.............................(off Calshot St.)
Calshot St. N1 .... 1F 7 (1B 62)
Calstock NW1 .... 5E 47
.............................(off Royal Coll. St.)
Calstock Ho. SE11 .... 1C 90
.............................(off Kennings Way)
Calthorpe St. WC1 ...3A 8 (3B 62)
Calton Av. SE21 .... 4A 106
Calverley Gro. N19 .... 3F 33
Calvert Av. E2 ...... 2E 11 (2A 64)
Calvert Ho. W12 .... 1D 71
.............................(off White City Est.)
Calverton SE5 .... 2A 92
.............................(off Albany Rd.)
Calvert Rd. SE10 .... 1B 96
Calvert's Bldgs. SE1 ...2B 26 (2F 77)
Calvert St. NW1 .... 5C 46
Calvin St. E1 ...... 4F 11 (3B 64)
Calydon Rd. SE7 .... 1D 97
Calypso Cres. SE15 .... 3B 92
Calypso Way SE16 .... 4B 80
Camarthen Grn. NW9 ...... 1A 28
Cambalt Rd. SW15 .... 3F 99
Cambay Ho. E1 .... 3A 66
.............................(off Harford St.)
Camber Ho. SE15 .... 2E 93
Camberley Ho. NW1 ...1E 5 (1D 61)
.............................(off Redhill St.)
Cambert Way SE3 .... 2D 111
CAMBERWELL 4F 91
Camberwell Bus. Cen. SE5 ...3F 91
Camberwell Chu. St. SE5 ...4F 91
Camberwell Glebe SE5 ...... 4A 92
CAMBERWELL GREEN 4F 91
Camberwell Grn. SE5 .... 4F 91
Camberwell Gro. SE5 .... 4F 91
Camberwell Leisure Cen. 4F 91
Camberwell New Rd. SE5 ...2C 90
Camberwell Pas. SE5 .... 4E 91
Camberwell Rd. SE5 .... 2E 91
Camberwell Sta. Rd. SE5 ...4E 91
Camberwell Trad. Est. SE5 ...4D 91
Cambisgate SW19 .... 5A 114
Cambium Apts. SW19 ...... 5F 99
.............................(off Beatrice Pl.)

Cambium Apts. W8 .... 4D 73
.... (off Beatrice Pl.)
Camborne M. SW18 .... 5C 100
Camborne M. W11 .... 5A 58
Camborne Rd. SW18 .... 5C 100
Cambray Rd. SW12 .... 1E 117
Cambria Ho. E14 .... 5A 66
.... (off Salmon La.)
Cambria Ho. SE26 .... 4C 120
.... (off High Level Dr.)
Cambrian Cl. SE27 .... 3D 119
Cambrian Grn. NW9 .... 1A 28
.... (off Snowdon Dr.)
Cambrian Rd. E10 .... 2C 38
Cambria Rd. SE5 .... 1E 105
Cambria St. SW6 .... 3D 87
Cambridge Av. NW6 .... 1C 58
Cambridge Cir. WC2 ... 3C 14 (5F 61)
Cambridge Cl. E17 .... 1B 38
Cambridge Cl. E2 .... 1D 65
.... (off Cambridge Heath Rd.)
Cambridge Cl. N16 .... 2A 36
.... (off Amhurst Pk.)
Cambridge Cl. NW6 .... 1C 58
.... (not continuous)
Cambridge Ct. W2 .... 4A 60
.... (off Edgware Rd.)
Cambridge Ct. W6 .... 5E 71
.... (off Shepherd's Bush Rd.)
Cambridge Cres. E2 .... 1D 65
Cambridge Dr. SE12 .... 3C 110
Cambridge Gdns. NW6 .... 1C 58
Cambridge Gdns. W10 .... 5F 57
Cambridge Ga. NW3 ... 3D 5 (3D 61)
Cambridge Ga. M.
NW1 .... 3E 5 (3D 61)
Cambridge Gro. W6 .... 5D 71
Cambridge Heath Rd. E1 ...... 4D 65
Cambridge Heath Rd. E2 ...... 3E 65
Cambridge Heath Station
(Overground) 1D 65
Cambridge Ho. W6 .... 5D 71
.... (off Cambridge Gro.)
Cambridge Pk. E11 .... 2C 40
Cambridge Pk. Rd. E11 .... 2C 40
.... (off Lonsdale Rd.)
Cambridge Pas. E9 .... 4E 51
Cambridge Pl. W8 .... 3D 73
Cambridge Rd. E11 .... 1B 40
Cambridge Rd. NW6 .... 1C 58
.... (not continuous)
Cambridge Rd. SW11 .... 4B 88
Cambridge Rd. SW13 .... 5B 84
Cambridge Rd. SW20 .... 5A 60
Cambridge Sq. W2 .... 5A 60
Cambridge St. SW1 .... 5D 75
Cambridge Ter. NW1...2D 5 (2D 61)
Cambridge Ter. M.
NW1 .... 2E 5 (2D 61)
Cambridge Theatre
.... 3D 15 (5A 62)
.... (off Earlham St.)
Cambus Rd. E16 .... 4C 68
Cam Ct. SE15 .... 2B 92
Camden Arts Cen. 2D 45
Camden Ct. NW1 .... 4E 47
.... (off Rousden St.)
Camden Gdns. NW1 .... 4D 47
Camden High St. NW1 .... 4D 47
Camden Hill Rd. SE19 .... 5A 120
Camden Ho. SE8 .... 1B 94
Camdenhurst St. E14 .... 5A 66
Camden La. N7 .... 2F 47
Camden Lock Market 4D 47
Camden Lock Pl. NW1 .... 4D 47
Camden Markets 4D 47

Camden M. NW1 .... 4E 47
CAMDEN MEWS DAY HOSPITAL
.... 4E 47
Camden Pk. Rd. NW1 .... 3F 47
Camden Pas. N1 .... 1D 63
Camden People's Theatre
.... 3F 5 (3E 61)
.... (off Hampstead Rd.)
Camden Rd. E11 .... 1D 41
Camden Rd. E17 .... 1B 38
Camden Rd. N7 .... 1A 48
Camden Rd. NW1 .... 4E 47
Camden Road Station
(Overground) 4E 47
Camden Row SE3 .... 5A 96
Camden Sq. NW1 .... 4F 47
.... (not continuous)
Camden Sq. SE15 .... 4E 92
Camden St. NW1 .... 4E 47
Camden Studios NW1 .... 5E 47
.... (off Camden St.)
Camden Ter. NW1 .... 3F 47
CAMDEN TOWN 5D 47
Camden Town Station
(Underground) 5D 47
Camden Wlk. N1 .... 5D 49
Camelford St. SW2 .... 5A 104
Camelford NW1 .... 5E 47
.... (off Royal Coll. St.)
Camelford Ct. W11 .... 5A 58
Camelford Ho. SE1 .... 1A 90
Camelford Wlk. W11 .... 5A 58
Camellia Cl. E10 .... 4C 38
Camellia Ho. SE8 .... 3B 94
.... (off Idonia St.)
Camellia St. SW11 .... 3D 89
Camellia St. SW8 .... 3A 90
.... (not continuous)
Camelot Cl. SW19 .... 4B 114
Camelot Ho. NW1 .... 3F 47
Camel Pl. E16 .... 2F 83
Camera Pl. SW10 .... 2F 87
Camera Press Gallery, The
.... 3F 27 (3B 78)
.... (off Queen Elizabeth St.)
Cameret Ct. W11 .... 3F 71
.... (off Holland Rd.)
Cameron Ho. NW8 .... 1A 60
.... (off St John's Wood Ter.)
Cameron Ho. SE5 .... 3E 91
Cameron Pl. E1 .... 5D 65
Cameron Pl. SW16 .... 2C 118
Cameron Rd. SE6 .... 2B 122
Cameron Ter. SE12 .... 3D 125
Camerton Cl. E8 .... 3B 50
Camgate Mans. SE5 .... 2E 91
.... (off Camberwell Rd.)
Camilla Rd. SE16 .... 5D 79
Camlan Rd. BR1: Broml... 4B 124
Camlet St. E2 .... 3F 11 (3B 64)
Camley St. N1 .... 1F 47
Camley Street Natural Pk.... 1A 62
Camley Street Natural Pk.
Vis. Cen. 1F 61
Camomile St. EC3 ...2D 19 (5A 64)
Campaign Ct. W9 .... 3B 58
.... (off Chantry Cl.)
Campana Rd. SW6 .... 4C 86
Campania Bldg. E1 .... 1F 79
.... (off Jardine Rd.)
Campbell Cl. SW16 .... 4F 117
Campbell Cl. SE22 .... 1C 120
Campbell Ct. SW7 .... 4E 73
.... (off Gloucester Rd.)
Campbell Gordon Way NW2 1D 43

Campbell Ho. SW1 .... 1E 89
.... (off Churchill Gdns.)
Campbell Ho. W12 .... 1D 71
.... (off White City Est.)
Campbell Ho. W2 .... 4F 59
.... (off Hall Pl.)
Campbell Ho. WC1 ... 3B 6 (3F 61)
Campbell Rd. E15 .... 1B 54
Campbell Rd. E3 .... 2C 66
Campbell Wlk. N1 .... 5A 48
.... (off Outram Pl.)
Campdale Rd. N7 .... 5F 33
Campden Gro. W8 .... 3C 72
Campden Hill W8 .... 3C 72
Campden Hill Ct. W8 .... 3C 72
Campden Hill Gdns. W8 .... 2C 72
Campden Hill Ga. W8 .... 3C 72
Campden Hill Mans. W8 ...... 2C 72
.... (off Edge St.)
Campden Hill Pl. W11 .... 2B 72
Campden Hill Rd. W8 .... 2C 72
Campden Hill Sq. W8 .... 2B 72
Campden Hill Towers W11 ... 2C 72
Campden Ho. NW6 .... 4F 45
.... (off Harben Rd.)
Campden Ho. W8 .... 2C 72
.... (off Sheffield Ter.)
Campden Ho. Cl. W8 .... 3C 72
Campden Ho's. W8 .... 2C 72
Campden Ho. Ter. W8 .... 2C 72
.... (off Kensington Chu. St.)
Campden Mans. W8 .... 2C 72
.... (off Kensington Mall)
Campen St. W8 .... 2C 72
Campen Cl. SW19 .... 2A 114
Camperdown St. E1 .... 5B 64
Campfield Rd. SE9 .... 5F 111
Campion Ho. E14 .... 5B 66
.... (off Frances Wharf)
Campion Ho. SE16 .... 3A 80
.... (off Blondin Way)
Campion Rd. E10 .... 2D 39
Campion Rd. SW15 .... 2E 99
Campion Ter. NW2 .... 5F 29
Camplin St. SE14 .... 3F 93
Camp Rd. SW19 .... 5D 113
Campshill Pl. SE13 .... 3E 109
Campshill Rd. SE13 .... 3E 109
Campus Rd. E17 .... 1B 38
Camp Vw. SW19 .... 5D 113
Cam Rd. E15 .... 5F 53
Canada Est. SE16.............. 4E 79
Canada Gdns. SE13 .... 3E 109
Canada House 1C 22 (2F 75)
.... (off Trafalgar Sq.)
Canada Memorial .. 3E 21 (3E 75)
Canada Pl. E14 .... 2C 81
.... (off Canada Sq.)
Canada Sq. E14 .... 2D 81
Canada St. SE16 .... 3F 79
Canada Water Bus Station
.... 3E 79
.... (off Surrey Quays)
Canada Water Station
(Underground & Overground)
.... 3E 79
Canada Way W12 .... 1D 71
Canada Wharf SE16 .... 2B 80
Canadian Av. SE6 .... 1D 123
Canal App. SE8 .... 1A 94
Canal Blvd. NW1 .... 3F 47
CANAL BRIDGE 2C 92
Canal Bldg. N1 .... 1E 63
Canal Cl. E1 .... 3A 66
Canal Cl. W10 .... 3F 57

Canal Cotts. E3 .... 5B 52
.... (off Parnell Rd.)
Canaletto EC1 .... 1F 9 (2E 63)
.... (off City Rd.)
Canal Gro. SE15 .... 2D 93
Canal Market 4D 47
.... (off Castlehaven Rd.)
Canal Mill Apts. E2 .... 5B 50
.... (off Boat La.)
Canal Path E2 .... 5B 50
Canal Reach N1 .... 5F 47
Canalside Activity Cen. 3F 57
Canalside Sq. N1 .... 5E 49
Canal Side Studios NW1 ....5F 47
.... (off St Pancras Way)
Canalside Studios N1 .... 5A 50
.... (off Orsman Rd.)
Canalside Wlk. W2 .... 4F 59
Canal St. SE5 .... 2F 91
Canal Wlk. N1 .... 5F 49
Canal Wlk. SE26 .... 5E 121
Canal Way W10 .... 3F 57
Canal Wharf E8 .... 5A 50
.... (off Kingsland Rd.)
Canary Vw. SE10 .... 2D 95
.... (off Dowells St.)
.... 2B 80
Canary Wharf Pier (River Bus)
.... 2B 80
Canary Wharf Station (Crossrail)
.... 2D 81
Canary Wharf Station
(Underground & DLR) 2C 80
Canberra Path E10 .... 2D 39
.... (off Whitney Rd.)
Canberra Rd. SE7 .... 2E 97
Canbury M. SE26 .... 3C 120
Cancell Rd. SW9 .... 4C 90
Candahar Rd. SW11 .... 5A 88
Candida Ct. NW1 .... 4D 47
Candid Ho. NW10 .... 2D 57
.... (off Trenmar Gdns.)
Candle Gro. SE15 .... 1D 107
Candlelight Ct. E15 .... 3B 54
.... (off Romford Rd.)
Candler St. N15 .... 1F 35
Candle St. E1 .... 4A 66
Candover St. W1 ...... 1F 13 (4E 61)
Candy St. E3 .... 5B 52
Candy Wharf E3 .... 3A 66
Caney M. NW2 .... 4F 29
Canfield Gdns. NW6 .... 4D 45
Canfield Ho. N15 .... 1A 36
.... (off Albert Rd.)
Canfield Pl. NW6 .... 3E 45
Canford Rd. SW11 .... 3C 102
Canham Rd. W3 .... 3A 70
CANN HALL 1A 54
Cann Hall Rd. E11 .... 1A 54
Cann Ho. W14 .... 4A 72
.... (off Russell Rd.)
Canning Cross SE5 .... 5A 92
Canning Ho. W12 .... 1D 71
.... (off Australia Rd.)
Canning Pas. W8 .... 4E 73
Canning Pl. W8 .... 4E 73
Canning Pl. M. W8 .... 4E 73
.... (off Canning Pl.)
Canning Rd. E15 .... 1A 68
Canning Rd. N5 .... 5D 35
CANNING TOWN 4A 68
CANNING TOWN 5B 68
Canning Town Bus Station
.... 5A 68
Canning Town Station
(Underground & DLR) 5A 68

Cannizaro Rd. SW19 ....5E 113
Cannock Ho. N4 .... 2E 35
Cannon Ct. EC1 .... 3D 9 (3D 63)
.... (off Brewhouse Yd.)
Cannon Dr. E14 .... 1C 80
Cannon Hill NW6 .... 2C 44
Cannon Ho. SE11 .... 5B 76
.... (off Beaufoy Wlk.)
Cannon La. NW3 .... 5F 31
Cannon Pl. NW3 .... 5F 31
Cannon St. EC4 .... 3F 17 (5E 63)
Cannon St. Rd. E1 .... 5D 65
Cannon Street Station (Rail &
Underground) 4B 18 (1F 77)
Cannon Wharf Bus. Cen.
SE8 .... 5A 80
.... (off Pell St.)
Cannon Wharf Development
SE8 .... 5A 80
.... (off Yeoman St.)
Cannon Workshops E14 .... 1C 80
.... (off Cannon Dr.)
Canoe Wlk. E14 .... 5B 66
Cannon All. EC4 .... 3F 17
.... (off Queen's Head Pas.)
Canon Beck Rd. SE16 .... 3E 79
Canonbie Rd. SE23 .... 5E 107
CANONBURY 3E 49
Canonbury Bus. Cen. N1 ...... 5E 49
Canonbury Ct. N1 .... 4D 49
.... (off Hawes St.)
Canonbury Cres. N1 .... 4E 49
Canonbury Gro. N1 .... 4E 49
Canonbury Hgts. N1 .... 3F 49
.... (off Dove St.)
Canonbury La. N1 .... 4D 49
Canonbury Pk. Nth. N1 .... 3E 49
Canonbury Pk. Sth. N1 .... 3E 49
Canonbury Pl. N1 .... 3D 49
.... (not continuous)
Canonbury Rd. N1 .... 3D 49
Canonbury Sq. N1 .... 4D 49
Canonbury Station (Overground)
.... 2E 49
Canonbury Vs. N1 .... 4D 49
Canon Ho. W10 .... 2B 58
.... (off Bruckner St.)
Canon Row SW1 ...... 4D 23 (3A 76)
.... (not continuous)
Canon's Cl. N2 .... 2F 31
Canons Ct. E15 .... 1A 54
Canon St. N1 .... 5E 49
Canrobert St. E2 .... 1D 65
Cantelowes Rd. NW1 .... 3F 47
Canterbury Cl. SE5 .... 5E 91
.... (off Lilford Rd.)
Canterbury Ct. NW6 .... 1C 58
.... (off Canterbury Rd.)
Canterbury Ct. SE12 .... 3D 125
Canterbury Ct. SE5 .... 3C 90
Canterbury Cres. SW9 .... 1C 104
Canterbury Gro. SE27 .... 4C 118
Canterbury Ho. E3 .... 2D 67
.... (off Bow Rd.)
Canterbury Ho. SE1 ... 5A 24 (4B 76)
Canterbury Ho. SE8 .... 1C 94
.... (off Wharf St.)
Canterbury Ind. Pk. SE15 .....2E 93
Canterbury Pl. SE17 .... 1D 91
Canterbury Rd. NW6:
.... Lon Carlton Va. 1B 58
Canterbury Rd. NW6:
.... Lon Princess Rd. 1C 58
Canterbury Rd. E10 .... 2E 39

Canterbury Ter. NW6 .... 1C 58
Canter Way E1 .... 5C 64
Cantium Retail Pk. 2C 92
Canto Ct. EC1 .... 3A 10 (3E 63)
.... (off Old St.)
Canton St. E14 .... 5C 66
Cantrell Rd. E3 .... 3B 66
Canute Gdns. SE16 .... 5F 79
Canvey St. SE1 .... 1F 25 (2E 77)
.... 2B 66
Canyon Gdn. E2 .... 2B 66
.... (off St Clements Av.)
Cape Henry Ct. E14 .... 1F 81
.... (off Jamestown Way)
Cape Ho. E16 .... 2D 83
.... (off Cunningham Av.)
Cape Ho. E8 .... 3B 50
.... (off Dalston La.)
Capel Ct. EC2 .... 3C 18 (5F 63)
.... (off Bartholomew La.)
Capel Ho. E9 .... 4E 51
.... (off Loddiges Rd.)
Capel Rd. E12 .... 1F 55
Capel Rd. E7 .... 1D 55
Capener's Cl. SW1 ... 4A 20 (3C 74)
.... (off Kinnerton St.)
Cape Yd. E1 .... 2C 78
Capital E. Apts. E16 .... 1C 82
.... (off Western Gateway)
Capital Ho. SW15 .... 3A 100
.... (off Plaza Gdns.)
Capital Mill Apts. E2 .... 5B 50
.... (off Whiston Rd.)
Capital Wharf E1 .... 2C 78
Capitol Bldg. SW11 .... 2F 89
.... (off New Union Sq.)
Capitol Wlk. SE23 .... 2E 121
.... (off London Rd.)
Capland Ho. NW8 .... 3F 59
.... (off Capland St.)
Capland St. NW8 .... 3F 59
Caple Ho. SW10 .... 3E 87
.... (off King's Rd.)
Caple Rd. NW10 .... 1B 56
Capper St. WC1 ...... 4A 6 (3E 61)
Capstan Ct. E1 .... 1E 79
.... (off Wapping Wall)
Capstan Ho. E14:
.... Lon Clove Cres. 1F 81
.... (off Clove Cres.)
Capstan Ho. E14:
.... Lon Stebondale St. 5E 81
.... (off Stebondale St.)
Capstan Ho. SE8 .... 5B 80
Capstan Sq. E14 .... 3E 81
Capstan Way SE16 .... 2A 80
Capstone Rd. BR1: Broml.. 4B 124
Captain St. SE8 .... 4F 97
.... (off Tellson Av.)
Capulet M. E16 .... 2C 82
Capulet Sq. E3 .... 2D 67
.... (off Talwin St.)
Capworth St. E10 .... 3C 38
Caradoc Cl. W2 .... 5C 58
Caradoc St. SE10 .... 1A 96
Caradon Cl. E11 .... 3A 40
Cara Ho. N1 .... 4C 48
.... (off Liverpool Rd.)
Caramel Ct. E3 .... 1D 67
.... (off Taylor Pl.)
Carandey Vs. W11 .... 2F 71
.... (off Norland Rd.)
Carat Ho. E14 .... 4C 66
.... (off Ursula Gould Way)
Caravel Cl. E14 .... 4C 80

Caravel Ho. E16.................3D **83**
Caravel M. SE8..................2C **94**
Caraway Apts. SE1 ..3F **27** (3B **78**)
(off Cayenne Ct.)
Caraway Cl. E13.................4D **69**
Caraway Hgts. E14...............1E **81**
(off Poplar High St.)
Carbis Rd. E14...................5B **66**
Carbrooke Ho. E9................5E **51**
(off Templecombe Rd.)
Carburton St. W1 ...5E **5** (4D **61**)
Cardale St. E14..................3E **81**
Cardamon Bldg. SE1 2F **27** (3B **78**)
(off Shad Thames)
Carden Rd. SE15...............1D **107**
Cardiff Ho. SE15.................2C **92**
(off Friary Est.)
Cardigan Pl. SE3................5F **95**
Cardigan Rd. E3.................1B **66**
Cardigan Rd. SW13.............5C **84**
Cardigan St. SE11...............1C **90**
Cardigan Wlk. N1................4E **49**
(off Ashby Gro.)
Cardinal Bourne St.
SE1...........................5C **26** (4F **77**)
Cardinal Cap All. SE1 1F **25** (2E **77**)
Cardinal Ct. E1...................1C **78**
(off Thomas More St.)
Cardinal Hinsley Cl. NW10....1C **56**
Cardinal Mans. SW1..............5E **75**
(off Carlisle Pl.)
Cardinal Pl. SW1 ....5F **21** (4E **75**)
(not continuous)
Cardinal Pl. SW15................2F **99**
Cardinals Way N19.............3F **33**
Cardinal Wlk. SW1 ..5F **21** (4E **75**)
(off Victoria St.)
Cardine M. SE15.................3D **93**
Cardington St. NW1 ..1A **6** (2E **61**)
Cardozo Rd. N7...................2A **48**
Cardross Ho. W6.................4D **71**
(off Cardross St.)
Cardross St. W6.................4D **71**
Cardwell Rd. N7..................1A **48**
Cardwell Ter. N7..................1A **48**
(off Cardwell Rd.)
Career Ct. SE16..................3E **79**
(off Christopher Cl.)
Carew Cl. N7......................4B **34**
Carew Ct. SE14...................2F **93**
(off Samuel Cl.)
Carew St. SE5.....................5E **91**
Carey Gdns. SW8................4E **89**
Carey La. EC2...........2F **17** (5E **63**)
Carey Mans. SW1.................5F **75**
(off Rutherford St.)
Carey Pl. SW1.....................5F **75**
Carey St. WC2.........3A **16** (5B **62**)
Carfax Pl. SW4..................2F **103**
Carfree Cl. N1.....................4C **48**
Cargill Rd. SW18..............1D **115**
Carholme Rd. SE23.............1B **122**
Carillon Ct. E1....................4C **64**
(off Greatorex St.)
Carina Ho. E20...................2E **53**
(off Cheering La.)
Carinthia Ct. SE16...............5A **80**
(off Plough Way)
Carisbrooke Ct. W1 ..1C **12** (4C **60**)
(off Weymouth St.)
Carisbrooke Gdns. SE15...3B **92**
Carker's La. NW5................2D **47**
Carleton Gdns. N19............2E **47**

Carleton Rd. N19................2F **47**
Carleton Rd. N7..................2F **47**
Carleton Vs. NW5................2E **47**
Carlile Cl. E3......................1B **66**
Carlile Ho. SE1 .....5C **26** (4F **77**)
(off Tabard St.)
Carlingford Rd. NW3............1F **45**
Carlisle Av. EC3........3E **19** (5A **64**)
Carlisle Av. W3...................5A **56**
Carlisle Gdns. IG1: Ilf 1F **41**
Carlisle Gdns. IG1: Ilf 1F **41**
Carlisle La. SE1 ......5A **24** (4B **76**)
Carlisle Mans. SW1..............5E **75**
(off Carlisle Pl.)
Carlisle Pl. SW1.......5F **21** (4E **75**)
Carlisle Rd. E10..................3C **38**
Carlisle Rd. N4....................2C **34**
Carlisle Rd. NW6.................5A **44**
Carlisle St. W1 ......3B **14** (5F **61**)
Carlisle Wlk. E8...................3B **50**
Carlisle Way SW17.............5C **116**
Carlos Pl. W1...........5C **12** (1C **74**)
Carlow St. NW1...................1E **61**
Carlson Ct. SW15...............2B **100**
Carlton Cl. NW3...................4C **30**
Carlton Ct. W9....................1D **59**
(off Maida Vale)
Carlton Dr. SW15................3F **99**
Carlton Gdns. SW1...1B **22** (2F **75**)
Carlton Gro. SE15...............4D **93**
Carlton Hill NW8.................1D **59**
Carlton Ho. NW6..................1C **58**
(off Canterbury Ter.)
Carlton Ho. SE16................3F **79**
(off Wolfe Cres.)
Carlton Ho. Ter.
SW1.......................2B **22** (2F **75**)
Carlton Lodge N4................2C **34**
(off Carlton Rd.)
Carlton Mans. N16..............3B **36**
Carlton Mans. NW6.............4C **44**
(off West End La.)
Carlton Mans. W14.............3A **72**
(off Holland Pk. Gdns.)
Carlton Mans. W9...............2D **59**
Carlton Mans. NW6.............2C **44**
(off West Cotts.)
Carlton Rd. E11...................3B **40**
Carlton Rd. E12...................1F **55**
Carlton Rd. N4....................2C **34**
Carlton Sq. E1.....................3F **65**
(not continuous)
Carlton St. SW1 .....5B **14** (1F **75**)
Carlton Ter. E7....................4E **55**
Carlton Ter. SE26...............3E **121**
Carlton Twr. Pl. SW1 ..5A **20** (4B **74**)
Carlton Va. NW6.................1B **58**
Carlton Vs. SW15...............3A **100**
Carlton Works, The SE15....3D **93**
Carlwell St. SW17.............5A **116**
Carlyle Cl. N2......................1E **31**
Carlyle Ct. SW10.................4D **87**
(off Chelsea Harbour Dr.)
Carlyle Ct. SW6..................4D **87**
(off Imperial Rd.)
Carlyle Ho. N16..................5A **36**
Carlyle Ho. SE5..................3E **91**
Carlyle Ho. SW3..................2F **87**
(off Old Church St.)
Carlyle Mans. SW3..............2A **88**
(off Cheyne Wlk.)
Carlyle Mans. W8................2C **72**
(off Kensington Mall)

Carlyle M. E1......................3F **65**
Carlyle Pl. SW15.................2F **99**
Carlyle Rd. E12...................1F **55**
Carlyle Rd. NW10...............5A **42**
Carlyle's House.................2A **88**
(off Cheyne Row)
Carlyle Sq. SW3.................1F **87**
Carly M. E2.........................2C **64**
(off Barnet Gro.)
Carmalt Gdns. SW15...........2E **99**
Carmarthen Pl. SE1 .3D **27** (3A **78**)
Carmel Ct. W8....................3D **73**
(off Holland St.)
Carmelite St. EC4......4C **16** (1C **76**)
Carmel Lodge SW6..............2C **86**
(off Lillie Rd.)
Carmelo M. E1.....................4F **65**
(off Maria Ter.)
Carmen St. E14...................5D **67**
Carmichael Cl. SW11...........1F **101**
Carmichael Cl. SW13...........5B **84**
(off Grove Rd.)
Carmichael Ho. E14.............1E **81**
(off Poplar High St.)
Carmichael M. SW18...........5F **101**
Carmine W2........................4F **59**
(off Nth. Wharf Rd.)
Carmine Wharf E14..............5B **66**
Carminia Rd. SW17.............2D **117**
Carnaby St. W1 ......3F **13** (5E **61**)
Carnac St. SE27.................4F **119**
Carnarvon Rd. E10..............1E **39**
Carnarvon Rd. E15..............3B **54**
Carnbrook M. SE3...............1F **111**
Carnbrook Rd. SE3.............1F **111**
Carnegie Pl. SW19..............3F **113**
Carnegie St. N1...................5B **48**
Carnell Apts. E14................5B **66**
(off St Anne's Row)
Carney Pl. SW9.................2C **104**
Carnie Lodge SW17...........3D **117**
Carnival Ho. SE1 .....3F **27** (3B **78**)
(off Gainsford St.)
Carnoustie Dr. N1...............4B **48**
(not continuous)
Carnwath Rd. SW6.............1C **100**
Carolean Cres. SE8.............5A **80**
Carole Ho. NW1..................5B **46**
(off Regent's Pk. Rd.)
Carolina Cl. E15..................2A **54**
Caroline Cl. SW16...........3B **118**
Caroline Cl. W2...................1D **73**
Caroline Ct. W2.................4F **123**
Caroline Gdns. E2 ....1E **11** (2A **64**)
Caroline Gdns. SE15...........3D **93**
(not continuous)
Caroline Ho. W2..................1D **73**
(off Bayswater Rd.)
Caroline Ho. W6..................1E **85**
(off Queen Caroline St.)
Caroline Pl. SW11...............5C **88**
Caroline Pl. W2...................1D **73**
Caroline Pl. M. W2...............1D **73**
Caroline St. E1....................5F **65**
Caroline Ter. SW1................5C **74**
Caroline Wlk. W6.................2A **86**
(off Lillie Rd.)
Carol St. NW1.....................5E **47**
Caronia Ct. SE16.................5A **80**
(off Plough Way)
Carpenter Ho. E1.................4F **65**
(off Trafalgar Gdns.)
Carpenter Ho. E14...............4C **66**
(off Burgess St.)
Carpenter Ho. NW11............1E **31**

Carpenters Arms Apts. SE1. 5C **78**
................................(off Welsford St.)
Carpenters Ct. NW1 ....5E **47**
................................(off Pratt St.)
Carpenters M. N7 ....2A **48**
Carpenters Pl. SW4 ....2F **103**
Carpenter's Rd. E15 ....4E **53**
Carpenter's Rd. E20 ....2C **52**
Carpenter St. W1 ....5D **13** (1D **75**)
Carp Ho. E3 ....5B **52**
................................(off Old Ford Rd.)
Carradale Ho. E14 ....5E **67**
................................(off St Leonard's Rd.)
Carrara Cl. SE24 ....2C **104**
Carrara Cl. SW9 ....2D **105**
Carrara M. E8 ....3C **50**
................................(off Dalston La.)
Carrara Wharf SW6 ....1A **100**
Carre M. SE5 ....4D **91**
................................(off Calais St.)
Carrera Twr. EC1 ......1F **9** (2E **63**)
................................(off Bollinder Pl.)
Carriage Dr. E. SW11 ....3D **88**
Carriage Dr. Nth. SW11: Lon
 Carriage Dr. E. 2C **88**
Carriage Dr. Nth. SW11: Lon The
 Parade 3B **88**
Carriage Dr. Sth. SW11. 4B **88**
................................(not continuous)
Carriage Dr. W. SW11 ....3B **88**
Carriage Ho. E15 ....3F **53**
................................(off Leyton Rd.)
Carriage Ho. N4 ....4C **34**
Carriage Pl. N16 ....5F **35**
Carriage Pl. SW16 ....5E **117**
Carriage Way SE8 ....3C **94**
................................(off Deptford High St.)
Carrick Ct. E3 ....2E **67**
................................(off Bolinder Way)
Carrick Ho. N7 ....3B **48**
................................(off Caledonian Rd.)
Carrick Ho. SE11 ....1C **90**
Carrick M. SE8 ....2C **94**
Carrington Ct. SW11 ....2A **102**
................................(off Barnard Rd.)
Carrington Gdns. E7 ....1C **54**
Carrington Ho. W1 ....2D **21** (2D **75**)
................................(off Carrington St.)
Carrington St. W1 ....2D **21** (2D **75**)
Carrol Cl. NW5 ....1D **47**
Carroll Cl. E15 ....2B **54**
Carroll Ho. W2 ....1F **73**
................................(off Craven Ter.)
Carronade Ct. N7 ....2B **48**
Carron Cl. E14 ....5D **67**
Carroun Rd. SW8 ....3B **90**
Carr St. E14 ....4A **66**
Carslake Rd. SW15 ....4E **99**
Carson Rd. E16 ....3C **68**
Carson Rd. SE21 ....2F **119**
Carson Ter. W11 ....2A **72**
................................(off Princes Pl.)
Carstairs Rd. SE6 ....3E **123**
Carston Cl. SE12 ....3B **110**
Carswell Rd. SE6 ....5E **109**
Carter Cl. NW9 ....1A **28**
Carter Ct. EC4 ....3D **17** (5D **63**)
................................(off Carter La.)
Carteret Ho. W12 ....1D **71**
................................(off White City Est.)
Carteret St. SW1 ......4B **22** (3F **75**)
Carteret Way SE8 ....5A **80**
Carter Ho. E1 ....1F **19** (4B **64**)
................................(off Brune St.)
Carter La. EC4 ....3E **17** (5D **63**)

Carter Pl. SE17 ....1E **91**
Carter Rd. E13 ....5D **55**
Carter Rd. SW19 ....5F **115**
Carters Cl. NW5 ....2F **47**
................................(off Torriano Av.)
Carters Hill Cl. SE9 ....1E **125**
Carter La. SE23 ....2A **122**
Carter Sq. E14 ....5D **67**
................................(off Bowen St.)
Carter St. SE17 ....2E **91**
Carter's Yd. SW18 ....3C **100**
Carthew Rd. W6 ....4D **71**
Carthew Vs. W6 ....4D **71**
Carthusian Ct. EC1 ....5F **9** (4E **63**)
................................(off Carthusian St.)
Carthusian St. EC1 ....5F **9** (4E **63**)
Cartier Circ. E14 ....2D **81**
Carting La. WC2 ....5E **15** (1A **76**)
Cartmel NW1 ....1F **5** (2E **61**)
................................(off Harrington St.)
Carton Ho. W11 ....1F **71**
................................(off St Ann's Rd.)
Cartoon Mus. 1F **13** (5E **61**)
Cartwright Gdns.
 WC1 ....2D **7** (2A **62**)
Cartwright Ho. SE1 ....4E **77**
................................(off County St.)
Cartwright St. E1 ....1B **78**
Cartwright Way SW13 ....3D **85**
Carvel Ho. E14 ....1E **95**
................................(off Manchester Rd.)
Carver Rd. SE24 ....4E **105**
Carville St. N4 ....4C **34**
Cary Av. SE16 ....5A **80**
Cary Rd. E11 ....1A **54**
Carysfort Rd. N16 ....5F **35**
Casbeard St. N4 ....4E **35**
Casby Ho. SE16 ....4C **78**
................................(off Marine St.)
Cascade Ct. SW11 ....3D **89**
Cascades Twr. E14 ....2B **80**
Casella Rd. SE14 ....3F **93**
Casewick Rd. SE27 ....5C **118**
Casey Cl. NW8 ....2A **60**
Casey Cl. SE14 ....4F **93**
................................(off Besson St.)
Cashmere Ho. E8 ....5B **50**
................................(off Pamela St.)
Casia Point E20 ....4E **53**
Casino Rd. E5 ....4E **37**
Casings Way E3 ....4C **52**
Casino Av. SE24 ....3E **105**
Caspian St. SE5 ....3F **91**
Caspian Wlk. E16 ....5F **69**
Caspian Wharf E3 ....4D **67**
................................(off Violet Rd.)
Casselden Ho. NW10 ....4A **42**
Cassell Ho. SW9 ....5B **90**
................................(off Stockwell Gdns. Est.)
Cass Ho. E9 ....3F **51**
................................(off Harrowgate Rd.)
Cassia Rd. E1 ....5C **64**
................................(off Piazza Wlk.)
Cassidy Rd. SW6 ....3C **86**
................................(not continuous)
Cassilis Rd. E14 ....3C **80**
Cassini Apts. E16 ....5C **68**
Cassiobury Rd. E17 ....1A **38**
Cassland Rd. E9 ....4F **51**
Casslee Rd. SE6 ....5B **108**
Casson Apts. E14 ....5C **66**
................................(off Upper Nth. St.)
Casson Ho. E1 ....4C **64**
................................(off Hanbury St.)
Casson Sq. SE1 ....2A **24** (2B **76**)

Casson St. E1 ....4C **64**
Castalia Sq. E14 ....3E **81**
Castellain Mans. W9 ....3D **59**
................................(off Castellain Rd.)
Castellain Rd. W9 ....3D **59**
Castell Ho. SE8 ....3C **94**
Castell Av. SW15 ....3E **98**
Castelnau SW13 ....2C **84**
CASTELNAU 2D **85**
Castelnau Gdns. SW13 ....2D **85**
Castelnau Mans. SW13 ......2D **85**
................................(off Castelnau)
Castelnau Row SW13 ....2D **85**
Casterbridge NW6 ....5D **45**
................................(off Abbey Rd.)
Casterbridge W11 ....5B **58**
................................(off Dartmouth Cl.)
Casterbridge Rd. SE3 ....1C **110**
Casterton St. E8 ....3D **51**
Castillon Rd. SE6 ....2A **124**
Casting Ho. SE14 ....2B **94**
Castlands Rd. SE6 ....2B **122**
Castleacre W2 ....5A **60**
................................(off Hyde Pk. Cres.)
Castle Baynard St.
 EC4 ....4E **17** (1D **77**)
Castlebrook Cl. SE11 ....5D **77**
Castle Cen., The 5D **77**
Castle Cinema, The 2F **51**
Castle Climbing Cen., The 4E **35**
Castle Cl. E9 ....2A **52**
Castle Cl. SW19 ....3F **113**
Castlecombe Dr. SW19 ......5F **99**
Castlecombe Rd. SE9 ....4F **125**
Castle Ct. EC3 ....3C **18** (5F **63**)
................................(off Birchin La.)
Castle Ct. SE26 ....4A **122**
Castle Ct. SW15 ....1A **100**
................................(off Brewhouse La.)
Castleden Ho. NW3 ....4F **45**
................................(off Hilgrove Rd.)
Castle Dr. IG4: Ilf 1F **41**
Castleford Ct. NW8 ....3F **59**
................................(off Henderson Dr.)
Castlehaven Rd. NW1 ....4D **47**
Castle Ho. SW8 ....3A **90**
................................(off Sth. Lambeth Rd.)
Castle La. SW1 ....5A **22** (4E **75**)
Castlemaine SW11 ....5B **88**
Castlemain St. E1 ....4D **65**
Castle Mead SE5 ....3E **91**
Castle M. NW1 ....3D **47**
Castle M. SW17 ....4A **116**
Castle M. W3 ....3A **70**
Castle Pl. W4 ....5A **70**
Castle Point E13 ....1E **69**
................................(off Boundary Rd.)
Castlereagh St. W1 ....5B **60**
Castle Rd. NW1 ....3D **47**
Castle Sq. SE17 ....5E **77**
Castle St. E13 ....1E **69**
Castle St. E6 ....1E **69**
Castleton Ho. E14 ....5E **81**
................................(off Pier St.)
Castleton Rd. SE9 ....4F **125**
Castletown Rd. W14 ....1A **86**
Castleview Cl. N4 ....4E **35**
Castle Way SW19 ....3F **113**
Castle Wharf E14 ....1A **82**
................................(off Orchard Pl.)
Castlewood Rd. N15 ....1C **36**
Castlewood Rd. N16 ....1C **36**
Castle Yd. N6 ....2C **32**
Castle Yd. SE1 ....1E **25** (2D **77**)
Castor La. E14 ....1D **81**

Catalina Ho. E1 .... 5C 64
(off Piazza Wlk.)
Catalpa Ct. SE13 .... 4F 109
Caterham Rd. SE13 .... 1F 109
Catesby Ho. E9 .... 4E 51
(off Frampton Pk. Rd.)
Catesby St. SE17 .... 5F 77
CATFORD 5D 109
Catford Bridge Station
(Rail) 5C 108
Catford B'way. SE6 .... 5D 109
CATFORD GYRATORY 5D 109
Catford Hill SE6 .... 1B 122
Catford Island SE6 .... 5D 109
Catford M. SE6 .... 5D 109
Catford Rd. SE6 .... 5D 109
Catford Station (Rail) 5C 108
Catford Trad. Est. SE6 ...... 2D 123
Cathall Rd. E11 .... 4F 39
Cathay Ho. SE16 .... 3D 79
Cathay St. SE16 .... 3D 79
Cathcart Hill N19 .... 5E 33
Cathcart Ho. SW10 .... 1E 87
(off Cathcart Rd.)
Cathcart Rd. SW10 .... 2D 87
Cathcart St. NW5 .... 3D 47
Cathedral Lodge
EC1 .... 5F 9 (4E 63)
(off Aldersgate St.)
Cathedral Mans. SW1 .... 5E 75
(off Vauxhall Bri. Rd.)
Cathedral Piazza
SW1 .... 5F 21 (4E 75)
Cathedral St. SE1 .. 1B 26 (2F 77)
Cathedral Wlk.
SW1 .... 5F 21 (4E 75)
Catherall Rd. N5 .... 5E 35
Catherine Ct. SW19 .... 5B 114
Catherine Ct. SW3 .... 2F 87
(off Callow St.)
Catherine Griffiths Ct.
EC1 .... 3C 8 (3C 62)
(off Northampton Rd.)
Catherine Gro. SE10 .... 4D 95
Catherine Ho. E3 .... 1C 66
(off Thomas Fyre Dr.)
Catherine Ho. N1 .... 5A 50
(off Whitmore St.)
Catherine Pl. SW1 .. 5F 21 (4E 75)
Catherine Pl. WC2 .. 4F 15 (1B 76)
Catherine Wheel All.
E1 .... 1E 19 (4A 64)
Catherine Wheel Yd.
SW1 .... 2F 21 (2E 75)
(off Lit. St James's St.)
Catherwood Ct. N1 .. 1B 10 (1F 63)
(off Murray Gro.)
Cathles Rd. SW12 .... 4D 103
Cathnor Rd. W12 .... 3D 71
Catkin Cl. E14 .... 5F 67
Catling Cl. SE23 .... 3E 121
Catlin St. SE16 .... 1C 92
Cato Rd. SW4 .... 1F 103
Cator St. SE15:
Lon Commercial Way 3B 92
Cator St. SE15: Lon Ebley Cl. .. 2B 92
Cato St. W1 .... 4A 60
Catton St. WC1 .... 1F 15 (4B 62)
Catwalk Pl. N15 .... 1F 35
Caudwell Ter. SW18 .... 4F 101
Caughley Ho. SE11 .... 4C 76
(off Lambeth Wlk.)
Caulfield Ct. NW1 .... 4E 47
(off Baynes St.)
Caulfield Rd. SE15 .... 5D 93

Causeway, The SW18 .... 3D 101
Causeway, The SW19 .... 5E 113
Causton Cotts. E14 .... 5A 66
(off Galsworthy Av.)
Causton Ho. SE5 .... 2E 91
Causton Ho. SW9 .... 4B 90
Causton Rd. N6 .... 2D 33
Causton St. SW1 .... 5F 75
Cautley Av. SW4 .... 3E 103
Cavalier Ter. SE2 .... 2E 97
Cavalry Gdns. SW15 .... 3B 100
Cavalry Sq. SW3 .... 1B 88
Cavatina Point SE8 .... 2D 95
(off Copperas St.)
Cavaye Ho. SW10 .... 2E 87
(off Cavaye Pl.)
Cavaye Pl. SW10 .... 1E 87
Cavell Ho. N1 .... 5A 50
(off Colville St.)
Cavell St. E1 .... 4D 65
Cavendish Av. NW8 .... 1F 59
Cavendish Cl. NW6 .... 3B 44
Cavendish Cl. NW8 .... 2F 59
Cavendish Ct. EC3 ... 2E 19 (5A 64)
(off Devonshire St.)
Cavendish Ct. SE6 .... 1D 123
(off Bromley Rd.)
Cavendish Dr. E11 .... 3F 39
Cavendish Gdns. SW4 .... 4E 103
Cavendish Ho. NW8 .... 1F 59
(off Wellington Rd.)
Cavendish Ho. SW1 .... 4F 75
(off Monck St.)
Cavendish Ho. W1 ... 1F 13 (4E 61)
(off Mortimer St.)
Cavendish Mans.
EC1 .... 4B 8 (3C 62)
(off Rosebery Av.)
Cavendish Mans. NW6 .... 2C 44
Cavendish M. Nth.
W1 .... 5E 5 (4D 61)
Cavendish M. Sth.
W1 .... 1E 13 (4D 61)
Cavendish Pde. SW4 .... 4D 103
(off Clapham Comn. Sth. Side)
Cavendish Pl. NW2 .... 3F 43
Cavendish Pl. SW4 .... 3F 103
Cavendish Pl. W1 ... 2E 13 (5D 61)
Cavendish Rd. N4 .... 1D 35
Cavendish Rd. NW6 .... 4A 44
Cavendish Rd. SW12 .... 4D 103
Cavendish Sq. W1 ... 2D 13 (5D 61)
Cavendish St. N1 .... 1F 63
Cavendish Ter. E3 .... 2B 66
Cave Rd. E13 .... 2D 69
Caversham Ho. SE15 .... 2C 92
(off Haymerle Rd.)
Caversham M. SW3 .... 2B 88
(off Caversham St.)
Caversham Rd. NW5 .... 3E 47
Caversham St. SW3 .... 2B 88
Caverswall St. W12 .... 5E 57
Cavesson Ho. E20 .... 2E 53
(off Ribbons Wlk.)
Cavour Ho. SE17 .... 1D 91
(off Alberta Est.)
Cawdor Wlk. E14 .... 5E 67
Cawnpore St. SE19 .... 5A 120
Cawston Av. W16 .... 5D 119
Caxton Cl. SW11 .... 5A 88
Caxton Gro. E3 .... 2C 66
Caxton Hall SW1 ... 5B 22 (4F 75)
(off Caxton St.)
Caxton Ho. 4C 22 (3F 75)
(off Tothill St.)

Caxton Rd. SW19 .... 5E 115
Caxton Rd. W12 .... 3F 71
Caxtons, The SW9 .... 3D 91
(off Langton Rd.)
Caxton St. SW1 ...... 5A 22 (4E 75)
Caxton St. Nth. E16 .... 5B 68
Caxton Wlk. WC2 ... 3C 14 (5F 61)
Cayenne Ct. SE1 ... 2F 27 (3B 78)
Cayton Pl. EC1 .... 2B 10 (2F 63)
(off Cayton St.)
Cayton St. EC1 .... 2B 10 (2F 63)
Cazenove Rd. N16 .... 4B 36
Cearns Ho. E6 .... 5F 55
Cecil Ct. NW6 .... 4D 45
Cecil Ct. SW10 .... 2E 87
(off Fawcett St.)
Cecil Ct. WC2 .... 4D 15 (1A 76)
Cecile Pk. N8 .... 1A 34
Cecil Gro. NW8 .... 5A 46
Cecilia Rd. E8 .... 2B 50
Cecil Mans. SW17 .... 2C 116
Cecil Rhodes Ho. NW1 .... 1F 61
(off Goldington St.)
Cecil Rd. E11 .... 5B 40
Cecil Rd. E13 .... 5C 54
Cecil Rd. NW10 .... 5A 42
Cecil Sharp House 5C 46
(off Gloucester Av.)
Cedar Cl. E3 .... 5B 52
Cedar Cl. SE21 .... 1E 119
Cedar Cl. E11 .... 1D 41
Cedar Ct. N1 .... 4E 49
Cedar Ct. SE1 .... 4D 27 (3A 78)
(off Royal Oak Yd.)
Cedar Ct. SE13 .... 2F 109
Cedar Ct. SE7 .... 2E 97
Cedar Ct. SW19 .... 3F 113
Cedar Hgts. NW2 .... 3B 44
Cedar Ho. E1 .... 3E 81
(off Manchester Rd.)
Cedar Ho. E2 .... 1D 65
(off Mowlem St.)
Cedar Ho. SE14 .... 4F 93
Cedar Ho. SE16 .... 3F 79
(off Woodland Cres.)
Cedar Ho. SW6 .... 5E 87
(off Lensbury Av.)
Cedar Ho. W8 .... 4D 73
(off Marloes Rd.)
Cedarhurst Dr. SE9 .... 3E 111
Cedar M. SE4 .... 1B 108
Cedar Mt. SE9 .... 3F 99
Cedar Mt. SE9 .... 1F 125
Cedarne Rd. SW6 .... 3D 87
Cedar Pk. Gdns. SW19 ...... 5D 113
Cedar Pl. SE7 .... 1E 97
Cedar Rd. NW2 .... 1E 43
Cedars, The E15 .... 4B 54
Cedars, The E9 .... 4F 51
(off Banbury Rd.)
Cedars Av. E17 .... 1C 38
Cedars Cl. SE13 .... 1F 109
Cedarside Apts. NW6 .... 1B 58
Cedars M. SW4 .... 2D 103
.... (not continuous)
Cedars Rd. E15 .... 3A 54
Cedars Rd. SW13 .... 5C 84
Cedars Rd. SW4 .... 1D 103
Cedar Tree Gro. SE27 .... 5D 119
Cedar Way N1 .... 4F 47
Cedar Way Ind. Est. N1 ...... 4F 47
Cedra Ct. N16 .... 3C 36
Cedric Chambers NW8 .... 3F 59
(off Northwick Cl.)
Celandine Cl. E14 .... 4C 66

Celandine Dr. E8 .... 4B 50
Celandine Way E15 .... 2A 68
Celbridge M. W2 .... 4D 59
Celebration Av. E20 .... 2E 53
Celestial Gdns. SE13 .... 2F 109
Celia Ho. N1 .... 1A 64
.... (off Arden Est.)
Celia Rd. N19 .... 1E 47
Cellini St. SW8 .... 3F 89
Celtic St. E14 .... 4D 67
Cemetery La. SE7 .... 2F 97
Cemetery Rd. E7 .... 2B 54
Cenacle Cl. NW3 .... 5C 30
Cenotaph 3D 23 (3A 76)
Centaur St. SE1 .... 5A 24 (4B 76)
Central Av. E11 .... 4F 39
Central Av. SW11 .... 3B 88
Central Av. SW6 .... 1E 101
Central Bus. Cen. NW10 ...... 2A 42
Central Cir. NW4 .... 1D 29
Central Ctyd. EC2 ..... 1E 19 (5A 64)
.... (off Cutlers Gdns.)
Central Criminal Court
  Old Bailey 2E 17 (5D 63)
Central Hill SE19 .... 5F 119
Central Ho. E15 .... 1D 67
Central Mall SW18 .... 4D 101
..... (within Southside Shop. Cen.)
Central Mans. NW4 .... 1D 29
.... (off Watford Way)
Central Mill Apts. E8 .... 5B 50
.... (off Samuel St.)
Central Pk. Rd. E6 .... 1F 69
Central St Giles Piazza
  WC2 .... 2C 14 (5A 62)
.... (off St Giles High St.)
Central St Martins College of Art
  & Design
  Back Hill Site 4C 8 (3C 62)
.... (off Back Hill)
Central St Martins College of Art
  & Design
  Byam Shaw Campus 4F 33
Central School of Speech &
  Drama, The 4F 45
Central Sq. NW11 .... 1D 31
Central St. EC1 .... 1F 9 (2E 63)
Central Walkway N19 .... 1F 47
.... (off Pleshey Rd.)
Centre Av. W3 .... 2A 70
Centre for Wildlife Gardening Vis.
  Cen. 1B 106
Centre Hgts. NW3 .... 4F 45
.... (off Finchley Rd.)
Centre Point SE1 .... 1C 92
Centrepoint WC2 ...... 2C 14 (5F 61)
.... (off St Giles High St.)
Centre Rd. E11 .... 4C 40
Centre Rd. E7 .... 4C 40
Centre St. E2 .... 1D 65
Centric Cl. NW1 .... 5C 46
Centurian Sq. SE18 .... 4F 97
Centurion Bldg. SW11 .... 2D 89
Centurion Cl. N7 .... 4B 48
Centurion La. E3 .... 5B 52
Century Cl. NW4 .... 1F 29
Century Ct. NW8 .... 2F 59
Century Ho. SW15 .... 2F 99
Century M. E5 .... 1E 51
Century M. N5 .... 5D 35
.... (off Conewood St.)

Century Way BR3: Beck 5B 122
Century Yd. SE23 .... 2E 121
.... (not continuous)
Cephas Av. E1 .... 3E 65
Cephas Av. E1 .... 3E 65
.... (off Doveton St.)
Cephas St. E1 .... 3E 66
.... (off Gunmaker's La.)
Cerise Apts. E3 .... 5A 52
Cerise Rd. SE15 .... 4C 92
Cerney M. W2 .... 1F 73
.... (off Gloucester Ter.)
Cervantes Ct. W11 .... 5A 58
.... (off Rushton M.)
Cervantes Ct. W2 .... 5D 59
Cervantes Theatre ... 3E 25 (3D 77)
Cester St. E2 .... 5C 50
Ceylon Ho. E1 .... 5C 64
.... (off Alie St.)
Ceylon Rd. W14 .... 4F 71
Ceylon Wharf Apts. SE16 .... 3E 79
.... (off St Marychurch St.)
CFGS Community Performing Arts
  & Sports Cen. 2B 66
Chabot Dr. SE15 .... 1D 107
Chadacre Ct. E15 .... 5C 54
.... (off Vicars Cl.)
Chadacre Ho. SW9 .... 2D 105
.... (off Loughborough Rd.)
Chadbourn St. E14 .... 4D 67
Chadd Grn. E13 .... 5C 54
.... (not continuous)
Chadston Ho. N1 .... 4D 49
.... (off Halton Rd.)
Chadswell WC1 .... 2E 7 (2A 62)
.... (off Cromer St.)
Chadwell Ho. SE17 .... 1F 91
.... (off Inville Rd.)
Chadwell St. EC1 ..... 1C 8 (2C 62)
Chadwick Av. SW19 .... 5C 114
Chadwick Ct. SW15 .... 5B 98
Chadwick Ct. E14 .... 5C 66
.... (off Jonzen Wlk.)
Chadwick Rd. E11 .... 1A 40
Chadwick Rd. NW10 .... 5B 42
Chadwick Rd. SE15 .... 5B 92
Chadwick St. SW1 .... 5B 22 (4F 75)
Chadwin Rd. E13 .... 4D 69
Chadworth Ho. EC1 ... 2F 9 (2E 63)
.... (off Lever St.)
Chadworth Ho. N4 .... 3E 35
Chagford Ho. E3 .... 2D 67
.... (off Talwin St.)
Chagford St. NW1 .... 4A 4 (3B 60)
Chailey St. E5 .... 5E 37
Chalbury Wlk. N1 .... 1B 62
Chalcot Cres. NW1 .... 5B 46
Chalcot Gdns. NW3 .... 3B 46
Chalcot M. SW16 .... 3A 118
Chalcot M. NW1 .... 4C 46
Chalcot Rd. NW1 .... 4C 46
Chalcot Sq. NW1 .... 4C 46
.... (not continuous)
Chalcroft Rd. SE13 .... 3A 110
Chaldon Rd. SW6 .... 3A 86
Chale Rd. SW2 .... 4A 104
Chalfont Ct. NW1 .... 4A 4 (3B 60)
.... (off Baker St.)
Chalfont Ho. SE16 .... 4D 79
.... (off Keetons Rd.)
Chalfont M. SW19 .... 1B 114
Chalford NW6 .... 4E 45
.... (off Finchley Rd.)
Chalford Rd. SE21 .... 4F 119

CHALK FARM 4C 46
Chalk Farm Pde. NW3 .... 4C 46
.... (off Adelaide Rd.)
Chalk Farm Rd. NW1 .... 4C 46
Chalk Farm Station
  (Underground) 4C 46
Chalk Hill Rd. W6 .... 5F 71
Chalk Rd. E13 .... 4D 69
Chalkwell Ho. E1 .... 5F 65
.... (off Pitsea St.)
Challenge Cl. NW10 .... 5A 42
Challenger Ho. E14 .... 1A 80
.... (off Victory Pl.)
Challice Way SW2 .... 1B 118
Challis Ho. SW11 .... 5B 88
Challoner Ct. W14 .... 1B 86
.... (off Challoner St.)
Challoner Cres. W14 .... 1B 86
Challoner Mans. W14 .... 1B 86
.... (off Challoner St.)
Challoner St. W14 .... 1B 86
Challoner Wlk. E1 .... 5C 64
.... (off Christian St.)
Chalmers Wlk. SE17 .... 2D 91
.... (off Hillingdon St.)
Chaloner Ct. SE1 ...... 3B 26 (3F 77)
.... (off Tennis St.)
Chalsey Rd. SE4 .... 2B 108
Chalton Dr. N2 .... 1F 31
Chalton Ho. NW1 ..... 1B 6 (2F 61)
.... (off Chalton St.)
Chalton St. NW1 ...... 1B 6 (1E 61)
.... (not continuous)
Chamberlain Cotts. SE5 .... 4F 91
Chamberlain Cl. SE16 .... 5E 79
.... (off Silwood St.)
Chamberlain Ho. E1 .... 1E 79
.... (off Cable St.)
Chamberlain Ho. EC2 3D 11 (3A 64)
.... (off Blackall St.)
Chamberlain Ho.
  NW1 .... 1B 6 (2F 61)
.... (off Ossulston St.)
Chamberlain Ho.
  SE1 .... 4B 24 (3C 76)
.... (off Westminster Bri. Rd.)
Chamberlain St. NW1 .... 4B 46
Chamberlayne Mans.
  NW10 .... 2F 57
.... (off Chamberlayne Rd.)
Chamberlayne Rd. NW10 ..... 5E 43
Chamberlens Garages W6 .... 5D 71
.... (off Dalling Rd.)
Chambers, The SW10 .... 4E 87
.... (off Chelsea Harbour Dr.)
Chambers La. NW10 .... 4D 43
Chambers Rd. N7 .... 1A 48
Chambers St. SE16 .... 3C 78
Chamber St. E1 .... 4F 19 (1B 78)
Chambers Wharf SE16 .... 3C 78
Chambon Pl. W6 .... 5C 70
Chambord Ho. E2 .... 2F 11 (2B 64)
.... (off Chambord St.)
Chambord St. E2 ..... 1F 11 (2B 64)
.... (off Yunus Khan Cl.)
Chamomile Ct. E17 .... 1C 38
Champion Gro. SE26 .... 4A 122
Champion Gro. SE5 .... 1F 105
Champion Hill SE5 .... 1F 105
Champion Hill Est. SE5 ...... 1A 106
Champion Hill Stadium 2A 106
Champion Ho. SE7 .... 2E 97
.... (off Charlton Rd.)
Champion Pk. SE5 .... 5F 91
Champion Rd. SE26 .... 4A 122

Champions Wlk. E20 ....2E 53
Champlain Ho. W12 ....1D 71
............................(off White City Est.)
Champness Cl. SE27..............4F 119
Chancel Ct. W1 ....4B 14 (1F 75)
........................(off Old Compton St.)
Chancel Ind. Est. NW10 ....2B 42
Chancellor Gro. SE21...........2E 119
Chancellor Ho. E1 ....2D 79
............................(off Green Bank)
Chancellor Ho. SW7 ....4E 73
............................(off Hyde Pk. Ga.)
Chancellor Pas. E14..................2C 80
Chancellors Ct. WC1 .....5F 7 (4B 62)
............................(off Orde Hall St.)
Chancellor's Rd. W6..................1E 85
Chancellor's St. W6..................1E 85
Chancellors Wharf W6..........1E 85
Chancel St. SE1 ....2D 25 (2D 77)
Chancery Bldg. SW11.............3F 89
Chancery Bldgs. E1 ....1D 79
............................(off Lowood St.)
Chancery La. WC2....1A 16 (5C 62)
Chancery Lane Station
(Underground) 1B 16 (4C 62)
Chancery M. SW17 ....2A 116
Chance St. E1...............3F 11 (3B 64)
Chance St. E2...............3F 11 (3B 64)
Chandler Av. E16......................4C 68
Chandler Ho. NW6....................5B 44
............................(off Willesden La.)
Chandler Ho. WC1 ....4E 7 (3A 62)
............................(off Colonnade)
Chandlers Av. SE10 ....3B 82
Chandlers Ct. SE12 ....1D 125
Chandlers M. E14 ....2C 80
Chandler St. E1 ....2D 79
Chandlers Way SW2 ....5C 104
Chandler Way SE15 ....2A 92
Chandlery, The
SE1 ....5C 24 (4C 76)
............................(off Gerridge St.)
Chandlery Ho. E1 ....5C 64
............................(off Gower's Wlk.)
Chandos Cl. W12.....5D 15 (1A 76)
Chandos Rd. E15......................2F 53
Chandos Rd. NW10 ....3A 56
Chandos Rd. NW2 ....2E 43
Chandos St. W1 ....1E 13 (4D 61)
Chandos Way NW11 ....3D 31
Change All. EC3........3C 18 (5F 63)
Chanin 4 TV...............5B 22 (4F 75)
............................(off Horseferry Rd.)
Channel Ga. Rd. NW10............2A 56
Channel Ho. SE16 ....3F 79
............................(off Water Gdns. Sq.)
Channel Islands Est. N1 ....3E 49
Channelsea Ho. E15.................1F 67
Channelsea Path E15...............5F 53
Channelsea Rd. E15.................5F 53
Chantelle Ct. SE8 ....5A 80
............................(off Yeoman St.)
Chantrey Rd. SW9.................1B 104
Chantry Cl. W9 ....3C 58
Chantry Cres. NW10................3B 42
Chantry Sq. W8 ....4D 73
Chantry St. N1..........................5D 49
Chant Sq. E15 ....4F 53
Chant St. E15 ....4F 53
............................(not continuous)
Chapel, The SW15.................4A 100
Chapel Cl. NW10 ....2B 42

Chapel Ct. E10 ....4D 39
............................(off Rosedene Ter.)
Chapel Ct. SE1 ....3B 26 (3F 77)
............................(off Bedford Rd.)
Chapel Ga. M. SW4 ....1A 104
Chapel Ho. St. E14 ....1D 95
Chapelier Ho. SW18................2C 100
Chapel Mkt. N1 ....1C 62
Chapel Path E11 ....1D 41
............................(off Woodbine Pl.)
Chapel Pl. EC2...........2D 11 (2A 64)
Chapel Pl. N1 ....1C 62
Chapel Pl. W1...............3D 13 (5D 61)
Chapel Rd. SE27 ....4D 119
Chapel Side W2 ....1D 73
Chapel St. NW1 ....1A 60
Chapel St. SW1 ....5C 20 (4C 74)
Chapel Way N7 ....5B 34
Chapel Yd. SW18 ....3D 101
............................(off Wandsworth High St.)
Chaplin Cl. SE1 ....3C 24 (3C 76)
Chaplin Cl. E3 ....3B 66
............................(off Joseph St.)
Chaplin Ct. SE14 ....4F 93
............................(off Besson St.)
Chaplin Ct. SE17 ....2D 91
............................(off Royal Rd.)
Chaplin Ho. N1 ....5F 49
............................(off Shepperton Rd.)
Chaplin Rd. E15........................1B 68
Chaplin Rd. NW2 ....3C 42
Chapman Ho. E1 ....5D 65
............................(off Bigland St.)
Chapman Pl. N4........................4D 35
Chapman Rd. E9 ....3B 52
Chapmans Pk. Ind. Est.
NW10...................................3B 42
Chapman Sq. SW19 ....2F 113
Chapman St. E1 ....1D 79
Chapone Pl. W1 ....3B 14 (5F 61)
Chapter Chambers SW1 ....5F 75
............................(off Chapter St.)
Chapter Ho. E2 ....3C 64
............................(off Dunbridge St.)
Chapter Rd. NW2 ....2C 42
Chapter Rd. SE17 ....1D 91
Chapter St. SW1 ....5F 75
Charcot Ho. SW15 ....4B 98
Charcroft Ct. W14 ....3F 71
............................(off Minford Gdns.)
Chardin Ho. SW9 ....4C 90
............................(off Gosling Way)
Chardin Rd. W4 ....5A 70
Chardmore Rd. N16 ....3C 36
Charecroft Way W14................3F 71
Charfield Ct. W9 ....3D 59
............................(off Shirland Rd.)
Charford Rd. E16 ....4C 68
Chargeable La. E13 ....3B 68
Chargeable St. E16 ....3B 68
Chargrove Cl. SE16 ....3F 79
Charing Cross SW1 ....1D 23 (2A 76)
CHARING CROSS HOSPITAL.2F 85
Charing Cross Rd.
WC2.....................2C 14 (5F 61)
Charing Cross Sports Club...2F 85
Charing Cross Station
(Rail & Underground)
London.....................1D 23 (2A 76)
Charing Cross Theatre
.................................1E 23 (2A 76)
............................(off Villiers St.)
Charing Cross. SE1 ....3C 24 (3C 76)
............................(off Windmill Wlk.)

Chariot Cl. E3 ....5C 52
Charis Ho. E3 ....2D 67
............................(off Grace St.)
Charlbert Ct. NW8 ....1A 60
............................(off Charlbert St.)
Charlbert St. NW8 ....1A 60
Charlbury Gro. SE26.............3D 121
Charlecote Gro. SE26............3D 121
Charles II Pl. SW3 ....1B 88
Charles II St. SW1....1B 22 (2F 75)
Charles Auffray Ho. E1 ....4E 65
............................(off Smithy St.)
Charles Baker Pl. SW17.......1A 116
Charles Barry Cl. SW4 ....1E 103
Charles Burton Ct. E5.............2A 52
............................(off Ashenden Rd.)
Charles Clowes Wlk. SW11 ...3F 89
Charles Coveney Rd. SE15 ...4B 92
Charles Darwin Ho. E16.........5B 68
............................(off Minnie Baldock St.)
Charles Darwin Ho. E2...........2D 65
............................(off Canrobert St.)
Charles Dickens Ho. E2 ....2C 64
............................(off Mansford St.)
Charles Dickens Mus., The
.................................3A 8 (3B 62)
............................(off Doughty St.)
Charlesfield SE9.....................3E 125
Charles Flemwell M. E16.......2C 82
Charles Gardner Ct.
N1 ....1C 10 (2F 63)
............................(off Haberdasher St.)
Charles Haller St. SW2 ....5C 104
Charles Harrod Ct. SW13.......2E 85
............................(off Somerville Av.)
Charles Ho. W14 ....5B 72
Charles Lamb Ct. N1 ....1D 63
............................(off Gerrard Rd.)
Charles La. NW8 ....1A 60
Charles Mackenzie Ho.
SE16.....................................5C 78
............................(off Linsey St.)
Charles Nex M. SE21............2E 119
Charles Pl. NW1 ....2A 6 (2E 61)
Charles Rd. E7 ....4E 55
Charles Rowan Ho.
WC1.............................2B 8 (2C 62)
............................(off Margery St.)
Charles Simmons Ho.
WC1.............................2A 8 (2B 62)
............................(off Margery St.)
Charles Sq. N1..........2C 10 (2F 63)
Charles Sq. Est. N1 ..2C 10 (2F 63)
............................(off Pitfield St.)
Charles St. E16 ....2E 83
Charles St. N19 ....3A 34
Charles St. SW13 ....5A 84
Charles St. W1 ....1D 21 (2D 75)
Charles Talbot M. SE22.......1D 121
Charles St. SE17 ....5E 77
Charles Townsend Ho.
EC1.............................2D 9 (2D 63)
............................(off Skinner St.)
Charles Uton Ct. E8.................1C 50
Charles Whincup Rd. E16.....2D 83
Charlesworth Ho. E14.............5C 66
............................(off Dod St.)
Charlesworth Pl. SW13 ....1A 98
Charleville Cir. SE26..............5C 120
Charleville Ct. W14..................1B 86
............................(off Charleville Rd.)
Charleville Mans. W14...........1A 86
............................(off Charleville Rd.)
Charleville Rd. W14 ....1A 86
Charlie Chaplin Adventure
Playground.........................3D 91

Charlie Chaplin Wlk.
SE1..........................1A **24** (2B **76**)
Charlmont Rd. SW17 .....5A **116**
Charlotte Ct. N8 ....1F **33**
Charlotte Ct. SE1..................5A **78**
.................................(off Old Kent Rd.)
Charlotte Ct. W6................5C **70**
Charlotte Despard Av.
SW11.....................................4C **88**
Charlotte Ho. E16................2D **83**
....................................(off Fairfax M.)
Charlotte Ho. W6................1E **85**
............................(off Queen Caroline St.)
Charlotte M. W1 ....5A **6** (4E **61**)
Charlotte M. W10...............5F **57**
Charlotte M. W14...............5A **72**
Charlotte Pl. SW1...............5E **75**
Charlotte Pl. W1 ....1A **14** (4E **61**)
Charlotte Rd. EC2....2D **11** (2A **64**)
Charlotte Rd. SW13...........4B **84**
Charlotte Row SW4...........1E **103**
Charlotte St. W1 ....5A **6** (4E **61**)
Charlotte Ter. N1................5B **48**
Charlow Cl. SW6................5E **87**
CHARLTON 3F **97**
Charlton Athletic FC 1E **97**
Charlton Chu. La. SE7.......1E **97**
Charlton Ct. E2...................5B **50**
Charlton Ct. NW5...............2F **47**
Charlton Dene SE7.............3E **97**
Charlton Ga. Bus. Pk. SE7 ...5E **83**
Charlton King's Rd. NW5....2F **47**
Charlton La. SE7.................5F **83**
Charlton Lido 3F **97**
Charlton Pk. La. SE7.........3F **97**
Charlton Pk. Rd. SE7 ....2F **97**
Charlton Pl. N1...................1D **63**
Charlton Riverside Pl. SE7...5D **83**
Charlton Rd. NW10............5A **42**
Charlton Rd. SE3................3C **96**
Charlton Rd. SE7................2D **97**
Charlton Station (Rail) 1E **97**
Charlton Ter. SE1................2C **90**
Charlton Way SE3..............4A **96**
Charlwood Ho. SW1...........5F **75**
.............................(off Vauxhall Bri. Rd.)
Charlwood Ho's.
WC1......................2E **7** (2A **62**)
..................................(off Midhope St.)
Charlwood Pl. SW1.............5E **75**
Charlwood Rd. SW15.........2F **99**
Charlwood St. SW1.............1E **89**
...................................(not continuous)
Charlwood Ter. SW15........7F **99**
Charmans Ho. SW8............3A **90**
............................(off Wandsworth Rd.)
Charmeuse Ct. E2...............1D **65**
...............................(off Silk Weaver Way)
Charmian Ho. N1.....1D **11** (1A **64**)
...................................(off Crondall St.)
Charminster Rd. SE9 ....4F **125**
Charmouth Ho. SW8..........3B **90**
Charnock Ho. W12.............1D **71**
................................(off White City Est.)
Charnock Rd. E5................5D **37**
Charnwood Gdns. E14.......5C **80**
Charnwood St. E5..............4D **37**
Charrington St. NW1..........1F **61**
...................................(not continuous)
Charsley Rd. SE6...............2D **123**
Charter Bldgs. SE10..........4D **95**
................................(off Catherine Gro.)
Charter Ct. N4......................3E **34**
Charter Ho. WC2 ......3E **15** (5A **62**)
...................................(off Crown Ct.)

Charterhouse 4E **9** (3D **63**)
Charterhouse Apts. SW18....2E **101**
Charterhouse Bldgs.
EC1........................4E **9** (3E **63**)
Charterhouse M.
EC1........................5E **9** (4D **63**)
Charterhouse Mus. ..5E **9** (4D **63**)
...........................(within Charterhouse)
Charterhouse Rd. E8............1C **50**
Charterhouse Sq.
EC1........................5E **9** (4D **63**)
Charterhouse St.
EC1........................1C **16** (4C **62**)
Charteris Community Sports Cen.
....5C **44**
Charteris Rd. N4..................3C **34**
Charteris Rd. NW6..............5B **44**
Charteris Rd. SE19............5A **120**
Charter St. E14...................2E **81**
Chartes Ho. SE1.......5E **27** (4A **78**)
...................................(off Stevens St.)
Chartfield Av. SW15...........3D **99**
Chartfield Sq. SW15...........3F **99**
Chartham Ct. SW9 ....1C **104**
.............................(off Canterbury Cres.)
Chartham Gro. SE27 ....3D **119**
Chartham Ho. SE1...5C **26** (4F **77**)
...................................(off Weston St.)
Chart Ho. E14...................1Q **95**
............................(off Burrells Wharf Sq.)
Chartley Av. NW2................5A **28**
Chartridge SE17.................2F **91**
............................(off Westmoreland St.)
Chart St. N1............1C **10** (2F **63**)
Chartwell Ct. NW2...............5C **28**
Chartwell Ho. SW10............4E **87**
.................................(off Ladbroke Gro.)
Chartwell Ho. W11.............2B **72**
...............................(off Ladbroke Rd.)
Charville Ct. SE10...............5F **89**
...................................(off Trafalgar Gro.)
Charwood SW16.................4C **118**
Chase, The E12...................1F **55**
Chase, The SW4 ....1D **103**
Chase Ct. SW3....................4B **74**
...............................(off Beaufort Gdns.)
Chasefield Rd. SW17..........4B **116**
Chase Ho. NW6...................2C **58**
..................................(off Hansel Rd.)
Chaseley Ct. E14................5A **66**
Chasemore Ho. SW6 ....3A **86**
..................................(off Williams Cl.)
Chase Rd. Trad. Est.
N10.......................................3A **56**
Chaseway Lodge E16..........5C **68**
................................(off Butchers Rd.)
Chaston Pl. NW5.................2C **46**
.................................(off Grafton Ter.)
Chater Ho. E2.....................2F **65**
...................................(off Roman Rd.)
Chatfield Rd. SW11.............1E **101**
Chatham Cl. NW11...............1C **30**
Chatham Pl. E9....................3E **51**
Chatham Rd. SW11.............4B **102**
Chatham St. SE17...............5F **77**
Chats Palace Arts Cen.........2F **51**
Chatsworth Av.
BR1: Broml 4D **125**
Chatsworth Ct. W8..............5C **72**
..................................(off Pembroke Rd.)
Chatsworth Est. E5..............1F **51**
Chatsworth Ho. E16............2D **83**
...................................(off Wesley Av.)
Chatsworth Ho.
SE1.........................2F **27** (2B **78**)
..................................(off Duchess Wlk.)

Chatsworth Lodge W4........1A **84**
..................................(off Bourne Pl.)
Chatsworth Rd. E5..............2B **54**
Chatsworth Rd. E15............5B **54**
Chatsworth Rd. NW2..........3E **43**
Chatsworth Way SE27.......3D **119**
Chatterton M. N4.................5D **35**
................................(off Chatterton Rd.)
Chatterton Rd. N4...............5D **35**
Chatto Rd. SW11................3B **102**
Chaucer Ct. N16.................1A **50**
Chaucer Ct. SW17..............3F **115**
...........................(off Lanesborough Way)
Chaucer Dr. SE1..................5B **78**
Chaucer Gdns. E1................5C **64**
....................................(off Piazza Wlk.)
Chaucer Ho. SW1................1E **89**
................................(off Churchill Gdns.)
Chaucer Mans. W14 ....2A **86**
...........................(off Queen's Club Gdns.)
Chaucer Rd. E11..................1C **40**
Chaucer Rd. E7...................3C **54**
Chaucer Rd. SE24..............3C **104**
Chaucer Rd. SW19.............5F **115**
Chaulden Ho. EC1....2C **10** (2F **63**)
..................................(off Cranwood St.)
Chauntler Cl. E16.................5D **69**
Cheadle Ct. NW8................3F **59**
................................(off Henderson Dr.)
Cheadle Ho. E14.................5B **66**
................................(off Copenhagen Pl.)
Cheam St. SE15.................1E **107**
Cheapside EC2........2F **17** (5E **63**)
Cheapside Pas.
EC2..3F **15** (5E **63**)
................................(off One New Change)
Cheddington Ho. E2.............5C **50**
.................................(off Whiston Rd.)
Cheering La. E20.................2E **53**
Cheesemans Ter. W14.........1B **86**
...................................(not continuous)
Chelford Rd. BR1: Broml ...5F **123**
Chelmer Rd. E9...................2F **51**
Chelmsford Cl. W6..............2F **85**
Chelmsford Ho. N7..............1B **48**
...................................(off Holloway Rd.)
Chelmsford Rd. E11.............3F **39**
Chelmsford Rd. E17.............1C **38**
Chelmsford Sq. NW10.........5E **43**
CHELSEA 1A **88**
CHELSEA & WESTMINSTER
HOSPITAL 2E **87**
CHELSEA BRI. 2D **89**
Chelsea Bri. Rd. SW1..........1C **88**
Chelsea Bri. Wharf SW11 ...2D **89**
Chelsea Cloisters SW3........5A **74**
Chelsea Cl. NW10................5A **42**
Chelsea Ct. SW3.................2B **88**
..............................(off Embankment Gdns.)
Chelsea Cres. NW2..............3B **44**
Chelsea Cres. SW10............4E **87**
Chelsea Emb. SW3..............2A **88**
Chelsea Farm Ho. Studios
SW10.....................................2F **87**
...................................(off Cremorne Est.)
Chelsea FC 3D **87**
Chelsea Gdns. SW1.............1C **88**
Chelsea Ga. SW1 ....1C **88**
...................................(off Ebury Bri. Rd.)
Chelsea Harbour SW10 ....4E **87**
Chelsea Harbour Design Cen.
SW10.....................................4E **87**
.............................(off Chelsea Harbour Dr.)
Chelsea Harbour Dr.
SW10.....................................4E **87**

Chelsea Harbour Pier
(River Bus) 4F 87
Chelsea Lodge SW3.....2B 88
.............................(off Tite St.)
Chelsea Mnr. St. SW3.....2A 88
Chelsea Mnr. Gdns. SW3.....1A 88
Chelsea Mnr. St. SW3.....1A 88
Chelsea Mnr. Studios SW3.....1A 88
.........................(off Flood St.)
Chelsea Pk. Gdns. SW3.....2F 87
Chelsea Physic Gdn. 2B 88
Chelsea Reach Twr. SW10.....3F 87
.................(off Worlds End Est.)
Chelsea Sports Cen. 1A 88
Chelsea Sq. SW3.....1F 87
Chelsea Studios SW6.....3D 87
.........................(off Fulham Rd.)
Chelsea, The Theatre.....3E 87
Chelsea Towers SW3.....2A 88
.................(off Chelsea Mnr.)
Chelsea Village 3D 87
.........................(off Fulham Rd.)
Chelsea Vista SW6.....4E 87
Chelsea Wharf SW10.....3F 87
.........................(off Lots Rd.)
Chelsfield Gdns. SE26.....3E 121
Chelsfield Ho. SE17.....5A 78
.................(off Massinger St.)
Chelsfield Point E9.....4F 51
.................(off Penshurst Rd.)
Chelsham Rd. SW4.....1F 103
Chelston Ct. E11.....1D 41
Cheltenham Gdns. E6.....1F 69
Cheltenham Rd. E10.....1E 39
Cheltenham Rd. SE15.....2E 107
Cheltenham Ter. SW3.....1B 88
Chelverton Rd. SW15.....2F 99
Chelwood Ho. W2.....4F 87
.................(off Westbridge Rd.)
Chelwood Ho. W2.....5F 59
.................(off Gloucester Sq.)
Chelwood Wlk. SE4.....2A 108
Chenappa Cl. E13.....2D 68
Cheney Ct. SE23.....1F 121
Cheneys Rd. E11.....5A 40
Chenies, The NW1.....1F 61
.................(off Pancras Rd.)
Chenies Ho. W2.....1D 73
.........................(off Moscow Rd.)
Chenies Ho. W4.....3B 84
.................(off Corney Reach Way)
Chenies M. WC1.....4B 6 (3F 61)
Chenies Pl. NW1.....1F 61
Chenies St. WC1.....5B 6 (4F 61)
Cheniston Gdns. W8.....4D 73
Chenla SE13.....5D 95
Cheping Ho. W10.....1F 71
.........................(off Shalfleet Dr.)
Chepstow Cl. SW15.....3A 100
Chepstow Cnr. W2.....5C 58
.........................(off Chepstow Pl.)
Chepstow Ct. W11.....1C 72
.........................(off Chepstow Vs.)
Chepstow Cres. W11.....1C 72
Chepstow Pl. W2.....5C 58
Chepstow Rd. W2.....5C 58
Chepstow Vs. W11.....1B 72
Chequers Ct. EC1.....4A 10 (3F 63)
.........................(off Chequer St.)
Chequers Ho. NW8.....3A 60
.........................(off Jerome Cres.)
Chequer St. EC1.....4A 10 (3E 63)
.............................(not continuous)
Cherbury Ct. N1.....1C 10 (1F 63)
.........................(off St John's Est.)

Cherbury St. N1.....1F 63
Cheriton Ct. SE12.....5C 110
Cheriton Sq. SW17.....2C 116
Cherry Cl. SW2.....5C 104
Cherry Cl. W3.....2A 84
Cherry Gdn. Ho. SE16.....3D 79
.........................(off Cherry Gdn. St.)
Cherry Gdn. St. SE16.....3D 79
Cherry Laurel Wlk. SW2.....4B 104
Cherry Orchard SE7.....2E 97
Cherry Pk. La. E20.....4E 53
Cherry Tree Cl. E9.....5E 51
Cherry Tree Ct. NW1.....4E 47
.........................(off Camden Rd.)
Cherry Tree Ct. SE7.....2E 97
Cherry Tree Dr. SW16.....3A 118
Cherry Tree Rd. E15.....2A 54
Cherry Tree Ter.
SE1.....4E 27 (3A 78)
.................(off Whites Grounds)
Cherry Tree Wlk.
EC1.....4A 10 (3E 63)
Cherry Tree Way W3.....3F 69
Cherrywood Cl. E3.....2A 66
Cherrywood Dr. SW15.....3F 99
Cherrywood Lodge SE13.....4F 109
.........................(off Birdwood Av.)
Chertsey Ho. E2.....2F 11 (2B 64)
.........................(off Arnold Cir.)
Chertsey Rd. E11.....4F 39
Chertsey St. SW17.....5C 116
Cherwell Ho. NW8.....3F 59
.........................(off Church St. Est.)
Cherwell M. SW11.....2A 102
Cheryls Cl. SW6.....4D 87
Cheseman St. SE26.....3D 121
Chesham Cl. SW1.....5B 20 (4C 74)
.........................(off Lyall St.)
Chesham Flats W1.....4C 12 (1C 74)
.........................(off Brown Hart Gdns.)
Chesham Ho. SE8.....4C 94
.........................(off Brookmill Rd.)
Chesham M. SW1.....5B 20 (4C 74)
.........................(off Belgrave M. W.)
Chesham Pl. SW1.....5B 20 (4C 74)
.............................(not continuous)
Chesham Rd. SW19.....5F 115
Chesham St. SW1.....5C 20 (4C 74)
Chesham St. NW10.....5A 42
Cheshire Cl. SE4.....5B 94
Cheshire Ct. EC4.....3C 16 (5C 62)
.........................(off Fleet St.)
Cheshire St. E2.....3B 64
Chesholm Rd. N16.....5A 36
Cheshunt Ho. NW6.....5D 45
.........................(off Mortimer Cres.)
Cheshunt Rd. E7.....3D 55
Chesil Ct. E2.....1E 65
Chesil Ct. SW3.....2A 88
Chesilton Rd. SW6.....4B 86
Chesley Gdns. E6.....1F 69
Chesney Ct. W9.....3C 58
.........................(off Shirland Rd.)
Chesney Ho. SE13.....2F 109
.........................(off Mercator Rd.)
Chesney St. SW11.....4C 88
Chessington Ho. SW8.....5F 89
Chessington Mans. E10.....2C 38
Chessington Mans. E11.....2A 40
Chessington Rd. W14.....2B 86
Chester Cl. SW1.....4D 21 (3D 75)
Chester Cl. SW13.....1D 99
Chester Cl. Nth. NW1.....1D 5 (2D 61)
Chester Cl. Sth. NW1.....2D 5 (2D 61)
Chester Cotts. SW1.....5C 74
.........................(off Bourne St.)

Chester Ct. NW1.....1E 5 (2D 61)
.............................(not continuous)
Chester Ct. SE5.....3F 91
.........................(off Lomond Gro.)
Chester Ct. SE8.....1F 93
Chester Ct. W6.....5F 71
.........................(off Wolverton Gdns.)
Chester Cres. E8.....2B 50
Chesterfield Gdns. N4.....1D 35
Chesterfield Gdns. SE10.....3F 95
Chesterfield Gdns.
W1.....1D 21 (2D 75)
Chesterfield Gro. SE22.....3B 106
Chesterfield Hill W1.....1D 21 (2D 75)
Chesterfield Ho. W1.....1C 20 (2C 74)
.........................(off Chesterfield Gdns.)
Chesterfield M. N4.....1D 35
Chesterfield Rd. E10.....1E 39
Chesterfield St. W1.....1D 21 (2D 75)
Chesterfield Wlk. SE10.....4F 95
Chesterfield Way SE15.....3E 93
Chesterford Gdns. NW3.....1D 45
Chesterford Ho. SE18.....4F 97
.........................(off Tellson Av.)
Chester Ga. NW1: Lon Regent's Pk.
.....2D 5 (2D 61)
Chester Ho. SE8.....2B 94
Chester Ho. SW1.....5D 75
.........................(off Eccleston Pl.)
Chester Ho. SW9.....3C 90
.........................(off Cranmer Rd.)
Chesterman Ct. W4.....3A 84
.................(off Corney Reach Way)
Chester M. SW1.....5D 21 (4D 75)
Chester Pl. NW1.....1D 5 (2D 61)
Chester Rd. E11.....1D 41
Chester Rd. E16.....3A 68
Chester Rd. E17.....1F 37
Chester Rd. E7.....4F 55
Chester Rd. N19.....4D 33
Chester Rd. NW1.....2C 4 (2C 60)
Chester Row SW1.....5C 74
Chester Sq. SW1.....5C 74
Chester Sq. M. SW1.....5D 21 (4D 75)
.........................(off Chester Sq.)
Chester St. E2.....3C 64
Chester St. SW1.....5C 20 (4C 74)
Chester St. SW1.....5D 21 (4D 75)
.............................(not continuous)
Chesterton Cl. SW18.....3C 100
Chesterton Cl. SW11.....1F 101
.........................(off Ingrave St.)
Chesterton Ho. W10.....4A 58
.........................(off Portobello Rd.)
Chesterton Rd. E13.....2C 68
Chesterton Rd. W10.....4F 57
Chesterton Sq. W8.....5C 72
Chesterton Ter. E13.....2C 68
Chester Way SE11.....5C 76
Chestnut All. SW6.....2B 86
Chestnut Apts. E3.....1D 67
.........................(off Alameda Pl.)
Chestnut Av. E7.....1D 55
Chestnut Cl. N16.....4F 35
Chestnut Cl. SE14.....4B 94
Chestnut Cl. SE6.....5E 123
Chestnut Cl. SW16.....4C 118
Chestnut Ct. SW6.....2B 86
Chestnut Ct. W8.....4D 73
.........................(off Abbots Wlk.)
Chestnut Dr. E11.....1C 40
Chestnut Gro. SW12.....5C 102
Chestnut Ho. E3.....5B 52
.........................(off Sycamore Av.)

Chestnut Ho. SW15................... 2B **98**
Chestnut Ho. W4......................... 5A **70**
.................................(off The Orchard)
Chestnut Pl. SE26.................... 4B **120**
Chestnut Plaza E20...................... 2A **53**
.................(within Westfield Shop. Cen.)
Chestnut Rd. SE27................... 3D **119**
Chestnuts, The N5......................... 1E **49**
..............................(off Highbury Grange)
Chestnuts Ho. E17....................... 1C **38**
....(off Hoe St.)
Chesworth Ct. E1.......................... 4E **65**
.................................(off Fulneck Pl.)
Chettle Cl. SE1............. 5B **26** (4F **77**)
................................(off Spurgeon St.)
Chettle Ct. N8................................ 1C **32**
Chetwode Ho. NW8...................... 3A **60**
.................................(off Grendon St.)
Chetwode Rd. SW17.................. 3B **116**
Chetwynd Rd. NW5...................... 1D **47**
Chetwynd Vs. NW5....................... 1D **47**
.................................(off Chetwynd Rd.)
Cheval Pl. SW7............................ 4A **74**
Cheval St. E14............................. 4C **80**
Chevening Rd. NW6..................... 1F **57**
Chevening Rd. SE10................... 1B **96**
Cheverell Ho. E2.......................... 1C **64**
.................................(off Pritchard's Rd.)
Cheverton Rd. N19....................... 3F **33**
Chevet St. E9............................... 2A **52**
Chevington NW2.......................... 3B **44**
Cheviot Ct. SE14......................... 2E **93**
.................................(off Avonley Rd.)
Cheviot Gdns. NW2...................... 4F **29**
Cheviot Gdns. SE27.................... 4D **119**
Cheviot Ga. NW2......................... 4A **30**
Cheviot Ho. E1............................. 5D **65**
.................................(off Commercial Rd.)
Cheviot Rd. SE27....................... 5C **118**
Chevron Cl. E16........................... 5C **68**
Cheylesmore Ho. SW1................. 1D **89**
.................................(off Ebury Bri. Rd.)
Cheyne Cl. NW4........................... 1E **29**
Cheyne Ct. SW3........................... 2B **88**
Cheyne Gdns. SW3...................... 2A **88**
Cheyne Ho. SW3.......................... 2B **88**
.................................(off Chelsea Emb.)
Cheyne M. SW3............................ 2A **88**
Cheyne Pl. SW3........................... 2B **88**
Cheyne Row SW3......................... 2A **88**
Cheyne Wlk. NW4......................... 1E **29**
Cheyne Wlk. SW10...................... 3F **87**
Cheyne Wlk. SW3......................... 2A **88**
.................................(not continuous)
Chichele Rd. NW2........................ 2F **43**
Chicheley St. SE1......... 3A **24** (3B **76**)
Chichester Cl. SE3....................... 3E **97**
Chichester Ct. NW1...................... 4E **47**
.................................(off Royal Coll. St.)
Chichester Ho. NW6..................... 1C **58**
Chichester Ho. SW9..................... 3C **90**
.................................(off Cranmer Rd.)
Chichester Lodge SE10............... 5C **82**
.................................(off Peartree Way)
Chichester M. SE27.................... 4C **118**
Chichester Rents
WC2.......................... 2B **16** (5C **62**)
.................................(off Chancery La.)
Chichester Rd. E11...................... 5A **40**
Chichester Rd. NW6..................... 1C **58**
Chichester Rd. W2....................... 4D **59**
Chichester St. SW1....................... 1E **89**
Chichester Way E14...................... 5F **81**
Chicksand Ho. E1......................... 4C **64**
.................................(off Chicksand St.)

Chicksand St. E1........................... 4B **64**
.................................(not continuous)
Chiddingstone SE13.................... 3E **109**
Chiddingstone St. SW6................ 5C **86**
Chigwell Ct. E9............................ 3A **52**
.................................(off Ballance Rd.)
Chigwell Hill E1............................ 1D **79**
Chilcombe Ho. SW15................... 5C **98**
.................................(off Fontley Way)
Chilcot Cl. E14............................. 5D **67**
Childebert Rd. SW17................... 2D **117**
Childeric Rd. SE14....................... 3A **94**
Childerley St. SW6....................... 4A **86**
Childers St. SE8........................... 2A **94**
Child La. SE10.............................. 4B **82**
CHILDREN'S HOSPITAL
(LEWISHAM), THE................ 3D **109**
.................(within Lewisham University
Hospital)
CHILD'S HILL................................ 5B **30**
Childs Hill Wlk. NW2.................... 5B **30**
.................................(off Cricklewood La.)
Child's M. SW5............................. 5C **72**
.................................(off Child's Pl.)
Child's Pl. SW5............................ 5C **72**
Child's Rd. SW5........................... 5C **72**
Child's Wlk. SW5......................... 5C **72**
.................................(off Child's St.)
Chilham Ho. SE1.............. 5C **26** (4F **77**)
Chilham Ho. SE15........................ 2E **93**
Chilham Rd. SE9.......................... 4F **125**
Chilianwallah Memorial............... 2C **88**
Chillerton Rd. SW17................... 5C **116**
Chillingford Ho. SW17................ 4E **115**
Chillington Dr. SW11.................. 2F **101**
Chillingworth Rd. N7.................... 2C **48**
Chill La. N1................................. 5F **47**
.................................(off Baker St.)
Chiltern Ct. SE14......................... 3E **93**
.................................(off Avonley Rd.)
Chiltern Gdns. NW2...................... 5F **29**
Chiltern Hgts. N1......................... 4B **48**
.................................(off Caledonian Rd.)
Chiltern Ho. SE17........................ 2F **91**
.................................(off Portland St.)
Chiltern Ho. W10........................... 4A **58**
.................................(off Telford Rd.)
Chiltern Rd. E3............................. 3C **66**
Chiltern St. W1............... 5B **4** (4C **60**)
Chilthorne Cl. SE6...................... 5B **108**
Chilton Gro. SE8.......................... 5F **79**
Chiltonian Ind. Est. SE12........... 4B **110**
Chiltonian M. SE13..................... 3F **109**
Chilton St. E2.............................. 3B **64**
Chilver St. SE10.......................... 1B **96**
Chilworth Ct. SW19.................... 1F **113**
Chilworth M. W2........................... 5F **59**
Chilworth St. W2........................... 5E **59**
Chimes Ter. N8............................. 1A **34**
Chimney Ct. E1............................ 2D **79**
.................................(off Brewhouse La.)
China Ct. E1................................ 2D **79**
.................................(off Asher Way)
China Hall M. SE16...................... 4E **79**
China M. SW2............................. 5B **104**
China Wharf SE1.......................... 3C **78**
Chinbrook Cres. SE12................ 3D **125**
Chinbrook Rd. SE12................... 3D **125**
Ching Ct. WC2................. 3D **15** (5A **62**)
.................................(off Monmouth St.)
Chingley Cl. BR1: Broml............. 5A **124**
Chinnock's Wharf E14................. 1A **80**
.................................(off Narrow St.)
Chipka St. E14............................. 3E **81**

.................................(not continuous)
Chipley St. SE14.......................... 2A **94**
Chippendale Ho. SW1.................. 1D **89**
.................................(off Churchill Gdns.)
Chippendale St. E5....................... 5F **37**
Chippenham Gdns. NW6.............. 2C **58**
Chippenham M. W9...................... 3C **58**
Chippenham Rd. W9.................... 3C **58**
Chipperfield Ho. SW3.................. 1A **88**
.................................(off Cale St.)
Chipstead Gdns. NW2.................. 4D **29**
Chipstead St. SW6...................... 4C **86**
Chip St. SW4............................... 1F **103**
Chisenhale Rd. E3........................ 1A **66**
Chisholm Ct. W6.......................... 1C **84**
Chisledon Wlk. E9....................... 3B **52**
.................................(off Osborne Rd.)
Chisley Rd. N15........................... 1A **36**
Chiswell Sq. SE3.......................... 5D **97**
Chiswell St. EC1............. 5A **10** (4E **63**)
Chiswell St. SE5........................... 3F **91**
.................................(off Edmund St.)
Chiswick Comn. Rd. W4................ 5A **70**
Chiswick Community Sports Hall
.... 3A **84**
Chiswick House & Gdns.............. 2A **84**
Chiswick Ho. Grounds W4............ 2A **84**
Chiswick La. W4........................... 1A **84**
Chiswick La. Sth. W4.................... 2B **84**
Chiswick Mall W4......................... 2B **84**
Chiswick Mall W6......................... 1C **84**
Chiswick Pier.............................. 3B **84**
Chiswick Sq. W4.......................... 2A **84**
Chiswick Wharf W4...................... 2B **84**
Chitty St. W1.................. 5A **6** (4E **61**)
Chivalry Rd. SW11....................... 3A **102**
Chivelston SW19.......................... 1F **113**
Chivers Pas. SW18...................... 3D **101**
Chobham Academy Sports Cen.
.... 2E **53**
Chobham Gdns. SW19................. 2F **113**
CHOBHAM MANOR........................ 2D **53**
Chobham Rd. E15......................... 2F **53**
Chocolate Studios
N1............................. 1B **10** (2F **63**)
.................................(off Shepherdess Pl.)
Cholmeley Cl. N6.......................... 2D **33**
Cholmeley Cres. N6...................... 2D **33**
Cholmeley Lodge N6.................... 3D **33**
Cholmeley Pk. N6......................... 3D **33**
Cholmley Gdns. NW6.................... 2C **44**
Cholmondeley Av. NW10.............. 1C **56**
Choppin's Ct. E1.......................... 2D **79**
Chopwell Ct. E15.......................... 4F **53**
Choudhury Mans. N1.................... 4A **48**
.................................(off Pembroke St.)
Choumert Gro. SE15.................... 5C **92**
Choumert M. SE15...................... 5C **92**
Choumert Rd. SE15.................... 1B **106**
Choumert Sq. SE15..................... 5C **92**
Chow Sq. E8................................. 2B **50**
Chrisp Ho. SE10........................... 2A **96**
.................................(off Maze Hill)
Chrisp St. E14............................. 4D **67**
.................................(not continuous)
Chris Pullen Way N7..................... 3A **48**
Christabel Pankhurst Ct.
SE5... 3F **91**
.................................(off Brisbane St.)
Christchurch Av. NW6................... 5F **43**
Christ Church Ct. NW10............... 5A **42**
Christchurch Ct. EC4 2E **17** (5D **63**)
.................................(off Warwick La.)
Christchurch Ct. NW6................... 4A **44**
.................................(off Willesden La.)

Christchurch Hill NW3 ....5F **31**
Christchurch Ho. SW2 .... 1B **118**
.... *(off Christchurch Rd.)*
Christchurch Pas.
  NW3: Lon Hampstead 5E **31**
Christchurch Pl. SW8 ....5F **89**
Christchurch Rd. N8 ..... 1A **34**
Christchurch Rd. SW2 .... 1B **118**
Christchurch Sq. E9 ....5E **51**
Christchurch St. SW3 .... 2B **88**
Christchurch Ter. SW3 ...... 2B **88**
.... *(off Christchurch St.)*
Christchurch Way SE10 ... 1A **96**
Christian Ct. SE16 .... 2B **80**
Christian Pl. E1 .... 5C **64**
.... *(off Burslem St.)*
Christian St. E1 .... 5C **64**
Christie Ct. N19 .... 4A **34**
Christie Ho. E16 .... 4C **68**
.... *(off Hammersley Rd.)*
Christie Ho. SE10 .... 1B **96**
.... *(off Blackwall La.)*
Christie Ho. W12 .... 5D **57**
.... *(off Du Cane Rd.)*
Christie Rd. E9 .... 3A **52**
Christina Sq. N4 .... 3D **35**
Christina St. EC2 ....3D **11** (3A **64**)
Christopher Bell Twr. E3 ..... 1C **66**
.... *(off Pancras Way)*
Christopher Boones Ct.
  SE13 ....2F **109**
.... *(off Bessington Rd.)*
Christopher Cl. SE16 ....3F **79**
Christopher Ct. E1 .... 5C **64**
.... *(off Leman St.)*
Christopher Pl. NW1 .. 1C **6** (2F **61**)
Christopher M. W11 ....2A **72**
Christopher St.
  EC2 ....4C **10** (3F **63**)
Chroma Mans. E20 ....3E **53**
.... *(off Penny Brookes St.)*
Chronicle Twr. N1 .... 1F **9** (2E **63**)
Chryssell Rd. SW9 .... 3C **90**
Chubworthy St. SE14 .... 2A **94**
Chudleigh Rd. NW6 ....4F **43**
Chudleigh Rd. SE4 .... 3B **108**
Chudleigh St. E1 ....5F **65**
Chulsa Rd. SE26 .... 5D **121**
Chumleigh Gdns. SE5 ...... 2A **92**
.... *(off Chumleigh St.)*
Chumleigh St. SE5 .... 2A **92**
Church App. SE21 ....3F **119**
Church Av. NW1 .... 3D **47**
Churchbury Rd. SE9 ....5F **111**
Church Cloisters
  EC3 ....5D **19** (1A **78**)
.... *(off Lovat La.)*
Church Cl. W8 .... 3D **73**
Church Ct. EC4 ....3B **16** (5C **62**)
Church Ct. SE16 .... 3B **80**
.... *(off Rotherhithe St.)*
Church Cres. E9 ....4F **51**
Churchcroft Cl. SW12 .... 5C **102**
Churchdown BR1: Broml ...4A **124**
CHURCH END 4A **42**
Church Entry EC4 .....3E **17** (5D **63**)
.... *(off Carter La.)*
Churchfield Ho. W2 ....3F **59**
.... *(off Hall Pl.)*
Churchfield Mans. SW6 ...... 5B **86**
.... *(off New Kings Rd.)*
Churchfields SE10 .... 2E **95**
Church Gth. N19 ....4F **33**
.... *(off St John's Gro.)*
Church Ga. SW6 .... 1A **100**

Church Grn. SW9 .... 4C **90**
Church Gro. SE13 .... 3D **109**
Church Hill SW19 .... 5B **114**
Church Ho. EC1 ....3E **9** (3D **63**)
.... *(off Compton St.)*
Church Ho. SW1 ....5C **22** (4F **75**)
.... *(off Gt. Smith St.)*
CHURCHILL CAMBIAN HOSPITAL
  ....5C **24** (4C **76**)
Churchill Cl. N4 .... 2C **34**
Churchill Gdns. SW1 ....1E **89**
.... *(off Churchill Gdns. Rd.)*
Churchill Gdns. Rd. SW1 ... 1D **89**
Churchill Pl. E14 .... 2D **81**
Churchill Rd. E16 ....5E **69**
Churchill Rd. NW2 .... 3D **43**
Churchill Rd. NW5 .... 1D **47**
Churchill Wlk. E9 ....1F **51**
Churchill War Rooms
  ....3C **22** (3F **75**)
Church La. E11 .... 3A **40**
Church La. SW17 .... 5B **116**
Churchley Rd. SE26 .... 4D **121**
Church Mead SE5 ....3E **91**
.... *(off Camberwell Rd.)*
Churchmead Rd. NW10 ..... 3C **42**
Church Mt. N2 ....1F **31**
Church Path N5:
  Lon Highbury 2D **49**
Church Path NW10:
  Lon Willesden 4A **42**
Church Path E11 .... 1C **40**
Church Pl. SW1 ....5A **14** (1E **75**)
Church Ri. SE23 ....2F **121**
Church Rd. SW19:
  Lon Courthorpe Rd. 5A **114**
Church Rd. E10 .... 3C **38**
Church Rd. E12 ....2F **55**
Church Rd. E5 ....3E **49**
Church Rd. N1 .... 3E **49**
Church Rd. N6 .... 1C **32**
Church Rd. NW10 .... 4A **42**
Church Rd. SW13 .... 5B **84**
Church Rd. Almshouses
  E10 .... 4D **39**
.... *(off Church Rd.)*
Church Rd. Ind. Est. E10 ..... 3C **38**
Church Row NW3 ....1E **45**
Church Row SW18 .... 3D **101**
Church Row SW6 .... 3D **87**
.... *(off Moore Pk. Rd.)*
Church St. E15 ....5A **54**
Church St. NW8 ....4F **59**
Church St. W2 ....4F **59**
.... *(not continuous)*
Church St. W4 .... 2B **84**
Church St. Est. NW8 ....3F **59**
Church St. Nth. E15 ....5A **54**
Church St. Pas. E15 ....5A **54**
.... *(off Church St.)*
Church Ter. SE13 .... 1A **110**
Church Va. SE23 ....2F **121**
Church Vw. Gro. SE26 ....5F **121**
Church Wlk. SW13:
  Lon Barnes 4C **84**
Church Wlk. N6:
  Lon Dartmouth Pk. 5C **32**
Church Wlk. SW15:
  Lon Putney 3D **99**
Church Wlk. N16 ....5F **35**
.... *(not continuous)*
Church Wlk. NW2 .... 5B **30**
Churchward Ho. SE17 .... 2D **91**
.... *(off Lorrimore Sq.)*
Churchward Ho. W14 .... 1B **86**
.... *(off Ivatt Pl.)*

Churchway NW1 .... 1C **6** (2F **61**)
.... *(not continuous)*
Churchwell Path E9 ....2E **51**
Churchwood Gdns. SE23 ...5E **107**
Churchyard Pas. SE5 ....5F **91**
Churchyard Row SE11 ...... 5D **77**
Churston Av. E13 ....5D **55**
Churston Cl. SW2 .... 1C **118**
Churston Mans. WC1 ....4A **8** (3B **62**)
.... *(off Gray's Inn Rd.)*
Churton Pl. SW1 ....5E **75**
Churton St. SW1 ....5E **75**
Chusan Pl. E14 .... 5B **66**
Chute Ho. SW9 ....5C **90**
.... *(off Stockwell Pk. Rd.)*
Chuter Ede Ho. SW6 .... 2B **86**
.... *(off Clem Attlee Ct.)*
Cibber Rd. SE23 ....2F **121**
Cicada Rd. SW18 ....4E **101**
Cicely Ho. NW8 ....1F **59**
.... *(off Cochrane St.)*
Cicely Rd. SE15 .... 4C **92**
Cinderella Path NW11 .... 3D **31**
Cinderford Way
  BR1: Broml 4A **124**
Ciné Lumière 5F **73**
.... *(off Queensberry Pl.)*
Cineworld Cinema Chelsea,
  Fulham Rd. 1E **87**
Cineworld Cinema Leicester Sq.
  ....4C **14** (1F **75**)
.... *(off Leicester Sq.)*
Cineworld Cinema The O2...2A **82**
.... *(within The O2)*
Cineworld Cinema Wandsworth
  ....3D **101**
Cineworld Cinema West India
  Quay 1C **80**
Cinnabar Wharf Central E1...2C **78**
.... *(off Wapping High St.)*
Cinnabar Wharf E. E1 .... 2C **78**
.... *(off Wapping High St.)*
Cinnabar Wharf W. E1 .... 2C **78**
.... *(off Wapping High St.)*
Cinnamon Cl. SE15 .... 3B **92**
Cinnamon Row SW11 ....1E **101**
Cinnamon St. E1 .... 2D **79**
Cinnamon Wharf SE1 .... 3B **78**
.... *(off Shad Thames)*
Cipher Ct. NW2 ....1F **43**
Circa Apts. NW1 .... 4C **46**
Circle, The NW2 .... 5A **28**
Circle, The SE1 ....3F **27** (3B **78**)
.... *(off Queen Elizabeth St.)*
Circus Lodge NW8 ....2F **59**
.... *(off Circus Rd.)*
Circus M. W1 .... 4B **60**
.... *(off Enford St.)*
Circus Pl. EC2 ....1C **18** (4F **63**)
Circus Rd. NW8 .... 2F **59**
Circus Rd. E. SW11 ....3E **89**
Circus Rd. N. SW11 .... 2D **89**
Circus Rd. S. SW11 .... 3D **89**
Circus Rd. W. SW11 .... 3D **89**
Circus St. SE10 .... 3E **95**
Circus W. SW11 .... 2D **89**
Cirencester St. W2 .... 4D **59**
Cirrus Apts. E1 ....3F **11** (3B **64**)
.... *(off Bacon St.)*
Cissbury Ho. SE26 .... 3C **120**
Cissbury Rd. N15 ....1F **35**
Citadel Pl. SE11 .... 1B **90**
Citius Apts. E1 .... 1C **66**
.... *(off Tredegar La.)*
Citius Wlk. E20 ....3E **53**

Citizen Ho. N7 ....1C 48
Citizen Ho. N7 ....1C 48
Citrine Apts. E3 ....5A 52
.... (off Gunmaker's La.)
Citrus Ho. SE8 ....1B 94
.... (off Alverton St.)
CITY & HACKNEY CENTRE FOR
MENTAL HEALTH 2F 51
City Apts. E1 ....5C 64
.... (off White Church La.)
City Bus. Cen. SE16 ....4E 79
City Bus. Library ...1A 18 (4E 63)
City Cross Bus. Pk. SE10 .....5A 82
City E. Bldg. E1 ....1D 79
.... (off Cable St.)
City Forum EC1 ....1F 9 (2E 63)
City Gdn. Row EC1 ..1F 9 (2E 63)
City Gdn. Row N1 .....1E 9 (1D 63)
City Gateway E1 ....1C 78
.... (off Ensign St.)
City Hall Southwark
.... 2E 27 (2F 78)
City Harbour E14 ....4D 81
.... (off Selsdon Way)
City Hgts. E8 ....5B 50
.... (off Kingsland Rd.)
City Island E14 ....5A 68
City Island Way E14 ....5A 68
City Lights SE11 ....1C 90
.... (off Bowden St.)
City Mill Apts. E8 ....5B 50
.... (off Lovelace St.)
City Mill River Path E15 ....5E 53
City Nth. E. Twr. N4 ....4C 34
.... (off City Nth. Pl.)
City Nth. Pl. N4 ....4C 34
City Nth. W. Twr. N4 ....4C 34
CITY OF LONDON 1A 18 (5F 63)
City of London Almshouses
SW9 ....2B 104
City of London Crematorium
.... 5F 41
City of London Distillery
.... 3D 17 (5D 63)
City of London Point N7 ....3F 47
.... (off York Way)
City of London Police Mus.
.... 2A 18 (5E 63)
City of London Tourist Info.
Cen. 3F 17 (5E 63)
City Pav. EC1 ....5D 9 (4D 63)
.... (off Britton St.)
City Pl. Ho. EC2 .....1A 18 (4F 63)
.... (off Basinghall St.)
Citypoint EC2 ....5B 10 (4F 63)
.... (off Ropemaker St.)
City Pride Development
E14 ....2C 80
City Rd. EC1 ....1D 9 (1D 63)
City Thameslink Station (Rail)
.... 2D 17 (5D 63)
City Twr. EC2 ....1B 18 (4F 63)
.... (off Basinghall St.)
City Twr. SW8 ....2A 90
City University London
Goswell Pl. 2E 9 (2D 63)
City University London
Northampton Square Campus
.... 2D 9 (2D 63)
City University London The
Saddlers Sports Cen.
.... 3E 9 (3D 63)
Cityview SE7 ....2E 97
City Vw. Apts. N1 ....4E 49
.... (off Essex Rd.)

City Vw. Apts. N4 ....2F 35
.... (off Devan Gro.)
City Vw. Ct. SE22 ....5C 106
City Wlk. SE1 ....4D 27 (3A 78)
City Wlk. Apts. EC1 ...3E 9 (2E 63)
.... (off Seward St.)
Civil Justice Cen.
Central London 4D 5 (3D 61)
.... (off Park Cres.)
Clabon M. SW1 ....4B 74
Clack St. SE16 ....3E 79
Clacton Rd. E17 ....1A 38
Clacton Rd. E6 ....2F 69
Claire Ct. NW2 ....3A 44
Claire Pl. E14 ....4C 80
Clairview Rd. SW16 ....5D 117
Clairville Point SE23 ....3F 121
.... (off Dacres Rd.)
Clancarty Rd. SW6 ....5C 86
Clandon Ho. SE1 ....4E 25 (3D 77)
.... (off Webber St.)
Clandon St. SE8 ....5C 94
Clanricarde Gdns. W2 ....1C 72
CLAPHAM 2E 103
CLAPHAM COMMON 2F 103
Clapham Comn. Northside
SW4 ....2E 103
Clapham Comn. Nth. Side
SW4 ....2B 102
Clapham Comn. Sth. Side
SW4 ....4D 103
Clapham Common Station
(Underground) 2B 102
Clapham Comn. W. Side
SW4 ....2B 102
.... (not continuous)
Clapham Cres. SW4 ....2F 103
Clapham High St. SW4 ....2F 103
Clapham High Street Station
(Overground) 1F 103
CLAPHAM JUNCTION 1A 102
Clapham Junction Station
(Rail & Overground) 1A 102
Clapham Leisure Cen. 1F 103
Clapham Mnr. Ct. SW4 ....1E 103
Clapham Mnr. St. SW4 ....1E 103
Clapham North Station
(Underground) 1A 104
CLAPHAM PK. 3F 103
Clapham Pk. Est. SW4 ....4F 103
Clapham Pk. Rd. SW4 ....2E 103
Clapham Pk. Ter. SW4 ....3A 104
.... (off Lyham Rd.)
Clapham Picturehouse 2E 103
Clapham Rd. SW9 ....1A 104
Clapham Rd. Est. SW4 ....1A 104
Clapham South Station
(Underground) 4D 103
Clapton Comn. E5 ....2B 36
.... (not continuous)
CLAPTON PK. 1F 51
Clapton Pk. Est. E5 ....1F 51
Clapton Pas. E5 ....2E 51
Clapton Sq. E5 ....2E 51
Clapton Station (Overground)
.... 4D 37
Clapton Ter. E5 ....3C 36
Clapton Way E5 ....1C 50
Clara Grant Ho. E14 ....4C 80
.... (off Mellish St.)
Clara Nehab Ho. NW11 ....1B 30
.... (off Leeside Cres.)
Clare Ct. W11 ....1A 72
.... (off Clarendon Rd.)

Clare Ct. WC1 ....2E 7 (2A 62)
.... (off Judd St.)
Claredale Ho. E2 ....1D 65
.... (off Claredale St.)
Claredale St. E2 ....1C 64
Clare Gdns. E7 ....1C 54
Clare Gdns. W11 ....5A 58
Clare Ho. E3 ....5B 52
Clare Ho. SE1 ....1B 92
.... (off Cooper's Rd.)
Clare La. N1 ....4E 49
Clare Mkt. WC2 ....3A 16 (5B 62)
Clare M. SW6 ....3D 87
Claremont Cl. N1 ......1C 8 (1C 62)
Claremont Cl. SW2 ....1A 118
Claremont Ct. E2: Lon Cambridge
Heath Rd. 1D 65
.... (off Cambridge Heath Rd.)
Claremont Ct. E2: Lon
Claredale St. 1C 64
.... (off Claredale St.)
Claremont Ct. W2 ....5D 59
.... (off Queensway)
Claremont Ct. W9 ....1B 58
.... (off Claremont Rd.)
Claremont Gro. W4 ....3A 84
Claremont Ho. SE16 ....3A 80
Claremont Rd. E11 ....5F 39
Claremont Rd. E7 ....2D 55
Claremont Rd. N6 ....2E 33
Claremont Rd. NW2 ....2F 29
Claremont Rd. W9 ....1B 58
Claremont Sq. N1 .....1B 8 (1C 62)
Claremont St. SE10 ....2D 95
Claremont Vs. SE5 ....3F 91
.... (off Southampton Way)
Claremont Way NW2 ....3E 29
Claremont Way Ind. Est.
NW2 ....3E 29
Clarence Av. SW4 ....5F 103
Clarence Ct. W6 ....5D 71
.... (off Cambridge Gro.)
Clarence Cres. SW4 ....4F 103
Clarence Gdns. NW1 ...2E 5 (2D 61)
Clarence Ga. Gdns.
NW1 ....4A 4 (3B 60)
.... (off Glentworth St.)
Clarence Ho. SE17 ....2F 91
.... (off Merrow St.)
Clarence House 3A 22 (3E 75)
.... (off St James's Pal.)
Clarence La. SW15 ....4A 98
Clarence M. E5 ....2D 51
Clarence M. SE16 ....2F 79
Clarence M. SW12 ....5D 103
Clarence Pl. E5 ....2D 51
Clarence Rd. E12 ....1E 55
Clarence Rd. E16 ....3A 68
Clarence Rd. E5 ....1D 51
Clarence Rd. NW6 ....4B 44
Clarence Rd. SE8 ....2D 95
Clarence Rd. SE9 ....2F 125
Clarence Rd. SW19 ....5D 115
Clarence Ter. NW1 ...3A 4 (3B 60)
Clarence Wlk. SW4 ....5A 90
Clarence Way NW1 ....4D 47
Clarendon Cl. E9 ....4E 51
Clarendon Cl. W2 ....1A 74
Clarendon Ct. EC1 ...4A 10 (3E 63)
.... (off Brackley St.)
Clarendon Ct. NW2 ....4E 43
Clarendon Ct. W9 ....3E 59
.... (off Maida Va.)
Clarendon Cross W11 ....1A 72

Clarendon Dr. SW15 ....2E **99**
Clarendon Flats W1 ..3C **12** (5C **60**)
..................................(off Balderton St.)
Clarendon Gdns. W9 ....3E **59**
Clarendon Gro. M1 ...1B **6** (2F **61**)
Clarendon Ho. NW1 ...1A **6** (1E **61**)
..................................(off Werrington St.)
Clarendon Ho. W2 ....1A **74**
..................................(off Strathearn Pl.)
Clarendon Lodge W11 ....1A **72**
..................................(off Clarendon Rd.)
Clarendon M. W2 ....1A **74**
Clarendon Pl. W2 ....1A **74**
Clarendon Ri. SE13 ....2E **109**
Clarendon Rd. E11 ....3F **39**
Clarendon Rd. E17 ....1D **39**
Clarendon Rd. W11 ....1A **72**
Clarendon St. SW1 ....1D **89**
Clarendon Ter. W9 ....3E **59**
Clarendon Wlk. W11 ....5A **58**
Clarens St. SE6 ....2B **122**
Clare Pl. SW15 ....5B **98**
Clare Point NW2 ....3F **29**
..................................(off Whitefield St.)
Clare Rd. E11 ....1F **39**
Clare Rd. NW10 ....4C **42**
Clare Rd. SE14 ....4B **94**
Clare St. E2 ....1D **65**
Clareville Ct. SW7 ....5E **73**
..................................(off Clareville St.)
Clareville Gro. SW7 ....5E **73**
Clareville Gro. M. SW7 ....5E **73**
Clareville St. SW7 ....5E **73**
Clarewood Ct. W1 ....4B **60**
..................................(off Seymour Pl.)
Clarewood Wlk. SW9 ....2C **104**
Clarges M. W1 ....1D **21** (2D **75**)
Clarges St. W1 ....1E **21** (2D **75**)
Claribel Rd. SW9 ....5D **91**
Claridge Ct. SW6 ....5B **86**
Clarion Ho. E3 ....1A **66**
..................................(off Roman Rd.)
Clarion Ho. SW1 ....1E **89**
..................................(off Moreton Pl.)
Clarion Ho. W1 ....3B **14** (5F **61**)
..................................(off St Anne's Ct.)
Clarissa Ho. E14 ....5D **67**
..................................(off Cordela St.)
Clarissa St. E8 ....5B **50**
Clarke Apts. E3 ....3B **66**
..................................(off Heath Pl.)
Clarke Path N16 ....3C **36**
Clarke's M. W1 ....5C **4** (4C **60**)
Clark Ho. SW10 ....3E **87**
..................................(off Coleridge Gdns.)
Clarkson Rd. E16 ....5B **68**
Clarkson Row NW1 ....1E **61**
..................................(off Mornington Ter.)
Clarkson St. E2 ....2D **65**
Clark St. E1 ....4D **65**
..................................(not continuous)
Clarnico La. E20 ....3C **52**
Clarson Ho. SE5 ....3D **91**
..................................(off Midnight Av.)
Clarson Ho. SE8 ....2A **94**
Classic Mans. E9 ....4D **51**
..................................(off Wells St.)
Claude Rd. E10 ....4E **39**
Claude Rd. E13 ....5D **55**
Claude Rd. SE15 ....5D **93**
Claude St. E14 ....5C **80**
Claudia Jones Way SW2 ....4A **104**
Claudia Pl. SW19 ....1A **114**
Claughton Rd. E13 ....1E **69**
Clavell St. SE10 ....2E **95**

Claverdale Rd. SW2 ....5B **104**
Clavering Av. SW13 ....2D **85**
Clavering Ho. SE13 ....2F **109**
..................................(off Blessington Rd.)
Clavering Pl. SW12 ....4C **102**
Clavering Rd. E12 ....3F **41**
Claverton St. SW1 ....1E **89**
Clave St. E1 ....2E **79**
Claxton Gro. W6 ....1F **85**
Claxton Path SE4 ....2F **107**
..................................(off Coston Wlk.)
Claybank Gro. SE13 ....1D **109**
Claybridge Rd. SE12 ....4E **125**
Claybrook Rd. W6 ....2F **85**
Clay Ct. SE1 ....5D **27** (4A **78**)
..................................(off Long La.)
Claydon Ho. SW10 ....4E **87**
Clayhall Ct. E3 ....1B **66**
..................................(off St Stephen's Rd.)
Clayhill Cres. SE9 ....4F **125**
Claylands Pl. SW8 ....3C **90**
Claylands Rd. SW8 ....2B **90**
Claypole Ct. E17 ....1C **38**
..................................(off Yunus Khan Cl.)
Claypole Rd. E15 ....1E **67**
Clay St. W1 ....1A **12** (4B **60**)
Clayton Cres. N1 ....5A **48**
Clayton Dr. SE8 ....1A **94**
Clayton Ho. E9 ....4E **51**
..................................(off Frampton Pk. Rd.)
Clayton Ho. SW13 ....3E **85**
..................................(off Trinity Chu. Rd.)
Clayton M. SE10 ....4F **95**
Clayton Rd. SE15 ....4C **92**
Clayton St. SE11 ....2C **90**
Clearbrook Way E1 ....5E **65**
Clearwater Ter. W11 ....3F **71**
Clearwater Yd. NW1 ....5D **47**
..................................(off Inverness St.)
Clearwell Dr. W9 ....3D **59**
Cleaver Ho. NW3 ....4B **46**
..................................(off Adelaide Rd.)
Cleaver Sq. SE11 ....1C **90**
Cleaver St. SE11 ....1C **90**
Cleeve Hill SE23 ....1D **121**
Cleeve Ho. E2 ....2E **11** (2A **64**)
..................................(off Calvert Av.)
Cleeve Way SW15 ....5B **98**
Cleeve Workshops
E2 ....2E **11** (2A **64**)
..................................(off Boundary Rd.)
Clegg Ho. SE16 ....4E **79**
..................................(off Moodkee St.)
Clegg St. E1 ....2D **79**
Clegg St. E13 ....1C **68**
Cleland Ho. E2 ....1E **65**
..................................(off Sewardstone Rd.)
Clematis Apts. E3 ....2B **66**
..................................(off Merchant St.)
Clematis St. W12 ....1C **70**
Clem Attlee Ct. SW6 ....2B **86**
Clem Attlee Pde. SW6 ....2B **86**
..................................(off North End Rd.)
Clemence St. E14 ....4B **66**
Clement Av. SW4 ....2F **103**
Clement Cl. NW6 ....4E **43**
Clement Danes Ho. W12 ....5D **57**
Clement Ho. SE8 ....5A **80**
Clement Ho. W10 ....4E **57**
..................................(off Dalgarno Gdns.)
Clementina Ct. E3 ....3A **66**
..................................(off Copperfield Rd.)
Clementina Rd. E10 ....3B **38**
Clement Rd. SW19 ....5A **114**
Clement's Av. E16 ....1C **82**

Clement's Inn
WC2 ....3A **16** (5B **62**)
Clements La. EC4 .....4C **18** (1F **77**)
Clements Rd. SE16 ....4C **78**
Clemson Ho. E8 ....5B **50**
Clennam St. SE1 ....3A **26** (3E **77**)
Clenston M. W1 ....2A **12** (5B **60**)
Cleopatra's Needle...1F **23** (1B **76**)
Clephane Rd. N1 ....3E **49**
Clephane Rd. Nth. N1 ....3E **49**
Clere Pl. EC2 ....3C **10** (3F **63**)
Clere St. EC2 ....3C **10** (3F **63**)
CLERKENWELL 2B **8** (2D **62**)
Clerkenwell Cl. EC1 ...3C **8** (3C **62**)
..................................(not continuous)
Clerkenwell Ct. N1 ....1O **63**
..................................(off Duncan St.)
Clerkenwell Grn.
EC1 ....4C **8** (3C **62**)
Clerkenwell Rd.
EC1 ....4B **8** (3C **62**)
Clerks Pl. EC3 ....2D **19** (5A **64**)
Clermont Rd. E9 ....5E **51**
Clevedon Cl. N16 ....5B **36**
Clevedon Ct. SW11 ....4A **88**
..................................(off Bolingbroke Wlk.)
Clevedon Mans. NW5 ....1C **46**
Clevedon Pas. N16 ....4B **36**
Cleve Ho. NW6 ....4D **45**
Cleveland Av. W4 ....5B **70**
Cleveland Gdns. N4 ....1E **35**
Cleveland Gdns. NW2 ....4F **29**
Cleveland Gdns. SW13 ....5B **84**
Cleveland Gdns. W2 ....5E **59**
Cleveland Gro. E1 ....3E **65**
Cleveland Mans. NW6 ....4B **44**
..................................(off Willesden La.)
Cleveland Mans. SW9 ....3C **90**
..................................(off Mowll St.)
Cleveland M. W1 ....5F **5** (4E **61**)
Cleveland Pl. SW1 ...1A **22** (2E **75**)
Cleveland Rd. N1 ....4F **49**
Cleveland Rd. SW13 ....5B **84**
Cleveland Row SW1 ...2A **22** (2E **75**)
Cleveland Sq. W2 ....5E **59**
Cleveland St. W1 ....4E **5** (3D **61**)
Cleveland Ter. W2 ....5E **59**
Cleveland Way E1 ....3E **65**
Cleveley Cl. SE7 ....5F **83**
Cleveley Ct. SE16 ....5A **80**
..................................(off Ashton Reach)
Cleveleys Rd. E5 ....5D **37**
Cleverly Est. W12 ....2C **70**
Cleve Rd. NW6 ....4C **44**
Cleves Ho. E16 ....2C **82**
..................................(off Southey M.)
Cleves Rd. E6 ....5F **55**
Clewer Ct. E10 ....3C **38**
..................................(off Leyton Grange Est.)
Cley Ho. SE4 ....2F **107**
Clichy Est. E1 ....4E **65**
Clichy Ho. E1 ....4E **65**
..................................(off Stepney Way)
Clifden M. E5 ....1F **51**
Clifden Rd. E5 ....2E **51**
Cliffe Ho. SE10 ....1B **96**
..................................(off Blackwall La.)
Clifford Ct. W2 ....4D **59**
..................................(off Westbourne Pk. Vs.)
Clifford Dr. SW9 ....2D **105**
Clifford Gdns. NW10 ....1E **57**
Clifford Haigh Ho. SW6 ....3F **85**
Clifford Ho. BR3: Beck. 5D **123**
..................................(off Calverley Cl.)

Clifford Ho. W14 . . . . .5B **72**
. . . . (off Edith Vs.)
Clifford Rd. E16 . . . . .3B **68**
Clifford Rd. N1 . . . . .5A **50**
Clifford's Inn EC4 . . . . . .3B 16 (5C 62)
. . . . (off Fetter La.)
Clifford's Inn Pas.
  EC4 . . . . .3B 16 (5C 62)
Clifford St. W1 . . . . .5F 13 (1E 75)
Clifford Way NW10 . . . . .1B **42**
Cliff Rd. NW1 . . . . .3F **47**
Cliffsend Ho. SW9 . . . . .4C **90**
. . . . (off Cowley Rd.)
Cliff Ter. SE8 . . . . .5C **94**
Cliffview Rd. SE13 . . . . .1C **108**
Cliff Vs. NW1 . . . . .3F **47**
Cliff Wlk. E16 . . . . .4B **68**
Clifton Av. W12 . . . . .2F **70**
Clifton Ct. N4 . . . . .4C **34**
Clifton Ct. NW8 . . . . .3F **59**
. . . . (off Maida Vale)
Clifton Ct. SE15 . . . . .3D **93**
Clifton Cres. SE15 . . . . .3D **93**
Clifton Est. SE15 . . . . .4D **93**
Clifton Gdns. N15 . . . . .1B **36**
Clifton Gdns. NW11 . . . . .1B **30**
Clifton Gdns. W4 . . . . .5A **70**
. . . . (not continuous)
Clifton Gdns. W9 . . . . .3E **59**
Clifton Ga. SW10 . . . . .2E **87**
Clifton Gro. E8 . . . . .3C **50**
Clifton Hill NW8 . . . . .1D **59**
Clifton Hill Studios NW8 . . . . . . .1E **59**
Clifton Ho. E11 . . . . .4A **40**
Clifton Ho. E2 . . . . .3F 11 (3B 64)
. . . . (off Club Row)
Clifton Pl. SE16 . . . . .3E **79**
Clifton Pl. SW10 . . . . .2E **87**
. . . . (off Hollywood Rd.)
Clifton Pl. W2 . . . . .5F **59**
Clifton Ri. SE14 . . . . .3A **94**
. . . . (not continuous)
Clifton Rd. E16 . . . . .4A **68**
Clifton Rd. E7 . . . . .3F **55**
Clifton Rd. N1 . . . . .3E **49**
Clifton Rd. N8 . . . . .1F **33**
Clifton Rd. NW10 . . . . .1C **56**
Clifton Rd. SW19 . . . . .5F **113**
Clifton Rd. W9 . . . . .3E **59**
Clifton St. EC2 . . . . . .4D 11 (3A **64**)
Clifton Ter. N4 . . . . .4C **34**
Clifton Vs. W9 . . . . .4E **59**
Cliftonville Ct. SE12 . . . . .1C **124**
Clifton Wlk. W6 . . . . .5D **71**
. . . . (off King St.)
Clifton Way SE15 . . . . .3D **93**
Climsland Ho. SE1 . . .1C 24 (2C **76**)
Clinger Ct. N1 . . . . .5A **50**
. . . . (off Hobbs Pl. Est.)
Clink Prison Mus.
. . . . .1B 26 (2F **77**)
. . . . (off Clink St.)
Clink St. SE1 . . . . .1A 26 (2F **77**)
Clink Wharf SE1 . . . . . . .1B 26 (2F **77**)
. . . . (off Clink St.)
Clinton Rd. E3 . . . . .2A **66**
Clinton Rd. E7 . . . . .1C **54**
Clinton Ter. SE8 . . . . .2C **94**
. . . . (off Watergate St.)
Clipper Apts. SE10 . . . . .2E **95**
. . . . (off Welland St.)
Clipper Cl. SE16 . . . . .3F **79**
Clipper Ho. E14 . . . . .1E **95**
. . . . (off Manchester Rd.)
Clipper Way SE13 . . . . .2E **109**

Clipstone M. W1 . . . . . . .5F 5 (4E **61**)
Clipstone St. W1 . . . . . . .5E 5 (4D **61**)
Clissold Ct. N4 . . . . .4E **35**
Clissold Cres. N16 . . . . .5F **35**
Clissold Leisure Cen. 5F **35**
Clissold Rd. N16 . . . . .5F **35**
Clitheroe Rd. SW9 . . . . .5A **90**
Clitterhouse Cres. NW2 . . . . .3E **29**
Clitterhouse Rd. NW2 . . . . .3E **29**
Clive Ct. W9 . . . . .3E **59**
Cliveden Ho. E16 . . . . .2C **82**
. . . . (off Fitzwilliam M.)
Cliveden Ho. SW1 . . . . .5C **74**
. . . . (off Cliveden Pl.)
Cliveden Pl. SW1 . . . . .5C **74**
Clive Ho. SE10 . . . . .2E **95**
. . . . (off Haddo St.)
Clive Lloyd Ho. N15 . . . . .1E **35**
. . . . (off Woodlands Pk. Rd.)
Clive Rd. SE21 . . . . .3F **119**
Clive Lodge NW4 . . . . .1F **29**
Clive Pas. SE21 . . . . .3F **119**
Cloak La. EC4 . . . . .4A 18 (1E **77**)
Clochar Ct. NW10 . . . . .5B **42**
Clock Ho. E3 . . . . .2E **67**
Clockhouse, The SW19 . . . . .3E **113**
Clockhouse Cl. SW19 . . . . .2E **113**
Clock Ho. Pde. E11 . . . . .1D **41**
Clockhouse Pl. SW15 . . . . .4A **100**
Clock Ho. Rd. E11 . . . . .1D **41**
Clock Pl. SE11 . . . . .5D **77**
. . . . (off Newington Butts)
Clock Twr. M. N1 . . . . .5E **49**
Clock Vw. Cres. N7 . . . . .3A **48**
Clockwork Apts.
  EC4 . . . . .3E 17 (5D **63**)
. . . . (off Ludgate Sq.)
Clockwork M. E5 . . . . .2F **51**
Cloister Rd. NW2 . . . . .5B **30**
Cloisters, The E1 . . . . . .4F 11 (4B **64**)
. . . . (off Commercial St.)
Cloisters, The SW9 . . . . .4C **90**
. . . . (off Battersea Pk. Rd.)
Cloisters Bus. Cen. SW8 . . . . .3D **89**
Clonbrock Rd. N16 . . . . .1A **50**
Cloncurry St. SW6 . . . . .5F **85**
Clonmel Rd. SW6 . . . . .3B **86**
Clonmore St. SW18 . . . . .1B **114**
Clorane Gdns. NW3 . . . . .5C **30**
Close, The SE3 . . . . .5F **95**
Cloth Ct. EC1 . . . . .1E 17 (4D **63**)
. . . . (off Cloth Fair)
Cloth Fair EC1 . . . . .1E 17 (4D **63**)
Cloth Ho. EC1 . . . . .5F 9 (4E **63**)
. . . . (off Cloth St.)
Clothier St. E1 . . . . .2E 19 (5A **64**)
Cloth St. EC1 . . . . .5F 9 (4E **63**)
Cloudesdale Rd. SW17 . . . . .2D **117**
Cloudesley Ho. N1 . . . . .5C **48**
. . . . (off Cloudesley St.)
Cloudesley Mans. N1 . . . . .5C **48**
. . . . (off Cloudesley Pl.)
Cloudesley Pl. N1 . . . . .5C **48**
Cloudesley Rd. N1 . . . . .5C **48**
. . . . (not continuous)
Cloudesley Sq. N1 . . . . .5C **48**
Cloudesley St. N1 . . . . .5C **48**
Clova Rd. E7 . . . . .3B **54**
Clove Cres. E14 . . . . .1E **81**
Clove Hitch Quay SW11 . . . . .1E **101**
Clovelly Ct. NW2 . . . . .2E **43**
Clovelly Ho. W2 . . . . .5E **59**
. . . . (off Hallfield Est.)
Clovelly Way E1 . . . . .5E **65**
Clover Cl. E11 . . . . .4F **39**

Clover Ct. E14 . . . . .4D **81**
. . . . (off Watergate Walk)
Clover M. SW3 . . . . .2B **88**
Clove St. E13 . . . . .3C **68**
Clowders Rd. SE6 . . . . .3B **122**
Cloysters Grn. E1 . . . . .2C **78**
Clubhouse, The E14 . . . . .5C **66**
Club Row E1 . . . . .3F 11 (3B **64**)
Club Row E2 . . . . .3F 11 (3B **64**)
Clunbury St. N1 . . . . .1F **63**
Clunie Ho. SW1 . . . . .5A 20 (4B **74**)
. . . . (off Hans Pl.)
Cluny Est. SE1 . . . . .5D 27 (4A **78**)
Cluny M. SW5 . . . . .5C **72**
Cluny Pl. SE1 . . . . .5D 27 (4A **78**)
Cluse Ct. N1 . . . . .1E **63**
. . . . (off St Peters St.)
Cluster Ho. W3 . . . . .2B **70**
Clutton St. E14 . . . . .4D **67**
Clyde Ct. NW1 . . . . .1F **61**
. . . . (off Hampden Cl.)
Clyde Flats SW6 . . . . .3B **86**
. . . . (off Rylston Rd.)
Clyde Ho. SW18 . . . . .2C **100**
. . . . (off Enterprise Way)
Clyde Pl. E10 . . . . .2D **39**
Clydesdale Ho. W11 . . . . .5B **58**
. . . . (off Clydesdale Rd.)
Clydesdale Rd. W11 . . . . .5B **58**
Clyde Sq. E14 . . . . .5B **66**
Clyde St. SE8 . . . . .2B **94**
Clyde Ter. SE23 . . . . .2E **121**
Clyde Va. SE23 . . . . .2E **121**
Clyde Wharf E16 . . . . .2C **82**
Clynes Ho. E2 . . . . .2F **65**
. . . . (off Knottisford St.)
Clyston St. SW8 . . . . .5E **89**
Coach & Horses Yd.
  W1 . . . . .4E 13 (1F **75**)
Coach Ho. La. N5 . . . . .1D **49**
Coach Ho. La. SW19 . . . . .4F **113**
Coach Ho. M. SE1 . . . .5D 27 (4A **78**)
. . . . (off Long La.)
Coach Ho. M. SE14 . . . . .5F **93**
Coach Ho. M. SE23 . . . . .4F **107**
Coach Ho. Yd. NW3 . . . . .1E **45**
. . . . (off Heath St.)
Coach Ho. Yd. SW18 . . . . .2D **101**
Coachmaker M. SW4 . . . . .1A **104**
. . . . (off Bedford Rd.)
Coach Yd. M. N19 . . . . .3A **34**
Coalbrookdale Gates 3F **73**
Coaldale Wlk. SE21 . . . . .5E **105**
Coalecroft Rd. SW15 . . . . .2E **99**
Coal La. SW9 . . . . .2C **104**
Coalmakers Wharf E14 . . . . .5C **66**
Coalport Ho. SE11 . . . . .5C **76**
. . . . (off Walnut Tree Wlk.)
Coalstore Ct. E1 . . . . .4A **66**
Coatbridge Ho. N1 . . . . .4B **48**
. . . . (off Carnoustie Dr.)
Coates Av. SW18 . . . . .4A **102**
Coate St. E2 . . . . .1C **64**
Cobalt Bldg., The EC2 . .4F 9 (4E **63**)
. . . . (off Bridgewater Sq.)
Cobalt Pl. SW11 . . . . .4F **87**
Cobalt Sq. SW8 . . . . .2B **90**
. . . . (off Sth. Lambeth Rd.)
Cobb St. E1 . . . . .2A **94**
Cobbetts Av. IG4: Ilf 1F **41**
Cobbett St. SW8 . . . . .3B **90**
Cobble La. N1 . . . . .4D **49**
Cobble M. N5 . . . . .5E **35**
Cobble M. N6 . . . . .3C **32**
. . . . (off Highgate West Hill)

Cobblestone Sq. E1..................2D **79**
Cobbold Ct. SW1.......................5F **75**
................................(off Elverton St.)
Cobbold Ind. Est. NW10...........3B **42**
Cobbold M. W12.......................3B **70**
Cobbold Rd. E11......................5B **40**
Cobbold Rd. NW10..................3B **42**
Cobbold Rd. W12.....................3A **70**
Cobb's Ct. EC4............3E **17** (5D **63**)
..................................(off Carter La.)
Cobb's Hall SW6......................2F **85**
..............................(off Fulham Pal. Rd.)
Cobbsthorpe Vs. SE26............4F **121**
Cob Stb. E1...................1F **19** (4B **64**)
Cobden Bldgs. WC1...1F **7** (2B **62**)
...............................(off King's Cross Rd.)
Cobden Ho. E2...........................2C **64**
................................(off Nelson Gdns.)
Cobden Ho. NW1.......................1E **61**
..................................(off Arlington Rd.)
Cobden M. SE26.......................5D **121**
Cobden Rd. E11.......................5A **40**
Cobham Cl. SW11....................4A **102**
Cobham M. NW1.......................4F **47**
Cobland Rd. SE12...................4E **125**
COBORN CENTRE FOR
  ADOLESCENT MENTAL HEALTH,
  THE 3F **69**
Coborn M. E3............................2B **66**
..................................(off Coborn St.)
Coborn Rd. E3..........................1B **66**
Coborn St. E3...........................2B **66**
Cobourg Rd. SE5.....................2B **92**
Cobourg St. NW1........2A **6** (2E **61**)
Coburg Cres. SW2..................1B **118**
Coburg Dwellings E1................5E **65**
...............................(off Hardinge St.)
Cochrane Cl. NW8....................1F **59**
.................................(off Cochrane St.)
Cochrane Cl. E10......................3C **38**
...............................(off Leyton Grange Est.)
Cochrane Ho. E14.....................3C **80**
................................(off Admirals Way)
Cochrane M. NW8....................1F **59**
Cochrane St. NW8....................1F **59**
Cockburn Ho. SW1...................1F **89**
................................(off Aylesford St.)
Cockerell Rd. E17.....................2A **38**
Cock Hill E1.................1E **19** (4A **64**)
Cock La. EC1...............1D **17** (4D **63**)
Cockpit Steps SW1....4B **22** (3F **75**)
...............................(off Birdcage Wlk.)
Cockpit Theatre 3A **60**
................................(off Gateforth St.)
Cockpit Yd. WC1.........5A **8** (4B **62**)
Cockspur Ct. SW1.....1C **22** (2F **75**)
Cockspur St. SW1.....1C **22** (2F **75**)
Coda Cen., The SW6................3A **86**
Coda Residences SW11.........1F **101**
.....................................(off York Place)
Code Ct. NW2...........................5C **28**
Code St. E1...............................3B **64**
Codicote Ho. SE8......................5F **79**
................................(off Chilton Gro.)
Codling Cl. E1...........................2C **78**
Codrington Ct. E1.....................3D **65**
Codrington Ct. SE16................1A **80**
Codrington Hill SE23..............5A **108**
Codrington M. W11.................5A **58**
Cody Rd. E16............................3F **67**
Cofferdam Way SE8................3D **95**
Coffey St. SE8...........................3C **94**
Coin St. SE1................1B **24** (2C **76**)
.................................(not continuous)

Coity Rd. NW5............................3C **46**
Cokers La. SE21.......................1F **119**
Coke St. E1................................5C **64**
Colas M. NW6............................5C **44**
Colbeck M. SE6............................5F **109**
Colbeck M. SW7........................5D **73**
Colberg Pl. N16........................2B **36**
Colbert SE5................................4A **92**
................................(off Sceaux Gdns.)
Colborne Ho. E14.....................1C **80**
...............................(off E. India Dock Rd.)
Colby M. SE19.........................5A **120**
Colby Rd. SE19.......................5A **120**
Colchester Ho. E3.....................5B **52**
....................................(off Parnell Rd.)
Colchester Rd. E10...................2E **39**
Colchester Rd. E17...................1C **38**
Coldbath Sq. EC1.......3B **8** (3C **62**)
Coldbath St. SE13....................4D **95**
Cold Blow La. SE14...................3F **93**
.................................(not continuous)
Coldharbour E14.......................3E **81**
Coldharbour Ind. Est. SE5......5E **91**
Coldharbour La. SE5..............1E **105**
Coldharbour La. SW9.............2C **104**
Coldharbour Pl. SE5................5E **91**
Coldstream Gdns. SW18.......4B **100**
Colebeck M. N1........................3D **49**
Colebert Av. E1.........................3E **65**
Colebert Ho. E1........................3E **65**
................................(off Colebert Av.)
Colebrook Cl. SW15................5F **99**
Colebrook Cl. SW3...................5A **74**
................................(off Makins St.)
Colebrooke Dr. E11..................2E **41**
Colebrooke Pl. N1....................5D **49**
Colebrooke Row
  N1.......................1D **9** (1D **63**)
Colebrook Ho. E14...................5D **67**
................................(off Ellesmere St.)
Coleby Path SE5.......................3F **91**
Colechurch Ho. SE1.................1C **92**
................................(off Avondale Sq.)
Colefax Bldgs. E1.....................5C **64**
................................(off Plumber's Row)
Coleford Rd. SW18................3E **101**
Colegrave Rd. E15....................2F **53**
Colegrove Rd. SE15.................2B **92**
Coleherne Ct. SW5..................1D **87**
Coleherne Mans. SW5.............1D **87**
................................(off Old Brompton Rd.)
Coleherne M. SW10.................1D **87**
Coleherne Rd. SW10................1D **87**
Colehill Gdns. SW6..................5A **86**
Colehill La. SW6.......................4A **86**
Cole Ho. SE1................4C **24** (3C **76**)
................................(off Baylis Rd.)
Coleman Ct. SW18...................5C **100**
Coleman Flds. N1.....................5E **49**
Coleman Mans. N8...................2A **34**
Coleman Rd. SE5......................3A **92**
Coleman St. EC2.......2B **18** (5F **63**)
Coleman St. Bldgs.
  EC2.....................2B **18** (5F **63**)
................................(off Coleman St.)
Colenso Rd. E5.........................1E **51**
Coleraine Rd. SE3.....................2B **96**
Coleridge Av. E12.....................3F **55**
Coleridge Cl. SW8....................5D **89**
Coleridge Ct. N1........................5E **49**
.................................(off Dibden St.)
Coleridge Ct. SW1....................5F **75**
.................................(off Regency St.)
Coleridge Ct. W14.....................4F **71**
.................................(off Blythe Rd.)

Coleridge Gdns. NW6..............4E **45**
Coleridge Gdns. SW10...........3D **87**
Coleridge Ho. SE17..................1E **91**
................................(off Browning St.)
Coleridge Ho. SW1....................1E **89**
................................(off Churchill Gdns.)
Coleridge La. N8.......................1A **34**
Coleridge Rd. N4......................4C **34**
Coleridge Rd. N8......................1F **33**
Coleridge Sq. SW10................3E **87**
................................(off Coleridge Gdns.)
Coles Grn. Ct. NW2.................4C **28**
Coles Grn. Rd. NW2................3C **28**
Coleshill Flats SW1..................5C **74**
.....................................(off Pimlico Rd.)
Colestown St. SW11...............5A **88**
Colet Gdns. W14............4A **26** (3E **77**)
Colet Ct. W6............................5F **71**
................................(off Hammersmith Rd.)
Colet Flats E1..........................5A **66**
.....................................(off Troon St.)
Colet Gdns. W14.....................5F **71**
Colet Ho. SE17.........................1D **91**
................................(off Doddington Gro.)
Colette Ct. SE16.......................3F **79**
.....................................(off Eleanor Cl.)
Coley St. WC1...............4A **8** (3B **62**)
Colfe & Hatcliffe Glebe
  SE13.....................................3D **109**
................................(off Lewisham High St.)
Colfe Rd. SE23........................1A **122**
Colfes Leisure Cen...............4C **110**
Colin Ct. SE6............................5B **108**
Colinette Rd. SW15.................2E **99**
Colin Rd. NW10.......................3C **42**
Colinsdale N1...........................5D **49**
................................(off Camden Wlk.)
Colin Winter Ho. E1.................3E **65**
................................(off Nicholas Rd.)
Coliseum Theatre London
  ....5D **15** (1A **76**)
................................(off St Martin's La.)
Coliston Pas. SW18................5C **100**
................................(off Coliston Rd.)
Coliston Rd. SW18.................5C **100**
Collamore Av. SW18..............1A **116**
Collard Pl. NW1........................4D **47**
Collection Pl. NW8...................5D **45**
.....................................(off Bolton Pl.)
College App. SE10..................2E **95**
College Cl. E9...........................2E **51**
College Ct. NW3.......................3F **45**
................................(off College Cres.)
College Ct. SW3.........................1B **88**
.....................................(off West Rd.)
College Ct. W6..........................1E **85**
................................(off Queen Caroline St.)
College Cres. NW3..................3E **45**
College Cross N1......................4C **48**
College E. E1..............1F **19** (4B **64**)
College Gdns. IG4: Ilf...........1F **41**
College Gdns. SE21...............1A **120**
College Gdns. SW17...............2A **116**
College Gro. NW1.....................5E **47**
College Hall WC1........4B **6** (3F **61**)
College Hill EC4...........4A **18** (1E **77**)
College Ho. SW15.....................3F **99**
College Mans. NW6................5A **44**
................................(off Salusbury Rd.)
College M. N1...........................4C **48**
................................(off College Cross)
College M. SW1.........5D **23** (4A **76**)
................................(off Gt. College St.)
College M. SW18......................3D **101**

College Pde. NW6 ....5A 44
.............(off Salusbury Rd.)
COLLEGE PK. 2D 57
College Pk. Cl. SE13 ....2F 109
College Pl. NW1 ....5E 47
College Pl. SW10 ....3E 87
College Point E15 ....3B 54
College Rd. E17 ....1E 39
College Rd. NW10 ....1E 57
College Rd. SE19 ....5B 120
College Rd. SE21 ....5A 106
College Row E9 ....2F 51
.............(off Homerton Gro.)
College St. EC4 ......4A 18 (1E 77)
College Ter. E3 ....2B 66
College Vw. SE9 ....1F 125
College Yd. NW5 ....1D 47
College Yd. NW6 ....5A 44
Collett St. E9 ....3E 51
Collerston Ho. SE10 ....1B 96
.............(off Armitage Rd.)
Colless Rd. N15 ....1B 36
Collett Rd. SE16 ....4C 78
Collier St. N1 ....1F 7 (1B 62)
Collingbourne Rd. W12........2D 71
Collingham Gdns. SW5 ......5D 73
Collingham Pl. SW5 ....5D 73
Collingham Rd. SW5 ....5D 73
Collington St. SE10 ....1F 95
Collingtree Rd. SE26 ....4E 121
Collingwood Ho. E1 ....3D 65
.............(off Darling Row)
Collingwood Ho. SE10 ....3D 79
.............(off Cherry Gdn. St.)
Collingwood Ho. SW1 ....1F 89
.............(off Dolphin Sq.)
Collingwood Ho. W1 ....5F 5 (4E 61)
.............(off Clipstone St.)
Collingwood Rd. E17 ....1C 38
Collingwood St. E1 ....3D 65
Collins Bldg. NW2 ....4E 29
Collins Ct. E8 ....3C 50
Collins Ho. E14 ....1E 81
.............(off Newby Pl.)
Collins Ho. SE10 ....1B 96
.............(off Armitage Rd.)
Collinson Ct. SE1 ....4F 25 (3E 77)
.............(off Gt. Suffolk St.)
Collinson Ho. SE15 ....3C 92
.............(off Peckham Pk. Rd.)
Collinson Ho. SE3 ....2D 111
.............(off Wallace Ct.)
Collinson St. SE1 ....4F 25 (3E 77)
Collinson Wlk. SE1 ..4F 25 (3E 77)
Collins Rd. N5 ....1E 49
Collins Sq. SE3 ....5B 96
Collins St. SE3 ....3A 96
.............(not continuous)
Collin's Yd. N1 ....5D 49
Collison Pl. N16 ....3A 36
Coll's Rd. SE15 ....4E 93
Collyer Pl. SE15 ....4C 92
Colman Rd. E16 ....4E 69
Colmans Wharf E14 ....4D 67
.............(off Morris Rd.)
Colmar Cl. E1 ....3F 65
Colmore M. SE15 ....4D 93
Colnbrook St. SE1....5D 25 (4D 77)
Colne Ho. NW8 ....3F 59
.............(off Penfold St.)
Colne Rd. E5 ....1A 52
Colne St. E13 ....2C 68
Colnmore Ct. E2 ....2F 65
.............(off Meath Cres.)
Cologne Rd. SW11 ....2F 101

Colombo Cen. 2D 25 (2D 77)
.............(off Colombo St.)
Colombo St. SE1 ......2D 25 (2D 77)
Colomb St. SE10 ....1A 96
Colonnade WC1..........4D 7 (3A 62)
Colonnade, The
SE1 ....3B 24 (3C 76)
.............(off Waterloo Rd.)
Colonnade, The SE8..............5B 80
Colonnade Gdns. W3............2B 70
Colonnades, The W2............5D 59
Colonnade Wlk. SW1............5D 75
Colony Mans. SW5................1D 87
Colony M. N1 ....2F 49
.............(off Mildmay Gro. Nth.)
Colorado Bldg. SE13............4D 95
.............(off Deal's Gateway)
Colosseum Apts. E2..............1F 65
.............(off Palmers Rd.)
Colosseum Ter. NW1..2E 5 (2D 61)
.............(off Albany St.)
Colour Ct. SW1 ......2A 22 (2E 75)
.............(off Marlborough Rd.)
Colour Ho. SE1 ....4E 27 (3A 78)
.............(off Bell Yd M.)
Colson Way SW16................4E 117
Colstead Ho. E1 ....5D 65
.............(off Watney Mkt.)
Colston Rd. E7 ....3F 55
Coltash Ct. EC1 ....3A 10 (3E 63)
.............(off Whitecross St.)
Colthurst Cres. N4 ....4D 35
Coltman Ho. SE10 ....2E 95
.............(off Welland St.)
Coltman St. E14 ....4A 66
Columbas Dr. NW3................3F 31
Columbia Gdns. SW6............2C 86
.............(off One Lillie Sq.)
Columbia Gdns. Nth. SW6....2C 86
.............(off Rickett St.)
Columbia Gdns. Sth. SW6....2C 86
.............(off Rickett St.)
Columbia Ho. E3 ....3B 66
.............(off Hamlets Way)
Columbia Point SE16............4E 79
Columbia Rd. E13 ....3B 68
Columbia Rd. E2 ....2F 11 (2B 64)
Columbia Rd. Flower Market
....................................1F 11 (2B 64)
.............(off Columbia Rd.)
Columbine Av. E6 ....4F 69
Columbine Way SE13............5E 95
Columbus Ct. SE16................2E 79
.............(off Rotherhithe St.)
Columbus Ctyd. E14............2C 80
Colva Wlk. N19......................4D 33
Colverson Ho. E1..................4E 65
.............(off Lindley St.)
Colvestone Cres. E8..............2B 50
Colview Ct. SE9 ....1F 125
Colville Est. N1 ....5A 50
Colville Est. W. E2 ....2B 64
.............(off Turin St.)
Colville Gdns. W11................5B 58
.............(not continuous)
Colville Ho. E2 ....1E 65
.............(off Waterloo Gdns.)
Colville Ho's. W11................5B 58
Colville Mans. E20 ....2D 53
.............(off Victory Pde.)
Colville M. W11......................5B 58
Colville Pl. W1 ....1A 14 (4F 61)

Colville Rd. E11 ....5E 39
Colville Rd. W11....................5B 58
Colville Rd. W3......................5B 58
Colville Sq. W11 ....5B 58
Colville Ter. W11 ....5B 58
Colvin Cl. SE26 ....5E 121
Colvin Ho. W10 ....5F 57
.............(off Kingsdown Cl.)
Colvin Rd. E6..........................4F 55
Colwell Rd. SE22 ....3B 106
Colwick Cl. N6........................2F 33
Colwith Rd. W6 ....2E 85
Colworth Gro. SE17..............5E 77
Colworth Rd. E11 ....1A 40
Colwyn Cl. SW16 ....5E 117
Colwyn Grn. NW9 ....1A 28
.............(off Snowdon Dr.)
Colwyn Ho. SE1 ......5B 24 (4C 76)
Colwyn Rd. NW2 ....5D 29
Colyton La. SW16................5C 118
Colyton Rd. SE22 ....3D 107
Combe, The NW1 ......2E 5 (2D 61)
Combe Av. SE3......................3B 96
Combedale Rd. SE10............1C 96
Combe Ho. W2 ....4C 58
.............(off Gt. Western Rd.)
Combemartin Rd. SW18 ....5A 100
Combe M. SE3 ....3B 96
Comber Cl. NW2 ....5D 29
Comber Gro. SE5..................3E 91
Comber Ho. SE5 ....3E 91
Combermere Rd. SW9 ....1B 104
Comberton Rd. E5................4D 37
Comedy Store 5B 14 (1F 75)
.............(off Oxendon St.)
Comeragh M. W14................1A 86
Comeragh Rd. W14..............1A 86
Comerford Rd. SE4..............2A 108
Comet Cl. E12 ....1F 55
Comet Pl. SE8 ....3C 94
.............(not continuous)
Comet St. SE8 ....3C 94
Comfort St. SE15..................2A 92
Commercial Rd. E1 ....5C 64
Commercial Rd. E14 ....5A 66
Commercial St. E1....4F 11 (3B 64)
Commercial Way SE10 ....5B 80
Commercial Way SE15 ....3B 92
Commercial Wharf E8 ....5A 50
.............(off Kingsland Rd.)
Commerell Pl. SE10 ....1B 96
Commerell St. SE10 ....1A 96
Commodity Quay
E1 ....5F 19 (1B 78)
Commodore Ct. SE8..............4C 94
.............(off Albyn Rd.)
Commodore Ho. E14 ....1E 81
.............(off Poplar High St.)
Commodore Ho. E16..............3D 83
.............(off Royal Crest Av.)
Commodore Ho. SW18........1E 101
Commodore St. E1 ....3A 66
Common, The E15..................3A 54
Commonfield La. SW17 ......5A 116
Common Mile Cl. SW4 ....3F 103
Common Rd. SW13 ....1D 99
Commonwealth Av. W12 ....1D 71
.............(not continuous)
Commonwealth Memorial Gates
....................................3D 21 (3D 75)
Community La. N7..................2F 47
Community Rd. E15 ....2F 53
Como Rd. SE23 ....2A 122
Compass Ct. SE1 ....2F 27 (2B 78)
.............(off Shad Thames)

Compass Ho. E1 .... 2D 79
................................(off Raine St.)
Compass Ho. SW18 .... 2D 101
Compass Point E14 .... 1B 80
................................(off Grenade St.)
Compayne Gdns. NW6 .... 4D 45
Compayne Mans. NW6 .... 3D 45
................................(off Fairhazel Gdns.)
Compter Pas. EC2 ....3A 18 (5E 63)
................................(off Wood St.)
Compton Av. E6 .... 1F 69
Compton Av. N1 .... 3D 49
Compton Av. N6 .... 2A 32
Compton Cl. E3 .... 4C 66
Compton Cl. NW1 ....2E 5 (2D 61)
................................(off Robert St.)
Compton Cl. NW11 .... 5F 29
Compton Cl. SE15 .... 3B 92
Compton Ct. SE19 .... 5A 120
Compton Ho. E20 .... 2D 53
................................(off Peloton Av.)
Compton Ho. SW10 .... 4E 87
Compton Ho. SW11 .... 4A 88
Compton Pas. EC1 ....3E 9 (3D 63)
Compton Pl. WC1 ......3D 7 (3A 62)
Compton Rd. N1 .... 3D 49
Compton Rd. N21 .... 2F 57
Compton Rd. SW19 .... 5B 114
Compton St. EC1 ......3D 9 (3D 63)
Compton Ter. N1 .... 3D 49
Compton Ter. N4 .... 1E 35
Comus Ho. SE17 .... 5A 78
................................(off Comus Pl.)
Comus Pl. SE17 .... 5A 78
Comyn Rd. SW11 .... 2A 102
Comyns Cl. E16 .... 4B 68
Conant Ho. SE11 .... 2D 91
................................(off St Agnes Pl.)
Conant M. E1 .... 1C 78
Concanon Rd. SW2 .... 2B 104
Concert Hall App.
SE1 .... 2A 24 (2B 76)
Concorde Way SE16 .... 5F 79
Concordia Wharf E14 .... 2E 81
................................(off Coldharbour)
Condell Rd. SW8 .... 4E 89
Conder St. E14 .... 5A 66
Condor Ho. E13 .... 5C 54
................................(off Brooks Rd.)
Condray Pl. SW11 .... 3A 88
Conduit Av. SE10 .... 4F 95
Conduit Ct. WC2 ......4D 15 (1A 76)
................................(off Floral St.)
Conduit M. W2 .... 5F 59
Conduit Pas. W2 .... 5F 59
................................(off Conduit Pl.)
Conduit Pl. W2 .... 5F 59
Conduit St. W1 ....4E 13 (1D 75)
Conewood St. N5 .... 5D 35
Coney Acre SE21 .... 1E 119
Coneybear Point SE10 .... 5C 82
Coney Way SW8 .... 2B 90
Confluence Plaza SE13 .... 1E 109
................................(off Station Rd.)
Congers Ho. SE8 .... 3C 94
Congreve Ho. N16 .... 2A 50
Congreve St. SE17 .... 5A 78
Congreve Wlk. E16 .... 4F 69
................................(off Fulmer Rd.)
Conifer Gdns. SW16 .... 3B 118
Conifer Ho. SE4 .... 2B 108
................................(off Brockley Rd.)
Coniger Rd. SW6 .... 5C 86
Coningham Ct. SW10 .... 3E 87
................................(off King's Rd.)

Coningham M. W12 .... 2C 70
Coningham Rd. W12 .... 3D 71
Coningsby Rd. N4 .... 2D 35
Conington Rd. SE13 .... 5D 95
Conisborough Cres. SE6 ....3E 123
Conisbrough NW1 .... 5E 47
................................(off Bayham St.)
Coniston NW1 ....1F 5 (2E 61)
................................(off Harrington St.)
Coniston Ct. SW13 .... 3B 84
Coniston Ct. SE16 .... 5F 79
................................(off Eleanor Cl.)
Coniston Ct. W2 .... 5A 60
................................(off Kendal St.)
Coniston Ho. E3 .... 3B 66
................................(off Southern Gro.)
Coniston Ho. SE5 .... 3E 91
................................(off Wyndham Rd.)
Coniston Rd. BR1: Broml....5A 124
Coniston Wlk. E9 .... 2E 51
Conlan St. W10 .... 3A 58
Conley Ho. NW10 .... 3A 42
Conley St. SE10 .... 1A 96
Connaught Bri. E16 .... 2F 83
Connaught Cl. E10 .... 4A 38
Connaught Cl. W2 .... 5A 60
Connaught St. W2 .... 5B 60
................................(off Connaught St.)
CONNAUGHT DAY CEN. 1A 40
................................(off James La.)
Connaught Hall WC1 ...3C 6 (3F 61)
Connaught Hgts. E16 .... 2F 83
................................(off Agnes George Wlk.)
Connaught Ho. NW10 .... 2D 57
Connaught Ho. W1 ....5D 13 (1D 75)
................................(off Davies St.)
Connaught Lodge N4 .... 2C 34
................................(off Connaught Rd.)
Connaught M. NW3 .... 1A 46
Connaught M. SW6 .... 4A 86
Connaught Pl. W2 .... 1B 74
Connaught Rd. E11 .... 3F 39
Connaught Rd. E16 .... 2F 83
Connaught Rd. E17 .... 1C 38
Connaught Rd. N4 .... 2C 34
Connaught Rd. NW10 .... 5A 42
CONNAUGHT RDBT. 1F 83
................................(off Victoria Dock Rd.)
Connaught Sq. W2 .... 5B 60
Connaught St. W2 .... 5A 60
Connaught Works E3 .... 5A 52
................................(off Old Ford Rd.)
Connell Ct. SE14 .... 2F 93
................................(off Myers La.)
Conning ham Ct. SE9 .... 3E 111
Connor Cl. E11 .... 2A 40
Connor Cl. SW11 .... 4D 89
Connor St. E9 .... 5F 51
Conrad Ct. SE16 .... 5A 80
................................(off Cary Av.)
Conrad Ho. E14 .... 1A 80
................................(off Victory Pl.)
Conrad Ho. E16 .... 2D 83
................................(off Wesley Av.)
Conrad Ho. E8 .... 3C 50
Conrad Ho. N16 .... 2A 50
................................(off Matthias Rd.)
Conrad Ho. SW8 .... 3A 90
................................(off Wyvil Rd.)
Consort Cl. W8 .... 4D 73
................................(off Wright's La.)
Consort Ho. E14 .... 1D 95
................................(off St Davids Sq.)

Consort Ho. SW6 .... 5E 87
................................(off Lensbury Av.)
Consort Ho. W2 .... 1D 73
................................(off Queensway)
Consort Lodge NW8 .... 5B 46
................................(off Prince Albert Rd.)
Consort Pk. 5D 93
................................(off Gordon Road)
Consort Rd. SE15 .... 4D 93
Cons St. SE1 ....3C 24 (3C 76)
Constable Av. E16 .... 2D 83
Constable Cl. NW11 .... 1D 31
Constable Ct. SE16 .... 1D 93
................................(off Stubbs Dr.)
Constable Ho. E14 .... 3C 80
................................(off Cassilis Rd.)
Constable Ho. NW3 .... 4B 46
Constable Wlk. SE21 .... 3A 120
Constance Allen Ho. W10 ....5F 57
................................(off Bridge Cl.)
Constance St. E16 .... 2F 83
Constant Ho. E14 .... 1D 81
................................(off Harrow La.)
Constantine Ct. E1 .... 5C 64
................................(off Fairclough St.)
Constantine Rd. NW3 .... 1A 46
Constitution Hill SW1 3D 21 (3D 75)
Consul Ho. E3 .... 3C 66
................................(off Wellington Way)
Container City 1 E14 .... 1A 82
Container City 2 E14 .... 1A 82
Contemporary Applied Arts
.................................2E 25 (2D 77)
................................(off Southwark St.)
Content St. SE17 .... 5F 77
Convent Gdns. W11 .... 5A 58
Conway Gro. W3 .... 4A 56
Conway Ho. E14 .... 5C 80
................................(off Cahir St.)
Conway Ho. SW3 .... 1B 88
................................(off Ormonde Ga.)
Conway M. W1 ....4F 5 (3E 61)
................................(off Conway St.)
Conway Rd. NW2 .... 4C 29
Conway St. W1 ....4F 5 (3E 61)
..............................(not continuous)
Conybeare NW3 .... 4A 46
Conyer's Rd. SW16 .... 5F 117
Conyer St. E3 .... 1A 66
Cook Ct. SE16 .... 2E 79
................................(off Rotherhithe St.)
Cook Ct. SE8 .... 1A 94
................................(off Evelyn St.)
Cookes Cl. E11 .... 4B 40
Cookham Cres. SE16 .... 3F 79
Cookham Ho. E2 ....3F 11 (3B 64)
................................(off Montclare St.)
Cooks Cl. E14 .... 2C 80
................................(off Cabot Sq.)
Cook's Rd. E15 .... 1D 67
Cooks Rd. SE17 .... 2D 91
Coolfin Rd. E16 .... 5C 68
Coolhurst Rd. N8 .... 1F 33
Coolhurst Tennis & Squash Club
.....................................1F 33
Cool Oak La. NW9 .... 2A 28
Coomassie Rd. W9 .... 3B 58
Coombe Ho. N7 .... 2F 47
Coombe Lodge SE7 .... 2E 97
Coomber Ho. SW6 .... 1D 101
................................(off Wandsworth Bri. Rd.)
Coombe Rd. SE26 .... 4D 121
Coombe Rd. W4 .... 1A 84
Coombrook Ct. SE16 .... 3A 80
................................(off Elgar St.)

Coombs St. N1 ....1E **9** (1D 63)
Coomer M. SW6 ....2B **86**
Coomer Pl. SW6 ....2B **86**
Coomer Rd. SW6 ....2B **86**
Cooperage, The
 SE1 ....2F **27** (3B 78)
 ....(off Gainsford St.)
Cooperage, The SW6 ....3B **90**
 ....(off Regent's Bri. Gdns.)
Cooperage Yd. E15 ....1E **67**
Co-operative Ho. SE15 ....1C **106**
Cooper Cl. SE1 ....4C **24** (3C 76)
Cooper Ho. NW8 ....3F **59**
 ....(off Lyons Pl.)
Cooper Ho. SE4 ....3F **107**
 ....(off St Norbert Rd.)
Cooper Rd. NW10 ....2C **42**
Cooper Rd. NW4 ....1F **29**
Coopersale Rd. E9 ....2F **51**
Coopers Cl. E1 ....3E **65**
Coopers Ct. E3 ....3B **66**
 ....(off Eric St.)
Cooper's La. SE12 ....2D **125**
Coopers La. E10 ....1D **39**
Coopers La. E20 ....2D **53**
Coopers La. NW1 ....1F **61**
Coopers Lodge SE1...3F **27** (3B 78)
 ....(off Tooley St.)
Cooper's Rd. SE1 ....1B **92**
Coopers Row EC3 ....4F **19** (1B 78)
Cooper St. E16 ....4B **68**
Coopers Wlk. E15 ....2A **54**
Cooper's Yd. SE19 ....5A **120**
Coopers Yd. N1 ....4D **49**
 ....(off Upper St.)
Cope Ho. EC1...........2A **10** (2E 63)
 ....(off Bath St.)
Copeland Dr. E14 ....5C **80**
Copeland Ho. SE11 ....4C **76**
 ....(off Lambeth Wlk.)
Copeland Ho. SW17 ....4F **115**
Copeland Rd. E17 ....1D **39**
Copeland Rd. SE15 ....5C **92**
Copeman Cl. SE26 ....5E **121**
Copenhagen Ct. SE8 ....5A **80**
 ....(off Pell St.)
Copenhagen Ho. N1 ....5B **48**
 ....(off Barnsbury Est.)
Copenhagen Pl. E14 ....5B **66**
 ....(not continuous)
Copenhagen St. N1 ....5A **48**
Cope Pl. W8 ....4C **72**
Cope St. SE16 ....5F **79**
Copford Wlk. N1 ....5E **49**
 ....(off Popham St.)
Copgate Path SW16 ....5B **118**
Copleston M. SE15 ....5B **92**
Copleston Pas. SE15 ....5B **92**
Copleston Rd. SE15 ....1B **106**
Copley Cl. SE17 ....2E **91**
Copley Pk. SW16 ....5B **118**
Copley St. E1 ....4F **65**
Coppelia Rd. SE3 ....2B **110**
Copperas St. SE8 ....2D **95**
Copperbeech Cl. NW3 ....2F **45**
Copper Box Arena 3C **52**
Copper Ct. E5 ....4E **37**
Copperfield Ho. SE1 ....3C **78**
 ....(off Wolseley St.)
Copperfield Ho. W1...5C **4** (4C **60**)
 ....(off Marylebone High St.)
Copperfield Ho. W11 ....2F **71**
 ....(off St Ann's Rd.)
Copperfield M. E2 ....1C **64**
 ....(off Claredale St.)

Copperfield Rd. E3 ....3A **66**
Copperfield St. SE1...3E **25** (3D **77**)
Copper La. N16 ....1F **49**
Copperlight Apts. SW18 ......3C **100**
 ....(off Buckhold Rd.)
Coppermead Cl. NW2 ....5E **29**
Copper Mill La. SW17 ....4F **115**
Coppermill La. E17 ....1E **37**
Copper Row SE1 .....2F **27** (2B 78)
 ....(off Horselydown La.)
Copperwood Pl. SE10 ....4E **95**
Copperworks, The N1 ....1A **62**
 ....(off Railway St.)
Coppice Dr. SW15 ....4D **99**
Coppock Cl. SW11 ....5A **88**
Copse Cl. SE7 ....2D **97**
Coptain Ho. SW18 ....2C **100**
Copthall Av. EC2 .....2C **18** (5F 63)
 ....(not continuous)
Copthall Bldgs.
 EC2 ....2B **18** (5F 63)
 ....(off Copthall Av.)
Copthall Cl. EC2 ......2B **18** (5F 63)
Copthorne Av. SW12 ....5C **103**
Coptic St. WC1 ....1D **15** (4A 62)
Coral Apts. E16 ....1C **82**
 ....(off Western Gateway)
Coral Ho. E1 ....3A **66**
 ....(off Harford St.)
Coral Mans. NW6 ....5C **44**
 ....(off Kilburn High Rd.)
Coral Row SW11 ....1E **101**
Coral St. SE1 ....4C **24** (3C 76)
Coram Ho. W4 ....1A **84**
 ....(off Wood St.)
Coram Ho. WC1 ....3D **7** (3A 62)
 ....(off Herbrand St.)
Coram Mans. WC1 ....4F **7** (3B 62)
 ....(off Millman St.)
Coram St. WC1 ....4D **7** (3A 62)
Corbden Cl. SE15 ....4B **92**
Corben M. SW8 ....5E **89**
Corbet Ct. EC3 ....3C **18** (5F 63)
Corbet Ho. N1 ....1C **62**
 ....(off Barnsbury Est.)
Corbet Pl. E1 ....5F **11** (4B 64)
Corbett Ct. SE26 ....4B **122**
Corbett Ho. SW10 ....2C **87**
 ....(off Cathcart Rd.)
Corbett Rd. E11 ....1E **41**
Corbetts La. SE16 ....5E **79**
 ....(not continuous)
Corbetts Pas. SE16 ....5E **79**
 ....(off Corbetts La.)
Corbetts Wharf SE16 ....3D **79**
 ....(off Bermondsey Wall E.)
Corbicum E11 ....2A **40**
Corbridge Ct. SE8 ....2D **95**
Corbiere Ho. N1 ....5F **49**
 ....(off De Beauvoir Est.)
Corbin Ho. E3 ....2D **67**
 ....(off Bromley High St.)
Corbridge Cres. E2 ....1D **65**
Corbyn St. N4 ....3A **34**
Corby Way E3 ....3C **66**
Cordage Ho. E1 ....2D **79**
 ....(off Cobblestone Sq.)
Cordelia Cl. SE24 ....2D **105**
Cordelia Ho. N1 ....1A **64**
 ....(off Arden Est.)
Cordelia St. E14 ....4D **67**
Cording St. E14 ....4D **67**
Cordwainer Ho. E8 ....5D **51**

Cordwainers Ct. E9 ....4E **51**
 ....(off St Thomas's Sq.)
Cordwainers Wlk. E13 ....1C **68**
Cord Way E14 ....1C **80**
Cordwell Rd. SE13 ....3A **110**
Corelli Ct. SW5 ....5D **73**
Corelli Ct. SW5 ....5C **72**
 ....(off W. Cromwell Rd.)
Corelli Rd. SE3 ....5F **97**
Corfe Ho. SW8 ....3B **90**
 ....(off Dorset Rd.)
Corfield St. E2 ....2D **65**
Coriander Av. E14 ....5F **67**
Coriander Ct. SE1 ....3B **78**
 ....(off Gainsford St.)
Corinne Rd. N19 ....1E **47**
Corker Wlk. N7 ....4B **34**
Cork Ho. SW19 ....4D **115**
Cork Sq. E1 ....2D **79**
Cork St. W1 ....5F **13** (1E 75)
Cork St. M. W1 ....5F **13** (1E 75)
 ....(off Cork St.)
Cork Tree Ho. SE27 ....5D **119**
 ....(off Lakeview Rd.)
Corlett St. NW1 ....4A **60**
Cormont Rd. SE5 ....4D **91**
Cormorant Ct. SE8 ....2B **94**
 ....(off Pilot Cl.)
Cormorant Lodge E1.............2C **78**
 ....(off Thomas More St.)
Cormorant Rd. E7 ....2B **54**
Cornbury Ho. SE8 ....2B **94**
 ....(off Evelyn St.)
Cornelia St. N7 ....3B **48**
Cornell Bldg. E1 ....5C **64**
 ....(off Coke St.)
Cornell Sq. SW8 ....4F **89**
Corner Ct. E2 ....2D **65**
 ....(off Three Colts La.)
Corner Fielde SW2 ....1B **118**
Corner Grn. SE3 ....5C **96**
Corner Ho. NW6 ....1D **59**
 ....(off Oxford Rd.)
Corner Ho. St.
 WC2 ....1D **23** (2A **76**)
 ....(off Northumberland St.)
Corney Reach Way W4 ....3A **84**
Corney Rd. W4 ....3A **84**
Cornflower Ter. SE22 ....4D **107**
Cornford Gro. SW12 ....2D **117**
Cornhill EC3 ....3C **18** (5F 63)
Cornick Ho. SE16 ....4D **79**
 ....(off Slippers Pl.)
Cornish Ho. SE17 ....2D **91**
 ....(off Brandon Est.)
Cornmill Ho. SE8 ....1C **94**
 ....(off Wharf St.)
Cornmill La. SE13 ....1E **109**
Cornmow Dr. NW10 ....2B **42**
Cornthwaite Rd. E5 ....5E **37**
Cornwall Av. E2 ....2E **65**
Cornwall Cres. W11 ....5A **58**
Cornwall Gdns. NW10 ....3D **43**
Cornwall Gdns. SW7 ....4D **73**
Cornwall Gdns. Wlk. SW7 ....4D **73**
Cornwall Gro. W4 ....1A **84**
Cornwall Ho. SW7 ....4D **73**
 ....(off Cornwall Gdns.)
Cornwallis Ct. SW8 ....4A **90**
 ....(off Lansdowne Grn.)
Cornwallis Ho. SE16 ....3D **79**
 ....(off Cherry Gdn. St.)
Cornwallis Ho. W12 ....1D **71**
 ....(off India Way)
Cornwallis Rd. N19 ....4A **34**

Cornwallis Sq. N19 .... 4A 34
Cornwall Mans. SW10 .... 3E 87
.... (off Cremorne Rd.)
Cornwall Mans. W14 .... 4F 71
.... (off Blythe Rd.)
Cornwall Mans. W8 .... 3D 73
.... (off Kensington Ct.)
Cornwall M. Sth. SW7 .... 4E 73
Cornwall M. W. SW7 .... 4D 73
Cornwall Rd. N15 .... 1F 35
Cornwall Rd. N4 .... 2C 34
Cornwall Rd. SE1 ...... 1B 24 (2C 76)
Cornwall Sq. SE11 .... 1D 91
.... (off Seaton Cl.)
Cornwall St. E1 .... 1D 79
Cornwall Ter. NW1 ...... 4A 4 (3B 60)
Cornwall Ter. M.
NW1 .... 4A 4 (3B 60)
.... (off Allsop Pl.)
Corn Way E11 .... 5F 39
Cornwell Gdns. E10 .... 2C 38
Cornwood Dr. E1 .... 5E 65
Corona Bldg. E14 .... 2E 81
.... (off Blackwall Way)
Corona Rd. SE12 .... 5C 110
Coronation Av. N16 .... 1B 50
Coronation Ct. E15 .... 3B 54
Coronation Ct. W10 .... 4E 57
.... (off Brewster Gdns.)
Coronation Rd. E13 .... 2E 69
Coroner's Court
City of London 4B 18 (1F 77)
Coroner's Court Poplar 1D 81
.... (off Poplar High St.)
Coroner's Court
Southwark 3B 26 (3F 77)
Coroner's Court St Pancras .. 5F 47
Coroner's Court
West London 4E 87
Coroner's Court Westminster
.... 5F 75
Coronet St. N1 .... 2D 11 (2A 64)
Corporation Row EC1 .. 3C 8 (3C 62)
Corporation St. E15 .... 1A 68
Corporation St. N7 .... 2A 48
Corrance Rd. SW2 .... 2A 104
Corringham St. NW11 .... 2C 30
Corringham Ho. E1 .... 5F 65
.... (off Pitsea St.)
Corringham Rd. NW11 .... 2C 30
Corringway NW11 .... 2D 31
Corris Grn. NW9 .... 1A 28
Corry Dr. SW9 .... 2D 105
Corry Ho. E14 .... 1D 81
.... (off Wade's Pl.)
Corsair Ho. E16 .... 3E 83
.... (off Starboard Way)
Corselitt St. SW16 .... 5E 117
Corsham St. N1 .... 2C 10 (2F 63)
Corsica St. N5 .... 3D 49
Corsley Way E9 .... 3B 52
Cortayne Rd. SW6 .... 5B 86
Cortis Rd. SW15 .... 4D 99
Cortis Ter. SW15 .... 4D 99
Corunna Rd. SW8 .... 4E 89
Corunna Ter. SW8 .... 4E 89
Corvette Sq. SE10 .... 2F 95
Coryton Path W9 .... 3B 58
Cosbycote Av. SE24 .... 3E 105
Cosgrove Ho. E2 .... 5C 50
.... (off Whiston Rd.)
Cosmo Pl. WC1 .... 5E 7 (4A 62)
Cosmur Cl. W12 .... 4B 70
Cossall Wlk. SE15 .... 5D 93

Cossar M. SW2 .... 3C 104
Cosser St. SE1 .... 5B 24 (4C 76)
Costa St. SE15 .... 5C 92
Costemonger Bldg.
SE16 .... 5F 27 (4B 78)
.... (off Arts La.)
Coster Av. N4 .... 3E 35
Coston Wlk. SE4 .... 2F 107
Cosway Mans. NW1 .... 4A 60
.... (off Shroton St.)
Cosway St. NW1 .... 4A 60
Cotall St. E14 .... 4C 66
Coteford St. SW17 .... 4B 116
Cotesbach Rd. E5 .... 5E 37
Cotes Ho. NW8 .... 3A 60
.... (off Broadley St.)
Cotham St. SE17 .... 5E 77
Cotherstone Ct. E2 .... 3D 65
.... (off Three Colts La.)
Cotherstone Rd. SW2 .... 1B 118
Cotleigh Rd. NW6 .... 4C 44
Cotman Cl. NW11 .... 1E 31
Cotman Cl. SW15 .... 4F 99
Cotman Ho. NW8 .... 1A 60
.... (off Townshend Est.)
Cotswold Ct. EC1 ...... 3F 9 (3E 63)
.... (off Gee St.)
Cotswold Gdns. E6 .... 2F 69
Cotswold Gdns. NW2 .... 4F 29
Cotswold Ga. NW2 .... 3A 30
Cotswold M. SW11 .... 4F 87
Cotswold St. SE27 .... 4D 119
Cottage Cl. E1 .... 3E 65
.... (off Mile End Rd.)
Cottage Grn. SE5 .... 3F 91
Cottage Gro. SW9 .... 1A 104
Cottage Pl. SW3 .... 4A 74
Cottage Rd. N7 .... 2B 48
.... (not continuous)
Cottage St. E14 .... 1D 81
Cottage Wlk. N16 .... 5B 36
Cottesbrook St. SE14 .... 3A 94
Cottesloe Ho. NW8 .... 3A 60
.... (off Jerome Cres.)
Cottesloe M. SE1 ..... 5C 24 (4C 76)
.... (off Emery St.)
Cottesmore Ct. W8 .... 4D 73
.... (off Stanford Rd.)
Cottesmore Gdns. W8 .... 4D 73
Cottingham Rd. SW8 .... 3B 90
Cottington St. SE11 .... 1C 90
Cottle Way SE16 .... 3D 79
.... (off Paradise St.)
Cotton Apts. E1 .... 4F 65
.... (off Killick Way)
Cotton Av. W3 .... 5A 56
Cotton Cl. E11 .... 4A 40
Cotton Hill BR1: Broml. 4E 123
Cotton Ho. SW2 .... 5A 104
Cotton Row SW11 .... 1E 101
Cottons Cen. SE1 .... 1D 27 (2A 78)
Cotton's Gdns. E2 ... 1E 11 (2A 64)
Cottons La. SE1 ...... 1C 26 (2F 77)
Cotton St. E14 .... 1E 81
Cottonworks Ho. N7 .... 5B 34
.... (off Seven Sisters Rd.)
Cottrell Ct. SE10 .... 5B 82
.... (off Hop St.)
Cottrill Gdns. E8 .... 3D 51
Coulgate St. SE4 .... 1A 108
Coulson St. SW3 .... 1B 88
Coulter Rd. W6 .... 4D 71
Councillor St. SE5 .... 3E 91
Counter Ct. SE1 ...... 2B 26 (2F 77)
.... (off Borough High St.)

Counter Ho. E1 .... 1C 78
Counters Ct. W14 .... 4A 72
.... (off Holland Rd.)
Counter St. SE1 ...... 1D 27 (2A 78)
Countess Rd. NW5 .... 2E 47
County Court
Central London 4D 5 (3D 61)
.... (off Park Cres.)
County Court Clerkenwell &
Shoreditch 3F 9 (3E 63)
County Court Wandsworth
.... 3A 100
County Court West London ... 1F 85
.... (off Talgarth Rd.)
County Court Willesden 1B 56
County Ground Beckenham, The
.... 5C 122
County Gro. SE5 .... 4E 91
County Hall Apts.
SE1 .... 3F 23 (3B 76)
.... (off Westminster Bri. Rd.)
County Hall (Former)
.... 3F 23 (3B 76)
.... (off Westminster Bri. Rd.)
County Ho. SW9 .... 4C 90
.... (off Brixton Rd.)
County St. SE1 .... 4E 77
Courland Gro. SW8 .... 4F 89
Courland St. SW8 .... 4F 89
Court Annexe 4A 26 (3E 77)
Courtauld Gallery 4F 15 (1B 76)
.... (off Strand)
Courtauld Ho. E2 .... 5C 50
.... (off Goldsmiths Row)
Courtauld Institute of Art, The
.... 4F 15 (1B 76)
.... (off Strand)
Courtauld Rd. N19 .... 3A 34
Court Cl. NW8 .... 4F 45
.... (off Boydell Ct.)
Courtenay Av. N6 .... 2A 32
Courtenay M. E17 .... 1A 38
Courtenay Rd. E11 .... 5B 40
Courtenay Sq. SE11 .... 1C 90
Courtenay St. SE11 .... 1C 90
Court Farm Rd. SE9 .... 2F 125
Courtfield Gdns. SW5 .... 5D 73
Courtfield Ho. EC1 ... 5B 8 (4C 62)
.... (off Baldwins Gdns.)
Courtfield M. SW5 .... 5E 73
Courtfield Rd. SW7 .... 5E 73
Court Gdns. N1 .... 3C 48
Court Gdns. N7 .... 3C 48
Courthill Rd. SE13 .... 2E 109
Courthope Ho. SE16 .... 4E 79
.... (off Lower Rd.)
Courthope Ho. SW8 .... 3A 90
.... (off Hartington Rd.)
Courthope Rd. NW3 .... 1B 46
Courthope Rd. SW19 .... 5A 114
Courthouse, The SW1 .... 4A 76
.... (off Horseferry Rd.)
Courthouse La. N16 .... 1B 50
Courthouse Way SW18 .... 3D 101
Courtland Rd. E6 .... 5F 55
Courtlands Av. SE12 .... 3D 111
Court La. SE21 .... 4A 106
Court La. Gdns. SE21 .... 5A 106
Courtleigh NW11 .... 1B 30
Court Lodge SW1 .... 5C 74
.... (off Sloane Sq.)
Courtmead Cl. SE24 .... 4E 105
Court M. SE13 .... 4A 110
Courtnell St. W2 .... 5C 58
Courtney Ct. N7 .... 2C 48

Courtney Ho. W14 .... 4A 72
Courtney Rd. N7 .... 2C 48
Courtrai Rd. SE23 .... 4A 108
Court Royal SW15 .... 3A 100
Courtside N8 .... 1F 33
Courtside SE26 .... 3D 121
Court St. E1 .... 4D 65
Courtville Ho. W10 .... 2A 58
.... (off Third Av.)
Courtyard SW3 .... 1B 88
.... (off Smith St.)
Courtyard, The E2 .... 2B 64
.... (off Ezra St.)
Courtyard, The EC3 .. 3C 18 (5F 63)
.... (within Royal Exchange)
Courtyard, The N1 .... 4B 48
Courtyard, The NW1 .... 4C 46
Courtyard, The SE14 .... 4F 93
.... (off Besson St.)
Courtyard, The SW3 .... 2F 87
Courtyard Apts. E1 .... 3F 11 (3B 64)
.... (off Sclater St.)
Courtyard Ho. SW6 .... 5E 87
.... (off Lensbury Av.)
Courtyard Theatre Hoxton
.... 2D 11 (2A 64)
Cousin La. EC4 .... 5B 18 (1F 77)
Couthurst Rd. SE3 .... 2D 97
Coutt's Cres. NW5 .... 5C 32
Couzens Ho. E3 .... 4B 66
.... (off Weatherley Cl.)
Covell Ct. SE8 .... 3C 94
COVENT GARDEN .. 3D 15 (1A 76)
Covent Gdn. WC2 ... 4E 15 (1A 76)
Covent Garden Piazza
WC2 .... 4E 15 (1A 76)
.... (off Covent Garden)
Covent Garden Station
(Underground) ... 3E 15 (1A 76)
Coventry Ho. NW6 .... 1C 58
Coventry Hall SW16 .... 5A 118
Coventry Rd. E1 .... 3D 65
Coventry Rd. E2 .... 3D 65
Coventry St. W1 ..... 5B 14 (1F 75)
Coverdale Rd. NW2 .... 4F 43
Coverdale Rd. W12 .... 3D 71
Coverham Ho. SE4 .... 2F 107
.... (off Billingford Cl.)
Coverley Cl. E1 .... 4C 64
Coverley Point SE11 .... 5B 76
.... (off Tyers St.)
Coverton Rd. SW17 .... 5A 116
Covington Way SW16 .... 5B 118
.... (not continuous)
Cowcross St. EC1 ...5D 9 (4D 63)
Cowdenbeath Path N1 .... 5B 48
Cowden St. SE6 .... 4C 122
Cowdrey M. SE6 .... 4C 122
Cowdrey Rd. SW19 .... 5D 115
Cowick Rd. SW17 .... 4B 116
Cowley La. E11 .... 5A 40
Cowley Rd. E11 .... 1D 41
Cowley Rd. SW14 .... 1A 98
Cowley Rd. SW9 .... 4C 90
.... (not continuous)
Cowley Rd. W3 .... 2B 70
Cowley St. SW1 ...5D 23 (4A 76)
Cowling Cl. W11 .... 2A 72
Cowper Av. E6 .... 4F 55
Cowper Ho. SE17 .... 1E 91
.... (off Browning St.)
Cowper Ho. SW1 .... 1F 89
.... (off Aylesford St.)

Cowper Rd. N16 .... 2A 50
Cowper Rd. SW19 .... 5E 115
Cowper's Ct. EC3 .... 3C 18 (5F 63)
.... (off Birchin La.)
Cowper St. EC2 .... 3C 10 (3F 63)
Cowper Ter. W10 .... 4F 57
Cowthorpe Rd. SW8 .... 4F 89
Cox Ho. W6 .... 2A 86
.... (off Field Rd.)
Coxmount Rd. SE7 .... 1F 97
Coxson Way SE1 .... 4F 27 (3B 78)
Cox's Wlk. SE21 .... 1C 120
Crabtree Cl. E2 .... 1B 64
Crabtree Hall SW6 .... 3E 85
.... (off Crabtree La.)
Crabtree La. SW6 .... 3E 85
.... (not continuous)
Crabtree Pl. W1 .... 1A 14 (4E 61)
Crace St. NW1 .... 1B 6 (2F 61)
Craddock St. NW5 .... 3C 46
Cradford Ho. Nth. E2 .... 2F 65
Cradford Ho. Sth. E2 .... 2F 65
Crafts Council & Gallery 1C 62
Cragie Ho. SE1 .... 5B 78
.... (off Balaclava Rd.)
Craigerne Rd. SE3 .... 3D 97
Craignair Rd. SW2 .... 5C 104
Craig's Ct. SW1 ..... 1D 23 (2A 76)
Craik Ct. NW6 .... 1B 58
.... (off Carlton Vale)
Crail Row SE17 .... 5F 77
Cramer St. W1 .... 1C 12 (4C 60)
Crammond Cl. W6 .... 2A 86
Crampton Ho. SW8 .... 4E 89
Crampton St. SE17 .... 5E 77
Cranberry La. E16 .... 3A 68
Cranbourn All.
WC2 .... 4C 14 (1F 75)
.... (off Cranbourn St.)
Cranbourne NW1 .... 4F 47
.... (off Agar Gro.)
Cranbourne Ct. SW11 .... 3A 88
.... (off Albert Bri. Rd.)
Cranbourne Ct. E12 .... 2F 55
Cranbourne Rd. E15 .... 1E 53
Cranbourne Ho. SE16 .... 3D 79
.... (off Marigold St.)
Cranbourn Pas. SE16 .... 3D 79
Cranbourn St. WC2 .. 4C 14 (1F 75)
Cranbrook 5E 47
.... (off Camden St.)
Cranbrook Est. E2 .... 1F 65
Cranbrook Rd. SE8 .... 4C 94
Cranbrook Rd. W4 .... 1A 84
Cranbrook St. E2 .... 1F 65
Cranbury Rd. SW6 .... 5D 87
Crandley Ct. SE8 .... 5A 80
.... (not continuous)
Crane Ct. EC4 .... 3C 16 (5C 62)
Crane Gro. N7 .... 3C 48
Crane Ho. E3 .... 1A 66
.... (off Roman Rd.)
Crane Ho. SE15 .... 4B 92
Crane Mead SE16 .... 1E 93
Crane St. SE10 .... 1F 95
Crane St. SE15 .... 4B 92
Cranfield Cl. SE27 .... 3E 119
Cranfield Ct. W1 .... 4A 60
.... (off Homer St.)
Cranfield Ho. WC1 .....5D 7 (4A 62)
.... (off Southampton Row)
Cranfield Rd. SE4 .... 1B 108
Cranfield Row SE1 .. 5C 24 (4C 76)
.... (off Gerridge St.)
Cranfield Wlk. SE3 .... 1D 111

Cranford Cotts. E1 .... 1F 79
.... (off Cranford St.)
Cranford St. E1 .... 1F 79
Cranhurst Rd. NW2 .... 2E 43
Cranleigh W11 .... 2B 72
.... (off Ladbroke Rd.)
Cranleigh Ho's. NW1 .... 1E 61
.... (off Cranleigh St.)
Cranleigh M. SW11 .... 5A 88
Cranleigh St. NW1 .... 1E 61
Cranley Gdns. SW7 .... 1E 87
Cranley M. SW7 .... 1E 87
Cranley Pl. SW7 .... 5F 73
Cranley Rd. E13 .... 4D 69
Cranmer Ct. SW3 .... 5A 74
Cranmer Ct. SW4 .... 1F 103
Cranmer Ho. SW11 .... 4A 88
.... (off Surrey La. Est.)
Cranmer Ho. SW9 .... 3C 90
.... (off Cranmer Rd.)
Cranmer Rd. E7 .... 1D 55
Cranmer Rd. SW9 .... 3C 90
Cranmer Ter. SW17 .... 5F 115
Cranmore Rd.
BR1: Broml 3B 124
Cranston Est. N1 .... 1F 63
Cranston Rd. SE23 .... 1A 122
Cranswick Rd. SE16 .... 1D 93
Crantock Rd. SE6 .... 2D 123
Cranwell Cl. E3 .... 3D 67
Cranwich Rd. N16 .... 2F 35
Cranwood St. EC1 ... 2C 10 (2F 63)
.... (off Vince St.)
Cranwood St. EC1 ... 2B 10 (2F 63)
Cranworth Gdns. SW9 .... 4C 90
Craster Rd. SW2 .... 5B 104
Crathie Rd. SE12 .... 4D 111
Craven Cl. N16 .... 2C 36
Craven Cottage 5F 85
Craven Ct. NW10 .... 5A 42
Craven Gdns. SW19 .... 5C 114
Craven Hill W2 .... 1E 73
Craven Hill Gdns. W2 .... 1E 73
.... (not continuous)
Craven Hill M. W2 .... 1E 73
Craven Lodge SW6 .... 4F 85
.... (off Harbord St.)
Craven Lodge W2 .... 1E 73
.... (off Craven Hill)
Craven M. SW11 .... 1C 102
Craven Pk. NW10 .... 5A 42
Craven Pk. M. NW10 .... 4A 42
Craven Pk. Rd. N15 .... 1B 36
Craven Pk. Rd. NW10 .... 5A 42
Craven Pas. WC2 ... 1D 23 (2A 76)
.... (off Craven St.)
Craven Rd. NW10 .... 5A 42
Craven Rd. W2 .... 1E 73
Craven St. WC2 ..... 1D 23 (2A 76)
Craven Ter. W2 .... 1E 73
Craven Wlk. N16 .... 2C 36
Crawford Bldgs. W1 .... 4A 60
.... (off Homer St.)
Crawford Est. SE5 .... 5E 91
Crawford Mans. W1 .... 4A 60
.... (off Crawford St.)
Crawford M. W1 ..... 1A 12 (4B 60)
Crawford Pas. EC1 ...4B 8 (3C 62)
Crawford Pl. W1 .... 5A 60
Crawford Rd. SE5 .... 4E 91
Crawford St. W1 .... 4A 60
Crawley Rd. E10 .... 3D 39
Crawshay Rd. SW9 .... 4C 90
Crawthew Gro. SE22 .... 2B 106
Crayford Cl. E6 .... 5F 69

Crayford Ho. SE1.............4C **26** (3F **77**)
............................(off Long La.)
Crayford M. N7..........................1A **48**
Crayford Rd. N7..........................1F **47**
Cray Ho. NW8..............................3D **89**
............................(off Penfold St.)
Crayle Ho. EC1...........3D **9** (3D **63**)
............................(off Malta St.)
Crealock St. SW18...................4D **101**
Creasy Est. SE1..........................4A **78**
Creative Ho. SE8.........................3D **89**
............................(off Prince of Wales Dr.)
Creative Rd. SE8.........................3D **95**
Crebor St. SE22..........................4C **106**
Crecy Cl. SE11.............................1C **90**
............................(off Hotspur St.)
Credenhill Ho. SE15..................3D **93**
Credenhill St. SW16...................5E **117**
Crediton Hgts. NW10..................5F **43**
............................(off Okehampton St.)
Crediton Hill NW6......................2D **45**
Crediton Rd. E16........................5C **68**
Crediton Rd. NW10....................5F **43**
Credon Rd. E13..........................1E **69**
Credon Rd. SE16.........................1D **93**
Creechurch La.
  EC3.........................3E **19** (5A **64**)
............................(not continuous)
Creechurch Pl.
  EC3.........................3E **19** (5A **64**)
............................(off Creechurch La.)
Creed Ct. E1...............................2A **66**
Creed Ct. EC4.............3E **17** (5D **63**)
............................(off Ludgate Sq.)
Creed La. EC4.............3E **17** (5D **63**)
Creed Pas. SE10.........................1A **96**
............................(off Hoskins St.)
Creek Ho. W14...........................4A **72**
............................(off Russell Rd.)
Creek Rd. SE10...........................2D **95**
Creek Rd. SE8.............................2C **94**
Creekside SE8.............................3D **95**
Creekside Foyer SE8...................2D **95**
............................(off Stowage)
Creeland Gro. SE6......................1B **122**
Crefeld Cl. W6............................2A **86**
Creighton Av. E6.........................1F **69**
Creighton Cl. W12.......................1C **70**
Creighton Rd. NW6....................1F **57**
Cremer Bus. Cen.
  E2...........................1F **11** (1B **64**)
............................(off Cremer St.)
Cremer Ho. SE8...........................3C **94**
............................(off Deptford Chu. St.)
Cremer St. E2............1F **11** (1B **64**)
Cremorne Est. SW10...................2F **87**
............................(not continuous)
Cremorne Riverside Cen......3F **87**
Cremorne Rd. SW10...................3E **87**
Creon Ct. SW9.............................3C **90**
............................(off Caldwell St.)
Crescent EC3................4F **19** (1B **78**)
Crescent, The E17........................1A **38**
Crescent, The NW2......................5D **29**
Crescent, The SE8........................4C **94**
............................(off Seager Pl.)
Crescent, The SW13....................5B **84**
Crescent, The SW19....................3C **114**
Crescent, The W12......................2E **71**
Crescent, The W3.........................5A **56**
Crescent Arc. SE10......................2E **95**
............................(off Creek Rd.)
Crescent Ct. SW4.........................5E **89**
............................(off Park Hill)
Crescent Ct. Bus. Cen. E16 ..3F **67**

Crescent Gdns. SW19................3C **114**
Crescent Gro. SW4.....................2E **103**
Crescent Ho. EC1.........4F **9** (3E **63**)
............................(off Golden La. Est.)
Crescent Ho. SE13......................5D **95**
Crescent La. SW4.......................2E **103**
Crescent Mans. SW3...................5A **74**
............................(off Fulham Rd.)
Crescent Mans. W11...................1A **72**
............................(off Elgin Cres.)
Crescent Pl. SW3.........................5A **74**
Crescent Rd. E10.........................4D **39**
Crescent Rd. E13.........................5C **54**
Crescent Rd. E6............................5E **55**
Crescent Rd. N8...........................1F **33**
Crescent Row EC1.......4F **9** (3E **63**)
Crescent Stables SW15...........3A **100**
Crescent St. N1............................4B **48**
Crescent Way SE4......................1C **108**
Crescent Wood Rd. SE26..3C **120**
Cresford Rd. SW6........................4D **87**
Crespigny Rd. NW4.....................1D **29**
Cressal Ho. E14...........................4C **80**
............................(off Tiller Rd.)
Cresset Ho. E9............................3E **51**
Cresset Rd. E9.............................3E **51**
Cresset St. SW4...........................1F **103**
Cressfield Cl. NW5......................2C **46**
Cressida Rd. N19.........................3E **33**
Cressingham Rd. SE13..........1E **109**
Cressington Cl. N16.....................2A **50**
Cress M. BR1: Broml................5B **123**
Cresswell Gdns. SW5................1E **87**
Cresswell Pk. SE13..................3B **110**
Cresswell Pl. SW10....................1E **87**
Cressy Ct. E1...............................4E **65**
Cressy Ct. W6..............................4D **71**
Cressy Ho. SW15.........................1D **99**
Cressy Ho's. E1............................1E **65**
............................(off Hannibal Rd.)
Cressy Pl. E1................................4E **65**
Cressy Rd. NW3...........................2B **46**
Cresta Ho. E3...............................3C **66**
............................(off Dimson Cres.)
Cresta Ho. NW3...........................4F **45**
............................(off Finchley Rd.)
Crested Ct. NW9..........................2B **28**
Crestfield St. WC1.......1E **7** (2A **62**)
Creston Ho. SW11......................1F **101**
............................(off Gartons Way)
Crest Rd. NW2..............................4B **28**
Creswick SW15............................4C **98**
Creswick Wlk. E3.........................2C **66**
Creukhorne Rd. NW10..............4A **42**
Crewdson Rd. SW9......................3C **90**
Crewe Pl. NW10...........................2B **56**
Crewkerne Ct. SW11..................1F **87**
............................(off Bolingbroke Wlk.)
Crews St. E14..............................5C **80**
Crewys Rd. NW2..........................4B **30**
Crewys Rd. SE15..........................5B **93**
Crichton St. SW8.........................5E **89**
Cricketers Ct. SE11.....................5D **77**
............................(off Kennington La.)
Cricketers M. SW18.................3D **101**
Cricketers Wlk. SE26...............5E **121**
Cricketfield Rd. E5......................1D **51**
Cricket La. BR3: Beck.............3A **122**
Crickett Ho. SE5.........................5D **109**
Cricklade Av. SW2...................2A **118**
CRICKLEWOOD........................1F **43**
Cricklewood B'way. NW2......5E **29**
Cricklewood La. NW2.................1F **43**
Cricklewood Station (Rail)....1F **43**
Cridland St. E15...........................5B **54**

Crieff Rd. SW18...........................4E **101**
Criffel Av. SW2...........................2F **117**
Crimscott St. SE1.........................4A **78**
Crimsworth Rd. SW8..................4F **89**
Crinan St. N1...............................1A **62**
Cringle St. SW11..........................3E **89**
Crinoline M. E1............1F **19** (4B **64**)
Cripplegate St. EC2....5A **10** (4E **63**)
Crispe Ho. N1..............................5B **48**
............................(off Barnsbury Est.)
Crispian Cl. NW10.......................1A **42**
Crispin Cl. SE17...........................5A **78**
Crispin Pl. E1..............5F **11** (4B **64**)
Crispin St. E1...............1F **19** (4B **64**)
Crisp Rd. W6................................1E **85**
Cristie Ct. E16.............................3B **68**
Cristowe Rd. SW6........................5B **86**
Criterion Ct. E8............................4B **50**
............................(off Middleton Rd.)
Criterion M. N19..........................4F **33**
Criterion M. SE24........................3D **105**
............................(off Shakespeare Rd.)
Criterion Theatre London...
....5B **14** (1F **75**)
............................(off Piccadilly Cir.)
Crockerton Rd. SW17..........2B **116**
Croft, The NW10.........................1B **56**
Croft Ct. SE13.............................4E **109**
Croftdown Rd. NW5....................5C **32**
Crofters Cl. SE8............................5A **80**
............................(off Croft St.)
Crofters Way NW1......................5F **47**
Croft Ho. W10..............................2A **58**
............................(off Third Av.)
Crofton Albion Sports Ground
....2C **110**
Croftongate Way SE4............3A **108**
CROFTON Ho. SW3.....................2A **88**
............................(off Old Church St.)
CROFTON PK...............................3B **108**
Crofton Pk. Rd. SE4..............4B **108**
Crofton Park Station (Rail)
....3B **108**
Crofton Rd. E13...........................3D **69**
Crofton Rd. SE5...........................4A **92**
Crofton Ter. E5.............................2A **52**
Crofts Ho. E2...............................1C **64**
............................(off Teale St.)
Crofts St. E1................................1C **78**
Croft St. SE8................................5A **80**
Croftway NW3.............................1C **44**
Crogsland Rd. NW1....................4C **46**
Cromartie Rd. N19.....................2F **33**
Cromarty Ct. SW2....................3B **104**
Cromarty Ho. E1..........................3A **66**
............................(off Ben Jonson Rd.)
Crombie M. SW11.......................5A **88**
Crome Rd. NW10.........................3A **42**
Cromer Rd. E10...........................2E **39**
Cromer St. WC1............2D **7** (2A **62**)
Cromer Ter. E8.............................2C **50**
Cromer Vs. Rd. SW18..........4B **100**
Cromford Path E5........................1F **51**
Cromford Rd. SW18.................3C **100**
Crompton Ct. SW3......................5A **74**
Crompton Ho. SE1......................4E **77**
............................(off County St.)
Crompton Ho. W2.......................3F **59**
............................(off Hall Pl.)
Crompton St. W2.........................3F **59**
Cromwell Av. N6..........................3D **33**
Cromwell Av. W6.........................1D **85**
CROMWELL BUPA HOSPITAL
....5D **73**
Cromwell Cl. E1...........................2C **78**

Cromwell Cres. SW5 ....5C **72**
Cromwell Gdns. SW7 ....4F **73**
Cromwell Gro. W6 ....4E **71**
Cromwell Highwalk
EC2 ....2A **10** (4E **63**)
.............................(off Silk St.)
Cromwell Ho. SW11 ....4C **88**
Cromwell Ind. Est. E10 ....3A **38**
.....................(off Cleveland Gro.)
Cromwell Lodge E1 ....3E **65**
.......................(off Cleveland Gro.)
Cromwell Mans. SW5 ....5C **72**
.......................(off Cromwell Rd.)
Cromwell M. SW7 ....5F **73**
Cromwell Pl. EC2 ....5A **10** (4E **63**)
.............................(off Silk St.)
Cromwell Pl. N6 ....3D **33**
Cromwell Pl. SW7 ....5F **73**
Cromwell Rd. E17 ....1E **39**
Cromwell Rd. E7 ....4E **55**
Cromwell Rd. SW19 ....5C **114**
Cromwell Rd. SW5 ....5C **72**
Cromwell Rd. SW7 ....5D **73**
Cromwell Rd. W6 ....4C **90**
Cromwell Twr. EC2 ....5A **10** (4E **63**)
.............................(off Silk St.)
Crondace Rd. SW6 ....4C **86**
Crondall Ct. N1 ....1C **10** (1A **64**)
.....................(off St John's Est.)
Crondall Ho. SW15 ....5C **98**
Crondall St. N1 ....1C **10** (1F **63**)
Crone Ct. NW6 ....1B **58**
.....................(off Denmark Rd.)
Cronin St. SE15 ....3B **92**
Crooked Billet Yd.
E2 ....1E **11** (2A **64**)
.....................(off Kingsland Rd.)
Crooke Rd. SE8 ....1A **94**
Crookham Rd. SW6 ....4B **86**
Croombs Rd. E16 ....4E **69**
Croom's Hill SE10 ....3E **95**
Croom's Hill Gro. SE10 ....3E **95**
Cropley Ct. N1 ....1F **63**
.........................(off Cropley St.)
Cropley St. N1 ....1B **10** (1F **63**)
Cropthorne Ct. W9 ....2E **59**
Crosby Ct. SE1 ....3B **26** (3F **77**)
Crosby Ho. E14 ....4E **81**
.....................(off Manchester Rd.)
Crosby Rd. E7 ....3C **54**
Crosby Rd. E7 ....3C **54**
Crosby Row SE1 ......4B **26** (3F **77**)
Crosby Sq. EC3 ....2D **19** (5A **64**)
Crosby Wlk. E8 ....3B **50**
Crosby Wlk. SW2 ....5C **104**
Crosby Way SW2 ....5C **104**
Crosier Cl. SE3 ....4F **97**
Crosland Pl. SW11 ....1C **102**
Cross Av. SE10 ....2F **95**
Crossbones Graveyard
...........................2A **26** (2E **77**)
.......................(off Redcross Way)
Crossbow Ho. N1 ....5A **50**
.....................(off Whitmore Est.)
Crossbrook Rd. SE3 ....5F **97**
Cross Cl. SE15 ....5D **93**
Crossfield Ct. W10 ....5F **57**
.....................(off Cambridge Gdns.)
Crossfield Ho. W11 ....1A **72**
.........................(off Mary Pl.)
Crossfield Rd. NW3 ....3F **45**
Crossfield St. SE8 ....3C **94**
........................(not continuous)
Crossford St. SW9 ....5B **90**
Crossharbour Plaza E14 ....4D **81**

Crossharbour Station
(Underground & DLR) 4D **81**
Cross Keys Cl. W1 ...1C **12** (4C **60**)
Cross Keys Sq.
EC1 ....1F **17** (4E **63**)
.......................(off Little Britain)
Cross La. EC3 ....5D **19** (1A **78**)
........................(not continuous)
Crossleigh Ct. SE14 ....3B **94**
.......................(off New Cross Rd.)
Crosslet St. SE17 ....5F **77**
Crosslet Va. SE10 ....4D **95**
Crossley St. N7 ....3C **48**
Crossmount Ho. SE5 ....3E **91**
.........................(off Bowyer St.)
Crosspoint Ho. SE8 ....3C **94**
.........................(off Watson's St.)
Crossrail Pl. E14 ....2D **81**
Crossrail Wlk. E14 ....2D **81**
Cross Rd. SE5 ....5A **92**
Cross St. N1 ....5D **49**
Cross St. SE5 ....1F **105**
Cross St. SW13 ....5A **84**
Crossthwaite Av. SE5 ....2F **105**
Crosstrees Ho. E14 ....4C **80**
.........................(off Cassilis Rd.)
Crosswall EC3 ....4F **19** (1B **78**)
Cross Way W10 ....4C **42**
Crossway N16 ....2A **50**
Crossway, The SE9 ....2F **125**
Crossway Ct. SE4 ....5A **94**
Crossways Ter. E5 ....1E **51**
Croston St. E8 ....5C **50**
CROUCH END 2F **33**
Crouch End Hill N8 ....2F **33**
Crouch Hall Ct. N19 ....3A **34**
Crouch Hall Rd. N8 ....1F **33**
Crouch Hill N4 ....2A **34**
Crouch Hill N8 ....2A **34**
Crouch Hill Station (Overground)
...................................2B **34**
Crouchman's Cl. SE26 ....3B **120**
Crowborough Rd. SW17 ....5C **116**
Crowder St. E1 ....1D **79**
Crowfield Ho. N5 ....1E **49**
Crowfoot Cl. E9 ....2B **52**
Crowhurst Cl. SW9 ....5C **90**
Crowhurst Ho. SW9 ....5B **90**
.........................(off Aytoun Rd.)
Crowland Ho. NW8 ....5E **45**
.......................(off Springfield Rd.)
Crowland Rd. N15 ....1B **36**
Crowland Ter. N1 ....4F **49**
Crowline Wlk. N1 ....3E **49**
Crowmarsh Gdns. SE23 ....5E **107**
Crown Cl. E3 ....5C **52**
Crown Cl. NW6 ....3D **45**
Crown Cl. Bus. Cen. E3 ....5C **52**
.........................(off Crown Cl.)

Crown Court
Blackfriars 3E **25** (3D **77**)
Crown Court
Inner London 5F **25** (4E **77**)

Crown Ct. EC2 ....3A **18** (5E **63**)
.........................(off Cheapside)
Crown Ct. NW8 ....2A **60**
.........................(off Park Rd.)
Crown Ct. SE12 ....4D **111**
Crown Ct. WC2 ....3E **15** (5A **62**)
Crown Dale SE19 ....5D **119**
........................(not continuous)
Crowndale Ct. NW1 ....1F **61**
.......................(off Crowndale Rd.)

Crowndale Rd. NW1 ....1E **61**
Crownfield Rd. E15 ....1F **53**
Crowngate Ho. E3 ....1B **66**
.........................(off Hereford Rd.)
Crownhill Rd. NW10 ....5B **42**
Crown La. SW16 ....5C **118**
Crown La. Gdns. SW16 ....5C **118**
Crown Lodge SW3 ....5A **74**
.........................(off Elystan St.)
Crown M. E1 ....4F **65**
.......................(off White Horse La.)
Crown M. E13 ....5E **55**
Crown M. W6 ....5C **70**

Crown Office Row
EC4 ....4B **16** (1C **76**)

Crown Pas. SW1 ....2A **22** (2E **75**)
Crown Pl. EC2 ....5D **11** (4A **64**)
Crown Pl. NW5 ....3D **47**
Crown Pl. SE16 ....1D **93**
Crown Point SE19 ....5D **119**
Crown Point Pde. SE19 ....5D **119**
.........................(off Crown Dale)
Crown Reach SW1 ....1F **89**
Crown Sq. SE1 ....2E **27** (2B **78**)
.........................(off Duchess Wlk.)
Crownstone Ct. SW2 ....3C **104**
Crownstone Rd. SW2 ....3C **104**
Crown St. SE5 ....3E **91**
Crown Wharf E14 ....2E **81**
.........................(off Coldharbour)
Crown Wharf SE8 ....1B **94**
.........................(off Grove St.)
Crown Yd. E2 ....1D **65**
Crown Yd. W6 ....5C **86**
Crows Rd. E3 ....2F **67**
Crowther Cl. SW6 ....2B **86**
.........................(off Bucklers All.)
Crowthorne Cl. SW18 ....5B **100**
Crowthorne Rd. W10 ....5F **57**
Croxley Rd. W9 ....2B **58**
Croxted Cl. SE21 ....5E **105**
Croxted M. SE24 ....4E **105**
Croxted Rd. SE21 ....5E **105**
Croxted Rd. SE24 ....5E **105**
Croxteth Ho. SW8 ....5F **89**
Croydon Ho. SE1 .....3C **24** (3C **76**)
.........................(off Wootton St.)
Croydon Rd. E13 ....3B **68**
Crozier Ho. SW8 ....3B **90**
.........................(off Wilkinson St.)
Crozier Ter. E9 ....2F **51**
Crucifix La. SE1 ......3D **27** (3A **78**)
Cruden Ho. E3 ....1B **66**
.........................(off Vernon Rd.)
Cruden Ho. SE17 ....2D **91**
.........................(off Brandon Est.)
Cruden St. N1 ....5D **49**
Cruikshank Ho. NW8 ....1A **60**
.......................(off Townshend Rd.)
Cruikshank Rd. E15 ....1A **54**
Cruikshank St. WC1 ..1B **8** (2C **62**)
Crummock Gdns. NW9 ....1A **28**
Crusader Ind. Est. N4 ....1E **35**
Crusoe M. N16 ....4F **35**
Crutched Friars EC3 ...4E **19** (1A **78**)
Crutchley Rd. SE6 ....2A **124**
Crystal, The 1C **82**
Crystal Ct. E8 ....5D **51**
Crystal Ct. SE19 ....5B **120**
.........................(off College Rd.)
CRYSTAL PALACE 5B **120**
Crystal Pal. Cvn. Club Site
SE19 ....5C **120**
Crystal Palace Mus. 5B **120**

Crystal Palace Nat. Sports Cen.
................................5C **120**
Crystal Palace Pde. SE19 ...5B **120**
Crystal Palace Pk. 5C **120**
Crystal Palace Pk. Rd.
  SE26.................................5C **120**
Crystal Palace Rd. SE22 ...4B **106**
Crystal Ter. SE19 ....5F **119**
Crystal Vw. Ct. BR1: Broml....4F **123**
Crystal Wharf N1 ....1D **63**
Cuba St. E14 ....3C **80**
Cube North East London
  Gymnastic Club, The.........1F **49**
Cube SE16...................5F **27** (4B **78**)
Cubitt Apts. SW11..................1E **101**
...................................(off Chatfield Rd.)
Cubitt Bldg. N1 ....1D **89**
Cubitt Ct. NW1...........1F **5** (1E **61**)
.............................(off Park Village E.)
Cubitt Ho. SW4....................4E **103**
Cubitt Steps E14...................2C **80**
Cubitt St. WC1...............2A **8** (2B **62**)
Cubitt Ter. SW4.....................1E **103**
CUBITT TOWN 5E **81**
Cudham St. SE6....................5E **109**
Cudweed Ct. E14 ....4D **81**
...............................(off Watergate Walk)
Cudworth Ho. SW8................4E **89**
Cudworth St. E1....................3D **65**
Cuff Cres. SE3 ....4F **111**
Cuffley Ho. W10 ....4E **57**
....(off Sutton Way)
Cuff Point E2.................1F **11** (2B **64**)
....................................(off Columbia Rd.)
Culand Ho. SE17 ....5A **78**
...................................(off Congreve St.)
Culford Gdns. SW3 ....5B **74**
Culford Gro. N1 ....3A **50**
Culford Mans. SW3 ....5B **74**
......................................(off Culford Gdns.)
Culford M. N1 ....3A **50**
Culford Rd. N1 ....4A **50**
Culford Ter. N1 ....3A **50**
...................................(off Balls Pond Rd.)
Culham Ho. E2.................2F **11** (2B **64**)
......................................(off Palissy St.)
Culham Ho. W2.......................4C **58**
...................................(off Gt. Western Rd.)
Culling Rd. SE16 ....4E **79**
Cullingworth Rd. NW10 ....2C **42**
Culloden Cl. SE16....................1C **92**
Culloden Cl. SE7....................2Q **97**
Culloden Ho. SE14 ....3A **94**
....(off Batavia Rd.)
Cullum St. EC3...........4D **19** (1A **78**)
Cullum Welch Ho.
  N1 ....1C **10** (2F **63**)
.................................(off Haberdasher St.)
Cullum Welch Ho.
  EC1.............................4F **9** (3E **63**)
...................................(off Golden La. Est.)
Culmore Rd. SE15 ....3D **93**
Culmstock Rd. SW11 ....3C **102**
Culpepper Ct. SE11................5C **76**
...................................(off Kennington Rd.)
Culross Ho. W10 ....5F **57**
....(off Bridge Cl.)
Culross St. W1................5B **12** (1C **74**)
Culverden Rd. SW12 ....2E **117**
Culverhouse WC1....1F **15** (4B **62**)
....(off Red Lion Sq.)
Culverhouse Gdns. SW16 ....3B **118**
Culverley Rd. SE6 ....1D **123**
Culvert Dr. E3..........................2E **67**
Culvert Pl. SW11 ....5C **88**

Culvert Rd. N15.......................1A **36**
....(not continuous)
Culvert Rd. SW11....................5B **88**
Culworth Ho. NW8..................1A **60**
....(off Allitsen Rd.)
Culworth St. NW8 ....1A **60**
Culzean Cl. SE27....................3D **119**
Cumberland Basin Primrose Hill
....5C **46**
Cumberland Basin NW1........5C **46**
Cumberland Cl. E8.................3B **50**
Cumberland Cl. SW1..............1D **89**
...................................(off Cumberland St.)
Cumberland Ct. W1...3A **12** (5B **60**)
..................................(off Gt. Cumberland Pl.)
Cumberland Cres. W14...........5A **72**
....(not continuous)
Cumberland Gdns.
  WC1.............................1B **8** (2C **62**)
Cumberland Ga. W1...4A **12** (1B **74**)
Cumberland Ho. E16...............2C **82**
....(off Wesley Av.)
Cumberland Ho. W8................3D **73**
..................................(off Kensington Ct.)
Cumberland Mans. W1 ....5B **60**
....(off George St.)
Cumberland Mkt.
  NW1...............................1E **5** (2D **61**)
Cumberland M. SE11 ....1C **90**
Cumberland Mills Sq. E14 .....1F **95**
Cumberland Pk. NW10............2C **56**
Cumberland Pl. NW1...1D **5** (2D **61**)
Cumberland Pl. SE6................1B **124**
Cumberland Rd. E12................1F **55**
Cumberland Rd. E13................4D **69**
Cumberland Rd. SW13............4B **84**
Cumberland St. SW1...............1D **89**
Cumberland Ter.
  NW1...................................1D **5** (1D **61**)
Cumberland Ter. M.
  NW1...................................1D **5** (1D **61**)
..................................(off Cumberland Ter.)
Cumberland Wharf SE16 ....3E **79**
...................................(off Rotherhithe St.)
Cumbrian Gdns. NW2 ....4F **29**
Cumming St. N1...........1A **8** (1B **62**)
Cumnor Cl. SW9......................5B **90**
....(off Robsart St.)
Cunard Pl. EC3...........3E **19** (5A **64**)
Cunard Rd. NW10....................2A **56**
Cunard Wlk. SE16...................5F **79**
Cundy Rd. E16..........................5E **69**
Cundy St. SW1........................5C **74**
Cunliffe St. SW16...................5E **117**
Cunningham Av. E16...............3D **83**
Cunningham Ct. E10...............5D **39**
....(off Oliver Rd.)
Cunningham Ct. W9.................3E **59**
....(off Maida Vale)
Cunningham Ho. SE5 ....3F **91**
....(off Elmington Est.)
Cunningham Pl. NW8...............3F **59**
Cupar Rd. SW11......................4C **88**
Cupola Cl. BR1: Broml...........5D **125**
Cureton St. SW1.....................5F **75**
Curlew Ho. SE15 ....4B **92**
Curlew Ho. SE4 ....2A **108**
....(off St Norbert Rd.)
Curlew St. SE1...........3F **27** (3B **78**)
Curlew St. SE18 ....4F **97**
....(off Tellson Av.)
Curness St. SE13 ....2E **109**
Curnick's La. SE27 ....4E **119**
Curran Ho. SW3 ....5A **74**
....(off Lucan Pl.)

Curricle St. W3.......................2A **70**
Currie Hill Cl. SW19 ....4B **114**
Cursitor St. EC4..............2B **16** (5C **62**)
Curtain Pl. EC2..............2E **11** (2A **64**)
Curtain Rd. EC2..............2E **11** (3A **64**)
Curtis & Staub Health Club
  Golders Green 2B **30**
Curtis Dr. W3............................5A **56**
Curtis Fld. Rd. SW16..............4B **118**
Curtis Ho. SE17 ....1F **91**
..................................(off Morecambe St.)
Curtis St. SE1 ....5B **78**
Curtis Way SE1 ....5B **78**
Curve, The W12.........................1C **70**
Curwen Av. E7 ....1D **55**
Curwen Rd. W12.......................3C **70**
Curzon Cinema Bloomsbury
....3D **7** (3A **62**)
Curzon Cinema Mayfair
....1D **21** (2D **75**)
....(off Curzon St.)
Curzon Cinema Soho
....4C **14** (1F **75**)
...................................(off Shaftesbury Av.)
Curzon Cinema Victoria
....5A **22** (4E **75**)
....(off Victoria St.)
Curzon Ct. SW6.......................4E **87**
....(off Imperial Rd.)
Curzon Cres. NW10................4A **42**
Curzon Ga. W1............2C **20** (2C **74**)
Curzon Sq. W1............2C **20** (2C **74**)
Curzon St. W1.............1D **21** (2C **74**)
Custance Ho. N1 ....1B **10** (1F **63**)
......................................(off Provost St.)
Custance St. N1 ....1B **10** (2F **63**)
Custom Ho. EC3...........5D **19** (1A **78**)
CUSTOM HOUSE 5E **69**
Custom House for ExCeL Station
  (DLR & Crossrail).............1D **83**
Custom Ho. Reach SE16........3B **80**
Custom Ho. Wlk. EC35D **19** (1A **78**)
Cut, The SE1...................3C **24** (3C **76**)
Cutbush Ho. N7........................2F **47**
Cutcombe Rd. SE5 ....5E **91**
Cuthbert Bell Twr. E3 ....1C **66**
....(off Pancras Way)
Cuthbert Harrowing Ho.
  EC1.............................4F **9** (3E **63**)
...................................(off Golden La. Est.)
Cuthbert Ho. W2.......................4F **59**
....(off Hall Pl.)
Cuthbert Rd. E17......................1B **38**
Cuthill Wlk. SE5.......................4F **91**
Cutlers Gdns. EC2......2E **19** (4A **64**)
Cutlers Gdns. Arc.
  EC2...................................2E **19** (5A **64**)
......................................(off Devonshire Sq.)
Cutlers Sq. E14 ....5C **80**
Cutlers Ter. N1 ....3A **50**
...................................(off Balls Pond Rd.)
Cutler St. E1..................2E **19** (5A **64**)
Cutter Ho. E16.........................3D **83**
....(off Admiralty Av.)
Cutter La. SE10 ....3A **82**
Cutty Sark 2E **95**
Cutty Sark for Maritime
  Greenwich Station (DLR)
....2E **95**
Cutty Sark Gdns. SE10 ....2E **95**
..................................(off King William Wlk.)
Cutty Sark Hall SE10 ....2E **95**
....(off Welland St.)
Cuxton Ho. SE17 ....1A **92**
....(off Mina Rd.)

Cyan Apts. E3................................5A 52
.....................(off Gunmaker's La.)
Cyclops M. E14.............................5C 80
Cygnet Cl. NW10..........................2A 42
CYGNET HOSPITAL, BLACKHEATH
....4E 95
Cygnet Ho. SE15..........................2C 92
Cygnet Ho. SW3...........................1A 88
....(off King's Rd.)
Cygnet Ho. Nth. E14....................5D 67
....(off Chrisp St.)
Cygnet Ho. Sth. E14....................5D 67
....(off Chrisp St.)
CYGNET LODGE 4E 109
Cygnet St. E1...............3F 11 (3B 64)
Cygnus Bus. Cen. NW10..............2B 42
Cynthia St. N1...............1A 8 (1B 62)
Cyntra Pl. E8................................4D 51
Cypress Cl. E5..............................4C 36
Cypress Gdns. SE4.......................3A 108
Cypress Ho. SE14........................4F 93
Cypress Ho. SE16.........................3F 79
..............................(off Woodland Cres.)
Cypress Pl. W1...............4A 6 (3E 61)
Cyprus Cl. N4................................1D 35
Cyprus Pl. E2................................1E 65
Cyprus St. E2................................1E 65
...................................(not continuous)
Cyrena Rd. SE22..........................4B 106
Cyril Mans. SW11........................4B 88
Cyrus Fld. St. SE10......................5A 82
Cyrus Ho. EC1..............3E 9 (3D 63)
....(off Cyrus St.)
Cyrus St. EC1................3E 9 (3D 63)
....(off Cyrus St.)
Czar St. SE8.................................2C 94

D

Dabbs La. EC1................4C 8 (3C 62)
....(off Farringdon Rd.)
Dabin Cres. SE10.........................4E 95
Dacca St. SE8..............................2B 94
Dace Rd. E3..................................5C 52
Dacre Gdns. SE13........................2A 110
Dacre Ho. SW3.............................2F 87
....(off Beaufort St.)
Dacre Pk. SE13.............................1A 110
Dacre Pl. SE13..............................1A 110
Dacre Rd. E11...............................3B 40
Dacre Rd. E13...............................5D 55
Dacres Est. SE23..........................3F 121
Dacres Ho. SW4...........................1D 103
Dacres Rd. SE23...........................2F 121
Dacre St. SW1.................5B 22 (4F 75)
Daffodil St. W12............................1B 70
Dafforne Rd. SW17.......................3C 116
Da Gama Pl. E14...........................1C 94
Dagenham Rd. E10.......................3B 38
Dagmar Ct. E14.............................4E 81
Dagmar Gdns. NW10....................1F 57
Dagmar Pas. N1............................5D 49
....(off Cross St.)
Dagmar Rd. N4..............................2C 34
Dagmar Rd. SE5............................4A 92
Dagmar Ter. N1.............................5D 49
Dagnall St. SW11.........................5B 88
Dagnan Rd. SW12........................5D 103
Dagobert Ho. E1............................4E 65
....(off Smithy St.)
Dagonet Gdns. BR1: Broml 3C 124
Dagonet Rd. BR1: Broml....3C 124
Dahomey Rd. SW16......................5E 117
Daimler Ho. E3..............................3C 66
....(off Wellington Way)

Dain Ct. W8...................................5C 72
....................................(off Lexham Gdns.)
Dainford Cl. BR1: Broml....5F 123
Dainton Ho. W2.............................4C 58
.................................(off Gt. Western Rd.)
Daintry Way E9.............................3B 52
Dairy Cl. NW10.............................5C 42
Dairy Cl. SW6...............................4C 86
Dairy Farm Pl. SE15....................4E 93
Dairyman Ct. NW2........................5F 29
Dairy M. SW9................................1A 104
Dairy Wlk. SW19..........................4A 114
Daisy Dobbings Wlk. N19.....2A 34
...........................(off Jessie Blythe La.)
Daisy La. SW6...............................1C 100
Daisy Rd. E16...............................3A 68
Dakin Pl. E1..................................4A 66
Dakota Bldg. SE13.......................4D 95
....(off Deal's Gateway)
Dalberg Rd. SW2..........................2C 104
...................................(not continuous)
Dalby Rd. SW18............................2E 101
Dalby St. NW5..............................3D 47
Dalebury Rd. SW17......................2B 116
Dale Cl. SE3..................................1C 110
Daleham Gdns. NW3....................2F 45
Daleham M. NW3..........................3F 45
Dalehead NW1...............1F 5 (1E 61)
.................................(off Hampstead Rd.)
Dale Ho. N1...................................5A 50
....(off Halcomb St.)
Dale Ho. NW8...............................5E 45
....(off Boundary Rd.)
Dale Ho. SE4................................2A 108
Dale Lodge N6...............................1E 33
Dalemain M. E16...........................2C 82
Dale Rd. NW5................................2C 46
Dale Rd. SE17...............................2D 91
Dale Row W11...............................5A 58
Daleside Rd. SW16......................5D 117
Dale St. W4...................................1A 84
Daleview Rd. N15..........................1A 36
Daley Ho. W12..............................5D 57
Daley St. E9..................................3F 51
Daley Thompson Way SW8...5D 89
Dalgarno Gdns. W10...................4E 57
Dalgarno Way W10......................3E 57
Dalgleish St. E14..........................5A 66
Daling Way E3...............................5A 52
Dalkeith Ct. SW1..........................5F 75
....(off Vincent St.)
Dalkeith Ho. SW9.........................4D 91
....(off Lothian Rd.)
Dalkeith Rd. SE21........................1E 119
Dallas Rd. NW4.............................2C 28
Dallas Rd. SE26...........................3D 121
Dallinger Rd. SE12.......................4B 110
Dalling Rd. W6..............................5D 71
Dallington Sq. EC1.....3E 9 (3D 63)
....(off Dallington St.)
Dallington St. EC1.....3E 9 (3D 63)
Dalmain Rd. SE23........................1F 121
Dalmeny Av. N7.............................1F 47
Dalmeny Rd. N7............................5F 33
...................................(not continuous)
Dalmeyer Rd. NW10.....................3B 42
Dalmore Rd. SE21........................2E 119
Dalo Lodge E3...............................4C 66
....(off Gale St.)
Dalrymple Rd. SE4.......................2A 108
Dalston La. E8...............................3B 50
Dalston Junction (Overground)
....3B 50
Dalston Kingsland Station
(Overground).................................2A 50

Dalston La. E8...............................3B 50
Dalston Sq. E8...............................3B 50
...................................(not continuous)
Dalton Ho. E3................................1A 66
....(off Ford St.)
Dalton Ho. SE14............................2F 93
....(off John Williams Cl.)
Dalton Ho. SW1.............................1D 89
....(off Ebury Bri. Rd.)
Dalton St. SE27.............................3D 119
Dalwood St. SE5...........................4A 92
Dalyell Rd. SW9............................1B 104
Damascene Wlk. SE21........1E 119
Damask Cres. E16........................3A 68
Damer Ter. SW10.........................3E 87
Dames Rd. E7................................5C 40
Dame St. N1..................................1E 63
Damien Ct. E1...............................5D 65
....(off Damien St.)
Damien St. E1................................5D 65
Damory Ho. SE16.........................5D 79
....(off Abbeyfield Est.)
Damsel Ho. SE4...........................1A 108
....(off Dragonfly Pl.)
Damsel Wlk. NW9.........................1C 28
....(off Perryfield Way)
Damson Ho. SW13.......................1B 28
Danbury St. N1.............................1D 63
Danby Ho. E9................................4E 51
.....................................(off Frampton Pk. Rd.)
Danby Ho. W10............................2A 58
....(off Bruckner St.)
Danby St. SE15.............................1B 106
Dance Ho. SE4.............................3F 107
....(off St Norbert Rd.)
Dancer Rd. SW6...........................4B 86
Dancers Way SE8.........................2D 95
Dance Sq. EC1..............2F 9 (2E 63)
Dandelion Ct. E14........................4D 81
....................................(off Watergate Wlk.)
Dandridge Cl. SE10.....................1B 96
Dandridge Ho. E1.....5F 11 (4B 64)
....(off Lamb St.)
Danebury Av. SW15.....................4A 98
Daneby Rd. SE6...........................3D 123
Danecroft Rd. SE24.....................3E 105
Danehurst St. SW6......................4A 86
Danemere St. SW15....................1E 99
Dane Pl. E3...................................1A 66
Danescombe SE12.......................1C 124
Danes Ct. NW8.............................5B 46
....(off St Edmund's Ter.)
Danescroft NW4...........................1F 29
Danescroft Av. NW4.....................1F 29
Danescroft Gdns. NW4................1F 29
Danesdale Rd. E9........................3A 52
Danesfield SE5.............................2A 92
....(off Albany Rd.)
Danes Ho. W10.............................4E 57
....(off Sutton Way)
Dane St. WC1...........1F 15 (4B 62)
Daneswood Av. SE6....................3E 123
Dane's Yd. E15.............................1E 67
Daneville Rd. SE5.........................4F 91
Danewood Dr. N2.........................2F 31
Dangan Rd. E11............................1C 40
Daniel Bolt Cl. E14.......................4D 67
Daniel Cl. SW17...........................5A 116
Daniel Gdns. SE15......................3B 92
Daniell Ho. N1...............................1F 63
....(off Cranston Est.)
Daniel Pl. NW4.............................2D 29
Daniels Rd. SE15..........................1E 107
Dan Leno Wlk. SW6.....................3D 87
DANNY FISZMAN BRI.............1C 48

Dansey Pl. W1 ....4B **14** (1F *75*)
............................(off Wardour St.)
Danson Rd. SE17 ....1D 91
Dante Pl. SE11 ....5D 77
Dante Rd. SE11 ....5D 77
Danube Ct. SE15 ....3B 92
............................(off Daniel Gdns.)
Danube St. SW3 ....1A 88
Danvers Av. SW11 ....2A 102
Danvers Ho. E1 ....5C 64
............................(off Christian St.)
Danvers St. SW3 ....2F 87
Dao Cl. E13 ....5D 55
Da Palma Ct. SW6 ....2C 86
............................(off Anselm Rd.)
Daphne St. SW18 ....4E 101
Daplyn St. E1 ....4C 64
Darbishire Pl. E1 ....1C 78
............................(off John Fisher St.)
D'Arblay St. W1 ......3A **14** (5E *61*)
Darcies M. N8 ....1A 34
Darcy Ho. E8 ....5D 51
............................(off London Flds. E. Side)
Darent Ho. BR1: Broml 5F **123**
Darent Ho. NW8 ....4F 59
............................(off Church St.)
Darenth Rd. N16 ....2B 36
Darfield NW1 ....5E 47
............................(off Bayham St.)
Darfield Rd. SE4 ....3B 108
Darfield Way W10 ....5F 57
Darfur St. SW15 ....1F 99
Darien Rd. SW11 ....1F 101
Daring Ho. E3 ....1A 66
............................(off Roman Rd.)

Dark Ho. Wlk.
EC3......................5C **18** (1F *77*)
Darlan Rd. SW6 ....3B 86
Darley Ho. SE11 ....1B 90
............................(off Laud St.)
Darley Rd. SW11 ....4B 102
Darling Rd. SE4 ....1C 108
Darling Row E1 ....3D 65
Darlington Ct. SE6 ....1B 124
Darlington Ho. SW8 ....3F 89
............................(off Hemans St.)
Darlington Rd. SE27 ....5D 119
Darnall Ho. SE10 ....4E 95
............................(off Royal Hill)
Darnaway Pl. E14 ....4E 67
............................(off Aberfeldy St.)
Darnay Apts. E15 ....3F 53
Darnley Ho. E14 ....5A 66
............................(off Camdenhurst St.)
Darnley Rd. E9 ....3E 51
Darnley Ter. W11 ....2F 71
Darrell Rd. SE22 ....3C 106
Darren Cl. N4 ....2B 34
Darren Ct. N7 ....1A 48
Darsley Dr. SW8 ....4F 89
Dartford Ho. SE1 ....5B 78
............................(off Longfield Est.)
Dartford St. SE17 ....2E 91
Dartington NW1 ....5E 47
............................(off Plender St.)
Dartington Ho. SW8 ....5F 89
............................(off Union Gro.)
Dartington Ho. W2 ....4D 59
............................(off Senior St.)
Dartle Ct. SE16 ....3C 78
............................(off Scott Lidgett Cres.)
Dartmoor Wlk. E14 ....5C 80
............................(off Severnake Cl.)
Dartmouth Cl. W11 ....5B 58
Dartmouth Ct. SE10 ....4E 95

Dartmouth Gro. SE10 ....4E 95
Dartmouth Hill SE10 ....4E 95
Dartmouth Ho. SE10 ....4D 95
............................(off Catherine Gro.)
DARTMOUTH PK. 5D 33
Dartmouth Pk. Av. NW5 ....5D 33
Dartmouth Pk. Hill N19 ....3D 33
Dartmouth Pk. Hill NW5 ....5D 33
Dartmouth Pk. Rd. NW5 ....1D 47
Dartmouth Pl. SE23 ....2E 121
Dartmouth Pl. W4 ....2A 84
Dartmouth Rd. NW2 ....3F 43
Dartmouth Rd. NW4 ....1C 28
Dartmouth Rd. SE23 ....3E 121
Dartmouth Rd. SE26 ....3D 121
Dartmouth Row SE10 ....5E 95

Dartmouth St.
SW1.........................4B **22** (3F *75*)
Dartmouth Ter. SE10 ....4F 95
Dartrey Twr. SW10 ....3E 87
............................(off Worlds End Est.)
Dartrey Wlk. SW10 ....3E 87
Dart St. W10 ....2A 58
Darvell Ho. SE17 ....1F 91
............................(off Inville Rd.)
Darville Rd. N16 ....5B 36
Darwen Pl. E2 ....1D 65
Darwin Cl. E13 ....2D 69
Darwin Cl. NW1 ....5D 47
............................(not continuous)
Darwin Ct. SE17 ....5F 77
............................(off Barlow St.)
Darwin Ho. SW1 ....2E 89
............................(off Grosvenor Rd.)
Darwin St. SE17 ....5F 77
............................(not continuous)
Darwood Ct. NW6 ....4E 45
............................(off Belsize Rd.)
Daryngton Ho. SE1 ...4B **26** (3F *77*)
............................(off Hankey Pl.)
Daryngton Ho. SW8 ....3A 90
............................(off Hartington Rd.)
Dashwood Rd. N8 ....1B 34
Dashwood Studios SE17 ....5E 77
............................(off Walworth St.)
Dassett Rd. SE27 ....5D 119
Data Point Bus. Cen. E16 .....3F 67
Datchelor Pl. SE5 ....4F 91
Datchet Ho. E2 ......2F **11** (2B *64*)
............................(off Virginia Rd.)
Datchet Ho. NW1....1E **5** (2D *61*)
............................(off Augustus St.)
Datchet Rd. SE6 ....2B 122
Datchworth Ho. N1 ....4D 49
............................(off The Sutton Est.)
Date St. SE17 ....1F 91
Daubeney Rd. E5 ....1A 52
Daubeney Twr. SE8 ....1B 94
............................(off Bowditch)
Dault Rd. SW18 ....4E 101
Dauncey Ho. SE1...4D **25** (3D *77*)
............................(off Webber Row)
Dave Adams Ho. E3 ....1B 66
............................(off Norman Gro.)
Davenant Ho. E1 ....4C 64
............................(off Old Montague St.)
Davenant Pl. SE26 ....5D 121
Davenant Rd. N19 ....4F 33
Davenant St. E1 ....4C 64
Davenport Ho. SE11 ....5C 76
............................(off Walnut Tree Wlk.)
Davenport Rd. SE6 ....4D 109
Daventry Av. E17 ....1C 38
Daventry St. NW1 ....4A 60
Daver Ct. SW3 ....1A 88

Davern Cl. SE10 ....5B 82
Davey Cl. N7 ....3B 48
Davey Rd. E9 ....4C 52
Davey's Ct. WC2 ....4D **15** (1A *76*)
............................(off Bedfordbury)
Davey St. SE15 ....2B 92
David Cl. E14 ....4D 67
............................(off Hillary M.)
Davidge Ho. SE1 ....4C **24** (3C *76*)
............................(off Coral St.)
Davidge St. SE1 .....4D **25** (3D *77*)
David Hewitt Ho. E3 ....4D 67
............................(off Watts Gro.)
David Ho. SW8 ....3A 90
............................(off Wyvil Rd.)
David Lee Point E15 ....5A 54
............................(off Leather Gdns.)

David Lloyd Leisure Fulham
....3C 86
(within Fulham Broadway Shop.Cen.)
David Lloyd Leisure Kidbrooke
....2D 111
David M. SE10 ....3E 95
David M. W1 ....5A **4** (4B *60*)
Davidson Gdns. SW8 ....3A 90
Davidson Terraces E7 ....2D 55
............................(off Claremont Rd.)
David's Rd. SE23 ....1E 121
David St. E15 ....3F 53
Davies La. E11 ....4A 40
Davies M. W1 ....4D **13** (1D *75*)
Davies St. W1 ....3D **13** (5D *61*)
Da Vinci Cl. SE16 ....1D 93
Da Vinci Lodge SE10 ....4B 82
............................(off W. Parkside)
Da Vinci Torre SE13 ....1D 109
............................(off Loampit Va.)
Davis Ho. W12 ....1D 71
............................(off White City Est.)
Davis Rd. W3 ....2B 70
Davis St. E13 ....1D 69
Davisville Rd. W12 ....3C 70
Dawes Ho. SE17 ....5F 77
............................(off Orb St.)
Dawes Rd. SW6 ....3A 86
Dawes St. SE17 ....1F 91
Dawkins Ct. SE1 ...5B **26** (4F *77*)
Dawlish Av. SW18 ....2D 115
Dawlish Rd. E10 ....3E 39
Dawlish Rd. NW2 ....3F 43
Dawnay Gdns. SW18 ....2F 115
Dawnay Rd. SW18 ....2E 115
Dawn Cres. E15 ....5F 53
Dawpool Rd. NW2 ....4B 28
Dawson Ho. E2 ....2E 65
............................(off Sceptre Rd.)
Dawson Pl. W2 ....1C 72
Dawson Rd. NW2 ....2E 43
Dawson St. E2 ....1B 64
Day Ho. SE5 ....3E 91
............................(off Bethwin Rd.)
Daylesford Av. SW15 ....2C 98
Daynor Ho. NW6 ....5C 44
............................(off Quex Ho.)
Daysbrook Rd. SW2 ....1B 118
Dayton Gro. SE15 ....4E 93
Deacon Ho. SE11 ....5B 76
............................(off Black Prince Rd.)
Deacon M. N1 ....4F 49
Deacon Rd. NW2 ....2C 42
Deacons Ter. N1 ....3E 49
............................(off Harecourt Rd.)
Deal Ho. SE15 ....2F 93
............................(off Lovelinch La.)

Deal Ho. SE17 .... 1A 92
.... (off Mina Rd.)
Deal Porters Wlk. SE16 .... 3F 79
Deal Porters Way SE16 .... 4E 79
Deal's Gateway SE10 .... 4C 94
Deal's Gateway SE13 .... 4C 94
Deal St. E1 .... 4C 64
Dealtry Rd. SW15 .... 2E 99
Deal Wlk. SW9 .... 3C 90
Dean Abbott Ho. SW1 .... 5F 75
.... (off Vincent St.)
Dean Bradley St. SW1 .... 4A 76
Dean Cl. E9 .... 2E 51
Dean Cl. SE16 .... 2F 79
Dean Cl. SW8 .... 3A 90
.... (off Thorncroft St.)
Deancross St. E1 .... 5E 65
Deanery M. W1 .... 1C 20 (2C 74)
.... (off Deanery St.)
Deanery Rd. E15 .... 3A 54
Deanery St. W1 .... 1C 20 (2C 74)
Dean Farrar St.
SW1 .... 5C 22 (4F 75)
Dean Ho. E1 .... 5E 65
.... (off Tarling St.)
Dean Ho. SE14 .... 3A 94
.... (off New Cross Rd.)
Dean Rd. NW2 .... 3E 43
Dean Ryle St. SW1 .... 5A 76
Dean's Bldgs. SE17 .... 5F 77
Dean's Ct. EC4 .... 3E 17 (5D 63)
Deans Ga. EC SE23 .... 3F 121
Deanshanger Ho. SE8 .... 5F 79
.... (off Chilton Gro.)
Dean's M. W1 .... 2E 13 (5D 61)
Dean Stanley St.
SW1 .... 5D 23 (4A 76)
Deanston Wharf E16 .... 3D 83
.... (not continuous)
Dean St. E7 .... 2C 54
Dean St. W1 .... 2B 14 (5F 61)
Dean's Yd. SW1 .... 5C 22 (4F 75)
Dean Trench St.
SW1 .... 5D 23 (4A 76)
Deauville Cl. E14 .... 5F 67
Deauville Ct. SE16 .... 3F 79
.... (off Eleanor Cl.)
Deauville Ct. SW4 .... 4E 103
De Barowe M. N5 .... 1D 49
Debdale Ho. E2 .... 5C 50
.... (off Whiston Rd.)
De Beauvoir Ct. N1 .... 4F 49
.... (off Northchurch Rd.)
De Beauvoir Cres. N1 .... 5A 50
De Beauvoir Est. N1 .... 5A 50
De Beauvoir Pl. N1 .... 5A 50
De Beauvoir Rd. N1 .... 5A 50
De Beauvoir Sq. N1 .... 4A 50
DE BEAUVOIR TOWN 5A 50
De Beauvoir Wharf N1 .... 5A 50
.... (off Hertford Rd.)
Debenham Ct. E8 .... 5C 50
.... (off Pownall Rd.)
Debham Ct. NW2 .... 5E 29
Debnams Rd. SE16 .... 5E 79
De Bruin Ct. E14 .... 1E 95
.... (off Ferry St.)
Decapod St. E15 .... 2F 53
Decima St. SE1 .... 5D 27 (4A 78)
Decima Studios SE1 .... 5D 27 (4A 78)
.... (off Decima St.)
Deck Cl. SE16 .... 2F 79
De Coubertin St. E20 .... 3E 53
De Crespigny Pk. SE5 .... 5F 91
Deeley Rd. SW8 .... 4F 89

Deepak Ho. SW17 .... 4A 116
Deepdale SW19 .... 4F 113
Deepdene Gdns. SW2 .... 5B 104
Deepdene Mans. NW6 .... 4B 86
.... (off Rostrevor Rd.)
Deepdene Point SE23 .... 3F 121
Deepdene Rd. SE5 .... 2F 105
Deerbrook Rd. SE24 .... 1D 119
Deerdale Rd. SE24 .... 2E 105
Deerfield Cotts. NW9 .... 1B 28
Deerhurst Ho. SE15 .... 2C 92
.... (off Haymerle Rd.)
Deerhurst Rd. NW2 .... 3F 43
Deerhurst Rd. SW16 .... 5B 118
Deering Ho. SE3 .... 2E 111
Deeside Rd. SW17 .... 3F 115
Dee St. E14 .... 5E 67
Defoe Cl. SE16 .... 3B 80
Defoe Cl. SW17 .... 5A 116
Defoe Ho. EC2 .... 5A 10 (4E 63)
.... (off Beech St.)
Defoe Pl. EC2 .... 5F 9 (4E 63)
.... (off Beech St.)
Defoe Rd. N16 .... 5A 36
Defoe Rd. SW17 .... 4B 116
De Frene Rd. SE26 .... 4F 121
Dehar Cres. NW9 .... 2B 28
Dehavilland Studios E5 .... 4E 37
.... (off Theydon Rd.)
Dekker Ho. SE5 .... 3F 91
.... (off Elmington Est.)
Dekker Rd. SE21 .... 4A 106
Delacourt Rd. SE3 .... 3D 97
Delafield Ho. E1 .... 5C 64
.... (off Christian St.)
Delafield Rd. SE7 .... 1D 97
Delaford Rd. SE16 .... 1D 93
Delaford St. SW6 .... 3A 86
Delahay Ho. SW3 .... 2B 88
.... (off Chelsea Emb.)
Delamare Cl. SE6 .... 3D 123
Delamere Rd. W2 .... 4D 59
Delamere Ter. W2 .... 4D 59
Delancey Pas. NW1 .... 5D 47
.... (off Delancey St.)
Delancey St. NW1 .... 5D 47
Delancey Studios NW1 .... 5D 47
.... (off Thames St.)
Delany Ho. SE10 .... 2E 95
Delarch Ho. SE1 .... 4D 25 (3D 77)
.... (off Webber Row)
De Laune St. SE17 .... 1D 91
Delaware Mans. W9 .... 3D 59
.... (off Delaware Rd.)
Delaware Rd. W9 .... 3D 59
Delawyk Cres. SE24 .... 4E 105
Delft Way SE22 .... 3A 106
Delhi St. N1 .... 5A 48
Delia St. SW18 .... 5D 101
Delius Gro. E15 .... 1F 67
Della Path E5 .... 5C 36
Dell Cl. E15 .... 5F 53
Dellow Ho. E1 .... 1D 79
.... (off Dellow St.)
Dellow St. E1 .... 1D 79
Dell's M. SW1 .... 5E 75
.... (off Churton Pl.)
Delmare Cl. SW9 .... 2B 104
Delme Cres. SE3 .... 5D 97
Delmerend Ho. SW3 .... 1A 88
.... (off Cale St.)
Deloraine Ho. SE8 .... 4C 94
Delorme St. W6 .... 2F 85
Delta Bldg. E14 .... 5E 67
.... (off Ashton St.)

Delta Ct. NW2 .... 4C 28
Delta Ct. SE8 .... 2A 94
.... (off Trundleys Rd.)
Delta Ho. N1 .... 1B 10 (2F 63)
.... (off Nile St.)
Delta Pk. SW18 .... 2D 101
Delta Point E2 .... 2C 64
.... (off Delta St.)
Delta St. E2 .... 2C 64
Delverton Ho. SE17 .... 1D 91
.... (off Delverton Rd.)
Delverton Rd. SE17 .... 1D 91
Delvino Rd. SW6 .... 4C 86
De Montfort Pde. SW16 .... 3A 118
De Montfort Rd. SW16 .... 3A 118
De Morgan Rd. SW6 .... 1D 101
Dempsey Ct. SE6 .... 5C 108
Dempster Rd. SW18 .... 3E 101
Den, The 1E 93
Denbigh Cl. W11 .... 1B 72
Denbigh Ct. E6 .... 2F 69
Denbigh Ho. SW1 .... 5A 20 (4B 74)
.... (off Hans Pl.)
Denbigh Ho. W11 .... 1B 72
Denbigh M. SW1 .... 5E 75
.... (off Denbigh St.)
Denbigh Pl. SW1 .... 1E 89
Denbigh Rd. E6 .... 2F 69
Denbigh Rd. W11 .... 1B 72
Denbigh St. SW1 .... 5E 75
.... (not continuous)
Denbigh Ter. W11 .... 1B 72
Denbury Ho. E3 .... 2D 67
.... (off Talwin St.)
Denby Cl. SE11 .... 5B 76
.... (off Lambeth Wlk.)
Dence Ho. E2 .... 2C 64
.... (off Turin St.)
Denchworth Ho. SW9 .... 5C 90
Dene Cl. E10 .... 4D 39
Dene Cl. SE4 .... 1A 108
Denehurst Gdns. NW4 .... 1E 29
Denesmead SE24 .... 3E 105
Denewood Rd. N6 .... 1B 32
Denford St. SE10 .... 1B 96
.... (off Glenforth St.)
Dengie Wlk. N1 .... 5E 49
.... (off Basire St.)
Denham Ct. NW6 .... 4E 45
.... (off Fairfax Rd.)
Denham Ct. SE26 .... 3D 121
.... (off Kirkdale)
Denham Ho. W12 .... 1D 71
.... (off White City Est.)
Denham St. SE10 .... 1C 96
Denholme Rd. W9 .... 2B 58
Denison Ho. E14 .... 4D 81
.... (off Dorset Rd.)
Denis Way SW4 .... 1F 103
Denland Ho. SW8 .... 3B 90
.... (off Dorset Rd.)
Denman Ho. N16 .... 4A 36
Denman Pl. W1 .... 4B 14 (1F 75)
.... (off Denman St.)
Denman Rd. SE15 .... 4B 92
Denman St. W1 .... 5B 14 (1F 75)
Denmark Gro. N1 .... 1C 62
Denmark Hill SE5 .... 4F 91
DENMARK HILL 1E 105
Denmark Hill Est. SE5 .... 2F 105
Denmark Hill Station (Rail &
Overground) 5F 91
Denmark Rd. SE5 .... 5F 83
Denmark Mans. SE5 .... 5E 91
.... (off Coldharbour La.)

Denmark Pl. E3 ....2C 66
Denmark Pl. WC2 ....2C 14 (5F 61)
Denmark Rd. NW6 ....1B 58
Denmark Rd. SE5 ....4E 91
Denmark St. E11 ....5A 40
Denmark St. E13 ....4D 69
Denmark St. WC2 ....2C 14 (5F 61)
Denmark Wlk. SE27 ....4E 119
Denmead Ho. SW15 ....4B 98
Denne Ter. E8 ....5B 50
Dennett's Gro. SE14 ....5F 93
Dennett's Rd. SE14 ....4E 93
Denning Cl. NW8 ....2E 59
Denning M. SW12 ....4C 102
Denning Point E1 ....2F 19 (5B 64)
            (off Commercial St.)
Denning Rd. NW3 ....1F 45
Dennington Cl. E5 ....4E 37
Dennington Pk. Rd. NW6 .....3C 44
Dennis Ho. E3 ....1B 66
            (off Roman Rd.)
Dennison Point E15 ....4E 53
Dennis Severs' House
            ....5E 11 (4A 64)
Dennis Way SW4 ....1F 103
Denny Cl. E6 ....4F 69
Denny Cres. SE11 ....1C 90
Denny St. SE11 ....1C 90
Densham Ho. NW8 ....1F 59
            (off Cochrane St.)
Densham Rd. E15 ....5A 54
Denstone Ho. SE15 ....2C 92
            (off Haymerle Rd.)
Dent Ho. SE17 ....5A 78
            (off Peacock St.)
Denton NW1 ....3C 46
Denton Ho. N1 ....4D 49
            (off Halton Rd.)
Denton Rd. N8 ....1B 34
Denton St. SW18 ....4D 101
Denton Way E5 ....5F 37
Dents Rd. SW11 ....4B 102
Denver Rd. N16 ....2A 36
Denwood SE23 ....3F 121
Denyer St. SW3 ....5A 74
Denys Ho. EC1 ....5B 8 (4C 62)
            (off Bourne Est.)
Denzil Rd. NW10 ....2B 42
Deodar Rd. SW15 ....2A 100
Department for Business, Energy
 & Industrial Strategy
            ....5C 22 (4F 75)
Department for Communities
            ....5F 21 (4E 75)
            (off Bressenden Pl.)
Department for Education
            ....5C 22 (4F 75)
            (off Gt. Smith St.)
Department for Energy & Climate
 Change 2D 23 (2A 76)
            (off Whitehall Pl.)
Department for Transport 5F 75
Department for Work & Pensions
            ....4C 22 (3F 75)
            (off Tothill St.)
Department of Environment Parks
 Department.............1D 5 (2C 60)
Depot App. NW2 ....1F 43
Depot Rd. W12 ....1E 71
Depot St. SE5 ....2F 91
DEPTFORD 3C 94
Deptford Bri. SE8 ....4C 94
Deptford Bridge Station (DLR)
            ....4C 94
Deptford B'way. SE8 ....4C 94

Deptford Bus. Pk. SE15 .....2E 93
Deptford Chu. St. SE8 ....2C 94
Deptford Ferry Rd. E14 ......5C 80
Deptford Grn. SE8 ....2C 94
Deptford High St. SE8 ....2C 94
Deptford Pk. Bus. Cen.
            ....1A 94
Deptford Station (Rail) 3C 94
Deptford Strand SE8 ....2B 94
Deptford Trad. Est. SE8 ......2A 94
Deptford Wharf SE8 ....5B 80
De Quincey Ho. SW1 ....1E 89
            (off Lupus St.)
De Quincey M. E16 ....2C 82
Derby Ga. SW1 ....3D 23 (3A 76)
            (not continuous)
Derby Hill SE23 ....2E 121
Derby Hill Cres. SE23 ....2E 121
Derby Ho. SE11 ....5C 76
            (off Walnut Tree Wlk.)
Derby Lodge WC1 ...1F 7 (2B 62)
            (off Britannia St.)
Derby Rd. E7 ....4F 55
Derby Rd. E9 ....5F 51
Derbyshire St. E2 ....2C 64
            (not continuous)
Derby St. W1 ....2C 20 (2C 74)
Dere Cl. SW6 ....4A 86
Dereham Ho. SE4 ....2F 107
            (off Frensbury Rd.)
Dereham Pl. EC2 ...2E 11 (2A 64)
Derek Walcott Cl. SE24 .....3D 105
Dericote St. E8 ....5D 51
Dering St. W1 ....3D 13 (5D 61)
Dering Yd. W1 ....3E 13 (5D 61)
Derinton Rd. SW17 ....4B 116
Dermody Gdns. SE13 ....3F 109
Dermody Rd. SE13 ....3F 109
Derry Av. E20 ....2D 53
Deronda Rd. SE24 ....1D 119
Derrick Gdns. SE7 ....4E 83
Derrycombe Ho. W2 ....4C 58
            (off Gt. Western Rd.)
Derry Ho. NW8 ....3F 59
            (off Church St. Est.)
Derry M. N19 ....4A 34
Derry St. W8 ....3D 73
Dersingham Rd. NW2 ....5A 30
Derwent NW1 ....2F 5 (2E 61)
            (off Robert St.)
Derwent Av. SW15 ....4A 112
Derwent Ct. SE16 ....3F 79
            (off Eleanor Cl.)
Derwent Gro. SE22 ....2B 106
Derwent Ho. E3 ....3B 66
            (off Southern Gro.)
Derwent Ho. SW7 ....5E 73
            (off Cromwell Rd.)
Derwent Point EC1 ...1D 9 (2D 63)
            (off Goswell Rd.)
Derwent Ri. NW9 ....1A 28
Derwent St. SE10 ....1A 96
Des Barres Ct. SE10...........4C 82
            (off Peartree Way)
Desborough Cl. W2 ....4D 59
Desborough Ho. W14 ....2B 86
            (off North End Rd.)
Desborough St. W2 ....4D 59
            (off Cirencester St.)
Desenfans Rd. SE21 ....4A 106
Desford Rd. E16 ....3A 68
Design Mus. 4B 72
Desmond St. E14 ....2D 95
Desmond Tutu Dr. SE23 ....1B 122
Despard Rd. N19.................3E 33

Desvignes Dr. SE13 ....4F 109
Dethick Ct. E3 ....5A 52
Detling Ho. SE17 ....5A 78
            (off Congreve St.)
Detling Rd. BR1: Broml.....5C 124
Detmold Rd. E5 ....4C 37
Devane Way SE27 ....3D 119
Devas Gro. N4 ....2F 35
Devas St. E3 ....3D 67
Devenay Rd. E15 ....4B 54
Deventer Cres. SE22 ....3A 106
De Vere Cotts. W8 ....4E 73
            (off Canning Pl.)
De Vere Gdns. W8 ....3E 73
Deverell St. SE1 .....5B 26 (4F 77)
De Vere M. W8 ....4E 73
            (off Canning Pl.)
Devereux Ct. WC2 ....3B 16 (5C 62)
            (off Essex St.)
Devereux La. SW13............3D 85
Devereux Rd. SW11 ....4B 102
Devitt Ho. E14 ....1D 81
            (off Wade's Pl.)
Devizes St. N1 ....5F 49
Devon Gdns. N4 ....1D 35
Devon Ho. N1 ....1D 63
            (off Upper St.)
Devonia Rd. N1 ....1D 63
Devon Mans. SE1 ....3F 27 (3B 78)
            (off Tooley St.)
Devonport W2 ....5A 60
Devonport Ho. W2 ....4C 58
            (off Gt. Western Rd.)
Devonport M. W12 ....3D 71
Devonport Rd. W12 ....2D 71
            (not continuous)
Devonport St. E1 ....5E 65
Devons Est. E3 ....2D 67
Devonshire Cl. E15 ....1A 54
Devonshire Cl. W1 ...5D 5 (4D 61)
Devonshire Cl. E1 ....2E 65
            (off Bancroft Rd.)
Devonshire Ct. WC1 ..5E 7 (4A 62)
            (off Boswell St.)
Devonshire Dr. SE10 ....3D 95
Devonshire Gro. SE15 ....2D 93
Devonshire Hall E9 ....3E 51
Devonshire Ho. E14 ....5C 80
            (off Westferry Rd.)
Devonshire Ho. NW6 ....3B 44
            (off Kilburn High Rd.)
Devonshire Ho.
 SE1 ....5F 25 (4E 77)
            (off Bath Ter.)
Devonshire Ho. SW1 ....1F 89
            (off Lindsay Sq.)
Devonshire Ho. SW15 ....3F 99
Devonshire Ho. W2 ....4F 59
            (off Adpar St.)
Devonshire M. SW10 ....2F 87
            (off Park Wlk.)
Devonshire M. W4 ....1A 84
Devonshire M. Nth.
 W1 ....5D 5 (4D 61)
Devonshire M. Sth.
 W1 ....5D 5 (4D 61)
Devonshire M. W.
 W1 ....4C 4 (3C 60)
Devonshire Pas. W4 ....1A 84
Devonshire Pl. NW2 ....5C 30
Devonshire Pl. W1 ...4C 4 (3C 60)
Devonshire Pl. W8 ....4D 73
Devonshire Pl. M.
 W1 ....4C 4 (4C 60)

Devonshire Rd. E16 .... 5D 69
Devonshire Rd. E17 .... 1C 38
Devonshire Rd. SE23 .... 1E 121
Devonshire Rd. SE9 .... 2F 125
Devonshire Rd. W4 .... 1A 84
Devonshire Road Nature Reserve
.... 5F 107
Devonshire Road Nature Reserve
Vis. Cen. 5F 107
Devonshire Row
EC2. .... 1E 19 (4A 64)
Devonshire Row M.
W1. .... 4E 5 (3D 61)
.... (off Devonshire St.)
Devonshire Sq. EC2... 1E 19 (5A 64)
Devonshire St. W1 ......5C 4 (4C 60)
Devonshire St. W4 .... 1A 84
Devonshire Ter. W2 .... 5E 59
Devons Rd. E3. .... 2D 67
Devons Road Station (DLR)
.... 3D 67
Devon St. SE15. .... 2D 93
De Walden Ho. NW8 .... 1A 60
.... (off Allitsen Rd.)
De Walden St. W1 ... 1C 12 (4C 60)
Dewar St. SE15 .... 1C 106
Dewberry Gdns. E6 .... 4F 69
Dewberry St. E14 .... 4E 67
Dewey La. SW2 .... 4C 104
.... (off Tulse Hill)
Dewey Rd. N1 .... 1C 62
Dewey St. SW17 .... 5B 116
Dewhurst Rd. W14 .... 4F 71
Dewsbury Rd. NW10 .... 2C 42
Dewsbury Ter. NW1 .... 5D 47
De Wyndsor Ct. SE16 .... 4C 78
.... (off Jamaica Rd.)
Dexter Apts. SE15 .... 4D 93
.... (off Queen's Rd.)
D'Eynsford Rd. SE5 .... 4F 91
Dhonau Ho. SE1 .... 5B 78
.... (off Longfield Est.)
Diadem Ct. W1 .... 2B 14 (5F 61)
.... (off Dean St.)
Dial Wlk., The W8 .... 3D 73
Diamond Est. SW17 .... 3A 116
Diamond Gdns. E3 .... 4B 66
Diamond Ho. E3 .... 1A 66
.... (off Roman Rd.)
Diamond St. SE15 .... 3A 92
Diamond Ter. SE10 .... 4E 95
Diamond Way SE8 .... 2C 94
Diana Cl. SE8 .... 2B 94
Diana Ho. SW13 .... 4B 84
Diana, Princess of Wales
Memorial Fountain 3A 74
Diana, Princess of Wales
Memorial Playground 2D 73
Diana, Princess of Wales
Memorial Wlk. Kensington
Gdns. 2D 73
Dianne Ct. SE12 .... 1C 124
Dibden Ho. SE5 .... 3A 92
Dibden St. N1 .... 5E 49
Dibdin Ho. W9 .... 1D 59
Dibdin Row SE1 ....5C 24 (4C 76)
Dicey Av. NW2 .... 1E 43
Dickens Ct. SW17 .... 3F 115
.... (off Grosvenor Way)
Dickens Est. SE1 .... 5C 78
Dickens Est. SE16 .... 4C 78
Dickens Ho. NW6 .... 2C 58
.... (off Malvern Rd.)
Dickens Ho. NW8 .... 3F 59
.... (off Fisherton St.)

Dickens Ho. SE17 .... 1D 91
.... (off Doddington Gro.)
Dickens Ho. WC1 ....3D 7 (3A 62)
.... (off Herbrand St.)
Dickens M. EC1 ....5D 9 (4D 63)
.... (off Turnmill St.)
Dickenson Rd. N8 .... 2A 34
Dickens Ho. E6. .... 1F 69
Dickens Sq. SE1 .... 5A 26 (4E 77)
Dickens St. SW8 .... 5D 89
Dickinson Ct. EC1 ....3E 9 (3D 63)
.... (off Brewhouse Yd.)
Dicksee Ho. NW8 .... 3F 59
.... (off Lyons Pl.)
Dickson Ho. E1 .... 5D 65
.... (off Philpot St.)
Dickson Ho. N1 .... 4C 48
.... (off Drummond Way)
Dieppe Cl. W14 .... 1B 86
Digby Bus. Cen. E9 .... 3F 51
.... (off Digby Rd.)
Digby Cres. N4 .... 4E 35
Digby Mans. W6 .... 1D 85
.... (off Hammersmith Bri. Rd.)
Digby Rd. E9 .... 3F 51
Digby St. E2 .... 2E 65
Diggon St. E1 .... 4F 65
Dighton Ct. SE5 .... 2E 91
Dighton Rd. SW18 .... 3E 101
Dignum St. N1 .... 1C 62
Dilhorne Cl. SE12 .... 3D 125
Dilke St. SW3 .... 2B 88
Dillwyn Cl. SE26 .... 4A 122
Dilston Gro. SE16 .... 5E 79
Dilton Gdns. SW15 .... 1C 112
Dimes Pl. W6 .... 5D 71
Dimond Cl. E7 .... 1C 54
Dimsdale Hgts. E1 .... 5D 65
.... (off Spencer Way)
Dimsdale Wlk. E13. .... 1C 68
Dimson Cres. E3 .... 2C 66
Dinerman Ct. NW8 .... 5E 45
Dingle Gdns. E14 .... 1C 80
Dingley La. SW16 .... 2F 117
Dingley Pl. EC1 ....1A 10 (2E 63)
Dingley Rd. EC1 ....1A 10 (2E 63)
Dingwall Gdns. NW11 .... 1C 30
Dingwall Rd. SW18 .... 5E 101
Dinmont Est. E2 .... 1C 64
Dinmont Ho. E2 .... 1C 64
.... (off Pritchard's Rd.)
Dinmont St. E2 .... 1D 65
Dinmore Ho. E9 .... 5E 51
.... (off Templecombe Rd.)
Dinnington Ho. E1 .... 3D 65
.... (off Coventry Rd.)
Dinsdale Rd. SE3 .... 2B 96
Dinsmore Rd. SW12 .... 5D 103
Dinton Ho. NW8 .... 3A 60
.... (off Lilestone St.)
Dinton Rd. SW19 .... 5F 115
Diprose Lodge SW17 .... 4F 115
Dirleton Rd. E15 .... 5B 54
Dirty La. SE1 .... 1A 26 (2E 77)
Disbrowe Rd. W6 .... 2A 86
Discover Stratford 4F 53
Discover Greenwich Visitor Cen.
.... 2E 95
Discovery Bus. Pk. SE16 ..... 4C 78
.... (off St St James's Rd.)
Discovery Dock Apts. E. E14 3D 81
.... (off Sth. Quay Sq.)

Discovery Dock Apts. W.
E14 .... 3D 81
.... (off Sth. Quay Sq.)
Discovery Ho. E14 .... 1E 81
.... (off Newby Pl.)
Discovery Twr. E16 .... 5B 68
.... (off Minnie Baldock St.)
Discovery Wlk. E1 .... 2D 79
Disney Pl. SE1 ...... 3A 26 (3E 77)
Disney St. SE1 ...... 3A 26 (3E 77)
Dispensary La. E8 .... 2D 51
Disraeli Gdns. SW15 .... 2B 100
Disraeli Rd. E7 .... 3C 54
Disraeli Rd. SW15 .... 2A 100
Diss St. E2 .... 1F 11 (2B 64)
Distaff La. EC4 .... 4F 17 (1E 77)
Distel Apts. SE10 .... 5A 82
.... (off Telegraph Av.)
Distillery La. W6 .... 1E 85
Distillery Rd. W6 .... 1E 85
Distillery Twr. SE8 .... 4C 94
Distillery Wharf W6 .... 2E 85
Distin St. SE11 .... 5C 76
Ditch All. SE13 .... 4D 95
Ditchburn St. E14 .... 1E 81
Dittisham Rd. SE9 .... 4F 125
Divis Way SW15 .... 4D 99
.... (off Dover Pk. Dr.)
Dixie St. SE6 .... 4C 108
Dixon Butler M. W9 .... 3C 58
Dixon Clark Ct. N1 .... 3D 49
Dixon Ho. W10 .... 5F 57
.... (off Darfield Way)
Dixon Rd. SE14 .... 4A 94
Dixon's All. SE16 .... 3D 79
Dixon Way NW10 .... 4A 42
Dobree Av. NW10 .... 4D 43
Dobson Cl. NW6 .... 4F 45
Dobson Ho. SE14 .... 2F 93
.... (off John Williams Cl.)
Dobson Wlk. SE5 .... 3F 91
Doby Ct. EC4 .... 4A 18 (1E 77)
.... (off Skinners La.)
Dock, The E1 .... 1D 79
Dock Cotts. E1 .... 1E 79
.... (off The Highway)
Dockers Tanner Rd. E14...... 4C 80
Dockhead SE1 .... 3B 78
Dockhead Wharf SE1 3F 27 (3B 78)
.... (off Shad Thames)
Dock Hill Av. SE16 .... 2F 79
Docklands Ct. E14 .... 5B 66
.... (off Wharf La.)
Docklands Sailing & Watersports
Cen. 4C 80
Dockley Rd. SE16 .... 4C 78
Dockley Rd. Ind. Est. S
E16. .... 4C 78
.... (off Dockley Rd.)
Dock Offices SE16 .... 4E 79
.... (off Surrey Quays Rd.)
Dock Rd. E16 .... 1B 82
Dockside Ct. E5 .... 4E 37
Dockside Rd. E16. .... 1F 83
Dock St. E1 .... 1C 78
Dockweed Ct. E14 .... 4D 81
.... (off Watergate Wlk.)
Dockyard La. E14. .... 5D 80
Dr Harold Moody Pk. 5D 93
Dr Johnson Av. SW17 .... 3D 117
Dr Johnson's House
.... 2C 16 (5C 62)
.... (off Pemberton Row)
Doctors Cl. SE26 .... 5E 121
Docura Ho. N7 .... 4B 34

Docwra's Bldgs. N1 ....3A **50**
Dodbrooke Rd. SE27 .....3C **118**
Dodd Ho. SE16 ....5D **79**
.............................(off Rennie Est.)
Doddington Gro. SE17 ......2D **91**
Doddington Pl. SE17 ....2D **91**
Dodds Ho. SE10 ....4C **82**
.............................(off Peartree Way)
Dodson St. SE1 ......4C **24** (3C **76**)
Dod St. E14 ....5B **66**
Dog & Duck Yd.
  WC1.....................5A **8** (4B **62**)
.........................(off Princeton St.)
Doggett Rd. SE6 ....5C **108**
Dog Kennel Hill SE22.......1A **106**
Dog Kennel Hill Est.
  SE22...............................1A **106**
.........................(off Albrighton Rd.)
Dog La. NW10 ....1A **42**
Doherty Rd. E13 ....3C **68**
Dolben Ct. SW1 ....5F **75**
.........................(off Montaigne Cl.)
Dolben St. SE1 ......2D **25** (2D **77**)
.........................(not continuous)
Dolby Rd. SW6 ....5B **86**
Dolland Ho. SE11 ....1B **90**
.........................(off Newburn St.)
Dolland St. SE11 ....1B **90**
Dollar Bay Pl. E14 ....3E **81**
DOLLIS HILL 4D **29**
Dollis Hill Av. NW2 ....5D **29**
Dollis Hill Est. NW2............5C **28**
Dollis Hill La. NW2 ....1B **42**
Dollis Hill Station (Underground)
  ....2C **42**
Dolman St. SW4 ....2B **104**
Dolphin Cl. SE16 ....3F **79**
Dolphin Ct. NW11 ....1A **30**
Dolphin Ho. SW18 ....2D **101**
Dolphin Ho. SW6 ....5E **87**
.........................(off Lensbury Av.)
Dolphin La. E14 ....1D **81**
Dolphin Sq. SW1 ....1E **89**
Dolphin Sq. W4 ....3A **84**
Dolphin Twr. SE8 ....2D **94**
.........................(off Abinger Gro.)
Dombey Ho. SE1 ....3C **78**
.........................(off Wolseley St.)
Dombey Ho. W11 ....2F **71**
.........................(off St Ann's Rd.)
Dombey St. WC1 ......5F **7** (4B **62**)
.........................(not continuous)
Domecq Ho. EC1 .....3E **9** (3D **63**)
.........................(off Dallington St.)
Dome Hill Pk. SE26 ....4B **120**
Domelton Ho. SW18............4D **101**
.........................(off Iron Mill Rd.)
Domett Cl. SE5 ....2F **105**
Domfe Pl. E5 ....1E **51**
Domingo St. EC1 .....3F **9** (3E **63**)
Dominica Cl. E13 ....1F **69**
Dominion Cl. E8 ....4B **50**
Dominion Dr. SE16 ....3F **79**
Dominion Ho. E14 ....1D **95**
.........................(off St Davids Sq.)
Dominion Ho. E1 ...1F **17** (4F **63**)
.........................(off Bartholomew Cl.)
Dominion St. EC2 ....5C **10** (4F **63**)
Dominion Theatre ...2C **14** (5F **61**)
.........................(off Tottenham Ct. Rd.)
Dominion Wlk. E14 ....1F **81**
.........................(off Fairmont Av.)
Domville Cl. SE17 ....1A **92**
.........................(off Bagshott St.)

Donald Hunter Ho. E7 ....2D **55**
.........................(off Woodgrange Rd.)
Donald Rd. E13 ....5D **55**
Donaldson Rd. NW6............5B **44**
Donato Dr. SE15 ....2A **92**
Doncaster Gdns. N4............1E **35**
Donegal Ho. E1 ....1D **65**
.........................(off Cambridge Heath Rd.)
Donegal St. N1 ....1B **62**
Doneraile Ho. SW1 ....1D **89**
.........................(off Ebury Bri. Rd.)
Doneraile St. SW6 ....5F **85**
Dongola Rd. E1 ....4A **66**
Dongola Rd. E13 ....2D **69**
Dongola Rd. W. E13 ....2D **69**
Don Gratton Ho. E1 ....4C **64**
.........................(off Old Montague St.)
Donkey All. SE22................5C **106**
Donkin Ho. SE16 ....5D **79**
.........................(off Rennie Est.)
Donmar Warehouse Theatre
  ....3D **15** (5A **62**)
.........................(off Earlham St.)
Donnatt's Rd. SE14.............4B **94**
Donne Ct. SE24 ....4E **105**
Donne Ho. E14 ....5C **66**
.........................(off Dod St.)
Donne Ho. SE14 ....2F **93**
.........................(off Samuel Cl.)
Donnelly Ct. SW6 ....3A **86**
.........................(off Dawes Rd.)
Donnelly Ho. SE1 ...5B **24** (4C **76**)
.........................(off McAuley Cl.)
Donne Pl. SW3 ....5A **74**
Donnington Ct. NW1 ....4D **47**
.........................(off Castlehaven Rd.)
Donnington Ct. NW10 ....4D **43**
.........................(off Donnington Rd.)
Donnington Mans. NW10....5E **43**
.........................(off Donnington Rd.)
Donnington Rd. NW10 ....4D **43**
.........................(off Old Ford Rd.)
Donnybrook Ct. E3 ....5B **52**
Donoghue Bus. Pk. NW2.....5F **29**
Donoghue Cotts. E14..........4A **66**
.........................(off Galsworthy Av.)
Donoghue Ct. SE1 ....3D **67**
.........................(off Barry Blandford Way)
Donovan Ct. SW10 ....1F **87**
.........................(off Drayton Gdns.)
Donovan Ho. E1 ....1E **79**
.........................(off Cable St.)
Don Phelan Cl. SE5 ....4F **91**
Doon St. SE1 ....1B **24** (2C **76**)
Dora Ho. E14 ....5B **66**
.........................(off Rhodeswell Rd.)
Dora Ho. W11 ....1F **71**
.........................(off St Ann's Rd.)
Dorando Cl. W12..................1D **71**
Doran Mnr. N2 ....1B **32**
Doran Wlk. E15 ....4E **53**
Dora Rd. SW19.....................5C **114**
Dora St. E14 ....5B **66**
Dora Way SW9 ....5C **90**
Dorchester Ct. N1 ....4A **50**
Dorchester Ct. NW2............5F **29**
Dorchester Ct. SE24............3E **105**
Dorchester Ct. SW1 ...5A **20** (4B **74**)
.........................(off Sloane St.)
Dorchester Dr. SE24 ....3D **105**
Dorchester Gro. W4 ....1A **84**
Dorchester Ter. NW2 ....5F **29**
.........................(off Needham Ter.)

Dordrecht Rd. W3 ....2A **70**
Doreen Av. NW9 ....3A **28**
Doreen Capstan Ho. E11......5A **40**
.........................(off Apollo Pl.)
Dorfman Theatre ...1A **24** (2C **76**)
.........................(within National Theatre)
Doria Rd. SW6 ....5B **86**
Doric Ho. E2 ....1F **65**
.........................(off Mace St.)
Doric Way NW1......1B **6** (2F **61**)
Doris Emmerton Ct. SW11...2E **101**
Doris Rd. E7 ....4C **54**
Dorking Cl. SE8 ....2B **94**
Dorking Ho. SE1 ....5C **26** (4F **77**)
Dorlcote Rd. SW18...............5A **102**
Dorman Way NW8................5F **45**
Dorma Trad. Pk. E10 ....3F **37**
Dormay St. SW18.................3D **101**
Dormer Cl. E15.....................3B **54**
Dormstone Ho. SE17............5A **78**
.........................(off Congreve St.)
Dornberg Cl. SE3..................3C **96**
Dornberg Rd. SE3 ....3D **97**
Dorncliffe Rd. SW6 ....5A **86**
Dorney NW3 ....4A **46**
Dornfell St. NW6 ....2B **44**
Dornoch Ho. E3 ....1B **66**
.........................(off Anglo Rd.)
Dornton Rd. SW12 ....2D **117**
Dorothy Rd. SW11 ....1B **102**
Dorrell Pl. SW9...................1C **104**
Dorrien Wlk. SW16...............2F **117**
Dorrington Point E3 ....2D **67**
.........................(off Bromley High St.)
Dorrington St. EC1 ...5B **8** (4C **62**)
Dorrit Ho. W11 ....2F **71**
.........................(off St Ann's Rd.)
Dorrit St. SE1 ....3A **26** (3E **77**)
Dorryn Ct. SE26....................5F **121**
Dorset Bldgs. EC4....3D **17** (5D **63**)
Dorset Cl. NW1 ....5A **4** (4B **60**)
Dorset Ct. N1 ....4A **50**
.........................(off Hertford Rd.)
Dorset Mans. W6 ....2F **85**
.........................(off Lille Rd.)
Dorset M. SW1 ....5D **21** (4D **75**)
Dorset Pl. E15 ....3F **53**
Dorset Ri. EC4.........3D **17** (5D **63**)
Dorset Rd. E7 ....4E **55**
Dorset Rd. SE9 ....2F **125**
Dorset Sq. NW1 ....3A **90**
Dorset Sq. NW1 ....4A **4** (3B **60**)
Dorset St. W1 ....1A **12** (4B **60**)
Dorset Wharf W6 ....3E **85**
.........................(off Rainville Rd.)
Dorsey Ho. N1 ....3D **49**
.........................(off Canonbury Rd.)
Dorton Cl. SE15....................3A **92**
Dorville Cres. W6 ....4D **71**
Dorville Rd. SE12 ....3B **110**
Doubletree Docklands • Nelson
  Dock Pier (River Bus) 2B **80**
Doughty Ct. E1 ....2D **79**
.........................(off Prusom St.)
Doughty Ho. SW10 ....2E **87**
.........................(off Netherton Gro.)
Doughty M. WC1 .....4F **7** (3B **62**)
Doughty St. WC1 .....3F **7** (3B **62**)
Douglas Ct. NW6 ....4C **44**
.........................(off Quex Rd.)
Douglas Eyre Sports Cen.....1F **37**
Douglas Johnstone Ho. SW6..2B **86**
.........................(off Clem Attlee Ct.)

Douglas M. NW2 ....5A **30**
Douglas Path E14 ....1E **95**
.....................(off Manchester Rd.)
Douglas Rd. E16 ....4C **68**
Douglas Rd. N1 ....4E **49**
Douglas Rd. NW6 ....5B **44**
Douglas Rd. Nth. N1 ....3E **49**
Douglas Rd. Sth. N1 ....3E **49**
Douglas Rd. SW1 ....5F **75**
Douglas Waite Ho. NW6....4C **44**
Douglas Way SE8:
  Lon Stanley St. 3B **94**
Douglas Way SE8:
  Lon Watsons St. 3C **94**
Doulton Ho. SE11 ....4B **76**
.......................(off Lambeth Wlk.)
Doulton M. NW6 ....3D **45**
Dounesforth Gdns. SW18 ..1D **115**
Douro Pl. W8 ....4D **73**
Douro St. E3 ....1C **66**
Douthwaite Sq. E1 ....2C **78**
Dove App. E6 ....4F **69**
Dove Commercial Cen.
  NW5 ....2E **47**
Dovecote Gdns. SW14 ....1A **98**
Dovecote Ho. SE16...............3F **79**
.......................(off Water Gdns. Sq.)
Dovedale Bus. Est. SE15.....5C **92**
.......................(off Blenheim Gro.)
Dovedale Rd. SE22...............3D **107**
Dovehouse St. SW3...............1F **87**
Dove M. SW5 ....5E **73**
Dover Cl. NW2 ....4F **29**
Dover Cl. EC1 ....3D **9** (3D **63**)
.................................(off St John St.)
Dover Ct. N1 ....4F **49**
.................................(off Southgate Rd.)
Dovercourt Est. N1...............3F **49**
Dovercourt Rd. SE22...........4A **106**
Doverfield Rd. SW2..............5A **104**
Dover Flats SE1.....................5A **78**
Dover Ho. SE15......................2E **93**
Dover Ho. Rd. SW15............2C **98**
Dover Rd. N1 ....3F **49**
Dover Row E2 ....5C **50**
Dover Pk. Dr. SW15 ....4D **99**
Dover Patrol SE3..................5D **97**
Dover Rd. E12 ....4E **41**
Dover Rd. SE19.......................5F **119**
Dover St. W1 ....5E **13** (1D **75**)
Dover Yd. W1 ....1F **21** (2E **75**)
.................................(off Berkeley St.)
Doves Yd. N1 ....5C **48**
Dovet Ct. SW9 ....4B **90**
Doveton Ho. E1 ....3E **65**
.................................(off Doveton St.)
Doveton St. E1 ....3E **65**
Dove Wlk. SW1.......................1C **88**
Dovey Lodge N1.....................4C **48**
.................................(off Bewdley St.)
Dovill Ct. SE16 ....4C **78**
.................................(off Old Jamaica Rd.)
Dowanhill Rd. SE6................1F **123**
Dowdeswell Cl. SW15...........2A **98**
Dowding Dr. SE9...................3E **111**
Dowding Ho. N6....................2C **32**
.................................(off Hillcrest)
Dowdney Cl. NW5 ....2E **47**
Dowe Ho. SE3.........................1A **110**
Dowells St. SE10...................2D **95**
Dower Ct. SE16.......................5E **79**
.................................(off Silwood Rd.)
Dowes Ho. SW16...................3A **118**
Dowgate Hill EC4 ....4B **18** (1F **77**)
Dowland St. W10 ....2A **58**

Dowlas St. SE5.......................3A **92**
Dowler Ho. E1 ....5C **64**
.................................(off Burslem St.)
Downbarton Ho. SW9...........4C **90**
.................................(off Gosling Way)
Downbury M. SW18 ....3C **100**
Downderry Rd.
  BR1: Broml 3F **123**
Downend Ct. SE15 ....2A **92**
.................................(off Bibury Cl.)
Downer's Cott. SW4.............2E **103**
Downesbury NW3 ....3B **46**
.................................(off Steele's Rd.)
Downey Ho. E1.......................3F **65**
.................................(off Globe Rd.)
Downfield Cl. W9 ....3D **59**
DOWNHAM 5F **123**
Downham Ct. N1....................4F **49**
.................................(off Downham Rd.)
Downham Ent. Cen. SE6.....2B **124**
Downham Health & Leisure Cen.
  ....4B **124**
Downham La. BR1: Broml....5F **123**
Downham Rd. N1...................4F **49**
Downham Way
  BR1: Broml..........................5F **123**
Downham Wharf N1 ....5A **50**
.................................(off Downham Rd.)
Downing Ct. WC1 .....4E **7** (3A **62**)
.................................(off Grenville St.)
Downing Ho. W10 ....5F **57**
.................................(off Cambridge Gdns.)
Downing St. SW1 .....3D **23** (3A **76**)
Downland Ct. E11 ....4A **40**
Down Pl. W6 ....5D **71**
Downs Ct. Pde. E8 ....2D **51**
.................................(off Amhurst Rd.)
Downsell Rd. E15 ....1E **53**
Downsfield Rd. E17 ....1A **38**
Downshire Hill NW3 ....1F **45**
Downside Cres. NW3 ....2A **46**
Downs La. E5 ....1D **51**
Downs Pk. Rd. E5 ....2C **50**
Downs Pk. Rd. E8 ....2B **50**
Downs Rd. E5 ....1C **50**
Down St. W1 ....2D **21** (2D **75**)
Down St. M. W1 ......2D **21** (2D **75**)
Downton Av. SW2 ....2A **118**
Downtown Rd. SE16 ....3A **80**
Downy Ho. W3 ....2A **70**
Dowrey St. N1 ....5C **48**
Dowson Cl. SE5......................2F **105**
Dowson Ho. E1.......................5F **65**
.................................(off Bower St.)
Doyce St. SE1 ....3F **25** (3E **77**)
Doyle Gdns. NW10 ....5C **42**
Doyle Ho. SW13.....................3E **85**
.................................(off Trinity Chu. Rd.)
D'Oyley St. SW1 ....5C **74**
Doynton St. N19.....................4D **33**
Draco Ga. SW15.....................1E **99**
Draco St. SE17 ....2E **91**
Dragmore St. SW4 ....4F **103**
Dragonfly Cl. E13 ....2D **69**
Dragonfly Pl. SE4 ....1A **108**
Dragon Rd. SE5......................2A **92**
Dragon Yd. WC1 ......2E **15** (5A **62**)
Dragoon Rd. SE8 ....1B **94**
Drake Cl. SE16 ....3F **79**
Drake Ct. SE1 ....4A **26** (3E **77**)
.................................(off Swan St.)
Drake Ct. SE19.......................5B **120**
Drake Ct. W12 ....3E **71**
.................................(off Scott's Rd.)
Drakefell Rd. SE14................5F **93**

Drakefell Rd. SE4.................1A **108**
Drakefield Rd. SW17............3C **116**
Drakefield E16 ....2D **83**
.................................(off Wesley Av.)
Drake Ho. E1 ....4E **65**
.................................(off Stepney Way)
Drake Ho. E14 ....1A **80**
.................................(off Victory Pl.)
Drake Ho. SW1 ....2F **89**
.................................(off Dolphin Sq.)
Drakeland Ho. W9 ....3B **58**
.................................(off Fernhead Rd.)
Drakeley Ct. N5......................1D **49**
Drake Rd. SE4 ....1C **108**
Drakes, The SE8 ....2C **94**
Drakes Ct. SE23.....................1E **121**
Drakes Ctyd. NW6.................4B **44**
Drake St. WC1 ....1F **15** (4B **62**)
Draper Ho. SE1 ....5D **77**
.................................(off Newington Butts)
Draper Pl. N1 ....5D **49**
.................................(off Dagmar Ter.)
Drapers Almshouses E3 ......2D **67**
.................................(off Rainhill Way)
Drapers Gdns. EC2...2C **18** (5F **63**)
Drapers Rd. E15.....................1F **53**
Drapers Yd. SW18 ....3D **101**
.................................(off Ryland Blvd.)
Drappers Way SE16 ....5C **78**
Drawdock Rd. SE10...............3F **81**
Draxmont SW19.....................5A **114**
Draycot Rd. E11 ....1D **41**
Draycott Av. SW3 ....5A **74**
Draycott Cl. NW2 ....5F **29**
Draycott Cl. SE5 ....3F **91**
.................................(not continuous)
Draycott Cl. SW11................4A **88**
.................................(off Westbridge Rd.)
Draycott M. SW6...................5B **86**
.................................(off Laurel Bank Gdns.)
Draycott Pl. SW3 ....5B **74**
Draycott Ter. SW3.................5B **74**
Drayford Cl. W9 ....3B **58**
Dray Gdns. SW2....................3B **104**
Draymans M. SE15 ....5B **92**
Drayson M. W8 ....3C **72**
Drayton Gdns. SW10 ....1E **87**
Drayton Ho. E11 ....3F **39**
Drayton Ho. SE5....................3F **91**
.................................(off Elmington St.)
Drayton Pk. N5.......................1C **48**
Drayton Pk. M. N5 ....2C **48**
Drayton Park Station (Rail) ..1C **48**
Drayton Rd. E11 ....3F **39**
Drayton Rd. NW10 ....5B **42**
Dray Wlk. E1 ....4F **11** (3B **64**)
Dreadnought Library 2E **95**
Dreadnought St. SE10 ....4A **82**
Dreadnought Wlk. SE10.......2D **95**
Dresden Cl. NW6...................3D **45**
Dresden Ho. SE11 ....5B **76**
.................................(off Lambeth Wlk.)
Dresden Ho. SW11................5C **88**
.................................(off Dagnall St.)
Dresden Rd. N19 ....3E **33**
Dressington Av. SE4 ....4C **108**
Drewery Ct. SE3 ....1A **110**
Drewett Ho. E1 ....5C **64**
.................................(off Christian St.)
Drew Ho. SW2 ....1C **94**
Drew Ho. SW16......................3A **118**
Drew Rd. E16 ....2F **83**
.................................(not continuous)

Drewstead La. SW16......2F **117**
Drewstead Rd. SW16......2F **117**
Driffield Rd. E3............1A **66**
Driftway Ho. E3............1B **66**
.................(off Stafford Rd.)
Drinkwater Ho. SE5........3F **91**
.................(off Picton St.)
Drive, The N7.............3B **48**
.................(not continuous)
Drive, The N10...........5B **42**
Drive, The NW11...........2A **30**
Drive, The SW6...........5A **86**
Drive Mans. SW6..........5A **86**
.................(off Fulham Rd.)
Droitwich Cl. SE26........3C **120**
Dromore Rd. SW15.........4A **100**
Dron Ho. E1...............4E **65**
.................(off Adelina Gro.)
Droop St. W10.............2F **57**
Drovers Pl. SE15.........3E **93**
Drovers Way N7...........3A **48**
Druce Rd. SE21...........4A **106**
Druid St. SE1............3E **27** (3A **78**)
.................(not continuous)
Drum Ct. N1..............4A **48**
.................(off Gifford St.)
Drummond Cres.
NW1................1B **6** (2F **61**)
Drummond Ga. SW1........1F **89**
Drummond Ho. E2..........1C **64**
.................(off Goldsmiths Row)
Drummond Rd. E11.........1E **41**
Drummond Rd. SE16........4D **79**
Drummond St. NW1....3F **5** (3E **61**)
Drummond Way N1..........4C **48**
Drury Cl. SW15...........4C **98**
Drury Ho. SW8............4E **89**
Drury La. WC2.....2E **15** (5A **62**)
Drury Lane Theatre Royal
.................3E **15** (5A **62**)
.................(off Catherine St.)
Dryad St. SW15...........1F **99**
Dryburgh Ho. SW1.........1D **89**
.................(part of Abbots Mnr.)
Dryburgh Rd. SW15........1D **99**
Dryden Bldg. E1..........5C **64**
.................(off Commercial Rd.)
Dryden Cl. SW4...........3F **103**
Dryden Ct. SE11..........5C **76**
Dryden Mans. W14.........2A **86**
.................(off Queen's Club Gdns.)
Dryden Rd. SW19..........5E **115**
Dryden St. WC2.....2E **15** (5A **62**)
Dryfield Wlk. SE8........2C **94**
Drylands Rd. N8..........1A **34**
Drysdale Dwellings E8....2B **50**
.................(off Dunn St.)
Drysdale Pl. N1.....1E **11** (2A **64**)
Drysdale St. N1.....1E **11** (2A **64**)
Dublin Av. E8............5C **50**
Ducaine Apts. E3.........2B **66**
.................(off Merchant St.)
Ducal St. E2.......2F **11** (2B **64**)
Du Cane Cl. W12..........5E **57**
Du Cane Ct. SW17.........1C **116**
Du Cane Rd. W12..........5B **56**
Ducavel Ho. SW2..........1B **118**
Duchess Dr. E13..........3D **69**
Duchess M. W1.......1E **13** (4D **61**)
Duchess of Bedford Ho.
W8....................3C **72**
.................(off Duchess of Bedford's Wlk.)
Duchess of Bedford's Wlk.
W8....................3C **72**
Duchess St. W1......1E **13** (4D **61**)

Duchess Theatre......4F **15** (1B **76**)
.................(off Catherine St.)
Duchess Wlk. SE1....2F **27** (2B **78**)
Duchy St. SE1.......1C **24** (2C **76**)
.................(not continuous)
Ducie St. SW4............2B **104**
Duckett M. N4............1D **35**
Duckett Rd. N4...........1D **35**
Duckett's Apts. E3.......4B **52**
.................(off Wick La.)
Duckett St. E1...........3F **65**
Duckham Ct. E14..........5D **81**
.................(off Nauticus Wlk.)
Duck La. W1.........3B **14** (5F **61**)
.................(off Broadwick St.)
Du Cros Rd. W3...........2A **70**
DUDDEN HILL.............2D **43**
Dudden Hill La. NW10.....1B **42**
Dudden Hill Pde. NW10....1B **42**
Duddington Cl. SE9.......4F **125**
Dudley Cl. W1............5B **60**
.................(off Up. Berkeley St.)
Dudley Ct. WC2.....2D **15** (5A **62**)
Dudley M. SW2............4C **104**
Dudley Rd. NW6...........1A **58**
Dudley Rd. SW19..........5C **114**
Dudley St. W2............4F **59**
Dudlington Rd. E5........4E **37**
Dudmaston M. SW3.........1F **87**
.................(off Fulham Rd.)
Dudrich M. SE22..........3B **106**
Duffell Ho. SE11.........1B **90**
.................(off Loughborough St.)
Dufferin Av. EC1....4B **10** (3F **63**)
.................(off Dufferin St.)
Dufferin Ct. EC1....4B **10** (3F **63**)
.................(off Dufferin St.)
Dufferin St. EC1....4A **10** (3E **63**)
Duff St. E14.............5D **67**
Dufour's Pl. W1.....3A **14** (5E **61**)
Dufton Dwellings E15.....1A **54**
.................(off High Rd. Leyton)
Dugard Way SE11..........5D **77**
Dugdale Ct. NW10.........2D **57**
.................(off Harrow Rd.)
Duggan Dr. BR7: Chst.....5F **125**
Duke Humphrey Rd. SE3...4A **96**
Duke of Clarence Ct. SE17...1E **91**
.................(off Manor Pl.)
Duke of Wellington Pl.
SW1................3C **20** (3C **74**)
Duke of York Column
.................1B **22** (2F **75**)
Duke of York Sq. SW3....1B **88**
Duke of York's Theatre
.................5D **15** (1A **76**)
.................(off St Martin's La.)
Duke of York St.
SW1................1A **22** (2E **75**)
Duke Rd. W4.............1A **84**
Duke's Av. W4...........1A **84**
Dukes Ct. SE13..........5E **95**
Dukes Ct. W2............1D **73**
.................(off Moscow Rd.)
Duke's Head Yd. N6.......3D **33**
Duke Shore Wharf E14....1B **80**
Duke's Ho. SW1..........5F **75**
.................(off Vincent St.)
Dukes La. W8............3D **73**
Duke's La. Chambers W8....3D **73**
.................(off Dukes La.)
Duke's La. Mans. W8......3D **73**
.................(off Dukes La.)
Dukes Lodge W8..........2B **72**
.................(off Holland Wlk.)

Duke's M. W1........2C **12** (5C **60**)
.................(off Duke St.)
Duke's Pl. EC3.....3E **19** (5A **64**)
Dukes Point N6...........3D **33**
Dukesthorpe Rd. SE26.....4F **121**
Duke St. W1........2C **12** (5C **60**)
Duke St. SW1......1A **22** (2E **75**)
Duke St. Hill SE1...1C **26** (2F **77**)
Duke St. Mans. W1...3C **12** (5C **60**)
Duke St. St James's
SW1................1A **22** (2E **75**)
Duke's Yd. W1......4C **12** (1C **74**)
Dulas St. N4.............3B **34**
Dulford St. W11..........1A **72**
Dulka Rd. SW11...........3B **102**
Dulverton NW1............5E **47**
.................(off Royal College St.)
Dulverton Mans.
WC1....................4A **8** (3B **62**)
.................(off Gray's Inn Rd.)
DULWICH.................2A **120**
Dulwich & Sydenham Hill Golf
Course................2B **120**
Dulwich Bus. Cen. SE23...1F **121**
Dulwich Comn. SE21......1A **120**
Dulwich Comn. SE22......1C **120**
DULWICH COMMUNITY HOSPITAL
.................2A **106**
Dulwich Hamlet FC......2A **106**
Dulwich Lawn Cl. SE22...3B **106**
Dulwich Leisure Cen.....2C **106**
Dulwich Oaks, The SE21...3B **120**
Dulwich Picture Gallery...5F **105**
Dulwich Ri. Gdns. SE22...3B **106**
Dulwich Rd. SE24........3C **104**
Dulwich Upper Wood Nature Pk.
.................5B **120**
Dulwich Village SE21....4A **106**
DULWICH VILLAGE.........5A **106**
Dulwich Wood Av. SE19...4A **120**
Dulwich Wood Pk. SE19...4A **120**
Dumain Ct. SE11.........5D **77**
.................(off Opal St.)
Dumbarton Ct. SW2.......4A **104**
Dumbarton Rd. SW2.......4A **104**
Dumont Rd. N16..........5A **36**
Dumpton Pl. NW1.........4C **46**
Dunbar Rd. E7...........3C **54**
Dunbar St. SE27.........3E **119**
Dunbar Twr. E8..........3B **50**
.................(off Dalston Sq.)
Dunbar Wharf E14........1B **80**
.................(off Narrow St.)
Dunboyne Rd. NW3........2B **46**
Dunbridge Ho. SW15......4B **98**
Dunbridge St. E2........3C **64**
Duncan Ct. E14..........4E **67**
.................(off Teviot St.)
Duncan Gro. W3..........5A **56**
Duncan Ho. E15..........5F **53**
Duncan Ho. NW3..........4B **46**
.................(off Fellows Rd.)
Duncan Ho. SW1..........1F **89**
.................(off Dolphin Sq.)
Duncannon Ho. SW1.......1F **89**
.................(off Lindsay Sq.)
Duncannon St.
WC2................5D **15** (1A **76**)
Duncan Rd. E8...........5D **51**
Duncan St. N1...........1D **63**
Duncan Ter. N1.....1D **9** (1D **63**)
.................(not continuous)

Duncombe Hill SE23 .... 5A 108
Duncombe Rd. N19 .... 3F 33
Duncrievie Rd. SE13 .... 4F 109
Dundalk Ho. E1 .... 5E 65
.... (off Clark St.)
Dundalk Rd. SE4 .... 1A 108
Dundas Ct. SE10 .... 2D 95
.... (off Dowells St.)
Dundas Ho. E2 .... 1E 65
.... (off Bishop's Way)
Dundas Rd. SE15 .... 5E 93
Dundas Rd. SW9 .... 4C 90
Dundee Ct. E1 .... 2D 79
.... (off Wapping High St.)
Dundee Ct. SE1 .... 5D 27 (4A 78)
.... (off Long La.)
Dundee Ho. W9 .... 2E 59
.... (off Maida Vale)
Dundee Rd. E13 .... 1D 69
Dundee St. E1 .... 2D 79
Dundee Wharf E14 .... 1B 80
Dundonald Rd. NW10 .... 5F 43
Dundry Ho. SE26 .... 3C 120
Dunedin M. SW2 .... 1A 118
Dunedin Rd. E10 .... 5D 39
Dunelm Gro. SE27 .... 3E 119
Dunelm St. E1 .... 5F 65
Dunfield Gdns. SE6 .... 5D 123
Dunfield Rd. SE6 .... 5D 123
.... (not continuous)
Dunford Rd. N7 .... 1B 48
Dungannon Ho. SW6 .... 3C 86
.... (off Vanston Pl.)
Dungarvan Av. SW15 .... 2C 98
Dunhill Point SW15 .... 1C 112
Dunkery Rd. SE9 .... 4F 125
Dunkirk St. SE11 .... 4C 26 (3F 77)
Dunkirk St. SE27 .... 4E 119
Dunlace Rd. E5 .... 1E 51
Dunlin Ho. SE16 .... 5F 79
.... (off Tawny Way)
Dunloe Ct. E2 .... 1B 64
Dunloe St. E2 .... 1B 64
Dunlop Pl. SE16 .... 4B 78
Dunmore Point E2 .... 1F 11 (2B 64)
.... (off Gascoigne Pl.)
Dunmore Rd. NW6 .... 5A 44
Dunmow Rd. SE11 .... 1B 90
.... (off Newburn St.)
Dunmow Rd. E15 .... 1F 53
Dunmow Wlk. N1 .... 5E 49
.... (off Popham St.)
Dunnage Cres. SE16 .... 5A 80
.... (not continuous)
Dunnett Ho. E3 .... 1B 66
.... (off Vernon Rd.)
Dunnico Ho. SE17 .... 1A 92
.... (off East St.)
Dunnock Ho. NW9 .... 1B 28
Dunnock M. E5 .... 5C 36
Dunn St. E8 .... 2B 50
Dunollie Pl. NW5 .... 2E 47
Dunollie Rd. NW5 .... 2E 47
Dunoon Gdns. SE23 .... 5F 107
Dunoon Ho. N1 .... 5B 48
.... (off Bemerton Est.)
Dunoon Rd. SE23 .... 5E 107
Dunraven Rd. W12 .... 2C 70
Dunraven St. W1 ...... 4A 12 (1B 74)
Dunsany Rd. W14 .... 4F 71
Dunsford Way SW15 .... 4D 99
Dunsmure Rd. N16 .... 3A 36
Dunstable M. W1 ...... 5C 4 (4C 60)
Dunstan Ho's. E1 .... 4E 65
.... (off Stepney Grn.)

Dunstan Rd. NW11 .... 3B 30
Dunstan's Gro. SE22 .... 4D 107
Dunster Ct. EC3 .... 4D 19 (1A 78)
Dunster Gdns. NW6 .... 4B 44
Dunster Ho. SE6 .... 3E 123
Dunsterville Way
SE1 .... 4C 26 (3F 77)
Dunston Ct. SE6 .... 5C 108
Dunston Rd. E8 .... 5B 50
Dunston Rd. SW11 .... 5C 88
Dunton Ct. SE23 .... 2D 121
Dunton Rd. E10 .... 2D 39
Dunton Rd. SE1 .... 1B 92
Dunthill Rd. SW18 .... 1D 115
Dunworth M. W11 .... 5B 58
Duplex Ride SW1 ..... 4A 20 (3B 74)
Dupree Rd. SE7 .... 1D 97
Durand Gdns. SW9 .... 4B 90
Durands Wlk. SE16 .... 3B 80
Durant St. E2 .... 1C 64
Durban Ct. E7 .... 4F 55
Durban Ho. W12 .... 1D 71
.... (off White City Est.)
Durban Rd. E15 .... 2A 68
Durban Rd. SE27 .... 4E 119
Durdans Ho. NW1 .... 4D 47
.... (off Farrier St.)
Durell Ho. SE16 .... 3F 79
.... (off Wolfe Cres.)
Durfey Pl. SE5 .... 3F 91
Durford Cres. SW15 .... 1D 113
Durham Ct. NW6 .... 1C 58
.... (off Kilburn Pk. Rd.)
Durham Hill BR1: Broml 4B 124
Durham Ho. NW8 .... 2A 60
.... (off Lorne Cl.)
Durham Ho. St.
WC2 .... 5E 15 (1A 76)
.... (off John Adam St.)
Durham Pl. SW3 .... 1B 88
Durham Rd. E12 .... 1F 55
Durham Rd. E16 .... 3A 68
Durham Rd. N7 .... 4B 34
Durham Row E1 .... 4A 66
Durham St. SE11 .... 1B 90
Durham Ter. W2 .... 5D 59
Durham Yd. E2 .... 2D 65
Durley Rd. N16 .... 2A 36
Durlston Rd. E5 .... 4C 36
Durnford Ho. SE6 .... 3E 123
Durnford St. N15 .... 1A 36
Durnford St. SE10 .... 2E 95
Durning Rd. SE19 .... 5F 119
Durnsford Av. SW19 .... 2C 114
Durnsford Rd. SW19 .... 2C 114
Durrant Ho. EC1 .... 5B 10 (4F 63)
.... (off Chiswell St.)
Durrell Rd. SW6 .... 4B 86
Durrels Ho. W14 .... 5B 72
.... (off Warwick Gdns.)
Durrington Rd. E5 .... 1A 52
Durrington Twr. SW8 .... 5E 89
Durrisdeer Ho. NW2 .... 1B 44
.... (off Lyndale)
Dursley Cl. SE3 .... 5E 97
Dursley Gdns. SE3 .... 4F 97
Dursley Rd. SE3 .... 5E 97
Durward Ho. W8 .... 3D 73
.... (off Kensington Ct.)
Durward St. E1 .... 4D 65
Durweston M. W1 .... 5A 4 (4B 60)
.... (off York St.)
Durweston St. W1 ... 1A 12 (4B 60)

Dutch Yd. SW18 .... 3C 100
Dutton St. SE10 .... 4E 95
Duval Ho. N19 .... 4F 33
.... (off Ashbrook Rd.)
Duval Ho. SW11 .... 1A 102
DW Fitness Waldorf Hotel
.... 3E 15 (5B 62)
.... (off Tavistock St.)
Dye Ho. La. E3 .... 5C 52
Dyer's Bldgs. EC1 ... 1B 16 (4C 62)
Dyers Hall Rd. E11 .... 3A 40
Dyers Hall Rd. Sth. E11 ...... 4F 39
Dyers La. SW15 .... 2D 99
Dylan Rd. SE24 .... 2D 105
Dylways SE5 .... 2F 105
Dymes Path SW19 .... 2F 113
Dymock St. SW6 .... 1D 101
Dyneley Rd. SE12 .... 3E 125
Dyne Rd. NW6 .... 4A 44
Dynevor Rd. N16 .... 5A 36
Dynham Rd. NW6 .... 4C 44
Dyott St. WC1 .... 2C 14 (5F 61)
Dysart St. EC2 .... 4C 10 (3F 63)
Dyson Cl. SW2 .... 3E 29
Dyson Ho. SE10 .... 1B 96
.... (off Blackwall La.)
Dyson Rd. E11 .... 1A 40
Dyson Rd. E15 .... 3B 54

E

Eade Rd. N4 .... 2E 35
Eagle Cl. SE16 .... 1E 93
Eagle Ct. EC1 .... 5D 9 (4D 63)
Eagle Dwellings
EC1 .... 1A 10 (2E 63)
.... (off City Rd.)
Eagle Hgts. SW11 .... 1A 102
Eagle Ho. E1 .... 3D 65
.... (off Headlam St.)
Eagle Ho. EC1 .... 1B 10 (2F 63)
.... (off City Rd.)
Eagle Ho. N1 .... 5F 49
.... (off Eagle Wharf Rd.)
Eagle Ho. M. SW4 .... 3E 103
Eagle Lodge NW11 .... 2B 30
Eagle Mans. N16 .... 2B 50
.... (off Salcombe Rd.)
Eagle M. N1 .... 3A 50
Eagle Pl. SW1 .... 5A 14 (1E 75)
.... (off Piccadilly)
Eagle Pl. SW7 .... 1E 87
Eagle Point EC1 .... 1B 10 (2F 63)
.... (off City Rd.)
Eagle St. WC1 .... 1F 15 (4B 62)
Eagle Wharf Ct.
SE1 .... 2F 27 (2B 78)
.... (off Lafone St.)
Eagle Wharf E. E14 .... 1A 80
.... (off Narrow St.)
Eagle Wharf Rd. N1 .... 1E 63
Eagle Wharf W. E14 .... 1A 80
.... (off Narrow St.)
Eagle Works E. E1.... 4F 11 (3B 64)
.... (off Quaker St.)
Eagle Works W. E1.... 4F 11 (3B 64)
.... (off Quaker St.)
Eagling Cl. E3 .... 2C 66
Ealdham Sq. SE9 .... 2E 111
Eamont Cl. NW8 .... 1A 60
.... (off Eamont St.)
Eamont St. NW8 .... 1A 60
Eardley Cres. SW5 .... 1C 86
Eardley Rd. SW16 .... 5E 117
Earldom Rd. SW15 .... 2E 99

Earle Ho. SW1 ....5F **75**
.............................(off Montaigne Cl.)
Earlham St. E11 ....2B **40**
Earlham Gro. E7 ....2B **54**
Earlham St. WC2 ......3C **14** (5A **62**)
Earl Ho. NW1 ....3A **60**
.....................................(off Lisson Gro.)
Earlom Ho. WC1 ....2B **8** (2C **62**)
.................................(off Margery St.)
EARL'S COURT 5D **73**
Earl's Ct. Gdns. SW5 ....5D **73**
Earl's Ct. Rd. SW5 ....5C **72**
Earl's Ct. Rd. W8 ....4C **72**
Earl's Ct. Sq. SW5 ....1D **87**
Earl's Court Station
(Underground) 5C **72**
Earlsferry Way N1 ....4A **48**
....(not continuous)
EARLSFIELD 1E **115**
Earlsfield Rd. SW18 ....1E **115**
Earlsfield Station (Rail) 1E **115**
Earlsmead Rd. NW10 ....2E **57**
Earls Ter. W8 ....4B **72**
Earlsthorpe M. SW12 ....4C **102**
Earlsthorpe Rd. SE26 ....4F **121**
Earlstoke St. EC1 .....1D **9** (2D **63**)
Earlston Gro. E9 ....5D **51**
Earl St. EC2 ....5C **10** (4F **63**)
Earls Wlk. W8 ....4C **72**
Earls Way SE1 ....2E **27** (2A **78**)
..................................(off Duchess Wlk.)
Earlswood Cl. SE10 ....2A **96**
Earlswood St. SE10 ....1A **96**
Early M. NW1 ....5D **47**
Early Rivers Ho. E20 ....2E **53**
....(off Ellis Way)
Earnshaw Ho. EC1 ......2E **9** (3D **63**)
................................(off Percival St.)
Earnshaw St. WC2 ....2C **14** (5F **61**)
Earsby St. W14 ....5A **72**
....(not continuous)
Eashing Point SW15 ....1D **113**
..............................(off Wanborough Dr.)
Easleys M. W1 ....2C **12** (5C **60**)
East 10 Ent. Pk. E10 ....3A **38**
EAST ACTON 1B **70**
East Acton Arc. W3 ....5A **56**
East Acton Ct. W3 ....1A **70**
East Acton La. W3 ....2A **70**
East Acton Station (Underground)
....5B **56**
East Arbour St. E1 ....5F **65**
East Bank N16 ....2A **36**
East Bay La. E20 ....2C **52**
East Block SE1 ....3A **24** (3B **76**)
....(off York Rd.)
Eastbourne M. W2 ....5E **59**
Eastbourne Rd. E15 ....5A **54**
Eastbourne Rd. N15 ....1A **36**
Eastbourne Ter. W2 ....5E **59**
Eastbrook Rd. SE3 ....4D **97**
Eastbury Gro. W4 ....1A **84**
Eastbury Ter. E1 ....3F **65**
Eastcastle St. W1 ....2F **13** (5E **61**)
Eastcheap EC3 ....4C **18** (1A **78**)
Eastcombe Av. SE7 ....2D **97**
Eastcote St. SW9 ....5B **90**
East Cross Route E9:
  Lon Crowfoot Cl. 2B **52**
East Cross Route E9:
  Lon Wansbeck Rd. 4B **52**
Eastdown Ct. SE13 ....2F **109**
Eastdown Ho. E8 ....1C **50**
Eastdown Pk. SE13 ....2F **109**
EAST DULWICH 2B **106**

East Dulwich Est. SE22 ..... 1A **106**
..................................(off Albrighton Rd.)
East Dulwich Gro. SE22 .... 3A **106**
East Dulwich Rd. SE15 ..... 2C **106**
East Dulwich Rd. SE22 ..... 2B **106**
....(not continuous)
East Dulwich Station (Rail)
....2A **106**
Eastern Av. E11 ....1D **41**
Eastern Av. IG4: Ilf.................1F **41**
Eastern Ct. E15 ....3A **54**
.................................(off Gt. Eastern Rd.)
Eastern Gateway E16 ....1E **83**
Eastern Ho. E2 ....2D **65**
.................................(off Bethnal Grn. Rd.)
Eastern Quay Apts. E16 ......2D **83**
..................................(off Portsmouth M.)
Eastern Rd. E13 ....1D **69**
Eastern Rd. E17 ....1E **39**
Eastern Rd. SE4 ....2C **108**
East Ferry Rd. E14 ....5D **81**
Eastfields Av. SW18 ....2C **100**
Eastfield St. E14 ....4A **66**
East Gdns. SW17 ....5A **116**
Eastgate Bus. Pk. E10 ....3A **38**
East Gro. SE17 ....1C **78**
EAST HAM CARE CENTRE & DAY
HOSPITAL 4F **55**
East Harding St.
  EC4 ....2C **16** (5C **62**)
East Heath Rd. NW3 ....5E **31**
East Hill SW18 ....3D **101**
East India Bldgs. E14 ....1C **80**
....(off Saltwell St.)
East India Ct. SE16 ....3E **79**
.................................(off St Marychurch St.)
East India Dock Basin Local
  Nature Reserve 1A **82**
East India Dock Ho. E14 .....5E **67**
East India Dock Rd. E14 .....5C **66**
East India Dock (DLR) 1F **81**
Eastlake Ho. NW8 ....3F **59**
..................................(off Frampton St.)
Eastlake Rd. SE5 ....5E **91**
Eastlands Cres. SE21 ....4B **106**
East La. SE16: Lon Chambers St.
....3C **78**
East La. SE16: Lon Scott Lidgett
  Cres. 3C **78**
Eastlea M. E16 ....3A **68**
Eastleigh Cl. NW2 ....5A **28**
Eastleigh Wlk. SW15 ....5C **98**
East Lodge E16 ....2C **82**
....(off Wesley Av.)
East London Crematorium ...2B **68**
EASTMAN DENTAL HOSPITAL
  New Site 4B **6** (3F **61**)
EASTMAN DENTAL HOSPITAL &
  DENTAL INSTITUTE Expected
  Close 2020 ....3F **7** (3B **62**)
Eastman Ho. SW4 ....4E **103**
Eastman Rd. W3 ....3A **70**
Eastmearn Rd. SE21 ....2E **119**
Eastmoor Pl. SE7 ....4F **83**
Eastmoor St. SE7 ....4F **83**
East Mt. St. E1 ....4D **65**
....(not continuous)
Eastney St. SE10 ....1F **95**
Eastone Apts. E1 ......1F **19** (4B **64**)
.................................(off Lolesworth Cl.)
Easton St. WC1 ......3B **8** (3C **62**)
East Parkside SE10 ....3A **82**
East Park Wlk. E20 ....2E **53**
East Pas. EC1 ....5E **9** (4E **63**)
....(off Cloth St.)

East Pl. SE27 ....4E **119**
East Point SE1 ....1C **92**
East Poultry Av.
  EC1 ....1D **17** (4D **63**)
East Putney Station
(Underground) 3A **100**
East Rd. E15 ....5C **54**
East Rd. N1 ....1C **10** (2F **63**)
East Rd. SW3 ....1C **88**
East Row E11 ....1G **40**
East Row W10 ....3A **58**
Eastry Ho. SW8 ....3A **90**
.................................(off Hartington Rd.)
Eastry Ho. W11 ....1A **72**
.................................(off Walmer Rd.)
East Side W12 ....2D **71**
.................................(off Shepherd's Bush Mkt.)
Eastside Halls SW7 ....4F **73**
.................................(off Prince's Gdns.)
Eastside M. E3 ....1C **66**
.................................(off Morville St.)
East Smithfield E1 ...5F **19** (1B **78**)
East Stand N5 ....5D **35**
East St. SE17 ....1E **91**
....(not continuous)
East Surrey Gro. SE15 ....3B **92**
East Tenter St. E1 ....5B **64**
East Twr. E14 ....3D **81**
.................................(off Pan Peninsula Sq.)
East Twr. SW10 ....3F **87**
EAST VILLAGE 2E **53**
Eastville Av. NW11 ....1B **30**
Eastway E9 ....3B **52**
....(not continuous)
Eastwell Ho. SE1 .....5C **26** (4F **77**)
.................................(off Weston St.)
East Wick E20 ....2C **52**
East Wintergarden E14 ....2D **81**
.................................(off Bank St.)
Eastwood Cl. N7 ....2C **48**
Eastwood Ho. E3 ....4C **66**
.................................(off Bow Comn. La.)
easyGym Fulham 2B **86**
Eatington Rd. E10 ....1F **39**
Eaton Cl. SW1 ....5C **74**
Eaton Dr. SW9 ....2D **105**
Eaton Ga. SW1 ....5C **74**
Eaton Ho. E14 ....1B **80**
.................................(off Westferry Cir.)
Eaton Ho. SW11 ....4F **87**
Eaton La. SW1 ....5E **21** (4D **75**)
Eaton Mans. SW1 ....5C **74**
.................................(off Bourne St.)
Eaton M. Nth. SW1 ....5C **74**
Eaton M. Sth. SW1 ....5C **74**
Eaton M. W. SW1 ....5C **74**
Eaton Pl. SW1 ....5C **74**
Eaton Row SW1 ......5D **21** (4D **75**)
Eaton Sq. SW1 ....5C **74**
Eaton Ter. E3 ....2A **66**
Eaton Ter. SW1 ....5C **74**
Eaton Ter. M. SW1 ....5C **74**
....(off Eaton Ter.)
Ebbett Ct. W3 ....4A **56**
Ebbisham Dr. SW8 ....2B **90**
Ebbsfleet Rd. NW2 ....2A **44**
Ebdon Way SE3 ....1D **111**
Ebenezer Ho. SE11 ....5D **77**
Ebenezer Mussel Ho. E2 .....1E **65**
.................................(off Patriot Sq.)
Ebenezer St. N1 ....1B **10** (2F **63**)
Ebley Cl. SE15 ....2B **92**

Ebner St. SW18 .... 3D **101**
Ebony Ho. E2 .... 2C **64**
.... (off Buckfast St.)
Ebor Cotts. SW15 .... 3A **112**
Ebor St. E1 .... 3F **11** (3B **64**)
Ebsworth St. SE23 .... 5F **105**
Eburne Rd. N7 .... 5A **34**
Ebury Bri. SW1 .... 1D **89**
Ebury Bri. Est. SW1 .... 1D **89**
Ebury Bri. Rd. SW1 .... 1C **88**
Ebury M. N5 .... 5E **35**
Ebury M. SE27 .... 3D **119**
Ebury Sq. SW1 .... 5D **75**
Ebury St. SW1 .... 5D **75**
Ebury M. E. SW1 .... 4D **75**
Ebury Sq. SW1 .... 5C **74**
Ebury St. SW1 .... 5C **74**
Ecclesbourne Apts. N1 .... 4F **49**
.... (off Ecclesbourne Rd.)
Ecclesbourne Rd. N1 .... 4E **49**
Eccles Rd. SW11 .... 2B **102**
Eccleston Bri. SW1 .... 5D **75**
Eccleston Ho. SW2 .... 4C **104**
Eccleston M. SW1 .... 5C **20** (4C **74**)
Eccleston Pl. SW1 .... 5D **75**
Eccleston Sq. SW1 .... 5D **75**
.... (not continuous)
Eccleston Sq. M. SW1 .... 5D **75**
Eccleston St. SW1 .... 4D **75**
Eccleston Yd. SW1 .... 5D **75**
.... (off Eccleston Pl.)
Echo Ct. E16 .... 3E **83**
.... (off Admiralty Av.)
Eckford St. N1 .... 1C **62**
Eckington Cl. SE14 .... 3F **93**
Eckington Ho. N15 .... 1F **35**
.... (off Fladbury Rd.)
Eckington La. SE14 .... 3F **93**
Eckstein Rd. SW11 .... 2A **102**
Eclipse Bldg. N1 .... 3C **48**
.... (off Laycock St.)
Eclipse Rd. E13 .... 4D **69**
Ecology Cen. & Arts Pavilion
.... 5E **51**
Eco Va. SE23 .... 4D **107**
Ector Rd. SE6 .... 2A **124**
Edans Ct. W12 .... 3B **70**
Edbrooke Rd. W9 .... 3C **58**
Eddington Ct. E16 .... 5B **68**
.... (off Silvertown Sq.)
Eddisbury Ho. SE26 .... 3C **120**
Eddiscombe Rd. SW6 .... 5B **86**
Eddystone Rd. SE4 .... 3A **108**
Eddystone Twr. SE8 .... 1A **94**
Eden Apts. E14 .... 5E **81**
.... (off Glengarnock Av.)
Edenbridge Cl. SE16 .... 1D **93**
.... (off Masters Dr.)
Edenbridge Rd. E9 .... 4F **51**
Eden Cl. NW3 .... 4C **30**
Eden Cl. W8 .... 4C **72**
Edencourt Rd. SW16 .... 5D **117**
Eden Gro. N7 .... 2B **48**
Eden Gro. NW10 .... 3D **43**
Edenham Way W10 .... 3B **58**
Eden Ho. NW8 .... 3A **60**
.... (off Church St.)
Eden Ho. SE16 .... 3F **79**
.... (off Water Gdns. Sq.)
Eden Ho. SE8 .... 3C **94**
.... (off Deptford High St.)
Edenhurst Av. SW6 .... 1B **100**
Eden Lodge NW6 .... 4F **43**
Eden M. SW17 .... 3E **115**
Eden Rd. SE27 .... 4D **119**
Edensor Gdns. W4 .... 3A **84**

Edensor Rd. W4 .... 3A **84**
Edenvale St. SW6 .... 5E **87**
Eden Way E3 .... 5B **52**
Edgar Ho. E11 .... 2C **40**
Edgar Ho. E9 .... 2A **52**
.... (off Homerton Rd.)
Edgar Ho. SW8 .... 3A **90**
.... (off Wyvil Rd.)
Edgar Kail Way SE22 .... 2A **106**
Edgarley Ter. SW6 .... 4A **86**
Edgar Myles Ho. E16 .... 4B **68**
.... (off Ordnance Rd.)
Edgar Rd. E3 .... 2D **67**
Edgar Wallace Cl. SE15 .... 3A **92**
Edgar Wright Ct. SW6 .... 3B **86**
.... (off Dawes Rd.)
Edgcott Ho. W10 .... 4E **57**
.... (off Sutton Way)
Edge Finsbury, The 2E **35**
Edge, The SE8 .... 3B **94**
.... (off Glenville Gro.)
Edge Apts. E15 .... 4F **53**
Edgecombe Ho. SE5 .... 5A **92**
Edgecombe Ho. SW19 .... 1A **114**
Edgehill Ho. SW9 .... 5D **91**
Edgeley La. SW4 .... 1F **103**
Edgeley Rd. SW4 .... 1F **103**
Edgel St. SW18 .... 2D **101**
Edge Point Cl. SE27 .... 5D **119**
Edge St. W8 .... 2C **72**
Edgeworth Ho. NW8 .... 5E **45**
.... (off Boundary Rd.)
Edgeworth Rd. SE9 .... 2E **111**
Edgson Ho. SW1 .... 1D **89**
.... (off Ebury Bri. Rd.)
Edgware Rd. NW2 .... 3D **29**
Edgware Rd. W2 .... 3F **59**
Edgware Road Station
(Underground) 4A **60**
Edicule Sq. E3 .... 2A **66**
Edinburgh Cl. E2 .... 1E **65**
Edinburgh Ct. SE16 .... 2F **79**
.... (off Rotherhithe St.)
Edinburgh Ga. SW1 ... 3A **20** (3B **74**)
Edinburgh Ho. W9 .... 2D **59**
.... (off Maida Vale)
Edinburgh Rd. E13 .... 1D **69**
Edinburgh Rd. E17 .... 1C **38**
Edington NW5 .... 3C **46**
Edison Bldg. E14 .... 3C **80**
Edison Ct. SE10 .... 4B **82**
.... (off Schoolbank Rd.)
Edison Ct. W3 .... 3A **70**
Edison Hgts. E1 .... 3F **11** (3B **64**)
.... (off Cygnet St.)
Edison Ho. SE1 .... 5F **77**
.... (off New Kent Rd.)
Edison M. SW18 .... 4D **101**
Edison Rd. N8 .... 1F **33**
Edis St. NW1 .... 5C **46**
Editha Mans. SW10 .... 2E **87**
.... (off Edith Gro.)
Edith Brinson Ho. E14 .... 5F **67**
.... (off Oban St.)
Edith Cavell Cl. N19 .... 2A **34**
Edith Cavell Ho. E14 .... 5D **67**
.... (off Sturry St.)
Edith Gro. SW10 .... 2E **87**
Edith Ho. W6 .... 1E **85**
.... (off Queen Caroline St.)
Edithna St. SW9 .... 1A **104**
Edith Neville Cotts.
NW1 .... 1B **6** (2F **61**)
.... (off Drummond Cres.)

Edith Ramsay Ho. E1 .... 4A **66**
.... (off Duckett St.)
Edith Rd. E15 .... 2F **53**
Edith Rd. E6 .... 4F **55**
Edith Rd. N4 .... 5D **19**
Edith Rd. SW19 .... 5D **115**
Edith Rd. W14 .... 5A **72**
Edith Row SW6 .... 4D **87**
Edith St. E2 .... 1C **64**
Edith Summerskill Ho. SW6 ... 3B **86**
.... (off Clem Attlee Ct.)
Edith Ter. SW10 .... 3E **87**
Edith Vs. W14 .... 5B **72**
Edith Yd. SW10 .... 3E **87**
Edmeston Cl. E9 .... 3A **52**
Edmond Cl. SE14 .... 4E **93**
Edmonton Ct. SE16 .... 4E **79**
.... (off Canada Est.)
Edmund Halley Way SE10 ... 3A **82**
Edmund Ho. SE17 .... 2D **91**
Edmundsbury Ct. Est.
SW9 .... 2B **104**
Edmund St. SE5 .... 3F **91**
Edmund St. SE15 .... 2C **92**
.... (off Haymerle Rd.)
Edna St. SW11 .... 4A **88**
Edred Ho. E9 .... 1A **52**
.... (off Lindisfarne Way)
Edrich Ho. SW4 .... 4A **90**
Edric Ho. SW1 .... 5F **75**
.... (off Page St.)
Edric Rd. SE14 .... 3F **93**
Education Sq. E1 .... 5C **64**
.... (off Alder St.)
Edward VII Mans. NW10 .... 2F **57**
.... (off Chamberlayne Rd.)
Edward Bond Ho.
WC1 .... 2E **7** (2A **62**)
.... (off Cromer St.)
Edward Clifford Ho. SE17 ..... 5F **77**
.... (off Elsted St.)
Edward Cl. NW2 .... 1F **43**
Edward Cl. E16 .... 4C **68**
Edward Dodd Ct.
N1 .... 1C **10** (1F **63**)
.... (off Chart St.)
Edward Edward's Ho.
SE1 .... 2D **25** (2D **77**)
.... (off Nicholson St.)
Edwardes Pl. W8 .... 4B **72**
Edwardes Sq. W8 .... 4B **72**
Edward Heylin Ct. E15 .... 1D **67**
.... (off High St.)
Edward Heylyn Ho. E3 .... 1C **66**
.... (off Thomas Fyre Dr.)
Edward Ho. SE11 .... 1B **90**
.... (off Newburn St.)
Edward Ho. W2 .... 3F **59**
.... (off Hall Pl.)
Edward Kennedy Ho. W10 ... 3A **58**
.... (off Wornington Rd.)
Edward Mann Cl. E. E1 .... 5F **65**
.... (off Pitsea St.)
Edward Mann Cl. W. E1 .... 5F **65**
.... (off Pitsea St.)
Edward M. NW1 .... 1E **5** (2D **61**)
Edward Mills Way E14 .... 5C **66**
Edward Pl. SE8 .... 2B **94**
Edward's Cotts. N1 .... 3D **49**
Edward's La. N16 .... 4A **36**
Edwards M. N1 .... 4D **49**
Edwards M. W1 .... 3B **12** (5C **60**)
Edwards Pas. E1 .... 4E **65**
.... (off Trinity Grn.)
Edward Sq. N1 .... 5B **48**
Edward Sq. SE16 .... 2A **80**

Edward St. E16 .... 3C 68
.... (not continuous)
Edward St. SE14 .... 3A 94
Edward St. SE8 .... 2B 94
Edwards Way SE4 .... 3C 108
Edward Temme Av. E15 .... 4B 54
Edward Tyler Rd. SE12 .....2E 125
Edwina Gdns. IG4: Ilf 1F 41
Edwin Hall Pl. SE13 ....4F 109
Edwin Ho. SE15 ....3C 92
Edwin's Mead E9 ....1A 52
Edwin St. E1 ....3E 65
Edwin St. E16 ....4C 68
Edwy Ho. E9 ....1B 52
.... (off Homerton Rd.)
Edwyn Ho. SW18 ....4D 101
.... (off Neville Gill Cl.)
Eel Brook Cl. SW6 .... 4D 87
Effie Pl. SW6 .... 3C 86
Effie Rd. SW6 .... 3C 86
Effingham Rd. SE12 .... 3A 110
Effort St. SW17 .... 5A 116
Effra Cl. SW19 .... 5D 115
Effra Ct. SW2 .... 3B 104
.... (off Brixton Hill)
Effra Pde. SW2 .... 3C 104
Effra Rd. SW19 .... 5D 115
Effra Rd. SW2 .... 2C 104
Effra Rd. Retail Pk. 3C 104
Egbert Ho. E9 .... 2A 52
.... (off Homerton Rd.)
Egbert St. NW1 .... 5C 46
Egbury Ho. SW15 .... 4B 98
.... (off Tangley Gro.)
Egeremont Rd. SE13 .... 5D 95
Egerton Ct. E11 .... 2F 39
Egerton Cres. SW3 .... 5A 74
Egerton Dr. SE10 .... 4D 95
Egerton Gdns. NW10 ....5E 43
Egerton Gdns. SW3 .... 5A 74
Egerton Gdns. M. SW3 ...... 4A 74
Egerton Pl. SW3 .... 4A 74
Egerton Rd. N16 .... 2B 36
Egerton Ter. SW3 .... 4A 74
Egham Cl. SW19 .... 2A 114
Egham Rd. E13 .... 4D 69
Eglantine Rd. SW18 ....3E 101
Egleton Ho. SW15 .... 5C 98
Eglington Ct. SE17 ....2E 91
Egliston M. SW15 .... 1E 99
Egliston Rd. SW15 .... 1E 99
Egmont St. SE14 .... 3F 93
Egremont Ho. E20 ....2E 53
.... (off Medals Way)
Egremont Ho. SE13 .... 5D 95
.... (off Russett Way)
Egremont Rd. SE27 .... 3C 118
Egret Ho. SE16 ....5F 79
.... (off Tawny Way)
Eider Cl. E7 .... 2B 54
Eider Cl. SE8 .... 2B 94
.... (off Pilot Cl.)
Ekarro Ho. SW8 .... 4A 90
.... (off Guildford Rd.)
Elaine Gro. NW5 .... 2C 46
Elam Cl. SE5 .... 5D 91
Elam St. SE5 .... 5D 91
Elan Ct. E1 .... 4D 65
Eland Rd. SW11 .... 1B 102
Elba Pl. SE17 ....5E 77
Elbe St. SW6 ....5E 87
Elborough St. SW18 ....1C 114
Elbourne Ct. SE16 ....4F 79
.... (off Worgan St.)

Elbourn Ho. SW3 .... 1A 88
.... (off Cale St.)
Elbury Dr. E16 .... 5C 68
Elcho St. SW11 .... 3A 88
Elcot Av. SE15 .... 3D 93
Elden Ho. SW3 .... 5A 74
.... (off Sloane Av.)
Elder Av. N8 .... 1A 34
Elderberry Gro. SE27 .... 4E 119
Elderfield Ho. E14 .... 1C 80
.... (off Pennyfields)
Elderfield Pl. SW17 ....4D 117
Elderfield Rd. E5 ....1F 51
Elderflower Way E15 .... 4A 54
Elder Gdns. SE27 ....5E 119
Elder Ho. E15 .... 2A 68
.... (off Manor Rd.)
Elder Ho. SE16 .... 4A 80
Elder Rd. SE27 ....5E 119
Elder St. E1 ....4F 11 (3B 64)
.... (not continuous)
Elderton Rd. SE26 .... 4A 122
Elder Wlk. N1 .... 5D 49
.... (off Popham St.)
Elder Wlk. SE13 ....1E 109
Elderwood Pl. SE27 ....5E 119
Eldon Ct. NW6 .... 5C 44
Eldon Gro. NW3 .... 2F 45
Eldon Rd. W8 .... 4D 73
Eldons Pas. E1 ....1C 78
.... (off Cable St.)
Eldon St. EC2 ....1C 18 (4F 63)
Eldridge Ct. SE16 .... 4C 78
Eleanor Cl. SE16 ....3F 79
Eleanor Ct. E2 ....5C 50
.... (off Whiston Rd.)
Eleanor Gro. SW13 .... 1A 98
Eleanor Ho. W6 ....1E 85
.... (off Queen Caroline St.)
Eleanor Rathbone Ho. N6 ...2F 33
.... (off Avenue Rd.)
Eleanor Rd. E15 .... 3B 54
Eleanor Rd. E8 ....3C 50
Eleanor St. E3 ....2C 66
Electra Bus. Pk. E16 ....4F 67
Electric Av. SW9 .... 2C 104
Electric Cinema Portobello, The ...5D 58
Electric Cinema Shoreditch
.................................3F 11 (3B 64)
.... (off Club Row)
Electric Empire, The SE14 ...4F 93
.... (off New Cross Rd.)
Electric Ho. E3 ....2C 66
.... (off Bow Rd.)
Electric La. SW9 .... 2C 104
.... (not continuous)
Elektron Twr. E14 ....1F 81
Elephant & Castle SE1 ....5D 77
ELEPHANT & CASTLE 4D 77
Elephant & Castle Station
(Rail & Underground) 5E 77
Elephant La. SE16 ....3E 79
Elephant Pk. Development
SE17 ....5E 77
Elephant Rd. SE17 ....5E 77
Elfindale Rd. SE24 ....3E 105
Elfin Oak 2D 73
Elford Cl. SE3 ....2E 111
Elford M. SW4 ....3E 103
Elfort Rd. N5 ....1C 48
Elfrida Cres. SE6 ....4C 122
Elf Row E1 ....1E 79
Elgar Cl. E13 ....1E 69
Elgar Cl. SE8 ....3C 94

Elgar Ct. NW6 .... 2C 58
Elgar Ct. W14 .... 4A 72
.... (off Blythe Rd.)
Elgar Ho. NW6 ....4E 45
.... (off Fairfax Rd.)
Elgar Ho. SW1 ....1D 89
.... (off Churchill Gdns.)
Elgar St. SE16 .... 4A 80
Elgin Av. W12 .... 3C 70
Elgin Av. W9 .... 3B 58
Elgin Cl. W12 .... 3D 71
Elgin Ct. W9 .... 3D 59
Elgin Cres. W11 .... 1A 72
Elgin Est. W9 .... 3D 59
.... (off Elgin Av.)
Elgin Ho. E14 .... 5D 67
.... (off Ricardo St.)
Elgin Mans. W9 .... 2D 59
Elgin M. W11 .... 5A 58
Elgin M. Nth. W9 .... 2D 59
Elgin M. Sth. W9 .... 2D 59
Elgood Cl. W11 .... 1A 72
Elgood Ho. NW8 ....1F 59
.... (off Wellington Rd.)
Elgood Ho. SE1 ....4B 26 (3F 77)
.... (off Tabard St.)
Elham Ho. E5 .... 2D 51
Elia M. N1 ....1D 9 (1D 63)
Elia Pl. N1 .... 2C 90
Elias St. N1 ....1E 9 (1D 63)
Elim Est. SE1 ....5D 27 (4A 78)
Elim St. SE1 ....5C 26 (4F 77)
.... (not continuous)
Eliot Way E13 .... 2B 68
Eliot Bank SE23 .... 2D 121
Eliot Cotts. SE3 .... 5A 96
Eliot Ct. SW18 .... 4D 101
Eliot Gdns. SW15 .... 2C 98
Eliot Hill SE13 ....5E 95
Eliot M. NW8 ....1E 59
Eliot Pk. SE13 ....5E 95
Eliot Pl. SE3 .... 5A 96
Eliot Va. SE3 ....5F 95
Elis Way E20 ....2E 53
Elizabeth Av. N1 ....5E 49
Elizabeth Barnes Ct.
SW6 ....5D 87
.... (off Marinefield Rd.)
Elizabeth Bates Ct. E1 ....4E 65
.... (off Fulneck Pl.)
Elizabeth Blount Ct. E14 ...5A 66
.... (off Carr St.)
Elizabeth Bri. SW1 .... 5D 75
Elizabeth Cl. E14 .... 5D 67
Elizabeth Cl. W9 ....3E 59
Elizabeth Cl. E10 .... 2D 39
Elizabeth Ct. NW1 .... 3A 60
.... (off Palgrave Gdns.)
Elizabeth Ct. SW1 ...5C 22 (4F 75)
.... (off Milmans St.)
Elizabeth Ct. SW10 ....2F 87
.... (off Milman's St.)
Elizabeth Croll Ho.
WC1 ....1A 8 (2B 62)
.... (off Penton Ri.)
Elizabeth Fry M. E8 .... 4D 51
Elizabeth Gdns. W3 .... 2B 70
Elizabeth Ho. SE11 .... 5C 76
.... (off Reedworth St.)
Elizabeth Ho. W6 ....1E 85
.... (off Queen Caroline St.)
Elizabeth Ind. Est. SE14 ....2F 93
Elizabeth M. E10 ....3E 39

Elizabeth M. E2 .... 1C 64
.... (off Kay St.)
Elizabeth M. NW3 .... 3A 46
Elizabeth Newcomen Ho.
SE1 .... 3B 26 (3F 77)
.... (off Newcomen St.)
Elizabeth Rd. E6 .... 5F 55
Elizabeth Rd. N15 .... 1A 36
Elizabeth Sq. SE16 .... 1A 93
.... (off Sovereign Cres.)
Elizabeth St. SW1 .... 5C 74
Elkington Point SE11 .... 5C 76
.... (off Lollard St.)
Elkington Rd. E13 .... 3D 69
Elkstone Rd. W10 .... 4B 58
Ellacott M. SW16 .... 2F 117
Ellaline Rd. W6 .... 2F 85
Ella M. NW3 .... 1B 46
Elland Ho. E14 .... 5B 66
.... (off Copenhagen Pl.)
Elland Rd. SE15 .... 2E 107
Ella Rd. N8 .... 2A 34
Ellenborough Ho. W12 .... 1D 71
.... (off White City Est.)
Ellenborough Pl. SW15 .... 2C 98
Ellen Julia Ct. E1 .... 3A 66
.... (off James Voller Way)
Ellen Phillips La. E2 .... 1C 64
Ellen St. E1 .... 5C 64
Ellen Terry Ct. NW1 .... 4D 47
.... (off Farrier St.)
Ellen Wilkinson Ho. E2 .... 2F 65
.... (off Usk St.)
Ellen Wilkinson Ho. SW6 ..... 2B 86
.... (off Clem Attlee Ct.)
Ellerby St. SW6 .... 4F 85
Ellerdale Cl. NW3 .... 1E 45
Ellerdale Rd. NW3 .... 2E 45
Ellerdale St. SE13 .... 2D 109
Ellerslie Gdns. NW10 .... 5C 42
Ellerslie Rd. W12 .... 2D 71
Ellerslie Sq. Ind. Est.
SW2 .... 3A 104
Ellerton Rd. SW13 .... 4C 84
Ellerton Rd. SW18 .... 1F 115
Ellery Ho. SE17 .... 5F 77
Ellery St. SE15 .... 5D 93
Ellesmere Cl. E11 .... 1B 40
Ellesmere Ct. SE12 .... 1C 124
Ellesmere Ho. SW10 .... 2E 87
.... (off Fulham Rd.)
Ellesmere Mans. NW6 .... 3E 45
.... (off Canfield Gdns.)
Ellesmere Rd. E3 .... 1A 66
Ellesmere Rd. NW10 .... 2C 42
Ellesmere St. E14 .... 5D 67
Ellie M. E13 .... 1E 69
Ellingfort Rd. E8 .... 4D 51
Ellingham Rd. E15 .... 1F 53
Ellingham Rd. W12 .... 3C 70
Ellington Ho. SE1 ...... 5A 26 (4E 77)
Ellington St. N7 .... 3C 48
Elliot Cl. E15 .... 4A 54
Elliot Ho. SW17 .... 3F 115
.... (off Grosvenor Way)
Elliot Ho. W1 .... 4A 60
.... (off Cato St.)
Elliot Rd. NW4 .... 1D 29
Elliott Rd. SW9 .... 4D 91
Elliott Rd. W4 .... 5A 70
Elliott's Pl. N1 .... 5D 49
Elliott Sq. NW3 .... 4A 46
Elliotts Row SE11 .... 5D 77
Ellis Cl. NW10 .... 3D 43
Elliscombe Mt. SE7 .... 2E 97

Elliscombe Rd. SE7 .... 2E 97
Ellis Ct. E1 .... 5E 65
.... (off James Voller Way)
Ellisfield Dr. SW15 .... 5C 98
Ellis Franklin Ct. NW8 .... 1E 59
.... (off Abbey Rd.)
Ellis Ho. SE17 .... 1F 91
.... (off Brandon St.)
Ellison Apts. E3 .... 2C 66
.... (off Merchant St.)
Ellison Ho. SE13 .... 5D 95
.... (off Lewisham Rd.)
Ellison Rd. SW13 .... 5B 84
Ellis St. SW1 .... 5C 74
Ellora Rd. SW16 .... 5F 117
Ellsworth St. E2 .... 2D 65
Ellwood Ct. W9 .... 3D 59
.... (off Clearwell Dr.)
Elm Bank Gdns.
SW13 .... 5A 84
Elmbourne Rd. SW17 .... 3D 117
Elmbridge Wlk. E8 .... 4C 50
Elm Cl. E11 .... 1D 41
Elm Cl. N19 .... 4E 33
Elm Cl. SE15 .... 5C 92
Elm Cl. EC4 .... 3B 16 (5C 62)
.... (off King's Bench Wlk.)
Elm Ct. SE1 .... 4D 27 (3A 78)
.... (off Royal Oak Yd.)
Elm Ct. SE13 .... 1F 109
Elm Ct. SW9 .... 4C 90
.... (off Cranworth Gdns.)
Elm Ct. W9 .... 4C 58
.... (off Admiral Wlk.)
Elmcourt Rd. SE27 .... 2D 119
Elmcroft N6 .... 2E 33
Elmcroft Av. NW11 .... 2B 30
Elmcroft Cres. NW11 .... 2A 30
Elmcroft St. E5 .... 1E 51
Elmer Ho. NW8 .... 4A 60
.... (off Penfold St.)
Elmer Rd. SE6 .... 5E 109
Elmfield Av. N8 .... 1A 34
Elmfield Ho. NW8 .... 1D 59
.... (off Carlton Hill)
Elmfield Ho. W9 .... 3C 58
.... (off Goldney Rd.)
Elmfield Rd. E17 .... 1F 37
Elmfield Rd. SW17 .... 2C 116
Elmfield Way W9 .... 4C 58
Elm Friars Wlk. NW1 .... 4F 47
Elm Grn. W3 .... 5A 56
Elmgreen Cl. E15 .... 5A 54
Elm Gro. N8 .... 1A 34
Elm Gro. NW2 .... 1F 43
Elm Gro. SE15 .... 5B 92
Elm Gro. Rd. SW13 .... 4C 84
Elm Hall Gdns. E11 .... 1D 41
.... (not continuous)
Elm Ho. E14 .... 3E 81
.... (off E. Ferry Rd.)
Elm Ho. E3 .... 5B 52
.... (off Sycamore Av.)
Elm Ho. W10 .... 3A 58
.... (off Briar Wlk.)
Elmhurst Mans. SW4 .... 1F 103
Elmhurst Rd. E7 .... 4D 55
Elmhurst Rd. SE9 .... 2F 125
Elmhurst St. SW4 .... 1F 103
Elmira St. SE13 .... 1D 109
Elm La. SE6 .... 2B 122
Elm Lodge SW6 .... 4E 85

Elmore Ho. N1 .... 4F 49
.... (off Elmore St.)
Elmore Ho. SW9 .... 5D 91
Elmore Rd. E11 .... 5E 39
Elmore St. N1 .... 4E 49
Elm Pk. SW2 .... 4B 104
Elm Pk. Av. N15 .... 1B 36
Elm Pk. Chambers SW10 .... 1F 87
.... (off Fulham Rd.)
Elm Pk. Gdns. NW4 .... 1F 29
Elm Pk. Gdns. SW10 .... 1F 87
Elm Pk. Ho. SW10 .... 1F 87
Elm Pk. La. SW3 .... 1F 87
Elm Pk. Mans. SW10 .... 2E 87
Elm Pk. Rd. E10 .... 3A 38
Elm Pk. Rd. SW3 .... 2F 87
Elm Pl. SW7 .... 1F 87
Elm Quay Ct. SW1 .... 2F 89
Elm Rd. E11 .... 4F 39
Elm Rd. E17 .... 1E 39
Elm Rd. E7 .... 3B 54
Elm Row NW3 .... 5E 31
Elms, The E12 .... 3F 55
Elms, The SW13 .... 1B 98
Elms Av. NW4 .... 1F 29
Elmscott Rd. BR1: Broml ... 5A 124
Elms Cres. SW4 .... 4E 103
Elmshaw Rd. SW15 .... 3C 98
Elmslie Point E3 .... 4B 66
.... (off Leopold St.)
Elms M. W2 .... 1F 73
Elms Rd. SW4 .... 3E 103
Elmstone Rd. SW6 .... 4C 86
Elm St. WC1 .... 4A 8 (3B 62)
Elm Ter. NW2 .... 5C 30
Elm Ter. NW3 .... 1A 46
Elmton Ct. NW8 .... 3F 59
.... (off Cunningham Pl.)
Elm Tree Cl. NW8 .... 2F 59
Elm Tree Ct. NW8 .... 2F 59
.... (off Elm Tree Rd.)
Elm Tree Ct. SE7 .... 2E 97
Elm Tree Rd. NW8 .... 2F 59
Elm Wlk. NW3 .... 4C 30
Elm Way NW10 .... 1A 42
Elmwood Ct. E10 .... 3C 38
.... (off Goldsmith Rd.)
Elmwood Ct. SW11 .... 4D 89
Elmwood Ho. NW10 .... 1D 57
.... (off All Souls Av.)
Elmwood Rd. SE24 .... 3F 105
Elmworth Gro. SE21 .... 2F 119
Elnathan M. W9 .... 3D 59
Elphinstone Ct. SW16 ...... 5A 118
Elphinstone St. N5 .... 1D 49
Erington Rd. E8 .... 3C 50
Elsa Cotts. E14 .... 4A 66
.... (off Halley St.)
Elsa St. E1 .... 4A 66
Elsdale St. E9 .... 3E 51
Elsden M. E2 .... 1E 65
Elsenham St. SW18 .... 1B 114
Elsham Rd. E11 .... 5A 40
Elsham Rd. W14 .... 3A 72
Elsham Ter. W14 .... 4A 72
.... (off Elsham Rd.)
Elsie La. Ct. W2 .... 4C 58
.... (off Westbourne Pk. Vs.)
Elsiemaud Rd. SE4 .... 3B 108
Elsie Rd. SE22 .... 2B 106
Elsinore Gdns. NW2 .... 5A 30
Elsinore Ho. N1 .... 5C 48
.... (off Denmark Gro.)
Elsinore Ho. SE5 .... 5E 91
.... (off Denmark Rd.)

Elsinore Ho. SE7............5F 83
Elsinore Ho. W6............1F 85
................(off Fulham Pal. Rd.)
Elsinore Rd. SE23............1A 122
Elsley Rd. SW11............1B 102
Elspeth Rd. SW11............2B 102
Elstead Ho. SW2............5B 104
................(off Redlands Way)
Elsted St. SE17............5F 77
Elstow Grange NW6............4F 43
Elswick Rd. SE13............5D 95
Elswick St. SW6............5E 87
Elsworthy Ct. NW3............4A 46
................(off Primrose Hill Rd.)
Elsworthy Ri. NW3............4A 46
Elsworthy Rd. NW3............5A 46
Elsworthy Ter. NW3............4A 46
Elsynge Rd. SW18............3F 101
Eltham Grn. SE9............3F 111
Eltham Grn. Rd. SE9............2E 111
Eltham Hill SE9............3F 111
Eltham Pal. Rd. SE9............4E 111
Eltham Rd. SE12............3B 110
Eltham Rd. SE9............3E 111
Elthiron Rd. SW6............4C 86
Elthorne Rd. N19............4F 33
Elthorne Way NW9............1A 28
Elthruda Rd. SE13............4F 109
Elton Ho. E3............5B 52
................(off Candy St.)
Elton Pl. N16............2A 50
Eltringham St. SW18............2E 101
Eluna Apts. E1............1D 79
................(off Wapping La.)
Elvaston M. SW7............4E 73
Elvaston Pl. SW7............4E 73
Elven M. SE15............4E 93
Elver Gdns. E2............2C 64
Elverson Rd. SE8............5D 95
Elverson Road Station (DLR)
............5D 95
Elverton St. SW1............5F 75
Elvino Rd. SE26............5A 122
Elvis Rd. NW2............3E 43
Elwin St. E2............2C 64
Elwood St. N5............5D 35
Elworth Ho. SW8............3B 90
................(off Oval Pl.)
Elwyn Gdns. SE12............5C 110
Ely Ct. EC1............1C 16 (4C 62)
................(off Ely Pl.)
Ely Ho. SE15............3C 92
................(off Friary Est.)
Elyne Rd. N4............1C 34
Ely Pl. EC1............1C 16 (4C 62)
Ely Rd. E10............1E 39
Elysian M. N7............3B 48
Elysium Apts. E1............3E 65
................(off Theven St.)
Elysium Pl. SW6............5B 86
................(off Elysium St.)
Elysium St. SW6............5B 86
Elystan Pl. SW3............5A 74
................(off Elystan St.)
Elystan Pl. SW3............1A 88
Elystan St. SW3............5A 74
Elystan Wlk. N1............5C 48
Ely's Yd. E1............5F 11 (4B 64)
Emanuel Ho. SW1............5B 22 (4F 75)
Embankment SW15............5F 85
Embankment Galleries
............4A 16 (1B 76)
................(within Somerset House)
Embankment Gdns. SW3............2B 88

Embankment Pier
WC2............1E 23 (2A 76)
Embankment Pier (River Bus
& Tours)............1E 23 (2A 76)
Embankment Pl.
WC2............1E 23 (2A 76)
Embankment Station
(Underground)............1E 23 (2A 76)
Embassy Apts. SE5............5E 91
................(off Coldharbour La.)
Embassy Ct. E2............3D 65
................(off Brady St.)
Embassy Ct. NW8............1F 59
................(off Wellington Rd.)
Embassy Ho. NW6............4D 45
Embassy of United States of
America............2F 89
Embassy Theatre Central School
of Speech & Drama............4F 45
Embassy Way SW11............2F 89
Emba St. SE16............3C 78
Emberton SE5............2A 92
................(off Albany Rd.)
Emberton Ct. EC1............2D 9 (2D 63)
................(off Tompion St.)
Embleton Rd. SE13............2D 109
Embry Rd. SE9............2E 111
Emden St. SW6............4D 87
Emerald Cl. E16............5F 69
Emerald Rd. NW10............5A 42
Emerald Sq. SW15............3C 98
Emerald St. WC1............5F 7 (4B 62)
Emerson St. SE1............1F 25 (2E 77)
Emery Hill St. SW1............5F 75
Emery St. SE1............5C 24 (4C 76)
Emery Walker Trust............1C 84
................(off Hammersmith Ter.)
Emily Ct. SE1............4F 25 (3E 77)
................(off Sudrey St.)
Emily Duncan Pl. E7............1D 55
Emily Ho. W10............3A 58
................(off Kensal Rd.)
Emily St. E16............5B 68
................(off Jude St.)
Emirates Air Line............3B 82
Emirates Greenwich Peninsula
............3B 82
Emirates Royal Docks............1C 82
Emlyn Gdns. W12............3A 70
Emlyn Rd. W12............3A 70
Emmanuel Ct. E10............2D 39
Emmanuel Rd. SE11............5C 76
Emmanuel Rd. SW12............1E 117
Emma Rd. E13............1B 68
Emma St. E2............1D 65
Emminster NW6............5D 45
................(off Abbey Rd.)
Emmott Cl. E1............3A 66
Emmott Cl. NW11............1E 31
Emperor Ho. E20............2E 53
................(off Napa Cl.)
Emperor Ho. SE4............1A 108
................(off Dragonfly Pl.)
Emperor's Ga. SW7............4E 73
Emperor Way NW9............1B 28
Empingham Ho. SE8............5F 79
................(off Chilton Gro.)
Empire Cinema Haymarket
............5B 14 (1F 75)
................(off Haymarket)
Empire Cl. SE7............2D 97
Empire Ho. SW7............4A 74
................(off Thurloe Pl.)
Empire M. SW16............5A 118

Empire Reach SE10............2D 95
................(off Dowells St.)
Empire Sq. N7............5A 34
Empire Sq. SE1............4B 26 (3F 77)
................(off Tabard St.)
Empire Sq. E. SE1............4B 26 (3F 77)
................(off Long La.)
Empire Sq. Sth. SE1............4B 26 (3F 77)
................(off Sterry St.)
Empire Sq. W. SE1............4B 26 (3F 77)
................(off Tabard St.)
Empire Wharf E3............5A 52
................(off Old Ford Rd.)
Empire Wharf Rd. E14............5F 81
Empress App. SW6............1C 86
Empress Av. E12............4E 41
Empress M. SE5............5E 91
Empress Pl. SW6............1C 86
Empress State Bldg. SW6............1C 86
Empress St. SE17............2E 91
Empson St. E3............3D 67
Emslie Horniman Pleasance
............3A 58
................(off Bosworth Road)
Emsworth Ct. SW16............3A 118
Emsworth St. SW2............2B 118
Emu Rd. SW8............5D 89
Enard Ho. E3............1B 66
................(off Cardigan Rd.)
Enbrook St. W10............2A 58
Enclave, The SW13............5B 84
Enclave Ct. EC1............3E 9 (3D 63)
................(off Dallington St.)
Endeavour Ho. E14............3C 80
................(off Cuba St.)
Endeavour Ho. SE16............5A 80
................(off Ashton Reach)
Endeavour Sq. E20............4E 53
Endeavour Way SW19............4D 115
Endell St. WC2............2D 15 (5A 62)
Enderby St. SE10............1F 95
Endlesham Rd. SW12............5C 102
Endsleigh Ct. WC1............3C 6 (3F 61)
................(off Endsleigh St.)
Endsleigh Gdns. WC1............3B 6 (3F 61)
Endsleigh Pl. WC1............3C 6 (3F 61)
Endsleigh St. WC1............3B 6 (3F 61)
Endwell Rd. SE4............5A 94
Endymion Rd. N4............2C 34
Endymion Rd. SW2............4B 104
Energen Cl. NW10............3A 42
énergie Fitness Old Street
............3B 10 (3F 63)
Energy Cen., The
N1............1D 11 (2A 64)
Enfield Cloisters N1............1D 11 (2A 64)
................(off Fanshaw St.)
Enfield Ho. SW9............5A 90
................(off Stockwell Rd.)
Enfield Rd. N1............4A 50
Enford St. W1............4B 60
Engadine St. SW18............1B 114
Engate St. SE13............2E 109
Engine Ct. SW1............2A 22 (2E 75)
................(off Ambassador's Ct.)
England's La. NW3............3B 46
Englefield NW1............2F 5 (2E 61)
................(off Clarence Gdns.)
Englefield Rd. N1............4F 49
Engleheart Rd. SE6............5D 109
Englewood Rd. SW12............4D 103
English Grounds
SE1............2D 27 (2A 78)
English St. E3............3B 66

Enid St. SE16 ....5F **27** (4B **78**)
Enmore Gdns. SW14 ....3A **98**
Enmore Rd. SW15 ....2E **99**
Ennerdale NW1 ....1F **5** (2E **61**)
...............................*(off Varndell St.)*
Ennerdale Ct. E11 ....2C **40**
...............................*(off Cambridge Rd.)*
Ennerdale Dr. NW9 ....1A **28**
Ennerdale Ho. E3 ....3B **66**
Ennersdale Rd. SE13 ....3F **109**
Ennis Ho. E14 ....5D **67**
...............................*(off Vesey Path)*
Ennismore Av. W4 ....5B **70**
Ennismore Gdns. SW7 ....3A **74**
Ennismore Gdns. M. SW7 ......4A **74**
Ennismore Gdns. SW7 ....4A **74**
Ennismore St. SW7 ....4A **74**
Ennis Rd. N4 ....3C **34**
Ensbury Ho. SW8 ....3B **90**
...............................*(off Carroun Rd.)*
Ensham Ho. SW17 ....5B **116**
Ensign Ho. E14 ....3C **80**
...............................*(off Admirals Way)*
Ensign Ho. SW18 ....1E **101**
Ensign St. E1 ....1C **78**
Ensign St. SE3 ....2D **111**
Ensor M. SW7 ....1F **87**
Enterprise Bus. Pk. E14........3D **81**
Enterprise Cen., The
  BR3: Beck.........................5A **122**
...............................*(off Cricket La.)*
Enterprise Ho. E14 ....1D **95**
...............................*(off St Davids Sq.)*
Enterprise Ho. E9...................4E **51**
...............................*(off Tudor Gro.)*
Enterprise Ind. Est. SE16......1E **93**
Enterprise Row N15................1B **36**
Enterprise Way NW10.............2B **56**
Enterprise Way SW18.............2C **100**
Enterprize Way SE8 ....5B **80**
Entertainment Av. SE10..........2A **82**
Epcot M. NW10 ....2F **57**
Epirus M. SW6.......................3C **86**
Epirus Rd. SW6 ....3B **86**
Epping Cl. E14.......................5C **80**
Epping Pl. N1 ....3C **48**
Epple Rd. SW6.......................4B **86**
Epsom Rd. E10 ....1E **39**
Epstein Ct. N1 ....5D **49**
...............................*(off Gaskin St.)*
Epstein Sq. E14......................5C **66**
...............................*(off Upper Nth. St.)*
Epworth St.
  EC2...........................4C **10** (3F **63**)
Equana Apts. SE8 ....1A **94**
...............................*(off Evelyn St.)*
Equiano Ho. SW9....................4B **90**
...............................*(off Lett Rd.)*
Equinox Sq. E14.....................5D **67**
Equity Sq. E2..........................2F **64**
...............................*(off Shacklewell St.)*
Erasmus St. SW1 ....5F **75**
Erconwald St. W12 ....5B **56**
Eresby Ho. SW7.....................3A **74**
...............................*(off Rutland Ga.)*
Eresby Pl. NW6......................4C **44**
Erica Ho. SE4 ....1B **108**
Erica St. W12 ....1C **70**
Eric Cl. E7 ....1C **54**
Ericcson Cl. SW18................3C **100**
Eric Fletcher Ct. N1................4E **49**
...............................*(off Essex Rd.)*
Eric Rd. E7 ....1C **54**
Eric Rd. NW10 ....3B **42**

Eric Shipman Ter. E13............3C **68**
...............................*(off Balaam St.)*
Ericson Ho. SE13..................2F **109**
...............................*(off Blessington Rd.)*
Eric St. E3 ....3B **66**
...............................*(not continuous)*
Eric Wilkins Ho. SE1 ....1C **92**
...............................*(off Old Kent Rd.)*
Eridge Rd. W4 ....4A **70**
Erin Cl. SW6 ....3C **86**
Erin Ct. NW2 ....3E **43**
Erin's Vs. SE14......................4F **93**
...............................*(off New Cross Rd.)*
Erlanger Rd. SE14 ....4F **93**
Erlich Cotts. E1 ....4E **65**
...............................*(off Sidney St.)*
Ermine Ho. E3 ....5D **52**
...............................*(off Parnell Rd.)*
Ermine M. E2..........................5B **50**
Ermine Rd. N15.......................1B **36**
Ermine Rd. SE13 ....2D **109**
Ernest Av. SE27.....................4D **119**
Ernest Harriss Ho. W9 ....3C **58**
...............................*(off Elgin Av.)*
Ernest Shackleton Lodge
  SE10.................................5A **82**
...............................*(off Christchurch Way)*
Ernest St. E1 ....3F **65**
Ernshaw Pl. SW15..................3A **100**
Ernst Bldg. SE1 ....2E **25** (2E **77**)
...............................*(off Union St.)*
Eros 5B **14** (1F **75**)
Eros Ho. Shops SE6 ....5D **109**
...............................*(off Brownhill Rd.)*
Erpingham Rd. SW15..............1E **99**
Errington Rd. W9 ....3B **58**
Errol St. EC1 ....4A **10** (3E **63**)
Erskine Ho. SW1 ....1E **89**
...............................*(off Churchill Gdns.)*
Erskine M. NW3 ....4B **46**
...............................*(off Erskine Rd.)*
Erskine Rd. NW3 ....4B **46**
Esam Way SW16 ....5C **118**
Esher Gdns. SW19 ....2F **113**
Eskdale NW1 ....1F **5** (1E **61**)
...............................*(off Stanhope St.)*
Esker Pl. E2...........................1D **65**
Esk Ho. E3 ....3B **66**
Esk Rd. E13 ....3C **68**
Esmar Cres. NW9 ....2C **28**
Esmeralda Rd. SE1 ....5C **78**
Esmond Ct. W8.......................4D **73**
...............................*(off Thackeray St.)*
Esmond Gdns. W4..................5A **70**
Esmond Rd. NW6 ....5B **44**
Esmond Rd. W4 ....5A **70**
Esmond St. SW15 ....2A **100**
Esparto St. SW18 ....5D **101**
Esprit Ct. E1 ....1F **19** (4B **64**)
...............................*(off Brune St.)*
Essence E3 ....1B **66**
...............................*(off Cardigan Rd.)*
Essendine Mans. W9 ....2C **58**
Essendine Rd. W9 ....2C **58**
Essex Ct. EC4 ....3B **16** (5C **62**)
...............................*(off Brick Ct.)*
Essex Ct. SW13 ....5B **84**
Essex Ct. W6 ....4E **71**
...............................*(off Hammersmith Gro.)*
Essex Gdns. N4 ....1D **35**
Essex Gro. SE19 ....5F **119**
Essex Ho. E14 ....5D **67**
...............................*(off Giraud St.)*
Essex Mans. E11....................2F **39**

Essex Pk. M. W3 ....2A **70**
Essex Rd. E10 ....1E **39**
Essex Rd. E17 ....1A **38**
Essex Rd. N1 ....5D **49**
Essex Rd. NW10....................4A **42**
Essex Rd. Sth. E11.................2F **39**
Essex Road Station (Rail)......4E **49**
Essex St. E7 ....2C **54**
Essex St. WC2 ....3B **16** (5C **62**)
Essex Vs. W8.........................3C **72**
Essex Wharf E5......................4F **37**
Essian St. E1 ....4A **66**
Estate Way E10 ....3B **38**
Estcourt Rd. SW6 ....3B **86**
Estella Apts. E15....................3F **53**
...............................*(off Grove Cres. Rd.)*
Estella Ho. W11......................1F **71**
...............................*(off St Ann's Rd.)*
Estelle Rd. NW3 ....1B **46**
Esterbrooke St. SW1 ....5F **75**
Este Rd. SW11.......................1A **102**
Esther Anne Pl. N1 ....5D **49**
Esther Randall Ct.
  NW1...........................3E **5** (3D **61**)
...............................*(off Lit. Albany St.)*
Esther Rd. E11 ....2A **40**
Estoria Cl. SW2 ....5C **104**
Estorick Collection of Modern
  Italian Art..........................3D **49**
Estreham Rd. SW16................5F **117**
Estuary Ho. E16.....................2F **83**
...............................*(off Agnes George Wlk.)*
Eswyn Rd. SW17....................4B **116**
Etal Ho. N1 ....4D **49**
...............................*(off The Sutton Est.)*
Etcetera Theatre 4D **47**
...............................*(off Camden High St.)*
Etchingham Rd. E15...............1E **53**
Eternit Wlk. SW6....................4E **85**
Ethelbert Ho. E9.....................1A **52**
...............................*(off Homerton Rd.)*
Ethelbert St. SW12................1D **117**
Ethelburga St. SW11..............4A **88**
Ethelburga Twr. SW11............4A **88**
...............................*(off Rosenau Rd.)*
Ethelden Rd. W12 ....2D **71**
Ethel Rd. E16.........................5D **69**
Ethel St. SE17 ....5E **77**
Etheridge Rd. NW4.................2E **29**
...............................*(not continuous)*
Etherow St. SE22 ....5C **106**
Etherstone Grn. SW16...........4C **118**
Etherstone Rd. SW16.............4C **118**
Ethnard Rd. SE15...................2D **93**
Ethos Sport Imperial..............3F **73**
Etloe Ho. E10 ....3C **38**
Etloe Rd. E10..........................4C **38**
Eton Av. NW3 ....4F **45**
Eton Cl. SW18........................5D **101**
Eton Coll. Rd. NW3.................3B **46**
Eton Ct. NW3 ....4F **45**
Eton Garages NW3 ....3A **46**
Eton Gro. SE13......................1A **110**
Eton Hall NW3 ....3B **46**
Eton Ho. N5...........................1D **49**
...............................*(off Leigh Rd.)*
ETON MANOR 1D **53**
Eton Mnr. Ct. E10...................4C **38**
...............................*(off Leyton Grange Est.)*
Eton M. N1 ....4B **48**
Eton Pl. NW3 ....4C **46**
Eton Ri. NW3 ....3B **46**
Eton Rd. NW3 ....4B **46**
Eton Vs. NW3.........................3B **46**
Etta St. SE8 ....2A **94**

Ettrick St. E14...............5E 67
.................(not continuous)
Eucalyptus M. SW16........5F 117
Eugene Cotter Ho. SE17.....5F 77
.......................(off Tatum St.)
Eugenia Rd. SE16............5E 79
Euro Cl. NW10................3C 42
Eurolink Bus. Cen. SW2....2C 104
Europa Pl. EC1.........2F 9 (2E 63)
Europa Trade Pk. E16........3A 68
Eustace Bldg. SW11..........2D 89
Eustace Ho. SE11............5B 76
..............(off Old Paradise St.)
Eustace Rd. SW6.............3C 86
Euston Cir. NW1......3A 6 (3E 61)
Euston Gro. NW1.......2B 6 (2F 61)
..........................(off Euston Sq.)
Euston Rd. N1.........1D 7 (2A 62)
Euston Rd. NW1.......2B 6 (3D 61)
Euston Sq. NW1.......2B 6 (2F 61)
..........................(not continuous)
Euston Square Station
(Underground).........3A 6 (3E 61)
Euston Sta. Colonnade
NW1....................2B 6 (2F 61)
Euston Station (Rail, Underground
& Overground).........2A 6 (2F 61)
Euston St. NW1.......2A 6 (2E 61)
Euston Twr. NW1......3F 5 (3E 61)
EUSTON UNDERPASS....3A 6 (3E 61)
Evan Cook Cl. SE15..........4E 93
Evandale Rd. SW9............5C 90
Evangelist Ho. EC4...3D 17 (5D 63)
..................(off Black Friars La.)
Evangelist Rd. NW5..........1D 47
Evan Ho. E16.................4C 68
....................(off Exeter Rd.)
Evans Apts. E2...............2F 65
Evans Cl. E8..................3B 50
Evans Ho. SW8...............3F 89
.................(off Wandsworth Rd.)
Evans Ho. W12...............1D 71
.....................(off White City Est.)
Evans Rd. SE6...............2A 124
Evanston Gdns. IG4: Ilf......1F 41
Evedon Ho. N1...............5A 50
.......................(off Halcomb St.)
EVELINA CHILDREN'S HOSPITAL
.....................5F 23 (4B 76)
...........(within St Thomas' Hospital)
Evelina Ct. W6...............4D 71
.......................(off Vinery Way)
Evelina Mans. SE5...........3F 91
Evelina Rd. SE15...........1E 107
Eveline Lowe Est. SE16.....4C 78
Evelyn Ct. E3.................4B 66
.......................(off Burdett Rd.)
Evelyn Ct. E8.................1C 50
Evelyn Ct. N1.........1B 10 (1F 63)
.......................(off Evelyn Wlk.)
Evelyn Denington Ct. N1.....4D 48
.......................(off The Sutton Est.)
Evelyn Fox Ct. W10..........4E 57
Evelyn Gdns. SW7...........1E 87
Evelyn Ho. SE14.............4A 94
.......................(off Loring Rd.)
Evelyn Ho. W12..............3B 70
.......................(off Cobbold Rd.)
Evelyn Ho. W8................3D 73
.......................(off Hornton Pl.)
Evelyn Mans. SW1...5F 21 (4E 75)
.......................(off Carlisle Pl.)
Evelyn Mans. W14............2A 86
.......................(off Queen's Club Gdns.)
Evelyn Rd. E16...............2C 82

Evelyn Rd. SW19...........5D 115
Evelyn St. SE8...............5A 80
Evelyn Wlk. N1......1B 10 (1F 63)
Everatt Cl. SW18............2B 14 (5F 61)
Eve Martin Ct. EC1....2E 9 (2D 63)
.......................(off Goswell Road)
Evenwood Cl. SW15.........3A 100
Everard Ho. E1...............5C 64
.......................(off Boyd St.)
Everatt Cl. SW18.............4B 100
Everdon Rd. SW13............2C 84
Everest Pl. E14...............4E 67
Everett Ho. SE17.............1F 91
.......................(off East St.)
Evergreen Sq. E8.............4B 50
Everilda St. N1...............5B 48
Evering Rd. E5................5C 36
Evering Rd. N16..............5B 36
Everington St. W6.............2F 85
Everitt Rd. NW10.............2A 56
Everleigh St. N4...............3B 34
Eve Rd. E11...................1A 54
Eve Rd. E15...................1A 68
Evershed Ho. E1......2F 19 (5B 64)
.......................(off Old Castle St.)
Eversholt St. NW1.....1A 6 (1E 61)
Evershot Rd. N4...............3B 34
Eversleigh Rd. E6.............5F 55
Eversleigh Rd. SW11.........1B 102
Eversley Ho. E2...............2C 64
.......................(off Gosset St.)
Eversley Pk. SW19..........5D 113
Eversley Rd. SE7.............2D 97
Everthorpe Rd. SE15.........1B 106
Everton M. NW1.......2F 5 (2E 61)
Everyman Cinema Baker St.
.....................5A 4 (4B 60)
.......................(off Baker St.)
Everyman Cinema Belsize Pk.
.....................2A 46
Everyman Cinema King's Cross
.....................5A 48
Everyman on the Corner Cinema
.....................5F 47
Everyman Screen on the Green
Cinema..................5D 49
.......................(off Upper St.)
Evesham Ho. E2..............1E 65
.......................(off Old Ford Rd.)
Evesham Ho. NW8...........5E 45
.......................(off Abbey Rd.)
Evesham Ho. SW1............1D 89
.......................(part of Abbots Mnr.)
Evesham Rd. E15.............4B 54
Evesham St. W11.............1F 71
Evesham Wlk. SE5............5F 91
Evesham Wlk. SW9...........5C 90
Evesham Way SW11.........1C 102
Ewald Rd. SW6...............5B 86
Ewart Pl. E3...................1B 66
Ewart Rd. SE23..............5F 107
Ewe Cl. N7...................3A 48
Ewehurst Rd. SE23...........1E 121
Ewen Cres. SW2.............5C 104
Ewen Henderson St. SE14...3A 94
.......................(off Goodwood Rd.)
Ewen Ho. N1.................5B 48
.......................(off Barnsbury Est.)
Ewer St. SE1........2F 25 (2E 77)
Ewhurst Cl. E1................4E 65
Ewhurst Rd. SE4.............4B 108
Exbury Ho. E9................4E 51
Exbury Ho. N1................1F 89
.......................(off Rampayne St.)
Exbury Rd. SE6..............2C 122

Excalibur Dr. SE6............2A 124
Excel Ct. WC2.........5C 14 (1F 75)
.......................(off Whitcomb St.)
Excel Marina E16.............1C 82
Excelsior Gdns. SE13.........5E 95
Excelsior Ind. Est. SE15......2E 93
Excel Waterfront E16..........1D 83
Exchange Arc.
.....................EC2.......5E 11 (4A 64)
Exchange Bldg. E1....4F 11 (3B 64)
.......................(off Commercial St.)
Exchange Ct. WC2....5E 15 (1A 76)
Exchange Gdns. SW8.........2A 90
Exchange Ho. E17.............1D 39
Exchange Ho. EC2....5E 11 (4A 64)
.......................(off Exchange Sq.)
Exchange Ho. NW10..........4D 43
Exchange Ho. SW1............5F 75
.......................(off Vauxhall Bri. Rd.)
Exchange Mans. NW11.......2B 30
Exchange Pl. EC2.....5D 11 (4A 64)
Exchange Sq. EC2....5D 11 (4A 64)
Exchange St. EC1.......2F 9 (2E 63)
Exeter Ct. NW6...............1C 58
.......................(off Cambridge Rd.)
Exeter Ho. E14...............4F 67
.......................(off St Ives Pl.)
Exeter Ho. N1................5A 50
.......................(off New Era Est.)
Exeter Ho. SE15..............2C 92
.......................(off Friary Est.)
Exeter Ho. SW15.............4E 99
Exeter Ho. W2................5E 59
.......................(off Hallfield Est.)
Exeter Mans. NW2............3A 44
Exeter M. NW6................3D 45
Exeter M. SW6................3C 86
Exeter Pl. SE26..............3C 120
Exeter Rd. E16...............4C 68
Exeter Rd. NW2..............2A 44
Exeter St. WC2.......4E 15 (1A 76)
Exeter Way SE14.............3B 94
Exford Ct. SW11..............4F 87
.......................(off Bolingbroke Wlk.)
Exford Gdns. SE12..........1D 125
Exford Rd. SE12.............2D 125
Exhibition Cl. W12.............1E 71
Exhibition Rd. SW7............3F 73
Exmoor Ho. E3................1A 66
.......................(off Gernon Rd.)
Exmoor St. W10..............3F 57
Exmouth Ho. E14.............5D 81
Exmouth Mkt. EC1...3B 8 (3C 62)
.......................(off Pine St.)
Exmouth M. NW1.....2A 6 (2E 61)
Exmouth Pl. E8...............4D 51
Exmouth Rd. E17.............1B 38
Exmouth St. E1...............5E 65
Exning Rd. E16...............3B 68
Exonbury NW8...............5D 45
.......................(off Abbey Rd.)
Exon St. SE17................1A 92
Explorers Ct. E14.............1F 81
.......................(off Newport Av.)
Export Ho. SE1.......4E 27 (3A 78)
.......................(off Tower Bri. Rd.)
Express Ho. SE8..............2A 94
.......................(off Rolt St.)
Express Newspapers
SE1...................1D 25 (2D 77)
.......................(off Blackfriars Rd.)
Express Wharf E14............3C 80
.......................(off Hutchings St.)

Exton St. SE1.................2B **24** (2C **76**)
Eyhurst Cl. NW2......................4C **28**
Eylewood Rd. SE27..............5E **119**
Eynella Rd. SE22................5B **106**
Eynham Rd. W12.....................5E **57**
Eynsford Ho. SE1....4B **26** (3F **77**)
...................................(off Crosby Row)
Eynsford Ho. SE15.................2E **93**
Eynsford Ho. SE17................5A **78**
.....................................(off East St.)
Eyot Gdns. W6.......................1B **84**
Eyot Grn. W4........................1B **84**
Eyot Ho. SE16.......................4C **78**
.....................................(off Frean St.)
Eyre Ct. NW8........................1F **59**
Eyre Rd. NW8........................2E **59**
Eyre St. Hill EC1....4B **8** (3C **62**)
Eythorne Rd. SW9...................4C **90**
Ezra St. E2.........................2B **64**

F

Faber Gdns. NW4....................1C **28**
Fabian Bell Twr. E1..................
...................................(off Pancras Way)
Fabian Rd. SW6.....................3B **86**
Fable Apts. N1 (2E **63**)
Facade, The SE23..................2E **121**
Factory Rd. E16....................2F **83**
Fairacres SW15.....................2B **98**
Fairbairn Grn. SW9.................4D **91**
Fairbank Est. N1...1B **10** (1F **63**)
Fairbourne Rd. SW4................4F **103**
Fairbriar Residence SW7...5E **73**
...............................(off Stanhope Gdns.)
Fairbridge Rd. N19.................4F **33**
Fairburn Ct. SW15.................3A **100**
Fairburn Ho. W14...................1B **86**
....................................(off Ivatt Pl.)
Fairby Ho. SE1.....................5B **78**
................................(off Longfield Est.)
Fairby Rd. SE12....................3D **111**
Fairchild Cl. SW11.................5F **87**
Fairchild Ho. E2...................1D **65**
..............................(off Cambridge Cres.)
Fairchild Ho. E9...................4E **51**
...........................(off Frampton Pk. Rd.)
Fairchild Ho. N1...1D **11** (2A **64**)
..................................(off Fanshaw St.)
Fairchild Pl. EC2....4E **11** (3A **64**)
..............................(off Gt. Eastern St.)
Fairchild St. EC2....3E **11** (3A **64**)
Fairclough St. E1..................5C **64**
Fairdale Gdns. SW15...............2D **99**
Fairfax Ct. NW6....................4E **45**
.................................(off Fairfax Rd.)
Fairfax Mans. NW6..................4E **45**
.................................(off Finchley Rd.)
Fairfax M. E16.....................2D **83**
Fairfax M. SW15....................2E **99**
Fairfax Pl. NW6....................4E **45**
Fairfax Pl. W14....................4A **72**
Fairfax Rd. NW6....................4E **45**
Fairfax Rd. W4.....................4A **70**
Fairfield E1........................4E **65**
..............................(off Redman's Rd.)
Fairfield NW1......................5E **47**
..............................(off Arlington Rd.)
Fairfield Av. NW4..................1D **29**
Fairfield Cl. NW10.................5C **42**
Fairfield Dr. SW18.................3D **101**
Fairfield Gdns. N8.................1A **34**
Fairfield Gro. SE3.................2F **97**
Fairfield Rd. E3...................1C **66**

Fairfield Rd. N8...................1A **34**
Fairfield Rd. SW18................3D **101**
Fairfoot Rd. E3....................3C **66**
Fairford SE6.......................1C **122**
Fairford Ho. SE11.................5C **76**
Fairhazel Gdns. NW6...............3D **45**
Fairhazel Mans. NW6...............4E **45**
............................(off Fairhazel Gdns.)
Fairholme Rd. W14..................1A **86**
Fairholt Cl. N16...................3A **36**
Fairholt Rd. N16...................3F **35**
Fairholt St. SW7...................4A **74**
Fairland Rd. E15...................3B **54**
Fairlawn SE7.......................3E **97**
Fairlawn Ct. SE7...................3E **97**
.................................(not continuous)
Fairlawn Mans. SE14...............4F **93**
Fairlawn Pk. SE26.................5A **122**
Fairlead Ho. E14...................4C **80**
..................................(off Alpha Gro.)
Fairlie Ct. E3.....................2D **67**
..............................(off Stroudley Wlk.)
Fairlie Gdns. SE23................5E **107**
Fairlight Av. NW10.................1A **56**
Fairlight Ct. NW10.................1A **56**
Fairlight Rd. SW17...............4F **115**
Fairlop Ct. E11....................3F **39**
Fairlop Rd. E11....................2F **39**
Fairmead Gdns. IG4: Ilf...........1F **41**
Fairmead Ho. E9....................1A **52**
Fairmead Rd. N19...................5F **33**
Fairmile Av. SW16................5F **117**
Fairmont Av. E14...................2F **81**
Fairmont Ho. E3....................3C **66**
..............................(off Wellington Way)
Fairmont Ho. SE8...................3F **79**
.............................(off Needleman St.)
Fairmont M. NW2....................4C **30**
Fairmount Rd. SW2................4B **104**
Fairstead Wlk. N1..................5E **49**
...............................(off Popham St.)
Fair St. SE1........3E **27** (3A **78**)
Fairthorne Vs. SE7.................1C **96**
.................................(off Felltram Way)
Fairthorn Rd. SE7..................1C **96**
Fairview Cl. SE26.................5A **122**
Fairview Ho. SW2.................5B **104**
Fairview Pl. SW2.................5B **104**
Fairview Rd. N15...................1B **36**
Fairwall Ho. SE5...................4A **92**
Fairwater Ho. E16.................3D **83**
................................(off Bonnet St.)
Fairway, The W3....................5A **56**
Fairway Cl. NW11...................2E **31**
Fairway Ct. E3.....................2D **67**
................................(off Culvert Dr.)
Fairway St. SE16...................3F **79**
..............................(off Christopher Cl.)
Fairways Bus. Pk. E10.............4A **38**
Fairweather Ho. N7................1A **48**
Fairweather Rd. N16...............1C **36**
Fairwyn Rd. SE26.................4A **122**
Faith Ct. E3.......................1C **66**
...............................(off Lefevre Wlk.)
Faith Ct. SE1......................1B **92**
..............................(off Cooper's Rd.)
Faith M. E12.......................1F **55**
Fakruddin St. E1...................3C **64**
Falcon WC1.........................5E **7** (4A **62**)
Falconberg M. W1...2B **14** (5F **61**)
Falcon Ct. EC4....3B **16** (5C **62**)
Falcon Ct. N1......1E **9** (1D **63**)
...............................(off City Gdn. Row)
Falconer Wlk. N7...................4B **34**

Falconet Ct. E1....................2D **79**
...........................(off Wapping High St.)
Falcon Gro. SW11.................1A **102**
Falcon Highwalk
EC2.......................1F **17** (4E **63**)
...........................(off Aldersgate St.)
Falcon Ho. E14.....................1D **95**
..............................(off St Davids Sq.)
Falcon Ho. NW6....................5D **45**
...........................(off Springfield Wlk.)
Falcon Ho. SW5....................1D **87**
..........................(off Old Brompton Rd.)
Falcon La. SW11..................1A **102**
Falcon Lodge W9....................4C **58**
................................(off Admiral Wlk.)
Falcon Pk. Community Sports
Cen..............................5B **88**
Falcon Pk. Ind. Est.
NW10..............................1A **42**
Falcon Point SE1....5E **17** (1D **77**)
Falcon St. E13.....................5A **88**
Falcon St. E13.....................3C **68**
Falcon Ter. SW11.................1A **102**
Falcon Way E14.....................5D **81**
Falcon Wharf SW11.................5F **87**
Falconwood Ct. SE3................5B **96**
..............................(off Montpelier Row)
Falkirk Ct. SE16...................2E **79**
...........................(off Rotherhithe St.)
Falkirk Ho. W9.....................1D **59**
Falkirk St. N1.....1E **11** (1A **64**)
..................................(off Maida Vale)
Falkland Ho. SE6.................4E **123**
Falkland Ho. W14...................1B **86**
................................(off Edith Vs.)
Falkland Ho. W8....................4D **73**
Falkland Pl. NW5...................2E **47**
Falkland Rd. NW5...................2E **47**
Fallodon Ho. W11...................4B **58**
.............................(off Tavistock Cres.)
Fallow Ct. SE16....................1C **92**
..................................(off Argyle Way)
Falmouth Cl. SE12................3B **110**
Falmouth Ho. SE11..................1C **90**
................................(off Seaton Cl.)
Falmouth Ho. W2....................1F **73**
..............................(off Clarendon Pl.)
Falmouth Rd. SE1...................4E **77**
Falmouth St. E15...................2F **53**
Falmouth Wlk. SW15...............4C **98**
Falmouth Way E17...................1B **38**
Falstaff Bldg. E1..................1D **79**
................................(off Cannon St. Rd.)
Falstaff Ct. SE11..................5D **77**
.................................(off Opal St.)
Falstaff Ho. N1...1D **11** (1A **64**)
................................(off Regan Way)
Fambridge Cl. SE26...............4B **122**
Family Court East London.....2C **80**
Fane St. W14.......................2B **86**
Fan Mus., The......................3E **95**
Fann St. EC1......4F **9** (3E **63**)
Fann St. EC2......4F **9** (3E **63**)
.................................(not continuous)
Fanshaw St. N1....1D **11** (2A **64**)
Fanthorpe St. SW15................1E **99**
Faraday Cl. N7.....................3B **48**
Faraday Ho. E14....................1B **80**
.............................(off Brightlingsea Pl.)
Faraday Ho. SE1....4B **26** (3F **77**)
................................(off Cole St.)
Faraday Ho. SW11...................2D **89**
Faraday Lodge SE10...............4B **82**
Faraday Mans. W14.................2A **86**
...........................(off Queen's Club Gdns.)

Faraday Mus., The 5F 13 (1E 75)
Faraday Rd. E15.......................3B 54
Faraday Rd. SW19................5C 114
Faraday Rd. W10.....................4A 58
Faraday Way SE18................4F 83
Faringford Rd. E15................4A 54
Farjeon Ho. NW6......................4F 45
..............................(off Hilgrove Rd.)
Farjeon Rd. SE3........................4F 97
Farleigh Ho. N1.........................4D 49
..................................(off Halton Rd.)
Farleigh Pl. N16.......................1B 50
Farleigh Rd. N16.....................1B 50
Farley Ct. NW1...............4A 4 (3B 60)
.....................................(off Allsop Pl.)
Farley Ct. W14.........................4B 72
Farley Ho. SE26......................3D 121
Farley M. SE6............................5E 109
Farley Rd. SE6.........................5D 109
Farlington Pl. SW15.............5D 99
Farlow Rd. SW15.....................1F 99
Farlton Rd. SW18................1D 115
Farm Av. NW2...........................5A 30
Farm Av. SW16......................4A 118
Farm Cl. SW6...........................3C 86
Farmcote Rd. SE12.............1C 124
Farmdale Rd. SE10................1C 96
Farmer Rd. E10.......................3D 39
Farmer's Rd. SE5...................3D 91
Farmer St. W8.........................2C 72
Farmfield Rd. BR1: Broml..5A 124
Farmilo Rd. E17......................2B 38
Farm La. SW6............................2C 86
Farm Pl. W8..............................2C 72
Farm Rd. NW10.......................5A 42
Farmstead Rd. SE6..............4D 123
Farm St. W1...............5D 13 (1D 75)
Farm Wlk. NW11.....................1B 30
Farnaby Ho. W10.....................2B 58
..............................(off Bruckner St.)
Farnaby Rd. SE9....................2E 111
Farnan Lodge SW16...........5A 118
Farnan Rd. SW16................5A 118
Farnborough Ho. SW15....1C 112
Farncombe St. SE16............3C 78
Farndale Ct. SE18..................3F 97
Farndale Ho. NW6..................5D 45
...............................(off Kilburn Vale)
Farnell M. SW5.........................1D 87
Farnham Ho. NW1..................3A 60
.........................(off Harewood Av.)
Farnham Pl. SE1....2F 25 (3E 77)
..................................(off Union St.)
Farnham Royal SE1..............1B 90
Farningham Ho. N4...............2F 35
Farnley Ho. SW8....................5F 89
Farnsworth Ct. SE10............4B 82
..............................(off West Parkside)
Farnworth Ho. E14...............5F 81
..........................(off Manchester Rd.)
Faroe Rd. W14.........................4F 71
Farquhar Rd. SE19..............5B 120
Farquhar Rd. SW19.............3C 114
Farrance St. E14...................5C 66
Farrell Ho. E1...........................5E 65
...............................(off Ronald St.)
Farren Rd. SE23...................2A 122
Farrer Ho. SE8.........................3C 94
Farrier Ct. E1.............................4F 65
..........................(off White Horse La.)
Farriers Ho. EC1........4A 10 (3E 63)
....................................(off Errol St.)
Farriers M. SE15....................1E 107
Farriers M. SW9....................2C 104

Farrier St. NW1.......................4D 47
Farriers Yd. W6.......................1F 85
..............................(off Smiths Sq.)
Farrier Wlk. SW10...................2E 87
Farringdon La. EC1...4C 8 (3C 62)
Farringdon Rd. EC1...3B 8 (3C 62)
Farringdon Station (Rail,
Underground & Crossrail)
.....................................5D 9 (4D 63)
Farringdon St. EC4...1D 17 (4D 63)
Farrins Rents SE16................2A 80
Farrow La. SE14......................3E 93
Farrow Pl. SE16......................4A 80
Farthingale Wlk. E15..............4F 53
Farthing All. SE1......................3C 78
Farthing Flds. E1.....................2D 79
Fashion & Textile Mus.
.....................................3E 27 (3A 78)
Fashion St. E1............1F 19 (4B 64)
Fassett Rd. E8..........................3C 50
Fassett Sq. E8..........................3C 50
Faulkner Ho. W6.......................2E 85
Faulkners All. EC1....5D 9 (4D 63)
Faulkner St. SE14....................4E 93
Faunce Ho. SE17......................2D 91
..........................(off Doddington Gro.)
Faunce St. SE17.......................1D 91
Fauret Rd. SW6........................4C 86
Faversham Ho. NW1.................5E 47
..................................(off Bayham Pl.)
Faversham Ho. SE17................1A 92
...............................(off Kinglake St.)
Faversham Rd. SE6...............5B 108
Fawcett Cl. SW11....................5F 87
Fawcett Cl. SW16................5C 118
Fawcett Cl. SW10.....................2E 87
...................................(off Fawcett St.)
Fawcett Est. E5.........................3C 36
Fawcett Rd. NW10...................4B 42
Fawcett St. SW10.....................2E 87
Fawe Pk. M. SW15.................2B 100
Fawe Pk. Rd. SW15..............2B 100
Fawe St. E14............................4D 67
Fawkham Ho. SE1...................5B 78
.............................(off Longfield Est.)
Fawley Lodge E14....................5F 81
..............................(off Millennium Dr.)
Fawley Rd. NW6.......................2D 45
Fawnbrake Av. SE24............3D 105
Fawn Rd. E13...........................1E 69
Faygate Rd. SW2...................2B 118
Fayland Av. SW16................5E 117
Fazeley Ct. W9.........................4C 58
..............................(off Elmfield Way)
Fearnley Ho. SE5.....................5A 92
Fearon St. SE10.......................1C 96
Feather M. E1............................4C 64
Feathers Pl. SE10....................2F 95
Featherstone Av. SE23........2D 121
Featherstone M. SE22.........2A 106
Featherstone St.
EC1.............................3B 10 (3F 63)
Featley Rd. SW9......................1D 105
Feeny Cl. NW10.......................1B 42
Felbridge Cl. SW16.............4C 118
Felbridge Ho. SE22..............1A 106
Felday Rd. SE13.....................4D 109
Felden St. SW6.........................4B 86
Feldman Cl. N16.......................3C 36
Felgate M. W6...........................5D 71
Felix Av. N8...............................1A 34
Felix Pl. SW2...........................3C 104
..................................(off Talma Rd.)
Felix Point E14.........................5C 66
.............................(off Upper Nth. St.)

Felixstowe Rd. NW10...........2D 57
Felix St. E2................................1D 65
Fellbrig Rd. SE22................3B 106
Fellbrig St. E1..........................1D 65
Fellmongers Path
SE1............................4F 27 (3B 78)
..................................(off Tower Bri. Rd.)
Fellows Ct. E2..........1F 11 (1B 64)
................................(not continuous)
Fellows Rd. NW3.....................4F 45
Feltham M. SE7.......................1C 96
Felltram Way SE7...................1C 96
Felmersham Cl. SW4..........2A 104
Felsberg Rd. SW2................4A 104
Felsham M. SW15...................1F 99
...............................(off Felsham Rd.)
Felsham Rd. SW15................1E 99
Felstead Gdns. E14...............1E 95
Felstead Rd. E11......................2C 40
Felstead Rd. E9.......................3B 52
Felstead St. E9.........................3B 52
Felstead Wharf E14................1E 95
Felsted Rd. E16.........................5F 69
Felton Hall Ho. SE16...............3C 78
...............................(off George Row)
Felton Ho. N1............................5F 49
..................................(off Colville Est.)
Felton St. N1.............................5F 49
Fenchurch Av. EC3...3D 19 (5A 64)
Fenchurch Bldgs.
EC3..............................3E 19 (5A 64)
Fenchurch Ho. EC3..3F 19 (5B 64)
......................................(off Minories)
Fenchurch M. E3.......................4B 66
.............................(off St Paul's Way)
Fenchurch Pl. EC3...3E 19 (5A 64)
Fenchurch St. EC3...4D 19 (1A 78)
Fenchurch Street Station (Rail)
.....................................4E 19 (1B 78)
Fen Ct. EC3..............3D 19 (5A 64)
Fendall St. SE1.......5E 27 (4A 78)
................................(not continuous)
Fendt Cl. E16..............................5B 68
Fenelon Pl. W14.......................5B 72
Fenham Rd. SE15...................3C 92
Fenland Ho. E5.........................4E 37
Fen La. SW13............................4D 85
Fennel Apts. SE1.....2F 27 (2B 78)
..................................(off Cayenne Ct.)
Fennel Cl. E16..........................3A 68
Fenner Cl. SE16.......................5D 79
Fenner Ho. E1...........................2D 79
..................................(off Watts St.)
Fenner Sq. SW11....................1F 101
Fennings Rd. SW4................4F 103
Fenning St. SE1......3D 27 (3A 78)
Fenn St. E9...............................2F 51
Fenstanton N4.........................3B 34
...............................(off Marquis Rd.)
Fen St. E16...............................1B 82
Fentiman Rd. SW8.................2A 90
Fenton Cl. E8...........................3B 50
Fenton Cl. SW9.......................5B 90
Fenton Cl. SW16....................3A 94
Fenton House
.............................(off Hampstead Gro.)
Fenton Pde. SE10...................1B 96
.........................(off Woolwich Rd.)
Fentons Av. E13......................2D 69
Fenton St. E1...........................5D 65
Fenwick Gro. SE15................1C 106
Fenwick Rd. EC1.......1E 17 (4D 63)
...............................(off Little Britain)
Fenwick Pl. SW9...................1A 104
Fenwick Rd. SE15................1C 106

Ferdinand Ct. SE6 .... 5C 108
.... (off Adenmore Rd.)
Ferdinand Dr. SE15 .... 3A 92
Ferdinand Ho. NW1 .... 4C 46
.... (off Ferdinand Pl.)
Ferdinand Magellan Ct.
E16 .... 3D 83
.... (Ferdinand Magellan Court)
Ferdinand Pl. NW1 .... 4C 46
Ferdinand St. NW1 .... 4C 46
FERGUSON LANE, THE 1A 38
Ferguson Cl. E14 .... 5C 80
Ferguson Dr. W3 .... 5A 56
Fergus Rd. N5 .... 2D 49
Fergusson M. SW4 .... 5A 90
Fergus St. SE10 .... 4C 82
Ferial Ct. SE15 .... 3C 92
.... (off Fenham St.)
Fermain Ct. E. N1 .... 5A 50
.... (off Hertford Rd.)
Fermain Ct. Nth. N1 .... 5A 50
.... (off De Beauvoir Est.)
Fermain Ct. W. N1 .... 5A 50
.... (off De Beauvoir Est.)
Ferme Pk. Rd. N4 .... 1B 34
Ferme Pk. Rd. N8 .... 1A 34
Fermor Rd. SE23 .... 1A 122
Fermoy Ho. W9 .... 3B 58
.... (off Fermoy Rd.)
Fermoy Rd. W9 .... 3B 58
.... (not continuous)
Fernbank M. SW12 .... 4E 103
Fernbrook Cres. SE13 .... 4A 110
.... (off Leahurst Rd.)
Fernbrook Rd. SE13 .... 3A 110
Ferncliff Rd. E8 .... 2C 50
Fern Cl. N1 .... 1A 64
Fern Ct. SE14 .... 5F 93
Ferncroft Av. NW3 .... 5C 30
Ferndale Community Sports Cen.
.... 1B 104
Ferndale Rd. E11 .... 4A 40
Ferndale Rd. E7 .... 4D 55
Ferndale Rd. N15 .... 1B 36
Ferndale Rd. SW4 .... 2A 104
Ferndale Rd. SW9 .... 2B 104
Ferndene Rd. SE24 .... 2E 105
Ferndown NW1 .... 4F 47
.... (off Camley St.)
Ferndown Lodge E14 .... 4E 81
.... (off Manchester Rd.)
Ferndown Rd. SE9 .... 5F 111
Fernhall Dri. IG4: Ilf 1F 41
Fernhead Rd. W9 .... 2B 58
Fernholme Rd. SE15 .... 3F 107
Fernhurst Rd. SW4 .... 4A 86
Fernlea Rd. SW12 .... 1D 117
Fernleigh Cl. W9 .... 2B 58
Fernsbury St. WC1 .... 2B 8 (2C 62)
Fernshaw Cl. SW10 .... 2E 87
Fernshaw Mans. SW10 .... 2E 87
.... (off Fernshaw Rd.)
Fernshaw Rd. SW10 .... 2E 87
Fernside NW11 .... 4C 30
Fernside Rd. SW12 .... 1B 116
Ferns Rd. E15 .... 3B 54
Fern St. E3 .... 3C 66
Fernthorpe Rd. SW16 .... 5E 117
Ferntower Rd. N5 .... 2F 49
Fern Wlk. SE16 .... 1C 92
Fernwood SW19 .... 1B 114
Fernwood Av. SW16 .... 4F 117
Ferranti Cl. SE18 .... 4F 83
Ferrers Rd. SW16 .... 5F 117
Ferrey M. SW9 .... 5C 90

Ferriby Cl. N1 .... 4C 48
Ferrier Ind. Est. SW18 .... 2D 101
.... (off Ferrier St.)
Ferrier Point E16 .... 4C 68
.... (off Forty Acre La.)
Ferrier St. SW18 .... 2D 101
Ferrings SE21 .... 3A 120
Ferris Rd. SE22 .... 2C 106
Ferron Rd. E5 .... 5D 37
Ferrybridge Ho. SE11 .... 4C 76
.... (off Lambeth Wlk.)
Ferry Ho. E5 .... 3D 37
.... (off Harrington Hill)
Ferry La. SW13 .... 2B 84
Ferryman's Quay SW6 .... 5C 87
Ferry Rd. SW13 .... 3C 84
Ferry St. E14 .... 1E 95
Festing Rd. SW15 .... 1F 99
Festival Ct. E8 .... 4B 50
.... (off Holly St.)
Festival Pier (River Tours)
.... 1F 23 (2B 76)
Festive Mans. E20 .... 2E 53
.... (off Napa Cl.)
Festive Wlk. SW15 .... 5F 85
Festoon Way E16 .... 1F 83
Festubert Pl. E3 .... 1B 66
Festuca Ho. E20 .... 2E 53
.... (off Mirabelle Gdns.)
Fetter La. EC4 .... 2B 16 (5C 62)
Fetter La. Apts.
EC4 .... 3B 16 (5C 62)
.... (off Fetter La.)
Fettes Ho. NW8 .... 1F 59
.... (off Wellington Rd.)
Fettle Ct. SE14 .... 2A 94
.... (off Moulding La.)
Ffinch St. SE8 .... 3C 94
Fiador Apts. SE10 .... 5A 82
.... (off Telegraph Av.)
Fidelis Ho. E1 .... 1F 19 (4B 64)
.... (off Gun St.)
Field Cl. NW2 .... 4C 28
Field Ct. SW19 .... 3C 114
Field Ct. WC1 .... 1A 16 (4B 62)
Fielder Apts. E3 .... 3B 66
.... (off Heath Pl.)
Fieldgate Mans. E1 .... 4C 64
.... (off Fieldgate St.)
Fieldgate St. E1 .... 4C 64
Field Ho. NW6 .... 2F 57
.... (off Harvist Rd.)
Fieldhouse Rd. SW12 .... 1E 117
Fielding Ct. WC2 .... 3D 15 (5A 62)
.... (off Earlham St.)
Fielding Ho. NW8 .... 5E 45
.... (off Ainsworth Way)
Fielding Ho. W4 .... 2A 84
.... (off Devonshire Rd.)
Fielding M. SW13 .... 2D 85
Fielding Rd. W14 .... 4F 71
Fielding Rd. W4 .... 4A 70
Fieldings, The SE23 .... 1E 121
Fielding St. SE17 .... 2E 91
Field Point E7 .... 1C 54
Field Rd. E7 .... 1B 54
Field Rd. W6 .... 1A 86
Fields Est. E8 .... 4C 50
Fieldside Rd. BR1: Brom! ... 5F 123
Field St. WC1 .... 1F 7 (2B 62)
Fields Wlk. SW11 .... 3D 89
Fieldsway Ho. N5 .... 2C 48
Fieldview SW18 .... 1F 115
Fieldway Cres. N5 .... 2C 48
Fife Rd. E16 .... 4C 68

Fife Ter. N1 .... 1B 62
Fifield Path SE23 .... 3F 121
Fifth Av. W10 .... 2A 58
Fig Tree Cl. NW10 .... 5A 42
Figure Ct. SW3 .... 1B 88
.... (off West Rd.)
Filament Wlk. SW18 .... 3C 100
.... (off Spectrum Way)
Filey Av. N16 .... 3C 36
Filigree Ct. SE16 .... 2E 81
Fillebrook Rd. E11 .... 3F 39
Filmer Chambers SW6 .... 4A 86
.... (off Filmer Rd.)
Filmer Ho. SW6 .... 4B 86
Filmer M. SW6 .... 4B 86
Filmer Rd. SW6 .... 4A 86
Filton Ct. SE14 .... 3E 93
.... (off Farrow La.)
Finborough Ho. SW10 .... 2E 87
.... (off Finborough Rd.)
Finborough Rd. SW10 .... 1D 87
Finborough Theatre, The ... 2D 87
.... (off Finborough Rd.)
Finch Av. SE27 .... 4F 119
Finchdean Ho. SW15 .... 5B 98
Finch Ho. E3 .... 5B 52
.... (off Jasmine Sq.)
Finch Ho. SE8 .... 3D 95
.... (off Bronze St.)
Finch La. EC3 .... 3C 18 (5F 63)
Finchley Pl. NW8 .... 1F 59
Finchley Rd. NW2 .... 5C 30
Finchley Rd. NW3 .... 1C 44
Finchley Rd. NW8 .... 5F 45
Finchley Road & Frognal Station
(Overground) 2E 45
Finchley Road Station
(Underground) 3E 45
Finch Lodge W9 .... 4C 58
.... (off Admiral Wlk.)
Finch M. SE15 .... 4B 92
Finch's Ct. E14 .... 1D 81
Finch's Ct. M. E14 .... 1D 81
.... (off Finch's Ct.)
Finden Rd. E7 .... 2E 55
Findhorn St. E14 .... 5E 67
Findlay Ho. E3 .... 2C 66
.... (off Trevithick Way)
Findon Cl. SW18 .... 4C 100
Findon Rd. W12 .... 3C 70
Fingal St. SE10 .... 1B 96
Fingest Ho. NW8 .... 3A 60
.... (off Lilestone St.)
Finland Rd. SE4 .... 1A 108
Finland St. SE16 .... 4A 80
Finlay St. SW6 .... 4F 85
Finley St. SE5 .... 3E 91
.... (off Redcar St.)
Finmere Ho. N4 .... 2E 35
Finnemore Ho. N1 .... 5E 49
.... (off Britannia Row)
Finn Ho. N1 .... 1C 10 (2F 63)
.... (off Bevenden St.)
Finnis St. E2 .... 2D 65
FINSBURY 1B 8 (2C 62)
Finsbury Av. EC2 .... 1C 18 (4F 63)
Finsbury Av. Sq.
EC2 .... 5D 11 (4A 64)
Finsbury Cir. EC2 ... 1C 18 (4F 63)
Finsbury Est. EC1 ... 2C 8 (2C 62)
Finsbury Leisure Cen.
.... 2F 9 (2E 63)
Finsbury Mkt. EC2 .. 4D 11 (3A 64)
.... (not continuous)

FINSBURY PK......................3C 34
Finsbury Pk. Av. N4...............1E 35
Finsbury Park Interchange
　(Bus Station)...................4C 34
Finsbury Pk. Rd. N4..............4D 35
Finsbury Park Station
　(Rail & Underground)......4C 34
Finsbury Pavement
　EC2.............................5C 10 (4F 63)
Finsbury Sq. EC2.........4C 10 (3F 63)
Finsbury St. EC2.........5B 10 (4F 63)
Finsen Rd. SE5....................2E 105
Finstock Rd. W10...................5F 57
Finwhale Ho. E14.................4D 81
　..........................(off Glengall Gro.)
Fiona Ct. NW6......................1C 58
Firbank Cl. E16.....................4F 69
Firbank Rd. SE15..................5D 93
Fircroft Rd. SW17..................2B 116
Firecrest Dr. NW3..................5D 31
Firefly Gdns. E6....................3F 69
Firehorn Ho. E15...................2A 68
　...............................(off Teasel Way)
Fire Station Sq.
　SE1........................2E 27 (2A 78)
　...............................(off Abbots La.)
Firewatch Ct. E1...................4A 66
　...............................(off Candle St.)
Firgrove Ct. SE6...................5C 108
Fir Gro. Rd. SW9..................5C 90
Firhill Rd. SE6......................4C 122
Fir Ho. W10...........................3A 58
　..................................(off Droop St.)
Firle Ho. W10.........................4F 57
　...............................(off Sutton Way)
Firs, The SE26:
　Lon Border Rd................5D 121
Firs, The SE26:
　Lon Waverley Ct..............5E 121
Firs, The E6.........................4F 55
Firsby Rd. N16......................3C 36
Firs Cl. SE23.......................5A 108
First Av. E13.........................2C 68
First Av. SW14......................1A 98
First Av. W10........................3B 58
First Av. W3..........................2B 70
First St. SW3........................5A 74
Firth Gdns. SW6....................4B 86
Firth Ho. E2..........................2C 64
　...................................(off Turin St.)
Fir Tree Cl. SW16................5E 117
Firtree Ho. SE13..................5F 109
　.............................(off Birdwood Av.)
Fir Trees Cl. SE16.................2A 80
Fisher Cl. E9........................2F 51
Fisher Cl. SE16.....................2F 79
Fisher Ho. E1.........................1E 79
　..................................(off Cable St.)
Fisher Ho. N1........................5C 48
　............................(off Barnsbury Est.)
Fishermans Dr. SE16...........3F 79
Fisherman's Pl. W4................2B 84
Fisherman's Wlk. E14...........2C 80
Fisher's Cl. SW16...............3F 117
Fishers Ct. SE14..................4F 93
Fisher's La. W4......................5A 70
Fisher St. E16.......................4C 68
Fisher St. WC1......1F 15 (4B 62)
Fisherton St. NW8.................3F 59
Fishmongers Hall Wharf
　EC4........................5B 18 (1F 77)
　..................................(off Swan La.)
Fishponds Rd. SW17...........4A 116
Fish St. Hill EC3....5C 18 (1F 77)
Fish Wharf EC3....5C 18 (1F 77)

Fitch Ct. SW2.......................3C 104
Fitness4Less Canning Town
　.......................................4B 68
Fitness First Angel . 1D 9 (1D 63)
Fitness First Baker Street
　......................1A 12 (4B 60)
Fitness First Beckenham . 5C 122
Fitness First Berkeley Square
　......................5E 13 (1D 75)
Fitness First Brixton..........1C 104
Fitness First Camden..........5D 47
Fitness First Clapham Junction
　.......................................2A 102
Fitness First Covent Garden
　......................5E 15 (1A 76)
　.............................(off Bedford St.)
Fitness First Fetter Lane
　......................2C 16 (5C 62)
　...............................(off Fetter La.)
Fitness First Gracechurch Street
　......................4C 18 (1A 78)
　.........................(off Gracechurch St.)
Fitness First Great Marlborough
　Street......................3F 13 (5E 61)
　.........................(off Gt. Marlborough St.)
Fitness First Hammersmith . 5E 71
　..........................(off Arena Shop. Pk.)
Fitness First Harringay.......1D 35
Fitness First High Holborn
　......................1F 15 (5B 62)
　.............................(off High Holborn)
Fitness First Highbury.........5D 35
Fitness First Kilburn...........5B 44
Fitness First Kingly Street
　......................4F 13 (1E 75)
　.................................(off Kingly St.)
Fitness First Leyton Mills . 5E 39
Fitness First London Bridge
　......................2C 26 (2F 77)
　.............................(off London Bri. St.)
Fitness First London Bridge,
　Cottons..........1C 26 (2A 78)
　.................................(off Tooley St.)
Fitness First Paternoster Square
　......................2E 17 (5D 63)
　.........................(off Paternoster Sq.)
Fitness First Queen Victoria
　Street................4F 17 (1E 77)
　.........................(off Queen Victoria St.)
Fitness First Streatham . 2A 118
Fitness First Thomas More
　Square...........................1C 80
　.........................(off Thomas More Sq.)
Fitness First Tooting Bec . 3C 116
Fittleton Gdns. E3.................3D 67
Fitzalan St. SE11..................5C 76
Fitzclarence Ho. W11............3A 72
　.........................(off Holland Park Av.)
Fitzgeorge Av. W14..............5A 72
Fitzgerald Av. SW14.............1A 98
Fitzgerald Ct. E10..................3D 39
　.........................(off Leyton Grange Est.)
Fitzgerald Ho. E14.................5D 67
　.........................(off E. India Dock Rd.)
Fitzgerald Ho. SW9...............3F 115
Fitzgerald Rd. E11.................1C 40
Fitzgerald Rd. SW14.............1A 98
Fitzhardinge Ho.
　W1..........................2B 12 (5C 60)
　.................................(off Portman Sq.)
Fitzhardinge St. W1..2B 12 (5C 60)
Fitzhugh Gro. SW18..........4F 101
Fitzjames Av. W14................5A 72
Fitzjohn's Av. NW3...............1E 45

Fitzmaurice Ho. SE16..........5D 79
　...............................(off Rennie Est.)
Fitzmaurice Pl.
　W1.........................1E 21 (2D 75)
Fitzneal St. W12....................5B 56
Fitzpatrick Rd. SW9..............4D 91
Fitzrovia Apts. W1......4E 5 (3D 61)
　.............................(off Bolsover St.)
FITZROY BRI........................5C 46
Fitzroy Cl. N6........................3B 32
Fitzroy Ct. N6.........................1E 33
Fitzroy Ct. W1..............4A 6 (3E 61)
　.........................(off Tottenham Ct. Rd.)
Fitzroy Ho. E14.....................4B 66
　.............................(off Wallwood St.)
Fitzroy Ho. SE1.....................1B 92
　.............................(off Cooper's Rd.)
Fitzroy House Mus.....4F 5 (3E 61)
Fitzroy M. W1.............4F 5 (3E 61)
　.............................(off Cleveland St.)
Fitzroy Pk. N6........................3B 32
Fitzroy Rd. NW1....................5C 46
Fitzroy Sq. W1............4F 5 (3E 61)
FITZROY SQUARE HOSPITAL
　......................4F 5 (3E 61)
Fitzroy St. W1..............4F 5 (3E 61)
　...............................(not continuous)
Fitzroy Yd. NW1....................5C 46
Fitzwarren Gdns. N19...........3E 33
Fitzwilliam Hgts. SE23.........2E 121
Fitzwilliam M. E16................2C 82
Fitzwilliam Rd. SW4...........1E 103
Five Bell All. E14..................5B 66
　.............................(off Three Colt St.)
Five Oaks M. BR1: Broml ...3C 124
Fives Ct. SE11......................4D 77
Fiveways Rd. SW9................5C 90
Fixie Bldg. E17.....................1B 38
　.................................(off Track St.)
Flack Ct. E10.........................2D 39
Fladbury Rd. N15..................1F 35
Fladgate Rd. E11..................1A 40
Flagship Ho. E16..................3D 83
　.............................(off Royal Crest Av.)
Flamborough Ho. SE15.........4C 92
　.............................(off Clayton Rd.)
Flamborough St. E14............5A 66
Flamborough Wlk. E14.........5A 66
　.........................(off Flamborough St.)
Flamingo Ct. SE17...............1E 91
　.............................(off Crampton St.)
Flamingo Ct. SE8...................3C 94
　.............................(off Hamilton St.)
Flamstead Ho. SW3..............1A 88
　.................................(off Cale St.)
Flamsteed Rd. SE7..............1F 97
Flanaghan Apts. E3..............3B 66
　.................................(off Portia Way)
Flanchford Rd. W12.............4B 70
Flanders Ct. E17...................2A 38
Flanders Mans. W4..............5B 70
Flanders Rd. W4...................5A 70
Flanders Way E9...................3F 51
Flank St. E1..........................1C 78
Flannery Ct. SE16.................4D 79
Flansham Ho. E14................5B 66
　.............................(off Clemence St.)
Flask Wlk. NW3....................1E 45
Flatford Ho. SE6..................4E 123
Flather Cl. SW16.................5E 117
Flat Iron Sq. SE1...2A 26 (2E 77)
　.........................(off Southwark Bri. Rd.)
Flatiron Yd. SE1....2A 26 (2E 77)
　.................................(off Ayres St.)
Flavell M. SE10.....................1A 96

Flaxley Ho. SW1 .... 1D **89**
.... (part of Abbots Mnr.)
Flaxman Ct. W1 ......3B **14** (5F **61**)
Flaxman Ct. WC1 ......2C **6** (2F **61**)
.... (off Flaxman Ter.)
Flaxman Ho. SE1 ....5D **25** (4D **77**)
.... (off London Rd.)
Flaxman Ho. W4 .... 1A **84**
.... (off Devonshire St.)
Flaxman Rd. SE5 .... 1D **105**
Flaxman Sports Cen. 5E **91**
Flaxman Ter. WC1 ....2C **6** (2F **61**)
Flecker Ho. SE5 .... 3F **91**
.... (off Lomond Gro.)
Fleece Wlk. N7 .... 3A **48**
Fleetbank Ho.
EC4 ....3C **16** (5C **62**)
.... (off Salisbury Sq.)
Fleetfield WC1 .... 1E **7** (2A **62**)
.... (off Birkenhead St.)
Fleet Ho. E14 .... 1A **80**
.... (off Victory Pl.)
Fleet Pl. EC4 ....2D **17** (5D **63**)
Fleet Rd. NW3 .... 2A **46**
Fleet Sq. WC1 ....2A **8** (2B **62**)
Fleet St. EC4 ....3B **16** (5C **62**)
Fleetway WC1 .... 1E **7** (2A **62**)
.... (off Birkenhead St.)
Fleetwood Cl. E16 ....4F **69**
Fleetwood Rd. NW10 ....2C **42**
Fleetwood St. N16 ....4A **36**
Fleming Cl. SW10 ....2E **87**
.... (off Winterton Pl.)
Fleming Cl. W9 ....3C **58**
Fleming Ct. W2 ....4F **59**
.... (off St Mary's Sq.)
Fleming Ho. N4 ....3E **35**
Fleming Ho. SE16 ....3C **78**
.... (off George Row)
Fleming Ho. SW17 ....3F **115**
Fleming Lodge W9 ....4C **58**
.... (off Admiral Wlk.)
Fleming Rd. SE17 ....2D **91**
Flempton Rd. E10 ....3A **38**
Fletcher Bldgs.
WC2 ....3E **15** (5A **62**)
.... (off Martlett Ct.)
Fletcher Ho. N1 ....5A **50**
.... (off Nuttall St.)
Fletcher St. SE15 ....3E **93**
.... (off Clifton Way)
Fletcher La. E10 ....2E **39**
Fletcher Path SE8 ....3C **94**
Fletcher St. E1 .... 1C **78**
Fletching Apts. E3 ....3B **66**
.... (off Siyah Gdn.)
Fletching Rd. E5 ....5E **37**
Fletching Rd. SE7 ....2E **97**
Fleur de Lis St. E1 ....4E **11** (3B **64**)
Fleur Gates SW19 ....5F **99**
Flight Ho. N1 ....5A **50**
.... (off Phillipp St.)
Flimwell Cl. BR1: Broml 5A **124**
Flinders Ho. E1 .... 2D **79**
.... (off Green Bank)
Flint Cl. E15 .... 4B **54**
Flintlock Cl. E1 .... 5D **65**
Flintmill Cres. SE3 ....5F **97**
Flinton St. SE17 .... 1A **92**
Flint St. SE17 ....5F **77**
Flip Out Brent Cross 3D **29**
Flip Out Wandsworth 1D **115**
Flitcroft St. WC2 ....3C **14** (5F **61**)
Flitton Ho. N1 .... 4D **49**
.... (off The Sutton Est.)

Flock Mill Pl. SW18 ....1D **115**
Flockton St. SE16 ....3C **78**
Flodden Rd. SE5 ....4E **91**
Flood St. SW3 .... 1A **88**
Flood Wlk. SW3 .... 2A **88**
Flora Cl. E14 .... 5D **67**
Flora Gdns. W6 ....5D **71**
.... (off Albion Gdns.)
Flora Ho. E3 .... 5C **52**
.... (off Garrison Rd.)
Floral Ct. WC2 ....4D **15** (1A **76**)
Floral Pl. N1 .... 2F **49**
Floral St. WC2 ....4D **15** (1A **76**)
Florence Cantwell Mus.
N19 .... 2A **34**
.... (off Jessie Blythe La.)
Florence Ct. N1 .... 4D **49**
.... (off Florence St.)
Florence Ct. SW19 ....5A **114**
Florence Ct. W9 ....2E **59**
.... (off Maida Vale)
Florence Ho. SE16 ....1D **93**
.... (off Rotherhithe New Rd.)
Florence Ho. W11 .... 1F **71**
.... (off St Ann's Rd.)
Florence Mans. NW4 .... 1D **29**
.... (off Vivian Av.)
Florence Mans. SW6 ....4B **86**
.... (off Rostrevor Rd.)
Florence Nightingale Mus.
.................................4A **24** (3B **76**)
Florence Rd. E13 .... 1C **68**
Florence Rd. E6 ....5E **55**
Florence Rd. N4 ....2B **34**
.... (not continuous)
Florence Rd. SE14 ....4B **94**
Florence Sq. E3 ....3D **67**
Florence St. E16 ....3B **68**
Florence St. N1 ....4D **49**
Florence Ter. SE14 ....4B **94**
Florence Way SW12 ....1B **116**
Florey Lodge W9 ....4C **58**
.... (off Admiral Wlk.)
Florfield Pas. E8 ....3D **51**
.... (off Reading La.)
Florfield Rd. E8 ....3D **51**
Florian SE5 ....4A **92**
Florian Ct. E16 .... 4D **68**
.... (off Hastings Rd.)
Florian Rd. SW15 ....2A **100**
Florida St. E2 .... 2C **64**
Florin Ct. EC1 ....5F **9** (4E **63**)
.... (off Charterhouse Sq.)
Florin Ct. SE1 ....4F **27** (3B **78**)
.... (off Tanner St.)
Floris Pl. SW4 ....1E **103**
Florys Ct. SW19 ....1A **114**
Floss St. SW15 ....5E **85**
Flotilla Ho. E16 ....3D **83**
.... (off Cable St.)
Flotilla Ho. SW18 ....1E **101**
Flounder Ho. SE8 ....3D **95**
.... (off Creative Rd.)
Flower & Dean Wlk.
E1 ....1F **19** (4B **64**)
Flower M. NW11 .... 1A **30**
Flower Pot Cl. N15 ....1B **36**
Flowers Cl. NW2 .... 5C **28**
Flowersmead SW17 ....2C **116**
Flowers Ho. N19 ....4E **33**
Flower Wlk., The SW7 ....3E **73**
Floyd Rd. SE7 .... 1E **97**
Fludyer St. SE13 ....2A **110**
Flutemakers M. SW4 ....3F **103**

Flying Angel Ho. E16 ....1D **83**
.... (off Victoria Dock Rd.)
Flynn Ct. E14 .... 1C **80**
.... (off Garford St.)
Foley Ho. E1 ....5E **65**
.... (off Tarling St.)
Foley St. W1 ....1F **13** (4E **61**)
Folgate St. E1 ....5E **11** (4A **64**)
.... (not continuous)
Foliot Ho. N1 .... 1B **62**
.... (off Priory Grn. Est.)
Foliot St. W12 ....5B **56**
Folkestone Ho. SE17 .... 1A **92**
.... (off Upnor Way)
Follett Ho. SW10 .... 3F **87**
.... (off Worlds End Est.)
Follett St. E14 ....5E **67**
Follingham Ct. N1 ...1E **11** (2A **64**)
.... (off Drysdale Pl.)
Folly M. W11 ....5B **58**
Folly Wall E14 .... 3E **81**
Fonda Ct. E14 .... 1C **80**
.... (off Premiere Pl.)
Fondant Ct. E3 .... 1D **67**
.... (off Taylor Pl.)
Fontarabia Rd. SW11 ....2C **102**
Fontenelle SE5 ....4A **92**
Fontenoy Ho. SE11 ....5D **77**
.... (off Kennington La.)
Fontenoy Rd. SW12 ....2D **117**
Fonthill Ho. SW1 .... 1D **89**
.... (part of Abbots Mnr.)
Fonthill Ho. W14 ....4A **72**
.... (off Russell Rd.)
Fonthill M. N4 ....4B **34**
Fonthill Rd. N4 ....3B **34**
Fontley Way SW15 ....5C **98**
Footpath, The SW15 ....4C **98**
Forber Ho. E2 ....2E **65**
.... (off Cornwall Av.)
Forbes Cl. NW2 ....5C **28**
Forbes Ho. E7 ....2E **55**
.... (off Romford Rd.)
Forbes St. E1 .... 5C **64**
Forburg Rd. N16 ....3C **36**
Forbury Rd. SE13 ....1A **110**
Ford Cl. E3 .... 1A **66**
Fordel Rd. SE6 ....1E **123**
Fordham Ho. SE14 ....3A **94**
.... (off Angus St.)
Fordham St. E1 .... 5C **64**
Fordie Ho. SW1 ....5A **20** (4B **74**)
.... (off Sloane St.)
Fordingley Rd. W9 ....2B **58**
Fordington Ho. SE26 ....3C **120**
Fordmill Rd. SE6 ....2C **122**
Ford Rd. E3 .... 1B **66**
Fords Pk. Rd. E16 ....4C **68**
Ford Sq. E1 .... 4D **65**
Ford St. E16 ....5B **68**
Ford St. E3 ....5A **52**
Fordwych Rd. NW2 ....1A **44**
Fordyce Rd. SE13 ....4E **109**
Foreign St. SE5 .... 5D **91**
Foreland Ho. W11 .... 1A **72**
.... (off Walmer Rd.)
Foreman Ho. SE4 ....2F **107**
.... (off Billingford Cl.)
Foreshore SE8 ....5B **80**
Forest Bus. Pk. E10 ....2F **37**
Forest Cl. E11 .... 1C **40**
Forest Cl. NW6 ....4A **44**
Forest Cft. SE23 ....2D **121**
Forest Dr. E12 ....5F **41**
Forest Dr. E. E11 ....2F **39**

Forest Dr. W. E11.....................2E **39**
Forester Ho. E14..................1A **80**
.............................(off Victory Pl.)
Forester Rd. SE15.............1D **107**
FOREST GATE.......................2C **54**
Forest Gate Learning Zone....1C **54**
.........................(off Woodford Rd.)
Forest Ga. Retreat E7.........2C **54**
.............................(off Odessa Rd.)
Forest Gate Station (Rail &
  Crossrail).........................2C **54**
Forest Glade E11..................1A **40**
Forest Gro. E8.......................3B **50**
FOREST HILL........................2E **121**
Forest Hill Bus. Cen.
  SE23.................................2E **121**
.............................(off Clyde Va.)
Forest Hill Ind. Est. SE23....2E **121**
Forest Hill Pools...................2E **121**
Forest Hill Rd. SE22..........3D **107**
Forest Hill Rd. SE23..........4E **107**
Forest Hill School Sports Cen.
  ....3F **121**
Forest Hill Station (Rail &
  Overground).....................2E **121**
Forestholme Cl. SE23.........2E **121**
Forest La. E15......................2A **54**
Forest La. E7.........................2B **54**
Forest Lodge SE23...............3E **121**
.........................(off Dartmouth Rd.)
Forest Point E7.....................2D **55**
.............................(off Windsor Rd.)
Fore St. EC2...............1A **18** (4E **63**)
Fore St. Av. EC2......1B **18** (4F **63**)
Forest Rd. E11......................2F **39**
Forest Rd. E7.........................1C **54**
Forest Rd. E8.........................3B **50**
Forest Side E7......................1D **55**
Forest St. E7.........................2C **54**
Forest Vw. E11......................2B **40**
Forest Vw. Av. E10................1F **39**
Forest Vw. Rd. E12...............1F **55**
Forest Way N19......................4E **33**
Forfar Rd. SW11....................4C **88**
Forge Pl. NW1........................3C **46**
Forge Sq. E14........................5D **81**
Forman Pl. N16......................1B **50**
Formby Ct. N7........................2C **48**
.............................(off Morgan Rd.)
Formosa Ho. E1.....................3A **66**
.............................(off Ernest St.)
Formosa St. W9......................3D **59**
Formunt Cl. E16...............4B **68**
Forres Gdns. NW11..............1C **30**
Forrester Path SE26............4E **121**
Forrester Way E15.................3F **53**
Forset Ct. W2.........................5A **60**
.............................(off Edgware Rd.)
Forset St. W1.........................5A **60**
.............................(not continuous)
Forster Ho. BR1: Broml...... 4F **123**
Forster Ho. SW17..................3F **115**
.........................(off Grosvenor Way)
Forster Rd. E17.....................1A **38**
Forster Rd. SW2....................5A **104**
Forston Apts. SW11..............2A **102**
.........................(off Monarch Square)
Forston St. N1........................1E **63**
Forsyte Ho. SW3...................1A **88**
.........................(off Chelsea Mnr. St.)
Forsyth Gdns. SE17.............2D **91**
Forsyth Ho. E9.......................4E **51**
.........................(off Frampton Pk. Rd.)
Forsyth Ho. SW1..................1E **89**
.............................(off Tachbrook St.)

Fortescue Av. E8...................4D **51**
Fortess Gro. NW5.................2E **47**
Fortess Rd. NW5...................2D **47**
Fortess Wlk. NW5.................2D **47**
Fortess Yd. NW5...................1D **47**
Forte St. SE18........................4F **97**
.............................(off Tellson Av.)
Forthbridge Rd. SW11........2C **102**
Forth Ho. E3...........................1B **66**
.............................(off Tredegar Rd.)
Fortis Cl. E16.........................5E **69**
Fortius Apts. E3.....................1C **66**
.............................(off Tredegar La.)
Fortius Wlk. E20....................3E **53**
Fortnam Rd. N19...................4F **33**
Fort Rd. SE1...........................5B **78**
Fortrose Cl. E14.....................5F **67**
Fortrose Gdns. SW2.............1A **118**
.............................(not continuous)
Fort St. E1.................1E **19** (4A **64**)
Fort St. E16...........................2D **83**
Fortuna Cl. N7........................3B **48**
Fortuna Ho. E20.....................2D **53**
.............................(off Scarlet Cl.)
Fortune Ct. E8.........................4B **50**
.............................(off Queensbridge Rd.)
Fortune Ga. Rd. NW10..........5A **42**
FORTUNE GREEN.................2C **44**
Fortune Grn. Rd. NW6..........1C **44**
Fortune Ho. EC1......4A **10** (3E **63**)
.............................(off Fortune St.)
Fortune Ho. SE11..................5C **76**
.............................(off Marylee Way)
Fortune Pl. SE1......................1B **92**
Fortune St. EC1.......4A **10** (3E **63**)
Fortune St. Pk........4A **10** (3E **63**)
Fortunes Wlk. E20.................2E **53**
Fortune Theatre........3E **15** (5A **62**)
.............................(off Russell St.)
Fortune Way NW10................2C **56**
Forty Acre La. E16.................4C **68**
Forum Cl. E3...........................5C **52**
Forum Magnum Sq.
  SE1..........................3A **24** (3B **76**)
.............................(off York Rd.)
Forward Bus. Cen., The
  ....1E **67**
Fosbrooke Ho. SW8...............3A **90**
.........................(off Davidson Gdns.)
Fosbury M. W2.......................1D **73**
Foscote Ct. W9.......................3C **58**
.............................(off Amberley Rd.)
Foscote M. W9.......................3C **58**
Foscote Rd. NW4...................1D **29**
Foskett M. E8..........................2B **50**
Foskett Rd. SW6....................5B **86**
Fossdene Rd. SE7...................1D **97**
Foss Ho. NW8.........................1D **59**
.............................(off Carlton Hill)
Fossil Ct. SE1............5D **27** (4A **78**)
.............................(off Long La.)
Fossil Rd. SE13....................1C **108**
Foss Rd. SW17.....................4F **115**
Foster Ct. E16.........................1B **82**
.............................(off Tarling Rd.)
Foster Ct. NW1.......................4E **47**
.............................(off Royal College St.)
Foster Ho. SE14.....................4B **94**
Foster La. EC2........2F **17** (5E **63**)
Foster Rd. E13........................3C **68**
Foster Rd. W3........................1A **70**
Foster Rd. W4........................1A **84**
Foster's Way SW18..............1D **115**
Fothergill Cl. E13...................1C **68**
Foubert's Pl. W1.......3F **13** (5E **61**)

Foulden Rd. N16.....................1B **50**
Foulden Ter. N16....................1B **50**
Foulis Ter. SW7......................1F **87**
Foulser Rd. SW17..................3B **116**
Founders Ct. EC2.......2B **18** (5F **63**)
.............................(off Lothbury)
Founders Ho. SW1.................1F **89**
.............................(off Aylesford St.)
Foundling Ct. WC1..........3D **7** (3A **62**)
.............................(off Brunswick Cen.)
Foundling Mus., The
  ....3E **7** (3A **62**)
.............................(off Brunswick Sq.)
Foundry, The EC2.....2E **11** (2A **64**)
.............................(off Dereham Pl.)
Foundry Cl. SE16...................2A **80**
Foundry Ho. E14....................4D **67**
.............................(off Morris Rd.)
Foundry Ho. E15....................3F **53**
.............................(off Forrester Way)
Foundry Ho. SW8...................4D **89**
.............................(off Lockington Rd.)
Foundry M. NW1......3A **6** (3E **61**)
Foundry M. SW13..................5B **84**
Foundry Pl. E1........................4E **65**
.............................(off Jubilee St.)
Foundry Pl. SW18..................5D **101**
Fountain Cl. E5.......................1D **51**
Fountain Ct. EC4......4B **16** (1C **76**)
Fountain Ct. SE23...................2F **121**
Fountain Ct. SW1....................5D **75**
.............................(off Buckingham Pal. Rd.)
Fountain Ct. W11....................3F **71**
.............................(off Clearwater Ter.)
Fountain Dr. SE19..................4B **120**
Fountain Grn. Sq. SE16.........3C **78**
Fountain Ho. E2.........3F **11** (3B **64**)
.............................(off Redchurch St.)
Fountain Ho. NW6...................4A **44**
Fountain Ho. SE16..................3C **78**
.............................(off Bermondsey Wall E.)
Fountain Ho. SW6...................5E **87**
Fountain Ho. W1.......1B **20** (2C **74**)
.............................(off Park St.)
Fountain M. N5.......................1E **49**
.............................(off Highbury Grange)
Fountain M. NW3...................3B **46**
Fountain Park Way W12........1E **71**
Fountain Pl. SW9....................4C **90**
Fountain Rd. SW17................5F **115**
Fountain Sq. SW1..................5D **75**
Fountayne Rd. N16................4C **36**
Fount St. SW8........................3F **89**
Fouracre NW1..........2F **5** (2E **61**)
.............................(off Stanhope St.)
Four Casson Sq. SE1..2A **24** (2B **76**)
Fournier St. E1.........5F **11** (4B **64**)
Fourscore Mans. E2...............4C **50**
.............................(off Shrubland Rd.)
Four Seasons Cl. E3...............1C **66**
Fourth Av. W10.......................3A **58**
Fovant Ct. SW8......................5E **89**
Fowey Cl. E1............................2D **79**
Fowey Ho. SE11......................1C **90**
.............................(off Kennings Way)
Fowler Cl. SW11......................1F **101**
Fowler Ho. N15.......................1F **35**
.............................(off South Gro.)
Fowler Ho. E7.........................1C **54**
Fowler Rd. N1..........................5D **49**
Fowlers M. N19........................4E **33**
.............................(off Holloway Rd.)
Fownes St. SW11.....................1A **102**
Fox & Knot St. EC1....5E **9** (4D **63**)
.............................(off Charterhouse Sq.)

Foxberry Rd. SE4 .... 1A 108
Foxborough Gdns. SE4 ..... 3C 108
Foxbourne Rd. SW17 .... 2C 116
Fox Cl. E1 ....3E 65
Fox Cl. E16 .... 4C 68
Foxcombe Cl. E6 ....1F 69
Foxcombe Rd. SW15 .... 1C 112
Foxcote SE5 .... 1A 92
Foxcroft WC1 .... 1A 8 (1B 62)
.... (off Penton Ri.)
Foxes Dale SE3 .... 1C 110
Foxfield NW1 .... 5D 47
.... (off Arlington Rd.)
Foxglove Ct. E3 .... 1C 66
.... (off Four Seasons Cl.)
Foxglove St. W12 .... 1B 70
Foxham Rd. N19 ....5F 33
Foxhole Rd. SE9 ....3F 111
Foxley Cl. E8 .... 2C 50
Foxley Ho. E3 .... 2D 67
.... (off Bow Rd.)
Foxley Rd. SW9 .... 3C 90
Foxley Sq. SW9 .... 3D 91
Foxmore St. SW11 .... 4B 88
Fox Rd. E16 .... 4B 68
Fox's Yd. E2 .... 3F 11 (3B 64)
.... (off Rhoda St.)
Foxwell M. SE4 .... 1A 108
Foxwell St. SE4 .... 1A 108
Foxwood Rd. SE3 .... 2B 110
Foyle Rd. SE3 .... 2B 96
Framfield Rd. N5 .... 2D 49
Framlingham Cl. E5 ....4E 37
Frampton NW1 ....4F 47
.... (off Wrotham Rd.)
Frampton Ho. NW8 ....3F 59
.... (off Frampton St.)
Frampton Pk. Est. E9 ....4E 51
Frampton Pk. Rd. E9 ....3E 51
Frampton St. NW8 ....3F 59
Francemary Rd. SE4 .... 3C 108
Frances Ct. E17 .... 1C 38
Frances Wharf E14 .... 5B 66
Franche Ct. Rd. SW17 ......3E 115
Francis Bacon Ct. SE16 .....5D 79
.... (off Galleywall Rd.)
Francis Barber Cl. SW16 ... 5B 118
Francis Bentley M. SW4 .....1E 103
Franciscan Rd. SW17 .... 5B 116
Francis Chichester Way
SW11 ....4C 88
Francis Cl. E14 ....5F 81
Francis Ct. EC1 ..... 5D 9 (4D 63)
.... (off Briset St.)
Francis Ct. SE14 ....2F 93
.... (off Myers La.)
Francis Harvey Way SE8 .... 4B 94
Francis Ho. N1 .... 5A 50
.... (off Colville St.)
Francis Ho. SW10 .... 3D 87
.... (off Coleridge Gdns.)
Francis Ho. SW18 .... 2E 101
.... (off Eltringham St.)
Francis M. SE12 .... 5C 110
Francis Pl. N6 .... 2D 33
.... (off Shepherd's Cl.)
Francis Rd. E10 ....3E 39
Francis St. E15 .... 2A 54
Francis St. SW1 ....5E 75
Francis Ter. N19 ....5E 33
Francis Ter. M. N19 ....5E 33
Francis Wlk. N1 .... 5B 48
Franck Ho. E1 .... 2E 9 (2D 63)
.... (off Goswell Road)
Franconia Rd. SW4 ....3F 103

Frank Beswick Ho. SW6 ..... 2B 86
.... (off Clem Attlee Ct.)
Frank Burton Cl. SE7 .... 1D 97
Frank Dixon Cl. SE21 .... 5A 106
Frank Dixon Way SE21 ...... 1A 120
Frankfurt Rd. SE24 ....3E 105
Frankham Ho. SE8 .... 3C 94
.... (off Frankham St.)
Frankham St. SE8 .... 3C 94
Frank Ho. SW8 .... 3A 90
.... (off Wyvil Rd.)
Frankland Cl. SE16 .... 4D 79
Frankland Rd. SW7 ....4F 73
Franklin Bldg. E14 .... 3C 80
Franklin Cl. SE13 .... 4D 95
Franklin Cl. SE27 .... 3D 119
Franklin Ho. E1 .... 2D 79
.... (off Watts St.)
Franklin Ho. E14 ....5F 67
.... (off E. India Dock Rd.)
Franklin Ho. NW6 .... 2C 58
.... (off Carlton Va.)
Franklin Pl. SE13 .... 4D 95
Franklin Sq. W14 .... 1B 86
Franklin's Row SW3 .... 1B 88
Franklin St. E3 .... 2D 67
Franklin St. N15 .... 1A 36
Franklyn Rd. NW10 .... 3B 42
Frank M. SE1 .... 5D 79
Frank Soskice Ho. SW6 ..... 2B 86
.... (off Clem Attlee Ct.)
Frank St. E13 .... 3C 68
Frank Whipple Pl. E14 .... 5A 66
.... (off Repton St.)
Frank Whymark Ho. SE16 ...3E 79
.... (off Rupack St.)
Fransfield Gro. SE26 .... 3D 121
Frans Hals Ct. E14 ....4F 81
Franthorne Way SE6 .... 2D 123
Fraserburgh Ho. E3 .... 1B 66
.... (off Vernon Rd.)
Fraser Cl. E6 ....5F 69
Fraser Cl. E14 ....1E 95
.... (off Ferry St.)
Fraser Ct. SE1 .... 5A 26 (4E 77)
.... (off Brockham St.)
Fraser Ct. SW11 .... 4A 88
.... (off Surrey La. Est.)
Fraser Rd. E17 .... 1D 39
Fraser St. W4 .... 1A 84
Frazier St. SE1 .... 4B 24 (3C 76)
Frean St. SE16 .... 4C 78
Frearson Ho. WC1 .... 1A 8 (2B 62)
.... (off Penton Ri.)
Freda Corbett Cl. SE15 ..... 3C 92
Freda St. SE16 .... 4C 78
Frederica Ct. SW2 .... 1D 119
Frederica St. N7 .... 4B 48
Frederick Charrington Ho.
E1 ....3E 65
.... (off Wickford St.)
Frederick Cl. W2 .... 1A 74
Frederick Ct. SW3 ....5B 74
.... (off Duke of York Sq.)
Frederick Cres. SW9 .... 3D 91
Frederick Dobson Ho. W11 . 1A 72
.... (off Cowling Cl.)
Frederick Ho. SE18 ....5F 83
.... (off Pett St.)
Frederick Pl. N8 ....1F 33
.... (off Crouch Hall Rd.)
Frederick's Pl. EC2 .. 3B 18 (5F 63)
.... (off Sovereign Cres.)

Frederick's Row EC1. 1D 9 (2D 63)
Frederick St. WC1 ..... 2F 7 (2B 62)
Frederick Ter. E8 ....4B 50
Frederic M. SW1 ..... 4A 20 (3B 74)
.... (off Kinnerton St.)
Frederic St. E17 .... 1A 38
Fred Styles Ho. SE7 .... 2E 97
Fred White Wlk. N7 .... 3A 48
Freedom St. SW11 .... 5B 88
Freegrove Rd. N7 .... 2A 48
.... (not continuous)
Freeling Ho. NW8 ....5F 45
.... (off Dorman Way)
Freeling St. N1: Lon Carnoustie Dr.
.... 4B 48
Freeling St. N1: Lon Pembroke St.
.... 4A 48
Freeman Ct. N7 .... 5A 34
Freeman Ho. SE11 .... 5D 77
.... (off George Mathers Rd.)
Freemantle St. SE17 .... 1A 92
Freeman Wlk. SE9 ....3E 111
Freemasons' Hall ..2E 15 (5A 62)
.... (off Gt. Queen St.)
Freemasons Rd. E16 .... 4D 69
Free Trade Wharf E1 ....1F 79
Freight La. N1 ....4F 47
Freightliners City Farm 3C 48
Freke Rd. SW11 .... 1C 102
Fremantle Ho. E1 ....3D 65
.... (off Somerford St.)
Fremont St. E9 .... 5D 51
.... (not continuous)
French Ordinary Ct.
EC3 .... 4E 19 (1A 78)
.... (off Crutched Friars)
French Pl. E2 .... 2E 11 (2A 64)
Frendsbury Rd. SE4 .... 2A 108
Frensham Dr. SW15 .... 3B 112
Frensham St. SE15 .... 2C 92
Frere St. SW11 .... 5A 88
Freshfield Av. E8 ....4B 50
Freshfield Cl. SE13 ....2F 109
Freshford St. SW18 ....3E 115
Freshwater Cl. SW17 .... 5C 116
Freshwater Ct. W1 .... 4A 60
.... (off Crawford St.)
Freshwater Rd. SW17 .... 5C 116
Freston Rd. W10 ....1F 71
Freston Rd. W11 ....1F 71
Freswick Ho. SE8 .... 5A 80
.... (off Chilton Gro.)
Freud Mus. 3E 45
Frewell Ho. EC1 ..... 5B 8 (4C 62)
.... (off Bourne Est.)
Frewin Rd. SW18 ....1F 115
Friar M. SE27 .... 3D 119
Friars Av. SW15 .... 3B 112
Friars Cl. SE1 .... 1E 25 (2D 77)
.... (off Bear La.)
Friars Mead E14 ....4E 81
Friars Mt. Ho. E2 .... 2F 11 (2B 64)
.... (off Rochelle St.)
Friars Pl. La. W3 .... 1A 70
Friars Rd. E6 ....5F 55
Friar St. EC4 .... 3E 17 (5D 63)
Friary Cl. SW1 ...... 2A 22 (2E 75)
.... (off Marlborough Rd.)
Friary Est. SE15 .... 2C 92
.... (not continuous)
Friary Rd. SE15 .... 3C 92
Friday St. EC4 .... 4F 17 (1E 77)
Frideswide Pl. NW5 ....2E 47
Friendly Pl. SE13 .... 4D 95
Friendly St. SE8 .... 4C 95

Friendly St. M. SE8 ....5C **94**
Friendship Ho. SE1...4E **25** (3D **77**)
.................*(off Belvedere Pl.)*
Friendship Way E15.............5E **53**
Friend St. EC1............1D **9** (2D **63**)
Friern Rd. SE22 ....5C **106**
.................*(not continuous)*
Frigate Ho. E14....................5E **81**
.................*(off Stebondale St.)*
Frigate M. SE8.....................2C **94**
Frimley Cl. SW19.................2A **114**
Frimley St. E1......................3F **65**
.................*(off Frimley Way)*
Frimley Way E1...................................
Frinstead Ho. W10................1F **71**
.................*(off Freston Rd.)*
Frinton Rd. E6......................2F **69**
Frinton Rd. N15...................1A **36**
Friston St. SW6....................5D **87**
Frith Ho. NW8.....................3F **59**
.................*(off Frampton St.)*
Frith Rd. E11.......................1E **53**
Frith St. W1.............3B **14** (5F **61**)
Frithville Ct. W12.................2E **71**
.................*(off Frithville Gdns.)*
Frithville Gdns. W12............2E **71**
Frobisher Ct. SE10...............2F **95**
.................*(off Old Woolwich Rd.)*
Frobisher Ct. SE23................2D **121**
Frobisher Ct. SE8 ....1A **94**
.................*(off Evelyn St.)*
Frobisher Ct. W12................3E **71**
.................*(off Lime Gro.)*
Frobisher Cres.
EC2 ....5A **10** (4E **63**)
.................*(off Silk St.)*
Frobisher Gdns. E10 ....2D **39**
Frobisher Ho. E1..................2D **79**
.................*(off Watts St.)*
Frobisher Ho. SW1................2F **89**
.................*(off Dolphin Sq.)*
Frobisher Pas. E14................2C **80**
Frobisher Pl. SE15................4E **93**
Frobisher St. SE10 ....2A **96**
Froebel Coll. 4B **98**
Frogley Rd. SE22.................2B **106**
Frogmore SW18....................3C **100**
Frogmore Ind. Est. N5..........2E **49**
Frognal NW3........................1E **45**
Frognal Cl. NW3..................2E **45**
Frognal Ct. NW3..................3E **45**
Frognal Gdns. NW3..............1E **45**
Frognal La. NW3..................2D **45**
Frognal Pde. NW3................3E **45**
Frognal Ri. NW3...................5E **31**
Frognal Way NW3................1E **45**
Frogwell Cl. N15..................1F **35**
Froissart Rd. SE9..................3F **111**
Frome Ho. SE15...................2D **107**
Frome St. N1.......................1E **63**
Frontenac NW10...................4D **43**
Frostic Wlk. E1.....................4C **64**
Froude St. SW8....................5D **89**
Fryday Gro. M. SW12............5E **103**
.................*(off Weir Rd.)*
Frye Ct. E3..........................2B **66**
.................*(off Benworth St.)*
Frye Ho. E20.......................3E **53**
.................*(off Penny Brookes St.)*
Fryent Cres. NW9.................1A **28**
Fryent Flds. NW9.................1A **28**
Fryent Gro. NW9..................1A **28**
Fryers Vw. SE4....................2F **107**
.................*(off Frendsbury Rd.)*
Fry Ho. E6 ....4E **55**

Frying Pan All. E1 ...1F **19** (4B **64**)
.................*(off Bell La.)*
Fry Rd. E6............................4F **55**
Fry Rd. NW10......................5B **42**
Frys Ct. SE10.......................2E **95**
.................*(off Durnford St.)*
Fulbeck Ho. N7....................3B **48**
.................*(off Sutterton St.)*
Fulbeck Rd. N19..................1E **47**
Fulbourne St. E1..................4D **65**
Fulbrook M. N19..................1E **47**
Fulcher Ho. N1....................5A **50**
.................*(off Colville Est.)*
Fulcher Ho. SE8 ....1B **94**
Fulford St. SE16..................3D **79**
FULHAM 4A **86**
Fulham B'way. SW6..............3C **86**
FULHAM BROADWAY 3C **86**
Fulham Broadway Station
(Underground) 3C **86**
Fulham Bus. Exchange SW6 4E **87**
.................*(off The Boulevard)*
Fulham Ct. SW6...................4C **86**
Fulham FC...........................4F **85**
Fulham High St. SW6............5A **86**
Fulham Island SW6 ....3C **86**
.................*(off Farm La.)*
Fulham Palace 5A **86**
Fulham Pal. Rd. SW6 ....2F **85**
Fulham Pal. Rd. W6 ....1E **85**
Fulham Pk. Gdns. SW6 ....5B **86**
Fulham Pk. Rd. SW6 ....5B **86**
Fulham Pools Virgin Active
.....................................2A **86**
Fulham Rd. SW10 ....3D **87**
Fulham Rd. SW3 ....1F **87**
Fulham Rd. SW6 ....5A **86**
.................*(not continuous)*
Fuller Cl. E2........................3C **64**
.................*(off Cheshire St.)*
Fuller's Griffin Brewery 2B **84**
Fullerton Rd. SW18..............3D **101**
Fullwood's M. N1...1C **10** (2F **63**)
Fulmar Ho. SE16..................5F **79**
.................*(off Tawny Way)*
Fulmead St. SW6..................4D **87**
Fulmer Ho. NW8..................3A **60**
.................*(off Mallory St.)*
Fulmer Rd. E16....................4F **69**
Fulneck E1...........................3E **65**
Fulready Rd. E10..................1F **39**
Fulthorp Rd. SE3..................5B **96**
Fulton M. W2.......................1E **73**
Fulwood Pl. WC1...1A **16** (4B **62**)
Fulwood Wlk. SW19..............1A **114**
Furber St. W6......................4D **71**
Furley Ho. SE15...................3C **92**
.................*(off Peckham Pk. Rd.)*
Furley Rd. SE15...................3C **92**
Furlong Rd. N7....................2D **48**
Furmage St. SW18................5D **101**
Furneaux Av. SE27................5D **119**
Furness Ho. SW1..................1D **89**
.................*(part of Abbots Mnr.)*
Furness Rd. NW10................1C **56**
Furness Rd. SW6..................5D **87**
Furnival Ct. E3.....................1C **66**
.................*(off Four Seasons Cl.)*
Furnival Mans. W1...1F **13** (4E **61**)
.................*(off Wells St.)*
Furnival St. EC4....2B **16** (5C **62**)
Furrow La. E9......................2E **51**
Fursecroft W1......................5B **60**
.................*(off George St.)*
Further Grn. Rd. SE6............5A **110**

FURZEDOWN 5D **117**
Furzedown Dr. SW17............5D **117**
Furzedown Recreation Cen.
.....................................5D **117**
Furzedown Rd. SW17............5D **117**
Furzefield Rd. SE3................2D **97**
Furze St. E3.........................4C **66**
Fusilier Mus., The .5F **19** (1B **78**)
Fusion Apts. SE14................2A **94**
.................*(off Moulding La.)*
Fye Foot La. EC4...4F **17** (1E **77**)
.................*(off Queen Victoria St.)*
Fyfield N4............................4C **34**
.................*(off Six Acres Est.)*
Fyfield Ct. E7.......................3C **54**
Fyfield Rd. SW9...................1C **104**
Fynes St. SW1......................5F **75**

G

Gable Ct. SE26....................4D **121**
Gables Cl. SE12...................1C **124**
Gables Ct. SE5.....................4A **92**
Gabriel Ct. E1......................4A **66**
.................*(off Elsa Street)*
Gabriel Ho. N1.....................5D **49**
.................*(off Islington Grn.)*
Gabriel Ho. SE11..................5B **76**
Gabriel Ho. SE16..................4B **80**
.................*(off Odessa St.)*
Gabrielle Ct. NW3.................3F **45**
Gabriel M. NW2...................4B **30**
Gabriel St. SE23...................5F **107**
Gabriels Wharf SE1 .1B **24** (2C **76**)
Gad Cl. E13.........................2D **69**
Gaddesden Ho. EC1....2C **10** (2F **63**)
.................*(off Cranwood St.)*
Gadebridge Ho. SW3.............1A **88**
.................*(off Cale St.)*
Gadsbury Cl. NW9................1B **28**
Gadsden Ho. W10.................3A **58**
.................*(off Hazlewood Cres.)*
Gadwall Cl. E16...................5D **69**
Gadwall Ho. NW9................1C **28**
.................*(off Perryfield Way)*
Gage Brown Ho. W10...........5F **57**
.................*(off Bridge Cl.)*
Gage Rd. E16......................4A **68**
Gage St. WC1.........5E **7** (4A **62**)
Gainford Ho. E2...................2D **65**
.................*(off Ellsworth St.)*
Gainford St. N1...................5C **48**
Gainsborough Ct. SE16........1D **93**
.................*(off Stubbs Dr.)*
Gainsborough Ct. SE21........2A **120**
Gainsborough Ct. W12........3E **71**
Gainsborough Gdns. NW11...2B **30**
Gainsborough Gdns. NW3.....5F **31**
Gainsborough Ho.
.....E14: Lon Cassilis Rd........3C **80**
.................*(off Cassilis Rd.)*
Gainsborough Ho.
.....E14: Lon Victory Pl.........1A **80**
.................*(off Victory Pl.)*
Gainsborough Ho. SW1........5F **75**
.................*(off Erasmus St.)*
Gainsborough Mans. W14 ....2A **86**
.................*(off Queen's Club Gdns.)*
Gainsborough M. SE26........3D **121**
Gainsborough Rd. E11.........2A **40**
Gainsborough Rd. E15.........2A **68**
Gainsborough Rd. W4..........5B **70**
Gainsborough St. E9............3B **52**
Gainsborough Studios E. N1 5F **49**
.................*(off Poole St.)*

Gainsborough Studios Nth.
N1 ....5F **49**
.................................(off Poole St.)
Gainsborough Studios Sth.
N1 ....5F **49**
Gainsborough Studios W. N15F **49**
.................................(off Poole St.)
Gainsford Ct. E11 ....5A **40**
Gainsford St. S.E.1 ...2F **27** (3B **78**)
Gairloch Ho. NW1...................4F **47**
.............................(off Stratford Vs.)
Gairloch Rd. SE5...................5A **92**
Gaisford St. NW5...................3E **47**
Gaitskell Ct. SW11 ....5A **88**
Gaitskell Ho. E6....................5F **55**
Gaitskell Ho. SE17................2A **92**
....(off Villa St.)
Gaitskell Way SE1...3A **26** (3E **77**)
...................................(off Weller St.)
Gala Bingo Surrey Quays 4F **79**
Gala Bingo Tooting 5A **116**
Galahad M. E3.........................1B **66**
Galahad Rd. BR1: Broml....4C **124**
Galata Sq. SW13....................3C **84**
Galatea Sq. SE15.................1D **107**
Galaxy Bldg. E14....................5C **80**
.................................(off Crews St.)
Galaxy Ho. EC2......3C **10** (3F **63**)
...............................(off Leonard St.)
Galbraith St. E14....................4E **81**
Galena Arches W6...................5D **71**
................................(off Galena Rd.)
Galena Hgts. E20...................3E **53**
.........................(off Mirabelle Gdns.)
Galena Rd. W6.......................5D **71**
Galen Pl. WC1...........1E **15** (4A **62**)
Galesbury Rd. SW18............4E **101**
Gales Gdns. E2.......................2D **65**
Gale St. E3..............................4C **66**
Galgate Cl. SW19...................1F **113**
Galleon Cl. SE16....................3F **79**
Galleon Ho. E14.....................5E **81**
............................(off Glengarnock Av.)
Galleons Vw. E14....................3E **81**
Galleria SE15.........................2B **92**
Galleries, The NW8................1E **59**
...................................(off Abbey Rd.)
Gallery, The E20.....................3E **53**
.........................(within Westfield Shop. Cen.)
Gallery, The SE14..................3B **94**
.............................(off New Cross Rd.)
Gallery Apts. E1 ....5E **65**
.............................(off Commercial Rd.)
Gallery Apts. SE1....4D **27** (3A **78**)
...................................(off Lamb Wlk.)
**Gallery at London Glassblowing,
The** 3D **27** (3A **78**)
.........................(off Bermondsey St.)
Gallery By The Pool 4E **79**
Gallery Cl. SE1........4B **26** (3F **77**)
...............................(off Pilgrimage St.)
Gallery Ct. SW10....................3D **51**
.................................(off Gunter Gro.)
Gallery Ho. E8.........................3D **51**
.................................(off Hackney Rd.)
Gallery Rd. SE21...................1F **119**
Galleywall Rd. SE16................5D **79**
Galleywall Rd. Trad. Est.
SE16.....................................5D **79**
Galleywood Ho. W10...............4E **57**
.................................(off Sutton Way)
Gallia Rd. N5...........................2D **49**
Gallions Rd. SE7.....................5D **83**
...............................(not continuous)

Gallon Cl. SE7.........................5E **83**
Galloway Rd. W12....................2C **70**
Gallus Sq. SE3.......................1D **111**
Galsworthy Av. E14.................5A **66**
Galsworthy Cl. NW2................1A **44**
Galsworthy Cres. SE3.............3E **97**
Galsworthy Ho. W11 ....5A **58**
.................................(off Elgin Cres.)
Galsworthy Rd. NW2...............1A **44**
Galsworthy Ter. N16................5F **35**
Galton St. W10.........................2A **58**
Galveston Ho. E1....................3A **66**
.................................(off Harford St.)
Galveston Rd. SW15...............3B **100**
Galway Cl. SE16....................1D **93**
.................................(off Masters Dr.)
Galway Ho. E1........................4F **65**
.............................(off White Horse La.)
Galway Ho. EC1.......2A **10** (2E **63**)
.................................(off Galway St.)
Galway St. EC1.......2A **10** (2E **63**)
Gambado Beckenham 5C **122**
Gambado Chelsea.................4E **87**
.................................(off Station Ct.)
Gambetta St. SW8...................5D **89**
Gambia St. SE1.......2E **25** (2D **77**)
Gambier Ho. EC1.....2A **10** (2E **63**)
.................................(off Mora St.)
Gamble Rd. SW17....................4A **116**
Gamlen Rd. SW15....................2F **99**
Gamuel Cl. E17........................1C **38**
Gandhi Cl. E17........................1C **38**
Gandolfi St. SE15....................2A **92**
Ganley Ct. SW11 ....1F **101**
.............................(off Winstanley Est.)
Ganton St. W1........4F **13** (1E **75**)
Gap Rd. SW19.........................5C **114**
Garand Ct. N7.........................2B **48**
Garbett Ho. SE17....................2D **91**
.............................(off Doddington Gro.)
Garbutt Pl. W1.......1C **12** (4C **60**)
Garda Ho. SE10.......................5A **82**
.................................(off Cable Wlk.)
Garden Cl. SE12......................3D **125**
Garden Cl. SW15.....................5C **99**
Garden Ct. EC4......4B **16** (1C **76**)
.................................(off Fountain Ct.)
Garden Ct. NW8......................2F **59**
.................................(off Garden Rd.)
Garden Ct. W11.......................1A **72**
.................................(off Clarendon Rd.)
Garden Halls, The
WC1..........................2D **7** (2A **62**)
Garden Ho. NW6......................1D **59**
.................................(off Oxford Rd.)
Garden Ho. SW4......................4D **73**
.............................(off Cornwall Gdns.)
Garden Ho's., The W6.............2F **85**
.................................(off Bothwell St.)
Garden La. SW2.......................1B **118**
Garden M. SE10.......................5A **82**
Garden M. W2..........................1C **72**
Garden Mus., The 4B **76**
Garden Pl. E8...........................5B **50**
Garden Pl. NW8.......................2E **59**
Garden Row SE1......5D **25** (4D **77**)
Garden Royal SW15.................4F **99**
Gardens, The E5......................2B **36**
Gardens, The SE22.................2C **106**
Garden Sq. SW1......................1C **88**
Garden St. E1..........................4F **65**
Garden Ter. SW1......................1F **89**
Garden Ter. SW7......................3A **74**
.................................(off Trevor Pl.)
Garden Wlk. EC2......2D **11** (2A **64**)

Gardiner Av. NW2....................2E **43**
Gardiner Ho. SW11..................4A **88**
Gardiner Cl. EC1......................1D **41**
Gardner Ct. EC1.......3D **9** (3D **63**)
.................................(off Brewery Sq.)
Gardner Ind. Est.
BR3: Beck........................5B **122**
Gardner Rd. E13......................3D **69**
Gardners La. EC4....4F **17** (1E **77**)
Gardnor Rd. NW3....................1F **45**
Gard St. EC1............1E **9** (2D **63**)
Gareth Ct. SW16.....................3F **117**
Gareth Gro. BR1: Broml.......4C **124**
Garfield Ct. NW6.....................4A **44**
.............................(off Willesden La.)
Garfield M. SW11.....................1C **102**
Garfield Rd. E13......................3B **68**
Garfield Rd. SW11...................1C **102**
Garfield Rd. SW19..................5E **115**
Garford St. E14........................1C **80**
Garganey Ct. NW10.................3A **42**
.................................(off Elgar Av.)
Garland Cl. SE1.......5A **26** (4E **77**)
Garland Ct. E14........................1C **80**
.................................(off Premiere Pl.)
Garland Ho. SE17....................5E **77**
.................................(off Wansey St.)
Garlands Ho. NW8...................1E **59**
.................................(off Carlton Hill)
Garlick Hill EC4........4A **18** (1E **77**)
Garlies Rd. SE23.....................3A **122**
Garlinge Ho. SW9....................4C **90**
.................................(off Gosling Way)
Garlinge Rd. NW2....................3B **44**
Garnault M. EC1........2C **8** (2C **62**)
.................................(off Rosebery Av.)
Garnault Pl. EC1.......2C **8** (2C **62**)
Garner St. E2...........................1C **64**
Garnet Ho. E1..........................2E **79**
.................................(off Garnet St.)
Garnet Rd. NW10.....................3A **42**
Garnet St. E1...........................1E **79**
Garnett Rd. NW3.....................2B **46**
Garnham Cl. N16......................4B **36**
Garnham St. N16......................4B **36**
Garnies Cl. SE15......................3B **92**
Garrad's Rd. SW16.................3F **117**
Garrard Wlk. NW10..................3A **42**
Garratt La. SW18.....................5D **101**
Garratt La. SW17.....................3E **115**
Garratt La. SW18.....................4D **101**
Garratt Ter. SW17....................4A **116**
Garraway Ct. SW13.................3E **85**
.................................(off Wyatt Dr.)
Garrett Cl. W3..........................4A **56**
Garrett Ho. SE1.......3D **25** (3D **77**)
.................................(off Burrows M.)
Garrett St. EC1.........3A **10** (3E **63**)
Garrick Av. NW11.....................1A **30**
Garrick Cl. SW18.....................2E **101**
Garrick Cl. E8..........................4B **50**
.................................(off Jacaranda Gro.)
Garrick Ho. W1.......2D **21** (2D **75**)
.................................(off Carrington St.)
Garrick Ho. W4........................2A **84**
Garrick Ind. Cen. NW9...........1B **28**
Garrick Rd. NW9......................1B **28**
Garrick St. WC2......4D **15** (1A **76**)
.................................(off Charing Cross Rd.)
Garrick Theatre.......5C **14** (1F **75**)
.................................(off St Martin's La.)
Garrison Rd. E3........................5C **52**
Garrison Sq. SW1....................1C **88**

Garsdale Ter. W14 .... 1B **86**
.... (off Aisgill Av.)
Garsington M. SE4 .... 1B **108**
Garson Ho. W2 .... 1F **73**
.... (off Gloucester Ter.)
Garston Ho. N1 .... 4D **49**
.... (The Sutton Est.)
Garter Way SE16 .... 3F **79**
Garth Ho. NW2 .... 4B **30**
Garthorne Rd. SE23 .... 5F **107**
Garthorne Road Nature Reserve
.... 5F **107**
Garth Rd. NW2 .... 4B **30**
Gartmoor Gdns. SW19 ...... 1B **114**
Garton Pl. SW18 .... 4E **101**
Gartons Way SW11 .... 1E **101**
Garvary Rd. E16 .... 5D **69**
Garway Ct. E3 .... 1C **66**
.... (off Matilda Gdns.)
Garway Rd. W2 .... 5D **59**
Gascoigne Pl. E2 ... 1F **11** (2B **64**)
.... (not continuous)
Gascony Av. NW6 .... 4C **44**
Gascony Pl. W12 .... 2F **71**
Gascoyne Ho. E9 .... 4A **52**
Gascoyne Rd. E9 .... 4F **51**
Gaselee St. E14 .... 2E **81**
.... (off Baffin Way)
Gasholder Pk. 5F **47**
Gaskarth Rd. SW12 .... 4D **103**
Gaskell Rd. N6 .... 1B **32**
Gaskell St. SW4 .... 5A **90**
Gaskin St. N1 .... 5D **49**
Gaspar Cl. SW5 .... 5D **73**
Gaspar M. SW5 .... 5D **73**
Gassiot Rd. SW17 .... 4B **116**
Gasson Ho. SE14 .... 2F **93**
.... (off John Williams Cl.)
Gastein Rd. W6 .... 2F **85**
Gastigny Ho. EC1 ... 2A **10** (2E **63**)
.... (off Pleydell Ct.)
Gataker Ho. SE16 .... 4D **79**
.... (off Slippers Pl.)
Gataker St. SE16 .... 4D **79**
Gatcombe Ho. SE22 .... 1A **106**
Gatcombe Rd. E16 .... 2C **82**
Gatcombe Rd. N19 .... 5F **33**
Gate Cinema 2C **72**
.... (off Notting Hill Ga.)
Gateforth St. NW8 .... 3A **60**
Gate Hill Ct. W11 .... 2B **72**
.... (off Ladbroke Ter.)
Gate Ho. E3 .... 5A **52**
.... (off Gunmakers La.)
Gate Ho. N1 .... 4F **49**
.... (off Ufton Rd.)
Gate Ho. NW6 .... 1D **59**
.... (off Oxford Rd.)
Gatehouse Sq.
SE1 .... 1A **26** (2F **77**)
.... (off Southwark Bri. Rd.)
Gateley Ho. SE4 .... 2F **107**
.... (off Coston Wlk.)
Gateley Rd. SW9 .... 1B **104**
Gate Lodge W9 .... 4C **58**
.... (off Admiral Wlk.)
Gately Ct. SE15 .... 3B **92**
Gate M. SW7 .... 3A **74**
.... (off Rutland Ga.)
Gatesborough St.
EC2 .... 3D **11** (3A **64**)
Gates Ct. SE17 .... 1E **91**
Gatesden WC1 ...... 1E **7** (2A **62**)
Gateside Rd. SW17 .... 3B **116**
Gate St. WC2 .... 2F **15** (5B **62**)

Gate Theatre, The 2C **72**
.... (off Pembridge Rd.)
Gateway SE17 .... 2E **91**
Gateway Arc. N1 .... 1E **9**
.... (off Upper St.)
Gateway Bus. Cen. SE26 .... 5A **122**
Gateway Ind. Est. NW10 ..... 2D **56**
Gateway M. E8 .... 2B **50**
Gateway Rd. E10 .... 5D **39**
Gateways, The SW3 .... 5A **74**
GATEWAY SURGICAL CEN. 3F **69**
Gathorne St. E2 .... 1F **65**
.... (off Mace St.)
Gatliff Cl. SW1 .... 1D **89**
.... (off Ebury Bri. Rd.)
Gatliff Rd. SW1 .... 1D **89**
Gatonby St. SE15 .... 4B **92**
Gattis Wharf N1 .... 1A **62**
.... (off New Wharf Rd.)
Gatton Rd. SW17 .... 4A **116**
Gatwick Ho. E14 .... 5B **66**
.... (off Clemence St.)
Gatwick Rd. SW18 .... 5B **100**
Gauden Cl. SW4 .... 1F **103**
Gauden Rd. SW4 .... 5F **89**
Gaugin Cl. SE16 .... 1D **93**
.... (off Stubbs Dr.)
Gaugin Sq. E1 .... 1C **78**
Gaumont Pl. SW2 .... 2A **118**
Gaumont Ter. W12 .... 3E **71**
.... (off Lime Gro.)
Gaunt St. SE1 .... 5F **25** (4E **77**)
Gautrey Rd. SE15 .... 5E **93**
Gavel St. SE17 .... 5F **77**
Gaverick M. E14 .... 5C **80**
Gavestone Cres. SE12 .... 5E **111**
Gavestone Rd. SE12 .... 5D **111**
Gaviller Pl. E5 .... 1D **51**
Gawber St. E2 .... 2E **65**
Gawsworth Cl. E15 .... 2B **54**
Gawthorne Ct. E3 .... 1C **66**
Gay Cl. NW2 .... 2D **43**
Gaydon Ho. W2 .... 4D **59**
.... (off Bourne Ter.)
Gayfere St. SW1 ..... 5D **23** (4A **76**)
Gayford Rd. W12 .... 3B **70**
Gay Ho. N16 .... 2A **50**
Gayhurst SE17 .... 2F **91**
.... (off Hopwood Rd.)
Gayhurst Ho. NW8 .... 3A **60**
.... (off Mallory St.)
Gayhurst Rd. E8 .... 4C **50**
Gaymead NW8 .... 5D **45**
.... (off Abbey Rd.)
Gaynesford Rd. SE23 .... 2F **121**
Gay Rd. E15 .... 1F **67**
Gaysley Ho. SE11 .... 5C **76**
.... (off Hotspur St.)
Gay St. SW15 .... 1F **99**
Gayton Cres. NW3 .... 1F **45**
Gayton Ho. E3 .... 3C **66**
.... (off Chiltern Rd.)
Gayton Rd. NW3 .... 1F **45**
Gayville Rd. SW11 .... 4B **102**
Gaywood Cl. SW2 .... 1B **118**
Gaywood St. SE1 ... 5D **25** (4D **77**)
Gaza St. SE17 .... 1D **91**
Gazelle Ho. E15 .... 3A **54**
Gean Ct. E11 .... 1F **53**
Gearing Cl. SW17 .... 4C **116**
Geary Rd. NW10 .... 2C **42**
Geary St. N7 .... 2B **48**
Gedling Pl. SE1 ..... 5F **27** (3B **78**)
.... (off Sweeney Cres.)

Gedling Pl. SE1 ..... 5F **27** (4B **78**)
Geere Rd. E15 .... 5B **54**
Gees Ct. W1 .... 3C **12** (5C **60**)
Gee St. EC1 .... 3F **9** (3E **63**)
Geffrye Ct. N1 ...... 1E **11** (1A **64**)
Geffrye Est. N1 .... 1A **64**
Geffrye Mus. 1F **11** (1B **64**)
Geffrye St. E2 .... 1F **11** (1B **64**)
Geldart Rd. SE15 .... 3D **93**
Geldeston Rd. E5 .... 4C **36**
Gellatly Rd. SE14 .... 5E **93**
Gem Ct. SE10 .... 3D **95**
.... (off Merryweather Pl.)
Gemini Apts. E1 .... 3F **11** (3B **64**)
.... (off Sclater St.)
Gemini Bus. Cen. E16 .... 3F **67**
Gemini Bus. Est. SE14 .... 1F **93**
Gemini Ct. E1 .... 1C **78**
.... (off Vaughan Way)
Gemini Ho. E3 .... 5C **52**
.... (off Garrison Rd.)
General Wolfe Rd. SE10 ...... 4F **95**
Geneva Dr. SW9 .... 2C **104**
Genoa Av. SW15 .... 3E **99**
Genoa Ho. E1 .... 3F **65**
.... (off Ernest St.)
Genoa Rd. SE20 .... 1E **121**
Gentry Gdns. E13 .... 3C **68**
Geoff Cade Way E3 .... 4B **66**
Geoffrey Chaucer Way E1 .... 4B **66**
Geoffrey Cl. SE5 .... 5E **91**
Geoffrey Ct. SE4 .... 5B **94**
Geoffrey Gdns. E6 .... 1F **69**
Geoffrey Ho. SE1 ... 5C **26** (4F **77**)
.... (off Pardoner St.)
Geoffrey Jones Ct. NW10 .... 5C **42**
Geoffrey Rd. SE4 .... 1B **108**
George Beard Rd. SE8 .... 5B **80**
George Belt Ho. E2 .... 2F **65**
.... (off Smart St.)
George Ct. WC2 ..... 5E **15** (1A **76**)
.... (off John Adam St.)
George Downing Est. N16 .... 4B **36**
George Eliot Ho. SE17 .... 1E **91**
.... (off Thrush St.)
George Eliot Ho. SW1 .... 5E **75**
.... (off Vauxhall Bri. Rd.)
George Elliston Ho. SE1 ...... 1C **92**
.... (off Old Kent Rd.)
George Eyre Ho. NW8 .... 1F **59**
.... (off Cochrane St.)
George Furness Ho. NW10 ...3D **43**
.... (off Grange Rd.)
George Gillett Ct.
EC1 ....3A **10** (3E **63**)
.... (off Banner St.)
George Hilsdon Ct. E14 ....5A **66**
.... (off Repton St.)
George Ho. NW6 .... 1B **58**
.... (off Albert Rd.)
George Hudson Twr. E15 ..... 1D **67**
.... (off High St.)
George Inn Yd. SE1 .. 2B **26** (2F **77**)
George La. SE13 .... 4D **109**
George La. SE6 .... 4D **109**
George Lansbury Ho. E3 ...... 2B **66**
.... (off Bow Rd.)
George Lansbury Ho. NW10 ..4A **42**
George Leybourne Ho. E1 .... 1C **78**
.... (off Fletcher St.)
George Lindgren Ho. SW6 .... 3B **86**
.... (off Clem Attlee Ct.)
George Loveless Ho.
E2 .... 1F **11** (2B **64**)
.... (off Diss St.)

George Lowe Ct. W2 ....4D 59
..........................(off Bourne Ter.)
George Mathers Rd. SE11 ...5D 77
George M. NW1 ....2A 6 (2E 61)
.............................(off Drummond St.)
George M. SW9 ....5C 90
George Padmore Ho. E8 ....5C 50
.............................(off Brougham Rd.)
George Peabody Ct. NW1....4A 60
..............................(off Burne St.)
George Peabody St. E13.......1E 69
George Potter Ho. SW11 ....5F 87
..........................(off George Potter Way)
George Potter Way SW11 ....5F 87
George Row SE16 ....3D 78
George Scott Ho. E1..............5F 65
............................(off W. Arbour St.)
George's Rd. N7 ....2B 48
George's Sq. SW6 ....2B 86
.............................(off North End Rd.)
George St. E14.........................2D 81
George St. E16 ....5B 68
George St. W1 ....5B 60
Georgetown Cl. SE19 ....5A 120
Georgette Pl. SE10 ....3E 95
George Vale Ho. E2 ....1C 64
............................(off Mansford St.)
George Vw. Ho. SW18.........1D 115
.........................(off Knaresborough Dr.)
George Walter Ct. SE16 ....5E 79
............................(off Millender Wlk.)
George Wyver Cl. SW19.....5A 100
George Yd. EC3 ....3C 18 (5F 63)
George Yd. W1 ....4C 12 (1C 74)
Georgia Cl. SE16 ....4C 78
.................................(off Priter Rd.)
Georgiana St. NW1................1E 47
Georgian Cl. E9 ....5E 51
Georgian Ct. NW4...............1D 29
Georgian Ct. SE16 ....4A 118
Georgian Ho. E16 ....2C 82
.................................(off Capulet M.)
Georgian Ho. N1 ....1A 50
.................................(off Hertford Rd.)
Georgina Gdns. E2 ...1F 11 (2B 64)
Geotgette Ct. SW18................3D 101
.................................(off Courthouse Way)
Geraint Rd. BR1: Broml 4C 124
Geraldine Rd. SW18.............3E 101
Geraldine St. SE11...5D 25 (4D 77)
Gerald M. SW1 ....5C 74
.................................(off Gerald Rd.)
Gerald Rd. E16 ....3B 68
Gerald Rd. SW1 ....5C 74
Gerard Pl. E9 ....4F 51
Gerard Rd. SW13....................4B 84
Gerards Cl. SE16....................1E 93
Gerards Pl. SW4.....................2F 103
Germander Way E15 ....2A 68
Gernigan Ho. SW18...............4F 101
Gernon Rd. E3 ....1A 66
Geron Way NW2 ....3D 29
Gerrard Ho. SE14 ....3E 93
.................................(off Briant St.)
Gerrard Pl. W1 ....4C 14 (1F 75)
Gerrard Rd. N1 ....1D 63
Gerrard St. W1 ....4B 14 (1F 75)
Gerrard Way SE3....................2E 111
Gerridge Ct. SE1.......5C 24 (4C 76)
.................................(off Gerridge St.)
Gerridge St. SE1.......5C 24 (4C 76)
Gerry Raffles Sq. E15 ....3F 53
Gertrude St. SW10 ....2E 87

Gervase St. SE15 ....3D 93
Ghent St. SE6..........................2C 122
Ghent Way E8..........................3B 50
Giant Arches Rd. SE24..........5E 105
Gibbings Ho. SE1 ....4E 25 (3D 77)
.............................(off King James St.)
Gibbins Rd. E15 ....4E 53
Gibbon Ho. NW8......................3F 59
.............................(off Fisherton St.)
Gibbon Rd. SE15 ....5E 93
Gibbon Rd. W3 ....1A 70
Gibbon's Rents SE1...2D 27 (2A 78)
.............................(off Magdalen St.)
Gibbons Rd. NW10.................3A 42
Gibbs Av. SE19........................5F 119
Gibbs Cl. SE19........................5F 119
Gibbs Grn. W14......................1B 86
..............................(not continuous)
Gibbs La. E2 ....1C 64
Gibbs Sq. SE19......................5F 119
Gibney Ter. BR1: Broml 4B 124
Gibraltar Wlk. E2....................2B 64
.............................(off Shacklewell St.)
Gibson Cl. E1..........................3E 65
Gibson Cl. SE9 ....3E 111
Gibson Gdns. N16 ....4B 36
Gibson Rd. SE11 ....5B 76
Gibson Sq. N1 ....5C 48
Gibson Sq. Gdns. 5C 48
.................................(off Gibson Sq.)
Gibson St. SE10 ....1A 96
Gideon Rd. SW11 ....1C 102
Gielgud Theatre 4B 14 (1F 75)
.............................(off Shaftesbury Av.)
Giesbach Rd. N19 ....4F 33
Giffin Sq. Mkt. 3C 94
.................................(off Giffin St.)
Giffin St. SE8..........................3C 94
Gifford Ho. SE10.....................1F 95
.................................(off Eastney St.)
Gifford Ho. SW1......................1E 89
.............................(off Churchill Gdns.)
Gifford Rd. NW10...................4A 42
Gifford St. N1 ....4A 48
Gift La. E15 ....5A 54
GILBERT BRI..............1A 18 (4E 63)
.................................(off Wood St.)
Gilbert Ho. E2 ....2F 65
.................................(off Usk St.)
Gilbert Ho. EC2........1A 18 (4E 63)
.................................(off Wood St.)
Gilbert Ho. SE8 ....2C 94
Gilbert Ho. SW1 ....1D 89
.............................(off Churchill Gdns.)
Gilbert Ho. SW13....................5A 84
.............................(off Trinity Chu. Rd.)
Gilbert Ho. SW8 ....3A 90
.................................(off Wyvil Rd.)
Gilbert Pl. WC1 ....1D 15 (4A 62)
Gilbert Rd. SE11 ....5C 76
Gilbert Scott Bldg. SW15 ...4A 100
Gilbert Scott Ho. W14 ....5B 72
.............................(off Warwick La.)
Gilbert Sheldon Ho. W2 ....4F 59
.............................(off Edgware Rd.)
Gilbertson Ho. E14 ....4C 80
.................................(off Mellish St.)
Gilbert St. E15........................1A 54
Gilbert St. W1 ....3C 12 (5C 60)
Gilbey Ho. NW1 ....4D 47
Gilbey Rd. SW17 ....4A 116
Gilbeys Rd. NW1....................4C 46
Gilby Ho. E9 ....3F 51
Gilda Cres. N16 ....3C 36

Gildea St. W1 ....1E 13 (4D 61)
Gilden Cres. NW5...................2C 46
Giles Coppice SE19...............4B 120
Giles Ho. E15..........................3F 53
.............................(off Forrester Way)
Giles Ho. W11 ....5C 58
.............................(off Westbourne Gro.)
Gilesmead SE5........................4F 91
Gilkes Cres. SE21...................4A 106
Gilkes Pl. SE21 ....4A 106
Gillan Ct. SE12 ....3D 125
Gill Av. E16 ....5C 68
Gillender St. E14 ....3E 67
Gillender St. E3.......................3E 67
Gillespie Pk. Local Nature
Reserve...............................5C 34
Gillespie Rd. N5 ....5C 34
Gillett Av. E6 ....1F 69
Gillett Pl. N16 ....2A 50
Gillett Sq. N16 ....2A 50
.................................(off Gillett St.)
Gillett St. N16..........................2A 50
Gillfoot NW1 ....1F 5 (1E 61)
.............................(off Hampstead Rd.)
Gillian Lynne Theatre
.................................2E 15 (5A 62)
.................................(off Parker St.)
Gillian St. SE13 ....3D 109
Gillies Ho. NW6 ....4F 45
.............................(off Hilgrove Rd.)
Gillies St. NW5 ....2C 46
Gilling Ct. NW3 ....3A 46
Gillingham M. SW1 ....5E 75
Gillingham Rd. NW2...............5A 30
Gillingham Row SW1 ....5E 75
Gillingham St. SW1...............5E 75
Gillison Wlk. SE16..................4D 79
Gillis Sq. SW15.......................4C 98
Gillman Dr. E15.......................5B 54
Gillman Ho. E2 ....1C 64
.............................(off Pritchard's Rd.)
Gillray Ho. SW10 ....2F 87
.................................(off Ann La.)
Gill St. E14..............................5B 66
Gilman Ho. N1 ....4C 48
.............................(off Drummond Way)
Gilmore Rd. SE13...................2F 109
Gilpin Av. SW14 ....2A 98
Gilpin Cl. W2 ....4E 59
.................................(off Porteus Rd.)
Gilpin Rd. E5 ....1A 52
Gilray Ho. W2 ....1F 73
.............................(off Gloucester Ter.)
Gilstead Rd. SW6 ....5D 87
Gilston Rd. SW10 ....1E 87
Gilton Rd. SE6 ....3A 124
Giltspur St. EC1.........1E 17 (5D 63)
Ginger Apts. SE1 ......3F 27 (3B 78)
.................................(off Cayenne Ct.)
Ginsburg Yd. NW3..................1E 45
Gipsy Hill SE19.......................4A 120
Gipsy Hill Station (Rail) 5A 120
Gipsy La. SW15......................1D 99
Gipsy Rd. SE27......................4E 119
Gipsy Rd. Gdns. SE27 ....4E 119
Giralda Cl. E16 ....4F 69
Giraud St. E14.........................5D 67
Girdler's Rd. W14...................5F 71
Girdlestone Wlk. N19.............4E 33
Girdwood Rd. SW18..............5A 100
Girling Ho. N1.........................5A 50
.............................(off Colville Est.)
Gironde Rd. SW6....................3B 86
Girton Rd. SE26......................5F 121
Girton Vs. W10 ....5F 57

Gisburn Ho. SE15............2C 92
............(off Friary Est.)
Gissing Wlk. N1............4C 48
Gittens Cl. BR1: Broml....4B 124
Given Wilson Wlk. E13.....1B 68
Giverny Ho. SE16...........3F 89
............(off Water Gdns. Sq.)
Glacier Ho. SW11..........3F 89
............(off Ponton Rd.)
Glacier Pl. E2.............1D 65
............(off Clare St.)
Gladding Rd. E12..........1F 55
Glade, The E8.............3C 50
Glade, The SE7............3E 97
Glade, The W12............3D 71
............(off Coningham Rd.)
Glade Apts. E14...........5E 81
............(off Stebondale St.)
Glade Path SE1....4D 25 (3D 77)
............(off Blackfriars Rd.)
Gladesmore Community School
& Sports Cen.............1C 36
Gladesmore Rd. N15........1B 36
Glade Wlk. E20............3D 53
Gladiator St. SE23........5A 108
Glading Ter. N16..........5B 36
Gladsmuir Rd. N19.........3E 33
Gladstone Ct. NW6.........4E 45
............(off Fairfax Rd.)
Gladstone Ct. SW1.........5F 75
............(off Regency St.)
Gladstone Ct. Bus. Cen.
SW8......................4D 89
............(off Pagden St.)
Gladstone Ho. E14.........5C 66
............(off E. India Dock Rd.)
Gladstone M. NW6..........4B 44
............(off Cavendish Rd.)
Gladstone Pde. NW2........4E 29
Gladstone Pk. Gdns. NW2..1D 43
Gladstone Pl. E3..........1B 66
Gladstone St. SE1...5D 25 (4D 77)
Gladstone Ter. SE27.......5E 119
............(off Bentons La.)
Gladstone Ter. SW8........4D 89
Gladwell Rd. BR1: Broml...5C 124
Gladwell Rd. N8...........1B 34
Gladwin Ho. NW1....1A 6 (1E 61)
............(off Werrington St.)
Gladwyn Rd. SW15.........1F 99
Gladys Ct. BR1: Broml.....2B 124
Gladys Dimson Ho. E7......2B 54
Gladys Rd. NW6............4C 44
Glaisher St. SE8..........2C 94
Glamis Pl. E1.............1E 79
Glamis Rd. E1.............1E 79
Glanville Rd. SW2.........3A 104
Glasbrook Rd. SE9.........5F 111
Glaserton Rd. N16.........2A 36
Glasford St. SW17.........5B 116
Glasgow Ho. W9............1D 59
............(off Maida Vale)
Glasgow Rd. E13...........1D 69
Glasgow Ter. SW1..........1E 89
Glasier Ct. E15...........4A 54
Glaskin M. E9.............3A 52
Glass Blowers Ho. E14.....5F 67
............(off Valencia Cl.)
Glass Bldg., The NW1......5D 47
............(off Jamestown Rd.)
Glass Foundry Yd. E13.....4D 69
............(off Denmark St.)
Glasshill St. SE1....3E 25 (3D 77)
Glass Ho. WC2.......3D 15 (5A 62)
............(off Shaftesbury Av.)

Glass Ho., The SE1...4D 27 (3A 78)
............(off Royal Oak Yd.)
Glasshouse Flds. E1.......1F 79
............(not continuous)
Glasshouse Gdns. E20......4D 53
Glasshouse Gdns. Development
E20.....................4D 53
Glasshouse St. W1...5A 14 (1E 75)
Glasshouse Wlk. SE11......1A 90
Glasshouse Yd. EC1...4F 9 (3E 63)
Glasslyn Rd. N8...........1F 33
Glass Mill Leisure Cen....1E 109
Glass St. E2..............3D 65
Glassworks Studios
E2.................1E 11 (2A 64)
............(off Basing Pl.)
Glastonbury Ct. SE14......3E 93
............(off Farrow La.)
Glastonbury Ho. SE12......3B 110
............(off Wantage Rd.)
Glastonbury Pl. E1........1E 79
Glastonbury St. NW6.......2B 44
Glaucus St. E3............4D 67
Glazbury Rd. W14..........5A 72
Glazebrook Cl. SE21.......2F 119
Glebe, The SE3............1A 110
Glebe, The SW16...........4F 117
Glebe Cl. W4..............1A 84
Glebe Ct. E3..............2D 67
............(off Rainhill Way)
Glebe Ct. SE3.............1A 110
Glebe Ho. SE16............4D 79
............(off Slippers Pl.)
Glebe Hyrst SE19..........4A 120
Glebelands E10............4D 39
Glebelands Cl. SE5........1A 106
Glebe Pl. SW3.............2A 88
Glebe Rd. E8..............4B 50
Glebe Rd. NW10............3C 42
Glebe Rd. SW13............5C 84
Glebe St. W4..............1A 84
Glebe Ter. W4.............1A 84
Gledhow Gdns. SW5.........5E 73
Gledstanes Rd. W14........1A 86
Glegg Pl. SW15............2F 99
Glenaffric Av. E14........5E 81
Glen Albyn Rd. SW19.......2F 113
Glenallan Ho. W14.........5B 72
............(off North End Cres.)
Glenalvon Way SE18........5F 83
Glenarm Rd. E5............1E 51
Glenavon Rd. E15..........4A 54
Glenbow Rd. BR1: Broml....5A 124
Glenbrook Rd. NW6.........2C 44
Glenburnie Rd. SW17.......3B 116
Glencairne Cl. E16........4F 69
Glencar Ct. SE19..........5D 119
Glencoe Mans. SW9.........3C 90
............(off Mowll St.)
Glendale Dr. SW19.........5B 114
Glendall St. SW9..........2B 104
Glendarvon St. SW15.......1F 99
Glendower Gdns. SW14......1A 98
Glendower Pl. SW7.........5F 73
Glendown Ho. E8...........2C 50
Glendun Ct. W3............1A 70
Glendun Rd. W3............1A 70
Gleneagle M. SW16.........5F 117
Gleneagle Rd. SW16........5F 117
Gleneagles Cl. SE16.......1D 93
Glenelden Ho. SW16........4A 118
Glenelden Rd. SW16........4A 118
Glenelg Rd. SW2...........3A 104

Glenfarg Rd. SE6..........1E 123
Glenfield Rd. SW12........1E 117
Glenfinlas Way SE5........3D 91
Glenforth St. SE10........1B 96
Glengall Bus. Cen. SE15...2B 92
Glengall Pas. E14.........4D 81
Glengall Pas. NW6.........5C 44
............(off Priory Pk. Rd.)
Glengall Rd. NW6..........5B 44
Glengall Rd. SE15.........1B 92
Glengall Ter. SE15........2B 92
Glengariff Mans. SW9......3C 90
............(off Sth. Island Pl.)
Glengarnock Av. E14.......5E 81
Glengarry Rd. SE22........3A 106
Glenhurst Av. NW5.........1C 46
Glenhurst Ct. SE19........5B 120
Glenilla Rd. NW3..........3A 46
Glenister Rd. SE10........1B 96
Glenkerry Ho. E14.........5E 67
............(off Burcham St.)
Glenloch Rd. NW3..........3A 46
Glenluce Rd. SE3..........2C 96
Glenmere Row SE12.........4C 110
Glen M. E17...............1B 38
Glenmore Rd. NW3..........3A 46
Glennie Ct. SE22..........1C 120
Glennie Rd. SE27..........3C 118
Glenparke Rd. E7..........3D 55
Glenridding NW1......1A 6 (1E 61)
............(off Ampthill Est.)
Glen Rd. E13..............3E 69
Glen Rd. E17..............1B 38
Glenrosa St. SW6..........5E 87
Glenrose Ct. SE1....5D 27 (4A 78)
............(off Long La.)
Glenroy St. W12...........5E 57
Glensdale Rd. SE4.........1B 108
Glenshaw Mans. SW9........3C 90
............(off Brixton Rd.)
Glentanner Way SW17.......3F 115
Glen Ter. E14.............3E 81
............(off Manchester Rd.)
Glentham Gdns. SW13.......2D 85
Glentham Rd. SW13.........2C 84
Glenthorne M. W6..........5D 71
Glenthorne Rd. W6.........5D 71
Glenthorpe Av. SW15.......2C 98
Glenton M. SE13...........2A 110
Glentworth St. NW1...4A 4 (3B 60)
Glenville Gro. SE8........3B 94
Glenville M. SW18.........5D 101
Glenville M. Ind. Est. SW18.5C 100
Glenwood Av. NW9..........3A 28
Glenwood Rd. N15..........1D 35
Glenwood Rd. SE6..........1B 122
Glenworth Av. E14.........5F 81
Gliddon Dr. E5............1D 51
Gliddon Rd. W14...........5A 72
Gliddon Rd. W14...........5A 72
Glisson Rd. E3............1E 67
Globe Apts. E3............2B 94
............(off Evelyn St.)
Globe Ho. E14.............5A 68
Globe Pond Rd. SE16.......2A 80
Globe Rd. E1..............2E 65
Globe Rd. E15.............2B 54
Globe Rd. E2..............2E 65
Globe St. SE1.......5B 26 (4F 77)
Globe Ter. E2.............2E 65
GLOBE TOWN................2F 65
Globe Town Mkt............2F 65
Globe Vw. EC4......4F 17 (1E 77)
............(off High Timber St.)
Globe Wharf SE16..........1F 79

Gloster Ridley Ct. E14......5B 66
..................(off St Anne's Row)
Gloucester W14.....................5B 72
............(off Kensington Village)
Gloucester Arc. SW7.............5E 73
Gloucester Av. NW1..............4C 46
Gloucester Cir. SE10.............3E 95
Gloucester Ct. SE1:
   Lon Rolls Rd...................1B 92
..............................(off Rolls Rd.)
Gloucester Ct. SE1:
   Lon Swan St.............5A 26 (4E 77)
....................................(off Swan St.)
Gloucester Ct. EC3....5E 19 (1A 78)
Gloucester Ct. NW11...............2B 30
..................(off Golders Grn. Rd.)
Gloucester Ct. SE22..............1C 120
Gloucester Cres. NW1............5D 47
Gloucester Gdns. NW11.........2B 30
Gloucester Gdns. W2.............5E 59
Gloucester Ga. NW1................1D 61
..................................(not continuous)
GLOUCESTER GA. BRI.............5D 47
....................(off Gloucester Gate)
Gloucester Ga. M. NW1..........1D 61
Gloucester Ho. E16................2C 82
..................(off Gatcombe Rd.)
Gloucester Ho. NW6...............1C 58
..................(off Cambridge Rd.)
Gloucester Ho. SW9................3C 90
Gloucester M. E10...................2C 38
Gloucester M. W2....................5E 59
Gloucester W. W2....................5E 59
Gloucester Pk. Apts. SW7.....5E 73
..................................(off Ashburn Pl.)
Gloucester Pl. NW1....3A 4 (3B 60)
Gloucester Pl. W1......5A 4 (4B 60)
Gloucester Pl. M.
   W1......................1A 12 (4B 60)
Gloucester Rd. E10..................2C 38
Gloucester Rd. E11.................1D 41
Gloucester Rd. SW7................4E 73
Gloucester Road Station
   (Underground)....................5E 73
Gloucester Sq. E2..................5C 50
Gloucester Sq. W2..................5E 59
..................................(not continuous)
Gloucester St. SW1................1E 89
Gloucester Ter. W2..................5D 59
Gloucester Wlk. W8................3C 72
Gloucester Way EC1...2C 8 (2C 62)
Glover Ho. NW6.......................4E 45
..................................(off Harben Rd.)
Glover Ho. SE15....................2D 107
Glycena Rd. SW11................1B 102
Glyn Cl. SW16......................3C 118
Glynde M. SW3.......................4A 74
..................................(off Walton St.)
Glynde Reach WC1.....2E 7 (2A 62)
..................................(off Harrison St.)
Glynde St. SE4.....................4B 108
Glynfield Rd. NW10...............4A 42
Glyn Mans. W14......................5A 72
............(off Hammersmith Rd.)
Glyn Rd. E5..............................1F 51
Glyn St. SE11.........................1B 90
Glynwood Ct. SE23...............2E 121
Goals Soccer Cen. Eltham....4E 111
Go Ape! Battersea Park.........4B 88
Goater's All. SW6..................3B 86
..................................(off Dawes Rd.)
Goby Ho. SE8.........................3D 95
..................................(off Creative Rd.)
Godalming Rd. E14................4D 67

Godbold Rd. E15....................3A 68
Goddard Ho. SE11.................5D 77
..................(off George Mathers Rd.)
Goddard Pl. N19.....................5E 33
Godfree Ct. SE1........3B 26 (3F 77)
..................................(off Long La.)
Godfrey Ho. EC1.......2B 10 (2F 63)
..................(off St Luke's Est.)
Godfrey Pl. E2.......2F 11 (2B 64)
..................................(off Austin St.)
Godfrey St. E15......................1E 67
Godfrey St. SW3....................1A 88
Goding St. SE11.....................1A 90
Godley Cl. SE14......................4E 93
Godley Rd. SW18..................1F 115
Godliman St. EC4.....3E 17 (5D 63)
Godman Rd. SE15..................5D 93
Godolphin Ho. NW3................4A 46
..................................(off Fellows Rd.)
Godolphin Pl. W3.....................1A 70
Godolphin Rd. W12................2D 71
..................................(not continuous)
Godson St. N1..........................1C 62
Godson Yd. NW6....................2C 58
Godstone Ho. SE1....5C 26 (4F 77)
..................................(off Pardoner St.)
Godward Sq. E1......................3F 65
Godwin Cl. N1.........................1E 63
Godwin Cl. NW1......................1E 61
..................................(off Chalton St.)
Godwin Ho. E2........................1B 64
..................................(off Thurtle Rd.)
Godwin Ho. SE1.......2F 27 (2B 78)
..................................(off Duchess Wlk.)
Godwin Rd. E7.......................1D 55
Goffers Rd. SE3.......................4A 96
Golborne Gdns. W10..............3A 58
..................................(not continuous)
Golborne M. W10...................4A 58
Golborne Rd. W10..................4A 58
Goldbeaters Ho. W1..3C 14 (5F 61)
..................................(off Manette St.)
Goldcrest Cl. E16....................4F 69
Goldcrest M. N16...................5C 36
Golden Anchor Ho. SE10.......4C 82
..................................(off Latimer Square)
Golden Bus. Pk. E10..............3A 38
Golden Cross M. W11.............5B 58
..................................(off Portobello Rd.)
Golden Hind Pl. SE8..............5B 80
..................................(off Grove St.)
GOLDEN JUBILEE
   BRIDGES...........1F 23 (2B 76)
..................................(off Belvedere Rd.)
Golden La. EC1.........3F 9 (3E 63)
Golden La. Campus
   EC1........................4A 10 (3E 63)
..................................(off Golden La.)
Golden La. Est. EC1...4F 9 (3E 63)
Golden Lane Sport & Fitness Cen.
   ....4F 9 (3E 63)
..................................(off Golden La. Est.)
Golden Plover Cl. E16............5C 68
Goldhall Rd. SW1......4A 14 (1E 75)
Golden Yd. NW3......................1E 45
..................................(off Holly Mt.)
Golders Ct. NW11....................2B 30
Golders Gdns. NW11..............2A 30
GOLDERS GREEN......................1A 30
Golders Grn. Crematorium....2C 30
Golders Grn. Cres. NW11......2B 30
Golders Grn. Rd. NW11.........1A 30
Golders Green Station
   (Underground)....................3C 30

Goldersea NW11.....................3C 30
Golders Mnr. Dr. NW11..........1F 29
Golders Pk. Cl. NW11.............3C 30
Golders Way NW11.................2B 30
Goldfinch Ct. E3.....................1C 66
..................(off Four Seasons Cl.)
Goldhawk M. W12.................3D 71
Goldhawk Rd. W12.................4C 70
Goldhawk Rd. W6..................5B 70
Goldhawk Road Station
   (Underground)....................3E 71
Goldhurst Ho. W6...................2E 85
Goldhurst Mans. NW6............3E 45
..................(off Goldhurst Ter.)
Goldhurst Ter. NW6................4D 45
Goldie Ho. N19.......................2F 33
Golding St. E1........................5C 64
..................................(not continuous)
Golding Ter. E1........................5C 64
..................(off Rope Wlk. Gdns.)
Golding Ter. SW11...................5C 88
Goldington Bldgs. NW1..........5F 47
..................(off Royal College St.)
Goldington Cres. NW1............1F 61
Goldington St. NW1................1F 61
Goldman Cl. E2........................3C 64
Goldney Rd. W9......................3C 58
Goldsboro' Rd. SW8...............4F 89
Goldsborough Ho. E14...........1D 95
..................(off St Davids Sq.)
Goldsmith Av. NW9................1A 28
Goldsmith Ct.
   WC2....................2E 15 (5A 62)
..................................(off Stukeley St.)
Goldsmith Est. SE15..............4C 92
Goldsmith Rd. E10.................3C 38
Goldsmith Rd. SE15...............4C 92
Goldsmith's Bldgs. W3...........2A 70
Goldsmith's Row E2...............2A 70
Goldsmiths Coll....................4A 94
Goldsmith's Pl. NW6..............5D 45
..................(off Springfield La.)
Goldsmith's Row E2...............1C 64
Goldsmith's Sq. E2.................1C 64
Goldsmith St. EC2....2A 18 (5E 63)
Goldsworthy Gdns. SE16.......1E 93
Goldthorpe NW1......................5E 47
..................................(off Camden St.)
Goldwell Ho. SE22.................1A 106
..................................(off Quorn Rd.)
Goldwin Cl. SE14.....................4E 93
Goldwing Cl. E16....................5C 68
Gollogly Ter. SE7....................1E 97
Gomm Rd. SE16......................4E 79
Gondar Gdns. NW6.................2B 44
Gonson St. SE8......................2D 95
Gonston Cl. SW19................2A 114
Gonville St. SW6...................1A 100
Gooch Ho. E5...........................5D 37
Gooch Ho. EC1..........5B 8 (4C 62)
..................(off Portpool La.)
Gooch Ho. SW11.....................3F 89
..................(off Malthouse Rd.)
Goodall Ho. SE4.....................2F 107
Goodall Rd. E11......................5E 39
Goodchild Rd. N4....................3E 35
Goodfaith Ho. E14..................1D 81
..................(off Simpson's Rd.)
Googe Pl. W1..........1A 14 (4E 61)
Googe St. W1..........1A 14 (4E 61)
Googe Street Station
   (Underground)........5A 6 (4F 61)
Goodhall St. NW10.................2B 56
..................................(not continuous)
Goodhart Pl. E14....................1A 80

Goodhope Ho. E14 .... 1D **81**
..................(off Poplar High St.)
Gooding Cl. N7 .... 3A **48**
Gooding Rd. N7 .... 3A **48**
Gooding Ho. SE7 ....1E **97**
Goodman Cres. SW2 .... 2A **118**
Goodman Rd. E10 .... 2E **39**
Goodman's Ct. E1 ... 4F **19** (1B **78**)
Goodman's Stile E1 .... 5C **64**
Goodmans Yd. E1 .. 4F **19** (1B **78**)
Goodrich Ct. W10 .... 5F **57**
Goodrich Ho. E2 .... 1E **65**
...................(off Sewardstone Rd.)
Goodrich Rd. SE22 .... 4B **106**
Goodson Rd. NW10 .... 4A **42**
Goodspeed Ho. E14 .... 1D **81**
...................(off Simpson's Rd.)
Goods Way N1 .... 1A **62**
Goodway Gdns. E14 .... 5F **67**
Goodwill Ho. E14 .... 1D **81**
...................(off Simpson's Rd.)
Goodwin Cl. SE16 .... 4B **78**
Goodwin Cl. W12 .... 3C **70**
Goodwins Ct.
   WC2 .... 4D **15** (1A **76**)
Goodwin St. N4 .... 4C **34**
Goodwood Cl. W1 .... 5E **5** (4D **61**)
...................(off Devonshire St.)
Goodwood Ho. SE14 .... 3A **94**
...................(off Goodwood Rd.)
Goodwood Rd. SE14 .... 3A **94**
Goodyear Pl. SE5 .... 2E **91**
Goodyer Ho. SW1 .... 1F **89**
...................(off Tachbrook St.)
Goodyers Gdns. NW4 .... 1F **29**
Goose Grn. Trad. Est.
   SE22 .... 2B **106**
Gophir La. EC4 .... 4B **18** (1F **77**)
Gopsall St. N1 .... 5F **49**
Gordian Apts. SE10 .... 5A **82**
...................(off Cable Wlk.)
Gordon Av. SW14 .... 2A **98**
Gordonbrook Rd. SE4 .... 3C **108**
Gordon Cl. E17 .... 1C **38**
Gordon Cl. N19 .... 5A **34**
Gordon Cotts. W8 .... 3D **73**
...................(off Dukes La.)
Gordondale Rd. SW19 .... 2C **114**
Gordon Gro. SE5 .... 5D **91**
GORDON HOSPITAL 5F **75**
Gordon Ho. E1 .... 1E **79**
...................(off Glamis Rd.)
Gordon Ho. SW1 .... 4C **75**
...................(off Greencoat Pl.)
Gordon Ho. Rd. NW5 .... 1C **46**
Gordon Mans. W14 .... 4F **71**
...................(off Addison Gdns.)
Gordon Mans. WC1 ... 4B **6** (3F **61**)
...................(off Torrington St.)
Gordon Pl. W8 .... 3C **72**
Gordon Rd. E11 .... 1C **40**
Gordon Rd. E15 .... 1E **53**
Gordon Rd. SE15 .... 5D **93**
Gordon Sq. WC1 ...... 3B **6** (3F **61**)
Gordon Sq. Gdn. 3B **6** (3F **61**)
...................(off Gordon Square)
Gordon St. E13 .... 2C **68**
Gordon St. WC1 .... 3B **6** (3F **61**)
Gorefield Ho. NW6 .... 1C **58**
...................(off Gorefield Pl.)
Gorefield Pl. NW6 .... 1C **58**
Gore Ho. N1 .... 4C **48**
...................(off Drummond Way)
Gore Rd. E9 .... 5E **51**
Gore St. SW7 .... 4E **73**

Gorham Ho. SE16 .... 3F **79**
...................(off Wolfe Cres.)
Gorham Pl. W11 .... 1A **72**
Goring St. EC3 .... 2E **19** (5A **64**)
...................(off Houndsditch)
Gorleston St. W14 .... 5A **72**
...................(not continuous)
Gorse Cl. E16 .... 5C **68**
Gorsefield Ho. E14 .... 1C **80**
...................(off E. India Dock Rd.)
Gorse Ri. SW17 .... 5C **116**
Gorst Rd. SW11 .... 4B **102**
Gorsuch Pl. E2 .... 1F **11** (2B **64**)
Gorsuch St. E2 .... 1F **11** (1B **64**)
Gosberton Rd. SW12 .... 1B **116**
Gosfield St. W1 ..... 1F **13** (4E **61**)
Gosford Ho. E3 .... 1B **66**
...................(off Tredegar Rd.)
Goshawk Ct. NW9 .... 2B **28**
Goslett Yd. WC2 ..... 3C **14** (5F **61**)
Gosling Ho. E1 .... 1E **79**
...................(off Sutton St.)
Gosling Way SW9 .... 4C **90**
GOSPEL OAK 1C **46**
Gospel Oak Station (Overground)
   .... 1C **46**
Gosport Rd. E17 .... 1B **38**
Gossamer Gdns. E2 .... 1D **65**
Gosse St. N1 .... 1A **64**
...................(off Downham Rd.)
Gosset St. E2 .... 2B **64**
Gosterwood St. SE8 .... 2A **94**
Goston Ga. SW8 .... 4B **90**
...................(off Hampson Way)
Goswell Pl. EC1 ...... 2E **9** (2D **63**)
...................(off Goswell Rd.)
Goswell Rd. EC1 .....1D **9** (1D **63**)
Gothenburg Ct. SE8 .... 5A **80**
...................(off Bailey St.)
Gothic Ct. SE5 .... 3E **91**
...................(off Wyndham Rd.)
Gottfried M. NW5 .... 1E **47**
Goudhurst Rd.
   BR1: Broml 5A **124**
Gough Ho. N1 .... 5D **49**
...................(off Windsor St.)
Gough Rd. E15 .... 1B **54**
Gough Sq. EC4 .... 2C **16** (5C **62**)
Gough St. WC1 .... 3A **8** (3B **62**)
Gough Wlk. E14 .... 5C **66**
Goulden Ho. SW11 .... 5A **88**
Goulden Ho. App. SW11 .... 5A **88**
Gouldman Ho. E1 .... 3E **65**
...................(off Wyllen Cl.)
Gould Ter. E8 .... 2D **51**
Goulston St. E1 ...... 2F **19** (5B **64**)
Goulton Rd. E5 .... 1D **51**
Gourley St. N15 .... 1A **36**
Gourley St. N15 .... 1A **36**
Govan St. E2 .... 5C **50**
Gover Ct. SW4 .... 5A **90**
Govier Cl. E15 .... 4A **54**
Gowan Av. SW6 .... 4A **86**
Gowan Ho. E2 .... 2F **11** (2B **64**)
...................(off Chambord St.)
Gowan Rd. NW10 .... 3D **43**
Gower Cl. SW4 .... 4E **103**
Gower Ct. WC1 .... 3A **6** (3F **61**)
Gower Ho. SE17 .... 1E **91**
...................(off Morecambe St.)
Gower M. WC1 .... 1B **14** (4F **61**)
Gower M. Mans. WC1 ...5C **6** (4F **61**)
...................(off Gower M.)
Gower Pl. WC1 .... 3A **6** (3F **61**)
Gower St. E7 .... 3C **54**

Gower St. WC1 .... 3A **6** (3E **61**)
Gower's Wlk. E1 .... 5C **64**
Gowlett Rd. SE15 .... 1C **106**
Gowrie Rd. SW11 .... 1C **102**
Gracechurch St.
   EC3 .... 4C **18** (1F **77**)
Gracedale Rd. SW16 .... 5D **117**
Gracefield Gdns. SW16 .... 3A **118**
Gracehill E1 .... 4E **65**
...................(off Hannibal Rd.)
Grace Ho. SE11 .... 2B **90**
...................(off Vauxhall St.)
Grace Jones Cl. E8 .... 3C **50**
Grace Path SE26 .... 4E **121**
Grace Pl. E3 .... 2D **67**
Graces All. 1C **78**
Grace's M. SE5 .... 5F **91**
Graces M. NW8 .... 1E **59**
Grace's Rd. SE5 .... 5A **92**
Grace St. E3 .... 2D **67**
Gradient, The SE26 .... 4C **120**
Graduate Pl. SE1 ...5D **27** (4A **78**)
...................(off Long La.)
Grafton Chambers
   NW1 .... 2C **6** (2F **61**)
...................(off Grafton Pl.)
Grafton Cres. NW1 .... 3D **47**
Grafton Gdns. N4 .... 1E **35**
Grafton Ho. E3 .... 2C **66**
...................(off Wellington Way)
Grafton Ho. SE8 .... 1B **94**
Grafton M. W1 .... 4F **5** (3E **61**)
Grafton Pl. NW1 ..... 2B **6** (2F **61**)
Grafton Rd. NW5 .... 2C **46**
Graftons, The NW2 .... 5C **30**
Grafton Sq. SW4 .... 1E **103**
Grafton St. W1 .... 5E **13** (1D **75**)
Grafton Ter. NW5 .... 2B **46**
Grafton Way W1 ..... 4F **5** (3E **61**)
...................(not continuous)
Grafton Way W1 ...... 4A **6** (3E **61**)
Grafton Yd. NW5 .... 3D **47**
Graham Ct. SE14 .... 2F **93**
...................(off Myers La.)
Graham Lodge NW4 .... 1D **29**
Graham Rd. E13 .... 3C **68**
Graham Rd. E8 .... 3C **50**
Graham Rd. N11 .... 1D **29**
Graham Rd. N1 .... 1F **9** (1D **63**)
Graham Ter. SW1 .... 5C **74**
Grail Rd. SE6 .... 2A **124**
Grainger Ct. SE5 .... 3E **91**
Grainstore, The E16 .... 1C **82**
Gramer Cl. E11 .... 4F **39**
Grampian Gdns. NW2 .... 3A **30**
Grampians, The W6 .... 3F **71**
...................(off Shepherd's Bush Rd.)
Gramsci Way SE6 .... 3D **123**
Granada St. SW17 .... 5B **116**
Granard Av. SW15 .... 3D **99**
Granard Ho. E9 .... 3F **51**
Granard Rd. SW12 .... 5B **102**
Granary Ct. E15 .... 3F **53**
...................(off Millstone Cl.)
Granary Rd. E1 .... 3D **65**
Granary Sq. N1 .... 5A **48**
Granary St. NW1 .... 5F **47**
Granby Pl. SE1 ...... 4B **24** (3C **76**)
...................(off Lwr. Marsh)
Granby St. E2 .... 3C **64**
...................(not continuous)
Grand Av. EC1 .... 5E **9** (4D **63**)
...................(not continuous)

Grand Canal Apts. N1 .... 5A 50
.... (off De Beauvoir Cres.)
Grand Canal Av. SE16 .... 5A 80
Grand Connaught Rooms
.... 2F 15 (5B 62)
.... (off Gt. Queen St.)
Grandfield Ct. W4 .... 2A 84
Grandison Rd. SW11 .... 3B 102
Grand Junc. Wharf E2 .... 2F 65
Grand Junc. Wharf N1 .... 1E 63
Grand Pde. N4 .... 1D 35
Grand Pde. M. SW15 .... 3A 100
.... (off Palmer's Rd.)
Grand Regent Twr. E2 .... 2F 65
Grand Twr. SW15 .... 3A 100
.... (off Plaza Gdns.)
Grand Union Cen. W10 .... 3F 57
.... (off West Row)
Grand Union Cl. W9 .... 4B 58
Grand Union Cres. E8 .... 5C 50
Grand Union Ho. N1 .... 5A 50
.... (off Hertford Rd.)
Grand Union Wlk. NW1 .... 4D 47
.... (off Kentish Town Rd.)
Grand Vitesse Ind. Cen.
SE1 .... 2E 25 (2D 77)
.... (off Gt. Suffolk St.)
Grand Wlk. E1 .... 3A 66
Granfield St. SW11 .... 4F 87
Grange, The E17 .... 1A 38
.... (off Lynmouth Rd.)
Grange, The SE1 ...... 5F 27 (4B 78)
Grange, The SW19 .... 5F 113
Grange, The W14 .... 5B 72
Grange Ct. NW10 .... 5A 28
.... (off Neasden La.)
Grange Ct. WC2 .... 3A 16 (5B 62)
Grangecourt Rd. N16 .... 3A 36
Grangefield NW1 .... 4F 47
.... (off Marquis Rd.)
Grange Gdns. NW3 .... 5D 31
Grange Gro. N1 .... 3E 49
Grange Ho. NW10 .... 4D 43
Grange Ho. SE1 .... 5F 27 (4B 78)
Grange La. SE21 .... 2B 120
Grange Lodge SW19 .... 5F 113
Grangemill Rd. SE6 .... 3C 122
Grangemill Way SE6 .... 2C 122
Grange Pk. Rd. E10 .... 3D 39
Grange Pl. NW6 .... 4C 44
Grange Rd. E10 .... 3C 38
Grange Rd. E13 .... 2B 68
Grange Rd. E17 .... 1A 38
.... (not continuous)
Grange Rd. N6 .... 1C 32
Grange Rd. NW10 .... 3D 43
Grange Rd. SE1 .... 5E 27 (4A 78)
Grange Rd. SW13 .... 4C 84
Grange St. N1 .... 5F 49
Grange Wlk. SE1 ...... 5E 27 (4A 78)
Grange Wlk. M. SE1 5E 27 (4A 78)
.... (off Grange Wlk.)
Grangeway NW6 .... 4C 44
Grangewood St. E6 .... 5F 55
Grange Yd. SE1 .... 5F 27 (4B 78)
Granite Apts. E15 .... 3A 54
Granite Apts. SE10 .... 1A 96
Granleigh Rd. E11 .... 4A 40
Gransden Av. E8 .... 4D 51
Gransden Ho. SE8 .... 1B 94
Gransden Rd. W12 .... 3B 70
Grantbridge St. N1 .... 1D 63
Grantham Ct. SE16 .... 3F 79
.... (off Eleanor Cl.)
Grantham Ho. E14 .... 3A 68

Grantham Ho. SE15 .... 2C 92
.... (off Friary Est.)
Grantham Pl. W1 ...... 2D 21 (2D 75)
Grantham Rd. SW9 .... 5A 90
Grantham Rd. W4 .... 3A 84
Grant Ho. SW9 .... 4B 90
.... (off Liberty St.)
Grantley Ho. SE14 .... 2F 93
.... (off Myers La.)
Grantley St. E1 .... 2F 65
Grant Mus. of Zoology
.... 4B 6 (3F 61)
Grant Rd. SW11 .... 2F 101
Grants Quay Wharf
EC3 .... 5C 18 (1F 77)
Grant St. E13 .... 2D 68
Grant St. N1 .... 1C 62
Grant Ter. N16 .... 2C 36
.... (off Castlewood Rd.)
Grantully Rd. W9 .... 2D 59
Granville Arc. SW9 .... 2C 104
Granville Ct. N1 .... 5A 50
Granville Ct. N4 .... 1B 34
Granville Ct. SE14 .... 3A 94
.... (off Nynehead St.)
Granville Gro. SE13 .... 1E 109
Granville Ho. E14 .... 5C 66
.... (off E. India Dock Rd.)
Granville Mans. W12 .... 3E 71
.... (off Shepherd's Bush Grn.)
Granville Pk. SE13 .... 1E 109
Granville Pl. SW6 .... 3D 87
Granville Pl. W1 .... 3B 12 (5C 60)
Granville Point NW2 .... 4B 30
Granville Rd. E17 .... 1D 39
Granville Rd. N4 .... 1B 34
Granville Rd. NW2 .... 4B 30
Granville Rd. NW6 .... 1C 58
.... (not continuous)
Granville Rd. SW18 .... 5B 100
Granville Sq. SE15 .... 3A 92
Granville Sq. WC1 .... 2A 8 (2B 62)
Granville St. WC1 ...... 2A 8 (2B 62)
Grape St. WC2 .... 2D 15 (5A 62)
Graphite Apts., The
N1 .... 1B 10 (1F 63)
.... (off Provost St.)
Graphite Point E2 .... 2F 65
.... (off Palmer's Rd.)
Graphite Sq. SE11 .... 1B 90
Grasmere NW1 .... 2E 5 (2D 61)
.... (off Osnaburgh St.)
Grasmere Av. SW15 .... 4A 112
Grasmere Ct. SE26 .... 5C 120
Grasmere Ct. SW13 .... 2C 84
.... (off Verdun Rd.)
Grasmere Point SE15 .... 3E 93
.... (off Old Kent Rd.)
Grasmere Rd. E13 .... 1C 68
Grasmere Rd. SW16 .... 5A 118
Grassmount SE23 .... 2D 121
Gratton Rd. W14 .... 4A 72
Gratton Ter. NW2 .... 5F 29
Gravel La. E1 .... 2F 19 (5B 64)
Gravely Ho. SE8 .... 5A 80
.... (off Chilton Gro.)
Gravenel Gdns. SW17 .... 5B 116
.... (off Nutwell St.)
Graveney Rd. SW17 .... 4A 116
Gravesend Rd. W12 .... 1C 70
Gray Ct. E1 .... 4A 66
Gray Ho. SE17 .... 1E 91
.... (off King & Queen St.)
Grayling Cl. E16 .... 3A 68
Grayling Rd. N16 .... 4F 35

Grayling Sq. E2 .... 2C 64
.... (off Nelson Gdns.)
Grayshott Rd. SW11 .... 5C 88
Gray's Inn Bldgs.
EC1 .... 4B 8 (3C 62)
.... (off Rosebery Av.)
Gray's Inn Pl. WC1 ....1A 16 (4B 62)
Gray's Inn Rd. WC1 .. 1E 7 (2A 62)
Gray's Inn Sq. WC1 ...5A 8 (4B 62)
Grayson Ho. EC1 ...... 2A 10 (2E 63)
.... (off Radnor St.)
Grays Ter. E7 .... 3E 55
Grayston Ho. SE3 .... 2E 111
Gray St. SE1 .... 4C 24 (3C 76)
Grayswood Point SW15 .... 1C 112
Gray's Yd. W1 .... 3C 12 (5C 60)
.... (off James St.)
Grazebrook Rd. N16 .... 4F 35
Grazeley Ct. SE19 .... 5A 120
Great Acre Ct. SW4 .... 2F 103
Great Arthur Ho.
EC1 .... 4F 9 (3E 63)
.... (off Golden La. Est.)
Great Bell All. EC2 .... 2B 18 (5F 63)
Great Brownings SE21 .... 4B 120
Great Castle St. W1 .. 2E 13 (5D 61)
Great Central St. NW1 .... 4B 60
Great Central Way NW10 .... 2A 42
Great Chapel St. W1 2B 14 (5F 61)
Great Chart St. SW11 .... 2F 101
Great Church La. W6 .... 5F 71
Great College St.
SW1 .... 5D 23 (4A 76)
Great Cft. WC1 .... 2E 7 (2A 62)
.... (off Cromer St.)
Great Cross Av. SE10 .... 3F 95
Great Cumberland M.
W1 .... 3A 12 (5B 60)
Great Cumberland Pl.
W1 .... 2A 12 (5B 60)
Great Dover St.
SE1 .... 4A 26 (3E 77)
Great Eastern Ent. Cen.
E14 .... 3D 81
Great Eastern Rd. E15 .... 4F 53
Great Eastern St.
EC2 .... 2D 11 (2A 64)
Great Eastern Wharf
SW11 .... 3A 88
Greater London Ho. NW1 ...... 1E 61
.... (off Hampstead Rd.)
Greatfield NW5 .... 2E 47
Greatfield Cl. N19 .... 1E 47
Greatfield Cl. SE4 .... 2C 108
Great George St.
SW1 .... 4C 22 (3F 75)
Great Guildford Bus. Sq.
SE1 .... 2F 25 (2E 77)
Great Guildford St.
SE1 .... 1F 25 (2E 77)
Great Hall SW11 .... 4C 88
.... (off Battersea Pk. Rd.)
Greatham Wlk. SW15 .... 1C 112
Great James St.
WC1 .... 5A 8 (4B 62)
Great Marlborough St.
W1 .... 3F 13 (5E 61)
Great Maze Pond
SE1 .... 3C 26 (3F 77)
Great Mill Apts. E2 .... 5B 50
.... (off Whiston Rd.)
Great Minster Ho. SW1 .... 5F 75
.... (off Marsham St.)
Great Newport St.
WC2 .... 4D 15 (1A 76)

Great New St. EC4 .....2C **16** (5C **62**)
.................(off New Fetter La.)
Great Nth. Rd. N6.................1B **32**
Greatorex Ho. E1.................4C **64**
.................(off Greatorex St.)
Greatorex St. E1.................4C **64**
Great Ormond St.
WC1.................5E **7** (4A **62**)
GREAT ORMOND STREET
HOSPITAL FOR CHILDREN
.................4E **7** (3A **62**)
Great Percy St. WC1....1A **8** (2B **62**)
Great Peter St.
SW1.................5B **22** (4F **75**)
Great Portland St.
W1.................4E **5** (3D **61**)
Great Portland Street Station
(Underground).....4E **5** (3D **61**)
Great Pulteney St.
W1.................4A **14** (1E **75**)
Great Queen St.
WC2.................2E **15** (5A **62**)
Great Russell Mans.
WC1.................1D **15** (4A **62**)
.................(off Gt. Russell St.)
Great Russell St.
WC1.................1C **14** (5F **61**)
Great St Helen's
EC3.................2D **19** (5A **64**)
Great St Thomas Apostle
EC4.................4A **18** (1E **77**)
Great Scotland Yd.
SW1.................2D **23** (2A **76**)
Great Smith St.
SW1.................5C **22** (4F **75**)
Great Spilmans SE22.....3A **106**
Great Suffolk St.
SE1.................2E **25** (2D **77**)
Great Sutton St.
EC1.................4E **9** (3D **63**)
Great Swan All.
EC2.................2B **18** (5F **63**)
Great Titchfield St.
W1.................4E **5** (3D **61**)
Great Tower St.
EC3.................4D **19** (1A **78**)
Great Trinity La.
EC4.................4A **18** (1E **77**)
Great Turnstile
WC1.................1A **16** (4B **62**)
Great Turnstile Ho.
WC1.................1A **16** (4B **62**)
.................(off Great Turnstile)
Great Western Rd. W11.....4B **58**
Great Western Rd. W2.....4B **58**
Great Western Rd. W9.....4B **58**
Great West Rd. W4: Lon
Dorchester Gro.................2B **84**
Great West Rd. W6.................1B **84**
Great Winchester St.
EC2.................2C **18** (5F **63**)
Great Windmill St.
W1.................4B **14** (1F **75**)
Great Yd. SE1.....3E **27** (3A **78**)
.................(off Crucifix La.)
Greaves Cotts. E14.................4A **66**
.................(off Maroon St.)
Greaves Pl. SW17.................4A **116**
Greaves Twr. SW10.................3E **87**
.................(off Worlds End Est.)
Grebe Cl. E7.................2B **54**
Grebe Cl. E14.................3E **81**
.................(off River Barge Cl.)
Grebe Ct. SE8.................2B **94**
.................(off Dorking Cl.)

Grecian Cres. SE19.................5D **119**
Greek Cl. W1.................3C **14** (5F **61**)
Greek Orthodox Cathedral
of St Sophia.................1D **73**
Greek St. W1.................3C **14** (5F **61**)
Green, The BR1: Broml.....3C **124**
.................(not continuous)
Green, The E11.................1D **41**
Green, The E15.................3A **54**
Green, The SW19.................5F **113**
Green, The W3.................5A **56**
Greenacres Ho. SW18.....1D **115**
.................(off Knaresborough Dr.)
Greenacre Sq. SE16.................3F **79**
Greenan Ct. E2.................2F **65**
.................(off Meath Cres.)
Green Arbour Ct.
EC1.................2D **17** (5D **63**)
.................(off Old Bailey)
Greenaway Gdns. NW3.....1D **45**
Greenaway Ho. NW8.................5E **45**
.................(off Boundary Rd.)
Greenaway Ho. WC1 ...2B **8** (2C **62**)
.................(off Fernsbury St.)
Green Bank E1.................2D **79**
Greenbanks Cl. SE13.....1D **109**
Greenbay Rd. SE7.................3F **97**
Greenberry St. NW8.................1A **60**
Green Cl. NW11.................2E **31**
Greencoat Mans. SW1.....4E **75**
.................(off Greencoat Row)
Greencoat Pl. SW1.................4E **75**
Greencoat Row SW1.................4E **75**
Greencourt Ho. E1.................3F **65**
.................(off Mile End Rd.)
Greencrest Pl. NW2.................5C **28**
Greencroft Cl. E6.................4F **69**
Greencroft Gdns. NW6.....4D **45**
Green Dale SE22.................3A **106**
Green Dale SE5.................2F **105**
Green Dale Cl. SE22.................3A **106**
Green Dragon Ct.
SE1.................1B **26** (2F **77**)
.................(off Bedale St.)
Green Dragon Ho.
WC2.................2E **15** (5A **62**)
.................(off Stukeley St.)
Green Dragon Yd. E1.................4C **64**
Greene Ct. SE14.................2F **93**
.................(off Samuel Cl.)
Greene Ho. SE1 .....5B **26** (4F **77**)
.................(off Burbage Cl.)
Greenend Rd. W4.................3A **70**
Greener Ho. SW4.................1F **103**
Greenfell Mans. SE8.................2D **95**
Greenfield Gdns. NW2.....4A **30**
Greenfield Ho. SW19.....1F **113**
Greenfield Rd. E1.................4C **64**
Greengate Lodge E13.....1D **69**
.................(off Hollybush St.)
Greengate St. E13.................1D **69**
Greenham Cl. SE1 ...4B **24** (3C **76**)
Greenham Ho. E9.................5E **51**
.................(off Templecombe Rd.)
Greenhill NW3.................1F **45**
Greenhill Gro. E12.................1F **55**
Greenhill Pk. NW10.................5A **42**
Greenhill Rd. NW10.................5A **42**
Greenhill's Rents
EC1.................5D **9** (4D **63**)
Greenhills Ter. N1.................3F **49**
Green Hundred Rd. SE15.....2C **92**
Greenhurst Rd. SE27.....5C **118**
Greenland Ho. E1.................3A **66**
.................(off Ernest St.)

Greenland M. SE8.................1F **93**
Greenland Pier (River Bus).....4B **80**
Greenland Pl. NW1.................5D **47**
Greenland Quay SE16.....5F **79**
Greenland Rd. NW1.................5E **47**
Greenland St. NW1.................5D **47**
Green Lanes N16.................5E **35**
Green Lanes N4.................3E **35**
Green Lanes Wlk. N4.................3E **35**
Greenleaf Cl. SW2.................5C **104**
Greenleaf Rd. E6.................5E **55**
Green Line Coach Station.....5D **75**
.................(off Bulleid Way)
GREEN MAN RDBT......2B **40**
Greenman St. N1.................4E **49**
Green M. N1.................1C **10** (2F **63**)
Greenoak Way SW19.....4F **113**
Green Pk. London 2E **21** (3D **75**)
Green Park Station (Underground)
.................1E **21** (2D **75**)
Green Pl. SE10.................3A **82**
Green Point E15.................3A **54**
Greenroof Way SE10.................4A **82**
Green's Ct. W1 .....4B **14** (1F **75**)
.................(off Brewer St.)
Green's Ct. W11.................2B **72**
.................(off Lansdowne M.)
Greenshank Ho. NW9.................1B **28**
Greenshields Ind. Est. E16.....3C **82**
Greenside Cl. SE6.................2F **123**
Greenside Rd. W12.................4C **70**
Greenstead Gdns. SW15.....3D **99**
Greenstone M. E11.................1C **40**
Green St. E13.................4E **55**
Green St. E7.................3D **55**
Green St. W1.................4A **12** (1C **74**)
Greenstreet Hill SE14.................5F **93**
Green Ter. EC1.................2C **8** (2C **62**)
Greenview Cl. W3.................2A **70**
Green Wlk. SE1.....5D **27** (4A **78**)
Greenway SE10.................3C **52**
Green Way E9.................3F **111**
Greenway Cl. N4.................4E **35**
Greenwell St. W1 ....4E **5** (3D **61**)
GREENWICH.................3E **95**
Greenwich Bus. Pk. SE10.....3D **95**
Greenwich Cen., The 1B **96**
.................(off Lambarde Sq.)
Greenwich Chu. St. SE10.....2E **95**
Greenwich Ct. E1.................5D **65**
.................(off Cavell St.)
GREENWICH FOOT TUNNEL.....1E **95**
Greenwich High Rd. SE10.....4D **95**
Greenwich Ho. SE13.................4F **109**
Greenwich Mkt. SE10.................2E **95**
GREENWICH MILLENNIUM
VILLAGE.................4B **82**
Greenwich Pk..................3F **95**
Greenwich Pk. St. SE10.....2F **95**
Greenwich Peninsula Ecology Pk.
.................4C **82**
Greenwich Peninsula Golf Driving
Range.................3F **81**
Greenwich Picturehouse 3E **95**
Greenwich Pier (River Bus &
Tours).................1E **95**
Greenwich Quay SE8.................2D **95**
Greenwich Shop. Pk.................5D **83**
Greenwich Sth. St. SE10.....4D **95**
Greenwich Station (Rail & DLR)
.................3D **95**
Greenwich Theatre.................3E **95**
Greenwich Tourist Info. Cen.
.................3E **95**
Greenwich Vw. Pl. E14.................4D **81**

Greenwich Yacht Club........4C 82
Greenwood NW5..................2E 47
....................(off Osney Cres.)
Greenwood Ho. EC1...2B 8 (2C 62)
....................(off Rosebery Av.)
Greenwood Ho. SE4............2F 107
Greenwood Pl. NW5.............2D 47
Greenwood Rd. E13............1B 68
Greenwood Rd. E8..............3C 50
Greenwood Ter. NW10........5A 42
Greenwood Theatre
....................3C 26 (3F 77)
Green Yd. WC1..............3A 8 (3B 62)
Green Yd., The EC3...3D 19 (5A 64)
....................(off Leadenhall Pl.)
Greet Ho. SE1..............4C 24 (3C 76)
....................(off Frazier St.)
Greet St. SE1..........2C 24 (2C 76)
Greg Cl. E10.....................1E 39
Gregor M. SE3...................3C 96
Gregory Cres. SE9.............5F 111
Gregory Pl. W8..................3D 73
Grehan M. SE14................3B 94
Greig Ter. SE17.................2D 91
Grenada Ho. E14................1B 80
....................(off Limehouse C'way.)
Grenada Rd. SE7................3E 97
Grenade St. E14................1B 80
Grenard Cl. SE15...............3C 92
Grendon Ho. E9.................4E 51
....................(off Shore Pl.)
Grendon Ho. N1.................1B 62
....................(off Calshot St.)
Grendon St. NW8................3A 60
Grenfell Ct. E3....................5D 67
....................(off Barry Blandford Way)
Grenfell Ho. SE5................3E 91
Grenfell Rd. W11...............1F 71
Grenfell Wlk. W11..............1F 71
Grenier Apts. SE15............3D 93
Grenville Ho. E3.................1A 66
....................(off Arbery Rd.)
Grenville Ho. SE8...............2C 94
....................(off New King St.)
Grenville Ho. SW1..............2F 89
....................(off Dolphin Sq.)
Grenville M. N19................3A 34
Grenville M. SW7...............5E 73
Grenville Pl. SW7...............4E 73
Grenville Rd. N19...............3A 34
Grenville St. WC1....4E 7 (3A 62)
Gresham Gdns. NW11........3A 30
Gresham Pl. E3..................4C 66
Gresham Pl. N19................4F 33
Gresham Rd. E16................5D 69
Gresham Rd. NW10.............2A 42
Gresham Rd. SW9...............1C 104
Gresham St. EC2....2F 17 (5E 63)
Gresham Way SW19...........3D 115
Gresham Way Ind. Est.
SW19.....................3D 115
....................(off Gresham Way)
Gresley Cl. E17.................1A 38
Gresley Rd. N19................1E 33
Gressenhall Rd. SW18.....4B 100
Gresse St. W1........1B 14 (5F 61)
Greswell St. SW6...............4F 85
Gretton Ho. E2.................2E 65
....................(off Globe Rd.)
Greville Ct. E5...................5D 37
....................(off Napoleon Rd.)
Greville Hall NW6..............1D 59
Greville Ho. SW1......5A 20 (4B 74)
....................(off Kinnerton St.)
Greville Lodge E13............5D 55

Greville M. NW6..................5D 45
....................(off Greville Rd.)
Greville Pl. NW6.................1D 59
Greville Rd. NW6...............1D 59
Greville St. EC1........1B 16 (4C 62)
....................(not continuous)
Grey Cl. NW11...................1E 31
Greycoat Gdns. SW1...........4F 75
....................(off Greycoat St.)
Greycoat Pl. SW1......5B 22 (4F 75)
Greycoat St. SW1................4F 75
Greycot Rd. BR3: Beck.......5C 122
Grey Eagle St. E1......4F 11 (3B 64)
Greyfriars SE26.................3C 120
....................(off Wells Pk. Rd.)
Greyfriars Pas. EC1...2E 17 (5D 63)
Greyhound Ct. WC2...4A 16 (1B 76)
Greyhound Mans. W6.........2A 86
....................(off Greyhound Rd.)
Greyhound Rd. NW10........2D 57
Greyhound Rd. W14...........2A 86
Greyhound Rd. W6............2F 85
Grey Ho. W12...................1D 71
....................(off White City Est.)
Greyladies Gdns. SE10.......5E 95
Greystead Rd. SE23...........5E 107
Greystoke Ho. SE15...........2C 92
....................(off Peckham Pk. Rd.)
Greystoke Pl. EC4......2B 16 (5C 62)
Greyswood St. SW16.........5D 117
Grey Turner Ho. W12.........5C 56
Grierson Ho. SW16............4E 117
Grierson Rd. SE23.............5F 107
Griffin Cl. NW10...............2D 43
Griffin Ct. W4...................1B 84
Griffin Ho. E14..................5D 67
....................(off Ricardo St.)
Griffin Ho. N1...................4A 50
....................(off Halcomb St.)
Griffin Ho. W6...................5F 71
....................(off Hammersmith Rd.)
Griffin M. SW12................1E 117
Griggs Ct. SE1......5E 27 (4A 78)
....................(off Grigg's Pl.)
Grigg's Pl. SE1......5E 27 (4A 78)
Griggs Rd. E10.................1E 39
Grimaldi Ho. N1................1B 62
....................(off Calshot St.)
Grimsby St. E2..................3B 64
Grimsel Path SE5..............3D 91
Grimshaw Cl. N6...............2C 32
Grimston Rd. SW6.............5B 86
Grimthorpe Ho. EC1...3D 9 (3D 63)
....................(off Agdon St.)
Grimwade Cl. SE15...........1E 107
Grindall Ho. E1..................3D 65
....................(off Darling Row)
Grindal St. SE1........4B 24 (3C 76)
Grindley Ho. E3.................4B 66
....................(off Leopold St.)
Grinling Pl. SE8.................2C 94
Grinstead Rd. SE8.............1A 94
Grisedale NW1..........1F 5 (2E 61)
....................(off Cumberland Mkt.)
Grittleton Rd. W9..............3C 58
Grizedale Ter. SE23...........2D 121
Grocer's Hall Ct.
EC2..................3B 18 (5F 63)
Grocer's Hall Gdns.
EC2..................3B 18 (5F 63)
....................(off Prince's St.)
Groombridge Ho. SE17......1A 92
....................(off Upnor Way)
Groombridge Rd. E9..........4F 51
Groom Cres. SW18............5F 101

Groome Ho. SE11..............5B 76
Groomfield Cl. SW17.........4C 116
Groom Pl. SW1........5C 20 (4C 74)
Grosse Way SW15.............4D 99
Grosvenor Av. N5..............2E 49
Grosvenor Av. SW14.........1A 98
Grosvenor Cotts. SW1........5C 74
Grosvenor Ct. E10..............3D 39
Grosvenor Ct. E14.............5B 66
....................(off Wharf La.)
Grosvenor Ct. NW6............5F 43
Grosvenor Ct. SE5.............2E 91
Grosvenor Ct. W14............4F 71
....................(off Irving Rd.)
Grosvenor Ct. Mans. W2....5B 60
....................(off Edgware Rd.)
Grosvenor Cres. SW1 4C 20 (3C 74)
Grosvenor Cres. M.
SW1...................4B 20 (3C 74)
Grosvenor Est. SW1...........5F 75
Grosvenor Gdns. E6...........2F 69
Grosvenor Gdns. NW11.....1B 30
Grosvenor Gdns. NW2.......3E 43
Grosvenor Gdns.
SW1......................5D 21 (4D 75)
Grosvenor Gdns. SW14......1A 98
Grosvenor Gdns. M. E.
SW1......................5E 21 (4D 75)
....................(off Beeston Pl.)
Grosvenor Gdns. M. Nth.
SW1......................5D 21 (4D 75)
....................(off Grosvenor Gdns.)
Grosvenor Gdns. M. Sth.
SW1......................5E 21 (4D 75)
....................(off Ebury St.)
Grosvenor Ga. W1......5B 12 (1C 74)
Grosvenor Hill SW19.........5A 114
Grosvenor Hill W1......4D 13 (1D 75)
Grosvenor Hill Ct.
W1......................4D 13 (1D 75)
....................(off Bourdon St.)
Grosvenor Pk. SE5.............3E 91
Grosvenor Pk. Rd. E17......1C 38
Grosvenor Pl. SW1...3C 20 (3C 74)
Grosvenor Ri. E. E17..........1D 39
Grosvenor Rd. E10.............3E 39
Grosvenor Rd. E11.............1D 41
Grosvenor Rd. E6..............5F 55
Grosvenor Rd. E7..............3D 55
Grosvenor Rd. SW1............2D 89
Grosvenor Sq. W1......4C 12 (1C 74)
Grosvenor St. W1......4C 12 (1D 75)
Grosvenor Studios SW1......5C 74
....................(off Eaton Ter.)
Grosvenor Ter. SE5............3E 91
Grosvenor Way E5.............4E 37
Grosvenor Way SW17.......3F 115
Grosvenor Wharf Rd. E14...5F 81
Grotes Bldgs. SE3.............5A 96
Grote's Pl. SE3.................5A 96
Groton Rd. SW18..............2D 115
Grotto Ct. SE1..........3E 25 (3D 77)
Grotto Pas. W1........5B 4 (4C 60)
Grove, The E15................3A 54
Grove, The N4.................2B 34
Grove, The N6.................3C 32
Grove, The N8.................1F 33
Grove, The NW11.............2A 30
GROVE, THE.....................1C 120
Grove Cl. SE23.................1A 122
Grove Cotts. SW3.............2A 88
....................(off Chelsea Mnr. St.)
Grove Cotts. W4...............2A 84
Grove Ct. NW8.................2F 59
....................(off Grove End Rd.)

Grove Ct. SE15 .... 3A **92**
.... (off Peckham Rd.)
Grove Ct. SW10 .... 1E **87**
.... (off Drayton Gdns.)
Grove Cres. Rd. E15 .... 3F **53**
Grove Dwellings E1 .... 4E **65**
Grove End NW5 .... 1D **47**
Grove End Gdns. NW8 ...... 1F **59**
Grove End Ho. NW8 .... 2F **59**
.... (off Grove End Rd.)
Grove End Rd. NW8 .... 1F **59**
Grove Gdns. NW8 .... 2A **60**
Grove Grn. Rd. E11 .... 5E **39**
Grove Hall Ct. E3 .... 1C **66**
.... (off Jebb St.)
Grove Hall Ct. NW8 .... 2E **59**
Grovehill Ct. BR1: Broml.... 5B **124**
Grove Hill Rd. SE5 .... 1A **106**
Grove Ho. SW3 .... 2A **88**
.... (off Chelsea Mnr. St.)
Groveland Ct. EC4 .... 3A **18** (5E **63**)
.... (off Bow La.)
Grovelands Cl. SE5 .... 5A **92**
Grovelands Rd. N15 .... 1C **36**
Grove La. SE5 .... 4F **91**
Grove La. Ter. SE5 .... 5F **91**
Grove Mans. W6 .... 3E **71**
.... (off Hammersmith Gro.)
Grove M. W6 .... 4E **71**
GROVE PK. 3D **125**
Grove Pk. SE5 .... 5A **92**
Grove Pk. Nature Reserve ..1B **124**
Grove Pk. Rd. SE9 .... 3E **125**
Grove Park Station (Rail) ...3D **125**
Grove Pas. E2 .... 1D **65**
Grove Pl. NW3 .... 5F **31**
Grove Pl. SW12 .... 5D **103**
Grover Ct. SE13 .... 5D **95**
Grover Ho. SE11 .... 1B **90**
Grove Rd. E11 .... 2B **40**
Grove Rd. E17 .... 1D **39**
Grove Rd. E3 .... 5F **51**
Grove Rd. N15 .... 1A **36**
Grove Rd. NW2 .... 3E **43**
Grove Rd. SW13 .... 5B **84**
Groveside Ct. SW11 .... 5F **87**
Grove St. SE8 .... 5B **80**
Grove Ter. NW5 .... 5D **33**
Grove Ter. M. NW5 .... 5D **33**
Grove Va. SE22 .... 2B **106**
Grove Vs. E14 .... 1D **81**
Groveway SW9 .... 4B **90**
Grummant Rd. SE15 .... 4B **92**
Grundy St. E14 .... 5D **67**
Grunwick Cl. NW2 .... 2C **42**
Gtec Ho. E15 .... 1F **67**
.... (off Canning Rd.)
Guardian Apts. E3 .... 3B **66**
.... (off Kevtar Gdn.)
Guardian Ct. SE12 .... 3A **110**
Guards Memorial ..2C **22** (2F **75**)
Guards' Mus., The ..4A **22** (3E **75**)
Gubyon Av. SE24 .... 3D **105**
Guerin Sq. E3 .... 2B **66**
Guernsey Gro. SE24 .... 5E **105**
Guernsey Ho. N1 .... 3E **49**
.... (off Channel Island Est.)
Guernsey Rd. E11 .... 3F **39**
Guglielmo Marconi M. E3 ... 1B **66**
Guibal Rd. SE12 .... 5D **111**
Guildford Ct. SW8 .... 3A **90**
.... (off Guildford Rd.)
Guildford Gro. SE10 .... 4D **95**

Guildford Rd. SW8 .... 4A **90**
Guildhall London 2A **18** (5E **63**)
.... (off Aldermanbury)
Guildhall Art Gallery 2B **18** (5F **63**)
.... (off Aldermanbury)
Guildhall Bldgs. EC2.2B **18** (5F **63**)
.... (off Gresham St.)
Guildhall Coll. 5D **65**
Guildhall Library ...2A **18** (5E **63**)
.... (off Aldermanbury)
Guildhall Offices EC2 2A **18** (5E **63**)
.... (off Basinghall St.)
Guildhall Yd. EC2 .... 2A **18** (5E **63**)
Guildhouse St. SW1 ....5E **75**
Guild Rd. SE7 .... 2F **97**
Guilford Pl. WC1 .... 4F **7** (3B **62**)
Guilford St. WC1 .... 4D **7** (3A **62**)
Guillemot Ct. SE8 .... 2B **94**
.... (off Alexandra Cl.)
Guinea Ct. E1 .... 1C **78**
.... (off Royal Mint St.)
Guinea Point E14 .... 5A **66**
.... (off Repton St.)
Guinness Cl. E9 .... 4A **52**
Guinness Cl. E3 .... 3F **19** (5H **64**)
.... (off Mansell St.)
Guinness Ct. EC1 .... 2A **10** (2E **63**)
.... (off Lever St.)
Guinness Ct. SE1 .... 3D **27** (3A **78**)
.... (off Snowsfields)
Guinness Ct. SW3 .... 5B **74**
Guinness Sq. SE1 .... 5A **78**
Guinness Trust SW3 .... 5B **74**
.... (off Cadogan St.)
Guinness Trust Bldgs. SE11 1D **91**
Guinness Trust Bldgs. W6....1E **85**
.... (off Fulham Pal. Rd.)
Guinness Trust Est., The
N16 .... 3A **36**
Guion Rd. SW6 .... 5B **86**
Gulland Wlk. N1 .... 3E **49**
.... (off Church Rd.)
Gullane Ho. E3 .... 1B **66**
.... (off Shetland Rd.)
Gulliver's Ho. EC1 .... 4F **9** (3E **63**)
.... (off Goswell Rd.)
Gulliver St. SE16 .... 4A **80**
Gullivers Wlk. SE8 .... 5B **80**
Gulston Wlk. SW3 .... 5B **74**
.... (off Blackland Ter.)
Gundulf St. SE11 .... 5C **76**
Gun Ho. E1 .... 2D **79**
.... (off Wapping High St.)
Gunmakers La. E3 .... 5A **52**
Gunnel Ct. E3 .... 2B **67**
.... (off Bolinder Way)
Gunnell Ct. SE26 .... 4C **120**
Gunners Rd. SW18 ....2F **115**
Gunpowder Sq.
EC4 ....2C **16** (5C **62**)
.... (off E. Harding St.)
Gunstor Rd. N16 .... 1A **50**
Gun St. E1 .... 1F **19** (4B **64**)
Gunter Gro. SW10 .... 2D **87**
Gunter Hall Studios
SW10 .... 2E **87**
.... (off Gunter Gro.)
Gunterstone Rd. W14 .... 5A **72**
Gunthorpe St. E1 .... 4B **64**
Gunton M. SE13 .... 3F **109**
Gunton Rd. E5 .... 5D **37**
Gunwhale Cl. SE16 .... 2F **79**
Gun Wharf E1 .... 2F **79**
.... (off Wapping High St.)
Gunyard M. SE18 .... 3F **97**

Gurdon Ho. E14 .... 5C **66**
.... (off Dod St.)
Gurdon Rd. SE7 .... 1C **96**
Gurney Cl. E15 .... 2A **54**
Gurney Ho. E2 .... 1C **64**
.... (off Goldsmiths Row)
Gurney Rd. E15 .... 2A **54**
Gurney Rd. SW6 .... 1E **101**
Gutenberg Ct. SE1... 5E **27** (4B **78**)
.... (off Grange Rd.)
Guthridge Cl. E14.............. 4C **66**
Guthrie Ct. SE1 .... 4C **24** (4C **76**)
.... (off Morley St.)
Guthrie St. SW3 .... 1F **87**
Gutter La. EC2 .... 2F **17** (5E **63**)
Guy Barnett Gro. SE3 .... 1C **110**
Guyscliff Rd. SE13 .... 3E **109**
GUY'S HOSPITAL 2B **26** (3F **77**)
GUY'S NUFFIELD HOUSE
.... 3B **26** (3F **77**)
.... (within Guy's Hospital)
Guy St. SE1 .... 3C **26** (3F **77**)
Guy St. Pk. 3C **26** (3F **77**)
Guy Townsley Sq. E3 .... 4D **67**
Gwalior Rd. SW15 .... 2F **99**
Gwendolen Av. SW15 .... 2F **99**
Gwendolen Cl. SW15 .... 3F **99**
Gwendoline Av. E13 .... 5D **55**
Gwendwr Rd. W14 .... 1A **86**
Gwen Morris Ho. SE5......... 3E **91**
Gwent Ct. SE16 .... 2F **79**
.... (off Rotherhithe St.)
Gwilym Maries Ho. E2 .... 2D **65**
.... (off Blythe St.)
Gwyn Cl. SW6.................... 3E **87**
Gwynne Cl. W4 .... 2B **84**
Gwynne Ho. E1 .... 4D **65**
.... (off Turner St.)
Gwynne Ho. SW1 .... 1C **88**
.... (off Lwr. Sloane St.)
Gwynne Ho. WC1 .... 2B **8** (2C **62**)
.... (off Lloyd Baker St.)
Gwynne Pl. WC1 ...... 2A **8** (2B **62**)
Gwynne Rd. SW11 .... 5F **87**
Gylcote Cl. SE5................. 2F **105**
Gym Bloomsbury, The
.... 4D **7** (3A **62**)
Gym Holborn Circus, The
.... 1C **16** (5C **62**)
.... (off Thavie's Inn)
Gym London Monument, The
.... 5C **18** (1F **77**)
Gym Walworth Road, The....1E **91**
Gymnasium, The N1 .... 1A **62**

H

Haarlem Rd. W14 ....4F **71**
Haberdasher Est. N1 1C **10** (2F **63**)
Haberdasher Pl. N1..1C **10** (2F **63**)
Haberdashers Ct. SE14........1F **107**
Haberdasher St. N1... 1C **10** (2F **63**)
Habitat Cl. SE15 .... 5D **93**
Habitat Sq. SE10 .... 4B **82**
.... (off Teal St.)
Hackford Rd. SW9 .... 4B **90**
Hackford Wlk. SW9............. 4C **90**
Hackington Cres.
BR3: Beck.................... 5C **122**
HACKNEY 3D **51**
Hackney Central Station
(Overground) 3D **51**
Hackney City Farm 1C **64**
Hackney Downs Station
(Overground) 2D **51**

Hackney Empire Theatre..... 3D 51
Hackney Fashion Hub E9......3E 51
Hackney Gro. E8 ....3D 51
Hackney Marshes Cen.....1B 52
Hackney Mus. 3D 51
Hackney Picturehouse 3D 51
............................(off Mare St.)
Hackney Rd. E2........ 1F 11 (2B 64)
Hackney St. E1 ....1E 11 (2A 64)
Hackney University Technical
Coll. 1E 11 (2A 64)
HACKNEY WICK 3A 52
HACKNEY WICK 3B 52
Hackney Wick Station
(Overground) 3C 52
Hackworth Point E3.............2D 67
.............................(off Rainhill Way)
Hacon Sq. E8......................4D 51
.................................(off Mare St.)
Haddington Rd.
BR1: Broml 3F 123
Haddo Ho. SE10 ....2D 95
.................................(off Haddo St.)
Haddon Ct. W3 ....1B 70
Haddonfield SE8 ....5F 79
Haddo St. SE10 ....2D 95
Haden Cl. N4.......................4C 34
Hadfield Ho. E1...................5C 64
.................................(off Ellen St.)
Hadleigh Cl. E1...................3E 65
Hadleigh St. NW2................3E 43
Hadleigh Ho. E1 ....3E 65
............................(off Hadleigh Cl.)
Hadleigh St. E2 ....2E 65
Hadley Cl. N16....................3C 36
Hadley St. NW1 ....3D 47
.............................(not continuous)
Hadlow Ho. SE17..............1A 92
............................(off Kinglake Est.)
Hadrian Cl. E3 ....5C 52
.............................(off Garrison Rd.)
Hadrian Est. E2 ....1C 64
Hadrian M. N7....................4B 48
Hadrian St. SE10...............1A 96
Hadstock Ho. NW1 ....1C 6 (2F 61)
............................(off Ossulston St.)
Hadyn Pk. Ct. W12.............3C 70
............................(off Curwen Rd.)
Hadyn Pk. Rd. W12.............3C 70
Hafer Rd. SW11.................2B 102
Hafton Rd. SE6.................1A 124
HAGGERSTON 4B 50
Haggerston Rd. E8.............4B 50
Haggerston Station (Overground)
....5B 50
Haggerston Studios E8........5B 50
............................(off Kingsland Rd.)
Hague St. E2 ....2C 64
Haider Cl. NW2...................4F 29
Haig Ho. E2 ....1C 64
............................(off Shipton St.)
Haig Rd. E. E13...................2E 69
Haig Rd. W. E13..................2E 69
Hailes Cl. SW19.................5E 115
Hailsham Av. SW2 ....2B 118
Hailsham Ho. NW8 ....3A 60
............................(off Salisbury St.)
Haimo Rd. SE9..................3F 111
Hainault Rd. E11.................3E 39
Haines Cl. N1 ....4A 50
Haines Ho. SW11...............3F 89
............................(off Ponton Rd.)
Haines St. SW11 ....3E 89
Hainford Cl. SE4.................2F 107
Hainthorpe Rd. SE27..........3D 119
Hainton Cl. E1....................5D 65

Halberd M. E5.....................4D 37
Halcomb St. N1 ....5A 50
Halcrow St. E1 ....4D 65
Halcyon Cl. SW13...............1C 98
Halcyon Wharf E1 ....2C 78
............................(off Hermitage Wall)
Haldane Pl. SW18...............1D 115
Haldane Rd. E6...................2F 69
Haldane Rd. SW6................3B 86
Haldon Rd. SW18...............4B 100
Hale Ho. SW1.....................1F 89
.............................(off Lindsay Sq.)
Hale Path SE27..................4D 119
Hales Prior N1..........1F 7 (1B 62)
............................(off Calshot St.)
Hales St. SE8.....................3C 94
Hale St. E14.......................1D 81
Halesworth Cl. E5...............4E 37
Halesworth Rd. SE13..........1D 109
Haley Rd. NW4...................1E 29
Half Moon Ct. EC1...1F 17 (4E 63)
............................(off Bartholomew Cl.)
Half Moon Cres. N1............1B 62
.............................(not continuous)
Half Moon La. SE24............4E 105
Half Moon Pas. E1 ...3F 19 (5B 64)
Half Moon St. W1 ....1E 21 (2D 75)
Halford Rd. E10...................1F 39
Halford Rd. SW6.................2C 86
Haliday Ho. N1 ....3F 49
............................(off Mildmay St.)
Haliday Wlk. N1 ....3F 49
Halidon Cl. E9.....................2E 51
Halifax St. SE26 ....3D 121
Haliwell Ho. NW6................5D 45
............................(off Mortimer Cres.)
Halkett Ho. E2 ....5E 51
............................(off Waterloo Gdns.)
Halkin Arc. SW1........5A 20 (4B 74)
Halkin M. SW1.........5B 20 (4C 74)
Halkin Pl. SW1.........5B 20 (4C 74)
Halkin St. SW1.........4C 20 (3C 74)
Hall, The SE3.....................1C 110
Hallam Ct. W1 ....5E 5 (4D 61)
............................(off Hallam St.)
Hallam Ho. SW1..................1E 89
............................(off Churchill Gdns.)
Hallam M. W1..........5E 5 (4D 61)
Hallam Rd. SW13...............1D 99
Hallam St. W1 ....4E 5 (4D 61)
Hallane Ho. SE27...............5E 119
Hall Apts. E3 ....4B 66
............................(off Geoff Cade Way)
Hall Dr. SE26.....................5E 121
Halley Gdns. SE13..............2F 109
Halley Ho. E2 ....1C 64
............................(off Pritchards Rd.)
Halley Ho. SE10.................1B 96
............................(off Armitage Rd.)
Halley Rd. E12....................3F 55
Halley Rd. E7......................3E 55
Halley St. E14.....................4A 66
Hallfield Est. W2.................5E 59
.............................(not continuous)
Hall Ga. NW8.....................2F 59
Halliday Ho. E1...................5C 64
............................(off Christian St.)
Halliford St. N1...................4E 49
Halling Ho. SE1 ....4C 26 (3F 77)
............................(off Long La.)
Hallings Wharf Studios
E15......................................5F 53
Halliwell Ct. SE22..............3C 106
Halliwell Rd. SW2...............4B 104

Hallmark Ho. E14...............4C 66
............................(off Ursula Gould Way)
Hall Oak Wlk. NW6..............3B 44
Hall Pl. W2.........................3F 59
.............................(not continuous)
Hall Rd. E15.......................1F 53
Hall Rd. NW8 ....2E 59
Hall St. EC1...............1E 9 (2D 63)
Hallsville Rd. E16................5B 68
Hallswelle Rd. NW11 ....1B 30
Hall Twr. W2.......................4F 59
.................................(off Hall Pl.)
Hall Vw. SE9.......................2F 125
Halo E15............................5E 53
Halpin Bldg. SE10...............4C 82
............................(off Rennie Street)
Halpin Pl. SE17..................5F 77
Halsbrook Rd. SE3..............1E 111
Halsbury Ho. N7.................1B 48
............................(off Biddestone Rd.)
Halsbury Rd. W12...............2D 71
Halsey Ho. WC1.......1F 15 (4B 62)
............................(off Red Lion Sq.)
Halsey M. SW3...................5B 74
Halsey St. SW3...................5B 74
Halsmere Rd. SE5...............4D 91
Halstead Ct. E17.................2B 38
Halstead Ct. N1........1C 10 (1F 63)
............................(off Murray Gro.)
Halstead Rd. E11.................1C 40
Halston Cl. SW11 ....4B 102
Halstow Rd. NW10..............2F 57
Halstow Rd. SE10...............1C 96
Halton Cl. SE3 ....1D 111
Halton Cross St. N1............5D 49
Halton Ho. N1.....................4D 49
............................(off Halton Rd.)
Halton Mans. N1.................4D 49
Halton Pl. N1......................5D 49
Halton Rd. N1 ....4D 49
Halyard Ho. E14.................4E 81
............................(off Manchester Rd.)
Halyard Pl. E14..................3D 83
Hamara Ghar E13...............3E 55
Hambalt Rd. SW4...............3E 103
Hambledon SE17................2F 91
..................................(off Villa St.)
Hambledon Ct. SE22...........2A 106
Hambledon Pl. SE21...........1A 120
Hambledon Rd. SW18.........5B 100
Hamble St. SW6 ....1D 101
Hambley Ho. SE16...............5D 79
............................(off Camilla Rd.)
Hambridge Way SW2...........5C 104
Hambro Rd. SW16..............5F 117
Hamella Ho. E9....................2A 52
............................(off Sadler Pl.)
Hamfrith Rd. E15................3B 54
Hamilton Cl. NW8................2F 59
Hamilton Cl. SE16...............3A 80
Hamilton Cl. SE6.................1B 124
Hamilton Cl. SW15..............1A 100
Hamilton Cl. W9..................2E 59
.................................(off Maida Vale)
Hamilton Gdns. NW8............2E 59
Hamilton Hall NW8..............1E 59
............................(off Hamilton Ter.)
Hamilton Ho. E14: Lon
St Davids Sq.......................1D 95
............................(off St Davids Sq.)
Hamilton Ho. E14: Lon Victory Pl.
....1B 80
.................................(off Victory Pl.)
Hamilton Ho. E3..................2B 66
............................(off British St.)

Hamilton Ho. NW8...................2F 59
..............................(off Hall Rd.)
Hamilton Ho. W4....................2A 84
Hamilton Ho. W8....................3D 73
..........................(off Vicarage Ga.)
Hamilton La. N5.....................1D 49
Hamilton Lodge E1.................3E 65
........................(off Cleveland Gro.)
Hamilton M. SW18..................1C 114
Hamilton M. W1............3D 21 (3D 75)
Hamilton Pk. N5......................1D 49
Hamilton Pk. W. N5.................1D 49
Hamilton Pl. N19....................5F 33
Hamilton Pl. W1............2C 20 (2C 74)
Hamilton Rd. E15....................2A 68
Hamilton Rd. NW10.................2C 42
Hamilton Rd. NW11.................2F 29
Hamilton Rd. SE27..................4F 119
Hamilton Rd. W4.....................3A 70
Hamilton Rd. Ind. Est.
   SE27.................................4F 119
Hamilton Sq. SE1.........1C 26 (3F 77)
Hamilton St. SE8....................2C 94
Hamilton Ter. NW8..................1D 59
Hamlea Cl. SE12.....................3C 110
Hamlet, The SE5.....................1F 105
Hamlet Cl. SE13.....................2A 110
Hamlet Cl. SE6.......................5D 109
Hamlet Ct. E3.........................2C 66
.............................(off Tomlin's Gro.)
Hamlet Ct. SE11.....................1D 91
...............................(off Opal St.)
Hamlet Ct. W6........................5C 70
Hamlet Gdns. W6....................5C 70
Hamlet Ind. Est. E9.................4C 52
Hamlet M. SE21.....................1F 119
Hamlet Sq. NW2.....................5A 30
Hamlets Way E3......................3B 66
Hamlet Way SE1..........3C 26 (3F 77)
Hammerfield Ho. SW3...............1A 88
.................................(off Cale St.)
Hammersley Ho. SE14..............3E 93
........................(off Pomeroy St.)
Hammersley Rd. E16................4C 68
HAMMERSMITH..................5E 71
Hammersmith Apollo The
   Eventim Apollo...................1E 85
HAMMERSMITH BRI................2D 85
Hammersmith Bri. Rd. W6.......1E 85
Hammersmith B'way. W6.........5E 71
HAMMERSMITH BROADWAY....5E 71
Hammersmith Bus Station.........5E 71
Hammersmith Emb. W6...........2E 85
Hammersmith Fitness & Squash
   Cen. 5F 71
.........................(off Chalk Hill Rd.)
Hammersmith Flyover W6........1E 85
HAMMERSMITH FLYOVER.........1E 85
Hammersmith Gro. W6.............3E 71
HAMMERSMITH HOSPITAL
   ....5C 56
................(within The Broadway Cen.)
Hammersmith Rd. W14............5F 71
Hammersmith Rd. W6..............5F 71
Hammersmith Station
   (Underground)....................5E 71
Hammersmith Ter. W6.............1C 84
Hammett St. EC3.........4F 19 (1B 78)
.........................(off Leyton Grange Est.)
Hammond Ct. E10...................4D 39
Hammond Ct. SE11.................1C 90
.............................(off Hotspur St.)
Hammond Ho. E14..................4C 80
...............................(off Tiller Rd.)

Hammond Ho. SE14.................3E 93
..........................(off Lubbock St.)
Hammond Lodge W9................4C 58
.........................(off Admiral Wlk.)
Hammond St. NW5..................3E 47
Hamond Sq. N1.......................1A 64
Ham Pk. Rd. E15.....................4B 54
Ham Pk. Rd. E7.......................4C 54
Hampden Cl. NW1...................1F 61
Hampden Gurney St.
   W1............................3A 12 (5B 60)
Hampden Ho. SW9..................5C 90
..........................(off Overton Rd.)
Hampden Rd. N19...................4F 33
Hampshire Hog La. W6............1D 85
Hampshire St. NW5.................3F 47
Hampson Way SW8.................4B 90
HAMPSTEAD.......................1F 45
Hampstead Cricket Club..........2D 45
.........................(off Lymington Rd.)
Hampstead Gdns. NW11..........1C 30
Hampstead Ga. NW3................2C 45
Hampstead Golf Course...........2F 31
Hampstead Grn. NW3...............2A 46
Hampstead Gro. NW3..............5E 31
Hampstead Heath.....................4F 31
Hampstead Heath Station
   (Overground)......................1A 46
Hampstead High St. NW3........1F 45
Hampstead Hill Gdns.
   NW3..................................1F 45
Hampstead Ho.
   NW1............................2F 5 (2E 61)
..........................(off William Rd.)
Hampstead La. N6...................2F 31
Hampstead La. NW3.................3F 31
Hampstead Lodge NW1............4A 60
..............................(off Bell St.)
Hampstead Mus........................1F 45
.........................(off New End Sq.)
Hampstead Rd. NW1...1F 5 (1E 61)
Hampstead Sq. NW3................5E 31
Hampstead Station
   (Underground)....................1E 45
Hampstead Theatre.................4F 45
Hampstead Wlk. E3.................5B 52
Hampstead Way NW11............1B 30
Hampstead W. NW6.................3C 44
Hampton Cl. NW6...................2C 58
Hampton Ct. N1......................3D 49
Hampton Ct. SE14..................3A 94
.........................(off Batavia Rd.)
Hampton Ct. SE16..................1F 79
.........................(off King & Queen Wharf)
Hampton Ho. SW8...................3B 89
..............................(off Ascalon St.)
Hampton Rd. E11....................3F 39
Hampton Rd. E7......................2D 55
Hampton St. SE1.....................5E 77
Hampton St. SE17...................5D 77
Hamston Ho. W8.....................4D 73
.........................(off Kensington Ct. Pl.)
Ham Yd. W1.................4B 14 (1F 75)
Hanameel St. E16...................2D 83
Hana M. E5.............................1D 51
Hanbury Dr. E11.....................2B 40
Hanbury Ho. E1......................4C 64
..............................(off Hanbury St.)
Hanbury Ho. SW8....................3A 90
.........................(off Regent's Bri. Gdns.)
Hanbury M. N1.......................5E 49
Hanbury St. E1............5F 11 (4B 64)
Hancock Nunn Ho. NW3..........3B 46
.........................(off Fellows Rd.)
Hancock Rd. E3......................2E 67

Hancock Rd. SE19..................5F 119
Handa Wlk. N1.......................3F 49
Hand Axe Yd. WC1.......1E 7 (2A 62)
Hand Ct. WC1..............1A 16 (4B 62)
Handel & Hendrix in London
   ....4D 13 (1D 75)
..............................(off Brook St.)
Handel Mans. SW13................3E 85
Handel Mans. WC1......3E 7 (3A 62)
.............................(off Handel St.)
Handel Pl. NW10....................3A 42
Handel St. WC1............3D 7 (3A 62)
Handen Rd. SE12...................3A 110
Handforth Rd. SW9.................3C 90
Handley Dr. SE3.....................1D 111
Handley Gro. NW2..................5F 29
Handley Rd. E9......................4E 51
Hands Wlk. E16......................5C 68
Handyside St. N1....................5F 47
Hanford Cl. SW18..................1C 114
Hanford Row SW19.................5E 113
Hanging Sword All.
   EC4.............................3C 16 (5C 62)
.........................(off Whitefriars St.)
Hankey Ho. SE1.........4B 26 (3F 77)
.............................(off Hankey Pl.)
Hankey Pl. SE1...........4C 26 (3F 77)
Hankins Ho. SE10...................4C 82
.........................(off Peartree Way)
Hanley Gdns. N4....................3B 34
Hanley Rd. N4........................3A 34
Hanmer Wlk. N7.....................4B 34
Hannaford Wlk. E3.................3D 67
Hannah Barlow Ho. SW8.........4B 90
Hannah Bldg. E1....................5D 65
.............................(off Watney St.)
Hannah Ct. E15......................1B 68
Hannah Mary Way SE1...........5C 78
Hannay Ho. SW15..................4A 100
Hannay La. N8.......................2F 33
Hannay Wlk. SW16.................2F 117
Hannell Rd. SW6....................3A 86
Hannen Rd. SE27...................3D 119
Hannibal Rd. E1.....................4E 65
Hannington Rd. SW4..............1D 103
Hanover Av. E16.....................2C 82
Hanover Ct. E8......................5B 50
.............................(off Stean St.)
Hanover Ct. SW15..................2B 98
Hanover Ct. W12....................2C 70
.........................(off Uxbridge St.)
Hanover Flats W1.........4C 12 (1C 74)
.............................(off Binney St.)
Hanover Gdns. SE11...............2C 90
Hanover Ga. NW1...................2A 60
Hanover Ga. Mans. NW1.........3A 60
Hanover Ho. E14....................2B 80
.........................(off Westferry Cir.)
Hanover Ho. NW8..................1A 60
.........................(off St John's Wood High St.)
Hanover Ho. SE16..................3F 79
.............................(off Dominion Rd.)
Hanover Ho. SW9...................1C 104
Hanover Mans. SW2................3C 104
.............................(off Barnwell Rd.)
Hanover Mead NW11..............1A 30
Hanover Pk. SE15...................4C 92
Hanover Pl. E3.......................2B 66
Hanover Pl. WC2.........3E 15 (5A 62)
Hanover Rd. NW10..................4E 43
Hanover Sq. W1..........3E 13 (5D 61)
Hanover Steps W2..................5A 60
.........................(off St George's Flds.)
Hanover St. W1..........3E 13 (5D 61)
Hanover Ter. NW1...................2B 60

Hanover Ter. M. NW1........2A 60
Hanover Trad. Est. N7........2A 48
Hanover Yd. N1..................1E 63
..............................(off Noel Rd.)
Hansard M. W14.................3F 71
Hanscomb M. SW4..........2E 95
Hans Ct. SW3......................4B 74
..............................(off Hans Rd.)
Hans Cres. SW1......5A 20 (4B 74)
Hansel Rd. NW6.................2C 58
Hansler Ct. SW19.............1A 114
..............................(off Princes Way)
Hansler Rd. SE22...............3B 106
Hansom M. SE11................1B 90
Hanson Cl. SW12..............5D 103
Hanson Ct. E17..................1D 39
Hanson Ho. E1....................1C 78
..............................(off Pinchin St.)
Hanson St. W1.........5F 5 (4E 61)
Hans Pl. SW1.........5A 20 (4B 74)
Hans Rd. SW3....................4B 74
Hans St. SW1.........5A 20 (4B 74)
Hanway Pl. W1........2B 14 (5F 61)
Hanway St. W1........2B 14 (5F 61)
Hanwell Ho. W2..................4C 58
..............................(off Gt. Western Rd.)
Hanworth Ho. SE5..............3D 91
Harad's Pl. E1.....................1C 78
Harben Pde. NW3...............4E 45
..............................(off Finchley Rd.)
Harben Rd. NW6................4E 45
Harberson Rd. E15............5B 54
Harberson Rd. SW12........1D 117
Harberton Rd. N19.............3E 33
Harbet Rd. W2....................4F 59
Harbinger Rd. E14..............5D 81
Harbledown Ho.
SE1....................4B 26 (3F 77)
..............................(off Manciple St.)
Harbledown Rd. SW6.........4C 86
Harbord Cl. SE5..................5F 91
Harbord Ho. SE16..............5F 79
..............................(off Cope St.)
Harbord St. SW6................4F 85
Harborough Rd. SW16......4B 118
Harbour Av. SW10..............6E 87
Harbour Club Chelsea.......5E 87
Harbour Club Kensington...5D 73
..............................(off Point West)
Harbour Club Notting Hill...4C 58
Harbour Exchange Sq. E14....3D 81
Harbour Reach SW6...........6E 87
Harbour Rd. SE5..............1E 105
Harbourside Ct. SE8.........5A 80
..............................(off Plough Way)
Harbour Way E14...............3D 81
Harbour Yd. SW10..............4E 87
Harbridge Av. SW15...........5B 98
Harbut Rd. SW11..............2F 101
Harcombe Rd. N16............5A 36
Harcourt Bldgs.
EC4..................4B 16 (1C 76)
..............................(off Middle Temple La.)
Harcourt Ho. W1.........2D 13 (5D 61)
..............................(off Cavendish Sq.)
Harcourt Rd. E15................1B 68
Harcourt Rd. SE4...............1B 108
Harcourt St. W1..................4A 60
Harcourt Ter. SW10............1D 87
Hardcastle Ho. SE14.........4A 94
..............................(off Loring Rd.)
Hardel Ri. SW2..................1D 119
Hardel Wlk. SW2................5C 104
Harden Ct. SE7...................5F 83
Harden Ho. SE5.................5A 92

Harden's Manorway SE7......4F 83
..............................(not continuous)
Harders Rd. SE15..............5D 93
Hardess St. SE24.............1E 105
Harding Cl. SE17................2E 91
Harding La. E1...................5E 65
..............................(not continuous)
Harding Rd. NW10..............5D 43
Hardinge St. E1: Lon Johnson St.
..............................5E 65
Hardinge St. E1: Lon Steel's La.
..............................5E 65
Harding Ho. SW13..............2D 85
..............................(off Wyatt Dr.)
Hardington NW1................4C 46
..............................(off Belmont St.)
Hardman Rd. SE7...............1D 97
Hardwicke M. WC1....2A 8 (2B 62)
..............................(off Lloyd Baker M.)
Hardwick Ho. NW8.............3A 60
..............................(off Lilestone St.)
Hardwicks Sq. SW18..........3C 100
Hardwick St. EC1....2C 8 (2C 62)
Hardwidge St. SE1...3D 27 (3A 78)
Hardy Av. E16....................2C 82
Hardy Cl. SE16...................3F 79
Hardy Cotts. SE10...............2F 95
Hardy Ho. SW17.................3F 115
..............................(off Grosvenor Way)
Hardy Ho. SW18.................5D 101
Hardy Rd. SW4...................5E 103
Hardy Rd. SE3....................3B 96
Hare & Billet Rd. SE3..........4F 95
Hare Ct. EC4..........3B 16 (5C 62)
..............................(off Church Ct.)
Harecourt Rd. N1................3E 49
Haredale Ho. SE16..............3C 78
..............................(off East La.)
Haredale Rd. SE24............2E 105
Haredon Cl. SE23..............5E 107
Harefield M. SE4...............1B 108
Harefield Rd. SE4..............1B 108
Hare Marsh E2...................3C 64
Hare Pl. EC4..........3C 16 (5C 62)
..............................(off Fleet St.)
Hare Row E2......................1D 65
Hare Wlk. N1......................1A 64
..............................(not continuous)
Harewood Av. NW1.............3A 60
Harewood Pl. W1.....3E 13 (5D 61)
Harewood Row NW1...........4A 60
Harfield Gdns. SE5...........1A 106
Harfleur Ct. SE11...............5D 77
..............................(off Opal St.)
Harford Ho. SE5.................2E 91
..............................(off Bethwin Rd.)
Harford Ho. W11.................4B 58
Harford M. N19..................5F 33
Harford St. E1....................3A 66
Hargood Rd. SE3...............4E 97
Hargrave Mans. N19...........4F 33
Hargrave Pk. N19...............4E 33
Hargrave Pl. N7..................2F 47
Hargrave Rd. N19...............4E 33
Hargraves Ho. W12...........1D 71
..............................(off White City Est.)
Hargreaves Ct. E3..............2C 82
..............................(off Bolinder Way)
Hargwyne St. SW9.............1B 104
Haringey Pk. N8.................1A 34
Harkness Ho. E1.................5C 64
..............................(off Christian St.)
Harland Rd. SE12..............1C 124
Harlequin Ct. E1.................1C 78
..............................(off Thomas More St.)

Harlequin Ct. NW10............3A 42
..............................(off Mitchellbrook Way)
Harlescott Rd. SE15..........2F 107
HARLESDEN.......................1B 56
Harlesden Gdns. NW10......5B 42
Harlesden La. NW10...........5C 42
Harlesden Plaza NW10......1B 56
Harlesden Rd. NW10..........5C 42
Harlesden Station (Underground
& Overground)...................1A 56
Harleston Cl. E5.................4E 37
Harley Ct. E11....................2C 40
Harleyford Ct. SE11............2B 90
..............................(off Harleyford Rd.)
Harleyford Rd. SE11...........2B 90
Harleyford St. SE11...........2C 90
Harley Gdns. SW10............1E 87
Harley Gro. E3....................2B 66
Harley Ho. E11...................2F 39
Harley Ho. E14...................5B 66
..............................(off Frances Wharf)
Harley Ho. NW1........4C 4 (3C 60)
..............................(off Marylebone Rd.)
Harley Pl. W1.........1D 13 (4D 61)
Harley Rd. NW3.................1A 56
Harley Rd. NW3.................4F 45
Harley St. W1.........4D 5 (3D 61)
HARLEY STREET CLINIC, THE
..............................5D 5 (4D 61)
Harlie Vs. NW10.................1A 56
Harlie Ct. SE6....................4C 108
Harling Ct. SW11...............5B 88
Harlinger St. SE18.............4F 83
Harlynwood SE5................3E 91
..............................(off Wyndham Rd.)
Harman Cl. NW2................5A 30
Harman Cl. SE1..................1C 92
Harman Dr. NW2................5A 30
Harmon Ho. SE8................5B 80
Harmont Ho. W1.....1D 13 (4D 61)
..............................(off Harley St.)
Harmony Cl. NW11.............1A 30
..............................(not continuous)
Harmony Pl. SE1................1B 92
Harmony Pl. SE8................2D 95
..............................(off Dancers Way)
Harmood Gro. NW1............4D 47
Harmood Ho. NW1..............4D 47
..............................(off Harmood St.)
Harmood St. NW1...............4D 47
Harmood St. NW1...............3D 47
Harmsworth M. SE11..........4D 77
Harmsworth St. SE17.........1D 91
Harold Ct. SE16.................3F 79
..............................(off Christopher Cl.)
Harold Est. SE1.......5E 27 (4A 78)
Harold Gibbons Ct. SE7......2E 97
Harold Ho. E2.....................1F 65
..............................(off Mace St.)
Harold Laski Ho. EC1..2E 9 (2D 63)
..............................(off Percival St.)
Harold Maddison Ho.
SE17..............................1D 91
..............................(off Penton Pl.)
Harold Pinter Theatre
..............................5B 14 (1F 75)
..............................(off Panton St.)
Harold Pl. SE11..................1C 90
Harold Rd. E11...................3A 40
Harold Rd. E13...................5D 55
Harold Wilson Ho. SW6......2B 86
..............................(off Clem Attlee Ct.)
Harp All. EC4.....................2D 63
Harp Bus. Cen., The NW2...4C 28
Harpenden Rd. E12.............4E 41

Harpenden Rd. SE27 .... 3D 119
Harpenmead Point NW2 .... 4B 30
Harper Ho. SW9 .... 1D 105
Harper M. SW17 .... 3E 115
Harper Rd. SE1 .... 5A 26 (4E 77)
Harp Island Cl. NW10 .... 4A 28
Harp La. EC3 .... 5D 19 (1A 78)
Harpley Sq. E1 .... 3F 65
Harpsden St. SW11 .... 4C 88
Harpur M. WC1 .... 5F 7 (4B 62)
Harpur St. WC1 .... 5F 7 (4B 62)
Harraden Rd. SE3 .... 4E 97
Harrier Av. E11 .... 1D 41
Harriet Cl. E8 .... 5C 50
Harriet Ct. SE14 .... 3E 93
.... (off Pomeroy St.)
Harriet Ho. SW6 .... 3D 87
.... (off Wandon Rd.)
Harriet St. SW1 .... 4A 20 (3B 74)
Harriet Tubman Cl. SW2 ... 5B 104
Harriet Wlk. SW1 ...... 4A 20 (3B 74)
HARRINGAY 1D 35
Harringay Green Lanes Station
(Overground) 1D 35
Harringay Station (Rail) 1C 34
Harrington Ct. SW7 .... 5F 73
.... (off Harrington Rd.)
Harrington Ct. W10 .... 2B 58
Harrington Gdns. SW7 .... 5D 73
Harrington Hill E5 .... 3D 37
Harrington Ho. NW1 .. 1F 5 (2E 61)
.... (off Harrington St.)
Harrington Rd. E11 .... 3A 40
Harrington Rd. SW7 .... 5F 73
Harrington Sq. NW1 .... 1E 61
Harrington St. NW1 .. 1F 5 (1E 61)
.... (not continuous)
Harrington Way SE18 .... 4F 83
Harriott Cl. SE10 .... 5B 82
Harriott Ho. E1 .... 4E 65
.... (off Jamaica St.)
Harris Bldgs. E1 .... 5C 64
.... (off Burslem St.)
Harris Clapham Sixth Form
College SW4 .... 3A 104
Harris Ho. E11 .... 3A 40
Harris Ho. E3 .... 2C 66
.... (off Alfred St.)
Harris Ho. SW9 .... 1C 104
...............(off St James's Cres.)
Harris Lodge SE6 .... 1E 123
Harrison Rd. E1 .... 5D 65
Harrison Ho. SE17 .... 1F 91
.... (off Brandon St.)
Harrison Rd. NW10 .... 5A 42
Harrisons Ct. SE14 .... 2F 93
.... (off Myers La.)
Harrison St. WC1 ...... 2E 7 (2A 62)
Harris Sports Cen. 3E 107
Harris St. E17 .... 2B 38
Harris St. SE5 .... 3F 91
Harrods 4B 74
Harrogate Ct. SE12 .... 5C 110
Harrogate Ct. SE26 .... 3C 120
.... (off Droitwich Cl.)
Harrold Ho. NW3 .... 4F 45
Harroway Rd. SW11 .... 5F 87
Harrowby Ho. W1 .... 5B 60
.... (off Harrowby St.)
Harrowby St. W1 .... 5A 60
Harrow Club W10 .... 1F 71
Harrowgate Ho. E9 .... 3F 51
Harrowgate Rd. E9 .... 3A 52
Harrow Grn. E11 .... 5A 40
Harrow La. E14 .... 1D 81

Harrow Lodge NW8 .... 3F 59
.... (off Northwick Ter.)
Harrow Pl. E1 .... 2E 19 (5A 64)
Harrow Rd. E11 .... 5A 40
Harrow Rd. NW10 .... 2D 57
Harrow Rd. W10 .... 3A 58
Harrow Rd. W2 .... 4E 59
.... (not continuous)
Harrow Rd. W9 .... 3B 58
HARROW RD. BRI. 4E 59
Harrow St. NW1 .... 4A 60
.... (off Daventry St.)
Harry Cole Ct. SE17 .... 1F 91
.... (off Thurlow St.)
Harry Day M. SE27 .... 3E 119
Harry Hinkins Ho. SE17 ...... 1E 91
.... (off Bronti Cl.)
Harry Lambourn Ho. SE15 .. 3D 93
.... (off Gervase St.)
Harry Zeital Way E5 .... 4E 37
Harston Wlk. E3 .... 3D 67
Hartfield Ter. E3 .... 1C 66
Hartham Cl. N7 .... 2A 48
Hartham Rd. N7 .... 2A 48
Harting Rd. SE9 .... 3F 125
Hartington Cl. SW8 .... 4A 90
Hartington Ho. SW1 .... 1F 89
.... (off Drummond Ga.)
Hartington Rd. E16 .... 5D 69
Hartington Rd. E17 .... 1A 38
Hartington Rd. SW8 .... 4A 90
Hartismere Rd. SW6 .... 3B 86
Hartlake Rd. E9 .... 3F 51
Hartland NW1 .... 5E 47
.... (off Royal College St.)
Hartland Rd. E15 .... 4B 54
Hartland Rd. NW1 .... 4D 47
Hartland Rd. NW6 .... 1B 58
Hartley Av. E6 .... 5F 55
Hartley Ho. SE1 .... 5B 78
.... (off Longfield Est.)
Hartley Rd. E11 .... 3B 40
Hartley St. E2 .... 2E 65
.... (not continuous)
Hartmann Rd. E16 .... 2F 83
Hartnoll St. N7 .... 2B 48
Harton Lodge SE8 .... 4C 94
.... (off Harton St.)
Harton St. SE8 .... 4C 94
Hartop Point SW6 .... 3A 86
.... (off Pellant Rd.)
Hartshorn All. EC3 .. 3E 19 (5A 64)
.... (off Leadenhall St.)
Hart's La. SE14 .... 4A 94
Hart St. EC3 .... 4E 19 (1A 78)
Hartswood Gdns. W12 .... 4B 70
Hartswood Rd. W12 .... 3B 70
Hartsworth Cl. E13 .... 1B 68
Hartwell Cl. SW2 .... 1B 118
Hartwell Ho. SE7 .... 1D 97
.... (off Troughton Rd.)
Hartwell St. E8 .... 3B 50
Harvard Cl. NW6 .... 2D 45
Harvard Ho. SE17 .... 2D 91
.... (off Doddington Gro.)
Harvard Rd. SE13 .... 3E 109
Harvey Ct. E17 .... 1C 38
Harvey Gdns. E11 .... 3B 40
Harvey Gdns. SE7 .... 1E 97
Harvey Ho. E1 .... 3D 65
.... (off Brady St.)
Harvey Ho. N1 .... 5F 49
.... (off Colville Est.)
Harvey Ho. SW1 .... 1F 89
.... (off Aylesford St.)

Harvey Lodge W9 .... 4C 58
.... (off Admiral Wlk.)
Harvey Rd. E11 .... 3A 40
Harvey Rd. SE5 .... 4F 91
Harvey's Bldgs.
WC2 .... 5E 15 (1A 76)
Harvey St. N1 .... 5F 49
Harvington Wlk. E8 .... 4C 50
Harvist Est. N7 .... 1C 48
Harvist Rd. NW6 .... 1F 57
Harwicke Ho. E3 .... 2D 67
.... (off Bow Rd.)
.... 5F 49
Harwood Ct. N1 .... 5F 49
.... (off Colville Est.)
Harwood Ct. SW15 .... 2E 99
Harwood M. SW6 .... 3C 86
Harwood Point SE16 .... 3B 80
Harwood Rd. SW6 .... 3C 86
Harwood Ter. SW6 .... 4D 87
Hascombe Ter. SE5 .... 5F 91
.... (off Love Wlk.)
Haseley End SE23 .... 5E 107
Haselrigge Rd. SW4 .... 2F 103
Haseltine Rd. SE26 .... 4B 122
Hasker St. SW3 .... 5A 74
Haslam Cl. N1 .... 4C 48
Haslam Ho. N1 .... 4E 49
.... (off Canonbury Rd.)
Haslam St. SE15 .... 3B 92
Haslemere Av. NW4 .... 1F 29
Haslemere Av. SW18 .... 2D 115
Haslemere Ind. Est.
SW18 .... 2D 115
Haslemere Rd. N8 .... 2F 33
Haslers Wharf E3 .... 5A 52
.... (off Old Ford Rd.)
Hassard St. E2 .... 1F 11 (1B 64)
Hassendean Rd. SE3 .... 3D 97
Hassett Rd. E9 .... 3F 51
Hassocks Cl. SE26 .... 3D 121
Hassop Rd. NW2 .... 1F 43
Hassop Wlk. SE9 .... 4F 125
Hasted Rd. SE7 .... 1F 97
Hastings Cl. SE15 .... 3C 92
Hastings Ho. W12 .... 1D 71
.... (off White City Est.)
Hastings Rd. E16 .... 4C 68
Hastings St. WC1 .... 2D 7 (2A 62)
.... (off Hastings St.)
Hastings St. WC1 .... 2D 7 (2A 62)
Hat & Mitre Ct. EC1 ... 4E 9 (3D 63)
.... (off St John St.)
Hatcham Mews Bus. Cen.
SE14 .... 4F 93
.... (off Hatcham Pk. Rd.)
Hatcham Pk. M. SE14 .... 4F 93
Hatcham Pk. Rd. SE14 .... 4F 93
Hatcham Rd. SE15 .... 2E 93
Hatcham St. SE26 .... 5B 122
Hatchard Rd. N19 .... 4F 33
Hatchers M. SE1 .... 4E 27 (3A 78)
.... (off Bermondsey St.)
Hatchfield Ho. N15 .... 1A 36
.... (off Albert Rd.)
Hatcliffe Almshouses SE10 . 1A 96
.... (off Tuskar St.)
Hatcliffe Cl. SE3 .... 1B 110
Hatcliffe St. SE10 .... 1B 96
Hatfield Cl. SE14 .... 3F 93
Hatfield Ct. SE3 .... 3C 96
Hatfield Ho. EC1 ...... 4F 9 (3E 63)
.... (off Golden La. Est.)
Hatfield Ho. SE10 .... 3D 95
Hatfield Rd. E15 .... 2A 54

Hatfield Rd. W4 .... 3A 70
Hatfields SE1 .... 1C 24 (2C 76)
Hathaway Ho. N1 ...... 1D 11 (1A 64)
Hatherley Ct. W2 .... 5D 59
.... (off Hatherley Gro.)
Hatherley Gdns. E6 .... 2F 69
Hatherley Gdns. N8 .... 1A 34
Hatherley Gro. W2 .... 5D 59
Hatherley St. SW1 .... 5E 75
Hathersage Ct. N1 .... 2F 49
Hathorne St. SE15 .... 5C 93
Hathway St. SE14 .... 5F 93
Hathway Ter. SE14 .... 5F 93
.... (off Hathway St.)
Hatley Rd. N4 .... 4B 34
Hatteraick St. SE16 .... 3E 79
Hatton Gdn. EC1 .... 5C 8 (4C 62)
Hatton Ho. E1 .... 1C 78
.... (off Hindmarsh Cl.)
Hatton Pl. EC1 .... 5C 8 (4C 62)
Hatton Row NW8 .... 3F 59
.... (off Hatton St.)
Hatton St. NW8 .... 3F 59
Hatton Wall EC1 .... 5C 8 (4C 62)
Haunch of Venison Yd.
    W1 .... 3D 13 (5D 61)
Hauteville Ct. Gdns. W6 .... 4B 70
.... (off South Side)
Havana Rd. SW19 .... 2C 114
Havannah St. E14 .... 3C 80
Havelock Cl. W12 .... 1D 71
Havelock Ho. SE1 .... 5B 78
.... (off Fort Rd.)
Havelock Ho. SE23 .... 1E 121
Havelock Ho. SW19 .... 5E 115
Havelock St. N1 .... 5A 48
Havelock Ter. SW8 .... 4D 89
Havelock Ter. Arches SW8 .... 4D 89
.... (off Havelock Ter.)
Havelock Wlk. SE23 .... 1E 121
Haven Cl. SW19 .... 3F 113
Haven M. E3 .... 4B 66
Haven M. N1 .... 4C 48
Havenpool NW8 .... 5D 45
.... (off Abbey Rd.)
Haven St. NW1 .... 4D 47
Haven Way SE1 .... 5F 27 (4B 78)
Haverfield Rd. E3 .... 2A 66
Haverhill Rd. SW12 .... 1E 117
Havering NW1 .... 4D 47
.... (off Castlehaven Rd.)
Havering St. E1 .... 5F 65
Haverley St. SE26 .... 5B 122
Haversham Pl. N6 .... 4B 32
Haverstock Hill NW3 .... 2A 46
Haverstock Pl. N1 ..... 1E 9 (2D 63)
.... (off Haverstock St.)
Haverstock Rd. NW5 .... 2C 46
Haverstock St. N1 .... 1E 9 (1D 63)
Havilland M. W12 .... 3D 71
Havil St. SE5 .... 3A 92
Havisham Apts. E15 .... 3F 53
.... (off Grove Cres. Rd.)
Havisham Ho. SE16 .... 3C 78
Hawarden Gro. SE24 .... 5E 105
Hawarden Hill NW2 .... 5C 28
Hawbridge Rd. E11 .... 3F 39
Hawes St. N1 .... 4D 49
Hawfinch Ho. NW9 .... 2B 28
Hawgood St. E3 .... 4C 66
Hawke Ho. E1 .... 3F 65
.... (off Ernest St.)
Hawke Pl. SE16 .... 3F 79
Hawker Ct. E3 .... 2E 67
.... (off Bolinder Way)

Hawke Rd. SE19 .... 5F 119
Hawkesbury Rd. SW15 .... 3D 99
Hawkesfield Rd. SE23 .... 2A 122
Hawkesley Ho. E17 .... 1D 39
Hawke Twr. SE14 .... 2A 94
Hawkins Ho. SE8 .... 2C 94
.... (off New King St.)
Hawkins Ho. SW1 .... 2E 89
.... (off Dolphin Sq.)
Hawkins Ho. NW10 .... 4A 42
Hawkins Way SE6 .... 5C 122
Hawkley Gdns. SE27 .... 2D 119
Hawkshaw Cl. SW2 .... 5A 104
.... (off Nebraska St.)
Hawkshead NW1 .... 1F 5 (2E 61)
.... (off Stanhope St.)
Hawkshead Rd. NW10 .... 4B 42
Hawkshead Rd. W4 .... 3A 70
Hawkslade Rd. SE15 .... 3F 107
Hawksley Rd. N16 .... 5A 36
Hawks M. SE10 .... 3E 95
Hawksmoor Cl. E6 .... 5F 69
Hawksmoor M. E1 .... 1D 79
Hawksmoor Pl. E2 .... 2C 64
.... (off Cheshire St.)
Hawksmoor St. W6 .... 2F 85
Hawkstone Rd. SE16 .... 5E 79
Hawkwell Wlk. N1 .... 5E 49
.... (off Maldon Cl.)
Hawkwood Mt. E5 .... 3D 37
Hawley Cres. NW1 .... 4D 47
Hawley M. NW1 .... 4D 47
Hawley Rd. NW1 .... 4D 47
.... (not continuous)
Hawley St. NW1 .... 4D 47
Hawstead Rd. SE6 .... 4D 109
Hawthorn Av. E3 .... 5B 52
Hawthorn Cres. SW17 .... 5C 116
Hawthorne Ho. N1 .... 3A 50
Hawthorne Cres. SE10 .... 1B 96
Hawthorne Ho. N15 .... 1C 36
Hawthorne Ho. SW1 .... 1E 89
.... (off Churchill Gdns.)
Hawthorn Ho. E15 .... 3F 53
.... (off Forrester Way)
Hawthorn Ho. SE16 .... 3A 80
.... (off Blondin Way)
Hawthorn Rd. NW10 .... 4C 42
Hawthorn Wlk. W10 .... 3A 58
Hawtrey Rd. NW3 .... 4A 46
Hay Cl. E15 .... 4A 54
Haycroft Gdns. NW10 .... 5C 42
Haycroft Rd. SW2 .... 3A 104
Hay Currie St. E14 .... 5D 67
Hayday Rd. E16 .... 4C 68
.... (not continuous)
Hayden Piper Ho. SW3 .... 2B 88
.... (off Caversham St.)
Hayden's Pl. W11 .... 5B 58
Hayden Twr. SW8 .... 3F 89
Haydon Pk. Rd. SW19 .... 5C 114
Haydon Rd. SW19 .... 5D 115
Haydon St. EC3 .... 4F 19 (1B 78)
Haydon Wlk. E1 .... 3F 19 (5B 64)
Haydon Way SW11 .... 2F 101
Hayes Cl. SE5 .... 3E 91
.... (off Camberwell New Rd.)
Hayes Cres. NW11 .... 1B 30
Hayesens Ho. SW17 .... 4E 115
Hayes Gro. SE22 .... 1B 106
Hayes M. SE8 .... 4B 94
Hayes Pl. NW1 .... 3A 60
Hayfield Pas. E1 .... 3E 65

Hayfield Yd. E1 .... 3E 65
Haygarth Pl. SW19 .... 5F 113
Hay Hill W1 .... 5E 13 (1D 75)
Hayhurst Ct. N1 .... 5D 49
.... (off Dibden St.)
Hayles Bldgs. SE11 .... 5D 77
.... (off Elliotts Row)
Hayles St. SE11 .... 5D 77
Haymans Point SE11 .... 5B 76
Hayman St. N1 .... 4D 49
Haymarket SW1 .... 5B 14 (1F 75)
Haymarket Arc.
    SW1 .... 5B 14 (1F 75)
.... (off Haymarket)
Haymarket Ct. E8 .... 4B 50
.... (off Jacaranda Gro.)
Haymarket Theatre Royal
    .... 5C 14 (1F 75)
.... (off Haymarket)
Haymerle Ho. SE15 .... 2C 92
.... (off Haymerle Rd.)
Haymerle Rd. SE15 .... 2C 92
Hayne Ho. W11 .... 2A 72
.... (off Penzance Pl.)
Haynes Cl. SE3 .... 1A 110
Hayne St. EC1 .... 5E 9 (4D 63)
.... (off Rotherhithe St.)
Hay's Ct. SE16 .... 3E 79
Hay's Galleria
    SE1 .... 1D 27 (2A 78)
Hays La. SE1 .... 1D 27 (2A 78)
Hay's M. W1 .... 1D 21 (2D 75)
Hay St. E2 .... 5C 50
Hayter Ct. E11 .... 4D 41
Hayter Rd. SW2 .... 3A 104
Hayton Cl. E8 .... 3B 50
Hayward Ct. SW9 .... 5A 90
.... (off Studley Rd.)
Hayward Gallery 1A 24 (2B 76)
Hayward Gdns. SW15 .... 4E 99
Hayward Ho. N1 .... 1C 62
.... (off Penton St.)
Hayward M. SE4 .... 3B 108
Hayward's Pl. EC1 .... 3D 9 (3D 63)
Hazelbank Rd. SE6 .... 2F 123
Hazelbourne Rd. SW12 .... 4D 103
Hazel Cl. N19 .... 4E 33
Hazel Cl. SE15 .... 5C 92
.... (off Bournemouth Cl.)
Hazeldean Rd. NW10 .... 4A 42
Hazeldon Rd. SE4 .... 3A 108
Hazel Gro. SE26 .... 4F 121
Hazel Ho. E3 .... 5B 52
.... (off Barge La.)
Hazelhurst Ct. SE6 .... 5E 123
.... (off Beckenham Hill Rd.)
Hazelhurst Rd. SW17 .... 4E 115
Hazel La. SE10 .... 1B 96
Hazellville Rd. N19 .... 2F 33
Hazelmere Ct. SW2 .... 1B 118
Hazelmere Rd. NW6 .... 5B 44
Hazel Rd. E15 .... 2A 54
Hazel Rd. NW10 .... 2D 57
.... (not continuous)
Hazel Way SE1 .... 5B 78
Hazelwood Ct. NW10 .... 5A 28
Hazelwood Ho. SE8 .... 5A 80
Hazelwood Rd. E17 .... 1A 38
Hazlebury Rd. SW6 .... 5D 87
Hazlewell Rd. SW15 .... 3E 99
Hazlewood Cl. E5 .... 5A 38
Hazlewood Cres. W10 .... 3A 58
Hazlewood M. SW9 .... 1A 104

Hazlewood Twr. W10 .... 3A **58**
.... (off Golborne Gdns.)
Hazlitt M. W14 .... 4A **72**
Hazlitt Rd. W14 .... 4A **72**
Headbourne Ho.
SE1 .... 5C **26** (4F **77**)
Headcorn Rd. BR1: Broml..5B **124**
Headfort Pl. SW1...... 4C **20** (3C **74**)
Headington Rd. SW18.......2E **115**
Headlam Rd. SW4................4F **103**
.... (not continuous)
Headlam St. E1 .... 3D **65**
Headley Ct. SE26................5E **121**
Headley M. SW18................3D **101**
Head's M. W11 .... 5C **58**
Head St. E1 .... 5F **65**
.... (not continuous)
Heald St. SE14 .... 4C **94**
Healey Ho. E3 .... 3C **66**
.... (off Wellington Way)
Healey Ho. SW9 .... 3C **90**
Healey St. NW1 .... 3D **47**
Hearn Pl. SW16 ....4C **118**
Hearn's Bldgs. SE17 ....5F **77**
Hearnshaw St. E14 ....5A **66**
Hearn St. EC2........... 4E **11** (3A **64**)
Hearnville Rd. SW12 ....1C **116**
Heath Brow NW3.................5E **31**
Heath Cl. NW11 .... 2D **31**
Heathcock Ct. WC2...5E **15** (1A **76**)
.... (off Exchange Ct.)
Heathcote Ga. SW6 ....1C **100**
Heathcote St. WC1 ... 3F **7** (3B **62**)
Heath Cft. NW11 .... 3D **31**
Heath Dr. NW3 .... 1D **45**
Heathedge SE26................ 2D **121**
Heather Cl. N7 .... 5B **34**
Heather Cl. SE13 ....5F **109**
Heather Cl. SW8 .... 1D **103**
HEATHER CLOSE REHABILITATION
CEN. 5F **109**
Heather Gdns. NW11 ....1A **30**
Heather Ho. E14 ....5E **67**
.... (off Dee St.)
Heatherley St. E5 .... 5C **36**
Heather Rd. NW2 .... 4B **28**
Heather Rd. SE12................2C **124**
Heather Wlk. W10 .... 3A **58**
Heatherwood Cl. E12 ....4E **41**
Heathfield Av. SW18 ....5F **101**
Heathfield Cl. E16 ....4F **69**
Heathfield Cl. E3 .... 1C **66**
.... (off Tredegar Rd.)
Heathfield Ct. SE14.............3E **93**
Heathfield Gdns. NW11 ......1F **29**
Heathfield Gdns. SE3 ....5A **96**
.... (off Baizdon Rd.)
Heathfield Gdns. SW18......4F **101**
Heathfield Ho. SE3 ....5A **96**
Heathfield Pk. NW2 ....3E **43**
Heathfield Rd. SW18............4E **101**
Heathfield Sq. SW18 ....5F **101**
Heathgate NW11 .... 1D **31**
Heathgate Pl. NW3 ....2B **46**
Heath Hurst Rd. NW3 ....1A **46**
Heathland Rd. N16................3A **36**
Heath La. SE3.......................5F **95**
.... (not continuous)
Heathlee Rd. SE3 ....2B **110**
Heathmans Rd. SW6 ....4B **86**
Heath Mead SW19 ....3F **113**
Heath Pas. NW3 ....4D **31**
Heath Pl. E3........................ 3D **66**
Heathpool Ct. E1 .... 3D **65**
Heath Ri. SW15 ....4F **99**

Heath Rd. SW8 .... 5D **89**
Heath Royal SW15 ....4F **99**
Heath Side NW3 .... 1F **45**
Heathside SW11 .... 3C **90**
Heathside SE13 ....5E **95**
Heathstan Rd. W12 ....5C **56**
Heath St. NW3 .... 1E **45**
Heathview NW5 .... 1C **46**
Heathview Gdns. SW15 ....5E **99**
Heath Vs. NW3 ....5F **31**
Heathville Rd. N19 .... 2A **34**
Heathwall St. SW11 ....1B **102**
Heathway SE3 .... 3C **96**
Heathway Ct. NW3 ....4C **30**
Heathwood Gdns. SE7 ....5B **83**
Heathwood Point SE23.........3F **121**
Heaton Ho. SW10 ....2E **87**
.... (off Fulham Rd.)
Heaton Rd. SE15 .... 5D **93**
Heaven Tree Cl. N1 ....3E **49**
Heaver Rd. SW11 ....1F **101**
Hebden St. E2 .... 5B **50**
Hebden St. SW8 .... 3F **89**
Hebdon Rd. SW17 ....3A **116**
Heber Mans. W14 .... 2A **86**
.... (off Queen's Club Gdns.)
Heber Rd. NW2 .... 2F **43**
Heber Rd. SE22 .... 4B **106**
Hebrides St. E1 .... 4A **66**
.... (off Ocean St.)
Hebron Rd. W6 ....4E **71**
Heckfield Pl. SW6 .... 3C **86**
Heckford Ho. E14 .... 5D **67**
.... (off Grundy St.)
Heckford St. E1 ....1F **79**
Heckford St. Bus. Cen. E1 ....1F **79**
.... (off Heckford St.)
Hector Ct. SW9.................... 3C **90**
.... (off Caldwell St.)
Hector Ho. E2 .... 1D **65**
.... (off Old Bethnal Grn. Rd.)
Heddington Gro. N7..............2B **48**
Heddon St. W1 .... 4F **13** (1E **75**)
Hedgegate Ct. W11 ....5B **58**
.... (off Powis Ter.)
Hedgers Gro. E9 ....3A **52**
Hedger St. SE11 .... 5D **77**
Hedge Wlk. SE6....................5D **123**
Hedgley M. SE12..................3B **110**
Hedgley St. SE12..................3B **110**
Hedingham Cl. N1.................4E **49**
Hedley Ho. E14.....................4E **81**
.... (off Stewart St.)
Hedley Row N5......................2F **49**
Hedsor Ho. E2 .... 3F **11** (3B **64**)
.... (off Ligonier St.)
Heer M. E2.......................... 1C **64**
.... (off Hackney Rd.)
Hega Ho. E14.......................4E **67**
.... (off Ullin St.)
Heidegger Cres. SW13.........3D **85**
Heigham Rd. E6 ....4F **55**
Heights, The SE7..................1E **97**
Heiron St. SE17 ....2D **91**
Heldar Ct. SE1 .... 4C **26** (3F **77**)
Helder Gro. SE12..................5B **110**
Helena Cl. SW19...................5F **99**
Helena Rd. NW6 ....4D **45**
.... (off Compayne Gdns.)
Helena Pl. E9........................5D **51**
Helena Rd. E13.....................1B **68**
Helena Rd. E17.....................1C **38**
Helena Rd. NW10..................2D **9**
Helena Sq. SE16...................1A **80**
.... (off Sovereign Cres.)

Helen Gladstone Ho.
SE1 ....3D **25** (3D **77**)
.... (off Surrey Row)
Helen Ho. E2......................1D **65**
.... (off Old Bethnal Grn. Rd.)
Helen Peele Cotts. SE16 .....4E **79**
.... (off Lower Rd.)
Helenslea Av. NW11.............3C **30**
Helen's Pl. E2.......................2E **65**
Helen Taylor Ho. SE16 ....4C **78**
.... (off Evelyn Lowe Est.)
Heligan Ho. SE16 ....3F **79**
.... (off Water Gdns. Sq.)
Helios, The 1E **71**
Heliport Ind. Est. SW11 ....5F **87**
Helix Ct. W11 ....2F **71**
.... (off Swanscombe Rd.)
Helix Gdns. SW2..................4B **104**
Helix Rd. SW2......................4B **104**
Helix Ter. SW19....................2F **113**
Hellings St. E1 ....2C **78**
Helme Cl. SW19....................5B **114**
Helmet Row EC1 .... 2A **10** (3E **63**)
Helmsdale Apts. SW11 ....2A **102**
.... (off Monarch Square)
Helmsdale Ho. NW6 ....1D **59**
.... (off Carlton Vale)
Helmsley Pl. E8 ....4D **51**
Helmsley St. E8 ....4D **51**
Helperby Rd. NW10...............4A **42**
Helsby St. NW8 ....3F **59**
.... (off Pollitt Dr.)
Helsinki Sq. SE16.................4A **80**
Helston NW1.........................5E **47**
.... (off Camden St.)
Helston Ct. N15.....................1A **36**
.... (off Culvert Rd.)
Helston Ho. SE11 ....1C **90**
.... (off Kennings Way)
Helvetia St. SE6...................2B **122**
Hemans St. SW8 ....3F **89**
Hemans St. Est. SW8 ....3A **90**
Hemberton Rd. SW9 ....1A **104**
Hemingford Rd. N1 ....5B **48**
Hemingway Cl. NW5..............1C **46**
Hemlock Ho. SE16 ....4A **80**
Hemlock Rd. W12 ....1B **70**
.... (not continuous)
Hemming St. E1 ....3C **64**
Hemp Wlk. SE17 ....5F **77**
Hemstal Rd. NW6..................4C **44**
Hemsworth Ct. N1 ....1A **64**
Hemsworth St. N1 ....1A **64**
Hemus Pl. SW3.....................1A **88**
Hen & Chicken Ct.
EC4........................3B **16** (5C **62**)
.... (off Fleet St.)
Hen & Chickens Theatre......3D **49**
.... (off St Paul's Rd.)
Henchman St. W12 ....5B **56**
Henderson Ct. NW3...............2F **45**
.... (off Fitzjohn's Av.)
Henderson Ct. SE14..............2F **93**
.... (off Myers La.)
Henderson Dr. NW8 ....3F **59**
Henderson Rd. E7 ....3E **55**
Henderson Rd. SW18 ....5A **102**
Hendham Rd. SW17 ....2A **116**
Hendon Central Station
(Underground) 1D **29**
Hendon Ho. NW4 ....1F **29**
Hendon Leisure Cen. 2F **29**
Hendon Pk. Mans. NW4 ....1E **29**
Hendon Pk. Row NW11 ....1B **30**
Hendon Station (Rail) 1C **28**

Hendon St. SE10 .... 4B **82**
Hendon Way NW2 .... 2F **29**
Hendon Way NW4 .... 1D **29**
Hendre Ho. SE1 .... 5A **78**
.... *(off Hendre Rd.)*
Hendre Rd. SE1 .... 5A **78**
Hendrick Av. SW12 .... 5B **102**
Heneage La. EC3 .... 2E **19** (5A **64**)
Heneage Pl. EC3 .... 3E **19** (5A **64**)
Heneage St. E1 .... 4B **64**
Henfield Cl. N19 .... 3E **33**
Hengist Rd. SE12 .... 5D **111**
Hengrave Rd. SE23 .... 4E **107**
Henley Cl. SE16 .... 3E **79**
.... *(off St Marychurch St.)*
Henley Ct. NW2 .... 3F **43**
Henley Dr. SE1 .... 5B **78**
Henley Hgts. N1 .... 4B **48**
.... *(off Caledonian Rd.)*
Henley Ho. E2 .... 3F **11** (3B **64**)
.... *(off Swanfield St.)*
Henley Prior N1 .... 1F **7** (1B **62**)
.... *(off Affleck St.)*
Henley Rd. NW10 .... 5E **43**
Henley St. SW11 .... 5C **88**
Hennel Cl. SE23 .... 3E **121**
Hennessy Ct. E10 .... 1E **39**
Henniker Gdns. E6 .... 2F **69**
Henniker M. SW3 .... 2F **87**
Henniker Point E15 .... 2A **54**
.... *(off Leytonstone Rd.)*
Henniker Rd. E15 .... 2F **53**
Henning St. SW11 .... 4A **88**
Henrietta Barnet Wlk.
   NW11 .... 1C **30**
Henrietta Cl. SE8 .... 2C **94**
Henrietta Ho. N15 .... 1A **36**
.... *(off St Ann's Rd.)*
Henrietta Ho. W6 .... 1E **85**
.... *(off Queen Caroline St.)*
Henrietta M. WC1 ...... 3E **7** (3A **62**)
Henrietta Pl. W1 .... 2D **13** (5D **61**)
Henrietta St. WC2 ..... 4E **15** (1A **76**)
Henriques St. E1 .... 5C **64**
Henry Chester Bldg. SW15 ...... 5E **99**
Henry Cooper Way SE9 .... 3F **125**
Henry Dent Cl. SE5 .... 1F **105**
Henry Dickens Ct. W11 .... 1F **71**
Henry Doulton Dr. SW17 .... 4C **116**
Henry Ho. SE1 .... 2B **24** (2C **76**)
Henry Ho. SW8 .... 3A **90**
.... *(off Wyvil Rd.)*
Henry Hudson Apts. SE10 .... 1A **96**
.... *(off Banning St.)*
Henry Jackson Rd. SW15 .... 1F **99**
Henry Moore Ct. SW3 .... 1A **88**
Henry Purcell Ho. E16 .... 2D **83**
.... *(off Evelyn Rd.)*
Henry Rd. N4 .... 3E **35**
Henry Rd. SW9 .... 4C **90**
Henryson Rd. SE4 .... 3C **108**
Henry Tate M. SW16 .... 5B **118**
Henry Wise Ho. SW1 .... 5E **75**
.... *(off Vauxhall Bri. Rd.)*
Hensford Gdns. SE26 .... 4D **121**
Henshall Point E3 .... 2D **67**
.... *(off Bromley High St.)*
Henshall St. N1 .... 3F **49**
Henshaw St. SE17 .... 5F **77**
Henslowe Rd. SE22 .... 3C **106**
Henslow Ho. SE15 .... 3C **92**
.... *(off Peckham Pk. Rd.)*
Henson Av. NW2 .... 2E **43**
Henstridge Pl. NW8 .... 5A **46**
Henty Cl. SW11 .... 3A **88**

Henty Wlk. SW15 .... 3D **99**
Henwick Rd. SE9 .... 1F **111**
Hepburn M. SW11 .... 3B **102**
Hepdon M. SW17 .... 5F **115**
Hepplestone Cl. SW15 .... 4D **99**
Hepscott Rd. E9 .... 3C **52**
Hepworth Ct. N1 .... 5D **49**
.... *(off Gaskin St.)*
Hepworth Ct. NW3 .... 2A **46**
Hepworth Ct. SW1 .... 1D **89**
Hera Ct. E14 .... 5C **80**
.... *(off Homer Dr.)*
Herald's Pl. SE11 .... 5D **77**
Herald St. E2 .... 3D **65**
Herbal Hill EC1 .... 4C **8** (3C **62**)
Herbal Hill Gdns.
   EC1 .... 4C **8** (3C **62**)
.... *(off Herbal Hill)*
Herbal Pl. EC1 .... 4C **8** (3C **62**)
Herbert Cres. SW1 ... 5A **20** (4B **74**)
Herbert Gdns. NW10 .... 1D **57**
Herbert Ho. E1 .... 2F **19** (5A **64**)
.... *(off Old Castle St.)*
Herbert M. SW2 .... 4C **104**
Herbert Morrison Ho.
   SW6 .... 2B **86**
.... *(off Clem Attlee Ct.)*
Herbert Rd. E12 .... 1F **55**
Herbert Rd. E17 .... 2B **38**
Herbert Rd. NW9 .... 1C **28**
Herbert Rd. SE18 .... 1C **68**
Herbert St. E13 .... 1C **68**
Herbert St. NW5 .... 3C **46**
Herbrand Est. WC1 .... 3D **7** (3A **62**)
Herbrand St. WC1 ..... 3D **7** (3A **62**)
Hercules Ct. SE14 .... 2A **94**
Hercules Ho. E14 .... 5A **68**
Hercules Pl. N7 .... 5A **34**
.... *(not continuous)*
Hercules Rd. SE1 ...... 5A **24** (4B **76**)
Hercules St. N7 .... 5A **34**
Hercules Wharf E14 .... 1A **82**
.... *(off Orchard Pl.)*
Hercules Yd. N7 .... 5A **34**
Here E. E20 .... 2C **52**
Hereford Bldgs. SW3 .... 2F **87**
.... *(off Old Church St.)*
Hereford Gdns. SE13 .... 3A **110**
Hereford Ho. NW6 .... 1C **58**
.... *(off Carlton Vale)*
Hereford Ho. SW10 .... 3D **87**
.... *(off Fulham Rd.)*
Hereford Ho. SW3 .... 4A **74**
.... *(off Ovington Gdns.)*
Hereford Mans. W2 .... 5C **58**
.... *(off Hereford Rd.)*
Hereford M. W2 .... 5C **58**
Hereford Pl. SE14 .... 3B **94**
Hereford Retreat SE15 .... 3C **92**
Hereford Rd. E11 .... 1D **41**
Hereford Rd. E3 .... 1B **66**
Hereford Rd. W2 .... 5C **58**
Hereford Sq. SW7 .... 5E **73**
Hereford St. E2 .... 3C **64**
Hereward Rd. SW17 .... 4B **116**
Heritage Cl. SW9 .... 1D **105**
Heritage Ct. SE8 .... 1F **93**
Heritage La. NW6 .... 3C **44**
Heritage Pl. SW18 .... 1E **115**
Herlwyn Gdns. SW17 .... 4B **116**
Her Majesty's Theatre
   .... 1B **22** (2F **75**)
.... *(off Haymarket)*
Hermes Cl. W9 .... 3C **58**
Hermes Ct. SW2 .... 4B **104**

Hermes Ct. SW9 .... 4C **90**
.... *(off Southey Rd.)*
Hermes St. N1 .... 1B **8** (1C **62**)
Herm Ho. N1 .... 3E **49**
.... *(off Clifton Rd.)*
Hermiston Av. N8 .... 1A **34**
Hermitage, The SE13 .... 5E **95**
Hermitage, The SE23 .... 1E **121**
Hermitage, The SW13 .... 4B **84**
Hermitage Basin 2C **78**
.... *(off Cromwell Cl.)*
Hermitage Ct. E1 .... 2C **78**
.... *(off Knighten St.)*
Hermitage Ct. NW2 .... 5C **30**
Hermitage Gdns. NW2 .... 5C **30**
Hermitage Ho. N1 .... 1D **63**
.... *(off Gerrard Rd.)*
Hermitage La. NW2 .... 5C **30**
Hermitage Moorings E1 .... 2C **78**
Hermitage Rd. N15 .... 1F **35**
Hermitage Rd. N4 .... 2D **35**
Hermitage Row E8 .... 2C **50**
Hermitage St. W2 .... 4F **59**
Hermitage Vs. SW6 .... 2C **86**
.... *(off Lillie Rd.)*
Hermitage Wall E1 .... 2C **78**
Hermitage Waterside E1 .... 2C **78**
.... *(off Thomas More St.)*
Hermit Pl. NW6 .... 5D **45**
Hermit Rd. E16 .... 4B **68**
Hermit St. EC1 .... 1D **9** (2D **63**)
Hermon Hill E11 .... 1C **40**
Herndon Rd. SW18 .... 3E **101**
Herne Cl. NW10 .... 2A **42**
Herne Hill SE24 .... 4E **105**
HERNE HILL 3E **105**
Herne Hill Ho. SE24 .... 4D **105**
.... *(off Railton Rd.)*
Herne Hill Rd. SE24 .... 1E **105**
Herne Hill Station (Rail) 4D **105**
Herne Hill Velodrome 4F **105**
Herne Pl. SE24 .... 3D **105**
Heron Cl. NW10 .... 3A **42**
Heron Ct. E14 .... 4E **81**
.... *(off New Union Cl.)*
Herondale Av. SW18 .... 1F **115**
Heron Dr. N4 .... 4E **35**
Herongate N1 .... 5E **49**
.... *(off Ridgewell Cl.)*
Herongate Rd. E12 .... 4E **41**
Heron Ho. E3 .... 5B **52**
.... *(off Sycamore Av.)*
Heron Ho. NW8 .... 1A **60**
.... *(off Newcourt St.)*
Heron Ho. SW11 .... 3A **88**
.... *(off Searles Cl.)*
Heron Ind. Est. E15 .... 1D **67**
Heron Pl. E16 .... 2E **83**
.... *(off Bramwell Way)*
Heron Pl. SE16 .... 2A **80**
Heron Pl. W1 .... 2C **12** (5C **60**)
.... *(off Thayer St.)*
Heron Quay E14 .... 2C **80**
Heron Quays Station (DLR)
   .... 2C **80**
Heron Rd. SE24 .... 2E **105**
Herons, The E11 .... 1B **40**
Heron's Lea N6 .... 1B **32**
Herrick Ho. N16 .... 1F **49**
.... *(off Howard Rd.)*
Herrick Ho. SE5 .... 3F **91**
.... *(off Elmington Est.)*
Herrick Rd. N5 .... 5E **35**
Herrick St. SW1 .... 5F **75**
Herries St. W10 .... 1A **58**

Herringham Rd. SE7 ....4E 83
Hersant Cl. NW10 ....5C 42
Herschell M. SE5............1E 105
Herschell Rd. SE23 ....5A 108
Hersham Cl. SW15 ....5C 98
Hertford Av. SW14 ....3A 98
Hertford Lock Ho. E3 ......5B 52
.................(off Parnell Rd.)
Hertford Pl. W1 ......4A 6 (3E 61)
Hertford Rd. N1 ....5A 50
.....................(not continuous)
Hertford St. W1 ....2D 21 (2D 75)
Hertford Wharf N1 ....5A 50
.................(off Hertford Rd.)
Hertslet Rd. N7................5B 34
Hertsmere Rd. E14..........2C 80
Hervey Rd. SE3 ....4D 97
Hesewall Cl. SW4............5E 89
Hesketh Pl. W11 ....1A 72
Hesketh Rd. E7 ....5C 40
Heslop Rd. SW12 ....1B 116
Hesper M. SW5 ....5D 73
Hesperus Cres. E14 ....5D 81
Hessel St. E1 ....1D 65
Hestercombe Av. SW6 .....5A 86
Hester Rd. SW11 ....1A 102
Hestia Ho. SE1....4D 27 (3A 78)
.....................(off City Wlk.)
Heston Ho. SE8 ....4C 94
Heston St. SE14 ....4C 94
Hetherington Rd. SW4 ....2A 104
Hethpool Ho. W2 ....3F 59
...........................(off Hall Pl.)
Hetley Rd. W12.................2D 71
Hevelius Cl. SE10............4B 82
Hever Ho. SE15 ....2F 93
..................(off Lovelinch Cl.)
Heversham Ho. SE15.......2E 93
Hevingham Sq. SE26......5D 121
Hewer St. W10 ....4F 57
Hewett St. EC2 ......4E 11 (3A 64)
Hewison St. E3 ....1B 66
Hewitt Rd. N8 ....1C 34
Hewlett Ho. SW8 ....3D 89
..................(off Havelock Ter.)
Hewlett Rd. E3 ....1A 66
Hewson Way SE17 ....5E 77
Hexagon, The N6 ....3B 32
Hexal Rd. SE6 ....3A 124
Hexham Rd. SE27 ....2E 119
Heybridge NW1 ....3D 47
.........................(off Lewis St.)
Heybridge Way E10..........2A 38
Heydon Ho. SE14 ....4E 93
.......................(off Kender St.)
Heyford Av. SW8 ....3A 90
Heyford Ter. SW8 ....3A 90
..............(off Old Sth. Lambeth Rd.)
Heygate St. SE17 ....5E 77
Heylyn Sq. E3 ....2B 66
Heysham La. NW3............5D 31
Heysham Rd. N15 ....1F 35
Heythorp St. SW18 ....1B 114
Heywood Ho. SE14...........2F 93
.......................(off Myers La.)
Heyworth Rd. E15 ....2B 54
Heyworth Rd. E5 ....1D 51
Hibbert Ho. E14 ....4C 80
.........................(off Tiller Rd.)
Hibbert Rd. E17 ....2B 38
Hibbert St. SW11 ....1F 101
Hibiscus Lodge E15 ....4A 54
....................(off Glenavon Rd.)
Hichisson Rd. SE15.........3E 107
Hicken Rd. SW2 ....3B 104

Hickes Ho. NW6 ....4F 45
Hickin Cl. SE7..................5F 83
Hickin St. E14 ....4E 81
Hickleton NW1 ....4E 47
...................(off Camden St.)
Hickling Ho. SE16............4D 79
....................(off Slippers Pl.)
Hickman Cl. E16 ....4F 69
Hickmore Wlk. SW4 ....1F 103
Hicks Bolton Ho. NW6......1B 58
...................(off Denmark Ho.)
Hicks Cl. SW11................1A 102
Hicks Gallery 5C 114
Hicks Ho. SE16................4C 78
.........................(off Spa Rd.)
Hicks St. SE8 ....1A 94
Hidcote Apts. SW11 ....2A 102
..................(off Danvers Av.)
Hide Pl. SW1....................5F 75
Hide Ct. SE3....................3E 97
Hides St. N7 ....3B 48
Hide Twr. SW1 ....5F 75
.....................(off Regency St.)
Hierro Ct. E1....................4A 66
.......................(off Ocean Est.)
Higgins Ho. N1 ....5A 50
.....................(off Colville Est.)
Higginson Ho. NW3..........4B 46
.......................(off Fellows Rd.)
Higgs Ind. Est. SE24 ......1D 105
Highbank Way N8 ....1C 34
High Bri. SE10.................1F 95
Highbridge Ct. SE14.........3E 93
......................(off Farrow La.)
High Bri. Wharf SE10 ....1F 95
.......................(off High Bri.)
Highbrook Rd. SE3...........1F 111
HIGHBURY 1D 49
Highbury & Islington Station
(Rail, Underground &
Overground) 3D 49
HIGHBURY CORNER 3D 49
Highbury Cres. N5.............2D 49
Highbury Est. N5...............2E 49
Highbury Gdns. N7...........2C 48
Highbury Grange N5 ....1E 49
Highbury Gro. N5...............2D 49
Highbury Gro. Ct. N5.........3E 49
Highbury Hill N5................5C 34
Highbury Leisure Cen. 3D 49
Highbury Mans. N1 ....4D 49
.......................(off Upper St.)
Highbury New Pk. N5 ....2E 49
Highbury Pk. N5.................5D 35
Highbury Pl. N5.................5D 35
Highbury Quad. N5 ....5D 35
Highbury Rd. SW19...........5A 114
Highbury Stadium Sq. N5...5D 35
Highbury Sta. Rd. N1 ....3C 48
Highbury Ter. N5...............5D 35
Highbury Ter. M. N5 ....2D 49
Highclere St. SE26...........4A 122
Highcliffe Dr. SW15 ....4B 98
Highcliffe Gdns. IG4: Ilf 1F 41
Highcombe SE7................2D 97
Highcombe Cl. SE9...........1F 125
Highcroft Est. N19 ....2A 34
Highcroft Gdns. NW11 ......1B 30
Highcroft Rd. N19 ....2A 34
Highcross Way SW15........1C 112
Highdown Rd. SW15..........4D 99
Highfield Av. NW11 ....2F 29
Highfield Cl. SE13.............4F 109
Highfield Ct. NW11............1A 30
Highfield Gdns. NW11 ....1A 30

Highfield M. NW6 ....4D 45
...............(off Compayne Gdns.)
Highfield Rd. NW11 ....1A 30
Highfields Gro. N6 ....3B 32
HIGHGATE 1C 32
Highgate Av. N6 ....2D 33
Highgate Cemetery 3C 32
Highgate Cl. N6 ....2C 32
Highgate Golf Course 1A 32
Highgate Hgts. N6..............1E 33
Highgate High St. N6.........3C 32
Highgate Hill N19...............3D 33
Highgate Hill N6.................3D 33
HIGHGATE HOSPITAL 1B 32
Highgate Ho. SE26............2D 120
HIGHGATE MENTAL HEALTH CEN.
....4D 33
Highgate Nth. NW5............5C 32
Highgate Spinney N8.........1F 33
Highgate Station (Underground)
....1D 33
Highgate Wlk. SE23 ....2E 121
Highgate W. Hill N6...........3C 32
High Hill Est. E5 ....3D 37
High Hill Ferry E5..............3D 37
High Ho. M. N16................4A 36
High Holborn WC1...2D 15 (5A 62)
High no. M. N16.................4A 36
Highland Cft. BR3: Beck.....5D 123
Highland Rd. SE19 ....5A 120
Highlands Cl. N4 ....2A 34
Highlands Cl. SE19 ....5A 120
Highlands Heath SW15......5E 99
Highland St. E15...............1D 67
Highland Ter. SE13 ....1D 109
...................(off Algernon Rd.)
High Level Dr. SE26 ....4C 120
Highlever Rd. W10 ....4E 57
High Meads Rd. E16 ....5F 69
Highmore Rd. SE3 ....3A 96
High Mt. NW4 ....1C 28
High Pde. SW16................3A 118
High Point, The N6.............2C 32
High Rd. NW10 ....3A 42
High Rd. Leyton E10 ....1D 39
High Rd. Leyton E15 ....1A 40
High Rd. Leytonstone E11...3A 40
High Rd. Leytonstone E15...1A 54
High Sheldon N6................1B 32
Highshore Rd. SE15...........5B 92
.....................(not continuous)
Highstone Av. E11 ....1C 40
Highstone Ct. E11 ....1B 40
.....................(off New Wanstead)
Highstone Mans. NW1........4E 47
.......................(off Camden Rd.)
High St. E13 ....1C 68
High St. E15 ....1F 67
High St. SW19..................5F 113
High St. Harlesden NW10 ...1B 56
High Street Kensington Station
(Underground) 3D 73
High St. M. SW19 ....5A 114
High St. Nth. E12 ....2F 55
High Timber St. EC4 4F 17 (1E 77)
High Trees SW2 ....1C 118
Hightrees Ho. SW12..........4C 102
Highview N6.......................1E 33
Highway, The E1................1C 78
Highway Trad. Cen., The E1 ...1F 79
...................(off Heckford St.)
Highwood Cl. SE22 ....1C 120
Highwood Rd. N19 ....5A 34
Highworth St. NW1............4A 60
...................(off Daventry St.)
Hi-Gloss Cen. E1 ....1A 94

Hilary Cl. SW6 ....3D **87**
Hilary M. SE1 ....3A **26** (3E **77**)
Hilary Rd. W12 ....5B **56**
........................(not continuous)
Hilborough Ct. E8 ....4B **50**
Hilda Lockert Wlk.
SW9 ....5D **91**
........................(off Loughborough Rd.)
Hilda Rd. E16 ....3A **68**
Hilda Rd. E6 ....4F **55**
Hilda Ter. SW9 ....5C **90**
Hildenborough Gdns.
BR1: Bromi 5A **124**
Hildreth St. SW12 ....1D **117**
Hildreth St. M. SW12 ....1D **117**
Hildyard Rd. SW6. ....2C **86**
Hiley Rd. NW10 ....2E **57**
Hilgrove Rd. NW6. ....4E **45**
Hillary Ct. W12 ....3E **71**
........................(off Titmuss St.)
Hillary M. E14. ....4D **67**
Hillbeck Cl. SE15. ....3E **93**
........................(not continuous)
Hillboro Ct. E11 ....2F **39**
Hillbrook Rd. SW17 ....3B **116**
Hillbury Rd. SW17 ....3D **117**
Hill Cl. NW11 ....1C **30**
Hill Cl. NW2 ....5D **29**
Hillcourt Est. N16. ....3F **35**
Hillcourt Rd. SE22 ....4D **107**
Hillcrest N6 ....2C **32**
Hillcrest SE24. ....2F **105**
Hillcrest W11 ....1B **72**
........................(off St John's Gdns.)
Hillcrest Cl. SE26 ....4C **120**
Hillcrest Gdns. NW2. ....5C **28**
Hillcrest Rd. BR1: Bromi.........5C **124**
Hilldrop Cres. N7 ....2F **47**
Hilldrop Est. N7 ....2F **47**
........................(not continuous)
Hilldrop La. N7 ....2F **47**
Hilldrop Rd. BR1: Bromi 5D **125**
Hilldrop Rd. N7. ....2F **47**
Hillersden Ho. SW1 ....1D **89**
........................(off Ebury Bri. Rd.)
Hillersdon Av. SW13. ....5C **84**
Hillery Cl. SE17 ....5F **77**
Hill Farm Rd. W10 ....4E **57**
Hillfield Ct. NW3. ....2A **46**
Hillfield Ho. N5. ....2E **49**
Hillfield Rd. NW6. ....2B **44**
Hillgate Pl. SW12 ....5D **103**
Hillgate Pl. W8 ....2C **72**
Hillgate St. W8 ....2C **72**
Hill Ga. Wlk. N6. ....1E **33**
Hill Ho. E5. ....3D **37**
........................(off Harrington Hill)
Hill Ho. N19 ....4E **33**
........................(off Highgate Hill)
Hill Ho. Apts. N1 ....1A **8** (1B **62**)
........................(off Pentonville Rd.)
Hill Ho. Rd. SW16. ....5B **118**
Hilliard Ho. E1 ....2D **79**
........................(off Prusom St.)
Hilliards Ct. E1 ....2E **79**
Hillier Ho. NW1. ....4F **47**
........................(off Camden Sq.)
Hillier Rd. SW11 ....4B **102**
Hillingdon St. SE17 ....2D **91**
Hillman Dr. W10 ....3E **57**
Hillman St. E8 ....3D **51**
Hillmarton Rd. N7 ....2A **48**
Hillmarton Ter. N7 ....2A **48**
........................(off Hillmarton Rd.)
Hillmead Dr. SW9 ....2D **105**

Hillmore Ct. SE13 ....1F **109**
........................(off Belmont Hill)
Hillmore Gro. SE26. ....5A **122**
Hill Path SW16 ....5B **118**
Hill Ri. SE23. ....1D **121**
Hillrise Mans. N19 ....2A **34**
........................(off Warltersville Rd.)
Hillrise Rd. N19. ....2A **34**
Hill Rd. NW8 ....1E **59**
Hillsboro' Rd. SE22 ....3A **106**
Hillsborough Ct. NW6 ....5D **45**
........................(off Mortimer Cres.)
Hillside N8 ....1F **33**
Hillside NW5. ....5C **32**
Hillside SE10. ....3F **95**
........................(off Croom's Hill)
Hillside Av. SE10. ....4E **95**
Hillside Cl. NW8 ....1D **59**
Hillside Gdns. N6 ....1D **33**
Hillside Gdns. SW2. ....2C **118**
Hillside Pas. SW2. ....2B **118**
Hillside Rd. N15 ....2A **36**
Hillside Rd. SW2 ....2B **118**
Hillsleigh Rd. W8 ....2B **72**
Hills Pl. W1 ....3F **13** (5E **61**)
Hillstone Ct. E3 ....3D **67**
........................(off Empson St.)
Hillstowe St. E5. ....5E **37**
Hill St. W1 ....1C **20** (2C **74**)
Hilltop Ct. NW8 ....4E **45**
........................(off Alexandra Rd.)
Hilltop Ho. N6. ....2F **33**
Hilltop Rd. NW6. ....4C **44**
Hill Vw. NW3 ....5B **46**
........................(off Ainger Rd.)
Hillway N6 ....4C **32**
Hillway NW9. ....3A **28**
Hill-Wood Ho. N1 ......1A **6** (1E **61**)
........................(off Polygon Rd.)
Hillworth Rd. SW2. ....5C **104**
Hillyard Ho. SW9. ....4C **90**
Hillyard St. SW9 ....4C **90**
Hillyfield Cl. E9 ....2A **52**
Hilly Flds. Cres. SE13. ....1C **108**
Hilly Flds. Cres. SE4. ....1C **108**
Hilsea Point SW15 ....1D **113**
Hilsea St. E5. ....1E **51**
Hilton Ho. SE4 ....2F **107**
Hilversum Cres. SE22 ....3A **106**
Himley Rd. SW17 ....5A **116**
Hinchinbrook Ho. NW6 ....5D **45**
........................(off Mortimer Cres.)
Hinckley Rd. SE15. ....2C **106**
Hind Ct. EC4 ....3C **16** (5C **62**)
Hinde Ho. W1 ....2C **12** (5C **60**)
........................(off Hinde St.)
Hinde M. W1 ....2C **12** (5C **60**)
........................(off Marlebone La.)
Hinde St. W1 ....2C **12** (5C **60**)
Hind Gro. E14. ....5C **66**
Hindhead Cl. N16. ....3A **36**
Hindhead Point SW15 ....1D **113**
Hind Ho. N7. ....1C **48**
Hind Ho. SE14 ....2F **93**
........................(off Myers La.)
Hindle Ho. E8. ....2B **50**
Hindmans Ho. SW8. ....4F **89**
Hindmans Rd. SE22 ....3C **106**
Hindmarsh Cl. E1 ....1C **78**
Hindon Ct. SW1 ....5E **75**
........................(off Guildhouse St.)
Hindrey Rd. E5. ....2D **51**
Hindsley's Pl. SE23. ....2E **121**
Hinstock NW6 ....5D **45**

Hinton Rd. E10 ....4D **39**
........................(off Leyton Grange Est.)
Hinton Rd. SE24 ....1E **105**
Hinton Rd. SW9 ....1D **105**
Hippodrome M. W11 ....1A **72**
Hippodrome Pl. W11 ....1A **72**
Hiroshima Prom. SE7 ....4E **83**
Hirst Ct. SW1 ....2D **89**
Hitcham Rd. E17. ....2B **38**
Hitchcock La. E20. ....3E **53**
Hitchin Sq. E3 ....1A **66**
Hithe Gro. SE16. ....4E **79**
Hither Farm Rd. SE3 ....1E **111**
Hitherfield Rd. SW16 ....2B **118**
HITHER GREEN 4F **109**
Hither Green Crematorium
....2B **124**
Hither Grn. La. SE13 ....3E **109**
Hither Green Station (Rail) 4A **110**
Hitherwood Dr. SE19 ....4B **120**
Hittard Ct. SE17 ....2F **91**
........................(off Red Lion Row)
HMP Brixton 4A **104**
HMP Pentonville 3B **48**
HMP Wandsworth 5F **101**
HMP Wormwood Scrubs 5A **56**
HMS Belfast 1D **27** (2A **78**)
Hoadly Ho. SE1. ....2F **25** (2E **77**)
........................(off Union St.)
Hoadly Rd. SW16 ....3F **117**
Hobart Pl. SW1 ....5D **21** (4D **75**)
Hobbes Wlk. SW15. ....3D **99**
Hobbs Ct. SE1 ....3B **78**
........................(off Mill St.)
Hobbs Pl. N1 ....1A **64**
Hobbs Pl. Est. N1 ....1A **64**
........................(off Hobbs Pl.)
Hobday St. E14 ....5D **67**
Hobby Ho. SE1 ....5D **79**
Hobhouse Ct. SW1 ....5C **14** (1F **75**)
........................(off Suffolk St.)
Hobson's Pl. E1 ....4C **64**
Hobury St. SW10. ....2E **87**
Hocker St. E2 ....2F **11** (2B **64**)
Hockett Cl. SE8 ....5B **80**
........................(off Grove St.)
Hockliffe Ho. W10 ....4E **57**
........................(off Sutton Way)
Hockney Ct. SE16 ....1D **93**
........................(off Rossetti Rd.)
Hocroft Av. NW2 ....5B **30**
Hocroft Ct. NW2 ....5B **30**
Hocroft Rd. NW2 ....1B **44**
Hocroft Wlk. NW2 ....5B **30**
Hodes Row NW3 ....1C **46**
Hodford Rd. NW11 ....3B **30**
Hodgkin Cl. SE5. ....3F **91**
........................(off Dobson Wlk.)
Hodister Cl. SE5. ....3E **91**
Hodnet Gro. SE16. ....5F **79**
Hoever Ho. SE6 ....4E **123**
Hoey Ct. E3. ....3D **67**
........................(off Barry Blandford Way)
Hoffman Sq. N1 ....1C **10** (2F **63**)
........................(off Chart St.)
Hofland Rd. W14 ....4A **72**
Hogan M. W2. ....4E **59**
Hogan Way E5. ....4C **36**
Hogarth Bus. Pk. W4 ....2A **84**
Hogarth Cl. E16. ....4F **69**
Hogarth Ct. E1 ....5C **64**
........................(off Batty St.)
Hogarth Ct. NW1 ....4E **47**
........................(off St Pancras Way)

Hogarth Ct. SE19................4B **120**
Hogarth Health Club, The
....5B **70**
Hogarth Ho. EC1.......1E **17** (4D **63**)
....................(off Bartholomew Cl.)
Hogarth Ho. SW1.................5F **75**
....................(off Erasmus Cl.)
Hogarth Ind. Est. NW10 ....3C **56**
Hogarth La. W4....................2A **84**
Hogarth Pl. SW5..................5D **73**
........................(off Hogarth Rd.)
Hogarth Rd. SW5.................5D **73**
HOGARTH RDBT..................2A **84**
Hogarth's House 2A **84**
........................(off Hogarth La.)
Holbeach Rd. SW12...........1D **117**
Holbeach Rd. SE6................5C **108**
Holbeck Row SE15..............3C **92**
Holbein Ho. SW1..................1C **88**
........................(off Holbein M.)
Holbein M. SW1...................1C **88**
Holbein Pl. SW1...................5C **74**
Holberton Gdns. NW10 ......2D **57**
Holborn EC1............1A **16** (4C **62**)
HOLBORN................1F **15** (5A **62**)
Holborn Bars EC1.....1B **16** (4C **62**)
........................(off Holborn)
Holborn Cir. EC1.....1C **16** (4C **62**)
Holborn Ho. W12.................5D **57**
Holborn Pl. WC1......1F **15** (4B **62**)
Holborn Rd. E13..................3D **69**
Holborn Station (Underground)
........................1F **15** (5B **62**)
Holborn Viaduct
EC1.........................1C **16** (4D **63**)
Holbrook Ho. SW1...............3D **33**
Holbrooke Ct. N7.................1A **48**
Holbrook Rd. E15.................1B **68**
Holburne Cl. SE3..................4E **97**
Holburne Gdns. SE3............4F **97**
Holburne Rd. SE3.................4E **97**
Holcombe Ho. SW9 ....1A **104**
........................(off Landor Rd.)
Holcombe Pl. SE4...............1A **108**
........................(off St Asaph Rd.)
Holcombe St. W6.................5D **71**
Holcroft Ct. W1.........5F **5** (4E **61**)
........................(off Clipstone St.)
Holcroft Ho. SW11..............1F **101**
Holcroft Rd. E9....................4E **51**
Holdenby Rd. SE4..............3A **108**
Holden Ho. N1......................5E **49**
........................(off Prebend St.)
Holden Ho. SE8....................3C **94**
Holden Point E15.................3F **53**
........................(off Waddington St.)
Holden St. SW11..................5C **88**
Holdernesse Rd. SW17 ....3B **116**
Holderness Ho. SE5............1A **106**
Holderness Way SE27 ....5D **119**
Holford Ho. SE16.................5D **79**
........................(off Camilla Rd.)
Holford Ho. WC1......1A **8** (2B **62**)
........................(off Gt. Percy St.)
Holford M. WC1........1B **8** (2C **62**)
........................(off Cruikshank St.)
Holford Pl. WC1.......1A **8** (2B **62**)
Holford Rd. NW3..................5E **31**
Holford St. WC1.......1A **8** (2B **62**)
Holford Way SW15..............4C **98**
Holford Yd. WC1.......1A **8** (1C **62**)
........................(off Cruikshank St.)
Holgate Av. SW11...............1F **101**
Holgate St. SE7...................4F **83**
Holland Dr. SE23................3A **122**

Holland Dwellings
WC2.........................2E **15** (5A **62**)
........................(off Newton St.)
Holland Gdns. W14...............4A **72**
Hollandgreen Pl. W8.............4C **72**
Holland Gro. SW9.................3C **90**
Holland Ho. NW10................1D **57**
........................(off Holland Rd.)
Holland Pk. W11...................2A **72**
Holland Pk. W11...................3B **72**
HOLLAND PK..........................2B **72**
Holland Pk. Av. W11..............3A **72**
Holland Pk. Ct. W14..............3A **72**
........................(off Holland Pk. Gdns.)
Holland Pk. Gdns. W14.........3A **72**
Holland Pk. Mans. W14.........2A **72**
........................(off Holland Pk. Gdns.)
Holland Pk. M. W11...............2A **72**
Holland Pk. Rd. W14..............4B **72**
HOLLAND PARK RDBT............3F **71**
Holland Park Station
(Underground)....................2B **72**
Holland Pk. Tennis Ground ..2A **72**
Holland Pk. Ter. W11.............1A **72**
........................(off Portland Rd.)
Holland Pk. Theatre (Open Air)
....3B **72**
Holland Pas. N1.....................5E **49**
........................(off Basire St.)
Holland Pl. W8......................3D **73**
........................(off Kensington Chu. St.)
Holland Pl. Chambers W8....3D **73**
........................(off Holland Pl.)
Holland Ri. Ho. SW9..............3B **90**
........................(off Clapham Rd.)
Holland Rd. E15....................2A **68**
Holland Rd. NW10.................5C **42**
Holland Rd. W14....................3F **71**
Holland Rd. SE1......1E **25** (2D **77**)
Holland St. W8.......................3C **72**
Holland Vs. Rd. W14..............3A **72**
Holland Wlk. W8: Lon Kensington
....2B **72**
Holland Wlk. N19: Lon Up.
Holloway..............................3F **33**
Holland Wlk. N19..................3F **33**
........................(off Calverley Gro.)
Hollar Rd. N16......................5B **36**
Hollen St. W1..........2B **14** (5F **61**)
Holles Ho. SW9.....................5B **90**
Holles St. W1..........2E **13** (5D **61**)
Holley Rd. W3.......................3A **70**
Holliday Sq. SW11...............1F **101**
........................(off Fowler Cl.)
Hollies, The E11.....................1C **40**
........................(off New Wanstead)
Hollies Way SW12................5C **102**
Hollingbourne Rd. SE24......3E **105**
Hollins Ho. N7......................1A **48**
Hollisfield WC1.........2E **7** (2A **62**)
........................(off Cromer St.)
Hollister Ho. NW6.................2C **58**
........................(off Kilburn Pk. Rd.)
HOLLOWAY.............................5A **34**
Holloway Ho. NW2................5E **29**
........................(off Stoll Cl.)
Holloway Rd. E11..................5F **39**
Holloway Rd. N19..................4F **33**
Holloway Rd. N7....................1B **48**
Holloway Road Station
(Underground)....................2B **48**
Hollyberry La. NW3...............1E **45**
Hollybush Cl. E11..................1C **40**
Hollybush Gdns. E2...............2D **65**
Holly Bush Hill NW3..............1E **45**

Hollybush Hill E11.................1B **40**
Hollybush Ho. E2..................2D **65**
Hollybush Pl. E2....................2D **65**
Holly Bush Steps NW3..........1E **45**
........................(off Holly Mt.)
Hollybush St. E13.................2D **69**
Holly Bush Va. NW3...............1E **45**
Hollybush Wlk. SW9............2D **105**
Holly Ct. SE10.......................4B **82**
Hollycroft Av. NW3...............5C **30**
Hollydale Rd. SE15...............4E **93**
Hollydene SE13.....................4F **109**
Hollydene SE15.....................4D **93**
Hollydown Way E11...............5F **39**
Holly Gro. SE15.....................5B **92**
Holly Hedge Ter. SE13..........3F **109**
Holly Hill NW3.......................1E **45**
Holly Ho. W10.......................3A **58**
........................(off Hawthorn Wlk.)
Holly Lodge W8.....................3C **72**
........................(off Thornwood Gdns.)
Holly Lodge Gdns. N6...........4C **32**
Holly Lodge Mans. N6...........4C **32**
Holly M. SW10......................1E **87**
Holly Mt. NW3......................1E **45**
Hollymount Cl. SE10.............4E **95**
Holly Pk. N4..........................2A **34**
........................(not continuous)
Holly Pk. Est. N4...................2B **34**
Holly Pl. NW3........................1E **45**
........................(off Holly Berry La.)
Holly Rd. E11........................2B **40**
Holly Rd. W4........................5A **70**
Holly St. E8...........................4B **50**
Holly Ter. N6.........................3C **32**
Holly Tree Cl. SW19............1F **113**
Holly Tree Ho. SE4..............1B **108**
........................(off Brockley Rd.)
Hollyview Cl. NW4................1C **28**
Holly Village N6....................4D **33**
Holly Vs. W6.........................4D **71**
........................(off Wellesley Av.)
Holly Wlk. NW3.....................1E **45**
Hollywood Bowl Surrey Quays
....4F **79**
Hollywood Bowl The O2 ......2A **82**
Hollywood Ct. SW10.............2E **87**
........................(off Hollywood Rd.)
Hollywood M. SW10..............2E **87**
Hollywood Rd. SW10.............2E **87**
Holman Ho. E2......................2F **65**
........................(off Roman Rd.)
Holman Hunt Ho. W6............1A **86**
........................(off Field Rd.)
Holman Rd. SW11..................5F **87**
Holmbrook NW1....................1E **61**
........................(off Eversholt St.)
Holmbury Ct. SW17.............3B **116**
Holmbury Vw. E5..................3D **37**
Holmbush Rd. SW15............4A **100**
Holmcote Gdns. N5...............2E **49**
Holm Cl. SE12.......................3D **125**
Holmdale Gdns. NW4............1F **29**
Holmdale Rd. NW6................2C **44**
Holmdale Ter. N15.................1A **36**
Holmdene Av. SE24..............3E **105**
Holmead Rd. SW6.................3D **87**
Holmefield Ho. W10.............3A **58**
........................(off Hazlewood Cres.)
Holme Ho. SE15...................3D **93**
........................(off Studholme St.)
Holme Lacey Rd. SE12........4B **110**
Holmes Cl. SE22..................2C **106**
Holmesdale Ho. NW6...........5C **44**
........................(off Kilburn Vale)

Holmesdale Rd. N6 .... 2D **33**
Holmesley Rd. SE23......... 4A **108**
Holmes Pl. SW10.................2E **87**
Holmes Rd. NW5.................2D **47**
Holmes Ter. SE1.......3B **24** (3C **76**)
.................................(off Waterloo Rd.)
Holmewood Gdns. SW2 ... 5B **104**
Holmewood Rd. SW2 .... 5B **104**
Holmfield Ct. NW3................2A **46**
Holmhurst SE13................4F **109**
Holmleigh Rd. N16.............. 3A **36**
Holmleigh Rd. Est. N16...... 3A **36**
Holm Oak Cl. SW15 .... 4B **100**
Holm Oak M. SW4 .... 3A **104**
Holmsdale Ho. E14................ 1D **81**
.................................(off Poplar High St.)
Holmshaw Cl. SE26............ 4A **122**
Holmside Rd. SW12 .... 4C **102**
Holmsley Ho. SW15............ 5B **98**
.................................(off Tangley Gro.)
Holm Wlk. SE3 ....5C **96**
Holmwood Vs. SE7.............. 1C **96**
Holne Chase N2 ....1E **31**
Holness Rd. E15.................. 3B **54**
Holocaust Memorial Gdn., The
.... 3A **20** (3B **74**)
Holroyd Rd. SW15 .... 2E **99**
Holsgrove Ho. W3 .... 2A **70**
Holst Ct. SE1........ 5B **24** (4C **76**)
.................................(off Kennington Rd.)
Holst Ho. W12.......................5D **57**
.................................(off Du Cane Rd.)
Holst Mans. SW13...............2E **85**
Holsworthy Ho. E3 ....2D **67**
.................................(off Talwin St.)
Holsworthy Sq. WC1 ... 4A **8** (3B **62**)
.................................(off Elm St.)
Holt Ct. SE10 ....2E **95**
.................................(off Horseferry Pl.)
Holt Gdns. SW17 .... 3A **116**
Holt Ho. SW2 ....4C **104**
Holton St. E1 ....3F **65**
Holwood Pl. SW4................. 2F **103**
Holybourne Av. SW15........ 5C **98**
Holyoake Ct. SE16.............. 3B **80**
Holyoak Rd. SE11................5D **77**
Holyport Rd. SW6 .... 3F **85**
Holyrood Ct. NW1 ....5D **47**
.................................(off Gloucester Av.)
Holyrood M. E16..................2C **82**
Holyrood St. SE1 ... 2D **27** (2A **78**)
.................................(off Phipp St.)
Holywell Cen. EC2...3D **11** (3A **64**)
.................................(off Phipp St.)
Holywell Cl. SE16............... 1D **93**
Holywell Cl. SE3..................2C **96**
Holywell La. EC2 ... 3E **11** (3A **64**)
Holywell Row EC2...4D **11** (3A **64**)
Homecroft Rd. SE26.......... 5E **121**
Homefield Ho. SE23.......... 3E **121**
Homefield Rd. SW19......... 5F **113**
Homefield Rd. W4 .... 1B **84**
Homefield St. N1...1D **11** (1A **64**)
Homeleigh Ct. SW16......... 3A **118**
Homeleigh Rd. SE15.......... 3F **107**
Mdmw. Mw. M. SE22 .... 3C **106**
Home Pk. Rd. SW19........... 4B **114**
Homer Dr. E14.....................5C **80**
Home Rd. SW11 .... 5A **88**
Homer Rd. E9 ....3A **52**
Homer Row W1 ....4A **60**
Homer St. W1 ....4A **60**
HOMERTON 2F **51**
Homerton Gro. E9 .... 2F **51**
Homerton High St. E9......... 2F **51**
Homerton Rd. E9..................2A **52**

Homerton Row E9 ....2E **51**
Homerton Station (Overground)
....3F **51**
Homerton Ter. E9.................3E **51**
.................................(not continuous)
**HOMERTON UNIVERSITY
HOSPITAL** 2F **51**
Homesdale Cl. E11.............. 1C **40**
Homestall Rd. SE22 .... 3E **107**
Homestead Pk. NW2........... 5B **28**
Homestead Rd. SW6 .... 3B **86**
Homewalk Ho. SE26 .... 4D **121**
Homewoods SW12............. 5E **103**
Homildon Ho. SE26 .... 3C **120**
Honduras St. EC1......... 3F **9** (3E **63**)
Honeybourne Rd. NW6...... 2D **45**
Honeybrook Rd. SW12...... 5E **103**
Honeyfield M. SE23 .... 3F **121**
Honeyghan Ct. SE17 .... 1A **92**
.................................(off Sedan Way)
Honey La. EC2...........3A **18** (5E **63**)
.................................(off Trump St.)
Honey La. Ho. SW10.......... 2D **87**
.................................(off Finborough Rd.)
Honeyman Cl. NW6............. 4F **43**
Honey M. SE27 ....4E **119**
.................................(off Norwood High St.)
Honeywell Rd. SW11......... 4B **102**
Honeywood Ho. SE15......... 4C **92**
.................................(off Goldsmith Rd.)
Honeywood Rd. NW10 .... 1B **56**
Honiton Gdns. SE15........... 5E **107**
.................................(off Gibbon Rd.)
Honiton Rd. NW6.................1B **58**
Honley Rd. SE6.................. 5D **109**
HONOR OAK 4E **107**
Honor Oak Crematorium 4F **107**
Honor Oak Pk. SE23........... 4E **107**
HONOR OAK RD. 5A **108**
Honor Oak Park Station
(Rail & Overground) 4F **107**
Honor Oak Ri. SE23............. 4E **107**
Honor Oak Rd. SE23 .... 1E **121**
Honour Lea Av. E20 ....2D **53**
Hood Ct. EC4.........3C **16** (5C **62**)
.................................(off Fleet St.)
Hood Ho. SE5 ....3F **91**
.................................(off Elmington St.)
Hood Ho. SW1.......................1F **89**
.................................(off Dolphin Sq.)
Hood Point SE16 ....3B **80**
.................................(off Rotherhithe St.)
Hooke Ct. SE10 ....4E **95**
.................................(off Winforton St.)
Hooke Ho. E3........................5A **52**
.................................(off Gernon Rd.)
Hookham Ct. SW8................4F **89**
Hooks Cl. SE15....................4D **93**
Hooper Rd. E16....................5C **68**
Hooper's Ct.
SW3.....................4A **20** (3B **74**)
Hooper Sq. E1.....................5C **64**
.................................(off Hooper St.)
Hooper St. E1......................5C **64**
Hoopers Yd. NW6................ 5B **44**
.................................(off Kimberley Rd.)
Hoop La. NW11....................2B **30**
Hope Cl. N1 ....3E **49**
Hope Cl. SE12......................3D **125**
Hope Ct. NW10.................... 2F **57**
.................................(off Chamberlayne Rd.)
Hope Ct. SE1........................1C **92**
.................................(off Avocet Cl.)
Hopedale Rd. SE7 ....2D **97**
Hopefield Av. NW6 .... 1A **58**

Hope Sq. EC2...........1D **19** (4A **64**)
.................................(off Sun St. Pas.)
Hope St. E14....................... 5A **68**
Hope St. SW11..................... 1F **101**
Hopetown St. E1 ....4B **64**
Hopewell St. SE5................. 3F **91**
Hopewell Yd. SE5................. 3F **91**
.................................(off Hopewell St.)
Hope Wharf SE16................3E **79**
Hop Gdns. WC2....... 5D **15** (1A **76**)
Hopgood St. W12 .... 2E **71**
Hopground Ho. E20............. 2E **53**
.................................(off De Coubertin St.)
Hopkins Ho. E14...................5C **66**
.................................(off Canton St.)
Hopkins M. E15 ....5B **54**
Hopkinsons Pl. NW1 .... 5C **46**
Hopkins Rd. E10 ....2D **39**
Hopkins St. W1 ...... 3A **14** (5E **61**)
Hopping La. N1 .... 3D **49**
Hops Ho. E17.......................1B **38**
.................................(off Old Brewery Way)
Hop St. SE10 ....5B **82**
Hopton Ho. SW9.................. 5A **118**
Hopton's Gdns.
SE1..........................1E **25** (2D **77**)
.................................(off Hopton St.)
Hopton St. SE1 ......1E **25** (1D **77**)
Hopwood Cl. SW17 .... 3E **115**
Hopwood Rd. SE17 .... 2F **91**
Hopwood Wlk. E8.................4C **50**
Horace Bldg. SW11............. 3D **89**
Horace Jones Ho.
SE1...........................2F **27** (2B **78**)
.................................(off Duchess Wlk.)
Horace Rd. E7 ....1D **55**
Horatio Ct. SE16..................2E **79**
.................................(off Rotherhithe St.)
Horatio Ho. E2.....................1B **64**
.................................(off Horatio St.)
Horatio Ho. W6 .... 1F **85**
.................................(off Fulham Pal. Rd.)
Horatio Pl. E14....................2E **81**
.................................(off Managers St.)
Horatio St. E2......................1B **64**
Horbury Cres. W11 .... 1C **72**
Horbury M. W11 .... 1B **72**
Horder Rd. SW6 ....4A **86**
Hordle Prom. Sth. SE15..... 3B **92**
.................................(off Quarley Way)
Horizon Bldg. E14............... 1C **80**
.................................(off Hertsmere Rd.)
Horizon Ho. SW18 .... 1E **101**
.................................(off Juniper Dr.)
Horizon Ind. Est. SE15....... 2C **92**
Horle Wlk. SE5....................5D **91**
Horley Rd. SE9 ....4F **125**
Hormead Rd. W9.................. 3B **58**
Hornbeam Cl. SE11............. 5C **76**
Hornbeam Ho. 3A **80**
Hornbeam Sq. E3 ....5B **52**
Hornbean Ho. E15................2A **68**
.................................(off Manor Rd.)
Hornblower Cl. SE16........... 4A **80**
Hornby Cl. NW3 ....4F **45**
Hornby Ct. NW10..................3B **42**
Hornby Ho. SE11..................2C **90**
.................................(off Clayton St.)
Horncastle Cl. SE12........... 5C **110**
Horncastle Rd. SE12.......... 5C **110**
Horndean Cl. SW15............. 1C **112**
Horner Ho. N1......................5A **50**
.................................(off Nuttall St.)
Horner Sq. E1........5F **11** (4B **64**)
.................................(within Old Spitalfields Mkt.)

Horne Way SW15 ....5E **85**
Hornfair Rd. SE7 ....2E **97**
Horniman Dr. SE23 ....1D **121**
Horniman Gdns. 1D **121**
Horniman Mus. 1D **121**
Horn La. SE10 ....1C **96**
    ....(not continuous)
Horn Link Way SE10 ....5C **82**
HORN PK. 3D **111**
Horn Pk. Cl. SE12 ....3D **111**
Horn Pk. La. SE12 ....3D **111**
Hornsey Cricket Club 1F **33**
Hornsey La. N6 ....3D **33**
Hornsey La. Est. N19 ....2F **33**
Hornsey La. Gdns. N6 ....2E **33**
Hornsey Ri. N19 ....2F **33**
Hornsey Ri. Gdns. N19 ....2F **33**
Hornsey Rd. N19 ....3A **34**
Hornsey Rd. N7 ....4B **34**
Hornsey St. N7 ....2B **48**
HORNSEY VALE 1B **34**
Hornshay St. SE15 ....2E **93**
Hornton Ct. W8 ....3C **72**
    ....(off Kensington High St.)
Hornton Pl. W8 ....3D **73**
Hornton St. W8 ....3C **72**
Horsa Rd. SE12 ....5E **111**
Horse & Dolphin Yd.
    W1 ....4C **14** (1F **75**)
    ....(off Macclesfield St.)
Horseferry Pl. SE10 ....2E **95**
Horseferry Rd. E14 ....1A **80**
Horseferry Rd.
    SW1 ....5B **22** (4F **75**)
Horseferry Rd. Est.
    SW1 ....5B **22** (4F **75**)
    ....(off Horseferry Rd.)
Horse Guards Av. S
    W1 ....2D **23** (2A **76**)
Horse Guards Parade
    ....2C **22** (2F **75**)
Horse Guards Rd.
    SW1 ....2C **22** (2F **75**)
Horseley Ct. E1 ....4A **66**
Horsell Rd. N5 ....2C **48**
    ....(not continuous)
Horselydown La.
    SE1 ....3F **27** (3B **78**)
Horselydown Mans.
    SE1 ....3F **27** (3B **78**)
    ....(off Lafone St.)
Horsemongers M.
    SE1 ....4A **26** (3E **77**)
    ....(off Cole St.)
Horse Ride SW1 ....2A **22** (2E **75**)
Horseshoe Ct. E14 ....1E **95**
Horseshoe Cl. NW2 ....4D **29**
Horseshoe Ct. EC1 ....3E **9** (3D **63**)
    ....(off Brewhouse Yd.)
Horseshoe M. SW2 ....2A **104**
Horseshoe Wharf
    SE1 ....1B **26** (2F **77**)
    ....(off Clink St.)
    ....(off Essex Rd.)
Horsfeld Gdns. SE9 ....3F **111**
Horsfeld Rd. SE9 ....3F **111**
Horsfield Ho. N1 ....4E **49**
    ....(off Northampton St.)
Horsford Rd. SW2 ....3B **104**
Horsley Ct. SW1 ....5F **75**
    ....(off Vincent St.)
Horsley St. SE17 ....2F **91**
Horsman Ho. SE5 ....2E **91**
    ....(off Bethwin Rd.)

Horsman St. SE5 ....2E **91**
Horsmonden Rd. SE4 ....3B **108**
Hornsell St. SE5 ....3F **91**
Hortensia Ho. SW10 ....3E **87**
    ....(off Gunter Gro.)
Hortensia Rd. SW10 ....3E **87**
Horton Av. NW2 ....1A **44**
Horton Halls SW17 ....3F **115**
Horton Ho. SE15 ....2E **93**
Horton Ho. SW8 ....3B **90**
Horton Ho. W6 ....1A **86**
    ....(off Field Rd.)
Horton Rd. E8 ....3D **51**
Horwood Ho. E2 ....2D **65**
    ....(off Pott St.)
Horwood Ho. NW8 ....3A **60**
    ....(off Paveley St.)
Hosack Rd. SW17 ....2C **116**
Hoser Av. SE12 ....2C **124**
Hosier La. EC1 ....1D **17** (4D **63**)
Hoskins Cl. E16 ....5E **69**
Hoskins St. SE10 ....1F **95**
HOSPITAL FOR TROPICAL
DISEASES 4A **6** (3E **61**)
    ....(off Mortimer Markey)
HOSPITAL OF ST JOHN &
ST ELIZABETH 1F **59**
Hospital Rd. E11 ....1F **39**
Hospital Rd. E9 ....2F **51**
Hospital Way SE13 ....5F **109**
Hotham Rd. SW15 ....1E **99**
Hotham St. E15 ....5A **54**
Hothfield Pl. SE16 ....4E **79**
Hotspur St. SE11 ....5C **76**
Houghton Cl. E8 ....3B **50**
Houghton Ct. EC1 ....4F **9** (3E **63**)
    ....(off Glasshouse Yd.)
Houghton Sq. SW9 ....5A **90**
    ....(off Clapham Rd.)
Houghton St. WC2 .....3A **16** (5B **62**)
    ....(not continuous)
Houlton Ho. SW3 ....1B **88**
    ....(off Walpole St.)
Houlton Pl. E3 ....3B **66**
    ....(off Hamlets Way)
Houndsditch EC3 .....2E **19** (5A **64**)
Household Cavalry Mus., The
    ....2C **22** (2F **75**)
House Mill, The 2E **67**
House of Illustration 5A **48**
Houses of Parliament
    ....4D **23** (4A **76**)
Houston Rd. SE23 ....2A **122**
Hove Av. E17 ....1B **38**
Hoveden Rd. NW2 ....2A **44**
Hove St. SE15 ....3E **93**
    ....(off Culmore Rd.)
Howard Bldg. SW11 ....2D **89**
Howard Cl. NW2 ....1A **44**
Howard Ho. E16 ....2D **83**
    ....(off Wesley Av.)
Howard Ho. SE8 ....2B **94**
    ....(off Evelyn St.)
Howard Ho. SW1 ....1E **89**
    ....(off Dolphin Sq.)
Howard Ho. SW9 ....1D **105**
    ....(off Barrington Rd.)
Howard Ho. W1 ....4E **5** (3D **61**)
    ....(off Cleveland St.)
Howard M. N5 ....1D **49**
Howard Rd. E11 ....5A **40**
Howard Rd. N15 ....1A **36**
Howard Rd. N16 ....1F **49**
Howard Rd. NW2 ....1F **43**
Howard's La. SW15 ....2D **99**

Howards Rd. E13 ....2C **68**
Howbury Rd. SE15 ....1E **107**
Howcroft Ho. E3 ....2B **66**
    ....(off Benworth St.)
Howden St. SE15 ....1C **106**
Howell Ct. E10 ....2D **39**
Howell Wlk. SE1 ....5D **77**
Howick Pl. SW1 ....5A **22** (4E **75**)
Howie St. SW11 ....3A **88**
Howitt Cl. N16 ....1A **50**
Howitt Cl. NW3 ....3A **46**
Howitt Rd. NW3 ....3A **46**
Howland Est. SE16 ....4E **79**
Howland Ho. SW16 ....3A **118**
Howland M. E. W1 .....5A **6** (4E **61**)
Howland St. W1 ....5A **6** (4E **61**)
Howland Way SE16 ....3A **80**
Howlett Apts. N1 ....4A **48**
    ....(off Caledonian Rd.)
Howlett's Rd. SE24 ....4E **105**
Howley Pl. W2 ....4E **59**
Howsman Rd. SW13 ....2C **84**
Howson Rd. SE4 ....2A **108**
How's St. E2 ....1B **64**
HOXTON 1C **10** (1A **64**)
Hoxton Hall Theatre 1A **64**
    ....(off Hoxton St.)
Hoxton Mkt. N1 ....2D **11** (2A **64**)
    ....(off Coronet St.)
Hoxton Sq. N1 ....1D **11** (2A **64**)
Hoxton Station (Overground)
    ....1B **64**
Hoxton St. N1 ....2E **11** (5A **50**)
Hoylake Rd. W3 ....5A **56**
Hoyland Cl. SE15 ....3D **93**
Hoyle Rd. SW17 ....5A **116**
Hoy St. E16 ....5B **68**
HQS Wellington 4B **16** (1C **76**)
    ....(off Victoria Embankment)
Hub Westminster, The
    ....1A **4** (1B **60**)
Hubbard Ho. SW10 ....3F **87**
    ....(off World's End Pas.)
Hubbard Rd. SE27 ....4E **119**
Hubbard St. E15 ....5A **54**
Huberd Ho. SE1 .....5C **26** (4F **77**)
    ....(off Manciple St.)
Hubert Gro. SW9 ....1A **104**
Hubert Ho. NW8 ....3A **60**
    ....(off Ashbridge St.)
Hubert Rd. E6 ....2F **69**
Hucknall Cl. NW8 ....3F **59**
    ....(off Cunningham Pl.)
Huddart St. E3 ....4B **66**
    ....(not continuous)
Huddleston Cl. E2 ....1E **65**
Huddlestone Rd. E7 ....1B **54**
Huddlestone Rd. NW2 ....3D **43**
Huddleston Rd. N7 ....5E **33**
Hudson Bldg. E1 ....4C **64**
    ....(off Chicksand St.)
Hudson Cl. E15 ....5C **54**
Hudson Cl. W12 ....1D **71**
Hudson Ct. E14 ....1C **94**
    ....(off Maritime Quay)
Hudson Ho. SW10 ....3E **87**
    ....(off Hortensia Rd.)
Hudson Ho. W11 ....5A **58**
    ....(off Ladbroke Gro.)
Hudson's Pl. SW1 ....5D **75**
Hudson Way NW2 ....5F **29**
Hugero Point SE10 ....4C **82**
Huggin Ct. EC4 ....4A **18** (1E **77**)
    ....(off Huggin Hill)
Huggin Hill EC4 ....4A **18** (1E **77**)

Huggins Ho. E3 .... 2C 66
.... (off Alfred St.)
Huggins Pl. SW2 .... 1B 118
Hughan Rd. E15 .... 2F 53
Hugh Astor Ct.
SE1 ....5E 25 (4D 77)
.... (off Keyworth St.)
Hugh Cubitt Ho. N1 .... 1B 62
.... (off Collier St.)
Hugh Dalton Av. SW6 .... 2B 86
Hughenden Ho. NW8 .... 3A 60
.... (off Jerome Cres.)
Hughendon Ter. E15 .... 1E 53
Hughes Ct. N7 .... 2F 47
Hughes Ho. E2 .... 2E 65
.... (off Sceptre Ho.)
Hughes Ho. E3 .... 2C 66
.... (off Trevithick Way)
Hughes Ho. SE17 .... 5D 77
.... (off Peacock St.)
Hughes Ho. SE5 .... 4E 91
.... (off Flodden Rd.)
Hughes Ho. SE8 .... 2C 94
.... (off Benbow St.)
Hughes Mans. E1 .... 3C 64
Hughes Ter. SW9 .... 1D 105
.... (off Styles Gdns.)
Hugh Gaitskell Cl. SW6 .... 2B 86
Hugh Gaitskell Ho. N16 .... 4B 36
Hugh M. SW1 .... 5D 75
Hugh Platt Ho. E2 .... 1D 65
.... (off Patriot Sq.)
Hugh St. SW1 .... 5D 75
Hugo Ho. SW1 .... 5A 20 (4B 74)
.... (off Sloane St.)
Hugon Rd. SW6 .... 1D 101
Hugo Rd. N19 .... 1E 47
Huguenot Pl. E1 .... 4B 64
Huguenot Pl. SW18 .... 3E 101
Huguenot Sq. SE15 .... 1D 107
Hullbridge M. N1 .... 5F 49
Hull Cl. SE16 .... 3F 79
Hull St. EC1 .... 2F 9 (2E 63)
Hulme Pl. SE1 .... 4A 26 (3E 77)
Hult Intl. Studios E1 .... 5C 64
.... (off Alder St.)
Hult Twr. E1 .... 5C 64
.... (off Alder St.)
Humber Dr. W10 .... 3F 57
Humber Rd. NW2 .... 4D 29
Humber Rd. SE3 .... 2B 96
Humberstone Rd. E13 .... 2E 69
Humberton Cl. E9 .... 2A 52
Humber Trad. Est. NW2 .... 4D 29
Humbolt Rd. W6 .... 2A 86
Hume Ct. N1 .... 4D 49
.... (off Hawes St.)
Hume Ho. W11 .... 2F 71
.... (off Queensdale Cres.)
Hume Ter. E16 .... 4D 69
Humphrey St. SE1 .... 1B 92
HUNGERFORD BRIDGE
.... 1F 23 (2B 76)
Hungerford Ho. SW1 .... 2E 89
.... (off Churchill Gdns.)
Hungerford La. WC2 ... 1D 23 (2A 76)
.... (off Craven St.)
Hungerford Rd. N7 .... 3F 47
Hungerford St. E1 .... 5D 65
Hunsdon Rd. SE14 .... 3F 93
Hunslett St. E2 .... 2E 65
Hunstanton Ho. NW1 .... 4A 60
.... (off Cosway St.)
Hunt Cl. W11 .... 2F 71
Hunter Cl. SE1 .... 5C 26 (4F 77)

Hunter Cl. SW12 .... 1C 116
HUNTERCOMBE HOSPITAL
ROEHAMPTON 5C 98
Hunter Ho. SE1 .... 4E 25 (3D 77)
.... (off King James St.)
Hunter Ho. SW5 .... 1C 86
.... (off Old Brompton Rd.)
Hunter Ho. SW8 .... 3F 89
.... (off Fount St.)
Hunter Ho. WC1 .... 3D 7 (3A 62)
.... (off Hunter St.)
Hunterian Mus. 2A 16 (5B 62)
Hunter Lodge W9 .... 4C 58
.... (off Admiral Wlk.)
Hunters Mdw. SE19 .... 4A 120
Hunter St. WC1 .... 3E 7 (3A 62)
Hunter Wlk. E13 .... 1C 68
Huntingdon St. E16 .... 5B 68
Huntingdon St. N1 .... 4B 48
Huntingfield Rd. SW15 .... 2C 98
Huntington Ho. SW11 .... 3D 89
.... (off Palmer Rd.)
Huntley Cl. SE10 .... 1A 96
Huntley St. WC1 .... 4A 6 (3E 61)
Huntloe Ho. SE14 .... 4E 93
.... (off Kender St.)
Hunton St. E1 .... 4C 64
Hunt's Cl. SE3 .... 5C 96
Hunt's Ct. WC2 .... 5C 14 (1F 75)
Huntshaw Ho. E3 .... 2D 67
.... (off Devons Rd.)
Hunts La. E15 .... 1E 67
Huntsman St. SE17 .... 5A 78
Huntspill St. SW17 .... 3E 115
Hunts Slip Rd. SE21 .... 3A 120
Huntsworth M. NW1 .... 3B 60
Hurdwick Ho. NW1 .... 1E 61
.... (off Harrington Sq.)
Hurdwick Pl. NW1 .... 1E 61
.... (off Hampstead Rd.)
Hurleston Ho. SE8 .... 1B 94
Hurley Ct. SW17 .... 5C 116
.... (off Mitcham Rd.)
Hurley Cres. SE16 .... 3F 79
Hurley Ho. SE11 .... 5D 77
HURLINGHAM 1D 101
Hurlingham Bus. Pk. SW6 ...1C 100
Hurlingham Club, The 1C 100
Hurlingham Ct. SW6 .... 1B 100
Hurlingham Gdns. SW6 .... 1B 100
Hurlingham Pk. 5B 86
Hurlingham Retail Pk. 1D 101
Hurlingham Rd. SW6 .... 5B 86
Hurlingham Rd. SW6 .... 1C 100
Hurlingham Sq. SW6 .... 1C 100
Hurlingham Yacht Club ... 1A 100
Hurlock St. N5 .... 5D 35
Huron Rd. SW17 .... 2C 116
Hurren Cl. SE3 .... 1A 110
Hurry Cl. E15 .... 4A 54
Hurst Av. N6 .... 1E 33
Hurstbourne Ho. SW15 .... 4B 98
.... (off Tangley Gro.)
Hurstbourne Rd. SE23 .... 1A 122
Hurst Cl. NW11 .... 1D 31
Hurst Ct. E6 .... 4F 69
.... (off Tollgate Rd.)
Hurstdene Gdns. N15 .... 2A 36
Hurst Ho. WC1 .... 1A 8 (1B 62)
.... (off Penton Ri.)
Hurst St. SE24 .... 4D 105
Hurstway Rd. W11 .... 1F 71
.... (off Hurstway Wlk.)
Hurstway Wlk. W11 .... 1F 71
Husborne Ho. SE8 .... 5A 80
.... (off Chilton Gro.)

Huson Cl. NW3 .... 4A 46
Hutchings St. E14 .... 3C 80
Hutchins Wharf E14 .... 3C 80
.... (off Hutchins St.)
Hutchins Cl. E15 .... 4E 53
Hutchinson Ho. NW3 .... 4B 46
Hutchinson Ho. SE14 .... 3E 93
Hutton Cl. N4 .... 3B 34
.... (off Victoria Rd.)
Hutton M. SW15 .... 3D 99
Hutton St. EC4 .... 3D 17 (5D 63)
Huxbear St. SE4 .... 3B 108
Huxley Ho. NW8 .... 3F 59
.... (off Fisherton St.)
Huxley Rd. E10 .... 4E 39
Huxley St. W10 .... 2A 58
Hyacinth Rd. SW15 .... 1C 112
Hybrid Ho. W3 .... 2A 70
.... (off Furze St.)
Hyde Cl. E13 .... 1C 68
Hyde Cres. NW9 .... 1A 28
Hyde Est. Rd. NW9 .... 1B 28
Hyde Farm M. SW12 .... 1F 117
Hyde Ho. E3 .... 4C 66
.... (off Furze St.)
Hyde Ind. Est., The NW9 ...... 1B 28
Hyde La. SW11 .... 4A 88
Hyde Pk. 1A 20 (2B 74)
HYDE PARK CORNER ... 2C 20 (3D 75)
Hyde Pk. Cnr. W1 ..... 3C 20 (3C 74)
Hyde Park Corner Station
(Underground) 3C 20 (3C 74)
Hyde Pk. Cres. W2 .... 5A 60
Hyde Pk. Gdns. W2 .... 1F 73
.... (not continuous)
Hyde Pk. Gdns. M. W2 .... 1F 73
Hyde Pk. Ga. SW7 .... 3E 73
.... (not continuous)
Hyde Pk. Ga. M. SW7 .... 3E 73
Hyde Pk. Mans. NW1 .... 4A 60
.... (off Cabbell St.)
Hyde Pk. Pl. W2 .... 1A 74
Hyde Pk. Sq. W2 .... 5A 60
Hyde Pk. Sq. M. W2 .... 5A 60
.... (off Southwick Pl.)
Hyde Pk. St. W2 .... 5A 60
Hyde Pk. Towers W2 .... 1E 73
Hyderabad Way E15 .... 4A 54
Hyde Rd. N1 .... 5A 50
Hyde's Pl. N1 .... 4D 49
Hyde St. SE8 .... 2C 94
Hydethorpe Rd. SW12 .... 1E 117
Hyde Va. SE10 .... 3E 95
Hydra Bldg., The
EC1 .... 2C 8 (2C 62)
.... (off Hardwick St.)
Hyndewood SE23 .... 3F 121
Hyndman St. SE15 .... 2D 93
Hyperion Ct. E16 .... 4C 68
.... (off Robertson St.)
Hyperion Ho. E3 .... 1A 66
.... (off Arbery Rd.)
Hyperion Ho. SW2 .... 4B 104
Hyson Rd. SE16 .... 1D 93
Hythe Ho. SE16 .... 3E 79
.... (off Swan Rd.)
Hythe Ho. W6 .... 5E 71
.... (off Shepherd's Bush Rd.)
Hythe Rd. NW10 .... 2B 56
Hythe Rd. Ind. Est. NW10 ... 2C 56

I

Ian Bowater Ct. N1 ...... 1C 10 (2F 63)
.... (off East Rd.)

Ian Ct. SE23..................................2E 121
Ibberton Ho. SW8.....................3B 90
..............................(off Meadow Rd.)
Ibberton Ho. W14.........................4A 72
..............................(off Russell Rd.)
Ibbotson Av. E16.......................5B 68
Ibbott St. E1.................................3E 65
Iberia Ho. N19...............................2F 33
Ibex Ho. E15.................................2A 54
..............................(off Forest La.)
Ibis Ct. SE8..................................2B 94
..............................(off Edward Pl.)
Ibsley Gdns. SW15....................1C 112
ICA Cinema 1C 22 (2F 75)
..............................(within ICA)
Icarus Ho. E3...............................2B 66
..............................(off British St.)
ICA Theatre 1C 22 (2F 75)
..............................(within ICA)
Iceland Rd. E3.............................5C 52
Iceland Wharf SE16.....................5A 80
Iceni Ct. E3..................................5B 52
..............................(off Parnell Rd.)
Ice Wharf N1..............................1A 62
Ice Wharf Marina N1...................1A 62
..............................(off New Wharf Rd.)
Ice Works, The NW1....................4D 47
..............................(off Jamestown Rd.)
Ickburgh Est. E5..........................4D 37
Ickburgh Rd. E5..........................5D 37
Icknield Ho. SW3........................1A 88
..............................(off Cale St.)
Icon Apts. SE1........5D 27 (4A 78)
..............................(off Cluny Pl.)
Icona Point E15...........................5E 53
..............................(off Warton Rd.)
Icon College of Technology &
Management 5C 64
..............................(off Adler St.)
Idaho Bldg. SE13.........................4D 95
..............................(off Deal's Gateway)
Ida St. E14...................................5E 67
..............................(not continuous)
Idea Store (Whitechapel) Library
....4D 65
Ide Mans. E1................................1F 79
..............................(off Cable St.)
Idlecombe Rd. SW17..................5C 116
Idmiston Ho. E15........................1B 54
Idmiston Rd. SE27.....................3E 119
Idol La. EC3..........5D 19 (1A 78)
Idonia St. SE8.............................3C 94
Iffley Rd. W6...............................4D 71
Ifield Ho. SE17............................1A 92
..............................(off Madron St.)
Ifield Rd. SW10...........................2D 87
Ifor Evans Pl. E1.........................3F 65
Ightham Ho. SE17.......................5A 78
..............................(off Beckway St.)
Ikon Ho. E1..................................1E 79
..............................(off Devonport St.)
Ilbert St. W10..............................2F 57
Ilchester Gdns. W2....................1D 73
Ilchester Mans. W8....................4C 72
..............................(off Abingdon Rd.)
Ilchester Pl. W14.........................4B 72
Ildersly Gro. SE21......................2F 119
Ilderton Rd. SE15........................2E 93
Ilderton Rd. SE16........................1E 93
Ilderton Wharf SE15...................2E 93
..............................(off Rollins St.)
Ilex Rd. NW10..............................3B 42
Ilex Way SW16...........................5C 118
Ilford Ho. N1................................3F 49
..............................(off Dove Rd.)

Ilfracombe Flats SE13A 26 (3E 77)
..............................(off Marshalsea Rd.)
Ilfracombe Rd.
BR1: Broml.................................3B 124
Iliffe St. SE17................................1D 91
Iliffe Yd. SE17...............................1D 91
..............................(off Crampton St.)
Ilkeston Ct. E5..............................1F 51
..............................(off Overbury St.)
Ilkley Rd. E16..............................4E 69
Illumina Ho. SW18......................3C 100
..............................(off Broomhill Rd.)
Ilminster Gdns. SW11................2A 102
Ilsley Ct. SW8..............................5E 89
Imani Mans. SW11.......................5F 87
IMAX (BFI) 2B 24 (2C 76)
Imber St. N1.................................5F 49
Imperial Av. N16..........................1A 50
Imperial Cl. NW2..........................2D 43
Imperial College London Charing
Cross Campus 2F 85
Imperial College London Chelsea
& Westminster Campus 2E 87
..............................(within Chelsea & Westminster
..............................Hospital)
Imperial College London
Hammersmith Campus 5C 56
Imperial College London
Royal Brompton Campus,
Emmanuel Kaye 1A 88
..............................(off Manresa Rd.)
Imperial College London
Royal Brompton Campus,
Guy Scadding Bldg..................1F 87
..............................(off Dovehouse St.)
Imperial College London
St Mary's Campus 5F 59
..............................(off Norfolk Pl.)
Imperial College London
Sth. Kensington Campus........4F 73
Imperial College London
Sth. Kensington Campus,
Ennismore Gdns. M................4F 73
..............................(off Ennismore Gdns. M.)
Imperial College London
Sth. Kensington Campus,
Kensington Gore 4F 73
Imperial Coll. Rd. SW7..............4F 73
Imperial Ct. N6............................1E 33
Imperial Ct. NW8.........................1A 60
..............................(off Prince Albert Rd.)
Imperial Cres. SW6.....................5E 87
Imperial Ho. E14.........................1B 80
..............................(off Victory Pl.)
Imperial Ho. E3...........................2A 66
..............................(off Grove Rd.)
Imperial M. E6..............................1F 69
Imperial Sq. SW9........................2B 104
..............................(off Brighton Ter.)
Imperial Rd. SW6........................4D 87
Imperial Sq. SW6........................3D 87
Imperial St. E3.............................2E 67
Imperial War Mus. London All
Saints Annexe 4C 76
..............................(off Austral St.)
Imperial War Mus. London Main
Museum 5C 24 (4C 76)
Imperial Wharf E2........................1D 65
..............................(off Darwen Pl.)
Imperial Wharf SW6....................5E 87
Imperial Wharf Station
(Overground) 4E 87
Imperium Ho. E1..........................5D 65
..............................(off Cannon St. Rd.)

Imre Cl. W12.................................2D 71
Inchmery Rd. SE6.......................2D 123
Independent Pl. E8......................2B 50
Independents Rd. SE3.............1B 110
Inderwick Rd. N8.........................1B 34
Indescon Ct. E14.........................3D 81
Indescon Sq. E14........................3C 80
Indiana Bldg. SE13.....................4C 94
..............................(off Deal's Gateway)
India Pl. WC2...........4F 15 (1B 76)
..............................(off Montreal Pl.)
India St. EC3.............3F 19 (5B 64)
India Way SW15..........................4C 98
India Way W12..............................1D 71
indigo at the O2..........................2A 82
Indigo M. E14..............................1E 81
Indigo M. N16..............................5F 35
Indus Ct. SE15.............................3B 92
..............................(off Amstel Ct.)
Indus Rd. SE7..............................3E 97
Infirmary Cl. SW3........................2B 88
..............................(off West Rd.)
Inforum M. SE15..........................3C 92
Ingal Rd. E13...............................3C 68
Ingate Pl. SW8............................4D 89
Ingatestone Rd. E12....................3E 41
Ingelow Ho. W8...........................3D 73
..............................(off Holland St.)
Ingelow Rd. SW8.........................5D 89
Ingersoll Rd. W12........................2D 71
Ingestre Pl. W1.....3A 14 (5E 61)
Ingestre Rd. E7...........................1C 54
Ingestre Rd. NW5.......................1D 47
Ingham Rd. NW6.........................1C 44
Inglebert St. EC1.....1B 8 (2C 62)
Ingleborough St. SW9.................5C 90
Ingleby Rd. N7.............................5A 34
Ingledene Cl. NW4......................1C 28
Inglefield Sq. E1..........................2D 79
..............................(off Prusom St.)
Inglemere Rd. SE23...................3F 121
Ingle M. EC1............1B 8 (2C 62)
Inglesham Wlk. E9......................3B 52
Ingleside Gro. SE3......................2B 96
Inglethorpe St. SW6...................4F 85
Ingleton St. SW9.........................5C 90
Inglewood Cl. E14.......................5C 80
Inglewood M. SE27...................5E 119
..............................(off Elder Rd.)
Inglewood Rd. NW6....................2C 44
Inglis St. SE5...............................4D 91
Ingoldisthorpe Gro. SE15.........2B 92
Ingot Twr. E14..............................4C 66
..............................(off Ursula Gould Way)
Ingram Av. NW11.........................2E 31
Ingram Cl. SE11...........................5B 76
Ingram Ho. E3..............................5A 52
Ingrave St. SW11.........................1F 101
Ingrebourne Apts. SW6 ....1D 101
Ingrebourne Ho.
BR1: Broml.................................5F 123
..............................(off Brangbourne Rd.)
Ingrebourne Ho. NW8................4F 59
..............................(off Broadley St.)
Ingress St. W4.............................1A 84
Inigo Jones Rd. SE7...................3F 97
Inigo Pl. WC2..........4D 15 (1A 76)
..............................(off Bedford St.)
Ink Bldg. W10..............................4F 57
Inkerman Rd. NW5......................3D 47
Inkerman Ter. W8.........................4C 72
..............................(off Allen St.)
Inkster Ho. SW11........................1A 102
Ink Works Ct. SE1......4E 27 (3A 78)
..............................(off Bell Yd. M.)

Inman Rd. NW10 ....5A **42**
Inman Rd. SW18 ....5E **101**
Inner Circ. NW1 ....2B **4** (2C **60**)
Inner Ct. SW3 ....2A **88**
Inner Pk. Rd. SW19 ....1F **113**
Inner Temple La.
EC4 ....3B **16** (5C **62**)
..................................(off Fleet St.)
Innes Gdns. SW15 ....4D **99**
Innes St. SE15 ....3A **92**
Innis Ho. SE17 ....1A **92**
................................(off East St.)
Inniskilling Rd. E13 ....1E **69**
Innova Pas. E1 ....3F **11** (3B **64**)
.............................(off Sclater St.)
Innovation Cen., The E14 ......3E **81**
.............................(off Marsh Wall)
Inns of Court & City Yeomanry
Mus. 1A **16** (4B **62**)
Insignia Point E20 ....2E **53**
Inskip Cl. E10 ....4D **39**
Insley Ho. E3 ....2D **67**
.................................(off Bow Rd.)
Institute for Arts in Therapy &
Education, The 5D **49**
..........................(off Britannia Row)
Institute of Archaeology
Collections 3B **6** (3F **61**)
Institute of Commonwealth
Studies 5C **6** (4F **61**)
............................(off Russell Sq.)
Institute of Contemporary Arts
(ICA)......................2C **22** (2F **75**)
.........................(off Carlton Ho. Ter.)
Institute of Germanic & Romance
Studies 5C **6** (4F **61**)
............................(off Russell Sq.)
Institute of Ophthalmology
................................2B **10** (2F **63**)
...........................(off Peerless St.)
Institute of Psychoanalysis, the
....3C **58**
.............................(off Elgin Av.)
Institute Pl. E8 ....2D **51**
Integer Gdns. E11 ....2F **39**
Interchange, The NW1 ....4D **47**
.........................(off Camden Lock Pl.)
International Bus. Pk. E15....5F **53**
International Hall
WC1 ....4E **7** (3A **62**)
.......................(off Lansdowne St.)
International Ho.
E1 ....5F **19** (1B **78**)
.....................(off St Katharine's Way)
INTERNATIONAL QUARTER, THE
....3E **53**
International Sq. E20 ....3E **53**
.................(within Westfield Shop. Cen.)
International Way E20 ....3E **53**
Inver Cl. E5 ....4E **37**
Inver Ct. W2 ....5D **59**
Inver Ct. W6 ....4C **70**
Inverforth Cl. NW3 ....4E **31**
Invergarry Ho. NW6 ....1D **59**
.............................(off Carlton Vale)
Inverine Rd. SE7 ....1D **97**
Invermead Cl. W6 ....4C **70**
Inverness Ct. SE6..................1B **124**
Inverness Gdns. W8 ....2D **73**
Inverness M. W2 ....1D **73**
Inverness Pl. W2 ....1D **73**
Inverness St. NW1 ....5D **47**
Inverness Ter. W2 ....5D **59**
Inverton Rd. SE15 ....2F **107**
Invicta Cl. E3 ....4C **66**

Invicta Plaza SE1 ......1D **25** (2D **77**)
Invicta Rd. SE3........................3C **96**
Inville Rd. SE17 ....1F **91**
...................................(not continuous)
Inville Wlk. SE17 ....1F **91**
Inwen Ct. SE8.........................1A **94**
..................................(not continuous)
Inwood Ct. NW1 ....4E **47**
.............................(off Rochester Sq.)
Inwood Ho. N1 ....5D **49**
..................................(off Elliott's Pl.)
Inworth St. SW11 ....5A **88**
Inworth Wlk. N1 ....5E **49**
.............................(off Popham St.)
Iona Cl. SE6............................5C **108**
Ion Ct. E2 ....1C **64**
Ionian Bldg. E14.....................1A **80**
.............................(off Narrow St.)
Ionian Ho. E1 ....3F **65**
.............................(off Duckett St.)
Ion Sq. E2 ....1C **64**
Ipsden Bldgs. SE1....2C **24** (2C **76**)
.............................(off Windmill Wlk.)
Ira Ct. SE27 ....2D **119**
Ireland Yd. EC4 ....3E **17** (5D **63**)
Irene Rd. SW6 ....4C **86**
Ireton Ho. SW15 ....3A **100**
..........................(off Stamford Sq.)
Ireton St. E3 ....3C **66**
Iris Ct. SE14 ....4E **93**
...............................(off Briant St.)
Iron Bri. Cl. NW10 ....2A **42**
Iron Bri. Ho. NW1 ....4B **46**
Iron Mill Pl. SW18 ....4D **101**
Iron Mill Rd. SW18 ....4D **101**
Ironmonger La. EC2.3A **18** (5E **63**)
Ironmonger Pas.
EC1 ....2A **10** (2E **63**)
.........................(off Ironmonger Row)
Ironmonger Row
EC1 ....2A **10** (2E **63**)
Ironmonger Row Baths
................................2A **10** (2E **63**)
.........................(off Ironmonger Row)
Ironmongers Pl. E14 ....5C **80**
Ironside Cl. SE16....................3F **79**
Ironside Ho. E9.......................1A **52**
Iron Works E3 ....5C **52**
Ironworks, The N1 ....1A **62**
..............................(off Albion Wlk.)
Ironworks Way E13 ....1F **69**
Irvine Cl. E14..........................4D **67**
Irvine Ct. W1 ....4A **6** (3E **61**)
.............................(off Whitfield St.)
Irvine Ho. N7 ....3B **48**
.............................(off Caledonian Rd.)
Irving Gro. SW9 ....5B **90**
Irving Ho. SE17 ....1D **91**
.........................(off Doddington Gro.)
Irving Mans. W14....................2A **86**
.......................(off Queen's Club Gdns.)
Irving M. N1 ....3D **49**
Irving Rd. W14 ....4F **71**
Irving St. WC2 ....5C **14** (1F **75**)
Irving Way NW9 ....1C **28**
Irwell Est. SE16.......................4E **79**
Irwin Gdns. NW10 ....5D **43**
Isaac Way SE1 ....3A **26** (3E **77**)
.............................(off Sanctuary St.)
Isabella Ho. SE11 ....1D **91**
.............................(off Othello Cl.)
Isabella Ho. W6.......................1E **85**
.....................(off Queen Caroline St.)
Isabella M. N1 ....3A **50**
Isabella Rd. E9........................2E **51**

Isabella St. SE1 ....2D **25** (2D **77**)
Isabel St. SW9.........................4B **90**
Isambard M. E14.....................4E **81**
Isambard Pl. SE16 ....2E **79**
Isel Way SE22 ....3A **106**
Isis Cl. SW15 ....2E **99**
Isis Ho. NW8 ....3F **59**
.............................(off Church St. Est.)
Isis St. SW18 ....2E **115**
Island Apts. N1 ....5E **49**
Island Gardens Station (DLR)
....1E **95**
Island Ho. E3 ....2E **67**
Island Ho. SE16......................5F **79**
Island Row E14.......................5B **66**
Islay Wlk. N1 ....4E **49**
.........................(off Douglas Rd. Sth.)
Isleden Ho. N1 ....5E **49**
.............................(off Prebend St.)
Isledon Rd. N7 ....5C **34**
ISLEDON VILLAGE 5C **34**
ISLE OF DOGS 3D **81**
Isley Ct. E14 ....3E **67**
.............................(off Teviot St.)
Islip Ct. SW8 ....5E **89**
ISLINGTON 4D **49**
Islington Bus. Cen. N1 ....5E **49**
.........................(off Coleman Flds.)
Islington Ecology Cen., The...5C **34**
Islington Grn. N1 ....5D **49**
...................................(not continuous)
Islington High St. N1 ....1C **62**
...................................(not continuous)
Islington Mus. 2D **9** (2D **63**)
Islington Pk. M. N1 ....4D **49**
Islington Pk. St. N1 ....4C **48**
Islington Pl. N1 ....5C **48**
Islington Sq. N1 ....5D **49**
Islington Tennis Cen. 3A **48**
Islip St. NW5 ....2E **47**
Ismailia Rd. E7 ....4D **55**
Isola Ct. N1 ....5E **49**
.............................(off Popham Rd.)
Isom Cl. E13 ....2D **69**
Issigonis Ho. W3 ....2B **70**
.............................(off Cowley Rd.)
Istra Ho. E20 ....2E **53**
.............................(off Logan Cl.)
Ivanhoe Ho. E3 ....1A **66**
.............................(off Grove Rd.)
Ivanhoe Rd. SE5......................1B **106**
Ivatt Pl. W14 ....1B **86**
Iveagh Cl. E9 ....5F **51**
Iveagh Ct. E1 ....3F **19** (5B **64**)
.............................(off Haydon St.)
Iveagh Ho. SW10 ....3E **87**
.............................(off King's Rd.)
Iveagh Ho. SW9.......................5C **90**
Ive Farm Cl. E10 ....4C **38**
Ive Farm La. E10 ....4C **38**
Iveley Rd. SW4 ....5E **89**
Iver Ho. N1 ....5A **50**
.............................(off Halcomb St.)
Iverna Ct. W8 ....4C **72**
Iverna Gdns. W8 ....4C **72**
Iverson Rd. NW6 ....3B **44**
Ives Rd. E16 ....4A **68**
Ives St. SW3 ....5A **74**
Ivestor Ter. SE23....................5E **107**
Ivimey St. E2 ....2C **64**
Ivinghoe Ho. N7 ....2F **47**
Ivo Pl. N19..............................5F **33**
Ivor Ct. N8 ....1A **34**
Ivor Ct. NW1 ....3B **60**
.........................(off Gloucester Pl.)

Ivories, The N1	4E 49
(off Northampton St.)	
Ivor Pl. NW1	3B 60
Ivor St. NW1	4E 47
Ivordown BR1: Broml	4C 124
Ivory Ho. E1	2B 78
Ivory Pl. W11	1A 72
(off Treadgold St.)	
Ivory Sq. SW11	1E 101
Ivybridge Ct. NW1	4D 47
(off Lewis St.)	
Ivybridge La. WC2	5E 15 (1A 76)
Ivychurch La. SE17	1B 92
Ivy Cotts. E14	1E 81
Ivy Ct. SE16	1C 92
(off Argyle Rd.)	
Ivydale Rd. SE15	1F 107
Ivyday Gro. SW16	3B 118
Ivy Gdns. N8	1A 34
Ivy Lodge W11	2C 72
(off Notting Hill Ga.)	
Ivymount Rd. SE27	3C 118
Ivy Rd. E16	5C 68
Ivy Rd. E17	1C 38
Ivy Rd. NW2	1E 43
Ivy Rd. SE4	2B 108
Ivy Rd. SW17	5A 116
Ivy St. N1	1A 64
Ixworth Pl. SW3	1A 88

J

Jacana Ct. E1	1B 78
(off Star Pl.)	
Jacaranda Gro. E8	4B 50
Jack Clow Rd. E15	1A 68
Jack Dash Way E6	3F 69
Jackman Ho. E1	2D 79
(off Watts St.)	
Jackman M. NW2	5A 28
Jackman St. E8	5D 51
Jackson & Joseph Bldg.	
E1	5F 11 (4B 64)
(off Princelet St.)	
Jackson Cl. E9	4E 51
Jackson Ct. E7	3D 55
Jackson N7	1B 48
Jacksons La. N6	2C 32
Jacksons Lane Theatre	1D 33
(off Archway Rd.)	
Jacks Pl. E1	5F 11 (4B 64)
(off Corbet Pl.)	
Jack the Ripper Mus.	1C 78
Jack Walker Ct. N5	1D 49
Jacobin Lodge N7	2A 48
Jacob Mans. E1	5D 65
(off Commercial Rd.)	
Jacobs Ct. E1	5C 64
(off Plumber's Row)	
Jacobs Ho. E13	2E 69
(off New City Rd.)	
Jacobs Island Ho. SE16	4B 78
(off Spa Rd.)	
Jacobs Island Pier	3C 78
(off Bermondsey Wall W.)	
Jacobs M. SW15	2A 100
Jacob St. SE1	3C 78
Jacob's Well M.	
W1	1C 12 (4C 60)
Jacotts Ho. W10	3E 57
(off Sutton Way)	
Jacquard Ct. SW18	3D 101
Jacqueline Creft Ter. N6	1C 32
(off Grange Rd.)	

Jacqueline Ho. NW1	5B 46
(off Regent's Pk. Rd.)	
Jade Cl. E16	5F 69
Jade Cl. NW2	2F 29
Jade Ter. NW6	4E 45
Jaffray Pl. SE27	4D 119
Jaggard Way SW12	5B 102
Jagger Ho. SW11	4B 88
(off Rosenau Rd.)	
Jago Wlk. SE5	3F 91
Jake Russell Wlk. E16	1E 83
Jamaica Rd. SE1	4F 27 (3B 78)
Jamaica Rd. SE16	4C 78
Jamaica St. E1	5E 65
James Allens School Swimming	
Pool	3A 106
James Anderson Ct. E2	1A 64
(off Kingsland Rd.)	
James Av. NW2	2E 43
James Boswell Cl. SW16	4B 118
James Brine Ho. E2	1F 11 (2B 64)
(off Ravenscroft St.)	
James Campbell Ho. E2	1E 65
(off Old Ford Rd.)	
James Cl. E13	1C 68
James Cl. NW11	1A 30
James Collins Cl. W9	3B 58
James Ct. N1	5E 49
(off Raynor Pl.)	
James Docherty Ho. E2	1D 65
(off Patriot Sq.)	
James Hammett Ho.	
E2	1F 11 (2B 64)
(off Ravenscroft St.)	
James Hill Ho. W10	3A 58
(off Kensal Rd.)	
James Ho. E1	3A 66
(off Solebay St.)	
James Ho. SE16	3F 79
(off Wolfe Cres.)	
James Ho. SW8	3A 90
(off Wyvil Rd.)	
James Ho. W10	3A 58
James Joyce Wlk. SE24	2D 105
James La. E10	2E 39
James La. E11	1F 39
James Lighthill Ho.	
WC1	1A 8 (1B 62)
(off Penton Ri.)	
James Lind Ho. SE8	5B 80
(off Grove St.)	
James Middleton Ho. E2	2D 65
(off Middleton St.)	
James Morgan M. N1	5E 49
Jameson Ct. E2	1E 65
(off Russia La.)	
Jameson Ho. SE11	1B 90
(off Glasshouse Wlk.)	
Jameson Lodge N6	1E 33
Jameson St. W8	2C 72
James Riley Point E15	5E 53
(off Carpenters Rd.)	
James Stewart Ho. NW6	4B 44
James St. W1	2C 12 (5C 60)
James St. WC2	3E 15 (1A 76)
James Stroud Ho. SE17	1E 91
(off Walworth St.)	
James Ter. SW14	1A 98
(off Church Path)	
Jamestown Rd. NW1	5D 47
Jamestown Way E14	1F 81
James Voller Way SE5	5E 65
Jam Factory, The	
SE1	5D 27 (4A 78)
(off Green Wlk.)	

Jamuna Cl. E14	4A 66
Jane Austen Hall E16	2D 83
(off Wesley Av.)	
Jane Austen Ho. SW1	1E 89
(off Churchill Gdns.)	
Jane St. E1	5D 65
Janet Adegoke Swimming Pool	
	1C 70
Janet St. E14	4C 80
Janeway Pl. SE16	3D 79
Janeway St. SE16	3C 78
Jansen Wlk. SW11	1F 101
Janson Cl. E15	2A 54
Janson Cl. NW10	5A 28
Janson Rd. E15	2A 54
Japan Cres. N4	2B 34
Jaquard Ct. E2	1E 65
(off Bishop's Way)	
Jardine Rd. E1	1F 79
Jarman Ho. E1	4E 65
(off Jubilee St.)	
Jarman Ho. SE16	5F 79
(off Hawkstone Rd.)	
Jarret Ho. E3	2C 66
(off Bow Rd.)	
Jarrett Cl. SW2	1D 119
Jarrow Rd. SE16	5E 79
Jarrow Way E9	1B 52
Jarvis Ho. SE15	4C 92
(off Goldsmith Rd.)	
Jarvis Rd. SE22	2A 106
Jasmin Cl. SE12	4C 110
Jasmine Cl. SW19	5C 114
Jasmine Ho. SW18	1E 101
Jasmine Sq. E3	5B 52
(off Hawthorn Av.)	
Jasmin Lodge SE16	1D 93
(off Sherwood Gdns.)	
Jason Ct. SW9	4C 90
(off Southey Rd.)	
Jason Ct. W1	2C 12 (5C 60)
(off Wigmore St.)	
Jasper Pas. SE19	5B 120
Jasper Rd. E16	5F 69
Jasper Rd. SE19	5B 120
Jasper Wlk. N1	1B 10 (2F 63)
Java Ho. E14	4A 68
Java Wharf SE1	3B 78
(off Shad Thames)	
Jay Ho. E3	5B 52
(off Hawthorn Av.)	
Jay M. SW7	3E 73
Jays St. N1	5B 48
Jean Darling Ho. SW10	2F 87
(off Milman's St.)	
Jean Ho. SW17	5A 116
Jeanne Ct. E14	4A 66
(off Pechora Way)	
Jean Pardies Ho. E1	4E 65
(off Jubilee St.)	
Jebb Av. SW2	4A 104
(not continuous)	
Jebb St. E3	1C 66
Jedburgh Rd. E13	2E 69
Jedburgh St. SW11	2C 102
Jeddo M. W12	3B 70
Jeddo Rd. W12	3B 70
Jeeyas Apts. E16	4B 68
Jefferson Bldg. E14	3C 80
Jefferson Plaza E3	3E 67
(off Hannaford Wlk.)	
Jeffrey Row SE12	3D 111
Jeffrey's Pl. NW1	4E 47
Jeffreys Rd. SW4	5A 90
Jeffrey's St. NW1	4E 47

Jeffreys Wlk. SW4 .... 5A 90
Jeger Av. E2.................... 5B 50
Jeken Rd. SE9.............. 2E 111
Jelf Rd. SW2................. 3C 104
Jelico Point SE16.......... 3B 80
.... (off Rotherhithe St.)
Jellicoe Ho. E2................ 1C 64
.... (off Ropley St.)
Jellicoe Rd. E13............ 3C 68
Jemma Knowles Cl. SW2... 1C 118
.... (off Tulse Hill)
Jemotts Ct. SE14.......... 2F 93
.... (off Myers La.)
Jenkinson Ho. E2........... 2D 65
.... (off Usk St.)
Jenkins Rd. E13............ 3D 69
Jenner Ho. WC1....... 3E 7 (3A 62)
.... (off Hunter St.)
Jenner Pl. SW13............ 2D 85
Jenner Rd. N16............ 5B 36
Jennifer Ho. E14........... 5E 67
Jennifer Ho. SE11......... 5C 76
.... (off Reedworth St.)
Jennifer Rd. BR1: Broml... 3B 124
Jenningsbury Ho. SW3... 1A 88
.... (off Cale St.)
Jennings Ho. SE10......... 1F 95
.... (off Old Woolwich Rd.)
Jennings Rd. SE22......... 4B 106
Jenny Hammond Cl. E11... 5B 40
Jensen Ho. E3................ 3C 66
.... (off Wellington Way)
Jenson Hgts. N1............ 4B 48
.... (off Caledonian Rd.)
Jephson Ct. SW4............ 5A 90
Jephson Ho. SE17.......... 2D 91
.... (off Doddington Gro.)
Jephson Rd. E7............. 4E 55
Jephson St. SE5............ 4F 91
Jephtha Rd. SW18......... 4C 100
Jepson Ho. SW6............ 4D 87
.... (off Pearscroft Rd.)
Jerdan Ho. SW6............. 3C 86
.... (off North End Rd.)
Jerdan Pl. SW6.............. 3C 86
Jeremiah St. E14........... 5D 67
Jeremy Bentham Ho. E2... 2C 64
.... (off Mansford St.)
Jermyn St. SW1...... 1A 22 (2E 75)
Jermyn Street Theatre
.... 5A 14 (1F 75)
.... (off Jermyn St.)
Jerningham Ct. SE14...... 4A 94
Jerningham Rd. SE14..... 5A 94
Jerome Cres. NW8......... 3A 60
Jerome Ho. NW1........... 4A 60
.... (off Lisson Gro.)
Jerome Ho. SW7............ 5F 73
.... (off Glendower Pl.)
Jerome St. E1......... 4F 11 (3B 64)
Jerrard St. SE13........... 1D 109
Jerrold St. N1......... 1E 11 (1A 64)
Jersey Ho. N1................ 3E 49
.... (off Jersey Rd.)
Jersey Rd. E11.............. 3F 39
Jersey Rd. E16.............. 5E 69
Jersey Rd. N1................ 3E 49
Jersey St. E2................. 2D 65
Jerusalem Pas. EC1...4D 9 (3D 63)
Jervis Ct. SE10.............. 4E 95
.... (off Blissett St.)
Jervis Ct. W1........... 3E 13 (5D 61)
.... (off Princes St.)
Jervis Rd. SW6.............. 2B 86
Jerviston Gdns. SW16... 5C 118

Jerwood Space Art Gallery
.... 3E 25 (3D 77)
.... (off Union St.)
Jesmond Dene NW3....... 3E 45
Jessam Av. E5............... 3D 37
Jessel Ho. SW1.............. 5F 75
.... (off Page St.)
Jessel Ho. WC1....... 2D 7 (2A 62)
.... (off Judd St.)
Jessel Mans. W14.......... 2A 86
.... (off Queen's Club Gdns.)
Jesse Rd. E10............... 3E 38
Jessica Rd. SW18.......... 4E 101
Jessie Blythe La. N19.... 2A 34
Jessie Duffett Ho. SE5... 3E 91
.... (off Pitman St.)
Jessie Wood Ct. SW9..... 3C 90
.... (off Caldwell St.)
Jesson Ho. SE17........... 5F 77
.... (off Orb St.)
Jessop Ct. N1................ 1D 63
Jessop Ho. W4.............. 5A 70
.... (off Kirton Cl.)
Jessop Rd. SE24........... 2D 105
Jessop Sq. E14.............. 2C 80
Jevington Way SE12...... 1D 125
Jevons Ho. NW8............ 4F 45
.... (off Hilgrove Rd.)
Jewel Sq. E1................. 1D 79
Jewel Tower 5D 23 (4A 76)
.... (off College M.)
Jewish Mus. 5D 47
Jewry St. EC3........ 3F 19 (5B 64)
Jew's Row SW18........... 2D 101
Jews' Wlk. SE26............ 4D 121
Jeymer Av. NW2............ 2D 43
Jeypore Rd. SW18......... 5E 101
Jeypore Rd. Pas. SW18 ...4E 101
Jim Griffiths Ho. SW6 .... 2B 86
.... (off Clem Attlee Ct.)
Jim Veal Dr. N7............. 3A 48
Joan Cres. SE9.............. 5F 111
Joanna Ho. W6.............. 1E 85
.... (off Queen Caroline St.)
Joan St. SE1.......... 2D 25 (2D 77)
Jocelin Ho. N1............... 5B 48
.... (off Barnsbury Est.)
Jocelyn St. SE15........... 4C 92
Jockey's Flds. WC1 ...5A 8 (4B 62)
Jodane St. SE8.............. 5B 80
Jodrell Rd. E3................ 5B 52
Joe Hunte Ct. SE27....... 5D 119
Johanna St. SE1...... 4B 24 (3C 76)
John Adam St.
.... WC2......... 5E 15 (1A 76)
John Aird Ct. W2............ 4E 59
.... (off Howley Pl.)
John Archer Way SW18... 4F 101
John Ashby Cl. SW2....... 4A 104
John Baird Ct. SE26....... 4E 121
John Barker Ct. NW6...... 4A 44
John Barnes Wlk. E15 .... 3B 54
John Bell Twr. E. E3....... 1C 66
.... (off Pancras Way)
John Bell Twr. W. E3...... 1C 66
.... (off Pancras Way)
John Betts' Ho. W12...... 4B 70
John Bond Ho. E3.......... 1B 66
.... (off Wright's Rd.)
John Bowles Ct. E1........ 1F 79
.... (off Schoolhouse La.)
John Brent Ho. SE8........ 5F 79
.... (off Haddonfield)
John Buck Ho. NW10...... 5B 42
John Campbell Rd. N16... 2A 50

John Carpenter St.
.... EC4......... 4D 17 (1D 77)
John Cartwright Ho. E2... 2D 65
.... (off Old Bethnal Grn. Rd.)
John Crane St. SE17...... 2F 91
John Donne Way SE10 ... 3D 95
.... (off Norman Rd.)
John Drinkwater Cl. E11... 2B 40
John Fearon Wlk. W10 .... 2A 58
.... (off Dart St.)
John Fielden Ho. E2....... 2D 65
.... (off Canrobert St.)
John Fisher St. E1......... 1C 78
John Harrison Way SE10... 4B 82
John Horner M. N1......... 1E 63
JOHN HOWARD CEN. 2A 52
John Hunter Av. SW17.... 3A 116
John Islip St. SW1.......... 5F 75
John Kennedy Ct. N1..... 3F 49
.... (off Newington Grn. Rd.)
John Kennedy Ho. SE16... 5F 79
.... (off Rotherhithe Old Rd.)
John Knight Lodge SW6... 3C 86
John McDonald Ho. E14... 4E 81
.... (off Glengall Gro.)
John McKenna Wlk. SE16... 4C 78
John Masefield Ho. N15... 1F 35
.... (off Fladbury Rd.)
John Maurice Cl. SE17... 5F 77
John Nash M. E14......... 5A 66
.... (off Commercial Rd.)
Johnny Andrews Ho. E1... 5F 65
.... (off Boulcott St.)
John Orwell Sports Cen. ... 2D 79
John Parker Sq. SW11....1F 101
John Parry Ct. N1.......... 1A 64
.... (off Hare Wlk.)
John Penn Ho. SE14...... 3B 94
.... (off Amersham Va.)
John Penn St. SE13....... 4D 95
John Penry Ho. SE1....... 1C 92
.... (off Marlborough Gro.)
John Prince's St.
.... W1.......... 2E 13 (5D 61)
John Pritchard Ho. E1 .... 3C 64
.... (off Buxton St.)
John Ratcliffe Ho. NW6 ... 2C 58
.... (off Chippenham Gdns.)
John Rennie Wlk. E1 ...... 1D 79
John Riley Ho. E3.......... 4B 66
.... (off Geoffrey Chaucer Way)
John Roll Way SE16....... 4C 78
John Ruskin St. SE5....... 3D 91
John Scurr Ho. E14........ 5A 66
.... (off Ratcliffe La.)
John Sessions Sq. E1 .... 5C 64
.... (off Alie St.)
John Silkin La. SE8.........1F 93
John's M. WC1........ 4A 8 (3B 62)
John Smith Av. SW6....... 3B 86
John Smith M. E14.........1F 81
Johnson Cl. E8.............. 5C 50
Johnson Ct. SE9.......... 2E 111
Johnson Ho. E2............. 2C 64
.... (off Roberta St.)
Johnson Ho. NW1.......... 1E 61
.... (off Cranleigh St.)
Johnson Ho. NW3.......... 4B 46
.... (off Adelaide Rd.)
Johnson Ho. SW1.......... 5C 74
.... (off Cundy St.)
Johnson Ho. SW8.......... 3F 89
.... (off Wandsworth Rd.)
Johnson Ho. W8............ 3C 72
.... (off Campden Hill)

Johnson Lock Ct. E1............4A 66
Johnson Lodge W9................4C 58
................(off Admiral Wlk.)
Johnson Mans. W14.........2A 86
................(off Queen's Club Gdns.)
Johnson's Ct. EC4....3C 16 (5C 62)
Johnson's Pl. SW1............1E 89
Johnson St. E1................1E 79
John Spencer Sq. N1........3D 49
John's Pl. E1..................5D 65
Johnston Cl. SW9..............4B 90
Johnston Ct. E10..............5D 39
Johnstone Ho. SE13........1F 109
................(off Belmont Hill)
Johnston Ter. NW2............5F 29
John Strachey Ho. SW6....2B 86
................(off Clem Attlee Ct.)
John St. E15..................5B 54
John St. WC1............4A 8 (3B 62)
John Strype Ct. E10...........3D 39
John Trundle Ct.
EC2.................5F 9 (4E 63)
................(off Aldersgate St.)
John Trundle Highwalk
EC2.................5F 9 (4E 63)
................(off Aldersgate St.)
John Tucker Ho. E14..........4C 80
................(off Mellish St.)
John Wesley Highwalk
EC2.................1F 17 (4E 63)
................(off Aldersgate St.)
John Wetherby Ct. E15......1D 67
................(off High St.)
John Wetherby Ct. E. E15...1D 67
................(off High St.)
John Wetherby Ct. W. E15...1D 67
................(off High St.)
John Wheatley Ho. SW6....2B 86
................(off Clem Attlee Ct.)
John Williams Cl. SE14......2F 93
John Woolley Cl. SE13.....2A 110
Joiners Arms Yd. SE5.........4E 91
Joiners M. E11................5A 40
Joiners Pl. N5.................1F 49
Joiner St. SE1.........2C 26 (2F 77)
Joiners Yd. N1.........1E 7 (1A 62)
................(off Caledonia St.)
Jolles Ho. E3..................2D 67
................(off Bromley High St.)
Jonathan St. SE11............1B 90
Jones Ho. E14.................5F 67
................(off Blair St.)
Jones M. SW15..............2A 100
Jones Rd. E13.................3D 69
Jones St. W1...........5D 13 (1D 75)
Jonson Ho. SE1.....5C 26 (4F 77)
................(off Burbage Cl.)
Jonzen Wlk. E14..............5C 66
Jordan Cl. SW15..............2F 99
Jordan Ho. N1.................5F 49
................(off Colville Est.)
Jordan Ho. SE4...............2F 107
................(off St Norbert Rd.)
Jordans Ho. NW8.............3F 59
................(off Capland St.)
Joscoyne Ho. E1...............5D 65
................(off Philpot St.)
Joseph Cl. N4.................4D 35
Joseph Conrad Ho. SW1 ....5E 75
................(off Tachbrook St.)
Joseph Ct. N16................1A 36
................(off Amhurst Pk.)
Joseph Grimaldi Pk.
.......................1A 8 (1B 62)
Joseph Hardcastle Cl. SE14 ...3F 93

Josephine Av. SW2...........3B 104
Joseph Irwin Ho. E14.......1B 80
................(off Gill St.)
Joseph Lister Ct. E7.........4C 54
Joseph M. N7..................3E 48
................(off Westbourne Rd.)
Joseph M. SE15..............3F 107
Joseph Powell Cl. SW12....4E 103
Joseph Priestley Ho.
E2.........................2D 65
................(off Canrobert St.)
Joseph Ray Rd. E11..........4A 40
Joseph St. E3.................3B 66
Joseph Trotter Cl.
EC1.................2C 8 (2C 62)
................(off Finsbury Est.)
Joshua Pedley M. E3.........1C 66
Joshua St. E14................5E 67
Joslings Cl. W12..............1C 70
Jossiline Ct. E3...............1A 66
................(off Ford St.)
Joubert Mans. SW3..........1A 88
................(off Jubilee Pl.)
Joubert St. SW11.............5B 88
Jowett St. SE15...............3B 92
Jowitt Ho. E2..................2F 65
................(off Morpeth St.)
Joyce Page Cl. SE7...........2F 97
Joyce Wlk. SW2..............4C 104
Joy of Life Fountain
.......................1B 20 (2C 74)
Jubb Powell Ho. N15.........1A 36
Jubilee, The SE10.............3D 95
Jubilee Bldgs. NW8...........5F 45
Jubilee Cl. NW10..............1A 56
Jubilee Cl. NW9...............1A 28
Jubilee Ct. E16................5B 68
................(off Silvertown Sq.)
Jubilee Ct. SE10...............2D 95
................(off Dowells St.)
Jubilee Cres. E14..............4E 81
Jubilee Hall Gym........4E 15 (1A 76)
................(within Jubilee Hall)
Jubilee Hgts. SE10............4E 95
................(off Parkside Av.)
Jubilee Ho. SE11..............5C 76
................(off Reedworth St.)
Jubilee Ho. WC1........3F 7 (3B 62)
................(off Gray's Inn Rd.)
Jubilee Mans. E1..............5E 65
................(off Jubilee St.)
Jubilee Mkt. WC2.....4E 15 (1A 76)
................(off Covent Garden)
Jubilee Mkt........4E 15 (1A 76)
................(off Covent Gdn.)
Jubilee Pl. SW3................1A 88
Jubilee St. E1..................5E 65
Jubilee Walkway
SE1.................5D 17 (1D 77)
Jubilee Yd. SE1.....3F 27 (3B 78)
................(off Lafone St.)
Judd St. WC1.........1D 7 (2A 62)
Jude St. E16...................5B 68
Judges Wlk. NW3..............5E 31
Juer St. SW11.................3A 88
Juett Lodge SE10..............5C 82
................(off Peartree Way)
Julia Ct. E17..................1D 39
Julia Garfield M. E16.........2D 83
................(not continuous)
Julian Ct. NW1................4E 47
................(off Rochester Sq.)
Julian Ho. SE21...........4A 120
Julian Pl. E14.................1D 95
Julian Taylor Path SE23 ...2D 121

Julia Scurr St. E3.............4C 66
Julia St. NW5.................1C 46
Juliet Ho. N1..................1A 64
................(off Arden Est.)
Juliette Rd. E13................1C 68
Julius Ho. E14................5F 67
................(off E. India Dock Rd.)
Julius Nyerere Cl. N1........5B 48
................(off Copenhagen St.)
Junction App. SE13........1E 109
Junction App. SW11......1A 102
Junction M. W2...............5A 60
Junction Pl. W2...............5F 59
................(off Praed St.)
Junction Rd. E13.............1D 69
Junction Rd. N19.............1E 47
Juniper Ct. W8................4D 73
................(off St Mary's Pl.)
Juniper Cres. NW1...........4C 46
Juniper Dr. SW18...........2E 101
Juniper Ho. SE14............3E 93
Juniper Ho. W10.............3A 58
................(off Fourth Av.)
Juno Ct. E1...................1E 79
Juno Ct. SW9.................3C 90
................(off Caldwell St.)
Juno Ent. Cen. SE14.........2F 93
Juno Ho. E3...................5C 52
................(off Garrison Rd.)
Juno Way SE14...............2F 93
Juno Way Ind. Est. SE14....2F 93
Jupiter Ct. E3.................1C 66
................(off Four Seasons Cl.)
Jupiter Ct. SW9...............3C 90
................(off Caldwell St.)
Jupiter Ho. E14...............1D 95
................(off St Davids Sq.)
Jupiter Ho. E16...............5B 68
................(off Turner St.)
Jupiter Way N7................3B 48
Jupp Rd. E15.................5F 53
Jupp Rd. W. E15..............5F 53
Jura Ho. SE16.................5A 79
................(off Plough Way)
Jurston Ct. SE1......4C 24 (3C 76)
................(off Gerridge St.)
Justice Apts. E1...............5F 65
................(off Aylward St.)
Justice Wlk. SW3.............2A 88
Justines Pl. E2.................2F 65
Jutland Cl. N19................3A 34
Jutland Ho. SE18.............5F 83
................(off Prospect Va.)
Jutland Ho. SE5...............5E 91
Jutland Rd. E13...............3C 68
Jutland Rd. SE6.............5E 109
Juxon Ho. EC4.......3E 17 (5D 63)
................(off St Paul's Chyd.)
Juxon St. SE11................5B 76
JVC Bus. Pk. NW2............3C 28

K

KALEIDOSCOPE.............4D 109
Kaleidoscope Ho. E20.......2E 53
................(off Mirabelle Gdns.)
Kambala Rd. SW11..........1F 101
Kamen Ho. SE1......2D 27 (2A 78)
................(off Magdalen St.)
Kane Ct. SE10.................5C 82
................(off Peartree Way)
Kangley Bri. Rd. SE26.......5B 122
Kangley Bus. Cen. SE26 ...5B 122
Kanli M. SE6..................3D 123
Kapuvar Cl. SE15............5C 92

Karachi Ho. E15 .... 3A 54
 .... (off Well St.)
Kara Way NW2 .... 1F 43
Karen Ter. E11 .... 4B 40
Karner Ho. E20 .... 2D 53
 .... (off Logan Cl.)
Kashmir Rd. SE7 .... 3F 97
Kassala Rd. SW11 .... 4B 88
Katherine Bell Twr. E3 ...... 1C 66
 .... (off Pancras Way)
Katherine Cl. N4 .... 2E 35
Katherine Cl. SE16 .... 2F 79
Katherine Cl. SE23 .... 1D 121
Katherine Gdns. SE9 .... 2F 111
Katherine Ho. W10 .... 3A 58
 .... (off Portobello Rd.)
Katherine Rd. E6 .... 4F 55
Katherine Rd. E7 .... 2E 55
Katherine Sq. W11 .... 2A 72
Kathleen Godfree Ct. SW195C 114
Kathleen Rd. SW11 .... 1B 102
Katial Ho. EC1 ....1E 9 (2D 63)
 .... (off Goswell Road)
Kayani Av. N4 .... 3E 35
Kayani Ho. E16 .... 5D 69
 .... (off Burrard St.)
Kay Rd. SW9 .... 5A 90
Kay St. E15 .... 4F 53
 .... (off New Mount St.)
Kay St. E2 .... 1C 64
Kean Ho. SE17 .... 2D 91
Kean St. WC2 ....3F 15 (5B 62)
Keats Apts. E1 .... 3B 66
 .... (off Wraxall Rd.)
Keats Av. E16 .... 2D 83
Keats Cl. NW3 .... 1A 46
Keats Cl. SE1 .... 5B 78
Keats Cl. SE7 .... 3E 97
Keats Cl. SW19 .... 5F 115
Keats Est. N16 .... 4B 36
 .... (off Kyverdale Rd.)
Keats Gro. NW3 .... 1A 46
Keats Ho. E2 .... 2E 65
 .... (off Roman Rd.)
Keats Ho. SE5 .... 3E 91
 .... (off Elmington St.)
Keats Ho. SW1 .... 2E 89
 .... (off Churchill Gdns.)
Keats House 1A 46
Keats Pl. EC2 ....1B 18 (4F 63)
 .... (off Moorfields)
Keats Rd. E10 .... 2D 39
Kebbell Ter. E7 .... 2D 55
 .... (off Claremont Rd.)
Keble Pl. SW13 .... 2D 85
Keble St. SW17 .... 4E 115
Kedge Ho. E14 .... 4C 80
 .... (off Tiller Rd.)
Kedleston Wlk. E2 .... 2D 65
Keedonwood Rd.
 BR1: Broml 5A 124
Keel Cl. SE16 .... 2F 79
Keel Ct. E14 .... 1F 81
 .... (off Newport Av.)
Keeley St. WC2 ....3F 15 (5B 62)
Keeling Ho. E2 .... 1D 65
 .... (off Claredale St.)
Keeling Rd. SE9 .... 3F 111
Keelson Ho. E14 .... 4C 80
 .... (off Mellish St.)
Keens Cl. SW16 .... 5F 117
Keen's Yd. N1 .... 3D 49
Keep, The SE3 .... 5C 96
Keepier Wharf E14 .... 1F 79
 .... (off Narrow St.)

Keeton's Rd. SE16 .... 4D 79
 .... (not continuous)
Keevil Dr. SW19 .... 5F 99
Keibs Way SE17 .... 1A 92
Keighley Cl. N7 .... 2A 48
Keildon Rd. SW11 .... 2B 102
Keir, The SW19 .... 5E 113
Keir Hardie Est. E5 .... 5D 37
Keir Hardie Ho. N19 .... 2F 33
Keir Hardie Ho. NW10 .... 4B 42
Keir Hardie Ho. W6 .... 2F 85
 .... (off Fulham Pal. Rd.)
Keirin Rd. E20 .... 2D 53
Keith Connor Cl. SW8 .... 1D 103
Keith Gro. W12 .... 3C 70
Keith Ho. NW6 .... 1C 58
 .... (off Carlton Vale)
Keith Ho. SW8 .... 3A 90
 .... (off Wheatsheaf La.)
Kelbrook Rd. SE3 .... 5F 97
Kelby Ho. N7 .... 3B 48
 .... (off Sutterton St.)
Kelceda Cl. NW2 .... 4C 28
Kelday Hgts. E1 .... 5D 65
 .... (off Spencer Way)
Kelfield Ct. W10 .... 5F 57
Kelfield Gdns. W10 .... 5E 57
Kelfield M. W10 .... 5F 57
Kelland Rd. E13 .... 3C 68
Kellaway Rd. SE3 .... 5F 97
Keller Cres. E12 .... 1F 55
Kellerton Rd. SE13 .... 3A 110
Kellet Ho's. WC1 ....2E 7 (2A 62)
 .... (off Tankerton St.)
Kellett Ho. N1 .... 5A 50
 .... (off Colville St.)
Kellett Rd. SW2 .... 2C 104
Kellino St. SW17 .... 4B 116
Kellow Ho. SE1 ....3B 26 (3F 77)
 .... (off Tennis St.)
Kell St. SE1 ....5E 25 (4D 77)
Kelly Av. SE15 .... 3B 92
Kelly Cl. NW10 .... 5A 28
Kelly Ct. E14 .... 1C 80
 .... (off Garford St.)
Kelly M. W9 .... 3B 58
Kelly St. NW1 .... 3D 47
Kelman Cl. SW4 .... 5F 89
Kelmore Gro. SE22 .... 2C 106
Kelmscott Gdns. W12 .... 4C 70
Kelmscott House 1D 85
Kelmscott Rd. SW11 .... 3A 102
Kelross Pas. N5 .... 1E 49
Kelross Rd. N5 .... 1E 49
Kelsall Cl. SE3 .... 5D 97
Kelsey St. E2 .... 3C 64
Kelson Ho. E14 .... 4E 81
Kelson Ho. E16 .... 3D 83
Kelso Pl. W8 .... 4D 73
Kelvedon Ho. SW8 .... 4A 90
Kelvedon Rd. SW6 .... 3B 86
Kelvin Cl. W11 .... 1C 72
 .... (off Kensington Pk. Rd.)
Kelvin Gro. SE26 .... 3D 121
Kelvington Rd. SE15 .... 3F 107
Kelvin Ho. SE26 .... 4B 122
 .... (off Worsley Bri. Rd.)
Kelvin Rd. N5 .... 1E 49
Kelway Ho. W14 .... 1B 86
Kember St. N1 .... 4B 48
Kemble Ho. SW9 .... 1D 105
 .... (off Barrington Rd.)
Kemble Rd. SE23 .... 1F 121
Kemble St. WC2 ....3F 15 (5B 62)
Kemerton Rd. SE5 .... 1E 105

Kemey's St. E9 .... 2A 52
Kemp Ct. SW8 .... 3A 90
 .... (off Hartington Rd.)
Kempe Ho. SE1 .... 4F 77
 .... (off Burbage Cl.)
Kempe Rd. NW6 .... 1F 57
Kemp Ho. E2 .... 1F 65
 .... (off Sewardstone Rd.)
Kemp Ho. W1 ....4B 14 (1F 75)
 .... (off Berwick St.)
Kempis Way SE22 .... 3A 106
Kemplay Rd. NW3 .... 1F 45
Kemps Ct. W1 ....3A 14 (5F 61)
 .... (off Hopkins St.)
Kemps Dr. E14 .... 1C 80
Kempsford Gdns. SW5 ...... 1C 86
Kempsford Rd. SE11 .... 5C 76
 .... (not continuous)
Kemps Gdns. SE13 .... 3E 109
Kempson Rd. SW6 .... 4C 86
Kempthorne Rd. SE8 .... 5B 80
Kempton Ct. E1 .... 4D 65
Kempton Ho. N1 .... 5A 50
 .... (off Hoxton St.)
Kemsing Ho. SE1 ....4C 26 (3F 77)
 .... (off Long La.)
Kemsing Rd. SE10 .... 1C 96
Kemsley SE13 .... 3D 109
Kenbrook Ho. NW5 .... 2E 47
Kenbrook Ho. W14 .... 4B 72
Kenbury Gdns. SE5 .... 5E 91
Kenbury Mans. SE5 .... 5E 91
 .... (off Kenbury St.)
Kenbury St. SE5 .... 5E 91
Kenchester Cl. SW8 .... 3A 90
Kendal NW1 ....1E 5 (2D 61)
 .... (off Augustus St.)
Kendal Cl. SW9 .... 3D 91
Kendale Rd. BR1: Broml 5A 124
Kendal Ho. E9 .... 5E 51
Kendal Ho. N1 .... 1B 62
 .... (off Priory Grn. Est.)
Kendall Ho. W14 .... 5B 72
 .... (off Warwick La.)
Kendall Pl. W1 ....1B 12 (4C 60)
Kendall Pl. SW15 .... 3B 100
Kendal Rd. NW10 .... 1C 42
Kendal Steps W2 .... 5A 60
 .... (off St George's Flds.)
Kendal St. W2 .... 5A 60
Kender Est. SE14 .... 4E 93
 .... (off Queen's Rd.)
Kender St. SE14 .... 3E 93
Kendoa Rd. SW4 .... 2F 103
Kendon Cl. E11 .... 1D 41
Kendon Ho. E15 .... 4F 53
 .... (off Bryant St.)
Kendrick Ct. SE15 .... 4D 93
 .... (off Colmore M.)
Kendrick M. SW7 .... 5F 73
Kendrick Pl. SW7 .... 5F 73
KEN FRIAR BRI. 1C 48
Keniford Rd. SW12 .... 5D 103
Kenilworth Av. SW19 .... 5C 114
Kenilworth Ct. SW15 .... 1A 100
 .... (off Lwr. Richmond Rd.)
Kenilworth Rd. E3 .... 1A 66
Kenilworth Rd. NW6 .... 5B 44
Kenley Wlk. W11 .... 1A 72
Kenlor Rd. SW17 .... 5F 115
Kenmont Gdns. NW10........ 2D 57
 .... (not continuous)
Kenmore Ct. NW6 .... 4D 45
 .... (off Acol Rd.)
Kenmure Rd. E8 .... 2D 51

Kenmure Yd. E8 .... 2D 51
Kennacraig Cl. E16 .... 2C 82
Kennard Ho. SW11 .... 5C 88
Kennard Rd. E15 .... 4F 53
Kennard St. SW11 .... 4C 88
Kennedy Cl. E13 .... 1C 68
Kennedy Cox Ho. E16 .... 4B 68
.... (off Burke St.)
Kennedy Ho. SE11 .... 1B 90
.... (off Vauxhall Wlk.)
Kennedy Wlk. SE17 ....5F 77
.... (off Elsted St.)
Kennet Cl. SW11 .... 2F 101
Kennet Ct. W9 .... 4C 58
.... (off Elmfield Way)
Kenneth Campbell Ho.
NW8 .... 3F 59
.... (off Orchardson St.)
Kenneth Ct. SE11 .... 5C 76
Kenneth Cres. NW2 .... 2D 43
Kennet Ho. NW8 .... 3F 59
.... (off Church St.)
Kennet Ho. SW18 .... 2C 100
.... (off Enterprise Way)
Kenneth Younger Ho.
SW6 .... 2B 86
.... (off Clem Attlee Ct.)
Kennet Rd. W9 .... 3B 58
Kennet St. E1 .... 2C 78
Kennett Wharf La.
EC4 .... 4A 18 (1E 77)
Kenninghall Rd. E5 .... 5C 36
Kenning Ho. N1 .... 5A 50
.... (off Colville St.)
Kenning St. SE16 .... 3E 79
Kennings Way SE11 .... 1C 90
Kenning Ter. N1 .... 5A 50
KENNINGTON 2C 90
Kennington Grn. SE11 .... 1C 90
Kennington La. SE11 .... 1B 90
Kennington Oval SE11 .... 2B 90
KENNINGTON OVAL 2C 90
Kennington Pal. Ct. SE11 ...... 1C 90
.... (off Sancroft St.)
Kennington Pk. Gdns.
SE11 .... 2D 91
Kennington Pk. Ho. SE11 ...... 1C 90
.... (off Kennington Pk. Pl.)
Kennington Pk. Pl. SE11 .... 2C 90
Kennington Pk. Rd. SE11 ...... 2C 90
Kennington Rd.
SE1 .... 5B 24 (4C 76)
Kennington Rd.
SE11 .... 5B 24 (4C 76)
Kennington Station
(Underground) 1D 91
Kennistoun Ho. NW5 ....2E 47
Kennoldes SE21 .... 2F 119
.... (off Croxted Rd.)
Kennyland Ct. NW4 .... 1D 29
.... (off Hendon Way)
Kenrick Pl. W1 ....1B 12 (4C 60)
KENSAL GREEN 2E 57
Kensal Green Station
(Underground & Overground)
....2E 57
Kensal Ho. W10 ....3F 57
.... (off Ladbroke Gro.)
KENSAL RISE 1F 57
Kensal Rise Station (Overground)
.... 1F 57
Kensal Rd. W10 .... 3A 58
KENSAL TOWN 3A 58
Kensal Wharf W10 ....3F 57
KENSINGTON 4C 72

Kensington Arc. W8 .... 3D 73
.... (off Kensington High St.)
Kensington Bus. Cen. SW3 ....4A 74
.... (off Brompton Rd.)
Kensington Cen. W14 .... 5A 72
.... (not continuous)
Kensington Chu. Ct. W8 .... 3D 73
Kensington Chu. St. W8 .... 2C 72
Kensington Chu. Wlk. W8 ..... 3D 73
.... (not continuous)
Kensington Ct. SE16 .... 2F 79
.... (off King & Queen Wharf)
Kensington Ct. W8 .... 3D 73
Kensington Ct. Gdns. W8 ..... 4D 73
.... (off Kensington Ct. Pl.)
Kensington Ct. Mans. W8 ..... 3D 73
.... (off Kensington Ct. Pl.)
Kensington Ct. M. W8 .... 4D 73
.... (off Kensington Ct. Pl.)
Kensington Ct. Pl. W8 .... 4D 73
Kensington Gdns. 2E 73
Kensington Gdns. Sq. W2 .....5D 59
Kensington Ga. W8 ....4E 73
Kensington Gore SW7 ....3E 73
Kensington Hall Gdns. W14 ..1B 86
Kensington Hgts. W8 .... 2C 72
Kensington High St. W14 ...... 4B 72
Kensington High St. W8 .... 4B 72
Kensington Ho. SW11 .... 3D 89
.... (off Palmer Rd.)
Kensington Ho. W14 .... 3F 71
Kensington Ho. W8 .... 3D 73
.... (off Kensington Ct.)
Kensington Leisure Cen. 1A 72
Kensington Mall W8 .... 2C 72
Kensington Mans. SW5 .... 1C 86
.... (off Trebovir Rd.)
Kensington Memorial Pk. 4F 57
.... (off St Mark's Road)
Kensington Olympia Station
(Rail, Underground &
Overground) 4A 72
Kensington Palace 2D 73
Kensington Pal. Gdns. W8 ....2D 73
Kensington Pk. Gdns. W11 ...1B 72
Kensington Pk. M. W11 ....5B 58
Kensington Pk. Rd. W11 ....5B 58
Kensington Path E10 .... 4D 39
.... (off Osborne Rd.)
Kensington Pl. W8 .... 2C 72
Kensington Rd. SW7 ....3E 73
Kensington Rd. W8 .... 3D 73
Kensington Sq. W8 .... 4D 73
Kensington Village W14 .... 5B 72
Kensington W. W14 .... 5A 72
Kensworth Ho. EC1 ..... 2C 10 (2F 63)
.... (off Cranwood St.)
Kent Bldg. E14 .... 5A 68
Kent Ct. E2 .... 1B 64
Kent Ho. SE1 .... 1B 92
Kent Ho. SW1 ....1F 89
.... (off Aylesford St.)
Kent Ho. W11 .... 2B 72
.... (off Boyne Ter. M.)
Kent Ho. W4 .... 1A 84
.... (off Devonshire St.)
Kent Ho. W8 .... 3D 73
.... (off Kensington Ct.)
Kent Ho. La. BR3: Beck 5A 122
Kent Ho. Rd. SE26 .... 5A 122
Kentish Bldgs. SE1 ..... 2B 26 (3F 77)
KENTISH TOWN 2D 47
Kentish Town Ind. Est. NW5 ..2D 47
Kentish Town Rd. NW1 .... 4D 47
Kentish Town Rd. NW5 .... 3D 47

Kentish Town Sports Cen.
.... 3D 47
Kentish Town Station (Rail &
Underground) 2E 47
Kentish Town West Station
(Overground) 2E 47
Kentmere Ho. SE15 ....2E 93
Kenton Ct. SE26 .... 4A 122
.... (off Adamsrill Rd.)
Kenton Ct. W14 .... 4B 72
Kenton Ho. E1 .... 3E 65
.... (off Mantus Cl.)
Kenton Rd. E9 ....3F 51
Kenton St. WC1 ....3D 7 (3A 62)
Kent Pk. Ind. Est. SE15 .... 2D 93
Kent Pas. NW1 .... 3B 60
Kent St. E13 ....2E 69
Kent St. E2 .... 1B 64
Kent Ter. NW1 .... 2A 60
Kent Wlk. SW9 .... 2D 105
Kentwell Cl. SE4 .... 2A 108
Kent Wharf SE8 .... 3D 95
.... (off Creekside)
Kentwode Grn. SW13 .... 3C 84
Kent Yd. SW7 .... 3A 74
Kenward Rd. SE9 ....3E 111
Kenward Way SW11 .... 5C 88
Kenway Rd. SW5 .... 5D 73
Ken Wilson Ho. E2 .... 1C 64
.... (off Pritchards St.)
Kenwood Cl. NW3 .... 3F 31
Kenwood House 3A 32
Kenwood Pl. N6 .... 3B 32
Kenwood Rd. N6 .... 1B 32
Kenworthy Rd. E9 .... 2A 52
Kenwrick Ho. N1 .... 5B 48
.... (off Barnsbury Est.)
Kenwyn Dr. NW2 .... 4A 28
Kenwyn Rd. SW4 ....2F 103
Kenya Rd. SE7 ....3F 97
Kenyon Ho. SE5 ....3E 91
.... (off Camberwell Rd.)
Kenyon Mans. W14 .... 2A 86
.... (off Queen's Club Gdns.)
Kenyon St. SW6 ....4F 85
Keogh Rd. E15 .... 3A 54
Kepler Ho. SE10 .... 1B 96
.... (off Armitage Rd.)
Kepler Rd. SW4 .... 2A 104
Keppel Ho. SE8 .... 1B 94
Keppel Ho. SW3 .... 5A 74
.... (off Elystan St.)
Keppel Row SE1 .... 2F 25 (2E 77)
Keppel St. WC1 .... 5C 6 (4F 61)
Kerbela St. E2 .... 3C 64
Kerbey St. E14 .... 5D 67
Kerfield Cres. SE5 ....4F 91
Kerfield Pl. SE5 ....4F 91
Kerridge Ct. N1 .... 3A 50
.... (off Balls Pond Rd.)
Kerrier Ho. SW10 ....3E 87
.... (off Stadium St.)
Kerrington Ct. W10 .... 3A 58
.... (off Wornington Rd.)
Kerrington Ct. W12 ....3E 71
.... (off Uxbridge Rd.)
Kerris Ho. SE11 .... 1C 90
.... (off Tavy Cl.)
Kerrison Rd. E15 .... 5F 53
Kerrison Rd. SW11 .... 1A 102
Kerry Cl. E16 ....5D 69
Kerry Ho. E1 .... 5E 65
.... (off Sidney St.)
Kerry Path SE14 .... 2B 94
Kerry Rd. SE14 .... 2B 94

Kerscott Ho. E3 .... 2D 67
Kersey Gdns. SE9............4F 125
Kersfield Ho. SW15..........4F 99
Kersfield Rd. SW15..........4F 99
Kershaw Cl. SW18............4F 101
Kersley M. SW11 .... 4B 88
Kersley Ho. N16 .... 4A 36
Kersley St. SW11 .... 5B 88
Kerswell Cl. N15 .... 1A 36
Kerwick Cl. N7 .... 4A 48
Keslake Mans. NW10.......1F 57
..................................(off Station Ter.)
Keslake Rd. NW6 .... 1F 57
.............................(off Kinglake Est.)
Keston Ho. SE17.............. 1A 92
Keston Rd. SE15 .... 1C 106
Kestrel Av. E6................... 4F 69
Kestrel Av. SE24 .... 3D 105
Kestrel Ct. E3 .... 1C 66
...............................(off Four Seasons Cl.)
Kestrel Ct. EC1 ...... 1F 9 (2E 63)
.................................(off Pickard St.)
Kestrel Ho. SE10 .... 4B 82
.............................(off Parkside Av.)
Kestrel Pl. SE14 .... 2A 94
Keswick Av. SW15..........5A 112
Keswick B'way. SW15.......3B 100
.....................(off Up. Richmond Rd.)
Keswick Ct. SE13...........3D 109
Keswick Ct. SE6............ 1B 124
Keswick Ho. SE5.............. 5E 91
Keswick Rd. SW15 ....3A 100
Kett Gdns. SW2 .... 3B 104
Kettlebaston Rd. E10 .... 3B 38
Kettleby Ho. SW9 ....1D 105
.............................(off Barrington Rd.)
Ketton Ho. W10 ....3E 57
.............................(off Sutton Way)
Kevan Ho. SE5.................3E 91
Kevtar Gdn. E3 .... 2B 66
Key Cl. E1 ....3E 65
Keyes Ho. SW1 ....1F 89
.............................(off Dolphin Sq.)
Keyes Rd. NW2.................2F 43
Keyham Ho. W2................4C 58
...........................(off Westbourne Pk. Rd.)
Key Ho. SE11 ....2C 90
Keymer Pl. E14 .... 5B 66
Keymer Rd. SW2 .... 2B 118
Keynsham Gdns. SE9........3F 111
Keynsham Rd. SE9............3F 111
Keyse Rd. SE1 .... 4B 78
Keystone Cres. N1 .. 1E 7 (1A 62)
Keyworth Cl. E5 .... 1A 52
Keyworth Pl. SE1 .. 5E 25 (4D 77)
.............................(off Keyworth St.)
Keyworth St. SE1 .. 5E 25 (4D 77)
Kezia M. SE8 .... 1A 94
Kezia St. SE8 .... 1A 94
Khama Rd. SW17 ....4A 116
Khartoum Rd. E13............2D 69
Khartoum Rd. SW17 ....4F 115
Khyber Rd. SW11 .... 5A 88
Kia, The Oval 2B 90
Kibworth St. SW8 .... 3B 90
KIDBROOKE 5D 97
Kidbrooke St. SE3 .... 1E 111
Kidbrooke Gdns. SE3........5C 96
Kidbrooke Green Nature Reserve
.................................1E 111
Kidbrooke Gro. SE3...........4C 96
Kidbrooke Pk. Cl. SE3....... 4D 97
Kidbrooke Pk. Rd. SE3...... 4D 97
Kidbrooke Station (Rail) 1D 111

Kidbrooke Way SE3 .... 5D 97
Kidderpore Av. NW3..........1C 44
Kidderpore Gdns. NW3 ...... 1C 44
Kiebs Way SE17 .... 1F 91
Kiffen St. EC2........... 3C 10 (3F 63)
Kilbrennan Ho. E14 ....5E 67
.............................(off Findhorn St.)
KILBURN.......................1B 58
Kilburn Bri. NW6 .... 5C 44
Kilburn Ga. NW6............... 1D 59
Kilburn High Rd. NW6 .... 4B 44
Kilburn High Road Station
(Overground) 5D 45
Kilburn Ho. NW6...............1B 58
.............................(off Malvern Pl.)
Kilburn La. W10 ....2F 57
Kilburn La. W9 .... 1A 58
Kilburn Library & Youth Cen.
.................................5D 45
Kilburn Pk. Rd. NW6 ....2C 58
Kilburn Park Station
(Underground) 1C 58
Kilburn Pl. NW6................5C 44
Kilburn Priory NW6 ....5D 45
Kilburn Sq. NW6...............5C 44
Kilburn Station (Underground)
.................................3B 44
Kilburn Va. NW6...............5D 45
Kilburn Va. Est. NW6.........5D 45
.............................(off Kilburn Vale)
Kilby Ct. SE10..................4B 82
.............................(off Greenroof Way)
Kildare Ct. W2..................5C 58
.............................(off Kildare Ter.)
Kildare Gdns. W2 ....5C 58
Kildare Rd. E16................4C 68
Kildare Ter. W2.................5C 58
Kildare Wlk. E14 ....5C 66
Kildoran Rd. SW2 ....3A 104
Kilgour Rd. SE23.............4A 108
Kilkie St. SW6 ....5E 87
Killarney Rd. SW18..........4E 101
Killearn Rd. SE6............. 1F 7 (1B 62)
Killick St. N1 .... 1F 7 (1B 62)
Killick Way E1 ....4F 65
Killieser Av. SW2 ....2A 118
Killip Cl. E16....................5B 68
Killoran Ho. E14 ....4E 81
.............................(off Galbraith St.)
Killowen Rd. E9 ....3F 51
Killyon Rd. SW8................5E 89
Killyon Ter. SW8...............5E 89
Kilmaine Rd. SW6 ....3A 86
Kilmarsh Rd. W6 ....5E 71
Kilmington Rd. SW13........2C 84
Kilmore Ho. E14 ....5D 67
.............................(off Vesey Path)
Kilmorie Rd. SE23 ....1A 122
Kilmuir Ho. SW1...............5C 74
.............................(off Bury St.)
Kiln Cinema 4B 44
Kiln Ct. E14 ....1B 80
.............................(off Newell St.)
Kilner Ho. E16...................4D 69
.............................(off Freemasons Rd.)
Kilner Ho. SE11 ....2C 90
.............................(off Clayton St.)
Kilner St. E14 ....4C 66
Kiln Ho. E1 ....4F 65
.............................(off Duckett St.)
Kiln M. SW17...................5F 115
Kiln Pl. NW5....................2C 46
Kiln Theatre 4B 44
Kilravock St. W10 ....2A 58
Kimbell Gdns. SW6 ....4A 86

Kimbell Pl. SE3.................2E 111
Kimber Ct. SE1 .... 5D 27 (4A 78)
.............................(off Long La.)
Kimberley Av. E6 ....1F 69
Kimberley Av. SE15 ....5D 93
Kimberley Ct. NW6............5A 44
.............................(off Kimberley Rd.)
Kimberley Gdns. N4...........1D 35
Kimberley Ho. E14 ....4E 81
.............................(off Galbraith St.)
Kimberley Rd. E11.............4F 39
Kimberley Rd. E16.............3B 68
Kimberley Rd. NW6...........5A 44
Kimberley Rd. SW9 ....5A 90
Kimber Rd. SW18..............5C 100
Kimble Ho. NW8 ....3A 60
.............................(off Lilestone St.)
Kimble Rd. SW19 ....5F 115
Kimbolton Cl. SE12...........4B 110
Kimbolton Ct. SW3............5A 74
.............................(off Fulham Rd.)
Kimbolton Row SW3 ....5A 74
.............................(off Fulham Rd.)
Kimmeridge Rd. SE9..........4F 125
Kimmins Ct. SE16..............4C 78
.............................(off Old Jamaica Rd.)
Kimpton Ho. SW15 ....5C 98
Kimpton Rd. SE5...............4F 91
Kinburn St. SE16...............3F 79
Kincaid Rd. SE15...............3D 93
Kincardine Gdns. W9 ....3C 58
.............................(off Harrow Rd.)
Kinder Ho. N1...................1F 63
.............................(off Cranston Est.)
Kindersley Ho. E1..............5C 64
.............................(off Pinchin St.)
Kinder St. E1 ....5D 65
Kinefold Ho. N7.................3A 48
.............................(off York Way Est.)
Kinfauns Rd. SW2..............2C 118
King Alfred Av. SE6............4C 122
.................................(not continuous)
King & Queen St. SE17 ......1E 91
King & Queen Wharf SE16...1F 79
King Arthur Cl. SE15 ....3E 93
KING CHARLES I ISLAND
................1D 23 (2A 76)
.............................(end of Whitehall)
King Charles Ct. SE17.........2D 91
.............................(off Royal Rd.)
King Charles Ho. SW6.........3D 87
.............................(off Wandon Rd.)
King Charles's Ct. SE10......2E 95
.............................(off Park Row)
King Charles St.
SW1 ....3C 22 (3F 75)
King Charles Ter. E1 ....1D 79
.............................(off Sovereign Cl.)
King Ct. E10 ....2D 39
King David La. E1 ....1E 79
Kingdom St. W2.................4E 58
Kingdon Ho. E14 ....4E 81
.............................(off Galbraith St.)
Kingdon Rd. NW6..............3C 44
King Edward Bldg.
EC1........................2E 17 (5D 63)
.............................(off King Edward St.)
King Edward Mans. E8 ....5D 51
.............................(off Mare St.)
King Edward M. SW13.........4C 84
King Edward Rd. E10..........3E 39
King Edwards Mans. SW6 ....3C 86
.............................(off Fulham Rd.)
King Edward's Rd. E9..........5D 51

King Edward St.
EC1..................2F **17** (5E **63**)
King Edward the Third M.
SE16........................3D **79**
KING EDWARD VII'S HOSPITAL SISTER AGNES....5C **4** (4C **60**)
King Edward Wlk.
SE1........................5C **24** (4C **76**)
Kingfield St. E14................5E **81**
Kingfisher Av. E11............1D **41**
Kingfisher Ct. E14.............3E **81**
.....................(off River Barge Cl.)
Kingfisher Ct. SE16....2A **26** (3E **77**)
.........................(off Swan St.)
Kingfisher Ct. SW19.........2F **113**
Kingfisher Hgts. E16.......2E **83**
....................(off Bramwell Way)
Kingfisher Ho. SW18.......1E **101**
Kingfisher Ho. W14...........4B **72**
........................(off Melbury Rd.)
Kingfisher M. SE13..........2D **109**
Kingfisher Sq. SE8.........2B **94**
..........................(off Clyde St.)
King Frederick IX Twr.
SE16........................4B **80**
King George IV Ct. SE17......1F **91**
.........................(off Dawes St.)
King George VI Memorial
.........................2B **22** (2F **75**)
King George Av. E16...........5E **69**
King George M. SW17.........5B **116**
King George's Fld.............4E **79**
........................(off Lower Road)
King George St. SE10.......3E **95**
Kingham Cl. SW18.........5E **101**
Kingham Cl. W11.............3A **72**
King Henry's Reach W6.......2E **85**
King Henry's Rd. NW3.......4A **46**
King Henry's Stairs E1......2D **79**
King Henry St. N16............2A **50**
King Henry's Wlk. N1.........3A **50**
King Henry Ter. E1...........1D **79**
.......................(off Sovereign Cl.)
Kinghorn St. EC1.....1F **17** (4E **63**)
King Ho. W12......................5D **57**
Kingisholt Ct. NW10...........2F **57**
......................(off Wellington Rd.)
King James Ct. SE1..4E **25** (3D **77**)
...........................(off King James St.)
King James St. SE1..4E **25** (3D **77**)
King John Ct. EC2....3E **11** (3A **64**)
King John St. E1................4F **65**
King John's Wlk. SE9.......5F **111**
Kinglake Est. SE17...........1A **92**
Kinglake St. SE17............1A **92**
.........................(not continuous)
Kinglet Cl. E7..................3C **54**
Kingly Ct. W1.........4A **14** (1E **75**)
.........................(off Beak St.)
Kingly St. W1........3F **13** (5E **61**)
Kingsand Rd. SE12.........2C **124**
Kings Arms Ct. E1............4C **64**
King's Arms Yd. SW18.....3D **101**
Kings Arms Yd. EC2..2B **18** (5F **63**)
Kings Av. SW12...............1F **117**
Kings Av. SW4...............5F **103**
King's Bench St.
SE1........................3E **25** (3D **77**)
King's Bench Wlk.
EC4........................3C **16** (5C **62**)
King's Blvd. N1.......1D **7** (1A **62**)
.......................(off Dockers Tanner Rd.)
Kingsbridge Ct. E14..........4C **80**
.......................(off Dockers Tanner Rd.)
Kingsbridge Rd. NW1......4D **47**
.......................(off Castlehaven Rd.)

Kingsbridge Rd. W10.........5E **57**
Kingsbury Rd. N1..............3A **50**
Kingsbury Ter. N1.............3A **50**
Kingsclere Ct. SW15.......5C **98**
Kingscliffe Gdns. SW19....1B **114**
Kings Cl. E10....................2D **39**
Kings Coll. Ct. NW3........4A **46**
KING'S COLLEGE DENTAL INSTITUTE.................5F **91**
KING'S COLLEGE HOSPITAL.5F **91**
King's College London
Denmark Hill Campus....5F **91**
King's College London
Guy's Campus....2B **26** (2F **77**)
.......................(within Guy's Hospital)
King's College London
Institute of Psychiatry, De
Crespigny Park..............5F **91**
King's College London
Maughan Library...2B **16** (5C **62**)
King's College London
St Thomas' Campus -
Lambeth Pal. Rd.....5E **23** (4B **76**)
.......................(off Lambeth Pal. Rd.)
King's College London
St Thomas' Campus - St Thomas'
House......................5F **23** (4B **76**)
King's College London
Strand Campus....4A **16** (1B **76**)
King's College London
Waterloo Campus...2B **24** (2C **76**)
King's Coll. Rd. NW3.......4A **46**
King's College School of Medicine & Dentistry......5E **91**
Kingscote St. EC4....4D **17** (1D **77**)
Kings Ct. E13...................5D **55**
Kings Ct. SE1.......3E **25** (3D **77**)
Kings Ct. N7....................4B **48**
.......................(off Caledonian Rd.)
Kings Ct. NW8.................5B **46**
.......................(off Prince Albert Rd.)
Kings Ct. W6....................5C **70**
Kings Ct. Mans. SW6........4B **86**
.......................(off Fulham Rd.)
Kings Ct. Nth. SW3..........1A **88**
Kingscourt Rd. SW16.......3F **117**
Kings Ct. Sth. SW3..........1A **88**
.......................(off Chelsea Mnr. Gdns.)
King's Cres. N4................5E **35**
Kings Cres. Est. N4..........4E **35**
Kingscroft SW4..............4A **104**
Kingscroft Rd. NW2.........3B **44**
KING'S CROSS................1A **62**
King's Cross Bri. N1.....1E **7** (2A **62**)
.......................(off Gray's Inn Rd.)
King's Cross Rd. WC1...1E **7** (2B **62**)
King's Cross St Pancras Station
(Underground)......1D **7** (2A **62**)
.......................(off Euston Rd.)
King's Cross Station (Rail & Underground)......1C **6** (1A **62**)
Kingsdale Gdns. W11......2F **71**
Kingsdown Av. W3...........1A **70**
Kingsdown Cl. SE16........1D **93**
.......................(off Masters Dr.)
Kingsdown Cl. W10.........5F **57**
Kingsdown Ho. E8...........2C **50**
Kingsdown Point SW2....2C **118**
Kingsdown Rd. E11.........5A **40**
Kingsdown Rd. N19........4A **34**
Kingsfield Ho. SE9..........3F **125**
Kingsford St. NW5.........2B **46**
King's Gdns. NW6............4C **44**

Kings Gth. M. SE23........2E **121**
Kingsgate Est. N1.............3A **50**
Kingsgate Ho. SW9..........4C **90**
Kingsgate Mans.
WC1......................1F **15** (4B **62**)
.......................(off Red Lion Sq.)
Kingsgate Pde. SW1.5A **22** (4E **75**)
.......................(off Victoria St.)
Kingsgate Pl. NW6..........4C **44**
Kingsgate Rd. NW6.........4C **44**
Kings Ga. Wlk. SW1...5A **22** (4E **75**)
.......................(off Victoria St.)
Kingsground SE9............5F **111**
King's Gro. SE15.............3D **93**
.........................(not continuous)
Kings Hall Leisure Cen.......2E **51**
Kings Hall M. SE13.........1E **109**
Kings Head Pas. SW4......2F **103**
.......................(off Clapham Pk. Rd.)
Kings Head Theatre..........5D **49**
.........................(off Upper St.)
King's Head Yd.
SE1........................2B **26** (2F **77**)
Kingshold Rd. E9..............4E **51**
Kingsholm Gdns. SE9......2F **111**
King's Ho. SW10................2F **87**
.........................(off King's Rd.)
Kings Ho. SW8.................3A **90**
.......................(off Sth. Lambeth Rd.)
King's Ho. Studios SW10....2F **87**
.......................(off Lamont Rd. Pas.)
Kingshurst Rd. SE12.......5C **110**
Kings Keep SW15.............3F **99**
KINGSLAND.....................3A **50**
Kingsland NW8................5A **46**
Kingsland Basin...............5A **50**
Kingsland Grn. E8............3A **50**
Kingsland High St. E8......3B **50**
Kingsland Pas. E8............3A **50**
Kingsland Rd. E13..........2E **69**
Kingsland Rd. E2....1E **11** (2A **64**)
Kingsland Rd. E8............5A **50**
Kingslawn Cl. SW15........5D **99**
Kingsley Cl. NW2.............3D **43**
Kingsley Flats SE1...........5A **78**
.......................(off Old Kent Rd.)
Kingsley Ho. SW3............2F **87**
.........................(off Beaufort St.)
Kingsley Ho. W14............5A **72**
.......................(off Avonmore Pl.)
Kingsley Mans. W14.......2A **86**
.......................(off Greyhound Rd.)
Kingsley M. E1................1D **79**
Kingsley M. W8................4D **73**
Kingsley Pl. N6................2C **32**
Kingsley Rd. E7...............4C **54**
Kingsley Rd. SW19.........5D **115**
Kingsley St. SW11.........1B **102**
Kings Mall W6.................5E **71**
Kings Mans. SW3.............2A **88**
.......................(off Lawrence St.)
Kingsmead Ct. N6............2F **33**
Kingsmead Ho. E9...........1A **52**
Kingsmead Rd. SW2......2C **118**
Kingsmead Way E9..........1A **52**
Kingsmere Cl. SW15........1F **99**
Kingsmere Pl. N16...........3F **35**
Kingsmere Rd. SW19......2F **113**
King's M. SW4.................3A **104**
King's M. WC1..........4A **8** (3B **62**)
Kingsmill NW8..................1F **59**
.......................(off Kingsmill Ter.)
Kingsmill Ho. SW3...........1A **88**
.........................(off Cale St.)

Kingsmill Ter. NW8 .... 1F 59
Kingsnorth Ho. W10 .... 5F 57
Kings Pde. NW10 .... 5E 43
Kings Pde. W12 .... 4C 70
Kings Pas. E11 .... 2A 40
King's Pl. SE1 .... 4A 26 (3E 77)
Kings Place 1A 62
King Sq. EC1 .... 2F 9 (2E 63)
Kings Quarter Apts. N1 .... 5B 48
.... (off Copenhagen St.)
King's Quay SW10 .... 4E 87
.... (off Chelsea Harbour Dr.)
Kings Reach Twr.
SE1 .... 1C 24 (2C 76)
.... (off Stamford St.)
Kingsridge SW19 .... 2A 114
King's Rd. E6 .... 5E 55
King's Rd. SW10 .... 3E 87
King's Rd. SW3 .... 2F 87
King's Rd. SW6 .... 3D 87
Kings Rd. E11 .... 2A 40
Kings Rd. NW10 .... 4D 43
Kings Rd. SW14 .... 1A 98
King's Scholars' Pas. SW1 .. 4E 75
.... (off Carlisle Pl.)
King Stairs Cl. SE16 .... 3D 79
King's Ter. NW1 .... 5E 47
Kingsthorpe Rd. SE26 .... 4F 121
Kingston Ho. NW1 .... 5E 47
.... (off Camden St.)
Kingston Ho. NW6 .... 4A 44
Kingston Ho. E. SW7 .... 3A 74
.... (off Prince's Ga.)
Kingston Ho. Nth. SW7 .... 3A 74
.... (off Prince's Ga.)
Kingston Ho. Sth. SW7 .... 3A 74
.... (off Ennismore Gdns.)
Kingston Mans. SW9 .... 4B 90
.... (off Clapham Rd.)
Kingston Rd. SW19: Lon
Norstead Pl. 1D 113
Kingston Rd. SW15 .... 2C 112
Kingston Sq. SE19 .... 5F 119
Kingston University
Roehampton Vale Cen. 3B 112
KINGSTON VALE 4A 112
Kingstown St. NW1 .... 5C 46
.... (not continuous)
King St. E13 .... 3C 68
King St. EC2 .... 2A 18 (5E 63)
King St. SW1 .... 2A 22 (2E 75)
King St. W6 .... 5C 70
King St. WC2 .... 4D 15 (1A 76)
King St. Cloisters W6 .... 5D 71
.... (off King St.)
Kingswater Pl. SW11 .... 3A 88
Kingsway WC2 .... 2F 15 (5B 62)
Kingsway Mans.
WC1 .... 5F 7 (4B 62)
.... (off Red Lion Sq.)
Kingsway Pde. N16 .... 5F 35
.... (off Albion Rd.)
Kingsway Pl. EC1 .... 3C 8 (3C 62)
.... (off Sans Wlk.)
Kingswear Rd. NW5 .... 5D 33
King's Wharf SE10 .... 2D 95
.... (off Wood Wharf)
Kings Wharf E8 .... 5A 50
.... (off Kingsland Rd.)
Kingswood E2 .... 1E 65
.... (off Cyprus St.)
Kingswood Av. NW6 .... 5A 44
Kingswood Cl. SW8 .... 3A 90
Kingswood Cl. NW6 .... 4C 44
.... (off West End La.)

Kingswood Ct. SE13 .... 4F 109
Kingswood Dr. SE19 .... 4A 120
Kingswood Est. SE21 .... 4A 120
Kingswood Library & Community
Cen. 4A 120
Kingswood Pl. SE13 .... 2A 110
Kingswood Rd. E11 .... 2A 40
Kingswood Rd. SW2 .... 4A 104
Kings Yd. SW15 .... 1E 99
.... (off Lwr. Richmond Rd.)
Kington Ho. NW6 .... 5D 45
.... (off Mortimer Cres.)
Kingward Ho. E1 .... 4C 64
.... (off Hanbury St.)
King Wardrobe Apts.
EC4 .... 3E 17 (5D 63)
.... (off Carter La.)
Kingweston Cl. NW2 .... 5A 30
King William La. SE10 .... 1A 96
King William's Ct. SE10 .... 2F 95
.... (off Park Row)
King William St. EC4 .. 3C 18 (5F 63)
King William Wlk. SE10 .... 2E 95
.... (not continuous)
Kingwood Gdns. E1 .... 5C 64
.... (off Piazza Wlk.)
Kingwood Rd. SW6 .... 4A 86
Kinloch Dr. NW9 .... 2A 28
Kinloch St. N7 .... 5B 34
Kinnaird Av. BR1: Brom1... 5B 124
Kinnaird Ho. SE17 .... 5F 77
Kinnear Rd. W12 .... 3B 70
Kinnerton Pl. Nth.
SW1 .... 4A 20 (3B 74)
.... (off Kinnerton St.)
Kinnerton Pl. Sth.
SW1 .... 4A 20 (3B 74)
.... (off Kinnerton St.)
Kinnerton St. SW1 .. 4B 20 (3C 74)
Kinnerton Yd. SW1 .. 4A 20 (3C 74)
.... (off Kinnerton St.)
Kinnoul Rd. W6 .... 2A 86
Kino Bermondsey 5E 27 (4A 78)
.... (off Bermondsey Sq.)
Kinross Cl. SE6 .... 1B 124
Kinross Ho. N1 .... 5B 48
.... (off Bemerton Est.)
Kinsale Rd. SE15 .... 1C 106
Kinsella Gdns. SW19 .... 5D 113
Kinsham Ho. E2 .... 3C 64
.... (off Ramsey St.)
Kintore Way SE1 .... 5B 78
Kintyre Ct. SW2 .... 5A 104
Kintyre Ho. E14 .... 2E 81
.... (off Coldharbour)
Kinveachy Gdns. SE7 .... 1F 97
Kipling Dr. SW19 .... 5F 115
Kipling Est. SE1 .... 4C 26 (3F 77)
Kipling Ho. N19 .... 3A 34
.... (off Charles St.)
Kipling Ho. SE5 .... 3E 91
.... (off Elmington Est.)
Kipling St. SE1 .... 4C 26 (3F 77)
Kippington Dr. SE9 .... 1F 125
Kira Bldg. E3 .... 2B 66
Kiran Apts. E1 .... 4B 64
.... (off Chicksand St.)
Kirby Est. SE16 .... 4D 79
Kirby Gro. SE1 .... 3D 27 (3A 78)
Kirby St. EC1 .... 5C 8 (4C 62)
Kirkby Apts. E3 .... 4B 66
.... (off St Paul's Way)
Kirkdale SE26 .... 2D 121

Kirkdale Cnr. SE26 .... 4E 121
Kirkdale Rd. E11 .... 3A 40
Kirkeby Ho. EC1 .... 5B 8 (4C 62)
.... (off Leather La.)
Kirkland Ter. E14: Lon
St Davids Sq. 1D 95
.... (off St Davids Sq.)
Kirkland Ho. E14: Lon
Westferry Rd. 1D 95
.... (off Westferry Rd.)
Kirkland Ter. BR3: Beck.... 5C 122
Kirkland Wlk. E8 .... 3B 50
Kirkman Pl. W1 .. 1B 14 (4F 61)
.... (off Tottenham Ct. Rd.)
Kirkmichael Rd. E14 .... 5E 67
Kirk Rd. E17 .... 1B 38
Kirkside Rd. SE3 .... 2C 96
Kirk's Place 4B 66
Kirkstall Gdns. SW2 .... 1A 118
Kirkstall Ho. SW1 .... 1D 89
.... (part of Abbots Mnr.)
Kirkstall Rd. SW2 .... 1F 117
Kirkstead Ct. E5 .... 1F 51
Kirkstone NW1 .... 1F 5 (2E 61)
.... (off Harrington St.)
Kirk St. WC1 .... 4A 8 (3B 62)
.... (off Northington St.)
Kirkwall Pl. E2 .... 2E 65
Kirkwood Pl. NW1 .... 4C 46
Kirkwood Rd. SE15 .... 5D 93
Kirtley Ho. SW8 .... 4E 89
Kirtley Rd. SE26 .... 4A 122
Kirtling St. SW11 .... 3E 89
Kirton Gdns. E2 .... 2F 11 (2B 64)
.... (not continuous)
Kirton Lodge SW18 .... 4D 101
Kirton Rd. E13 .... 1E 69
Kirwyn Way SE5 .... 3D 91
Kitcat Ter. E3 .... 2C 66
Kitchen Ct. E10 .... 4D 39
Kitchener Rd. E7 .... 3D 55
Kite Ho. SW11 .... 5D 79
Kite Ho. SE3 .... 2D 111
Kite Pl. E2 .... 2C 64
.... (off Warner Pl.)
Kite Yd. SW11 .... 4B 88
.... (off Cambridge Rd.)
Kitson Rd. SE5 .... 3F 91
Kitson Rd. SW13 .... 4C 84
Kittiwake Ct. SE1 .. 4A 26 (3E 77)
.... (off Gt. Dover St.)
Kittiwake Ct. SE8 .... 2B 94
.... (off Abinger Gro.)
Kitto Rd. SE14 .... 5F 93
Kiver Rd. N19 .... 4F 33
Klea Av. SW4 .... 4E 103
Kleine Wharf N1 .... 5A 50
Klein's Wharf E14 .... 4C 80
.... (off Westferry Rd.)
Knapdale Cl. SE23 .... 2D 121
Knapmill Rd. SE6 .... 2C 122
Knapmill Way SE6 .... 2D 123
Knapp Cl. NW10 .... 3A 42
Knapp Rd. E3 .... 3C 66
Knapton M. SW17 .... 5C 116
Knaresborough Dr.
SW18 .... 1D 115
Knaresborough Pl. SW5 ...... 5D 73
Knatchbull Ho. NW10 ...... 5A 42
Knatchbull Rd. SE5 .... 5D 91
Knebworth Ho. SW8 .... 5F 89
Knebworth Rd. N16 .... 1A 50
Kneller Rd. SE4 .... 2A 108
Knighten St. E1 .... 2D 79
Knighthead Point E14 .... 3C 80

Knight Ho. SE17 .... 5A 78
.... (off Tatum St.)
Knightland Rd. E5.................... 4D 37
Knightleas Ct. NW2................3E 43
Knightleys Ct. E10 ....3A 38
.... (off Wellington Rd.)
Knightley Wlk. SW18 ...... 2C 100
Knighton Pk. SE26......5F 121
Knighton Rd. E7....................5C 40
Knightrider Ct. EC4... 4E 17 (1E 77)
.... (off Knightrider St.)
Knightrider St. EC4... 3E 17 (5D 63)
.... (off Knightsbridge)
Knights Arc. SW1..... 4A 20 (3B 74)
Knightsbridge SW1 ... 4A 20 (3B 74)
Knightsbridge SW7 ....3B 74
KNIGHTSBRIDGE 3A 74
Knightsbridge Apts., The
SW7.......................................3B 74
.... (off Knightsbridge)
Knightsbridge Ct.
SW1.....................4A 20 (3B 74)
.... (off Sloane St.)
Knightsbridge Grn. SW1 .... 3B 74
.... (not continuous)
Knightsbridge Station
(Underground) 4A 20 (3B 74)
Knights Cl. E9 ....2E 51
Knights Ct. BR1: Broml... 3B 124
Knights Hill SE27 .... 5D 119
Knight's Hill Sq. SE27... 4D 119
Knight's Ho. SW10 ....3E 87
.... (off Hortensia Rd.)
Knight's Ho. W14 .... 1B 86
.... (off Baron's Ct. Rd.)
Knights Ho. SW8 .... 3A 90
.... (off Sth. Lambeth Rd.)
Knight's Rd. E16 .... 3C 82
Knights Twr. SE8 .... 1C 94
Knight's Wlk. SE11 .... 5D 77
.... (not continuous)
Knightswood Ct. N6...........2F 33
Knivet Rd. SW6 ....2C 86
Knockholt Rd. SE9 ....3F 111
Knoll Ct. SE19 .... 5B 120
.... (off Farquhar Rd.)
Knoll Rd. NW8 .... 1E 59
.... (off Carlton Hill)
Knoll Rd. SW18 .... 3E 101
Knollys Cl. SW16................. 3C 118
Knolly's Ho. WC1........3D 7 (3A 62)
.... (off Tavistock Pl.)
Knollys Rd. SW16.............. 3B 118
Knot Ho. SE1 .... 2F 27 (2B 78)
.... (off Brewery Sq.)
Knottisford St. E2.................2E 65
Knotts Grn. M. E10.............. 1D 39
Knotts Grn. Rd. E10 .... 1D 39
Knowlden Ho. E1.................1E 79
.... (off Cable St.)
Knowle Cl. SW9 ....1C 104
Knowles Hill Cres. SE13 ... 3F 109
Knowles Ho. SW18.............4D 101
.... (off Neville Gill Cl.)
Knowles Wlk. SW4..............1E 103
Knowles Wharf NW1...........5E 47
.... (off St Pancras Way)
Knowlton Ho. SW9 ....4C 90
.... (off Cowley Rd.)
Knowsley Rd. SW11............. 5B 88
Knox Ct. SW4 .... 5A 90
Knox Rd. E7..............................3B 54
Knox St. W1..............5A 4 (4B 60)
Knoyle Ho. W14 .... 4A 72
.... (off Russell Rd.)

Knoyle St. SE14.....................2A 94
Kohat Rd. SW19....................5D 115
Koops Mill M. SE1 .... 4B 78
Kossuth St. SE10 .... 1A 96
Kotata Ho. E20......................4E 53
.... (off Ravens Wlk.)
Kotree Way SE1 .... 5C 78
Kramer M. SW5 ....1C 86
Kreedman Wlk. E8 .... 2C 50
Krupnik Pl. EC2 ...... 3E 11 (3A 64)
.... (shown as Curtain Pl.)
Kubrick Bus. Est. E7 .... 1D 55
.... (off Station App.)
Kuhn Way E7 ....2C 54
Kurdish Mus........................... 5C 70
Kurland Ho. SW9.................. 5C 90
Kwesi M. SE27 .... 5C 118
Kyle Ho. NW6.........................5C 44
Kylemore Cl. E6....................1F 69
Kylemore Rd. NW6...............4C 44
Kylestrome Ho. SW1 .... 5C 74
.... (off Cundy St.)
Kynance M. SW7 .... 4D 73
Kynance Pl. SW7 .... 4E 73
Kynaston Av. N16 .... 5B 36
Kynaston Rd. BR1: Broml... 5C 124
Kynaston Rd. N16 .... 5A 36
Kyrle Rd. SW11 ....4C 102
Kyverdale Rd. N16 .... 2B 36

L

Laban Cen. 2D 95
Laban Wlk. SE8......................2D 95
.... (off Copperas St.)
Laburnum Cl. SE15 ....3E 93
Laburnum Cl. E2....................5B 50
Laburnum Cl. SE16................3E 79
.... (off Albion St.)
Laburnum La. E2....................1B 64
Laburnum St. E2....................5B 50
Labyrinth Twr. E8 .... 3B 50
.... (off Dalston Sq.)
Lace Ct. E1 ....4F 65
.... (off Master's St.)
Lacewing Cl. E13................. 2C 68
Lacey M. E3.............................1C 66
Lacine Ct. SE16....................3F 79
.... (off Christopher Cl.)
Lackington St. EC2.. 5C 10 (4F 63)
Lackland Ho. SE1 .... 1B 92
.... (off Rowcross St.)
Lacland Ho. SW10................3F 87
.... (off Worlds End Est.)
Lacon Ho. WC1........ 5F 7 (4B 62)
.... (off Theobald's Rd.)
Lacon Rd. SE22 ....2C 106
Lacy Rd. SW15.......................2F 99
Ladas Rd. SE27 ....4E 119
Ladbroke Cl. E1 .... 1F 19 (5B 64)
Ladbroke Cres. W11 .... 5A 58
Ladbroke Gdns. W11 .... 1B 72
Ladbroke Gro. W10...............3F 57
Ladbroke Gro. W11.............. 5A 58
Ladbroke Gro. W11..............1B 72
.... (off Ladbroke Gro.)
Ladbroke Grove Memorial...3F 57
Ladbroke Grove Station
(Underground) 5A 58
Ladbroke M. W11................... 2A 72
Ladbroke Rd. W11 .... 2B 72
Ladbroke Sq. W11 .... 1B 72
Ladbroke Ter. W11 .... 1B 72
Ladbroke Wlk. W11 .... 2B 72
Ladbrook Cl. BR1: Broml... 5A 124
Ladlands SE22 ....5C 106

Ladycroft Rd. SE13 .... 1D 109
Lady Dock Path SE16 .... 3A 80
Ladyfern Ho. E3 .... 4C 66
.... (off Gail St.)
Lady Florence Ctyd. SE8..... 3C 94
Lady Margaret Ho. SE17....2F 91
.... (off Queen's Row)
Lady Margaret Rd. N19....... 1E 47
Lady Margaret Rd. NW5......2E 47
Lady May Ho. SE5..................3E 91
.... (off Pitman St.)
Lady Micos Almshouses E1... 5E 65
.... (off Aylward St.)
Ladyship Ter. SE22 .... 5C 106
Ladysmith Av. E6 ....1F 69
Ladysmith Rd. E16................ 2B 68
Lady Somerset Rd. NW5..... 1D 47
LADYWELL 3D 109
Ladywell Arena (Running Track)
.... 4C 108
Ladywell Cl. SE4 .... 3C 108
Ladywell Hgts. SE4............. 4B 108
Ladywell Rd. SE13 .... 3C 108
Ladywell Station (Rail) 3D 109
Ladywell St. E15 .... 5B 54
Ladywell Water Twr.
SE4..3C 108
Lafone St. SE1......... 3F 27 (3B 78)
Lagado M. SE16 ....2F 79
Lagare Apts. SE1 ... 3E 25 (3D 77)
.... (off Surrey Row)
Lagonda Ho. E3..................... 3C 66
.... (off Tidworth Rd.)
Lagonier Ho. EC1 ... 2A 10 (2E 63)
.... (off Ironmonger Row)
Laing Ho. SE5......................... 3E 91
Lainson St. SW18................. 5C 100
Lairdale Cl. SE21................... 1E 119
Laird Ho. SE5 ....3E 91
.... (off Redcar St.)
Lairs Cl. N7 ....2A 48
Laitwood Rd. SW12 .... 1D 117
Lakanal SE5 .... 4A 92
.... (off Sceaux Gdns.)
Lake Av. BR1: Broml 5C 124
Lake Cl. SW19....................... 5B 114
Lake Ho. SE1 .... 4F 25 (3E 77)
.... (off Southwark Bri. Rd.)
Lake Ho. Rd. E11 .... 5C 40
Lakenham Pl. E3.................... 3B 66
Laker Ct. SW4 .... 4A 90
Laker Ho. E16........................ 3D 83
Laker Ind. Est. BR3: Beck...5A 122
Lake Rd. E10 ....2D 39
Lake Rd. SW19...................... 5B 114
Lakerr Pl. SW15 ....4A 100
Lakeside Cl. N4......................4E 35
Lakeside Rd. W14 ....4F 71
Lakeside Ter. EC2... 5A 10 (4E 63)
.... (off Silk St.)
Lake Vw. Est. E3.................... 1A 66
Lakeview Rd. SE27 .... 5C 118
Lakis Cl. NW3.........................1E 45
Laleham Ho. E2...... 3F 11 (3B 64)
.... (off Camlet St.)
Laleham Rd. SE6....................5E 109
Lalor St. SW6 ....5A 86
Lambarde Sq. SE10 .... 1B 96
Lambard Ho. SE10 .... 3E 95
.... (off Langdale St.)
Lamb Ct. E14...........................1A 80
.... (off Narrow St.)
Lamberhurst Ho. SE15.........2E 93
Lamberhurst Rd. SE27.......4C 118

Lambert Ho. SW11 ....1F 101
..............................(off Gartons Way)
Lambert Jones M.
EC2.................................5F 9 (4E 63)
..................................(off Beech St.)
Lambert Rd. E16 ....5D 69
Lambert Rd. SW2 ....3A 104
Lambert St. N1 ....4C 48
LAMBETH 5A 24 (4B 76)
Lambeth Bri. SW1 ....5A 76
LAMBETH COMMUNITY CARE
CEN. 5C 76
............................(off Monkton St.)
Lambeth Crematorium 4E 115
Lambeth High St. SE1 ....5B 76
Lambeth Hill EC4 ......4F 17 (1E 77)
LAMBETH HOSPITAL 1B 104
Lambeth North Station
(Underground) 4C 24 (4C 76)
Lambeth Palace .5F 23 (4B 76)
Lambeth Pal. Rd.
SE1 ....5F 23 (4B 76)
Lambeth Pier 4A 76
Lambeth Rd. SE1 ....5B 76
Lambeth Rd. SE11 ...5A 24 (4B 76)
Lambeth Towers
SE11 ....5B 24 (4C 76)
.............................(off Kennington Rd.)
Lambeth Wlk. SE11...5B 24 (5B 76)
...................................(not continuous)
Lambfold Ho. N7 ....3A 48
.................................(off North Rd.)
Lamb Ho. SE10 ....2E 95
.................................(off Haddo St.)
Lamb Ho. SE5 ....3E 91
..........................(off Elmington Est.)
Lamb La. E8 ....4D 51
Lamble St. NW5 ....2C 46
Lambolle Pl. NW3 ....3A 46
Lambolle Rd. NW3 ....3A 46
Lambourn Cl. NW5 ....1E 47
Lambourne Av. SW19 ....4B 114
Lambourne Gro. SE16 ....1F 93
Lambourne Ho. NW8 ....4F 59
..............................(off Broadley St.)
Lambourne Pl. SE3 ....4D 97
Lambourne Rd. E11 ....2E 39
Lambourn Rd. SW4 ....1D 103
Lambrook Ho. SE15 ....4C 92
Lambrook Ter. SW6 ....4A 86
Lamb's Bldgs. EC1...4B 10 (3F 63)
Lamb's Conduit Pas.
WC1.................................5F 7 (4B 62)
Lamb's Conduit St.
WC1.................................4F 7 (3B 62)
...................................(not continuous)
Lambscroft Av. SE9 ....3E 125
Lamb's M. N1 ....5D 49
Lambs Pas. EC1 ......4B 10 (3F 63)
Lamb St. E1 ....5F 11 (4B 64)
Lambton M. N19 ....3A 34
...............................(off Lambton St.)
Lambton Pl. W11 ....1B 72
Lambton Rd. N19 ....3A 34
Lamb Wlk. SE1...4D 27 (3A 78)
Lamerock Rd. BR1: Broml...4B 124
Lamerton St. SE8 ....2C 94
Lamington St. W6 ....5D 71
Lamlash St. SE11 ....5D 77
Lamley Ho. SE10 ....3D 95
..........................(off Ashburnham Pl.)
Lammas Grn. SE26 ....2D 121
Lammas Rd. E10 ....4A 38
Lammas Rd. E9 ....4F 51
Lammermoor Rd. SW12...5D 103

Lamont Rd. SW10 ....2F 87
Lamont Rd. Pas. SW10 ....2F 87
...................................(off Lamont Rd.)
Lampard Gro. N16 ....3B 36
Lampern Sq. E2 ....2C 64
Lampeter Cl. NW9 ....1A 28
Lampeter Sq. W6 ....2A 86
Lamplighter Cl. E1 ....3E 65
Lampmead Rd. SE12 ....3B 110
Lamp Office Ct. WC1...4F 7 (3B 62)
...................................(off Conduit St.)
Lampton Ho. Cl. SW19...4F 113
Lanain Ct. SE12 ....5B 110
Lanark Ho. SE1 ....1C 92
.................................(off Old Kent Rd.)
Lanark Mans. W12 ....3E 71
...................................(off Pennard Rd.)
Lanark Mans. W9 ....3E 59
.................................(off Lanark Rd.)
Lanark Pl. W9 ....3E 59
Lanark Rd. W9 ....1D 59
Lanark Sq. E14 ....4D 81
Lanbury Rd. SE15 ....2F 107
Lancashire Ct. W1 ...4D 13 (1D 75)
Lancaster Av. SE27..................2D 119
Lancaster Av. SW19................5F 113
Lancaster Cl. N1 ....4A 50
Lancaster Cl. W2 ....1D 73
.........................(off St Petersburgh Pl.)
Lancaster Ct. SE27 ....2D 119
Lancaster Ct. SW6 ....3B 86
Lancaster Ct. W2 ....1E 73
.................................(off Lancaster Ga.)
Lancaster Dr. E14 ....2E 81
Lancaster Dr. NW3 ....3A 46
Lancaster Gdns. SW19 ....5A 114
Lancaster Ga. W2 ....1E 73
Lancaster Gate Station
(Underground) 1F 73
Lancaster Gro. NW3................3F 45
Lancaster Hall E16 ....2C 82
.....................................(off Wesley Av.)
Lancaster Ho. E11 ....4B 40
Lancaster House 3A 22 (3E 75)
.................................(off Stable Yd. Rd.)
Lancaster Lodge W11 ....5A 58
...................................(off Lancaster Rd.)
Lancaster M. SW18..................3D 101
Lancaster M. W2 ....1E 73
Lancaster Pl. SW19 ....5F 113
Lancaster Pl. WC2 ...4F 15 (1B 76)
Lancaster Rd. E11 ....4A 40
Lancaster Rd. E7 ....4C 54
Lancaster Rd. N4 ....2B 34
Lancaster Rd. NW10................2C 42
Lancaster Rd. SW19................5F 113
Lancaster Rd. W11 ....5A 58
Lancaster Stables NW3 ....3A 46
Lancaster St. SE1 ....4D 25 (3D 77)
Lancaster Ter. W2 ....1F 73
Lancaster Wlk. W2....................2E 73
Lancefield Ho. SE15................2D 107
Lancefield St. W10 ....2B 58
Lancell St. N16 ....4A 36
Lancelot Pl. SW7 ....3B 74
Lancer Sq. W8 ....3D 73
...........................(off Kensington Chu. St.)
Lancey Cl. SE7 ....5F 83
Lanchester Rd. W2 ....5B 60
..................................(off Seymour St.)
Lanchester Way SE14..............4E 93
Lancing St. NW1 ......2B 6 (2F 61)
Lancresse Ct. N1 ....5A 50
.............................(off De Beauvoir Est.)

Landale Ho. SE16 ....4E 79
...................................(off Lower Rd.)
Landau Apts. SW6 ....2C 86
Landcroft Rd. SE22..................3B 106
Landells Rd. SE22 ....4B 106
Landford Rd. SW15....................1E 99
Landgrove Rd. SW19...............5C 114
Landing Waiters Ho. E14........5F 67
.............................(off New Village Av.)
Landin Ho. E14 ....5C 66
...............................(off Thomas Rd.)
Landleys Fld. N7 ....2F 47
................................(off Long Mdw.)
Landmann Ho. SE16 ....5D 79
...................................(off Rennie Est.)
Landmann Point SE10 ....4C 82
Landmann Way SE14...............1F 93
Landmark East Twr. E14.........3C 80
.................................(off Marsh Wall)
Landmark Hgts. E5 ....1A 52
Landmark Ho. W6 ....1E 85
.........................(off Hammersmith Bri. Rd.)
Landmark Sq. E14 ....3C 80
Landmark West Twr. E14.......3C 80
.................................(off Marsh Wall)
London Pl. SW1.........5A 20 (4B 74)
London's Cl. E14.........................2E 81
London Wlk. E14 ....1D 81
Landor Ho. SE5 ....3F 91
.........................(off Elmington Est.)
Landor Ho. W2 ....4C 58
.........................(off Westbourne Pk. Rd.)
Landor Rd. SW9 ....1A 104
Landor Space 1A 104
Landor Wlk. W12 ....3C 70
Landrake NW1 ....5E 47
.................................(off Plender St.)
Landridge Rd. SW6 ....5B 86
Landrock Rd. N8 ....1A 34
Landsdowne Ct. N19 ....3A 34
.................................(off Fairbridge Rd.)
Landseer Ho. NW8 ....3F 59
.................................(off Frampton St.)
Landseer Ho. SW1....................5F 75
.................................(off Herrick St.)
Landseer Ho. SW11..................4C 88
Landseer Rd. N19 ....5A 34
...................................(not continuous)
Landulph Ho. SE11 ....1C 90
.............................(off Kennings Way)
Landward Ct. W1 ....5A 60
.............................(off Harrowby St.)
Lane, The NW8 ....1E 59
Lane, The SE3 ....1C 110
Lane Cl. NW2...............................5D 29
Lane End SW15 ....4F 99
Lanercost Cl. SW2 ....2C 118
Lanercost Rd. SW2 ....2C 118
Lanesborough Ct.
N1 ....1D 11 (2A 64)
................................(off Fanshaw St.)
Lanesborough Pl.
SW1...........................3C 20 (3C 74)
.............................(off Grosvenor Pl.)
Lanesborough Way SW17...3F 115
Laneway SW15 ....3D 99
Laney Ho. EC1 ....5B 8 (4C 62)
.................................(off Leather La.)
Lanfranc Rd. E3 ....1A 66
Lanfrey Pl. W14.........................1B 86
Langan Ho. E14 ....5B 66
.................................(off Keymer Pl.)
Langbourne Av. N6 ....4C 32
Langbourne Cl. E17..................1A 38
Langbourne Mans. N6 ....4C 32

Langbourne Pl. E14 .... 1D 95
Langbrook Rd. SE3 ....1F 111
Langdale NW1 .... 1F 5 (2E 61)
.... (off Stanhope St.)
Langdale Cl. SE17 ....2E 91
Langdale Ho. SW1 ....1E 89
.... (off Churchill Gdns.)
Langdale Rd. SE10 ....3E 95
Langdale St. E1 ....5D 65
Langdon Ct. EC1 .... 1E 9 (1D 63)
.... (off City Rd.)
Langdon Ct. NW10 ....5A 42
Langdon Ho. E14 ....5E 67
.... (off Ida St.)
Langdon Pk. Rd. N6 ....2E 33
Langdon Park Station (DLR)
....5D 67
Langdon Way SE1 ....5C 78
Langford Cl. E8 ....2C 50
Langford Cl. N15 ....1A 36
Langford Cl. NW8 ....1E 59
Langford Ct. NW8 ....1E 59
.... (off Abbey Rd.)
Langford Gdn. 4D 87
.... (off Pearscroft Road)
Langford Grn. SE5 ....1A 106
Langford Ho. SE8 ....2C 94
Langford M. N1 ....4C 48
Langford M. SW11 ....2F 101
.... (off St John's Hill)
Langford Pl. NW8 ....1E 59
Langford Rd. SW6 ....5D 87
Langham Ho. E15 ....3F 53
.... (off Forrester Way)
Langham Mans. SW5 ....1D 87
.... (off Earl's Ct. Sq.)
Langham Pl. W1 .... 1E 13 (4D 61)
Langham Pl. W4 ....2A 84
Langham St. W1 .... 1E 13 (4D 61)
Langholm Cl. SW12 ....5F 103
Langhorne Ct. NW8 ....1F 59
.... (off Dorman Way)
Lang Ho. SW8 ....3A 90
.... (off Hartington Rd.)
Langland Gdns. NW3 ....2D 45
Langland Ho. SE5 ....3F 91
.... (off Edmund St.)
Langler Rd. NW10 ....1E 57
Langley Ct. WC2 ....4D 15 (1A 76)
Langley Cres. E11 ....2E 41
Langley Dr. E11 ....2D 41
Langley Ho. W2 ....4C 58
.... (off Alfred Rd.)
Langley La. SW8 ....2B 90
Langley Mans. SW8 ....2B 90
.... (off Langley La.)
Langley St. WC2 ....3D 15 (5A 62)
Langmead Ho. E3 ....2D 67
.... (off Bruce Rd.)
Langmead St. SE27 ....4D 119
Langmore Ho. E1 ....5C 64
.... (off Stutfield St.)
Langport Ho. SW9 ....5D 91
Langroyd Rd. SW17 ....2B 116
Langside Av. SW15 ....2C 98
Langston Hughes Cl.
SE24 ....2D 105
Lang St. E1 ....3E 65
Langthorn Ct. EC2 ......2B 18 (5F 63)
Langthorne Ct. BR1: Broml.... 4E 123
Langthorne Ho. E3 ....2B 66
.... (off Merchant St.)
Langthorne Rd. E11 ....5E 39
.... (not continuous)
Langthorne St. SW6 ....3F 85

Langton Cl. WC1 .... 3A 8 (3B 62)
Langton Ho. SE11 ....5B 76
.... (off Lambeth Wlk.)
Langton Pl. SW18 ....1C 114
Langton Rd. SW9 ....3D 91
Langton Rd. NW2 ....5E 29
Langton Rd. SW9 ....3D 91
Langton St. SW10 ....2E 87
Langton Way SE3 ....4B 96
Langtry Pl. SW6 ....2C 86
Langtry Rd. NW8 ....5D 45
Langtry Wlk. NW8 ....5D 45
Lanhill Rd. W9 ....3C 58
Lanier Rd. SE13 ....4F 109
Lannoy Point SW6 ....3A 86
.... (off Pellant Rd.)
Lanrick Rd. E14 ....5F 67
Lansbury Est. E14 ....5D 67
Lansbury Gdns. E14 ....5F 67
Lanscombe Wlk. SW8 ....4A 90
Lansdell Ho. SW2 ....4C 104
Lansdowne Ct. W11 ....1A 72
.... (off Lansdowne Ri.)
Lansdowne Cres. W11 ....1A 72
Lansdowne Dr. E8 ....3C 50
Lansdowne Gdns. SW8 ....4A 90
Lansdowne Grn. SW8 ....4A 90
Lansdowne Gro. NW10 ....1A 42
Lansdowne Hill SE27 ....3D 119
Lansdowne Ho. W11 ....2B 72
.... (off Ladbroke Rd.)
Lansdowne La. SE7 ....2F 97
Lansdowne M. SE7 ....1F 97
Lansdowne M. W11 ....2B 72
Lansdowne Pl. SE1 ..... 5C 26 (4F 77)
Lansdowne Ri. W11 ....1A 72
Lansdowne Rd. E11 ....4B 40
Lansdowne Rd. E17 ....1C 38
Lansdowne Rd. W11 ....1A 72
Lansdowne Row N1 ... 1E 21 (2D 75)
Lansdowne Ter.
WC1 ....4E 7 (3A 62)
Lansdowne Wlk. W11 ....2B 72
Lansdowne Way SW8 ....4F 89
Lansdowne Wood Cl.
SE27 ....3D 119
Lansdowne Workshops
SE7 ....1E 97
Lansdown Rd. E7 ....4E 55
Lanson Apts. SW11 ....3D 89
Lantan Hgts. E20 ....4E 53
Lantern 1 .... 3F 25 (3E 77)
.... (off Lant St.)
Lantern Cl. SW15 ....2C 98
Lanterns Way E14 ....3C 80
Lant Ho. SE1 .... 4F 25 (3E 77)
.... (off Toulmin St.)
Lant St. SE1 .... 3F 25 (3E 77)
Lanvanor Rd. SE15 ....5E 93
Lanward Apts. N1 ....4B 48
.... (off Caledonian Rd.)
Lanyard Ho. SE8 ....5B 80
Lapford Cl. W9 ....3B 58
Lapidge Dr. SW17 ....3F 115
Lapis M. E15 ....2E 53
Lapse Wood Wlk. SE23 ....1D 121
Lapwing Ct. SE1 .... 4A 26 (3E 77)
.... (off Swan St.)
Lapwing Ter. E7 ....2F 55
Lapwing Twr. SE8 ....2B 94
.... (off Taylor Cl.)
Lapworth Ct. W2 ....4D 59
.... (off Delamere Ter.)
Lara Cl. SE13 ....4E 109
Larch Av. W3 ....2A 70

Larch Cl. E13 ....3D 69
Larch Cl. N19 ....4E 33
Larch Cl. SE8 ....2B 94
Larch Cl. SW12 ....2D 117
Larch Ct. SE1 .... 4D 27 (3A 78)
.... (off Royal Oak Yd.)
Larch Ct. W9 ....4C 58
.... (off Admiral Wlk.)
Larch Ho. SE16 ....3E 79
.... (off Ainsty Est.)
Larch Ho. W10 ....3A 58
.... (off Rowan Wlk.)
Larch Rd. E10 ....4C 38
Larch Rd. NW2 ....1E 43
Larcom St. SE17 ....5E 77
Larden Rd. W3 ....2A 70
Lariat Apts. SE10 ....5A 82
.... (off Cable Wlk.)
Larissa St. SE17 ....1F 91
Larkbere Rd. SE26 ....4A 122
Larkhall La. SW4 ....5F 89
Larkhall Ri. SW4 ....1E 103
.... (not continuous)
Lark Row E2 ....5E 51
Larkspur Cl. E6 ....4F 69
Larkwood Av. SE10 ....4E 95
Larnach Rd. W6 ....2F 85
Larpent Av. SW15 ....3E 99
Larson Wlk. E14 ....4C 80
Lascar Wharf Bldg. E14 ....5A 66
.... (off Parnham St.)
Lascelles Cl. E11 ....4F 39
Lascelles Ho. NW1 ....3A 60
.... (off Harewood Av.)
Lassell St. SE10 ....1F 95
Lasseter Pl. SE3 ....2B 96
Latchmere Leisure Cen. 5B 88
Latchmere Pas. SW11 ....5A 88
Latchmere Rd. SW11 ....5B 88
Latchmere St. SW11 ....5B 88
Latham Ct. SW5 ....5C 72
.... (off W. Cromwell Rd.)
Latham Ho. E1 ....5F 65
.... (off Chudleigh St.)
Latimer Ho. E9 ....3F 51
Latimer Ho. W11 ....1B 72
.... (off Kensington Pk. Rd.)
Latimer Ind. Est. W10 ....5E 57
Latimer Pl. W10 ....5E 57
Latimer Rd. E7 ....1D 55
Latimer Rd. N15 ....1A 36
Latimer Rd. W10 ....4E 57
.... (not continuous)

Latimer Road Station
(Underground) 1F 71
Latitude Ho. NW1 ....5D 47
Latona Cl. SW9 ....3C 90
.... (off Caldwell St.)
Latona Rd. SE15 ....2C 92
Lattimer Pl. W4 ....3A 84
Latvia St. SE17 ....1E 91
Latymer Ct. W6 ....5F 71
Lauderdale Ho. SW9 ....4C 90
Lauderdale House Community
Arts Cen. 3D 33
.... (within Lauderdale House)
Lauderdale Mans. W9 ....2D 59
.... (off Lauderdale Rd.)
Lauderdale Pde. W9 ....3D 59
Lauderdale Pl. EC2 .... 5F 9 (4E 63)
.... (off Beech St.)

Lauderdale Rd. W9..............2D 59
Lauderdale Twr. EC2....5F 9 (4E 63)
..............................(off Beech St.)
Laud St. SE11......................1B 90
Laugan Wlk. SE17................1E 91
Launcelot Ho. BR1: Broml....4C 124
Launcelot St. SE1....4B 24 (3C 76)
Launceston Pl. W8...............4E 73
Launch St. E14.....................4E 81
Laundress La. N16................5C 36
Laundry La. N1.....................5E 49
Laundry M. SE23...............5A 108
Laundry Rd. W6...................2A 86
Laura Pl. E5.........................1E 51
Laura Ter. N4.......................4D 35
Laurel Apts. SE17................5A 78
..............................(off Townsend St.)
Laurel Bank Gdns. SW6......5B 86
Laurel Cl. N19.....................4E 33
Laurel Cl. SW17..................5A 116
Laurel Ct. SE1..........5B 26 (4F 77)
..............................(off Garland Cl.)
Laurel Gro. SE26................4F 121
Laurel Ho. E3......................5B 52
..............................(off Hornbeam Sq.)
Laurel Ho. SE8....................2B 94
Laurel M. SE5......................1E 105
..............................(off Harbour Rd.)
Laurel Rd. SW13...................5C 84
Laurels, The NW10..............5D 43
Laurels, The SW9................3D 91
..............................(off Langton Rd.)
Laurel St. E8.......................3B 50
Laurence Ct. E10.................2D 39
Laurence Ct. W11.................1A 72
..............................(off Lansdowne Rd.)
Laurence M. W12.................3C 70
Laurence Pountney Hill
EC4............................4B 18 (1F 77)
Laurence Pountney La.
EC4............................4B 18 (1F 77)
Laurie Gro. SE14..................4A 94
Laurie Ho. SE1..........5E 25 (4D 77)
..............................(off St George's Rd.)
Laurie Ho. W8......................2C 72
..............................(off Airlie Gdns.)
Laurier Rd. NW5.................5D 33
Lauriston Ho. E9.................4E 51
..............................(off Lauriston Rd.)
Lauriston Rd. E9..................4E 51
Lauriston Rd. SW19..........5F 113
Lausanne Rd. SE15..............4E 93
Lavell St. N16......................1F 49
Lavender Cl. SW3.................2F 87
Lavender Gdns. SW11.........2B 102
Lavender Gro. E8................4C 50
Lavender Hill SW11...........2A 102
Lavender Ho. SE16...............2F 79
..............................(off Rotherhithe St.)
Lavender Pond Nature Pk.
....2A 80
Lavender Rd. SE16..............2A 80
Lavender St. E15..................1F 101
Lavender Sq. SW9...............4B 90
..............................(off Printers Rd.)
Lavender St. E15..................3A 54
Lavender Sweep SW11......2B 102
Lavender Ter. SW11..........1A 102
Lavender Wlk. SW11...........2B 102
Lavendon Ho. NW8..............5A 60
..............................(off Paveley St.)
Lavengro Rd. SE27..............2E 119
Lavenham Rd. SW18..........2B 114
Lavers Rd. N16.....................5A 36
Laverstoke Gdns. SW15......5B 98

Laverton M. SW5.................5D 73
Laverton Pl. SW5.................5D 73
Lavette Ho. E3.....................2C 66
..............................(off Rainhill Way)
Lavina Gro. N1.....................1B 62
Lavington Cl. E9...................3B 52
Lavington St. SE1....2E 25 (2D 77)
Lavisham Ho.
BR1: Broml.....................5D 125
Lawes Ho. W10.....................2B 58
..............................(off Lancefield St.)
Lawford Rd. N1.....................4A 50
Lawford Rd. NW5.................3E 47
Lawfords Wharf NW1.........4E 47
..............................(off Lyme St.)
Lawless Ho. E14..................1E 81
..............................(off Bazely St.)
Lawless St. E14...................1D 81
Lawley St. E5........................1E 51
Lawnfield Ct. NW6...............4F 43
..............................(off Coverdale Rd.)
Lawn Cl. N9........................(off White City Est.)
Lawn Ho. Cl. E14.................3E 81
Lawn La. SW8......................2B 90
Lawn Rd. NW3......................2B 46
Lawns, The SW3...................1B 110
Lawns, The SW19................5B 114
Lawn Ter. SE3.....................1A 110
Lawnside SE3.....................2B 110
Lawrence Bldgs. N16..........5B 36
Lawrence Cl. E3...................2C 66
Lawrence Cl. W12...............1D 71
Lawrence Ct. N16.................5B 36
..............................(off Smalley Rd. Est.)
Lawrence Ct. SE6.................4C 108
Lawrence Ho. N1.................4D 47
..............................(off Hawley Cres.)
Lawrence Ho. SW1...............5F 75
..............................(off Cureton St.)
Lawrence La. EC2....2A 18 (5E 63)
Lawrence Mans. SW3...........2A 88
..............................(off Lordship Pl.)
Lawrence M. SW15...............2E 99
Lawrence M. SW8.................3A 90
Lawrence Pl. N1....................5A 48
..............................(off Brydon Wlk.)
Lawrence Rd. E13.................5D 54
Lawrence Rd. E6...................5F 55
Lawrence St. E16.................4B 68
Lawrence St. SW3.................2A 88
Lawrence Trad. Est. SE10....5A 82
Lawrie Ho. SW19................5D 115
..............................(off Durnsford Rd.)
Lawrie Pk. Av. SE26............5D 121
Lawrie Pk. Cres. SE26.........5C 121
Lawrie Pk. Gdns. SE26........4D 121
Lawrie Pk. Rd. SE26...........5D 121
Lawson Cl. E16.....................4E 69
Lawson Cl. SW19...............3F 113
Lawson Ct. N4......................3B 34
..............................(off Lorne Rd.)
Lawson Ho. W12..................1D 71
..............................(off White City Est.)
Lawson Ter. SE15................2E 107
Law St. SE1..............5C 26 (4F 77)
Lawton Rd. E10.....................3E 39
Lawton Rd. E3......................2A 66
..............................(not continuous)
Laxfield Ct. E8.....................5C 50
..............................(off Pownall Rd.)
Laxford Ho. SW1..................5C 74
..............................(off Cundy St.)
Laxley Cl. SE5......................3D 91
Laxton Pl. NW1........3E 5 (3D 61)
Layard Rd. SE16..................5D 79
Layard Sq. SE16..................5D 79

Laybourne Ho. E14..............3C 80
..............................(off Admirals Way)
Laycock St. N1....................3C 48
Layfield Cl. NW4..................2D 29
Layfield Cres. NW4..............2D 29
Layfield Ho. SE10................1C 96
..............................(off Kemsing Rd.)
Layfield Rd. NW4.................2D 29
Laystall St. WC1........4B 8 (3C 62)
..............................(off Mt. Pleasant)
Laystall St. EC1........4B 8 (3C 62)
Layzell Wlk. SE9..................1F 125
Lazar Wlk. N7......................4B 34
Lazenby Ct. WC2....4D 15 (1A 76)
..............................(off Floral St.)
Leabank Sq. E9....................3C 52
Leabank Vw. N15.................1C 36
Lea Bon Ct. E15...................5B 54
..............................(off Plaistow Gro.)
Leabourne Rd. N16..............2C 36
LEA BRIDGE..........................5F 37
Lea Bri. Ind. Cen. E10.........3A 38
Lea Bri. Rd. E10...................2C 38
Lea Bri. Rd. E5.....................2C 38
Lea Ct. E13..........................2C 68
Leacroft Av. SW12.............5B 102
Leadale Rd. N15..................1C 36
Leadale Rd. N16..................1C 36
Leadenhall Mkt.....3D 19 (5A 64)
Leadenhall Pl. EC3...3D 19 (5A 64)
Leadenhall St. EC3...3D 19 (5A 64)
Leadenham Ct. E3................3C 66
Leadmill La. E20..................1D 53
Leaf Gro. SE27...................5C 118
Leaf Wlk. N7........................1F 47
Leafy Oak Rd. SE12............4E 125
Leagrave St. E5....................5E 37
Lea Hall Gdns. E10..............3C 38
Lea Hall Rd. E10..................3C 38
Lea Ho. NW8........................3A 60
..............................(off Salisbury St.)
Leahurst Rd. SE13..............3F 109
LEA INTERCHANGE...............2C 52
Leake Ct. SE1..........4A 24 (3B 76)
Leake St. SE1..........3A 24 (3B 76)
..............................(not continuous)
Lealand Rd. N15..................1B 36
Leamington Av. BR1: Broml.5E 125
Leamington Av. E17.............1C 38
Leamington Cl. BR1: Broml..4E 125
Leamington Ct. SE3..............2A 96
Leamington Ho. W11...........4B 58
..............................(off Tavistock Rd.)
Leamington Rd. Vs. W11.....4B 58
Leamore St. E2....................2F 65
Leamore St. W6...................5E 71
LEAMOUTH.............................1A 82
Leamouth Rd. E14................5F 67
Leamouth Rd. E6..................4F 69
Leander Ct. E9......................4F 51
..............................(off Lauriston Rd.)
Leander Ct. SE8...................4C 94
Leander Rd. SW2................4B 104
Lea Pk. Trad. Est. E10.........2B 38
Leary Ho. SE11....................1B 90
Leaside Rd. E5......................3E 37
Leasowes Rd. E10................3C 38
Lea Sq. E3.............................5B 52
Leatherdale St.
E1: Lon Portelet Rd............2F 65
Leather Gdns. E15................5A 54
Leatherhead Cl. N16............3B 36
Leather La. EC1.........4B 8 (4C 62)
..............................(not continuous)

Leather Mkt., The
SE1....................4D **27** (3A **78**)
...................................(off Weston St.)
Leathermarket Ct.
SE1....................4D **27** (3A **78**)
Leathermarket St.
SE1....................4D **27** (3A **78**)
Leather Pl. SE1....................4A **78**
...................................(off Crimscott St.)
Leather Rd. SE16....................5F **79**
Leather St. E1....................1F **79**
Leathwaite Rd. SW11....................2B **102**
Leathwell Rd. SE8....................5D **95**
Lea Valley Bus. Pk. E10....................4A **38**
Lea Vw. Ho. E5....................3D **37**
Leaway E10....................3F **37**
Lebanon Gdns. SW18....................4C **100**
Lebanon Rd. SW18....................3C **100**
Lebus Ho. NW8....................1A **60**
...................................(off Cochrane St.)
Lechmere Rd. NW2....................3D **43**
Leckford Rd. SW18....................2E **115**
Leckhampton Pl. SW2....................5C **104**
Lecky St. SW7....................1F **87**
Leconfield Av. SW13....................1B **98**
Leconfield Ho. SE5....................2A **106**
Leconfield Rd. N5....................1F **49**
Leda Ct. SW9....................3C **90**
...................................(off Caldwell St.)
Ledam Ho. EC1....................5B **8** (4C **62**)
...................................(off Bourne Est.)
Ledbury Ho. SE22....................1A **106**
Ledbury Ho. W11....................5B **58**
...................................(off Colville Rd.)
Ledbury M. Nth. W11....................1C **72**
Ledbury M. W. W11....................1C **72**
Ledbury Rd. W11....................5B **58**
Ledbury St. SE15....................3C **92**
Ledger M. E17....................1C **38**
LEE....................4C **110**
Lee Bri. SE13....................1E **109**
Lee Chu. St. SE13....................2A **110**
Lee Conservancy Rd. E9....................2E **52**
Lee Ct. E3....................3E **67**
...................................(off Navigation Rd.)
Lee Ct. SE13....................2F **109**
...................................(off Lee High Rd.)
Leeds Ct. EC1....................3D **9** (3D **63**)
...................................(off St John St.)
Leeds Pl. N4....................3B **34**
Leefern Rd. W12....................3C **70**
Leegate SE12....................3B **110**
LEE GREEN....................3B **110**
Lee High Rd. SE12....................2B **110**
Lee High Rd. SE13....................1E **109**
Leeke St. WC1....................1F **7** (2B **62**)
Leeland Way NW10....................1B **42**
Lee Pk. SE3....................2B **110**
Leerdam Dr. E14....................4E **81**
Lee Rd. SE3....................1B **110**
Lees Ct. W1....................4B **12** (1C **74**)
...................................(off Lees Pl.)
Lees Ho. SE17....................1F **91**
...................................(off Orville Rd.)
Leeside Ct. SE16....................2F **79**
...................................(off Rotherhithe St.)
Leeside Cres. NW11....................1A **30**
Leeson Rd. SE24....................2C **104**
Lees Pl. W1....................4B **12** (1C **74**)
Lee Station (Rail)....................4C **110**
Lee St. E8....................5B **50**
Lee Ter. SE13....................1A **110**
Lee Ter. SE3....................1A **110**
Lee Valley Hockey & Tennis Cen.
...................................1D **53**

Lee Valley Ice Cen.....................4F **37**
Lee Valley VeloPark....................2D **53**
Leeve Ho. W10....................2B **58**
...................................(off Lancefield St.)
Leeward Ct. E1....................2C **78**
Leeward Ct. SE8....................5A **80**
...................................(off Yeoman St.)
Leeward Gdns. SW19....................5A **114**
Leeward Ho. N1....................5A **50**
...................................(off Halcomb St.)
Leeway SE8....................1B **94**
Leewood Cl. SE12....................4C **110**
Lefevre Wlk. E3....................1C **66**
Leff Ho. NW6....................5A **44**
Lefroy Ho. SE1....................4F **25** (3E **77**)
...................................(off Southwark Bri. Rd.)
Lefroy Rd. W12....................3B **70**
Legacy Bldg. SW11....................2F **89**
Legacy Wharf E15....................1D **67**
Leggatt Rd. E15....................1E **67**
Legge St. SE13....................3E **109**
Leghorn Rd. NW10....................1B **56**
Legion Cl. N1....................4C **48**
Legion Ter. E3....................5B **52**
Leg O'Mutton Reservoir Local
Nature Reserve....................3B **84**
Leicester Ct. W9....................4C **58**
...................................(off Elmfield Way)
Leicester Ct. WC2....................4C **14** (1F **75**)
...................................(off Lisle St.)
Leicester Flds....................5C **14** (1F **75**)
...................................(off Leicester Sq.)
Leicester Ho. SW9....................1D **105**
...................................(off Loughborough Rd.)
Leicester Pl. WC2....................4C **14** (1F **75**)
Leicester Rd. NW10....................4A **42**
Leicester Sq. SW2....................5C **14** (1F **75**)
Leicester Square Station
(Underground)....................4C **14** (1A **76**)
Leicester Square Theatre
...................................4C **14** (1F **75**)
...................................(off Leicester Pl.)
Leicester St. WC2....................4C **14** (1F **75**)
Leigham Av. SW16....................3A **118**
Leigham Cl. SW16....................3B **118**
Leigham Ct. Rd. SW16....................2A **118**
Leigham Hall Pde.
SW16....................3A **118**
...................................(off Streatham High Rd.)
Leigham Va. SW16....................3B **118**
Leigham Va. SW16....................2C **118**
Leigh Ct. W14....................5B **72**
...................................(off Avonmore Pl.)
Leigh Gdns. NW10....................1E **57**
Leigh Orchard Cl. SW16....................3B **118**
Leigh Pl. EC1....................5B **8** (4C **62**)
Leigh Rd. E10....................2E **39**
Leigh Rd. N5....................1D **49**
Leigh St. WC1....................2D **7** (2A **62**)
Leighton Cres. NW5....................2E **47**
Leighton Gdns. NW10....................1D **57**
Leighton Gro. NW5....................2E **47**
Leighton Ho. SW1....................5F **75**
...................................(off Herrick St.)
Leighton House Mus.....................4B **72**
Leighton Mans. W14....................2A **86**
...................................(off Greyhound Rd.)
Leighton Pl. NW5....................2E **47**
Leighton Rd. NW5....................2E **47**
Leila Parnell Pl. SE7....................2E **97**
Leinster Gdns. W2....................5E **59**
Leinster M. W2....................1E **73**
Leinster Pl. W2....................5E **59**

Leinster Sq. W2....................5C **58**
...................................(not continuous)
Leinster Ter. W2....................1E **73**
Leirum St. N1....................5B **48**
Leitch Ho. NW8....................4F **45**
...................................(off Hilgrove Rd.)
Leithcote Gdns. SW16....................4B **118**
Leithcote Path SW16....................3B **118**
Leith Mans. W9....................2D **59**
...................................(off Grantully Rd.)
Leith Yd. NW6....................5C **44**
...................................(off Quex Rd.)
Lelitia Cl. E8....................5C **50**
Leman St. E1....................5B **64**
Le Mare Ter. E3....................4C **66**
Le May Av. SE12....................3D **125**
Lemmon Rd. SE10....................2A **96**
Lemna Rd. E11....................2B **40**
Le Moal Ho. E1....................4E **65**
...................................(off Stepney Way)
Lemon Tree Ho. E3....................2B **66**
...................................(off Bow Rd.)
Lemsford Cl. N15....................1C **36**
Lemsford Ct. N4....................4E **35**
Lemuel St. SW18....................4E **101**
Lena Gdns. W6....................4E **71**
Lenanton Steps E14....................3C **80**
...................................(off Manilla St.)
Len Bishop Ct. E1....................1F **79**
...................................(off Schoolhouse La.)
Lendal Ter. SW4....................1F **103**
Len Freeman Pl. SW6....................2B **86**
Lenham Ho. SE1....................4C **26** (4F **77**)
...................................(off Staple St.)
Lenham Rd. SE12....................2B **110**
Lennard Rd. SE20....................5F **121**
Lennon Rd. NW2....................2E **43**
Lennox Gdns. NW10....................1B **42**
Lennox Gdns. SW1....................4B **74**
Lennox Gdns. M. SW1....................4B **74**
Lennox Ho. E17....................1B **38**
Lennox Rd. N4....................4B **34**
Lennox Rd. SW9....................4D **91**
Lensbury Av. SW6....................5E **87**
Lens Rd. E7....................4E **55**
Lenthall Ho. SW1....................1E **89**
...................................(off Churchill Gdns.)
Lenthall Rd. E8....................4C **50**
Lenthorp Rd. SE10....................5B **82**
Lentmead Rd. BR1: Broml....................3B **124**
Lenton Ter. N4....................4C **34**
Len Williams Ct. NW6....................1C **58**
Leof Cres. SE6....................5D **123**
Leonard Cir. EC2....................3C **10** (3F **63**)
Leonard Ct. W8....................4C **72**
Leonard Ct. WC1....................3C **6** (3F **61**)
Leonard Pl. N16....................1A **50**
Leonard Rd. E7....................1C **54**
Leonard St. EC2....................3C **10** (3F **63**)
Leonora Ho. W9....................3E **59**
...................................(off Lanark Rd.)
Leonora Tyson M. SE21....................2F **119**
Leontine Cl. SE15....................3C **92**
Leopards Ct. EC1....................5B **8** (4C **62**)
...................................(off Baldwins Gdns.)
Leopold Av. SW19....................5B **114**
Leopold Bldgs. E2....................1F **11** (2B **64**)
...................................(off Columbia Rd.)
Leopold M. E9....................5E **51**
Leopold Rd. E17....................1C **38**
Leopold Rd. NW10....................4A **42**
Leopold Rd. SW19....................4B **114**
Leopold St. E3....................4B **66**
Leopold Ter. SW19....................5B **114**
Leo St. SE15....................3D **93**

Leo Yd. EC1 ....4E **9** (3D **63**)
................................(off St John St.)
Leppoc Rd. SW4 ....3F **103**
Leroy St. SE1 ....5D **27** (5A **78**)
Lerry Cl. W14 ....2B **86**
Lescombe Cl. SE23 ....3A **122**
Lescombe Rd. SE23 ....3A **122**
Lesley Ct. SW1 ....5B **22** (4F **75**)
................................(off Strutton Ground)
Leslie Ho. SW8 ....3A **90**
................................(off Wheatsheaf La.)
Leslie Prince Ct. SE5 ....3F **91**
Leslie Rd. E11 ....1E **53**
Leslie Rd. E16 ....5D **69**
Lesney Av. E20 ....2C **52**
Lessar Av. SW4 ....4E **103**
Lessingham Av. SW17 ....4B **116**
Lessing St. SE23 ....5A **108**
Lester Av. E15 ....3A **68**
Lester Ct. E3 ....2D **67**
................................(off Bruce Rd.)
Leswin Pl. N16 ....5B **36**
Leswin Rd. N16 ....5B **36**
Letchford Gdns. NW10 ....2C **56**
Letchford Ho. E3 ....1C **66**
................................(off Thomas Fyre Dr.)
Letchford M. NW10 ....2C **56**
Letchmore Ho. W10 ....3E **57**
................................(off Sutton Way)
Letchworth St. SW17 ....4B **116**
Lethbridge Cl. SE10 ....4E **95**
Letterstone Rd. SW6 ....3B **86**
Lettice St. SW6 ....4B **86**
Lett Rd. E15 ....4F **53**
Lett Rd. SW9 ....4B **90**
Lettsom St. SE5 ....5A **92**
Lettsom Wlk. E13 ....1C **68**
Leucha Rd. E17 ....1A **38**
Levana Cl. SW19 ....1A **114**
Levant Ho. E1 ....1F **65**
................................(off Ernest St.)
Levehurst Ho. SE27 ....5E **119**
Levendale Rd. SE23 ....2A **122**
Levenhurst Way SW4 ....5A **90**
Leven Rd. E14 ....4E **67**
Leverett St. SW3 ....5A **74**
Leverington Pl. N1 ....2C **10** (2F **63**)
Leverstock Ho. SW3 ....1A **88**
................................(off Cale St.)
Lever St. EC1 ....2E **9** (2D **63**)
Leverton Pl. NW5 ....2E **47**
Leverton St. NW5 ....2E **47**
Levett Buildging, The
    EC1.............................1E **17** (4D **63**)
................................(off Little Britain)
Levison Way N19 ....3F **33**
Levita Ho. NW1 ....1C **6** (2F **61**)
................................(off Ossulston St.)
Levyne Ct. EC1 ....3B **8** (3C **62**)
................................(off Pine St.)
Lewesdon Cl. SW19 ....1F **113**
Lewes Ho. SE1 ....3E **27** (3A **78**)
................................(off Druid St.)
Lewes Ho. SE15 ....2C **92**
................................(off Friary Est.)
Leweston Pl. N16 ....2B **36**
Lew Evans Ho. SE22 ....3C **106**
Lewey Ho. E3 ....3B **66**
................................(off Joseph St.)
Lewington Apts. SE16 ....5E **79**
................................(off Alpine Rd.)
Lewington Cen. SE16 ....5E **79**
................................(off Alpine Rd.)
Lewin Rd. SW14 ....1A **98**
Lewin Rd. SW16 ....5F **117**

Lewis Ct. SE16 ....1D **93**
................................(off Stubbs Dr.)
Lewis Cubitt Pk. 5A **48**
Lewis Cubitt Sq. N1 ....5A **48**
Lewis Cubitt Wlk. N1 ....5A **48**
Lewis Gdns. N16 ....1B **36**
Lewis Gro. SE13 ....1E **109**
LEWISHAM 1E **109**
Lewisham Hgts. SE23 ....1E **121**
Lewisham High St. SE13 ....1E **109**
................................(not continuous)
Lewisham Hill SE13 ....5E **95**
Lewisham Indoor Bowls Cen.
....5B **122**
Lewisham Lions Cen. 1E **93**
Lewisham Model Mkt. 2E **109**
................................(off Lewisham High St.)
Lewisham Pk. SE13 ....3E **109**
Lewisham Rd. SE13 ....4D **95**
Lewisham Station (Rail & DLR)
....1E **109**
Lewisham St. SW1 ....1C **22** (2F **75**)
Lewisham Way SE14 ....4B **94**
Lewisham Way SE4 ....4B **94**
Lewis Ho. E14 ....2E **81**
................................(off Coldharbour)
Lewis Ho. N1 ....3D **49**
................................(off Canonbury Rd.)
Lewis Pl. E8 ....2C **50**
Lewis Silkin Ho. SE15 ....2E **93**
................................(off Lovelinch Cl.)
Lewis St. NW1 ....3D **47**
................................(not continuous)
Lexham Gdns. W8 ....5C **72**
Lexham Gdns. M. W8 ....4D **73**
Lexham M. W8 ....5D **73**
................................(off Lexham Gdns.)
Lexham M. W8 ....4D **73**
Lexham Wlk. W8 ....4D **73**
Lexington Apts. EC1 3B **10** (3F **63**)
Lexington Bldg. E3 ....5C **66**
Lexington St. W1 ....3A **14** (1E **75**)
Lexton Gdns. SW12 ....1F **117**
Leybourne Ho. E14 ....5B **66**
................................(off Dod St.)
Leybourne Ho. SE15 ....2E **93**
Leybourne Rd. E11 ....3B **40**
Leybourne Rd. NW1 ....4D **47**
Leybourne St. NW1 ....4D **47**
Leybridge Ct. SE12 ....3C **110**
Leyden Mans. N19 ....2A **34**
Leyden St. E1 ....1F **19** (4B **64**)
Leydon Cl. SE16 ....2F **79**
Leyes Rd. E16 ....5F **69**
Ley Ho. SE1 ....4F **25** (3E **77**)
................................(off Scovell Rd.)
Leyland Ct. SE15 ....3B **92**
................................(off Shield Street)
Leyland Ho. E14 ....1D **81**
................................(off Hale St.)
Leyland Rd. SE12 ....3C **110**
Leylands SW18 ....4B **100**
Leylang Rd. SE14 ....3F **93**
Leys Cl. SW9 ....5C **90**
Leysdown Ho. SE17 ....1A **92**
................................(off Madron St.)
Leysfield Rd. W12 ....4C **70**
Leyspring Rd. E11 ....3B **40**
LEYTON 4E **39**
Leyton Bus. Cen. E10 ....4C **38**
Leyton Ct. SE23 ....1E **121**
Leyton Grange E10 ....3C **38**
Leyton Grn. Rd. E10 ....1E **39**
Leyton Grn. Twr. E10 ....1E **39**
................................(off Leyton Grn. Rd.)

Leyton Ho. E2 ....2F **11** (2B **64**)
................................(off Calvert Av.)
Leyton Ind. Village E10 ....2F **37**
Leyton Leisure Cen. 2E **39**
Leyton Link Est. E10 ....2A **38**
Leyton Mnr. Pk. 2D **39**
Leyton Midland Road Station
    (Overground) 2E **39**
Leyton Mills E10 ....5E **39**
Leyton Orient FC 5D **39**
Leyton Pk. Rd. E10 ....5E **39**
Leyton Rd. E15 ....2E **53**
Leyton Station (Underground)
....5E **39**
LEYTONSTONE 3A **40**
Leytonstone High Road Station
    (Overground) 4A **40**
Leytonstone Ho. E11 ....2B **40**
................................(off Hanbury Dr.)
Leytonstone Leisure Cen. 4A **40**
Leytonstone Rd. E15 ....3A **54**
Leytonstone Station
    (Underground) 3A **40**
Leyton Way E11 ....2A **40**
Leywick St. E15 ....1A **68**
Lianne Gro. SE9 ....3E **125**
Liardet St. SE14 ....2A **94**
Libari Mans. E20 ....2E **53**
................................(off Victory Pde.)
Liberia Rd. N5 ....3D **49**
Liberty Bri. Rd. E15 ....2E **53**
Liberty Bri. Rd. E20 ....2E **53**
Liberty Ho. E1 ....1C **78**
................................(off Ensign St.)
Liberty Ho. E13 ....1C **68**
Liberty M. SW12 ....4D **103**
Liberty St. SW9 ....4B **90**
Libra Mans. E3 ....1B **66**
................................(off Libra Rd.)
Libra Rd. E13 ....1C **68**
Libra Rd. E3 ....5B **52**
Library & Mus. of Freemasonry,
    The 2E **15** (5A **62**)
................................(off St. Queen St.)
Library Mans. W12 ....3E **71**
................................(off Pennard Rd.)
Library Pde. NW10 ....5A **42**
................................(off Craven Pk. Rd.)
Library Pl. E1 ....1D **79**
Library Sq. E1 ....3A **66**
Library St. SE1 ....4D **25** (3D **77**)
Lichfield Rd. E3 ....2A **66**
Lichfield Rd. E6 ....2F **69**
Lichfield Rd. NW2 ....1A **44**
Lickey Ho. W14 ....2B **86**
................................(off North End Rd.)
Lidcote Gdns. SW9 ....5B **90**
Liddell Gdns. NW10 ....1E **57**
Liddell Pl. NW6 ....3C **44**
Liddell Rd. NW6 ....3C **44**
Liddiard Ho. W11 ....1A **72**
................................(off Lansdowne Rd.)
Liddington Rd. E15 ....5B **54**
Liden Ho. E13 ....2D **69**
Liden Cl. E17 ....2B **38**
Lidfield Rd. N16 ....1F **49**
Lidgate Rd. SE15 ....3B **92**
Lidiard Rd. SW18 ....2E **115**
Lidlington Pl. NW1 ....1E **61**
Lidyard Rd. N19 ....3E **33**
Lifestyle Club @ Charlton, The
....3F **97**
Liffords Pl. SW13 ....5B **84**
Lifford St. SW15 ....2F **99**
Lighter Cl. SE16 ....5A **80**

Lighterman Ho. E14 ....1E 81
Lighterman M. E1 ....5F 65
Lighterman Point E14 ....5F 67
...............(off New Village Av.)
Lightermans Rd. E14 ....3C 80
Lightermans Wlk. SW16 ....2C 100
Lightfoot Vs. N1 ....4C 48
...............(off Augustas La.)
Light Horse Ct. SW3 ....1C 88
...............(off Royal Hospital Rd.)
Lighthouse, The 3E 91
Lighthouse Apts. E1 ....5E 65
...............(off Commercial Rd.)
Lighthouse Vw. SE10 ....2A 82
Ligonier St. E2 ....3F 11 (3B 64)
Lilac Cl. E13 ....5E 55
Lilac Ho. SE4 ....1C 108
Lilac La. E2 ....2F 65
Lilac Pl. SE11 ....5B 76
Lilac St. W12 ....1C 70
Lilestone Ho. NW8 ....3F 59
...............(off Frampton St.)
Lilestone St. NW8 ....3A 60
Lilford Ho. SE5 ....5E 91
Lilford Rd. SE5 ....5D 91
Lilian Barker Cl. SE12 ....3C 110
Lilian Cl. N16 ....5A 36
Lilian Knowles Ho.
E1 ....1F 19 (4B 64)
...............(off Crispin St.)
Lilium M. E10 ....2C 38
Lilley Cl. E1 ....2C 78
Lillian Rd. SW13 ....2C 84
Lillie Bri. Dpt. W14 ....1B 86
...............(off Aisgill Av.)
Lillie Mans. SW6 ....2A 86
...............(off Lillie Rd.)
Lillie Rd. SW6 ....2A 86
Lillie Road Fitness Cen. 3F 85
Lillieshall Rd. SW4 ....1D 103
Lillie Sq. SW6 ....2C 86
Lillie Yd. SW6 ....2C 86
Lillingston Ho. N7 ....1C 48
Lillington Gdns. Est.
SW1 ....5E 75
...............(off Vauxhall Bri. Rd.)
Lilliput Ct. SE12 ....3D 111
Lilliput Rd. E15 ....5A 54
Lily Cl. W14 ....5F 71
Lily M. SE11 ....5D 77
Lily Nichols Ho. E16 ....2F 83
...............(off Connaught Rd.)
Lily Pl. EC1 ....5C 8 (4C 62)
Lily Rd. E17 ....1C 38
Lilyville Rd. SW6 ....4B 86
Limasol St. SE16 ....5F 27 (4B 78)
Limborough Ho. E14 ....4C 66
...............(off Thomas Rd.)
Limburg Rd. SW11 ....2A 102
Limeburner La. EC4 .3D 17 (5D 63)
Lime Cl. E1 ....2C 78
Lime Cl. E11 ....4A 40
...............(off Trinity Cl.)
Lime Ct. E17 ....1E 39
Lime Gro. W12 ....3E 71
Limeharbour E14 ....4D 81
LIMEHOUSE 5B 66
Limehouse C'way. E14 ....1B 80
Lime Ho. Ct. E14 ....5B 66
...............(off Wharf La.)
Limehouse Cut. E14 ....5C 66
Limehouse Cut E14 ....4D 67
...............(off Morris Rd.)
Limehouse Flds. Est. E14 ...4A 66
Limehouse Link E14 ....5A 66

Limehouse Lodge E5 ....4E 37
...............(off Harry Zeital Way)
Limehouse Station (Rail & DLR)
....5A 66
Lime Kiln Dr. SE7 ....2D 97
Limekiln Wharf E14 ....1B 80
Limelight Ho. SE11 ....5D 77
...............(off Dugard Way)
Lime Quay E14 ....3E 67
Limerick Cl. SW12 ....5E 103
Limerston St. SW10 ....2E 87
Limes, The W1 ....4C 100
Limes, The W2 ....1C 72
Limes Av. NW11 ....2A 30
Limes Av. SW13 ....5B 84
Limes Ct. NW6 ....4A 44
...............(off Brondesbury Pk.)
Limes Fld. Rd. SW13 ....1A 98
Limesford Rd. SE15 ....2F 107
Limes Gdns. SW18 ....4C 100
Limes Gro. SE13 ....2E 109
Lime St. EC3 ....4D 19 (1A 78)
Lime St. Pas. EC3 ....3D 19 (5A 64)
Lime St. Sq. EC3 ....3D 19 (5A 64)
Limes Wlk. SE15 ....2E 107
Limetree Cl. SW2 ....1B 118
Lime Tree Cl. E3 ....4C 66
...............(off Whitehorn St.)
Lime Tree Ct. SE17 ....1E 91
...............(off Walworth Rd.)
Limetree Ter. SE6 ....1B 122
Limetree Wlk. SW17 ....5C 116
Lime View Apts. E14 ....5A 66
...............(off Commerical Rd.)
Lime Wlk. E15 ....5A 54
Limpsfield Av. SW19 ....2F 113
Limscott Ho. E3 ....2D 67
...............(off Bruce Rd.)
Linacre Cl. SE15 ....1D 107
Linacre Ct. W6 ....1F 85
Linacre Rd. NW2 ....3D 43
Linale Ho. N1 ....1B 10 (1F 63)
...............(off Murray Gro.)
Linberry Wlk. SE8 ....5B 80
Linchmere Rd. SE12 ....5B 110
Lincoln Apts. W12 ....1E 71
...............(off Fountain Park Way)
Lincoln Av. SW19 ....3F 113
Lincoln Ct. N16 ....2F 35
Lincoln Ct. SE12 ....3D 125
Lincoln Ho. SE5 ....3C 90
Lincoln Ho. SW3 ....4A 20 (3B 74)
Lincoln M. NW6 ....5B 44
Lincoln M. SE21 ....2F 119
Lincoln Plaza E14 ....3D 81
...............(off Lightermans Rd.)
Lincoln Rd. E13 ....3D 69
Lincoln Rd. E7 ....3F 55
Lincoln's Inn Flds.
WC2 ....2F 15 (5B 62)
Lincoln's Inn Hall 2A 16 (5B 62)
Lincoln St. E11 ....4A 40
Lincoln St. SW3 ....5B 74
Lincombe Rd. BR1: Broml ...3B 124
Lindal Rd. SE4 ....3B 108
Linden Av. NW10 ....1F 57
Linden Ct. W12 ....2E 71
Linden Gdns. W2 ....1A 84
Linden Gro. SE15 ....1D 107
Linden Ho. SE8 ....2B 94
...............(off Abinger Gro.)
Linden Lea N2 ....1E 31
Linden Mans. N6 ....3D 33
...............(off Hornsey La.)

Linden M. N1 ....2F 49
Linden M. W2 ....1C 72
Linden Wlk. N19 ....4E 33
Lindfield Gdns. NW3 ....2D 45
Lindfield St. E14 ....5C 66
Lindisfarne Way E9 ....1A 52
Lindley Est. SE15 ....3C 92
Lindley Ho. E1 ....4E 65
...............(off Lindley St.)
Lindley Ho. SE15 ....3C 92
...............(off Peckham Pk. Rd.)
Lindley Rd. E10 ....4E 39
Lindley St. E1 ....4E 65
Lindop Ho. E1 ....3A 66
...............(off Mile End Rd.)
Lindore Rd. SW11 ....2B 102
Lindo St. SE15 ....5E 93
Lindrop St. SW6 ....5E 87
Lindsay Ct. SE13 ....1D 109
...............(off Loampit Va.)
Lindsay Ct. SW11 ....4F 87
...............(off Battersea High St.)
Lindsay Ho. SW7 ....4E 73
...............(off Gloucester Rd.)
Lindsay Sq. SW1 ....1F 89
Lindsell St. SE10 ....4E 95
Lindsey M. N1 ....4E 49
Lindsey St. EC1 ....5E 9 (4D 63)
Lind St. SE8 ....5C 94
Lindway SE27 ....5D 119
Linear Pk. 2F 89
Linen Ho., The W10 ....1A 58
Linen M. W12 ....3B 70
Liner Ho. E16 ....3E 83
Linfield WC1 ....2F 7 (2B 62)
...............(off Sidmouth St.)
Linford Christie Stadium
....4C 56
Linford Ho. E16 ....4C 68
...............(off Hammersley Rd.)
Linford Ho. E2 ....5C 50
...............(off Whiston Rd.)
Linford St. SW8 ....4E 89
Linford St. Bus. Est. SW8 ...4E 89
...............(off Linford St.)
Lingard Ho. E14 ....4E 81
...............(off Marshfield St.)
Lingards Rd. SE13 ....2E 109
Lingfield Ho. SE1 ......4E 25 (3D 77)
...............(off Lancaster St.)
Lingfield Rd. SW19 ....5F 113
Lingham Ct. SW9 ....5A 90
Lingham St. SW9 ....5A 90
Ling Rd. E16 ....4C 68
Lings Coppice SE21 ....2F 119
Lingwell Rd. SW17 ....3A 116
Lingwood Rd. E5 ....2C 36
Linhope St. NW1 ....3B 60
Link, The NW2 ....3C 28
Linkenholt Mans. W6 ....5B 70
...............(off Stamford Brook Av.)
Link Ho. E3 ....2D 67
Link Ho. W10 ....1F 57
...............(off Kingsdown Cl.)
Link Rd. E1 ....1C 78
Links Rd. NW2 ....4B 28
Link St. E9 ....3E 51
Linksview N2 ....1B 32
Links Yd. E1 ....4C 64
...............(off Spelman St.)
Linkway N4 ....2E 35
Linkwood Wlk. NW1 ....4F 47
Linnell Cl. NW11 ....1D 31
Linnell Dr. NW11 ....1D 31

Linnell Ho. E1..............5F **11** (4B **64**)
...................................(off Folgate St.)
Linnell Ho. NW8........................5E **45**
...................................(off Ainsworth Way)
Linnell Rd. SE5.............................5A **92**
Linnet Cl. SW15.........................4E **99**
Linnet M. SW12..........................5C **102**
Linom Rd. SW4..........................2A **104**
Linscott Rd. E5...............................1E **51**
Linsey Ct. E10..............................3C **38**
...................................(off Grange Rd.)
Linsey St. SE16...............................5C **78**
...................................(not continuous)
Linslade Ho. E2...............................5C **50**
Linslade Ho. NW8......................3A **60**
...................................(off Paveley St.)
Linstead St. NW6.........................4C **44**
Linstead Way SW18.............5A **100**
Lintaine Cl. W6............................2A **86**
Linthorpe Rd. N16.......................2A **36**
Linton Cl. SE7................................1E **97**
Linton Ct. NW1.............................4E **47**
...................................(off Agar Gro.)
Linton Gdns. E6...........................5F **69**
Linton Gro. SE27........................5D **119**
Linton Ho. E3...............................4C **66**
...................................(off St Paul's Way)
Linton St. N1.................................5E **49**
...................................(not continuous)
Linver Rd. SW6............................5C **86**
Linwood Cl. SE5..........................5B **92**
Lion Apts. SE16...........................1D **93**
...................................(off Rotherhithe New Rd.)
Lion Cl. SE4.................................4C **108**
Lion Ct. E1......................................1F **79**
...................................(off The Highway)
Lion Ct. SE1.....................................5B **48**
...................................(off Copenhagen St.)
Lion Ct. SE1.................2D **21** (2D **75**)
...................................(off Magdalen St.)
Lionel Gdns. SE9.....................3F **111**
Lionel Mans. W14......................4F **71**
...................................(off Haarlem Rd.)
Lionel M. W10.............................4A **58**
Lionel Rd. SE9...........................3F **111**
Lion Ga. SW18...........................5C **100**
Lion Mills E2.................................1C **64**
Lions Cl. SE9..............................3E **125**
Lion Yd. SW4...............................2F **103**
Liphook Cres. SE23...................5E **107**
Lipton Rd. E1..................................5F **65**
Lisburne Rd. NW3........................1B **46**
Lisford St. SE15...........................4B **92**
Lisgar Ter. W14.............................5B **72**
Liskeard Gdns. SE3....................4C **96**
Liskeard Ho. SE11......................1C **90**
...................................(off Kennings Way)
Lisle Cl. SW17.............................4D **117**
Lisle Ct. NW2.................................5A **30**
Lisle St. WC2............4B **14** (1F **75**)
Lismore SW19...............................5B **114**
...................................(off Woodside)
Lismore Cir. NW5........................2C **46**
Lismore Wlk. N1............................3E **49**
...................................(off Clephane Rd. Nth.)
Lissenden Gdns. NW5..............1C **46**
...................................(not continuous)
Lissenden Mans. NW5.............1C **46**
Lisson Grn. Est. NW8................3A **60**
...................................(off Tresham Cres.)
Lisson Gro. NW1.........................3A **60**
Lisson Gro. NW8.........................3F **59**
LISSON GROVE 4A **60**
Lisson Ho. NW1...........................4A **60**
...................................(off Lisson St.)

Lisson St. NW1.............................4A **60**
Lister Cl. W3.................................4A **56**
Lister Cl. N16..............................4A **36**
Listergate Ct. SW15...................2E **99**
LISTER HOSPITAL, THE 1D **89**
Lister Ho. E1..................................4C **64**
...................................(off Lomas St.)
Lister Lodge W9...........................4C **58**
...................................(off Admiral Wlk.)
Lister Rd. E11...............................3A **40**
Liston Rd. SW4...........................1E **103**
Listowel Cl. SW9..........................3C **90**
Listria Pk. N16.............................4A **36**
Litcham Ho. E1.............................2F **65**
...................................(off Longnor Rd.)
Litchfield Av. E15.........................3A **54**
Litchfield Ct. E17.........................1C **38**
Litchfield Gdns. NW10..............3C **42**
Litchfield St. WC2.....4C **14** (1F **75**)
Lithos Rd. NW3.............................3D **45**
Little Albany St.
  NW1.............................3E **5** (3D **61**)
...................................(off Longford St.)
Little Angel Theatre 5D **49**
...................................(off Dagmar Ter.)
Little Argyll St. W1......3F **13** (5E **61**)
Little Boltons, The SW10.........1D **87**
Little Bolton, The SW5..............1D **87**
Little Bornes SE21.....................4A **120**
Littlebourne SE13.......................5A **110**
Littlebourne Ho. SE17...............1A **92**
...................................(off Upnor Way)
Little Britain EC1.........1E **17** (4D **63**)
Little Brownings SE23................2D **121**
Littlebury Rd. SW4.....................1F **103**
Little Chelsea Ho. SW10...........2E **87**
...................................(off Edith Gro.)
Little Chester St.
  SW1..........................5D **21** (4D **75**)
Little Cloisters SW1....5D **23** (4A **76**)
Little College La.
  EC4................................4B **18** (1F **77**)
...................................(off College St.)
Little College St.
  SW1..........................5D **23** (4A **76**)
Littlecombe SE7..........................2D **97**
Littlecombe Cl. SW15................4F **99**
Littlecote Cl. SW19.....................5A **100**
Little Cottage Pl. SE10...............3D **95**
Little Dean's Yd.
  SW1..........................5D **23** (4A **76**)
...................................(off Dean's Yd.)
Little Dimocks SW12................2D **117**
Little Dorrit Ct. SE1....3A **26** (3E **77**)
Little Edward St.
  NW1................................1E **5** (2D **61**)
Little Essex St.
  WC2..............................4B **16** (1C **76**)
...................................(off Essex St.)
Littlefield Cl. N19.........................1E **47**
Little George St.
  SW1..........................4D **23** (3A **76**)
Little Green St. NW5...................1D **47**
Little Heath SE7...........................2F **97**
Little Holt E11...............................1C **40**
Little London Ct. SE1.................3B **78**
...................................(off Wolseley St.)
Little Marlborough St.
  W1...............................3F **13** (5E **61**)
...................................(off Kingly St.)
Little Newport St.
  WC2..............................2C **14** (1F **75**)
Little New St. EC4......2C **16** (5C **62**)
Little Portland St.
  W1...............................2E **13** (5E **61**)

Little Russell St.
  WC1...............................1D **15** (4A **62**)
Little St James's St.
  SW1...............................2F **21** (2E **75**)
Little Sanctuary
  SW1..............................4C **22** (3F **75**)
Little Smith St. SW1 ....5C **22** (4F **75**)
Little Somerset St.
  E1.................................3F **19** (5B **64**)
Little South St. SE5.....................4A **92**
Little Thames Wlk. SE8.............2D **95**
...................................(off Dancers Way)
Little Titchfield St.
  W1..................................1F **13** (4E **61**)
Littleton Ho. SW1......................1E **89**
...................................(off Lupus St.)
Littleton St. SW18......................2E **115**
Little Trinity La.
  EC4..................................4A **18** (1E **77**)
Little Turnstile WC1...1F **15** (4B **62**)
LITTLE VENICE 4E **59**
Little Venice Sports Cen.........4F **59**
Littlewood SE13.........................4E **109**
Livermere Ct. E8..........................5B **50**
...................................(off Queensbridge Rd.)
Livermere Rd. E8.........................5B **50**
Liverpool Gro. SE17....................1E **91**
Liverpool Rd. E10.......................1E **39**
Liverpool Rd. E16.......................4A **68**
Liverpool Rd. N1...........................4C **48**
Liverpool Rd. N7...........................2C **48**
Liverpool St. EC2.......1D **19** (4A **64**)
Liverpool Street Station
  (Rail, Underground & Crossrail)
  ....1D **19** (4A **64**)
Livesey Pl. SE15..........................2C **92**
Livingstone Cl. E10.....................1E **39**
Livingstone Ho. SE5...................3E **91**
...................................(off Wyndham Rd.)
Livingstone Lodge W9..............4C **58**
...................................(off Admiral Wlk.)
Livingstone Mans. W14............2A **86**
...................................(off Queen's Club Gdns.)
Livingstone Pl. E14.....................1E **95**
Livingstone Rd. E17....................1D **39**
Livingstone Rd. SW11...............1F **101**
Livonia St. W1.............3A **14** (5E **61**)
Lizard St. EC1..............2A **10** (2E **63**)
Lizban St. SE3...............................3D **97**
Lizmans Ter. W8...........................4C **72**
...................................(off Earl's Ct. Rd.)
Llandovery Ho. E14.....................3E **81**
...................................(off Chipka St.)
Llanelly Rd. NW2.........................4B **30**
Llanvanor Rd. NW2....................4B **30**
Llewellyn Mans. W14................5A **72**
...................................(off Hammersmith Rd.)
Llewellyn St. SE16.......................3C **78**
Lloyd Baker St. WC1 ...2A **8** (2B **62**)
...................................(not continuous)
Lloyd Ct. SW15............................5B **88**
...................................(off Roydon Cl.)
Lloyd's Av. EC3 ....3E **19** (5A **64**)
Lloyd's Pl. SE3.............................5A **96**
Lloyd Sq. WC1..............1B **8** (2C **62**)
Lloyd's Row EC1..........2C **8** (2C **62**)
Lloyd St. WC1...............1B **8** (2C **62**)
Lloyds Wharf SE1........................3B **78**
...................................(off Mill St.)
Lloyd Vs. SE4................................5C **94**
Loampit Hill SE13........................5C **94**
Loampit Va. SE13........................1D **109**
LOAMPIT VALE 1E **109**
Loanda Cl. E8...............................5B **50**
Loats Rd. SW2............................4A **104**

Locarno Ct. SW16 ....5E **117**
Lochaber Rd. SE13 ....2A **110**
Lochaline St. W6 ....2E **85**
Lochinvar St. SW12 ....5D **103**
Lochmore Ho. SW1 ....5C **74**
......................(off Cundy St.)
Lochnagar St. E14 ....4E **67**
Lockbridge Ct. W9 ....4C **58**
......................(off Woodfield Rd.)
Lock Bldg., The E15.........1E **67**
Lock Chase SE3 ....1A **110**
Lock Ct. E5 ....4F **37**
Locke Hgts. N1 ....4B **48**
.....................(off Caledonian Rd.)
Locke Ho. SW8 ....4E **89**
......................(off Wadhurst Rd.)
Lockesfield Pl. E14 ....1D **95**
Lockgate St. E9 ....2B **52**
Lockhart Cl. N7 ....3B **48**
Lockhart St. E3 ....3B **66**
Lockhouse, The NW1 ....5C **46**
Lockhurst St. E5 ....1F **51**
Lockington Rd. SW8 ....4D **89**
Lock Keepers Hgts. SE16 ....4F **79**
......................(off Brunswick Quay)
Lockmead Rd. N15 ....1C **36**
Lockmead Rd. SE13.........1E **109**
Lock M. NW1 ....3F **47**
......................(off Northpoint Sq.)
Lock Mill Apts. E2 ....5B **50**
......................(off Whiston Rd.)
Locksfields SE17 ....5F **77**
......................(off Catesby St.)
Lockside E14 ....1A **80**
......................(off Narrow St.)
Locksley Est. E14 ....5B **66**
Locksley Ho. E15 ....3F **53**
......................(off Forrester Way)
Locksley St. E14 ....4B **66**
Locksons Cl. E14 ....4D **67**
Lockton St. W10 ....1F **71**
......................(off Bramley Rd.)
Lock Vw. Ct. E14 ....1A **80**
......................(off Narrow St.)
Lockwood Ct. SE26..........4F **121**
Lockwood Ho. E5 ....4E **37**
Lockwood Ho. SE11 ....2C **90**
Lockwood Sq. SE16 ....4D **79**
Lockyer Est. SE1 ...3C **26** (3F **77**)
......................(off Kipling St.)
Lockyer Ho. SE10 ....1B **96**
......................(off Armitage Rd.)
Lockyer Ho. SW15 ....1F **99**
Lockyer Ho. SW8 ....3F **89**
......................(off Wandsworth Rd.)
Lockyer St. SE1 ...4C **26** (3F **77**)
Locton Grn. E3 ....5B **52**
Loddiges Ho. E9 ....4E **51**
Loddiges Rd. E9 ....4E **51**
Loddon Ho. NW8 ....3F **59**
......................(off Church St. Est.)
Loder St. SE15 ....3E **93**
Lodge, The W12 ....3F **71**
......................(off Richmond Way)
Lodge Av. SW14 ....1A **98**
Lodge M. N5 ....1E **49**
Lodge Rd. NW8 ....2F **59**
Lodore Gdns. NW9 ....1A **28**
Lodore St. E14 ....5E **67**
Loft, The W12 ....2F **71**
Loft Ho. E1 ....2F **19** (5B **64**)
......................(off Middlesex St.)
Loftie St. SE16 ....3C **78**
Lofting Ho. N1 ....4C **48**
......................(off Liverpool Rd.)

Lofting Rd. N1 ....4B **48**
Lofts on the Pk. E9 ....3F **51**
......................(off Cassland Rd.)
Loftus Rd. W12 ....2D **71**
Loftus Vs. W12 ....2D **71**
......................(off Loftus Rd.)
Logan Cl. E20 ....2E **53**
Logan M. W8 ....5C **72**
Logan Pl. W8 ....5C **72**
Loggetts SE21 ....2A **120**
Lohmann Ho. SE11 ....2C **90**
......................(off Kennington Oval)
Lolesworth Cl. E1 ....1F **19** (4B **64**)
Lolland Ho. SE7 ....5F **83**
Lollard St. SE11 ....5B **76**
......................(not continuous)
Loman St. SE1 ....3E **25** (3D **77**)
Lomas Dr. E8 ....4B **50**
Lomas St. E1 ....4C **64**
Lombard Ct. EC3 ...4C **18** (1F **77**)
Lombard La. EC4 ...3C **16** (5C **62**)
Lombard Pl. E3 ....1A **66**
Lombard Rd. SW11 ....5F **87**
Lombard St. EC3 ...3C **18** (5F **63**)
Lombard Trad. Est. SE7......5D **83**
Lombard Wall SE7 ....4D **83**
Lombard Wharf SW11 ....5F **87**
Lombardy Pl. W2 ....1D **73**
Lomond Gro. SE5 ....3F **91**
Lomond Ho. SE5 ....3F **91**
Loncroft Rd. SE5 ....2B **92**
Londesborough Rd. N16 .....1A **50**
Londinium Twr. E1 ....4F **19** (1B **78**)
......................(off W. Tenter St.)
LONDON...............1D **23** (2A **76**)
London Aquatics Cen. Queen
     Elizabeth Olympic Pk......4E **53**
London Bri. E14 ...1C **26** (1F **77**)
London Bri. SE1 ...1C **26** (2F **77**)
London Bridge City Pier (River
     Bus).................1C **26** (2A **78**)
London Bridge Experience
     ....1C **26** (2F **77**)
......................(off Tooley St.)
LONDON BRIDGE HOSPITAL
     ....1C **26** (2F **77**)
London Bridge Station (Rail &
     Underground) 2C **26** (2F **77**)
London Bri. St. SE1...2C **26** (2F **77**)
London Bri. Wlk. SE1...1C **26** (2F **77**)
......................(off Duke St. Hill)
London Business School
     ....3A **4** (3B **60**)
London Canal Mus............1A **62**
London Central Markets
     ....1D **17** (4D **63**)
......................(off West Smithfield)
London City Coll. 2B **24** (2C **76**)
......................(off Waterloo Rd.)
LONDON COLISEUM....4C **4** (3C **60**)
London Coliseum .5D **15** (1A **76**)
......................(off St Martin's La.)
London College of Fashion, The
     John Prince's St....2E **13** (5D **61**)
London College of Fashion, The
     Mare St............................4E **51**
London Dock E1..................1C **78**
London Dungeon 3F **23** (3B **76**)
London Eye 3F **23** (3B **76**)
LONDON EYE HOSPITAL
     ....2D **13** (5D **61**)
......................(off Harley St.)
London Eye Millennium Pier
     (River Bus & Tours)
     ....3F **23** (3B **76**)

London Flds. East Side E8...4D **51**
London Fields Lido 4D **51**
London Fields Station
     (Overground) 4D **51**
London Flds. West Side E8...4C **50**
London Film Mus......4E **15** (1A **76**)
......................(off Wellington St.)
London Fruit Exchange
     E1.........................1F **19** (4B **64**)
......................(off Brushfield St.)
London Group Bus. Pk.
     NW2..3B **28**
London Heliport, The 5E **87**
London Ho. EC1 .....1F **17** (4E **63**)
......................(off Aldersgate St.)
London Ho. NW8 ....1A **60**
......................(off Avenue Rd.)
London Ho. WC1 .....3F **7** (3B **62**)
LONDON INDEPENDENT BMI
     HOSPITAL 4F **65**
London Info. Cen. ...5C **14** (1F **75**)
......................(off Leicester Sq.)
London International Gallery of
     Children's Art..................3D **33**
......................(within Waterloo Pk. Cen.)
London La. E8 ....4D **51**
London Marathon Community
     Track...............................5D **53**
London Master Bakers
     Almshouses E10...........1D **39**
London Mercantile Court
     ....2B **16** (5C **62**)
London Metropolitan Archives
     ....3C **8** (3C **62**)
......................(off Northampton Rd.)
London Metropolitan University
     London City Campus, Calcutta
     House & Goulston St.
     ....2F **19** (5B **64**)
London Metropolitan University
     London City Campus, Central
     House 5C **64**
......................(off Whitechapel High St.)
London Metropolitan University
     London City Campus,
     Commercial Rd..................5C **64**
London Metropolitan University
     London City Campus, Moorgate
     ....1B **18** (4F **63**)
......................(off Moorgate)
London Metropolitan University
     North London Campus,
     Eden Grove 2B **48**
London Metropolitan University
     North London Campus,
     Stapleton House..............2B **48**
London Metropolitan University
     North London Campus, Tower
     Bldg. & Graduate Cen. 2C **48**
London M. W2 ....5F **59**
London Mill Apts. E2 ....5B **50**
......................(off Whiston Rd.)
London Mithraeum ...3B **18** (5F **63**)
......................(off Queen Victoria Street)
London Oxford St. Youth Hostel
     W1.......................3A **14** (5E **61**)
......................(off Noel St.)
London Palace, The 5E **77**
......................(within Elephant & Castle
     Shopping Centre)
London Palladium....3F **13** (5E **61**)
London Plane Ho. E15 ......2A **68**
......................(off Teasel Way)
London Regatta Cen........1F **83**

London Rd. E13................................1C 68
London Rd. SE1........5D 25 (4D 77)
London Rd. SE23..............................1D 121
London School of Economics &
  Political Science....3A 16 (5B 62)
London Scottish Golf Course
  ....3D 113
London South Bank University
  Keyworth St...............5E 25 (4D 77)
London South Bank University
  Southwark Campus5E 25 (4D 77)
London South Bank University
  Technopark..........5E 25 (4D 77)
              (off London Rd.)
London's Roman Amphitheatre
  ....2B 18 (5F 63)
          (off Aldermanbury)
London Stadium Queen Elizabeth
  Olympic Pk...............................4D 53
London St. EC3............4E 19 (1A 78)
London St. W2.................................5F 59
London Ter. E2.................................1C 64
              .4E 15 (1A 76)
London Trocadero....4B 14 (1F 75)
London Wall EC2......1A 18 (4E 63)
London Wall Bldgs.
  EC2............................1C 18 (4F 63)
          (off London Wall)
London Wall Pl. EC2..1A 18 (4E 63)
          (off St Alphage Gdn.)
LONDON WELBECK HOSPITAL
  ....1C 12 (4C 60)
          (off Welbeck St.)
London Wetland Cen.........4D 85
London Wetland Cen. Vis. Cen.
  ....4D 85
London Wharf E2.......................5D 51
              (off Wharf Pl.)
London Zoo..............1B 4 (1C 60)
Long Acre WC2.........3D 15 (1A 76)
Longbeach Rd. SW11...........1B 102
Longberrys NW2......................5B 30
Longbow Apts. E3...................3B 66
          (off St Clements Av.)
Longbow Ho. EC1....5B 10 (4F 63)
           (off Chiswell St.)
Longbridge Way SE13 ....3E 109
Longdown Rd. SE6...............4C 122
Long Dr. W3...............................5A 56
Longfellow Rd. E17..............1B 38
Longfellow Way SE1 ....5B 78
Longfield Cres. SE26 ......3E 121
Longfield Est. SE1..................5B 78
Longfield St. SW18 ....5C 100
Longford Ct. E5........................1F 51
             (off Pedro St.)
Longford Ho. BR1: Broml....5F 123
        (off Brangbourne Rd.)
Longford Ho. E1.....................5E 65
           (off Jubilee St.)
Longford St. NW1......3E 5 (3D 61)
Longford Wk. SW2..............5C 104
Longhedge Ho. SE26..........4C 120
        (off High Level Dr.)
Longhedge St. SW11..........5C 88
Longhill Rd. SE6.....................2F 123
Longhope Cl. SE15...............2A 92
Longhurst Ho. W10..............2B 58
         (off Lancefield St.)
Longhurst Rd. SE13............3F 109
Longland Ct. E9........................2A 52
           (off Mabley St.)
Longland Ct. SE1....................1C 92
Longlands Ct. W11................1B 72

Long La. EC1..................1E 17 (4D 63)
Long La. SE1.................4B 26 (3F 77)
Longleat Ho. SW1................1F 89
         (off Rampayne St.)
Longleigh Ho. SE5................4A 92
         (off Peckham Rd.)
Long Lents Ho. NW10........5A 42
       (off Shrewsbury Rd.)
Longley Ct. SW8....................4A 90
Longley Rd. SW17...............5A 116
Longley St. SE1.......................5C 78
Longley Way NW2..................5E 29
Longman Ho. E2.....................1F 65
           (off Mace St.)
Longman Ho. E8.....................5B 50
        (off Haggerston Rd.)
Long Mark Rd. E16................4F 69
Longmead Ho. SE27..........5E 119
Long Mdw. NW5.....................2F 47
Longmead Rd. SW17.........5B 116
Long Mill SE10.......................4D 95
       (off Greenwich High Rd.)
Longmoore St. SW1............5E 75
Longmoor Point SW15......1D 113
          (off Norley Va.)
Longmore Gdns. Est. SW1..5E 75
        (off Vauxhall Bri. Rd.)
Longnor Est. E1......................2F 65
Longnor Rd. E1........................2F 65
Long Pond Rd. SE3................4A 96
Longridge Ho. SE1 ..5A 26 (4E 77)
Longridge Rd. SW5...............5C 72
Long Rd. SW4..........................2D 103
Long's Ct. WC2............5C 14 (1F 75)
           (off Orange St.)
Longshore SE8.........................5B 80
Longshott Ct. SW5...............5C 72
       (off W. Cromwell Rd.)
Longstaff Cres. SW18.........4C 100
Longstaff Rd. SW18...........4C 100
Longstone Av. NW10..........4B 42
Longstone Ct. SE1 ..4A 26 (3E 77)
         (off Gt. Dover St.)
Longstone Rd. SW17.........5D 117
Long St. E2..................1F 11 (2B 64)
Longthorpe Ct. W6...............5C 70
Longton Av. SE26.................4C 120
Longton Gro. SE26...............4D 121
Long Wlk. SE1........................5D 77
Long Wlk.
  SW13: Lon Barnes................5A 84
Long Wlk. SE1.............5E 27 (4A 78)
Long Wall E15..........................2F 67
Longwood Dr. SW15...........4C 98
Long Yd. WC1...............4F 7 (3B 62)
Lonsdale Av. E6......................3F 69
Lonsdale Cl. E6.......................4F 69
Lonsdale Cl. SE9....................3F 125
Lonsdale Ho. W11.................5B 58
           (off Lonsdale Rd.)
Lonsdale M. W11...................5B 58
           (off Colville M.)
Lonsdale Pl. N1.......................4C 48
Lonsdale Rd. E11...................1B 40
Lonsdale Rd. NW6.................1B 58
Lonsdale Rd. SW13...............2C 84
Lonsdale Rd. W11..................5B 58
Lonsdale Rd. W4....................5B 70
Lonsdale Road Reservoir Local
  Nature Reserve...................3B 84
Lonsdale Sq. N1.....................4C 48
Lonsdale Yd. W11.................1C 72
Lookout La. E14.....................5A 68
Loop Ct. SE10.........................5A 82
         (off Telegraph Av.)

Lopez Ho. SW9......................1A 104
Loraine Cotts. N7..................1B 48
Loraine Rd. N7........................1B 48
Lord Amory Way E14...........3E 81
Lordell Pl. SW19.................5E 113
Lorden Wlk. E2.......................2C 64
Lord Hills Bri. W2.................4D 59
Lord Hills Rd. W2...................4D 59
Lord Holland La. SW9..........5C 90
Lord Kensington Ho. W14....5B 72
          (off Radnor Ter.)
Lord Napier Pl. W6...............1C 84
Lord Nth. St. SW1 ....5D 23 (4A 76)
Lord Roberts M. SW6...........3D 87
Lord's..2F 59
Lords Cl. SE21........................2E 119
Lordship Gro. N16..................4F 35
Lordship La. SE22................2B 106
Lordship La. Est. SE21........5C 106
Lordship Pk. N16....................4E 35
Lordship Pk. M. N16..............4E 35
Lordship Pl. SW3...................2A 88
Lordship Rd. N16...................3F 35
Lordship Ter. N16...................4F 35
Lords Vw. NW8.......................2F 59
        (not continuous)
Loreburn Ho. N7.....................1B 48
Lorenzo St. WC1.........1F 7 (2B 62)
Loring Rd. SE14.......................4A 94
Loris Rd. W6............................4E 71
Lorn Ct. SW9............................5C 90
Lorne Cl. NW8........................2A 60
Lorne Gdns. W11...................3F 71
Lorne Ho. E1.............................4A 66
        (off Ben Jonson Rd.)
Lorne Rd. E7.............................1C 38
Lorne Rd. E17..........................1D 55
Lorne Rd. N4.............................3B 34
Lorn Rd. SW9...........................5B 90
Lorraine Ct. NW1....................4D 47
Lorrimore Rd. SE17................2D 91
Lorrimore Sq. SE17................2D 91
Lorton Ho. NW6......................5C 44
        (off Kilburn Vale)
Lost Theatre...........................4F 89
Lothair Rd. Nth. N4...............1D 35
Lothair Rd. Sth. N4................2C 34
Lothair St. SW11...................1A 102
Lothbury EC2...............2B 18 (5F 63)
Lothian Rd. SW9.....................4D 91
Lothrop St. W10.....................2A 58
Lots Rd. SW10.........................3E 87
Lotus Cl. SE21........................3F 119
Lotus M. N19...........................4A 34
Loubet St. SW17..................5B 116
Loudoun Rd. NW8.................5E 45
Loughborough Est. SW9....1D 105
Loughborough Junction Station
  (Rail)......................................1D 105
Loughborough Pk. SW9.....2D 105
Loughborough Rd. SW9......5C 90
Loughborough St. SE11......1B 90
Lough Rd. N7............................2B 48
Louisa Cl. E9.............................5F 51
Louisa Gdns. E1......................3F 65
Louisa St. E1.............................3F 65
Louise Aumonier Wlk. N19...2A 34
        (off Jessie Blythe La.)
Louise Bennett Cl. SE24....2D 105
Louise Ct. E11..........................1D 41
Louise De Marillac Ho. E1....4E 66
          (off Smithy St.)
Louise Rd. E15.........................3A 54
Louise White Ho. N19..........3F 33
Louisville Rd. SW17............3C 116

Lourdes Cl. SE13.................1F **109**
Louvaine Rd. SW11............2F **101**
Lovat Cl. E14........................5B **66**
Lovat Cl. NW2......................5B **28**
Lovat La. EC3...........4D **19** (1A **78**)
Lovatt Ct. SW12..................1D **117**
Lovegrove St. SE1..............1C **92**
Lovegrove Wlk. E14.............2E **81**
Lovejoy Cl. SE11.................2C **90**
.........................(off Pownell Ter.)
Lovelace Rd. SE21..............2E **119**
Lovelace St. E8...................5B **50**
Loveland Cl. SE1................3B **78**
.........................(off Jamaica Rd.)
Love La. EC2.............2A **18** (5E **63**)
Lovelinch Cl. SE15..............2E **93**
Lovell Ho. E8......................5C **50**
.........................(off Shrubland Rd.)
Lovell Pl. SE16....................1A **80**
Loveridge M. NW6...............3B **44**
Loveridge Rd. NW6..............3B **44**
Lovers Wlk. SE10................2F **95**
Lovers' Wlk. W1....1B **20** (2C **74**)
Lovett's Pl. SW18...............2D **101**
Love Wlk. SE5.....................5F **91**
Lovibond La. SE10..............3D **95**
.........................(off Norman Rd.)
Low Cross Wood La. SE21 3B **120**
Lowden Rd. SE24................2D **105**
Lowder Ho. E1.....................2D **79**
.........................(off Wapping La.)
Lowe Av. E16......................4C **68**
Lowell Ho. SE5....................3E **91**
.........................(off Wyndham Est.)
Lowell St. E14.....................5A **66**
Lower Addison Gdns. W14...3A **72**
Lower Belgrave St.
 SW1......................5D **21** (4D **75**)
LOWER CLAPTON................1D **51**
Lower Clapton Rd. E5..........5D **37**
Lower Clarendon Wlk. W11...5A **58**
.........................(off Clarendon Rd.)
Lower Common St. SW15...1D **99**
Lower Grosvenor Pl.
 SW1......................5D **21** (4D **75**)
LOWER HOLLOWAY.............2B **48**
Lower James St.
 W1.........................4A **14** (1E **75**)
Lower John St. W1....4A **14** (1E **75**)
Lower Lea Crossing E14......1A **82**
Lower Lea Crossing E16......1A **82**
Lower Mall W6....................1D **85**
Lower Marsh SE1....4A **24** (3C **76**)
Lower Merton Ri. NW3.........4A **46**
Lower New Change Pas.
 EC4........................3A **18** (5D **63**)
.........................(off One New Change)
Lower Richmond Rd.
 SW15...............................1D **99**
Lower Rd. SE1........3B **24** (3C **76**)
Lower Rd. SE16...................3E **79**
.........................(not continuous)
Lower Rd. SE8.....................5F **79**
Lower Robert St.
 WC2......................5E **15** (1A **76**)
.........................(off Robert St.)
Lower Sloane St. SW1.........5C **74**
Lower Stable St. N1.............5A **48**
.........................(off Stable Street)
LOWER SYDENHAM.............4F **121**
Lower Sydenham Ind. Est.
 SE26.................................5B **122**
Lower Sydenham Station (Rail)
 ....5B **122**
Lower Ter. NW3...................5E **31**

Lower Ter. SE27..................5D **119**
.........................(off Woodcote Pl.)
Lower Thames St.
 EC3......................5C **18** (1F **77**)
Lowerwood Ct. W11.............5A **58**
.........................(off Westbourne Pk. Rd.)
Lowestoft Cl. E5..................4E **37**
.........................(off Theydon Rd.)
Loweswater Ho. E3..............3B **66**
Lowfield Rd. NW6................4C **44**
Low Hall La. E17..................1A **38**
Low Hall Mnr. Bus. Cen.
 E17...................................1A **38**
Lowman Rd. N7...................1B **48**
Lowndes Cl. SW1....5C **20** (4C **74**)
Lowndes Ct. SW1....5A **20** (4B **74**)
Lowndes Ct. W1.......3F **13** (5E **61**)
.........................(off Carnaby St.)
Lowndes Lodge
 SW1......................5A **20** (4B **74**)
.........................(off Cadogan Pl.)
Lowndes M. SW16...............2A **118**
Lowndes Pl. SW1....5B **20** (4C **74**)
Lowndes Sq. SW1...4A **20** (3B **74**)
Lowndes St. SW1....5A **20** (4C **74**)
Lowood Ct. SE19..................5B **120**
.........................(off Farquhar Rd.)
Lowood Ho. E1....................1E **79**
.........................(off Bewley St.)
Lowood St. E1......................1D **79**
Lowry Ct. SE16....................1D **93**
.........................(off Stubbs Dr.)
Lowry Ho. E14.....................3C **80**
.........................(off Cassilis Rd.)
Lowther Hill SE23................5A **108**
Lowther Ho. E8....................1B **89**
.........................(off Churchill Gdns.)
Lowther Rd. N7...................2C **48**
Lowther Rd. SW13...............4B **84**
Lowth Rd. SE5.....................4E **91**
Loxford Av. E6.....................1F **69**
Loxford Gdns. N5.................1D **49**
Loxham St. WC1.....2E **7** (2A **62**)
Loxley Cl. SE26...................5F **121**
Loxley Rd. SW18.................1F **115**
Loxton St. SE23..................1F **121**
LSO St Lukes.........3A **10** (3E **63**)
.........................(off Old St.)
Lubbock Ho. E14.................1D **81**
.........................(off Poplar High St.)
Lubbock St. SE14................3E **93**
Lucan Ho. N1......................5F **49**
.........................(off Colville St.)
Lucan Pl. SW3....................5A **74**
Lucas Av. E13.....................5D **55**
Lucas Ct. NW10..................4C **42**
Lucas Ct. SE26...................5A **122**
Lucas Ct. SW11...................4C **88**
Lucas Ho. SW10..................3D **87**
.........................(off Coleridge Gdns.)
Lucas Ho. WC1.......2D **7** (2A **62**)
.........................(off Argyle Wlk.)
Lucas Sq. NW11..................1C **30**
Lucas St. SE8.....................4C **94**
Lucent Ho. SW18.................3C **100**
.........................(off Hardwicks Sq.)
Lucerne M. W8....................3C **72**
Lucerne Rd. N5...................1D **49**
Lucey Rd. SE16...................4C **78**
Lucey Way SE16..................4C **78**
Lucia Hgts. E20...................2E **53**
.........................(off Logan Cl.)
Lucien Ho. SW17.................4C **116**
Lucien Rd. SW19.................2D **115**
Lucorn Cl. SE12...................4B **110**

Lucy Brown Ho.
 SE1......................2A **26** (2E **77**)
.........................(off Park St.)
Ludgate B'way.
 EC4.........................3D **17** (5D **63**)
Ludgate Cir. EC4....3D **17** (5D **63**)
Ludgate Hill EC4....3D **17** (5D **63**)
Ludgate Sq. EC4....3E **17** (5D **63**)
Ludham NW5.......................2B **46**
Ludlow St. EC1.........3F **9** (3E **63**)
Ludovick Wlk. SW15.............2A **98**
Ludwell Ho. W14.................4A **72**
.........................(off Russell Rd.)
Ludwick M. SE14.................3A **94**
Luff Ct. E3..........................4C **66**
.........................(off Shellmerdine Cl.)
Luffman Rd. SE12................3D **125**
Lugard Ho. W12...................2D **71**
.........................(off Bloemfontein Rd.)
Lugard Rd. SE15..................5D **93**
Luke Ho. E1........................5D **65**
.........................(off Tillman St.)
Lukes Cl. NW2....................4C **28**
Luke St. EC2...........3D **11** (3A **64**)
Lukin St. E1........................5E **65**
Luli Ct. SE14......................2B **94**
Lullingstone Ho. SE15..........2E **93**
.........................(off Lovelinch Cl.)
Lullingstone La. SE13...........4F **109**
Lulot Gdns. N19..................4D **33**
Lulsgate M. E3....................3B **66**
Lulworth NW1......................4F **47**
.........................(off Wrotham Rd.)
Lulworth SE17.....................1F **91**
.........................(off Portland St.)
Lulworth Ct. N1....................4A **50**
.........................(off St Peter's Way)
Lulworth Ho. SW8................3B **90**
Lulworth Rd. SE15...............5D **93**
Lulworth Rd. SE9.................2F **125**
Lumiere Apts. SW11.............2F **101**
Lumiere Bldg., The E7..........2F **55**
.........................(off Romford Rd.)
Lumiere Ct. SW17................2C **116**
Lumina Bldgs. E14...............2E **81**
.........................(off Prestons Rd.)
Lumina Loft Apts.
 SE1.........................4E **27** (3A **78**)
.........................(off Tower Bri. Rd.)
Lumley Ct. WC2....................1A (1A **76**)
Lumley Flats SW1................1C **88**
.........................(off Holbein Pl.)
Lumley St. W1.........3C **12** (5C **60**)
Lumsdon NW8.....................5D **45**
.........................(off Abbey Rd.)
Luna Ho. SE16....................3C **78**
Lunan Ho. E3......................1B **66**
.........................(off Shetland Rd.)
Lunaria Ho. E20..................2E **53**
.........................(off Elis Way)
Lund Point E15....................5E **53**
Lundy Wlk. N1.....................3E **49**
Lunham Rd. SE19................5A **120**
Luntley Pl. E1......................4C **64**
.........................(off Chicksand St.)
Lupin Cl. SW2.....................2D **119**
Lupin Cl. SE11....................5B **76**
Lupin Point SE1...................3B **78**
.........................(off Abbey St.)
Lupton Cl. SE12..................3D **125**
Lupton St. NW5...................1E **47**
.........................(not continuous)
Lupus St. SW1....................1D **89**
Luralda Wharf E14...............1F **95**
Lurgan Av. W6....................2F **85**

Lurline Gdns. SW11............4C **88**
Luscombe Way SW8..........3A **90**
Lushington Rd. NW10..........1D **57**
Lushington Rd. SE6............4D **123**
Lushington Ter. E8...............2C **50**
Luther King Cl. E17...............1B **38**
Luton Ho. E13.......................3C **68**
..............................(off Luton Rd.)
Luton Pl. SE10....................3E **95**
Luton Rd. E13.....................3C **68**
Luton St. NW8....................3F **59**
Lutton Ter. NW3....................1E **45**
..................................(off Lakis Cl.)
Luttrell Av. SW15................3D **99**
Lutwyche M. SE6................2B **122**
Lutwyche Rd. SE6...............2B **122**
Lutyens Ho. SW1..................1E **89**
........................(off Churchill Gdns.)
Lux Apts. SW18...................3C **100**
Luxborough Ho. W1..5B 4 (4C **60**)
........................(off Luxborough St.)
Luxborough St. W1....4B 4 (4C **60**)
Luxborough Twr. W1..5B 4 (4C **60**)
........................(off Luxborough St.)
Luxemburg M. E15.............2A **54**
Luxemburg Gdns. W6........5F **71**
Luxfield Rd. SE9..................1F **125**
Luxford St. SE16.................5F **79**
Luxmore St. SE4.................4B **94**
Luxor St. SE5.....................1E **105**
Lyall Av. SE21....................4A **120**
Lyall M. SW1..........5B **20** (4C **74**)
Lyall M. W. SW1....................4C **74**
Lyall St. SW1..........5B **20** (4C **74**)
Lyal Rd. E3.........................1A **66**
Lycett Pl. W12....................3C **70**
Lyceum Theatre London
....................4F **15** (1B **76**)
........................(off Wellington St.)
Lydden Gro. SW18.............5D **101**
Lydden Rd. SW18...............5D **101**
Lydford NW1.........................5E **47**
........................(off Royal College St.)
Lydford Cl. N16....................2A **50**
..................................(off Pellerin Rd.)
Lydford Rd. N15...................1F **35**
Lydford Rd. NW2..................3E **43**
Lydford Rd. W9...................3B **58**
Lydhurst Av. SW2...............2B **118**
Lydney Cl. SW19................2A **114**
Lydon Rd. SW4...................1E **103**
Lyell St. E14.......................5A **68**
Lyford Rd. SW18................5F **101**
Lygon Ho. E2........................2B **64**
....................................(off Gosset St.)
Lygon Ho. SW6....................4A **86**
........................(off Fulham Pal. Rd.)
Lygon Pl. SW1........5D **21** (4D **75**)
Lyham Cl. SW2...................4A **104**
Lyham Rd. SW2..................3A **104**
Lyly Ho. SE1...........5C **26** (4F **77**)
..................................(off Burbage Cl.)
Lyme Farm Rd. SE12.........2C **110**
Lyme Gro. E9........................4E **51**
Lyme Gro. Ho. E9................4E **51**
..................................(off Lyme Gro.)
Lymer Av. SE19.................5B **120**
Lyme St. NW1.......................4E **47**
Lyme Ter. NW1.....................4E **47**
Lyminge Gdns. SW18........1A **116**
Lymington Lodge E14...........4F **81**
..................................(off Schooner Cl.)
Lymington Rd. NW6............3D **45**
Lympstone Gdns. SE15.......3C **92**

Lynbrook Gro. SE15...........3A **92**
Lynch Cl. SE3.....................5B **96**
Lynch Wlk. SE8...................2B **94**
..................................(off Prince St.)
Lyncott Cres. SW4..............2D **103**
Lyncourt SE3.......................5F **95**
Lyncroft Gdns. NW6...........2C **44**
Lyncroft Mans. NW6...........2C **44**
Lyndale NW2......................1B **44**
Lyndale Av. NW2.................5B **30**
Lyndale Cl. SE3..................2B **96**
Lynde Ho. SW4...................1F **103**
Lynden Ho. E1.....................2F **65**
..................................(off Westfield Way)
Lyndhurst Cl. NW10............5A **28**
Lyndhurst Cl. NW8...............5F **45**
..................................(off Finchley Rd.)
Lyndhurst Dr. E10................2E **39**
Lyndhurst Gdns. NW3.........2F **45**
Lyndhurst Gro. SE15...........5A **92**
Lyndhurst Lodge E14..........5F **81**
........................(off Millennium Dr.)
Lyndhurst Rd. NW3.............2F **45**
Lyndhurst Sq. SE15............4B **92**
Lyndhurst Ter. NW3.............2F **45**
Lyndhurst Way SE15...........4B **92**
Lyndon Yd. SW17...............4E **115**
Lyneham Wlk. E5................2A **52**
Lynette Av. SW4..................4D **103**
Lynford French Ho. SE17.....1E **91**
..................................(off Thrush St.)
Lyn M. E3.............................2B **66**
Lyn M. N16...........................1A **50**
Lynmouth Rd. E17...............1A **38**
Lynmouth Rd. N16...............3B **36**
Lynne Cl. SE23..................5B **108**
Lynne Ct. NW6...................4D **45**
..................................(off Priory Rd.)
Lynette Ct. E9.....................3A **52**
..................................(off Annis Rd.)
Lynn Ho. SE15.....................2D **93**
..................................(off Friary Est.)
Lynn M. E11........................4A **40**
Lynn Rd. E11......................4A **40**
Lynn Rd. SW12..................5D **103**
Lynsted Gdns. SE9............2F **111**
Lynton Cl. NW10................2A **42**
Lynton Est. SE1...................5C **78**
Lynton Ho. W2....................5E **59**
..................................(off Hallfield Est.)
Lynton Mans. SE1...5B **24** (4C **76**)
........................(off Westminster Bri. Rd.)
Lynton Rd. N8.....................1F **33**
..................................(not continuous)
Lynton Rd. NW6..................1B **58**
Lynton Rd. SE1...................5B **78**
Lynwood Rd. SW17.............3B **116**
Lynx Way E16.......................1F **83**
Lyon Ho. NW8......................3A **60**
..................................(off Broadley St.)
Lyon Ind. Est. NW2.............4D **29**
Lyons Pl. NW8....................3F **59**
Lyon St. N1..........................4B **48**
Lyons Wlk. W14..................5A **72**
Lyric Ct. E8..........................4B **50**
..................................(off Holly St.)
Lyric M. SE26.....................4E **121**
Lyric Rd. SW13...................4B **84**
Lyric Sq. W6........................5E **71**
..................................(off King St.)
Lyric Theatre Hammersmith
..............................5E **71**
Lyric Theatre Westminster
....................4B **14** (1F **75**)
........................(off Shaftesbury Av.)

Lysander Gro. N19................3F **33**
Lysander Ho. E2...................1D **65**
..................................(off Temple St.)
Lysander M. N19...................3E **33**
Lysia Ct. SW6......................3F **85**
..................................(off Lysia St.)
Lysias Rd. SW12................4D **103**
Lysia St. SW6......................3F **85**
Lysons Wlk. SW15..............2C **98**
Lytcott Gro. SE22...............3A **106**
Lytham St. SE17...................1F **91**
Lyttelton Cl. NW3................4A **46**
Lyttelton Ho. E9...................4E **51**
..................................(off Well St.)
Lyttelton Rd. E10.................5D **39**
Lyttelton Theatre .. 1A **24** (2C **76**)
..................(within National Theatre)
Lytton Cl. N2........................1F **31**
Lytton Ct. WC1......1E **15** (4A **62**)
..................................(off Barter St.)
Lytton Gro. SW15.................3F **99**
Lytton Rd. E11.....................2A **40**
Lyveden Rd. SE3.................3D **97**

M

Mabledon Pl. WC1....2C **6** (2F **61**)
Mablethorpe Rd. SW6........3A **86**
Mabley St. E9.......................2A **52**
Macarthur Cl. E7...................3C **54**
Macarthur Ter. SE7..............2F **97**
Macartney Ho. SE10............3F **95**
........................(off Chesterfield Wlk.)
Macartney Ho. SW9............4C **90**
..................................(off Gosling Way)
Macaulay Ct. SW4...............1D **103**
Macaulay Rd. E6...................1F **69**
Macaulay Rd. SW4..............1D **103**
Macaulay Sq. SW4..............2D **103**
Macaulay Wlk. SW9.............4B **90**
..................................(off Lett Rd.)
McAuley Cl. SE1.......5B **24** (4C **76**)
Macauley Ho. W10...............4A **58**
..................................(off Portobello Rd.)
Macauley M. SE13...............5E **95**
McAusland Ho. E3...............1B **66**
..................................(off Wright's Rd.)
Macbeth Ho. N1...................1A **64**
Macbeth St. W6...................1D **85**
McBride Ho. E3....................1B **66**
..................................(off Libra Rd.)
McCabe Ct. E16...................4B **68**
..................................(off Barking Rd.)
McCall Cl. SW4...................5A **90**
McCall Cres. SE7.................1F **97**
McCall Ho. N7......................5A **48**
Macclesfield Apts. N1..........5F **49**
..................................(off Branch Pl.)
Macclesfield Ho. EC1..2F **9** (2E **63**)
..................................(off Central St.)
Macclesfield Rd. EC1...1F **9** (2E **63**)
Macclesfield St. W1...4C **14** (1F **75**)
McCoid Way SE1......4F **25** (3E **77**)
McCrone M. NW3.................3F **45**
McCullum Rd. E3..................5B **52**
McDermott Cl. SW11...........1A **102**
McDermott Rd. SE15...........1C **106**
Macdonald Ho. SW11..........5C **88**
..................................(off Dagnall St.)
McDonald Ho. NW6.............2C **58**
..................................(off Malvern Rd.)
Macdonald Rd. E7................1C **54**
Macdonald Rd. N19...............4E **33**
McDowall Cl. E16................4B **68**
McDowall Rd. SE5................4E **91**

Macduff Rd. SW11 .... 4C 88
Mace Cl. E1 .... 2D 79
Mace St. E2 .... 1F 65
McEwan Ho. E3 .... 1B 66
.... (off Roman Rd.)
McEwen Way E15 .... 5F 53
.... (off Rokeby St.)
Macey Ho. SW11 .... 4A 88
Macey St. SE10 .... 2E 95
.... (off Thames St.)
McFadden Ct. E10 .... 5D 39
.... (off Buckingham Rd.)
Macfarland Gro. SE15 ...... 3A 92
Macfarlane Rd. W12 .... 2E 71
Macfarren Pl. NW1 .... 4C 4 (3C 60)
Macfarron Ho. W10 .... 2A 58
.... (off Parry Rd.)
McGlashon Ho. E1 .... 3C 64
.... (off Hunton St.)
McGrath Rd. E15 .... 2B 54
McGregor Ct. N1 .... 1E 11 (2A 64)
.... (off Hoxton St.)
Macgregor Rd. E16 .... 4E 69
McGregor Rd. W11 .... 5B 58
Machell Rd. SE15 .... 1E 107
McIndoe Ct. N1 .... 5F 49
.... (off Sherborne St.)
Macintosh Ho. W1 .... 5C 4 (4C 60)
.... (off Beaumont St.)
McIntosh Ho. SE16 .... 5E 79
.... (off Millender Wlk.)
Mackay Ho. W12 .... 1D 71
.... (off White City Est.)
Mackay Rd. SW4 .... 1D 103
McKeever Ho. E16 .... 4C 68
.... (off Hammersley Rd.)
McKenna Ho. E3 .... 1B 66
.... (off Wright's Rd.)
Mackennal St. NW8 .... 1A 60
Mackenzie Cl. W12 .... 1D 71
Mackenzie Ho. NW2 .... 5C 28
Mackenzie Rd. N7 .... 3B 48
Mackenzie Wlk. E14 .... 2C 80
McKerrell Rd. SE15 .... 4C 92
Mackeson Rd. NW3 .... 1B 46
Mackie Rd. SW2 .... 5C 104
Mackintosh La. E9 .... 2F 51
Macklin St. WC2 ..... 2E 15 (5A 62)
Mackonochie Ho.
EC1 .... 5B 8 (4C 62)
.... (off Baldwins Gdns.)
Mackrow Wlk. E14 .... 1E 81
Mack's Rd. SE16 .... 5C 78
Mackworth Ho. NW1 ...1F 5 (2E 61)
.... (off Augustus St.)
Mackworth St. NW1 ...1F 5 (2E 61)
McLaren Ho. SE1 ....4D 25 (4D 77)
.... (off St Georges Cir.)
Maclaren M. SW15 .... 2E 99
Maclean Rd. SE23 .... 4A 108
McLeod Ct. SE22 .... 1C 120
McLeod's M. SW7 .... 5D 73
Macleod St. SE17 .... 1E 91
Maclise Ho. SW1 .... 5A 76
.... (off Marsham St.)
Maclise Rd. W14 .... 4A 72
Macmillan Ho. NW8 .... 2A 60
.... (off Lorne Cl.)
McMillan Ho. SE14 .... 4A 94
McMillan Ho. SE4 .... 1A 108
.... (off Arica Rd.)
McMillan St. SE8 .... 2C 94
McMillan Student Village
SE8 .... 2C 94
Macmillan Way SW17 ...... 4D 117

Macnamara Ho. SW10 ...... 3F 87
.... (off Worlds End Est.)
McNeil Rd. SE5 .... 5A 92
Maconochies Rd. E14 ...... 1D 95
MacOwan Theatre 5C 72
Macquarie Way E14 .... 5D 81
Macready Ho. W1 .... 4A 60
.... (off Crawford St.)
Macready Pl. N7 .... 1A 48
.... (not continuous)
Macrea Ho. E3 .... 2B 66
.... (off Bow Rd.)
Macroom Ho. W9 .... 2B 58
.... (off Macroom Rd.)
Macroom Rd. W9 .... 2B 58
Mac's Pl. EC4 ....2B 16 (5C 62)
.... (off Greystoke Pl.)
Madame Tussaud's
.... 4B 4 (3C 60)
Maddams St. E3 .... 3D 67
Maddison Ct. E16 .... 4C 68
.... (off Hastings Rd.)
Maddocks Ho. E1 .... 1D 79
.... (off Cornwall St.)
Maddock Way SE17 .... 2D 91
Maddox St. W1 .... 4E 13 (1D 75)
Madoc Cl. NW2 .... 4A 30
Madeira Rd. E11 .... 3F 39
Madeira Ho. SW16 .... 5A 118
Madeira St. E14 .... 4D 67
Madeira Twr. SW11 .... 3F 89
Madinah Rd. E8 .... 3C 50
Madison, The SE1 ... 3B 26 (3F 77)
.... (off Long La.)
Madison Bldg. SE10 .... 4D 95
.... (off Blackheath Rd.)
Madison Ho. E14 .... 1B 80
.... (off Victory Pl.)
Madison Way E20 .... 2D 53
Madras Cl. NW2 .... 4C 30
Madras Pl. N7 .... 3C 48
Madrid Rd. SW13 .... 4C 84
Madrigal La. SE5 .... 3D 91
Madron St. SE17 .... 1A 92
Mafeking Av. E6 .... 1F 69
Mafeking Rd. E16 .... 3B 68
Magazine Ga. W2 .... 2A 74
Magdala Av. N19 .... 4E 33
Magdalene Cl. SE15 .... 5D 93
Magdalen Ho. E16 .... 2D 83
.... (off Keats Av.)
Magdalen M. NW3 .... 3E 45
.... (off Frognal)
Magdalen Pas. E1 .... 1B 78
Magdalen Rd. SW18 .... 1E 115
Magdalen St. SE1 .... 2D 27 (2A 78)
Magee St. SE11 .... 2C 90
Magellan Ho. E1 .... 3F 65
.... (off Ernest St.)
Magellan Pl. E14 .... 5C 80
Magic Circle 3A 6 (3E 61)
.... (off Stephenson Way)

Magistrates' Court
City of London ...3B 18 (5F 63)
.... (off Queen Victoria St.)
Magistrates' Court Hendon ...1B 28
Magistrates' Court Highbury
Corner 3C 48
Magistrates' Court Lavender Hill
.... 1B 102
Magistrates' Court Stratford ...4F 53
Magistrates' Court Thames ...2C 66
Magistrates' Court Westminster
.... 4A 60
Magistrates' Court Willesden
.... 3B 42
Magistrates' Court Wimbledon
.... 5C 114

Magnin Cl. E8 .... 5C 50
Magnolia Cl. E10 .... 4C 38
Magnolia Gdns. E10 .... 4C 38
Magnolia Ho. SE8 .... 2B 94
.... (off Evelyn St.)
Magnolia Lodge W8 .... 4D 73
.... (off St Mary's Ga.)
Magnolia Pl. SW4 .... 3A 104
Magpie All. EC4 ......3C 16 (5C 62)
Magpie Cl. E7 .... 2B 54
Magpie Ho. E3 .... 5B 52
.... (off Sycamore Av.)
Magpie Pl. SE14 .... 2A 94
Magri Wlk. E1 .... 4E 65
Maguire Apts. E3 .... 4B 66
.... (off Geoff Cade Way)
Maguire St. SE1 .....3F 27 (3B 78)
Maha Bldg. E3 .... 2C 66
.... (off Merchant St.)
Mahatma Gandhi Ind. Est.
SE24 .... 2D 105
Mahogany Cl. SE16 .... 2A 80
Mahoney Ho. SE14 .... 4B 94
.... (off Heald St.)
Maida Av. W2 .... 4E 59
MAIDA HILL 3B 58
Maida Va. W9 .... 1D 59
MAIDA VALE 3D 59
Maida Vale Station
(Underground) 2D 59
Maiden La. NW1 .... 4F 47
Maiden La. SE1 ...... 2A 26 (2E 77)
Maiden La. WC2 ...... 4E 15 (1A 76)
Maiden Pl. NW5 .... 5E 33
Maiden Rd. E15 .... 4A 54
Maidenstone Hill SE10 ..... 4E 95
Maidstone Bldgs. M.
SE1 .... 2A 26 (2E 77)
Maidstone Ho. E14 .... 5D 67
.... (off Carmen St.)
Mailcoach Yd. E2 ....1E 11 (2A 64)
Maine Twr. E14 .... 3D 81
Main Mill SE10 .... 3D 95
.... (off Greenwich High St.)
Mais Ho. SE26 .... 2D 121
Maismore St. SE15 .... 2C 92
Maitland Cl. SE10 .... 3D 95
Maitland Ct. W2 .... 1F 73
.... (off Lancaster Ter.)
Maitland Ho. E2 .... 1E 65
.... (off Waterloo Gdns.)
Maitland Ho. SW1 .... 2E 89
.... (off Churchill Gdns.)
Maitland Pk. Est. NW3 ..... 3B 46
Maitland Pk. Rd. NW3 ...... 3B 46
Maitland Pk. Vs. NW3 ...... 3B 46
Maitland Pl. E5 .... 1D 51
Maitland Rd. E15 .... 3B 54
Maitland Rd. SE26 .... 5F 121
Maize Row E14 .... 1B 80
Major Cl. SW9 .... 1D 105
Major Rd. E15 .... 2F 53
Major Rd. SE16 .... 4C 78
Makepeace Av. N6 .... 4C 32
Makepeace Mans. N6 ...... 4C 32
Makers' Yd. E20 .... 3C 52
Makins St. SW3 .... 5A 74
Malabar Ct. W12 .... 1D 71
.... (off India Way)
Malabar St. E14 .... 3C 80
Malam Ct. SE11 .... 5C 76
Malam Gdns. E14 .... 1D 81
Malbrook Rd. SW15 .... 2D 99

Malcolm Ct. E7....................3B **54**
Malcolm St. NW4..................1C **28**
Malcolm Cres. NW4...............1C **28**
Malcolm Ho. N1....................1A **64**
......................(off Arden Est.)
Malcolm Pl. E2.....................3E **65**
Malcolm Rd. E1....................3E **65**
Malcolm Sargent Ho. E16....2D **83**
......................(off Evelyn Rd.)
Malcolmson Ho. SW1...........1F **89**
......................(off Aylesford St.)
Malden Ct. N4......................1E **35**
Malden Cres. NW1................3C **46**
Malden Pl. NW5...................2C **46**
Malden Rd. NW5..................2B **46**
Maldon Cl. E15....................2A **54**
Maldon Cl. N1......................5E **49**
Maldon Cl. SE5....................1A **106**
Malet Pl. WC1............4B **6** (3F **61**)
Malet St. WC1.............4B **6** (3F **61**)
Maley Av. SE27....................2D **119**
Malfort Rd. SE5...................1A **106**
Malham Rd. SE23.................1F **121**
Malham Rd. Ind. Est. SE23...1F **121**
Malibu Cl. SE26...................3D **121**
Mall, The E15.......................4F **53**
Mall, The SW1...........3A **22** (3E **75**)
Mallams M. SW9..................1D **105**
Mallard Cl. E9.....................3B **52**
Mallard Cl. NW6..................1C **58**
Mallard Ho. NW8.................1A **60**
......................(off Bridgeman St.)
Mallard Ho. SW6..................4E **87**
......................(off Station Cl.)
Mallard Point E3.................2D **67**
......................(off Rainhill Way)
Mallards E11.......................2C **40**
......................(off Blake Hall Rd.)
Mall Chambers W8...............2C **72**
......................(off Kensington Mall)
Mallet Rd. SE13..................4F **109**
Mall Galleries......1C **22** (2F **75**)
......................(off The Mall)
Malling SE13.......................3D **109**
Mallinson Rd. SW11.............3A **102**
Mallinson Sports Cen........2B **32**
Mallon Gdns. E1......1F **19** (5B **64**)
......................(off Commercial St.)
Mallord St. SW3...................2F **87**
Mallory Bldgs. EC1....4D **9** (3D **63**)
......................(off St John St.)
Mallory Cl. E14....................4D **67**
Mallory Cl. SE4..................2A **108**
Mallory Cl. SE12................5D **111**
Mallory St. NW8.................3A **60**
Mallow Way SE3................2D **111**
Mallow St. EC1.......3B **10** (3F **63**)
Mall Rd. W6.......................1D **85**
Mall Vs. W6........................1D **85**
......................(off Mall Rd.)
Malmesbury E2..................1E **65**
......................(off Cyprus St.)
Malmesbury Rd. E16...........4A **68**
Malmesbury Rd. E3.............2B **66**
Malmesbury Ter. E16...........4B **68**
Malmo Twr. SE8..................5A **80**
Malmsey Ho. SE11..............1B **90**
Malmsmead Ho. E9.............2B **52**
......................(off Homerton Rd.)
Malpas Rd. E8....................2D **51**
Malpas Rd. SE4...................5B **94**
Malswick Ct. SE15..............3A **92**
......................(off Tower Mill Rd.)
Malta Rd. E10.....................3C **38**
Malta St. EC1.........3D **9** (3D **63**)

Maltby Ho. SE1..........5F **27** (4B **78**)
......................(off Maltby St.)
Maltby Ho. SE3..................2E **111**
Maltby St. SE1...........4F **27** (3B **78**)
Malt Ho. E17......................1B **38**
......................(off Old Brewery Way)
Malthouse Dr. W4................2B **84**
Malthouse Pas. SW13..........5B **84**
......................(off Clevelands Gdns.)
Malthouse Rd. SW11...........3F **89**
......................(off Oak La.)
Maltings Cl. E3...................2E **67**
Maltings Cl. SW13...............5B **84**
Maltings Lodge W4..............2A **84**
......................(off Corney Reach Way)
Maltings Pl. SE1.......3E **27** (3A **78**)
......................(off Roper La.)
Malton M. W10....................5F **57**
Malton Rd. W10..................5A **58**
Maltravers St. WC2....4A **16** (1B **76**)
Malt St. SE1.......................2C **92**
Malva Cl. SW18..................3D **101**
Malvern Cl. W10.................4B **58**
Malvern Ct. SW7.................5F **73**
......................(off Onslow Sq.)
Malvern Ct. W12.................3C **70**
......................(off Hadyn Pk. Rd.)
Malvern Gdns. NW2.............4A **30**
Malvern Ho. N16.................3B **36**
Malvern Ho. SE17...............1E **91**
......................(off Liverpool Gro.)
Malvern M. NW6.................2C **58**
Malvern Pl. NW6................2B **58**
Malvern Rd. E11.................4A **40**
Malvern Rd. E6...................5F **55**
Malvern Rd. E8...................4C **50**
Malvern Rd. NW6................1B **58**
......................(not continuous)
Malvern Ter. N1..................5C **48**
Malwood Rd. SW12.............4D **103**
Malyons Rd. SE13..............4D **109**
Malyons Ter. SE13..............3D **109**
Managers St. E14................2E **81**
Manaton Cl. SE15...............1D **107**
Manbey Gro. E15................3A **54**
Manbey M. E15..................3A **54**
Manbey Pk. Rd. E15...........3A **54**
Manbey Rd. E15.................3A **54**
Manbey St. E15.................3A **54**
Manbre Rd. W6..................2E **85**
Manchester Ct. E16............5D **69**
......................(off Garvary Rd.)
Manchester Dr. W10............3A **58**
Manchester Gro. E14...........1E **95**
Manchester Ho. SE17..........1E **91**
......................(off East St.)
Manchester M. W1....1B **12** (4C **60**)
......................(off Manchester St.)
Manchester Rd. E14............1E **95**
Manchester Rd. N15...........1F **35**
Manchester Sq. W1....2B **12** (5C **60**)
Manchester St. W1....1B **12** (4C **60**)
Manchuria Rd. SW11...........4C **102**
Manciple St. SE1......4B **26** (3F **77**)
Mancroft Ct. NW8...............5F **45**
......................(off St John's Wood Pk.)
Mandalay Rd. SW4..............3E **103**
Mandara Pl. SE8.................5A **80**
......................(off Yeoman St.)
Mandarin Ct. NW10.............3A **42**
......................(off Mitchellbrook Way)
Mandarin St. E8.................2B **94**
Mandarin St. E14................1C **80**

Mandarin Wharf N1............5A **50**
......................(off De Beauvoir Cres.)
Mandela Cl. W12.................1D **71**
Mandela Ho. E2........1F **11** (2B **64**)
......................(off Virginia Rd.)
Mandela Ho. SE5................5D **91**
Mandela Rd. E16................5C **68**
Mandela St. NW1................5E **47**
Mandela St. SW9................3C **90**
......................(not continuous)
Mandela Way SE1...............5A **78**
Mandeley M. E11................1B **40**
Mandel Ho. SW18..............2C **100**
Manderley W14...................4B **72**
......................(off Oakwood La.)
Mandeville Cl. SE3..............3B **96**
Mandeville Ho. SE1..............1B **92**
......................(off Rolls Rd.)
Mandeville Ho. SW4............3E **103**
Mandeville M. SW4.............2A **104**
Mandeville Pl. W1.....2C **12** (5C **60**)
Mandeville St. E5...............5A **38**
Mandrake Rd. SW17...........3B **116**
Mandrake Way E15.............4A **54**
Mandrell Rd. SW2..............3A **104**
Manet Gdns. W3.................1A **70**
Manette St. W1........3C **14** (5F **61**)
Manfred Rd. SW15.............3B **100**
Manger Rd. N7...................3A **48**
Manhattan Bldg. E3............1C **66**
Manhattan Loft Gdns. E20...3E **53**
Manilla St. E14...................3C **80**
Manilla Wlk. SE10...............5A **82**
Manitoba Ct. SE16..............3E **79**
......................(off Canada Est.)
Manley Ct. N16..................5B **36**
Manley Ho. SE11................5C **76**
Manley St. NW1.................5C **46**
Manna Ho. E20...................3E **53**
......................(off Glade Wlk.)
Mannan Ho. E3...................1B **66**
......................(off Roman Rd.)
Manneby Prior N1......1A **8** (1B **62**)
......................(off Cumming St.)
Manningford Cl. EC1...1D **9** (2D **63**)
Manning Ho. W11...............5A **58**
......................(off Westbourne Pk. Rd.)
Manningtree Cl. SW19........1A **114**
Manningtree St. E1.............5C **64**
Manns Ter. SE27................3E **119**
Manny Shinwell Ho. SW6....2B **86**
......................(off Clem Attlee Ct.)
Manor Av. SE4...................5B **94**
Manorbrook SE3................2C **110**
Manor Ct. E10....................3D **39**
Manor Ct. N2.....................1B **32**
Manor Ct. SW16................3A **118**
Manor Ct. SW2..................3B **104**
Manor Ct. SW3..................1A **88**
......................(off Hemus Pl.)
Manor Ct. SW6..................4D **87**
Manor Est. SE16................5D **79**
Manorfield Cl. N19..............1E **47**
......................(off Fulbrook M.)
Manor Flds. SW15..............4F **99**
Manor Gdns. N7.................5A **34**
Manor Gdns. SW4...............5E **89**
......................(off Larkhall Ri.)
Manor Gdns. W4.................1A **84**
Manor Gro. SE15................2E **93**
Manorhall Gdns. E10...........3C **38**
Manor Ho. NW1.................4A **60**
......................(off Lisson Gro.)
MANOR HOUSE.................2E **35**
MANOR HOUSE...................2F **35**

Manor Ho. Ct. W9 ....3E **59**
................(off Warrington Gdns.)
Manor Ho. Dr. NW6 ....4F **43**
Manor Ho. Gdn. E11 ....1D **41**
Manor House Station
(Underground) 2E **35**
Manor La. SE12 ....3A **110**
Manor La. SE13 ....3A **110**
Manor La. Ter. SE13 ....2A **110**
Manor Lodge NW6 ....4F **43**
................(off Willesden La.)
Manor M. NW6 ....1C **58**
................(off Cambridge Av.)
Manor M. SE4 ....5B **94**
Manor Mt. SE23 ....1E **121**
Manor Pde. N16 ....4B **36**
Manor Pde. NW10 ....1B **56**
................(off High St. Harlesden)
MANOR PK. 1F **55**
Manor Pk. SE13 ....2F **109**
Manor Pk. Crematorium 1E **55**
Manor Pk. Pde. SE13 ....2F **109**
................(off Lee High Rd.)
Manor Pk. Rd. E12 ....1F **55**
................(not continuous)
Manor Pk. Rd. NW10 ....5B **42**
Manor Park Station (Rail &
Crossrail) 1F **55**
Manor Rd. SE17 ....1D **91**
Manor Rd. E10 ....2C **38**
Manor Rd. E15 ....1A **68**
Manor Rd. E16 ....3A **68**
Manor Rd. N16 ....4F **35**
Manor Way SE23 ....5E **107**
Manor Way SE3 ....2B **110**
Manresa Rd. SW3 ....1A **88**
Mansard Beeches SW17 .....5C **116**
Mansbridge Ho. SW8 ....4D **89**
................(off Patcham Ter.)
Mansell St. E1 ....2F **19** (5B **64**)
Manse Rd. N16 ....5B **36**
Mansell Ct. E2 ....5B **50**
................(off Whiston Rd.)
Mansfield Ct. SE15 ....3B **92**
................(off Sumner Rd.)
Mansfield Hgts. N2 ....1A **32**
Mansfield Ho. N1 ....5A **50**
................(off Halcomb St.)
Mansfield M. W1 ....1D **13** (4D **61**)
Mansfield Rd. NW3 ....1E **45**
Mansfield Rd. E11 ....1D **41**
Mansfield Rd. NW3 ....2B **46**
Mansfield St. W1 ....1D **13** (4D **61**)
Mansford St. E2 ....1C **64**
Mansion Cl. SW9 ....4C **90**
................(not continuous)
Mansion Gdns. NW3 ....5D **31**
Mansion Ho. Pl.
EC4 ....3B **18** (5F **63**)
Mansion House Station
(Underground) 3A **18** (1E **77**)
Mansion Ho. St. EC4 .3B **18** (5F **63**)
Mansion Lock Ho. NW1 ....4D **47**
................(off Hawley Cres.)
Mansions, The SW5: Lon
Earl's Ct. Rd. 1D **87**
Mansions, The SW5: Lon
Old Brompton Rd. 1D **87**
................(off Old Brompton Rd.)
Manson Vw. E15 ....5F **53**
................(off High St.)
Manson Ho. N1 ....4C **48**
................(off Drummond Way)
Manson M. SW7 ....5F **73**

Manson Pl. SW7 ....5F **73**
Manston NW1 ....4E **47**
................(off Agar Gro.)
Manstone Rd. NW2 ....2A **44**
Manston Ho. W14 ....4F **71**
................(off Russell Rd.)
Mantilla Rd. SW17 ....4C **116**
Mantle Ct. SW18 ....4D **101**
................(off Mapleton Rd.)
Mantle Rd. SE4 ....1A **108**
Mantle Way E15 ....4A **54**
Mantua St. SW11 ....1F **101**
Mantus Cl. E1 ....3E **65**
Mantus Rd. E1 ....3E **65**
Manuka Hgts. E20 ....2E **53**
................(off Napa Cl.)
Manville Gdns. SW17 ....3D **117**
Manville Rd. SW17 ....2C **116**
Manwood Rd. SE4 ....3B **108**
Manygates SW12 ....2D **117**
Mapesbury Ct. NW2 ....2A **44**
Mapesbury M. NW4 ....1C **28**
Mapesbury Rd. NW2 ....4A **44**
Mapeshill Pl. NW2 ....3E **43**
Mapes Ho. NW6 ....4A **44**
Mape St. E2 ....3D **65**
................(not continuous)
Maple Av. W3 ....2A **70**
Maple Cl. N16 ....1C **36**
Maple Cl. SW4 ....4F **103**
Maple Cl. E3 ....1C **66**
................(off Four Seasons Cl.)
Maple Ct. SE6 ....1D **123**
Maplecroft Cl. E6 ....5F **69**
Mapledene Est. E8 ....4C **50**
Mapledene Rd. E8 ....4B **50**
Maple Ho. N19 ....5E **33**
Maple Ho. SE8 ....3B **94**
................(off Idonia St.)
Maple Leaf Sq. SE16 ....3F **79**
Maple Lodge SE18 ....4D **73**
................(off Abbots Wlk.)
Maple M. NW6 ....1D **59**
Maple M. SE16 ....3F **79**
Maple M. SW16 ....5B **118**
Maple Pl. W1 ....4A **6** (3E **61**)
Maple Rd. E11 ....1A **40**
Maple Rd. E1 ....4D **65**
Maplestead Rd. SW2 ....5B **104**
Maple St. E2 ....1D **65**
Maple St. W1 ....5F **5** (4E **61**)
Mapleton Cres. SW18 ....4D **101**
Mapleton Rd. SW18 ....4C **100**
................(not continuous)
Maple Tree Pl. SE3 ....4F **97**
Maple Wlk. W10 ....2F **57**
Maple Way SE16 ....3A **80**
Maplewood Apts. N4 ....2E **35**
................(off Katherine Cl.)
Maplin Rd. E16 ....5C **68**
Maplin St. E3 ....2B **66**
Mapperley Cl. E11 ....1B **40**
Marabou Cl. E12 ....2F **55**
Mara Ho. E20 ....2D **53**
................(off Victory Pde.)
Marathon Ho.
NW1 ....5A **4** (4B **60**)
................(off Marylebone Rd.)
Marban Rd. W9 ....2B **58**
Marble Arch 4A **12** (1B **74**)
Marble Arch 4A **12** (1B **74**)
................(off Cumberland Ga.)
MARBLE ARCH 4A **12** (1B **74**)
Marble Arch Apts. W1 ....5B **60**
................(off Harrowby St.)

Marble Arch Station
(Underground) 3A **12** (5B **60**)
Marble Dr. NW2 ....3F **29**
Marble Ho. W9 ....3B **58**
Marble Quay E1 ....2C **78**
Marbles Ho. SE5 ....2E **91**
................(off Grosvenor Ter.)
Marbrook Ct. SE12 ....3E **125**
Marcella Rd. SW9 ....5C **90**
Marchant Ho. N1 ....5A **50**
................(off Halcomb St.)
Marchant Rd. E11 ....4F **39**
Marchbank Rd. W14 ....2B **86**
March Ct. SW15 ....2D **99**
Marchmont St. WC1 ...3D **7** (3A **62**)
Marchwood Cl. SE5 ....3A **92**
Marcia Ct. SE1 ....5A **78**
................(off Marcia Rd.)
Marcia Rd. SE1 ....5A **78**
Marcilly Rd. SW18 ....3F **101**
Marcon Ct. E8 ....2D **51**
................(off Amhurst Rd.)
Marconi Rd. E10 ....3C **38**
Marcon Pl. E8 ....3D **51**
Marco Rd. W6 ....4E **71**
Marcus Ct. E15 ....5A **54**
Marcus Garvey M. SE22 .....4D **107**
Marcus Garvey Way SE24 ...2C **104**
Marcus St. E15 ....5B **54**
Marcus St. SW18 ....4D **101**
Marcus Ter. SW18 ....4D **101**
Mardale Dr. NW9 ....1A **28**
Marden Ho. E8 ....2D **51**
Marden Sq. SE16 ....4D **79**
Mardyke Ho. SE17 ....5F **77**
................(off Mason St.)
Maresfield Gdns. NW3 ....2E **45**
Mare St. E8 ....2D **51**
Margaret Bondfield Ho. E3 ...1A **66**
................(off Driffield Rd.)
MARGARET CENTRE (HOSPICE)
....1A **40**
Margaret Ct. W1 ....2F **13** (5E **61**)
................(off Margaret St.)
Margaret Herbison Ho. SW6...2B **86**
................(off Clem Attlee Ct.)
Margaret Ho. W6 ....1E **85**
................(off Queen Caroline St.)
Margaret Ingram Cl. SW6 ......2B **86**
Margaret McMillan Ho. E16...5E **69**
Margaret McMillan Pk. 3B **94**
Margaret Rd. E11 ....1A **40**
Margaret Rd. N16 ....3B **36**
Margaret Rutherford Pl.
SW12 ....1E **117**
Margaret St. W1 ....2E **13** (5D **61**)
Margaretta Ter. SW3 ....2A **88**
Margaretting Rd. E12 ....3E **41**
Margaret Way IG4: Ilf 1F **41**
Margaret White Ho.
NW1 ....1B **6** (2F **61**)
................(off Chalton St.)
Margate Rd. SW2 ....3A **104**
Margerie Ct. E2 ....1D **65**
................(off Esker Pl.)
Margery Fry Ct. N7 ....5A **34**
Margery Pk. Rd. E7 ....3C **54**
Margery St. WC1 ....2B **8** (2C **62**)
Margery Ter. E7 ....3C **54**
................(off Margery Pk. Rd.)
Margin Dr. SW19 ....5F **113**
Margravine Gdns. W6 ....1F **85**
Margravine Rd. W6 ....1F **85**
Marham Gdns. SW18 ....1A **116**

Maria Cl. SE1 ....5D **79**
Marian Ct. E9 ....2E **51**
Marianne Cl. SE5 ....4A **92**
Marian Pl. E2 ....1D **65**
Marian St. E2 ....1D **65**
Marian Way NW10 ....4B **42**
Maria Ter. E1 ....4F **65**
Maribor SE10 ....3E **95**
                        (off Burney St.)
Marie Curie SE5 ....4B **92**
MARIE CURIE HOSPICE
Hampstead 2F **45**
Marie Lloyd Gdns. N19 ....2A **34**
Marie Lloyd Ho. N1....1B **10** (1F **63**)
                        (off Murray Gro.)
Marie Lloyd Wlk. E8 ....3B **50**
Marigold All. SE1 ......5D **17** (1D **77**)
Marigold St. SE16 ....3D **79**
Marina Ct. E3 ....2B **66**
                        (off Alfred St.)
Marina One N1 ....1A **62**
                        (off New Wharf Rd.)
Marina Point E14 ....4D **81**
                        (off Lanark Sq.)
Marina Point SW6 ....5E **87**
Marine Ct. E11 ....4A **40**
Marinefield Rd. SW6 ....5D **87**
Marinel Ho. SE5 ....3E **91**
Mariners M. E14 ....5F **81**
Mariners Pl. SE16 ....5A **80**
                        (off Plough Way)
Marine St. SE16 ....4C **78**
Marine Twr. SE8 ....2B **94**
                        (off Abinger Gro.)
Marion Ho. NW1 ....5B **46**
                        (off Regent's Pk. Rd.)
Marion M. SE21 ....3F **119**
Marischal Rd. SE13 ....1F **109**
Maritime Quay E14 ....1C **94**
Maritime St. E3 ....3B **66**
Maritime St. SE16 ....4F **79**
Marius Mans. SW17 ....2C **116**
Marius Rd. SW17 ....2C **116**
Marjorie Gro. SW11 ....2B **102**
Marjorie M. E1 ....5F **65**
Market App. W12 ....3E **71**
Market Ct. W1 ....2F **13** (5E **61**)
                        (off Market Pl.)
Market Dr. W4 ....3A **84**
Market Est. N7 ....3A **48**
Market La. W12 ....3E **71**
Market M. W1 ....2D **21** (2D **75**)
Market Pde. E10 ....1E **39**
                        (off High Rd. Leyton)
Market Pde. N16 ....2C **36**
                        (off Oldhill St.)
Market Pav. E10 ....5C **38**
Market Pl. SE16 ....5C **78**
                        (not continuous)
Market Pl. W1 ....2F **13** (5E **61**)
Market Rd. N7 ....3A **48**
Market Row SW9 ....2C **104**
Market Sq. E14 ....5D **67**
Market St. E1 ....5F **11** (4B **64**)
Market Way E14 ....5D **67**
Market Yd. SE8 ....3C **94**
Market Yd. M. SE1....4D **27** (3A **78**)
Markfield Beam Engine & Mus.
                                            .1C **36**
Markham Pl. SW3 ....1B **88**
Markham Sq. SW3 ....1B **88**
Markham St. SE17 ....1A **92**
Markham St. SW3 ....1A **88**
Mark Ho. E2 ....1F **65**
                        (off Sewardstone Rd.)

Markhouse Av. E17 ....1A **38**
Markhouse Pas. E17 ....1B **38**
                        (off Downsfield Rd.)
Markhouse Rd. E17 ....1B **38**
Markland Ho. W10 ....1F **71**
                        (off Darfield Way)
Mark La. EC3............4E **19** (1A **78**)
Markmanor Av. E17...................2A **38**
Mark Sq. EC2 ....3D **11** (3A **64**)
Markstone Ho. SE1....4D **25** (3D **77**)
                        (off Lancaster St.)
Mark St. E15 ....4A **54**
Mark St. EC2 ....3D **11** (3A **64**)
Mark Twain Dr. NW2 ....1D **43**
Markwell Cl. SE26 ....4D **121**
Markyate Ho. W10 ....3E **57**
                        (off Sutton Way)
Marland Ho. SW1 .....5A **20** (4B **74**)
                        (off Sloane St.)
Marlborough SW19 ....1F **113**
                        (off Inner Pk. Rd.)
Marlborough W9 ....2E **59**
                        (off Maida Vale)
Marlborough Av. E8 ....5C **50**
                        (not continuous)
Marlborough Cl. SE17..............5E **77**
Marlborough Ct.
    W1............................3A **14** (1E **75**)
                        (off Carnaby St.)
Marlborough Ct. W8 ....5C **72**
                        (off Pembroke Rd.)
Marlborough Cres. W4..............4A **70**
Marlborough Flats SW3 ....5A **74**
                        (off Walton St.)
Marlborough Ga. Ho. W2 ....1F **73**
                        (off Elms M.)
Marlborough Gro. SE1 ....1C **92**
Marlborough Hill NW8 ....1E **59**
Marlborough Ho. E16 ....2C **82**
                        (off Hardy Av.)
Marlborough House
                                       2A **22** (2E **75**)
Marlborough La. SE7 ....2E **97**
Marlborough Lodge NW8 ....1E **59**
                        (off Hamilton Ter.)
Marlborough Mans. NW6.........2D **45**
                        (off Canon Hill)
Marlborough M. SW2................2B **104**
Marlborough Pl. NW8 ....1E **59**
Marlborough Rd. E15 ....1A **54**
Marlborough Rd. E7 ....4E **55**
Marlborough Rd. N19 ....4F **33**
Marlborough Rd.
    SW1............................2A **22** (2E **75**)
Marlborough Yd. N19 ....4F **33**
Marlbury NW8 ....5D **45**
                        (off Abbey Rd.)
Marler Rd. SE23 ....1A **122**
Marley Ho. W11 ....1F **71**
                        (off St Ann's Rd.)
Marley St. SE16 ....5F **79**
Marley Wlk. NW2 ....2E **43**
Marloes Rd. W8 ....4D **73**
Marlow Ct. NW6 ....4F **43**
Marlowe Ct. SE19 ....5B **120**
Marlowe Ct. SW3 ....5A **74**
                        (off Petyward)
Marlowe Path SE8 ....2C **94**
Marlowes, The NW8 ....5F **45**
Marlow Ho. E2 ....2F **11** (2B **64**)
                        (off Calvert Av.)
Marlow Ho. SE1 ....5F **27** (4B **78**)
                        (off Abbey St.)

Marlow Ho. W2 ....5D **59**
                        (off Hallfield Est.)
Marlow Way SE16.....................3F **79**
Marlow Workshops
    E2.............................2F **11** (2B **64**)
                        (off Virginia Rd.)
Marl Rd. SW18 ....2E **101**
Marlston NW1 ....2E **5** (2D **61**)
                        (off Munster Sq.)
Marlton St. SE10 ....1B **96**
Marlu Ct. SE14 ....4F **93**
                        (off Hatcham Pk. M.)
Marlu Ho. SE14 ....4F **93**
                        (off Hatcham Pk. M.)
Marmara Apts. E16...................1C **82**
                        (off Western Gateway)
Marmion M. SW11 ....1C **102**
Marmion Rd. SW11 ....2C **102**
Marmont Rd. SE15 ....4C **92**
Marmora Rd. SE22....................4E **107**
Marner Point E3........................3E **67**
Marne St. W10 ....2A **58**
Marney Rd. SW11 ....2C **102**
Marnfield Cres. SW2...............1C **118**
Marnham Av. NW2....................1A **44**
Marnock Ho. SE17 ....1F **91**
                        (off Brandon St.)
Marnock Rd. SE4 ....3B **108**
Maroon St. E14 ....4A **66**
Maroons Way SE6.....................5C **122**
Marqueen Ct. W8 ....3D **73**
                        (off Kensington Chu. St.)
Marques Rd. N1 ....3F **49**
Marquis Ct. N4 ....3B **34**
                        (off Marquis Rd.)
Marquis Rd. N4 ....3B **34**
Marquis Rd. NW1 ....3F **47**
Marrick Cl. SW15 ....2C **98**
Marrick Ho. NW6 ....5D **45**
                        (off Mortimer Cres.)
Marriett Ho. SE6.......................4E **123**
Marriott Rd. E15 ....5A **54**
Marriott Rd. N4 ....3B **34**
Marriotts Cl. NW9 ....1B **28**
Marryat Ho. SW1 ....1E **89**
                        (off Churchill Gdns.)
Marryat Pl. SW19 ....4A **114**
Marryat Rd. SW19 ....5F **113**
Marryat Sq. SW6 ....4A **86**
Marsala Rd. SE13 ....2D **109**
Marsalis Ho. E3 ....2C **66**
                        (off Rainhill Way)
Marsden Rd. SE15 ....1B **106**
Marsden St. NW5 ....3C **46**
Marshall Bldg. W2 ....4F **59**
                        (off Hermitage St.)
Marshall Cl. SW18 ....4E **101**
Marshall Ct. SW6 ....4F **43**
                        (off Coverdale Rd.)
Marshall Ho. N1 ....1F **63**
                        (off Cranston Est.)
Marshall Ho. SE1 .....5E **27** (4A **78**)
                        (off Page's Wlk.)
Marshall Ho. SE17 ....1F **91**
                        (off East St.)
Marshall Rd. E10 ....5D **39**
Marshall's Pl.
    SE16........................5F **27** (4B **78**)
Marshall St. W1 ....3A **14** (5E **61**)
Marshall Street Leisure Cen.
                                       3A **14** (5E **61**)
Marshalsea Rd. SE1 .3A **26** (3E **77**)
Marsham Ct. SW1 ....5F **75**
Marsham St. SW1 .....5C **22** (4F **75**)
Marshbrook Cl. SE3..................1F **111**

Marsh Cen., The E1......2F **19** (5B **64**)
.... (off Whitechapel High St.)
Marsh Ct. E8 ....3C **50**
Marsh Ct. SE17 ....1F **91**
.... (off Thurlow St.)
Marsh Dr. NW9.......................1B **28**
Marshfield St. E14.................4E **81**
Marshgate Bus. Cen. E15....5E **53**
Marshgate La. E15...............5D **53**
Marshgate La. E20.................3C **52**
Marsh Hill E9..........................2A **52**
Marsh Ho. SW1....................1F **89**
.... (off Aylesford St.)
Marsh Ho. SW8....................4E **89**
Marsh La. E10........................4B **38**
Marsh St. E14.......................5D **81**
Marsh Wall E14.....................2C **80**
Marshwood Apts. SW11.....2A **102**
.... (off Eckstein Road)
Marshwood Ho. NW6.........5C **44**
.... (off Kilburn Vale)
Marsland Cl. SE17.................1D **91**
Marsom Ho. N1.......1B **10** (1F **63**)
.... (off Provost St.)
Marston Cl. NW6.....................4E **45**
Marston Ho. SW9..................5C **90**
Marsworth Ho. E2..................5C **50**
.... (off Whiston Rd.)
Martaban Rd. N16..................4B **36**
Martara M. SE17.....................1E **91**
Martello St. E8........................4D **51**
Martello Ter. E8......................4D **51**
Martell Rd. SE21.................3F **119**
Martel Pl. E8...........................3B **50**
Martha Rd. E15.......................3A **54**
Martha's Bldgs. EC1 3B **10** (3F **63**)
Martha St. E1.........................5E **65**
Martin Ct. E14........................3E **81**
.... (off River Barge Cl.)
Martindale Av. E16.................1C **82**
Martindale Ho. E14.................1D **81**
.... (off Poplar High St.)
Martindale Rd. SW12.........5D **103**
Martineau Est. E1...................1E **79**
Martineau Ho. SW1.................1E **88**
.... (off Churchill Gdns.)
Martineau M. N5....................1D **49**
Martineau Rd. N5...................1D **49**
Martineau Sq. E1....................1C **78**
Martingale Ho. E1..................2D **79**
.... (off Raine St.)
Martin Ho. E3.........................5B **52**
.... (off Old Ford Rd.)
Martin Ho. SE1..........5A **26** (4E **77**)
Martin Ho. SW8.......................3A **90**
.... (off Wyvil Rd.)
Martin La. EC4............4C **18** (1F **77**)
.... (not continuous)
Martins, The SE26................5D **121**
Martlett Ct. WC2......3E **15** (5A **62**)
Marton Cl. SE6.....................3C **122**
Marton Rd. N16......................4A **36**
Martys Yd. NW3....................1F **45**
Marula Ho. E1........................5C **64**
.... (off Boulevard Walkway)
Marvell Ho. SE5.....................3F **91**
.... (off Camberwell Rd.)
Marvels Cl. SE12..................2D **125**
Marvels La. SE12..................2D **125**
Marville Rd. SW6....................3B **86**
Marvin St. E8..........................3D **51**
Mary Adelaide Cl. SW15....4A **112**
Mary Ann Gdns. SE8.............2C **94**
Mary Bayly Ho. W11............2A **72**

Mary Boast Wlk. SE5..............5F **91**
Mary Datchelor Cl. SE5.........4F **91**
Mary Datchelor Ho. SE5........4F **91**
.... (off Grove La.)
Mary Flux Ct. SW5.................1D **87**
.... (off Bramham Gdns.)
Mary Grn. NW8.......................5D **45**
Mary Holben Ho. SW16.......5E **117**
Mary Ho. W6............................1E **85**
.... (off Queen Caroline St.)
Mary Jones Ct. E14................1C **80**
.... (off Garford St.)
Maryland Ind. Est. E15..........2A **54**
Maryland Pk. E15...................2A **54**
.... (not continuous)
Maryland Point E15...............3A **54**
.... (off The Grove)
Maryland Rd. E15...................2F **53**
Maryland Sq. E15...................2A **54**
Marylands Rd. W9..................3C **58**
.... (not continuous)
Maryland Station (Rail &
Crossrail)............................3A **54**
Maryland St. E15....................2F **53**
Maryland Wlk. N1...................5E **49**
.... (off Popham St.)
Mary Lawrenson Pl. SE3......3C **96**
MARYLEBONE..........1A **12** (4C **60**)
Marylebone Cricket Club.....2F **59**
.... (shown as Lord's)
Marylebone Fly-Over W2......4F **59**
MARYLEBONE FLYOVER......4A **60**
Marylebone High St.
W1..............................5C **4** (4C **60**)
Marylebone La. W1...1C **12** (4C **60**)
Marylebone M. W1..1D **13** (4D **61**)
Marylebone Pas. W1 ..2A **14** (5E **61**)
Marylebone Rd. NW1.............4A **60**
Marylebone Station (Rail &
Underground).....................3B **60**
Marylebone St. W1...1C **12** (4C **60**)
Le Bow Way E3.....................4D **67**
Marylee Way SE11.................5B **76**
Mary Macarthur Ho. E2........2F **65**
.... (off Warley St.)
Mary Macarthur Ho. W6........2A **86**
Maryon Ho. NW6....................4E **45**
.... (off Goldhurst Ter.)
Maryon M. NW3......................1A **46**
Maryon Rd. SE18....................5F **83**
Maryon Rd. SE7.....................5F **83**
Mary Pl. W11...........................1A **72**
Mary Rose Sq. SE16..............5A **80**
.... (off Cary Av.)
Marys Ct. NW1.......................3A **60**
.... (off Palgrave Gdns.)
Mary Seacole Cl. E8..............5B **50**
Mary Seacole Ho. W6...........4C **70**
.... (off Invermead Cl.)
Mary Smith Ct. SW5..............5C **72**
.... (off Trebovir Rd.)
Marysmith Ho. SW1..............1F **89**
.... (off Cureton St.)
Mary St. E16...........................4B **68**
Mary St. N1.............................5E **49**
Mary Ter. NW1........................5D **47**
Mary Wharrie Ho. NW3.........4B **46**
.... (off Fellows Rd.)
Marzell Ho. W14...................1B **86**
.... (off North End Rd.)
Masbro' Rd. W14....................4F **71**
Mascalls Ct. SE7....................2E **97**
Mascalls Rd. SE7...................2E **97**
Mascotte Rd. SW15...............2F **99**
Mascotts Cl. NW2..................5D **29**

Masefield Ho. NW6................2C **58**
.... (off Stafford Rd.)
Masey M. SE3.......................3C **104**
Mashie Rd. W3........................5A **56**
Masjid La. E14.........................4B **66**
Maskall Cl. SW2...................1C **118**
Maskell Rd. SW17................3E **115**
Maskelyne Cl. SW11.............4A **88**
Mason Cl. E16.........................1C **82**
Mason Cl. SE16......................1C **92**
Mason Ho. E9.........................4E **51**
.... (off Frampton Pk. Rd.)
Mason Ho. SE1.......................5C **78**
.... (off Simms Rd.)
Masonry Ho. SE14.................4F **93**
.... (off Fishers Ct.)
Mason's Arms M.
W1...............................3E **13** (5D **61**)
Mason's Av. EC2......2B **18** (5F **63**)
Masons Pl. EC1.......1E **9** (2E **63**)
Mason St. SE17......................5F **77**
Mason's Yd. SW1.....1A **22** (2E **75**)
Mason's Yd. SW19................5F **113**
Masons Yd. EC1......1E **9** (2D **63**)
Massey Ct. E6.........................5E **55**
.... (off Florence Rd.)
Massie Rd. E8.........................3C **50**
Massingberd Way SW17.....4D **117**
Massinger St. SE17...............5A **78**
Massingham St. E1................3F **65**
Mast Ct. SE16.........................5A **80**
.... (off Boat Lifter Way)
Master Gunner Pl. SE18.......3F **97**
Masterhead Ho. E16..............3D **83**
.... (off Royal Crest Av.)
Masterman Ho. SE5...............3F **91**
.... (off Elmington Est.)
Masterman Rd. E6..................2F **69**
Masters Cl. SW16................5E **117**
Masters Dr. SE16...................1D **93**
Masters Lodge E1..................5E **65**
.... (off Johnson St.)
Masters St. E1........................4F **65**
Mast Ho. Ter. E14..................5C **80**
.... (not continuous)
Masthouse Terrace Pier (River
Bus)....................................1C **94**
Mastmaker Ct. E14................3C **80**
Mastmaker Rd. E14................3C **80**
Matcham Rd. E11...................5A **40**
Match Ct. E3...........................1C **66**
.... (off Blondin St.)
Matching Ct. E3......................2B **66**
.... (off Merchant St.)
Matham Gro. SE22...............2B **106**
Matheson Lang Ho.
SE1.......................4B **24** (3C **76**)
.... (off Baylis Rd.)
Matheson Rd. W14................5B **72**
Mathews Pk. Av. E15.............3B **54**
Mathews Yd. WC2....3D **15** (5A **62**)
Mathieson Ct. SE1....4E **25** (3D **77**)
.... (off King James St.)
Mathison Ho. SW10................3E **87**
.... (off Coleridge Gdns.)
Matilda Gdns. E3....................1C **66**
Matilda Ho. E1........................2C **78**
.... (off St Katherine's Way)
Matilda St. N1.........................5B **48**
Matisse Ct. EC1.......3B **10** (3F **63**)
.... (off Featherstone St.)
Matlock Cl. SE24..................2E **105**
Matlock Cl. NW8....................1E **59**
.... (off Abbey Rd.)
Matlock Ct. SE5.....................2F **105**

Matlock Ct. W11 ....1C **72**
.................(off Kensington Pk. Rd.)
Matlock Ho. E15..................3F **53**
.................(off Forrester Way)
Matlock Rd. E10.................1E **39**
Matlock St. E14.................5A **66**
Maton Ho. SW6 ....3B **86**
.................(off Estcourt Rd.)
Matrimony Pl. SW8 ....5E **89**
Matson Ho. SE16 ....4D **79**
Matthew Cl. W10 ....3C **57**
Matthew Parker St.
SW1.................4C **22** (3F **75**)
Matthews Ho. E14...............4C **66**
.................(off Burgess St.)
Matthews St. SW11 ....5B **88**
Matthias Apts. N1 ....4F **49**
.................(off Northchurch Rd.)
Matthias Rd. N16 ....2A **50**
Mattison Rd. N4 ....1C **34**
Maud Chadburn Pl. SW4...4D **103**
Maude Ho. E2....................1C **64**
.................(off Ropley St.)
Maude Rd. SE5 ....4A **92**
Maud Gdns. E13 ....5B **54**
Maudlins Grn. E1 ....2C **78**
Maud Rd. E10...................5E **39**
Maud Rd. E13 ....3E **69**
MAUDSLEY HOSPITAL, THE...5F **91**
Maud St. E16...................4B **68**
Maud Wilkes Cl. NW5..........2E **47**
Mauleverer Rd. SW2 ....3A **104**
Maundeby Wlk. NW10 ....3A **42**
Maunsel St. SW1................5F **75**
Maurer Ct. SE10................4B **82**
Mauretania Bldg. E1 ....1F **79**
.................(off Jardine Rd.)
Maurice Ct. E1 ....2F **65**
Maurice Drummond Ho.
SE10.................4D **95**
.................(off Catherine Gro.)
Maurice St. W12 ....5D **57**
Mauritius Rd. SE10 ....5A **82**
Maury Rd. N16 ....4C **36**
Maverton Rd. E3 ....5C **52**
Mavor Ho. N1 ....5B **48**
.................(off Barnsbury Est.)
Mawbey Ho. SE1 ....1C **92**
Mawbey Pl. SE1 ....1B **92**
Mawbey Rd. SE1 ....1B **92**
Mawbey St. SW8................3A **90**
Mawdley Ho. SE1....4C **24** (3D **77**)
.................(off Webber Row)
Mawson Ct. N1 ....5F **49**
.................(off Gopsall St.)
Mawson Ho. EC1....5B **8** (4C **62**)
.................(off Baldwins Gdns.)
Mawson La. W4 ....5B **70**
Maxden Ct. SE15...............1B **106**
Maxilla Wlk. W10 ....5F **57**
Maxted Rd. SE15...............1B **106**
Maxwell Ct. SE22...............1C **120**
Maxwell Ct. SW4................3F **103**
Maxwell Rd. SW6................3D **87**
Maya Apts. E20...................2E **53**
.................(off Victory Pde.)
Maya Cl. SE15...................5D **93**
Mayall Rd. SE24................3D **105**
Maybourne Cl. SE26 ....5D **121**
Maybury Ct. W1 ....1C **12** (4C **60**)
.................(off Marylebone St.)
Maybury Gdns. NW10 ....3D **43**
Maybury M. N6 ....2E **33**
Maybury Rd. E13 ....3E **69**
Maybury St. SW17 ....5A **116**

Mayday Gdns. SE3 ....5F **97**
Maydew Ho. SE16 ....5E **79**
.................(off Abbeyfield Est.)
Maydwell Ho. E14................4C **66**
.................(off Thomas Rd.)
Mayerne Rd. SE9................3F **111**
Mayeswood Rd. SE12........4E **125**
MAYFAIR 5C **12** (1D **75**)
Mayfair M. NW1 ....4B **46**
.................(off Regents Pk. Rd.)
Mayfair Pl. W1.........1D **117**
Mayfair Pl. W1 ....1E **21** (2D **75**)
Mayfair Row W1.....2D **21** (2D **75**)
Mayfield Av. W4 ....5A **70**
Mayfield Cl. E8..................3B **50**
Mayfield Cl. SW4................3F **103**
Mayfield Gdns. NW4 ....1F **29**
Mayfield Ho. E2..................1D **65**
.................(off Cambridge Heath Rd.)
Mayfield Mans. SW15........3B **100**
Mayfield Rd. E13................3B **68**
Mayfield Rd. E8..................4B **50**
Mayfield Rd. N8 ....1B **34**
Mayfield Rd. W12................3A **70**
Mayfield Rd. Flats N8 ....1B **34**
Mayflower Cl. SE16 ....5F **79**
Mayflower Ho. E14 ....3C **80**
.................(off Westferry Rd.)
Mayflower Rd. SW9 ....1A **104**
Mayflower St. SE16 ....3E **79**
Mayford NW1 ....1E **61**
.................(not continuous)
Mayford Cl. SW12 ....5B **102**
Mayford Rd. SW12 ....5B **102**
Maygood Ho. N1 ....1B **62**
.................(off Maygood St.)
Maygood St. N1 ....1C **62**
Maygrove Rd. NW6 ....3B **44**
Mayhew Ct. SE5.................2F **105**
Mayhill Rd. SE15 ....3A **92**
Mayhill Rd. SE7 ....2D **97**
May Ho. E3........................1C **66**
.................(off Thomas Fyre Dr.)
Maylands Ho. SW3 ....5A **74**
.................(off Cale St.)
Maylie Ho. SE16.................3D **79**
.................(off Marigold St.)
Maynard Cl. SW6................3D **87**
Maynard Rd. E17................1E **39**
Maynards Quay E1..............1E **79**
Mayne Ct. SE26..................5D **121**
Mayo Ho. E1.......................4E **65**
.................(off Lindley St.)
Mayola Rd. E5.....................1E **51**
Mayo Rd. NW10..................3A **42**
Mayor's & City of London Court,
The.................2B **18** (5F **63**)
.................(off Basinghall St.)
Mayow Rd. SE23.................3F **121**
Mayow Rd. SE26.................4F **121**
May Rd. E13.......................1C **68**
May's Bldgs. M. SE10..........3E **95**
May's Ct. SE10...................3E **95**
Mays Ct. WC2.........5D **15** (1A **76**)
Maysoule Rd. SW11............2F **101**
Mayston M. SE10................1C **96**
.................(off Ormiston Rd.)
May St. W14: Lon Kelway Ho.1B **86**
May St. W14: Lon
Orchard Sq.................1B **86**
Maythorne Cotts. SE13........3F **109**
Mayton St. N7 ....5B **34**
May Tree Ho. SE4................1B **108**
.................(off Wickham Rd.)

Maytree Wlk. SW2 ....2C **118**
Mayville Est. N16 ....2A **50**
Mayville Rd. E11 ....4A **40**
.................(not continuous)
May Wlk. E13......................1D **69**
Mayward Ho. SE5................4A **92**
.................(off Peckham Rd.)
May Wynne Ho. E16............1D **83**
.................(off Murray Sq.)
Maze Hill SE10...................2A **96**
Maze Hill SE3....................3B **96**
Maze Hill Lodge SE10..........2F **95**
.................(off Park Vista)
Maze Hill Station (Rail) 2A **96**
Mazenod Av. NW6...............4C **44**
MCC Cricket Mus. & Tours...2F **59**
Meadbank Studios SW11 .....3A **88**
.................(off Parkgate Rd.)
Mead Cl. NW1....................3C **46**
Meadcroft Rd. SE11 ....2D **91**
.................(not continuous)
Meadcroft Rd. SE17............2D **91**
Meade Ho. E14 ....5A **68**
.................(off Lyell St.)
Meade M. SW1 ....1F **89**
.................(off Causton St.)
Mead Ho. W11....................2B **72**
.................(off Ladbroke Rd.)
Meadowbank NW3 ....4B **46**
Meadowbank SE3 ....1B **110**
Meadowbank Cl. SW6..........3F **85**
Meadow Cl. E9....................3B **52**
Meadow Cl. SE6 ....5C **122**
Meadow Cl. E16 ....2E **83**
.................(off Booth Rd.)
Meadow Cl. N1 ....1A **64**
Meadowcourt Rd. SE3.........2B **110**
Meadowcroft Cl. E10...........2D **39**
Meadowcroft M. E1.............1C **78**
.................(off Cable St.)
Meadowcroft M. SE6...........4D **109**
Meadow La. SE12................3D **125**
Meadowlark Ho. NW9..........2B **28**
Meadow M. SW8.................3A **90**
Meadow Pl. SW8.................3A **90**
Meadow Pl. W4...................3A **84**
Meadow Rd. SW8................3B **90**
Meadow Row SE1................4E **77**
Meadows Cl. E10 ....4C **38**
Meadowside SE3 ....2E **111**
Meadowside SE9 ....2E **111**
Meadows Way SE4 ....1A **108**
Meadowsweet Cl. E16.........4F **69**
Meadow Rd. SE6 ....5B **122**
Mead Path SW17 ....4E **115**
Mead Pl. E9........................3E **51**
Mead Row SE1......5B **24** (4C **76**)
Meads Ct. E15....................3B **54**
Medway NW11 ....1C **30**
Medway, The SE3 ....5F **95**
Medway Cl. NW11 ....1D **31**
Medway Ga. NW11 ....1C **30**
Meakin Est. SE1......5D **27** (4A **78**)
Meander Ho. E20.................2D **53**
.................(off Logan Cl.)
Meard St. W1 ....3B **14** (5F **61**)
.................(not continuous)
Mears Cl. E1.......................4C **64**
.................(off Settles St.)
Meath Cres. E2....................2F **65**
Meath Ho. SE24.................4D **105**
.................(off Dulwich Rd.)
Meath Rd. E15....................1B **68**
Meath St. SW11 ....4D **89**

Mecca Bingo Camden 5D **47**
.... (off Arlington Rd.)
Mecca Bingo Catford 5D **109**
Mecklenburgh Pl.
WC1 .... 3F **7** (3B **62**)
Mecklenburgh Sq.
WC1 .... 3F **7** (3B **62**)
Mecklenburgh St.
WC1 .... 3F **7** (3B **62**)
Medals Way E20 .... 2E **53**
Medburn St. NW1 .... 1F **61**
Medebourne Cl. SE3 ...... 1C **110**
Mede Ho. BR1: Broml 5D **125**
.... (off Pike Cl.)
Medfield St. SW15 .... 5C **98**
Medhurst Cl. E3 .... 1A **66**
.... (not continuous)
Medhurst Dr. BR1: Broml .. 5A **124**
Median Rd. E5 .... 2E **51**
Medina Gro. N7 .... 5C **34**
Medina Pl. E14 .... 4C **66**
Medina Rd. N7 .... 5C **34**
Medland Ho. E14 .... 1A **80**
Medlar St. SE5 .... 4E **91**
Medley Rd. NW6 .... 3C **44**
Medora Rd. SW2 .... 5B **104**
Medusa Rd. SE6 .... 4D **109**
Medway Bldgs. E3 .... 1A **66**
.... (off Medway Rd.)
Medway M. NW11 .... 1D **31**
Medway Ct. WC1 ..... 2D **7** (2A **62**)
.... (off Judd St.)
Medway Ho. NW8 .... 3A **60**
Medway Ho. SE1 ..... 4C **26** (3F **77**)
.... (off Hankey Pl.)
Medway M. E3 .... 1A **66**
Medway Rd. E3 .... 1A **66**
Medway St. SW1 .... 4F **75**
Medwin St. SW4 .... 2B **104**
Meerbrook Rd. SE3 .... 1E **111**
Meeson Rd. E15 .... 4B **54**
Meeson St. E5 .... 1A **52**
Meeson's Wharf E15 .... 1E **67**
Meeting Fld. Path E9 .... 3E **51**
Meeting Ho. All. E1 .... 2D **79**
Meeting Ho. La. SE15 .... 4D **93**
Megan Ct. SE14 .... 3E **93**
.... (off Pomeroy St.)
Mehetabel Rd. E9 .... 2E **51**
Melba Way SE13 .... 4D **95**
Melbourne Cl. E5 .... 1A **52**
.... (off Daubeney Rd.)
Melbourne Ct. W9 .... 3E **59**
.... (off Randolph Av.)
Melbourne Gro. SE22 ...... 2A **106**
Melbourne Ho. W8 .... 2C **72**
.... (off Kensington Pl.)
Melbourne Mans. W14 ...... 2A **86**
.... (off Musard Rd.)
Melbourne M. SE6 .... 5E **109**
Melbourne M. SW9 .... 4C **90**
Melbourne Pl.
WC2 .... 3A **16** (5B **62**)
Melbourne Rd. E10 .... 2D **39**
Melbourne Sq. SW9 .... 4C **90**
Melbourne Ter. SW6 .... 3D **87**
.... (off Moore Pk. Rd.)
Melbray M. SW6 .... 5B **86**
Melbreak Ho. SE22 .... 1A **106**
Melbury Ct. W8 .... 4B **72**
Melbury Dr. SE5 .... 3A **92**
Melbury Ho. SW8 .... 3B **90**
.... (off Richborne Ter.)
Melbury Rd. W14 .... 4B **72**

Melchester W11 .... 5B **58**
.... (off Ledbury Rd.)
Melchester Ho. N19 .... 5F **33**
.... (off Wedmore St.)
Melcombe Ct. NW1 ...... 5A **4** (4B **60**)
.... (off Melcombe Pl.)
Melcombe Ho. SW8 .... 3B **90**
.... (off Dorset Rd.)
Melcombe Pl. NW1 .... 4B **60**
Melcombe Regis Ct.
W1 .... 1C **12** (4C **60**)
.... (off Weymouth St.)
Melcombe St. NW1 ..... 4A **4** (3B **60**)
Meldon Cl. SW6 .... 4D **87**
Melfield Gdns. SE6 .... 4E **123**
Melford Ct. SE1 ...... 5E **27** (4A **78**)
.... (off Fendall St.)
Melford Ct. SE22 .... 1C **120**
.... (not continuous)
Melford Pas. SE22 .... 5C **106**
Melford Rd. E11 .... 4A **40**
Melford Rd. SE22 .... 5C **106**
Melgund Rd. N5 .... 2C **48**
Melina Ct. NW8 .... 2F **59**
.... (off Grove End Rd.)
Melina Ct. SW15 .... 1C **98**
Melina Pl. NW8 .... 2F **59**
Melina Rd. W12 .... 3D **71**
Melior Ct. N6 .... 1E **33**
Melior Pl. SE1 .... 3D **27** (3A **78**)
Melior St. SE1 .... 3D **27** (3A **78**)
Meliot Rd. SE6 .... 2F **123**
Meller Ho. E20 .... 3E **53**
.... (off Champions Wlk.)
Mellish Flats E10 .... 2C **38**
Mellish Ho. E1 .... 5D **65**
.... (off Varden St.)
Mellish Ind. Est. SE18 ...... 4F **83**
Mellish St. E14 .... 4C **80**
Mellison Rd. SW17 .... 5A **116**
Mellitus St. W12 .... 4B **56**
Mell St. SE10 .... 1A **96**
Melody La. N5 .... 2E **49**
Melody Rd. SW18 .... 3E **101**
Melon Pl. W8 .... 3C **72**
Melon Rd. E11 .... 5A **40**
Melon Rd. SE15 .... 4C **92**
Melrose Av. NW2 .... 2D **43**
Melrose Av. SW19 .... 2B **114**
Melrose Cl. SE12 .... 1C **124**
Melrose Gdns. W6 .... 4E **71**
Melrose Ho. NW6 .... 2C **58**
Melrose Ho. SW1 .... 1D **89**
.... (part of Abbots Mnr.)
Melrose Rd. SW13 .... 5B **84**
Melrose Rd. SW18 .... 4B **100**
Melrose Ter. W6 .... 4E **71**
Melthorpe Gdns. SE3 .... 4F **97**
Melton Ct. SW7 .... 5F **73**
Melton St. NW1 ...... 2A **6** (2E **61**)
Melville Ct. W12 .... 4D **71**
.... (off Goldhawk Rd.)
Melville Pl. N1 .... 4E **49**
Melville Rd. SW13 .... 4C **84**
Melwood Ho. E1 .... 5D **65**
.... (off Watney Mkt.)
Melyn Cl. N7 .... 1E **47**
Memel Ct. EC1 .... 4F **9** (3E **63**)
.... (off Memel St.)
Memel St. EC1 .... 4F **9** (3E **63**)
Memorial Av. E15 .... 2A **68**
Menai Pl. E3 .... 1C **66**
.... (off Blondin St.)

Menard Ct. EC1 .... 2A **10** (2E **63**)
.... (off Galway St.)
Mendez Way SW15 .... 4C **98**
Mendham Ho. SE1 ... 5D **27** (4A **78**)
.... (off Cluny Pl.)
Mendip Cl. SE26 .... 4E **121**
Mendip Ct. SE14 .... 2E **93**
.... (off Avonley Rd.)
Mendip Ct. SW11 .... 1E **101**
Mendip Dr. NW2 .... 4A **30**
Mendip Ho's. E2 .... 2E **65**
.... (off Welwyn St.)
Mendip Rd. SW11 .... 1E **101**
Mendora Rd. SW6 .... 3A **86**
Menelik Rd. NW2 .... 1A **44**
Menier Chocolate Factory
.... 2A **26** (2E **77**)
.... (off Southwark St.)
Menotti St. E2 .... 3C **64**
Menteath Ho. E14 .... 5C **66**
.... (off Dod St.)
Mentmore Ter. E8 .... 4D **51**
Mentone Mans. SW10 .... 3D **87**
.... (off Fulham Rd.)
Mepham St. SE1 ..... 2A **24** (2C **76**)
Meranti Ho. E1 .... 5C **64**
.... (off Goodman's Stile)
Merbury Cl. SE13 .... 3E **109**
Mercator Pl. E14 .... 1C **94**
Mercator Rd. SE13 .... 2F **109**
Mercer Bldg.
EC2 .... 3E **11** (3A **64**)
.... (off New Inn Yd.)
Mercer Ct. E1 .... 4A **66**
Mercer Ho. SW1 .... 1D **89**
.... (off Ebury Bri. Rd.)
Mercer Ho. SW8 .... 4D **89**
.... (off Gladstone Ter.)
Merceron Ho's. E2 .... 2E **65**
.... (off Globe Rd.)
Merceron St. E1 .... 3D **65**
Mercers Cl. SE10 .... 5B **82**
Mercer's Cotts. E1 .... 5A **66**
.... (off White Horse Rd.)
Mercers M. N19 .... 5F **33**
Mercers Pl. W6 .... 5F **71**
Mercers Rd. N19 .... 5F **33**
.... (not continuous)
Mercer St. WC2 ..... 3D **15** (5A **62**)
Mercer Wlk. WC2 ... 3D **15** (5A **62**)
.... (off Mercer St.)
Merchant Ct. E1 .... 2E **79**
.... (off Wapping Wall)
Merchant Ho. E14 .... 4D **81**
.... (off Selsdon Way)
Merchant Navy Memorial
.... 5E **19** (1B **78**)
Merchants Ho. E14 .... 5F **67**
.... (off New Village Av.)
Merchants Ho. E15 .... 3F **53**
.... (off Forrester Way)
Merchants Ho. SE10 .... 1F **95**
.... (off Collington St.)
Merchants Pl. SE13 .... 2A **110**
Merchant Sq. W2 .... 4F **59**
Merchant Sq. E. W2 .... 4F **59**
.... (off Harbet Road)
Merchant Sq. W. W2 .... 4F **59**
.... (off North Wharf Road)
Merchants Row SE10 .... 1F **95**
.... (off Hoskins St.)
Merchant St. E3 .... 2B **66**
Merchiston Rd. SE6 .... 2F **123**
Mercia Gro. SE13 .... 2E **109**

Mercia Ho. SE5....................5E **91**
................................*(off Denmark Rd.)*
Mercier Ct. E16........................2E **83**
................................*(off Starboard Way)*
Mercier Rd. SW15..............3A **100**
Mercury Ct. E14........................5C **80**
................................*(off Homer Dr.)*
Mercury Ct. SW9.......................4C **90**
................................*(off Southey Rd.)*
Mercury Ho. E16.......................5B **68**
................................*(off Jude St.)*
Mercury Ho. J3..........................5C **52**
................................*(off Garrison Rd.)*
Mercury Way SE14...................2F **93**
Mercy Ter. SE13......................3D **109**
Mere Cl. SW15.........................5F **99**
Meredith Av. NW2......................2E **43**
Meredith Ho. N16....................2A **50**
Meredith M. SE4......................2B **108**
Meredith St. E13.......................2C **68**
Meredith St. EC1.........2D **9** (2D **63**)
Meredyth Rd. SW13..............5C **84**
Meretone Cl. SE4...................2A **108**
Mereton Mans. SE8...................4C **94**
................................*(off Brookmill Rd.)*
Mereworth Ho. SE15...............2E **93**
Merganser Ct. E1......................1C **78**
................................*(off Star Pl.)*
Merganser Ct. SE8....................2B **94**
................................*(off Edward St.)*
Meriden Ct. SW3.......................1A **88**
................................*(off Chelsea Mnr. St.)*
Meriden Ho. N1.......................5A **50**
................................*(off Wilmer Gdns.)*
Meridia Ct. E15........................5E **53**
................................*(off Biggerstaff Rd.)*
Meridian Ct. SE16....................3D **93**
................................*(off Gervase St.)*
Meridian Ct. SE16....................3C **78**
................................*(off East La.)*
Meridian Ga. E14.....................3D **81**
Meridian Ho.
SE10: Lon Azof St..............5A **82**
................................*(off Azof St.)*
Meridian Ho.
SE10: Lon Royal Hill..........3E **95**
................................*(off Royal Hill)*
Meridian Ho. NW1....................4E **47**
................................*(off Baynes St.)*
Meridian Ho. SW18................2E **101**
................................*(off Juniper Dr.)*
Meridian Pl. E14......................3D **81**
Meridian Point SE8.................2D **95**
Meridian Rd. SE7....................3F **97**
Meridian Sq. E15......................4F **53**
Meridian Trad. Est. SE7........5D **83**
Merifield Rd. SE9......................2E **111**
Merino Ct. EC1...........2A **10** (2E **63**)
................................*(off Lever St.)*
Merival Rd. SW15..................2A **100**
Merle Mans. E20.......................3E **53**
................................*(off Glade Wlk.)*
Merlin Ct. SE3.........................2D **111**
Merlin Gdns.
BR1: Broml........................3C **124**
Merlin Rd. E12..........................4F **41**
Merlins Ct. WC1.........2B **8** (2C **62**)
................................*(off Margery St.)*
Merlin St. WC1...........2B **8** (2C **62**)
................................*(off Celandine Dr.)*
Mermaid Ct. E8.........................4B **50**
Mermaid Ct. SE1.........3B **26** (3F **77**)
Mermaid Ct. SE16....................2B **80**

Mermaid Ho. E14......................1E **81**
................................*(off Bazely St.)*
Mermaid Twr. SE8.....................2B **94**
................................*(off Abinger Gro.)*
Meroe Ct. N16..........................4A **36**
Merredene St. SW2.................4B **104**
Merriam Av. E9.........................3B **52**
Merrick Sq. SE1.........5B **26** (4F **77**)
Merriman Rd. SE3.....................4E **97**
Merrington Rd. SW6.................2C **86**
Merritt Rd. SE4.......................3B **108**
Merrivale NW1..........................5E **47**
................................*(off Camden St.)*
Merrow Bldgs. SE1...3E **25** (3D **77**)
................................*(off Rushworth St.)*
Merrow St. SE17......................1F **91**
Merrow Wlk. SE17.....................1F **91**
Merryfield SE3.........................5B **96**
Merryfield Ct. SW11...............5B **88**
Merryfield Ho. SE9................3E **125**
................................*(off Grove Pk. Rd.)*
Merryfields Way SE9.............5D **109**
Merryweather Ct. N19............5E **33**
Merryweather Pl. SE10...........3D **95**
Merthyr Ter. SW13....................2D **85**
Merton Av. W4..........................5B **70**
Merton Ri. NW3........................4A **46**
Merton La. N6..........................4B **32**
Merton Rd. E17..........................1E **39**
Merton Rd. SW18...................4C **100**
Mertoun Ter. W1.......................4B **60**
................................*(off Seymour Pl.)*
Merttins Rd. SE15..................3F **107**
Meru Cl. NW5............................1C **46**
Mervan Rd. SW2.....................2C **104**
Messenger Ct. SE16.................4C **78**
................................*(off Spa Rd.)*
Messent Rd. SE9....................3E **111**
Messina Av. NW6......................4C **44**
Messiter Ho. N1........................5B **48**
................................*(off Barnsbury Est.)*
Metcalfe Ct. SE10.....................4B **82**
Meteor St. SW11....................2C **102**
Methley St. SE11......................1C **90**
Methwold Rd. W10....................4F **57**
Metro Bus. Cen. SE26..........5B **122**
Metro Central Hgts.
SE1.............................5F **25** (4E **77**)
................................*(off Newington C'way.)*
Metropolis SE11........................4D **77**
................................*(off Oswin St.)*
Metropolis Plaza E3.................3A **66**
................................*(off Copperfield Rd.)*
Metropolitan Bldg. SW10......3E **87**
Metropolitan Bus. Cen. N1...4A **50**
................................*(off Enfield Rd.)*
Metropolitan Cl. E14...............4C **66**
Metropolitan Cres. SW4.......3F **103**
Metropolitan Sta. Bldgs. W6....5E **71**
................................*(off Beadon Rd.)*
Metropolitan Wharf E1...........2E **79**
................................*(off Wapping Wall)*
Mews, The IG4: Ilf.................1F **41**
Mews, The N1...........................5E **49**
Mews St. E1..............................2C **78**
Mexborough NW1......................5E **47**
Mexfield Rd. SW15.................3B **100**
Meymott St. SE1.........2D **25** (2D **77**)
Meynell Cres. E9......................4F **51**
Meynell Gdns. E9.....................4F **51**
Meynell Rd. E9..........................4F **51**
Meyrick Ho. E14.......................4C **66**
................................*(off Burgess St.)*
Meyrick Rd. NW10....................3D **42**
Meyrick Rd. SW11...................1F **101**
MFA Bowl Lewisham...............1E **109**

Miah Ter. E1..............................2C **78**
Miall Wlk. SE26......................4A **122**
Mica Ho. N1..............................4C **48**
Micawber Ct. N1.........1A **10** (2E **63**)
................................*(off Windsor Ter.)*
Micawber Ho. SE16.................3C **78**
................................*(off Llewellyn St.)*
Micawber St. N1.........1A **10** (2E **63**)
Michael Cliffe Ho.
EC1.............................2C **8** (2D **63**)
................................*(off Finsbury Est.)*
Michael Cl. E3..........................3B **66**
Michael Edwards Studio Theatre,
The..2E **95**
................................*(within Cutty Sark)*
Michael Faraday Ct. SE17 . 1A **92**
................................*(off Beaconsfield Rd.)*
Michael Haines Ho. SW9 ....3C **90**
................................*(off Sth. Island Pl.)*
Michael Manley Ind. Est.
SW8...4E **89**
Michael Rd. E11.......................3A **40**
Michael Rd. SW6......................4D **87**
Michaels Cl. SE13...................2A **110**
Michael Stewart Ho. SW6.....2B **86**
................................*(off Clem Attlee Ct.)*
Michelangelo Ct. SE16...........1D **93**
................................*(off Stubbs Dr.)*
Micheldever Rd. SE12..........4A **110**
Michelle Ct. W3......................1A **70**
Michelson Ho. SE11...............5B **76**
................................*(off Black Prince Rd.)*
Michigan Bldg. E14..................2F **81**
................................*(off Biscayne Av.)*
Michigan Ho. E14.....................4C **80**
Mickleboro NW1...........1A **6** (1E **61**)
................................*(off Ampthill Est.)*
Micklethwaite Rd. SW6..........2C **86**
Mickleton Ho. W2......................4C **58**
................................*(off Westbourne Pk. Rd.)*
Middle Dartrey Wlk. SW10...3E **87**
................................*(off Worlds End Est.)*
Middlefield NW8........................5F **45**
Middle La. N8...........................1A **34**
Middle La. M. N8.....................1A **34**
Middle New St.
EC4.............................2C **16** (5C **62**)
................................*(off Pemberton Row)*
Middle Pk. Av. SE9................4F **111**
Middle Rd. E13.........................1C **68**
Middle Row W10.......................3A **58**
Middlesex Bldg.
E1...............................1E **19** (4A **64**),
................................*(off Artillery La.)*
Middlesex CCC.........................2F **59**
Middlesex Ct. W4.....................5B **70**
Middlesex Filter Beds Nature
Reserve...................................5F **37**
Middlesex Guildhall ...4C **22** (3A **76**)
................................*(off Lit. George St.)*
Middlesex Pl. E9......................3E **51**
................................*(off Elsdale St.)*
Middlesex St. E1.......1E **19** (4A **64**)
Middlesex University Archway
Campus..................................3E **33**
Middlesex Wharf E5................4E **37**
Middle St. EC1..........5F **9** (4E **63**)
Middle Temple Hall .. 4B **16** (1C **76**)
Middle Temple La.
EC4.............................3B **16** (5C **62**)
Middleton Dr. SE16..................3F **79**
Middleton Green 2D **65**
................................*(off Old Bethnal Green Road)*
Middleton Gro. N7....................2A **48**
Middleton Ho. E8......................4C **50**

Middleton Ho. SE1 ...5B **26** (4F **77**)
...............................*(off Burbage Cl.)*
Middleton Ho. SW1 ....5F **75**
...............................*(off Causton St.)*
Middleton M. N7 ....2A **48**
Middleton Pl. W1..... 1F **13** (4E **61**)
...............................*(off Langham St.)*
Middleton Rd. E8 ....4B **50**
Middleton Rd. NW11 ....2C **30**
Middleton St. E2 ....2D **65**
Middleton Way SE13.......2F **109**
Middleway NW11 ....1D **31**
Middle Yd. SE1 ....1D **27** (2A **78**)
Midford Pl. W1 ....4A **6** (3E **61**)
Midhope Ho. WC1 ...2E **7** (2A **62**)
...............................*(off Midhope St.)*
Midhope St. WC1 ...2E **7** (2A **62**)
Midhurst SE26 ....5E **121**
Midhurst Ho. E14 ....5B **66**
...............................*(off Salmon La.)*
Midhurst Way E5 ....1C **50**
Midland Goods Shed N1 ...5A **48**
...............................*(off Handyside St.)*
Midland Pde. NW6 ....3D **45**
Midland Rd. E10 ....1E **95**
Midland Rd. NW1 ....2E **39**
Midland Rd. NW11 .... 1C **6** (1F **61**)
Midland Ter. NW10 ....3A **56**
Midland Ter. NW2 ....5F **29**
Midlothian Rd. E3 ....3B **66**
...............................*(off Burdett Rd.)*
Midmoor Rd. SW12 ....1E **117**
Midnight Av. SE5 ....3D **91**
Midship Cl. SE16 ....2F **79**
Midship Point E14 ....3C **80**
...............................*(off The Quarterdeck)*
Midstrath Rd. NW10 ....1A **42**
Midway Ho. EC1 ......1D **9** (2D **63**)
...............................*(off Manningford Cl.)*
Midwood Cl. NW2 ....5D **29**
Mighell Av. IG4: Ilf..................1F **41**
Mikardo Ct. E14 ....1E **81**
...............................*(off Poplar High St.)*
Milborne Gro. SW10..........1E **87**
Milborne St. E9 ....3E **51**
Milborough Cres. SE12......4A **110**
Milcote St. SE1 ....4D **25** (3D **77**)
Mildenhall Rd. E5 ....1E **51**
Mildmay Av. N1 ....3F **49**
Mildmay Gro. Nth. N1 ....2F **49**
Mildmay Gro. Sth. N1 ....2F **49**
MILDMAY HOSPITAL..2F **11** (2B **64**)
Mildmay Pk. N1 ....2F **49**
Mildmay Pl. N16 ....2A **50**
Mildmay Rd. N1 ....2F **49**
Mildmay St. N1 ....3F **49**
Mildrose Ct. NW6 ....2C **58**
...............................*(off Malvern M.)*
MILE END 3B **66**
Mile End Climbing Wall 2A **66**
MILE END HOSPITAL............3F **65**
Mile End Pk. 1A **66**
Mile End Pk. Leisure Cen....4A **66**
Mile End Pl. E1 ....3F **65**
Mile End Rd. E1 ....4E **65**
Mile End Rd. E3 ....3A **66**
Mile End Stadium 4A **66**
Mile End Station (Underground)
....3B **66**
Miles Bldgs. NW1 ....4A **60**
...............................*(off Penfold Pl.)*
Miles Ct. E1 ....5D **65**
...............................*(off Tillman St.)*
Miles Ho. SE10 ....1A **96**
...............................*(off Tuskar St.)*

Miles Lodge E15 ....2F **53**
...............................*(off Colegrave Rd.)*
Miles Pl. NW8 ....4F **59**
...............................*(off Broadley St.)*
Miles St. SW8 ....2A **90**
...............................*(not continuous)*
Milestone Ct. E10 ....2D **39**
Milfoil St. W12 ....1C **70**
Milford La. WC2 ....2A **16** (1C **76**)
Milford M. SW16 ....3B **118**
Milford Towers SE6 ....5D **109**
Milk St. BR1: Broml 5D **125**
Milk St. EC2 ....2A **18** (5E **63**)
Milkwell Yd. SE5..................4E **91**
Milkwood Rd. SE24 ....3D **105**
Milk Yd. E1 ....1E **79**
Millais Ho. SW1 ....5A **76**
...............................*(off Marsham St.)*
Millais Rd. E11 ....1E **53**
Millard Cl. N16 ....2A **50**
Millard Rd. SE8 ....1B **94**
Millbank SW1 ....5D **23** (4A **76**)
Millbank Ct. SW1 ....5A **76**
...............................*(off John Islip St.)*
Millbank Millennium Pier
(River Bus) 5A **76**
Millbank Twr. SW1 ....5A **76**
Millbank Way SE12 ....3C **110**
Millbrooke Ct. SW15...........3A **100**
...............................*(off Keswick Rd.)*
Millbrook Ho. SE15 ....2C **92**
...............................*(off Peckham Pk. Rd.)*
Millbrook Pas. SW9 ....1D **105**
Millbrook Pl. NW1 ....1E **61**
...............................*(off Hampstead Rd.)*
Millbrook Rd. SW9 ....1D **105**
Mill Ct. E10 ....5E **39**
Mill Ct. E15 ....4E **37**
Millcroft Ho. SE6 ....4E **123**
...............................*(off Melfield Gdns.)*
Millender Wlk. SE16 ....5E **79**
...............................*(off New Rotherhithe Rd.)*
MILLENNIUM BRIDGE
SOUTHWARK.....5E **17** (1E **77**)
Millennium Bri. Ho.
EC4............................2F **17** (1E **77**)
...............................*(off Up. Thames St.)*
Millennium Bus. Cen. NW2...4D **29**
Millennium Cl. E16................5D **69**
Millennium Dr. E14 ....5F **81**
Millennium Ho. SW15 ....3A **100**
...............................*(off Plaza Gdns.)*
Millennium Pl. E2 ....1D **65**
Millennium Sq. SE1...3F **27** (3B **78**)
Millennium Way SE10 ....3A **82**
Miller Cl. BR1: Broml 5D **125**
Miller Ho. E1 ....4F **65**
...............................*(off Shandy St.)*
Miller Ho. W10 ....2F **57**
...............................*(off Harrow Rd.)*
Miller Rd. SW19 ....5F **115**
Miller's Av. E8 ....2B **50**
Miller's House Visitor Cen....2E **67**
...............................*(off Three Mill La.)*
Millers Mdw. Cl. SE3 ....2B **110**
Millers Row E20...................2D **53**
Miller's Ter. E8 ....2B **50**
Miller St. NW1 ....1E **61**
...............................*(not continuous)*
Millers Way W6 ....3E **71**
Millers Wharf Ho. E1 ....2C **78**
...............................*(off St Katherine's Way)*
Milles Sq. SW9 ....2C **104**
Millfield N4..............................4C **34**

Millfield La. N6......................3A **32**
Millfield Pl. N6 ....4C **32**
Millfields Rd. E5 ....1E **51**
Mill Gdns. SE26 ....3D **121**
Millgrove St. SW11 ....4C **88**
Millharbour E14 ....3D **81**
Mill Hill SW13 ....5C **84**
Mill Hill Rd. SW13 ....5C **84**
Millhouse Pl. SE27 ....4D **119**
Millicent Rd. E10 ....3B **38**
Milligan St. E14 ....1B **80**
Milliner Ho. SW10 ....3E **87**
...............................*(off Hortensia Rd.)*
Milliners Ho. SE1......4E **27** (3A **78**)
...............................*(off Bermondsey St.)*
Milliners Ho. SW18 ....2C **100**
Millington Ho. N16..............5F **35**
Mill La. NW6 ....2B **44**
Mill La. SE8 ....4C **94**
...............................*(off Deptford Bri.)*
Millman Ct. WC1 ..... 4F **7** (3B **62**)
...............................*(off Millman St.)*
Millman M. WC1 ......4F **7** (3B **62**)
Millman Pl. WC1 ....4A **8** (3B **62**)
...............................*(off Millman St.)*
Millman St. WC1 ......4F **7** (3B **62**)
Millmark Gro. SE14 ....5A **94**
MILL MEADS 1F **67**
Mill Pl. E14 ....5A **66**
Mill Pond Cl. SW8 ....3F **89**
Millpond Est. SE16 ....3D **79**
Mill Rd. E16 ....2D **83**
Mill Row N1 ....5A **50**
Mills Gro. EC2 ....2D **11** (2A **64**)
...............................*(off Curtain Rd.)*
Mills Gro. E14 ....5E **67**
Millshott Cl. SW6 ....4E **85**
Mills Ho. SW8 ....4E **89**
...............................*(off Thessaly Rd.)*
Millstone Cl. E15 ....3F **53**
Millstream Ho. SE16 ....3D **79**
...............................*(off Jamaica Rd.)*
Millstream Rd. SE1 ..4F **27** (3B **78**)
Mill St. SE1 ....3B **78**
Mill St. W1 ....4E **13** (1D **75**)
Mill Yd. SW6 ....1D **101**
MILLWALL 5D **81**
Millwall Dock Rd. E14 ....1C **80**
Millwall F.C. 1E **93**
Millwall Pk. 5E **81**
Millwood St. W10.................4A **58**
Mill Yd. E1 ....1C **78**
Milman Rd. NW6 ....1F **57**
Milman's Ho. SW10 ....2F **87**
...............................*(off Milman's St.)*
Milman's St. SW10 ....2F **87**
Milne Gdns. SE9 ....1F **111**
Milner Ct. SE15 ....3B **92**
...............................*(off Colegrove Rd.)*
Milner Ho. N1 ....5C **48**
Milner Pl. SE1 ....2A **24** (3B **76**)
Milner Rd. E15 ....2A **68**
Milner Sq. N1 ....5C **48**
Milner St. SW3 ....5B **74**
Milo Gdns. SE22 ....4B **106**
Milo Rd. SE22 ....4B **106**
Milroad Ho. E1 ....4C **64**
...............................*(off Stepney Grn.)*
Milroy Wlk. SE1 .....1D **25** (2D **77**)
Milson Rd. W14....................4F **71**
Milstead Ho. E5 ....2D **51**
Milton Av. E6 ....4F **55**
Milton Av. N6 ....2E **33**
Milton Cl. N2 ....1E **31**
Milton Cl. SE1 ....5B **78**

Milton Ct. EC2 ....5B **10** (4F **63**)
Milton Ct. SE14 ....2B **94**
....(not continuous)
Milton Ct. SW18 ....3C **100**
Milton Court Concert Hall
..............................5B **10** (4F **63**)
......................................(off Milton Ct.)
Milton Ct. Rd. SE14............2A **94**
Milton Gdn. Est. N16...........1F **49**
Milton Gro. N16....................1F **49**
Milton Ho. E2................................3D **65**
......................................(off Roman Rd.)
Milton Ho. SE5 ....3F **91**
......................................(off Elmington Est.)
Milton Mans. W14.................2A **86**
......................................(off Queen's Club Gdns.)
Milton Pk. N6 ....2E **33**
Milton Pl. N7 ....2C **48**
......................................(off Eastwood Cl.)
Milton Rd. N6 ....4E **65**
Milton Rd. NW9......................2C **28**
Milton Rd. SE24 ....3D **105**
Milton Rd. SW19 ....5E **115**
Milton St. EC2 ....5B **10** (4F **63**)
Milverton Ho. SE6................3A **122**
Milverton Pl. BR1: Broml....5E **125**
Milverton Rd. NW6................4E **43**
Milverton St. SE11................1C **90**
Milward St. E1 ....4D **65**
Mimosa Ho. E20 ....2E **53**
......................................(off Liberty Bri. Rd.)
Mimosa Lodge NW10............2B **42**
Mimosa St. SW6....................4B **86**
Minard Rd. SE6 ....5A **110**
Mina Rd. SE17.......................1A **92**
Minchin Ho. E14.....................5C **66**
......................................(off Dod St.)
Mincing La. EC3........4D **19** (1A **78**)
Minehead Rd. SW16 ....5B **118**
Minera M. SW1.......................5C **74**
Minerva Cl. SW9....................3C **90**
Minerva Ct. EC1 ....4C **8** (3C **62**)
......................................(off Bowling Grn. La.)
Minerva Lodge N7.................3B **48**
Minerva St. E2.......................1D **65**
Minerva Wlk. EC1 ....2E **17** (5D **63**)
Minet Av. NW10.....................1A **56**
Minet Gdns. NW10...............1A **56**
Minet Rd. SW9......................5D **91**
Minford Gdns. W14................3F **71**
Minford Ho. W14....................3F **71**
......................................(off Minford Gdns.)
Mingard Wlk. N7...................4B **34**
Ming St. E14 ....1C **80**
Miniver Pl. EC4........4A **18** (1E **77**)
......................................(off Garlick Hill)
Minnie Baldock St. E16.......5B **68**
Minnow St. SE17 ....5A **78**
Minnow Wlk. SE17................5A **78**
Minories EC3..............3F **19** (5B **64**)
MINOR INJURIES UNIT (GUY'S
HOSPITAL)...............3C **26** (3F **77**)
MINOR INJURIES UNIT
(ROEHAMPTON) 4C **98**
MINOR INJURIES UNIT (ST
BARTHOLOMEW'S HOSPITAL)
..............................1E **17** (4D **63**)
Minshill St. SW8...................4F **89**
Minson Rd. E9.......................5F **51**
Minstead Gdns. SW15 ....5B **98**
Minster Ct. EC3 ....4E **19** (1A **78**)
......................................(off Mincing La.)
Minster Pavement
EC3...........................4E **19** (1A **78**)
......................................(off Mincing La.)
Minster Rd. NW2...................2A **44**
Mint Bus. Pk. E16................4D **69**
Mintern St. N1.......................1F **63**
Minton Apts. SW8 ....3A **90**
Minton Ho. SE11 ....5C **76**
......................................(off Walnut Tree Wlk.)
Minton M. NW6 ....3D **45**
Mint St. E2..............................3D **65**
......................................(off Three Colts La.)
Mint St. SE1 ....3F **25** (3E **77**)
Mirabelle Gdns. E20 ....2E **53**
Mirabel Rd. SW6...................3B **86**
Mira Ho. E20..........................2E **53**
......................................(off Prize Wlk.)
Miranda Cl. E1 ....4E **65**
Miranda Ho. N1 ....1D **11** (1A **64**)
......................................(off Crondall St.)
Miranda Rd. N19...................3E **33**
Mirfield St. SE7 ....5F **83**
Mirror Path SE9 ....3E **125**
Missenden SE17 ....1F **91**
......................................(off Roland Way)
Missenden Ho. NW8.............3A **60**
......................................(off Jerome Cres.)
Mission, The E14.................5B **66**
......................................(off Commercial Rd.)
Mission Pl. SE15 ....4C **92**
Mistral SE5.............................4A **92**
Mitali Pas. E1 ....5C **64**
Mitcham Ho. SE5 ....4E **91**
Mitcham Rd. SW17 ....5B **116**
Mitchell Ho. N1 ....4D **49**
......................................(off College Cross)
Mitchell Ho. W12...................1D **71**
......................................(off White City Est.)
Mitchell's Pl. SE21...............4A **106**
......................................(off Aysgarth Rd.)
Mitchell St. EC1 ......3F **9** (3E **63**)
......................................(not continuous)
Mitchell Wlk. E6: Lon
Allhallows M. 4F **69**
......................................(off Allhallows Rd.)
Mitchison Rd. N1...................3F **49**
Mitford Bldgs. SW6..............3C **86**
......................................(off Dawes Rd.)
Mitford Rd. N19 ....4A **34**
Mitre, The E14......................5C **66**
Mitre Bri. Ind. Pk. W10.......3D **57**
......................................(not continuous)
Mitre Ho. SW3 ....1B **88**
......................................(off King's Rd.)
Mitre Pas. EC3 ....3E **19** (5A **64**)
......................................(off Mitre Sq.)
Mitre Pas. SE10.....................3A **82**
Mitre Rd. E15.........................1A **68**
Mitre Rd. SE1 ....3C **24** (3C **76**)
Mitre Sq. EC3 ....3E **19** (5A **64**)
Mitre St. EC3 ....3E **19** (5A **64**)
Mitre Way W10.......................3D **57**
Mitre Yd. SW3 ....5A **74**
Mitten Ho. SE8 ....3D **95**
......................................(off Creative Rd.)
Mizen Ct. E14........................3C **80**
......................................(off Alpha Gro.)
Moat Dr. E13..........................1E **69**
Moatfield NW6 ....4A **44**
Moatlands Ho.
WC1.........................2E **7** (2A **62**)
......................................(off Cromer St.)
Moat Pl. SW9..........................1B **104**
Moat St. SW11.......................3E **89**
Moberly Rd. SW4 ....5F **103**
Moberly Sports Cen............2F **57**
Mobil Ct. WC2 ....3A **16** (5B **62**)
......................................(off Clement's Inn)
Mocatta Ho. E1......................3D **65**
......................................(off Brady St.)
Mocha Ct. E3...........................1D **67**
......................................(off Taylor Pl.)
Modbury Gdns. NW5.............3C **46**
Modder Pl. SW15 ....2F **99**
Modena Ho. E14.....................5A **68**
......................................(off Lyell St.)
Modern Ct. EC4........2D **17** (5D **63**)
......................................(off Farringdon St.)
Modling Ho. E2......................1F **65**
......................................(off Mace St.)
Moelwyn N7 ....2F **47**
Moffat Ct. SW19...................5C **114**
Moffat Ho. SE5 ....3E **91**
Moffat Rd. SW17 ....4B **116**
Mogul Bldg. E15...................2E **53**
......................................(off Property Row)
Mohawk Ho. E3......................1A **66**
......................................(off Gernon Rd.)
Mohmmad Khan Rd. E11....3B **40**
Moira Ho. SW9.......................4C **90**
......................................(off Gosling Way)
Molasses Ho. SW11.............1E **101**
......................................(off Clove Hitch Quay)
Molasses Row SW11...........1E **101**
Mole Ho. NW8.........................3F **59**
......................................(off Church St. Est.)
Molesford Rd. SW6..............4C **86**
Molesworth Ho. SE17..........2D **91**
......................................(off Brandon Est.)
Molesworth St. SE13...........2E **109**
Mollis Ho. E3..........................4C **66**
......................................(off Gale St.)
Molly Huggins Cl. SW12 ....5E **103**
Molten Ct. SE14 ....2B **94**
......................................(off Moulding La.)
Molton Ho. N1 ....5B **48**
......................................(off Barnsbury Est.)
Molyneux Dr. SW17 ....4D **117**
Molyneux St. W1...................4A **60**
Monarch Dr. E16 ....4F **69**
Monarch Ho. W8 ....4C **72**
......................................(off Kensington High St.)
Monarch M. E17.....................1D **39**
Monarch M. SW16 ....5C **118**
Monarch Point SW6 ....5E **87**
Monarch Sq. SW11 ....2A **102**
Mona Rd. SE15......................5E **93**
Mona St. E16..........................4B **68**
Monck Ho. SE1 ......4A **26** (3E **77**)
......................................(off Cole St.)
Moncks Row SW18..............4B **100**
Monck St. SW1 ....5C **22** (4F **75**)
Monckton Ct. W14.................4B **72**
......................................(off Strangways Ter.)
Monclar Rd. SE5...................2F **105**
Moncorvo Cl. SW7................3A **74**
Moncrieff Pl. SE15...............5C **92**
Moncrieff St. SE15................5C **92**
Monday All. N16....................4B **36**
......................................(off High St.)
Mondragon Ho. SW8............4A **90**
......................................(off Guildford Rd.)
Monega Rd. E12....................3F **55**
Monega Rd. E7.......................3E **55**
Monet Ct. SE16 ....1D **93**
......................................(off Stubbs Dr.)
Moneyer Ho. N1 ....1B **10** (2F **63**)
......................................(off Provost St.)
Mongers Almshouses E9.....4F **51**
......................................(off Church Cres.)
Monica Shaw Ct.
NW1 ....1C **6** (1F **61**)
......................................(off Purchese St.)

Monier Rd. E3 .... 4C **52**
Monk Ct. W12 .... 2C **70**
Monk Dr. E16 .... 1C **82**
Monkton Ho. E5 .... 2D **51**
Monkton Ho. SE16 ....3F **79**
.....................(off Wolfe Cres.)
Monkton St. SE11 .... 5C **76**
Monkwell Sq. EC2.... 1A **18** (4E **63**)
Monmouth Pl. W2 .... 5D **59**
...............(off Monmouth St.)
Monmouth Rd. W2 .... 5C **58**
Monmouth St. WC2...3D **15** (5A **62**)
Monnery Rd. N19...............5E **33**
Monnow Rd. SE1............... 1C **92**
Monolulu St. SE17 ....1F **91**
..........................(off East St.)
Monro Ct. E16.................... 2D **83**
Monroe Ho. NW8................ 2A **60**
........................(off Lorne Cl.)
Monro Way E5.................... 1C **50**
Monsell Ct. N4 .... 5D **35**
Monsell Rd. N4.................. 5C **34**
Monsey Pl. E1 .... 3A **66**
Monson Rd. NW10 .... 1C **56**
Monson Rd. SE14.............. 3F **93**
Montacute Rd. SE6 .... 5B **108**
Montagu Ct. W1 ..... 1A **12** (4B **60**)
........................(off Montagu Pl.)
Montague Av. SE4 .... 2B **108**
Montague Cl. SE1 .. 1B **26** (2F **77**)
Montague Ct. N7................ 4C **48**
.................(off St Clements St.)
Montague Ho. E16 .... 2D **83**
......................(off Wesley Av.)
Montague Ho. N1................ 5A **50**
.......................(off Halcomb St.)
Montague M. E3.................. 2B **66**
.......................(off Tredegar Ter.)
Montague Pl. WC1 .... 5C **6** (4F **61**)
Montague Rd. E11 .... 4B **40**
Montague Rd. E8 .... 2C **50**
Montague Sq. SE15........... 3E **93**
Montague St. EC1 .... 1F **17** (4E **63**)
Montague St. WC1 ...5D **7** (4A **62**)
Montagu Mans. W1 ...5A **4** (4B **60**)
Montagu M. Nth.
W1.................... 1A **12** (4B **60**)
Montagu M. Sth.
W1................................2A **12** (5B **60**)
Montagu M. W. W1....2A **12** (5B **60**)
Montagu Pl. W1 ...... 1A **12** (4B **60**)
Montagu Rd. NW4.............. 1C **28**
Montagu Row W1 .... 1A **12** (4B **60**)
Montagu Sq. W1 ..... 1A **12** (4B **60**)
Montagu St. W1 ...... 2A **12** (5B **60**)
Montaigne Cl. SW1 ....5F **75**
Montana Bldg. SE13 .... 4D **95**
...................(off Deal's Gateway)
Montana Gdns. SE26 .... 5B **122**
Montana Rd. SW17 .... 3C **116**
Montanaro Ct. N1...............5E **49**
...................(off Coleman Flds.)
Montcalm Ho. E14 .... 5B **80**
Montcalm Rd. SE7 ....3F **97**
Montclare St. E2 .... 2F **11** (3B **64**)
Monteagle Ct. N1 .... 1A **64**
Monteagle Way E5 .... 5C **36**
Monteagle Way SE15........ 1D **107**
Montefiore Ct. N16 .... 3R **36**
Montefiore St. SW8 .... 5D **89**
Montego Cl. SE24................ 2C **104**
Montem Rd. SE23 .... 5B **108**
Montem St. N4 .... 3B **34**
Montenotte Rd. N8.............1E **33**
Monterey Studios W10 ..... 1A **58**

Montevetro SW11 ....4F **87**
Montfichet Rd. E20.............4E **53**
Montford Pl. E15................1E **67**
Montford Pl. SE11 .... 1C **90**
Montfort Ho. E14................4E **81**
.................(off Galbraith St.)
Montfort Ho. E2.................. 2E **65**
..................(off Victoria Pk. Sq.)
Montfort Pl. SW19.............. 1F **113**
Montgomerie M. SE23 ....5E **107**
Montgomery Ho. W2...........4F **59**
........................(off Harrow Rd.)
Montgomery Lodge E1 ......3E **65**
.....................(off Cleveland Gro.)
Montgomery Sq. E14 .... 2D **81**
Montgomery St. E14 .... 2D **81**
Montholme Rd. SW11 .... 4B **102**
Monthope Rd. E1 .... 4C **64**
Montolieu Gdns. SW15 ..... 3D **99**
Montpelier Gdns. E6 .... 2F **69**
Montpelier Gro. NW5 .... 2E **47**
Montpelier M. SW7 .... 4A **74**
Montpelier Pl. E1 .... 5E **65**
Montpelier Pl. SW7 .... 4A **74**
Montpelier Ri. NW11 .... 2A **30**
..........................(not continuous)
Montpelier Rd. SE15......... 4D **93**
Montpelier Row SE3 .... 5B **96**
Montpelier Sq. SW7 .... 3A **74**
Montpelier St. SW7 .... 4A **74**
Montpelier Ter. SW7 .... 3A **74**
Montpelier Va. SE3 .... 5B **96**
Montpelier Wlk. SW7 .... 4A **74**
Montpelier Way NW11 ...... 2A **30**
Montreal Ho. SE16 ....3F **79**
........................(off Maple M.)
Montreal Pl. WC2.... 4F **15** (1B **76**)
Montrell Rd. SW2 .... 1A **118**
Montrose Av. NW6 .... 1A **58**
Montrose Ct. SE6 .... 2B **124**
Montrose Ct. SW7 .... 3F **73**
Montrose Ho. E14 .... 4C **80**
Montrose Ho.
SW1.......................4C **20** (3C **74**)
Montrose Pl. SW1 ...4C **20** (3C **74**)
Montrose Way SE23...........1F **121**
Montserrat Cl. SE19 ....5F **119**
Montserrat Rd. SW15 .... 2A **100**
Monument, The......4C **18** (1F **77**)
Monument Gdns. SE13 ......3E **109**
Monument Station (Underground)
.........................3C **18** (1F **77**)
Monument St. EC3... 4C **18** (1F **77**)
Monza St. E1 ....1E **79**
Moodkee St. SE16..............4E **79**
Moody Rd. SE15................. 4B **92**
Moody St. E1 ....2F **65**
Moon Ct. SE12................... 2C **110**
Moonlight Dr. SE23............ 5D **107**
Moonraker Point
SE1....................... 3E **25** (3E **77**)
Moon St. N1 .... 5D **49**
Moorcroft Rd. SW16 .... 3A **118**
Moore Ct. N1 .... 5D **49**
.........................(off Gaskin St.)
Moorehead Way SF3.......... 1C **110**
Moore Ho. E1.....................1E **79**
..........................(off Cable St.)
Moore Ho. E14................... 3C **80**
Moore Ho. E2..................... 2E **65**
......................(off Roman Rd.)
Moore Ho. SE10 ....1B **96**
.....................(off Armitage Rd.)

Moore Ho. SW1 .... 1D **89**
............................(off Gatliff Rd.)
Moore Pk. Rd. SW6............3C **86**
Moore Rd. SE19 ....5E **119**
Moore Wlk. E7................... 1C **54**
Moorey Cl. E15...................5B **54**
Moorfields EC2...... 1B **18** (4F **63**)
MOORFIELDS EYE HOSPITAL
...........................1D **10** (2F **63**)
Moorfields Highwalk
EC2...................... 1B **18** (4F **63**)
......................(off New Union St.)
Moorgate EC2 .... 2B **18** (5F **63**)
Moorgate Pl. EC2 ... 2B **18** (5F **63**)
Moorgate Station (Rail &
Underground) 1B **18** (4F **63**)
Moorgreen Ho. EC1...1D **9** (2D **63**)
......................(off Wynyatt St.)
Moorhen Dr. NW9 .... 1B **28**
Moorhen Ho. E3 .... 5B **52**
......................(off Old Ford Rd.)
Moorhouse Rd. W2 .... 5C **58**
Moorings, The E16..............4E **69**
....................(off Prince Regent La.)
Moorland Rd. SW9 .... 2D **105**
Moor La. EC2....... 1B **18** (4F **63**)
..........................(not continuous)
Moor Pl. EC2........ 1B **18** (4F **63**)
Moorside Rd.
BR1: Broml 3A **124**
Moor St. W1 .... 3C **14** (5F **61**)
Moran Ho. E1 .... 2D **79**
.....................(off Wapping La.)
Morant St. E14................... 1C **80**
Mora Rd. NW2 ....1E **43**
Mora St. EC1 .... 2A **10** (2E **63**)
Morat St. SW9.................... 4B **90**
Moravian Cl. SW10 ....2F **87**
Moravian Pl. SW10.............2F **87**
Moravian St. E2 ....1E **65**
Moray Ho. E1 .... 3A **66**
..........................(off Harford St.)
Moray M. N7 .... 4B **34**
Moray Rd. N4 .... 4B **34**
Mordaunt Ho. NW10........... 5A **42**
..........................(off Stracey Rd.)
Mordaunt St. SW9.............. 1B **104**
Morden Hill SE13 ....5E **95**
Morden La. SE13 ....5E **95**
Morden Rd. SE3 .... 5C **96**
Morden Rd. M. SE3 .... 5C **96**
Morden St. SE13 .... 4D **95**
Morden Wharf SE10........... 4A **82**
...................(off Morden Wharf Rd.)
Morden Wharf Rd. SE10 .... 4A **82**
Mordern Ho. NW1...............3A **60**
..................(off Harewood Av.)
Morea M. N5 ....2E **49**
Morecambe Cl. E1 ....4F **65**
Morecambe St. SE17 ....5E **77**
More Cl. E16.......................5B **68**
More Cl. W14......................5F **71**
More Copper Ho.
SE1.......................2D **27** (2A **78**)
....................(off Magdalen St.)
Moreland Cotts. E3 .... 1C **66**
.........................(off Fairfield Rd.)
Moreland Ct. NW2..............5C **30**
Moreland St. EC1 ..... 1E **9** (2D **63**)
Morella Rd. SW12 .... 5B **102**
More London Pl.
SE1.......................2D **27** (2A **78**)
..........................(not continuous)

More London Riverside
SE1.................2E **27** (2A **78**)
..........................(not continuous)
Moremead Rd. SE6............4B **122**
Morena St. SE6..................5D **109**
Moreno Ho. E2.....................1D **65**
..........................(off Esker Pl.)
Moresby Rd. E5....................3D **37**
Moresby Wlk. SW8..............5E **89**
More's Gdn. SW3..................2F **87**
..........................(off Cheyne Wlk.)
Moreton Cl. E5.....................4D **37**
Moreton Cl. N15..................1F **35**
Moreton Cl. SW1.................1E **89**
..........................(off Moreton Ter.)
Moreton Ho. SE16..............4D **79**
Moreton Pl. SW1.................1E **89**
Moreton Rd. N15.................1F **35**
Moreton St. SW1.................1E **89**
Moreton Ter. SW1..............1E **89**
Moreton Ter. M. Nth. SW1..1E **89**
Moreton Ter. M. Sth. SW1..1E **89**
Morgan Ho. SW1..................5E **75**
..........................(off Vauxhall Bri. Rd.)
Morgan Ho. SW8..................4E **89**
..........................(off Wadhurst Rd.)
Morgan Mans. N7.................2C **48**
..........................(off Morgan Rd.)
Morgan Rd. N7......................2C **48**
Morgan Rd. W10..................4B **58**
Morgans La. SE1.....2D **27** (2A **78**)
..........................(off Tooley St.)
Morgan St. E16.....................4B **68**
Morgan St. E3......................2A **66**
..........................(not continuous)
Moriarty Cl. N7.....................1A **48**
Morie St. SW18...................3D **101**
Morieux Rd. E10...................3B **38**
Moring Rd. SW17...............4C **116**
Morkyns Wlk. SE21...........3A **120**
Morland Cl. NW11...............3D **31**
Morland Ct. W12..................3D **71**
..........................(off Coningham Rd.)
Morland Est. E8....................4C **50**
Morland Ho. NW1.....1A **6** (1E **61**)
..........................(off Werrington St.)
Morland Ho. NW6.................5C **44**
Morland Ho. SW1.................5A **76**
..........................(off Marsham St.)
Morland Ho. W11.................4B **58**
..........................(off Lancaster Rd.)
Morland M. N1.....................4C **48**
Morland Rd. E17..................1F **37**
Morley Ho. SE15..................3B **92**
..........................(off Commercial Way)
Morley Rd. E10.....................3E **39**
Morley Rd. E15.....................1B **68**
Morley Rd. SE13..................2E **109**
Morley St. SE1.......5C **24** (4C **76**)
Morna Rd. SE5......................5E **91**
Morning La. E9......................3E **51**
Mornington Av. W14.............5B **72**
Mornington Av. Mans. W14..5B **72**
..........................(off Mornington Av.)
Mornington Ct. NW1............1E **61**
..........................(off Mornington Cres.)
Mornington Cres. NW1........1E **61**
Mornington Crescent Station
(Underground).....................1E **61**
Mornington Gro. E3..............2C **66**
Mornington M. SE5...............4E **91**
Mornington Pl. NW1.............1E **61**
Mornington Pl. SE8..............3B **94**
..........................(off Mornington Rd.)
Mornington Rd. E11.............2B **40**

Mornington Rd. SE8.............3B **94**
Mornington St. NW1.............1D **61**
Mornington Ter. NW1...........5D **47**
Moro Apts. E14......................5C **66**
..........................(off New Festival Av.)
Morocco St. SE1.....4D **27** (3A **78**)
Morocco Wharf E1...............2D **79**
..........................(off Wapping High St.)
Morpeth Gro. E9..................5F **51**
Morpeth Mans. SW1.............5E **75**
..........................(off Morpeth Ter.)
Morpeth Rd. E9....................5F **51**
Morpeth St. E2....................2E **65**
Morpeth Ter. SW1................4E **75**
Morrel Cl. E2.........................1C **64**
..........................(off Goldsmiths Row)
Morrells Yd. SE11.................1C **90**
..........................(off Cleaver St.)
Morris Blitz Ct. N16.............1B **50**
Morris Gdns. SW18..............5C **100**
Morris Ho. E2.......................2E **65**
..........................(off Roman Rd.)
Morris Ho. NW8...................3A **60**
..........................(off Salisbury St.)
Morris Ho. W3......................3B **70**
Morrish Rd. SW2.................5A **104**
Morris M. SW19..................5C **114**
Morrison Bldgs. Nth. E1......5C **64**
..........................(off Commercial Rd.)
Morrison Ct. SW1...5C **22** (4F **75**)
..........................(off Gt. Smith St.)
Morrison Ho. SW2...............1C **118**
..........................(off Tulse Hill)
Morrison Rd. SW9...............5C **90**
Morrison St. SW11...............1C **102**
Morris Pl. N4........................4C **34**
Morris Rd. E14......................4D **67**
Morris Rd. E15......................1A **54**
Morris Rd. SE16...................3D **79**
..........................(off Cherry Gdn. St.)
Morris St. E1.........................5D **65**
Morse Cl. E13.......................2C **68**
Morshead Mans. W9.............2C **58**
..........................(off Morshead Rd.)
Morshead Rd. W9.................2C **58**
Mortain Ho. SE16.................5D **79**
..........................(off Roseberry St.)
Morten Cl. SW4...................4F **103**
Mortham St. E15..................5A **54**
Mortimer Cl. NW2................4B **30**
Mortimer Ct. NW8................1E **59**
..........................(off Abbey Rd.)
Mortimer Cres. NW6.............5D **45**
Mortimer Est. NW6...............5D **45**
..........................(off Mortimer Pl.)
Mortimer Ho. W11................2F **71**
Mortimer Ho. W14................5A **72**
..........................(off North End Rd.)
Mortimer Mkt. WC1....4A **6** (3E **61**)
Mortimer Pl. NW6.................5D **45**
Mortimer Rd. N1...................4A **50**
..........................(not continuous)
Mortimer Rd. NW10.............2F **57**
Mortimer Sq. W11................1F **71**
Mortimer St. W1....1F **13** (5E **61**)
Mortimer Ter. NW5..............1D **47**
MORTLAKE...........................1A **98**
Mortlake Rd. E16.................5D **69**
Mortlock Cl. SE15................4D **93**
Mortlock Ct. E7....................1F **55**
Morton Cl. E1.......................5E **65**
Morton Ho. SE17.................2D **91**
Morton M. SW5....................5D **73**
Morton Pl. SE1.......5B **24** (4C **76**)

Morton Rd. E15....................4B **54**
Morton Rd. N1......................4E **49**
Morval Rd. SW2..................3C **104**
Morven Rd. SW17...............3B **116**
Morville Ho. SW18..............4F **101**
..........................(off Fitzhugh Gro.)
Morville St. E3.....................1C **66**
Morwell St. WC1....1B **14** (4F **61**)
Moscow Mans. SW5.............5C **72**
..........................(off Cromwell Rd.)
Moscow Pl. W2....................1D **73**
Moscow Rd. W2...................1C **72**
Mosedale NW1.......2E **5** (2E **61**)
..........................(off Cumberland Mkt.)
Moseley Row SE10..............5B **82**
Mosque Ter. E1....................4D **64**
..........................(off Whitechapel Rd.)
Mosque Twr. E1....................4C **64**
..........................(off Fieldgate St.)
Mosque Twr. E3....................1A **66**
..........................(off Ford St.)
Mossbury Rd. SW11............1A **102**
Moss Cl. E1..........................4C **64**
Mossford St. E3....................3B **66**
Mossington Gdns. SE16......5E **79**
Mossop St. SW3..................5A **74**
Mostyn Gdns. NW10.............2F **57**
Mostyn Gro. E3.....................1C **66**
Mostyn Rd. SW9...................4C **90**
Motcomb St. SW1....5B **20** (4C **74**)
Mothers Sq. E5.....................1D **51**
Motley Av. EC2.......3D **11** (3A **64**)
..........................(off Phipp St.)
Mottingham Gdns. SE9.......1F **125**
Mottingham La. SE12.........1E **125**
Mottingham La. SE9...........1E **125**
Mottingham Rd. SE9...........2F **125**
Moulding La. SE14...............2A **94**
Moules Ct. SE5.....................3E **91**
Moulins Rd. E9.....................4E **51**
Moulsford Ho. N7.................2F **47**
Moulsford Ho. W2................4C **58**
..........................(off Westbourne Pk. Rd.)
Moundfield Rd. N16.............1C **36**
Mounsey Ho. W10...............2A **58**
..........................(off Third Av.)
Mount, The NW3..................4D **37**
..........................(not continuous)
Mount, The NW3...................5E **31**
Mount, The W8....................2C **72**
..........................(off Bedford Gdns.)
Mountacre Cl. SE26............4B **120**
Mount Adon Pk. SE22..........5C **106**
Mountague Pl. E14...............1E **81**
Mountain Ho. SE11...............5B **76**
Mount Angelus Rd. SW15...5B **98**
Mount Ash Rd. SE26............3D **121**
Mountbatten Cl. SE19.........5A **120**
Mountbatten Cl. SE16..........2E **79**
..........................(off Rotherhithe St.)
Mountbatten Ho. N6.............2C **32**
..........................(off Hillcrest)
Mountbatten M. SW18.........5E **101**
Mount Carmel Chambers
W8.......................................3C **72**
..........................(off Dukes La.)
Mount Ct. SW15...................1A **100**
Mounteari Gdns. SW16.......3B **118**
Mount Ephraim La. SW16...3F **117**
Mount Ephraim Rd. SW16...3F **117**
Mountfield Cl. SE6...............5F **109**
Mountfield Ter. SE6.............5F **109**
Mountford Mans. SW11........4C **88**
..........................(off Battersea Pk. Rd.)
Mountfort Cres. N1..............4C **48**

Mountfort Ho. N1 .... 4C 48
.... (off Barnsbury Sq.)
Mountfort Ter. N1 .... 4C 48
Mount Gdns. SE26 .... 3D 121
Mountgrove Rd. N5 .... 5D 35
Mountjoy Cl. EC2 ... 1A 18 (4E 63)
.... (off Monkwell Sq.)
Mountjoy Ho. EC2 ... 1F 17 (4E 63)
.... (off Monkwell Sq.)
Mount Lodge N6 .... 1E 33
Mount Mills EC1 ...... 2E 9 (2D 63)
Mount Nod Rd. SW16 .... 3B 118
Mount Pleasant SE27 .... 4E 119
Mount Pleasant
WC1 .... 4B 8 (3C 62)
Mount Pleasant Cres. N4 ..... 3B 34
Mount Pleasant Hill E5 .... 4D 37
Mount Pleasant La. E5 .... 3D 37
Mount Pleasant M. N4 .... 3B 34
.... (off Mt. Pleasant Cres.)
Mount Pleasant Rd. NW10 ....4E 43
Mount Pleasant Rd. SE13...4D 109
Mount Pleasant Vs. N4 .... 2B 34
Mount Rd. NW2 .... 5D 29
Mount Rd. NW4 .... 1C 28
Mount Rd. SW19 .... 2C 114
Mount Row W1 ...... 5D 13 (1D 75)
Mountsfield Ct. SE13 .... 4F 109
Mountsfield Ho. SE10 .... 4E 95
.... (off Primrose Way)
Mounts Pond Rd. SE3 .... 5F 95
.... (not continuous)
Mount Sq., The NW3 .... 5E 31
Mount St. W1 ...... 5B 12 (1C 74)
Mount St. M. W1 ... 5D 13 (1D 75)
Mount Ter. E1 .... 4D 65
Mount Vernon NW3 .... 1E 45
Mountview Cl. NW11 .... 3D 31
Mount Vw. Rd. N4 .... 2A 34
Mount Vs. SE27 .... 3D 119
Mowatt Cl. N19 .... 3F 33
Mowbray Rd. NW6 .... 4A 44
Mowlem St. E2 .... 1D 65
Mowll St. SW9 .... 3C 90
Moxon Cl. E13 .... 1B 68
Moxon St. W1 ...... 1B 12 (4C 60)
Moye Cl. E2 .... 1C 64
Moyers Rd. E10 .... 2E 39
Moylan Rd. W6 .... 2A 86
Moyle Ho. SW1 .... 1E 89
.... (off Churchill Gdns.)
Moyser Rd. SW16 .... 5D 117
Mozart St. W10 .... 2B 58
Mozart Ter. SW1 .... 5C 74
MTV Europe 4D 47
Mudchute Pk. & Farm 5E 81
Mudchute Station (DLR) 5D 81
Mudlarks Blvd. SE10 .... 4B 82
Mudlarks Way SE10 .... 4C 82
Muir Dr. SW18 .... 4A 102
Muirfield W3 .... 5A 56
Muirfield Cl. SE16 .... 1D 93
Muirfield Cres. E14 .... 4D 81
Muirkirk Rd. SE6 .... 1E 123
Muir Rd. E5 .... 5C 36
Mulberry Apts. N4 .... 3E 35
.... (off Coster Av.)
Mulberry Cl. NW3 .... 1F 45
Mulberry Cl. SE22 .... 3C 106
Mulberry Cl. SE7 .... 2F 97
Mulberry Cl. SW16 .... 4E 117
Mulberry Cl. SW3 .... 2F 87
.... (off Beaufort St.)
Mulberry Cl. E11 .... 1F 53
.... (off Langthorne Rd.)

Mulberry Ct. EC1 ...... 2E 9 (2D 63)
.... (off Tompion St.)
Mulberry Ct. SW3 .... 2F 87
.... (not continuous)
Mulberry Ct. W9 .... 2B 58
Mulberry Ho. E2 .... 2E 65
.... (off Victoria Pk. Sq.)
Mulberry Ho. SE10 .... 4E 95
.... (off Parkside Av.)
Mulberry Ho. SE8 .... 2B 94
Mulberry Housing Co-operative
SE1 .... 1C 24 (2C 76)
.... (off Upper Rd.)
Mulberry M. SE14 .... 4B 94
Mulberry Pl. E14 .... 1E 81
.... (off Clove Cres.)
Mulberry Pl. SE9 .... 2F 111
Mulberry Pl. W6 .... 1C 84
Mulberry Rd. E8 .... 4B 50
Mulberry St. E1 .... 5C 64
Mulberry Wlk. SW3 .... 2F 87
Mulgrave Rd. NW10 .... 1B 42
Mulgrave Rd. SW6 .... 2B 86
Mulkern Rd. N19 .... 3F 33
.... (not continuous)
Mullen Twr. WC1 ...... 4B 8 (3C 62)
.... (off Mt. Pleasant)
Mullet Gdns. E2 .... 2C 64
Mulletsfield WC1 ...... 2E 7 (2A 62)
.... (off Cromer St.)
Mull Ho. E3 .... 1B 66
.... (off Stafford Rd.)
Mulligans Apts. NW6 .... 4C 44
.... (off Kilburn High Rd.)
Mullins Pl. SW4 .... 5A 104
Mull Wlk. N1 .... 3E 49
.... (off Clephane Rd.)
Mulready Ho. SW1 .... 5A 76
.... (off Marsham St.)
Mulready St. NW8 .... 3A 60
Multi Way W3 .... 3A 70
Multon Ho. E9 .... 4E 51
Multon Rd. SW18 .... 5F 101
Mulvaney Way SE1.....4C 26 (3F 77)
.... (not continuous)
Mumford Mills SE10 .... 4D 95
.... (off Greenwich High Rd.)
Mumford Rd. SE24 .... 3D 105
Muncaster Rd. SW11 .... 3B 102
Muncies M. SE6 .... 2E 123
Mundania Ct. SE22 .... 4D 107
Mundania Rd. SE22 .... 4D 107
Munday Ho. SE1.....5B 26 (4F 77)
.... (off Burbage Cl.)
Munday Rd. E16 .... 1C 82
Munden Ho. E3 .... 2D 67
.... (off Bromley High St.)
Munden St. W14 .... 5A 72
Mundford Rd. E5 .... 4E 37
Mund St. W14 .... 1B 86
Mundy Ho. W10 .... 2A 58
.... (off Dart St.)
Mundy St. N1 ...... 1D 11 (2A 64)
Munkenbeck Bldg. W2 .... 4F 59
.... (off Hermitage St.)
Munnings Ho. E16 .... 2D 83
.... (off Portsmouth M.)
Munro Ho. SE1 ...... 4B 24 (3C 76)
Munro M. W10 .... 4A 58
.... (not continuous)
Munro Ter. SW10 .... 3F 87
Munster Cres. SW6 .... 5B 86
Munster M. SW6 .... 3A 86
Munster Rd. SW6 .... 3A 86

Munster Sq. NW1 ...... 2E 5 (2D 61)
Munster Ter. E13 .... 2E 69
Munton Rd. SE17 .... 5E 77
Muratori Ho. WC1.....2B 8 (2C 62)
.... (off Margery St.)
Murchison Ho. W10 .... 4A 58
.... (off Ladbroke Gro.)
Murchison Rd. E10 .... 4E 39
Murdoch Ho. SE16 .... 4E 79
.... (off Moodkee St.)
Murdock Cl. E16 .... 5B 68
Murdock St. SE15 .... 2D 93
Murfett Cl. SW19 .... 2A 114
Muriel St. N1 .... 1B 62
.... (not continuous)
Murillo Rd. SE13 .... 2F 109
Murphy Ho. SE1 ...... 5E 25 (4D 77)
.... (off Borough Rd.)
Murphy St. SE1 ...... 4B 24 (3C 76)
Murrain Rd. N4 .... 4E 35
Murray Cl. E3 .... 4B 66
.... (off Geoff Cade Way)
Murray Gro. N1 ...... 1A 10 (1E 63)
Murray M. NW1 .... 4F 47
Murray Rd. SW19 .... 5F 113
Murray Sq. E16 .... 5C 68
Murray St. NW1 .... 4F 47
Murray Ter. NW3 .... 1E 45
Mursell Est. SW8 .... 4B 90
Musard Rd. W14 .... 2A 86
Musard Rd. W6 .... 2A 86
Musbury St. E1 .... 5E 65
Muscal W6 .... 2A 86
.... (off Field Rd.)
Muscatel Pl. SE5 .... 4A 92
Muschamp Rd. SE15 .... 1B 106
Muscovy Cl. E2 .... 5C 50
.... (off Whiston Rd.)
Muscovy St. EC3 ...... 4E 19 (1A 78)
Museum Chambers
WC1 .... 1D 15 (4A 62)
.... (off Bury Pl.)
Museum Ho. E2 .... 2E 65
.... (off Burnham St.)
Museum La. SW7 .... 4F 73
Museum Mans. WC1...1D 15 (4A 62)
.... (off Gt. Russell St.)
Museum of Brands, Packaging &
Advertising 5A 58
.... (off Lancaster Rd.)
Museum of Comedy ....
1D 15 (4A 62)
.... (off Bloomsbury Way)
Museum of London ...1F 17 (4E 63)
Museum of London Docklands
.... 1C 80
Museum of The Order of St John
.... 4D 9 (3D 63)
Museum of Wimbledon 5A 114
Museum Pas. E2 .... 2E 65
Museum St. WC1 ... 1D 15 (4A 62)
Musgrave Cl. SW11 .... 4A 88
Musgrave Cres. SW6 .... 3C 86
Musgrove Rd. SE14 .... 4F 93
Musjid Rd. SW11 .... 5F 87
Mustang Ho. N1 .... 3D 49
.... (off Canonbury Rd.)
Muston Rd. E5 .... 4D 37
Muston Pl. SW6 .... 5B 86
Muswell Hill Rd. N10 .... 1D 33
Muswell Hill Rd. N6 .... 1C 32
Mutrix Rd. NW6 .... 5C 44
Mutton Pl. NW1 .... 3C 46

Myatt Rd. SW9 ....4D 91
Myatts Fld. Sth. SW9 ....5C 90
Mycenae Rd. SE3 ....3C 96
Myddelton Pas. EC1 ...1C 8 (2C 62)
Myddelton Sq. EC1 .....1C 8 (2C 62)
Myddelton St. EC1 ......2C 8 (2C 62)
Myddleton Av. N4 ....4E 35
Myddleton Ho. N1 ...1B 8 (1C 62)
..............................(off Pentonville Rd.)
Myers Ho. SE5.......................3E 91
.................................(off Bethwin Rd.)
Myers La. SE14 ....2F 93
Myers Wlk. E14 ....2E 81
Myles Ct. SE16 ....4E 79
...................................(off Neptune St.)
Mylis Cl. SE26 ....4D 121
Mylius St. SE14 ....3E 93
Mylne Cl. W6 ....1C 84
Mylne St. EC1 ....1B 8 (2C 62)
Myrdle Ct. E1 ....5C 64
......................................(off Myrdle St.)
Myrdle St. E1 ....4C 64
Myron Pl. SE13 ....1E 109
Myrtleberry Cl. E8 ....3B 50
..............................(off Beechwood Rd.)
Myrtle Rd. E17 ....1A 38
Myrtle Wlk. N1 ....1D 11 (1A 64)
Mysore Rd. SW11 ....1B 102
Myton Rd. SE21 ....3F 119
Mytton Ho. SW8 ....3B 90
.............................(off St Stephens Ter.)

N

Nadine St. SE7 ....1E 97
Nagasaki Wlk. SE7 ....4D 83
NAG'S HEAD 5A 34
Nags Head Ct.
   EC1 ....4A 10 (3E 63)
....(off Golden La.)
Nainby Ho. SE11 ....5C 76
......................................(off Hotspur St.)
Nairne Gro. SE24..................3E 105
Nairn St. E14 ....4E 66
Naldera Gdns. SE3 ....2C 96
Nalton Ho. NW6....................4E 45
...................................(off Belsize Rd.)
Namba Roy Cl. SW16 ....4B 118
Nankin St. E14 ....5C 66
Nansen Rd. SW11 ....1C 102
Nant Ct. NW2.......................4B 30
Nantes Cl. SW18 ....2E 101
Nantes Pas. E1 ....1F 11 (4B 64)
Nant Rd. NW2 ....4B 30
Nant St. E2 ....2D 65
Naomi St. SE8 ....5A 80
Naoroji St. WC1 ......2B 8 (2C 62)
Napa Cl. E20.........................2E 53
Napier Av. E14 ....1C 94
Napier Av. SW6 ....1B 100
Napier Cl. SE8 ....3B 94
Napier Cl. W14 ....4A 72
Napier Ct. N1 ....1F 63
.....................................(off Cropley St.)
Napier Ct. SE12....................3D 125
Napier Ct. SW6 ....1B 100
.................................(off Ranelagh Gdns.)
Napier Gro. N1 ....1E 63
Napier Ho. E3 ....2C 66
..............................(off Campbell Rd.)
Napier Ho. SE17 ....2D 91
...................................(off Cooks Rd.)
Napier Ho. W3 ....2A 70
Napier Pl. W14 ....4B 72
Napier Rd. E11 ....1A 54

Napier Rd. E15 ....1A 68
....(not continuous)
Napier Rd. NW10..................2D 57
Napier Rd. W14 ....4B 72
Napier St. SE8 ....3B 94
....(off Napier Cl.)
Napier Ter. N1 ....4D 49
Napoleon Rd. E5 ....5D 37
Nara SE13 ....5D 95
Narbonne Av. SW4 ....3E 103
Narborough St. SW6 ....5D 87
Narcissus Rd. NW6 ....2C 44
Narford Rd. E5 ....5C 36
Narrow St. E14 ....1A 80
Narvic Ho. SE5 ....5E 91
Narwhal Inuit Art Gallery 1A 84
Nascot St. W12 ....5E 57
Naseby Cl. NW6 ....4E 45
Naseby Rd. SE19..................5F 119
Nashe Ho. SE1 ....5B 26 (4F 77)
....(off Burbage Cl.)
Nash Ho. E14 ....3C 80
...................................(off Alpha Gro.)
Nash Ho. NW1 ....1D 61
..............................(off Park Village E.)
Nash Ho. SW1 ....1D 89
....(off Lupus St.)
Nash Pl. E14 ....2D 81
Nash Rd. SE4 ....2A 108
Nash St. NW1 ....1E 5 (2D 61)
Nasmyth St. W6 ....4D 71
Nassau Rd. SW13 ....4B 84
Nassau St. W1 ....1F 13 (4E 61)
Nassington Rd. NW3 ....1B 46
Natal Rd. SW16 ....5F 117
Natasha M. SE1 ....2E 107
Nathan Ho. SE11 ....5C 76
...............................(off Reedworth St.)
Nathaniel Cl. E1 ....1F 19 (4B 64)
Nathaniel Ct. E17 ....2A 38
National Army Mus...............2B 88
National Gallery 5C 14 (1F 75)
NATIONAL HOSPITAL FOR
   NEUROLOGY & NEUROSURGERY
   ....4E 7 (3A 62)
National Maritime Mus.........2F 95
National Portrait Gallery
   ....5C 14 (1F 75)
.................................(off St Martin's Pl.)
National Tennis Cen. 3A 98
National Ter. SE16 ....3E 79
.............................(off Bermondsey Wall E.)
National Theatre 1A 24 (2C 76)
Natural History Mus. London
   ....4F 73
Nature Gdn. 1E 93
...............................(off Bramcote Gro.)
Nautical Dr. E16....................3D 83
Nautical Ho. SW18................2E 101
....................................(off Juniper Dr.)
Nauticus Wlk. E14 ....5D 81
Nautilus Bldg., The
   EC1 ....1C 8 (2C 62)
...............................(off Myddelton Pas.)
Naval Ho. E14 ....1F 81
....................................(off Quixley St.)
Naval Row E14 ....1E 81
Navarino Gro. E8 ....3C 50
Navarino Mans. E8 ....3C 50
Navarino Rd. E8 ....3C 50
Navarre Rd. SW9..................4D 91
Navarre St. E2 ....3F 11 (3B 64)
Navenby Wlk. E3 ....3C 66
Navigation Ho. SE16 ....5A 80
...............................(off Grand Canal Av.)

Navigation Rd. E3 ....3E 67
Navigator Sq. N19................4E 33
Navy St. SW4........................1F 103
Naxos Bldg. E14....................3B 80
Nayim Pl. E8 ....2D 51
Nayland Ho. SE6 ....4E 123
Naylor Bldg. E. E1 ....5C 64
...................................(off Assam St.)
Naylor Bldg. W. E1 ....5C 64
....(off Adler St.)
Naylor Ho. SE17 ....5F 77
....(off Flint St.)
Naylor Ho. W10 ....2A 58
....(off Dart St.)
Naylor Rd. SE15 ....3D 93
Nazareth Gdns. SE15............5D 93
Nazrul St. E2 ....1E 11 (2B 64)
NCR Bus. Cen. NW10 ....2A 42
Neagle Ho. NW2 ....5E 29
....(off Stoll Cl.)
Nealden St. SW9 ....1B 104
Neal St. SE10 ....4B 82
Neal St. WC2 ....3D 15 (5A 62)
Neal's Yd. WC2 ......3D 15 (5A 62)
Neap Ct. E3 ....3E 67
...............................(off Navigation Rd.)
NEASDEN 5A 28
Neasden Cl. NW10 ....2A 42
NEASDEN JUNC. 1A 42
Neasden La. NW10 ....1A 42
Neasden Station (Underground)
   ....2A 42
Neate Ho. SW1 ....1E 89
....(off Lupus St.)
Neate St. SE5 ....2A 92
Neathouse Pl. SW1 ....5E 75
Neatscourt Rd. E6..................4F 69
Nebraska Bldg. SE13.............4D 95
...............................(off Deal's Gateway)
Nebraska St. SE1 ....4B 26 (3F 77)
Nebula Ct. E13 ....1C 68
....................................(off Umbriel Pl.)
Neckinger SE16 ....5F 27 (4B 78)
Neckinger Est. SE16 5F 27 (4B 78)
Neckinger St. SE1 ....3B 78
Nectarine Way SE13 ....5D 95
Needham Ho. SE11 ....1C 90
..................................(off Marylee Way)
Needham Rd. W11 ....5C 58
Needham Ter. NW2................5F 29
Needleman St. SE16 ....3F 79
Needwood Ho. N4 ....3E 35
Neeld Cres. NW4 ....1D 29
Neeld Pl. W9.........................4B 58
Neil Wates Cres. SW2 ....1C 118
Nelgarde Rd. SE6 ....5C 108
Nella Rd. W6 ....2F 85
Nelldale Rd. SE16 ....5E 79
Nell Gwynn Ho. SW3 ....5A 74
Nellie Cressall Way E3..........4B 66
Nello James Gdns. SE27......4F 119
Nelson Arc. SE10 ....2E 95
...................................(off Nelson Rd.)
Nelson Cl. NW6 ....2C 58
Nelson Cl. SE16 ....2E 79
...................................(off Brunel Rd.)
Nelson Gdns. E2....................2C 64
Nelson Ho. SW1 ....2E 89
...................................(off Dolphin Sq.)
Nelson Mandela Ho. N16 ......4C 36
Nelson Mandela Rd. SE3 ....1E 111
Nelson Pas. EC1 ......1A 10 (2E 63)
Nelson Pl. N1 ....1E 9 (1D 63)
Nelson Rd. N8 ....1B 34
Nelson Rd. SE10...................2E 95

Nelson's Column..... 1D 23 (2A 76)
Nelson Sq. SE1.............3D 25 (3D 77)
Nelson's Row SW4...................2F 103
Nelson St. E1...........................5D 65
Nelson St. E16.........................5B 68
Nelsons Yd. NW1........................1E 61
.........................(off Mornington Cres.)
Nelson Ter. N1..............1E 9 (1D 63)
Nelson Wlk. E3: Lon
  Bromley-by-Bow.................3D 67
Nelson Wlk. SE16: Lon Canada
  Water..................................2A 80
Nemus Apts. SE8.....................5F 79
Nepaul Rd. SW11.....................5A 88
Nepean St. SW15....................4C 98
Neptune Ct. E14......................5C 80
.................................(off Homer Dr.)
Neptune Ct. E16......................4C 68
.........................(off Hammersley Rd.)
Neptune Development SE8....1A 94
.............................(off Garrison Rd.)
Neptune Ho. E3........................5C 52
.............................(off Garrison Rd.)
Neptune Ho. SE16....................4E 79
..........................(off Moodkee St.)
Neptune St. SE16.....................4E 79
Nero Ho. E20............................3E 53
............................(off Anthems Way)
Neroli Ho. E1............................5C 64
.......................(off Boulevard Walkway)
Nesbit Ct. SE17.........................2D 91
...................................(off Cook's Rd.)
Nesbit Rd. SE9.........................2F 111
Nesbitt Cl. SE3.......................1A 110
Nesham Ho. N1........................5A 50
...................................(off Hoxton St.)
Nesham St. E1..........................1C 78
Ness St. SE16..........................4C 78
Nestor Ho. E2...........................1D 65
......................(off Old Bethnal Grn. Rd.)
Netheravon Rd. W4..................5B 70
Netheravon Rd. Sth. W4 .....1B 84
Netherby Rd. SE23.................5E 107
Nethercott Ho. E3.....................2D 67
.................................(off Bruce Rd.)
Netherfield Rd. SW17...........3C 116
Netherford Rd. SW4................5E 89
Netherhall Gdns. NW3.............3E 45
Netherhall Way NW3................2E 45
Netherleigh Cl. N6..................3D 33
Netherton Gro. SW10.............2E 87
Netherton Rd. N15..................1F 35
Netherwood Pl. W14................4F 71
.........................(off Netherwood Rd.)
Netherwood Rd. W14...............4F 71
Netherwood St. NW6...............4B 44
Netley SE5................................4A 92
........................(off Redbridge Gdns.)
Netley Rd. E17.........................1B 38
Netley St. NW1...........2F 5 (2E 61)
................................(off Agar Gro.)
Nettlecombe NW1.....................4F 47
......................................(off Agar Gro.)
Nettleden Ho. SW3..................5A 74
...................................(off Cale St.)
Nettlefold Pl. SE27................3D 119
Nettleton Ct. EC2........1F 17 (4E 63)
.............................(off London Wall)
Nettleton Rd. SE14..................4F 93
Neuchatel Rd. SE6..................2B 122
Neutron Twr. E14......................1F 81
Nevada Bldg. SE10..................4E 95
...........................(off Blackheath Rd.)
Nevada St. SE10......................2E 95
Nevern Mans. SW5..................1C 86
............................(off Warwick Rd.)
Nevern Pl. SW5.......................5C 72

Nevern Rd. SW5.......................5C 72
Nevern Sq. SW5......................5C 72
Nevil Ho. SW9.........................5D 91
............................(off Loughborough Rd.)
Nevill Ct. SW10........................3E 87
..................................(off Edith Ter.)
Neville Cl. E11.........................5B 40
Neville Cl. NW1.........................1F 61
Neville Cl. NW6.......................1B 58
Neville Cl. SE15......................4C 92
Neville Ct. NW8........................1F 59
...................................(off Abbey Rd.)
Neville Dr. N2...........................1E 31
Neville Gill Cl. SW18..............4C 100
Neville Ho. NW6......................1B 58
..............................(off Denmark Rd.)
Neville Rd. E7..........................4C 54
Neville Rd. NW6......................1B 58
Nevilles Ct. NW2.....................5C 28
Neville St. SW7........................1F 87
Neville Ter. SW7.......................1F 87
Nevill La. EC4.................2C 16 (5C 62)
..........................(off New Fetter La.)
Nevill Rd. N16..........................1A 50
Nevinson Cl. SW18..................4F 101
Nevis Cl. E13............................1D 69
Nevis Rd. SW17......................2C 116
Nevitt Ho. N1............................1F 63
............................(off Cranston Est.)
Newall Ho. SE1..............5A 26 (4E 77)
..................................(off Bath Ter.)
Newark Ho. SW9.....................5D 91
Newark St. E1.........................4D 65
.............................(not continuous)
New Atlas Wharf E14.............4C 80
..................................(off Arnhem Pl.)
New Baltic Wharf SE8 ....1A 94
.................................(off Evelyn St.)
New Barn St. E13.....................3C 68
Newbridge Point SE23.........3F 121
New Bri. St. EC4..........3D 17 (5D 63)
New Broad St. EC2...1C 18 (4A 64)
Newburgh St. W1.........3A 14 (5E 63)
New Burlington M.
  W1.................................4F 13 (1E 75)
New Burlington Pl.
  W1.................................4F 13 (1E 75)
New Burlington St.
  W1.................................4F 13 (1E 75)
Newburn Ho. SE11..................1B 90
.............................(off Newburn St.)
Newburn St. SE11...................1B 90
Newbury Cl. E5.........................2A 52
............................(off Daubeney Rd.)
Newbury Ho. SW9...................5D 91
Newbury Ho. W2......................5D 59
.............................(off Hallfield Est.)
Newbury M. NW5.....................3C 46
Newbury St. EC1........1F 17 (4E 63)
New Bus. Cen., The
  NW10....................................2B 56
New Butt La. SE8......................3C 94
New Butt La. Nth. SE8.............3C 94
..................................(off Hales St.)

Newby NW1.....................2F 5 (2E 61)
.................................(off Robert St.)
Newby Ho. E14..........................1E 81
..................................(off Newby Pl.)
Newby Pl. E14..........................1E 81
Newby St. SW8.........................1D 103
New Caledonian Mkt.
  ....5E 27 (4A 78)
.........................(off Bermondsey Sq.)
New Caledonian Wharf
  SE16.....................................4B 80
Newcastle Cl. EC4...2D 17 (5D 63)
Newcastle Ct. EC4 ...4A 18 (1E 77)
.................................(off College Hill)
Newcastle Ho. W1.......5B 4 (4C 60)
...........................(off Luxborough St.)
Newcastle Pl. W2....................4F 59
Newcastle Row EC1...3C 8 (3C 62)
New Cavendish St.
  W1..................................1C 12 (4C 60)
New Century Ho. E16................5B 68
.................................(off Jude St.)
New Change EC4........3F 17 (5E 63)
New Change Pas.
  EC4..................................3F 17 (5E 63)
.........................(off New Change)
New Charles St.
  EC1..................................1E 9 (2D 63)
NEW CHARLTON.......................5E 83
New Chiswick Pool...................3A 84
New Church Rd. SE5................3E 91
.................................(not continuous)
New City Rd. E13.....................2E 69
New Claremont Apts. SE1 .....5B 78
.............................(off Setchell Rd.)
New Clocktower Pl. N7............3A 48
New College Ct. NW3..............3E 45
............................(off College Cres.)
New College M. N1..................4C 48
New College Pde. NW3...........3F 45
..................................(off Finchley Rd.)
Newcombe Gdns. SW16 ....4A 118
Newcombe Ho. E5...................5D 37
Newcombe St. W8..................2C 72
Newcomen Rd. E11.................5B 40
Newcomen Rd. SW11..............1F 101
Newcomen St. SE1....3B 26 (3F 77)
New Compton St.
  WC2...................................3C 14 (5F 61)
New Concordia Wharf SE1....3C 78
New Ct. EC4...................3B 16 (1C 76)
.................................(off Fountain Ct.)
Newcourt Ho. E2......................2D 65
...................................(off Pott St.)
Newcourt St. NW8....................1A 60
New Covent Garden Market...3F 89
New Covent Garden Market
  Entrance SW8.......................5E 89
New Crane Pl. E1.....................2E 79
New Crane Wharf E1...............2E 79
.............................(off New Crane Pl.)
New Cres. Yd. NW10................1B 56
NEW CROSS................................3B 94
NEW CROSS................................4B 94
NEW CROSS GATE.....................4F 93
NEW CROSS GATE.....................4F 93
New Cross Gate Station (Rail &
  Overground).........................3A 94
New Cross Rd. SE14................3E 93
New Cross Station (Rail &
  Overground).........................3B 94
Newdigate Ho. E14..................5B 66
.............................(off Norbiton Rd.)
New Diorama Theatre
  ....3E 5 (3D 61)

New Drum St. E1 .... 5B **64**
.... (off Aldgate Pl.)
Newell St. E14 .... 5B **66**
New End NW3 .... 5E **31**
New End Sq. NW3 .... 1F **45**
Newent Cl. SE15 .... 3A **92**
New Era Est. N1 .... 5A **50**
.... (off Halcomb St.)
New Era Ho. N1 .... 5A **50**
.... (off Halcomb St.)
New Festival Av. E14 .... 5C **66**
New Fetter La. EC4 .... 2C 16 (5C **62**)
Newfield Ri. NW2 .... 5C **28**
Newgate St. EC1 ...... 2E 17 (5D **63**)
New Globe Wlk. SE1 1F 25 (2E **77**)
New Goulston St. E1 2F 19 (5B **64**)
New Grn. Pl. SE19 .... 5A **120**
New Gun Wharf E3 .... 5A **52**
.... (off Gunmaker's La.)
Newhall Cl. N1 .... 5E **49**
.... (off Popham Rd.)

Newham Academy of Music
.... 5F **55**

NEWHAM CENTRE FOR MENTAL
HEALTH 3F **69**
Newham City Farm 5B **54**
Newham Leisure Cen. 3E **69**
Newham's Row
SE1 .... 4E 27 (4A **78**)

NEWHAM UNIVERSITY HOSPITAL
.... 3E **69**
Newham Way E16 .... 4B **68**
Newham Way E6 .... 3F **69**
Newhaven Gdns. SE9 .... 2F **111**
Newhaven La. E16 .... 3B **68**
New Hope Cl. NW10 .... 2D **57**
Newick Rd. E5 .... 1D **51**

NEWINGTON 5A 26 (4E **77**)
Newington Barrow Way N7 .... 5B **34**
Newington Butts SE1 .... 5D **77**
Newington Butts SE11 .... 5D **77**
Newington C'way.
SE1 .... 5E 25 (4D **77**)
Newington Cl. N16 .... 1E **49**
.... (off Green Lanes)
Newington Ct. Bus. Cen.
SE1 .... 5F 25 (4E **77**)
.... (off Newington C'way.)
Newington Grn. N1 .... 2F **49**
Newington Grn. N16 .... 2F **49**
Newington Grn. Community Gdns.
.... 2F **49**
.... (off Newington Grn.)
Newington Grn. Mans. N16 ....2F **49**
Newington Grn. Rd. N1 .... 3F **49**
Newington Ind. Est. SE17 .... 5D **77**
New Inn B'way.
EC2 .... 3E 11 (3A **64**)
New Inn Pas. WC2 ....3A 16 (5B **62**)
.... (off Houghton St.)
New Inn Sq. EC2 .... 3E 11 (3A **64**)
.... (off Bateman's Row)
New Inn St. EC2 .... 3E 11 (3A **64**)
New Inn Yd. EC2 .... 3E 11 (3A **64**)
New Jubilee Wharf E1 .... 2E **79**
.... (off Wapping Wall)
New Kent Rd. SE1 .... 4E **77**
New Kings Rd. SW6 .... 5B **86**
New King St. SE8 .... 2C **94**
Newland Ct. EC1 ..... 2B 10 (3F **63**)
.... (off St Luke's Est.)
Newland Ho. SE14 .... 2F **93**
.... (off John Williams Cl.)
Newlands NW1 .... 1F 5 (2E **61**)
.... (off Harrington St.)

Newlands 3F **107**
Newlands Pk. SE26 .... 5E **121**
Newlands Quay E1 .... 1E **79**
New Lion Way SE17 .... 5E **77**
New London St.
EC3 .... 4E 19 (1A **78**)
.... (off Hart St.)
New Lydenburg Commercial Est.
SE7 .... 4E **83**
New Lydenburg St. SE7 .... 4E **83**
Newlyn NW1 .... 5E **47**
.... (off Plender St.)
Newman Cl. NW10 .... 3D **43**
Newman Cl. SE26 .... 4E **121**
Newman Ho. SE1 ....5D 25 (4D **77**)
Newman Pas. W1 ....1A 14 (4E **61**)
Newman Rd. E13 .... 2D **69**
Newman's Ct. EC3 ...3C 18 (5F **63**)
.... (off Cornhill)

Newman's Row
WC2 .... 1A 16 (4B **62**)
Newman St. W1 ......1A 14 (4E **61**)
Newmarket Grn. SE9 .... 5F **111**
Newmill Ho. E3 .... 3E **67**
New Mill Rd. SW11 .... 2F **89**
New Mt. St. E15 .... 4F **53**
Newnes Path SW15 .... 2D **99**
Newnham Ter. SE1 ...5B 24 (4C **76**)
New Nth. Pl. EC2 .....3D 11 (3A **64**)
New Nth. Rd. N1 ......1C 10 (3F **49**)
New Nth. St. WC1 .....5F 7 (4B **62**)
Newnton Cl. N4 .... 2F **35**
New Orleans Wlk. N19 .... 2F **33**
New Oxford St. WC1 ..2C 14 (5F **61**)
New Paragon Wlk. SE17 .... 5F **77**
New Pk. Pde. SW2 .... 5A **104**
.... (off New Pk. Rd.)
New Pk. Rd. SW2 .... 1F **117**
New Pl. Sq. SE16 .... 4D **79**
New Plaistow Rd. E15 .... 5A **54**
Newport Av. E13 .... 3D **69**
Newport Av. E14 .... 1F **81**
Newport Ct. WC2 .....4C 14 (1F **75**)
Newport Ho. E3 .... 2A **66**
.... (off Strahan Rd.)
Newport Pl. WC2 .....4C 14 (1F **75**)
Newport Rd. E10 .... 4E **39**
Newport Rd. SW13 .... 4C **84**
Newport St. SE11 .... 5B **76**
Newport Street Gallery 5B **76**
New Priory Ct. NW6 .... 4C **44**
.... (off Mazenod Av.)
New Providence Wharf E14 ....2F **81**
Newquay Ho. SE11 .... 1C **90**
Newquay Rd. SE6 .... 2D **123**
New Quebec St. W1 ..3A 12 (5B **60**)
New Ride SW7 .... 3A **74**
New River Av. N8 .... 1E **34**
New River Head EC1 ..1C 8 (2C **62**)
New River Wlk. N1 .... 3E **49**
.... (not continuous)
New River Way N4 .... 2D **35**
New Rd. E1 .... 4D **65**
New Rd. N8 .... 1A **34**
New Rochford St. NW5 .... 2B **46**
New Row WC2 .... 4D 15 (1A **76**)
New Spitalfields Mkt. E10 ...... 5C **38**
New Spring Gdns. Wlk.
SE11 .... 1A **90**
New Sq. WC2 .... 2B 16 (5C **62**)
New Sq. Pas. WC2 ...2B 16 (5C **62**)
.... (off Star Yd.)
Newstead Ho. N1 .... 1C **62**
.... (off Tolpuddle St.)

Newstead Rd. SE12 .... 5B **110**
Newstead Way SW19 .... 4F **113**
New St. EC2 .... 1E 19 (4A **64**)
New St. Hill BR1: Broml 5D **125**
New St. Sq. EC4 ......2C 16 (5C **62**)
.... (not continuous)
Newton Cl. E17 .... 1A **38**
Newton Cl. E3 .... 4C **66**
Newton Cl. NW6 .... 4E **45**
.... (off Fairfax Rd.)
Newton Cl. SW17 .... 3F **115**
.... (off Grosvenor Way)
Newton Ct. W8 .... 3C **72**
.... (off Kensington Chu. St.)
Newton Gro. W4 .... 5A **70**
Newton Ho. E1 .... 1D **79**
.... (off Cornwall St.)
Newton Ho. NW8 .... 5D **45**
.... (off Abbey Rd.)
Newton Lodge SE10 .... 4B **82**
.... (off Teal St.)
Newton Mans. W14 .... 2A **86**
.... (off Queen's Club Gdns.)
Newton Pl. E14 .... 5C **80**
Newton Rd. E15 .... 2F **53**
Newton Rd. NW2 .... 1E **43**
Newton Rd. W2 .... 5D **59**
Newton's Yd. SW18 .... 3C **100**
New Tower Bldgs. E1 .... 2D **79**
Newtown St. SW11 .... 4D **89**
New Turnstile WC1 ...1F 15 (4B **62**)
.... (off High Holborn)
New Union Cl. E14 .... 4E **81**
New Union Sq. SW11 .... 2F **89**
New Union St.
EC2 .... 1B 18 (4F **63**)
New Village Av. E14 .... 5F **67**
New Wanstead E11 .... 1B **40**
New Wharf Rd. N1 .... 1A **62**
New Willow Ho. E13 .... 1C **68**
.... (off Plaistow Rd.)
New Zealand Way W12 .... 1D **71**
Nexus Cl. E11 .... 3A **40**
Nexus Ct. NW6 .... 2C **58**
NHS WALK-IN CENTRE (CLAPHAM
JUNCTION) 1A **102**
NHS WALK-IN CENTRE
(CRICKLEWOOD HEALTH
CENTRE) 1F **43**
NHS WALK-IN CENTRE (EARL'S
COURT) 5D **73**
NHS WALK-IN CENTRE (ISLE OF
DOGS) 3C **80**
NHS WALK-IN CENTRE (PARSONS
GREEN) 4C **86**
NHS WALK-IN CENTRE (SOHO)
.... 3B 14 (5F **61**)
.... (off Frith St.)
Niagara Cl. N1 .... 1E **63**
Niagra Ct. SE16 .... 4E **79**
.... (off Canada Est.)
Nice Bus. Pk. SE15 .... 2D **93**
Nicholas Cl. E13 .... 2D **69**
Nicholas Ct. N7 .... 2B **48**
Nicholas Ct. SE12 .... 1C **124**
Nicholas Ct. W4 .... 2A **84**
.... (off Corney Reach Way)
Nicholas La. EC4 .....4C 18 (1F **77**)
.... (not continuous)
Nicholas M. W4 .... 2A **84**
Nicholas Pas. EC4 ...4C 18 (1F **77**)
.... (off Nicholas La.)
Nicholas Rd. E1 .... 3E **65**
Nicholas Rd. W11 .... 1F **71**

Nicholas Stacey Ho. SE7 ..... 1D 97
.................(off Frank Burton Cl.)
Nicholay Rd. N19 ....3F 33
.................(not continuous)
Nicholl Ho. N4 ....3E 35
Nichollsfield Wlk. N7 .... 2B 48
Nicholls M. SW16 .... 4A 118
Nicholls Point E15............... 5C 54
.................(off Park Gro.)
Nicholl St. E2 .... 5C 50
Nichols Cl. N4 .... 3C 34
.................(off Osborne Rd.)
Nichols Ct. E2 ...... 1F 11 (1B 64)
Nicholson Ho. SE17............. 1F 91
Nicholson Sq. E3.................. 2E 67
.................(off Bolinder Way)
Nicholson St. SE1 ....2D 25 (2D 77)
Nickeby Apts. E15 .... 3F 53
.................(off Grove Cres. Rd.)
Nickleby Ho. SE16............... 3C 78
Nickleby Ho. W11 .... 2F 71
.................(off St Ann's Rd.)
Nickols Wlk. SW18............... 2D 101
Nicoll Ct. NW10 .... 5A 62
Nicoll Pl. NW4 .... 1D 29
Nicoll Rd. NW10 .... 5A 62
Nicosia Rd. SW18................ 5A 102
Niederwald Rd. SE26........ 4A 122
Nigel Ho. EC1 ....5B 8 (4C 62)
.................(off Portpool La.)
Nigel Playfair Av. W6.......... 5D 71
Nigel Rd. E7 .... 2E 55
Nigel Rd. SE15 .... 1C 106
Nigeria Rd. SE7 .... 3E 97
Nightingale Cl. E14.............. 3E 81
.................(off Ovex Cl.)
Nightingale Ct. N4 .... 4B 34
.................(off Tollington Pk.)
Nightingale Gro. SE13.........3F 109
NIGHTINGALE HOSPITAL 4A 60
Nightingale Ho. E1............... 2C 78
.................(off Thomas More St.)
Nightingale Ho. E2............... 5A 50
.................(off Kingsland Rd.)
Nightingale Ho. NW8............ 3A 60
.................(off Samford St.)
Nightingale Ho. W12............ 5E 57
.................(off Du Cane Rd.)
Nightingale La. SW12 .... 5B 102
Nightingale La. SW4 .... 4D 103
Nightingale Lodge W9 .... 4C 58
.................(off Admiral Wlk.)
Nightingale M. E11 .... 1C 40
Nightingale M. E3................. 1F 65
Nightingale M. SE11 .... 5D 77
Nightingale Pl. SW10 .... 2E 87
Nightingale Rd. E5................ 5D 37
Nightingale Rd. N1............... 3E 49
Nightingale Rd. NW10.......... 1B 58
Nightingale Sq. SW12 .... 5C 102
Nightingale Wlk. N1.............. 3E 49
Nightingale Wlk. SW4 .... 4D 103
Nile Cl. N16........................... 5B 36
Nile Ho. N1 ....1B 10 (2F 63)
.................(off Nile St.)
Nile Rd. E13........................... 1E 69
Nile St. N1 ....1A 10 (2E 63)
Nile Ter. SE15....................... 1B 92
Nimegen Way SE22............. 3A 106
Nimrod Ho. E16.................... 4D 69
.................(off Vanguard Cl.)
Nimrod Pas. N1 .... 3A 50
Nimrod Rd. SW16 .... 5D 117
Nina Mackay Cl. E15 .... 5A 54

NINE ELMS 3E 89
Nine Elms La. SW11.............3E 89
Nine Elms La. SW8................2F 89
Nine Elms Station (Underground)
....3A 90
Nipponzan Myohoji Peace
   Pagoda 2B 88
Nisbet Ho. E9 ....2F 51
Nita Ct. SE12 ....1C 124
Niton St. SW6........................3F 85
Niveda Cl. W12......................3C 70
Noah's Yd. N1 ....1E 7 (1A 62)
Nobel Ho. SE5.......................5E 91
Noble Ct. E1 ....1D 79
Noblefield Hgts. N2..............1A 32
Noble M. N16.........................5F 35
.................(off Albion Rd.)
Noble St. EC2 ....2F 17 (5E 63)
Noble Yd. N1 ....5D 49
.................(off Camden Pas.)
Nocavia Ho. SW6..................5E 87
.................(off Townmead Rd.)
Noel Coward Ho. SW1.........5E 75
.................(off Vauxhall Bri. Rd.)
Noel Coward Theatre
.................................4D 15 (1A 76)
.................(off St Martin's La.)
Noel Ho. NW6 ....4F 45
Noel Rd. E6.............................3F 69
Noel Rd. N1 ....1D 63
Noel St. W1 ....3A 14 (5E 61)
Noel Ter. SE23......................2E 121
Noko W10................................2F 57
Nolan Mans. E20...................2D 53
.................(off Honour Lea Av.)
Nolan Way E5.........................1C 50
Noll Ho. N7 ....4B 34
.................(off Tomlins Wlk.)
Nook Apts. E1 ....5B 64
.................(off Scarborough St.)
Nora Leverton Ct. NW1 ....4E 47
.................(off Randolph St.)
Norbiton Ho. NW1 ....5E 47
.................(off Camden St.)
Norbiton Rd. E14...................5B 66
Norbroke St. W12.................1B 70
Norburn St. W10 ....4A 58
Norcombe Ho. N19................5F 33
.................(off Wedmore St.)
Norcott Rd. N16.....................4C 36
Norcroft Gdns. SE22.............5C 106
Norden Ho. E2 ....2D 65
.................(off Pott St.)
Norfolk Av. N15......................1B 36
Norfolk Cres. W2...................5A 60
Norfolk Ho. EC4....4F 17 (1E 77)
.................(off Trig La.)
Norfolk Ho. SE8.....................4C 94
.................(off Brookmill Rd.)
Norfolk Ho. SW1....................5F 75
.................(off Page St.)
Norfolk Ho. Rd. SW16...........3F 117
Norfolk Mans. SW11.............4B 88
.................(off Prince of Wales Dr.)
Norfolk M. W10......................4A 58
.................(off Blagrove Rd.)
Norfolk Pl. W2 ....(not continuous)
Norfolk Rd. NW10 ....4A 42
Norfolk Rd. NW8 ....5F 45
Norfolk Row SE1...................5B 76
Norfolk Sq. W2......................5F 59
Norfolk Sq. M. W2.................5F 59
.................(off London St.)

Norfolk St. E7........................2C 54
Norfolk Ter. W6.....................1A 86
Norgrove St. SW12...............5C 102
Norland Ho. W11...................2F 71
.................(off Queensdale Cres.)
Norland Pl. W11....................2A 72
Norland Rd. W11...................2F 71
.................(not continuous)
Norland Sq. W11...................2A 72
Norland Sq. Mans. W11........2A 72
.................(off Norland Sq.)
Norlem Ct. SE8......................5A 80
.................(off Seafarer Way)
Norley Va. SW15...................1C 112
Norlington Rd. E10................3E 39
Norlington Rd. E11................3F 39
Norman Butler Ho. W10........3F 57
.................(off Ladbroke Gro.)
Normanby Cl. SW15.............3B 100
Normanby Rd. NW10 ....1B 42
Norman Ct. N4.......................2C 34
Norman Ct. NW10 ....4C 42
Normand Gdns. W14.............2A 86
.................(off Greyhound Rd.)
Normand Mans. W14............2A 86
.................(off Normand M.)
Normand M. W14...................2B 86
Normandy Cl. SE26...............3A 122
Normandy Ho. E14................3E 81
.................(off Plevna St.)
Normandy Pl. W12.................2F 71
Normandy Rd. SW9...............4C 90
Normandy Ter. E16................5D 69
Norman Gro. E3.....................1A 66
Norman Ho. SE1....5E 27 (4A 78)
.................(off Riley Rd.)
Norman Ho. SW8...................3A 90
.................(off Wyvil Rd.)
Normanhurst Rd. SW2..........2B 118
Norman Rd. E11.....................4F 39
Norman Rd. SE10..................3D 95
Norman St. EC1.....2A 10 (2E 63)
Norman Ter. NW6..................2B 44
Normanton Av. SW19............2C 114
Normanton St. SE23.............2F 121
Normanton Way SE16...........5C 108
Norrice Lea N2.......................1F 31
Norris Ho. E9 ....5E 51
.................(off Handley Rd.)
Norris Ho. N1........................5A 50
.................(off Colville Est.)
Norris Ho. SW8.....................1B 94
.................(off Grove St.)
Norris St. SW1 ......5B 14 (1F 75)
Norroy Rd. SW15...................2F 99
Norstead Pl. SW15................2C 112
Northam Rd. E11...................1F 37
North Acton Station
   (Underground)...................4A 56
Northampton Gro. N1 ....2F 49
Northampton Pk. N1 ....3E 49
Northampton Rd. EC1 ...3C 8 (3C 62)
Northampton Row
   EC1 ....2C 8 (3C 62)
.................(off Rosoman Pl.)
Northampton Sq. EC1 2D 9 (2D 63)
Northampton St. N1................4E 49
North Audley St. W1 3B 12 (1C 74)
Northaw Ho. W10...................3E 57
.................(off Sutton Way)
North Bank NW8....................2A 60
North Birkbeck Rd. E11........5F 39
North Block SE1.....3A 24 (3B 76)
.................(off Chickeley St.)

Northbourne Rd. SW4........3F 103
Northbrook Rd. SE13........3A 110
Northburgh St. EC1....4E 9 (3D 63)
North Carriage Dr. W2........1A 74
..................(off Bayswater St.)
Northchurch SE17................1F 91
..........................(not continuous)
Northchurch Ho. E2..........5C 50
..................(off Whiston Rd.)
Northchurch Rd. N1..........4F 49
..........................(not continuous)
Northchurch Ter. N1..........4A 50
North Circular Rd. NW11....2F 29
North Circular Rd. NW2......5A 28
North Circular Rd. NW4.....2E 29
North Colonnade, The E14...2C 80
..........................(not continuous)
Northcote Rd. NW10..........4A 42
Northcote Rd. SW11..........3A 102
North Ct. SE24..................1D 105
North Ct. SW1.........5D 23 (4A 76)
..................(off Gt. Peter St.)
North Ct. W1..................5A 6 (4E 61)
North Cres. E16..................3F 67
North Cres. WC1..........5B 6 (4F 61)
Northcroft Ct. W12............3C 70
North Crofts SE23............1D 121
North Cross Rd. SE22........3B 106
Northdene Gdns. N15........1B 36
Northdown St. N1......1F 7 (1A 62)
North Dr. SW16................4E 117
..................................3F 105

NORTH END........................4E 31
North End Av. NW3............4E 31
North End Av. NW3............4E 31
North End Cres. W14........5B 72
North End Ho. W14............5A 72
North End Pde. W14...........5A 72
..................(off North End Rd.)
North End Rd. NW11..........3C 30
North End Rd. SW6.............2B 86
North End Rd. W14.............5A 72
North End Way NW3..........4E 31
Northern Hgts. N8..............2F 33
..................(off Crescent Rd.)
Northern Rd. E13................1D 69
Northesk Ho. E1................3D 65
..................................(off Tent St.)
North Eyot Gdns. W6.........1B 84
Northey St. E14................1A 80
Northfield Ho. SE15..........2C 92
Northfield Rd. N16............2A 36
Northfields SW18..............2C 100
Northfields Prospect Bus. Cen.
SW18..............................2C 100
Northfleet Ho. SE1...3B 26 (3F 77)
..................(off Tennis St.)
Northflock St. SE16............3C 78
North Gdn. E14................2B 80
North Ga. NW8................1A 60
..................(off Prince Albert Rd.)
Northgate Ct. SW9............1C 104
Northgate Dr. NW9............1A 28
Northgate Ho. E14.............1C 80
..................(off E. India Dock Rd.)
North Gower St. NW1....2A 6 (2E 61)
North Greenwich Pier (River Bus
& Tours)........................2B 82
North Greenwich Station
(Underground)................3A 82
North Gro. N15................1F 35
North Gro. N6....................2C 32
North Hill N6....................1B 32
North Hill Av. N6..............1C 32

North Ho. SE8..................1B 94
Northiam WC1............2E 7 (2A 62)
..................(off Cromer St.)
Northiam St. E9..................5D 51
Northington St. WC1....4A 8 (3B 62)
..................(off Southside Shop. Cen.)
North M. WC1..........4A 8 (3B 62)
North Mill Apts. E8............5B 50
..................(off Lovelace St.)
Northolme Rd. N5..............1E 49
Northover BR1: Brom........3B 124
North Pas. SW18................3C 100
Northpoint Ho. N1..............2F 49
..................(off Essex Rd.)
Northpoint Sq. NW1............3F 47
North Pole Rd. W10............4E 57
Northport St. N1................5F 49
North Quay Pl. E14.............1D 81
North Ride W2..................1A 74
North Ri. W2....................5A 60
North Rd. N6....................2C 32
North Rd. N7....................3A 48
North Rd. W4............4A 12 (1B 74)
North Row Bldgs.
W1..................4B 12 (1C 74)
..................(off North Row)
North Several SE3...............5F 95
Northside Studios E8..........5D 51
..................(off Andrew's Rd.)
North Side Wandsworth Comn.
SW18..............................3F 101
North Sq. NW11................1C 30
North Stand N5..................5D 35
Northstead Rd. SW2..........2C 118
North St. E13..................1D 69
North St. SW4..................1E 103
North St. Pas. E13.............1D 69
North Tenter St. E1...3F 19 (5B 64)
North Ter. SW3................4A 74
North Ter. WC2............1C 22 (2F 75)
..................(off Trafalgar Sq.)
Northumberland All.
EC3.................3E 19 (5A 64)
..........................(not continuous)
Northumberland Av. E12....3E 41
Northumberland Av.
WC2.................1D 23 (2A 76)
Northumberland Ho.
SW1.................1D 23 (2A 76)
..................(off Northumberland Av.)
Northumberland Pl. W2......5C 58
Northumberland Rd. E17....2C 38
Northumberland St.
WC2.................1D 23 (2A 76)
Northumbria St. E14..........5C 66
North Verbena Gdns. W6....1C 84
North Vw. SW19................5E 113
Northview Cres. NW10........1B 42
Northview Pde. N7.............5A 34
North Vs. NW1..................3F 47
Northwall Rd. E20..............2C 52
Northway NW11................1D 31
Northway Rd. SE5.............1E 105
Northways NW3................4F 45
..................(off College Cres.)
Northways Pde. NW3.........4F 45
..................(off College Cres.)

Northwest Pl. N1................1C 62
North Wharf E14................2E 81
..................(off Coldharbour)
North Wharf Rd. W2..........4F 59
Northwick Cl. NW8.............3F 59
Northwick Ho. NW8...........3E 59
..................(off St John's Wood Rd.)
Northwick Ter. NW8..........3F 59
Northwold Rd. E5..............4C 36
Northwold Rd. N16.............4B 36
Northwood Est. E5..............4C 36
Northwood Hall N6.............2E 33
Northwood Ho. SE27..........4F 119
Northwood Ho. N6.............2D 33
Northwood Rd. SE23.........1B 122
Northwood Way SE19........5F 119
North Woolwich Rd. E16......2B 82
Norton Folgate E1.....5E 11 (4A 64)
Norton Folgate Ho.
E1..................5F 11 (4B 64)
..................(off Puma Ct.)
Norton Ho. E1................5D 65
..................(off Bigland St.)
Norton Ho. E2..................1F 65
..................(off Mace St.)
Norton Ho. SW1........5C 22 (4F 75)
..................(off Arneway St.)
Norton Ho. SW9................5B 90
..................(off Aytoun Rd.)
Norton Rd. E10..................3B 38
Norval Grn. SW9................5C 90
Norway Ga. SE16................4A 80
Norway Ho. N1..................5A 50
..................(off Hertford Rd.)
Norway Pl. E14................5B 66
Norway St. SE10................2D 95
Norway Wharf E14.............5B 66
Norwegian War Memorial....2A 74
Norwich Ho. E14................5D 67
..................(off Cordelia St.)
Norwich Rd. E7................2C 54
Norwich St. EC4....2B 16 (5C 62)
Norwood Cl. NW2..............5A 30
Norwood High St. SE27......3D 119
Norwood Ho. E14...............1D 81
..................(off Poplar High St.)
NORWOOD NEW TOWN.....5E 119
Norwood Pk. Rd. SE27......5E 119
Norwood Rd. SE24............1D 119
Norwood Rd. SE27............2D 119
Notley Pl. SW4................5A 104
Notley St. SE5..................3F 91
Notting Barn Rd. W10.........3F 57
Nottingdale Sq. W11..........2A 72
Nottingham Av. E16............4E 69
Nottingham Ct. WC2...3D 15 (5A 62)
Nottingham Ho. WC2...3D 15 (5A 62)
..................(off Shorts Gdns.)
Nottingham Pl. W1.....4B 4 (4C 60)
Nottingham Rd. E10...........1E 39
Nottingham Rd. SW17.......1B 116
Nottingham St. W1.....5B 4 (4C 60)
Nottingham Ter. NW1....4B 4 (3C 60)
..................(off York Ter. W.)
NOTTING HILL....................1B 72
Notting Hill Ga. W11..........2C 72
Notting Hill Gate Station
(Underground)................2C 72
Nottingwood Ho. W11.........1A 72
..................(off Clarendon Rd.)
Nova Bldg. E14................5C 80
Nova Ct. E. E14................2E 81
..................(off Yabsley St.)
Nova Ct. W. E14................2E 81
..................(off Yabsley St.)

Novello Ct. N1 ....5E **49**
.................*(off Dibden St.)*
Novello St. SW6 ....4C **86**
Novello Theatre West End
.................4F **15** (1B **76**)
.................*(off Aldwych)*
Novem Ho. E1 ....4C **64**
.................*(off Chicksand St.)*
Nowell Rd. SW13 ....2C **84**
Noyna Rd. SW17 ....3B **116**
Nubia Way BR1: Broml.....3A **124**
Nucleus Apts. SW15 ....5F **99**
.................*(off W. Hill)*
Nuding Cl. SE13 ....1C **108**
Nuffield Health Battersea .5B **88**
.................*(within Latchmere Leisure Cen.)*
Nuffield Health Bloomsbury
.................3F **7** (3B **62**)
.................*(off Mecklenburgh Pl.)*
Nuffield Health Cannon Street
.................4B **18** (1F **77**)
.................*(off Cousin La.)*
Nuffield Health Covent Garden
.................3E **15** (5A **62**)
.................*(off Endell St.)*
Nuffield Health Fulham 4F **85**
Nuffield Health Hendon ...1E **29**
Nuffield Health Islington ..5D **49**
Nuffield Health Paddington .4E **59**
Nuffield Health Wandsworth
.................5D **101**
Nuffield Health Wandsworth,
Southside Shop. Cen...3D **101**
Nuffield Health Willesden Green
.................4E **43**
Nuffield Lodge N6 ....1E **33**
Nuffield Lodge W9 ....4C **58**
.................*(off Admiral Wlk.)*
Nugent Rd. N19 ....3A **34**
Nugent Ter. NW8 ....1E **59**
No. One EC1 ....4A **10** (3E **63**)
Nun Ct. EC2 ....2B **18** (5F **63**)
.................*(off Coleman St.)*
NUNHEAD 1D **107**
Nunhead Cemetery Local Nature
Reserve 2E **107**
Nunhead Cres. SE15 ....1D **107**
Nunhead Est. SE15 ....2D **107**
Nunhead Grn. SE15 ....1D **107**
Nunhead Gro. SE15 ....1D **107**
Nunhead La. SE15 ....1D **107**
Nunhead Pas. SE15 ....1C **106**
Nunhead Station (Rail) 5E **93**
Nursery Cl. SE4 ....5B **94**
Nursery Cl. SW15 ....2F **99**
Nursery La. E2 ....5B **50**
Nursery La. E7 ....3C **54**
Nursery La. W10 ....4F **57**
Nursery Rd. E9 ....3E **51**
Nursery Rd. SW9 ....2B **104**
Nursery Row SE17 ....5F **77**
Nutbourne St. W10 ....2A **58**
Nutbrook St. SE15 ....1C **106**
Nutcroft Rd. SE15 ....3D **93**
Nutfield Rd. E15 ....1E **53**
Nutfield Rd. NW2 ....5C **28**
Nutfield Rd. SE22 ....2B **106**
Nutford Pl. W1 ....5B **60**
Nuthurst Av. SW2 ....2B **118**
Nutley Ter. NW3 ....3E **45**
Nutmeg Cl. E16 ....3A **68**
Nutmeg La. E14 ....5F **67**
Nuttall St. N1 ....1A **64**
Nutter La. E11 ....1E **41**
Nutt St. SE15 ....3B **92**

Nutwell St. SW17 ....5A **116**
Nye Bevan Est. E5 ....5F **37**
Nye Bevan Ho. SW6 ....3B **86**
.................*(off St Thomas's Way)*
Nyland Ct. SE8 ....5A **80**
.................*(off Naomi St.)*
Nynehead St. SE14 ....3A **94**
Nyon Gro. SE6 ....2B **122**
Nyton Cl. N19 ....3A **34**

O

O2, The 2A **82**
O2 Brixton Academy 1C **104**
O2 Forum Kentish Town ...2D **47**
O2 Shepherd's Bush Empire
Theatre 3E **71**
Oak Apple Ct. SE12 ....1C **124**
Oakbank Gro. SE24 ....2E **105**
Oakbrook Cl. BR1: Broml ..4D **125**
Oakbury Rd. SW6 ....5D **87**
Oak Cott. Cl. SE6 ....1B **124**
Oak Ct. SE15 ....3B **92**
.................*(off Sumner Rd.)*
Oak Cres. E16 ....4A **68**
Oakcroft Rd. SE13 ....5F **95**
Oakdale Rd. E11 ....4F **39**
Oakdale Rd. E7 ....4D **55**
Oakdale Rd. N4 ....1E **35**
Oakdale Rd. SE15 ....1E **107**
Oakdale Rd. SW16 ....5A **118**
Oakden St. SE11 ....4D **93**
Oakden St. SE11 ....5C **76**
Oake Ct. SW15 ....3A **100**
Oakeford Ho. W14 ....4A **72**
.................*(off Russell Rd.)*
Oakeshott Av. N6 ....4C **32**
Oakes M. E14 ....4F **67**
.................*(off Nairn St.)*
Oakey La. SE1 .....5B **24** (4C **76**)
Oakfield Ct. N8 ....2A **34**
Oakfield Ct. NW2 ....2F **29**
Oakfield Gdns. SE19 ....5A **120**
.................*(not continuous)*
Oakfield Ho. E3 ....4C **66**
.................*(off Gale St.)*
Oakfield Rd. E6 ....5F **55**
Oakfield Rd. N4 ....1C **34**
Oakfield Rd. SW19 ....3F **113**
Oakfields Rd. NW11 ....1A **30**
Oakfield St. SW10 ....2E **87**
Oakford Rd. NW5 ....1E **47**
Oak Gro. NW2 ....1A **44**
Oakhall Ct. E11 ....1D **41**
Oak Hall Rd. E11 ....1D **41**
Oakham Cl. SE6 ....2B **122**
Oakham Ho. W10 ....3E **57**
.................*(off Sutton Way)*
Oakhill Av. NW3 ....1D **45**
Oakhill Ct. SE23 ....4E **107**
Oak Hill Pk. NW3 ....1D **45**
Oak Hill Pk. M. NW3 ....1E **45**
Oakhill Pl. SW15 ....3C **100**
Oak Hill Pk. SW15 ....3B **100**
Oak Hill Way NW3 ....1D **45**
.................*(not continuous)*
Oak Ho. E14 ....3E **81**
.................*(off Stewart St.)*
Oak Ho. W10 ....3A **58**
.................*(off Sycamore Wlk.)*
Oakhurst Gro. SE22 ....2C **106**
Oakington Rd. W9 ....3C **58**
Oakington Way N8 ....2A **34**
Oakland Quay E14 ....4D **81**
Oakland Rd. E15 ....1F **53**

Oaklands Ct. NW10 ....5A **42**
.................*(off Nicoll Rd.)*
Oaklands Est. SW4 ....4E **103**
Oaklands Gro. W12 ....2C **70**
Oaklands M. NW2 ....1F **43**
.................*(off Oaklands Rd.)*
Oaklands Pas. NW2 ....1F **43**
.................*(off Oaklands Rd.)*
Oaklands Pl. SW4 ....2E **103**
Oaklands Rd. NW2 ....1F **43**
Oak La. E14 ....1B **80**
Oakleigh Ct. N1 ......1B **10** (1F **63**)
.................*(off Murray Gro.)*
Oakley Cres. EC1 ....1E **9** (1D **63**)
Oakley Dr. SE13 ....4F **109**
Oakley Gdns. SW3 ....2A **88**
Oakley Ho. SE11 ....5C **76**
.................*(off Hotspur St.)*
Oakley Ho. SW1 ....5B **74**
Oakley Pl. SE1 ....1B **92**
Oakley Rd. N1 ....4F **49**
Oakley Sq. NW1 ....1E **61**
Oakley St. SW3 ....2A **88**
Oakley Studios SW3 ....2A **88**
.................*(off Up. Cheyne Row)*
Oakley Wlk. W6 ....2F **85**
Oakley Yd. E2 ....3B **64**
Oak Lock M. W4 ....1A **84**
Oak Lodge E11 ....1C **40**
Oak Lodge W8 ....4D **72**
.................*(off Chantry Sq.)*
Oakman Ho. SW19 ....1F **113**
Oakmead Rd. SW12 ....1C **116**
Oak Pk. Gdns. SW19 ....1F **113**
Oak Pk. M. N16 ....5B **36**
Oak Pl. SW18 ....3D **101**
Oakridge La. BR1: Broml ..5F **123**
Oakridge Rd. BR1: Broml ..4F **123**
Oaks, The NW10 ....4D **43**
Oaks, The NW6 ....4F **43**
.................*(off Brondesbury Pk.)*
Oaks Av. SE19 ....5A **120**
Oaksford Av. SE26 ....3D **121**
Oakshade Rd. BR1: Broml .4F **123**
Oakshaw Rd. SW18 ....5D **101**
Oakshott Ct. NW1 ...1B **6** (1F **61**)
.................*(not continuous)*
Oaks Pavilion M. SE19 .....5A **120**
Oak Sq. SW9 ....5B **90**
Oak Tree Gdns. BR1: Broml 5D **125**
Oak Tree Ho. W9 ....3C **58**
.................*(off Shirland Rd.)*
Oak Tree M. NW2 ....3C **42**
Oak Tree Rd. NW8 ....2A **60**
Oakview Lodge NW11 ....2B **30**
.................*(off Beechcroft Av.)*
Oakview Rd. SE6 ....5D **123**
Oak Village NW5 ....1C **46**
Oak Vs. NW11 ....1B **30**
.................*(off Hendon Pk. Row)*
Oakville Ho. SE16 ....3F **79**
.................*(off Dominion Dr.)*
Oak Way W3 ....2A **70**
Oakwood Cl. SE13 ....4F **109**
Oakwood Ct. W14 ....4B **72**
Oakwood Dr. SE19 ....5F **119**
Oakwood Ho. E9 ....3E **51**
.................*(off Frampton Pk. Rd.)*
Oakwood La. W14 ....4B **72**
Oakwood Mans. W14 ....4B **72**
.................*(off Oakwood Ct.)*
Oakworth Rd. W10 ....4E **57**
Oasis Sports Cen. ...2D **15** (5A **62**)
Oast Ct. E14 ....1B **80**
.................*(off Newell St.)*

Oast Lodge W4..................3A 84
..................(off Corney Reach Way)
Oatfield Ho. N15..................1A 36
..................(off Perry Ct.)
Oat La. EC2..................2F 17 (5E 63)
Oatwell Ho. SW3..................1A 88
..................(off Cale St.)
Oban Cl. E13..................3E 69
Oban Ho. E14..................5F 67
..................(off Oban St.)
Oban Rd. E13..................2E 69
Oban St. E14..................5F 67
Oberon Ct. E6..................4F 55
Oberon Ho. N1..................1A 64
..................(off Arden Est.)
Oberstein M. SW11..................2F 101
Oborne Cl. SE24..................3D 105
O'Brien Ho. E2..................2F 65
..................(off Roman Rd.)
Observatory Gdns. W8..................3C 72
Observatory M. E14..................5F 81
Observatory Rd. SW7..................4F 73
Occupation Rd. SE17..................1E 91
Ocean Est. E1: Lon
Ben Jonson Rd...................4A 66
Ocean Est. E1: Lon Ernest St...3R 66
Oceanis Apts. E16..................1C 82
..................(off Seagull La.)
Ocean St. E1..................4A 66
Ocean Wharf E14..................3B 80
Ockbrook E1..................4E 65
..................(off Hannibal Rd.)
Ockendon M. N1..................3F 49
Ockendon Rd. N1..................3F 49
Ockham Bldg. SE16...5F 27 (4B 78)
..................(off Arts La.)
Ockley Rd. SW16..................4A 118
Octagon, The SW10..................3D 87
..................(off Coleridge Gdns.)
Octagon Arc. EC2....1D 19 (4A 64)
Octagon Ct. SE16..................2F 79
..................(off Rotherhithe St.)
Octavia Ho. SW1..................4F 75
..................(off Medway St.)
Octavia Ho. W10..................3A 58
Octavia M. W9..................3B 58
Octavia St. SW11..................4A 88
Octavius St. SE8..................3C 94
Odelia Ct. E15..................5E 53
..................(off Biggerstaff Rd.)
Odell Ho. E14..................5C 66
..................(off New Festival Av.)
Odell Wlk. SE13..................1E 109
Odeon Cinema Camden Town
..................5D 47
..................(off Parkway)
Odeon Cinema Covent Gdn.
..................3C 14 (5F 61)
..................(off Shaftesbury Av.)
Odeon Cinema Greenwich...5B 82
Odeon Cinema Haymarket,
Panton St...........5C 14 (1F 75)
..................(off Panton St.)
Odeon Cinema Holloway...5A 34
Odeon Cinema IMAX (BFI)
..................2B 24 (2C 76)
Odeon Cinema Leicester Sq.
..................5C 14 (1F 75)
..................(off Leicester Sq.)
Odeon Cinema Putney.......1A 100
Odeon Cinema Streatham...3A 118
Odeon Cinema Surrey Quays
..................4F 79
Odeon Cinema Swiss Cottage
..................4F 45

Odeon Cinema Tottenham Ct. Rd.
..................1B 14 (4F 61)
..................(off Tottenham Ct. Rd.)
Odeon Cinema Whiteleys...5D 59
Odeon Ct. E16..................4C 68
Odeon Ct. NW10..................5A 42
..................(off St Albans Rd.)
Odeon Pde. N7..................5A 34
..................(off Holloway Rd.)
Odessa Rd. E7..................5B 40
Odessa Rd. NW10..................1C 56
Odessa St. SE16..................3B 80
Odessa Wharf SE16..................4B 80
..................(off Odessa St.)
Odessey Ho. E15..................3F 53
..................(off Leyton Rd.)
Odette Duval Ho. E1..................4E 65
..................(off Stepney Way)
Odger St. SW11..................5B 88
Odhams Wlk. WC2...3E 15 (5A 62)
Odin Ho. SE5..................5E 91
O'Donnell Ct. WC1.....3E 7 (3A 62)
O'Driscoll Ho. W12..................5D 57
Offa's Mead E9..................1B 52
Offenbach Ho. E2..................1F 65
..................(off Mace St.)
Offenham Rd. SW9..................4C 90
Offerton Rd. SW4..................1E 103
Offham Ho. SE17..................5A 78
..................(off Beckway St.)
Offley Rd. SW9..................3C 90
Offord Rd. N1..................4B 48
Offord St. N1..................4B 48
Ogilvie Ho. E1..................5F 65
..................(off Stepney C'way.)
Oglander Rd. SE15..................2B 106
Ogle St. W1..................5F 5 (4E 61)
O'Gorman Ho. SW10..................3E 87
..................(off King's Rd.)
Ohio Bldg. SE13..................4D 95
..................(off Deal's Gateway)
Ohio Rd. E13..................3B 68
Oil Mill La. W6..................1C 84
Okeburn Rd. SW17..................5C 116
Okehampton Rd. NW10...5E 43
Olaf Ct. W8..................3C 72
..................(off Kensington Chu. St.)
Olaf St. W11..................1F 71
Old Abbey La. SE16..................4B 78
..................(off Vauban St.)
Oldacre M. SW12..................5C 102
Old Aeroworks, The NW8...3F 59
..................(off Hatton St.)
Old Bailey EC4.....3E 17 (5D 63)
Old Bailey..........2E 17 (5D 63)
Old Barge Ho. All.
SE1..................5C 16 (1C 76)
..................(off Barge Ho. St.)
Old Barracks W8..................3D 73
Old Barrack Yd.
SW1..................4B 20 (3C 74)
..................(not continuous)
Old Barrowfield E15..................5A 54
Old Bellgate Pl. E14..................4C 80
Old Bethnal Grn. Rd. E2.......2C 64
Old Billingsgate Mkt.
EC3..................5C 18 (1A 78)
..................(off Lwr. Thames St.)
Old Billingsgate Wlk.
EC3..................5D 19 (1A 78)
Old Bond St. W1.....5F 13 (1E 75)
Old Brewer's Yd.
WC2..................3D 15 (5A 62)
Old Brewery M. NW3..................1F 45
Old Brewery Way E17..................1B 38

Old Broad St. EC2...2C 18 (5F 63)
OLD BROAD STREET PRIVATE
MEDICAL CEN.....2D 19 (5A 64)
..................(off Old Broad St.)
Old Bromley Rd.
BR1: Broml..................5F 123
Old Brompton Rd. SW5........1C 86
Old Brompton Rd. SW7........1E 87
Old Bldgs. WC2.......2B 16 (5C 62)
..................(off Chancery La.)
Old Burlington St.
W1..................4F 13 (1E 75)
Oldbury Ct. E9..................2A 52
Oldbury Ho. W2..................4D 59
..................(off Harrow Rd.)
Oldbury Pl. W1..........4C 4 (4C 60)
Old Canal M. SE15..................1B 92
..................(off Trafalgar Av.)
Old Castle St. E1......1F 19 (5B 64)
Old Cavendish St.
W1..................2D 13 (5D 61)
Old Change Ct. EC4...3F 17 (5E 63)
..................(off Distaff La.)
Old Chapel Pl. SW9..................5C 90
Old Chelsea M. SW3..................2A 88
Old Chiswick Yd. W4..................2A 84
..................(off Pumping Sta. Rd.)
Old Church Rd. E1..................5F 65
Old Church St. SW3..................1F 87
Old Compton St. W1...4B 14 (1F 75)
Old Cople La. SE19..................5B 120
Old Ct. Ho. W8..................3D 73
..................(off Old Court Pl.)
Old Ct. Pl. W8..................3D 73
Old Curiosity Shop....2A 16 (5B 62)
..................(off Portsmouth St.)
Old Dairy N15..................1A 36
Old Dairy NW5..................3D 47
Old Dairy SW12..................1C 116
Old Dairy Ms. SW12...........2A 104
..................(off Tintern St.)
Old Devonshire Rd. SW12...5D 103
Old Dover Rd. SE3..................3C 96
Old Farm Cl. E6..................4F 55
Old Farm Cl. SW17..................2A 116
Old Farm La. SW19..................5D 115
Oldfield Gro. SE16..................5F 79
Oldfield Ho. W4..................1A 84
..................(off Devonshire St.)
Oldfield M. N6..................2E 33
Oldfield Rd. N16..................5A 36
Oldfield Rd. NW10..................4B 42
Oldfield Rd. SW19..................5A 114
Oldfield Rd. W3..................3B 70
Old Fish St. Hill EC4....4F 17 (1E 77)
..................(off Queen Victoria St.)
Old Fleet La. EC4.....2D 17 (5D 63)
OLD FORD..................5B 52
OLD FORD..................5C 52
Old Ford Rd. E2..................2E 65
Old Ford Rd. E3..................1A 66
Old Ford Trading Cen. E3 ...5C 52
..................(off Maverton Rd.)
Old Forge M. W12..................3D 71
Old Forge Rd. N19..................4F 33
Old Gloucester St.
WC1..................5E 7 (4A 62)
Old Goods Yd., The W2..........4E 59
Old Highwayman Pl. SW15 1D 113
Oldhill St. N16..................3C 36
Old Hospital Cl. SW12........1B 116
Old Ho. Cl. SW19..................5A 114
Old Jamaica Bus. Est. SE16 4B 78
Old Jamaica Rd. SE16..........4C 78

Old James St. SE15............1D 107
Old Jewry EC2............3B 18 (5F 63)
Old Kent Rd. SE1............5A 78
Old Kent Rd. SE15............2C 92
Old Library Ho. E3............1A 66
............(off Roman Rd.)
Old Mnr. Ct. NW8............1E 59
Old Manor Yd. SW5............5D 73
Old Mkt. Sq. E2............1F 11 (2B 64)
Old Marylebone Rd. NW1............4A 60
Old Mitre Ct. EC4............3C 16 (5C 62)
Old Montague St. E1............4C 64
Old Nichol St. E2............3F 11 (3B 64)
Old North St. WC1............5F 7 (4B 62)
Old Nursery Ct. E2............1B 64
............(off Dawson St.)
OLD OAK COMMON............4A 56
Old Oak Comn. La. NW10............4A 56
Old Oak Comn. La. W3............4A 56
Old Oak La. NW10............2A 56
Old Oak Rd. W3............1B 70
Old Operating Theatre Mus. &
Herb Garret, The...2C 26 (2F 77)
............(off St Thomas St.)
Old Orchard, The NW3............1B 46
Old Palace Yd. SW1...5D 23 (4A 76)
Old Paradise St. SE11............5B 76
Old Pk. Av. SW12............4C 102
Old Pk. La. W1............2C 20 (2D 75)
Old Pearson St. SE10............3D 95
Old Police Sta., The SW17...2B 116
Old Post Office La. SE3............1D 111
Old Pye St. SW1............5B 22 (4F 75)
Old Pye St. SW1...5B 22 (4F 75)
............(off Old Pye St.)
Old Quebec St. W1...3A 12 (5B 60)
............(not continuous)
Old Queen St. SW1...4C 22 (3F 75)
Old Red Lion Theatre.1C 8 (1C 62)
............(off St John St.)
Oldridge Rd. SW12............5C 102
Old Rd. SE13............2A 110
Old Royal Free Pl. N1............5C 48
Old Royal Free Sq. N1............5C 48
Old Royal Naval College............1F 95
Old School, The WC1...5A 8 (4B 62)
............(off Princeton St.)
Old School Cl. SE10............4A 82
Old School Cres. E7............3C 54
Old School Sq. E14............5C 66
............(off Pelling St.)
Old Seacoal La. EC4...2D 17 (5D 63)
Old Sessions Ho., The
EC1............4C 8 (3D 63)
Old Sth. Lambeth Rd. SW8.. 3A 90
Old Spitalfields Market
............5F 11 (4B 64)
Old Sq. WC2............2A 16 (5B 62)
Old Stable M. N5............5E 35
Old Stables Ct. SE5............4E 91
............(off Camberwell New Rd.)
Old Station Ho. SE17............1E 91
Old Sta. Way SW4............1F 103
............(off Voltaire Rd.)
Old Station Way SW4............1F 103
............(off Voltaire Road)
Oldstead Rd. BR1: Broml....6B 123
Old St. E13............1D 69
Old St. EC1............3F 9 (3E 63)
OLD STREET............2B 10 (3F 63)
Old Street Station (Rail &
Underground)............2C 10 (3F 63)
Old St. Yd. EC1............3B 10 (3F 63)
............(off City Rd.)

Old Sun Wharf E14............1A 80
............(off Narrow St.)
Old Swan Wharf SW11............4F 87
Old Theatre Ct. SE1 .. 1A 26 (2F 77)
............(off Porter St.)
Old Town SW4............1E 103
Old Town Hall Apts.
SE16............5F 27 (4B 78)
Old Vic Theatre, The
............3C 24 (3C 76)
............(off The Cut)
Old Willow Cl. E3............2C 66
Old Woolwich Rd. SE10............2F 95
Old York Rd. SW18............3D 101
Oleander Ho. SE15............1B 92
O'Leary Sq. E1............4E 65
Olga St. E3............1A 66
Olinda Rd. N16............1B 36
Oliphant St. E14............1E 81
Oliphant St. W10............2F 57
Olive Blythe Ho. W10............3A 58
............(off Ladbroke Gro.)
Olive Ct. E5............4E 37
............(off Woodmill Rd.)
Olive Ct. N1............5C 48
............(off Liverpool Rd.)
Olive Haines Lodge SW15....3B 100
Olive Ho. EC1............3C 8 (3C 62)
............(off Bowling Grn. La.)
Oliver Goldsmith Est. SE15.....4C 92
Oliver Ho. SE14............3B 94
............(off New Cross Rd.)
Oliver Ho. SE16............3C 78
............(off George Row)
Oliver Ho. SW8............3A 90
............(off Wyvil Rd.)
Oliver M. SE15............5C 92
Olive Rd. E13............2E 69
Olive Rd. NW2............1D 43
Oliver Rd. E10............4D 39
Olivers Row N8............1A 34
Olivers Wharf E1............2D 79
............(off Wapping High St.)
Olivers Yd. EC1............3C 10 (3F 63)
Olive Tree Ho. SE15............2E 93
............(off Sharratt St.)
Olivette St. SW15............1F 99
Olive Waite Ho. NW6............4C 44
Olivier Theatre............1A 24 (2C 76)
............(within National Theatre)
Ollerton Grn. E3............5B 52
Ollgar Cl. W12............2B 70
Olliffe St. E14............4E 81
Olmar St. SE1............2C 92
Olney Ho. NW8............3A 60
............(off Tresham Cres.)
Olney Rd. SE17............2D 91
............(not continuous)
Olympia............4A 72
Olympia M. W14............1D 73
Olympian Ct. E14............5C 80
............(off Homer Dr.)
Olympian Ct. E3............1C 66
............(off Wick La.)
Olympian Way SE10............2A 82
............(not continuous)
Olympia Way W14............4A 72
Olympic Ho. W10............1B 50
Olympic M. SW18............3E 101
Olympic Pk. Av. E20............2D 53
Olympus Sq. E5............5C 36
O'Mahoney Ct. SW17............3E 115
Oman Av. NW2............1E 43
Oman Way E14............5A 66

O'Meara St. SE1............2A 26 (2E 77)
Omega Cl. E14............4D 81
Omega Ho. SW10............3E 87
............(off King's Rd.)
Omega PL. N1............1E 7 (1A 62)
............(off Caledonian Rd.)
Omega St. SE14............4C 94
Omega Works E3............4C 52
Ommaney Rd. SE14............4F 93
Omnium Ct. WC1............5F 7 (4B 62)
............(off Princeton St.)
Ondine Rd. SE15............2B 106
One Blackfriars SE1 .. 1D 25 (2D 77)
............(off Rennie St.)
One Casson Sq. SE1 2A 24 (2B 76)
............(off Casson Sq.)
Onedin Ct. E1............1C 78
............(off Ensign St.)
Onega Ga. SE16............4A 80
One Hyde Pk. SW1 ..3A 20 (3B 74)
O'Neill Ho. NW8............1A 60
............(off Cochrane St.)
One Lillie Sq. SW6............2C 86
One Owen St. EC1 ....1D 9 (1D 63)
............(off Goswell St.)
One Southbank Pl.
SE1............3A 24 (3B 76)
............(off York Rd.)
One The Elephant SE1............5D 77
............(off Brook Dr.)
One Tree Cl. SE23............4E 107
One Tree Hill Local Nature
Reserve............4E 107
Ongar Rd. SW6............2C 86
Onra Rd. E17............2C 38
Onslow Cl. W10............2B 58
Onslow Cres. SW10............1E 87
............(off Drayton Gdns.)
Onslow Cres. SW7............5F 73
Onslow Gdns. SW7............5F 73
Onslow M. E. SW7............5F 73
Onslow M. W. SW7............5F 73
Onslow Sq. SW7............5F 73
Onslow St. EC1 ....4C 8 (3C 62)
Ontario Point SE16............3E 79
............(off Surrey Quays Rd.)
Ontario St. SE1....5E 25 (4D 77)
Ontario Twr. E14............1F 81
Ontario Way E14............1C 80
............(not continuous)
Onyx M. E15............3B 54
Opal Apts. W7............5C 58
............(off Hereford Rd.)
Opal Cl. E16............5F 69
Opal Ct. SE15............1E 53
Opal M. NW6............5B 44
Opal St. SE11............1D 91
Open Air Stage............3A 32
Openview SW18............1E 115
............(off Wedmore St.)
Opera Ct. N19............5F 33
............(off Wedmore St.)
Ophelia Gdns. NW2............5A 30
Ophelia Ho. W6............1F 85
............(off Fulham Pal. Rd.)
Ophir Ter. SE15............4C 92
Opie Ho. NW8............1A 60
............(off Townshend Est.)
Oppenheim Rd. SE13............5E 95
Oppidan Apts. NW6............4C 44
............(off Netherwood St.)
Oppidans Rd. NW3............4B 46
Orange Gro. E11............5A 40
Orange Pl. SE16............4E 79
Orangery Gallery, The............3B 72
Orange St. WC2............5C 14 (1F 75)

Orange Tree Ct. SE5............ 3A 92
....................................(off Havil St.)
Orange Yd. W1 ....3C 14 (5F 61)
.................................(off Manette Ct.)
Oransay Rd. N1.........................3E 49
Oratory La. SW3.......................1F 87
Orbain Rd. SW6........................3A 86
Orbel St. SE17.......................... 4A 88
Orbis Wharf SW11.................1F 101
Orb St. SE17...............................5F 77
Orchard, The NW11................. 1C 30
Orchard, The SE3..................... 5F 95
Orchard, The W4.......................5A 70
Orchard Bus. Cen. SE26 ...5B 122
Orchard Cl. N1..........................4E 49
Orchard Cl. NW2 ....5C 28
Orchard Cl. SE23.....................4E 107
Orchard Cl. W10....................... 4B 58
Orchard Cl. E10........................ 3D 39
Orchard Ct. SE26 ....4B 122
Orchard Ct. W1 ....2B 12 (5C 60)
............................(off Fitzhardinge St.)
Orchard Dr. SE3........................ 5F 95
Orchard Hill SE13.....................5D 95
Orchard Ho. SE16.....................4E 79
Orchard Ho. SE5.......................4E 91
...................................(off County Gro.)
Orchard Ho. SW6......................3B 86
..................................(off Varna Rd.)
Orchard Ho. W12......................2C 70
Orchard Mead Ho. NW2 ....4C 30
Orchard M. N1...........................4F 49
Orchard M. N6 ....2D 33
Orchard M. SW17....................3E 115
Orchard Pl. E14......................... 1A 82
..................................(not continuous)
Orchard Pl. E5.......................... 2D 51
Orchard Pl. W4.........................5A 70
Orchard Rd. N6..........................2D 33
Orchard Rd. SE3 ....5A 96
Orchardson Ho. NW8...............3F 59
..........................(off Orchardson St.)
Orchardson St. NW8...............3F 59
Orchard Sq. SW1......................1C 88
Orchard Sq. W14...................... 1B 86
Orchard Sq. W1.........3B 12 (5C 60)
Orchard Studios W6................5F 71
....................................(off Brook Grn.)
Orchard Ter. NW10..................1B 42
Orchard Wharf E14..................1A 82
..................................(off Orchard Pl.)
Orchid Cl. E6..............................4F 69
Orchid Cl. SE13......................3F 109
Orchid Cl. W12..........................1C 70
Orde Hall St. WC1 .....4F 7 (3B 62)
Ordell Cl. E3.............................. 1B 66
..................................(off Ordell Rd.)
Ordell Rd. E3............................. 1B 66
Ordnance Cres. SE10..............3A 82
Ordnance Hill NW8..................5F 45
Ordnance M. NW8....................1F 59
Ordnance Rd. E16....................4B 68
Oregano Dr. E14.......................5E 67
Oregon Bldg. SE13..................4D 95
..............................(off Deal's Gateway)
Oreilly St. SE1...........................5B 78
..................................(off Willow Wlk.)
Orestes M. NW6.......................2C 44
Orford Cl. SE27 ....2D 119
Orford Rd. E17..........................1C 38
Orford Rd. SE6.........................3D 123
Oriana Ho. E10..........................4D 39
............................(off Grange Pk. Rd.)
Oriana Ho. E14.........................1B 80
..................................(off Victory Pl.)

Oriel Ct. NW3............................1E 45
Oriel Dr. SW13..........................2E 85
Oriel Ho. NW6..........................5C 44
..................................(off Priory Pk. Rd.)
Oriel Pl. NW3............................1E 45
..................................(off Heath St.)
Oriel Rd. E9...............................3F 51
Oriens M. E20............................2E 53
Oriental Rd. E16.......................2F 83
Oriental St. E14........................1C 80
..................................(off Pennyfields)
Orient Ho. SW6.........................4E 87
..................................(off Station Ct.)
Orient Pk. E10.........................4C 38
Orient St. SE11.........................5D 77
Orient Way E10.........................3A 38
Orient Way E5...........................5F 37
Orient Wharf E1 ....2D 79
..............................(off Wapping High St.)
Orion E14...................................5C 80
..................................(off Crews St.)
Orion Bus. Cen. SE14.............1F 93
Orion Ho. E1..............................3D 65
..................................(off Coventry Rd.)
Orkney Ct. E1............................4A 66
..................................(off Ocean Est.)
Orkney Ho. N1...........................5B 48
..................................(off Bemerton Est.)
Orkney St. SW11......................5C 88
Orlando Rd. SW4....................1E 103
Orleston M. N7..........................3C 48
Orleston Rd. N7........................3C 48
Orlop St. SE10..........................1A 96
Ormanton Rd. SE26 ....4C 120
Orme Ct. W2..............................1D 73
Orme Ct. M. W2........................1D 73
..................................(off Orme La.)
Orme Ho. E8.............................5B 50
Orme La. W2.............................1D 73
Ormeley Rd. SW12.................1D 117
Orme Sq. W2.............................1D 73
Ormiston Gro. W12..................2D 71
Ormiston Rd. SE10..................1C 96
Ormond Cl. WC1 ....5E 7 (4A 62)
Ormonde Ct. NW8 ....5B 46
..................................(off St Edmund's Cl.)
Ormonde Ct. SW15..................2E 99
Ormonde Ga. SW3...................1B 88
Ormonde Mans. WC1 ....5E 7 (4A 62)
..........................(off Southampton Row)
Ormonde Pl. SW1.....................5C 74
Ormonde Ter. NW8..................5B 46
Ormond Ho. N16.......................4F 35
Ormond M. WC1 ......4E 7 (3A 62)
Ormond Rd. N19........................3A 34
Ormond Yd. SW1 ...1A 22 (2E 75)
Ormrod Ct. W11........................5A 58
................................(off Westbourne Pk. Rd.)
Ormsby Lodge W4 ....4A 70
Ormsby Pl. N16.........................5B 36
Ormsby St. E2............................1B 64
Ormside St. SE15......................2E 93
Ornan Rd. NW3.........................2A 46
Orpen Ho. SW5.........................5C 72
..................................(off Trebovir Rd.)
Orpen Wlk. N16.........................5A 36
Orpheus Ho. W10 ....3B 58
..................................(off Harrow Rd.)
Orpheus St. SE5.......................4F 91
Orsett M. W2.............................5D 59
..................................(not continuous)
Orsett St. SE11.........................1B 90
Orsett Ter. W2..........................5D 59
Orsman Rd. N1..........................5A 50

Orton St. E1...............................2C 78
Orville Rd. SW11......................5F 87
Orwell Cl. E8............................. 5C 50
..................................(off Pownall Rd.)
Orwell Ct. N5.............................1E 49
Orwell Ct. SE13.......................1D 109
Orwell Ct. SW17......................3F 115
..................................(off Grosvenor Way)
Orwell Rd. E13..........................1E 69
Osbaldeston Rd. N16...............4C 36
Osberton Rd. SE12..................3C 110
Osbert St. SW1.........................5F 75
Osborn Cl. E8............................5C 50
Osborne Ct. E10........................2D 39
Osborne Ho. E16.......................2C 82
..................................(off Wesley Av.)
Osborne Rd. E10.......................4D 39
Osborne Rd. E7.........................2D 55
Osborne Rd. E9.........................3B 52
Osborne Rd. N4.........................3C 34
Osborne Rd. NW2.....................3D 43
Osborne Ter. SW17................5B 116
..................................(off Church La.)
Osborn La. SE23.......................5A 108
Osborn St. E1............................4B 64
Osborn Ter. SE3.......................2B 110
Oscar Ct. SE16.........................3A 80
Oscar Faber Pl. N1..................4A 50
Oscar St. SE8............................5C 94
..................................(not continuous)
Oseney Cres. NW5 ....2E 47
Osier Ct. E1...............................3F 65
..................................(off Osier St.)
Osier Ho. SE16.........................4A 80
Osier La. SE10..........................4B 82
Osier M. W4..............................2A 84
Osiers Rd. SW18 ....2C 100
Osiers Twr. SW18 ....2C 100
..................................(off Enterprise Way)
Osier St. E1...............................3E 65
Osier Way E10..........................5D 39
Oslac Rd. SE6..........................5D 123
Oslo Ct. NW8.............................1A 60
..................................(off Prince Albert Rd.)
Oslo Ho. E9...............................3B 52
..................................(off Felstead St.)
Oslo Ho. SE5.............................5E 91
..................................(off Carew St.)
Oslo Sq. SE16...........................4A 80
Oslo Twr. SE8............................5A 80
..................................(off Naomi St.)
Osman Cl. N15..........................1F 35
Osmani Youth Cen..................4C 64
Osman Rd. W6..........................4E 71
Osmington Ho. SW8 ....3B 90
..................................(off Dorset Rd.)
Osmunda Ct. E1........................5C 64
..................................(off Myrdle St.)
Osmund St. W12.......................4A 56
Osnaburgh St. NW1: Lon
  Euston St..........................3E 5 (3D 61)
Osnaburgh St. NW1: Lon
  Robert St........................2E 5 (2D 61)
..................................(off Robert St.)
Osnaburgh Ter. NW1...3E 5 (3D 61)
Osprey Cl. E6.............................4F 69
Osprey Ct. E1............................1C 78
..................................(off Star Pl.)
Osprey Est. SE16.......................5F 79
Osprey Ho. E14.........................1A 80
..................................(off Victory Pl.)
Osprey Ho. SE1........................1D 93
..................................(off Lynton Rd.)
Ospringe Ho. SE1 .....3C 24 (3C 76)
..................................(off Wootton St.)

Ospringe Rd. NW5..............1E 47
Osram Ct. W6.....................4E 71
Osric Path N1....................1A 64
Ossel Ct. SE10..................5A 82
Ossian M. N4.....................2B 34
Ossian Rd. N4....................2B 34
Ossington Bldgs. W1...5B 4 (4C 60)
Ossington Cl. W2.................1C 72
Ossington St. W2................1C 72
Ossory Rd. SE1..................2C 92
Ossulston St. NW1...1B 6 (1F 61)
Ostade Rd. SW2.................5B 104
Ostend Pl. SE1...................5E 77
Osten M. SW7....................4D 73
Osterley Ho. E14................5D 67
..........................(off Giraud St.)
Osterley Rd. N16................1A 50
Ostro Twr. E14..................3D 81
Oswald Bldg. SW11.............2D 89
Oswald's Mead E9.............1A 52
Oswald St. E5...................5F 37
Oswald Ter. SW2...............5E 29
Osward Rd. SW17..............2B 116
Oswell Ho. E1....................2D 79
.........................(off Farthing Flds.)
Oswin St. SE11..................5D 77
Oswyth Rd. SE5.................5A 92
Otford Cres. SE4...............4B 108
Otford Ho. SE1........4C 26 (3F 77)
.............................(off Staple St.)
Otford Ho. SE15................2E 93
.........................(off Lovelinch Cl.)
Othello Cl. SE11.................1D 91
Other Place Theatre, The....5F 21
(4E 75)................(off Palace St.)
Otley Ho. N5.....................5C 34
Otley Rd. E16...................5E 68
Otley Ter. E5....................5F 37
Ottawa Ho. SE16...............1F 93
.......................(off Province Dr.)
Ottaway St. E5..................5C 36
Otterburn Ho. SE5..............3E 91
..............................(off Sultan St.)
Otterburn St. SW17..........5B 116
Otter Cl. E15....................5C 53
Otterden St. SE6...............4C 122
Otterden Ter. SE1.............5B 78
.............................(off Lynton Rd.)
Ottley Dr. SE3..................2E 111
Otto Cl. SE26....................3D 121
Otto St. SE17...................2D 91
Ott's Yd. N19....................1E 47
.........................(off Southcote Rd.)
Oulton Cl. E5....................4E 37
Our Lady's Cl. SE19..........5F 119
Ouseley Rd. SW12............1B 116
Outer Circ. NW1...............1A 60
Outgate Rd. NW10.............4B 42
Outram Pl. N1....................5A 48
Outram Rd. E6..................5F 55
Outwich St. EC3.....2E 19 (5A 64)
.........................(off Camomile St.)
Outwood Ho. SW2.............5B 104
.........................(off Deepdene Gdns.)
Oval Surrey CCC, The........2B 90
Oval, The E1.....................1D 65
Oval Mans. SE11...............2B 90
Oval Pl. SW8.....................3B 90
Oval Rd. NW1...................5C 46
Oval Station (Underground)...2C 90
Oval Way SE11..................1B 90
Ovanna M. N1...................3A 50
Overbrae BR3: Beck..........5C 122
Overbury Rd. N15..............1F 35
Overbury St. E5.................1F 51

Overcliff Rd. SE13.............1C 108
Overdown Rd. SE6.............4C 122
Overhill Rd. SE22..............5C 106
Overlea Rd. E5..................2C 36
Oversley Ho. W2................4C 58
.........................(off Alfred Rd.)
Overstone Ho. E14.............5C 66
.........................(off E. India Dock Rd.)
Overstone Rd. W6..............4E 71
Overstrand Mans. SW11....4B 88
Overton Cl. E11.................2C 40
Overton Dr. E11.................2C 40
Overton Ho. SW15..............5B 98
.........................(off Tangley Gro.)
Overton Rd. E10.................3A 38
Overton Rd. SW9................5C 90
Overy Ho. SE1..........4D 25 (3D 77)
Ovex Cl. E14......................3E 81
Ovington Ct. SW3..............4A 74
.........................(off Brompton Rd.)
Ovington Gdns. SW3...........4A 74
Ovington M. SW3...............4A 74
.........................(off Ovington Gdns.)
Ovington Sq. SW3..............4A 74
Ovington St. SW3..............5A 74
Owen Mans. W14................2A 86
.........................(off Queen's Club Gdns.)
Owens M. E11....................4A 40
Owen's Row EC1.......1D 9 (2D 63)
Owen St. EC1..........1D 9 (1D 63)
Owens Way SE23...............5A 108
Owgan Cl. SE5..................3F 91
Oxberry Av. SW6...............5A 86
Oxborough Ho. SW18........2E 101
.........................(off Eltringham St.)
Oxendon St. SW1....5B 14 (1F 75)
Oxenford St. SE15.............1B 106
Oxenham Ho. SE8..............2C 94
.........................(off Benbow St.)
Oxenholme NW1......1A 6 (1E 61)
.........................(off Hampstead Rd.)
Oxestall's Rd. SE8..............1A 94
Oxford & Cambridge Mans.
NW1.............................4A 60
.........................(off Old Marylebone Rd.)
Oxford Cir. W1....3F 13 (5E 61)
.............................(off Oxford St.)
Oxford Cir. Av. W1...3F 13 (5E 61)
Oxford Circus Station
(Underground)....2F 13 (5E 61)
Oxford Ct. EC4.......4B 18 (1F 77)
.........................(off Cannon St.)
Oxford Ct. W9....................4C 58
.........................(off Elmfield Way)
Oxford Dr. SE1.......2D 27 (2A 78)
Oxford Gdns. W10.............5E 57
Oxford Ga. W6..................5F 71
Oxford Ho. E3...................4B 66
.........................(off William Whiffin Sq.)
Oxford Ho. N4..................1C 58
.............................(off Oxford Rd.)
Oxford Pl. NW10...............5A 28
.............................(off Press Rd.)
Oxford Rd. E15.................3F 53
.........................(not continuous)
Oxford Rd. N4..................3C 34
Oxford Rd. NW6................1C 58
Oxford Rd. SE19...............5F 119
Oxford Rd. SW15..............2A 100
Oxford Sq. W2..................5A 60
Oxford St. W1......3A 12 (5C 60)
Oxford Ter. NW6...............1D 59
.............................(off Oxford Rd.)
Oxgate Cen. NW2..............4D 29
Oxgate Ct. NW2................4C 28

Oxgate Ct. Pde. NW2.........4C 28
Oxgate Gdns. NW2............5D 29
Oxgate La. NW2................4D 29
Oxgate Pde. NW2..............4C 28
Oxley Cl. SE1....................1B 92
Oxley Sq. E3.....................3D 67
.........................(off Truman Wlk.)
Oxleys Rd. NW2................5D 28
Oxonian St. SE22..............2B 106
Oxo Tower Wharf....5C 16 (1C 76)
Oxygen, The E16................1C 82
Oystercatcher Cl. E16........5D 69
Oyster Ct. SE17................5E 77
.........................(off Crampton St.)
Oyster M. E7.....................3F 55
Oyster Row E1..................5E 65
Oyster Wharf SW11...........5F 87
Ozolins Way E16................5C 68

P

Pablo Neruda Cl. SE24.......2D 105
Pace Pl. E1......................5D 65
Pacific Bldg. E15...............2F 53
.........................(off Property Row)
Pacific Ct. E1....................4E 65
Pacific Ho. E1...................3F 65
.............................(off Ernest St.)
Pacific M. SW9..................2C 104
Pacific Rd. E16.................5C 68
Pacific Wharf SE16............2F 79
Packenham Ho. E2............2B 64
.........................(off Wellington Row)
Packenham Ho. W10.........1F 71
.........................(off Shalfleet Dr.)
Packington Sq. N1.............5E 49
.........................(not continuous)
Packington St. N1..............5D 49
Padbury SE17...................1A 92
.............................(off Bagshot St.)
Padbury Ct. E2.......2F 11 (2B 64)
Padbury Ho. NW8..............3A 60
.........................(off Tresham Cres.)
Paddenswick Rd. W6.........4C 70
PADDINGTON.....................5F 59
Paddington Gdns. W2........4F 59
Paddington Grn. W2...........4F 59
Paddington Sports Club......3D 59
Paddington Station (Rail,
Underground & Crossrail)...5F 59
Paddington St. W1...5B 4 (4C 60)
Paddock Cl. SE26..............4F 121
Paddock Cl. SE3................5C 96
Paddock Rd. NW2..............5C 28
Paddock Way SW15...........5E 99
Padfield Rd. SE5...............1E 105
Padstone Ho. E3................2D 67
.............................(off Talwin St.)
Padstow Ho. E14...............1B 80
.........................(off Three Colt St.)
Pageant St. SW8...............4D 89
Pageant Cres. SE16...........2A 80
Pageantmaster Ct.
EC4.........................3D 17 (5D 63)
.............................(off Ludgate Hill)
Page Grn. Rd. N15.............1C 36
Page Grn. Ter. N15............1B 36
Page Ho. SE10..................2E 95
.............................(off Welland St.)
Page M. SW11...................5C 88
Page St. SW1....................5F 75
Page's Wlk. SE1................5A 78
Pages Yd. W4....................2B 84
Paget Ho. E2.....................1E 65
.............................(off Bishop's Way)

Paget Rd. N16 ....3F 35
Paget St. EC1 ....1D 9 (2D 63)
Pagham Ho. W10 ....3E 57
............(off Sutton Way)
Pagnell St. SE14 ....3B 94
Pagoda Gdns. SE3 ....5F 95
Pagoda Gro. SE27 ....2E 119
Paignton Rd. N15 ....1A 36
Painsthorpe Rd. N16 ....5A 36
Painted Hall Greenwich 2E 95
Painters M. SE16 ....5C 78
Pakefield M. SW22 ....1B 118
Pakeman Ho. SE1 ...3E 25 (3D 77)
............(off Surrey Row)
Pakeman St. N7 ....5B 34
Pakenham Cl. SW12 ....1C 116
Pakenham St. WC1 ...2A 8 (2B 62)
Pakington Ho. SW9 ....5A 90
............(off Stockwell Gdns. Est.)
Palace Av. W8 ....3D 73
Palace Cl. E9 ....3B 52
Palace Ct. NW3 ....2C 46
Palace Ct. W2 ....1D 73
............(not continuous)
Palace Ct. W8 ....2D 73
Palace Gdns. M. W8 ....2D 73
Palace Gdns. Ter. W8 ......2C 72
Palace Ga. W8 ....3E 73
Palace Grn. W8 ....2D 73
Palace Mans. W14 ....5A 72
............(off Hammersmith Rd.)
Palace M. SW1 ....5C 74
............(off Eaton Ter.)
Palace M. SW6 ....3B 86
Palace Pl. SW1 ....5F 21 (4E 75)
Palace Pl. Mans. W8 ....3D 73
............(off Kensington Ct.)
Palace Rd. N8 ....1F 33
............(not continuous)
Palace Rd. SW2 ....1B 118
Palace St. SW1 ....5F 21 (4E 75)
Palace Superbowl 2D 73
(within Elephant & Castle Shop. Cen.)
Palace Theatre London
............3C 14 (5F 61)
............(off Shaftesbury Av.)
Palace Vw. SE12 ....2C 124
Palace Wharf W6 ....3E 85
............(off Rainville Rd.)
Palamos Rd. E10 ....3C 38
Palatine Av. N16 ....1A 50
Palatine Rd. N16 ....1A 50
Palazzo Apts. N1 ....4A 50
............(off Ardleigh Rd.)
Palemead Cl. SW6 ....4F 85
Palermo Rd. NW10 ....1C 56
Palestra Ho. SE1 ...2D 25 (2D 77)
............(off Blackfriars Rd.)
Palewell Comn. Dr. SW14 ...3A 98
Palfrey Pl. SW8 ....3B 90
Palgrave Gdns. NW1 ....3A 60
Palgrave Ho. SE5 ....3E 91
............(off Wyndham Est.)
Palgrave Rd. W12 ....4B 70
Palissy St. E2 ....2F 11 (2B 64)
............(not continuous)
Palladian Gdns. W4 ....2A 84
Palladino Ho. SW17 ....5A 116
............(off Laurel Cl.)
Palladio Ct. SW18 ....4D 101
............(off Mapleton Rd.)
Palladium Ct. E8 ....4B 50
............(off Queensbridge Rd.)
Pallant Ho. SE1 ...5C 26 (4F 77)
............(off Tabard St.)
Pallet Way SE18 ....4F 97

Palliser Rd. W14 ....1A 86
............(off Palliser Rd.)
Palliser Ho. E1 ....3F 65
............(off Ernest St.)
Palliser Ho. SE10 ....2F 95
............(off Trafalgar Rd.)
Palliser Rd. W14 ....1A 86
Palliser Ter. SW15 ....3B 112
Pall Mall SW1 .....2A 22 (2E 75)
Pall Mall E. SW1 ...1C 22 (2F 75)
Pall Mall Pl. SW1 ..2A 22 (2E 75)
............(off Pall Mall)
Palm Cl. E10 ....5D 39
Palm Ct. SE15 ....3B 92
............(off Garnies Cl.)
Palmer Ho. SE14 ....3F 93
............(off Lubbock St.)
Palmer Pl. N7 ....2C 48
Palmer Rd. E13 ....3D 69
Palmer Rd. SW11 ....3D 89
Palmer's Rd. E2 ....1F 65
Palmerston Ct. E3 ....1F 65
............(off Old Ford Rd.)
Palmerston Ho.
SE1 ....4B 24 (3C 76)
............(off Westminster Bri. Rd.)
Palmerston Ho. W8 ....2C 72
............(off Kensington Pl.)
Palmerston Mans. W14 ....2A 86
............(off Queen's Club Gdns.)
Palmerston Rd. E7 ....3D 55
Palmerston Rd. NW6 ......4B 44
............(not continuous)
Palmerston Way SW8 ......3D 89
Palmer St. SW1 ....5B 22 (4F 75)
............(not continuous)
Palyn Ho. EC1 ....2A 10 (2E 63)
............(off Radnor St.)
Pamela St. E8 ....5D 50
Panama Ho. E1 ....4F 65
............(off Beaumont Sq.)
Pancras La. EC4 ...3A 18 (5E 63)
Pancras Rd. N1 ....1D 7 (1A 62)
Pancras Rd. NW1 ....1F 61
Pancras Sq. N1 ....1A 62
Pancras Square Leisure Cen.
............1A 62
Pancras Way E3 ....1C 66
Pandangle Ho. E8 ....5B 50
............(off Kingsland Rd.)
Pandian Way NW1 ....3F 47
Pandora Ct. E16 ....4C 68
............(off Robertson Rd.)
Pandora Rd. NW6 ....3C 44
Pangbourne NW1 ...2F 5 (2E 61)
............(off Stanhope St.)
Pangbourne Av. W10 ......4E 57
Pankhurst Av. E16 ....2D 83
Pankhurst Av. E3 ....4D 67
Pankhurst Cl. SE14 ....3F 93
Pankhurst Ho. W12 ....5D 57
Panmure Cl. N5 ....1D 49
Panmure Rd. SE26 ....3D 121
Panmure Rd. SE26 ....3D 121
Panorama Ct. N6 ....1E 33
Panoramic Twr. E14 ......5D 67
............(off Burcham St.)
Pan Peninsula Sq. E14 .....3D 81
Pansy Gdns. W12 ....1C 70
Panton St. SW1 ....5B 14 (1F 75)
Panyer All. EC1 ...2F 17 (5E 63)
Paper Bldgs. EC4 ...4C 16 (1C 76)
............(off King's Bench Wlk.)
Paper Mill Wharf E14 ......1A 80

Papillons Wlk. SE3 ....5C 96
Papworth Gdns. N7 ....2B 48
Papworth Way SW2 ....5C 104
Papyrus Ho. N1 ......1F 9 (2E 63)
............(off Wells Pk. Rd.)
Parade, The SE26 ....3D 121
Parade, The SE4 ....5B 94
............(off Up. Brockley Rd.)
Parade, The SW11 ....3B 88
Parade Mans. NW4 ....1D 29
Parade M. SE27 ....2D 119
Paradise Gdns. W6 ....5D 71
Paradise Pas. N7 ....2C 48
Paradise Rd. SW4 ....5A 90
Paradise Row E2 ....2D 65
Paradise St. SE16 ....3D 79
Paradise Wlk. SW3 ....2B 88
Paragon, The SE3 ....5B 96
Paragon Cl. E16 ....5C 68
Paragon M. SE1 ....5F 77
Paragon M. SW8 ....2B 90
Paragon Pl. SE3 ....5B 96
Paragon Rd. E9 ....3E 51
Paramount Bldg.
EC1 ....3D 9 (3D 63)
............(off St John St.)
Paramount Ct. WC1 ...4A 6 (3E 61)
............(off University St.)
Parbury Rd. SE23 ....4A 108
Pardoe Rd. E10 ....2D 39
Pardoner Ho. SE1 ...5C 26 (4F 77)
............(off Pardoner St.)
Pardoner St. SE1 ...5C 26 (4F 77)
............(not continuous)
Pardon St. EC1 ....3E 9 (3D 63)
Parfett St. E1 ....4C 64
............(not continuous)
Parfitt Cl. NW3 ....3E 31
Parfrey St. W6 ....2E 85
Paris Corte SE13 ....1D 109
............(off Loampit Va.)
Paris Gdn. SE1 ....1D 25 (2D 77)
Paris Ho. E2 ....1D 65
............(off Old Bethnal Grn. Rd.)
Park, The N6 ....1C 32
Park, The NW11 ....3D 31
Park, The SE23 ....1E 121
Park App. SE16 ....4D 79
Park Av. NW10: Lon
Park Av. Nth. 2D 43
Park Av. E15 ....3A 54
Park Av. NW11 ....3D 31
Park Av. NW2 ....3D 43
Park Av. Nth. NW10 ......2D 43
Park Central SE17 ....5E 77
Park Central Bldg. E3 .....1C 66
............(off Talwin St.)
Park Cl. E9 ....5E 51
Park Cl. NW2 ....5D 29
Park Cl. SW1 ....3B 74
Park Cl. W14 ....4B 72
Park Cl. W4 ....2A 84
Park Club Acton, The 2A 70
Park Ct. E17 ....1D 39
Park Ct. SE21 ....3E 119
Park Ct. SE26 ....5D 121
Park Ct. SW11 ....4D 89
Park Ct. W6 ....5C 70
Park Cres. W1 ....4D 5 (3D 61)
Park Cres. M. E. W1 ...4E 5 (3D 61)
Park Cres. M. W.
W1 ....4D 5 (3D 61)
Parkcroft Rd. SE12 ......5B 110
Park Dr. E14 ....2E 81
Park Dr. NW11 ....3D 31
Park Dr. SW14 ....3A 98

Park Dwellings – Parolles Rd.

Park Dwellings NW3........2B 46
Park E. Bldg. E3.............1C 66
.............(off Fairfield Rd.)
Park End NW3.................1A 46
Parker Bldg. SE16...........4C 78
.............(off Old Jamaica Rd.)
Parker Cl. E16................2F 83
Parker Ct. N1.................5E 49
.............(off Basire St.)
Parker Ho. E14...............3C 80
.............(off Admirals Way)
Parker M. WC2......2E 15 (5A 62)
Parke Rd. SW13..............4C 84
Parkers Row SE1.............3C 78
Parker St. E16................2F 83
Parker St. WC2......2E 15 (5A 62)
Parkes St. E20................3C 52
Parkfield Av. SW14..........2A 98
Parkfield Ct. SE14...........4B 94
.............(off Parkfield Rd.)
Parkfield Ind. Est. SW11...5C 88
Parkfield Rd. NW10..........4D 43
Parkfield Rd. SE14..........4B 94
Parkfield Rd. SW4...........4F 103
.............(not continuous)
Parkfields SW15..............2E 99
Parkfields Av. NW9..........3A 28
Parkfield St. N1..............1C 62
Park Gdns. E10...............3C 38
Parkgate N1...................5F 49
.............(off Southgate Rd.)
Parkgate SE3.................1B 110
Parkgate M. N6...............5F 47
Parkgate Rd. SW11..........3A 88
Park Gro. E15.................5C 54
Park Gro. Rd. E11...........4A 40
Park Hall SE10................3F 95
.............(off Croom's Hill)
Park Hall Rd. SE21..........3E 119
Park Hall Trad. Est. SE21..3E 119
Parkham St. SW11...........4A 88
Park Hgts. Ct. E14...........5B 66
.............(off Wharf La.)
Park Hill SE23................2D 121
Park Hill SW4.................3F 103
Park Hill Ct. SW17..........3B 116
Parkhill Rd. NW3.............2B 46
Parkhill Wlk. NW3............2B 46
Parkholme Rd. E8............3C 50
Park Ho. E9...................4E 51
.............(off Shore Rd.)
Park Ho. SE5..................4F 91
.............(off Camberwell Grn.)
Park Ho. W1.........3B 12 (5C 60)
.............(off Oxford St.)
Park Ho. Pas. N6.............2C 32
Parkhouse St. SE5...........3F 91
Parkhurst Ct. N7..............1A 48
Parkhurst Rd. N7.............1A 48
Parkinson Ct. N1......2C 10 (2F 63)
.............(off Charles Sq. Est.)
Parkinson Ho. E9.............4E 51
.............(off Frampton Pk. Rd.)
Parkinson Ho. SW1...........5E 75
.............(off Tachbrook St.)
Parkland Ct. E15..............2A 54
Parkland Ct. W14..............3A 72
.............(off Holland Pk. Av.)
Parkland Gdns. SW19........1F 113
Parklands N6..................2D 33
Parklands Rd. SW16.........5D 117
Parkland Wlk. Local Nature
Reserve......................2A 34
Park La. E15..................5F 53

Park La. W1...........4A 12 (1B 74)
Park Lee Ct. N16..............2A 36
Park Lodge NW8..............4F 45
Park Lodge W14..............4B 72
.............(off Melbury Rd.)
Park Lofts SW2...............3A 104
.............(off Lyham Rd.)
Park Lorne NW8..............2A 60
.............(off Park Rd.)
Park Mans. NW4..............1D 29
Park Mans. NW8..............1A 60
.............(off Allitsen Rd.)
Park Mans. SW1......4A 20 (3B 74)
.............(off Knightsbridge)
Park Mans. SW11............4B 88
.............(off Prince of Wales Dr.)
Park Mans. SW8..............2A 90
Parkmead SW15..............4D 99
Park M. N8....................1A 34
Park M. SE10................1B 96
Park M. SE24.................5E 105
Park M. W10..................1A 58
Park Pde. NW10...............1B 56
Park Piazza SE13.............4F 109
Park Pl. E14...................2C 80
Park Pl. N1...................4F 49
.............(off Downham Rd.)
Park Pl. Vs. W2......2F 21 (2E 75)
Park Ri. SE23.................1A 122
Park Ri. Rd. SE23............1A 122
Park Rd. E10..................3C 38
Park Rd. E12..................3D 41
Park Rd. E15..................5C 54
Park Rd. E17..................1B 38
Park Rd. E6...................5E 55
Park Rd. NW1.........3A 4 (3B 60)
Park Rd. NW10................5A 42
Park Rd. NW4..................2C 28
Park Rd. NW8..................2A 60
Park Rd. Nth. W4..............1A 84
Park Rd. Pools & Fitness...1F 33
Park Row SE10................2F 95
Park St James NW8..........5B 46
.............(off St James's Ter. M.)
Parkside SE3.................3B 96
Parkside SW1.........3A 20 (3B 74)
.............(off Knightsbridge)
Parkside SW19................3F 113
Parkside W3...................2A 70
Park Side NW2.................5C 28
Parkside Av. SE10............4E 95
Parkside Av. SW19............5F 113
Parkside Bus. Est. SE8: Lon
Blackhorse Rd...............2A 94
.............(not continuous)
Parkside Ct. E11...............1C 40
.............(off Wanstead Pl.)
Parkside Ct. E16..............3E 83
.............(off Booth Rd.)
Parkside Cres. N7.............5C 34
Parkside Est. E9...............5E 51
.............(not continuous)
Parkside Gdns. SW19........4F 113
PARKSIDE HOSPITAL.........3F 113
Parkside Rd. SW11............4C 88
Parkside Sq. E14..............5E 81
Parkside Sq. SE10.............4E 95
Parks Info. Cen................2A 74
Park Sth. SW11................4C 88
.............(off Austin Rd.)
Park Sq. E. NW1.......3D 5 (3D 61)
Park Sq. M. NW1......4D 5 (3D 61)
Park Sq. W. NW1......3D 5 (3D 61)
Parkstead Rd. SW15.........3C 98

Park Steps W2.................1A 74
.............(off St George's Flds.)
Parkstone Rd. SE15..........5C 92
Park St. SE1.........1F 25 (2E 77)
Park St. SW6..................4E 87
Park St. W1..........4B 12 (1C 74)
Park Ter. SE3.................1E 111
Park Theatre.................4C 34
Parkthorne Rd. SW12.......5F 103
Park Towers W1......2D 21 (2D 75)
.............(off Brick St.)
Park Vw. N5...................1E 49
Park Vw. SE8..................1F 93
.............(off Trundleys Rd.)
Park Vw. Apts. SE16.........4D 79
.............(off Banyard Rd.)
Parkview Apts. E14...........5D 67
.............(off Chrisp St.)
Park Vw. Ct. E3...............4C 66
Park Vw. Ct. SE12...........3E 125
Parkview Ct. SW18...........4C 100
Parkview Ct. SW6.............5A 86
Park Vw. Est. E2..............1F 65
Park Vw. Gdns. NW4..........1E 29
Park Vw. Ho. SE24...........4D 105
.............(off Hurst St.)
Park Vw. Mans. E20..........2D 53
.............(off Olympic Pk. Av.)
Park Vw. Mans. N4...........1D 35
Park Vw. M. SW9.............5B 90
Park Vw. Rd. NW10..........1B 42
Park Village E. NW1...1E 5 (1D 61)
Park Village W. NW1.........1D 61
Parkville Rd. SW6............3B 86
Park Vista SE10..............2F 95
Park Wlk. N6..................2C 32
Park Wlk. SE10...............3F 95
Park Wlk. SW10...............2E 87
Parkway NW1..................5D 47
Park Way NW11................1A 30
Parkway Cres. E15...........2E 53
Park W. W2....................5A 60
.............(off Park West Pl.)
Park W. Bldg. E3.............1C 66
Park W. Pl. W2................5A 60
Park Wharf SE8...............1A 94
.............(off Evelyn St.)
Parkwood NW8................5B 46
.............(off St Edmund's Ter.)
Parkwood M. N6...............1D 33
Parkwood Rd. SW19.........5B 114
Parliament Ct. E1....1E 19 (4A 64)
.............(off Artillery La.)
Parliament Hill..............5B 32
Parliament Hill Mans. NW5..1A 46
Parliament Hill Fields......5C 32
Parliament Hill Lido........1C 46
Parliament Hill Mans. NW5..1C 46
Parliament Sq.
SW1.................4D 23 (3A 76)
Parliament St.
SW1.................3D 23 (3A 76)
Parliament Vw. SE1..........5B 76
Parma Cres. SW11............2B 102
Parmiter St. E2................1D 65
Parmoor Ct. EC1.......3F 9 (3E 63)
.............(off Gee St.)
Parnell Cl. W12................4D 71
Parnell Ho. WC1.....1C 14 (4F 61)
Parnell Ho. N1.................3D 49
.............(off Canonbury Rd.)
Parnell Rd. E3.................5B 52
Parnham St. E14..............5A 66
.............(not continuous)
Parolles Rd. N19..............3E 33

Parr Ct. N1 ....1F 63
..................................(off New North Rd.)
Parr Ho. E16 ....2D 83
..................................(off Beaulieu Av.)
Parrington Ho. SW4 ....4F 103
Parr Rd. E6 ....5F 55
Parr St. N1 ....1F 63
Parrs Way W6 ....2E 85
Parry Ho. E1 ....2D 79
..................................(off Green Bank)
Parry Rd. W10 ....2A 58
Parry St. SW8 ....2A 90
Parsifal Rd. NW6 ....2C 44
Parsonage St. E14 ....5E 81
Parsons Ga. M. SW6 ....5C 86
Parson's Grn. SW6 ....4C 86
PARSONS GREEN 5B 86
Parson's Grn. La. SW6 ....4C 86
Parsons Green Station
(Underground) 4C 86
Parsons Ho. W2 ....3F 59
..................................(off Hall Pl.)
Parsons Lodge NW6 ....4D 45
..................................(off Priory Rd.)
Parsons M. SW18 ....3E 101
Parson's Rd. E13 ....1E 69
Parthenia Rd. SW6 ....4C 86
Partington Cl. N19 ....3F 33
Partridge Cl. E16 ....4F 69
Partridge Ct. EC1 ....3D 9 (3D 63)
..................................(off Cyrus St.)
Partridge Ho. E3 ....1B 66
..................................(off Stafford Rd.)
Pascall Ho. SE17 ....2E 91
..................................(off Draco St.)
Pascal St. SW8 ....3F 89
Pascoe Rd. SE13 ....3F 109
Pasley Cl. SE17 ....1D 91
Passfield Dr. E14 ....4D 67
Passfield Hall WC1 .....3C 6 (3F 61)
..................................(off Endsleigh Pl.)
Passfields SE6 ....3D 123
Passfields W14 ....1B 86
..................................(off Star Rd.)
Passing All. EC1 ....4E 9 (4D 63)
..................................(off St John St.)
Passmore Ct. E14 ....5C 66
Passmore Ho. E2 ....5B 50
..................................(off Kingsland Rd.)
Passmore St. SW1 ....1C 88
Pastel Ct. E1 ....1F 65
..................................(off Shandy St.)
Paston Cl. E5 ....5F 37
Paston Cres. SE12 ....5D 111
Pastor Ct. N6 ....1E 33
Pastor St. SE11 ....5D 77
Pasture Rd. SE6 ....1B 124
Pastures Path E11 ....3B 40
Patcham Ter. SW8 ....4D 89
Patent Ho. E14 ....4D 67
..................................(off Morris Rd.)
Paternoster Ct. EC4 ...3E 17 (5D 63)
Paternoster Row
EC4 ....3F 17 (5E 63)
Paternoster Sq. EC4 ...2E 17 (5D 63)
Paterson Ct. EC1 ......2B 10 (2F 63)
..................................(off St Luke's Est.)
Pater St. W8 ....4C 72
Patience Rd. SW11 ....5A 88
Patina Mans. E20 ....2E 53
..................................(off Mirabelle Gdns.)
Patio Cl. SW4 ....4F 103
Patmore Est. SW8 ....4E 89
Patmore Ho. N16 ....2A 50

Patmore St. SW8 ....4E 89
Patmos Lodge SW9 ....4D 91
..................................(off Elliott Rd.)
Patmos Rd. SW9 ....3D 91
Paton Cl. E3 ....2C 66
Paton Ho. SW9 ....5B 90
..................................(off Stockwell Rd.)
Paton St. EC1 ....2F 9 (2E 63)
Patrick Coman Ho.
EC1 ....2D 9 (2D 63)
..................................(off St John St.)
Patrick Connolly Gdns. E3 ...2D 67
Patrick Ct. SE1 ....4E 25 (3D 77)
..................................(off Webber St.)
Patrick Pas. SW11 ....5A 88
Patrick Rd. E13 ....2E 69
Patriot Sq. E2 ....1D 65
Patrol Pl. SE6 ....4D 109
Patroni Ct. E15 ....2A 68
..................................(off Durban Rd.)
Pat Shaw Ho. E1 ....3F 65
..................................(off Globe Rd.)
Patshull Pl. NW5 ....3E 47
Patshull Rd. NW5 ....3E 47
Pattenden Rd. SE6 ....1B 122
Patten Ho. N4 ....3E 35
Patten Rd. SW18 ....5A 102
Patterdale NW1 ....2E 5 (2D 61)
..................................(off Osnaburgh St.)
Patterdale Rd. SE15 ....3E 93
Pattern Rd. EC1 ....3D 9 (3D 63)
Pattina Wlk. SE16 ....2A 80
..................................(off Silver Wlk.)
Pattison Ho. E1 ....1F 65
..................................(off Wellesley St.)
Pattison Ho. SE1 ....3A 26 (3E 77)
..................................(off Redcross Way)
Pattison Rd. NW2 ....5C 30
Paul Cl. E15 ....5A 54
Paul Daisley Ct. NW6 ....4A 44
..................................(off Christchurch Av.)
Paulet Rd. SE5 ....5D 91
Paulet Way NW10 ....4A 42
Paul Ho. W10 ....3A 58
..................................(off Ladbroke Gro.)
Pauline Ho. E1 ....4C 64
..................................(off Old Montague St.)
Paul Julius Cl. E14 ....1F 81
Paul Robeson Ho.
WC1 ....1A 8 (1B 62)
..................................(off Penton Ri.)
Paul St. E15 ....5A 54
Paul St. EC2 ....4C 10 (3F 63)
Paul's Wlk. EC4 ....4E 17 (1E 77)
Paultons Ho. SW3 ....2F 87
..................................(off Paultons Sq.)
Paultons Sq. SW3 ....2F 87
Paultons St. SW3 ....2F 87
Pauntley St. N19 ....3E 33
Pavan Ct. E2 ....2E 65
..................................(off Sceptre Rd.)
Paveley Dr. SW11 ....3A 88
Paveley Ho. N1 ....1E 62
..................................(off Priory Grn. Est.)
Paveley St. NW8 ....2A 60
Pavement, The E11 ....3E 39
..................................(off Hainault Rd.)
Pavement, The SW19 ....5B 114
..................................(off Worple Rd.)
Pavement, The SW4 ....2E 103
Pavers Way E3 ....1F 65
Pavilion, The SW8 ....3F 89
Pavilion Apts. NW8 ....2F 59
Pavilion Ct. NW6 ....2C 58
..................................(off Stafford Rd.)

Pavilion Pde. W12 ....5E 57
..................................(off Wood La.)
Pavilion Rd. SW1 ....4A 20 (4B 74)
Pavilion Rd. SW3 ....5B 74
Pavilion Sq. SW17 ....3B 116
Pavilion St. E13 ....1E 69
Pavilion St. SW1 ....5A 20 (4B 74)
Pavilion Ter. W12 ....5E 57
..................................(off Wood La.)
Pavilion Wlk. E10 ....4C 38
Pavilion Way SE10 ....3A 82
Pavillion Ho. SE16 ....3F 79
..................................(off Water Gdns. Sq.)
Pavillion M. N4 ....4B 34
..................................(off Tollington Pk.)
Pawsey Cl. E13 ....5D 55
Paxton Cl. N7 ....3C 48
..................................(off Westbourne Rd.)
Paxton Ct. SE12 ....3E 125
Paxton Ct. SE26 ....4A 122
..................................(off Adamsrill Rd.)
Paxton Ho. SE17 ....1F 91
..................................(off Morecambe St.)
Paxton Pl. SE27 ....4A 120
Paxton Point SE10 ....3D 95
Paxton Rd. SE23 ....3A 122
Paxton Rd. W4 ....2A 84
Paxton Ter. SW1 ....2D 89
Paymal Ho. E1 ....4E 65
..................................(off Stepney Way)
Payne Ho. N1 ....5B 48
..................................(off Barnsbury Est.)
Payne Rd. E3 ....1D 67
Paynell Ct. SE3 ....1A 110
Paynesfield Av. SW14 ....1A 98
Payne St. SE8 ....3B 94
Paynes Wlk. W6 ....2A 86
Peabody Av. SW1 ....1D 89
Peabody Bldgs. E1 ....1C 78
..................................(off John Fisher St.)
Peabody Bldgs. EC1 ...4A 10 (3E 63)
..................................(off Banner St.)
Peabody Bldgs. SW3 ....2A 88
..................................(off Cheyne Row)
Peabody Cl. SE10 ....4D 95
Peabody Cl. SW1 ....1D 89
Peabody Ct. EC1 ....4A 10 (3E 63)
..................................(off Roscoe St.)
Peabody Ct. SE5 ....4F 91
..................................(off Kimpton Rd.)
Peabody Est. SE1: Lon
 Duchy St. 2C 24 (2C 76)
Peabody Est. EC1: Lon
 Dufferin St. 4A 10 (3E 63)
..................................(off Dufferin St.)
Peabody Est. EC1: Lon
 Farringdon La. 4C 8 (3C 62)
..................................(off Farringdon La.)
Peabody Est. SE1: Lon
 Marshalsea Rd. 3A 26 (3E 77)
..................................(off Marshalsea Rd.)
Peabody Est. SE1: Lon
 Southwark St. 1F 25 (2E 77)
Peabody Est. E1 ....1F 79
..................................(off Brodlove La.)
Peabody Est. E2 ....1D 65
..................................(off Minerva St.)
Peabody Est. N1 ....5E 49
Peabody Est. SE24 ....5D 105
Peabody Est. SE5 ....4F 91
..................................(off Camberwell Grn.)
Peabody Est. SW1 ....5E 75
..................................(off Vauxhall Bri. Rd.)
Peabody Est. SW3 ....2A 102
Peabody Est. SW3 ....2A 88

Peabody Est. SW6 .... 2C **86**
.... (off Lillie Rd.)
Peabody Est. W10 ....4E **57**
Peabody Est. W6 ....1E **85**
Peabody Hill SE21 .... 1D **119**
Peabody Ho. N1 ....5E **49**
.... (off Greenman St.)
Peabody Sq. N1 ....5E **49**
.... (off Peabody Est.)
Peabody Sq. SE1 ...... 4D **25** (3D **77**)
.... (not continuous)
Peabody Ter. EC1 ...... 4C **8** (3C **62**)
.... (off Farringdon La.)
Peabody Twr. EC1 ... 4A **10** (3E **63**)
.... (off Golden La.)
Peabody Trust SE17 ....5F **77**
Peabody Yd. N1 ....5E **49**
.... (off Harmony Pl.)
Peace Ct. SE1 ....1C **92**
.... (off Harmony Pl.)
Peachey Ho. SW18 ....2E **101**
.... (off Eltringham St.)
Peach Gro. E11 ....5F **39**
Peach Rd. W10 ...."........2F **57**
Peachum Rd. SE3 ....2B **96**
Peachwalk M. E3 ....1F **65**
Peacock Ho. SE5 ....4A **92**
.... (off St Giles Rd.)
Peacock Pl. N1 ....3C **48**
Peacock St. SE17 ....5D **77**
Peacock Theatre 3F **15** (5B **62**)
.... (off Portugal St.)
Peacock Wlk.
N6: Lon Highgate 2D **33**
Peacock Yd. SE17 ....1D **91**
.... (off Iliffe St.)
Peak, The SE26 ....3E **121**
Peak Hill SE26 ....4E **121**
Peak Hill Av. SE26 ....4E **121**
Peak Hill Gdns. SE26 ....4E **121**
Pearcefield Av. SE23 ....1E **121**
Pearce Ho. SW1 ....5F **75**
.... (off Causton St.)
Pear Cl. SE14 ....3A **94**
Pear Ct. SE15 ....2A **93**
.... (off Thruxton Way)
Pearcroft Rd. E11 ....4F **39**
Peardon St. SW8 ....5D **89**
Pearfield Rd. SE23 ....3A **122**
Pearl Cl. NW2 ....7F **29**
Pearl St. E1 ....2D **79**
Pearmain Ct. W6 ....4D **71**
.... (off Vinery Way)
Pearman St. SE1 ...... 5C **24** (4C **76**)
Pear Pl. SE1 ....3B **24** (3C **76**)
Pear Rd. E11 ....5F **39**
Pearscroft Ct. SW6 ....4D **87**
Pearscroft Rd. SW6 ....4D **87**
Pearse St. SE15 ....2A **92**
Pearson Cl. SE5 ....4E **91**
.... (off Camberwell New Rd.)
Pearson M. SW4 ....1F **103**
.... (off Edgeley Rd.)
Pearson's Av. SE14 ....4C **94**
Pearson Sq. W1 .... 1A **14** (4E **61**)
Pearson St. E2 ....1B **64**
Peartree SE26 ....5A **122**
Peartree Av. SW17 ....3E **115**
Pear Tree Cl. E2 ....5B **50**
Pear Tree Ct. EC1 ...... 4C **8** (3C **62**)
Pear Tree Ct. SE26 ....3B **122**
Pear Tree Ho. SE4 ....1B **108**
Peartree La. E1 ....1E **79**
Pear Tree St. EC1 ...... 3E **9** (3E **63**)
Peartree Way SE10 ....5C **82**
Peary Pl. E2 ....2E **65**

Pechora Way E14 ....4A **66**
Peckarmans Wood SE26 ... 3C **121**
Peckett Sq. N5 ....1E **49**
Peckford Pl. SW9 ....5C **90**
PECKHAM 4C **92**
Peckham Bus Station 4C **92**
Peckham Gro. SE15 ....3A **92**
Peckham High St. SE15 ....4C **92**
Peckham Hill St. SE15 ....3C **92**
Peckham Pk. Rd. SE15 ....3C **92**
Peckhamplex 5C **92**
Peckham Pulse Leisure Cen.
....4C **92**
Peckham Rd. SE5 ....4B **92**
Peckham Rd. SE15 ....4A **92**
Peckham Rye SE15 ....1C **106**
Peckham Rye SE22 ....2C **106**
Peckham Rye Station (Rail &
Overground) 5C **92**
Pecks Yd. E1 ....5F **11** (4B **64**)
.... (off Hanbury St.)
Peckwater St. NW5 ....2E **47**
Pedlar's Wlk. N7 ....2B **48**
Pedley St. E1 ....3C **64**
Pedro St. E5 ....5F **37**
Pedworth Gdns. SE16 ....5E **79**
Peebles Ho. NW6 ....1D **59**
.... (off Carlton Vale)
Peek Cres. SW19 ....5F **113**
Peel Gro. E2 ....1E **65**
Peel Pas. W8 ....2C **72**
Peel Pct. NW6 ....1C **58**
Peel St. W8 ....2C **72**
Peerless St. EC1 ...... 2B **10** (2F **63**)
Pegasus Cl. N16 ....1F **49**
Pegasus Cl. NW10 ....2D **57**
.... (off Trenmar Gdns.)
Pegasus Ho. E1 ....3F **65**
.... (off Beaumont Sq.)
Pegasus Ho. E13 ....2D **69**
Pegasus Pl. SE11 ....2C **90**
Pegasus Pl. SW6 ....4C **86**
Pegler Sq. SE3 ....1D **111**
Pegley Gdns. SE12 ....1C **124**
Pegswood Ct. E1 ....1C **78**
.... (off Cable St.)
Pekin Cl. E14 ....5C **66**
.... (off Pekin St.)
Pekin St. E14 ....5C **66**
Peldon Wlk. N1 ....5D **49**
.... (off Popham St.)
Pelham Cl. SE5 ....1A **106**
Pelham Ct. SW3 ....5A **74**
.... (off Fulham Rd.)
Pelham Cres. SW7 ....5A **74**
Pelham Ho. SW1 ...... 5C **22** (4F **75**)
.... (off Gt. Peter St.)
Pelham Ho. W14 ....5B **72**
.... (off Mornington Av.)
Pelham Pl. SW7 ....5A **74**
Pelham St. SW7 ....5F **73**
Pelican Est. SE15 ....4B **92**
Pelican Ho. SE5 ....4B **92**
Pelican Ho. SE8 ....5B **80**
Pelican Pas. E1 ....3E **65**
Pelican Wlk. SW9 ....2D **105**
Pelican Wharf E1 ....2E **79**
.... (off Wapping Wall)
Pelier St. SE17 ....2E **91**
Pelinore Rd. SE6 ....2A **124**
Pella Ho. SE11 ....1B **90**
Pellatt Rd. SE22 ....3A **86**
Pellatt Rd. SW22 ....3B **106**

Pellerin Rd. N16 ....2A **50**
Pellew Ho. E1 ....3D **65**
.... (off Somerford St.)
Pelling St. E14 ....5C **66**
Pell St. SE8 ....5A **80**
Pelly Rd. E13 ....5C **54**
.... (not continuous)
Peloton Av. E20 ....2D **53**
Pelter St. E2 ....1F **11** (2B **64**)
Pelton Rd. SE10 ....1A **96**
Pember Rd. NW10 ....2F **57**
Pemberton Ct. E1 ....2F **65**
.... (off Portelet Rd.)
Pemberton Gdns. N19 ....5E **33**
Pemberton Ho. SE26 ....4C **120**
.... (off High Level Dr.)
Pemberton Pl. E8 ....4D **51**
Pemberton Rd. N4 ....1C **34**
Pemberton Row EC4 ... 2C **16** (5C **62**)
Pemberton Ter. N19 ....5E **33**
Pembridge Cres. W11 ....1C **72**
Pembridge Gdns. W2 ....1C **72**
PEMBRIDGE PALLIATIVE CARE
CEN. 4F **57**
.... (within St Charles Hospital)
Pembridge Pl. SW15 ....3C **100**
Pembridge Pl. W2 ....1C **72**
Pembridge Rd. W11 ....1C **72**
Pembridge Sq. W2 ....1C **72**
Pembridge Studios W11 .... 1C **72**
.... (off Pembridge Vs.)
Pembridge Vs. W11 ....1C **72**
Pembridge Vs. W2 ....5C **58**
Pembroke W14 ....5B **72**
.... (off Kensington Village)
Pembroke Av. N1 ....5A **48**
Pembroke Bldgs. NW10 ....2C **56**
Pembroke Cl. SW1 ... 4C **20** (3C **74**)
Pembroke Cotts. W8 ....4C **72**
.... (off Pembroke Sq.)
Pembroke Ct. W8 ....4C **72**
.... (off Sth. Edwardes Sq.)
Pembroke Gdns. W8 ....5B **72**
Pembroke Gdns. Cl. W8 ....4C **72**
Pembroke Ho. SW1 ... 5B **20** (4C **74**)
.... (off Chesham St.)
Pembroke Ho. W2 ....5D **59**
.... (off Hallfield Est.)
Pembroke Mans. NW6 ....3E **45**
.... (off Canfield Gdns.)
Pembroke M. E3 ....2A **66**
Pembroke Pl. W8 ....4C **72**
Pembroke Rd. W8 ....5B **72**
Pembroke Sq. W8 ....4C **72**
Pembroke St. N1 ....4A **48**
.... (not continuous)
Pembroke Studios W8 ....4B **72**
Pembroke Ter. NW8 ....5F **45**
.... (off Queen's Ter.)
Pembroke Vs. W8 ....5C **72**
Pembroke Wlk. W8 ....5C **72**
Pembrook M. SW11 ....2F **101**
Pembry Cl. SW9 ....4C **90**
Pembury Cl. E5 ....2D **51**
Pembury Pl. E5 ....2D **51**
Pembury Rd. E5 ....2D **51**
Pemell Cl. E1 ....3E **65**
Pemell Ho. E1 ....3E **65**
.... (off Pemell Cl.)
Penally Pl. N1 ....5F **49**
Penang Ho. E1 ....2D **79**
.... (off Prusom St.)
Penang St. E1 ....2D **79**

Penarth Cen. SE15 ....2E 93
Penarth St. SE15 ....2E 93
Penberth Rd. SE6 ....2E 123
Pencombe M. W11 ....1B 72
Pencraig Way W9 ....2D 93
Penda's Mead E9 ....1A 52
Pendennis Ho. SE8 ....5A 80
Pendennis Rd. SW16 ....4A 118
Penderry Ri. SE6 ....2F 123
Penderyn Way N7 ....1F 47
Pendle Ho. SE26 ....3C 120
Pendle Rd. SW16 ....5D 117
Pendlestone Rd. E17 ....1D 39
Pendley Ho. E2 ....5C 50
.... (off Whiston Rd.)
Pendragon Rd.
   BR1: Brom 3B 124
Pendragon Wlk. NW9 ....1A 28
Pendrell Ho. WC2 ......3C 14 (5F 61)
.... (off New Compton St.)
Pendrell Rd. SE4 ....5A 94
Penerley Rd. SE6 ....1D 123
Penfield Lodge W9 ....4C 58
.... (off Admiral Wlk.)
Penfields Ho. N7 ....3A 48
.... (off York Way Est.)
Penfold Pl. NW1 ....4A 60
Penfold St. NW1 ....4A 60
Penfold St. NW8 ....3F 59
Penford Gdns. SE9 ....1F 111
Penford St. SE5 ....5D 91
Penge East Station (Rail) ...5E 121
Penge Ho. SW11 ....1F 101
Pengelly Apts. E14 ....1D 95
.... (off Bartlett M.)
Penge Rd. E13 ....5E 55
Penhall Rd. SE7 ....5F 83
Penhurst Mans. SW6 ....4B 86
.... (off Rostrevor Rd.)
Penhurst Pl. SE1 ....5A 24 (4B 76)
.... (off Carlisle La.)
Peninsula Apts. N1 ....5E 49
.... (off Basire St.)
Peninsula Apts. W2 ....4F 59
.... (off Praed St.)
Peninsula Ct. E14 ....4D 81
.... (off E. Ferry Rd.)
Peninsula Ct. N1 ....5E 49
.... (off Basire St.)
Peninsula Hgts. SE1 ....1A 90
Peninsular Pk. 5C 82
Peninsular Pk. Rd. SE7 ....5C 82
Peninsula Sq. SE10 ....3A 82
Penley Ct. WC2 ....4A 16 (1B 76)
Penmayne Ho. SE11 ....1C 90
.... (off Kennings Way)
Pennack Rd. SE15 ....2B 92
Penn Almshouses SE10 ....4E 95
.... (off Greenwich Sth. St.)
Pennant M. W8 ....5D 73
Pennard Mans. W12 ....3E 71
.... (off Goldhawk Rd.)
Pennard Rd. W12 ....3E 71
Penner Cl. SW19 ....2A 114
Pennethorne Cl. E9 ....5E 51
Pennethorne Ho. SW11 ....1F 101
Pennethorne Rd. SE15 ....3D 93
Penn Ho. NW8 ....3A 60
.... (off Mallory St.)
Pennine Dr. NW2 ....4F 29
Pennine La. NW2 ....4A 30
Pennine Pde. NW2 ....4A 30
Pennington Cl. SE27 ....4F 119
Pennington St. SE16 ....2A 80

Pennington St. E1 ....1D 79
Pennington Way SE12 ....2D 125
Penn Rd. N7 ....2A 48
Penn St. N1 ....5F 49
Penny Brookes St. E20 ....3E 53
Pennyfields E14 ....1C 80
.... (not continuous)
Penny Flds. Ho. SE8 ....4B 94
.... (off Francis Harvey Way)
Pennyford Ct. NW8 ....3F 59
.... (off St John's Wood Rd.)
Penny M. SW12 ....5D 103
Pennymoor Wlk. W9 ....3B 58
.... (off Fernhead Rd.)
Penpoll Rd. E8 ....3D 51
Penrith Cl. SW15 ....3A 100
Penrith Pl. SE27 ....2D 119
Penrith St. SW16 ....5E 117
Penrose Ct. SW12 ....1C 116
Penrose Gdns. NW3 ....1C 44
Penrose Gro. SE17 ....1E 91
Penrose Ho. SE17 ....1E 91
Penrose St. SE17 ....1E 91
Penrose Way SE10 ....2A 82
Penryn Ho. SE11 ....1D 91
.... (off Seaton Cl.)
Penryn St. NW1 ....1F 61
Penry St. SE1 ....5A 78
Pensbury Pl. SW8 ....5E 89
Pensbury St. SW8 ....5E 89
Penshurst NW5 ....3C 46
Penshurst Ho. SE15 ....2E 93
.... (off Lovelinch Cl.)
Penshurst Rd. E9 ....4F 51
Pentagram Yd. W11 ....5C 58
.... (off Needham Rd.)
Pentland Cl. NW11 ....4A 30
Pentland Gdns. SW18 ....4E 101
Pentland Rd. NW6 ....2C 58
Pentland St. SW18 ....4E 101
Pentlow St. SW15 ....1E 99
Pentney Rd. SW12 ....1E 117
Penton Gro. N1 ....1C 62
Penton Ho. N1 ....1B 8 (1C 62)
.... (off Pentonville Rd.)
Penton Pl. SE17 ....1D 91
Penton Ri. WC1 ....1A 8 (2B 62)
Penton St. N1 ....1C 62
PENTONVILLE 1B 62
Pentonville Rd. N1 .....1A 8 (1A 62)
Pentridge St. SE15 ....3B 92
Penwith Rd. SW18 ....2C 114
Penwood Ho. SW15 ....4B 98
Penwortham Rd. SW16 ....5D 117
Penywern Rd. SW5 ....1C 86
Penzance Pl. W11 ....2A 72
Penzance St. W11 ....2A 72
Peony Ct. SW10 ....2E 87
Peony Gdns. W12 ....1C 70
Peperfield WC1 ....2F 7 (2B 62)
.... (off Cromer St.)
Pepler Ho. W10 ....3A 58
.... (off Wornington Rd.)
Pepler M. SE5 ....1B 92
Peploe Rd. NW6 ....1F 57
Peppermead Sq. SE13 ....3C 108
Peppermint Pl. E11 ....5A 40
Pepper St. E14 ....4D 81
Pepper St. SE1 ....3F 25 (3E 77)
Peppie Cl. N16 ....4A 36
Pepys Cres. E16 ....2C 82
Pepys Ho. E2 ....2E 65
.... (off Kirkwall Pl.)
Pepys Rd. SE14 ....4F 93
Pepys St. EC3 ....4E 19 (1A 78)

Perceval Av. NW3 ....2A 46
Perch St. E8 ....1B 50
Percival Ho. EC1 ......1E 17 (4D 63)
.... (off Bartholomew Cl.)
Percival M. SE11 ....2B 90
Percival St. EC1 ....2D 9 (3D 63)
Percy Cir. WC1 ....1A 8 (2B 62)
Percy Laurie Ho. SW15 ....2F 99
.... (off Nursery Cl.)
Percy M. W1 ....1B 14 (4F 61)
.... (off Rathbone Pl.)
Percy Rd. E11 ....2A 40
Percy Rd. E16 ....4A 68
Percy Rd. W12 ....3C 70
Percy St. W1 ....1B 14 (4F 61)
Percy Yd. WC1 ....1A 8 (2B 62)
Peregrine Cl. NW10 ....2A 42
Peregrine Ct. SE8 ....2C 94
.... (off Edward St.)
Peregrine Ct. SW16 ....4B 118
Peregrine Ho. EC1 .....1E 9 (2D 63)
.... (off Hall St.)
Perham Rd. W14 ....1A 86
Peridot Ct. E2 ....2F 11 (2B 64)
.... (off Virginia Rd.)
Perifield SE21 ....1E 119
Perilla Ho. E1 ....5C 64
.... (off Boulevard Walkway)
Periton Rd. SE9 ....2F 111
Perkins Ho. E14 ....4B 66
.... (off Wallwood St.)
Perkin's Rents SW1 ....5B 22 (4F 75)
Perkins Sq. SE1 ....1A 26 (2E 77)
Perks Cl. SE3 ....1A 110
Perley Ho. E3 ....4B 66
.... (off Weatherley Cl.)
Perran Rd. SW2 ....1D 119
Perren St. NW5 ....3D 47
Perrers Rd. W6 ....5D 71
Perrin Apts. N1 ....4A 48
.... (off Caledonian Rd.)
Perring Est. E3 ....4C 66
.... (off Gale St.)
Perrin Ho. NW6 ....2C 58
Perrin's Ct. NW3 ....1E 45
Perrin's La. NW3 ....1E 45
Perrin's Wlk. NW3 ....1E 45
Perronet Ho. SE1 ......5E 25 (4D 77)
.... (off Princess St.)
Perry Av. W3 ....5A 56
Perry Ct. E14 ....1C 94
.... (off Maritime Quay)
Perry Ct. N15 ....1A 36
Perryfield Way NW9 ....1B 28
Perry Hill SE6 ....3B 122
Perry Lodge E12 ....3F 41
Perrymead St. SW6 ....4C 86
Perryn Ho. W3 ....1A 70
Perryn Rd. SE16 ....4D 79
Perry Ri. SE23 ....3A 122
Perry's Pl. W1 ....1B 14 (5F 61)
Perry Va. SE23 ....2E 121
Persant Rd. SE6 ....2A 124
Perseverance Pl. SW9 ....3C 90
Perseverance Works
   E2 ....1E 11 (2A 64)
.... (off Kingsland Rd.)
Perth Av. NW9 ....2A 28
Perth Cl. SE5 ....2F 105
Perth Ho. N1 ....1B 48
.... (off Bemerton Est.)
Perth Rd. E10 ....3A 38
Perth Rd. E13 ....1D 69
Perth Rd. N4 ....3C 34
Peruvian Wharf E16 ....2C 82

Perystreete SE23 ....2E **121**
Peter Av. NW10 ....4D **43**
Peter Best Ho. E1 ....5D **65**
.........................*(off Nelson St.)*
Peterboat Cl. SE10 ....5A **82**
Peterborough Ct.
EC4 ....2C **16** (5C **62**)
Peterborough M. SW6 ....5C **86**
Peterborough Rd. E10 ......1E **39**
Peterborough Rd. SW6 .....5C **86**
Peterborough Vs. SW6 .....4D **87**
Peter Butler Ho. SE1 ....3C **78**
.......................*(off Wolseley St.)*
Peterchurch Ho. SE15.......2D **93**
.......................*(off Commercial Way)*
Petergate SW11 ....2E **101**
Peter Harrison Planetarium..3F **95**
Peter Heathfield Ho. E15 .....5F **53**
.............................*(off Wise Rd.)*
Peter Hills Ho. SE16 ....5C **78**
...........................*(off Alexis St.)*
Peter Ho. SW8 ....3A **90**
.....................*(off Luscombe Way)*
Peterley Bus. Cen. E2 ....1D **65**
Peter Pan Statue................2F **73**
Peters Ct. W2 ....5D **59**
.......................*(off Porchester Rd.)*
Petersfield Ri. SW15 ....1D **113**
Petersham Ho. SW7 ....5F **73**
.......................*(off Kendrick M.)*
Petersham La. SW7 ....4E **73**
Petersham M. SW7 ....4E **73**
Petersham Pl. SW7 ....4E **73**
Peter's Hill EC4 ....4F **17** (1E **77**)
Peter Shore Ct. E1 ....4F **65**
.......................*(off Beaumont Sq.)*
Peter's La. EC1 ....5D **9** (4D **63**)
.........................(not continuous)
Peter's Path SE26 ....4D **121**
Peterstow Cl. SW19 ....2A **114**
Peter St. W1 ....4B **14** (1F **75**)
Petherton Ct. NW10 ....5F **43**
.........................*(off Tiverton Rd.)*
Petherton Rd. N5 ....2E **49**
Petiver Cl. E9 ....4E **51**
Petley Rd. W6 ....2F **85**
Peto Pl. NW1 ....3E **5** (3D **61**)
Peto St. Nth. E16...............5B **68**
Petra Way E16 ....4B **68**
Petrie Cl. NW2 ....3A **44**
Petrie Mus. of Egyptian
Archaeology 4B **6** (3F **61**)
Petros Gdns. NW3 ....3D **45**
Petticoat Lane Market
.................................1E **19** (4A **64**)
Petticoat Sq. E1 ....2F **19** (5B **64**)
Petticoat Twr. E1 ......2F **19** (5B **64**)
.......................*(off Petticoat Sq.)*
Pettiward Cl. SW15............3E **99**
Pett St. SE18 ....5F **83**
Petty France SW1 .....5A **22** (4E **75**)
Petty Wales EC3.......5E **19** (1A **78**)
Petworth St. SW11 ....4A **88**
Petyt Pl. SW3 ....2A **88**
Petyward SW3 ....5A **74**
Pevensey Ct. SW16 ....3C **118**
Pevensey Ho. E1 ....4F **65**
.......................*(off Ben Jonson Rd.)*
Pevensey Rd. E7 ....1B **54**
Pevensey Rd. SW17 ....4F **115**
Peverill Ho. SE1 ....5C **26** (4F **77**)
.......................*(off Rephidim St.)*
Peyton Pl. SE10.................3E **95**
Pharamond NW2.................3F **43**
Pheasant Cl. E16 ....5D **69**

Pheasantry Ho. SW3 ....1A **88**
.............................*(off Jubilee Pl.)*
Pheasant Sq. NW9 ....1B **28**
Phelps Lodge N1................5B **48**
Phelp St. SE17 ....2F **91**
Phene St. SW3 ....2A **88**
Philadelphia Ct. SW10 ....3E **87**
.........................*(off Uverdale Rd.)*
Philbeach Gdns. SW5 ....1C **86**
Phil Brown Pl. SW8............1D **103**
.......................*(off Daley Thompson Way)*
Philchurch Pl. E1 ....5C **64**
Philia Ho. NW1 ....4E **47**
.............................*(off Farrier St.)*
Philip Ct. W2 ....4F **59**
.............................*(off Hall Pl.)*
Philip Ho. NW6 ....5D **45**
.........................*(off Mortimer Pl.)*
Philip Jones Ct. N4 ....3B **34**
Philip Mole Ho. W9 ....3C **58**
.......................*(off Chippenham Rd.)*
Philippa Gdns. SE9 ....3F **111**
Philip Sq. SW8 ....5D **89**
Philip St. E13....................3C **68**
Philip Wlk. SE15................1C **106**
.........................(not continuous)
Phillimore Ct. W8 ....3C **72**
.......................*(off Kensington High St.)*
Phillimore Gdns. NW10.......3C **42**
Phillimore Gdns. W8 ....5E **43**
Phillimore Gdns. Cl. W8 .....3C **72**
Phillimore Pl. W8 ....4C **72**
Phillimore Ter. W8 ....4C **72**
.............................*(off Allen St.)*
Phillimore Wlk. W8 ....4C **72**
Phillip Ho. E1 ....4B **64**
.........................*(off Heneage St.)*
Phillip St. N1 ....5A **50**
Philpot La. EC3........4D **19** (1A **78**)
Philpot Sq. SW6 ....1D **101**
Philpot St. E1 ....5D **65**
Phipps Ho. SE7 ....1D **97**
.......................*(off Woolwich Rd.)*
Phipps Ho. W12 ....1D **71**
.......................*(off White City Est.)*
Phipp's M. SW1 ....4D **75**
.......................*(off Buckingham Palace Rd.)*
Phipp St. EC2 ....3D **11** (3A **64**)
Phoebeth Rd. SE4 ....3C **108**
Phoebe Wlk. E16...............5D **69**
Phoenix Av. SE10...............3A **82**
Phoenix Cl. E8 ....5B **50**
Phoenix Cl. W12.................1D **71**
Phoenix Ct. E1 ....3D **65**
.......................*(off Buckhurst St.)*
Phoenix Ct. E14.................5C **80**
Phoenix Ct. NW1 ......1C **6** (1F **61**)
.........................*(off Purchese St.)*
Phoenix Ct. SE14...............2A **94**
.............................*(off Chipley St.)*
Phoenix Fitness Cen..........1C **70**
Phoenix Hgts. E. E14 ....3C **80**
.............................*(off Byng St.)*
Phoenix Hgts. W. E14 ....3C **80**
.......................*(off Mastmaker Ct.)*
Phoenix Lodge Mans. W6....5F **71**
.........................*(off Brook Grn.)*
Phoenix Pk. NW2 ....4C **28**
Phoenix Pl. WC1.......3A **8** (3B **62**)
Phoenix Rd. NW1 .....1B **6** (1F **61**)
Phoenix St. WC2 ....3C **14** (5F **61**)
Phoenix Theatre........3C **14** (5F **61**)
.......................*(off Charing Cross Rd.)*
Phoenix Way E16................4B **68**
.........................*(off Barking Rd.)*

Phoenix Way SW18............3E **101**
Phoenix Wharf E1 ....2D **79**
.......................*(off Wapping High St.)*
Phoenix Wharf Rd.
SE1 ....4F **27** (3B **78**)
.............................*(off Tanner St.)*
Phoenix Yd. WC1........2A **8** (2B **62**)
.......................*(off King's Cross Rd.)*
Photographers' Gallery
.................................3F **13** (5E **61**)
.......................*(off Ramillies St.)*
Phyllis Hodges Ho.
NW1 ....1B **6** (1F **61**)
.......................*(off Aldenham St.)*
Physical Energy Statue 2E **73**
Physic Pl. SW3..................2B **88**
Piano La. N16....................5F **35**
Piano Yd. N16 ....2D **47**
Piazza, The WC2 ......4E **15** (1A **76**)
.........................*(off Covent Gdn.)*
Piccadilly W1 ....2D **21** (2D **75**)
Piccadilly Arc. SW1 ...1F **21** (2E **75**)
.............................*(off Piccadilly)*
Piccadilly Circus........5B **14** (1F **75**)
Piccadilly Circus Station
(Underground)..........5A **14** (1F **75**)
Piccadilly Ct. N7 ....3B **48**
.......................*(off Caledonian Rd.)*
Piccadilly Pl. W1 ......5A **14** (1E **75**)
.............................*(off Piccadilly)*
Piccadilly Theatre.....4A **14** (1E **75**)
.......................*(off Denman St.)*
Pickard Gdns. E3 ....4B **66**
Pickard St. EC1 ....1E **9** (2D **63**)
Pickering Cl. E9 ....4F **51**
Pickering Ho. W2 ....5C **58**
.......................*(off Hallfield Est.)*
Pickering M. W2 ....5D **59**
Pickering Pl. SW1 ....2A **22** (2E **75**)
.......................*(off St James's St.)*
Pickering St. N1.................5D **49**
Picketts St. SW12 ....5D **103**
Picketts Ter. SE22 ....3C **106**
Pickfords Wharf N1 ...1F **9** (1E **63**)
Pickfords Wharf
SE1 ....1B **26** (2F **77**)
Pickle M. SW9....................3C **90**
Pickle Sq. SE1...................4A **78**
.......................*(off The Tannery)*
Pickwick Ho. SE16.............3C **78**
.............................*(off George Row)*
Pickwick Ho. W11..............2F **71**
.............................*(off St Ann's Rd.)*
Pickwick Rd. SE21.............5F **105**
Pickwick St. SE1......4F **25** (3E **77**)
Pickworth Cl. SW8 ....3A **90**
Picton Pl. W1 ....3C **12** (5C **60**)
Picton St. SE5...................3F **91**
Picture Ho. SW16..............2A **118**
Picturehouse Central
.................................4B **14** (1F **75**)
.......................*(off Shaftesbury Av.)*
Pied Bull Ct. WC1 ....1D **15** (4A **62**)
.............................*(off Bury Pl.)*
Pied Bull Yd. N1.................5D **49**
.......................*(off Theberton St.)*
Pied Bull Yd. WC1 ....1D **15** (4A **62**)
.............................*(off Bury Pl.)*
Pier Head E1 ....2D **79**
.........................(not continuous)
Pierhead Wharf E1.............2D **79**
.......................*(off Wapping High St.)*
Pier Ho. SW3....................2A **88**
Piermont Grn. SE22 ....3D **107**

Piermont Rd. SE22...............3D 107
Pierpoint Bldg. E14................3B 80
Pierrepont Arc. N1.................1D 63
     (off Islington High St.)
Pierrepont Row N1.................1D 63
     (off Camden Pas.)
Pier St. E14.............................5E 81
     (not continuous)
Pier Ter. SW18.......................2D 101
Pier Wlk. SE10........................3A 82
Pietra Lara Bldg.
EC1......................3F 9 (3E 63)
     (off Pear Tree St.)
Piggott Ho. E2.........................1F 65
     (off Sewardstone Rd.)
Pigott St. E14..........................5C 66
Pike Cl. BR1: Broml...............5D 125
Pikemans Ct. SW5..................5C 72
     (off W. Cromwell Rd.)
Pikethorne SE23.....................2F 121
Pilgrimage St. SE1...4B 26 (3F 77)
Pilgrim Hill SE27....................4E 119
Pilgrim Ho. SE1.........5C 26 (4F 77)
     (off Tabard St.)
Pilgrim Ho. SE16.....................3E 79
     (off Brunel Rd.)
Pilgrims Cloisters SE5............3A 92
     (off Sedgmoor Pl.)
Pilgrims Cnr. NW6..................1C 58
     (off Chichester Rd.)
Pilgrim's La. NW3....................1F 45
Pilgrims M. E14.......................1A 82
Pilgrim's Pl. NW3....................1F 45
Pilgrim St. EC4............3D 17 (5D 63)
Pilgrims Way N19.....................3F 33
Pilkington Rd. SE15................5D 93
Pill Box Studios E2.................2D 65
     (off Coventry Rd.)
Pillfold Ho. SE11.....................5B 76
     (off Old Paradise St.)
Pilot Cl. SE8...........................2B 94
Pilot Ind. Cen. NW10..............3A 56
Pilot Wlk. SE10.......................3B 82
Pilsdon Cl. SW19....................1F 113
Pilton Pl. SE17........................1E 91
PIMLICO.................................1E 89
Pimlico Ho. SW1.....................1D 89
     (off Ebury Bri. Rd.)
Pimlico Rd. SW1......................1C 88
Pimlico Sq. SW1......................1C 88
Pimlico Station (Underground)
....1F 89
Pinchin & Johnsons Yd. E1 ...1C 78
     (off Pinchin St.)
Pinchin St. E1..........................1C 78
Pincombe Ho. SE17................1F 91
     (off Orb St.)
Pincott Pl. SE4.........................1E 107
Pindar St. EC2..........5D 11 (4A 64)
Pindock M. W9.........................3D 59
Pindoria M. E1...........4F 11 (3B 64)
     (off Quaker St.)
Pineapple Ct. SW1.....5A 22 (4E 75)
     (off Castle La.)
Pine Av. E15.............................2F 53
Pine Cl. E10.............................4D 39
Pine Cl. N19.............................4E 33
Pinedene SE15........................4D 93
Pinefield Cl. E14.....................1C 80
Pine Gro. N4............................4A 34
Pine Gro. SW19.......................5B 114
Pine Ho. E3..............................5A 52
     (off Barge La.)
Pine Ho. SE16..........................3E 79
     (off Ainsty Est.)

Pine Ho. W10...........................3A 58
     (off Droop St.)
Pinehurst Ct. W11....................5B 58
     (off Colville Gdns.)
Pinelands Cl. SE3....................3B 96
Pinemartin Cl. NW2.................5E 29
Pine M. NW10.........................1F 57
     (off Clifford Gdns.)
Pine Rd. NW2..........................1E 43
Pine St. EC1...............3B 8 (3C 62)
Pine Tree Way SE13...............1D 109
Pinewood Ct. SW4...................4F 103
Pinfold Rd. SW16....................4A 118
Pinkerton Pl. SW16.................4F 117
Pinnace Ho. E14......................4E 81
     (off Manchester Rd.)
Pinnacle Ho. SW18..................2E 101
Pinnacle Way E14....................5A 66
     (off Commercial Rd.)
Pinnell Rd. SE9........................2F 111
Pinner Ct. NW8........................3F 59
     (off St John's Wood Rd.)
Pintail Cl. E6............................4F 69
Pintail Ct. SE8.........................2B 94
     (off Pilot Cl.)
Pinter Ho. SW9........................5A 90
     (off Grantham Rd.)
Pintle Pl. E3.............................2E 67
Pinto Twr. SW8........................3A 90
Pinto Way SE3.........................2D 111
Pioneer Cen., The SE15.........4E 93
Pioneer Cl. E14.......................4D 67
Pioneer Ct. E16.......................4C 68
     (off Hammersley Rd.)
Pioneer Ho. WC1......1F 7 (2B 62)
     (off Britannia St.)
Pioneer St. SE15.....................4C 92
Pioneer Way W12....................5D 57
Piper Bldg., The SW6.............1D 101
Piper Cl. N7.............................3B 48
Pipers Ho. SE10......................1F 95
     (off Collington St.)
Pippin Ct. SW19......................4E 99
Pippin Cl. NW2........................5C 28
Pippin Ct. SW8........................2D 89
     (off Vauxhall Gro.)
Pippin Ho. W10........................1F 71
     (off Freston Rd.)
Pippin Mans. E20....................2E 53
     (off Mirabelle Gdns.)
Pique M. E1..............................1F 79
     (off Glasshouse Flds.)
Pirbright Rd. SW18.................1B 114
Pirie Cl. SE5............................1F 105
Pirie St. E16............................2D 83
Pissaro Ho. N1........................4C 48
     (off Augustas La.)
Pitcairn Ho. E9........................4E 51
Pitchford St. E15.....................4F 53
Pitfield Est. N1..........1D 11 (2A 64)
Pitfield St. N1............1D 11 (2A 64)
Pitfold Cl. SE12.......................4D 111
Pitfold Rd. SE12......................4C 110
Pitlochry Ho. SE27..................2D 119
     (off Elmcourt Rd.)
Pitman Bldg. SE16...................4C 78
     (off Old Jamaica Rd.)
Pitman Ho. SE8.......................4C 94
Pitman St. SE5.........................3E 91
Pitmaston Ho. SE13................5E 95
     (off Lewisham Rd.)
Pitmaston Rd. SE13.................5E 95
Pitsea Pl. E1............................5F 65
Pitsea St. E1............................5F 65
Pitt Cres. SW19.......................4D 115

Pitt's Head M. W1 ....2C 20 (2C 74)
Pitt St. W8..............................3C 72
Pitwell M. E8............................3C 50
Pixley St. E14..........................5B 66
Place London, The....2C 6 (2F 61)
Place, The SE1..........2C 26 (2F 77)
Plaisterers Highwalk
EC2...........................1F 17 (4E 63)
     (off London Wall)
PLAISTOW.................................1C 68
Plaistow Gro. E15....................5B 54
Plaistow Pk. Rd. E13...............1D 69
     (not continuous)
Plaistow Rd. E13.....................1C 68
Plaistow Rd. E15.....................5B 54
Plaistow Station (Underground)
....1B 68
Plaistow Wharf E16.................3C 82
Plane St. SE26.........................3D 121
Planetree Ct. W6......................5F 71
     (off Brook Grn.)
Plane Tree Ho. SE8.................3A 94
     (off Etta St.)
Plane Tree Ho. W8..................3B 72
     (off Duchess of Bedford's Wlk.)
Plane Tree Wlk. SE19.............5A 120
Plantain Gdns. E11..................5F 39
     (off Hollydown Way)
Plantain Pl. SE1.......3B 26 (3F 77)
Plantation, The SE3.................5C 96
Plantation Cl. SW4..................3A 104
Plantation La. EC3....4D 19 (1A 78)
     (off Rood La.)
Plantation Pl. EC3....4D 19 (1A 78)
     (off Mincing La.)
Plantation Wharf SW11...........1E 101
Plantation Wharf Pier (River Bus)
....1E 101
Plasel Ct. E13..........................5D 55
     (off Pawsey Cl.)
Plashet Gro. E6.......................5E 55
Plashet Rd. E13.......................5C 54
Plassy Rd. SE6........................5D 109
Plate Ho. E14..........................1D 95
     (off Burrells Wharf Sq.)
Platform Theatre......................5A 48
Platina St. EC2........3C 10 (3F 63)
     (off Tabernacle St.)
Platinum Ct. E1.......................3E 65
     (off Cephas Av.)
Platinum M. N15......................1B 36
Plato Rd. SW2.........................2A 104
Platt, The SW15......................1F 99
Platt's La. NW3........................1C 44
Platt St. NW1...........................1F 61
Plaxdale Ho. SE17...................5A 78
     (off Congreve St.)
Plaxton Cl. E11.......................5B 40
Playfair Ho. E14......................5C 66
     (off Saracen St.)
Playfair Mans. W14.................2A 86
     (off Queen's Club Gdns.)
Playfair St. W6........................1E 85
Playfield Cres. SE22...............3B 106
Playford Rd. N4.......................4B 34
     (not continuous)
Playgreen Way SE6.................3C 122
Playground Gdns. E22F 11 (2B 64)
     (off Rochelle St.)
Playhouse Ct. SE1....2F 25 (2E 77)
     (off Southwark Bri. Rd.)
Playhouse Theatre London
....1E 23 (2A 76)
     (off Northumberland Av.)
Playhouse Yd. EC4...3D 17 (5D 63)

Plaza Gdns. SW15 ....3A **100**
Plaza Hgts. E10 ....5E **39**
Plaza Pde. NW6 ....1D **59**
Pleasance, The SW15 ....2D **99**
Pleasance Rd. SW15 ....3D **99**
Pleasance Theatre London....3A **48**
............................(off Carpenters M.)
Pleasant Pl. N1 ....4D **49**
Pleasant Row NW1 ....5D **47**
Pleasaunce Mans. SE10 ....1C **96**
................................(off Halstow Rd.)
Plender Ct. NW1 ....5E **47**
....................................(off College Pl.)
Plender St. NW1 ....5E **47**
Pleshey Rd. N7 ....1F **47**
Plessey Bldg. E14 ....5C **66**
....(off Dod St.)
Plevna Cres. N15 ....1A **36**
Plevna St. E14 ....4E **81**
Pleydell Av. W6 ....5B **70**
Pleydell Ct. EC4 ....3C **16** (5C **62**)
................................(off Pleydell St.)
Pleydell Est. EC1 ....2A **10** (2E **63**)
................................(off Radnor St.)
Pleydell Ho. EC4 ....3C **16** (5C **62**)
................................(off Pleydell St.)
Pleydell St. EC4 ....3C **16** (5C **62**)
................................(off Bouverie St.)
Plimley Pl. W12 ....3F **71**
............................(off Shepherd's Bush Pl.)
Plimsoll Cl. E14 ....5D **67**
Plimsoll Rd. N4 ....5C **34**
Plough Cl. NW10 ....2D **57**
Plough Ct. EC3 ....4C **18** (1F **77**)
Plough La. SE22 ....4B **106**
Plough La. SW17 ....4E **115**
Plough La. SW19 ....5D **115**
Ploughmans Cl. NW1 ....5F **47**
Plough M. SW11 ....2F **101**
Plough Pl. EC4 ....2C **16** (5C **62**)
Plough Rd. SW11 ....1F **101**
Plough St. E1 ....5B **64**
....................................(off Buckle St.)
Plough Ter. SW11 ....2F **101**
Plough Way SE16 ....5F **79**
Plough Yd. EC2 ....4E **11** (3A **64**)
Plover Ho. SW9 ....3C **90**
....................................(off Brixton Rd.)
Plover Way SE16 ....4A **80**
Plowden Bldgs.
EC4 ....4B **16** (1C **76**)
................................(off Middle Temple La.)
Plumber's Row E1 ....1C **64**
Plumbridge St. SE10 ....4E **95**
Plume Ho. SE10 ....2D **95**
....................................(off Creek Rd.)
Plummer Rd. SW4 ....5F **103**
Plumtree Ct. EC4 ....2D **17** (5D **63**)
Plum Tree M. SW16 ....5A **118**
Plymouth Ho. SE10 ....4D **95**
............................(off Devonshire Dr.)
Plymouth Rd. E16 ....4C **68**
Plymouth Ter. NW2 ....3E **43**
................................(off Sidmouth Rd.)
Plymouth Wharf E14 ....5F **81**
Plympton Av. NW6 ....4B **44**
Plympton Pl. NW8 ....3A **60**
Plympton Rd. NW6 ....4B **44**
Plympton St. NW8 ....3A **60**
Pocklington Cl. W12 ....4C **70**
............................(off Ashchurch Pk. Vs.)
Pocklington St. SW15 ....1C **112**
Pocklington Lodge W12 ....4C **70**
Pocock St. SE1 ....3D **25** (3D **77**)
Podmore Rd. SW18 ....2E **101**

Poet Ct. E1 ....4F **65**
....................................(off Shandy St.)
Poet's Rd. N5 ....2F **49**
Point, The W2 ....4F **59**
................................(off Nth. Wharf Rd.)
Point Cl. SE10 ....4E **95**
Pointers Cl. E14 ....1D **95**
Point Hill SE10 ....3E **95**
Point Pleasant SW18 ....2C **100**
Point Ter. E7 ....2D **55**
................................(off Claremont Rd.)
Point W. SW7 ....3D **73**
Poland St. W1 ....2A **14** (5E **61**)
Poldo Ho. SE10 ....5A **82**
....................................(off Cable Wlk.)
Polebrook Rd. SE3 ....1E **111**
Polecroft La. SE6 ....2B **122**
Polesworth Ho. W2 ....4C **58**
....................................(off Alfred Rd.)
Pollard Cl. E16 ....1C **82**
Pollard Cl. N7 ....1B **48**
Pollard Ho. N1 ....1F **7** (1B **62**)
................................(off Northdown St.)
Pollard Ho. SE16 ....4B **78**
....................................(off Spa Rd.)
Pollard Row E2 ....2C **64**
Pollard St. E2 ....2C **64**
Pollen St. W1 ....3E **13** (5E **61**)
Pollitt Dr. NW8 ....3F **59**
Pollock Ho. W10 ....3A **58**
....................................(off Kensal Rd.)
Pollock's Toy Mus. Pollocks
....5A **6** (4E **61**)
Polperro Ho. W2 ....4C **58**
................................(off Westbourne Pk. Rd.)
Polperro M. SE11 ....5D **77**
Polsted Rd. SE6 ....5B **108**
Polworth Rd. SW16 ....5A **118**
Polychrome Ct. SE1 ....2D **25** (3D **77**)
................................(off Waterloo Rd.)
Polydamas Cl. E3 ....1C **66**
Polygon, The NW8 ....5F **45**
....................................(off Avenue Rd.)
Polygon, The SW4 ....2E **103**
Polygon Rd. NW1 ....1B **6** (1F **61**)
................................(not continuous)
Pomell Way E1 ....2F **19** (5B **64**)
Pomeroy Ho. E2 ....1F **65**
................................(off St James's Av.)
Pomeroy Ho. W11 ....5A **58**
................................(off Lancaster Rd.)
Pomeroy St. SE14 ....3E **93**
Pomfret Pl. E14 ....1D **81**
................................(off Bullivant St.)
Pomfret Rd. SE5 ....1D **105**
Pomoja La. N19 ....4A **34**
Pomona Ho. SE8 ....5A **80**
....................................(off Evelyn St.)
Pond Cl. SE3 ....5C **96**
Pond Cotts. SE21 ....1A **120**
Ponder St. N7 ....4B **48**
Pond Farm Est. E5 ....5E **37**
Pondfield Ho. SE27 ....5E **119**
Pond Ho. SW3 ....5A **74**
Pond Mead SE21 ....4F **105**
Pond Pl. SW3 ....5A **74**
Pond Rd. E15 ....1A **68**
Pond Rd. SE3 ....5B **96**
Pond Sq. N6 ....3C **32**
Pond St. NW3 ....2A **46**
Ponler St. E1 ....5D **65**
Ponsard Rd. NW10 ....2D **57**
Ponsford St. E9 ....3E **51**
Ponsonby Ho. E2 ....1E **65**
................................(off Bishop's Way)

Ponsonby Pl. SW1 ....1F **89**
Ponsonby Rd. SW15 ....5D **99**
Ponsonby Ter. SW1 ....1F **89**
Ponsonby Vs. E2 ....1E **65**
................................(off Lark Row)
Pontefract Rd.
BR1: Broml 5B **124**
Pontifex Apts. SE1 ....1B **26** (2F **77**)
................................(off Stoney St.)
Ponton Rd. SW11 ....2F **89**
Pontoon Dock Station (DLR)
....2E **83**
Pontoon Reach E16 ....2F **83**
Pont St. SW1 ....5A **20** (4B **74**)
Pont St. M. SW1 ....4B **74**
Pontypool Pl. SE1 ....3D **25** (3D **77**)
Pooja Cl. NW1 ....4E **47**
................................(off Agar Gro.)
Pool Cl. BR3: Beck. 5C **122**
Pool Ct. SE6 ....2C **122**
Poole Ct. N1 ....4A **50**
................................(off St Peter's Way)
Poole Ho. SE11 ....4C **76**
................................(off Lambeth Wlk.)
Poole Rd. E9 ....3F **51**
Pooles Bldgs. WC1 ....4B **8** (3C **62**)
................................(off Mt. Pleasant)
Pooles La. SW10 ....3E **87**
Pooles Pk. N4 ....4C **34**
Poole St. N1 ....5F **49**
Pooley Ho. E1 ....2F **65**
Pool Ho. NW8 ....4F **59**
................................(off Penfold St.)
Poolmans St. SE16 ....3F **79**
Pool St. E20 ....4E **53**
Poonah St. E1 ....5E **65**
Pope Cl. SW19 ....5F **115**
Pope Ho. SE16 ....5D **79**
................................(off Manor Est.)
Pope Ho. SE5 ....3F **91**
................................(off Elmington Est.)
Pope's Head All.
EC3 ....3C **18** (5F **63**)
Pope's Rd. SW9 ....1C **104**
Pope St. SE1 ....4E **27** (3A **78**)
Popham Rd. N1 ....5E **49**
Popham St. N1 ....5D **49**
................................(not continuous)
POPLAR 1D **81**
Poplar Baths Leisure Cen. 1D **81**
Poplar Bath St. E14 ....5D **67**
Poplar Bus. Pk. E14 ....1E **81**
Poplar Cl. E9 ....2B **52**
Poplar Ct. SW19 ....5C **114**
Poplar Gro. W6 ....3E **71**
Poplar High St. E14 ....1D **81**
Poplar Ho. SE16 ....3F **79**
................................(off Woodland Cres.)
Poplar M. W12 ....2B **108**
................................(off Wickham Rd.)
Poplar M. W12 ....2E **71**
Poplar Pl. W2 ....1D **73**
Poplar Rd. SE24 ....2E **105**
Poplars Av. NW2 ....3E **43**
Poplars Rd. E17 ....1D **39**
Poplar Station (DLR) 1D **81**
Poplar Wlk. SE24 ....1E **105**
Poppins Ct. EC4 ....3D **17** (5D **63**)
Poppleton Rd. E11 ....1A **40**
Poppy M. SE22 ....3C **106**
Poppy Pl. SE13 ....4F **109**
Porchester Cl. SE5 ....2E **105**
Porchester Ct. W2 ....1D **73**
................................(off Porchester Gdns.)

Porchester Gdns. W2 .... 1D 73
Porchester Gdns. M. W2 ...... 5D 59
Porchester Ga. W2 .... 1D 73
.... (off Bayswater Rd.)
Porchester Ho. E1 .... 5D 65
.... (off Philpot St.)
Porchester Leisure Cen. 5D 59
Porchester Mead
    BR3: Beck. 5D 123
Porchester Pl. W2 .... 5A 60
Porchester Rd. W2 .... 5D 59
Porchester Sq. W2 .... 5D 59
Porchester Sq. M. W2 .... 5D 59
Porchester Ter. W2 .... 1E 73
Porchester Ter. Nth. W2 ...... 5D 59
Porden Rd. SW2 .... 2B 104
Porlock Ho. SE26 .... 3C 120
Porlock St. SE1 .... 3C 26 (3F 77)
Portal Cl. SE27 .... 3C 118
Portbury Cl. SE15 .... 4C 92
Port Cres. E13 .... 3D 69
Portcullis Ho. SW1 ... 4D 23 (3A 76)
.... (off Bridge St.)
Port East Apts. E14 .... 1C 80
.... (off Hertsmere Rd.)
Portelet Ct. N1 .... 5A 50
.... (off De Beauvoir Est.)
Portelet Rd. E1 .... 2F 65
Porten Ho's. W14 .... 4A 72
.... (off Porten Rd.)
Porten Rd. W14 .... 4A 72
Porters Lodge, The SW10 ... 3E 87
.... (off Coleridge Gdns.)
Porter Sq. N19 .... 3A 34
Porter St. SE1 .... 1A 26 (2E 77)
Porter St. W1 .... 5A 4 (4B 60)
Porters Wik. E1 .... 1D 79
Porteus Pl. SW4 .... 1E 103
Porteus Rd. W2 .... 4E 59
Portfleet Pl. N1 .... 5A 50
.... (off De Beauvoir Rd.)
Portgate Cl. W9 .... 3B 58
Porthcawe Rd. SE26 .... 4A 122
Port Ho. E14 .... 1D 95
.... (off Burrells Wharf Sq.)
Portia Ct. SE11 .... 1D 91
.... (off Opal St.)
Portia Way E3 .... 3B 66
Porticos, The SW3 .... 2F 87
.... (off King's Rd.)
Portinscale Rd. SW15 .... 3A 100
Portishead Ho. W2 .... 4C 58
.... (off Westbourne Pk. Rd.)
Portland Av. N16 .... 2B 36
Portland Ct. N1 .... 4A 50
.... (off St Peter's Way)
Portland Ct. SE1 ...... 5B 26 (4F 77)
.... (off Gt. Dover St.)
Portland Ct. SE14 .... 2A 94
.... (off Whitcher Cl.)
Portland Cres. SE9 .... 2F 125
Portland Gdns. N4 .... 1D 35
Portland Ho. SW8 .... 4B 90
PORTLAND HOSPITAL FOR
    WOMEN & CHILDREN
.... 4E 5 (3D 61)
Portland Ho. SW11 .. 5F 21 (4E 75)
.... (off Bressenden Pl.)
Portland Ho. SW15 .... 3F 99
Portland Mans. W1 .... 2F 59
.... (off Addison Bri. Pl.)
Portland M. W1 .... 3A 14 (5E 61)
Portland Pl. W1 .... 4D 5 (4D 61)
Portland Ri. N4 .... 3D 35
.... (not continuous)

Portland Rd. BR1: Broml 4E 125
Portland Rd. SE9 .... 2F 125
Portland Rd. W11 .... 1A 72
Portland Sq. E1 .... 2D 79
Portland St. SE17 .... 1F 91
Portland Wlk. SE17 .... 2F 91
Portman Cl. W1 ...... 2A 12 (5B 60)
Portman Ga. NW1 .... 3A 60
Portman Mans. W1 .. 5A 4 (4B 60)
.... (off Chiltern St.)
Portman M. Sth.
    W1 .... 3B 12 (5C 60)
Portman Pl. E2 .... 2E 65
Portman Sq. W1 .... 2A 12 (5C 60)
Portman St. W1 .... 3B 12 (5C 60)
Portman Towers
    .... 2A 12 (5B 60)
Portmeers Cl. E17 .... 1B 38
Portnall Ho. W9 .... 2B 58
.... (off Portnall Rd.)
Portnall Rd. W9 .... 1B 58
Portobello Ct. W11 .... 5B 58
Portobello Grn. W10 .... 4A 58
.... (off Portobello Rd.)
Portobello Lofts W10 .... 3A 58
.... (off Kensal Rd.)
Portobello Mkt. 5B 58
Portobello M. W11 .... 1C 72
Portobello Rd. W10 .... 4A 58
Portobello Rd. W11 .... 5B 58
Portobello Road Market 1B 72
.... (off Portobello Rd.)
Portpool La. EC1 ..... 5B 8 (4C 62)
Portree St. E14 .... 5F 67
Portsdown Av. NW11 .... 1B 30
Portsdown M. NW11 .... 1B 30
Portsea Hall W2 .... 5B 60
.... (off Portsea Pl.)
Portsea M. W2 .... 5A 60
.... (off Portsea Pl.)
Portsea Pl. W2 .... 5A 60
Portslade Rd. SW8 .... 5E 89
Portsmouth M. E16 .... 2D 83
Portsmouth Rd. SW15 .... 5D 99
Portsmouth St.
    WC2 .... 2F 15 (5B 62)
Portsoken Pavs. EC3 .. 3F 19 (5B 64)
.... (off Aldgate Sq.)
Portsoken St. E1 ...... 4F 19 (1B 78)
Portswood Pl. SW15 .... 4B 98
Portugal St. WC2 ..... 3F 15 (5B 62)
Portway N15 .... 5B 54
Portway Gdns. SE18 .... 3F 97
Pory Ho. SE11 .... 5B 76
Poseidon Ct. E14 .... 5C 80
.... (off Homer Dr.)
Postal Mus., The 3A 8 (3B 62)
Postern, The EC2 .... 1A 18 (4E 63)
.... (off Wood St.)
Postmark Development
    EC1 .... 3A 8 (3B 62)
Post Office App. E7 .... 2D 55
Post Office Ct. EC3 .. 3C 18 (5F 63)
.... (off King William St.)
Post Office Way SW11 .... 3F 89
Potier St. SE1 .... 5C 26 (4F 77)
Potter Cl. SE15 .... 3A 92
Potter Ho. E1 .... 4E 65
.... (off Beaufort Gdns.)
Potterne Cl. SW19 .... 5F 99
Potters Flds. SE1 .. 2E 27 (2A 78)
Potter's La. SW16 .... 5F 117
Potters Lodge E14 .... 1E 95
.... (off Ferry St.)
Potters Rd. SW6 .... 5E 87

Potters Row E20 .... 2D 53
.... (off Keirin Rd.)
Pottery Café 4B 86
.... (off Fulham Rd.)
Pottery La. W11 .... 2A 72
Pottery M. SW6 .... 5B 86
Pottery St. SE16 .... 3D 79
Pott St. E2 .... 2D 65
Poulton Cl. E8 .... 3D 51
Poultry EC2 .... 3B 18 (5F 63)
Pound La. NW10 .... 3C 42
Pound Pk. Rd. SE7 .... 5F 83
Pound Path E3 .... 1F 65
.... (off Stoneway Wlk.)
Pountney Rd. SW11 .... 1C 102
Povey Ho. SE17 .... 5A 78
.... (off Beckway St.)
Powell Ho. W2 .... 1F 73
.... (off Gloucester Ter.)
Powell Rd. E5 .... 5D 37
Powell's Wlk. W4 .... 2A 84
Powergate Bus. Pk. NW10 .. 2A 56
Powerleague Battersea 3E 89
Powerscroft Rd. E5 .... 1E 51
Powis Cl. W11 .... 5B 58
.... (off Powis Gdns.)
Powis Gdns. NW11 .... 2B 30
Powis Gdns. W11 .... 5B 58
Powis Ho. WC2 .... 2E 15 (5A 62)
.... (off Macklin St.)
Powis M. W11 .... 5B 58
Powis Pl. WC1 .... 4E 7 (3A 62)
Powis Rd. E3 .... 2D 67
Powis Sq. W11 .... 5B 58
.... (not continuous)
Powis Ter. W11 .... 5B 58
Powlesland Ct. E1 .... 5A 66
.... (off White Horse Rd.)
Powlett Ho. NW1 .... 3D 47
.... (off Powlett Pl.)
Powlett Pl. NW1 .... 4C 46
Pownall Rd. E8 .... 5B 50
Pownall Ter. SE11 .... 2C 90
Powster Rd. BR1: Broml...... 5C 124
Poynders Ct. SW4 .... 4E 103
Poynders Gdns. SW4 .... 5E 103
Poynders Pde. SW4 .... 4F 103
Poynders Rd. SW4 .... 4E 103
Poynings Rd. N19 .... 5E 33
Poynter Ho. NW8 .... 3F 59
.... (off Fisherton St.)
Poynter Ho. W11 .... 2F 71
.... (off Queensdale Cres.)
Poyntz Rd. SW11 .... 5B 88
Poyser St. E2 .... 1D 65
Praed M. W2 .... 5F 59
Praed St. W2 .... 5F 59
Pragel St. E13 .... 1E 69
Pragnell Rd. SE12 .... 2D 125
Prague Pl. SW2 .... 3A 104
Prah Rd. N4 .... 4C 34
Prairie Bldg. E15 .... 2F 53
.... (off Property Row)
Prairie St. SW8 .... 5C 88
Praline Ct. E3 .... 1D 67
.... (off Taylor Pl.)
Pratt M. NW1 .... 5E 47
Pratt St. NW1 .... 5E 47
Pratt Wlk. SE11 .... 5B 76
Prayle Gro. NW2 .... 3F 29
Preachers Ct. EC1 ... 4E 9 (3D 63)
.... (off Charterhouse Sq.)
Prebend Gdns. W4 .... 5B 70
Prebend Gdns. W6 .... 5B 70
.... (not continuous)

Prebend Mans. W4 .... 5B **70**
.... (off Chiswick High Rd.)
Prebend St. N1 .... 5E **49**
Precinct, The N1 .... 5E **49**
Premier Cnr. W9 .... 1B **58**
Premiere Pl. E14 .... 1C **80**
Premier Ho. N1 .... 4D **49**
.... (off Waterloo Ter.)
Premier Pl. SW15 .... 2A **100**
Prendergast Rd. SE3 ...... 1A **110**
Prentice Ct. SW19 .... 5B **114**
Prentis Rd. SW16 .... 4F **117**
Prentiss Ct. SE7 .... 5F **83**
Presburg St. E5 .... 5F **37**
Prescot St. E1 ...... 4F **19** (1B **78**)
Prescott Ho. SE17 .... 2D **91**
.... (off Hillingdon St.)
Prescott Pl. SW4 .... 1F **103**
Presentation M. SW2 ...... 2B **118**
President Dr. E1 .... 2D **79**
President Ho. EC1 ...... 2E **9** (2D **63**)
President Quay E1 .... 2B **78**
.... (off St Katherine's Way)
President St. EC1 ...... 1F **9** (2E **63**)
.... (off Central St.)
Press Ct. SE1 .... 1C **92**
Press Ho. E1 .... 4F **65**
.... (off Trafalgar Gdns.)
Press Ho. NW10 .... 5A **28**
Press Rd. NW10 .... 5A **28**
Prestage Way E14 .... 1E **81**
Prestbury Rd. E7 .... 4E **55**
Prested Rd. SW11 .... 2A **102**
Preston Cl. SE1 .... 5A **78**
Preston Dr. E11 .... 1E **41**
Preston Gdns. NW10 ...... 3B **42**
Preston Ho. SE1: Lon
    Preston Cl. 5A **78**
    .... (off Preston Cl.)
Preston Ho. SE1: Lon
    St Saviour's Est. ... 5F **27** (4B **78**)
    .... (off St Saviour's Est.)
Preston Pl. NW2 .... 3C **42**
Preston Rd. E11 .... 1A **40**
Preston Rd. SE19 .... 5D **119**
Preston's Rd. E14 .... 1E **81**
Preston St. E2 .... 1F **65**
Prestwich Ter. SW4 .... 3E **103**
Prestwood Ho. SE16 ...... 4D **79**
.... (off Drummond Rd.)
Prestwood St. N1 ... 1A **10** (1E **63**)
Pretoria Rd. E11 .... 3F **39**
Pretoria Rd. E16 .... 3B **68**
Pretoria Rd. SW16 .... 5D **117**
Priam Ho. E2 .... 1D **65**
.... (off Old Bethnal Grn. Rd.)
Price Cl. SW17 .... 3B **116**
Price Ho. N1 .... 5E **49**
.... (off Britannia Row)
Price's Ct. SW11 .... 1F **101**
Price's M. N1 .... 5B **48**
Price's St. SE1 ...... 1E **25** (2D **77**)
Prichard Ct. N7 .... 2B **48**
Prichard Ho. SE11 .... 5C **76**
.... (off Kennington Rd.)
Prideaux Ho. WC1 ... 1A **8** (2B **62**)
.... (off Prideaux Pl.)
Prideaux Pl. W3 .... 1A **70**
Prideaux Pl. WC1 ... 1A **8** (2B **62**)
Prideaux Rd. SW9 .... 1A **104**
Priestfield Rd. SE23 ...... 3A **122**
Priestley Cl. N16 .... 2B **36**
Priestley Ho. EC1 ... 3A **10** (3E **63**)
.... (off Old St.)
Priestley Way NW2 .... 3C **28**

Priestman Point E3 .... 2D **67**
.... (off Rainhill Way)
Priests Bri. SW14 .... 1A **98**
Priests Bri. SW15 .... 1A **98**
Priest's Ct. EC2 ...... 2F **17** (5E **63**)
.... (off Foster La.)
Prima Rd. SW9 .... 3C **90**
Prime Meridian Line 3F **95**
Prime Meridian Wlk. E14 ... 1F **81**
Primezone M. N8 .... 1A **34**
Primrose Cl. E3 .... 1C **66**
Primrose Cl. SE6 .... 5E **123**
Primrose Cl. NW8 .... 1B **60**
.... (off Prince Albert Rd.)
Primrose Ct. SW12 .... 5F **103**
Primrose Gdns. NW3 ...... 3A **46**
Primrose Hill EC4 ... 3C **16** (5C **62**)
PRIMROSE HILL. 5C **46**
Primrose Hill Ct. NW3 ...... 4B **46**
Primrose Hill Rd. NW3 ...... 4B **46**
Primrose Hill Studios
    NW1 .... 5C **46**
Primrose Ho. SE15 .... 4C **92**
.... (off Peckham Hill St.)
Primrose Ho. SE16 .... 3A **80**
.... (off Blondin Way)
Primrose Mans. SW11 ...... 4C **88**
Primrose M. NW1 .... 4B **46**
.... (off Sharpleshall St.)
Primrose M. SE3 .... 3C **96**
Primrose Rd. E10 .... 3D **39**
Primrose Sq. E9 .... 4E **51**
Primrose St. EC2 ... 5D **11** (4A **64**)
Primrose Wlk. SE14 .... 3A **94**
Primrose Way SE10 .... 5C **56**
Primula St. W12 .... 5C **56**
Prince Albert Ct. NW8 ...... 5B **46**
.... (off Prince Albert Rd.)
Prince Albert M. SW11 ...... 3A **88**
Prince Albert Rd. NW1 ...... 2A **60**
Prince Albert Rd. NW8 ...... 2A **60**
Prince Arthur M. NW3 ...... 1E **45**
Prince Arthur Rd. NW3 ...... 2E **45**
Prince Charles Cinema
    .... 4C **14** (1F **75**)
    .... (off Leicester Pl.)
Prince Charles Dr. NW4 ...... 2E **29**
Prince Charles Rd. SE3 ...... 5B **96**
Prince Consort Rd. SW7 ...... 4E **73**
Princedale Rd. W11 .... 2A **72**
Prince Edward Mans. W2 ... 1C **72**
.... (off Moscow Rd.)
Prince Edward Rd. E9 ...... 3B **52**
Prince Edward Theatre
    .... 3C **14** (5F **61**)
    .... (off Old Compton St.)
Prince George Rd. N16 ...... 1A **50**
Prince Henry Rd. SE7 ...... 3F **97**
Prince John Rd. SE9 ...... 3F **111**
Princelet St. E1 ...... 5F **11** (4B **64**)
Prince of Orange Ct. SE16 ... 4F **79**
.... (off Lower Rd.)
Prince of Orange La. SE10 ... 3E **95**
Prince of Wales Dr. SW11 ... 4A **88**
Prince of Wales Dr. SW8 ... 3D **89**
Prince of Wales Mans.
    SW11 .... 4C **88**
Prince of Wales Pas.
    NW1 .... 2F **5** (2E **61**)
    .... (off Hampstead Rd.)
Prince of Wales Rd. E16 ...... 5E **69**
Prince of Wales Rd. NW5 ... 3C **46**
Prince of Wales Rd. SE3 ...... 5B **96**
Prince of Wales Ter. W4 ...... 1A **84**
Prince of Wales Ter. W8 ...... 3D **73**

Prince of Wales Theatre
    .... 5B **14** (1F **75**)
    .... (off Coventry St.)
Prince Regent Ct. NW8 ...... 1A **60**
    .... (off Avenue Rd.)
Prince Regent Ct. SE16 ...... 1A **80**
    .... (off Edward Sq.)
Prince Regent La. E13 ...... 2D **69**
Prince Regent La. E16 ...... 4E **69**
Prince Regent M.
    NW1 .... 2F **5** (2E **61**)
    .... (off Hampstead Rd.)
Prince Regent Station (DLR)
    .... 1E **83**
Princes Arc. SW1 ... 1A **22** (2E **75**)
    .... (off Piccadilly)
Princes Cir. WC2 ... 2D **15** (5A **62**)
Princes Cl. N4 .... 3D **35**
Princes Cl. SW4 .... 1E **103**
Prince's Ct. SE16 .... 4B **80**
Prince's Ct. SW3 .... 4B **74**
    .... (off Brompton Rd.)
Princes Ct. Bus. Cen. E1 ... 1D **79**
Prince's Gdns. SW7 .... 4F **73**
Prince's Ga. SW7 .... 3F **73**
    .... (not continuous)
Prince's Ga. Ct. SW7 ...... 3F **73**
Prince's Ga. M. SW7 ...... 4F **73**
Princes Ho. W11 .... 1B **72**
Prince's M. W2 .... 1D **73**
Prince's M. W6 .... 1D **85**
    .... (off Down Pl.)
Princes Pde. NW11 .... 1A **30**
    .... (off Golders Grn. Rd.)
Princes Pk. Av. NW11 ...... 1A **30**
Princes Pl. SW1 ... 1A **22** (2E **75**)
    .... (off Duke St.)
Princes Pl. W11 .... 2A **72**
Prince's Ri. SE13 .... 5E **95**
Princes Riverside Rd.
    SE16 .... 2F **79**
Prince's Rd. SW19 .... 5C **114**
Princes Rd. SW14 .... 1A **98**
Princess Alice Ho. W10 ...... 3E **57**
Princess Ct. N6 .... 2E **33**
Princess Ct. NW6 .... 3D **45**
    .... (off Compayne Gdns.)
Princess Ct. W1 .... 4B **60**
    .... (off Bryanston Pl.)
Princess Ct. W2 .... 1D **73**
    .... (off Queensway)
Princess Cres. N4 .... 4D **35**
PRINCESS GRACE HOSPITAL
    .... 4B **4** (3C **60**)
Princess Louise Bldg. SE8 ... 3C **94**
    .... (off Hales St.)
Princess Louise Cl. W2 ...... 4F **59**
Princess Louise Wlk. W10 ... 4F **57**
    .... (off Vincent St.)
Princess May Ho. SW1 ...... 5F **75**
    .... (off Vincent St.)
Princess May Rd. N16 ...... 1A **50**
Princess M. NW3 .... 2F **45**
Princess Sq. W2 .... 1D **73**
    .... (not continuous)
Princess Rd. NW1 .... 5C **46**
Princess Rd. NW6 .... 1C **58**
Princess St. SE1 ... 5E **25** (4D **77**)
Prince's St. EC2 ... 3B **18** (5F **63**)
Princes St. W1 ... 3E **13** (5D **61**)
Princes Ter. E13 .... 5D **55**
Prince's Twr. SE16 .... 3E **79**
    .... (off Elephant La.)
Prince St. SE8 .... 2B **94**
Princes Way SW19 .... 5F **99**
Prince's Yd. W11 .... 2A **72**

Princethorpe Ho. W2..............4D 59
.....................(off Woodchester Sq.)
Princethorpe Rd. SE26.........4F 121
Princeton Ct. SW15..............1F 99
Princeton St. WC1 1F 15 (4B 62)
Principal Pl. EC2....4E 11 (3A 64)
.....................(off Shoreditch High St.)
Principal Sq. E9......................2F 51
Pringle Gdns. SW16............4E 117
......................(not continuous)
Printers Inn Ct.
EC4...................2B 16 (5C 62)
Printers M. E3........................5A 52
Printers Rd. SW9..................4B 90
Printer St. EC4.....2C 16 (5C 62)
Printing Ho. Yd. E2...1E 11 (2A 64)
Printon Ho. E14......................4B 66
.......................(off Wallwood St.)
Print Room, The...................5C 58
.......................(off Hereford Rd.)
Print Room at the Coronet ..2C 72
.......................(off Notting Hill Ga.)
Print Village SE15..................5B 92
Printwork Apts.
SE1...................5D 27 (4A 78)
.......................(off Long La.)
Printwork Apts. SE5...............5E 91
.......................(off Coldharbour La.)
Priolo Rd. SE7........................1E 97
Prior Bolton St. N1...............3D 49
Prioress Ho. E3......................2D 67
.......................(off Bromley High St.)
Prioress Rd. SE27................3D 119
Prioress St. SE1 ....5C 26 (4A 78)
Priors, The NW3....................5F 31
Prior St. SE10........................3E 95
Priory, The SE3.....................2B 110
Priory Apts., The SE6.........1D 123
Priory Av. W4........................5A 70
Priory Ct. E6..........................5E 55
Priory Ct. E9..........................2F 51
Priory Ct. EC4.......3E 17 (5D 63)
.......................(off Pilgrim St.)
Priory Ct. SW8......................4F 89
Priory Gdns. N6...................1D 33
Priory Gdns. SW13...............1B 98
Priory Gdns. W4...................5A 70
Priory Grn. N1.......................1B 62
Priory Grn. Est. N1...............1B 62
Priory Gro. SW8....................4A 90
Priory Hgts. N1.....................1B 62
.......................(off Wynford Rd.)
PRIORY HOSPITAL ROEHAMPTON
....2B 98
Priory Ho. E1........5F 11 (4B 64)
.......................(off Folgate St.)
Priory Ho. EC1.........3D 9 (3D 63)
.......................(off Sans Wlk.)
Priory Ho. SW1......................1F 89
.......................(off Rampayne St.)
Priory La. SW15....................4A 98
Priory Mans. SW10...............1F 87
.......................(off Drayton Gdns.)
Priory M. SW8......................4A 90
Priory Pk. SE3......................1B 110
Priory Pk. Rd. NW6...............5B 44
Priory Rd. E6..........................5F 55
Priory Rd. NW6.....................5D 45
Priory St. E3..........................2D 67
Priory Ter. NW6....................5D 45
Priory Wlk. SW10...................1E 87
Pritchard Ho. E2.....................1D 65
.......................(off Ada Pl.)
Pritchard's Rd. E2................5C 50
Priter Rd. SE16......................4C 78

Priter Rd. Hostel SE16..........4C 78
.......................(off Dockley Rd.)
Priter Way SE16.....................4C 78
Prize Wlk. E20........................2E 53
Probert Rd. SW2...................3C 104
Probyn Ho. SW1.....................5F 75
.......................(off Page St.)
Probyn Rd. SW2..................2D 119
Procter Ho. SE1....................1C 92
.......................(off Avondale Sq.)
Procter Ho. SE5.....................3F 91
.......................(off Picton St.)
Procter St. WC1.....1F 15 (4B 62)
Project Pk. E16......................3F 67
Prologis Pk. E3......................3E 67
Promenade, The W4...............5A 84
Promenade App. Rd. W4 .....3A 84
Prospect Cl. SE26...............4D 121
Prospect Cotts. SW18..........2C 100
Prospect Ho. E3.....................2C 66
.......................(off Campbell Rd.)
Prospect Ho. N1.....................1C 62
.......................(off Donegal St.)
Prospect Ho. SE1 ...5D 25 (4D 77)
.......................(off Gaywood St.)
Prospect Ho. SE16.................4C 78
.......................(off Frean St.)
Prospect Ho. W10..................5F 57
.......................(off Bridge Cl.)
Prospect Pk. 3D 67
.......................(off Reeves Rd.)
Prospect Pl. E1......................2E 79
.......................(not continuous)
Prospect Pl. N7......................1A 48
Prospect Pl. NW2..................5B 30
Prospect Pl. NW3..................1E 45
Prospect Pl. SE8....................2B 94
.......................(off Evelyn St.)
Prospect Pl. SW11................3D 89
Prospect Quay SW18...........2C 100
.......................(off Lightermans Wlk.)
Prospect Rd. NW2.................5B 30
Prospect Row E15.................2E 53
Prospect Row Ho's. E15.......2E 53
.......................(off Property Row)
Prospect St. SE16..................4D 79
Prospect Wharf E1.................1E 79
Prospero Ho. E1.....4F 19 (1B 78)
.......................(off Portsoken St.)
Prospero Rd. N19..................3F 33
Protea Cl. E16........................3B 68
Protea Pl. E9..........................4E 51
.......................(off Lyme Gro.)
Prothero Rd. SW6..................3A 86
Proton Twr. E14......................1F 81
Proud Ho. E1..........................5D 65
.......................(off Amazon St.)
Prout Gro. NW10...................1A 42
Prout Rd. E5...........................5D 37
Provence St. N1......................1E 63
Providence Cl. E9...................5F 51
Providence Ct.
W1..........................4C 12 (1C 74)
Providence Ho. E14...............5B 66
.......................(off Three Colt St.)
Providence Pl. N1..................5D 49
Providence Pl. SE10...............1A 96
Providence Row N1 ...1F 7 (1B 62)
.......................(off Pentonville Rd.)
Providence Row Cl. E2.........2D 65
Providence Sq. SE1...............3C 78
Providence Twr. E14...............1F 81
.......................(off Fairmont Av.)
Providence Twr. SE16............3C 78
.......................(off Bermondsey Wall W.)

Providence Yd. E2..................2C 64
.......................(off Ezra St.)
Province Dr. SE16..................3E 79
Province Sq. E14....................2E 81
.......................(off Blackwall Way)
Provost Ct. NW3....................3B 46
.......................(off Eton Rd.)
Provost Est. N1......1B 10 (1F 63)
.......................(off Provost St.)
Provost Rd. NW3....................4B 46
Provost St. N1........1B 10 (1F 63)
Prowse Pl. NW1......................4D 47
Prudent Pas. EC2....2A 18 (5E 63)
.......................(off King St.)
Prusom's Island E1................2E 79
.......................(off Wapping High St.)
Prusom St. E1.........................2D 79
Pryce Ho. E3...........................2C 66
.......................(off Campbell Rd.)
Pudding La. EC3......5C 18 (1F 77)
Pudding Mill La. E15...............5D 53
Pudding Mill Lane Station (DLR)
....5D 53
Puddle Dock EC4 ...4D 17 (1D 77)
.......................(not continuous)
Pugin Cl. SW19....................4D 115
Pugin Ct. N1...........................4C 48
.......................(off Liverpool Rd.)
Pulborough Rd. SW18.........5B 100
Pulford Rd. N15.....................1F 35
Pulham Ho. SW8...................3B 90
.......................(off Dorset Rd.)
Pullen's Bldgs. SE17............1D 91
.......................(off Iliffe St.)
Pullman Ct. SW2..................1A 118
Pullman Gdns. SW15............4E 99
Pullman M. SE12..................3D 125
Pulross Rd. SW9...................1B 104
Pulse Apts. NW6...................2D 45
.......................(off Lymington Rd.)
Pulteney Cl. E3.......................5B 52
Pulteney Ter. N1.....................5B 48
.......................(not continuous)
Pultney St. N1.........................5B 48
Pulton Rd. SE4......................2A 108
.......................(off Turnham Rd.)
Pulton Pl. SW6.......................3C 86
Puma Ct. E1..........5F 11 (4B 64)
Pump Ct. EC4........3B 16 (5C 62)
Pump Ho. Cl. SE16................3E 79
Pump House Gallery..............3C 88
Pump Ho. La. SW11...............3E 89
Pump Ho. M. E1.....................1C 78
.......................(off Hooper St.)
Pumping Ho. E14...................1F 81
.......................(off Naval Row)
Pumping Station Rd. W4 .....3A 84
Pump La. SE14.......................3E 93
Punderson's Gdns. E2..........2D 65
Purbeck Dr. NW2...................4F 29
Purbeck Gdns. SE26.............5B 122
Purbeck Ho. SW8...................3B 90
.......................(off Bolney St.)
Purbrook Est. SE1...4E 27 (3A 78)
Purbrook St. SE1....5E 27 (4A 78)
Purcell Cres. SW6.................3F 85
Purcell Ho. SW10...................2F 87
.......................(off Milman's St.)
Purcell Mans. W14................2A 86
.......................(off Queen's Club Gdns.)
Purcell M. NW10....................4A 42
Purcell Room 1A 24 (2B 76)
.......................(in Southbank Cen.)
Purcell St. N1.........................1A 64
Purchese St. NW1 ...1C 6 (1F 61)

Purday Ho. W10 .... 2A 58
.... (off Bruckner St.)
Purdon Ho. SE15 .... 4C 92
.... (off Oliver Goldsmith Est.)
Purdy St. E3 .... 3D 67
PureGym Aldgate 2F 19 (5B 64)
.... (off Houndsditch)
PureGym Bayswater 1D 73
.... (off Moscow Pl.)
PureGym Canary Wharf 1C 80
PureGym East India Dock ... 1E 81
.... (off Clove Cres.)
PureGym Hallam St. 5E 5 (4D 61)
.... (off Hallam St.)
PureGym Hammersmith Palais
.... 5E 71
PureGym Holborn 5F 7 (4B 62)
.... (off Theobald's Rd.)
PureGym Limehouse 5A 66
PureGym London Wall
.... 1B 18 (4F 63)
.... (off London Wall)
PureGym Marylebone,
Balcombe St. 5A 4 (4B 60)
PureGym Piccadilly ..1B 22 (2F 75)
.... (off Regent St.)
PureGym Putney 2A 100
PureGym South Kensington
.... 5A 74
PureGym St Pauls ... 1F 17 (4E 63)
.... (off Little Britain)
PureGym Tottenham 4E 121
PureGym Tower Hill .. 4F 19 (1B 78)
.... (off America Sq.)
Purelake M. SE13 .... 1F 109
.... (off Marischal Rd.)
Purley Av. NW2 .... 4A 30
Purley Pl. N1 .... 4D 49
Purneys Rd. SE9 .... 2F 111
Purser Ho. SW2 .... 4C 104
Pursers Cross Rd. SW6 .... 4B 86
Purves Rd. NW10 .... 2D 57
Pusey Ho. E14 .... 5C 66
.... (off Saracen St.)
Puteaux Ho. E2 .... 1F 65
.... (off Mace St.)
PUTNEY 2F 99
Putney Arts Theatre 2F 99
PUTNEY BRI. 1A 100
Putney Bri. App. SW6 .... 1A 100
Putney Bri. Rd. SW15 .... 2A 100
Putney Bri. Rd. SW18 .... 2C 100
Putney Bridge Station
(Underground) 1B 100
Putney Comn. SW15 .... 1E 99
Putney Heath SW15 .... 5D 99
PUTNEY HEATH 4E 99
Putney Heath La. SW15 .... 4F 99
Putney High St. SW15 .... 2F 99
Putney Hill SW15 .... 5F 99
.... (not continuous)
Putney Leisure Cen. 2E 99
Putney Pk. Av. SW15 .... 2C 98
Putney Pk. La. SW15 .... 2D 99
.... (not continuous)
Putney Pier (River Bus) 1A 100
Putney Station (Rail) 2A 100
PUTNEY VALE 3C 112
Putney Va. Crematorium 2D 113
Putney Wharf SW15 .... 1A 100
Putt in the Pk. 2B 100
Pymers Mead SE21 .... 1E 119
Pyne Ter. SW19 .... 1A 114
.... (off Windlesham Gro.)
Pynfolds SE16 .... 3D 79

Pynnersmead SE24 .... 3E 105
Pyrland Rd. N5 .... 2F 49
Pyrmont Gro. SE27 .... 3D 119
Pytchley Rd. SE22 .... 1A 106

Q

Q Bldg., The E15 .... 3A 54
.... (off The Grove)
Quad Ct. SE1 .... 5E 27 (4A 78)
.... (off Grigg's Pl.)
Quadrangle, The E15 .... 3A 54
Quadrangle, The SE24 .... 3E 105
Quadrangle, The SW10 .... 4E 87
Quadrangle, The W6 .... 3A 86
Quadrangle, The W2 .... 5A 60
Quadrangle Cl. SE1 .... 5A 78
Quadrant, The W10 .... 2F 57
Quadrant Arc. W1 .... 5A 14 (1E 75)
.... (off Regent St.)
Quadrant Bus. Cen. NW6 ...... 5A 44
Quadrant Gro. NW5 .... 2B 46
Quadrant Ho. E1 .... 1C 78
.... (off Nesham St.)
Quadrant Ho. E15 .... 2A 68
.... (off Durban Rd.)
Quadrant Ho. SE1 .... 1D 25 (2D 77)
.... (off Burrell St.)
Quadrant Wlk. E14 .... 4D 81
.... (off Lanterns Way)
Quaggy Wlk. SE3 .... 2C 110
Quain Mans. W14 .... 2A 86
.... (off Queen's Club Gdns.)
Quaker Ct. E1 .... 4F 11 (3B 64)
.... (off Quaker St.)
Quaker Ct. EC1 .... 3A 10 (3E 63)
.... (off Banner St.)
Quakers Pl. E7 .... 2F 55
Quaker St. E1 .... 4F 11 (3B 64)
Quality Ct. WC2 .... 2B 16 (5C 62)
.... (off Chancery La.)
Quantock Gdns. NW2 .... 4F 29
Quantock Ho. N16 .... 3B 36
Quantock M. SE15 .... 5C 92
Quantum Ct. E1 .... 1E 79
.... (off King David La.)
Quarrendon St. SW6 .... 5C 86
Quarry Rd. SW18 .... 4E 101
Quarterdeck, The E14 .... 3C 80
Quarter Ho. SW18 .... 2E 101
Quartz Apts. SE14 .... 2A 94
.... (off Moulding La.)
Quastel Ho. SE1 .... 4B 26 (3F 77)
.... (off Long La.)
Quay Ho. E14 .... 3C 80
.... (off Admirals Way)
Quayside Cotts. E1 .... 2C 78
.... (off Mews St.)
Quayside Ct. SE16 .... 2F 79
.... (off Abbotshade Rd.)
Quayside Ho. E14 .... 2B 80
Quayside Ho. E16 .... 5B 68
.... (off Tarling Rd.)
Quayside Ho. W10 .... 4C 80
Quay Vw. Apts. E14 .... 4C 80
.... (off Arden Cres.)
Quebec M. W1 .... 3A 12 (5B 60)
Quebec Way SE16 .... 3F 79
Quebec Wharf E14 .... 5B 66
Quebec Wharf E8 .... 5A 50
.... (off Kingsland Rd.)
Quedgeley Ct. SE15 .... 2B 92
.... (off Ebley Cl.)
Queen Alexandra Mans.
WC1 .... 1D 7 (2A 62)
.... (off Bidborough St.)

Queen Alexandra's Ct.
SW19 .... 5B 114
Queen Anne Ho. E16 .... 2C 82
.... (off Hardy Av.)
Queen Anne M. W1 ...1D 13 (4D 61)
Queen Anne Rd. E9 .... 3F 51
Queen Anne's Ct. SE10 .... 1F 95
.... (off Park Row)
Queen Anne's Gdns. W4 .... 4A 70
Queen Anne's Ga.
SW1 .... 4B 22 (3F 75)
Queen Anne's Gro. W4 .... 4A 70
Queen Annes Sq. SE1 .... 5C 78
.... (off Monnow Rd.)
Queen Anne St. W1 ..2D 13 (5D 61)
Queen Anne Ter. E1 .... 1D 79
.... (off Sovereign Cl.)
Queen Caroline's Temple 2F 73
Queen Caroline M. SW6 .... 1E 85
Queen Catherine Ho. SW6 .... 3D 87
.... (off Wandon Rd.)
QUEEN CHARLOTTE'S & CHELSEA
HOSPITAL 5C 56
Queen Ct. WC1 .... 4E 7 (3A 62)
.... (off Queen Sq.)
Queen Elizabeth Bldgs.
EC4 .... 4B 16 (1C 76)
.... (off Middle Temple La.)
Queen Elizabeth Hall
.... 1A 24 (2B 76)
Queen Elizabeth Ho.
SW12 .... 5C 102
Queen Elizabeth Olympic Pk.
.... 4D 53
Queen Elizabeth's Cl. N16 ....4F 35
Queen Elizabeth's Coll.
SE10 .... 3E 95
Queen Elizabeth St.
SE1 .... 3E 27 (3A 78)
Queen Elizabeth's Wlk. N16 ... 3F 35
Queen Elizabeth's Wlk. SW13 ...4C 84
Queenhithe EC4 .... 4A 18 (1E 77)
Queen Isabella Way
EC1 .... 2E 17 (5D 63)
.... (off King Edward St.)
Queen Margaret Flats E2 ..... 2D 65
.... (off St Jude's Rd.)
Queen Margaret's Gro. N1 .... 2A 50
Queen Mary Ho. E16 .... 2D 83
.... (off Wesley Av.)
Queen Mary Rd. SE19 .... 5D 119
Queen Marys Bldgs. SW1 ..... 5E 75
.... (off Stillington St.)
Queen Mary's Ct. SE10 .... 2F 95
.... (off Park Row)
QUEEN MARY'S HOSPITAL,
ROEHAMPTON 4C 98
Queen Mary's Ho. SW15 ...... 4C 98
Queen Mary University of London
Charterhouse Sq. ... 4E 9 (3D 63)
Queen Mary University of London
Lincoln's Inn Flds. Campus ... 2F 15
(5B 62) .... (off Remnant St.)
Queen Mary University of London
Mile End Campus 3A 66
Queen Mary University of London
W. Smithfield Campus
.... 1E 17 (4D 63)
.... (off Giltspur St.)
Queen Mother Sports Cen., The
.... 5E 75
.... (off Vauxhall Bri. Rd.)
Queen of Denmark Ct.
SE16 .... 4B 80
Queensberry M. W. SW7 ...... 5F 73
Queensberry Pl. E12 .... 2F 55

Queensberry Pl. SW7 ....5F **73**
Queensberry Way SW7 ....5F **73**
Queensborough M. W2 ....1E **73**
Queensborough Pas. W2 .....1E **73**
.... (off Queensborough M.)
Queensborough Studios W2...1E **73**
.... (off Queensborough M.)
Queensbridge Ct. E2 ....5B **50**
.... (off Queensbridge Rd.)
Queensbridge Rd. E2 ....5B **50**
Queensbridge Rd. E8 ....3B **50**
Queensbridge Sports &
  Community Cen. 4B **50**
Queensbury St. N1 ....4E **49**
Queen's Cir. SW11 ....3D **89**
Queen's Club Gdns. W14 ....2A **86**
Queen's Club (Tennis Courts),
  The 1A **86**
Queens Club Ter. W14 ....2B **86**
.... (off Normand Rd.)
Queen's Ct. NW8 ....1F **59**
.... (off Queen's Ter.)
Queens Ct. E11.....................2A **40**
Queens Ct. NW11 ....1B **30**
Queens Ct. NW6 ....2C **45**
Queens Ct. SE16 ....4B **78**
.... (off Old Jamaica Rd.)
Queens Ct. SE23 ....2E **121**
Queens Ct. W2 ....1D **73**
.... (off Queensway)
Queen's Cres. NW5 ....3C **46**
Queenscroft Rd. SE9............3F **111**
Queensdale Cres. W11.........2F **71**
.... (not continuous)
Queensdale Pl. W11..............2A **72**
Queensdale Rd. W11............2F **71**
Queensdale Wlk. W11...........2A **72**
Queen's Diamond Jubilee
  Galleries, The ..... 5D **23 (4A 76)**
Queensdown Rd. E5.............1D **51**
Queen's Dr. N4 ....4D **35**
Queens Dr. E10 ....2C **38**
Queen's Elm Pde. SW3 ....1F **87**
.... (off Old Church St.)
Queen's Elm Sq. SW3 ....1F **87**
Queen's Gallery...........4E **21 (3D 75)**
Queen's Gdns. NW4 ....1E **29**
Queen's Gdns. W2................1D **73**
Queen's Ga. SW7 ....3E **73**
Queen's Ga. Gdns. SW7 ....3E **73**
Queens Ga. Gdns. SW15 ......2D **99**
Queensgate Ho. E3 ....1B **66**
.... (off Hereford Rd.)
Queen's Ga. M. SW7 ....4E **73**
Queen's Ga. Pl. SW7 ....4E **73**
Queen's Ga. Pl. M. SW7 ....4E **73**
Queen's Ga. Ter. SW7 ....4E **73**
Queens Ga. Vs. E9...............4A **52**
Queen's Gro. NW8................5F **45**
Queen's Gro. Studios
  NW8 ....5F **45**
Queen's Head Pas.
  EC4..........................2F **17 (5E 63)**
Queen's Head St. N1 ....5D **49**
Queen's Head Yd.
  SE1......................2B **26 (2F 77)**
.... (off Borough High St.)
Queens Ho. SE17..................2F **91**
.... (off Merrow St.)
Queens Ho. SW8 ....3A **90**
.... (off Sth. Lambeth Rd.)
Queens Ho. W2.....................1D **73**
.... (off Queensway)

Queen's House, The 2F **95**
.... (within National Maritime Mus.)
Queen's Ice & Bowl 1D **73**
Queensland Rd. N7 ....1C **48**
Queen's Mans. W6................5F **71**
.... (off Brook Grn.)
Queen's Mkt. E13..................1E **69**
Queensmead NW8.................5F **45**
Queensmere Cl. SW19 ....2F **113**
Queensmere Ct. SW13 ....3B **84**
Queensmere Rd. SW19 ....2F **113**
Queen's M. W2.....................1D **73**
Queensmill Rd. SW6 ....3F **85**
Queen's Pde. NW2 ....3E **43**
.... (off Willesden La.)
Queens Pde. NW4 ....1E **29**
.... (off Queens Rd.)
QUEENS PK. 1A **58**
Queen's Pk. Ct. W10............2F **57**
Queen's Pk. Rangers FC.....2D **71**
Queen's Park Station
  (Underground & Overground)
  ....1B **58**
Queen Sq. WC1 ....4E **7 (3A 62)**
Queen Sq. Pl. WC1 ......4E **7 (3A 62)**
Queen's Quay EC4......4A **18 (1E 77)**
.... (off Up. Thames St.)
Queens Ride SW13................1C **98**
Queen's Rd. E11...................1B **38**
Queen's Rd. SE14 ....4E **93**
Queen's Rd. SE15 ....4D **93**
Queen's Rd. SW14 ....1A **98**
Queens Rd. E11....................2F **39**
Queens Rd. E13....................5D **55**
Queens Rd. E17 ....1A **38**
Queens Rd. NW4..................1E **29**
Queens Road Station, Peckham
  (Rail & Overground) 4E **93**
Queen's Rd. W. E13.............1C **68**
Queen's Row SE17...............2F **91**
Queen's Ter. E13..................5D **55**
Queen's Ter. NW8................5F **45**
Queens Ter. E1.....................3E **65**
.... (off Cephas St.)
Queen's Theatre London
  ....4B **14 (1F 75)**
.... (off Shaftesbury Av.)
Queensthorpe M. SE26.........4F **121**
Queensthorpe Rd. SE26.......4F **121**
Queen's Tower 4F **73**
.... (within Imperial College London)
Queenstown M. SW8.............5D **89**
Queenstown Rd. SW11 ....2D **89**
Queenstown Rd. SW8 ....4D **89**
Queenstown Road Station,
  Battersea (Rail) 4D **89**
Queen St. EC4 ....4A **18 (1E 77)**
.... (not continuous)
Queen St. W1 ....1D **21 (2D 75)**
Queen St. Pl. EC4......4A **18 (1E 77)**
Queensville Rd. SW12.........5F **103**
Queen's Wlk. SW1: Lon
  Green Pk...............1F **21 (2E 75)**
Queen's Wlk. N5: Lon
  Highbury............................2D **49**
Queen's Wlk., The
  SE1......................1A **24 (2B 76)**
Queen's Way NW4................1E **29**
Queensway W2 ....5D **59**
Queensway M. SE6 ....4E **123**
.... (off Whitefoot La.)
Queensway Station
  (Underground).....................1D **73**
Queenswood Ct. SE27 ....4F **119**
Queenswood Rd. SW4 ....3A **104**

Queenswood Gdns. E11.......3D **41**
Queens Wood Rd. N10.........1D **33**
Queenswood Rd. SE23.........3F **121**
Queen's Yd. WC1 ....4A **6 (4E 61)**
Queens Yd. E9......................3C **52**
Queen Victoria Memorial
  ....3F **21 (3E 75)**
Queen Victoria Seaman's Rest
  E14...................................5D **67**
.... (off E. India Dock Rd.)
Queen Victoria Statue 2D **73**
Queen Victoria St.
  EC4.................................3E **17 (1D 77)**
Queen Victoria Ter. E1.........1D **79**
.... (off Sovereign Cl.)
Quemerford Rd. N7...............2B **48**
Quendon Ho. W10 ....3E **57**
.... (off Sutton Way)
Quenington Ct. SE15............2B **92**
Quentin Ho. SE1 ....3D **25 (3D 77)**
.... (off Chaplin Cl.)
Quentin Pl. SE13 ....1A **110**
Quentin Rd. SE13 ....1A **110**
Quernmore Cl.
  BR1: Broml 5C **124**
Quernmore Rd. N4 ....1C **34**
Querrin St. SW6 ....5E **87**
Quest, The W11....................1A **72**
.... (off Clarendon Rd.)
Quested Ct. E8 ....2D **51**
.... (off Brett Rd.)
Quex Ct. NW6.......................5D **45**
.... (off West End La.)
Quex M. NW6........................5C **44**
Quex Rd. NW6......................5C **44**
Quiberon Ct. E13..................5C **54**
.... (off Pelly Rd.)
Quick Rd. W4.......................1A **84**
Quick St. N1 ....1D **63**
Quick St. M. N1....................1D **63**
Quickswood NW3.................4A **46**
Quill Ho. E2 ....3C **64**
.... (off Cheshire St.)
Quill La. SW15.....................2F **99**
Quill St. N4 ....5C **34**
Quilp St. SE1 ....3F **25 (3E 77)**
.... (not continuous)
Quilter St. E2........................2C **64**
Quilting Ct. SE16..................3F **79**
.... (off Garter Way)
Quince Ho. SE13 ....5D **95**
.... (off Quince Rd.)
Quince Rd. SE13 ....5D **95**
Quinn Cl. E2 ....1E **65**
Quinton Ct. SE16..................5A **80**
.... (off Plough Way)
Quinton Ho. SW8..................3A **90**
.... (off Wyvil Rd.)
Quinton St. SW18.................2E **115**
Quixley St. E14.....................1F **81**
Quorn Rd. SE22 ....2A **106**

R

Rabbit Row W8.....................2C **72**
Raby St. E14.........................5A **66**
Racine SE5...........................4A **92**
.... (off Sceaux Gdns.)
Rackham M. SW16 ....5E **117**
Rackstraw Ho. NW3..............4B **46**
Racton Rd. SW6 ....2C **86**
RADA Chenies St......5B **6 (4F 61)**
.... (off Chenies St.)
RADA Gower St.........5B **6 (4F 61)**
.... (off Gower St.)

RADA Studios............5B 6 (4F 61)
............(off Chenies St.)
Radbourne Cl. E5.................1F 51
Radbourne Rd. SW12.......5E 103
Radcliff Ct. E3.......................3E 66
............(off Jospeh St.)
Radcliffe Av. NW10..............1C 56
Radcliffe Ho. SE16.............5D 89
............(off Anchor St.)
Radcliffe Path SW8.............5D 89
Radcliffe Rd. SE1....5E 27 (4A 78)
Radcliffe Sq. SW15...............4F 99
Radcot Point SE23...............3F 121
Radcot St. SE11...................1C 90
Raddington Rd. W10.............4A 58
Raddon Twr. E8.....................3B 50
............(off Dalston Sq.)
Radford St. SE15..................3D 93
............(off Old Kent Rd.)
Radford Est. NW10...............2A 56
Radford Ho. E14...................4D 67
............(off St Leonard's Rd.)
Radford Ho. N7.....................2B 48
Radford Rd. SE13..............4E 109
Radipole Rd. SW6...............4B 86
Radisson Ct. SE1....5D 27 (4A 78)
............(off Long La.)
Radius Apts. N1.......1E 7 (1B 62)
............(off Omega Pl.)
Radland Rd. E16..................5B 68
Radlet Av. SE26..................3D 121
Radlett Cl. E7.......................3B 54
Radlett Pl. NW8...................5A 46
Radley Ct. SE16...................3F 79
Radley Ho. NW1.....3A 4 (3B 60)
............(off Gloucester Pl.)
Radley M. W8.......................4C 72
Radley Sq. E5........................4E 37
Radley Ter. E16....................4B 68
............(off Hermit Rd.)
Radlix Rd. E10......................3C 38
Radnor Ho. EC1......2A 10 (2E 63)
............(off Radnor St.)
Radnor Lodge W2.................5F 59
............(off Sussex Pl.)
Radnor M. W2.......................5F 59
Radnor Pl. W2.......................5A 60
Radnor Rd. NW6....................5A 44
Radnor Rd. SE15...................3C 92
Radnor St. EC1.......2A 10 (2E 63)
Radnor Ter. W14..................5B 72
Radnor Wlk. E14...................5C 80
............(off Barnsdale Av.)
Radnor Wlk. SW3.................1A 88
Radstock St. SW11...............3A 88
............(not continuous)
Radway Ho. W2.....................4C 58
............(off Alfred Rd.)
Raeburn Cl. NW11................1E 31
Raeburn St. SW2.................2A 104
RAF Bomber Command Memorial
............3D 21 (3D 75)
Ragged School Mus..............4A 66
Raglan Ct. E17....................1E 39
Raglan Ct. SE12..................3C 110
Raglan St. NW5....................3D 47
Ragwort Ct. SE26...............5D 121
Rahere Ct. E1.......................1A 66
............(off Toby La.)
Railey M. NW5.....................2D 47
Railton Rd. SE24................2C 104
Railway App. N4...................1C 34
Railway App. SE1....1C 26 (2F 77)
Railway Arches E1: Lon
   Barnardo St..................5F 65
............(off Barnardo St.)
Railway Arches E1: Lon
   Chapman St...................1D 79
............(off Chapman St.)
Railway Arches E2: Lon
   Cremer St........1F 11 (1B 64)
............(off Cremer St.)
Railway Arches E2: Lon
   Geffrye St.....................1B 64
............(off Geffrye St.)
Railway Arches E2: Lon
   Laburnum St...................5B 50
............(off Laburnum St.)
Railway Arches E8: Lon
   Martello Ter..................4D 51
............(off Martello Ter.)
Railway Arches E8: Lon
   Mentmore Ter.................4D 51
............(off Mentmore Ter.)
Railway Arches E10.............3E 39
Railway Arches E11.............3F 39
............(off Grove Grn. Rd.)
Railway Arches E16.............2C 82
Railway Arches E3...............3B 66
............(off Cantrell Rd.)
Railway Arches E7...............1C 54
............(off Winchelsea Rd.)
Railway Arches W12.............3E 71
............(off Shepherd's Bush Mkt.)
Railway Arches W6...............4E 71
Railway Av. SE16.................3E 79
............(not continuous)
Railway Children Wlk.
   Reserve.......................1D 35
Railway Cotts. E15..............1A 68
............(off Baker's Row)
Railway Cotts. SW19....4D 115
Railway Cotts. W6................3E 71
............(off Sulgrave Rd.)
Railway Fields Local Nature
   Reserve.......................1D 35
Railway Gro. SE14..............3B 94
Railway M. W10....................5A 58
Railway Ri. SE22................2A 106
Railway Side SW13..............1A 98
Railway Sidings Rd.
   SE16..........................4C 78
Railway Sta. Bri. E7..........2D 55
Railway St. N1.....................1A 62
Railway Ter. SE13..............3D 109
Rainbow Av. E14.................1D 95
Rainbow Ct. SE14.............2A 94
............(off Chipley St.)
Rainbow Quay SE16............4A 80
............(not continuous)
Rainbow St. SE5................3A 92
Raines Ct. N16.....................4B 36
Raine St. E1.......................2D 79
Rainham Cl. SW11..............4A 102
Rainham Ho. NW1...............5E 47
............(off Bayham Pl.)
Rainham Rd. NW10............2E 57
Rainhill Way E3..................2C 66
Rainsborough Av. SE8........5A 80
Rainsborough Ho. SW15...3A 100
............(off Stamford Sq.)
Rainsborough Sq. SW6......2C 86
Rainsford St. W2................5A 60
Rainton Rd. SE7.................1C 96
Rainville Rd. W6.................2E 85
Rajsee Apts. E1.................2C 64
............(off Bethnal Grn. Rd.)
Raleana Rd. E14................2E 81
Raleigh St. SE16...............2F 79
............(off Clarence M.)
Raleigh Ct. SE8..................1A 94
............(off Evelyn St.)
Raleigh Ct. W12.................3E 71
............(off Scott's Rd.)
Raleigh Gdns. SW2............4B 104
Raleigh Ho. E14..................3D 81
............(off Admirals Way)
Raleigh Ho. SW1.................2F 89
............(off Dolphin Sq.)
Raleigh M. N1.....................5D 49
............(off Packington St.)
Raleigh St. N1.....................5D 49
Rally Bldg. E17....................1B 38
Ralph Bayer Ct. E3.............4C 66
............(off Geoff Cade Way)
Ralph Brook Ct. N1...1C 10 (2F 63)
............(off Chart St.)
Ralph Ct. W2.......................5D 59
............(off Queensway)
Ralston St. SW3..................1B 88
Ramac Ind. Est. SE7...........5D 83
Ramac Way SE7..................5D 83
Ramar Ho. E1......................4C 64
............(off Hanbury St.)
Rambert.............1B 24 (2C 76)
............(off Upper Ground)
Rambler Cl. SW16..............4E 117
Rame Cl. SW17...................5C 116
Ramilles Cl. SW2...............4A 104
Ramillies Pl. W1....3F 13 (5E 61)
Ramillies Rd. W4.................5A 70
Ramillies St. W1....3F 13 (5E 61)
Rampart St. E1....................5D 65
Rampayne St. SW1..............1F 89
Ram Pl. E9...........................3E 51
Ram Quarter SW18.............3D 101
Ramsay Ho. NW8................1A 60
............(off Townshend St.)
Ramsay M. SW3..................2A 88
Ramsay Rd. E7....................1A 54
Ramsdale Rd. SW17...........5C 116
Ramsden Rd. SW12............4C 102
Ramsey Cl. NW9.................1B 28
Ramsey Ho. SW9.................3C 90
Ramsey Ho. SW11...............3C 90
............(off Maysoule Rd.)
Ramsey St. E2.....................3C 64
Ramsey Wlk. N1..................3F 49
Ramsfort Ho. SE16............5D 79
............(off Camilla Rd.)
Ramsgate Cl. E16................2D 83
Ramsgate St. E8..................3B 50
Ram St. SW18....................3D 101
Ram Twr. SW18...................3D 101
Rancliffe Gdns. SE9..........2F 111
Randall Av. NW2..................4A 28
Randall Cl. SW11................4A 88
Randall Pl. SE10.................3E 95
Randall Rd. SE11................1B 90
Randall Row SE11...............5B 76
Randalls Rents SE16..........4B 80
............(off Gulliver St.)
Randell's Rd. N1.................5A 48
Randisbourne Gdns. SE6...3D 123
Randlesdown Rd. SE6........4C 122
............(not continuous)
Randolph App. E16...............5E 69
Randolph Av. W9..................1D 59
Randolph Cl. NW8................5E 45
Randolph Cres. W9...............3E 59
Randolph Gdns. NW6...........1D 59
Randolph M. W9...................3E 59
Randolph Rd. W9..................3E 59
Randolph St. NW1................4E 47
Ranelagh Av. SW13.............5C 84
Ranelagh Av. SW6...............1B 100
Ranelagh Bri. W2.................4D 59

Ranelagh Cotts. SW1............1D **89**
.... (off Ebury Bri. Rd.)
Ranelagh Gdns. SW6 ....1A **100**
.... (not continuous)
Ranelagh Gdns. W6 ....5B **70**
Ranelagh Gdns. Mans.
SW6 ....1A **100**
.... (off Ranelagh Gdns.)
Ranelagh Gro. SW1 ....1C **88**
Ranelagh Ho. SW3 ....1E **88**
.... (off Elystan Pl.)
Ranelagh Rd. E11 ....1A **54**
Ranelagh Rd. E15 ....1A **68**
Ranelagh Rd. NW10 ....1B **56**
Ranelagh Rd. SW1 ....1E **89**
Rangbourne Ho. N7 ....2A **48**
Rangefield Rd. BR1: Broml...5A **124**
Ranger's House 4F **95**
Rangers Sq. SE10 ....4F **95**
Rangoon St. EC3....3F **19** (5B **64**)
.... (off Crutched Friars)
Rankine Ho. SE1 ......5F **25** (4E **77**)
.... (off Bath Ter.)
Ranmere St. SW12............1D **117**
Rannoch Rd. W6 ....2E **85**
Rannock Av. NW9 ....2A **28**
Ransome's Dock Bus. Cen.
SW11 ....3A **88**
Ransom Rd. SE7 ....5E **83**
Ranston St. NW1 ....4A **60**
Ranulf Rd. NW2 ....1B **44**
Ranwell Cl. E3 ....5B **52**
Ranwell Ho. E3....................5B **52**
.... (off Ranwell Cl.)
Raphael Ct. SE16 ....1D **93**
.... (off Stubbs Dr.)
Raphael St. SW7 ....3B **74**
Raphen Apts. E3 ....1A **66**
.... (off Medway Rd.)
Rapley Ho. E2.......................2C **64**
.... (off Turin St.)
Raquel Ct. SE1 ....3D **27** (3A **78**)
.... (off Snowfields)
Rashleigh Ct. SW8 ....5D **89**
Rashleigh Ho. WC1....2D **7** (2A **62**)
.... (off Thanet St.)
Rashleigh St. SW8 ....5D **89**
.... (off Peardon St.)
Rastell Av. SW2...................2F **117**
RATCLIFF 4A **66**
Ratcliffe Cl. SE12................5C **110**
Ratcliffe Cl. SE1 ....4A **26** (3E **77**)
.... (off Gt. Dover St.)
Ratcliffe Cross St. E1 ....5F **65**
Ratcliffe Ho. E14..................5A **66**
.... (off Barnes St.)
Ratcliffe La. E14 ....5A **66**
Ratcliffe Orchard E1 ....1F **79**
Ratcliff Rd. E7 ....2E **55**
Rathbone Ho. E16 ....5B **68**
.... (off Rathbone St.)
Rathbone Ho. NW6 ....5C **44**
Rathbone Mkt. E16 ....4B **68**
Rathbone Pl. W1 .....1B **14** (4F **61**)
Rathbone Sq. W1 .....2A **14** (5E **61**)
Rathbone St. E16 ....5B **68**
Rathbone St. W1 .....1A **14** (4E **61**)
Rathfern Rd. SE6 ....1B **122**
Rathgar Rd. SW9 ....1D **105**
Rathmell Dr. SW4 ....4F **103**
Rathmore Rd. SE7................1D **97**
Rathnew Ct. E2.....................2F **65**
.... (off Meath Cres.)
Rattray Ct. SE6.....................2B **124**
Rattray Rd. SW2..................2C **104**

Raul Rd. SE15 ....5C **92**
Raveley St. NW5...................1E **47**
.... (not continuous)
Ravel Ho. SW11...................1F **101**
.... (off York Place)
Ravenet St. SW11.................4A **89**
.... (not continuous)
Ravensford St. SW8 ....1A **90**
Ravensfield Rd. SW17 ....3B **116**
Ravenhill Rd. E13.................1E **69**
Raven Ho. SE16...................5E **79**
.... (off Tawny Way)
Ravenna Rd. SW15...............3F **99**
Raven Row E1 ....4D **65**
Raven Row Contemporary Art
Cen. 1F **19** (4B **64**)
Ravensbourne Apts. SW6...1E **101**
.... (off Central Av.)
Ravensbourne Ct. SE6.........5C **108**
Ravensbourne Ho.
BR1: Broml.....................5F **123**
Ravensbourne Ho. E15.........3F **53**
.... (off Forrester Way)
Ravensbourne Ho. NW8........4A **60**
.... (off Broadley St.)
Ravensbourne Mans. SE8.....2C **94**
.... (off Berthon St.)
Ravensbourne Pk. SE6 ....5C **108**
Ravensbourne Pk. Cres.
SE6 ....5B **108**
Ravensbourne Pl. SE13.......5D **95**
Ravensbourne Pl. SE8 ....4C **94**
Ravensbourne Rd. SE6 ....5B **108**
Ravensbury Rd. SW18 ....2D **115**
Ravensbury Ter. SW18 ....2D **115**
Ravenscar NW1....................5E **47**
.... (off Bayham St.)
Ravenscar Rd. BR1: Broml.4A **124**
Ravenscourt Av. W6 ....5C **70**
Ravenscourt Gdns. W6 ....5C **70**
Ravenscourt Pk. W6 ....4C **70**
Ravenscourt Pk. Mans. W6...4D **71**
.... (off Paddenswick Rd.)
Ravenscourt Park Station
(Underground) 5D **71**
Ravenscourt Pl. W6 ....5D **71**
Ravenscourt Rd. W6 ....5D **71**
Ravenscourt Sq. W6 ....4C **70**
Ravenscroft Av. NW11..........2B **30**
.... (not continuous)
Ravenscroft Cl. E16 ....4C **68**
Ravenscroft Rd. E16..............4C **68**
Ravenscroft St. E2 ....1F **11** (1B **64**)
Ravensdale Ind. Est. N16 ....1C **36**
Ravensdale Mans. N8...........1A **34**
.... (off Haringey Pk.)
Ravensdale Rd. N16 ....2B **36**
Ravensdon St. SE11.............1C **90**
Ravensdown St. NW6 ....2B **44**
Ravenslea Rd. SW12...........5B **102**
Ravensleigh Gdns.
BR1: Broml 5D **125**
Ravensmede Way W4 ....5B **70**
Ravens M. SE12 ....3C **110**
Ravenstone SE17.................1A **92**
Ravenstone Rd. NW9 ....1B **28**
Ravenstone St. SW12 ....1C **116**
Ravens Wlk. E20 ....3D **53**
Ravens Way SE12 ....3C **110**
Ravenswood Rd. SW12........5D **103**
Ravensworth Ct. SW6 ....3C **86**
.... (off Fulham Rd.)
Raven Wharf SE1 .....3F **27** (3B **78**)
.... (off Lafone St.)
Ravey St. EC2.........3D **11** (3A **64**)
Ravine Way SW11.................2F **89**
Rav Pinter Cl. N16.................2A **36**
Rawchester Cl. SW18 ....1B **114**
Rawlings St. SW3 ....5B **74**
Rawlinson Ct. NW2 ....2E **29**
Rawlinson Ho. SE13.............2F **109**
.... (off Mercator Rd.)
Rawreth Wlk. N1...................5E **49**
.... (off Basire St.)
Rawson St. SW11..................4C **88**
.... (not continuous)
Rawstone Wlk. E13................1C **68**
Rawstorne Pl. EC1...1D **9** (2D **63**)
Rawstorne St. EC1...1D **9** (2D **63**)
.... (not continuous)
Rayburne Ct. W14................4A **72**
Raydon St. N19.....................4D **33**
Rayford Av. SE12.................5B **110**
Ray Gunter Ho. SE17...........1D **91**
.... (off Marsland Cl.)
Ray Ho. N1 ....5A **50**
.... (off Colville St.)
Ray Ho. W10.........................5F **57**
.... (off Cambridge Gdns.)
Rayleigh Rd. E16..................2D **83**
.... (off Treverton St.)
Raymede Towers W10..........4F **57**
Raymond Bldgs. WC1....5A **8** (4B **62**)
Raymond Chadburn Ho. E7 ....1D **55**
Raymond Cl. SE26 ....5E **121**
Raymond Rd. E13 ....5C **55**
Raymond Rd. SW19 ....5A **114**
Raymouth Rd. SE16..............5D **79**
Raynald Ho. SW16 ....3A **118**
Rayne Ho. SW12..................4C **102**
Rayne Ho. W9 ....3D **59**
.... (off Delaware Rd.)
Rayner Ct. W12.......................3E **71**
.... (off Bamborough Gdns.)
Rayners Rd. SW15................3A **100**
Rayners Ter. E14..................5A **66**
.... (off Carr St.)
Rayner Towers E10...............2C **38**
.... (off Albany Rd.)
Raynes Av. E11......................2E **41**
Raynham W2 ....5A **60**
.... (off Norfolk Cres.)
Raynham Ho. E1 ....3F **65**
.... (off Harpley Sq.)
Raynham Rd. W6 ....5D **71**
Raynor Pl. N1 ....4E **49**
Ray St. EC1..............4C **8** (3C **62**)
RAY ST. BRI. 4C **8** (3C **62**)
.... (off Farringdon Rd.)
Ray Wlk. N7 ....4B **34**
Raywood Mans. E20 ....3E **53**
.... (off West Pk. Wlk.)
Reachview Cl. NW1..............4E **47**
Read Ct. E17 ....1C **38**
Reader Ho. SE5 ....4E **91**
.... (off Badsworth Rd.)
Read Ho. SE11......................2C **90**
.... (off Clayton St.)
Reading Cl. SE22 ....4C **106**
Reading Ho. SE15 ....2C **92**
.... (off Friary Est.)
Reading Ho. W2 ....5E **59**
.... (off Hallfield Est.)
Reading La. E8......................3D **51**
Ream Apts. SE23 ....2E **121**
.... (off Clyde Ter.)
Reapers Cl. NW1...................5F **47**
Reardon Ho. E1....................2D **79**
.... (off Reardon St.)

Reardon Path. E1 ....2D **79**
.... (not continuous)
Reardon St. E1 ....2D **79**
Reaston St. SE14 ....3F **93**
Rebecca Ho. E3 ....3B **66**
.... (off Brokesley St.)
Reckitt Rd. W4 ....1A **84**
Record St. SE15 ....2E **93**
Recovery St. SW17 ....5A **116**
Recreation Rd. SE26 ......4F **121**
Rector St. N1 ....5E **49**
Rectory Chambers SW3 ....2A **88**
.... (off Old Church St.)
Rectory Cres. E11 ....1E **41**
.... (not continuous)
Rectory Field 3D **97**
Rectory Fld. Cres. SE7 ......3E **97**
Rectory Gdns. SW4 ....1E **103**
Rectory Gro. SW4 ....1E **103**
Rectory La. SW17 ....5C **116**
Rectory Orchard SW19 .....4A **114**
Rectory Rd. N16 ....4B **36**
Rectory Rd. SW13 ....5C **84**
Rectory Road Station
 (Overground) 5B **36**
Rectory Sq. E1 ....4F **65**
Reculver Ho. SE15 ....2E **93**
.... (off Lovelinch Cl.)
Reculver Rd. SE16 ....1F **93**
Red Anchor Cl. SW3 ....2F **87**
Redan Pl. W2 ....5D **59**
Redan St. W14 ....4F **71**
Redan Ter. SE5 ....5D **91**
Redberry Gro. SE26 ....3E **121**
Redbourne Ho. E14 ....5B **66**
.... (off Norbiton Rd.)
Redbourn Ho. W10 ....3E **57**
.... (off Sutton Way)
REDBRIDGE **1F 41**
Redbridge Gdns. SE5 ....3A **92**
Redbridge La. E. IG4: Ilf 1F **41**
Redbridge La. W. E11 ....1D **41**
REDBRIDGE RDBT. 1F **41**
Redbridge Station (Underground)
 ....**1F 41**
Redburn St. SW3 ....2B **88**
Redcar St. SE5 ....3E **91**
Redcastle Cl. E1 ....1E **79**
Redchurch St. E2 ...3F **11** (3B **64**)
Redcliffe Cl. SW5 ....1D **87**
.... (off Old Brompton Rd.)
Redcliffe Ct. E5 ....5D **37**
.... (off Napoleon Rd.)
Redcliffe Gdns. SW10 ....1D **87**
Redcliffe Gdns. SW5 ....1D **87**
Redcliffe M. SW10 ....1D **87**
Redcliffe Pl. SW10 ....2D **87**
Redcliffe Rd. SW10 ....1E **87**
Redcliffe Sq. SW10 ....2D **87**
Redcliffe Rd. E6 ....5E **55**
Redclyf Ho. E1 ....3E **65**
.... (off Cephas St.)
Red Cow La. EC1 ....3F **9** (3E **63**)
Red Cross Cotts.
 SE1 ....3A **26** (3E **77**)
.... (off Ayres St.)
Redcross Way
 SE1 ....3A **26** (3E **77**)
Redding Ho. SE18 ....4F **83**
Reddins Rd. SE15 ....2C **92**
Redenham Ho. SW15 ....5C **98**
.... (off Ellisfield Dr.)
Rede Pl. W2 ....5C **58**
Redesdale St. SW3 ....2A **88**

Redfern Ho. E13 ....5B **54**
.... (off Redriffe Rd.)
Redfern Ho. NW8 ....5F **45**
.... (off Dorman Way)
Redfern Rd. NW10 ....4A **42**
Redfern Rd. SE6 ....5E **109**
Redfield La. SW5 ....5C **72**
Redfield M. SW5 ....5D **73**
Redford Wlk. N1 ....5E **49**
.... (off Popham St.)
Redgate Ter. SW15 ....1F **99**
Redgrave Rd. SW15 ....1F **99**
Redgrave Ter. E2 ....2C **64**
.... (off Derbyshire St.)
Redhill Ct. SW2 ....2C **118**
Redhill St. NW1 ....1E **5** (1D **61**)
Red Ho. Sq. N1 ....4E **49**
Redington Gdns. NW3 ....1D **45**
Redington Ho. N1 ....1B **62**
.... (off Priory Grn. Est.)
Redington Rd. NW3 ....5D **31**
Redlands Way SW2 ....5B **104**
Red Lion Cl. SE17 ....2F **91**
.... (off Red Lion Row)
Red Lion Ct. EC4 ....3C **16** (5C **62**)
Red Lion Ct. SE1 ....1A **26** (2E **77**)
Red Lion Row SE17 ....2E **91**
Red Lion Sq. WC1 ...3C **16** (5C **62**)
Red Lion St. WC1 ...1F **15** (4B **62**)
Red Lion St. WC1 ....5A **8** (4B **62**)
Red Lion Yd. W1 ....1C **20** (2D **75**)
.... (off Waverton St.)
Redlynch Ct. W14 ....3A **72**
.... (off Addison Cres.)
Redlynch Ho. SW9 ....4C **90**
.... (off Gosling Way)
Redman Ho. EC1 ....5B **8** (4C **62**)
.... (off Bourne Est.)
Redman Ho. SE1 ....4A **26** (3E **77**)
.... (off Borough High St.)
Redman's Rd. E1 ....4E **65**
Redmead La. E1 ....2C **78**
Redmill Ho. E1 ....3D **65**
.... (off Headlam St.)
Redmond Ho. N1 ....5B **48**
.... (off Barnsbury Est.)
Redmore Rd. W6 ....5D **71**
Red Path E9 ....3A **52**
Redpath Way SE10 ....3A **82**
Red Pl. W1 ....4B **12** (1C **74**)
Red Post Hill SE21 ....3F **105**
Red Post Hill SE24 ....2F **105**
Red Post Ho. E6 ....4F **55**
Redriffe Rd. E13 ....5B **54**
Redriff Est. SE16 ....4B **80**
Redriff Rd. SE16 ....5F **79**
RED ROVER 2C **98**
Redrup Ho. SE14 ....2F **93**
.... (off John Williams Cl.)
Redruth Rd. E9 ....5E **51**
Redshank Ho. SE1 ....1B **92**
.... (off Avocet Cl.)
Redstart Cl. SE14 ....3A **94**
Redvers St. N1 ......1E **11** (2A **64**)
Redwald Rd. E5 ....1F **51**
Redwing Cl. SE1 ....4A **26** (3E **77**)
.... (off Swan St.)
Redwing M. SE5 ....5E **91**
Redwood Cl. E3 ....1C **66**
Redwood Cl. SE16 ....2A **80**
Redwood Cl. N19 ....2F **33**
Redwood Ct. NW6 ....4A **44**
Redwood Ho. EC1 ...1F **9** (2E **63**)
.... (off Bollinder Pl.)

Redwood Mans. W8 ....4D **73**
.... (off Chantry Sq.)
Redwood M. SW4 ....1D **103**
Redwoods SW15 ....1C **112**
Reece M. SW7 ....5F **73**
Reed Cl. E16 ....4C **68**
Reed Cl. SE12 ....3C **110**
Reedham St. SE15 ....5C **92**
Reedholm Vs. N16 ....1F **49**
Reed Ho. SW19 ....4D **115**
Reed Pl. SW4 ....2F **103**
Reed's Pl. NW1 ....4E **47**
Reedworth St. SE11 ....5C **76**
Reef Ho. E14 ....4E **81**
.... (off Manchester St.)
Rees St. N1 ....5E **49**
Reets Farm Cl. NW9 ....1A **28**
Reeves Ho. SE1 ....4B **24** (3C **76**)
.... (off Baylis Rd.)
Reeves M. W1 ....5B **12** (1C **74**)
Reeves Rd. E3 ....3D **67**
Reflection Ho. E2 ....3C **64**
.... (off Cheshire St.)
Reform St. SW11 ....5B **88**
Regal Bldg. W10 ....2F **57**
Regal Cl. E1 ....4C **64**
Regal Cl. NW6 ....1B **58**
.... (off Malvern Rd.)
Regal Ct. SW6 ....3C **86**
.... (off Dawes Rd.)
Regal Ho., The SW6 ....5E **87**
Regalia Ho. E1 ....3D **83**
Regalia Point E2 ....2F **65**
.... (off Palmer's Rd.)
Regal La. NW1 ....5C **46**
Regal Pl. E3 ....2B **66**
Regal Pl. SW6 ....3D **87**
Regal Row SE15 ....4E **93**
Regal Wharf Apts. N1 ....5A **50**
.... (off De Beauvoir Cres.)
Regan Way N1 .....1D **11** (1A **64**)
Regatta La. W6 ....2E **85**
Regatta Point E14 ....3C **80**
.... (off Westferry Rd.)
Regency Ct. E3 ....1B **66**
.... (off Norman Gro.)
Regency Ct. E9 ....5E **51**
.... (off Park Cl.)
Regency Ct. SE8 ....3B **94**
.... (off Glenville Gro.)
Regency Ho. E16 ....2C **82**
.... (off Pepys Cres.)
Regency Ho. SW1 ....5F **75**
.... (off Regency St.)
Regency Ho. SW6 ....4E **87**
.... (off The Boulevard)
Regency Lawn NW5 ....5D **33**
Regency Lodge NW3 ....4F **45**
.... (off Adelaide Rd.)
Regency M. NW10 ....3D **42**
Regency M. SW9 ....3D **91**
Regency Pde. NW3 ....4F **45**
.... (off Finchley Rd.)
Regency Pl. SW1 ....5F **75**
Regency St. NW10 ....3A **56**
Regency St. SW1 ....5F **75**
Regency Ter. SW7 ....1F **87**
.... (off Fulham Rd.)
Regeneration House 5A **48**
Regeneration Rd. SE16 ....5F **79**
Regent Cl. NW6 ....4B **44**
.... (off Cavendish Rd.)
Regent Cl. NW8 ....2A **60**
.... (off North Bank)
Regent Ct. W6 ....4D **71**
.... (off Vinery Way)

Regent Ct. W8 .... 4D **73**
   (off Wright's La.)
Regent Ho. W14 .... 5A **72**
   (off Windsor Way)
Regent Pl. SW19 .... 5E **115**
Regent Pl. W1 .... 4A **14** (1F **75**)
Regent Rd. SE24 .... 4D **105**
Regent's Bri. Gdns. SW8 .. 3A **90**
Regents Canal Ho. E14 ..... 5A **66**
   (off Commercial Rd.)
Regents Ct. E8 .... 5C **50**
Regents Ga. Ho. E14 .... 1A **80**
   (off Horseferry Rd.)
Regents Ho. E3 .... 4C **66**
   (off Bow Common La.)
Regents M. NW8 .... 1E **59**
Regent's Pk. 1A **4** (1B **60**)
REGENT'S PK. 1B **4** (2D **61**)
Regent's Pk. Barracks
   .... 1E **5** (1D **61**)
   (off Albany St.)
Regents Pk. Est. NW1 1F **5** (2E **61**)
   (off Robert St.)
Regent's Pk. Gdns. M. NW1 ...5B **46**
Regent's Pk. Ho. NW8 .... 2A **60**
   (off Park Rd.)
Regent's Pk. Open Air Theatre
   .... 2B **4** (2C **60**)
Regent's Pk. Rd. NW1 .... 4B **46**
   (not continuous)
Regent's Park Station
(Underground) .... 4D **5** *(3D* **61***)*
Regent's Pk. Ter. NW1 .... 5D **47**
Regent's Pl. SE3 .... 5C **96**
Regents Pl. NW1 .... 3F **5** (3E **61**)
Regent's Pl. Plaza
   NW1 .... 3F **5** (3E **61**)
Regents Plaza NW6 .... 1D **59**
   (off Kilburn High Rd.)
Regent Sq. E3 .... 2D **67**
Regent Sq. WC1 .... 2E **7** (2A **62**)
Regent's Row E8 .... 5C **50**
Regents Studios E8 .... 5D **51**
Regent St. NW10 .... 2C **57**
Regent St. SW1 .... 5B **14** (1F **75**)
Regent St. W1 .... 2E **13** (5D **61**)
Regent Street Cinema
   .... 2E **13** (5D **61**)
Regent's University London
   .... 3A **4** (3B **60**)
Regents Wharf E2 .... 5D **51**
   (off Wharf Pl.)
Regents Wharf N1 .... 1B **62**
Regent Ter. SW8 .... 2A **90**
Reginald Pl. SE8 .... 3C **94**
   (off Deptford High St.)
Reginald Rd. E7 .... 4C **54**
Reginald Rd. SE8 .... 3C **94**
Reginald Sorenson Ho. E11...2F **39**
Reginald Sq. SE8 .... 3C **94**
Regina Point SE16 .... 4E **79**
   (off Canada Est.)
Regina Rd. N4 .... 3B **34**
Regis Ct. NW1 .... 4B **60**
   (off Melcombe Pl.)
Regis Ho. W1 .... 5C **4** (4C **60**)
   (off Beaumont St.)
Regis Pl. SW2 .... 2B **104**
Regis Rd. NW5 .... 2D **47**
Regnart Bldgs. NW1 ...2A **6** (2E **61**)
   (off Euston St.)
Regnas Ho. E15 .... 3B **54**
   (off Carnarvon Rd.)
Regnum Apts. E1 ...... 4F **11** (3B **64**)
   (off Wheler St.)

Reid Bldg. E3 .... 3B **66**
   (off Eric St.)
Reigate Rd. BR1: Broml.... 3B **124**
Reighton Rd. E5 .... 5C **36**
Reindeer Cl. E13 .... 5C **54**
Reizel Cl. N16 .... 3B **36**
Relay Rd. W12 .... 1F **71**
Relf Rd. SE15 .... 1C **106**
Reliance Arc. SW9 .... 2C **104**
Reliance Wharf N1 .... 5A **50**
Relton M. SW7 .... 4A **74**
Rembrandt Cl. E14 .... 4F **81**
Rembrandt Cl. SW1 .... 1C **88**
   (off Graham Ter.)
Rembrandt Ct. SE16 .... 1D **93**
   (off Stubbs Dr.)
Rembrandt Rd. SE13 .... 2A **110**
Reminder La. SE10 .... 4B **82**
   (not continuous)
Remington Rd. E6 .... 5F **69**
Remington Rd. N15 .... 1F **35**
Remington St. N1 ..... 1E **9** (1D **63**)
Remnant St. WC2.... 2F **15** (5B **62**)
Remsted Ho. NW6 .... 5D **45**
   (off Mortimer Cres.)
Remus Bldg., The
   EC1........................ 2C **8** (2C **62**)
   (off Hardwick St.)
Remus Rd. E3 .... 4C **52**
Renaissance Sq. W4 .... 2A **84**
Renaissance Wlk. SE10...... 4B **82**
   (off Teal St.)
Renbold Ho. SE10 .... 4E **95**
   (off Blissett St.)
Rendle Ho. W10 .... 3A **58**
   (off Wornington Rd.)
Rendlesham Rd. E5 .... 1C **50**
Renforth St. SE16 .... 4E **79**
Renfrew Ho. NW6 .... 1D **59**
   (off Carlton Vale)
Renfrew Rd. SE11 .... 5D **77**
Renmuir St. SW17 .... 5B **116**
Rennell St. SE13 .... 1E **109**
Rennie Cotts. E1 .... 3E **65**
   (off Pernell Cl.)
Rennie Ct. SE1 .... 1D **25** (2D **77**)
   (off Upper Ground)
Rennie Est. SE16 .... 5D **79**
Rennie Ho. SE1 ...... 5F **25** (4E **77**)
   (off Bath Ter.)
Rennie St. SE1 .... 1D **25** (2D **77**)
   (not continuous)
Rensburg Rd. E17 .... 1F **37**
Renshaw Cl. SE6 .... 5C **108**
Renters Av. NW4 .... 1E **29**
Renton Cl. SW2 .... 4B **104**
Rephidim St. SE1...5D **27** (4A **78**)
Replingham Rd. SW18 ...... 1B **114**
Reporton Rd. SW6 .... 3A **86**
Repton Cl. BR1: Broml......5F **125**
Repton Ho. E16 .... 3D **83**
   (off Royal Crest Av.)
Repton Ho. SW1 .... 5E **75**
   (off Charlwood St.)
Repton St. E14 .... 5A **66**
Reservoir Rd. SE4 .... 5A **94**
Reservoir Studios E1 .... 5F **65**
   (off Cable St.)
Reservoir Way N10 .... 4C **42**
Residence Twr. N4 .... 2E **35**
Resolution Plaza E1. 2F **19** (5B **64**)
   (off Old Castle St.)

Resolution Way SE8............ 3C **94**
   (off Deptford High St.)
Restell Cl. SE3 .... 2A **96**
Reston Pl. SW7................... 3E **73**
Restoration Sq. SW11........ 4F **87**
Restormel Ho. SE11 .... 5C **76**
   (off Chester Way)
Retcar Pl. N19..................... 4D **33**
Retford St. N1 .... 1E **11** (1A **64**)
Retreat, The SW14 .... 1A **98**
Retreat Ho. E9 .... 3E **51**
Retreat Pl. E9 .... 3E **51**
Reuters Plaza E14 .... 2D **81**
   (off The South Colonnade)
Reveley Sq. SE16 .... 3A **80**
Revelon Rd. SE4 .... 2A **108**
Revelstoke Rd. SW18........ 2B **114**
Reverdy Rd. SE1 .... 5C **78**
Review Rd. NW2 .... 4B **28**
Revolution Karting 4B **66**
Rewell St. SW6.................... 3E **87**
Rex Pl. W1 .... 5C **12** (1C **74**)
Reydon Av. E11 .... 1E **41**
Reynard Cl. SE4 .... 1A **108**
Reynard Pl. SE14 .... 2A **94**
Reynham Gdns. SE7............ 1D **97**
Reynolds Cl. NW11 .... 2D **31**
Reynolds Ho. E2 .... 1E **65**
   (off Approach Rd.)
Reynolds Ho. NW8 .... 1F **59**
   (off Wellington Rd.)
Reynolds Ho. SW1 .... 5F **75**
   (off Erasmus St.)
Reynolds Pl. SE3 .... 3D **97**
Reynolds Rd. SE15............. 2E **107**
Rheidol M. N1 .... 1E **63**
Rheidol Ter. N1 .... 5E **49**
Rhoda St. E2 .... 3F **11** (3B **64**)
Rhodes Ho. N1 .... 1B **10** (2F **63**)
   (off Provost St.)
Rhodesia Rd. E11............... 4F **39**
Rhodesia Rd. SW9 .... 5A **90**
Rhodes St. N7 .... 2B **48**
Rhodeswell Rd. E14........... 4A **66**
   (not continuous)
Rhodium Ct. E14 .... 4C **66**
   (off Thomas Rd.)
Rhondda Gro. E3................. 2A **66**
RHS Lawrence Hall 4F **75**
RHS Lindley Hall 5F **75**
   (off Vincent Sq.)
Rhyl St. NW5 .... 3C **46**
Ribblesdale Ho. NW6 .... 5C **44**
   (off Kilburn Vale)
Ribblesdale Rd. SW16...... 5D **117**
Ribbon Dance M. SE4........ 4F **91**
Ribbons Wlk. E20................ 2E **53**
Ricardo St. E14................... 5D **67**
Ricards Rd. SW19.............. 5B **114**
Riceyman Ho. WC1 ...2B **8** (2C **62**)
   (off Lloyd Baker St.)
Richard Anderson Ct. SE14...3F **93**
   (off Monson Rd.)
Richard Burbidge Mans.
   SW13......................... 2E **85**
   (off Brasenose Dr.)
RICHARD DESMOND CHILDREN'S
   EYE CEN..........2B **10** (2F **63**)
   (within Moorfields Eye Hospital)
Richard Fielden Ho. E1 ...... 2A **66**
Richard Ho. SE16............... 5E **79**
   (off Silwood St.)
RICHARD HOUSE CHILDREN'S
   HOSPICE 1F **83**
Richard Ho. Dr. E16........... 5F **69**

Richard Neale Ho. E1 .... 1D 79
.... (off Cornwall St.)
Richard Robert Residence, The
E15..3F 53
.... (off Salway Rd.)
Richardson Cl. E8 ....5B 50
Richardson Ct. SW4 ....5A 90
.... (off Studley Rd.)
Richardson Rd. E15 ....1A 68
Richardson's M. W1......4F 5 (3E 61)
.... (off Warren St.)
Richard's Pl. SW3 ....5A 74
Richard St. E1 ....5D 65
Richard Tress Way E3 ....3B 66
Richbell WC1.............5E 7 (4B 62)
.... (off Boswell St.)
Richbell Pl. WC1 ....5F 7 (4B 62)
Richborne Ter. SW8 ....3B 90
Richborough Ho. SE15..........2E 93
.... (off Sharratt St.)
Richborough Rd. NW2 ....1A 44
Richbourne Ct. W1..................5A 60
.... (off Harrowby St.)
Richford Ga. W6.......................4E 71
Richford Rd. E15....................5B 54
Richford St. W6......................3E 71
Rich Ind. Est. SE1 ....5A 78
Rich Ind. Est. SE15 ....2D 93
Richland Ho. SE15..................4C 92
.... (off Goldsmith Rd.)
Rich La. SW5.............................1D 87
Richman Ho. SE8 ....1B 94
.... (off Grove St.)
Richmix Sq. E1 ....3F 11 (3B 64)
.... (off Bethnal Grn. Rd.)
**Richmond, The American
International University in
London** Kensington Campus,
Ansdell Street 4D 73
.... (off Ansdell St.)
**Richmond, The American
International University in
London** Kensington Campus, St
Albans Grove 4D 73
**Richmond, The American
International University in
London** Kensington Campus,
Young Street........................3D 73
Richmond Av. N1 ....5B 48
Richmond Av. NW10 ....3E 43
Richmond Bldgs.
W1..........................3B 14 (5F 61)
Richmond Cl. E17 ....1B 38
Richmond Cotts. W14 ....5A 72
.... (off Hammersmith Rd.)
Richmond Ct. E8 ....4D 51
.... (off Mare St.)
Richmond Ct. NW6...................4F 43
.... (off Willesden La.)
Richmond Ct. SW1....4A 20 (3B 74)
.... (off Sloane St.)
Richmond Ct. W14..................5A 72
.... (off Hammersmith Rd.)
Richmond Cres. N1 ....5B 48
Richmond Gro. N1 ....4D 49
.... (not continuous)
Richmond Ho. E3 ....4C 66
.... (off Bow Common La.)
Richmond Ho. NW1....1E 5 (1D 61)
.... (off Park Village E.)
Richmond Ho. SE17 ....1F 91
.... (off Portland St.)
Richmond Mans. SW5 ....5D 87
.... (off Old Brompton Rd.)
Richmond M. SE6 ....1D 123

Richmond M. W1 ......3B 14 (5F 61)
Richmond Pk. Golf Course 5A 98
Richmond Rd. E11 ....4F 39
Richmond Rd. E7 ....2D 55
Richmond Rd. E8 ....4B 50
Richmond Rd. N15..................1A 36
Richmond Rd. E13 ....1C 68
Richmond Ter. SW1...3D 23 (3A 76)
Richmond Way E11 ....4C 40
Richmond Way W12 ....3F 71
Richmond Way W14 ....4F 71
Richmount Gdns. SE3............1C 110
Rich St. E14 ....1B 80
Rickard Cl. SW2 ....1C 118
Rickett St. SW6 ....2C 86
Rickman Ho. E1 ....2E 65
.... (off Rickman St.)
Rickman St. E1 ....3E 65
Rick Roberts Way E15...........5E 53
Rickthorne Rd. N19 ....4A 34
Riddell Cl. SE5 ....1B 92
.... (off Albany Rd.)
Riddons Rd. SE12 ....3E 125
Ridgdale St. E3 ....1D 67
Ridgebrook Rd. SE3................1F 111
Ridge Cl. SE22 ....5C 106
Ridge Hill NW11 ....3A 30
Ridge Rd. N8 ....1B 34
Ridge Rd. NW2 ....5B 30
Ridge Way SE15 ....5A 120
Ridgeway, The NW11...............2A 30
Ridgeway Dr. BR1: Broml...4D 125
Ridgeway Gdns. N6 ....2E 33
Ridgewell Cl. N1 ....5E 49
Ridgewell Cl. SE26..................4B 122
Ridgmount Gdns.
WC1..........................4B 6 (4F 61)
Ridgmount Pl. WC1....5B 6 (4F 61)
Ridgmount St. SW18...............3D 101
Ridgmount St. WC1....5B 6 (4F 61)
Ridgway Pl. SW19...................5A 114
Ridgway Rd. SW9 ....1D 105
Ridgwell Rd. E16 ....4E 69
Riding, The NW11 ....2B 30
Riding Ho. St. W1....1E 13 (4D 61)
Ridings Cl. N6 ....2E 33
Ridley Ct. SW16 ....5A 118
Ridley Ho. SW1.........5C 22 (4F 75)
.... (off Monck St.)
Ridley Rd. E7...........................1E 55
Ridley Rd. E8 ....3B 50
Ridley Rd. NW10 ....1C 56
Riffel Rd. NW2 ....2E 43
Rifle St. E14 ....4D 67
Riga M. E1 ....5C 64
.... (off Commercial Rd.)
Rigault Rd. SW6 ....5A 86
Rigden St. E14 ....5D 67
Rigeley Rd. NW10 ....2C 56
Rigg App. E10 ....3F 37
Rigge Pl. SW4.........................2F 103
Riggindale Rd. SW16 ....5F 117
Riley Ho. E3 ....3C 66
.... (off Ireton St.)
Riley Ho. SW10........................3F 87
.... (off Riley St.)
Riley Rd. SE1...........5E 27 (4B 78)
Riley St. SW10.........................2F 87
Rill Ho. SE5..............................3F 91
.... (off Harris St.)
Rima Ho. SW3 ....2F 87
.... (off Callow St.)
Rinaldo Rd. SW12 ....5D 103
Ring, The SW7.........................3F 73
Ring, The W2............................1F 73

Ring Ct. SE1 ....3D 25 (3D 77)
.... (off The Cut)
Ringcroft St. N7 ....2C 48
Ringcross Youth Cen...........2B 48
.... (off Lough Rd.)
Ringford Rd. SW18 ....3B 100
Ring Ho. E1 ....1E 79
.... (off Sage St.)
Ringlet Cl. E16 ....4D 69
Ringmer Av. SW6.....................4A 86
Ringmer Gdns. N19 ....4A 34
Ringmore Ri. SE23..................5D 107
Ringmore Vw. SE23................5D 107
Ring Rd. W12 ....2E 71
.... (not continuous)
Ringsfield Ho. SE17 ....1E 91
.... (off Bronti Cl.)
Ringstead Rd. SE6..................5D 109
Ringwood Gdns. E14 ....5C 80
Ringwood Gdns. SW15 ....1C 112
Ringwood Rd. E17 ....1B 38
Rio Cinema Dalston................2A 50
.... (off Kingsland High St.)
Ripley Bldgs. SE1.....3E 25 (3D 77)
.... (off Rushworth St.)
Ripley Gdns. SW14..................1A 98
Ripley Ho. SW1........................2E 89
.... (off Churchill Gdns.)
Ripley M. E11 ....1A 40
Ripley Rd. E16 ....5E 69
Ripon Gdns. IG1: Ilf 1F 41
Ripplevale Gro. N1 ....4B 48
Risborough Ho. NW8...............3A 60
.... (off Mallory St.)
Risborough St. SE1....3E 25 (3D 77)
Risdon Ho. SE16.....................3E 79
.... (off Risdon St.)
Risdon St. SE16 ....4E 79
Rise, The NW10 ....1A 42
Riseholme Ct. E9.....................3B 52
Riseldine Rd. SE23..................4A 108
Risinghill St. N1 ....1B 62
Rising Sun Ct. EC1...1E 17 (4D 63)
.... (off Cloth Fair)
Rita Rd. SW8 ....2A 90
Ritchie Ho. E14 ....5F 67
.... (off Blair St.)
Ritchie Ho. N19 ....3F 33
Ritchie Ho. SE16 ....4E 79
.... (off Howland Est.)
Ritchie St. N1...........................1C 62
Ritherdon Rd. SW17................2C 116
Ritson Ho. N1...........................5B 48
.... (off Barnsbury Est.)
Ritson Rd. E8 ....2C 50
Ritzy Picturehouse 2C 104
.... (off Coldharbour La.)
Riva Bldg. SE13........................2F 109
Rivaz Pl., The E9......................3E 51
Riven Ct. W2............................5D 59
.... (off Inverness Ter.)
Riverbank Rd. BR1: Broml...3C 124
River Barge Cl. E14.................3E 81
River Cl. E11.............................1E 41
River Ct. SE1 ....5D 17 (1D 77)
Rivercourt Rd. W6....................5D 71
Riverdale SE13.........................2E 109
Riverdale Dr. SW18.................1D 115
Riverdale Rd. SE13 ....2E 109
Riverfleet WC1 ....1E 7 (2A 62)
.... (off Birkenhead St.)
Riverford Ho. W2......................4C 58
.... (off Westbourne Pk. Rd.)
River Gdns. Wlk. SE10...........1A 96
River Hgts. E15........................5E 53

River Ho. SE26 ....3D **121**
Riverlight Quay SW11 ....2E **89**
River Lodge SW1 ....2E **89**
................(off Grosvenor Rd.)
Rivermead Ct. SW6 ....1B **100**
Rivermead Ho. E9 ....2A **52**
River Mill One SE13 ....1E **109**
................(off Station Rd.)
River Mill Two SE13 ....1E **109**
................(off Station Rd.)
River Pl. N1 ....4E **49**
Riversdale Rd. N5 ....5D **35**
Riverside E3 ....5C **52**
Riverside NW4 ....2D **29**
Riverside SE7 ....4D **83**
Riverside SW11 ....3A **88**
Riverside W6 ....2E **85**
Riverside WC1 ....1E **7** (2A **62**)
................(off Birkenhead St.)
Riverside Apts. N4 ....2F **35**
................(off Goodchild Rd.)
Riverside Bus. Cen. SW18 ...1D **115**
Riverside Cl. E5 ....3E **37**
Riverside Ct. SE3 ....2B **110**
Riverside Ct. SW8 ....2F **89**
Riverside Dr. NW11 ....1A **30**
Riverside Dr. W4 ....3A **84**
Riverside Gdns. W6 ....1D **85**
Riverside Ho. N1 ....4E **49**
................(off Canonbury St.)
Riverside Mans. E1 ....2E **79**
................(off Milk Yd.)
Riverside Rd. E15 ....1E **67**
Riverside Rd. N15 ....1C **36**
Riverside Rd. SW17 ....4D **115**
Riverside Studios 1E **85**
Riverside Twr. SW6 ....5E **87**
................(off The Boulevard)
Riverside Wlk. W4: Lon Chiswick
................................2B **84**
................(off Chiswick Wharf)
Riverside Wharf E3 ....5C **52**
Riverside Yd. SW17 ....4E **115**
River St. EC1 ....1B **8** (2C **62**)
River St. M. EC1 ....1B **8** (2C **62**)
................(off River St.)
River Ter. WC2 ....5F **15** (1B **76**)
................(off Lancaster Pl.)
Riverton Cl. W9 ....2B **58**
River Twr. SW8 ....2A **90**
Riverview Ct. E14 ....4B **80**
Riverview Gdns. SW13 ....2D **85**
River Vw. Hgts. SE16 ....3C **78**
................(off Bermondsey Wall W.)
Riverview Pk. SE6 ....2C **122**
Riverview Wlk. SE6 ....3B **122**
River Wlk. W6 ....3E **85**
................(not continuous)
Riverwalk SW1 ....1A **90**
Riverwalk Apts. SW6 ....1E **101**
................(off Central Av.)
River Way SE10 ....4B **82**
Rivet Ho. SE1 ....1B **92**
................(off Cooper's Rd.)
Riviera Ct. E1 ....2C **78**
................(off St Katharine's Way)
Rivington Ct. NW10 ....5C **42**
Rivington Pl. EC2 ......2E **11** (2A **64**)
Rivington St. EC2 .....2D **11** (1A **64**)
Rivington Wlk. E8 ....5C **50**
Rivulet Apts. N4 ....2F **35**
Rixon St. N7 ....5C **34**
Roach Rd. E3 ....4C **52**
Roads Pl. N19 ....4A **34**
Roan St. SE10 ....2E **95**

Robert Adam St. W1 ...2B **12** (5C **60**)
Roberta St. E2 ....2C **64**
Robert Bell Ho. SE16 ....5C **78**
................(off Rouel Rd.)
Robert Burns M. SE24 ....3D **105**
Robert Cl. W9 ....3E **59**
Robert Cl. SE15 ....5C **92**
Robert Dashwood Way SE1 75E **77**
Robert Gentry Ho. W14 ......1A **86**
................(off Gledstanes Rd.)
Robert Jones Ho. SE16 ....5C **78**
................(off Rouel Rd.)
Robert Keen Cl. SE15 ....4C **92**
Robert Lowe Cl. SE14 ....3F **93**
Robert Morton Ho. NW8 .....4E **45**
Robert Owen Ho. E2. 1F **11** (2B **64**)
................(off Baroness Rd.)
Robert Owen Ho. SW6 ....4F **85**
Robert Runcie Ct. SW2 ......2B **104**
Roberts Cl. SE16 ....3F **79**
Roberts St. N1 ....5D **49**
................(off Essex Rd.)
Roberts M. SW1 ....5B **20** (4C **74**)
Robertson Gro. SW17 ....5A **116**
Robertson Rd. E16 ....4C **68**
Robertson St. SW8 ....1D **103**
Roberts Pl. EC1 ....3C **8** (3C **62**)
Robert Sq. SE13 ....2E **109**
Robert St. NW1 ....2E **5** (2D **61**)
Robert St. WC2 ....5E **15** (1A **76**)
Robert Sutton Ho. E1 ....5E **65**
................(off Tarling St.)
Robeson St. E3 ....4B **66**
Robin Ct. E14 ....3E **81**
Robin Ct. SE16 ....5C **78**
Robin Cres. E6 ....4F **69**
Robin Gro. N6 ....4C **32**
ROBIN HOOD 3A **112**
Robin Hood Ct. EC4..2C **16** (5C **62**)
................(off Shoe La.)
Robin Hood Gdns. E14 ....1E **81**
................(off Woolmore St.)
Robin Hood La. E14 ....1E **81**
Robin Hood La. SW15 ....3A **112**
Robin Hood Rd. SW19 ....5C **112**
Robin Hood Way SW15 ....3A **112**
Robin Hood Way SW20 ......5A **112**
Robin Ho. NW8 ....1A **60**
................(off Newcourt St.)
Robin Howard Dance Theatre
(The Place) 2C **6** (2F **61**)
................(off Duke's Rd.)
Robinia Cres. E10 ....4D **39**
Robinia Ho. SE16 ....3A **80**
................(off Blondin Way)
Robins Ct. SE12 ....3E **125**
Robinscroft M. SE10 ....4E **95**
Robinson Cl. E11 ....5A **40**
Robinson Ct. N1 ....5D **49**
................(off St Mary's Path)
Robinson Ho. E14 ....4C **66**
................(off Selsey St.)
Robinson Ho. W10 ....5F **57**
................(off Bramley Rd.)
Robinson Rd. E2 ....1E **65**
Robinson Rd. SE1 ....1D **25** (2D **77**)
Robinson Rd. SW17 ....5A **116**
Robinson St. SW3 ....2B **88**
Robinson Way SE14 ....3F **93**
Robinswood M. N5 ....2D **49**
Robinwood Pl. SW15 ....4A **112**
Robsart St. SW9 ....5B **90**
Robson Av. NW10 ....4C **42**
Robson Cl. E6 ....5F **69**

Robson Rd. SE27 ....3E **119**
Roby Ho. EC1 ....3F **9** (3E **63**)
................(off Mitchell St.)
Rocastle Rd. SE4 ....3A **108**
Rochdale Rd. E17 ....2C **38**
Rochdale Way SE8 ....3C **94**
................(not continuous)
Roche Ho. E14 ....1B **80**
................(off Beccles St.)
Rochelle Cl. SW11 ....2F **101**
Rochelle St. E2 ....2F **11** (2B **64**)
................(off Rouel Rd.)
Rochemont Wlk. E8 ....5C **50**
................(off Pownall Rd.)
Rochester Av. E13 ....5E **55**
Rochester Ct. E2 ....3D **65**
................(off Wilmot St.)
Rochester Ct. NW1 ....4E **47**
................(off Rochester Sq.)
Rochester Ho. SE1 .. 4B **26** (3F **77**)
................(off Manciple St.)
Rochester Ho. SE15 ....2E **93**
................(off Sharratt St.)
Rochester M. NW1 ....4E **47**
Rochester Pl. NW1 ....3E **47**
Rochester Rd. NW1 ....3E **47**
Rochester Row SW1 ....5E **75**
Rochester Sq. NW1 ....4E **47**
Rochester Ter. NW1 ....3E **47**
Rochester Wlk. SE1.. 1B **26** (2F **77**)
Rochester Way SE3 ....4D **97**
Rochester Way Relief Rd.
SE3 ....4D **97**
Rochford Cl. E6 ....1F **69**
Rochford Wlk. E8 ....4C **50**
Rochfort Ho. SE8 ....1B **94**
Rock Av. SW14 ....1A **98**
Rockbourne M. SE23 ....1F **121**
Rockbourne Rd. SE23 ....1F **121**
Rockell's Pl. SE22 ....4D **107**
Rockfield Ho. SE10 ....2E **95**
................(off Welland St.)
Rock Gro. Way SE16 ....5C **78**
................(not continuous)
Rockhall Rd. NW2 ....1F **43**
Rockhall Way NW2 ....2F **29**
Rockhampton Cl. SE27 ......4C **118**
Rockhampton Rd. SE27 ......4C **118**
Rock Hill SE26 ....4B **120**
................(not continuous)
Rockingham Cl. SW15 ....2B **98**
Rockingham St. SE1...5F **25** (4E **77**)
Rockland Rd. SW15 ....2A **100**
Rockley Ct. W14 ....3F **71**
................(off Rockley Rd.)
Rockley Rd. W14 ....3F **71**
Rocks La. SW13 ....4C **84**
Rock St. N4 ....4C **34**
Rockwell Gdns. SE19 ....5A **120**
Rockwood Pl. W12 ....3E **71**
Rocliffe St. N1 ....1D **63**
Rocombe Cres. SE23 ....5E **107**
Rocque Ho. SW6 ....3B **86**
................(off Estcourt Rd.)
Rocque La. SE3 ....1B **110**
Rodale Mans. SW18 ....4D **101**
Rodborough Cl. W9 ....3C **58**
................(off Hermes Cl.)
Rodborough Rd. NW11 ....3C **30**
Roden St. N6 ....2F **33**
Rodenhurst Rd. SW4...........4E **103**
Roden St. N7 ....5B **34**
Roderick Ho. SE16 ....5E **79**
................(off Raymouth Rd.)

Roderick Rd. NW3..............1B 46
Rodgers Ho. SW4..............5F 103
............................(off Clapham Pk. Est.)
Rodin Ct. N1......................5D 49
....(off Essex Rd.)
Roding Ho. N1....................5C 48
............................(off Barnsbury Est.)
Roding M. E1.....................2C 78
Roding Rd. E5....................1F 51
Rodmarton St. W1 ..1A 12 (4B 60)
Rodmell WC1..............2E 7 (2A 62)
............................(off Regent Sq.)
Rodmere St. SE10.............1A 96
Rodmill La. SW2...............5A 104
Rodney Ct. W9...................5E 59
Rodney Ho. E14..................5D 81
............................(off Cahir St.)
Rodney Ho. N1....................1B 62
............................(off Donegal St.)
Rodney Ho. SW1.................1E 89
............................(off Dolphin Sq.)
Rodney Ho. W11..................1C 72
............................(off Pembridge Cres.)
Rodney Pl. SE17................5E 77
Rodney Point SE16 ....3B 80
............................(off Rotherhithe St.)
Rodney Rd. SE17 ....5E 77
............................(not continuous)
Rodney St. N1 ....1A 8 (1B 62)
Rodway Rd. SW15...............5C 98
Rodwell Rd. SE22..............4B 106
Roedean Cres. SW15..........4A 98
ROEHAMPTON.....................5C 98
Roehampton Cl. SW15.........2C 98
Roehampton Ga. SW15........4A 98
Roehampton Golf Course 2B 98
Roehampton High St. SW15 5C 98
Roehampton La. SW15.........2C 98
ROEHAMPTON LANE 1D 113
Roehampton Sport & Fitness Cen.
....5C 98
Roehampton University
  Digby Stuart College 3C 98
Roehampton University
  Main Site 3C 98
Roehampton University
  Southlands College 3C 98
Roehampton University
  Whitelands Site 5C 98
Roehampton Va. SW15 ......3B 112
Roffey St. E14 ....3E 81
Roffo Ct. SE17 ....2F 91
............................(off Boundary La.)
Rogan Ho. SW8.................4D 89
............................(off St Joseph's St.)
Rogate Ho. E5....................5C 36
Roger Dowley Ct. E2...........1E 65
Roger Harriss Almshouses
  E15.................................5B 54
............................(off Gift La.)
Rogers Ct. E14 ....1C 80
............................(off Premiere Pl.)
Rogers Est. E2...................2E 65
............................(not continuous)
Rogers Ho. SW1.................5F 75
............................(off Page St.)
Rogers Rd. E16 ....5B 68
Rogers Rd. SW17..............4F 115
Roger St. WC1..........4A 8 (3B 62)
Rohere Ho. EC1 ....1F 9 (2E 63)
Rojack Rd. SE23................1F 121
Rokeby Ho. SW12.............5D 103
............................(off Lochinvar St.)
Rokeby Ho. WC1........4F 7 (3B 62)
............................(off Lamb's Conduit St.)

Rokeby Rd. SE4 ....5B 94
Rokeby St. E15...................5F 53
Rokell Ho. BR3: Beck 5D 123
............................(off Beckenham Hill Rd.)
Roland Gdns. SW10............1E 87
Roland Gdns. SW7..............1E 87
Roland Ho. SW7.................1E 87
............................(off Old Brompton Rd.)
Roland Mans. SW7..............1E 87
............................(off Old Brompton Rd.)
Roland M. E1.....................4F 65
Roland Way SE17................1F 91
Roland Way SW7................1E 87
Rolfing Mills M. E14............5A 66
Rollins Ho. SE15.................2E 93
............................(off Rollins St.)
Rollins St. SE15.................2E 93
Rollit St. N7.......................2C 48
Rolls Bldgs. EC4......2B 16 (5C 62)
Rollscourt Av. SE24.............3E 105
Rolls Pas. EC4.........2B 16 (5C 62)
............................(off Chancery La.)
Rolt St. SE8......................2A 94
............................(not continuous)
Roma Corte SE13................1D 109
............................(off Elmira St.)
Roman Apts. E8 ....4D 51
............................(off Silesia Bldgs.)
Roman Ct. N7.....................3B 48
Romanfield Rd. SW2...........5B 104
Roman Ho. EC2 ....1A 18 (4E 63)
............................(off Wood St.)
Roman Ri. SE19 ....5F 119
Roman Rd. NW2: Lon
  Edgware Rd. 5E 29
Roman Rd. NW2: Lon
  Temple Rd. 5E 29
Roman Rd. E2 ....2E 65
Roman Rd. E3 ....1A 66
Roman Rd. E6 ....3F 69
Roman Rd. W4 ....5A 70
Roman Rd. Mkt...................5B 52
............................(off Roman Rd.)
Roman Way N7 ....3B 48
Roman Way SE15................3B 92
Roman Way Ind. Est. N7 ......4B 48
............................(off Roman Way)
Roma Read Cl. SW15..........5D 99
Romayne Ho. SW4 ....1F 103
Romberg Rd. SW17............3C 116
Romborough Gdns. SE13....3E 109
Romborough Way SE13......3E 109
Romero Cl. SW9 ....1B 104
Romeyn Rd. SW16 ....3B 118
Romford Rd. E12..................2F 55
Romford Rd. E15..................3A 54
Romford Rd. E7...................3B 54
Romford St. E1 ....4C 64
Romilly Ho. W11.................1A 72
............................(off Wilsham St.)
Romilly Rd. N4...................4D 35
Romilly St. W1 ....1C 14 (1F 75)
Romilly Ct. SW6.................5B 86
Rommany Rd. SE27............4F 119
............................(not continuous)
Romney Cl. NW11..............3E 31
Romney Cl. SE14...............3E 93
Romney Cl. NW3...............3A 46
Romney Ct. W12................3F 71
............................(off Shepherd's Bush Grn.)
Romney Ho. SW1................4F 75
............................(off Marsham St.)
Romney M. W1 ....5B 4 (4C 60)
Romney Rd. SE10...............2F 95

Romney Row NW2...............4F 29
............................(off Brent Ter.)
Romney St. SW1 ....4A 76
Romola Rd. SE24...............1D 119
Ronald Av. E15...................2A 68
Ronald Buckingham Ct.
  SE16.............................3E 79
............................(off Kenning St.)
Ronaldshay N4..................2C 34
Ronalds Rd. N5..................2C 48
............................(not continuous)
Ronald St. E1 ....5E 65
Ronar Ho. NW3..................1C 46
Rona Wlk. N1 ....3F 49
Rondu Rd. NW2..................2A 44
Ronver Rd. SE12 ....5B 110
Rood La. EC3...........4D 19 (1A 78)
Roof Ter. Apts, The
  EC1..........................4E 9 (3D 63)
............................(off Gt. Sutton St.)
Rookery Cl. E10 ....5D 39
Rookery Rd. SW4...............2E 103
Rookery Way NW9 ....1B 28
Rooke Way SE10.................1B 96
Rookstone Rd. SW17..........5B 116
Rook Wlk. E6......................5F 69
Rookwood Rd. N16............2B 36
Rookwood Way 3...............4C 52
Roosevelt Memorial ...4C 12 (1C 74)
Rootes Dr. W10 ....4F 57
Ropemaker Rd. SE16 ....3A 80
Ropemaker's Flds. E14.......1B 80
Ropemaker St. EC2 ..5B 10 (4F 63)
Roper La. SE1...........3E 27 (3A 78)
Ropers Orchard SW3 ....2A 88
............................(off Danvers St.)
Ropers Wlk. SW2 ....5C 104
Ropery Bus. Pk. SE7 ....5E 83
Ropery St. E3 ....3B 66
Rope St. SE16 ....5A 80
Rope Ter. E16.....................3D 83
Ropewalk Gdns. E1.............5C 64
Ropewalk M. E8.................4C 50
Ropley St. E2 ....1C 64
Rosa Alba M. N5 ....1E 49
Rosalind Ho. N1 ....1A 64
............................(off Arden Est.)
Rosaline Rd. SW6..............3A 86
Rosaline Ter. SW6...............3A 86
............................(off Rosaline Rd.)
Rosamond St. SE26 ....3D 121
Rosa Parks Ho. SE17 ....5E 77
............................(off Munton Rd.)
Rosary Gdns. SW7 ....5E 73
Rosaville Rd. SW6...............3B 86
Roscoe St. EC1.........4A 10 (3E 63)
............................(not continuous)
Roscoe St. Est. EC1 ..4A 10 (3E 63)
Rosea Apts. SW11 ....2A 102
............................(off Danvers Av.)
Rose All. EC2.............1E 19 (4A 64)
............................(off Bishopsgate)
Rose All. SE1.............1A 26 (2E 77)
Rose & Crown Ct.
  EC2......................2A 18 (5E 63)
............................(off Foster La.)
Rose & Crown Yd.
  SW1.......................1A 22 (2E 75)
............................(off St Agnes Pl.)
Rosebank SW6 ....3D 85
Rosebank Gdns. E3.............1B 66
Rosebank Gdns. Nth. E3.....1B 66
Rosebank Rd. E17 ....1D 39
Rosebank Wlk. NW1 ....4F 47

Rosebay Ho. E3.................4C 66
..............(off Hawgood St.)
Roseberry Gdns. N4............1D 35
Roseberry Mans. N1...........5A 48
.................(off Tapper Wlk.)
Roseberry M. SW2..............4A 104
Roseberry Pl. E8................3B 50
Roseberry St. SE16............5D 79
Rosebery Av. EC1..........4B 8 (3C 62)
Rosebery Ct. EC1.........3B 8 (3C 62)
.................(off Rosebery Av.)
Rosebery Ct. W1........1D 21 (2D 75)
.................(off Charles St.)
Rosebery Gdns. N8.............1A 34
Rosebery Ho. E2..................1E 65
.................(off Sewardstone Rd.)
Rosebery Rd. SW2...............4A 104
Rosebery Sq. EC1..........4B 8 (3C 62)
.................(off Rosebery Av.)
Rosebury Rd. SW6..............5D 87
Rose Bush Ct. NW3.............2B 46
Rose Ct. E1...................1F 19 (4B 64)
.................(off Wentworth St.)
Rose Ct. E8......................4B 50
.................(off Richmond Rd.)
Rose Ct. N1......................5D 49
.................(off Collin's Yd.)
Rose Ct. SE8....................5F 79
Rosecroft Av. NW3.............5C 30
Rosecroft Gdns. NW2..........5C 28
Rosedale Ct. N5................1D 49
Rosedale Ho. N16..............3F 35
Rosedale Rd. E7................2E 55
Rosedale Ter. W6...............4D 71
.................(off Dalling Rd.)
Rosedene NW6...................5F 43
Rosedene Av. SW16............3B 118
Rosedene Ter. E10.............4D 39
Rosedew Rd. W6................2F 85
Rosefield Gdns. E14...........1C 80
Roseford Ct. W12...............3F 71
.................(off Shepherd's Bush Grn.)
Rosegate Ho. E3................1B 66
.................(off Hereford Rd.)
Rosehart M. W11................5C 58
Rosehill Rd. SW18.............4E 101
Rose Joan M. NW6..............1C 44
Rosekey Ct. SE8...............3B 94
.................(off Baildon St.)
Roseleigh Av. N5...............1D 49
Rose Lipman Bldg..............5A 50
Rosemary Branch Theatre ...5F 49
.................(off Rosemary St.)
Rosemary Ct. SE15.............3A 92
Rosemary Ct. SE8..............2B 94
.................(off Dorking Cl.)
Rosemary Dr. E14..............5F 67
Rosemary Dr. IG4: Ilf..........1F 41
Rosemary Ho. N1................5F 49
.................(off Colville Est.)
Rosemary Ho. NW10............5D 43
.................(off Uffington Rd.)
Rosemary Rd. SE15.............3B 92
Rosemary Rd. SW17...........3E 115
Rosemary St. N1................5F 49
Rosemary Works N1............5F 49
.................(off Branch Pl.)
Rosemont Rd. NW3.............3E 45
Rosemoor St. SW3..............5B 74
Rosemount Point SE23.........3F 121
Rosenau Cres. SW11...........4B 88
Rosenau Rd. SW11..............4A 88
Rosendale Rd. SE21............5E 105
Rosendale Rd. SE24...........5E 105
Roseneath Pl. SW16...........4B 118
.................(off Curtis Fld. Rd.)

Roseneath Rd. SW11...........4C 102
Rosenthal Rd. SE6.............4D 109
Rosenthorpe Rd. SE15.........3F 107
Rose Pl. N8....................1A 34
Rose Playhouse 1A 26 (2E 77)
.................(off Park St.)
Roserton St. E14...............3E 81
Rose Sq. SW3...................1F 87
Rose Stapleton Ter.
SE1..................5E 27 (4A 78)
.................(off Page's Wlk.)
Rose St. EC4.............2E 17 (5D 63)
Rose St. WC2.............4D 15 (1A 76)
.................(not continuous)
Rosethorn Cl. SW12............5F 103
Rosetta Cl. SW8.................3A 90
.................(off Kenchester Cl.)
Roseveare Rd. SE12............4E 125
Rose Way SE12..................3C 110
Roseway SE21...................4F 105
Rosewood Ct. E11..............1F 53
Rosewood Gdns. SE13..........5E 95
Rosewood Ho. SW8.............2D 90
Rosewood Sq. W12.............5C 56
Rosher Cl. E15..................4F 53
Roshni Ho. SW17...............5A 116
Rosina St. E9...................3F 51
Roskell Rd. SW15..............1F 99
Rosler Bldg. SE1 ......2F 25 (2E 77)
.................(off Ewer St.)
Roslin Ho. E1...................1F 79
.................(off Brodlove La.)
Roslin Way BR1: Broml 1C 163
Rosmead Rd. W11..............1A 72
Rosoman Pl. EC1.........3C 8 (3C 62)
Rosoman St. EC1........2C 8 (2C 62)
Ross Apts. E16.................1C 82
.................(off Seagull La.)
Ross Ct. E5....................1D 51
.................(off Napoleon Rd.)
Ross Ct. SW15..................5F 99
Rosscourt Mans.
SW1..................5E 21 (4D 75)
.................(off Buckingham Pal. Rd.)
Rossdale Rd. SW15............2E 99
Rosse Gdns. SE13.............4F 109
Rosse M. SE3..................4D 97
Rossendale St. E5.............4D 37
Rossendale Way NW1.........4E 47
Rossetti Ct. WC1.........5B 6 (4F 61)
.................(off Ridgmount Pl.)
Rossetti Gdn. Mans. SW3....2B 88
.................(off Flood St.)
Rossetti Ho. SW1...............5F 75
.................(off Erasmus St.)
Rossetti M. NW8................5F 45
Rossetti Rd. SE16.............1D 93
Rossetti Studios SW3.........2A 88
.................(off Flood St.)
Ross Ho. E1....................2D 79
.................(off Prusom St.)
Rossington St. E5.............4C 36
Rossiter Gro. SW9.............1C 104
Rossiter Rd. SW12............1D 117
Rosslyn Av. SW13..............1A 98
Rosslyn Hill NW3...............1F 45
Rosslyn Mans. NW6............4E 45
.................(off Goldhurst Ter.)
Rosslyn M. NW3................1F 45
Rosslyn Pe. M. NW3............2F 45
Rossmore Cl. NW1..............3A 60
.................(off Rossmore Rd.)
Rossmore Rd. NW1.............3B 60
Rossmore Rd. NW1.............3A 60
Ross Wlk. SE27................3F 119

Ross Way E14...................5A 66
Ross Way SE9..................1F 111
Rostella Rd. SW17.............4F 115
Rostrevor Av. N15..............1B 36
Rostrevor Mans. SW6.........4B 86
.................(off Rostrevor Rd.)
Rostrevor M. SW6..............4B 86
Rostrevor Rd. SW19...........5C 114
Rostrevor Rd. SW6.............4B 86
Roswell Apts. E3...............4B 66
.................(off Joseph St.)
Rotary St. SE1...........5D 25 (4D 77)
Rothay NW1 ....1E 5 (2D 61)
.................(off Albany St.)
Rothbury Cotts. SE10..........5A 82
.................(off Maritius Rd.)
Rothbury Rd. E9................4B 52
Rotheley Ho. E9.................4E 51
.................(off Balcorne St.)
Rotherfield Ct. N1..............4F 49
.................(off Rotherfield St.)
Rotherfield St. N1..............4E 49
Rotherham Wlk. SE12D 25 (2D 77)
.................(off Nicholson St.)
ROTHERHITHE 3E 79
Rotherhithe Bus. Est. SE16 .5D 79
Rotherhithe New Rd. SE16 ..1D 93
Rotherhithe Old Rd. SE16....5F 79
Rotherhithe Sands Film Studios
.................................3E 79
.................(off Tunnel Rd.)
Rotherhithe Station (Overground)
.................................3E 79
Rotherhithe St. SE16..........3E 79
ROTHERHITHE TUNNEL 2D 79
Rother Ho. SE15...............2D 107
Rotherwick Ho. E1.............1C 78
.................(off Thomas More St.)
Rotherwick Rd. NW11.........2C 30
Rotherwood Rd. SW15........1F 99
Rothery St. N1..................5D 49
.................(off St Marys Path)
Rothery Ter. SW9..............3D 91
.................(off Foxley Rd.)
Rothesay Ct. SE11............2C 90
.................(off Harleyford St.)
Rothesay Ct. SE12............3D 125
Rothesay Ct. SE6..............2B 124
.................(off Cumberland Pl.)
Rothley Ct. NW8...............3F 59
.................(off St John's Wood Rd.)
Rothsay Rd. E7................4E 55
Rothsay St. SE1.........5D 27 (4A 78)
Rothsay Wlk. E14..............5C 80
.................(off Charnwood Gdns.)
Rothschild St. SE27..........4D 119
Roth Wlk. N7...................4B 34
Rothwell St. NW1..............5B 46
Rotten Row NW3: Lon Hampstead
Heath.........................3E 31
Rotten Row SW7: Lon
Hyde Pk.......................3F 73
Rotterdam Dr. E14.............4E 81
Rotunda, The SW10...........3E 87
Rotunda Ct. BR1: Broml 5D 125
.................(off Burnt Ash La.)
Rouel Rd. SE16................5C 78
Roundacre SW19..............2F 113
Roundel Cl. SE4...............2B 108
Roundhay Cl. SE23...........2F 121
Round Hill SE26...............2E 121
.................(not continuous)
Roundhouse, The 4C 46
Roundhouse La. E20..........3E 53
.................(off International Way)

Roundtable Rd. BR1: Broml....3B 124	
Roundwood Ct. E2...............2F 65	
Roundwood Rd. NW10.........3B 42	
Rounton Rd. E3....................3C 66	
Roupell Rd. SW2.................1B 118	
Roupell St. SE1.........2C 24 (2C 76)	
Rousden St. NW1................4E 47	
Rouse Gdns. SE21............4A 120	
Routemaster Cl. E13...........2D 69	
Routh Rd. SW18.................5A 102	
Rover Ho. N1......................5A 50	
........................(off Whitmore Est.)	
Rowallan Rd. SW6...............3A 86	
Rowan Ct. E13....................1D 69	
.................................(off High St.)	
Rowan Ct. SE15..................3B 92	
...............................(off Garnies Cl.)	
Rowan Ct. SW11.................4B 102	
Rowan Ho. E3......................5B 52	
...........................(off Hornbeam Sq.)	
Rowan Ho. SE16...................3F 79	
..........................(off Woodland Cres.)	
Rowan Lodge W8.................4D 73	
..............................(off Chantry Sq.)	
Rowan Rd. W6.....................5F 71	
Rowans Tenpin....................4C 34	
Rowan Ter. W6....................5F 71	
Rowan Wik. N19..................4E 33	
Rowan Wik. N2....................1E 31	
Rowan Wik. W10..................3A 58	
Rowberry Cl. SW6...............3E 85	
Rowcross St. SE1................1B 92	
Rowditch La. SW11..............5C 88	
Rowdon Av. NW10................4D 43	
Rowe Ho. E9........................3E 51	
Rowe La. E9........................2E 51	
Rowena Cres. SW11.............5A 88	
Rowenhurst Mans. NW6........3E 45	
...............................(off Canfield Gdns.)	
Rowfant Rd. SW17.............1C 116	
Rowhill Rd. E5.....................1D 51	
Rowington Cl. W2................4D 59	
Rowland Ct. E16.................3B 68	
Rowland Gro. SE26.............3D 121	
.............................(not continuous)	
Rowland Hill Ho.	
SE1.......................3D 25 (3D 77)	
Rowland Hill St. NW3...........2A 46	
Rowlands Cl. N6...................1C 32	
Rowley Gdns. N4.................2E 35	
Rowley Ho. SE8...................1C 94	
..............................(off Watergate St.)	
Rowley Rd. N15...................1E 35	
Rowley Way NW8................5D 45	
Rowntree Clifford Cl. E13.....3C 68	
Rowntree Cl. NW6...............3C 44	
Rowse Cl. E15....................5E 53	
Rowstock Gdns. N7..............2F 47	
Roxburghe Mans. W8...........3D 73	
...........................(off Kensington Ct.)	
Roxburgh Rd. SE27............5D 119	
Roxby Pl. SW6....................2C 86	
Roxford Ho. E3....................3D 67	
...................................(off Devas St.)	
Roxley Rd. SE13................4D 109	
Roxwell NW1.......................3D 47	
................................(off Hartland Rd.)	
Roxwell Rd. W12..................3C 70	
Roxwell Trad. Pk. E10........2A 38	
Royal Academy of Arts	
(Burlington House)	
...........................5F 13 (1E 75)	
Royal Academy of Music Mus.	
...........................4C 4 (3C 60)	
..........................(off Marylebone Rd.)	

Royal Air Force Memorial	
...........................2E 23 (2A 76)	
Royal Albert Hall................3F 73	
ROYAL ALBERT RDBT..........1F 83	
.........................(on Royal Albert Way)	
Royal Albert Station (DLR)...1F 83	
Royal Albert Way E16...........1E 83	
Royal Arc. W1..........5F 13 (1E 75)	
...............................(off Old Bond St.)	
Royal Archer SE14...............3F 93	
...............................(off Egmont St.)	
Royal Av. SW3....................1B 88	
Royal Av. Ho. SW3...............1B 88	
.................................(off Royal Av.)	
Royal Belgrave Ho. SW1......5D 75	
.................................(off Hugh St.)	
ROYAL BROMPTON HOSPITAL	
Sydney St....................1A 88	
ROYAL BROMPTON HOSPITAL	
(OUTPATIENTS)..............1F 87	
Royal Cir. SE27................3C 118	
Royal Cl. N16.....................3A 36	
Royal Cl. SE8.....................2B 94	
Royal Cl. SW19................3F 113	
Royal College of Music.........4F 73	
Royal College of Nursing	
...........................2E 13 (5D 61)	
................................(off Dean's M.)	
Royal College of Physicians Mus.	
...........................3E 5 (3D 61)	
Royal Coll. St. NW1..............4E 47	
Royal Connaught Apts. E16...2F 83	
...........................(off Connaught Rd.)	
Royal Ct. EC3.........3C 18 (5F 63)	
...................................(off Cornhill)	
Royal Ct. SE16....................4D 80	
Royal Courts of Justice	
...........................3A 16 (5B 62)	
....................................(off Strand)	
Royal Court Theatre London 5C 74	
................................(off Sloane Sq.)	
Royal Cres. W11..................2F 71	
Royal Cres. M. W11..............2F 71	
Royal Crest Av. E16..............3D 83	
Royal Duchess M. SW12.....5D 103	
Royal Exchange...3C 18 (5F 63)	
Royal Exchange Av.	
EC3......................3C 18 (5F 63)	
.........................(off Threadneedle St.)	
Royal Exchange Bldgs.	
EC3......................3C 18 (5F 63)	
.........................(off Threadneedle St.)	
Royal Festival Hall ..2A 24 (2B 76)	
ROYAL FREE HOSPITAL.......2A 46	
Royal George M. SE5..........2F 105	
Royal Hill SE10....................3E 95	
Royal Hill Ct. SE10...............3E 95	
.........................(off Greenwich High St.)	
Royal Holloway (University of	
London) Gower Street	
...........................5C 6 (4F 61)	
..................................(off Gower St.)	
Royal Hospital Chelsea.........1C 88	
Royal Hospital Chelsea Great Hall	
......................................1B 88	
Royal Hospital Chelsea Mus.	
......................................1C 88	
ROYAL HOSPITAL FOR NEURO-	
DISABILITY....................4A 100	
Royal Hospital Rd. SW3........2B 88	
Royal Institution.......5E 13 (1E 75)	
Royal Langford Apts. NW6....1D 59	
................................(off Greville Rd.)	
Royal London Bldgs. SE15....2D 93	
..............................(off Old Kent Rd.)	

ROYAL LONDON HOSPITAL, THE	
......................................4D 65	
Royal London Hospital Archives	
& Mus............................4D 65	
..................................(off Newark St.)	
ROYAL LONDON HOSPITAL FOR	
INTEGRATED MEDICINE	
...........................4E 7 (3A 62)	
Royal London Ind. Est.	
NW10.............................1A 56	
ROYAL MARSDEN HOSPITAL	
Fulham, THE...................1F 87	
Royal M. SW1..........5E 21 (4D 75)	
Royal Mews, The......4E 21 (3D 75)	
Royal Mint Ct. EC3...5F 19 (1B 78)	
Royal Mint Pl. E1................1C 78	
Royal Mint St. E1.....4F 19 (1B 78)	
ROYAL NAT. ORTHOPAEDIC	
HOSPITAL Central London	
Outpatient Dept.....4E 5 (3D 61)	
ROYAL NATIONAL THROAT, NOSE	
& EAR HOSPITAL Expected	
Close 2020.......1F 7 (2B 62)	
ROYAL NATIONAL THROAT, NOSE	
& EAR HOSPITAL New Site	
..................................4B 6 (3F 61)	
Royal Naval Pl. SE14...........3B 94	
Royal Oak Ct. N1......1D 11 (2A 64)	
...................................(off Pitfield St.)	
Royal Oak Pl. SE22............4D 107	
Royal Oak Rd. E8................3D 51	
Royal Oak Station (Underground)	
......................................4D 59	
Royal Oak Yd. SE1...4D 27 (3A 78)	
Royal Observatory Greenwich	
......................................3A 96	
Royal Opera Arc.	
SW1.......................1B 22 (2F 75)	
Royal Opera House...3E 15 (5A 62)	
Royal Orchard Cl. SW18......5A 100	
Royal Pde. SE3....................5B 96	
Royal Pde. SW6...................3A 86	
Royal Pde. M. SW6...............5B 96	
.................................(off Royal Pde.)	
Royal Pl. SE10....................3E 95	
Royal Rd. E16.....................5F 69	
Royal Rd. SE17...................2D 91	
Royal St. SE1..........5A 24 (4B 76)	
Royal Twr. Lodge E1............1C 78	
...............................(off Cartwright St.)	
Royalty Mans. W1....3B 14 (5F 61)	
................................(off Meard St.)	
Royalty M. W1..........3B 14 (5F 61)	
Royalty Studios W11............5A 58	
...............................(off Lancaster Rd.)	
Royal Veterinary Coll.	
Camden Town.................5F 47	
Royal Victoria Dock E16......1D 83	
Royal Victoria Gdns. SE16...5A 80	
................................(off Whiting Way)	
Royal Victoria Patriotic Bldg.	
SW18.............................4F 101	
Royal Victoria Pl. E16..........2D 83	
Royal Victoria Sq. E16.........1D 83	
Royal Victoria Station (DLR) 1C 82	
Royal Victor Pl. E3...............1F 65	
Royal Westminster Lodge	
SW1...............................5F 75	
................................(off Elverton St.)	
Royal Wharf E16..................3D 83	
Royal Wharf Pier (River Bus)	
......................................3D 83	
Royal Wharf Wlk. E16...........3D 83	
Royal Wimbledon Golf Course	
......................................5D 113	

Roycroft Cl. SW2 .... 1C 118
Roydon Cl. SW11 .... 5B 88
Royle Bldg. N1 .... 1E 63
.... (off Wenlock Rd.)
Royley Ho. EC1 .... 3A 10 (3E 63)
.... (off Old St.)
Roy Sq. E14 .... 1A 80
Royston Ct. E13 .... 5C 54
.... (off Stopford Rd.)
Royston Ct. SE24 .... 4E 105
Royston Ct. W8 .... 2C 72
.... (off Kensington Chu. St.)
Royston Gdns. IG1: Ilf. 1F 41
Royston Ho. SE15 .... 2D 93
.... (off Friary Est.)
Royston Pde. IG1: Ilf. 1F 41
Royston St. E2 .... 1E 65
Rozel Ct. N1 .... 5A 50
Rozel Rd. SW4 .... 1E 103
RQ33 SW18 .... 2C 100
Rubens Gdns. SE22 .... 5C 106
.... (off Lordship La.)
Rubens Pl. SW4 .... 2A 104
Rubens St. SE6 .... 2B 122
Rubicon Ct. N1 .... 5A 48
Ruby Cl. E5 .... 5F 37
Ruby Ct. E15 .... 5E 53
.... (off Warton Rd.)
Ruby St. SE15 .... 2D 93
Ruby Triangle SE15 .... 2D 93
Ruckholt Cl. E10 .... 5D 39
Ruckholt Rd. E10 .... 1C 52
Rucklidge Av. NW10 .... 1B 56
Rucklidge Pas. NW10 .... 1B 56
.... (off Rucklidge Av.)
Rudall Cres. NW3 .... 1F 45
Rudbeck Ho. SE15 .... 3C 92
.... (off Peckham Pk. Rd.)
Ruddington Cl. E5 .... 1A 52
Rudge Ho. SE16 .... 4C 78
.... (off Jamaica Rd.)
Rudgwick Ter. NW8 .... 5A 46
Rudloe Rd. SW12 .... 5E 103
Rudolph Ct. E13 .... 1B 68
Rudolph Rd. NW6 .... 1C 58
Rudstone Ho. E3 .... 2D 67
.... (off Bromley High St.)
Rudyard Ct. SE1 ...... 4C 26 (3F 77)
.... (off Long La.)
Rufford St. N1 .... 5A 48
Rufford St. M. N1 .... 4A 48
Rufus Bus. Cen. SW18 ..... 2D 115
Rufus Ho. SE1 ...... 5F 27 (4B 78)
.... (off St Saviour's Est.)
Rufus St. N1 .... 2D 11 (2A 64)
.... (off Bishop King's Rd.)
Rugby Mans. W14 .... 5A 72
Rugby Rd. W4 .... 3A 70
Rugby St. WC1 .... 4F 7 (3B 62)
Rugg St. E14 .... 1C 80
Rugless Ho. E14 .... 3E 81
.... (off E. Ferry Rd.)
Rugmere NW1 .... 4C 46
.... (off Ferdinand St.)
Ruislip St. SW17 .... 4B 116
Rumball Ho. SE5 .... 3A 92
.... (off Harris St.)
Rumbold Rd. SW6 .... 3D 87
Rum Cl. E1 .... 1E 79
Rumford Ho. SE1 ... 5F 25 (4E 77)
.... (off Tiverton St.)
Rumsey M. N4 .... 5D 35
Rumsey Rd. SW9 .... 1B 104
Runacres Ct. SE17 .... 1E 91
Runbury Circ. NW9 .... 5A 28

Runcorn Pl. W11 .... 1A 72
Rundell Cres. NW4 .... 1D 29
Rundell Twr. SW8 .... 4B 90
Runnymede Cl. SW15 .... 1C 112
Runnymede Ho. E9 .... 1A 52
Rupack St. SE16 .... 3E 79
Rupert Ct. W1 .... 4B 14 (1F 75)
Rupert Gdns. SW9 .... 5D 91
Rupert Ho. SE11 .... 5C 76
Rupert Ho. SW5 .... 5C 72
.... (off Nevern Sq.)
Rupert Rd. N19 .... 5F 33
.... (not continuous)
Rupert Rd. NW6 .... 1B 58
Rupert Rd. W4 .... 4A 70
Rupert St. W1 .... 4B 14 (1F 75)
Rusbridge Cl. E8 .... 2C 50
Ruscoe Rd. E16 .... 5B 68
Ruscombe NW1 .... 5D 47
.... (off Delancey St.)
Rusham Rd. SW12 .... 4B 102
Rush Comn. M. SW2 .... 5B 104
Rushcroft Rd. SW2 .... 2C 104
Rushcutters Ct. SE16 .... 5A 80
.... (off Boat Lifter Way)
Rushey Grn. SE6 .... 5D 109
Rushey Mead SE4 .... 3C 108
Rushford Rd. SE4 .... 4B 108
Rushgrove Pde. NW9 .... 1A 28
Rush Hill M. SW11 .... 1C 102
.... (off Rush Hill Rd.)
Rush Hill Rd. SW11 .... 1C 102
Rushmead E2 .... 2D 65
Rushmere Pl. SW19 .... 5F 113
Rushmere Cres. SE5 .... 1F 51
Rushmore Ho. SW15 .... 5C 98
Rushmore Ho. W14 .... 4A 72
.... (off Russell Rd.)
Rushmore Rd. E5 .... 1E 51
.... (not continuous)
Rusholme Gro. SE19 .... 5A 120
Rusholme Rd. SW15 .... 4F 99
Rushton Ho. SW8 .... 5F 89
Rushton St. N1 .... 1F 63
Rushton Wlk. E3 .... 3B 66
.... (off Hamlets Way)
Rushworth St. SE1 ... 3E 25 (3D 77)
Ruskin Cl. NW11 .... 1D 31
Ruskin Ct. SE5 .... 1F 105
.... (off Champion Hill)
Ruskin Ho. SW1 .... 5F 75
.... (off Herrick St.)
Ruskin Mans. W14 .... 2A 86
.... (off Queen's Club Gdns.)
Ruskin Pk. Ho. SE5 .... 1F 105
Ruskin Wlk. SE24 .... 3E 105
Rusper Cl. NW2 .... 5E 29
Rusper Ct. SW9 .... 5A 90
.... (off Clapham Rd.)
Russell Chambers
   WC1 .... 1E 15 (4A 62)
.... (off Bury Pl.)
Russell Cl. SE7 .... 3E 97
Russell Cl. W4 .... 2B 84
Russell Ct. E10 .... 2D 39
Russell Ct. SE15 .... 5D 93
.... (off Heaton Rd.)
Russell Ct. SW1 ...... 2A 22 (2E 75)
.... (off Cleveland Row)
Russell Ct. SW6 .... 5B 118
Russell Ct. WC1 ...... 4D 7 (3A 62)
.... (off Woburn Pl.)
Russell Flint Ho. E16 .... 2D 83
.... (off Pankhurst Av.)
Russell Gdns. NW11 .... 1A 30

Russell Gdns. W14 .... 4A 72
Russell Gdns. M. W14 .... 3A 72
Russell Gro. SW9 .... 3C 90
Russell Ho. E14 .... 5C 66
.... (off Saracen St.)
Russell Ho. SW1 .... 1E 89
.... (off Cambridge St.)
Russell Lodge SE1 ... 5B 26 (4F 77)
.... (off Spurgeon St.)
Russell Mans. WC1 ... 5E 7 (4A 62)
.... (off Southampton Row)
Russell Pde. NW11 .... 1A 30
.... (off Golders Grn. Rd.)
Russell Pl. NW3 .... 2A 46
Russell Pl. SE16 .... 4A 80
Russell Rd. E10 .... 1D 39
Russell Rd. E16 .... 5C 68
Russell Rd. N15 .... 1A 36
Russell Rd. N8 .... 1F 33
Russell Rd. NW9 .... 1B 28
Russell Rd. W14 .... 4A 72
Russell's Footpath SW16 ... 5A 118
Russell Sq. WC1 ...... 4D 7 (4A 62)
Russell Sq. Mans.
   WC1 .... 5E 7 (4A 62)
Russell Square Station
(Underground) 4D 7 (3A 62)
Russell St. WC2 ...... 4E 15 (1A 76)
Russell's Wharf Flats
   W10 .... 3B 58
Russet Sq. SW15 .... 2A 100
Russet Cres. N7 .... 2B 48
Russett Way SE13 .... 5D 95
Russia Dock Rd. SE16 .... 2A 80
Russia La. E2 .... 1E 65
Russia Row EC2 ...... 3A 18 (5E 63)
Russia Wlk. SE16 .... 3A 80
Rusthall Av. W4 .... 5A 70
Rustic Wlk. E16 .... 5D 69
.... (off Lambert Rd.)
Ruston M. W11 .... 5A 58
Ruston Rd. SE18 .... 4F 83
Ruston St. E3 .... 5B 52
Rust Sq. SE5 .... 3F 91
Rutford Rd. SW16 .... 5A 118
Ruth Ct. E3 .... 1A 66
Rutherford Ho. E1 .... 3D 65
.... (off Brady St.)
Rutherford Ho. SW11 .... 5B 88
.... (off Battersea Pk. Rd.)
Rutherford St. SW1 .... 5F 75
Ruth Ho. W10 .... 3A 58
.... (off Kensal Rd.)
Ruthin Cl. NW9 .... 1A 28
Ruthin Rd. SE3 .... 2C 96
Ruthven St. E9 .... 5F 51
Rutland Cl. SE5 .... 2F 105
Rutland Ct. SW7 .... 3A 74
.... (off Rutland Gdns.)
Rutland Gdns. N4 .... 1D 35
Rutland Gdns. SW7 .... 3A 74
Rutland Gdns. M. SW7 .... 3A 74
Rutland Ga. SW7 .... 3A 74
Rutland Ga. M. SW7 .... 3A 74
.... (off Rutland Ga.)
Rutland Gro. W6 .... 5D 71
Rutland Ho. NW10 .... 2C 56
Rutland Ho. W8 .... 4D 73
.... (off Marloes Rd.)
Rutland M. NW8 .... 5D 45
Rutland M. E. SW7 .... 4A 74
.... (off Ennismore St.)
Rutland M. Sth. SW7 .... 4A 74
.... (off Ennismore St.)

Rutland M. W. SW7 .... 4A **74**
.... (off Rutland Ga.)
Rutland Pk. NW2 ....3E **43**
Rutland Pk. SE6 .... 2B **122**
Rutland Pk. Gdns. NW2 ....3E **43**
.... (off Rutland Pk.)
Rutland Pk. Mans. NW2 ....3E **43**
Rutland Pl. EC1 .... 4E **9** (3D **63**)
Rutland Rd. E17 .... 1C **38**
Rutland Rd. E7 .... 4F **55**
Rutland Rd. E9 .... 5F **51**
Rutland St. SW7 .... 4B **44**
Rutland Wlk. SE6 .... 2B **122**
Rutley Cl. SE17 .... 2D **91**
Rutt's Ter. SE14 .... 4F **93**
Ruvigny Gdns. SW15 .... 1F **99**
Ryan Cl. SE3 .... 2E **111**
Rycott Path SE22 .... 5C **106**
Rycuff Sq. SE3 .... 5B **96**
Rydal Gdns. SW15 .... 5A **112**
Rydal Rd. SW16 .... 4F **117**
Rydal Water NW1 ...... 2F **5** (2E **61**)
Ryde Ho. NW6 .... 5C **44**
.... (off Priory Pk. Rd.)
Rydens Ho. SE9 ....3E **125**
Ryder Av. E10 .... 2D **39**
Ryder Cl. BR1: Brom! 5D **125**
Ryder Ct. E10 .... 4D **39**
Ryder Ct. SW1 .... 1A **22** (2E **75**)
.... (off Ryder St.)
Ryder Dr. SE16 .... 1D **93**
Ryder Ho. E1 ....3E **65**
.... (off Colebert Av.)
Ryder M. E9 .... 2E **51**
Ryder's Ter. NW8 .... 1E **59**
Ryder St. SW1 .... 1A **22** (2E **75**)
Ryde Va. Rd. SW12 .... 2E **117**
Rydons Cl. SE9 .... 1F **111**
Rydon St. N1 ....5E **49**
Rydston Cl. N7 .... 4A **48**
Ryecotes Mead SE21 .... 1A **120**
Ryecroft Rd. SE13 .... 3E **109**
Ryecroft Rd. SW16 .... 5C **118**
Ryecroft St. SW6 .... 4D **87**
Ryedale SE22 .... 4D **107**
Ryefield Path SW15 .... 1C **112**
Ryefield Rd. SE19 ....5E **119**
Ryegates SE15 .... 5D **93**
.... (off Caulfield Rd.)
Rye Hill Pk. SE15 .... 2E **107**
Rye Ho. SE16 ....3E **79**
.... (off Swan Rd.)
Rye Ho. SW1 .... 1D **89**
.... (off Ebury Bri. Rd.)
Ryeland Blvd. SW18 .... 3D **101**
Ryelands Cres. SE12 ....4E **111**
Rye La. SE15 .... 4C **92**
Rye Mans. E20 .... 2E **53**
.... (off Napa Cl.)
Rye Pas. SE15 .... 1C **106**
Rye Rd. SE15 .... 2F **107**
Rye Wlk. SW15 .... 3F **99**
Ryfold Rd. SW19 .... 3C **114**
Rylandes Rd. NW2 .... 5C **28**
Ryland Rd. NW5 .... 3D **47**
Rylett Cres. W12 .... 3B **70**
Rylett Rd. W12 .... 3B **70**
Rylston Rd. SW6 .... 2B **86**
Rymer St. SE24 .... 4D **105**
Rysbrack St. SW3 ..... 5A **20** (4B **74**)

S

Saatchi Gallery 1B **88**
Sabella Ct. E3 .... 1B **66**

Sabine Rd. SW11 .... 1B **102**
Sable Ho. E20 .... 2D **53**
.... (off Scarlet Cl.)
Sable St. N1 .... 4D **49**
Sach Rd. E5 .... 4D **37**
Sackville Ho. SW16 .... 3A **118**
Sackville St. W1 .... 5A **14** (1E **75**)
Saddlers Ho. E20 .... 2E **53**
.... (off Ribbons Wlk.)
Saddlers Mall SW8 .... 4A **90**
Saddle Yd. W1 .... 1D **21** (2D **75**)
Sadler Hgts. N1 .... 4B **48**
.... (off Caledonian Rd.)
Sadler Ho. E3 .... 2D **67**
.... (off Bromley High St.)
Sadler Ho. EC1 .... 1C **8** (2D **63**)
.... (off Spa Grn. Est.)
Sadler Pl. E9 .... 2A **52**
Sadlers Ct. SE1 .... 5D **27** (4A **78**)
.... (off Wilds Rents)
Sadlers Ga. M. SW15 .... 1E **99**

Sadler's Wells Theatre
.... 1C **8** (2C **62**)
Safara Ho. SE5 .... 4A **92**
.... (off Dalwood St.)
Saffron Av. E14 .... 1F **81**
Saffron Cl. NW11 .... 1B **30**
Saffron Ct. E15 .... 2A **54**
.... (off Maryland St.)
Saffron Hill EC1 ..... 5C **8** (4C **62**)
Saffron St. EC1 .... 5C **8** (4C **62**)
Saffron Wharf SE1 .... 3B **78**
.... (off Shad Thames)
Sage M. SE22 .... 3B **106**
Sage St. E1 .... 1E **79**
Sage Way W1 .... 2F **7** (2B **62**)
.... (off Cubitt St.)
Saigasso Cl. E16 ....5F **69**
Sailacre Ho. SE10 .... 1B **96**
Sail Ct. E14 .... 1F **81**
.... (off Newport Av.)
Sailmakers Ct. SW6 ....1E **101**
Sailors Ho. E14 ....5F **67**
.... (off Deauville Cl.)
Sail St. SE11 .... 5B **76**
Sainfoin Rd. SW17 .... 2C **116**
Sainsbury Rd. SE19 .... 5A **120**
Sainsbury Wing 5C **14** (1F **75**)
.... (within National Gallery)
St Agnes Cl. E9 ....5E **51**
St Agnes Ho. E3 .... 1C **66**
.... (off Ordell Rd.)
St Agnes Pl. SE11 .... 2D **91**
St Agnes Quad. SE11 .... 2C **90**
St Agnes Well EC1 .... 3C **10** (3D **63**)
.... (off City Rd.)
St Aidan's Rd. SE22 .... 4D **107**
St Albans Cl. NW11 .... 3C **30**
St Albans Ct. EC2 ..... 1A **18** (5E **63**)
.... (off Wood St.)
St Albans Gro. W8 .... 4D **73**
St Alban's La. NW11 .... 3C **30**
St Albans Mans. W8 .... 4D **73**
.... (off Kensington Ct. Pl.)
St Albans Pl. N1 .... 5D **49**
St Albans Rd. NW10 .... 5A **42**
St Albans Rd. NW5 .... 5C **32**
St Alban's St. SW1 .....5B **14** (1F **75**)
St Albans Studios W8 .... 4D **73**
.... (off St Albans Gro.)
St Albans Ter. W6 .... 2A **86**
St Albans Vs. NW5 .... 5C **32**
St Alfege Pas. SE10 .... 2E **95**
St Alfege Rd. SE7 .... 2F **97**
St Alphage Gdn. EC2 .. 1A **18** (4E **63**)

St Alphage Highwalk
EC2 .... 1A **18** (4E **63**)
.... (off Wood St.)
St Alphonsus Rd. SW4 .... 2E **103**
St Amunds Cl. SE6 .... 4C **122**
St Andrews Chambers
W1 .... 1A **14** (4E **61**)
.... (off Wells St.)
St Andrew's Cl. NW2 .... 5D **29**
St Andrews Cl. SE16 .... 1D **93**
St Andrews Cl. SW19 .... 5D **115**
St Andrew's Ct. SW18 .... 2E **115**
St Andrew's Gro. N16 ....3F **35**
St Andrew's Hill EC4 .. 3E **17** (5D **63**)
.... (not continuous)
St Andrews Ho. SE16 .... 4D **79**
.... (off Southwark Pk. Rd.)
St Andrews Mans.
W1 .... 1B **12** (4C **60**)
.... (off Dorset St.)
St Andrews Mans. W14 ...... 2A **86**
.... (off St Andrew's Rd.)
St Andrew's M. N16 .... 3A **36**
St Andrew's M. SE3 .... 3C **96**
St Andrew's M. SW12 ....1F **117**
St Andrew's Pl. NW1 ...3D **5** (3D **61**)
St Andrew's Rd. E11 .... 1A **40**
St Andrew's Rd. E13 .... 2D **69**
St Andrews Rd. NW10 .... 3D **43**
St Andrew's Rd. NW11 .... 1B **30**
St Andrew's Rd. W14 .... 2A **86**
St Andrew's Rd. W3 .... 1A **70**
St Andrews Sq. W11 .... 5A **58**
St Andrew's St. EC4 ... 1C **16** (4C **62**)
St Andrews Way E3 .... 3D **67**
St Andrew's Wharf
SE1 .... 3F **27** (3B **78**)
St Anne's Cl. N6 .... 5C **32**
St Anne's Ct. NW6 .... 5A **44**
St Anne's Ct. W1 ...... 3B **14** (5F **61**)
.... (off Doric Way)
St Anne's Flats NW1 ... 1B **6** (2F **61**)
St Anne's Pas. E14 .... 5B **66**
St Anne's Rd. E11 ....4F **39**
St Anne's Row E14 .... 5B **66**
St Anne's Trad. Est. E14 ..... 5B **66**
.... (off St Anne's Row)
St Anne St. E14 .... 5B **66**
St Ann's Cres. SW18 .... 4D **101**
St Ann's Gdns. NW5 .... 3C **46**
St Ann's Hill SW18 .... 3D **101**
St Ann's Ho. WC1 ...... 2B **8** (2C **62**)
.... (off Margery St.)
St Ann's La. SW1 ..... 5C **22** (4F **75**)
St Ann's Pk. Rd. SW18 .... 4E **101**
St Ann's Pas. SW13 .... 1A **98**
St Ann's Rd. N15 .... 1D **35**
St Ann's Rd. SW13 .... 5B **84**
St Ann's Rd. W11 .... 1F **71**
St Ann's Rd. SW1 ..... 5C **22** (4F **75**)
St Ann's Ter. NW8 .... 1F **59**
St Ann's Vs. W11 ....2F **71**
St Anselms Cl. SW16 .... 5A **118**
St Anselm's Pl. W1 ...4D **13** (1D **75**)
St Anthony's Cl. E1 .... 2C **78**
St Anthony's Cl. E9 .... 3B **52**
.... (off Wallis Rd.)
St Anthony's Cl. SW17 .... 2A **116**
St Anthony's Ct. SW17 .... 2C **116**
St Anthony's Flats
NW1 .... 1B **6** (1F **61**)
.... (off Aldenham St.)
St Antony's Rd. E7 .... 4D **55**

St Asaph Rd. SE4 ....1F 107
St Aubins Ct. N1 ....5F 49
St Aubyn's Av. SW19 ....5B 114
St Augustine's Ct. SE1 ....1D 93
...........................(off Lynton Rd.)
St Augustine's Ho.
NW1 ....1B 6 (2F 61)
...................(off Werrington St.)
St Augustine's Mans. SW1 .....5E 75
...........................(off Bloomburg St.)
St Augustine's Path N5 ....1E 49
St Augustine's Rd. NW1 ....4F 47
St Augustine's Sports Cen. 1C 58
St Austell Rd. SE13 ....5E 96
St Barnabas Cl. SE22 ....3A 106
St Barnabas M. SW1 ....1C 88
...........................(off St Barnabas St.)
St Barnabas Rd. E17 ....1C 38
St Barnabas St. SW1 ....1C 88
St Barnabas Ter. E9 ....2F 51
St Barnabas Vs. SW8 ....4A 90
St Bartholomew's Cl. SE26 4D 121
ST BARTHOLOMEW'S HOSPITAL
.................................1E 17 (4D 63)
St Bartholomew's Hospital Mus.
.................................1E 17 (4D 63)
........(in St Bartholomew's Hospital)
St Benedict's Cl. SW17 ....5C 116
St Benet's Cl. SW17 ....2A 116
St Benet's Pl. EC3 ....4C 18 (1F 77)
St Bernard's Ct. SE27 ....4F 119
St Bernards Ho. E14 ....4F 81
.............................(off Galbraith St.)
St Bernard's Rd. E6 ....5F 55
St Botolph Row EC3 .3F 19 (5B 64)
St Botolphs E1 ....2F 19 (5B 64)
.............................(off St Botolph St.)
St Botolph St. EC3 ...2F 19 (5B 64)
St Brelades Ct. N1 ....5A 50
St Bride's Av. EC4 ....3D 17 (5D 63)
.................................(off Bride La.)
St Bride's Crypt Mus.
.................................3D 17 (5D 63)
.................................(off Fleet St.)
St Bride's Ho. E3 ....1C 66
.................................(off Ordell Rd.)
St Bride's Pas. EC4 ....3D 17 (5D 63)
.................................(off Salisbury Ct.)
St Bride St. EC4 ....2D 17 (5D 63)
.................................(off Bow Rd.)
St Catherine's Apts. E3 ....2D 67
St Catherine's Cl. SW17 ....2A 116
St Catherine's Ct. W4 ....4A 70
St Catherine's Dr. SE14 ....5F 93
St Catherines M. SW3 ....5B 74
St Cecilia Pl. SE3 ....1C 96
St Chad's Pl. WC1 ....1E 7 (2A 62)
St Chad's St. WC1 ......1E 7 (2A 62)
.................................(not continuous)
ST CHARLES HOSPITAL 4F 57
St Charles Pl. W10 ....4A 58
St Charles Sq. W10 ....4F 57
St Chloe's Ho. E3 ....1C 66
.................................(off Ordell Rd.)
ST CHRISTOPHER'S HOSPICE
(SYDENHAM) 5E 121
St Christopher's Ho.
NW1 ....1A 6 (1E 61)
...................(off Bridgeway St.)
St Christopher's Pl.
W1 ....2C 12 (5C 60)
St Clair Ho. E3 ....2B 66
.................................(off British St.)
St Clair Rd. E13 ....1D 69
St Clare St. EC3 ....3F 19 (5B 64)

St Clements Av. E3 ....2B 66
St Clement's Ct. EC4 ....4C 18 (1F 77)
.................................(off Clements La.)
St Clement's Ct. N7 ....3C 48
St Clements Ct. SE14 ....2F 93
.................................(off Myers La.)
St Clements Ct. W11 ....1F 71
.................................(off Stoneleigh St.)
St Clement's Development
E3 ....2B 66
St Clements Hgts. SE26 ....4C 120
St Clements Ho. E1 ...1F 19 (4B 64)
.................................(off Leyden St.)
St Clement's La.
WC2 ....3A 16 (5B 62)
St Clements Mans. SW6 ....2F 85
.................................(off Lillie Rd.)
St Clements St. N7 ....3C 48
St Clements Yd. SE22 ....2B 106
St Cloud Rd. SE27 ....4E 119
St Columba's Ct. E15 ....1A 54
.................................(off Janson Rd.)
St Columb's Ho. W10 ....4A 58
.................................(off Blagrove Rd.)
St Crispin's Cl. NW3 ....1A 46
St Cross St. EC1 ....5C 8 (4C 62)
St Cuthbert's Rd. NW2 ....3B 44
St Cyprian's St. SW17 ....4B 116
St Davids Cl. SE16 ....1D 93
.................................(off Masters Dr.)
St Davids M. E3 ....2A 66
.................................(off Morgan St.)
St David's Pl. NW4 ....2D 29
St Davids Sq. E14 ....1D 95
St Denis Rd. SE27 ....4F 119
St Dionis Rd. SW6 ....5B 86
St Donatt's Rd. SE14 ....4B 94
St Dunstan's All.
EC3 ....4D 19 (1A 78)
.................................(off St Dunstans Hill)
St Dunstan's Ct.
EC4 ....3C 16 (5C 62)
St Dunstan's Enterprises 1C 122
St Dunstans Hill
EC3 ....5D 19 (1A 78)
St Dunstan's Ho.
WC2 ....2B 16 (5C 62)
.................................(off Chancery La.)
St Dunstan's La.
EC3 ....5D 19 (1A 78)
St Dunstans M. E1 ....4A 66
.................................(off White Horse Rd.)
St Dunstan's Rd. E7 ....3D 55
St Dunstan's Rd. W6 ....1F 85
St Edmund's Cl. NW8 ....5B 46
St Edmund's Ct. SW17 ....2A 116
St Edmund's Ct. NW8 ....5B 46
.................................(off St Edmund's Ter.)
St Edmunds Sq. SW13 ....2E 85
St Edmund's Ter. NW8 ....5A 46
St Edward's Cl. NW11 ....1C 30
St Edwards Ct. NW11 ....1C 30
St Elmo Rd. W12 ....2B 70
St Elmos Rd. SE16 ....3A 80
St Ermin's Hill SW1 ....5B 22 (4F 75)
.................................(off Broadway)
St Ervan's Rd. W10 ....4B 58
.................................(off Salisbury Rd.)
St Eugene Ct. NW6 ....5A 44
.................................(off Salusbury Rd.)
St Faith's Rd. SE21 ....1D 119
St Fillans Rd. SE6 ....1E 123
St Francis' Ho. NW1 ....1F 61
.................................(off Bridgeway St.)
St Francis Cl. SW12 ....4D 103
St Francis Rd. SE22 ....2A 106

St Frideswide's M. E14 ....5E 67
St Gabriel's Cl. E11 ....4D 41
St Gabriel's Cl. E14 ....4D 67
.................................(off Cormont Rd.)
St Gabriels Mnr. SE5 ....4D 91
.................................(off Cormont Rd.)
St Gabriels Rd. NW2 ....2F 43
St Gabriel Wlk. SE1 ....5D 77
.................................(off Elephant & Castle)
St George's Antiochian Orthodox
Cathedral 1E 5 (2D 61)
St George's Av. E7 ....4D 55
St George's Av. N7 ....1F 47
St George's Bldgs.
SE1 ....5D 25 (4D 77)
.................................(off St George's Rd.)
St George's Cir.
SE1 ....5D 25 (4D 77)
St George's Cl. NW11 ....1B 30
St George's Cl. SW8 ....4E 89
St George's Cl. SE1 ...5D 25 (4D 77)
.................................(off Garden Row)
St George's Ct. SW1 ....1E 89
.................................(off St George's Dr.)
St George's Ct. SW15 ....2B 100
St George's Ct. SW3 ....5A 74
.................................(off Brompton Rd.)
St George's Ct. SW7 ....4E 73
St Georges Ct. EC4 ...2D 17 (5D 63)
St George's Dr. SW1 ....5D 75
ST GEORGE'S FIELD 1A 74
St George's Flds. W2 ....5A 60
St George's Gro. SW17 ....3F 115
ST GEORGE'S HOSPITAL
(TOOTING) 5F 115
St George's Ho. NW1 ....1F 61
.................................(off Bridgeway St.)
St Georges Ho. SW11 ....4C 88
.................................(off Charlotte Despard Av.)
St George's La. EC3 .4C 18 (1F 77)
.................................(off Pudding La.)
St George's Leisure Cen. 1D 79
St George's Mans. SW1 ....1F 89
.................................(off Causton St.)
St George's M. NW1 ....4B 46
St George's M. SE1 ...5C 24 (4C 76)
.................................(off Westminster Bri. Rd.)
St George's M. SE8 ....5B 80
St Georges Pde. SE6 ....2B 122
.................................(off Perry Hill)
St George's Path SE4 ....2C 108
.................................(off Adelaide Av.)
St George's Rd. E10 ....5E 39
St George's Rd. E7 ....4D 55
St George's Rd. NW11 ....1B 30
St George's Rd. SE1 ...5C 24 (4C 76)
St George's Rd. W4 ....3A 70
St George's Rd. W7 ....4D 55
St George's Sq. E7 ....4D 55
St George's Sq. SE8 ....5B 80
.................................(not continuous)
St George's Sq. SW1 ....1F 89
St Georges Sq. E14 ....1A 80
St George's Sq. M. SW1 ....1F 89
St George's Ter. E6 ....2F 69
.................................(off Masterman Rd.)
St George's Ter. NW1 ....4B 46
St George's Ter. SE15 ....3C 92
St George St. W1 ....3E 13 (1D 75)
St George's University of London
....5F 115
St George's Way SE15 ....2A 92
St George's Wharf
SE1 ....3F 27 (3B 78)
.................................(off Shad Thames)
St George Wharf SW8 ....2A 90

St George Wharf Pier (River Bus)
................................2A **90**
St Gerards Cl. SW4 ......3E **103**
St German's Pl. SE3........ 4C **96**
St German's Rd. SE23 ...... 1A **122**
St Giles Churchyard
EC2................1A **18** (4E **63**)
St Giles Cir. W1 ...... 2C **14** (5F **61**)
St Giles High St.
WC2................2C **14** (5F **61**)
St Giles Ho. SE5 .... 4A **92**
St Giles Rd. SE5 .... 3A **92**
St Giles Sq. WC2 ... 2C **14** (5F **61**)
St Giles Ter. EC2 .... 1A **18** (4E **63**)
................................(off Wood St.)
St Giles Twr. SE5 .... 4A **92**
................................(off Gables Cl.)
St Gilles Ho. E2 .... 1F **65**
................................(off Mace St.)
St Gothard Rd. SE27 .... 4F **119**
................................(not continuous)
St Helena Ho. WC1 .... 2B **8** (2C **62**)
................................(off Margery St.)
St Helena Rd. SE16............ 5F **79**
St Helena St. WC1 .... 2B **8** (2C **62**)
St Helen's Gdns. W10........4F **57**
St Helen's Pl. EC3 ... 2D **19** (5A **64**)
St Helens Pl. E10 .... 2A **38**
St Helier Ct. N1 .... 5A **50**
................................(off De Beauvoir Est.)
St Helier Ct. SE16............ 3F **79**
................................(off Poolmans St.)
St Helier's Rd. E10............ 1E **39**
St Hilda's Cl. NW6............ 4F **43**
St Hilda's Cl. SW17 ...... 2A **116**
St Hilda's Rd. SW13............ 2D **85**
St Hilda's Wharf E1............ 2E **79**
................................(off Wapping High St.)
St Hubert's Ho. E14............ 4C **80**
................................(off Janet St.)
St Hughes Cl. SW17 ...... 2A **116**
St Ives Pl. E14.................. 4E **67**
St James Ct. E12 .... 4E **41**
St James Ct. E2 .... 2C **64**
................................(off Bethnal Grn. Rd.)
St James Ct. SE3 .... 4D **97**
St James' Ct. SW1 ... 5A **22** (4E **75**)
St James Gro. SW11 .... 5B **88**
St James Hall N1 .... 5E **49**
................................(off Prebend St.)
St James Ind. M. SE1 .... 1C **92**
St James Mans. SE1 5B **24** (4C **76**)
................................(off McAuley Cl.)
St James' Mans. NW6........ 4C **44**
................................(off West End La.)
St James M. E14 .... 4E **81**
St James M. E17................ 1A **38**
St James Path E17............ 1A **38**
St James Residences
W1................4B **14** (1F **75**)
................................(off Brewer St.)
St James' Rd. E15.............. 2B **54**
St James's SE14................ 4A **94**
ST JAMES'S 1A **22** (2F **75**)
St James's App.
EC2................4D **11** (3A **64**)
St James's Av. E2................ 1E **65**
St James's Chambers
SW1................1A **22** (2E **75**)
................................(off Jermyn St.)
St James's Cl. NW8............ 5B **46**
................................(off St James's Ter. M.)
St James's Cl. SW17........ 2B **116**
St James's Cres. SW9 ...... 1C **104**
St James's Dr. SW12........ 1B **116**

St James's Dr. SW17 .... 1B **116**
St James's Gdns. W11........ 2A **72**
................................(not continuous)
St James's Ho. SE1............ 5C **78**
................................(off Strathnairn St.)
St James's Mkt.
SW1................5B **14** (1F **75**)
St James's Palace ... 2A **22** (3E **75**)
St James's Pk. 3B **22** (3F **75**)
St James's Park Station
(Underground) 4B **22** (3F **75**)
St James's Pas. E
C3................3E **19** (5A **64**)
................................(off Duke's Pl.)
St James's Pl. SW1 .. 2F **21** (2E **75**)
St James's Rd. SE1 .... 2C **92**
St James's Rd. SE16............ 4C **78**
St James's Sq. SW1 .. 1A **22** (2E **75**)
St James's St. E17 .... 1A **38**
St James's St. SW1 .. 1F **21** (2E **75**)
St James's Ter. NW8............ 5B **46**
................................(off Prince Albert Rd.)
St James's Ter. M. NW8........ 5B **46**
St James St. W6 .... 1E **85**
St James Street Station
(Overground) 1A **38**
St James's Wlk. EC1 ...3D **9** (3D **63**)
St James Ter. SW12............ 1C **116**
St Joan's Ho. NW1 ...... 1B 6 (2F **61**)
................................(off Phoenix Rd.)
ST JOHNS 5C **94**
St John's Av. NW10............ 5B **42**
St John's Av. SW15............ 3F **99**
St Johns Chu. Rd. E9........ 2E **51**
St John's Cl. SW6 .... 3C **86**
St John's Ct. E1 .... 2D **79**
................................(off Scandrett St.)
St John's Ct. N4................ 4D **35**
St John's Ct. SE13............ 5E **95**
St John's Ct. W6 .... 5D **71**
................................(off Glenthorne Rd.)
St Johns Ct. SW10............ 3E **87**
................................(off Ashburnham Rd.)
St John's Cres. SW9 .... 1C **104**
St Johns Dr. SW18............ 1D **115**
St John's Est. N1 ... 1C **10** (1F **63**)
St John's Est. SE1 ...3F **27** (3B **78**)
................................(off Fair St.)
St John's Gdns. W11 .... 1A **72**
St John's Gate 4D **9** (3D **63**)
................................(off St John's La.)
St John's Gro. N19............ 4E **33**
St John's Gro. SW13........ 5B **84**
St John's Hill SW11 .... 3F **101**
St John's Hill Gro. SW11 .. 2F **101**
ST JOHN'S HOSPICE London 1F **59**
................................(within Hospital of St John &
St Elizabeth)
St John's Ho. E14................ 5E **81**
................................(off Pier St.)
St Johns Ho. SE17................ 2F **91**
St John's La. EC1.......4D **9** (3D **63**)
St John's Lodge NW3 .... 4A **46**
................................(off King Henry's Rd.)
St John's Mans. EC1..1D **9** (2D **63**)
................................(off St John St.)
St John's M. W11................ 5C **58**
St John Smith Square
................................5D **23** (4A **76**)
................................(off Smith Sq.)
St John's Pk. SE3 .... 3B **96**
St John's Pk. Mans. N19......5E **33**
St John's Path EC1 ...4D **9** (3D **63**)

St Johns Pathway SE23 ......1E **121**
St John's Pl. EC1......4D 9 (3D **63**)
St John's Rd. E16 .... 5C **68**
St John's Rd. N15................ 1A **36**
St John's Rd. NW11............ 1B **30**
St John's Rd. SW11 .... 2A **102**
St John's Sq. EC1 ......4D 9 (3D **63**)
St John's Station (Rail) 5C **94**
St John's Ter. E7 .... 3D **55**
St John's Ter. SW15........ 3A **112**
................................(off Kingston La.)
St John's Ter. W10.............. 3F **57**
St John's Va. SE8 .... 5C **94**
St John's Vs. N19................ 4F **33**
St John's Vs. W8................ 4D **73**
................................(off St Mary's Pl.)
ST JOHN'S WOOD 1F **59**
St John's Wood Ct. NW8...... 2F **59**
................................(off St John's Wood Rd.)
St John's Wood High St.
NW8................................ 1F **59**
St John's Wood Pk. NW8...... 5F **45**
St John's Wood Rd. NW8...... 3F **59**
St John's Wood Station
(Underground) 1F **59**
St John's Wood Ter. NW8...... 1F **59**
St Josephs Almshouses W6.. 5F **71**
................................(off Brook Grn.)
St Joseph's Cl. W10............ 4A **58**
St Joseph's College Sports Cen.
................................5D **119**
St Joseph's Cotts. SW3 ...... 5B **74**
................................(off Cadagon St.)
St Josephs Ct. SE7 .... 2D **97**
St Joseph's Flats
NW1................................ 1B 6 (2F **61**)
................................(off Drummond Cres.)
ST JOSEPH'S HOSPICE London
................................5D **51**
St Joseph's Ho. W6............ 5F **71**
................................(off Brook Grn.)
St Joseph's St. SW8 .... 4D **89**
St Joseph's Va. SE3............ 1F **109**
St Jude's Rd. E2 .... 1D **65**
St Jude St. N16.................. 2A **50**
St Julian's Cl. SW16 .... 4C **118**
St Julian's Farm Rd. SE27 ..4C **118**
St Julian's Rd. NW6............ 5C **44**
St Katharine Docks ..5F **19** (1B **78**)
................................(off St Katharine's Way)
St Katharine's Pier (Boat Tours)
................................1F **27** (2B **78**)
St Katharine's Pct. NW1 .... 1D **61**
St Katharine's Way
E1................1F **27** (2B **78**)
St Katharine's Yacht Haven 2B **78**
................................(off St Katharine's Way)
St Katherine's Row
EC3................3E **19** (1A **78**)
................................(off Fenchurch St.)
St Katherines Wlk. W11......2F **71**
St Kilda's Rd. N16................ 3F **35**
St Kitts Ter. SE19................ 5A **120**
St Laurence Cl. NW6............ 5F **43**
St Lawrence Cotts. E14 ...... 2E **81**
................................(off St Lawrence St.)
St Lawrence Ct. N1.............. 4F **49**
St Lawrence Ho. SE1 ...5E **27** (4A **78**)
................................(off Purbrook St.)
St Lawrence St. E14............ 2E **81**
St Lawrence Ter. W10 ...... 4A **58**
St Lawrence Way SW9 .... 4C **90**

St Leger Ct. NW6...............4F 43
St Leonard M. N1 ....1A 64
................(off Coverdale Rd.)
St Leonard's Ct. N1...1C 10 (2F 63)
................(off New North Rd.)
St Leonard's Rd. E14...........4D 67
................(not continuous)
St Leonard's Rd. NW10........3A 56
St Leonards Sq. NW5............3C 46
St Leonard's St. E3..............2D 67
St Leonard's Studios SW3...1B 88
................(off Smith St.)
St Leonard's Ter. SW3.........1B 88
St Loo Av. SW3 ....2A 88
St Loo Ct. SW3 ....2A 88
................(off St Loo Av.)
St Louis Rd. SE27................4F 119
St Lucia Dr. E15...................5B 54
ST LUKE'S 3A 10 (3E 63)
St Luke's Av. SW4 ....2F 103
St Luke's Cl. EC1 ....3A 10 (3E 63)
St Lukes Cl. E10 ....2D 39
................(off Capworth St.)
St Lukes Ct. W11 ....5B 58
................(off St Luke's Rd.)
St Luke's Est. EC1...2B 10 (2F 63)
ST LUKE'S HEALTHCARE FOR THE
CLERGY 4F 5 (3E 61)
(within Fitzroy Square BMI Hosp.)
St Luke's M. W11 ....5B 58
St Lukes M. E14...................3C 80
................(off Strafford St.)
St Luke's Rd. W11 ....4B 58
St Luke's Sq. E16.................5B 68
St Luke's SW3 ....1A 88
St Luke's Yd. W9 ....1B 58
................(not continuous)
St Margaret's Ct. EC2...2B 18 (5F 63)
St Margarets Ct.
SE1 ....2A 26 (2E 77)
St Margarets Ct. SW15.........2D 99
St Margaret's Cres. SW15....3B 99
St Margaret's Gro. E11........5B 40
St Margaret's Ho.
NW1 ....1B 6 (1F 61)
................(off Polygon Rd.)
St Margaret's La. W8.............4D 73
St Margaret's Pas. SE13...1A 110
................(not continuous)
St Margaret's Rd. E12...........4E 41
St Margaret's Rd. NW10.....2E 57
St Margarets Rd. SE4...........2B 108
................(not continuous)
St Margaret St. SW1 4D 23 (3A 76)
St Mark's Cl. SE10...............3E 95
St Mark's Cl. W11 ....5A 58
St Marks Cl. SW6.................4C 86
St Marks Ct. NW8.................1E 59
................(off Abercorn Pl.)
St Mark's Cres. NW1 ....5C 46
St Mark's Ga. E9 ....4B 52
St Mark's Gro. SW10 ....3D 87
St Marks Ho. SE17...............2F 91
................(off Lytham St.)
St Marks Ind. Est. E16.........2F 83
St Mark's Pl. SW19...............5B 114
St Mark's Pl. W11 ....5A 58
St Mark's Ri. E8 ....2B 50
St Mark's Rd. W10................5F 57
St Mark's Rd. W11 ....5A 58
St Mark's Sq. NW1 ....5C 46
St Mark St. E1......................5B 64
St Mark's Vs. N4...................4B 34
................(off Moray Rd.)

St Martin-in-the-Fields Chu. Path
WC2...................5D 15 (1A 76)
................(off St Martin's Pl.)
St Martin's Almshouses
NW1 ....5E 47
St Martin's Av. E6 ....1F 69
St Martin's Cl. NW1 ....5E 47
St Martin's Ct. EC4....2F 17 (5E 63)
................(off Newgate St.)
St Martin's Ct. WC2...4D 15 (1A 76)
St Martins Ct. N1..................5A 50
................(off De Beauvoir Est.)
St Martin's Ctyd.
WC2...................4D 15 (1A 76)
................(off Up. St Martin's La.)
St Martins Est. SW2.............1C 118
St Martin's Ho. NW1 ...1B 6 (2F 61)
................(off Polygon Rd.)
St Martin's La. WC2...4D 15 (1A 76)
St Martin's Le-Grand
EC1.....................2F 17 (5E 63)
St Martin's Pl. WC2...5D 15 (1A 76)
St Martin's Rd. SW9 ....5B 90
St Martin's St. WC2...5C 14 (1F 75)
................(not continuous)
St Martin's Theatre ...1D 15 (1A 76)
................(off West St.)
St Martins Way SW17 ....3E 115
St Mary Abbot's Ct. W14.....4B 72
St Mary Abbot's Pl. W8 ....4B 72
................(off Warwick Gdns.)
St Mary Abbot's Ter. W14....4B 72
St Mary at Hill EC3...5D 19 (1A 78)
St Mary Axe EC3......3D 19 (5A 64)
St Marychurch St. SE16 ....3E 79
St Mary Graces Ct. E1 ....1B 78
St Marylebone Cl. NW10......5A 42
St Mary le-Park Ct. SW11....3A 88
................(off Parkgate Rd.)
St Mary Magdalene Gdns.
N7 ....3C 48
St Mary Newington Cl. SE17...1A 92
................(off Surrey Sq.)
St Mary's Av. E11 ....2D 41
St Mary's Community Gdn. ...1B 64
................(off Appleby St.)
St Mary's Ct. E3 ....5F 53
................(off Bow Rd.)
St Mary's Ct. SE7 ....5F 97
St Mary's Ct. W6...................4B 70
St Mary's Est. SE16 ....3E 79
................(off Elephant La.)
St Mary's Flats NW1 ...1B 6 (2F 61)
................(off Drummond Cres.)
St Mary's Gdns. SE11..........5C 76
St Mary's Ga. W8 ....4D 73
St Mary's Gro. N1 ....3D 49
St Mary's Gro. SW13............1D 99
ST MARY'S HOSPITAL London
....5F 59
St Mary's Ho. N1 ....5D 49
................(off St Mary's Path)
St Mary's Mans. W2 ....4F 59
St Mary's M. NW6 ....4D 45
St Marys Open Space 5A 42
St Mary's Path N1................5D 49
St Mary's Pl. W8 ....4D 73
St Mary's Rd. E10 ....5E 39
St Mary's Rd. E13 ....1D 69
St Mary's Rd. NW10.............5A 42
St Mary's Rd. NW11.............2A 30
St Mary's Rd. SE15..............4E 93
St Mary's Rd. SW19.............5A 114
St Mary's Sq. W2 ....4F 59

St Mary's Ter. W2 ....4F 59
St Mary's Twr. EC1 ...4A 10 (3E 63)
................(off Fortune St.)
St Mary's Wlk. SE11 ....5C 76
St Matthews Cl. E10.............2D 39
St Matthews Ct. SE1............4E 77
................(off Meadow Row)
St Matthews Ho. SE17.........2F 91
................(off Phelp St.)
St Matthew's Lodge NW1 ....1E 61
................(off Oakley Sq.)
St Matthew's Rd. SW2.........2B 104
St Matthew's Row E2 ....2C 64
St Matthew St. SW1 ...5B 22 (4F 75)
St Maur Rd. SW6..................4B 86
St Michael's All. EC3 3C 18 (5F 63)
St Michaels Cl. E16..............4E 69
St Michael's Ct. SE1 4A 26 (3E 77)
................(off Trinity St.)
St Michaels Ct. E14..............4E 67
................(off St Leonard's Rd.)
St Michael's Flats
NW1 ....1B 6 (1F 61)
................(off Aldenham St.)
St Michael's Gdns. W10 ......4A 58
St Michael's M. SW1.............5C 74
St Michael's Rd. NW2...........1E 43
St Michael's Rd. SW9...........5B 90
St Michael's St. W2...............5F 59
St Michaels Ter. N6...............3C 32
................(off South Gro.)
St Mildred's Ct. EC2. 3B 18 (5F 63)
St Mildreds Rd. SE12...........5B 110
St Mildreds Rd. SE6..............5A 110
St Nicholas' Flats
NW1 ....1B 6 (1F 61)
................(off Werrington St.)
St Nicholas Glebe SW17......5C 116
St Nicholas Ho. SE8.............2C 94
................(off Deptford Grn.)
St Nicholas St. SE8 ....4B 94
St Norbert Grn. SE4.............2A 108
St Norbert Rd. SE4...............3F 107
St Olaf Ho. SE1.........1C 26 (2F 77)
................(off Tooley St.)
St Olaf's Rd. SW6.................3A 86
St Olaf Stairs SE1 ....1C 26 (2F 77)
................(off Tooley St.)
St Olave's Ct. EC2.....3B 18 (5F 63)
St Olave's Est. SE1...3E 27 (3A 78)
St Olave's Gdns. SE11 ....5C 76
St Olave's Mans. SE11.........5C 76
................(off Walnut Tree Wlk.)
St Olave's Mans. SE11.........5C 76
................(off Walnut Tree Wlk.)
St Olav's Sq. SE16................3E 79
St Oswald's Pl. SE11 ....1B 90
St Oswalds Studios SW6 .....2C 86
................(off Sedlescombe Rd.)
St Oswulf St. SW1................5F 75
St Owen Ho. SE1 ......5E 27 (4A 78)
................(off St Saviour's Est.)
ST PANCRAS 2D 7 (2A 62)
St Pancras Commercial Cen.
NW1 ....5E 47
................(off Pratt St.)
St Pancras Gdns. NW1..........1F 61
................(off Pancras Rd.)
St Pancras Gdns. 1F 61
ST PANCRAS HOSPITAL......5F 47
St Pancras International Station
(Rail) 1D 7 (1A 62)
St Pancras Way NW1 ....4E 47
St Paul's All. EC4......3E 17 (5D 63)
................(off St Paul's Chyd.)

St Paul's Av. NW2 .... 3E 43
St Paul's Av. SE16 .... 2F 79
St Paul's Bldgs. EC1 ...... 3E 9 (3D 63)
 (off Dallington St.)
St Paul's Cathedral
 .... 3E 17 (5E 63)
St Paul's Churchyard
EC4 .... 3E 17 (5D 63)
St Pauls Cl. SE7 .... 1F 97
St Pauls Ct. SW4 .... 3F 103
St Pauls Ctyd. SE8 .... 3C 94
 (off Crossfield St.)
St Paul's Cres. NW1 .... 4F 47
 (not continuous)
St Paul's Dr. E15 .... 2F 53
St Pauls Ho. SE8 .... 3C 94
 (off Market Yd.)
St Paul's M. NW1 .... 4F 47
St Paul's Pl. N1 .... 3F 49
St Paul's Rd. N1 .... 3D 49
St Paul's Shrubbery N1 .... 3F 49
St Paul's Station (Underground)
 .... 2F 17 (5E 63)
St Paul's Studios W14 .... 1A 86
 (off Talgarth Rd.)
St Pauls Ter. SE17 .... 2D 91
St Paul St. N1 .... 5E 49
 (not continuous)
St Pauls Vw. Apts.
EC1 .... 2B 8 (2C 62)
 (off Amwell St.)
St Paul's Way E3 .... 4B 66
St Peter's All. EC3 .... 3C 18 (5F 63)
 (off Gracechurch St.)
St Peter's Av. E2 .... 1C 64
St Petersburgh M. W2 .... 1D 73
St Petersburgh Pl. W2 .... 1D 73
St Peter's Cen. E1 .... 2D 79
 (off Reardon St.)
St Peters Chu. Ct. N1 .... 5D 49
 (off St Peter's St.)
St Peter's Cl. E2 .... 1C 64
St Peter's Cl. SW17 .... 2A 116
St Peter's Ct. WC1 ...... 2E 7 (2A 62)
 (off Seaford St.)
St Peters Ct. E1 .... 3E 65
 (off Cephas St.)
St Peters Ct. SE12 .... 3B 110
St Peter's Gdns. SE27 .... 3C 118
St Peter's Gro. W6 .... 5C 70
St Peter's Ho. WC1 ..... 2E 7 (2A 62)
 (off Regent Sq.)
St Peters Ho. SE17 .... 2F 91
St Peters M. N4 .... 1D 35
St Peters M. N8 .... 1C 34
St Peter's Pl. W9 .... 3D 59
St Peter's Rd. W6 .... 1C 84
St Peter's Sq. E2 .... 1C 64
St Peter's Sq. W6 .... 5B 70
St Peter's St. N1 .... 5D 49
St Peter's St. M. N1 .... 1D 63
 (off St Peters St.)
St Peter's Ter. SW6 .... 3B 86
St Peter's Vs. W6 .... 5C 70
St Peter's Way N1 .... 4A 50
St Peter's Wharf W4 .... 1C 84
St Philip Ho. WC1 ...... 2B 8 (2C 62)
 (off Lloyd Baker St.)
St Philip Sq. SW8 .... 5D 89
St Philip's Rd. E8 .... 3C 50
St Philip St. SW8 .... 5D 89
St Philip's Way N1 .... 5E 49
St Quentin Ho. SW18 .... 4F 101
St Quintin Av. W10 .... 4E 57
St Quintin Gdns. W10 .... 4E 57

St Quintin Ho. W10 .... 4F 57
 (off Princess Louise Wlk.)
St Quintin Rd. E13 .... 2D 69
St Quintin Vw. W10 .... 4E 57
St Regis Hgts. NW3 .... 5E 31
St Richard's Ho. NW1 1B 6 (2F 61)
 (off Eversholt St.)
St Rule St. SW8 .... 5E 89
St Saviour's Est.
SE1 .... 4F 27 (3B 78)
St Saviour's Rd. SW2 .... 3B 104
St Saviour's Wharf SE1: Lon
 Mill St. 3F 27 (3B 78)
 (off Mill St.)
St Saviour's Wharf SE1: Lon Shad
 Thames 3F 27 (3B 78)
 (off Shad Thames)
Saints Ct. SE27 .... 4D 119
Saints Dr. E7 .... 2F 55
St Silas Pl. NW5 .... 3C 46
St Simon's Av. SW15 .... 3E 99
St Stephen's Av. E17 .... 1E 39
St Stephen's Av. W12 .... 2D 71
 (not continuous)
St Stephen's Cl. E17 .... 1D 39
St Stephen's Cl. NW8 .... 5A 46
St Stephens Cl. NW5 .... 2B 46
 (off Malden Rd.)
St Stephens Ct. N8 .... 1B 34
St Stephen's Cres. W2 .... 5C 58
St Stephen's Gdns. SW15 ... 3B 100
St Stephen's Gdns. W2 .... 5C 58
 (not continuous)
St Stephens Gro. SE13 .... 1E 109
St Stephens Ho. SE17 .... 2F 91
 (off Lytham St.)
St Stephen's M. W2 .... 4C 58
St Stephens Pde. E7 .... 4E 55
St Stephen's Rd. E17 .... 1D 39
St Stephen's Rd. E3 .... 5A 52
St Stephen's Rd. E6 .... 4E 55
St Stephen's Row
EC4 .... 3B 18 (5F 63)
 (off Walbrook)
St Stephen's Ter. SW8 .... 3B 90
St Stephen's Wlk. SW7 .... 5E 73
 (off Southwell Gdns.)
St Swithins La. EC4 .. 4B 18 (1F 77)
St Swithun's Rd. SE13 .... 4F 109
St Theresa's Cl. E9 .... 1C 52
St Thomas Ct. E10 .... 2D 39
 (off Lake Rd.)
St Thomas Ct. NW1 .... 4E 47
 (off Wrotham Rd.)
ST THOMAS' HOSPITAL
 .... 4F 23 (4B 76)
St Thomas Ho. E1 .... 5E 65
 (off W. Arbour St.)
St Thomas M. SW18 .... 3C 100
St Thomas Rd. E16 .... 5C 68
St Thomas's Gdns. NW5 .... 3C 46
St Thomas's Pl. E9 .... 4E 51
St Thomas's Rd. N4 .... 4C 34
St Thomas's Rd. NW10 .... 5A 42
St Thomas's Sq. E9 .... 4E 51
St Thomas St. SE1 .. 2B 26 (2F 77)
St Thomas's Way SW6 .... 3B 86
St Vincent Cl. SE27 .... 5D 119
St Vincent De Paul Ho. E1 .... 4E 65
 (off Jubilee St.)
St Vincent Ho. SE1 .. 5F 27 (4B 78)
 (off St Saviour's Est.)
St Vincent St. W1 .. 1C 12 (4C 60)
St Williams Ct. N1 .... 4A 48
Salamanca Pl. SE1 .... 5B 76

Salamanca Sq. SE1 .... 5B 76
 (off Salamanca Pl.)
Salamanca St. SE1 .... 5B 76
Salamanca St. SE11 .... 5B 76
Salcombe Ct. E14 .... 4E 67
 (off St Ives Pl.)
Salcombe Rd. E17 .... 2B 38
Salcombe Rd. N16 .... 2A 50
Salcott Rd. SW11 .... 3A 102
Salehurst Rd. SE4 .... 4B 108
Salem Rd. W2 .... 1D 73
Sale Pl. W2 .... 4A 60
Sale St. E2 .... 3C 64
Salford Ho. E14 .... 5E 81
 (off Seyssel St.)
Salford Rd. SW2 .... 1F 117
Salisbury Cl. SE17 .... 5F 77
Salisbury Ct. E9 .... 2A 52
 (off Mabley St.)
Salisbury Ct. EC4 ..... 3D 17 (5D 63)
Salisbury Ct. SE16 .... 4C 78
 (off Stork's Rd.)
Salisbury Ho. E14 .... 5D 67
 (off Hobday St.)
Salisbury Ho. EC2 .... 1C 18 (4F 63)
 (off London Wall)
Salisbury Ho. N1 .... 5D 49
 (off St Mary's Path)
Salisbury Ho. SW1 .... 1F 89
 (off Drummond Ga.)
Salisbury Ho. SW9 .... 3C 90
 (off Cranmer Rd.)
Salisbury Mans. N15 .... 1D 35
Salisbury M. SW6 .... 3B 86
Salisbury Pas. SW6 .... 3B 86
 (off Dawes Rd.)
Salisbury Pavement SW6 ...... 3B 86
 (off Dawes Rd.)
Salisbury Pl. SW9 .... 3D 91
Salisbury Pl. W1 .... 5A 4 (4B 60)
Salisbury Rd. E10 .... 4E 39
Salisbury Rd. E12 .... 2F 55
Salisbury Rd. E17 .... 1E 39
Salisbury Rd. E7 .... 3C 54
Salisbury Sq. EC4 ...... 3C 16 (5C 62)
Salisbury St. NW8 .... 3A 60
Salisbury Ter. SE15 .... 1E 107
Salisbury Wlk. N19 .... 4E 33
Salmen Rd. E13 .... 1B 68
Salmon La. E14 .... 5A 66
Salmon M. NW6 .... 2C 44
Salmon St. E14 .... 5B 66
Salomons Rd. E13 .... 4E 69
Salop Rd. E17 .... 1F 37
Salsabil Apts. E3 .... 3B 66
Saltcoats Rd. W4 .... 3A 70
Saltdene N4 .... 3B 34
Salterford Rd. SW17 .... 5C 116
Salter Rd. SE16 .... 2F 79
Salters Ct. EC4 .... 3A 18 (5E 63)
 (off Bow La.)
Salter's Hall Ct. EC4 4B 18 (1F 77)
 (off Cannon St.)
Salter's Hill SE19 .... 5F 119
Salters Rd. W10 .... 3F 57
Salters Row N1 .... 3F 49
 (off Tilney Gdns.)
Salter St. E14 .... 1B 80
 (not continuous)
Salter St. NW10 .... 2C 56
Salterton Rd. N7 .... 5B 34
Saltoun Rd. SW2 .... 2C 104
Saltram Cres. W9 .... 2B 58

Saltwell St. E14...................1C 80
Saltwood Gro. SE17..............1F 91
Saltwood Ho. SE15..............2E 93
..................................(off Lovelinch Cl.)
Salusbury Rd. NW6...............5A 44
Salutation Rd. SE10..............5A 82
Salvador SW17.....................5B 116
Salvin Rd. SW15...................1F 99
Salway Pl. E15......................3F 53
Salway Rd. E15.....................3F 53
Samantha Cl. E17..................2B 38
Samaras Mans. E20................2E 53
..................................(off Liberty Bri. Rd.)
Sam Bartram Cl. SE7..............1E 97
Sambourne Family Home, The
....4C 72
..................................(off Stafford Ter.)
Sambrook Ho. E1...................4E 65
..................................(off Jubilee St.)
Sambrook Ho. SE11................5C 76
..................................(off Hotspur St.)
Sambruck M. SE6..................1D 123
Samels Ct. W6......................1C 84
Samford Ho. N1.....................5C 48
..................................(off Barnsbury Est.)
Samford St. NW8...................3F 59
Samira Cl. E17......................1C 38
Sam King Wlk. SE5.................3F 91
..................................(off Edmund St.)
Sam Manners Ho. SE10..........1A 96
..................................(off Tuskar St.)
Sam March Ho. E14................5F 67
..................................(off Blair St.)
Samphire Hgts. E20................2E 53
..................................(off Napa Cl.)
Sampson Ho. SE1......1D 25 (2D 77)
Sampson St. E1.....................2C 78
Samson St. E13.....................1E 69
Samuda Est. E14....................4E 81
Samuel Cl. E8.......................5B 50
Samuel Cl. SE14....................2F 93
Samuel Cl. N1..............2D 11 (2A 64)
..................................(off Pitfield St.)
Samuel Johnson Cl. SW16......4B 118
Samuel Jones Ct. SE15...........3A 92
Samuel Lewis Bldgs. N1..........3C 48
Samuel Lewis Trust Dwellings
E8.....................................2C 50
..................................(off Amhurst Rd.)
Samuel Lewis Trust Dwellings
N16....................................1A 36
Samuel Lewis Trust Dwellings
SW3...................................5A 74
..................................(off Vanston Pl.)
Samuel Lewis Trust Dwellings
SW6...................................3C 86
..................................(off Vanston Pl.)
Samuel Lewis Trust Dwellings
W14...................................5B 72
..................................(off Lisgar Ter.)
Samuel Lewis Trust Est.
SE5....................................4E 91
..................................(off Warner Rd.)
Samuel Richardson Ho.
W14...................................5B 72
..................................(off North End Cres.)
Samuel's Cl. W6....................5E 71
Samuel St. E8.......................5B 50
Samuel St. SE15....................3B 92
Samuel Wallis Lodge SE10...5A 82
..................................(off Banning St.)
Samuel Wallis Lodge SE3..1B 110
..................................(off Banning St.)
Sanchia Cl. E2......................2C 64
..................................(off Wellington Row)
Sancroft Cl. NW2..................5D 29

Sancroft Ho. SE11.................1B 90
..................................(off Sancroft St.)
Sancroft St. SE11..................1B 90
Sanctuary, The
SW1........................5C 22 (4F 75)
..................................(off Broad Sanctuary)
Sanctuary M. E8....................3B 50
Sanctuary St. SE1......3A 26 (3E 77)
Sandale Cl. N16.....................5F 35
Sandall Ho. E3......................1A 66
Sandall Rd. NW5....................3E 47
Sandal St. E15......................5A 54
Sandalwood Cl. E1..................3A 66
Sandalwood Mans. W8............4D 73
..................................(off Stone Hall Gdns.)
Sandbourne NW8...................5D 45
..................................(off Abbey Rd.)
Sandbourne W11...................5C 58
..................................(off Dartmouth Cl.)
Sandbourne Rd. SE4..............5A 94
Sandbrook Rd. N16.................5A 36
Sandby Ct. NW10...................2D 57
..................................(off Plough Cl.)
Sandby Ho. NW6....................5C 44
..................................(off Abbey Rd.)
Sandell St. SE1.........3B 24 (3C 76)
Sanderling Ct. SE8.................2B 94
..................................(off Abinger Gro.)
Sanderling Lodge E1..............1B 78
..................................(off Star Pl.)
Sanders Ho. WC1..........1B 8 (2B 62)
..................................(off Gt. Percy St.)
Sanderson Bldg. NW2.............2E 29
Sanderson Cl. NW5.................1D 47
Sanderson Ho. E16.................4C 68
..................................(off Hammersley Rd.)
Sanderson Ho. SE8.................1B 94
..................................(off Grove St.)
Sandersons La. W4.................1A 84
..................................(off Chiswick High Rd.)
Sanderstead Av. NW2.............4A 30
Sanderstead Cl. SW12.............5E 103
Sanderstead Rd. E10..............3A 38
Sanders Way N19...................4F 33
Sandfield WC1............2E 7 (2A 62)
..................................(off Cromer St.)
Sandford Ct. N16...................3A 36
Sandford St. SW6..................3D 87
Sandgate Ho. E5....................2D 51
Sandgate La. SW18................1A 116
Sandgate St. SE15.................2D 93
Sandgate Trad. Est. SE15.......2D 93
..................................(off Sandgate St.)
Sandham Ct. SW4..................4A 90
Sandhills, The SW10..............2E 87
..................................(off Limerston St.)
Sandhurst Ho. E1...................4E 65
..................................(off Wolsy St.)
Sandhurst Mkt. SE6................1E 123
..................................(off Sandhurst Rd.)
Sandhurst Rd. SE6.................1F 123
Sandilands Rd. SW6...............4D 87
Sandison St. SE15.................1C 106
Sandland St. WC1......1A 16 (4B 62)
Sandlings Cl. SE15.................5D 93
Sandmere Rd. SW4................2A 104
Sandover Ho. SE16................4C 78
..................................(off Spa Rd.)
Sandown Ct. SE26..................3D 121
Sandpiper Cl. SE16................3B 80
Sandpiper Ct. E1....................1C 78
..................................(off Thomas More St.)
Sandpiper Ct. E14..................4E 81
..................................(off New Union Cl.)

Sandpiper Ct. SE8..................2C 94
..................................(off Edward Pl.)
Sandpit Rd. BR1: Broml.........5A 124
Sandridge St. N19..................4E 33
Sandringham Bldgs. SE17......5F 77
..................................(off Balfour St.)
Sandringham Cl. SW19..........1F 113
Sandringham Cl. SE16...........2F 79
..................................(off King & Queen Wharf)
Sandringham Ct. W13A 14 (5E 61)
..................................(off Dufour's Pl.)
Sandringham Ct. W9...............2E 59
..................................(off Maida Vale)
Sandringham Flats
WC2...........................4C 14 (1F 75)
..................................(off Charing Cross Rd.)
Sandringham Gdns. N8........1A 34
Sandringham Ho.
SE1.............................2E 27 (2A 78)
..................................(off Potters Flds.)
Sandringham Ho. W14...........5A 72
..................................(off Windsor Way)
Sandringham Rd.
BR1: Broml...................5C 124
Sandringham Rd. E10............1F 39
Sandringham Rd. E7...............2E 55
Sandringham Rd. E8...............2B 50
Sandringham Rd. NW11.........2A 30
Sandringham Rd. NW2............3D 43
Sandrock Rd. SE13................1C 108
SANDS END...........................4E 87
Sand's End La. SW6..............4D 87
Sandstone La. E16.................1D 83
Sandstone Pl. N19..................4D 33
Sandstone Rd. SE12..............2D 125
Sandtoft Rd. SE7...................2D 97
Sandwell Cres. NW6..............3C 44
Sandwich Ho. SE16................3E 79
..................................(off Swan Rd.)
Sandwich Ho. WC1.....2D 7 (2A 62)
..................................(off Sandwich St.)
Sandwich St. WC1......2D 7 (2A 62)
Sandy Rd. NW3......................4D 31
Sandys Row E1.........1E 19 (4A 64)
Sanford La. N16.....................5B 36
Sanford St. SE14...................2A 94
Sanford Ter. N16...................5B 36
Sanford Wlk. N16...................4B 36
Sanford Wlk. SE14.................2A 94
Sangley Ho. SE6....................5D 109
Sangora Rd. SW11.................2F 101
Sankey Ho. E2.......................1E 65
..................................(off St James's Av.)
Sansom Rd. E11....................4B 40
Sansom St. SE5.....................4F 91
Sans Wlk. EC1.............3C 8 (3C 62)
Santa Maria Ct. E1.................4A 66
..................................(off Ocean Est.)
Sant Ho. SE17......................5E 77
..................................(off Browning St.)
Santiago Ct. E1.....................4A 66
..................................(off Ocean Est.)
Santley Ho. SE1..........4C 24 (3C 76)
Santley St. SW4....................2B 104
Santos Rd. SW18...................3C 100
Sapcote Trad. Cen.
NW10.................................3B 42
Saperton Wlk. SE11...............5B 76
..................................(off Juxon St.)
Saphire Ct. E15.....................5E 53
Sapperton Ct. EC1......3F 9 (3E 63)
..................................(off Gee St.)
Sapperton Ho. W2..................4C 58
..................................(off Westbourne Pk. Rd.)

Sapphire Ct. E1 .... 1C 78
.... (off Cable St.)
Sapphire Rd. SE8 .... 5A 80
Saracens Head Yd.
EC3 .... 3F 19 (5B 64)
.... (off Jewry St.)
Saracen St. E14 .... 5C 66
Sarah Ho. E1 .... 5D 65
.... (off Commercial Rd.)
Sarah Swift Ho.
SE1 .... 3C 26 (3F 77)
.... (off Kipling St.)
Sara La. Ct. N1 .... 1A 64
.... (off Stanway St.)
Saratoga Rd. E5 .... 1E 51
Saravia Ct. SE13 .... 4A 110
Sardinia St. WC2 .... 2F 15 (5B 62)
Sarjant Path SW19 .... 2F 113
.... (off Blincoe Cl.)
Sark Wlk. E16 .... 5D 69
Sarnesfield Ho. SE15 .... 2D 93
.... (off Pencraig Way)
Sarratt Ho. W10 .... 4E 57
.... (off Sutton Way)
Sarre Rd. NW2 .... 2B 44
Sarsfeld Rd. SW12 .... 2B 116
Sartor Rd. SE15 .... 2F 107
Sarum Ho. W11 .... 1B 72
.... (off Portobello Rd.)
Sarum Ter. E3 .... 3B 66
Saskia M. SE15 .... 5D 93
Satanita Cl. E16 .... 5F 69
Satchwell Rd. E2 .... 2C 64
Satchwell St. E2 .... 2C 64
Satin Ho. E1 .... 5C 64
.... (off Piazza Wlk.)
Sattar M. N16 .... 5F 35
Saturn Ho. E15 .... 5F 53
.... (off High St.)
Saturn Ho. E3 .... 5C 52
.... (off Garrison Rd.)
Sauls Grn. E11 .... 5A 40
Saundby La. SE3 .... 2D 111
Saunders Apts. E3 .... 2C 66
.... (off Marchant St.)
Saunders Cl. E14 .... 1B 80
.... (off Limehouse C'way.)
Saunders Ho. SE16 .... 3F 79
.... (off Quebec Way)
Saunders Ness Rd. E14 .... 1E 95
Saunders St. SE11 .... 5C 76
Savage Gdns. EC3.... 4E 19 (1A 78)
.... (not continuous)
Savannah Cl. SE15 .... 3B 92
Savernake Ho. N4 .... 2E 35
Savernake Rd. NW3 .... 1B 46
Savile Row W1 .... 4F 13 (1E 75)
Savill Ho. SW4 .... 4F 103
Savona Ho. SW8 .... 3E 89
.... (off Savona St.)
Savona St. SW8 .... 3E 89
Savoy Bldgs. WC2.... 5F 15 (1B 76)
.... (off Strand)
SAVOY CIRCUS 1B 70
Savoy Cl. E15 .... 5A 54
Savoy Cl. NW3 .... 5E 31
Savoy Ct. SW5 .... 5C 72
.... (off Cromwell Rd.)
Savoy Ct. WC2.... 5E 15 (1B 76)
Savoy Hill WC2.... 5F 15 (1B 76)
Savoy M. SW9 .... 1A 104
Savoy Pl. W12 .... 2F 71
Savoy Pl. WC2.... 5E 15 (1A 76)
Savoy Row WC2.... 4F 15 (1B 76)
.... (off Savoy St.)

Savoy Steps WC2.... 5F 15 (1B 76)
.... (off Savoy St.)
Savoy St. WC2.... 4F 15 (1B 76)
Savoy Theatre 5E 15 (1A 76)
.... (off Strand)
Savoy Way WC2.... 5F 15 (1B 76)
.... (off Savoy Hill)
Sawkins Cl. SW19 .... 2A 114
Sawley Rd. W12 .... 2C 70
Saw Mill Way N16 .... 1C 36
Sawmill Pl. SE13 .... 5A 52
Sawyer Cl. NW10 .... 4A 42
Sawyers Apts. SW11 .... 2A 102
.... (off Danvers Avenue)
Sawyer St. SE1 .... 3F 25 (3E 77)
Saxby Rd. SW2 .... 5A 104
Saxonbury Ct. N7 .... 2A 48
Saxon Chase N8 .... 1B 34
Saxon Cl. E17 .... 2C 38
Saxon Ct. N1 .... 5A 48
Saxonfield Cl. SW2 .... 5B 104
Saxon Hall W2 .... 1D 73
.... (off Palace Ct.)
Saxon Ho. E1 .... 1F 19 (4B 64)
.... (off Thrawl St.)
Saxon Lea Ct. E3 .... 1B 66
.... (off Saxon Rd.)
Saxon Rd. E3 .... 1B 66
Saxon Ter. SE6 .... 2B 122
Saxton Cl. SE13 .... 1F 109
Sayer Ho. SE17 .... 5E 77
Sayes Ct. SE8 .... 2B 94
Sayes Ct. St. SE8 .... 2B 94
Scafell NW1 .... 1F 5 (2E 61)
.... (off Stanhope St.)
Scala 1E 7 (2A 62)
.... (off Pentonville Rd.)
Scala St. W1 .... 5A 6 (4E 61)
Scampston M. W10 .... 5F 57
Scandrett St. E1 .... 2D 79
Scarab Cl. E16 .... 1B 82
Scarba Wlk. N1 .... 3F 49
.... (off Essex Rd.)
Scarborough Rd. E11 .... 3F 39
Scarborough Rd. N4 .... 2C 34
Scarborough St. E1 .... 5B 64
Scarlet Cl. E20 .... 2D 53
Scarlet Rd. SE6 .... 3A 124
Scarlette Mnr. Way SW2.... 5C 104
Scarsbrook Rd. SE3 .... 1F 111
Scarsdale Pl. W8 .... 4D 73
Scarsdale Studios W8 .... 4C 72
.... (off Stratford Rd.)
Scarsdale Vs. W8 .... 4C 72
Scarth Rd. SW13 .... 1B 98
Scawen Rd. SE8 .... 1A 94
Scawfell St. E2 .... 1B 64
Sceaux Gdns. SE5 .... 4A 92
Scena Way SE5 .... 3E 91
Sceptre Ct. EC3.... 4F 19 (1B 78)
.... (off Tower Hill)
Sceptre Ho. E1 .... 3E 65
.... (off Malcolm Rd.)
Sceptre Rd. E2 .... 2E 65
Schafer Ho. NW1 .... 2F 5 (2E 61)
Schofield Wlk. SE3 .... 3C 96
Scholars Ho. NW6 .... 5C 44
.... (off Glengall Rd.)
Scholars Pl. N16 .... 5A 36
Scholars Rd. SW12 .... 1E 117
Scholefield Rd. N19 .... 4F 33
Scholey Ho. SW11 .... 1A 102
Schomberg Ho. SW1 .... 5F 75
.... (off Page St.)
Schonfeld Sq. N16 .... 4F 35

School App. E2 .... 1E 11 (2A 64)
.... (off Kingsland Rd.)
Schoolbank Rd. SE10 .... 4B 82
Schoolbell M. E3 .... 1A 66
School Ho. SE1 .... 5A 78
.... (off Page's Wlk.)
Schoolhouse La. E1 .... 1F 79
School La. SE23 .... 2D 121
School M. E1 .... 1D 79
.... (off Hawksmoor M.)
School Nook E5 .... 4F 37
School of Oriental & African
Studies Vernon Sq. Campus
.... 1A 8 (2B 62)
School of Pharmacy, The
.... 3E 7 (3A 62)
.... (off Brunswick Sq.)
School Rd. NW10 .... 3A 56
School Sq. SE10 .... 4B 82
Schooner Cl. E14 .... 4F 81
Schooner Cl. SE16 .... 3F 79
Schooner Rd. E16 .... 3D 83
Schubert Rd. SW15 .... 3B 100
Schwartz Wharf E9 .... 4C 52
Science Mus. 4F 73
Sclater St. E1 .... 3F 11 (3B 64)
Scoble Pl. N16 .... 1B 50
Scoles Cres. SW2 .... 1D 119
Scoop, The 2E 27 (2A 78)
Score Complex Leyton, The
.... 5D 39
Scoresby St. SE1.... 2D 25 (2D 77)
Scorton Ho. N1 .... 1A 64
.... (off Whitmore Est.)
SCOTCH HOUSE 4A 20 (3B 74)
Scoter Ct. SE8 .... 2B 94
.... (off Abinger Gro.)
Scotia Bldg. E1 .... 1F 79
.... (off Jardine Rd.)
Scotia Ct. SE16 .... 3E 79
.... (off Canada Est.)
Scotia Rd. SW2 .... 5C 104
Scotland Pl. SW1 .... 1D 23 (2A 76)
Scotney Ho. E9 .... 3E 51
Scotsdale Rd. SE12 .... 3D 111
Scotson Ho. SE11 .... 5C 76
.... (off Marylee Way)
Scotswood St. EC1 .... 3C 8 (3C 62)
Scott Av. SW15 .... 4A 100
Scott Ellis Gdns. NW8 .... 2F 59
Scott Ho. E13 .... 1C 68
.... (off Queens Rd. W.)
Scott Ho. E14 .... 5C 80
.... (off Admirals Way)
Scott Ho. N7 .... 3B 48
Scott Ho. NW8 .... 3A 60
.... (off Broadley St.)
Scott Ho. SE8 .... 1B 94
.... (off Grove St.)
Scott Lidgett Cres. SE16.... 3C 78
Scott Russell Pl. E14 .... 1D 95
Scotts Ct. W12 .... 3E 71
.... (off Scott's Rd.)
Scott's Rd. E10 .... 3E 39
Scott's Rd. W12 .... 3D 71
Scott's Sufferance Wharf
SE1 .... 4F 27 (3B 78)
.... (off Mill St.)
Scotts Ter. SE9 .... 2F 125
Scott St. E1 .... 3D 65
Scott's Yd. EC4.... 4B 18 (1F 77)
Scoulding Ho. E14 .... 4C 80
.... (off Mellish St.)
Scoulding Rd. E16 .... 5C 68

Scouler St. E14 ....1E 81
Scout App. NW10 ....1A 42
Scout La. SW4 ....1E 103
Scovell Cres. SE1 .... 4F 25 (3E 77)
....(off McCoid Way)
Scovell Rd. SE1 .... 4F 25 (3E 77)
Screenworks N1 ....2E 49
Scrimgeour Pl. N4 ....3E 35
Scriven Ct. E8 ....5B 50
Scriven St. E8 ....5B 50
Scrooby St. SE6 ....4D 109
Scrope Ho. EC1 .... 5B 8 (4C 62)
....(off Bourne Est.)
Scrubs La. NW10 ....2C 56
Scrubs La. W10 ....4D 57
Scrutton Cl. SW12 ....5F 103
Scrutton St. EC2 ....4D 11 (3A 64)
Sculpture Ho. E1 ....4F 65
....(off Duckett St.)
Scutari Rd. SE22 ....3E 107
Scylla Rd. SE15 ....1C 106
......................................(not continuous)
Seaborne Wharf E3 ....4C 66
....(off Invicta Cl.)
Seabright St. E2 ....2D 65
Sea Containers Ho.
SE1 ....5C 16 (1C 76)
.................................(off Upper Ground)
Seacon Twr. E14 ....3B 80
Seafarer Way SE16 ....5A 80
Seaford Ho. SE16 ....3E 79
....(off Swan Rd.)
Seaford St. WC1 .... 2E 7 (2A 62)
Seaforth Cres. N5 ....2E 49
Seaforth Pl. SW1 .... 5A 22 (4E 75)
...............................(off Buckingham La.)
Seager Pl. SE8 ....4C 94
....(off Deptford Rd.)
Seagrave Cl. E1 ....4F 65
Seagrave Lodge SW6 ....2C 86
....(off Seagrave Rd.)
Seagrave Rd. SW6 ....2C 86
Seagry Rd. E11 ....2C 40
Seagull La. E16 ....1C 82
Seahorse Sailing Club 4A 28
Seal Ho. SE1 .... 5C 26 (4F 77)
....(off Weston St.)
Sea Life London 3F 23 (3B 76)
Seal St. E8 ....1B 50
Searle Ho. NW8 ....5A 46
....(off Cecil Gro.)
Searle Ho. SW11 ....4C 88
....(off Macduff Rd.)
Searle Pl. N4 ....3B 34
Searles Cl. SW11 ....3A 88
Searles Rd. SE1 ....5F 77
Searson Ho. SE17 ....5D 77
....(off Canterbury Pl.)
Sears St. SE5 ....3F 91
Seasalter Ho. SW9 ....4C 90
....(off Gosling Way)
Seasons Ho. E20 ....3E 53
....................................(off Mirabelle Gdns.)
Seaton Cl. E13 ....3C 68
Seaton Cl. SE11 ....1C 90
Seaton Cl. SW15 ....1D 113
Seaton Point E5 ....1C 50
Sebastian Ho. N1 ....1D 11 (1A 64)
....(off Hoxton St.)
Sebastian St. EC1 .... 2E 9 (2D 63)
Sebbon St. N1 ....4D 49
Sebert Rd. E7 ....2D 55
Sebright Ho. E2 ....1C 64
....(off Coate St.)
Sebright Pas. E2 ....1C 64

Secker Ho. SW9 ....5D 91
.................................(off Loughborough Est.)
Secker St. SE1 .... 2B 24 (2C 76)
Second Av. E13 ....2C 68
Second Av. SW14 ....1A 98
Second Av. W3 ....3A 58
Second Av. W3 ....2B 70
Sedan Way SE17 ....1A 92
Sedding St. SW1 ....5C 74
Sedding Studios SW1 ....5C 74
....(off Sedding St.)
Seddon Highwalk EC25F 9 (4E 63)
.................................(off Aldersgate St.)
Seddon Ho. EC2 .... 5F 9 (4E 63)
.................................(off Aldersgate St.)
Seddon St. WC1 ....2A 8 (2B 62)
Sedgebrook Rd. SE3 ....5F 97
Sedgeford Rd. W12 ....2B 70
Sedgehill Rd. SE6 ....4C 122
Sedgeway SE6 ....1B 124
Sedgmoor Pl. SE5 ....3A 92
Sedgwick Ho. E3 ....4C 66
....(off Gale St.)
Sedgwick Rd. E10 ....4E 39
Sedgwick St. E9 ....2F 51
Sedleigh Rd. SW18 ....4B 100
Sedlescombe Rd. SW6 ....2C 86
Sedley Ct. SE26 ....2D 121
Sedley Ho. SE11 ....1B 90
....(off Newburn St.)
Sedley Pl. W1 ....3D 13 (5D 61)
Sedona Ho. E20 ....3D 53
....(off Victory Pde.)
Seeley Dr. SE21 ....4A 120
Seelig Av. NW9 ....2C 28
Seely Rd. SW17 ....5C 116
Seething La. EC3 ....4E 19 (1A 78)
Sefton St. SW15 ....1E 99
Segal Cl. SE23 ....5A 108
Sekforde St. EC1 ....4D 9 (3D 63)
Selbie Av. NW10 ....2B 42
Selborne Rd. SE5 ....5F 91
Selbourne Ho. SE1 .... 4B 26 (3F 77)
....(off St. Dover St.)
Selby Ho. E6 ....4F 69
Selby Rd. E11 ....5A 40
Selby Rd. E13 ....4D 69
Selby Sq. W10 ....2A 58
....(off Dowland St.)
Selby St. E1 ....3C 64
Selcroft Ho. SE10 ....1B 96
....(off Glenister Rd.)
Selden Ho. SE15 ....5E 93
....(off Selden Rd.)
Selden Rd. SE15 ....5E 93
Selden Wlk. N7 ....4B 34
Seldon Ho. SW1 ....1E 89
....(off Churchill Gdns.)
Seldon Ho. SW8 ....3E 89
....(off Stewart's Rd.)
Selfridges 3C 12 (5C 60)
....(off Oxford St.)
Selhurst Cl. SW19 ....1F 113
Selig Ct. NW11 ....2A 30
Selina Ho. NW8 ....3F 59
....(off Frampton St.)
Selkirk Ho. N1 ....5B 48
....(off Bingfield St.)
Selkirk Rd. SW17 ....4A 116
Sellincourt Rd. SW17 ....5A 116
Sellons Av. NW10 ....5B 42
Selman Ho. E9 ....3A 52
Selsdon Ho. E11 ....2C 40
Selsdon Rd. E13 ....5E 55
Selsdon Rd. NW2 ....4B 28

Selsdon Rd. SE27 ....3C 118
Selsdon Way E14 ....4D 81
Selsea Pl. N16 ....2A 50
Selsey WC1 .... 2E 7 (2A 62)
....(off Tavistock Pl.)
Selsey St. E14 ....4C 66
Selway Ho. SW8 ....4A 90
....(off Sth. Lambeth Rd.)
Selwood Pl. SW7 ....1F 87
Selwood St. SW2 ....5C 104
Selwood Ter. SW7 ....1F 87
Selworthy Cl. E11 ....1C 40
Selworthy Ho. SW11 ....4F 87
.................................(off Battersea Church Rd.)
Selworthy Rd. SE6 ....3B 122
Selwyn Ct. E17 ....1C 38
....(off Yunus Khan Cl.)
Selwyn Ct. SE3 ....1B 110
Selwyn Rd. E13 ....5D 55
Selwyn Rd. E3 ....1B 66
Selwyn Rd. NW10 ....4A 42
Semley Ga. E9 ....3B 52
....(not continuous)
Semley Ho. SW1 ....5D 75
....(off Semley Pl.)
Semley Pl. SW1 ....5C 74
Senate St. SE15 ....5E 93
Senators Lodge E3 ....1A 66
....(off Roman Rd.)
Sendall Cl. SW11 ....1F 101
.................................(off Winstanley Rd.)
Senior St. W2 ....4D 59
Senlac Rd. SE12 ....1D 125
Senrab St. E1 ....5F 65
Sentamu Cl. SE24 ....1D 119
Sentinel Bldg. E15 ....2F 53
....(off Property Row)
Seraph Ct. EC1 .... 1F 9 (2E 63)
....(off Moreland St.)
Serbin Cl. E10 ....2E 39
Serenaders Rd. SW9 ....5C 90
Serenity Apts. E17 ....1D 39
Serenity Apts. SW11 ....2A 102
....(off Monarch Sq.)
Seren Pk. Gdns. SE3 ....2A 96
Sergeant Ind. Est. SW18...4D 101
Serica Ct. SE10 ....3E 95
Serjeants Inn EC4 ....3C 16 (5C 62)
Serlby Cl. W14 ....4B 72
....(off Somerset Sq.)
Serle St. WC2 ....2A 16 (5B 62)
Sermon La. EC4 ....3F 17 (5E 63)
....(off Carter La.)
Serpentine, The 2A 74
Serpentine Ct. SE16 ....3F 79
....(off Christopher Cl.)
Serpentine Gallery 3F 73
Serpentine Lido, The 2A 74
Serpentine Rd. W2 ....2A 74
Serpentine Sackler Gallery...2F 73
Setchell Rd. SE1 ....5B 78
Setchell Way SE1 ....5B 78
Seth St. SE16 ....3E 79
Settle Point E13 ....1C 68
Settlers Ct. E14 ....1F 81
Settles St. E1 ....4C 64
Settrington Rd. SW6 ....5D 87
Seven Dials WC2 ....3D 15 (5A 62)
Seven Dials Ct. WC2 ...3D 15 (5A 62)
....(off Shorts Gdns.)
Seven Islands Leisure Cen.....4E 79
Sevenoaks Rd. SE4 ....4A 108
Seven Sea Gdns. E3 ....4D 67
Seven Sisters Rd. N15 ....1F 35
Seven Sisters Rd. N4 ....4C 34

Seven Sisters Rd. N7 .... 5B **34**
Seven Stars Cnr. W12.......... 4C **70**
Seven Stars Yd. E1.... 5F **11** (4B **64**)
.... (off Brick La.)
Severin Cl. SE17 .... 1A **92**
.... (off East St.)
Severnake Cl. E14................. 5C **80**
Severn Av. W10.................... 2A **58**
Severn Ho. SW18 .... 2C **100**
.... (off Enterprise Way)
Severn Way NW10 .... 2B **42**
Severus Rd. SW11 .... 2A **102**
Seville Ho. E1 .... 2C **78**
.... (off Wapping High St.)
Seville M. N1 .... 4A **50**
Seville St. SW1.......... 4A **20** (3B **74**)
Sevington Rd. NW4 .... 1D **29**
Sevington St. W9 .... 3D **59**
Sewardstone Rd. E2 .... 1E **65**
Seward St. EC1...... 2E **9** (2D **63**)
Sewdley St. E5....................... 5F **37**
Sewell St. E13 .... 2C **68**
Sextant Av. E14...................... 5F **81**
Sexton Ct. E14 .... 1F **81**
.... (off Newport Av.)
Sextons Ho. SE10................. 2E **95**
.... (off Bardsley La.)
Seymore M. SE14................. 3B **94**
.... (off New Cross Rd.)
Seymour Ct. NW2 .... 4D **29**
Seymour Gdns. SE4 .... 1A **108**
Seymour Ho. E16 .... 2C **82**
.... (off De Quincey M.)
Seymour Ho. NW1 ..... 1C **6** (2F **61**)
.... (off Churchway)
Seymour Ho. WC1 ...... 3D **7** (3A **62**)
.... (off Tavistock Pl.)
Seymour Leisure Cen. 4B **60**
Seymour M. W1....... 2B **12** (5C **60**)
Seymour Pl. W1 .... 5A **4** (4B **60**)
Seymour Rd. E10 .... 3B **38**
Seymour Rd. E6 .... 1F **69**
Seymour Rd. N8...................... 1C **34**
Seymour Rd. SW18 .... 5B **100**
Seymour Rd. SW19 .... 3F **113**
Seymour Rd. W1 .... 3A **12** (5B **60**)
Seymour Rd. W2 .... 5B **60**
Seymour Wlk. SW10 .... 2E **87**
Seyssel St. E14 .... 5E **81**
Shaa Rd. W3............................ 1A **70**
Shabana Rd. W12 .... 2D **71**
Shackleton Cl. SE23 .... 2D **121**
Shackleton Ct. E14 .... 1C **94**
.... (off Maritime Quay)
Shackleton Ct. W12.............. 3D **71**
.... (off Scott's Rd.)
Shackleton Ho. E1 .... 2E **79**
.... (off Prusom St.)
Shacklewell Grn. E8 .... 1B **50**
Shacklewell Ho. E8 .... 1B **50**
Shacklewell La. E8 .... 2B **50**
Shacklewell La. N16.............. 1B **50**
Shacklewell Rd. N16............. 1B **50**
Shacklewell Row E8 .... 1B **50**
Shacklewell St. E2................. 2B **64**
Shad Thames SE1: Lon Anchor
Brewhouse............ 2F **27** (2B **78**)
Shad Thames SE1: Lon Jamaica
Rd................................ 4F **27** (3B **78**)
SHADWELL 1D **79**
Shadwell Gdns. E1................. 1E **79**
Shadwell Pierhead E1 .... 1E **79**
Shadwell Pl. E1 .... 1E **79**
.... (off Sutton St.)
Shadwell Station (Overground &
DLR) 1D **79**
Shaftesbury Av. W1.... 4B **14** (1F **75**)
Shaftesbury Av.
WC1................... 2D **15** (5A **62**)
Shaftesbury Av.
WC2................... 2D **15** (5A **62**)
Shaftesbury Cen. W10......... 3F **57**
.... (off Barlby Rd.)
Shaftesbury Ct. N1 .... 1F **63**
.... (off Shaftesbury St.)
Shaftesbury Ct. SE1 ... 5B **26** (4F **77**)
.... (off Alderney M.)
Shaftesbury Ct. SE5.............. 2F **105**
Shaftesbury Ct. SW16........... 3F **117**
Shaftesbury Gdns. NW10.... 3A **56**
Shaftesbury Lodge E14 .... 5D **67**
.... (off Upper Nth. St.)
Shaftesbury M. SW4 .... 3E **103**
Shaftesbury M. W8 .... 4C **72**
Shaftesbury Pl. EC2....1F **17** (4E **63**)
.... (off London Wall)
Shaftesbury Pl. W14 .... 5B **72**
.... (off Warwick Rd.)
Shaftesbury Point E13.......... 1C **68**
.... (off High St.)
Shaftesbury Rd. E10............. 3C **38**
Shaftesbury Rd. E17 .... 1D **39**
Shaftesbury Rd. E7................ 4E **55**
Shaftesbury Rd. N19............. 3A **34**
Shaftesbury Row SE8 .... 3C **94**
.... (off Speedwell St.)
Shaftesbury St. N1................. 1E **63**
.... (not continuous)
Shaftesbury Theatre London
.... 2D **15** (5A **62**)
.... (off Shaftesbury Av.)
Shaftesbury Vs. W8 .... 4C **72**
.... (off Allen St.)
Shafto M. SW1 .... 4B **74**
Shafton M. E9 .... 5F **51**
Shafton Rd. E9 .... 5F **51**
Shafts Ct. EC3 .... 3D **19** (5A **64**)
Shaftswood Ct. SW17........... 3B **116**
.... (off Lynwood Rd.)
Shahjalal Ho. E2 .... 1C **64**
.... (off Pritchards Rd.)
Shakespeare Ct. NW6 .... 4E **45**
.... (off Fairfax Rd.)
Shakespeare Ho. E9 .... 4E **51**
Shakespeare Rd. SE24 .... 3D **105**
Shakespeare's Globe & Exhibition
.... 1F **25** (2E **77**)
Shakespeare Twr.
EC2..................... 5A **10** (4E **63**)
.... (off Beech St.)
Shakspeare M. N16 .... 1A **50**
Shakspeare Wlk. N16........... 1A **50**
Shalbourne Sq. E9 .... 3B **52**
Shalcomb St. SW10 .... 2E **87**
Shalden Ho. SW15 .... 4B **98**
Shalfleet Dr. W10.................... 1F **71**
Shalford Ct. N1 .... 1D **63**
Shalford Ho. SE1 ...... 5C **26** (4F **77**)
Shamrock Ho. SE26.............. 4C **120**
.... (off Talisman Sq.)
Shamrock St. SW4 .... 1F **103**
Shandon Rd. SW4 .... 4E **103**
Shand St. SE1 .... 3D **27** (3A **78**)
Shandy St. E1 .... 4F **65**
Shan Ho. WC1 .... 4F **7** (3B **62**)
.... (off Millman St.)
Shanklin Rd. N8...................... 1F **33**
Shannon Cl. NW2 .... 5F **29**

Shannon Ct. N16.................... 5A **36**
Shannon Ct. SE15.................. 3B **92**
.... (off Garnies Cl.)
Shannon Gro. SW9................ 2B **104**
Shannon M. SE3..................... 2B **110**
Shannon Pl. NW8 .... 1A **60**
Shanti Ct. SW18 .... 1C **114**
Shardcroft Av. SE24 .... 3D **105**
Shardeloes Rd. SE14 .... 5B **94**
Shardeloes Rd. SE4 .... 1B **108**
Shard's Sq. SE15 .... 2C **92**
Sharman Way E3.................... 4D **67**
Sharnbrook Ho. W14............. 2C **86**
Sharon Gdns. E9 .... 5E **51**
Sharp Ho. SW8 .... 1D **103**
Sharpleshall St. NW1........... 4B **46**
Sharpley Ct. SE1 ...... 3D **25** (3D **77**)
.... (off Pocock St.)
Sharratt St. SE15................... 2E **93**
Sharsted St. SE17 .... 1D **91**
Sharwood WC1 .... 1A **8** (1B **62**)
.... (off Penton Ri.)
Shaver's Pl. SW1....... 5B **14** (1F **75**)
.... (off Coventry St.)
Shawbrooke Rd. SE9............ 3E **111**
Shawbury Rd. SE22 .... 3B **106**
Shaw Cres. E14...................... 4A **66**
Shawfield St. SW3 .... 1A **88**
Shawford Ct. SW15................ 5C **98**
Shaw Path BR1: Broml 3B **124**
Shaw Rd. BR1: Broml 3B **124**
Shaw Rd. SE22...................... 2A **106**
Shaws Cotts. SE23................ 3A **122**
Shaw Theatre........... 1C **6** (2F **61**)
.... (off James Voller Way)
Shead Ct. E1........................... 5D **65**
Shearling Way N7 .... 3A **48**
Shearman Rd. SE3................. 2B **110**
Shearsmith Ho. E1 .... 1C **78**
.... (off Hindmarsh Cl.)
Shearwater Ct. E1 .... 1C **78**
.... (off Star Pl.)
Shearwater Ct. SE8............... 2B **94**
.... (off Abinger Gro.)
Shearwater Dr. NW9.............. 2C **28**
Sheba Pl. E1 .... 4F **11** (3B **64**)
Sheenewood SE26................ 4D **121**
Sheen Gro. N1 .... 5C **48**
Sheepcote La. SW11............. 5B **88**
Sheep La. E8 .... 5D **51**
Sheep Wlk. M. SW19..............5F **113**
Sheerwater Rd. E16............... 4F **69**
Sheffield Sq. E3 .... 2B **66**
Sheffield St. WC2..... 3F **15** (5B **62**)
Sheffield Ter. W8 .... 2C **72**
Shelburne Rd. N7................... 1B **48**
Shelbury Rd. SE22 .... 3D **107**
Sheldon Av. N2....................... 1B **32**
Sheldon Av. N6....................... 2A **32**
Sheldon Cl. SE12................... 3D **111**
Sheldon Ct. SW8 .... 3A **90**
.... (off Lansdowne Grn.)
Sheldon Ho. N1 .... 5A **50**
.... (off Kingsland Rd.)
Sheldon Pl. E2........................ 1C **64**
.... (not continuous)
Sheldon Rd. NW2 .... 1F **43**
Sheldon Sq. W2...................... 4E **59**
Sheldrake Ho. SE16 .... 5F **79**
.... (off Tawny Way)
Sheldrake Pl. W8 .... 3C **72**
Shelduck Cl. E15.................... 2B **54**
Shelduck Ct. SE8 .... 2B **94**
.... (off Pilot Cl.)
Shelford Pl. N16..................... 5F **35**

Shelgate Rd. SW11 .... 3A **102**
Shelley Av. E12 .... 3F **55**
Shelley Cl. SE15 .... 5D **93**
Shelley Ct. E10 .... 2D **39**
.... (off Skelton's La.)
Shelley Ct. N19 .... 3B **34**
Shelley Ct. SW3 .... 2B **88**
.... (off Tite St.)
Shelley Ho. E2 .... 2E **65**
.... (off Cornwall Av.)
Shelley Ho. N16 .... 1A **50**
Shelley Ho. SE17 .... 1E **91**
.... (off Browning St.)
Shelley Ho. SW1 .... 2E **88**
.... (off Churchill Gdns.)
Shelley Pl. N1 .... 5D **49**
Shelley Way SW19 .... 5F **115**
Shellness Rd. E5 .... 2D **51**
Shell Rd. SE13 .... 1D **109**
Shell Twr. SE1 ..... 2A **24** (3B **76**)
.... (off Milner Pl.)
Shellwood Rd. SW11 .... 5B **88**
Shelmerdine Cl. E3 .... 4C **66**
Shelton St. WC2 .....3D **15** (5A **62**)
.... (not continuous)
Shene Ho. EC1 ....5B **8** (4C **62**)
.... (off Bourne Est.)
Shene Sports & Fitness Cen.
.... 2A **98**
Shenfield Ho. SE18 .... 4F **97**
.... (off Portway Gdns.)
Shenfield St. N1 .... 1E **11** (1A **64**)
.... (not continuous)
Shenley Rd. SE5 .... 4A **92**
Shenstone Ho. SW16 ....5E **117**
Shepherdess Pl. N1 .. 1A **10** (2E **63**)
Shepherdess Wlk.
N1 .... 1A **10** (1E **63**)
Shepherd Ho. E14 .... 5D **67**
.... (off Annabel Cl.)
Shepherd Mkt. W1 ...1D **21** (2D **75**)
SHEPHERD'S BUSH 3E **71**
Shepherd's Bush Empire Theatre
.... 3E **71**
Shepherd's Bush Grn. W12 ..3E **71**
Shepherd's Bush Mkt. W12...3E **71**
.... (not continuous)
Shepherd's Bush Market Station
(Underground) 2F **71**
Shepherd's Bush Pl. W12...3F **71**
Shepherd's Bush Rd. W6.....5E **71**
Shepherd's Bush Station (Rail,
Underground & Overground)
.... 3F **71**
Shepherd's Cl. N6 .... 1D **33**
Shepherds Cl. W1 ....4B **12** (1C **74**)
.... (off Lees Pl.)
Shepherds Ct. W12 .... 3F **71**
.... (off Shepherd's Bush Grn.)
Shepherd's Hill N6 .... 1D **33**
Shepherds La. E9 .... 3F **51**
Shepherd's Path NW3 .... 2F **45**
.... (off Lyndhurst Rd.)
Shepherds Pl. W1 ....4B **12** (1C **74**)
Shepherd St. W1 ....2D **21** (2D **75**)
Shepherd's Wlk. NW3 .... 2F **45**
Shepherds Wlk. NW2 .... 4C **28**
Shepperd Dr. SE16 .... 1D **93**
Sheppard Ho. E2 .... 1C **64**
.... (off Warner Pl.)
Sheppard Ho. SW2 .... 1C **118**
Sheppard St. E16 .... 3B **68**
Shepperton Rd. N1 .... 5E **49**
Shepton Ho's. E2 .... 2E **65**
.... (off Welwyn St.)

Sherard Ct. N7 .... 5A **34**
Sherard Ho. E9 .... 4E **51**
.... (off Frampton Pk. Rd.)
Sheraton Ho. SW1 .... 2D **88**
.... (off Churchill Gdns.)
Sheraton St. W1 .....3B **14** (5F **61**)
Sherborne Ho. SW1 .... 1D **89**
.... (off Agar Gro.)
Sherborne Ho. SW1 .... 1D **89**
.... (part of Abbots Mnr.)
Sherborne Ho. SW8 .... 3B **90**
.... (off Bolney St.)
Sherborne La. EC4 ....4B **18** (1F **77**)
Sherborne St. N1 .... 5F **49**
Sherboro Rd. N15 .... 1B **36**
Sherbourne Ct. SW5 .... 5D **73**
.... (off Cromwell Rd.)
Sherbrooke Ho. E2 .... 1E **65**
.... (off Bonner Rd.)
Sherbrooke Ho. SW1 .... 4F **75**
.... (off Monck St.)
Sherbrooke Rd. SW6 .... 3A **86**
Sherbrooke Ter. SW6 .... 3A **86**
.... (off Sherbrooke Rd.)
Sherbrook Ho. SE16 .... 3E **79**
.... (off Albatross Way)
Shere Ho. SE1 .... 5B **26** (4F **77**)
.... (off Gt. Dover St.)
Sherfield Gdns. SW15 .... 4B **98**
Sheridan Bldgs.
WC2 .... 3E **15** (5A **62**)
.... (off Martlett Ct.)
Sheridan Ct. NW6 .... 4E **45**
.... (off Belsize Rd.)
Sheridan Ct. SW5 .... 5D **73**
.... (off Barkston Gdns.)
Sheridan Hgts. E1 .... 5D **65**
.... (off Watney St.)
Sheridan Ho. SE11 .... 5C **76**
.... (off Wincott St.)
Sheridan M. E11 .... 1D **41**
Sheridan Pl. SW13 .... 1B **98**
Sheridan Rd. E7 .... 5B **40**
Sheridan Wlk. NW11 .... 1C **30**
Sheringham NW8 .... 5F **45**
Sheringham Ho. NW1 .... 4A **60**
.... (off Lisson St.)
Sheringham Rd. N7 .... 3B **48**
Sherington Rd. SE7 .... 2D **97**
Sherlock Ct. NW8 .... 5F **45**
.... (off Dorman Way)
Sherlock Holmes Mus.
.... 4A **4** (3B **60**)
.... (off Baker St.)
Sherlock M. W1 ....5B **4** (4C **60**)
Sherman Ho. E14 ....5E **67**
.... (off Dee St.)
Sherrard Rd. E12 .... 2F **55**
Sherrard Rd. E7 .... 3E **55**
Sherren Ho. E1 .... 3E **65**
Sherrick Grn. Rd. NW10 ..... 2D **43**
Sherriff Ct. NW6 .... 3C **44**
.... (off Sherriff Rd.)
Sherriff Rd. NW6 .... 3C **44**
Sheringham Ct. E16 .... 5B **68**
.... (off Silvertown Sq.)
Sherrington Ct. E16 .... 4B **68**
.... (off Rathbone St.)
Sherston Ho. E10 .... 1D **53**
Sherston Ct. SE1 .... 5D **77**
.... (off Newington Butts)
Sherston Ct. WC1 ....2B **8** (2C **62**)
.... (off Attneave St.)
Sherwin Ho. SE11 .... 2C **90**
.... (off Kennington Rd.)

Sherwin Rd. SE14 .... 4F **93**
Sherwood NW6 .... 4A **44**
Sherwood Ct. SW13 .... 1D **99**
Sherwood Ct. SW11 .... 1E **101**
Sherwood Ct. W1 .... 4B **60**
.... (off Bryanston Pl.)
Sherwood Gdns. E14 .... 5C **80**
Sherwood Gdns. SE16 .... 1C **92**
Sherwood St. W1 .....4A **14** (1E **75**)
Sherwood Ter. E16 .... 5E **69**
.... (off Bingley Rd.)
Shetland Rd. E3 .... 1B **66**
Shield St. SE15 .... 3B **92**
Shifford Path SE23 .... 3F **121**
Shillaker Ct. W3 .... 2B **70**
Shilliber Pl. W1 .... 4A **60**
.... (off Harcourt St.)
Shillingford Ho. E3 .... 2D **67**
.... (off Talwin St.)
Shillingford St. N1 .... 4D **49**
Shillingshaw Lodge E16...... 5C **68**
.... (off Butchers Rd.)
Shillingstone Ho. W14 .... 4A **72**
.... (off Russell Rd.)
Shillington St. Open Space .. 1A **102**
Shinfield St. W12 .... 5E **57**
Ship & Mermaid Row
SE1 .... 3C **26** (3F **77**)
Shipbuilding Way E13 ....1F **69**
Shipka Rd. SW12 .... 1D **117**
Shiplake Ho. E2 ...... 2F **11** (2B **64**)
.... (off Arnold Cir.)
Shipman Rd. E16 .... 5D **69**
Shipman Rd. SE23 .... 2F **121**
Ship St. SE8 .... 4C **94**
Ship Tavern Pas.
EC3 .... 4D **19** (1A **78**)
.... (off Shipton St.)
Shipton Ho. E2 .... 1B **64**
.... (off Shipton St.)
Shipton St. E2 .... 1B **64**
Shipwright Rd. SE16 .... 3A **80**
Shipwright St. E16 .... 3D **83**
Shipwright Yd. SE1 ...2D **27** (2A **78**)
Ship Yd. E14 .... 1D **95**
Shirburn Cl. SE23 ....5E **107**
Shirebrook Rd. SE3 .... 1F **111**
Shirehall Cl. NW4 ....1F **29**
Shirehall Gdns. NW4 ....1F **29**
Shirehall La. NW4 ....1F **29**
Shirehall Pk. NW4 ....1F **29**
Shire Ho. E3 .... 2D **67**
.... (off Talwin St.)
Shire Ho. EC1 .... 4A **10** (3E **63**)
.... (off Lambs Pas.)
Shire Pl. SW18 ....5E **101**
Shirland M. W9 .... 2B **58**
Shirland Rd. W9 .... 2B **58**
Shirlbutt St. E14 .... 1D **81**
Shirley Gro. SW11 .... 1C **102**
Shirley Ho. SE5 .... 3E **91**
.... (off Picton St.)
Shirley Ho. Dr. SE7 .... 3E **97**
Shirley Rd. E15 .... 4A **54**
Shirley Rd. W4 .... 3A **70**
Shirley St. E16 .... 5B **68**
Shirlock Rd. NW3 .... 1B **46**
Shobroke Cl. NW2 ....5E **29**
Shoe La. EC4 .... 2C **16** (5C **62**)
Shona Ho. E13 .... 4E **69**
Shooters Hill Rd. SE10 .... 4F **95**
Shooters Hill Rd. SE18 .... 4F **97**
Shooters Hill Rd. SE3 .... 3E **97**
Shoot Up Hill NW2 .... 2A **44**
Shore Bus. Cen. E9 .... 4E **51**
SHOREDITCH 1D **11** (2A **64**)

Shoreditch Ct. E8 .... 4B **50**
Shoreditch High St.
  E1 .... 2E **11** (3A **64**)
Shoreditch High Street Station
  (Overground) 3F **11** (3B **64**)
Shoreditch Ho. N1 ...... 2C **10** (2F **63**)
  .... (off Charles Sq.)
Shoreham Cl. SW18 .... 3D **101**
Shore Ho. SW8 .... 1D **103**
Shore M. E9 .... 4E **51**
  .... (off Shore Rd.)
Shore Pl. E9 .... 4E **51**
Shore Rd. E9 .... 4E **51**
Shore Way SW9 .... 5C **90**
  .... (off Crowhurst Cl.)
Shorncliffe Rd. SE1 .... 1B **92**
Shorndean St. SE6 .... 1E **123**
Shorrold's Rd. SW6 .... 3B **86**
Shorter St. E1 .... 4F **19** (1B **78**)
Shortlands W6 .... 5F **71**
Shortlands Rd. E10 .... 2D **39**
Short Rd. E11 .... 4A **40**
Short Rd. W4 .... 2A **84**
Shorts Gdns. WC2 .... 3D **15** (5A **62**)
Short St. SE1 .... 3C **24** (3C **76**)
Short Wall E15 .... 2E **67**
Short Way SW9 .... 1F **111**
Shottendane Rd. SW6 .... 4C **86**
Shottfield Av. SW14 .... 2A **98**
Shottsford W2 .... 5C **58**
  .... (off Talbot Rd.)
Shoulder of Mutton All. E14 .. 1A **80**
Shouldham St. W1 .... 4A **60**
Shrek's Adventure! ..3F **23** (3B **76**)
Shrewsbury Ct. EC1 ... 4A **10** (3E **63**)
  .... (off Whitecross St.)
Shrewsbury Ho. SW3 .... 2A **88**
  .... (off Cheyne Wlk.)
Shrewsbury Ho. SW8 .... 2B **90**
  .... (off Kennington Oval)
Shrewsbury M. W2 .... 4C **58**
  .... (off Chepstow Rd.)
Shrewsbury Rd. E7 .... 2F **55**
Shrewsbury Rd. N2 .... 5C **58**
Shrewsbury St. W10 .... 3E **57**
Shroffold Rd. BR1: Broml .. 4A **124**
Shropshire Pl. WC1 ... 4A **6** (3E **61**)
Shroton St. NW1 .... 4A **60**
Shrubbery, The E11 .... 1D **41**
Shrubbery Cl. N1 .... 5E **49**
Shrubbery Rd. SW16 .... 4A **118**
Shrubland Rd. E10 .... 2C **38**
Shrubland Rd. E17 .... 1C **38**
Shrubland Rd. E8 .... 5B **50**
Shrublands Cl. SE26 .... 3E **121**
Shuna Wlk. N1 .... 3F **49**
Shurland Gdns. SE15 .... 3B **92**
Shushan Cl. N16 .... 2A **36**
Shuters Sq. W14 .... 1B **86**
Shuttle St. E1 .... 3C **64**
Shuttleworth Rd. SW11 .... 5A **88**
Sibella Rd. SW4 .... 5F **89**
Sibthorpe Rd. SE12 .... 4D **111**
Sicilian Av. WC1 ...... 1E **15** (4A **62**)
  .... (off Vernon Pl.)
Sidbury St. SW6 .... 4A **86**
Sidcup Rd. SE12 .... 4E **111**
Siddons La. NW1 ...... 4A **4** (3B **60**)
Siddons St. SE23 .... 2A **122**
Sidford Ho. SE1 .... 5A **24** (4C **76**)
  .... (off Cosser St.)
Sidford Pl. SE1 .... 5A **24** (4C **76**)
Sidgwick Ho. SW9 .... 5B **90**
  .... (off Stockwell Rd.)

Sidings, The E11 .... 3E **39**
Sidings M. N7 .... 5C **34**
Siding St. E20 .... 5D **53**
Sidlaw Ho. N16 .... 3B **36**
Sidmouth Ho. SE15 .... 3C **92**
  .... (off Lindsey Est.)
Sidmouth Ho. W1 .... 5A **60**
  .... (off Cato St.)
Sidmouth M. WC1 ...... 2F **7** (2B **62**)
Sidmouth Pde. NW2 .... 4E **43**
Sidmouth Rd. E10 .... 5E **39**
Sidmouth Rd. NW2 .... 4E **43**
Sidmouth St. WC1 ..... 2E **7** (2A **62**)
Sidney Boyd Ct. NW6 .... 4C **44**
Sidney Est.
  E1: Lon Bromhead St. 5E **65**
Sidney Est.
  E1: Lon Jubilee St. 4E **65**
  .... (off Digby St.)
Sidney Godley (VC) Ho. E2....2E **65**
  .... (off Digby St.)
Sidney Gro. EC1 .... 1D **9** (1D **63**)
Sidney Ho. E2 .... 1E **65**
  .... (off Old Ford Rd.)
Sidney Rd. E7 .... 5C **40**
Sidney Rd. SW9 .... 5B **90**
Sidney Sq. E1 .... 4E **65**
Sidney St. E1 .... 4D **65**
  .... (not continuous)
Sidney Webb Ho.
  SE1 .... 5C **26** (4F **77**)
  .... (off Tabard St.)
Sidonie Apts. SW11 .... 2A **102**
  .... (off Danvers Av.)
Sidworth St. E8 .... 4D **51**
Siebert Rd. SE3 .... 2C **96**
Siege Ho. E1 .... 5D **65**
  .... (off Sidney St.)
Siemens Brothers Way E16...1C **82**
Siemens Rd. SE18 .... 4F **83**
Sienna Alto SE13 .... 1E **109**
  .... (off Cornmill La.)
Sienna Ho. E20 .... 3D **53**
  .... (off Victory Pde.)
Sienna Ter. NW2 .... 4C **28**
Sigdon Pas. E8 .... 2C **50**
Sigdon Rd. E8 .... 2C **50**
Sigmund Freud Statue 3F **45**
Signal Ho. E8 .... 4D **51**
  .... (off Martello Ter.)
Signal Ho. SE1 .... 4F **25** (3E **77**)
  .... (off Gt. Suffolk St.)
Signmakers Yd. NW1 .... 5D **47**
  .... (off Delancey St.)
Sikorski Mus. 3F **73**
Silbury Ho. SE26 .... 3C **120**
Silbury St. N1 .... 1B **10** (2F **63**)
Silchester Rd. W10 .... 5F **57**
Silesia Bldgs. E8 .... 4D **51**
Silex St. SE1 .... 4E **25** (3D **77**)
Silicon M. E3 .... 5C **52**
Silicon Way N1 .... 2C **10** (2F **63**)
Silk Cl. SE12 .... 3C **110**
Silk Ct. E2 .... 2C **64**
  .... (off Squirries St.)
Silk Ho. E1: Lon Leman St. ... 5C **64**
  .... (off Leman St.)
Silk Ho.
  E1: Lon Trafalgar Gdns. 4F **65**
  .... (off Trafalgar Gdns.)
Silk Ho. E2 .... 1B **64**
  .... (off How's St.)
Silkin M. SE15 .... 3C **92**
Silkin M. SE11 .... 1C **90**
  .... (off Kennington Rd.)

Silk Mills Pas. SE13 .... 5D **95**
Silk Mills Path SE13 .... 5E **95**
  .... (not continuous)
Silk Mills Sq. E9 .... 3B **52**
Silk St. E11 .... 3B **40**
Silk St. EC2 .... 5A **10** (4E **63**)
Silk Weaver Way E2 .... 1D **65**
Sillitoe Ho. N1 .... 5F **49**
  .... (off Colville St.)
Silsoe Ho. NW1 .... 1D **61**
Silver Birch Cl. SE6 .... 3B **122**
Silverbirch Wlk. NW3 .... 3B **46**
Silverburn Ho. SW9 .... 4D **91**
  .... (off Lothian Rd.)
Silver Cl. SE14 .... 3A **94**
Silverdale NW1 .... 1F **5** (2E **61**)
  .... (off Harrington St.)
Silverdale SE26 .... 4E **121**
Silverdale Ct. EC1 ... 3E **9** (3D **63**)
  .... (off Goswell Rd.)
Silverdale Dr. SE9 .... 2F **125**
Silvermere Rd. SE6 .... 5D **109**
Silver Pl. W1 .... 3A **14** (5E **61**)
Silver Rd. SE13 .... 1D **109**
Silver Rd. W12 .... 1F **71**
Silverthorn NW8 .... 5D **45**
  .... (off Abbey Rd.)
Silverthorne Loft Apts. SE5..2F **91**
  .... (off Albany Rd.)
Silverthorne Rd. SW8 .... 5D **89**
Silverton Rd. W6 .... 2F **85**
SILVERTOWN 2E **83**
Silvertown Quay Development
  E16 ....2E **83**
Silvertown Sq. E16 .... 5B **68**
Silvertown Viaduct E16 .... 5B **68**
Silvertown Way E16: Lon
  Clarkson Rd. 5A **68**
Silvertown Way E16: Lon
  Hanover Av. 2C **82**
Silver Wlk. SE16 .... 2A **80**
Silverwood Pl. SE10 .... 4E **95**
Silvester Ho. E1 .... 5D **65**
  .... (off Varden St.)
Silvester Ho. E2 .... 2E **65**
  .... (off Sceptre Rd.)
Silvester Ho. W11 .... 5B **58**
  .... (off Basing St.)
Silvester Rd. SE22 .... 3B **106**
Silvester St. SE1 ..... 4B **26** (3F **77**)
Silvocea Way E14 .... 5F **67**
Silwood Est. SE16 .... 5E **79**
Silwood St. SE16 .... 5E **79**
  .... (off Rotherhithe New Rd.)
Simkins Cl. SW2 .... 2A **104**
Simla Cl. N7 .... 4A **48**
Simla Ho. SE1 .... 4C **26** (3F **77**)
  .... (off Kipling Est.)
Simmonds Ct. SW5 .... 5D **73**
  .... (off Earl's Ct. Gdns.)
Simms Rd. SE1 .... 5C **78**
Simnel Rd. SE12 .... 5D **111**
Simon Cl. W11 .... 1B **72**
Simon Ct. W9 .... 2C **58**
  .... (off Saltram Cres.)
Simonds Rd. E10 .... 4C **38**
Simone Ct. SE26 .... 3E **121**
Simons Cl. N16 .... 4B **36**
Simons Wlk. E15 .... 2F **53**
Simpson Dr. W3 .... 5A **56**
Simpson Ho. NW8 .... 3A **60**
Simpson Ho. SE11 .... 1B **90**
Simpson's Rd. E14 .... 1D **81**
Simpson St. SW11 .... 5A **88**

Simrose Ct. SW18 ....3C **100**
Sim St. N4 ....4E **35**
Sims Wlk. SE3 ....2B **110**
Sinclair Gdns. W14 ....3F **71**
Sinclair Gro. NW11 ....1F **29**
Sinclair Ho. E15 ....3F **53**
................................(off Leyton Rd.)
Sinclair Ho. WC1 ......2D **7** (2A **62**)
................................(off Sandwich St.)
Sinclair Mans. W12 ....3F **71**
................................(off Richmond Way)
Sinclair Pl. SE4 ....4C **108**
Sinclair Rd. W14 ....3F **71**
Sinclairs Ho. E3 ....1B **66**
................................(off St Stephen's Rd.)
Sindercombe M. W12 ....4C **70**
Singer M. SW4 ....5A **90**
Singer St. EC2 ....2C **10** (2F **63**)
Siobhan Davies Dance Studios
................................5D **25** (4D **77**)
................................(off St George's Rd.)
Sir Abraham Dawes Cotts.
SW15 ....2A **100**
Sir Alexander Cl. W3 ....2B **70**
Sir Alexander Rd. W3 ......2B **70**
Sir Christopher France Ho.
E1 ....2A **66**
Sirdar Rd. W11 ....1F **71**
Sireen Apts. E3 ....3B **66**
Sir Francis Drake Ct. SE10 ..1F **95**
Sirinham Point SW8 ....2B **90**
................................(off Meadow Rd.)
Sirius Bldg. E1 ....1F **79**
................................(off Jardine Rd.)
Sirius Ho. SE16 ....5A **80**
................................(off Seafarer Way)
Sir James Black Ho. SE5 ...5F **91**
................................(off Coldharbour La.)
Sir John Kirk Cl. SE5 ....3E **91**
Sir John Lyon Ho.
EC4 ....4F **17** (1E **77**)
................................(off High Timber St.)
Sir John Morden Wlk. SE3 ..5C **96**
Sir John Soane's Mus.
................................2A **16** (5B **62**)
Sir Nicholas Garrow Ho.
W10 ....3A **58**
Sirocco Twr. E14 ....3D **81**
Sir Oswald Stoll Mans.
SW6 ....3D **87**
................................(off Fulham Rd.)
Sir Simon Milton Sq.
SW1 ....5E **21** (4D **75**)
Sir Walter Raleigh Ct. SE10 ..1A **96**
Sir William Powell's Almshouses
SW6 ....5A **86**
Sise La. EC4 ....3B **18** (5F **63**)
Siskin Ho. SE16 ....5F **79**
................................(off Tawny Way)
Sispara Gdns. SW18 ....4B **100**
Sissinghurst Cl.
BR1: Broml 5A **124**
Sissinghurst Ho. SE15 .....2E **93**
................................(off Sharratt St.)
Sissulo Ct. E6 ....5E **55**
Sister Mabel's Way SE15 ...3C **92**
Sistova Rd. SW12 ....1D **117**
Sisulu Pl. SW9 ....1C **104**
Sitarey Ct. W12 ....2D **71**
Sitka Ho. SE16 ....3A **80**
Sivill Ho. E2 ....1F **11** (2B **64**)
................................(off Columbia Rd.)
Siward Rd. SW17 ....3E **115**

Six Acres Est. N4 ....4B **34**
Six Bridges Ind. Est. SE1 ...1C **92**
................................(not continuous)
Sixth Av. W10 ....2A **58**
Siyah Gdn. E3 ....2B **66**
Skardu Rd. NW2 ....2A **44**
Skeena Hill SW15 ....5A **100**
Skeggs Ho. E14 ....4E **81**
................................(off Glengall St.)
Skegness Ho. N7 ....4B **48**
................................(off Sutterton St.)
Skelbrook St. SW18 ....2E **115**
Skelgill Rd. SW15 ....2B **100**
Skelley Rd. E15 ....4B **54**
Skelton Cl. E8 ....3B **50**
Skelton Lodge SE14 ....4A **94**
................................(off Billinghurst Way)
Skelton Rd. E7 ....3C **54**
Skelton's La. E10 ....2D **39**
Skelwith Rd. W6 ....2E **85**
Skenfrith Ho. SE15 ....2D **93**
................................(off Commercial Way)
Sketch Apts. E1 ....4F **65**
................................(off Shandy St.)
Sketchley Gdns. SE16 ......1F **93**
Skiers St. E15 ....5A **54**
Skiffington Cl. SW2 ....1C **118**
Skinner Ct. E3 ....3D **67**
................................(off Barry Blandford Way)
Skinner Pl. SW1 ....5C **74**
................................(off Bourne St.)
Skinners La. EC4 .....4A **18** (1E **77**)
Skinner's Row SE10 ....4D **95**
Skinner St. EC1 ......2C **8** (2C **62**)
Skipsea Ho. SW18 ....4A **102**
Skipton Ho. SE4 ....2A **108**
Skipwith Ho. EC1 .....5B **8** (4C **62**)
................................(off Bourne Est.)
Skipworth Rd. E9 ....5E **51**
Skua Cl. SE8 ....2B **94**
................................(off Dorking Cl.)
Sky Gdn. Wlk. EC3 ...4D **19** (1A **78**)
................................(off Philpot La.)
Skylark Ct. SE1 ......4A **26** (3E **77**)
................................(off Swan St.)
Skylark Ct. SW15 ....4E **99**
Skyline Apts. N4 ....2F **35**
................................(off Devan Gro.)
Skyline St. SW1 ......5F **27** (4B **78**)
Skyline Plaza Bldg. E1 .....5C **64**
................................(off Commercial Rd.)
Skylines E14 ....3E **81**
Skylines Village E14 ....3E **81**
Sky View Twr. E15 ....1D **67**
................................(off High Street)
Sladebrook Rd. SE3 ....1F **111**
Sladen Pl. E5 ....1D **51**
Slade Twr. E10 ....4C **38**
................................(off Leyton Grange Est.)
Slade Wlk. SE17 ....2D **91**
Slagrove Pl. SE13 ....3C **108**
Slaidburn St. SW10 ....2E **87**
Slaithwaite Rd. SE13 ......2C **109**
Slaney Cl. NW10 ....4E **43**
Slaney Pl. N7 ....2C **48**
Slate Ho. E14 ....5B **66**
................................(off Keymer Pl.)
Slater M. SW4 ....1E **103**
Sleaford Ho. E3 ....3C **66**
................................(off Fern St.)
Sleaford Ind. Est. SW8 ....3E **89**
Sleaford St. SW8 ....3E **89**
Sleat Ho. E3 ....1B **66**
................................(off Saxon Rd.)

Sleigh Ho. E2 ....2E **65**
................................(off Bacton St.)
Slide, The 4D **53**
Slievemore Cl. SW4 ....1F **103**
Sligo Ho. E1 ....3F **65**
................................(off Beaumont Gro.)
Slindon Ct. N16 ....5B **36**
Slingsby Pl. WC2 ....4D **15** (1A **76**)
Slippers Pl. SE16 ....4D **79**
Slipway Ho. E14 ....1D **95**
................................(off Burrells Wharf Sq.)
Sloane Av. SW3 ....5A **74**
Sloane Av. Mans. SW3 .....5B **74**
Sloane Ct. E. SW3 ....1C **88**
Sloane Ct. W. SW3 ....1C **88**
Sloane Gdns. SW1 ....5C **74**
Sloane Ga. Mans. SW1 .....5C **74**
................................(off D'Oyley St.)
Sloane Ho. E9 ....4E **51**
................................(off Loddiges Rd.)
Sloane M. N8 ....1A **34**
Sloane Sq. SW1 ....5C **74**
Sloane Square Station
(Underground) 5C **74**
Sloane St. SW1 ......4A **20** (3B **74**)
Sloane Ter. SW1 ....5C **74**
Sloane Ter. Mans. SW1 .....5C **74**
................................(off Sloane Ter.)
Sly St. E1 ....5D **65**
Smallbrook M. W2 ....5F **59**
Smalley Cl. N16 ....5B **36**
Smalley Rd. Est. N16 ....5B **36**
................................(off Smalley Cl.)
Smallwood Rd. SW17 ......4F **115**
Smart's Pl. WC2 ......2E **15** (5A **62**)
Smart St. E2 ....2F **65**
Smead Way SE13 ....1D **109**
Smeaton Ct. SE1 ......5F **25** (4E **77**)
Smeaton Rd. SW18 ....5C **100**
Smeaton St. E1 ....2D **79**
Smedley St. SW4 ....5F **89**
Smedley St. SW8 ....5F **89**
Smeed Rd. E3 ....4C **52**
Smikle Ct. SE14 ....4E **93**
................................(off Hatcham Pk. M.)
Smiles Pl. SE13 ....1E **109**
Smith Cl. SE16 ....2F **79**
Smithfield Ct. E1 ....1C **78**
................................(off West Smithfield)
Smithfield Market ...1D **17** (4D **63**)
................................(off West Smithfield)
Smithfield St. EC1 ...1D **17** (4D **63**)
Smith's Ct. W1 ....4A **14** (1F **75**)
................................(off Gt. Windmill St.)
Smiths Point E13 ....5C **54**
................................(off Brooks Rd.)
Smiths Sq. SW1 ......5D **23** (4A **76**)
Smiths Way SW6 ....1F **85**
Smith St. SW3 ....1B **88**
Smiths Yd. SW18 ....2E **115**
Smith Ter. SW3 ....1B **88**
Smithwood Cl. SW19 ....1A **114**
Smithy St. E1 ....4E **65**
Smokehouse Yd. EC1 ...5E **9** (4D **63**)
................................(off St John St.)
Smugglers Way SW18 .....2D **101**
Smugglers Yd. W12 ....2D **71**
................................(off Devonport Rd.)
Smyrk's Rd. SE17 ....1A **92**
Smyrna Mans. NW6 ....4C **44**
................................(off Smyrna Rd.)
Smyrna Rd. NW6 ....4C **44**
Smythe St. E14 ....1D **81**
Snaresbrook Station
(Underground) 1C **40**

Snarsgate St. W10..........4E 57
Sneath Av. NW11...............2B 30
Sneyd Rd. NW2................1E 43
Snowberry Cl. E15.........1F 53
Snowbury Rd. SW6.........5D 87
Snowden St. EC2....4D 11 (3A 64)
Snowdon Aviary..............5B 46
...............(in London Zoo)
Snowdon Dr. NW9...............1A 28
Snow Hill EC1.........1D 17 (4D 63)
Snow Hill Ct. EC1....2E 17 (5D 63)
Snowman Ho. NW6...........5D 45
Snowsfields SE1....3C 26 (3F 77)
Snowshill Rd. E12............2F 55
Soames Ct. SE15..............1B 106
Soane Ct. NW1.................4E 47
...............(off St Pancras Way)
Soane Ho. SE17...............1F 91
...............(off Roland Way)
Sobell Leisure Cen..........5B 34
Soda Studios E8..............5B 50
...............(off Kingsland Rd.)
SOHO..................3A 14 (5E 61)
Soho Ho. W12.................1E 71
Soho Sq. W1.........2B 14 (5F 61)
Soho St. W1..........2B 14 (5F 61)
Soho Theatre........3B 14 (5F 61)
...............(off Dean St.)
Sojourner Truth Cl. E8.......3D 51
Solander Gdns. E1: Lon Cable St.
...............1D 79
...............(off Cable St.)
Solander Gdns. E1: Lon
The Highway...............1E 79
Solar Ct. SE16................3C 78
...............(off Chambers St.)
Solar Rd. E15..................3A 54
...............(off Romford Rd.)
Solarium Ct. SE1.............5B 78
...............(off Alscot Rd.)
Soldene Ct. N7................3B 48
Solebay St. E1.................3A 66
Solent Ho. E1.................4A 66
...............(off Ben Jonson Rd.)
Solent Ri. E13.................2C 68
Solent Rd. NW6...............2C 44
Soley M. WC1.......1B 8 (2C 62)
Solna Av. SW15..............3E 99
Solomon's Pas. SE15......2D 107
Solomon Way E1..............4A 66
Solon New Rd. SW4.......2A 104
Solon New Rd. Est. SW4...2A 104
Solon Rd. SW2...............2A 104
Solway Cl. E8.................3B 50
...............(off Queensbridge Rd.)
Solway Ho. E1................3F 65
...............(off Ernest St.)
Solway Rd. SE22............2C 106
Somali Rd. NW2..............2B 44
Sombourne Ho. SW15.......5C 98
...............(off Fontley Way)
Somer Ct. SW6................2C 86
...............(off Anselm Rd.)
Somerfield Rd. N4..............4D 35
...............(not continuous)
Somerfield St. SE16.........1F 93
Somerford Gro. N16..........1B 50
Somerford Gro. Est. N16.....1B 50
Somerford St. E1..............3D 65
Somerford Way SE16.......3A 80
Somerleyton Pas. SW9....2D 105
Somerleyton Rd. SW9.....2C 104
Somers Cl. NW1................1F 61
Somers Cres. W2...............5A 60
Somerset Ct. NW1.....1B 6 (1F 61)

Somerset Est. SW11..........4F 87
Somerset Gdns. N6...........2C 32
Somerset Gdns. SE13........5D 95
Somerset Ho. SW19..........3F 113
Somerset House....4A 16 (1B 76)
Somerset Rd. E17.............1C 38
Somerset Rd. SW19.........3F 113
Somerset Sq. W14...........3A 72
Somers Pl. SW2...............5B 104
Somers Rd. SW2..............4B 104
Somerston Ho. NW1..........5E 47
...............(off St Pancras Way)
SOMERS TOWN........1B 6 (1F 61)
Somers Town Community Sports
Cen..........................1F 61
Somerton Ho. WC1....2C 6 (2F 61)
...............(off Euston Rd.)
Somerton Rd. NW2............5F 29
Somerton Rd. SE15..........2D 107
Somertrees Av. SE12........2D 125
Somerville Av. SW13.........2D 85
Somerville Cl. SW9..........4B 90
Somerville Point SE16......3B 80
Sonderburg Rd. N7..........4B 34
Sondes St. SE17...............2F 91
Sonesta Apts. SE15..........4D 93
Sonia Gdns. NW10............1B 42
Sonning Ho. E2.....2F 11 (2B 64)
...............(off Swanfield St.)
Soper Cl. SE23................1F 121
Sophia Cl. N7...................3B 48
Sophia Ho. W6.................1E 85
...............(off Queen Caroline St.)
Sophia Rd. E10.................3D 39
Sophia Rd. E16.................5D 69
Sophia Sq. SE16...............1A 80
...............(off Sovereign Cres.)
Sophora Ho. SW11...........3D 89
Soprano Ho. E15..............5B 54
...............(off Plaistow Rd.)
Sopwith Way SW11..........3D 89
Sorensen Ct. E10..............4D 39
...............(off Leyton Grange Est.)
Sorrel Gdns. E6.................4F 69
Sorrel La. E14...................5F 67
Sorrell Cl. SE14................3A 94
Sorrell Cl. SW9.................5C 90
Sorrel Mead NW9..............2C 28
Sotheby Rd. N5.................5D 35
Sotheran Cl. E8.................5C 50
Sotherby Lodge E2............1E 65
...............(off Sewardstone Rd.)
Sotheron Pl. SW6.............3D 87
Soudan Rd. SW11.............4B 88
Souldern Rd. W14.............4F 71
Soul St. SE6..................1E 123
Sounding All. E3................5C 52
South Access Rd. E17.......2A 38
Southacre W2..................5A 60
...............(off Hyde Pk. Cres.)
South Africa Rd. W12........2D 71
Southall Pl. SE1....4B 26 (3F 77)
Southam Ho. W10.............3A 58
...............(off Southam St.)
Southampton Bldgs.
WC2................1B 16 (4C 62)
Southampton M. E16.........2D 83
Southampton Pl.
WC1.................1E 15 (4A 62)
Southampton Rd. NW5......2B 46
Southampton Row
WC1..................5E 7 (4A 62)
Southampton St.
WC2..................4E 15 (1A 76)
Southampton Way SE15.....3A 92

Southampton Way SE5......3F 91
South Audley St. W1 5C 12 (1C 74)
South Bank SE1...............3B 76)
Southbank Bus. Cen. SW11...4B 88
Southbank Cen.....1A 24 (2B 76)
South Bermondsey Station (Rail)
.................................1E 93
South Birkbeck Rd. E11......5F 39
South Black Lion La. W6....1C 84
South Block SE1.....4F 23 (3B 76)
...............(off Belvedere Rd.)
South Bolton Gdns. SW5.....1D 87
Southborough Ho. SE17.....1A 92
...............(off Kinglake Est.)
Southborough Rd. E9.........5F 51
Southbourne Gdns. SE12...3D 111
SOUTH BROMLEY..............1E 81
Southbrook M. SE12..........4B 110
Southbrook Rd. SE12........4B 110
Southbury NW8.................5E 45
...............(off Loudoun Rd.)
South Carriage Dr. SW7.....3F 73
South City Ct. SE15..........3A 92
South Cl. N6.....................1D 33
South Colonnade, The E14...2C 80
...............(not continuous)
Southcombe St. W14.........5A 72
Southcote Rd. N19.............1E 47
Southcott Ho. E3...............2D 67
...............(off Devons Rd.)
Southcott Ho. W9..............3E 59
...............(off Clifton Gdns.)
Southcroft Rd. SW16.........5D 117
Southcroft Rd. SW17.........5C 116
South Croxted Rd. SE21....3F 119
Southdean Gdns. SW19.....2B 114
South Eaton Pl. SW1.........5C 74
South Edwardes Sq. W8....4B 72
SOUTHEND......................4F 123
South End W8...................4D 73
South End Cl. NW3............1A 46
South End Grn. NW3..........1A 46
Southend La. SE6.............4B 122
South End Rd. NW3...........1A 46
South End Row W8.............4D 73
Southerngate Way SE14....3A 94
Southern Gro. E3...............2B 66
Southern Rd. E13..............1D 69
Southern Row W10............3A 58
Southern St. N1................1B 62
Southern Ter. W12.............2E 71
Southern Way SE10...........5B 82
Southernwood Retail Pk....1E 92
Southerton Rd. W6............5E 71
South Esk Rd. E7...............3E 55
Southey Ho. SE17.............1E 91
...............(off Browning St.)
Southey M. E16.................2C 82
Southey Rd. N15...............1A 36
Southey Rd. SW9...............4C 90
Southfield Ct. E11..............5B 40
SOUTHFIELDS...................1B 114
Southfields M. SW18.........4C 100
Southfields Pas. SW18......4C 100
Southfields Rd. SW18........4C 100
Southfields Station
(Underground)................1B 114
Southgate Gro. N1.............4F 49

South Gdns. SE17 ....5E **77**
Southgate Ct. N1..................4F **49**
..................*(off Downham Rd.)*
Southgate Gro. N1 ....4F **49**
Southgate Ho. N1 ....5F **49**
South Gro. E17..................1B **38**
South Gro. N15..................1F **35**
South Gro. N6..................3C **32**
South Gro. Ho. N6..................3C **32**
SOUTH HACKNEY 5F **51**
SOUTH HAMPSTEAD 4E **45**
South Hampstead Station
(Overground) 4E **45**
South Hill Pk. NW3..................1A **46**
South Hill Pk. Gdns. NW3 ....5A **32**
Southill St. E14 ....5D **67**
South Island Pl. SW9 ....3B **90**
SOUTH KENSINGTON 5F **73**
South Kensington Sta. Arc.
SW7..................5F **73**
..................*(off Pelham St.)*
South Kensington Station
(Underground) 5F **73**
SOUTH LAMBETH 3A **90**
South Lambeth Pl. SW8..................2A **90**
South Lambeth Rd. SW8..................2A **90**
Southlands Coll. Roehampton
University 3C **98**
Southlands Dr. SW19..................2F **113**
South Lodge E16..................2D **83**
..................*(off Audley Dr.)*
South Lodge NW8 ....1F **59**
South Lodge SW7 ....3A **74**
..................*(off Knightsbridge)*
South London Gallery 4A **92**
South London Theatre 3D **119**
..................*(off Norwood High St.)*
South Mall SW18 ....4D **101**
Southmead Rd. SW19..................1A **114**
Southmere Ho. E15..................1D **67**
..................*(off Highland Street)*
South Mill Apts. E2..................5B **50**
..................*(off Hebden St.)*
South Molton La.
W1..................3D **13** (5D **61**)
South Molton Rd. E16..................5C **68**
South Molton St. W1..................3D **13** (5D **61**)
Southmoor Way E9..................3B **52**
South Oak Rd. SW16..................4B **118**
Southolm St. SW11..................4D **89**
Southover BR1: Broml..................5C **124**
South Pde. SW3 ....1F **87**
South Pk. Cres. SE6..................1A **124**
South Pk. M. SW6 ....1D **101**
South Pl. EC2 ....5C **10** (4F **63**)
South Pl. M. EC2 ....1C **18** (4F **63**)
South Quay Plaza E14 ....3D **81**
South Quay Sq. E14 ....3D **81**
South Quay Station (DLR) 3D **81**
South Ri. W2 ....1A **74**
..................*(off St George's Flds.)*
South Rd. SE23 ....2F **121**
South Row SE3 ....5B **96**
South Sea St. SE16..................4B **80**
Southside N7..................1F **47**
South Side W6 ....4B **70**
Southside Comn. SW19..................5E **113**
Southside Halls SW7 ....4F **73**
..................*(off Prince's Gdns.)*
Southside Ind. Est. SW8 ....4E **89**
..................*(off Havelock Ter.)*
South Sq. NW11 ....1D **31**
South Sq. WC1 ....1B **16** (4C **62**)
South Stand N5..................1D **49**
South St. W1 ....1C **20** (2C **74**)

South Tenter St. E1..................1B **78**
South Ter. SW7 ....5A **74**
SOUTH TOTTENHAM 1B **36**
South Tottenham Station
(Overground) 1B **36**
Southvale Rd. SE3 ....5A **96**
Southview Av. NW10 ....2B **42**
Southview Cl. SW17..................5C **116**
Southview Rd. BR1: Broml..................4F **123**
South Vs. NW1 ....3F **47**
Southville SW8 ....4F **89**
SOUTHWARK 2D **25** (2D **77**)
Southwark Bri. SE1 ....5A **18** (1E **77**)
Southwark Bri. Bus. Cen.
SE1..................2A **26** (2E **77**)
..................*(off Southwark Bri. Rd.)*
Southwark Bri. Rd.
SE1..................5E **25** (4D **77**)
Southwark Cathedral
..................1B **26** (2F **77**)
Southwark Pk...................3D **79**
Southwark Pk. Est. SE16..................5D **79**
..................*(off Southwark Pk. Rd.)*
Southwark Pk. Rd. SE16 ....5B **78**
Southwark Pk. Sports Cen. Track
..................5E **79**
Southwark Pk. Sports Complex
..................5E **79**
Southwark Playhouse
..................5F **25** (4E **77**)
Southwark St George's RC
Cathedral..................5C **24** (4C **76**)
Southwark Station (Underground)
..................5E **25** (2D **77**)
Southwark St. SE1..................1D **25** (2D **77**)
Southway Cl. E14..................5B **66**
Southway NW11..................1D **31**
Southway Cl. W12..................3D **71**
Southwell Gdns. SW7 ....5E **73**
Southwell Gro. Rd. E11..................4A **40**
Southwell Ho. SE16 ....5D **79**
..................*(off Anchor St.)*
Southwell Rd. SE5..................1E **105**
South W. India Dock Entrance
E14..................3E **81**
Southwest Rd. E11 ....3F **39**
South Wharf Rd. W2 ....5F **59**
Southwick M. W2..................5F **59**
Southwick Pl. W2 ....5A **60**
Southwick St. W2 ....5A **60**
Southwick Yd. W2 ....5A **60**
..................*(off Titchborne Row)*
Southwold Mans. W9 ....2C **58**
..................*(off Widley Rd.)*
Southwold Rd. E5 ....4D **37**
Southwood Av. N6 ....2D **33**
Southwood Ct. EC1 ....1D **9** (2D **63**)
..................*(off Wynyatt St.)*
Southwood Ct. NW11..................1D **31**
South Woodford to Barking
Relief Rd. E11..................1F **41**
Southwood Hall N6..................1D **33**
Southwood Hgts. N6..................2D **33**
Southwood Ho. W11 ....1A **72**
..................*(off Avondale Pk. Rd.)*
Southwood La. N6..................2C **32**
Southwood Lawn Rd. N6..................2C **32**
Southwood Mans. N6..................1C **32**
..................*(off Southwood La.)*
Southwood Pk. N6..................2C **32**
Southwood Smith Ho. E2..................2D **65**
..................*(off Florida St.)*
Southwood Smith St. N1..................5D **49**
South Worple Av. SW14..................1A **98**

Southwyck Ho. SW9 ....2D **105**
Sovereign Cl. E1..................1D **79**
Sovereign Ct. W8 ....4D **73**
..................*(off Wright's La.)*
Sovereign Cres. SE16 ....1A **80**
Sovereign Ho. E1 ....3D **65**
..................*(off Cambridge Heath Rd.)*
Sovereign M. E2..................1B **64**
Spa Bus. Pk. SE16 ....4C **78**
Space Arts Cen., The 5C **80**
..................*(off Westferry Rd.)*
Spaces Bus. Cen. SW8..................4E **89**
Spa Ct. SE16 ....4C **78**
Spa Ct. SW16 ....4B **118**
Spafield St. EC1 ....3B **8** (3C **62**)
Spa Grn. Est. EC1..................1C **8** (2D **63**)
Spalding Ho. SE4 ....2A **108**
Spalding Rd. NW4..................2E **29**
Spalding Rd. SW17 ....5D **117**
Spanby Rd. E3..................3C **66**
Spaniards Cl. NW11 ....3F **31**
Spaniards End NW3..................3E **31**
Spaniards Rd. NW3..................4E **31**
Spanish Pl. W1..................2C **12** (5C **60**)
Spanish Rd. SW18 ....3E **101**
Spare St. SE17 ....5E **77**
Sparkes Cotts. SW1 ....5C **74**
..................*(off Graham Ter.)*
Sparkford Ho. SW11 ....4F **87**
..................*(off Battersea Church Rd.)*
Spa Rd. SE16..................5F **27** (4B **78**)
Sparrick's Row SE1...................3C **26** (3F **77**)
Sparrow Ho. E1 ....3E **65**
..................*(off Cephas Av.)*
Sparsholt Rd. N19..................3B **34**
Sparta St. SE10..................4E **95**
Speakers' Corner 4A **12** (1B **74**)
Speakman Ho. SE4 ....1A **108**
..................*(off Arica Rd.)*
Spearman Ho. E14..................5C **66**
..................*(off Upper Nth. St.)*
Spear M. SW5..................5C **72**
Spears Rd. N19..................3A **34**
Spectacle Works E13..................2E **69**
Spectrum Bldg., The
N1..................1C **10** (2F **63**)
..................*(off East Rd.)*
Spectrum Pl. SE17..................2F **91**
..................*(off Lytham St.)*
Spectrum Way SW18..................3C **100**
Spedan Cl. NW3..................5E **31**
Speechly Ho. E8..................2B **50**
Speed Highwalk EC2 5A **10** (4F **63**)
..................*(off Silk St.)*
Speed Ho. EC2..................5A **10** (4F **63**)
..................*(off Silk St.)*
Speedwell St. SE8..................3C **94**
Speedy Pl. WC1..................2D **7** (2A **62**)
..................*(off Cromer St.)*
Speke's Monument 2F **73**
Speldhurst Rd. E9..................4F **51**
Speldhurst Rd. W4 ....4A **70**
Spelbrook Wlk. N1..................5E **49**
Spelman Ho. E1...................4C **64**
..................*(off Spelman St.)*
Spelman St. E1 ....4C **64**
..................*(not continuous)*
Spence Cl. SE16 ....3B **80**
Spencer Ct. NW8..................1E **59**
..................*(off Marlborough Pl.)*
Spencer Dr. N2..................1E **31**
Spencer House 2F **21** (2E **75**)
..................*(off St James's Pl.)*
Spencer Mans. W14..................2A **86**
..................*(off Queen's Club Gdns.)*

Spencer M. SW8 .... 4B 90
............(off Lansdowne Way)
Spencer M. W6 .... 2A 86
Spencer Pk. SW18 .... 3F 101
SPENCER PK. 3F 101
Spencer Pl. N1 .... 1D 49
Spencer Ri. NW5 .... 1D 47
Spencer Rd. E6 .... 5F 55
Spencer Rd. N8 .... 1B 34
........................(not continuous)
Spencer Rd. SW18 .... 2F 101
Spencer St. EC1 ....2D 9 (2D 63)
Spencer Wlk. NW3 .... 1F 45
Spencer Wlk. SW15 .... 2F 99
Spencer Way E1 .... 5D 65
Spencer Yd. SE3 .... 5B 96
....................(off Tranquil Va.)
Spenlow Ho. SE16 .... 4C 78
....................(off Jamaica Rd.)
Spenser Gro. N16 .... 2A 50
Spenser M. SE21 .... 2F 119
Spenser Rd. SE24 .... 3D 105
Spenser St. SW1 ....5A 22 (4E 75)
Spens Ho. WC1 .... 4F 7 (3B 62)
....................(off Lamb's Conduit St.)
Spensley Wlk. N16 .... 5F 35
Spert St. E14 .... 1A 80
Spey St. E14 .... 4E 67
Spezia Rd. NW10 .... 1C 56
Sphere, The E16 .... 5B 68
....................(off Hallsville Rd.)
Spice Ct. E1 .... 1C 78
....................Spice Quay Hgts.
SE1 .... 2F 27 (2B 78)
Spicer Cl. SW9 .... 5D 91
Spindrift Av. E14 .... 5C 80
Spinnaker Ho. E14 .... 3C 80
....................(off Byng St.)
Spinnaker Ho. E16 .... 3D 83
....................(off Waypoint Way)
Spinnaker Ho. SW18 .... 2E 101
....................(off Juniper Dr.)
Spinner Ho. E8 .... 5B 50
....................(off Lovelace St.)
Spinney, The SW13 .... 3D 85
Spinney, The SW16 .... 3E 117
Spinney Gdns. SE19 .... 5B 120
Spire Ho. W2 .... 1E 73
....................(off Lancaster Ga.)
Spirit Quay E1 .... 2C 78
SPITALFIELDS 5F 11 (4B 64)
Spitalfields City Farm 3C 64
Spital Sq. E1 ....5E 11 (4A 64)
Spital St. E1 .... 4C 64
Spital Yd. E1 ....5E 11 (4A 64)
Spitfire Bldg. N1 ....1F 7 (1B 62)
....................(off Collier St.)
Splendour Wlk. SE16 .... 1E 93
....................(off Verney Rd.)
Spode Ho. SE11 ....5B 24 (4C 76)
....................(off Lambeth Wlk.)
Spode Wlk. NW6 .... 2D 45
Sporle Rd. SW11 .... 1F 101
Sports Academy (LSBU)
....................5E 25 (4D 77)
....................(off London Rd.)
Sportsbank St. SE6 .... 5E 109
Sportsman Pl. E2 .... 5C 50
Spratt Hall Rd. E11 .... 1C 40
Spriggs Ho. N1 .... 4D 49
....................(off Canonbury Rd.)
Sprimont Pl. SW3 .... 1B 88
Springall St. SE15 .... 3D 93
Springalls Wharf SE16 .... 3C 78
....................(off Bermondsey Wall W.)

Spring Apts. E14 .... 5E 81
....................(off Stebondale St.)
Springbank Rd. SE13 .... 4F 109
Springbank Wlk. NW1 .... 4F 47
Spring Ct. NW6 .... 3B 44
Springdale M. N16 .... 1F 49
Springdale Rd. N16 .... 1F 49
Springer Ct. E3 .... 3E 67
....................(off Navigation Rd.)
Springett Ho. SW2 .... 3C 104
....................(off St Matthews Rd.)
Springfield E5 .... 3D 37
Springfield Cl. NW3 .... 4A 46
....................(off Eton Av.)
Springfield Dr. SW17 .... 2A 116
Springfield Gdns. E5 .... 3D 37
Springfield Gdns. NW9 .... 1A 28
Springfield Gro. SE7 .... 2E 97
Springfield La. NW6 .... 5D 45
Springfield Pl. E5 .... 2F 115
Springfield Ri. SE26 .... 3D 121
Springfield Rd. E15 .... 2A 68
Springfield Rd. E17 .... 1B 38
Springfield Rd. NW8 .... 5E 45
Springfield Rd. SE26 .... 5D 121
Springfield Rd. SW19 .... 5B 114
SPRINGFIELD UNIVERSITY
HOSPITAL 2A 116
Springfield Wlk. NW6 .... 5D 45
Spring Gdns. N5 .... 2E 49
Spring Gdns. SW11 ....1C 22 (2F 75)
....................(not continuous)
Spring Hill E5 .... 2D 37
Spring Hill SE26 .... 4E 121
Springhill Cl. SE5 .... 1F 105
Spring Ho. WC1 ....2B 8 (2C 62)
....................(off Margery St.)
Spring La. E5 .... 2D 37
Spring M. SE11 .... 1B 90
Spring M. W1 ....5A 4 (4B 60)
Spring Pk. Dr. N4 .... 3E 35
Spring Pas. SW15 .... 1F 99
Spring Path NW3 .... 2F 45
Spring Pl. NW5 .... 2D 47
Springrice Rd. SE13 .... 4F 109
Spring St. W2 .... 5F 59
Spring Tide Cl. SE15 .... 4D 93
Springvale Ter. W14 .... 4F 71
Spring Wlk. E1 .... 4C 64
Springwater WC1 ....5F 7 (4B 62)
....................(off New North St.)
Spring Way SE5 .... 4E 91
Springwell Av. NW10 .... 5B 42
Springwell Cl. SW16 .... 4B 118
Springwell Rd. SW16 .... 4C 118
Springwood Cl. E3 .... 1C 66
Sprowston M. E7 .... 2C 54
Sprowston Rd. E7 .... 2C 54
Spruce Ho. SE16 .... 3F 79
....................(off Woodland Cres.)
Sprules Rd. SE4 .... 5A 94
Spurgeon St. SE1 ....5B 26 (4F 77)
Spurling Rd. SE22 .... 2B 106
Spur Rd. SE1 ....3B 24 (3C 76)
Spur Rd. SW1 ....4F 21 (3E 75)
Spurstowe Rd. E8 .... 3D 51
Spurstowe Ter. E8 .... 2C 50
Square, The E1 .... 1C 78
Square, The W6 .... 1E 85
Square Rigger Row SW11 ....1E 101
Squarey St. SW17 .... 3E 115
Squire Gdns. NW8 .... 2F 59
....................(off Grove End Rd.)
Squires Ct. SW19 .... 4C 114
Squires Ct. SW4 .... 4A 90

Squires Mt. NW3 .... 5F 31
Squirels, The SE13 .... 1F 109
Squirries St. E2 .... 2C 64
SS Robin 3F 83
Stable Cl. EC1 ....4E 9 (3D 63)
....................(off Clerkenwell Rd.)
Stable M. NW5 .... 3D 47
Stable M. SE6 .... 1A 124
Stable Pl. N4 .... 4D 35
Stables Gallery & Arts Cen.
....................5C 28
Stables Lodge E8 .... 4D 51
....................(off Mare St.)
Stables Mkt., The NW1 .... 4D 47
Stables Row E11 .... 1C 40
Stable St. N1 .... 5A 48
Stables Way SE11 .... 1C 90
Stables Yd. SW18 .... 4C 100
....................(off Stable Yd. Rd.)
Stable Vs. BR1: Broml 5F 125
Stable Wlk. E1 .... 1C 78
....................(off Boulevard Walkway)
Stable Way W10 .... 5E 57
Stable Yd. SW1 ....3F 21 (3E 75)
....................(off Stable Yd. Rd.)
Stable Yd. SW15 .... 1E 99
Stable Yd. Rd. SW1 ...2A 22 (3E 75)
....................(not continuous)
Stacey Cl. E10 .... 1F 39
Stacey St. N7 .... 5C 34
Stacey St. WC2 ....3C 14 (5F 61)
....................Stack Ho. SW1 .....5C 74
....................(off Cundy St.)
Stackhouse St. SW3 ...5A 20 (4B 74)
....................(off Rysbrack St.)
Stacy Path SE5 .... 3A 92
Stadium M. N5 .... 5C 34
Stadium Rd. E. NW4 .... 2D 29
Stadium St. SW10 .... 3E 87
Staffa Rd. E10 .... 3A 38
Stafford Cl. E17 .... 1B 38
....................(not continuous)
Stafford Cl. NW6 .... 2C 58
Stafford Cl. W8 .... 3A 90
Stafford Cl. W8 .... 4C 72
Stafford Cripps Ho. E2 .... 2E 65
....................(off Globe Rd.)
Stafford Cripps Ho. SW6 .... 2B 86
....................(off Clem Attlee Ct.)
Stafford Ho. SE1 .... 1B 92
....................(off Cooper's Rd.)
Stafford Mans. SW1: SF 21 (4E 75)
....................(off Stafford Pl.)
Stafford Mans. SW11 .... 3B 88
....................(off Albert Bri. Rd.)
Stafford Mans. SW4 .... 2A 104
Stafford Mans. W14 .... 4F 71
....................(off Haarlem Rd.)
Stafford Pl. SW1 ....5F 21 (4E 75)
Stafford Rd. E3 .... 1B 66
Stafford Rd. E7 .... 4E 55
Stafford Rd. NW6 .... 2C 58
Staffordshire St. SE15 .... 4C 92
Stafford St. W1 ....1F 21 (2E 75)
Stafford Ter. W8 .... 4C 72
Staff St. EC1 ....2C 10 (2F 63)
Stag La. SW15 .... 3B 112
STAG LANE 2B 112
Staining La. EC2 ....2A 18 (5E 63)
Stainsbury St. E2 .... 1E 65
Stainsby Rd. E14 .... 5C 66
Stainton Rd. SE6 .... 4F 109
Staith Ct. E3 .... 3E 67
....................(off Bolinder Way)

Stalbridge Flats W1...3C 12 (5C 60)
..........................(off Lumley St.)
Stalbridge Ho. NW1... 1F 5 (1E 61)
..........................(off Hampstead Rd.)
Stalbridge St. NW1 ......4A 60
Stalham St. SE16.............4D 79
Stamford Bri. Studios SW6.. 3D 87
Stamford Brook Arches W6 5C 70
..........................(off Wandon Rd.)
Stamford Brook Av. W6......4B 70
Stamford Brook Gdns. W6...4B 70
Stamford Brook Mans. W6...5B 70
..........................(off Goldhawk Rd.)
Stamford Brook Rd. W6......4B 70
Stamford Brook Station
  (Underground) 5B 70
Stamford Bldgs. SW8 ......3A 90
..........................(off Meadow Pl.)
Stamford Cl. NW3 ....5E 31
..........................(off Heath St.)
Stamford Cotts. SW10 ....3D 87
..........................(off Billing St.)
Stamford Ct. W6 ....5C 70
Stamford Ga. SW6 ....3D 87
Stamford Ga. Ho. SW6 ......3D 87
..........................(off Stamford Ga.)
Stamford Gro. E. N16..........3C 36
Stamford Gro. W. N16..........3C 36
Stamford Hill N16 ....4B 36
STAMFORD HILL..................3B 36
Stamford Hill Station
  (Overground) 2A 36
Stamford Lodge N16..........2B 36
Stamford Rd. E6...............5F 55
Stamford Rd. N1 ....4A 50
Stamford Sq. SW15............3A 100
Stamford St. SE1 ......2B 24 (2C 76)
Stamp Pl. E2 ......1F 11 (1B 64)
Stanard Cl. N16....................2A 36
Stanborough Ho. E3............3D 67
..........................(off Empson St.)
Stanborough Pas. E8..........3B 50
Stanbridge Rd. SW15..........1E 99
Stanbury Ct. NW3 ....3B 46
Stanbury Rd. SE15..............4D 93
..........................(not continuous)
Standard Pl. EC2...... 2E 11 (2A 64)
..........................(off Rivington St.)
Standen Rd. SW18..............5B 100
Standish Ho. W6 ....5C 70
..........................(off St Peter's Gro.)
Standish Rd. W6 ....5C 70
Standlake Point SE23......3F 121
Stane Gro. SW9.................5A 90
Stanesgate Ho. SE15.........3C 92
..........................(off Friary Est.)
Stane Way SE18..................3F 97
Stanfield Ho. NW8.............5F 59
..........................(off Frampton St.)
Stanfield Rd. E3.................1A 66
Stanford Ct. SW6 ....4D 87
Stanford Ct. W8.................4D 73
..........................(off Cornwall Gdns.)
Stanford M. E8..................2C 50
Stanford Pl. SE17...............5A 78
Stanford Rd. W8.................4D 73
Stanford St. SW1 ....5E 75
Stangate SE1.........5A 24 (4B 76)
..........................(off Royal St.)
Stanhope Cl. SE16..............3F 79
Stanhope Gdns. N4.............1D 35
Stanhope Gdns. N6.............1D 33
Stanhope Gdns. SW7...........5E 73
Stanhope Ga. W1 ......1C 20 (2C 74)

Stanhope Ho. SE8 ....3B 94
..........................(off Adolphus St.)
Stanhope M. E. SW7 ....5E 73
Stanhope M. Sth. SW7.........5E 73
Stanhope M. W. SW7 ....5E 73
Stanhope Pde. NW1... 1F 5 (2E 61)
Stanhope Pl. W2 ....1B 74
Stanhope Rd. E17 ....1D 39
Stanhope Rd. N6..................1E 33
Stanhope Row N1 ...2D 21 (2D 75)
Stanhope St. NW1... 1F 5 (1E 61)
Stanhope Ter. W2 ....1F 73
Stanier Cl. W14 ....1B 86
Stanlake M. W12.................2E 71
Stanlake Rd. W12................2E 71
Stanlake Vs. W12.................2E 71
Stanley Bri. Studios SW6.....3D 87
..........................(off King's Rd.)
Stanley Cl. SW8.................2B 90
Stanley Cohen Ho.
  EC1...................4A 10 (3E 63)
..........................(off Golden La.)
Stanley Cres. W11 ....1B 72
Stanley Gdns. NW2.............2E 43
Stanley Gdns. W11.............1B 72
Stanley Gdns. W3................3A 70
Stanley Gdns. M. W11 ....1B 72
..........................(off Kensington Pk. Rd.)
Stanley Gro. SW8 ....5C 88
Stanley Holloway Ct. E16 ....5C 68
..........................(off Coolfin Rd.)
Stanley Ho. E14.................5C 66
..........................(off Saracen St.)
Stanley Ho. SW10 ....3E 87
..........................(off Coleridge Gdns.)
Stanley Mans. SW10............2E 87
..........................(off Park Wlk.)
Stanley M. SW10................2E 87
..........................(off Coleridge Gdns.)
Stanley Rd. E10..................1D 39
Stanley Rd. E12..................2F 55
Stanley Rd. NW9 ....2C 28
Stanley Rd. SW14...............1A 98
Stanley St. SE8 ....3B 94
Stanley Studios SW10..........2E 87
..........................(off Park Wlk.)
Stanley Ter. N19..................4A 34
Stanliff Ho. E14...................4C 80
Stanmer St. SW11...............4A 88
Stanmore Pl. NW1...............5D 47
Stanmore Rd. E11...............3B 40
Stanmore St. N1 ....5B 48
Stannard Cotts. E1..............3E 65
..........................(off Fox Cl.)
Stannard Ct. SE6................1D 123
Stannard Ho. SW19............4E 115
Stannard Rd. E8..................2C 50
..........................(off Stannard Rd.)
Stannard Rd. E8.................3C 50
Stannary Pl. SE11 ....1C 90
Stannary St. SE11 ....1C 90
Stansbury Sq. W10 ....2A 58
Stansfeld Ho. SE1 ....5B 78
..........................(off Longfield Est.)
Stansfeld Rd. E16...............1F 83
Stansfeld Rd. E6.................4F 69
Stansfield Rd. SW9 ....1B 104
Stanstead WC1.......2E 7 (2A 62)
..........................(off Tavistock Pl.)
Stanstead Gro. SE6.............1B 122
Stanstead Ho. E3.................3E 67
..........................(off Devas St.)
Stanstead Rd. SE23.............1F 121
Stanstead Rd. SE6..............1B 122

Stanswood Gdns. SE5 ....3A 92
Stanthorpe Cl. SW16..........5A 118
Stanthorpe Rd. SW16.........5A 118
Stanton Ho. SE10................2E 95
..........................(off Thames St.)
Stanton Ho. SE16................3B 80
..........................(off Rotherhithe St.)
Stanton Rd. SE26...............4B 122
Stanton Rd. SW13...............5B 84
Stanton Sq. SE26...............4B 122
Stanton Way SE26..............4B 122
Stanway Ct. N1 ......1E 11 (1A 64)
..........................(off Shenfield St.)
Stanway St. N1 ....1A 64
Stanwick Rd. W14...............5B 72
Stanworth St. SE1.... 4F 27 (4B 78)
Staplefield Cl. SW2.............1A 118
Stapleford Cl. SW19............5A 100
Staplehurst Rd. SE13..........3F 109
Staple Inn WC1 ......1B 16 (4C 62)
Staple Inn Bldgs.
  WC1...................1B 16 (4C 62)
Staples Cl. SE16..................2A 80
STAPLES CORNER...............3D 29
Staples Cnr. Bus. Pk. NW2 ...3D 29
Staples Cnr. Retail Pk. 3D 29
Staple St. SE1.........4C 26 (3F 77)
Stapleton Hall Rd. N4.........3B 34
Stapleton Ho. E2.................2D 65
..........................(off Ellsworth St.)
Stapleton Rd. SW17............3C 116
Stapleton Vs. N16...............1A 50
..........................(off Wordsworth Rd.)
Star All. EC3.........4E 19 (1A 78)
..........................(off Mark La.)
Starboard Way E14..............4C 80
Starcross St. NW1...... 2A 6 (2E 61)
Starfield Rd. W12.................3C 70
Star La. E16.......................3A 68
Star Lane Station (DLR).......3A 68
Starling Ho. NW8................1A 60
..........................(off Charlbert St.)
Star Pl. E1..........................1B 78
Star Rd. W14......................2B 86
Star St. W2.........................5A 60
Star Wharf NW1..................5E 47
..........................(off St Pancras Way)
Star Yd. WC2.........2B 16 (5C 62)
Staten Bldg. E3...................1C 66
..........................(off Fairfield Rd.)
Statham Ct. N19.................5A 34
..........................(off Alexander Rd.)
Statham Gro. N16................1F 49
Statham Ho. SW8................4E 89
..........................(off Wadhurst Rd.)
Station App. SW16: Lon
  Gleneagle Rd....................5F 117
Station App. SE26: Lon Lower
  Sydenham.........................
Station App. E7...................1D 55
Station App. N16..................4B 36
..........................(off Stamford Hill)
Station App. NW1......4A 4 (3B 60)
Station App. NW10..............2B 56
Station App. NW11..............2F 29
Station App. SE12...............4C 110
..........................(off Burnt Ash Hill)
Station App. SW6................3B 86
Station App. Rd.
  SE1...................4A 24 (3C 76)
..........................(off Gt. Portland St.)
Station Arc. W1...................4E 5 (3D 61)
..........................(off Gt. Portland St.)

Station Av. SW9..............1D 105
Station Ct. N15.................1B 36
Station Ct. SW6................4E 87
Station Cres. SE3.............1C 96
Stationer's Hall Ct.
EC4..................3E 17 (5D 63)
Station Ho. SE8................3C 94
..............(off Deptford High St.)
Station M. Ter. SE3............1C 96
Station Pde. E13...............1F 69
...............................(off Green St.)
Station Pde. E5.................5D 37
.........................(off Up. Clapton Rd.)
Station Pde. NW2...............3E 43
Station Pde. SW12..............1C 116
Station Pas. E20................3E 53
Station Pas. SE15..............4E 93
Station Path SW6: Lon Putney
Bridge......................1B 100
Station Pl. N4..................4C 34
Station Ri. SE27...............2D 119
Station Rd. E12.................1E 55
Station Rd. E17................1A 38
Station Rd. E7.................1C 54
Station Rd. N19................5E 33
Station Rd. NW10...............1B 56
Station Rd. NW4................1C 28
Station Rd. SE13..............1E 109
Station Rd. SE20..............5E 121
Station Rd. SW13...............5B 84
Station St. E15.................4F 53
Station Ter. NW10..............1F 57
Station Ter. SE5...............4E 91
Station Wlk. W11................1F 71
.............................(off Bramley Rd.)
Station Way SE15...............5C 92
Staton Ct. E10.................2D 39
..............................(off Kings Cl.)
Staunton Ho. SE17.............5A 78
.............................(off Wansey St.)
Staunton St. SE8..............2B 94
Stave Hill Ecological Pk.
..............................3A 80
Staveley NW1.........1F 5 (2E 61)
............................(off Varndell St.)
Staveley Cl. E9................2E 51
Staveley Cl. N7................1A 48
Staveley Cl. SE15..............4D 93
Staveley Gdns. W4..............4A 84
Stavers Ho. E3.................1B 66
.............................(off Tredegar Rd.)
Staverton Rd. NW2..............4E 43
Stave Yd. Rd. SE16.............2A 80
Stavordale Lodge W14...........4B 72
.............................(off Melbury Rd.)
Stavordale Rd. N5..............1D 49
Stayner's Rd. E1...............5F 65
Steadman Ct. EC1...3A 10 (3E 63)
................................(off Old St.)
Stead St. SE17.................5F 77
Stean St. E8...................5B 50
Stebbing Ho. W11...............2F 71
.........................(off Queensdale Cres.)
Stebondale St. E14............5E 81
Stedham Pl. WC1...2D 15 (5A 62)
.........................(off New Oxford St.)
Steedman St. SE17..............5E 77
Steele Ho. E15.................1A 68
...............................(off Eve Rd.)
Steele Rd. E11.................1A 54
Steele's M. Nth. NW3...........3B 46
Steele's M. Sth. NW3...........3B 46
Steele's Rd. NW3...............3B 46
Steele's Studios NW3...........3B 46
Steel's La. E1.................5E 65

Steelyard Pas. EC4...5B 18 (1F 77)
.............................(off Cousin La.)
Steen Way SE22................3A 106
Steep Hill SW16................3F 117
Steeple Cl. SW19...............5A 114
Steeple Cl. SW6................5A 86
Steeple Ct. E1.................3D 65
Steeple Wlk. N1................5E 49
.............................(off New Nth. Rd.)
Steerforth St. SW18...........2E 115
Steers Way SE16................3A 80
Stelfox Ho. WC1......1A 8 (2B 62)
.................................(off Penton Ri.)
Stella Rd. SW17...............5B 116
Stellman Cl. E5................5C 36
Stephan Cl. E8.................5C 50
Stephendale Rd. SW6...........1D 101
Stephendale Yd. SW6...........1D 101
.........................(off Stephendale Rd.)
Stephen Fox Ho. W4.............1A 84
..............................(off Chiswick La.)
Stephen M. W1.........1B 14 (4F 61)
Stephen Pl. SW4...............1E 103
Stephens Cl. E16...............3B 68
Stephens Ct. SE4...............1A 108
Stephenson Cl. E3..............2D 67
Stephenson Ho. SE1...5F 25 (4E 77)
Stephenson Rd. E17.............1A 38
Stephenson St. E16.............3A 68
Stephenson St. NW10............2A 56
Stephenson Way
NW1................3A 6 (3E 61)
Stephen's Rd. E15..............5A 54
Stephen St. W1.......1B 14 (4F 61)
STEPNEY..........................4F 65
Stepney C'way. E1..............5F 65
Stepney City Apts. E1..........4E 65
Stepney City Farm.............4F 65
Stepney Grn. E1................4E 65
Stepney Grn. Ct. E1............4E 65
............................(off Stepney Grn.)
Stepney Green Station
(Underground).................3F 65
Stepney High St. E1............4F 65
Stepney Way E1.................4D 65
Sterling Cl. NW10..............4C 42
Sterling Gdns. SE14...........2A 94
Sterling St. SW7...............4A 74
Sterling Way N7................3B 48
Stern Ct. E3...................2E 67
.................................(off Culvert Dr.)
Sterndale Rd. W14..............4F 71
Sterne St. W12.................3F 71
Sternhall La. SE15............1C 106
Sternhold Av. SW2.............2F 117
Sterry St. SE1......4B 26 (3F 77)
Steucers La. SE23.............1A 122
Steve Biko Ct. W10.............3F 57
.............................(off St John's Ter.)
Steve Biko La. SE6.............4C 122
Steve Biko Lodge E13..........1C 68
.............................(off London Rd.)
Steve Biko Rd. N7..............5C 34
Stevedore St. E1...............2D 79
Stevenage Rd. SW6..............3F 85
Stevens Av. E9.................3E 51
Stevenson Cl. SE8.............2B 124
Stevenson Cres. SE16...........1C 92
Stevenson Ho. NW8..............5E 45
.........................(off Boundary Rd.)
Stevens St. SE1......5E 27 (4A 78)
Steventon Rd. W12..............1B 70
Steward Ho. E3.................2C 66
.........................(off Trevithick Way)
Steward St. E1......1E 19 (4A 64)

Stewart Rd. E15................1F 53
Stewart's Gro. SW3............1F 87
Stewart's Pl. SW2.............4B 104
Stewart's Rd. SW8.............3E 89
Stewart St. E14................3E 81
Stew La. EC4........4F 17 (1E 77)
Stibbington Ho. NW1............1E 61
.........................(off Cranleigh St.)
Stickle Ho. SE8................3D 95
.........................(off Creative Rd.)
Stifford Ho. E1................4E 65
.........................(off Stepney Way)
Stileman Ho. E3................4B 66
.........................(off Ackroyd Dr.)
Stillingfleet Rd. SW13.........2C 84
Stillington St. SW1...........5E 75
Stillness Rd. SE23............4A 108
Still Wlk. SE1.......2E 27 (2B 78)
.........................(off Duchess Wlk.)
Stirling Ct. EC1.....3D 9 (3D 63)
.............................(off St John St.)
Stirling Cl. E13...............1D 69
Stirling Rd. SW9...............5A 90
Stockbeck NW1.........1A 6 (1E 61)
.........................(off Ampthill Est.)
Stockbridge Ho. SW18..........2E 101
.........................(off Eltringham St.)
Stockfield Rd. SW16...........3B 118
Stockholm Apts. NW1............4C 46
.........................(off Chalk Farm Rd.)
Stockholm Ho. E1...............1C 78
.........................(off Swedenborg Gdns.)
Stockholm Rd. SE16............1E 93
Stockholm Way N1...............2C 78
Stockhurst Cl. SW15............5E 85
Stockleigh Hall NW8............1A 60
.........................(off Prince Albert Rd.)
Stock Orchard Cres. N7.........2B 48
Stock Orchard St. N7...........2B 48
Stocks Pl. E14.................1B 80
Stock St. E13..................1C 68
Stockton Ct. SW1...............4F 75
.........................(off Greycoat St.)
Stockton Ho. E2................2D 65
.........................(off Ellsworth St.)
STOCKWELL.......................5B 90
Stockwell Av. SW9.............1B 104
Stockwell Gdns. SW9............4B 90
Stockwell Gdns. Est. SW9.......5A 90
Stockwell Grn. SW9.............5B 90
Stockwell Grn. Ct. SW9.........5B 90
Stockwell M. SW9...............5B 90
Stockwell Pk. Cres. SW9........5B 90
Stockwell Pk. Est. SW9.........5B 90
Stockwell Pk. Rd. SW9..........4B 90
Stockwell Pk. Wlk. SW9........1C 104
Stockwell Rd. SW9..............5B 90
Stockwell Station (Underground)
..............................4A 90
Stockwell St. SE10.............2E 95
Stockwell Ter. SW9.............4B 90
Stoddart Ho. SW8...............2B 90
Stodmarsh Ho. SW9..............4C 90
.........................(off Cowley Rd.)
Stofield Gdns. SE9.............3F 125
Stoford Cl. SW19..............5A 100
Stokenchurch St. SW6..........4D 87
STOKE NEWINGTON.................5B 36
Stoke Newington Chu. St.
..............................5F 35
Stoke Newington Comn.
N16.............................5B 36
Stoke Newington High St.
N16.............................5B 36

Stoke Newington Rd. N16....2B 50
Stoke Newington Station
    (Overground)...............4B 36
Stoke Pl. NW10...................2B 56
Stokesley St. W12...............5B 56
Stokes Rd. E6......................3F 69
Stoll Cl. NW2......................5E 29
Stoms Path SE6..................5C 122
    ....(off Maroons Way)
Stondon Pk. SE23............4A 108
Stondon Wlk. E6.................1F 69
Stonebridge Cen. N15.......1B 36
Stonebridge Gdns..............5B 50
    ....(off Arbutus St.)
Stonebridge Rd. N15..........1B 36
Stone Bldgs. WC2...1A 16 (4B 62)
    ....(off Chancery La.)
Stonechat M. SW15............2C 98
Stone Cl. SW4.....................5E 89
Stonecutter St. EC4.2D 17 (5D 63)
Stonefield N4.....................4B 34
Stonefield Mans. N1...........5C 48
    ....(off Cloudesley St.)
Stonefield St. N1.................5C 48
Stonefield Way SE7............3F 97
Stone Hall W8.....................4D 73
    ....(off Stone Hall Gdns.)
Stonehall Av. IG1: Ilf...........1F 41
Stone Hall Gdns. W8...........4D 73
Stone Hall Pl. W8................4D 73
Stonehills Ct. SE21...........3A 120
Stonehouse NW1................5E 47
    ....(off Plender St.)
Stonehouse Ho. W2............4C 58
    ....(off Westbourne Pk. Rd.)
Stone Lake Ind. Pk. SE7.....5E 83
Stone Lake Retail Pk..........5E 83
Stoneleigh M. E3...............1A 66
Stoneleigh Pl. W11.............1F 71
Stoneleigh St. W11.............1F 71
Stoneleigh Ter. N19...........4D 33
Stonell's Rd. SW11.............4B 102
Stonemason Ct. SE1...4F 25 (3E 77)
    ....(off Borough Rd.)
Stonemason Ho. SE14........4F 93
    ....(off Fishers Ct.)
Stonemasons Yd. SW18....5F 101
Stonenest St. N4................3B 34
Stones End St. SE1...4F 25 (3E 77)
Stoneway Wlk. E3...............1F 65
Stoneyard La. E14..............1D 81
Stoneycroft Cl. SE12..........5B 110
Stoney La. E1........2E 19 (5B 64)
Stoney St. SE1.......1B 26 (2F 77)
Stonhouse St. SW4............2F 103
Stonor Rd. W14..................5B 72
Stopes St. SE15..................3B 92
Stopford Rd. E13................5C 54
Stopford Rd. SE17..............1D 91
Stopher Ho. SE1.....4E 25 (3D 77)
    ....(off Webber St.)
Storehouse M. E14..............1C 80
Storers Quay E14................5F 81
Store St. E15......................2F 53
Store St. WC1..........1B 14 (4F 61)
Storey Ct. NW8...................2F 59
    ....(off St John's Wood Rd.)
Storey Ho. E14....................1D 81
    ....(off Cottage St.)
Storey Rd. N6......................1B 32
Storey's Ga. SW1....4C 22 (3F 75)
Stories M. SE5....................5A 92
Stories Rd. SE5.................1A 106
Stork Rd. E7.......................3B 54
Stork's Rd. SE16.................4C 78

Stormont Lawn Tennis & Squash
    Club............................1B 32
Stormont Rd. N6.................2B 32
Stormont Rd. SW11..........1C 102
Storrington WC1........2E 7 (2A 62)
    ....(off Regent Sq.)
Story St. N1........................4B 48
Stothard Ho. E1..................3E 65
    ....(off Amiel St.)
Stothard Pl. E1......5E 11 (4A 64)
Stothard St. E1...................3E 65
Stott Cl. SW18....................4F 101
Stoughton Cl. SE11............5B 76
Stoughton Cl. SW15..........1C 112
Stourcliffe Cl. W1...............5B 60
Stourcliffe St. W1...............5B 60
Stourhead Cl. SW19...........5F 99
Stourhead Ho. SW1.............1F 89
    ....(off Tachbrook St.)
Stour Rd. E3.......................4C 52
Stowage SE8......................2C 94
Stowe Ho. NW11................1E 31
Stowe Rd. W12...................3D 71
Stracey Rd. E7....................1C 54
Stracey Rd. NW10...............5A 42
Stradbroke Rd. N5..............1E 49
Stradella Rd. SE24...........4E 105
Strafford Ho. SE8...............1B 94
    ....(off Grove St.)
Strafford St. E14................3C 80
Strahan Rd. E3...................2A 66
Straightsmouth SE10..........3E 95
Strakers Rd. SE15...........2D 107
Strale Ho. N1......................5A 50
    ....(off Whitmore Est.)
Strand WC2.............1D 23 (1A 76)
Strand E. Twr. E15...............1E 67
Strand La. WC2......4A 16 (1B 76)
Strang Ho. N1.....................5E 49
Strangways Ter. W14..........4B 72
Stranraer Way N1................4A 48
Strasburg Rd. SW11...........4C 88
Strata SE1...........................5E 77
    ....(off Walworth Rd.)
STRATFORD........................4F 53
Stratford Bus Station..........4F 53
Stratford Circus (Performing Arts
    Cen.)..........................3F 53
Stratford City Bus Station...3E 53
Stratford Eye E15................3E 53
Stratford Gro. SW15....2F 99
Stratford High Street Station
    (DLR).........................5F 53
Stratford International Station
    (Rail & DLR)................4E 53
STRATFORD NEW TOWN....3F 53
Stratford Office Village, The
    E15.............................4A 54
Stratford One E20.............3D 53
Stratford Picturehouse London
    ....3F 53
Stratford Pl. E20................3E 53
    ....(within Westfield Shop. Cen.)
Stratford Pl. W1.......3D 13 (5D 61)
Stratford Rd. E13................5B 54
    ....(not continuous)
Stratford Rd. W8................4C 72
Stratford Station (Rail,
    Underground, Overground,
    DLR & Crossrail)..........4E 53
Stratford Studios W8.........4C 72
Stratford Vs. W14...............4E 47
Stratford Workshops E15....5F 53
    ....(off Burford Rd.)

Strathan Cl. SW18.............4A 100
Strathaven Rd. SE12.........4D 111
Strathblaine Rd. SW11.......3F 101
Strathdale SW16...............5B 118
Strathdon Dr. SW17...........3F 115
Strathearn Ho. W2.............1A 74
    ....(off Strathern Pl.)
Strathearn Pl. W2...............5A 60
Strathearn Rd. SW19.........5C 114
Stratheden Pde. SE3..........3C 96
Stratheden Rd. SE3............4C 96
Strathleven Rd. SW2..........3A 104
Strathmore Ct. NW8...........2A 60
    ....(off Park Rd.)
Strathmore Gdns. W8.........2C 72
Strathmore Rd. SW19.........3C 114
Strathnairn St. SE1.............5C 78
    ....(not continuous)
Strathray Gdns. NW3..........3A 46
Strath Ter. SW11................2A 102
Strathville Rd. SW18..........2C 114
    ....(not continuous)
Stratosphere Twr. E15........4F 53
    ....(off Gt. Eastern Rd.)
Stratton Ct. N1...................4A 50
    ....(off Hertford Rd.)
Strattondale St. E14............4E 81
Stratton St. W1......1E 21 (2D 75)
Strauss Rd. W4...................3A 76
Streakes Fld. Rd. NW2.........4C 28
Streamline Ct. SE22............1C 120
    ....(off Streamline M.)
Streamline M. SE22...........1C 120
STREATHAM.......................3A 118
Streatham Cl. SW16............2A 118
Streatham Comn. Nth.
    SW16...........................5A 118
Streatham Ct. SW16...........3A 118
Streatham Green...............4F 117
    ....(off Streatham High Road)
Streatham High Rd. SW16..4A 118
Streatham Hill SW2............2A 118
STREATHAM HILL...............2A 118
Streatham Hill Station (Rail)
    ....2A 118
Streatham Ice & Leisure Cen.
    SW16..........................5A 118
STREATHAM PK.................5E 117
Streatham Pl. SW2.............5A 104
Streatham Station (Rail)....5F 117
Streatham St. WC1...2D 15 (5A 62)
Streatley Pl. NW3...............1E 45
Streatley Rd. NW6..............4B 44
Street, The E20...................3E 53
    ....(within Westfield Shop. Cen.)
Streetfield M. SE3...............1C 110
Streimer Rd. E15................1F 67
Strelley Way W3.................1A 70
Stretton Mans. SE8............1C 94
Strickland Ct. SE15...........1C 106
Strickland Ho. E2.....2F 11 (2B 64)
    ....(off Chambord St.)
Strickland Row SW18.........5F 101
Strickland St. SE8..............5C 94
Stride Rd. E13....................1B 68
Stringer Ho. N1..................5A 50
    ....(off Whitmore Est.)
Strode Cl. E7......................1C 54
Strode Rd. NW10................3C 42
Strode Rd. SW6.................3A 86
Strome Ho. NW6................1D 59
    ....(off Carlton Vale)
Strone Rd. E12...................3F 55
Strone Rd. E7.....................3E 55

Stronsa Rd. W12..............3B 70
Strood Ho. SE1.......4C 26 (3F 77)
..................................(off Staple St.)
Stroud Cres. SW15............3C 112
STROUD GREEN..................2B 34
Stroud Grn. Rd. N4............3B 34
Stroudley Ho. SW8...............4E 89
Stroudley Wlk. E3................2D 67
Stroud Rd. SW19................3C 114
Strouts Pl. E2...........1F 11 (2B 64)
Strudwick Ct. SW4.............4A 90
...............................(off Binfield Rd.)
Strutton Ct. SW1.......5B 22 (4F 75)
...............................(off Gt. Peter St.)
Strutton Ground
   SW1....................5B 22 (4F 75)
Strype St. E1............1F 19 (4B 64)
Stuart Av. NW9...................2C 28
Stuart Ho. E16...................2D 83
............................(off Beaulieu Av.)
Stuart Ho. E9.......................3F 51
........................(off Queen Anne Rd.)
Stuart Ho. W14..................5A 72
.............................(off Windsor Way)
Stuart Mill Ho. N1.....1F 7 (1B 62)
...............................(off Killick St.)
Stuart Rd. NW6...................2C 58
Stuart Rd. SE15................2E 107
Stuart Rd. SW19................3C 114
Stuart Twr. W9...................2E 59
.............................(off Maida Vale)
Stubbs Dr. SE16................1D 93
Stubbs Ho. E2...................2F 65
..............................(off Bonner St.)
Stubbs Ho. N1....................5F 75
.............................(off Erasmus St.)
Stubbs Point E13................3C 68
Stucley Pl. NW1.................4D 47
Studdridge St. SW6.............5C 86
Studd St. N1.....................5D 49
Studholme Ct. NW3.............1C 44
Studholme St. SE15.............3D 93
Studio Pl. SW1........4A 20 (3B 74)
...........................(off Kinnerton St.)
Studios, The SW4...............2E 103
...........................(off Crescent La.)
Studios, The W8.................2C 72
..................................(off Edge St.)
Studland SE17....................1F 91
..............................(off Portland St.)
Studland Rd. SE26.............5F 121
Studland St. W6.................5D 71
Studley Cl. E5....................2A 52
Studley Ct. E14..................1F 81
........................(off Jamestown Way)
Studley Dr. IG4: Ilf..............1F 41
Studley Est. SW4...............4A 90
Studley Rd. E7...................2D 55
Studley Rd. SW4................4A 90
Stukeley Rd. E7.................4D 55
Stukeley St. WC2.......2E 15 (5A 62)
Stumps Hill La. BR3: Beck...5C 122
Stunell Ho. SE14................2F 93
..........................(off John Williams Cl.)
Sturdee Ho. E2...................2C 64
..............................(off Horatio St.)
Sturdy Ho. E3....................1A 66
..............................(off Gernon Rd.)
Sturdy Rd. SE15................5D 93
Sturgeon Rd. SE17..............1E 91
Sturgess Av. NW4...............2D 29
Sturge St. SE1.........3F 25 (3E 77)
Sturmer Way N7................2B 48
Sturminster NW1................1E 47
..................................(off Agar Gro.)
Sturminster Ho. SW8...........3B 90
..................................(off Dorset Rd.)
Sturry St. E14...................5D 67
Sturts Apts. N1...................5F 49
..................................(off Branch Pl.)
Sturt St. N1..............1A 10 (1E 63)
Stutfield St. E1..................1C 64
Stuttle Ho. E1....................5C 64
..................................(off Buxton St.)
Styles Gdns. SW9..............1D 105
Styles Ho. SE1........2D 25 (2D 77)
..................................(off Hatfields)
Stylus Ho. E1....................5E 65
..................................(off Cooper's St.)
Success Ho. SE1................1B 92
..................................(off Cooper's St.)
Succession Wlk. E3............4C 52
Sudbourne Rd. SW2............3A 104
Sudbrooke Rd. SW12...........4B 102
Sudbury Ct. SW8................4F 89
.........................(off Allen Edwards Dr.)
Sudbury Cres. BR1: Broml....5C 124
Sudbury Ho. SW18...............3D 101
Sudeley St. N1..........1E 9 (1D 63)
Sudlow Rd. SW18...............3C 100
Sudrey St. SE1.........4F 25 (3E 77)
Suffield Ho. SE17...............1D 91
...............................(off Berryfield Rd.)
Suffolk Ct. E10...................2C 38
Suffolk La. EC4........4B 18 (1F 77)
Suffolk Pl. SW1........1C 22 (2F 75)
Suffolk Rd. E13..................2C 68
Suffolk Rd. N15..................1F 35
Suffolk Rd. NW10...............4A 42
Suffolk Rd. SW13...............3B 84
Suffolk St. E7...................5C 54
Suffolk St. SW1.........5C 14 (1F 75)
Sugar Bakers Ct.
   EC3.....................3E 19 (5A 64)
..............................(off Creechurch La.)
Sugar Ho. E1....................5C 64
..................................(off Leman St.)
Sugar Ho. Island Development
   E15.............................1E 67
Sugar Ho. La. E15...............1E 67
Sugar La. SE16..................3C 78
Sugar Loaf Wlk. E2.............2E 65
Sugar Quay EC3.......5E 19 (1A 78)
..........................(off Sugar Quay Wlk.)
Sugar Quay Wlk.
   EC3.....................5E 19 (1A 78)
Sugden Rd. SW11...............1C 102
Sulby Ho. SE4...................2A 108
..............................(off Turnham Rd.)
Sulgrave Gdns. W6..............3E 71
Sulgrave Rd. W6.................4E 71
Sulina Rd. SW2.................5A 104
Sulivan Ct. SW6.................5C 86
Sulivan Ent. Cen. SW6........1D 101
Sulivan Rd. SW6................1C 100
Sulkin Ho. E2....................2F 65
...........................(off Knottisford St.)
Sullivan Av. E16.................4F 69
Sullivan Cl. SW11..............1A 102
Sullivan Ct. E3...................3B 66
..................................(off Eric St.)
Sullivan Ct. N16.................2B 36
Sullivan Ct. SW5................5C 72
...............................(off Earls Ct. Rd.)
Sullivan Ho. SE11...............5B 76
...............................(off Vauxhall St.)
Sullivan Ho. SW1................2D 89
..........................(off Churchill Gdns.)
Sullivan Rd. SE11...............5C 76
Sultan Ho. SE1...................1C 92
...........................(off St James's Rd.)
Sultan St. SE5....................3E 91
Sultan Rd. NW6.................2C 44
Sumburgh Rd. SW12...........4C 102
Sumeria Ct. SE16...............5E 79
..........................(off Rotherhithe New Rd.)
Summerbee Ho. SW18.........2E 101
.............................(off Eltringham St.)
Summercourt Rd. E1............5E 65
Summerfield Av. NW6...........1A 58
Summerfield St. SE12.........5B 110
Summerhouse Rd. N16........4A 36
Summerley St. SW18..........2D 115
Summersby Rd. N6..............1D 33
Summerskill Cl. SE15...........1D 107
Summers St. EC1.......4B 8 (3C 62)
SUMMERSTOWN...................3E 115
Summerton Ho. E16..............3E 83
..............................(off Starboard Way)
Summit Ct. NW2.................2A 44
Summit Est. N16.................2C 36
Summit Av. SE15.................4B 92
Sumner Bldgs. SE1...1F 25 (2E 77)
..............................(off Sumner St.)
Sumner Ct. SW8..................3A 90
Sumner Est. SE15...............3B 92
Sumner Ho. E3...................4D 67
..................................(off Watts Gro.)
Sumner Pl. M. SW7..............5F 73
Sumner Pl. SW7..................5F 73
Sumner Rd. SE15................2B 92
Sumner St. SE15................2B 92
Sumner St. SE1........1E 25 (2D 77)
Sumpter Cl. NW3.................3E 45
Sunbeam Cres. W10.............3E 57
Sunbury Av. SW14...............2A 98
Sunbury Av. Pas. SW14........2A 98
Sunbury Ho. E2........2F 11 (2B 64)
...........................(off Swanfield St.)
Sunbury Ho. SE14................2F 93
..................................(off Myers La.)
Sunbury La. SW11...............4F 87
.................................(not continuous)
Sunbury Workshops
   E2......................2F 11 (2B 64)
...........................(off Swanfield St.)
Sun Ct. E3.........................3E 67
................................(off Navigation St.)
Sun Ct. EC3..............3C 18 (5F 63)
..................................(off Cornhill)
Suncroft Pl. SE26................3E 121
Sunderland Ct. SE22............5C 106
Sunderland Ho. W2..............4C 58
........................(off Westbourne Pk. Rd.)
Sunderland Mt. SE23.......2F 121
Sunderland Rd. SE23.........1F 121
Sunderland Ter. W2............5D 59
Sunderland Way E12...........4F 41
Sundew Av. W12.................1C 70
Sundew Cl. W12.................1C 70
Sundial Ct. EC1.......5A 10 (4E 63)
................................(off Chiswell St.)
Sundorne Rd. SE7...............1E 97
Sundra Wlk. E1...................3F 65
Sundridge Ho. E9................4F 51
..............................(off Church Cres.)
Sunfields Pl. SE3................3D 97
Sunflower Ct. NW2..............4B 30
Sunguard Ct. SE1....1D 25 (2D 77)
SUN-IN-THE-SANDS...............3D 97
Sun La. SE3........................3D 97
Sunlight Cl. SW19...............5E 115
Sunlight M. SW6.................5D 87
Sunlight Sq. E2...................2D 65
Sunningdale Av. W3.............1A 70
Sunningdale Cl. SE16...........1D 93

Sunningdale Gdns. W8 . . . . .4C **72**
    (off Stratford Rd.)
Sunninghill Rd. SE13 . . . . . .5D **95**
Sunnydale Rd. SE12 . . . . . . .3D **111**
Sunnydene St. SE26 . . . . . . .4A **122**
Sunnyhill Cl. E5. . . . . .1A **52**
Sunnyhill Rd. SW16 . . . . . . .4A **118**
Sunnymead Rd. SW15 . . . . . .3D **99**
Sunny M. NW1 . . . . .4C **46**
Sunnyside NW2. . . . . .5B **30**
Sunnyside SE6 . . . . .5B **108**
    (off Blythe Hill)
Sunnyside SW19. . . . . .5A **114**
Sunnyside Ho's. SW2 . . . . . .5B **30**
    (off Sunnyside)
Sunnyside Pl. SW19. . . . . . . .5A **114**
Sunnyside Rd. E10. . . . . .3C **38**
Sunnyside Rd. N19 . . . . .2F **33**
Sun Pas. SE16. . . . . .4C **78**
    (off Old Jamaica Rd.)
Sunray Av. SE24 . . . . .2F **105**
Sunrise Cl. E20 . . . . .2E **53**
Sun Rd. W14 . . . . .1B **86**
Sunset Lodge NW10 . . . . . . .4E **43**
    (off Hanover Rd.)
Sunset Rd. SE5 . . . . .2E **105**
Sunset Rd. SW19 . . . . .5D **113**
Sun St. EC2: Lon Finsbury Sq.
    . . . . .5C **10** (4F **63**)
Sun St. EC2: Lon Primrose St.
    . . . . .5D **11** (4A **64**)
Sun St. Pas. EC2 .1D **19** (4A **64**)
Sun Wlk. E1 . . . . .1B **78**
Sunwell Cl. SE15. . . . . .4D **93**
Sun Wharf SE8 . . . . .3D **95**
    (off Creekside)
Supreme Court 4D **23** (3A **76**)
Supreme Point E16. . . . . . . .4C **68**
    (off Butchers Rd.)
Surma Cl. E1 . . . . .3D **65**
Surrendale Pl. W9. . . . . .3C **58**
Surrey Canal Rd. SE14. . . . . .2F **93**
Surrey Canal Trade Pk.
    SE14. . . . . .2F **93**
Surrey County Cricket Club .2B **90**
Surrey Docks Farm. 3B **80**
Surrey Docks Watersports Cen.
    .4A **80**
Surrey Gdns. N4. . . . . .1E **35**
Surrey Gro. SE17. . . . . .1A **92**
Surrey Ho. SE16 . . . . .2F **79**
    (off Rotherhithe St.)
Surrey La. SW11 . . . . .4A **88**
Surrey La. Est. SW11 . . . . . .4A **88**
Surrey M. SE27 . . . . .4A **120**
Surrey Mt. SE23 . . . . .1D **121**
Surrey Quays Rd. SE16 . . . . .4E **79**
Surrey Quays Station
    (Overground). 5F **79**
Surrey Rd. SE15 . . . . .3F **107**
Surrey Row SE1 . . . .3D **25** (3D **77**)
Surrey Sq. SE17 . . . . .1A **92**
Surrey Steps WC2. . .4A **16** (1B **76**)
    (off Surrey St.)
Surrey St. E13. . . . . .2D **69**
Surrey St. WC2. . . . .4A **16** (1B **76**)
Surrey Ter. SE17 . . . . .1A **92**
Surrey Water Rd. SE16 . . . . .2F **79**
Surridge Ct. SW9 . . . . .5A **90**
    (off Clapham Rd.)
Surr St. N7 . . . . .2A **48**
Susan Constant Ct. E14. . . . .1F **81**
    (off Newport Av.)
Susan Lawrence Ho. E3. . . . .1A **66**
    (off Zealand Rd.)

Susannah St. E14 . . . . .5D **67**
Susan Rd. SE3. . . . . .5D **97**
Sussex Cl. N19 . . . . .4A **34**
Sussex Ct. SE10 . . . . .2E **95**
    (off Roan St.)
Sussex Ct. W2 . . . . .5F **59**
    (off Spring St.)
Sussex Gdns. N4. . . . . .1E **35**
Sussex Gdns. N6. . . . . .1B **32**
Sussex Gdns. W2 . . . . .1F **73**
Sussex Ga. N6. . . . . .1B **32**
Sussex Ho. NW1 . . . . .1F **61**
    (off Chalton St.)
Sussex Lodge W2 . . . . .5F **59**
    (off Sussex Pl.)
Sussex Mans. W2. . . . . .5F **73**
    (off Old Brompton Rd.)
Sussex Mans.
    WC2. . . . . .4E **15** (1A **76**)
    (off Maiden La.)
Sussex M. SE6 . . . . .5C **108**
Sussex M. E. W2. . . . . .5F **59**
    (off Clifton Pl.)
Sussex M. W. W2 . . . . .1F **73**
Sussex Pl. NW1 . . . . .3A **4** (3B **60**)
Sussex Pl. W2 . . . . .5F **59**
Sussex Pl. W6 . . . . .1E **85**
Sussex Sq. W2 . . . . .1F **73**
Sussex St. E13 . . . . .2D **69**
Sussex St. SW1 . . . . .1D **89**
Sussex Way N19. . . . . .3F **33**
    (not continuous)
Sussex Way N7 . . . . .4A **34**
Sutcliffe Cl. NW11. . . . . .1D **31**
Sutcliffe Pk. Athletics Track
    .3E **111**
Sutherland Av. W9 . . . . .3C **58**
Sutherland Ct. N16 . . . . .5F **35**
Sutherland Ct. W9. . . . . .3C **58**
    (off Marylands Rd.)
Sutherland Gdns. SW14. . . . .1A **98**
Sutherland Gro. SW18 . . . . .4A **100**
Sutherland Ho. W8. . . . . . . .4D **73**
Sutherland Pl. W2 . . . . .5C **58**
Sutherland Rd. E3. . . . . .1B **66**
Sutherland Rd. W4. . . . . .2A **84**
Sutherland Row W1 . . . . .1D **89**
Sutherland Sq. SE17 . . . . . . .1E **91**
Sutherland St. SW1 . . . . .1D **89**
Sutherland Wlk. SE17. . . . . .1E **91**
Sutlej Rd. SE7 . . . . .3B **48**
Sutterton St. N7 . . . . .3B **48**
Sutton Ct. Rd. SE13 . . . . . . .2E **69**
Sutton Est. EC1 . . . .2C **10** (2F **63**)
    (off Old St.)
Sutton Est. SW3 . . . . .1A **88**
Sutton Est. W10. . . . . .4E **57**
Sutton Est., the N1 . . . . .4D **49**
Sutton La. EC1 . . . . .4E **9** (3D **63**)
    (off G. Sutton St.)
Sutton Pl. E9. . . . . .2E **51**
Sutton Rd. E13 . . . . .3B **68**
Sutton Row W1. . . . .2B **14** (5F **61**)
Sutton Sq. E9 . . . . .2E **51**
Sutton St. E1 . . . . .1E **79**
Sutton's Way EC1 . . .4A **10** (3E **63**)
    (off Lambs Pas.)
Suttons Wharf E2 . . . . .2F **65**
Sutton Wlk. SE1 . . . .2A **24** (2B **76**)
Sutton Way W10 . . . . .4F **57**
Swaby Rd. SW18 . . . . .1E **115**
Swaffield Rd. SW18. . . . . . . .5D **101**
Swain's La. N6. . . . . .3C **32**
Swainson Rd. W3. . . . . .3B **70**
Swain St. NW8 . . . . .3A **60**

Swallands Rd. SE6. . . . . .3C **122**
    (not continuous)
Swallow Cl. SE14. . . . . .4F **93**
Swallow Ct. SE1 . . . .4A **26** (3E **77**)
    (off Swan St.)
Swallow Ct. SE12 . . . . .5C **110**
Swallow Ct. W9. . . . . .4C **58**
    (off Admiral Wlk.)
Swallow Dr. NW10 . . . . .3A **42**
Swallowfield NW1. . . .2E **5** (2D **61**)
    (off Munster Sq.)
Swallowfield Rd. SE7 . . . . . .1D **97**
Swallow Gdns. SW16. . . . . . .5F **117**
Swallow Ho. NW8 . . . . .1A **60**
    (off Allitsen Rd.)
Swallow Pas. W1 . .3E **13** (5D **61**)
    (off Swallow Pl.)
Swallow Pl. E14. . . . . .5B **66**
    (off Newell St.)
Swallow Pl. W1 . . . .3E **13** (5D **61**)
Swallow St. W1 . . . .5A **14** (1E **75**)
Swallowtail Ho. E20. . . . . . . .2E **53**
    (off Sunrise Cl.)
Swanage Ct. N1 . . . . .4A **50**
    (off Hertford Rd.)
Swanage Ho. SW8. . . . . .3B **90**
    (off Dorset Rd.)
Swanage Rd. SW18 . . . . .4E **101**
Swan App. E6. . . . . .4F **69**
Swanbourne Ho. NW8. . . . . . .3A **60**
    (off Capland St.)
Swan Cen., The SW17. . . . . .3D **115**
Swan Ct. E1 . . . . .1C **78**
    (off Star Pl.)
Swan Ct. E14. . . . . .5B **66**
    (off Agnes St.)
Swan Ct. SW3 . . . . .1A **88**
Swan Ct. SW6 . . . . .3C **86**
    (off Fulham Rd.)
Swandon Way SW18. . . . . . . .2D **101**
Swanfield St. E2 . . . .2F **11** (2B **64**)
Swan Ho. E15. . . . . .4A **54**
    (off Broadway)
Swan Ho. N1 . . . . .4F **49**
    (off Oakley Rd.)
Swan La. EC4. . . . . .5B **18** (1F **77**)
Swan La. N4. . . . . .3E **35**
Swanley Ho. SE17 . . . . .1A **92**
    (off Kinglake Est.)
Swan Mead SE1. . . .5D **27** (4A **78**)
Swan M. SW6 . . . . .4B **86**
Swan M. SW9. . . . . .5B **90**
Swanne Ho. SE10 . . . . .3E **95**
    (off Gloucester Cir.)
Swannell Way NW2. . . . . .3F **29**
Swan Pas. E1 . . . . .1B **78**
    (off Cartwright St.)
Swan Pl. SW13. . . . . .5B **84**
Swan Rd. SE16. . . . . .3E **79**
Swan Rd. SE18. . . . . .4F **83**
Swanscombe Ho. W11. . . . . .2F **71**
    (off St Ann's Rd.)
Swanscombe Rd. W11. . . . . .2F **71**
Swanscombe Rd. W4. . . . . . .1A **84**
Swan St. SE1. . . . . .5A **26** (4E **77**)
Swanton Ct. SE13 . . . . .1D **109**
Swanton Gdns. SW19 . . . . . .1F **113**
Swan Wlk. SW3. . . . . .2B **88**
Swanwick Cl. SW15. . . . . . . .5B **98**
Swan Yd. N1 . . . . .3D **49**
Swathling Ho. SW15 . . . . . . .4B **98**
    (off Tunworth Cres.)
Swaton Rd. E3 . . . . .3C **66**
Swedeland Ct. E1 . . .1E **19** (4A **64**)
    (off Bishopsgate)

Swedenborg Gdns. E1 .... 1D **79**
Sweden Ga. SE16. .... 4A **80**
Swedish Quays SE16. .... 4A **80**
.... (not continuous)
Sweeney Cres. SE1 ... 4F **27** (3B **78**)
Sweetwater E20. .... 4C **52**
Swell Ct. E17. .... 1C **38**
Swete St. E13. .... 1C **68**
Sweyn Pl. SE3. .... 5C **96**
Swift Ho. E3 .... 5B **52**
.... (off Old Ford Rd.)
Swift Ho. NW6 .... 1B **58**
.... (off Albert Rd.)
Swift La. SE13. .... 2A **110**
Swift Lodge W9. .... 4C **58**
.... (off Admiral Wlk.)
Swiftsden Way BR1: Broml 5A **124**
Swiftstone Ter. SE10 .... 4C **82**
Swift St. SW6. .... 4B **86**
Swimmers La. E2 .... 5B **50**
Swinbrook Rd. W10 .... 4A **58**
Swinburne Ct. SE5 .... 2F **105**
.... (off Basingdon Way)
Swinburne Ho. E2 .... 2E **65**
.... (off Roman Rd.)
Swinburne Rd. SW15 .... 2C **98**
Swindon St. W12 .... 2D **71**
Swinford Gdns. SW9 .... 1D **105**
Swingfield Ho. E9 .... 5E **51**
.... (off Templecombe Rd.)
Swinley Ho. NW1 .... 1E **5** (2D **61**)
.... (off Redhill St.)
Swinnerton St. E9 .... 2A **52**
Swinton Pl. WC1 .... 1F **7** (2B **62**)
Swinton St. WC1 .... 1F **7** (2B **62**)
SWISS COTTAGE 4F **45**
Swiss Cottage Sports Cen. ... 4F **45**
Swiss Cottage Station
(Underground). 4F **45**
Swiss Ct. W1 .... 5C **14** (1F **75**)
.... (off Panton St.)
Swiss Ter. NW6. .... 4F **45**
Switch Ho. E14. .... 1F **81**
Sybil M. N4. .... 1D **35**
Sybil Phoenix Cl. SE8. .... 1F **93**
Sybil Thorndike Casson Ho.
SW5. .... 1C **86**
.... (off Kramer M.)
Sybourn St. E17. .... 2B **38**
Sycamore Av. E3. .... 5B **52**
Sycamore Cl. E16. .... 3A **68**
Sycamore Cl. W3. .... 2A **70**
Sycamore Ct. E7 .... 3C **54**
Sycamore Ct. NW6 .... 5C **44**
.... (off Bransdale Cl.)
Sycamore Ct. SE1 .... 4D **27** (3A **78**)
.... (off Royal Oak Yd.)
Sycamore Gdns. W6 .... 3D **71**
Sycamore Gro. SE6 .... 4E **109**
Sycamore Ho. SE16 .... 3F **79**
.... (off Woodland Cres.)
Sycamore Ho. W6 .... 3D **71**
Sycamore Lodge W8 .... 4D **73**
.... (off Stone Hall Pl.)
Sycamore M. SW4 .... 1E **103**
Sycamore Path E17 .... 1D **39**
.... (off Poplars Rd.)
Sycamore Rd. SW19 .... 5E **113**
Sycamore St. EC1 ...... 4F **9** (3E **63**)
Sycamore Wlk. W10 .... 3A **58**
Sydcote SE21 .... 1C **119**
SYDENHAM. 4E **121**
Sydenham Av. SE26 .... 5D **121**
Sydenham Cotts. SE12 .... 2E **125**
Sydenham Hill SE23 .... 1D **121**

Sydenham Hill SE26 .... 4B **120**
Sydenham Hill Station (Rail)
.... 3B **120**
Sydenham Hill Wood & Cox's
Walk Nature Reserve..... 2C **120**
Sydenham Pk. SE26. .... 3E **121**
Sydenham Pk. Mans. SE26 3E **121**
.... (off Sydenham Pk.)
Sydenham Pl. SE27. .... 3D **119**
Sydenham Ri. SE23 .... 2D **121**
Sydenham Rd. SE26 .... 5F **121**
Sydenham Sta. App. SE26:
Lon Sydenham. 4E **121**
*Sydenham Station (Rail &
Overground).* 4E **121**
Sydmons Cl. SE23 .... 5E **107**
Sydner M. N16 .... 1B **50**
Sydner Rd. N16 .... 1B **50**
Sydney Cl. SW3. .... 5F **73**
Sydney Gro. NW4. .... 1E **29**
Sydney M. SW3. .... 5F **73**
Sydney Pl. SW7. .... 5F **73**
Sydney Rd. E11. .... 1B **40**
Sydney St. SW3. .... 1A **88**
Sylva Cotts. SE8. .... 4C **94**
Sylvan Ct. NW6. .... 5D **45**
.... (off Abbey Rd.)
Sylvan Gro. NW2. .... 1F **43**
Sylvan Gro. SE15. .... 2D **93**
Sylvan Rd. E7. .... 3D **55**
Sylvan Rd. SE19. .... 5A **120**
Sylvan Ter. SE15. .... 2D **93**
.... (off Sylvan Gro.)
Sylvester Path E8. .... 3D **51**
Sylvester Rd. E17. .... 2B **38**
Sylvester Rd. E8. .... 3D **51**
.... (off Wenlock St.)
Sylvia Ct. N1. .... 1F **63**
Sylvia Pankhurst St. E16..... 5B **68**
Symes M. NW1 .... 1E **61**
Symington Ho. SE1 .. 5B **26** (4F **77**)
.... (off Deverell St.)
Symington M. E9. .... 2F **51**
Symister M. N1 ...... 2D **11** (2A **64**)
.... (off Coronet St.)
Symons Cl. SE15. .... 5E **93**
Symons St. SW3. .... 5B **74**
Symphony M. W10 .... 2A **58**
Syon Ct. E11. .... 1D **41**
Syon Lodge SE12 .... 5C **110**
Syringa Ho. SE4 .... 1B **108**

T

Tabard Ct. E14 .... 5E **67**
.... (off Lodore St.)
Tabard Gdn. Est.
SE1. .... 4B **26** (4F **77**)
Tabard Ho. SE1 .... 5C **26** (4F **77**)
.... (off Manciple St.)
Tabard St. SE1 .... 3A **26** (3F **77**)
Tabard Theatre 5A **70**
Tabernacle, The 5B **58**
.... (off Powis Sq.)
Tabernacle Av. E13. .... 3C **68**
Tabernacle Gdns. E2 2F **11** (2B **64**)
.... (off Hackney Rd.)
Tabernacle St. EC2... 4C **10** (3F **63**)
Tableer Av. SW4. .... 3E **103**
Tabley Rd. N7 .... 1A **48**
Tabor Rd. W6 .... 4D **71**
TA Cen. 3F **45**
.... (off College Cres.)
TA Cen. 1A **100**
.... (off Ranelagh Gdns.)

Tachbrook Est. SW1 .... 1F **89**
Tachbrook M. SW1 .... 5E **75**
Tachbrook St. SW1 .... 5E **75**
Tack M. SE4 .... 1C **108**
Tadema Ho. NW8 .... 3F **59**
.... (off Penfold St.)
Tadema Rd. SW10 .... 3E **87**
Tadmor St. W12 .... 2F **71**
Tadworth Ho. SE1 .... 4D **25** (3D **77**)
.... (off Webber St.)
Tadworth Rd. NW2. .... 4C **28**
Taeping St. E14. .... 5D **81**
Taffeta Ho. E20 .... 3E **53**
.... (off De Coubertin St.)
Taffrail Ho. E14 .... 1D **95**
.... (off Burrells Wharf Sq.)
Taft Way E3 .... 2D **67**
Tagwright Ho. N1...... 1B **10** (2F **63**)
.... (off Westland Pl.)
Tailor Ho. WC1 .... 4D **7** (3A **62**)
.... (off Colonnade)
Tailworth St. E1 .... 4C **64**
.... (off Chicksand St.)
Tait Ct. E3. .... 5B **52**
.... (off St Stephen's Rd.)
Tait Ct. SW8 .... 4A **90**
.... (off Lansdowne Grn.)
Tait Ho. SE1 .... 2C **24** (2C **76**)
.... (off Greet St.)
Tait Ho. E1 .... 5D **65**
.... (off Brick La.)
Taj Apts. E1 .... 4B **64**
.... (off Brick La.)
Takhar M. SW11 .... 5A **88**
Talacre Community Sports Cen.
.... 3C **46**
.... 3C **46**
Talbot Ct. EC3 .... 4C **18** (1F **77**)
.... (off Gracechurch St.)
Talbot Cres. NW4 .... 1C **28**
Talbot Gro. Ho. W11. .... 5A **58**
.... (off Lancaster Rd.)
Talbot Ho. E14. .... 5D **67**
.... (off Giraud St.)
Talbot Ho. N7 .... 5C **34**
Talbot Ho. SW11 .... 1F **101**
.... (off York Place)
Talbot Pl. SE3. .... 5A **96**
Talbot Rd. E7. .... 1C **54**
Talbot Rd. N6. .... 1C **32**
Talbot Rd. SE22 .... 2A **106**
Talbot Rd. W11 .... 5B **58**
.... (not continuous)
Talbot Rd. W2 .... 5C **58**
Talbot Sq. W2 .... 5F **59**
Talbot Wlk.
NW10: Lon Church End 3A **42**
Talbot Wlk.
W11: Lon Notting Hill 5A **58**
.... (off St Mark's Rd.)
Talbot Yd. SE1........... 2B **26** (2F **77**)
Talcott Path SW2 .... 1C **118**
Talfourd Pl. SE15. .... 4B **92**
Talfourd Rd. SE15. .... 4B **92**
Talgarth Mans. W14 .... 1A **86**
.... (off Talgarth Rd.)
Talgarth Rd. W14. .... 1F **85**
Talgarth Rd. W6. .... 1F **85**
Talgarth Wlk. NW9. .... 1A **28**
Talia Ho. E14. .... 4E **81**
.... (off Manchester Rd.)
Talina Cen. SW6. .... 4E **87**
Talisman Sq. SE26 .... 4C **120**
Tallack Rd. E10. .... 3B **38**
Talleyrand Ho. SE5 .... 5E **91**
.... (off Lilford Rd.)

Tallis Cl. E16 ....5D **69**
Tallis Gro. SE7.....................2D **97**
Tallis St. EC4............4C **16** (1C **76**)
Tallis Vw. NW10...................3A **42**
Talmage Cl. SE23.................5E **107**
Talma Rd. SW2....................2C **104**
Talwin St. E3........................2D **67**
Tamar Cl. E3.........................5B **52**
Tamar Ho. E14......................3E **81**
..............................*(off Plevna St.)*
Tamar Ho. SE11....................1C **90**
..........................*(off Kennington La.)*
Tamarind Cl. SE1....3F **27** (3B **78**)
.............................*(off Gainsford St.)*
Tamarind Ct. W8...................4D **73**
.........................*(off Stone Hall Gdns.)*
Tamarind Ho. SE15................3C **92**
.............................*(off Reddins Rd.)*
Tamarind Yd. E1....................2C **78**
.................................*(off Kennet St.)*
Tamarisk Sq. W12................1B **70**
Tamar St. SE7......................4F **83**
Tamworth St. SW6................2C **86**
Tancred Rd. N4....................1D **33**
Tanfield Av. NW2.................1B **42**
Tangerine Ho. SE1....4C **26** (3F **77**)
..................................*(off Long La.)*
Tangley Gro. SW15...............4B **98**
Tangmere WC1........2F **7** (2B **62**)
.............................*(off Sidmouth St.)*
Tan Ho. E9...........................2A **52**
..................................*(off Sadler Pl.)*
Tanhouse Fld. NW5...............2F **47**
.............................*(off Torriano Av.)*
Tanhurst Ho. SW2.................5B **104**
..........................*(off Redlands Way)*
Tankerton Ho's. WC1.2E **7** (2A **62**)
.............................*(off Tankerton St.)*
Tankerton St. WC1...2E **7** (2A **62**)
Tankridge Rd. NW2...............4D **29**
Tanner Ho. E1.......................4F **65**
.........................*(off White Horse La.)*
Tanner Ho. SE1.......4E **27** (3A **78**)
.................................*(off Tanner St.)*
Tanneries, The E1.................3E **65**
.................................*(off Cephas Av.)*
Tanner Point E13...................5C **54**
..................................*(off Pelly Rd.)*
Tanner's Hill SE8..................4B **94**
Tanners M. SE8....................4B **94**
.............................*(off Tanner's Hill)*
Tanner St. SE1........4E **27** (3A **78**)
Tanners Yd. E2.....................1D **65**
.............................*(off Treadway St.)*
Tannery, The
   SE1: Lon Grange Rd............4A **78**
Tannery, The SE1: Lon Whites
   Grounds..............3E **27** (3A **78**)
.........................*(off Black Swan Yd.)*
Tannery Ho. E1.....................4C **64**
..................................*(off Deal St.)*
Tannery Sq. SE1...................4A **78**
.............................*(off Tannery Way)*
Tannery Way SE1..................4B **78**
Tannington Ter. N5................5D **35**
Tannoy Sq. SE27..................4F **119**
Tannsfeld Rd. SE26...............5F **121**
Tansley Cl. N7......................2F **47**
Tanswell St. SE1.....4B **24** (3C **76**)
Tantallon Rd. SW12...............1C **116**
Tant Av. E16........................5B **68**
Tanza Rd. NW3.....................1B **46**
Tapestry Apts. N1.................5E **47**
Tapestry Bldg. EC2..1E **19** (4A **64**)
.................................*(off New St.)*

Tapley Cl. E14.....................5E **67**
Tapley Ho. SE1.....................3C **78**
.............................*(off Wolseley St.)*
Taplow NW3.........................4F **45**
Taplow SE17.........................1F **91**
..............................*(off Thurlow St.)*
Taplow Ho. E2..........2F **11** (2B **64**)
.................................*(off Palissy St.)*
Taplow St. N1..........1A **10** (1E **63**)
Tapper Wlk. N1.....................5A **48**
Tappesfield Rd. SE15............1E **107**
Tapp St. E1..........................3D **65**
Tara Arts Cen.......................1D **115**
Tara Ho. E14........................5C **80**
.........................*(off Deptford Ferry Rd.)*
Tara M. N8...........................1A **34**
Taransay Wlk. N1..................3F **49**
Tarbert Rd. SE22.................3A **106**
Tarbert Wlk. E1....................1E **79**
Tarbuck Ho. SE10..................5A **82**
.............................*(off Manilla Wlk.)*
Tariff Cres. SE8....................5B **80**
Tarleton Gdns. SE23.............2D **121**
Tarling Rd. E16....................5B **68**
Tarling St. E1.......................5D **65**
Tarling St. Est. E1.................5E **65**
Tarnbrook Ct. SW1................5C **74**
..................................*(off Holbein Pl.)*
Tarns, The NW1.......1F **5** (2E **61**)
.............................*(off Varndell St.)*
Tarn St. SE1...........5F **25** (4E **77**)
Tarplett Ho. SE14.................2F **93**
.........................*(off John Williams Cl.)*
Tarquin Ho. SE26.................4C **120**
.............................*(off High Level Dr.)*
Tarragon Cl. SE14...............3A **94**
Tarragon Gro. SE26.............5F **121**
Tarrant Ho. E2.....................2E **65**
..................................*(off Roman Rd.)*
Tarrant Ho. W14...................4A **72**
..................................*(off Russell Rd.)*
Tarrant Pl. W1.....................4B **60**
Tarrington Cl. SW16.............3F **117**
Tartan Ho. E14.....................5E **67**
..................................*(off Dee St.)*
Tarver Rd. SE17...................1D **91**
Tarves Way SE10: Lon Lit.
   Cottage Pl........................3D **95**
Tarves Way SE10: Lon
   Norman Rd.......................3D **95**
Tasker Ho. E14....................4B **66**
.............................*(off Wallwood St.)*
Tasker Lodge W8.................3C **72**
.............................*(off Campden Hill)*
Tasker Rd. NW3...................2B **46**
Tasman Ct. E14....................5D **81**
.............................*(off Westferry Rd.)*
Tasman Ho. E1.....................2D **79**
..................................*(off Clegg St.)*
Tasman Rd. SW9.................1A **104**
Tasman Wlk. E16.................5F **69**
Tasso Rd. W6......................2A **86**
Tasso Yd. W6.......................2A **86**
..................................*(off Tasso Rd.)*
Tatchbury Ho. SW15.............4B **98**
.........................*(off Tunworth Cres.)*
Tate Apts. E1.......................5D **65**
..................................*(off Sly St.)*
Tate Britain.........................5A **76**
Tate Ho. E2..........................1F **65**
..................................*(off Mace St.)*
Tate Modern.............1E **25** (2D **77**)
Tatham Pl. NW8....................1F **59**
Tatnell Rd. SE23..................4A **108**

Tatsfield Ho. SE1.....5C **26** (4F **77**)
.............................*(off Pardoner St.)*
Tatton Cres. N16...................2B **36**
Tatum St. SE17.....................5F **77**
Tauheed Cl. N4.....................4E **35**
Taunton Ho. W2....................5E **59**
.............................*(off Hallfield Est.)*
Taunton M. NW1....................3B **60**
Taunton Pl. NW1...................3B **60**
Taunton Rd. SE12................3A **110**
Tavern Ct. SE1.....................4E **77**
.............................*(off New Kent Rd.)*
Taverners Cl. W11................2A **72**
Taverners Ct. E3..................2A **66**
..................................*(off Grove Rd.)*
Taverner Sq. N5....................1E **49**
Tavern La. SW9....................5C **90**
Tavern Quay SE16.................5A **80**
Tavistock Cl. N16..................2A **50**
Tavistock Cl. WC1.....3C **6** (3F **61**)
.............................*(off Tavistock Sq.)*
Tavistock Ct. WC2.....4E **15** (1A **76**)
.............................*(off Tavistock Street)*
Tavistock Cres. W11.............4B **58**
............................*(not continuous)*
Tavistock Ho. WC1...3C **6** (3F **61**)
.............................*(off Tavistock Sq.)*
Tavistock M. N19..................5A **34**
.............................*(off Tavistock Ter.)*
Tavistock M. W11..................5B **58**
Tavistock Pl. WC1...3D **7** (3A **62**)
Tavistock Rd. E15.................3B **54**
Tavistock Rd. E7...................1B **54**
Tavistock Rd. N4...................1F **35**
Tavistock Rd. NW10..............1B **56**
Tavistock Rd. W11.................5B **58**
............................*(not continuous)*
Tavistock Sq. WC1....3C **6** (3F **61**)
Tavistock St. WC2....4E **15** (1A **76**)
Tavistock Ter. N19................5F **33**
Tavistock Twr. SE16..............4A **80**
Tavistock Youth Cen............1B **56**
.............................*(off Tavistock Rd.)*
Taviton St. WC1........3B **6** (3F **61**)
Tavy Cl. SE11.......................1C **90**
.............................*(off White Hart St.)*
Tawny Way SE16...................5F **79**
Tayberry Ho. E20..................3D **53**
.............................*(off Ravens Wlk.)*
Taybridge Rd. SW11..............1C **102**
Tay Bldgs. SE1.........5D **27** (4A **78**)
.............................*(off Decima St.)*
Tayburn Cl. E14....................5E **67**
Tay Ct. E2.............................2F **65**
..................................*(off Meath Cres.)*
Tay Ct. SE1..............5D **27** (4A **78**)
.............................*(off Decima St.)*
Tay Ho. E3............................1B **66**
.............................*(off St Stephen's Rd.)*
Tayler Ct. NW8......................5F **45**
Taylor Cl. SE8.......................2B **94**
Taylor Ho. E14......................1C **80**
.............................*(off Storehouse M.)*
Taylor Pl. E3.........................1D **67**
Taylor's La. SE26.................4D **121**
Taylors La. NW10..................3A **42**
Taylors Yd. E1......................3B **64**
..................................*(off Brick La.)*
Taymount Grange SE23.........2E **121**
Taymount Ri. SE23...............2E **121**
Tayport Cl. N1......................4A **48**
Tayside Ct. SE5....................2F **105**
Tazzeta Ho. E20...................2E **53**
..................................*(off Victory Pde.)*
Teak Cl. SE16......................2A **80**

Tealby Ct. N7.....................3B 48
Teal Cl. E16........................4F 69
Teal Ct. E1.........................1C 78
........................(off Star Pl.)
Teale St. E2........................1C 64
Teal St. SE10......................4B 82
TeamSport Indoor Karting
Southwark.........................4D 79
Teasel Way E15..................2A 68
Tea Trade Wharf SE1..........3B 78
........................(off Shad Thames)
Ted Roberts Ho. E2............1D 65
........................(off Parmiter St.)
Tedworth Gdns. SW3..........1B 88
Tedworth Sq. SW3..............1B 88
Tee, The W3........................5A 56
Teesdale Cl. E2...................1C 64
Teesdale Rd. E11................1B 40
Teesdale St. E2...................1D 65
Teesdale Yd. E2..................1D 65
........................(off Teesdale St.)
Teign M. SE9......................2F 125
Teignmouth Cl. SW4...........2F 103
Teignmouth Rd. NW2..........2F 43
Telcon Way SE10................5A 82
Telegraph Av. SE10.............5A 82
Telegraph Hill NW3.............5D 31
Telegraph Pas. SW2............5A 104
........................(off New Pk. Rd.)
Telegraph Pl. E14...............5D 81
Telegraph St. SW15............5D 99
Telegraph St.
EC2..........................2B 18 (5F 63)
Telemann Sq. SE3...............2D 111
Telephone Pl. SW6..............2B 86
Telfer Ho. EC1..................2E 9 (2E 63)
........................(off Lever St.)
Telferscot Rd. SW12............1F 117
Telford Av. SW2..................1F 117
Telford Cl. E17...................2A 38
Telford Ho. SE1..............5F 25 (4E 77)
........................(off Tiverton St.)
Telford Rd. W10.................4A 58
Telfords Yd. E1...................1C 78
Telford Ter. SW1................2E 89
Telford Way W3..................4A 56
Tell Eco. SE22...................2B 106
Tellson Av. SE18................4F 97
Temair Ho. SE10................3D 95
........................(off Tarves Way)
Temeraire St. SE16.............3E 79
Tempelhof Av. NW4.............2E 29
Temperley Rd. SW12...........5C 102
Templar Ct. NW8.................2F 59
........................(off St John's Wood Rd.)
Templar Ho. SE15...............3F 53
........................(off Leyton Rd.)
Templar Ho. NW2................3B 44
Templars Av. NW11.............1B 30
Templar St. SE5..................5D 91
Temple Av. EC4..............4C 16 (1C 76)
Temple Bar..................3B 16 (5C 62)
Temple Bar Gate..........3E 17 (5D 63)
........................(off Paternoster Sq.)
Temple Chambers
EC4..........................4C 16 (1C 76)
........................(off Temple Av.)
Temple Cl. E11...................2A 40
Templecombe Rd. E9...........5E 51
Temple Ct. E1.....................4F 65
........................(off Rectory Sq.)
Temple Ct. SW8..................3A 90
........................(off Thorncroft St.)

Temple Dwellings E2...........1D 65
........................(off Temple St.)
Temple Fortune Hill NW11...1C 30
Temple Fortune La. NW11....1B 30
Temple Fortune Pde. NW11..1B 30
Temple Gdns. EC4.......4B 16 (1C 76)
........................(off Middle Temple La.)
Temple Gdns. NW11............1B 30
Temple Gro. NW11...............1C 30
Temple La. EC4............3C 16 (5C 62)
Templemead Cl. W3............5A 56
Templemead Ho. E9............1A 52
TEMPLE MILLS.....................1D 53
Temple Mills La. E10...........1D 53
Temple Mills La. E15...........2E 53
Temple Mills La. E20...........1E 53
Temple Pl. WC2...........4A 16 (1B 76)
Temple Rd. E6.....................5F 55
Temple Rd. NW2..................1E 43
Temple Station (Underground)
..........................4A 16 (1B 76)
Temple St. E2......................1D 65
Templeton Cl. N15...............1F 35
Templeton Cl. N16...............2A 50
Templeton Pl. SW5..............5C 72
Templeton Rd. N15..............1F 35
Temple W. M. SE11...5D 25 (4D 77)
Templewood Av. NW3...........5D 31
Templewood Gdns. NW3.......5D 31
Templewood Point NW2.......4B 30
........................(off Granville Rd.)
Temple Yd. E2.....................1D 65
........................(off Temple St.)
Tempus Apts. EC1......1D 9 (1D 63)
........................(off Goswell Rd.)
Tempus Wharf SE16.............3C 78
........................(off Bermondsey Wall W.)
Tenbury Cl. E7....................2F 55
Tenbury Ct. SW2.................1F 117
Tenby Ho. W2.....................5E 59
........................(off Hallfield Est.)
Tenby Mans. W1...........5C 4 (4C 60)
........................(off Nottingham St.)
Tench St. E1........................2D 79
Tenda Rd. SE16...................5D 79
Tenham Av. SW2.................1F 117
Tenison Ct. W1............4F 13 (1E 75)
Tenison Way SE1.........2B 24 (2C 76)
........................(off York Rd.)
Tenniel Cl. W2.....................1E 73
Tennis St. SE1............3B 26 (3F 77)
Tennyson Av. E11................2C 40
Tennyson Av. E12................4E 55
Tennyson Cl. NW1.......4A 4 (3B 60)
........................(off Dorset Sq.)
Tennyson Ho. SE17..............1E 91
........................(off Browning St.)
Tennyson Mans. SW3...........2A 88
........................(off Lordship Pl.)
Tennyson Mans. W14...........2B 86
........................(off Queen's Club Gdns.)
Tennyson Rd. E10................3D 39
Tennyson Rd. E15................4A 54
Tennyson Rd. E17................1B 38
Tennyson Rd. NW6..............5B 44
Tennyson Rd. SW19.............5E 115
Tennyson St. SW8...............5D 89
Tenterden Ho. SE17.............1A 92
........................(off Surrey Gro.)
Tenterden St. W1........3E 13 (5D 61)
Tenter Ground E1........1F 19 (4B 64)
Tent St. E1..........................3D 65
Tenzing Ct. E14...................4D 67
........................(off Hillary M.)
Tequila Wharf E14...............5A 66

Terborch Way SE22.............3A 106
Tercelet Ter. NW3................1E 45
Teredo St. SE16..................4F 79
Terence McMillan Stadium....3E 69
Terence Messenger Twr.
E10...............................4D 39
........................(off Alpine Rd.)
Terling Cl. E11....................5B 40
Terling Ho. W10..................4E 57
........................(off Sutton Way)
Terling Wlk. N1...................5E 49
........................(off Popham St.)
Terminus Pl. SW1.......5E 21 (4D 75)
Terrace, The E2...................2E 65
........................(off Old Ford Rd.)
Terrace, The EC4.........3B 16 (5C 62)
........................(off King's Bench Wlk.)
Terrace, The NW6................5C 44
Terrace, The SE23...............5A 108
Terrace, The SE8.................5B 80
........................(off Longshore)
Terrace, The SW13..............5A 84
Terrace Apts. N5.................2C 48
Terrace Gdns. SW13............5B 84
Terrace Rd. E13..................1C 68
Terrace Rd. E9....................4E 51
Terraces, The E2.................1C 64
........................(off Garner St.)
Terraces, The NW8..............1F 59
........................(off Queen's Ter.)
Terrace Wlk. SW11..............3B 88
Terrapin Rd. SW17..............3D 117
Terretts Pl. N1....................4D 49
........................(off Upper St.)
Terrick St. W12...................5D 57
Territorial Ho. SE11.............5C 76
........................(off Reedworth St.)
Terry Spinks Pl. E16............4B 68
........................(off Barking Rd.)
Tesla Ct. W3.......................3A 56
Tessa Sanderson Pl. SW8..1D 103
........................(off Daley Thompson Way)
Testerton Rd. W11...............1F 71
........................(off Hurstway Wlk.)
Testerton Wlk. W11..............1F 71
Tetbury Pl. N1....................5D 49
Tetcott Rd. SW10................3E 87
........................(not continuous)
Tevatree Ho. SE1................1C 92
........................(off Old Kent Rd.)
Teversham La. SW8.............4A 90
Teviot Est. E14...................4D 67
Teviot St. E14.....................4E 67
Tewkesbury Av. SE23........1D 121
Tewkesbury Cl. N15.............1F 35
Tewkesbury Rd. N15............1F 35
Texryte Ho. N1...................5F 49
........................(off Southgate Rd.)
Textile Ho. E1.....................4F 65
........................(off Duckett St.)
Thackeray Ho. NW6.............4E 45
........................(off Fairfax Rd.)
Thackeray Cl. SW3..............1B 88
........................(off Elystan Pl.)
Thackeray Cl. W14..............4A 72
........................(off Blythe Rd.)
Thackeray Ho. WC1....3D 7 (3A 62)
........................(off Herbrand St.)
Thackeray M. E8..................3C 50
Thackeray Rd. E6................1F 69
Thackeray Rd. SW8.............5D 89
Thackeray St. W8................4D 73
Thackery Ct. EC1........5D 9 (4D 63)
........................(off Turnmill St.)
Thakeham Cl. SE26.............4D 121

Thalia Cl. SE10.................2F 95
Thalia Ct. E8.....................4B 50
.................................(off Albion Dr.)
Thame Rd. SE16...............3F 79
Thames Av. SW10.............4E 87
Thames Barrier................3F 83
Thames Barrier Ind. Area
SE18..............................4F 83
.................................(off Faraday Way)
Thames Barrier Info. Cen...4F 83
Thames Barrier Pk............3E 83
Thamesbrook SW3.............1A 88
.................................(off Dovehouse St.)
Thames Circ. E14.............5C 80
Thames Ct. NW6................1B 58
.................................(off Albert Rd.)
Thames Ct. SE15.............3B 92
.................................(off Daniel Gdns.)
Thames Cres. W4.............3A 84
Thames Exchange Bldg.
EC4...............................4A 18 (1E 77)
.................................(off Queen St. Pl.)
Thames Hgts. SE1...3F 27 (3B 78)
.................................(off Gainsford St.)
Thames Ho. EC4.......4A 18 (1E 77)
.................................(off Queen St. Pl.)
Thames Ho. SW1...............5A 76
.................................(off Millbank)
Thameside Ind. Est. E16.....3F 83
Thames Path SE10.............4C 82
Thames Pl. SW15...............1F 99
Thames Point SW6.............5E 87
Thames Police Mus..........2D 79
Thames Quay E14.............3D 81
Thames Quay SW10...........4E 87
.................................(off Chelsea Harbour)
Thames Reach W6.............2E 85
.................................(off Rainville Rd.)
Thames Rd. E16..................2F 83
Thames Rd. Ind. Est. E16....2F 83
Thames St. SE10...............2D 95
Thames Tunnel Mills SE16...3E 79
Thames Wharf Studios W6...2E 85
.................................(off Rainville Rd.)
Thanet Ho. WC1.....2D 7 (2A 62)
.................................(off Thanet St.)
Thanet Lodge NW2.............3A 44
.................................(off Mapesbury Rd.)
Thanet St. WC1.......2D 7 (2A 62)
Thanet Wharf SE8.............2D 95
.................................(off Copperas St.)
Thane Vs. N7....................5B 34
Thane Works N7................5B 34
Thant Cl. E10....................5D 39
Thavie's Inn EC4.......2C 16 (5C 62)
Thaxted Ct. N1......1C 10 (1F 63)
.................................(off Murray Gro.)
Thaxted Ho. SE16...............5E 79
.................................(off Abbeyfield Est.)
Thaxton Rd. W14..............2B 86
Thayer St. W1........1C 12 (5C 60)
Theatre Hackney Wick, The...2C 52
Theatre Bldg. E3...............2C 66
.................................(off Paton Cl.)
Theatre Pl. SE8.................3C 94
.................................(off Speedwell Cl.)
Theatre-Rites..........4D 25 (3D 77)
.................................(off Blackfriars Rd.)
Theatre Royal Drury Lane
.................................3E 15 (5A 62)
.................................(off Catherine St.)
Theatre Royal Haymarket
.................................5C 14 (1F 75)
.................................(off Haymarket)

Theatre Royal Stratford East
.................................4F 53
Theatre Sq. E15................3F 53
Theatre St. SW11...............1B 102
Theatre Vw. Apts.
SE1........................3C 24 (3D 77)
.................................(off Short St.)
Theatro Technis................5E 47
.................................(off Crowndale Rd.)
Theatro Twr. E8.................2C 94
Theberton St. N1...............5C 48
Theed St. SE1.........2B 24 (2C 76)
Thelbridge Ho. E3.............2D 67
.................................(off Bruce Rd.)
Thelma Gdns. SE3.............4F 97
Theobald Rd. E17..............2B 38
Theobalds Ct. N4...............5C 35
Theobald's Rd. WC1 1E 15 (4B 62)
Theobald St. N4................4F 77
Theodore Ct. SE13............4F 109
Theodore Rd. SE13............4F 109
Therapia Rd. SE22............4E 107
Theresa Rd. W6.................5C 70
Therfield Ct. N4.................4E 35
Thermopylae Ga. E14........5D 81
Theseus Wlk. N1.......1E 9 (1D 63)
.................................(off City Gdn. Row)
Thessaly Ho. SW8.............3E 89
.................................(off Thessaly Rd.)
Thessaly Rd. SW8.............3E 89
.................................(not continuous)
Thesus Ho. E14................5E 67
.................................(off Blair St.)
Thetford Ho. SE1....5F 27 (4B 78)
.................................(off St Saviour's Est.)
Theven St. E1...................3E 65
Theydon Rd. E5.................4E 37
Theydon St. E17...............2B 38
Third Av. E13....................2C 68
Third Av. E17....................1C 38
Third Av. W10...................2A 58
Third Av. W3....................2D 70
Thirleby Rd. SW1.......5A 22 (4E 75)
Thirlmere NW1...........1E 5 (2D 61)
.................................(off Cumberland Mkt.)
Thirlmere Ho. N16..............1F 49
.................................(off Howard Rd.)
Thirlmere Rd. SW16..........4F 117
Thirsk Rd. SW11................1C 102
Thirty Casson Sq.
SE1........................2A 24 (2B 76)
.................................(off Casson Sq.)
Thirza Ho. E1....................5C 65
.................................(off Devonport St.)
Thistle Ct. SE12................2C 124
Thistle Gro. SW10.............1E 87
Thistle Ho. E14.................5C 67
.................................(off Dee St.)
Thistlewaite Rd. E5............5D 37
Thistlewood Cl. N7............4B 34
Thistley Ct. SE8.................2D 95
Thomas Baines Rd. SW11..1F 101
Thomas Burt Ho. E2..........2D 65
.................................(off Canrobert St.)
Thomas Coulter Ho. E16....3D 83
.................................(off Shipwright Street)
Thomas Darby Ct. W11......5A 58
.................................(off Lancaster Rd.)
Thomas Dean Rd. SE26.....4B 122
Thomas Dinwiddy Rd.
SE12.............................2D 125
Thomas Doyle St.
SE1........................5D 25 (4D 77)
Thomas Earle Ho. W14......5B 72
.................................(off Warwick La.)

Thomas Frye Ct. E15.........1D 67
.................................(off High St.)
Thomas Fyre Dr. E3..........1C 68
Thomas Hardy M. SW16....5E 117
Thomas Hollywood Ho. E2...1E 65
.................................(off Approach Rd.)
Thomas Joseph Ho. SE4....3F 107
.................................(off St Norbert Rd.)
Thomas La. SE6................5C 108
Thomas More Highwalk
EC2........................1F 17 (4E 63)
.................................(off Aldersgate St.)
Thomas More Ho.
EC2........................1F 17 (4E 63)
.................................(off Aldersgate St.)
Thomas More Sq. E1.........1C 78
Thomas More St. E1..........1C 78
Thomas Pl. W8..................4D 73
Thomas Rd. E14................5B 66
Thomas Rd. Ind. Est. E14...4C 66
.................................(not continuous)
Thomas Tallis Sports Cen.
.................................1D 111
Thomas Twr. E8.................3B 50
.................................(off Dalston Sq.)
Thompson Ho. SE14..........2F 93
.................................(off John Williams Cl.)
Thompson Ho. W10............3A 58
.................................(off Wornington Rd.)
Thompson Rd. SE22..........4B 106
Thompson's Av. SE5..........3E 91
Thomson Ho. E14...............5C 66
.................................(off Saracen St.)
Thomson Ho. SE17.............5A 78
.................................(off Tatum St.)
Thomson Ho. SW1..............1F 89
.................................(off Bessborough Pl.)
Thorburn Ho. SW1....4A 20 (3B 74)
.................................(off Kinnerton St.)
Thorburn Sq. SE1..............5C 78
Thoresby St. N1.......1A 10 (2E 63)
Thornaby Ho. E2................2D 65
.................................(off Canrobert St.)
Thorn Apts. E3..................4C 66
.................................(off St Paul's Way)
Thornbill Ho. SE15.............3C 92
.................................(off Bird in Bush Rd.)
Thornbury Cl. N16.............2A 50
Thornbury Ct. W11............1C 72
.................................(off Chepstow Vs.)
Thornbury Rd. SW2..........4A 104
Thornbury Sq. N6..............3E 33
Thornby Rd. E5.................5E 37
Thorncliffe Rd. SW2..........4A 104
Thorncombe Rd. SE22.......3A 106
Thorncroft St. SW8............3A 90
Thorndean St. SW18.........2E 115
Thorndike Cl. SW10...........3E 87
Thorndike Ho. SW1............1F 89
.................................(off Vauxhall Bri. Rd.)
Thorndike Rd. N1...............3F 49
Thorndike St. SW1.............5F 75
Thorne Cl. E11..................1F 53
Thorne Cl. E16..................5C 68
Thorne Ho. E14.................4E 81
.................................(off Launch St.)
Thorne Ho. E2...................2E 65
.................................(off Roman Rd.)
Thorne Pas. SW13.............5A 84
Thorne Rd. SW8.................3A 90
Thornes Ho. SW11.............3F 89
.................................(off Ponton Rd.)
Thorne St. SW13...............1A 98
Thornewill Ho. E1...............1E 79
.................................(off Cable St.)

Thorney Ct. W8 ....3E **73**
............................(off Palace Ga.)
Thorney Cres. SW11 ....3F **87**
Thorney St. SW1 ....5A **76**
Thornfield Ho. E14 ....1C **80**
.........................(off Rosefield Gdns.)
Thornfield Rd. W12 ....3D **71**
....................................(not continuous)
Thornford Rd. SE13 ....3E **109**
Thorngate Rd. W9 ....3C **58**
Thorngrove Rd. E14 ....5D **55**
Thornham Gro. E15.............2F **53**
Thornham Ind. Est. E15.......2F **53**
Thornham St. SE10 ....2D **95**
Thornhaugh M. WC1 ... 4C **6** (3F **61**)
Thornhaugh St. WC1 ... 4C **6** (3F **61**)
THORNHILL BRI. 1B **62**
........................(off Caledonian Rd.)
Thornhill Bri. Wharf N1.......5B **48**
Thornhill Cres. N1 ....4B **48**
Thornhill Gdns. E10 ....4D **39**
Thornhill Gro. N1 ....4B **48**
Thornhill Ho. W4 ....1A **84**
...................................(off Wood St.)
Thornhill Ho's. N1 ....4C **48**
.........................(off Thornhill Rd.)
Thornhill M. SW15 ....2B **100**
Thornhill Rd. E10 ....4D **39**
Thornhill Rd. N1 ....4C **48**
Thornhill Sq. N1 ....4B **48**
Thornicroft Ho. SW9 ....5B **90**
.........................(off Stockwell Rd.)
Thornlaw Rd. SE27 ....4C **118**
Thornley Pl. SE10................1A **96**
Thornsbeach Rd. SE6 ....1E **123**
Thornsett Rd. SW18..........1D **115**
Thorn Ter. SE15 ....1E **107**
Thornton Av. SW2 ....1F **117**
Thornton Av. W4 ....5A **70**
Thornton Gdns. SW12 ....1F **117**
Thornton Ho. SE17 ....5A **78**
..............................(off Townsend St.)
Thornton Pl. W1 ......5A **4** (4B **60**)
Thornton Rd. BR1: Broml .. 5C **124**
Thornton Rd. E11 ....4F **39**
Thornton Rd. SW12 ....5F **103**
Thornton St. SW9 ....5C **90**
Thornton Way NW11 ....1D **31**
Thorntree Rd. SE7 ....1F **97**
Thornville St. SE8 ....4C **94**
Thornwood Gdns. W8 ....3C **72**
Thornwood Lodge W8 ....3C **72**
..........................(off Thornwood Gdns.)
Thornwood Rd. SE13 ....3A **110**
Thornycroft Ho. W4.............1A **84**
....................................(off Fraser St.)
Thorogood Gdns. E15 ....2A **54**
Thorold Ho. SE1 ...... 3F **25** (3E **77**)
....................................(off Pepper St.)
Thorparch Rd. SW8 ....4F **89**
Thorpebank Rd. W12...........2C **70**
Thorpe Cl. SE26 ....4F **121**
Thorpe Cl. W10 ....5A **58**
Thorpedale Rd. N4 ....4A **34**
Thorpe Ho. N1 ....5B **48**
............................(off Barnsbury Est.)
Thorpe Rd. E7 ....1B **54**
Thorpe Rd. N15 ....1A **36**
Thorpewood Av. SE26 ....2D **121**
Thorsden Way SE19 ....5A **120**
Thorverton Rd. NW2 ....5A **30**
Thoydon Rd. E3 ....1A **66**
Thrale Rd. SW16 ....4E **117**
Thrale St. SE1 .... 2A **26** (2E **77**)

Thrasher Cl. E8 ....5B **50**
Thrawl St. E1 .... 1F **19** (4B **64**)
Thrayle Ho. SW9.................1B **104**
............................(off Benedict Rd.)
Threadgold Ho. N1 ....3F **49**
............................(off Dovercourt Est.)
Threadneedle St.
EC2...................... 3B **18** (5F **63**)
Threadneedle Wlk.
EC2...................... 2C **18** (5F **63**)
............................(off Throgmorton St.)
Three Colts La. E2...............3D **65**
Three Colt St. E14 ....5B **66**
Three Cups Yd. WC1... 1A **16** (4B **62**)
.............................(off Sandland St.)
Three Kings Yd. W1...4D **13** (1D **75**)
Three Mill La. E3 ....2E **67**
Three Mills Studios 2E **67**
Three Oak La. SE1 ... 3F **27** (3B **78**)
Three Quays EC3.... 5E **19** (1A **78**)
.....................................(off Tower Hill)
Three Quays Wlk.
.................................5E **19** (1A **78**)
Threshers Pl. W11 ....1A **72**
Thriffwood SE26 ....3E **121**
Thring Ho. SW9...................5B **90**
............................(off Stockwell Rd.)
Throckmorton Rd. E16 ....5D **69**
Throgmorton Av.
EC2...................... 2C **18** (5F **63**)
....................................(not continuous)
Throgmorton St. EC2 2C **18** (5F **63**)
Thrush St. SE17 ....1E **91**
Thunderer St. E13...............1E **69**
Thurbarn Rd. SE6................5D **123**
Thurland Ho. SE16 ....5D **79**
.................................(off Camilla Rd.)
Thurland Rd. SE16...............4C **78**
Thurlby Rd. SE27 ....4C **118**
Thurleigh Av. SW12 ....4C **102**
Thurleigh Ct. SW12 ....4C **102**
Thurleigh Rd. SW12 ....5B **102**
Thurlestone Rd. SE27 ....3C **118**
Thurloe Cl. SW7 ....5A **74**
Thurloe Ct. SW3 ....5A **74**
.................................(off Fulham Rd.)
Thurloe Pl. SW7 ....5F **73**
Thurloe Pl. M. SW7 ....5F **73**
..................................(off Thurloe Pl.)
Thurloe Sq. SW7 ....5A **74**
Thurloe St. SW7 ....5F **73**
Thurlow Hill SE21 ....1E **119**
Thurlow Ho. SW16 ....3A **118**
Thurlow Pk. Rd. SE21 ....2D **119**
Thurlow Rd. NW3 ....2F **45**
Thurlow St. SE17 ....1F **91**
....................................(not continuous)
Thurlow Ter. NW5................2C **46**
Thurlow Wlk. SE17 ....1A **92**
....................................(not continuous)
Thurnscoe NW1 ....5E **47**
..................................(off Pratt St.)
Thursley Gdns. SW19.........2F **113**
Thursley Ho. SW2................5B **104**
..........................(off Holmewood Gdns.)
Thurso Ho. NW6..................1D **59**
Thurso St. SW17 ....4F **115**
Thurstan Dwellings
WC2...................... 2E **15** (5A **62**)
..................................(off Newton St.)
Thurston St. SW6 ....4E **87**
Thurston Ho. N1 ....5B **48**
..........................(off Barnsbury Est.)
Thurston Rd. SE13 ....5D **95**
Thurtle Rd. E2 ....5B **50**

Thyme Cl. SE3 ....1E **111**
Thyme Wlk. E5......................1F **51**
Tibbatt's Rd. E3 ....3D **67**
Tibbenham Pl. SE6...............2C **122**
Tibbenham Wlk. E13.............1B **68**
Tibberton Sq. N1 ....5E **49**
Tibbet's Cl. SW19...............1F **113**
Tibbet's Ride SW15 ....5F **99**
TIBBET'S CORNER 5F **99**
Tibbet's Ride SW15 ....5F **99**
Tiber Cl. E3 ....5C **52**
Tiber Gdns. N1 ....5A **48**
Ticehurst Rd. SE23 ....2A **122**
Tickford Ho. NW8.................2A **60**
Tidal Basin Rd. E16 ....1B **82**
....................................(not continuous)
Tidbury Ct. SW8 ....3E **89**
.............................(off Stewart's Rd.)
Tidemill Sq. SE10 ....5A **82**
Tidemill Way SE8 ....3D **94**
Tideswell Rd. SW15 ....2E **99**
Tidewaiters Ho. E14.............5F **67**
....................................(off Blair St.)
Tideway Ct. SE16.................2F **79**
Tideway Ho. E14 ....3C **80**
.............................(off Strafford St.)
Tideway Wlk. SW11 ....2E **89**
Tidey St. E3 ....4C **66**
Tidworth Rd. E3 ....3C **66**
Tierney La. W6 ....2E **85**
Tierney Rd. SW2 ....1A **118**
Tiffany Hgts. SW18 ....5C **100**
Tiger Ho. WC1 .... 2C **6** (2F **61**)
...................................(off Burton St.)
Tiger Way E5........................1D **51**
Tiggap Ho. SE10..................5A **82**
Tilbrook Rd. SE3 ....1E **111**
Tilbury Cl. SE15 ....3B **92**
Tilbury Ho. SE14 ....2F **93**
.................................(off Myers La.)
Tilbury Rd. E10 ....2E **39**
Tildesley Rd. SW15 ....4E **99**
Tile Ho. N1.........................1A **62**
.........................(off Beaconsfield St.)
Tilehurst NW1 .... 2E **5** (2D **61**)
............................(off Lit. Albany St.)
Tilehurst Rd. SW18 ....1F **115**
Tile Kiln La. N6....................3D **33**
Tile Kiln Studios N6..............2E **33**
Tilemakers Yd. SW18 ....2E **115**
Tileyard Rd. N7 ....4A **48**
Tilford Gdns. SW19 ....1F **113**
Tilford Ho. SW2...................5B **104**
..........................(off Holmewood Gdns.)
Tilia Rd. E5...........................1D **51**
Tilia Wlk. SW9 ....2D **105**
Tiller Ho. N1 ....5A **50**
.........................(off Whitmore Est.)
Tiller Leisure Cen. 4C **80**
Tiller Rd. E14......................4C **80**
Tillett Sq. SE16 ....3A **80**
Tillett Way E2 ....2C **64**
Tilling Rd. NW2 ....3E **29**
Tillings Cl. SE5....................4E **91**
Tillman St. E1......................5D **65**
Tilloch St. N1 ....4B **48**
Tillotson Ct. SW8 ....3F **89**
.........................(off Wandsworth Rd.)
Tilney Ct. EC1........... 3A **10** (3E **63**)
Tilney Gdns. N1 ....3F **49**
Tilney St. W1 .... 1C **20** (2C **74**)
Tilson Cl. SE5......................3A **92**
Tilson Gdns. SW2 ....5A **104**
Tilson Ho. SW2 ....5A **104**
Tilston Cl. E11.....................5B **40**
Tiltman Pl. N7 ....5B **34**

Tilton St. SW6 .... 2A **86**
Timberland Cl. SE15 .... 3C **92**
Timberland Rd. E1 .... 5D **65**
Timber Mill Way SW4 ..... 1F **103**
Timber Pond Rd. SE16 ...... 2F **79**
Timber St. EC1 .... 3F **9** (3E **63**)
Timber Wharf 2 .... 5B **50**
Timberwharf Rd. N16 .... 1C **36**
Timber Wharves Est. E14 .... 5C **80**
.... *(off Copeland St.)*
Timber Yd., The N1 .. 2E **11** (2A **64**)
.... *(off Drysdale St.)*
Timbrell Pl. SE16 .... 2F **79**
Time Sq. E8 .... 2B **50**
Times Sq. E1 .... 5C **64**
Timians Way BR1: Brom! .. 4D **125**
Timmins Apts. E2 .... 2F **65**
Timor Ho. E1 .... 3A **66**
.... *(off Duckett St.)*
Timothy Cl. SW4 .... 3E **103**
Timperley Cl. SW19 .... 1A **114**
Timsbury Wlk. SW15 .... 1C **112**
Tina St. SE6 .... 5B **108**
Tindal St. SW9 .... 4D **91**
Tinderbox All. SW14 .... 1A **98**
Tinderbox Ho. SE8 .... 3C **94**
.... *(off Octavius St.)*
Tinniswood Cl. N5 .... 2C **48**
Tinsley Rd. E1 .... 4E **65**
Tintagel Ct. EC1 ..... 3D **9** (3D **63**)
.... *(off St John St.)*
Tintagel Cres. SE22 .... 2B **106**
Tintagel Gdns. SE22 .... 2B **106**
Tintern Cl. SW15 .... 3A **100**
Tintern Ho. NW1 ...... 1E **5** (1D **61**)
.... *(off Augustus St.)*
Tintern Ho. SW1 .... 5D **75**
.... *(part of Abbots Mnr.)*
Tintern Path NW9 .... 1A **28**
.... *(off Fryent Gro.)*
Tintern St. SW4 .... 2A **104**
Tinto Rd. E16 .... 3C **68**
Tinworth St. SE17 .... 2D **91**
.... *(off Royal Rd.)*
Tinworth St. SE11 .... 1A **90**
Tipper Wlk. E15 .... 2F **53**
Tipthorpe Rd. SW11 .... 1C **102**
Tiptree NW1 .... 4D **47**
.... *(off Castlehaven Rd.)*
Tisbury Ct. W1 ..... 4B **14** (1F **75**)
.... *(off Wardour St.)*
Tisdall Ho. SE17 .... 5F **77**
.... *(off Barlow St.)*
Tisdall Pl. SE17 .... 5F **77**
Tissington Ct. SE16 .... 5E **79**
Titan Bus. Est. SE8 .... 3C **94**
.... *(off Ffinch St.)*
Titan Ho. E20 .... 2E **53**
.... *(off Napa Cl.)*
Titanium Point E2 .... 2F **65**
.... *(off Palmer's Rd.)*
Titchborne Row W2 .... 5A **60**
Titchfield Rd. NW8 .... 5A **46**
Titchwell Rd. SW18 .... 1F **115**
Tite St. SW3 .... 1B **88**
Titian Hgts. E20 .... 2D **53**
.... *(off Scarlet Cl.)*
Titmuss St. W12 .... 3E **71**
Tiverton Rd. N15 .... 1F **35**
Tiverton Rd. NW10 .... 5F **43**
Tiverton St. SE1 ... 5F **25** (4E **77**)
Tivoli Ct. SE16 .... 2B **80**
Tivoli Gdns. SE18 .... 5F **83**
.... *(not continuous)*
Tivoli M. E14 .... 5B **66**

Tivoli Rd. N8 .... 1F **33**
Tivoli Rd. SE27 .... 5E **119**
Tivoli Way E14 .... 5B **66**
Tizzard Gro. SE3 .... 2D **111**
Tobacco Dock 1D **79**
Tobago St. E14 .... 3C **80**
Tobin Cl. NW3 .... 4A **46**
Toby La. E1 .... 3A **66**
Todber Ho. W14 .... 4A **72**
.... *(off Russell Rd.)*
Todds Wlk. N7 .... 4B **34**
Tokenhouse Yd. EC2 2B **18** (5F **63**)
Token Yd. SW15 .... 2A **100**
Toland Sq. SW15 .... 3C **98**
Tolchurch W11 .... 5B **58**
.... *(off Dartmouth Cl.)*
Tolhurst Dr. W10 .... 2A **58**
Tollard Ho. W14 .... 4B **72**
.... *(off Kensington High St.)*
Tollbridge Cl. W10 .... 3A **58**
Tollet St. E1 .... 3F **65**
Tollgate Dr. SE21 .... 2A **120**
Tollgate Gdns. NW6 .... 1D **59**
Tollgate Ho. NW6 .... 1D **59**
.... *(off Tollgate Gdns.)*
Tollgate Rd. E16 .... 4E **69**
Tollgate Rd. E6 .... 4E **69**
Tollhouse Way N19 .... 4E **33**
Tollington Pk. N4 .... 4B **34**
Tollington Pl. N4 .... 4B **34**
Tollington Rd. N7 .... 1B **48**
Tollington Way N7 .... 5A **34**
Tolmers Sq. NW1 ... 3A **6** (3E **61**)
.... *(not continuous)*
Tolpaide Ho. SE11 .... 5C **76**
.... *(off Marylee Way)*
Tolpuddle Av. E13 .... 5E **55**
Tolpuddle St. N1 .... 1C **62**
Tolsford Rd. E5 .... 2D **51**
Tom Groves Cl. E15 .... 2F **53**
Tom Hood Cl. E15 .... 2F **53**
Tom Jenkinson Rd. E16 .... 2C **82**
Tomkyns Ho. SE11 .... 5C **76**
.... *(off Distin St.)*
Tomline Ho. SE1 .... 2F **25** (2E **77**)
.... *(off Union St.)*
Tomlin's Gro. E3 .... 2C **66**
Tomlinson Cl. E2 .. 2F **11** (2B **64**)
Tomlins Ter. E14 .... 5A **66**
Tomlins Wlk. N7 .... 4B **34**
Tom Nolan Cl. E15 .... 1A **68**
Tompion Ho. EC1 .... 3E **9** (3D **63**)
.... *(off Percival St.)*
Tompion St. EC1 .... 2D **9** (2D **63**)
.... *(not continuous)*
Tom Smith Cl. SE10 .... 2A **96**
Tomson Ho. SE1 ... 5F **27** (4B **78**)
.... *(off St Saviour's Est.)*
Tom Williams Ho. SW6 .... 2B **86**
.... *(off Clem Attlee Ct.)*
Tonbridge Ho's. WC1 .. 2D **7** (2A **62**)
.... *(off Tonbridge St.)*
Tonbridge St. WC1 .. 1D **7** (2A **62**)
Toneborough NW8 .... 5D **45**
.... *(off Abbey Rd.)*
Tonsley Hill SW18 .... 3D **101**
Tonsley Pl. SW18 .... 3D **101**
Tonsley Rd. SW18 .... 3D **101**
Tonsley St. SW18 .... 3D **101**
Tony Cannell M. E3 .... 2B **66**
Took's Ct. EC4 ..... 2B **16** (5C **62**)
Tooley St. SE1 ..... 1C **26** (2F **77**)
TOOTING 5A **116**
TOOTING BEC 3B **116**

Tooting Bec Gdns.
SW16 .... 4F **117**
.... *(not continuous)*
Tooting Bec Lido. 4E **117**
Tooting Bec Rd. SW16 .... 4D **117**
Tooting Bec Rd. SW17 .... 3C **116**
Tooting Bec Station
(Underground) 3C **116**
Tooting B'way. Station
(Underground) 5A **116**
Tooting Broadway Station
(Underground) 5A **116**
TOOTING GRAVENEY 5B **116**
Tooting Gro. SW17 .... 5A **116**
Tooting High St. SW17 .... 5A **116**
Tooting Leisure Cen. 4F **115**
Tooting Mkt. SW17 .... 4B **116**
Topaz Ct. E11 .... 3A **40**
Topaz Wlk. NW2 .... 2F **29**
Topham Ho. SE10 .... 3E **95**
.... *(off Prior St.)*
Topham St. EC1 ..... 3B **8** (3C **62**)
Topley St. SE9 .... 2E **111**
Topmast Point E14 .... 3C **80**
Topp Wlk. NW2 .... 4E **29**
Topsfield Cl. N8 .... 1F **33**
Topsfield Pde. N8 .... 1A **34**
.... *(off Tottenham La.)*
Topsfield Rd. N8 .... 1A **34**
Topsham Rd. SW17 .... 3B **116**
Torbay Ct. NW1 .... 4D **47**
.... *(off Willesden La.)*
Torbay Mans. NW6 .... 5B **44**
Torbay Rd. NW6 .... 4B **44**
Torbay St. NW1 .... 4D **47**
Tor Ct. W8 .... 3C **72**
Torcross Dr. SE23 .... 2E **121**
Toreno Mansion E20 .... 2D **53**
.... *(off Olympic Pk. Av.)*
Tor Gdns. W8 .... 3C **72**
Tor Ho. N6 .... 1D **33**
Tornay Ho. E9 .... 4E **51**
Tornay Ho. N1 .... 1B **62**
.... *(off Priory Grn. Est.)*
Toronto Ho. SE16 .... 3F **79**
Torquay Ct. E14 .... 4E **67**
.... *(off St Ives Pl.)*
Torquay St. W2 .... 4D **59**
Torrance Cl. SE7 .... 2E **97**
Torrens Ct. SE5 .... 1F **105**
Torrens Rd. E15 .... 3B **54**
Torrens Rd. SW2 .... 3B **104**
Torrens Sq. E15 .... 3B **54**
Torrens St. EC1 .... 1C **62**
Torrent Lodge SE10 .... 3D **95**
.... *(off Merryweather Pl.)*
Torres Sq. E14 .... 1C **94**
Torre Vista SE13 .... 1E **109**
.... *(off Loampit Va.)*
Torrey Dr. SW9 .... 5C **90**
Torriano Av. NW5 .... 2F **47**
Torriano Cotts. NW5 .... 2E **47**
Torriano M. NW5 .... 2F **47**
Torridge Gdns. SE15 ...... 2E **107**
Torridon Ho. NW6 .... 1D **59**
.... *(off Randolph Gdns.)*
Torridon Rd. SE13 .... 5A **110**
Torridon Rd. SE6 .... 5F **109**
Torrington Ct. SE26 .... 5C **120**
.... *(off Crystal Palace Pk. Rd.)*
Torrington Pl. E1 .... 2C **78**
Torrington Pl. WC1 .. 4B **6** (4F **61**)
Torrington Sq. WC1 .. 4C **6** (3F **61**)
Tortington Ho. SE15 .... 3C **92**
.... *(off Friary Est.)*
Torwood Rd. SW15 .... 3C **98**

Tothill Ho. SW1 ....5F **75**
............................*(off Page St.)*
Tothill St. SW1 ....4B **22** (3F **75**)
Tottan Ter. E1 ....5F **65**
Tottenhall NW1 ....4C **46**
......................*(off Ferdinand St.)*
Tottenham Ct. Rd.
  W1 ....3A **6** (3E **61**)
Tottenham Court Road Station
(Underground & Crossrail)
.............................2B **14** (5F **61**)
Tottenham Ct. Rd. N8 ....1A **34**
Tottenham M. W1 ......5A **6** (4E **61**)
Tottenham Rd. N1 ....3A **50**
Tottenham St. W1 ......1A **14** (4E **61**)
Totterdown St. SW17 ....4B **116**
Totteridge Ho. SW11 ....5F **87**
......................*(off Yelverton Rd.)*
Totters Ct. SE17 ....2F **91**
......................*(off Westmorland Rd.)*
Touchard Ho. N1 ....2C **10** (2F **63**)
......................*(off Chart St.)*
Toulmin St. SE1 ....4F **25** (3E **77**)
Toulon St. SE5 ....3E **91**
Toulouse Ct. SE16 ....1D **93**
......................*(off Rossetti Rd.)*
Tounson Ct. SW1 ....5F **75**
......................*(off Montaigne Cl.)*
Tourers Ho. E17 ....1B **38**
......................*(off Track St.)*
Tournay Rd. SW6 ....3B **86**
Tours Pas. SW11 ....2E **101**
Toussaint Wlk. SE16 ....4C **78**
Tovy Ho. SE1 ....1C **92**
......................*(off Avondale Sq.)*
Towcester Rd. E3 ....3D **67**
......................*(off Potters Flds.)*
Tower, The SE1 ....2E **27** (2B **78**)
Tower, The SW8 ....2A **90**
TOWER BRIDGE 1F **27** (2B **78**)
Tower Bri. App. E1 ....1F **27** (2B **78**)
Tower Bri. Bus. Complex
  SE16 ....4C **78**
Tower Bri. Bus. Sq. SE16 .....5D **79**
Tower Bridge Exhibition
......................1F **27** (2B **78**)
......................*(off Tower Bri.)*
Tower Bri. Plaza SE12F **27** (2B **78**)
Tower Bri. Rd. SE1 ...5D **27** (4A **78**)
Tower Bri. Sq. SE1 ...3F **27** (3B **78**)
......................*(off Queen Elizabeth St.)*
Tower Bri. Wharf E1 ....2C **78**
Tower Bldgs. E1 ....2D **79**
......................*(off Brewhouse La.)*
Tower Cl. NW3 ....2F **45**
Tower Ct. N1 ....4E **49**
......................*(off Canonbury St.)*
Tower Ct. NW8 ....1A **60**
......................*(off Mackennal St.)*
Tower Ct. WC2 ....3D **15** (5A **62**)
......................*(off Tower St.)*
Towergate SE1 ....5A **78**
......................*(off Page's Wlk.)*
Towergate Ho. E3 ....1B **66**
......................*(off Ordell Rd.)*
Tower Gateway Station (DLR)
......................4F **19** (1B **78**)
TOWER HAMLETS CENTRE FOR
MENTAL HEALTH 3F **65**
Tower Hamlets Rd. E7 ....1B **54**
TOWER HILL 4F **19** (1B **78**)
Tower Hill EC3 ....5E **19** (1B **78**)
Tower Hill Memorial5E **19** (1B **78**)
Tower Hill Station (Underground)
......................4F **19** (1B **78**)

Tower Hill Ter. EC3....5E **19** (1A **78**)
......................*(off Tower Hill)*
Tower Ho. E1 ....4C **64**
......................*(off Fieldgate St.)*
Tower Ho. SE13......................1E **109**
Tower Mans. SE1 ....4B **78**
......................*(off Grange Rd.)*
Tower M. E5 ....1A **52**
Tower Millennium Pier (River Bus
& Tours) 1E **27** (2A **78**)
Tower Mill Rd. SE15 ....3A **92**
Tower of London, The
......................5F **19** (1B **78**)
Tower of London Jewel House
......................5F **19** (1B **78**)
Tower of London Welcome Cen.
......................5E **19** (1A **78**)
Tower Pier EC3 ....5E **19** (1A **78**)
Tower Pl. EC3 ....5E **19** (1A **78**)
Tower Pl. E. EC3.........5E **19** (1A **78**)
......................*(off Lwr. Thames St.)*
Tower Pl. W. EC3 ....5E **19** (1A **78**)
......................*(off Lwr. Thames St.)*
Tower Rd. NW10 ....4C **42**
Tower Rd. WC2 ....3C **14** (5A **62**)
Tower Wlk. SE1 ....5A **78**
......................*(off Leroy St.)*
Tower Wharf SE1 ......3F **27** (3B **78**)
......................*(off Tooley St.)*
Tower Workshops
  SE1 ....4F **27** (3B **78**)
......................*(off Riley Rd.)*
Town Hall App. N16 ....1F **49**
......................*(off Albion Rd.)*
Town Hall Rd. SW11 ....1B **102**
Townhouse M. W12 ....3D **71**
Townley Ct. E15 ....3B **54**
Townley Rd. SE22 ....3A **106**
Townley St. SE17 ....1F **91**
Townmead Bus. Cen. SW6 ...1E **101**
Townmead Rd. SW6 ....1D **101**
Townsend Ho. SE1 ....5C **78**
......................*(off Strathnairn St.)*
Townsend La. NW9 ....2A **28**
Townsend M. SW18...............2E **115**
Townsend Rd. N15 ....1B **36**
Townsend Rd. SE1 ....2E **111**
Townsend St. SE17 ....5A **78**
Townsend Yd. N6 ....3D **33**
Townshend Ct. NW8 ....1A **60**
......................*(off Townshend Rd.)*
Townshend Est. NW8.............1A **60**
Townshend Rd. NW8 ....5A **46**
......................*(not continuous)*
Towns Ho. SW4 ....1F **103**
Towpath, The SW10 ....4F **87**
Towpath Wlk. E9 ....2B **52**
Towton Rd. SE27.....................2E **119**
Toynbee St. E1 ....1F **19** (4B **64**)
Toynbee Studios 2F **19** (5B **64**)
......................*(off Commercial St.)*
Toyne Way N6 ....1B **32**
Tracey Av. NW2.......................2E **43**
Tracey Bellamy Ct. E14 ....5A **66**
......................*(off Repton St.)*
Track St. E17 ....1B **38**
Tracy Ho. E3 ....2B **66**
......................*(off Mile End Rd.)*
Tradescant Ho. E9 ....4E **51**
......................*(off Frampton Pk. Rd.)*
Tradescant Rd. SW8 ....3A **90**
Tradewind Hgts. SE16 ....2F **79**
......................*(off Rotherhithe St.)*
Tradewinds Ct. E1 ....1C **78**

Trafalgar Av. SE15..................1B **92**
Trafalgar Chambers SW3 .....1F **87**
......................*(off South Pde.)*
Trafalgar Cl. SE16 ....4A **80**
Trafalgar Ct. E1 ....2E **79**
......................*(off Wapping Wall)*
Trafalgar Gdns. E1 ....1F **65**
Trafalgar Gdns. W8.................4D **73**
Trafalgar Gro. SE10 ....2F **95**
Trafalgar Ho. SE17.................1E **91**
......................*(off Bronti Cl.)*
Trafalgar Ho. SW18...............2E **101**
Trafalgar M. E9 ....3B **52**
Trafalgar Point N1 ....4F **49**
......................*(off Downham Rd.)*
Trafalgar Quarters SE10.......2F **95**
......................*(off Park Row)*
Trafalgar Rd. SE10 ....2F **95**
Trafalgar Sq. SW1....1C **22** (2F **75**)
Trafalgar Sq. WC2....1C **22** (2F **75**)
Trafalgar Square......1C **22** (2F **75**)
Trafalgar St. SE17...................1F **91**
Trafalgar Studios 1D **23** (2A **76**)
......................*(off Whitehall)*
Trafalgar Way E14...................2E **81**
Trafford Ho. N1 ....1F **63**
......................*(off Cranston Est.)*
Trahorn Cl. E1 ....3D **65**
Trail St. E17 ....1B **38**
Traitors' Gate 1F **27** (2B **78**)
......................*(in The Tower of London)*
Tralee Ct. SE16 ....1D **93**
......................*(off Masters Dr.)*
Tram Cl. SE24 ....1D **105**
......................*(off Milkwood Rd.)*
Tramway Av. E15 ....4A **54**
Tramway Ct. E1 ....4A **66**
Tranby M. E9 ....2E **51**
......................*(off Brooksby's Wlk.)*
Tranley M. NW3 ....1A **46**
......................*(off Fleet Rd.)*
Tranmere Rd. SW18..............2E **115**
Tranquil Pas. SE3 ....5B **96**
......................*(off Montpelier Va.)*
Tranquil Va. SE3 ....5A **96**
Transenna Works N1 ....3D **49**
......................*(off Laycock St.)*
Transept St. NW1 ....4A **60**
Transom Cl. SE16 ....5A **80**
Transom Sq. E14 ....1D **95**
Tranton Rd. SE16....................4C **78**
Trappes Ho. SE16...................5D **79**
......................*(off Camilla Rd.)*
Travellers Path E6 ....5F **55**
Travers Ho. SE10 ....2F **95**
......................*(off Trafalgar Gro.)*
Travers Rd. N7 ....5C **34**
Trays Hill Cl. N19 ....1E **33**
Treadgold Ho. W11 ....1F **71**
......................*(off Bomore Rd.)*
Treadgold St. W11 ....1F **71**
Treadway St. E2......................1D **65**
Treasury Pas. SW1...3D **23** (3A **76**)
......................*(off Downing St.)*
Treaty St. N1 ....5B **48**
Trebeck St. W1 ....1D **21** (2D **75**)
Trebovir Rd. SW5 ....1C **86**
Treby St. E3 ....3B **66**
Trecastle Way N7....................1F **47**
Tredegar Ho. E3 ....2C **66**
......................*(off Bow Rd.)*
Tredegar M. E3 ....2B **66**
Tredegar Rd. E3 ....1B **66**
Tredegar Sq. E3 ....2B **66**
Tredegar Ter. E3 ....2B **66**

Trederwen Rd. E8 ....5C 50
Tredown Rd. SE26 ....5E 121
Tredwell Cl. SW2.................2B 118
Tredwell Rd. SE27 ....4D 119
Treen Av. SW13...................1B 98
Tree Rd. E16.........................5E 69
Treetop M. NW6 ....4A 44
Treewall Gdns.
　BR1: Broml 4D 125
Trefil Wlk. N7 ....1A 48
Trefoil Ho. SE10 ....5A 82
Trefoil Rd. SW18.................3E 101
Tregaron Av. N8...................1A 34
Tregarvon Rd. SW11 ....2C 102
Trego Rd. E9 ....4C 52
Tregothnan Rd. SW9 ....1A 104
Tregunter Rd. SW10.............2D 87
Treherne Ct. SW17..............4C 116
Trehern Rd. SW14.................1A 98
Trehurst St. E5.....................2A 52
Trelawney Est. E9 ....3E 51
Trelawney Ho. SE1...2F 25 (3E 77)
　...................................(off Union St.)
Trelawn Rd. E10 ....5E 39
Trelawn Rd. SW2 ....3C 104
Trellick Twr. W10..................3B 58
　...............................(off Golborne Rd.)
Trellis Sq. E3.......................2B 66
Tremadoc Rd. SW4 ....2F 103
Tremaine Cl. SE4 ....5C 94
Trematon Bldg. N1 ....1A 62
　.............................(off Trematon Wlk.)
Trematon Ho. SE11 ....1C 90
　...............................(off Kennings Way)
Trematon M. N1 ....1A 62
Trematon Wlk. N1 ....1A 62
　.................................(off Trematon M.)
Tremlett Gro. N19 ....5E 33
Tremlett M. N19....................5E 33
Trenchard Ct. NW4 ....1C 28
Trenchard St. SE10 ....1F 95
Trenchold St. SW8 ....2A 90
Trendell Ho. E14...................5C 66
　.....................................(off Dod St.)
Trenmar Gdns. NW10...........2D 57
Trent Ct. E11 ....1C 40
Trentham St. SW18 ....1C 114
Trent Ho. SE15 ....2E 107
Trent Rd. SW2 ....3B 104
Treport St. SW18 ....5D 101
Tresco Ho. SE11 ....1C 90
　................................(off Sancroft St.)
Tresco Rd. SE15..................2D 107
Tresham Cres. NW8 ....3A 60
Tresham Ho. WC1......5F 7 (4B 62)
　................................(off Red Lion Sq.)
Tresham Wlk. E9 ....2E 51
Tresidder Ho. SW4 ....5F 103
Tressell Cl. N1 ....1D 49
Tressillian Cres. SE4 ....1C 108
Tressillian Rd. SE4 ....2B 108
Tress Pl. SE1......................1D 25 (2D 77)
　..........................(off Blackfriars Rd.)
Trevanion Rd. W14 ....5A 72
Trevelyan Gdns. NW10 ....5E 43
Trevelyan Ho. E2...................2F 65
　..............................(off Morpeth St.)
Trevelyan Ho. SE5.................3D 91
　............................(off John Ruskin St.)
Trevelyan Rd. E15.................1B 54
Trevelyan Rd. SW17 ....5A 116
Trevenna Ho. SE23..............3F 121
　....................................(off Dacres Rd.)
Treveris St. SE1 ......2E 25 (2D 77)
Treverton St. W10................3F 57

Treverton Towers W10..........4F 57
　.............................(off Treverton St.)
Treves Ho. E1 ....3C 64
　.................................(off Vallance Rd.)
Treville St. SW15..................5D 99
Treviso Ho. SE23..................2F 121
Trevithick Ho. SE16 ....5D 79
　..................................(off Rennie Est.)
Trevithick St. SE8 ....2C 94
Trevithick Way E3.................2C 66
Trevor Pl. SW7 ....3A 74
Trevor Sq. SW7 ....3B 74
Trevor St. SW7 ....3A 74
Trevor Wlk. SW7 ....3B 74
　...............................(off Lancelot Pl.)
Trevose Ho. SE11 ....1B 90
　...................................(off Orsett St.)
Trewint St. SW18.................2E 115
Trewsbury Rd. SE26 ....5F 121
Tria Apts. E2 ....2C 64
　.....................................(off Durant St.)
Triangle, The E8 ....1A 50
Triangle, The EC1......3E 9 (3D 63)
　..................................(off Goswell Rd.)
Triangle Bus. Cen., The
　NW10..............................2B 56
Triangle Ct. E16 ....4F 69
Triangle Ct. SE1 ......2A 26 (2E 77)
　..............................(off Redcross Way)
Triangle Est. SE11................1C 90
　...........................(off Kennington Rd.)
Triangle Ho. SE1 ......3F 27 (3B 78)
　...............................(off Three Oak La.)
Triangle Pl. SW4 ....2F 103
Triangle Rd. E8 ....5D 51
Tribeca Apts. E1 ....4B 64
　..................................(off Heneage St.)
Trident Bus. Cen. SW17......5B 116
Trident Ho. E14 ....5E 67
　.....................................(off Blair St.)
Trident Pl. SW3 ....2F 87
　..............................(off Old Church St.)
Trident St. SE16...................5F 79
Trig La. EC4..............4F 17 (1E 77)
Trigon Rd. SW8 ....3B 90
Trilby Rd. SE23 ....2F 121
Trimdon NW1 ....5E 47
Trim St. SE14 ....2B 94
Trinder Gdns. N19 ....3A 34
Trinder M. SW12 ....1C 116
Trinder Rd. N19.....................3A 34
Trinidad Ho. E14 ....1B 80
　.......................................(off Gill St.)
Trinidad St. E14 ....1B 80
Trinity Buoy Wharf E14 ....1A 82
Trinity Chu. Pas. SW13 ....2D 85
Trinity Chu. Rd. SW13.........2D 85
Trinity Chu. Sq. SE1...4A 26 (4E 77)
Trinity Cl. E11 ....4A 40
Trinity Cl. E8 ....3B 50
Trinity Cl. NW3 ....1F 45
Trinity Cl. SE13 ....2F 109
Trinity Cl. SW4 ....2E 103
Trinity Cl. N1........................5A 50
　..............................(off Downham Rd.)
Trinity Cl. NW2 ....2E 43
Trinity Cl. SE26 ....3E 121
Trinity Cl. SE7 ....5F 83
Trinity Cl. SE8 ....1A 94
　..................................(off Evelyn St.)
Trinity Cl. SW9 ....1B 104
Trinity Cl. W2 ....5E 59
　..............................(off Gloucester Ter.)
Trinity Ct. W9 ....2B 58
　..................................(off Croxley Rd.)

Trinity Ct. WC1 ....3A 8 (3B 62)
　..............................(off Gray's Inn Rd.)
Trinity Cres. SW17 ....2B 116
Trinity Gdns. E16 ....4B 68
　...................................(not continuous)
Trinity Gdns. SW9 ....2B 104
Trinity Grn. E1 ....3E 65
Trinity Gro. SE10..................4E 95
TRINITY HOSPICE 2D 103
Trinity Hospital SE10 ....1F 95
TRINITY HOSPITAL 1F 95
Trinity Ho. SE1 ......5A 26 (4E 77)
　.................................(off Bath Ter.)
Trinity Ho. W14 ....4B 72
Trinity Laban.........................2E 95
　........(within Old Royal Naval College)
Trinity M. E1 ....4E 65
　..............................(off Redman's Rd.)
Trinity M. W10......................5F 57
Trinity Path SE26 ....3E 121
　...................................(not continuous)
Trinity Pl. EC3 ....4F 19 (1B 78)
Trinity Ri. SW2 ....1C 118
Trinity Rd. SW17 ....1A 116
Trinity Rd. SW18 ....2E 101
Trinity Rd. SW19 ....5C 114
Trinity Sq. E14 ....5A 68
Trinity Sq. EC3 ......4E 19 (1A 78)
Trinity St. E16 ....4B 68
Trinity St. SE1 ......4A 26 (3E 77)
　...................................(not continuous)
Trinity Twr. E1 ....1C 78
　..............................(off Vaughan Way)
Trinity Twr. E14 ....4D 81
Trinity Wlk. NW3 ....3E 45
Trinity Way W3.....................1A 70
Trio Pl. SE1.............4A 26 (3E 77)
Triptych Ho. SE8 ....3C 94
　..................................(off Watson's St.)
Tristan Ct. SE8 ....2B 94
　..................................(off Dorking Cl.)
Tristan Sq. SE3 ....1A 110
Tristram Rd. BR1: Broml 4B 124
Triton Ct. E16.......................4C 68
　..............................(off Robertson Rd.)
Triton Ho. E14 ....5D 81
　.....................................(off Cahir St.)
Triton Sq. NW1 ....3F 5 (3E 61)
Triton St. NW1............3E 5 (3D 61)
Tritton Rd. SE21...................3F 119
Trocette Mans.
　SE1...............5D 27 (4A 78)
　..........................(off Bermondsey St.)
Trojan Ct. NW6.....................4A 44
Trojan Ind. Est. NW10...........3B 42
Troon Cl. SE16 ....1D 93
Troon Ho. E1 ....5A 66
　..............................(off White Horse Rd.)
Troon St. E1 ....5A 66
Tropical Ct. W10...................2F 57
　..................................(off Kilburn La.)
Trossachs Rd. SE22 ....3A 106
Trothy Rd. SE1 ....5C 78
Trotman Ho. SE14 ....4E 93
　..............................(off Pomeroy St.)
Trott St. SW11 ....4A 88
Trotwood Ho. SE16 ....3D 79
　..............................(off Wilson Gro.)
Troughton Rd. SE7 ....1D 97
Troutbeck NW1 ......2E 5 (2D 61)
　..................................(off Albany St.)
Troutbeck Rd. SE14 ....4A 94
Trouville Rd. SW4 ....4E 103
Trowbridge Est. E9 ....3B 52
　..................................(off Osborne Rd.)

Trowbridge Ho. E9 ....3B **52**
Trowbridge Rd. E9 ....3B **52**
(off Felstead St.)
Troy Ct. W8 ....4C **72**
(off Kensington High St.)
Troy Town SE15 ....1C **106**
Trumans Rd. N16 ....2B **50**
Truman Wlk. E3 ....3D **67**
Trumpington Rd. E7 ....1B **54**
Trump St. EC2 ....3A **18** (5E **63**)
Trundle Ho. SE1 ......3F **25** (3E **77**)
(off Trundle St.)
Trundle St. SE1 ....3F **25** (3E **77**)
Trundleys Rd. SE8 ....1F **93**
Trundley's Ter. SE8 ....5F **79**
Truro Ho. W2 ....4C **59**
(off Westbourne Pk. Rd.)
Truro St. NW5 ....3C **46**
Truslove Rd. SE27 ....5C **118**
Trussley Rd. W6 ....4E **71**
Trust Wlk. SE21 ....1D **119**
Tryfan Cl. IG4: Ilf 1F **41**
Tryon Cres. E9 ....5E **51**
Tryon St. SW3 ....1B **88**
Tubbs Rd. NW10 ....1B **56**
Tucana Ct. E1 ....3F **11** (3B **64**)
(off Cygnet St.)
Tucana Hgts. E20 ....2E **53**
(off Cheering La.)
Tucklow Wlk. SW15 ....5B **98**
Tudor Cl. N6 ....2E **33**
Tudor Cl. NW3 ....2A **46**
Tudor Cl. SW2 ....4B **104**
Tudor Ct. E17 ....2B **38**
Tudor Ct. N1 ....3A **50**
Tudor Ct. SE16 ....2F **79**
(off Princes Riverside Rd.)
Tudor Gdns. SW13 ....1A **98**
Tudor Gro. E9 ....4E **51**
Tudor Ho. E16 ....2D **83**
(off Wesley Av.)
Tudor Ho. E9 ....4E **51**
Tudor Ho. SE1 ....2F **27** (2B **78**)
(off Duchess Wlk.)
Tudor Ho. W14 ....5F **71**
(off Windsor Way)
Tudor Rd. E6 ....5E **55**
Tudor Rd. E9 ....5D **51**
Tudor Stacks SE24 ....2E **105**
Tudor St. EC4 ....4C **16** (1C **76**)
Tudway Rd. SE3 ....2E **111**
Tufnell Ct. E3 ....5B **52**
(off Old Ford Rd.)
TUFNELL PK. 1E **47**
Tufnell Pk. Hall N7 ....5E **33**
Tufnell Pk. Rd. N19 ....1E **47**
Tufnell Pk. Rd. N7 ....1E **47**
Tufnell Park Station
(Underground) 1E **47**
Tufton Ct. SW1 ....5D **23** (4A **76**)
(off Tufton St.)
Tufton St. SW1 ....5C **22** (4A **76**)
Tugela St. SE6 ....2B **122**
Tullis Ho. E9 ....4E **51**
(off Frampton Pk. Rd.)
Tulse Hill SW2 ....4C **104**
TULSE HILL 1D **119**
Tulse Hill Est. SW2 ....4C **104**
Tulse Hill Station (Rail) 2D **119**
Tulse Ho. SW2 ....4C **104**
Tulsemere Rd. SE27 ....2E **119**
Tunbridge Ho. EC1 ...1C **8** (2D **63**)
(off St John St.)
Tunis Rd. W12 ....2E **71**
Tunley Grn. E14 ....4B **66**

Tunley Rd. NW10 ....5A **42**
Tunley Rd. SW17 ....1C **116**
Tunmarsh La. E13 ....2D **69**
Tunnel App. E14 ....1A **80**
Tunnel App. SE10 ....3A **82**
Tunnel Av. SE16 ....3E **79**
Tunnel Av. SE10 ....3F **81**
Tunnel Av. Trad. Est. SE10 ...3F **81**
Tunnel Rd. SE16 ....3E **79**
Tunstall Rd. SW9 ....2B **104**
Tunworth Cres. SW15 ....4B **98**
Tun Yd. SW8 ....5D **89**
(off Peardon St.)
Tupelo Rd. E10 ....4D **39**
Tupman Ho. SE16 ....3C **78**
(off Scott Lidgett Cres.)
Turenne Cl. SW18 ....2E **101**
Turing St. E20 ....4E **53**
Turin St. E2 ....2C **64**
Turk's Head Yd. EC1 ...5D **9** (4D **63**)
Turk's Row SW3 ....1B **88**
Turle Rd. N4 ....4B **34**
Turlewray Cl. N4 ....3B **34**
Turley Cl. E15 ....5A **54**
Turnagain La. EC4 ...2D **17** (5D **63**)
(off Farringdon St.)
Turnberry Cl. SE16 ....1D **93**
Turnberry Quay E14 ....4D **81**
Turnberry Rd. N1 ....5D **49**
Turnchapel M. SW4 ....1D **103**
Turner Cl. NW11 ....1D **31**
Turner Cl. SW9 ....3D **91**
Turner Ct. SE16 ....3E **79**
(off Albion St.)
Turner Dr. NW11 ....1D **31**
Turner Ho. E14 ....3C **80**
(off Cassilis Rd.)
Turner Ho. NW6 ....2E **45**
(off Dresden Cl.)
Turner Ho. NW8 ....1A **60**
(off Townshend Est.)
Turner Ho. SW1 ....5F **75**
(off Herrick St.)
Turner Pde. N1 ....4C **48**
(off Barnsbury Pk.)
Turner Pl. SW11 ....3A **102**
Turners Ct. E15 ....1E **53**
(off Drapers Rd.)
Turners Rd. N15 ....1F **35**
Turners Rd. E3 ....4B **66**
Turner St. E1 ....4D **65**
Turner St. E16 ....5B **68**
Turners Wood NW11 ....2E **31**
Turneville Rd. W14 ....2B **86**
Turney Rd. SE21 ....5E **105**
TURNHAM GREEN 5A **70**
Turnham Green Station
(Underground) 5A **70**
Turnham Grn. Ter. W4 ....5A **70**
Turnham Grn. Ter. M. W4 .....5A **70**
Turnham Rd. SE4 ....3A **108**
Turnmill St. EC1 ....4C **8** (3D **63**)
Turnour Ho. E1 ....5D **65**
(off Walburgh St.)
Turnpike Cl. SE8 ....3B **94**
Turnpike Ho. EC1 ...2E **9** (2D **63**)
Turnpin La. SE10 ....2E **95**
Turnstone Cl. E13 ....2C **68**
Turnstone Ho. E1 ....1C **78**
(off Star Pl.)
Turpentine La. SW1 ....1D **89**
Turpin Cl. E1 ....1F **79**
Turpin Ho. SW11 ....4D **89**
Turpins Yd. NW2 ....2F **43**
Turpins Yd. SE10 ....3E **95**

Turpin Way N19 ....4F **33**
Turquand St. SE17 ....5E **77**
Turret Gro. SW4 ....1E **103**
Turville Ho. NW8 ....3A **60**
(off Grendon St.)
Turville St. E2 ....3F **11** (3B **64**)
Tuscan Ho. E2 ....2E **65**
(off Knottisford St.)
Tuscany Corte SE13 ....1D **109**
(off Loampit Va.)
Tuskar St. SE10 ....2A **96**
Tussah Ho. E2 ....1E **65**
(off Russia La.)
Tustin Est. SE15 ....2E **93**
Tuttle Ho. SW1 ....1F **89**
(off Aylesford St.)
Tweedmouth Rd. E13 ....1D **69**
Tweed Wlk. E14 ....3E **67**
Tweezer's All. WC2 ...4B **16** (1C **76**)
(off Milford La.)
Twelvetrees Bus. Pk. E3 ....3F **67**
Twelvetrees Cres. E3 ....3E **67**
(not continuous)
Twickenham Rd. E11 ....4E **39**
Twig Folly Cl. E2 ....1F **65**
Twilley St. SW18 ....5D **101**
Twine Cl. E1 ....1E **79**
Twine Ter. E3 ....3B **66**
(off Ropery St.)
Twisden Rd. NW5 ....1D **47**
Twist Ho. SE1 ....5E **27** (4A **78**)
Two Southbank Pl.
SE1 ....3A **24** (3B **76**)
(off York Rd.)
Twycross M. SE10 ....1A **96**
Twyford Ho. N15 ....1A **36**
(off Chisley Rd.)
Twyford Ho. N5 ....5D **35**
Twyford Pl. WC2 ....2F **15** (5B **62**)
Twyford St. N1 ....5B **48**
Twynholm Mans. SW6 ....3A **86**
(off Lillie Rd.)
Tyas Rd. E16 ....3B **68**
Tyburn Ho. NW8 ....3F **59**
(off Fisherton St.)
Tyburn Tree (site of)
...................................3A **12** (1B **74**)
(off Marble Arch)
Tyburn Way W1 ....4A **12** (1B **74**)
Tyers Est. SE1 ....3D **27** (3A **78**)
(off Bermondsey St.)
Tyers St. SE11 ....1B **90**
Tyers Ter. SE11 ....1B **90**
Tyler Cl. E2 ....1B **64**
Tyler Ct. SE17 ....5F **77**
(off New Paragon Wlk.)
Tyler's Ct. W1 ....3B **14** (5F **61**)
(off Wardour St.)
Tyler St. SE10 ....1A **96**
(not continuous)
Tylney Av. SE19 ....5B **120**
Tylney Ho. E1 ....5D **65**
(off Nelson St.)
Tylney Rd. E7 ....1E **55**
Tyndale Ct. E14 ....1D **95**
(off Transom Sq.)
Tyndale Ho. E2 ....3A **52**
(off Brookfield Rd.)
Tyndale Ho. SW1 ....4D **49**
(off Tyndale La.)
Tyndale La. N1 ....4D **49**
Tyndale Mans. N1 ....4D **49**
(off Upper St.)

Tyndale Ter. N1 .... 4D 49
Tyndall Gdns. E10 ....4E 39
Tyndall Rd. E10 ....4E 39
Tyneham Cl. SW11 ....1C 102
Tyneham Rd. SW11 ....5C 88
Tynemouth St. SW6 ....5E 87
Tyne St. E1 ....2F 19 (5B 64)
Tynte Ct. E14 ....3E 67
.... (off Teviot St.)
Tynsdale Rd. NW10 ....4A 42
Tynte Ct. E9 ....2A 52
.... (off Mabley St.)
Tynwald Ho. SE26 ....3C 120
Type St. E2 ....1F 65
Tyrawley Rd. SW6 ....4D 87
Tyrell Ho. BR3: Beck. 5D 123
.... (off Beckenham Hill Rd.)
Tyrian Pl. E1 ....4C 64
Tyrols Rd. SE23 ....1F 121
Tyrrell Ho. SW1 ....2E 89
.... (off Churchill Gdns.)
Tyrrell Rd. SE22 ....2C 106
Tyrwhitt Rd. SE4 ....1C 108
Tysoe St. EC1 ....2B 8 (2C 62)
Tyson Gdns. SE23 ....5E 107
Tyson Rd. SE23 ....5E 107
Tyssen Pas. E8 ....3B 50
Tyssen Rd. N16 ....5B 36
Tyssen St. E8 ....3B 50
Tyssen St. N1 ....1A 64
Tytherton E2 ....1E 65
.... (off Cyprus St.)
Tytherton Rd. N19 ....5F 33

U

UAL (London College of Fashion)
...................................1A 16 (4B 62)
.... (off High Holborn)
Uamvar St. E14 ....4D 67
UCH MACMILLAN CANCER CEN.
...................................4A 6 (3E 61)
Udall St. SW1 ....5E 75
Udimore Ho. W10 ....4E 57
.... (off Sutton Way)
Uffington Rd. NW10 ....1C 42
Uffington Rd. SE27 ....4C 118
Ufford St. SE1 ....3C 24 (3C 76)
Ufton Gro. N1 ....4F 49
Ufton Rd. N1 ....4F 49
.... (not continuous)
Uhura Sq. N16 ....5A 36
Ujima Ct. SW16 ....4A 118
Ullathorne Rd. SW16 ....4E 117
Ullin St. E14 ....4E 67
Ullswater Cres. SW15 ....4A 112
Ullswater Ho. SE15 ....2E 93
.... (off Hillbeck Cl.)
Ullswater Rd. SE27 ....2D 119
Ullswater Rd. SW13 ....3C 84
Ulster Pl. NW1 ....4D 5 (3D 61)
Ulster Ter. NW1 ....3C 4 (3D 61)
Ulundi Rd. SE3 ....2A 96
Ulva Rd. SW15 ....3F 99
Ulverscroft Rd. SE22 ....3B 106
Ulverstone Rd. SE27 ....2D 119
Ulysses Rd. NW6 ....2B 44
Umberston St. E1 ....5C 64
Umbria St. SW15 ....4C 98
Umbriel Pl. E13 ....1C 68
Umfreville Rd. N4 ....1D 35
Undercliff Rd. SE13 ....1C 108
Underhill Ho. E14 ....4C 66
.... (off Burgess St.)
Underhill Pas. NW1 ....5D 47
.... (off Camden High St.)

Underhill Rd. SE22 ....3C 106
Underhill St. NW1 ....5D 47
Undershaft EC3 ....3D 19 (5A 64)
Undershaw Rd.
  BR1: Broml. 3B 124
Underwood Bldg., The
  EC1 ....1F 17 (4E 63)
.... (off Bartholomew Cl.)
Underwood Ct. E10 ....3D 39
.... (off Leyton Grange Est.)
Underwood Ho. W6 ....4D 71
.... (off Sycamore Gdns.)
Underwood Rd. E1 ....3C 64
Underwood Row N1 ..1A 10 (2E 63)
Underwood St. N1 ....1A 10 (2E 63)
Undine Rd. E14 ....5D 81
Undine St. SW17 ....5B 116
Unex Twr. E15 ....4F 53
.... (off Station St.)
Unicorn Bldg. E1 ....1F 79
.... (off Jardine Rd.)
Unicorn Theatre London
...................................2E 27 (2A 78)
Union Cl. E11 ....1F 53
Union Cotts. E15 ....4A 54
Union Ct. EC2 ....2D 19 (5A 64)
.... (off Old Broad St.)
Union Ct. SW4 ....5A 90
Union Ct. W9 ....4C 58
.... (off Elmfield Way)
Union Dr. E1 ....3A 66
Union Gro. SW8 ....5F 89
Union M. SW4 ....5A 90
Union Mills Apts. E8 ....5B 50
.... (off Samuel St.)
Union Pk. SE10 ....1B 96
Union Rd. E17 ....1B 38
Union Rd. SW4 ....5F 89
Union Rd. SW8 ....5F 89
Union Sq. N1 ....5E 49
Union St. SE1 ....2D 25 (2D 77)
Union Theatre 2E 25 (3D 77)
Union Wlk. E2 ....1E 11 (2A 64)
Union Wharf
  N1: Lon Arlington Av. 5E 49
Union Wharf
  N1: Lon Wenlock Rd. 1E 63
.... (off Wenlock Rd.)
Union Yd. W1 ....3E 13 (5D 61)
.... (off Brunel Rd.)
United Ho. SE16 ....3E 79
Unit Workshops E1 ....5C 64
.... (off Adler St.)
Unity Cl. NW10 ....3C 42
Unity Cl. SE19 ....5E 119
Unity Ct. SE1 ....1B 92
.... (off Fortune Pl.)
Unity M. NW1 ....1F 61
Unity Way SE18 ....4F 83
Unity Wharf SE1 ....3B 78
.... (off Mill St.)
UNIVERSITY COLLEGE HOSPITAL
  Main Site 3A 6 (3E 61)
UNIVERSITY COLLEGE HOSPITAL
  Maternity Department
...................................4A 6 (3E 61)
UNIVERSITY COLLEGE HOSPITAL
  Westmoreland Street
...................................1C 12 (4C 60)
University College London Art
  Mus. 3B 6 (3E 61)
.... (off Gower St.)
University College London
  Bloomsbury Campus
...................................3B 6 (3F 61)

University College London
  Department of Geological
  Collections 4B 6 (3F 61)
.... (off Gower St.)
University College London
  Institute of Neurology
...................................4E 7 (3A 62)
.... (off Queen Sq.)
University College London
  Slade School of Fine Art
...................................3B 6 (3F 61)
.... (off Gower St.)
University College London The
  Institute of Cancer Research
....1E 87
University College London
  Wolfson Ho. 2A 6 (2E 61)
.... (off Stephenson Way)
University College London
  Medical School University
  Hospital Campus 4E 33
.... (within Whittington Hospital)
UNIVERSITY HOSPITAL,
  LEWISHAM 3D 109
University of East London
  Stratford Campus. 3A 54
University of Greenwich
  Greenwich Campus,
  King William Wlk. 2F 95
University of Greenwich
  Maritime Greenwich Campus
....2E 95
University of London
  Birkbeck College 4C 6 (4F 61)
University of London
  Heythrop College 4D 73
.... (off Kensington Sq.)
University of London Institutes
  of Education & Advanced Legal
  Studies 4C 6 (3F 61)
University of London School of
  Hygiene & Tropical Medicine
...................................5C 6 (4F 61)
.... (off Gower St.)
University of London School of
  Oriental & African Studies
...................................4C 6 (3F 61)
.... (off Torrington Sq.)
University of London Senate
  House 5C 6 (4F 61)
University of London Warburg
  Institute 4C 6 (3F 61)
University of North London
  Hornsey Rd. 1C 48
University of North London
  Ladbrooke Ho. 2E 49
University of North London North
  London Campus, Spring House
....3C 48
University of the Arts London
  Camberwell College of Arts,
  Peckham Rd. 4A 92
University of the Arts London
  Camberwell College of Arts,
  Wilson Rd. 4A 92
University of the Arts London
  Chelsea College of Art & Design
....1F 89
University of the Arts
  London London College of
  Communication 5D 77
University of the Arts London
  London College of Fashion,
  Curtain Rd. 3E 11 (3A 64)
.... (off Curtain Rd.)

University of the Arts London
London College of Fashion,
Golden La............4F 9 (3E 63)
.................(off Golden La.)
University of the Arts London
London College of Fashion,
Mare St..........................4E 51
University of Westminster
Cavendish Campus, Hanson St.
.........................5F 5 (4E 61)
University of Westminster
Cavendish Campus, Lit.
Titchfield St........1F 13 (4E 61)
.................(off Lit. Titchfield St.)
University of Westminster
Marylebone Campus
........................5B 4 (4C 60)
University of Westminster Regent
Campus, Regent St.
........................2E 13 (5D 61)
.......................(off Regent St.)
University of Westminster
Regent Campus, Wells St...1A 14 (4E 61)
......................(off Wells St.)
University St. WC1.....4A 6 (3E 61)
Unwin Cl. SE15...................2C 92
Unwin Mans. W14...............2B 86
..................(off Queen's Club Gdns.)
Unwin Rd. SW7...................4F 73
Up at The O2........................2A 82
Upbrook M. W2....................5E 59
Upcerne Rd. SW10...............3E 87
Upcott Ho. E3.......................2D 67
.......................(off Bruce Rd.)
Upcott Ho. E9........................4E 51
.....................(off Frampton Pk. Rd.)
Upgrove Mnr. Way SW2....5C 104
Upham Pk. Rd. W4...............5A 70
Upland M. SE22...................3C 106
Upland Rd. E13....................3C 68
Upland Rd. SE22..................3C 106
.....................(not continuous)
Uplands Rd. N8.....................1B 34
Upnall Ho. SE15...................2E 93
Upnor Way SE17..................1A 92
Upper Addison Gdns. W14...3A 72
Upper Bank St. E14..............2D 81
.....................(not continuous)
Upper Bardsey Wlk. N1......3E 49
.....................(off Douglas Rd. Nth.)
Upper Belgrave St.
SW1.....................5C 20 (4C 74)
Upper Berenger Wlk. SW10...3F 87
.....................(off Worlds End Est.)
Upper Berkeley St. W1......5B 60
Upper Blantyre Wlk. SW10...3F 87
.....................(off Worlds End Est.)
Upper Brockley Rd. SE4...1B 108
.....................(not continuous)
Upper Brook St. W1....4B 12 (1C 74)
Upper Caldy Wlk. N1...........3E 49
.....................(off Caldy Wlk.)
Upper Camelford Wlk. W11...5A 58
Upper Cheyne Row SW3.....2A 88
UPPER CLAPTON..................4D 37
Upper Clapton Rd. E5...........3D 37
Upper Clarendon Wlk. W11...5A 58
.....................(off Clarendon Rd.)
Upper Dartrey Wlk. SW10....3E 87
.....................(off Worlds End Est.)
Upper Dengie Wlk. N1...........5E 49
.....................(off Baddow Wlk.)

Upper Feilde W1..........4B 12 (1C 74)
.....................(off Park St.)
Upper Grosvenor St.
W1.....................5C 12 (1C 74)
Upper Ground SE1....1B 24 (2C 76)
Upper Gulland Wlk. N1.........4E 49
.....................(off Church Rd.)
Upper Hampstead Wlk. NW3...1E 45
Upper Handa Wlk. N1...........3F 49
.....................(off Handa Wlk.)
Upper Hawkwell Wlk. N1......5E 49
.....................(off Maldon Cl.)
UPPER HOLLOWAY................4E 33
Upper Holloway Station
(Overground)......................4F 33
Upper James St. W1...4A 14 (1E 75)
Upper John St. W1......4A 14 (1E 75)
Upper Lismore Wlk. N1.........3E 49
.....................(off Clephane Rd.)
Upper Lodge W8.....................2D 73
.....................(off Palace Grn.)
Upper Mall W6.....................1C 84
.....................(not continuous)
Upper Marsh SE1.....5A 24 (4B 76)
Upper Montagu St.
W1.....................5A 4 (4B 60)
Upper Nth. St. E14................4C 66
Upper Pk. Rd. NW3...............2B 46
Upper Phillimore Gdns.
W8.......................................3C 72
Upper Ramsey Wlk. N1........3F 49
.....................(off Ramsey Wlk.)
Upper Rawreth Wlk. N1........5E 49
.....................(off Basire St.)
Upper Richmond Rd. SW15...2B 98
Upper Rd. E13....................2C 68
Upper St Martin's La.
WC2.....................4D 15 (1A 76)
Upper St. N1....................1C 62
UPPER SYDENHAM................3D 121
Upper Tachbrook St. SW1....5E 75
Upper Talbot Wlk. W11........5A 58
.....................(off Talbot Wlk.)
Upper Ter. NW3....................5E 31
Upper Thames St.
EC4.....................4E 17 (1D 77)
Upper Tollington Pk. N4......3C 34
.....................(not continuous)
Upperton Rd. E. E13.............2E 69
Upperton Rd. W. E13............2E 69
UPPER TOOTING.....................4B 116
Upper Tooting Pk. SW17...2B 116
Upper Tooting Rd. SW17...4B 116
Upper Tulse Hill SW2..........5B 104
Upper Whistler Wlk. SW10...3E 87
.....................(off Worlds End Est.)
Upper Wimpole St.
W1.....................5C 4 (4C 60)
Upper Woburn Pl. WC1...2C 6 (2F 61)
Upstairs at the Gatehouse
Theatre Highgate...............3C 32
Upstall St. SE5.....................4D 91
UPTON....................................4C 54
Upton Av. E7........................4C 54
Upton Cl. NW2......................5A 30
Upton Hgts. E7......................4C 54
Upton Ho. E9.........................2A 52
.....................(off Ward La.)
Upton La. E7..........................4C 54
Upton Lodge E7....................3C 54
UPTON PK.............................5F 55
Upton Pk. Boleyn Cinema...1F 69
Upton Pk. Rd. E7..................4D 55
Upton Park Station
(Underground)......................5E 55
Upwey Ho. N1.......................5A 50

Upwood Rd. SE12................4C 110
Urbanest King's Cross N1....5A 48
Urban M. N1..........................1D 35
Urdang, The......................2C 8 (2C 62)
.....................(off Rosebery Av.)
URGENT CARE CENTRE (ANGEL
MEDICAL PRACTICE)........1C 62
URGENT CARE CENTRE (CHELSEA
& WESTMINSTER HOSPITAL)
....2E 87
URGENT CARE CENTRE (FULHAM)
....1F 85
URGENT CARE CENTRE
(HAMMERSMITH HOSPITAL)
....5C 56
URGENT CARE CENTRE
(HAMPSTEAD)....................2A 46
URGENT CARE CENTRE
(HOMERTON UNIVERSITY
HOSPITAL)........................2F 51
URGENT CARE CENTRE
(NEWHAM)........................3E 69
URGENT CARE CENTRE (ST
CHARLES CENTRE).........4F 57
URGENT CARE CENTRE (ST
GEORGE'S HOSPITAL)....5A 116
URGENT CARE CENTRE (ST
MARY'S HOSPITAL).........5F 59
URGENT CARE CENTRE
(UNIVERSITY COLLEGE
HOSPITAL)...............3A 6 (3E 61)
URGENT CARE CENTRE
(UNIVERSITY HOSPITAL
LEWISHAM)......................3D 109
URGENT CARE CENTRE (WHIPPS
CROSS UNIVERSITY HOSPITAL)
....1F 39
URGENT CARE CENTRE
(WHITTINGTON HOSPITAL)...4E 33
Urlwin St. SE5......................2E 91
Urlwin Wlk. SW9...................4C 90
Urmston Dr. SW19...............1A 114
Urmston Ho. E14....................5E 81
.....................(off Seyssel St.)
Ursa Mans. E20....................2E 53
.....................(off Cheering La.)
Ursula Gould Way E14.........4C 66
Ursula M. N4.........................4C 34
Ursula St. SW11...................4A 88
Urswick Rd. E9.....................2E 51
Usborne M. SW8..................3B 90
Usher Rd. E3.........................5B 52
.....................(not continuous)
Usk Rd. SW11......................2E 101
Usk St. E2............................2F 65
Utah Bldg. SE13...................4D 95
.....................(off Deal's Gateway)
Utopia Village NW1..............4C 46
Uverdale Rd. SW10..............3E 87
Uxbridge Rd. W12................2C 70
Uxbridge St. W8...................2C 72

V

Vaine Ho. E9.........................3A 52
Vaizeys Wharf SE7...............4D 83
Vale, The NW11....................5F 29
Vale, The SW3......................2F 87
Vale Cl. W9..........................2E 59
Vale Cotts. SW15.................3A 112
Vale Cl. W3..........................2B 70
Vale Cl. W9..........................2E 59
Vale Cres. SW15..................4A 112
Vale End SE22....................2B 106
Vale Est., The W3.................2A 70

Vale Gro. N4 ....2E 35
Vale Lodge SE23 ....2E 121
Valencia Cl. E14 ....5F 67
Valencia Twr. EC1...... 1F 9 (2E 63)
................(off Bollinder Place)
Valentia Pl. SW9 ....2C 104
Valentine Ct. SE23 ....2F 121
..........................(not continuous)
Valentine Ho. E3 ....5B 52
................(off Garrison Rd.)
Valentine Pl. SE1....3D 25 (3D 77)
Valentine Rd. E9 ....3F 51
Valentine Row SE1 .4D 25 (3D 77)
Vale of Health NW3.................5F 31
VALE OF HEALTH 5E 31
Vale Pde. SW15.......................3A 112
Valerian Way E15.......................2A 68
Valerio M. N1 ....3F 49
Vale Ri. NW11 ....3B 30
Vale Rd. E7 ....3D 55
Vale Rd. N4 ....2E 35
Vale Row N5 ....5D 35
Vale Royal N7............................4A 48
Vale Royal Ho. WC2....4C 14 (1F 75)
................(off Charing Cross Rd.)
Vale St. SE27 ....3F 119
Valeswood Rd. BR1: Broml 5B 124
Vale Ter. N4 ....1E 35
Valetta Gro. E13 ....1C 68
Valetta Ho. SW11 ....3D 89
Valetta Rd. W3 ....3A 70
Valette Ho. E9 ....3E 51
Valette St. E9 ....3E 51
Valiant Ho. E14 ....3E 81
................(off Plevna St.)
Valiant Ho. SE7 ....1E 97
Vallance Rd. E1 ....3C 64
Vallance Rd. E2 ....2C 64
Valley, The 1E 97
Valleyfield Rd. SW16 ....5B 118
Valley Gro. SE7........................1E 97
Valley Rd. SW16 ....5B 118
Valley Side SE7 ....1F 97
Valliere Rd. NW10....................2C 56
Val McKenzie Av. N7 ....5C 34
Valmar Rd. SE5 ....4E 91
Valmar Trad. Est. SE5..............4E 91
Valnay St. SW17 ....5B 116
Valois Ho. SE1 ....5F 27 (4B 78)
................(off St Saviour's Est.)
Valonia Gdns. SW18 ....4B 100
V&A Mus. of Childhood 2E 65
Vanbrugh Castle SE10 ....2A 96
................(off Maze Hill)
Vanbrugh Cl. E16 ....4F 69
Vanbrugh Ct. SE11 ....5C 76
................(off Wincott St.)
Vanbrugh Flds. SE3 ....2B 96
Vanbrugh Hill SE10 ....1B 96
Vanbrugh Pk. SE3 ....2A 96
Vanbrugh Pk. Rd. E9 ....4E 51
................(off Loddiges Rd.)
Vanbrugh M. E15 ....1A 54
Vanbrugh Pk. SE3 ....3B 96
Vanbrugh Pk. Rd. SE3 ....3B 96
Vanbrugh Pk. Rd. W. SE3 ....3B 96
Vanbrugh Rd. W4 ....4A 70
Vanbrugh Ter. SE3 ....3B 96
Vanburgh Ho. E1 .....5F 11 (4B 64)
................(off Folgate St.)
Vancouver Ho. E1 ....2D 79
................(off Reardon Path)
Vancouver Rd. SE16 ....5F 79
................(off Needleman St.)
Vancouver Rd. SE23 ....2A 122

Vanderbilt Rd. SW18............... 1D 115
Vanderbilt Vs. W12 ....3F 71
................(off Sterne St.)
Vandervell Ct. W3 ....3A 70
................(off Amber Way)
Vandome Cl. E16 ....5D 69
Vandon Ct. SW1 .....5A 22 (4E 75)
................(off Petty France)
Vandon Pas. SW1....5A 22 (4E 75)
Vandon St. SW1 .....5A 22 (4E 75)
Vandyke Cl. SW15.....................5F 99
Vandyke Cross SE9..................3F 111
Vandy St. EC2 ....4D 11 (3A 64)
Vane Cl. NW3 ....2F 45
Vane St. SW1...........................5E 75
Vange Ho. W10.........................4E 57
................(off Sutton Way)
Van Gogh Ct. E14 ....4F 81
Vanguard Bldg. E14 ....3B 80
Vanguard Cl. E16 ....4C 68
Vanguard Ct. SE5 ....4A 92
Vanguard Ho. E8 ....4D 51
Vanguard St. SE8 ....4C 94
Vanilla & Sesame Ct.
   SE1 ....3F 27 (3B 78)
................(off Curlew St.)
Vanneck Sq. SW15...................3C 98
Vanoc Gdns. BR1: Broml 4C 124
Vansittart Rd. E7 ....1B 54
Vansittart St. SE14 ....3A 94
Vanstone Ct. N7 ....3C 48
................(off Blackthorn Av.)
Vanston Pl. SW6 ....3C 86
Vantage M. E14 ....2E 81
................(off Coldharbour)
Vantage Pl. W8 ....4C 72
Vantrey Ho. SE11 ....5C 76
................(off Marylee Way)
Vant Rd. SW17 ....5B 116
Varcoe Rd. SE16 ....1D 93
Vardens Rd. SW11...................2F 101
Varden St. E1 ....5D 65
Vardon Cl. W3 ....5A 56
Varley Ho. NW6 ....5C 44
Varley Ho. SE1..........................4E 77
................(off County St.)
Varley Rd. E16 ....5D 69
Varna Rd. SW6 ....3A 86
Varndell St. NW1 .... 1F 5 (2E 61)
Varnishers Yd. N1 .....1E 7 (1A 62)
................(off York Way)
Vartry Rd. N15 ....1F 35
Vassall Rd. E3 ....2A 66
................(off Antill Rd.)
Vassall Rd. SW9 ....3C 90
Vat Ho. SW8 ....3A 90
................(off Rita Rd.)
Vauban Est. SE16 ....4B 78
Vauban St. SE16 ....4B 78
Vaudeville Theatre...5E 15 (1A 76)
................(off Strand)
Vaughan Av. NW4 ....1C 28
Vaughan Av. W6 ....5C 70
Vaughan Est. E2........1F 11 (2B 64)
................(off Diss St.)
Vaughan Ho. SE1 .....3D 25 (3D 77)
................(off Blackfriars Rd.)
Vaughan Ho. SW4.....................5E 103
Vaughan Rd. E15 ....3B 54
Vaughan Rd. SE5 ....5E 91
Vaughan St. SE16 ....3B 80
Vaughan Way E1 ....1C 78
Vaughan Williams Cl. SE8....3C 94
VAUXHALL 2A 90
Vauxhall Bri. SW1 ....1A 90

Vauxhall Bri. Rd. SW1..............4E 75
Vauxhall Bus Station 2A 90
Vauxhall City Farm 1B 90
................(off Tyers St.)
VAUXHALL CROSS 1A 90
Vauxhall Gro. SW8 ....2A 90
Vauxhall Leisure Cen. SW8 ....2A 90
Vauxhall Station (Rail &
   Underground) 1A 90
Vauxhall St. SE11 ....1B 90
Vauxhall Wlk. SE11 ....1B 90
VauxWall East Climbing Cen.
....5B 76
VauxWall West Climbing Cen.
....2A 90
................(off Sth. Lambeth Rd.)
Vawdrey Cl. E1..........................3E 65
Veda Rd. SE13 ....2C 108
Vega Ho. E20.............................2E 53
................(off Prize Wlk.)
Velde Way SE22........................3A 106
Velletri Ho. E2 ....1F 65
................(off Mace St.)
Velodrome Queen Elizabeth
   Olympic Pk.............................2D 53
Velo Pl. E20..............................2D 53
Velvet Ho. E2 ....1B 64
................(off Whiston Rd.)
Venables St. NW8 ....3F 59
Vencourt Pl. W6 ....5C 70
Venerable Ho. E3 ....3B 66
................(off Portia Way)
Venetian Ho. E20 ....3D 53
................(off Victory Pde.)
Venetian Rd. SE5 ....5E 91
Venetia Rd. N4 ....1D 35
Venice Corte SE13 ....1E 109
................(off Elmira St.)
Venice Ct. SE5..........................3E 91
................(off Bowyer St.)
Venice Wlk. W2 ....4E 59
Venner Rd. SE26 ....5E 121
..........................(not continuous)
Venn Ho. N1 ....5B 48
................(off Barnsbury Est.)
Venn St. SW4 ....2E 103
Ventnor Rd. SE14.....................3F 93
Venture Ct. SE1 ....5E 27 (4A 78)
................(off Market Yd. M.)
Venture Ct. SE12......................5C 110
Venture Ho. W10.......................5F 57
................(off Bridge Cl.)
Venue St. E14...........................4E 67
Venus Ho. E14..........................5C 80
................(off Westferry Rd.)
Venus Ho. E3............................5C 52
................(off Garrison Rd.)
Vera Ct. E3 ....2D 67
................(off Grace Pl.)
Vera Lynn Cl. E7 ....1C 54
Vera Rd. SW6 ....4A 86
Verbena Cl. E16 ....3B 68
Verbena Gdns. W6 ....1C 84
Verdant Cl. SE6........................5A 110
................(off Verdant La.)
Verdant La. SE6 ....5A 110
Verdi Cres. W10 ....1A 58
Verdun Rd. SW13 ....2C 84
Vere Ct. W2 ....5D 59
................(off Westbourne Gdns.)
Vereker Rd. W14.......................1A 86
Verity Cl. W11 ....1A 72
Verity Ho. E3 ....2B 66
................(off Merchant St.)

Vermeer Ct. E14................4F 81
Vermeer Gdns. SE15........2E 107
Vermilion Apts. E3............5A 52
..................(off Gunmaker's La.)
Vermont Rd. SW18............4D 101
Verna Ho. E20....................2E 53
..........................(off Sunrise Cl.)
Verney Ho. NW8................3A 60
..........................(off Jerome Cres.)
Verney Rd. SE16................2C 92
Verney Way SE16..............1D 93
Vernon Ct. NW2................5B 30
Vernon Ho. SE11..............1B 90
..........................(off Vauxhall St.)
Vernon Ho. WC1.....1E 15 (4A 62)
..........................(off Vernon Pl.)
Vernon Mans. W14..............2B 86
..........................(off Queen's Club Gdns.)
Vernon M. W14..................5A 72
Vernon Pl. WC1.....1E 15 (4A 62)
Vernon Rd. WC1....1A 8 (2B 62)
Vernon Rd. E11..................3A 40
Vernon Rd. E15..................4A 54
Vernon Rd. E3....................1B 66
Vernon Sq. WC1....1A 8 (2B 62)
Vernon St. W14..................5A 72
Vernon Yd. W11..................1B 72
Verona Ct. SE14................2F 93
..........................(off Myers La.)
Verona Ct. W4..................1A 84
Verona Rd. E7..................4C 54
Veronica Ho. E3................2D 67
..........................(off Talwin St.)
Veronica Ho. SE4..............1B 108
Veronica Rd. SW17............2D 117
Verran Rd. SW12..............5D 103
Verulam Av. E17................1B 38
Verulam Bldgs.
WC1....................5A 8 (4B 62)
..........................(off Grays Inn)
Verulam Ct. NW9..............2C 28
Verulam Ho. W6................3E 71
..........................(off Hammersmith Gro.)
Verulam St. WC1.....5B 8 (4C 62)
Vervian Ho. SE15..............3C 92
..........................(off Reddins Rd.)
Verwood Ho. SW8..............3B 90
..........................(off Cobbett St.)
Verwood Lodge E14..........4F 81
..........................(off Manchester Rd.)
Veryan Ct. N8..................1F 33
Vesage Ct. EC1....1C 16 (4C 62)
..........................(off Leather La.)
Vesey Path E14................5D 67
Vespan Rd. W12................3C 70
Vespucci Ct. E14..............4A 66
..........................(off Oman Way)
Vesta Ct. SE1.....4D 27 (3A 78)
..........................(off City Wlk.)
Vesta Ho. E20..................2E 53
..........................(off Liberty Bri. Rd.)
Vesta Ho. E3....................5C 52
..........................(off Garrison Rd.)
Vesta Rd. SE4..................5A 94
Vestris Rd. SE23..............2F 121
Vestry Ct. SW1..................4F 75
..........................(off Monck St.)
Vestry M. SE5..................4A 92
Vestry M. SW18................3F 101
Vestry Rd. SE5..................4A 92
Vestry St. N1.....1B 10 (2F 63)
Vesuvius Apts. E3..............1B 66
..........................(off Centurion La.)
Vevey St. SE6..................2B 122
Viaduct Bldgs. EC1...1C 16 (4C 62)

Viaduct Gdns. SW11: Lon Ace
Way.................................2F 89
Viaduct Gdns. SW11: Lon Nine
Elms La.........................3E 89
Viaduct Pl. E2..................2D 65
Viaduct St. E2..................2D 65
Vian St. SE13..................1D 109
Vibart Gdns. SW2............5B 104
Vibart Wlk. N1..................5A 48

Vibeca Apts. E1................4B 64
..........................(off Chicksand St.)
Vicarage Av. SE3..............3C 96
Vicarage Ct. W8................3D 73
Vicarage Cres. SW11........4F 87
Vicarage Gdns. W8............2C 72
Vicarage Ga. W8................2D 73
Vicarage Gro. SE5............4F 91
Vicarage La. E15................4A 54
Vicarage M. W4..................2A 84
..........................(off Bennett St.)
Vicarage Path N8..............2A 34
Vicarage Rd. E10..............2C 38
Vicarage Rd. E15..............4B 54
Vicarage Rd. NW4..............1C 28
Vicarage Wlk. SW11..........4F 87
Vicarage Way NW10..........5A 28
Vicars Cl. E15..................5E 51
Vicars Cl. E15..................5C 54
Vicars Hill SE13................2D 109
Vicars Oak Rd. SE19........5A 120
Vicar's Rd. NW5................2C 46
Vicary Ho. EC1......1F 17 (4E 63)
..........................(off Bartholomew Cl.)
Vicentia Ct. SW11............1E 101
Viceroy Ct. NW8................1A 60
..........................(off Prince Albert Rd.)
Viceroy Rd. SW8................4A 90
Vicinity Ho. E14................1C 80
..........................(off Storehouse M.)
Vic Johnson Ho. E3..........5B 52
..........................(off Armagh Rd.)
Vickery Ct. EC1.....3A 10 (3E 63)
..........................(off Mitchell St.)
Vickery's Wharf E14..........5C 66
Victor Cazalet Ho. N1........5D 49
..........................(off Gaskin St.)
Victor Ho. SE7..................2E 97
Victoria & Albert Mus.........4F 73
Victoria Arc. SW1.....5E 21 (4D 75)
..........................(off Victoria St.)
Victoria Av. E6..................5F 55
Victoria Av. EC2....1E 19 (4A 64)
Victoria Bldgs. E8..............5D 51
..........................(off Mare St.)
Victoria Chambers
EC2....................3D 11 (3A 64)
..........................(off Paul St.)
Victoria Cl. SE22..............3C 106
Victoria Coach Station........5D 75
Victoria Colonnade
WC1....................1E 15 (4A 62)
..........................(off Southampton Row)
Victoria Cotts. E1..............4C 64
..........................(off Deal St.)
Victoria Ct. SE1................5A 78
..........................(off Hendre Rd.)
Victoria Cres. SE26............5E 121
Victoria Cres. N15............1A 36
Victoria Cres. SE19..........5A 120
Victoria Dock Rd. E16........1B 82
Victoria Dr. SW19..............5F 99
Victoria Emb. EC4...4B 16 (1C 76)
Victoria Emb. SW1..3E 23 (3A 76)

Victoria Emb. WC2....1E 23 (2A 76)
Victoria Embankment Gdns.
WC2............................1E 23 (2A 76)
..........................(off Victoria Embankment)
Victoria Gdns. W11............2C 72
Victoria Gro. W8................4E 73
Victoria Gro. M. W2..........1C 72
Victoria Hall E16................2C 82
..........................(off Wesley Av.)
Victoria Ho. SW1: Lon Ebury
Bri. Rd.........................1D 89
..........................(off Ebury Bri. Rd.)
Victoria Ho. SW1: Lon Francis St.
....................................5E 75
..........................(off Francis St.)
Victoria Ho. SE16..............3E 79
..........................(off Surrey Quays Rd.)
Victoria Ho. SW8..............3A 90
..........................(off Sth. Lambeth Rd.)
Victoria Ind. Est. W3..........4A 56
Victoria Mans. NW10........4D 43
Victoria Mans. SW8..........3A 90
..........................(off Sth. Lambeth Rd.)
Victoria Mans. W14..........2B 86
..........................(off Queen's Club Gdns.)
Victoria M. E8..................3C 50
Victoria M. NW6................3C 44
Victoria M. SW18..............1E 115
Victoria M. SW4................2D 103
Victoria M. W11................2C 72
Victoria Mills Studios E15...5F 53
..........................(off Burford Rd.)
Victorian Gro. N16............1A 50
Victorian Hgts. SW8..........5D 89
..........................(off Thackeray Rd.)
Victorian Rd. N16..............5A 36
Victoria Palace Theatre
....................................5F 21 (4E 75)
..........................(off Victoria St.)
Victoria Pde. SE10............2D 95
Victoria Pk. Hackney........5F 51
Victoria Pk. Ct. E9............4E 51
..........................(off Well St.)
Victoria Pk. Ind. Cen. E9...4C 52
..........................(off Rothbury Rd.)
Victoria Pk. Rd. E9............5E 51
Victoria Pk. Sq. E2............2E 65
Victoria Pk. Studios E9......3E 51
..........................(off Milborne St.)
Victoria Pas. NW8..............3F 59
..........................(off Fisherton St.)
Victoria Point E13..............1C 68
..........................(off Victoria Rd.)
Victoria Ri. NW6................4E 45
..........................(off Hilgrove Rd.)
Victoria Ri. SW4..............1D 103
Victoria Rd. E11................1A 54
Victoria Rd. E13................1C 68
Victoria Rd. N4..................2B 34
Victoria Rd. NW10............4A 56
Victoria Rd. NW6..............1B 58
Victoria Rd. W8..................4E 73
Victoria Sq. SW1.....5E 21 (4D 75)
Victoria Station (Rail &
Underground)..................5D 75
Victoria St. E15................4A 54
Victoria St. SW1.....5E 21 (4E 75)
Victoria Ter. N4..................3C 34
Victoria Ter. NW10............3B 56
Victoria Way SE7..............1D 97
Victoria Wharf E14............1A 80
Victoria Wharf E2..............1F 65
..........................(off Palmers Rd.)
Victoria Wharf SE8............1B 94
..........................(off Dragoon Rd.)

Victoria Works NW2.............. 4D 29
Victoria Yd. E1........................ 5C 64
Victor Rd. NW10.................... 2D 57
Victor Wharf SE1...... 1B 26 (2F 77)
................................(off Clink St.)
Victory Pde. E20.................... 3D 53
Victory Pl. E14....................... 1A 80
Victory Pl. SE17................... 5F 77
Victory Wlk. SE8................... 4C 94
Victory Way SE16................. 3A 80
Vida Ho. SE8........................ 1F 93
Video Ct. N4......................... 2B 34
View Cl. N6.......................... 2B 32
View Cres. N8...................... 1F 33
Viewfield Rd. SW18............. 4B 100
View Rd. N6........................ 2B 32
View Tube, The..................... 5D 53
................................(off Greenway)
Vigers Ct. NW10.................. 2D 57
................................(off Harrow Rd.)
Vigilant Cl. SE26.................. 4C 120
Vigo St. W1............. 5F 13 (1E 75)
Viking Cl. E3........................ 1A 66
Viking Ct. SW6.................... 2C 86
Viking Gdns. E6.................... 3F 69
Viking Ho. SE18................... 5F 83
................................(off Pett St.)
Viking Ho. SE5..................... 5E 91
................................(off Denmark Rd.)
Viking Pl. E10...................... 3B 38
Village, The NW3................. 4E 31
Village, The SE7.................. 2E 97
Village Cl. NW3.................... 2F 45
................................(off Belsize La.)
Village Ct. SE3.................... 1A 110
................................(off Hurren Cl.)
Village Ctyd. SW11.............. 2D 88
................................(off Arches La.)
Village M. SW18.................. 1B 114
................................(off Elsenham St.)
Village Mt. NW3................... 1E 45
................................(off Perrins Ct.)
Village Way NW10................ 1A 42
Village Way SE21................. 4F 105
Villa Rd. SW9...................... 1C 104
Villas on the Heath NW3......5E 31
Villa St. SE17...................... 1F 91
Villa Wlk. SE17.................... 1F 91
................................(off Villa St.)
Villiers Cl. E10..................... 4C 38
Villiers Ct. SW11................. 4A 88
................................(off Battersea Bri. Rd.)
Villiers Gdns. E20................ 2D 53
Villiers Rd. NW2.................. 3C 42
Villiers Rd. NW2.................. 3C 42
Villiers St. WC2...... 1E 23 (2A 76)
Vimy Ridge Ct. E3................ 1A 80
................................(off Festubert Pl.)
Vince Ct. N1............ 2C 10 (2F 63)
Vincennes Est. SE27............ 4F 119
Vincent Cl. SE16.................. 3A 80
Vincent Ct. N4...................... 3A 34
Vincent Ct. SW9.................. 4B 90
Vincent Ct. W1........ 2A 12 (5B 60)
................................(off Seymour Pl.)
Vincent Gdns. NW2.............. 5B 28
Vincent Ho.
    SW1: Lon Regency St......5F 75
................................(off Regency St.)
Vincent Ho.
    SW1: Lon Vincent Sq.......5F 75
................................(off Vincent Sq.)
Vincent M. E3....................... 1C 66

Vincent Sq. SW1.................. 5F 75
Vincent Sq. Mans. SW1........5F 75
................................(off Walcott St.)
Vincent St. E16.................... 4B 68
Vincent St. SW1.................. 5F 75
Vincent's Yd. SW9............... 4C 90
................................(off Alphabet M.)
Vincent Ter. N1.................... 1D 63
Vince St. EC1.......... 2C 10 (2F 63)
Vine Cl. E5.......................... 1C 50
Vine Cotts. E1...................... 5E 65
................................(off Sidney Sq.)
Vine Ct. E1.......................... 4C 64
Vinegar St. E1..................... 2D 79
Vinegar Yd. SE1......3D 27 (3A 78)
Vine Hill EC1............ 4B 8 (3C 62)
Vine La. SE1............ 2E 27 (2A 78)
Vineries, The SE6................. 1C 122
Vine Rd. E15........................ 4B 54
Vine Rd. SW13..................... 1B 98
Vinery, The SW8.................. 3A 90
................................(off Regent's Bri. Gdns.)
Vinery Way W6..................... 4D 71
Vinery Way W14.................... 1B 86
................................(off Star Rd.)
Vine St. EC3............ 3F 19 (5B 64)
Vine St. W1............ 5A 14 (1E 75)
Vine St. Bri. EC1........ 4C 8 (3C 62)
Vine Yd. SE1........... 3A 26 (3E 77)
................................(off Sanctuary St.)
Vineyard Cl. SE6................. 1C 122
Vineyard Hill Rd. SW19.........4B 114
Vineyard Wlk. EC1.....3B 8 (3C 62)
Viney Rd. SE13..................... 1D 109
Vining St. SW9.................... 2C 104
Vinson Ho. N1..................... 1F 63
................................(off Cranston Est.)
Vintner's Ct. EC4.....4A 18 (1E 77)
Vintner's Pl. EC4.....4A 18 (1E 77)
Vintry Ct. SE1....... 4C 26 (3F 77)
................................(off Porlock St.)
Viola Sq. W12....................... 1B 70
Violet Cl. E16...................... 3A 68
Violet Cl. SE8...................... 2B 94
Violet Ct. E15...................... 4A 54
................................(off Victoria St.)
Violet Hill NW8.................... 1E 59
Violet Hill Ho. NW8.............. 1E 59
................................(off Violet Hill)
Violet Rd. E17..................... 1C 38
Violet Rd. E3....................... 3D 67
Violet St. E2....................... 3D 65
VIP Trading Est. SE7............ 5E 83
Virgil Pl. W1........................ 4B 60
Virgil St. SE1........... 5A 24 (4B 76)
Virgin Active Aldersgate
................................1F 17 (4E 63)
................................(off Aldersgate St.)
Virgin Active Bank...2C 18 (5F 63)
................................(off Aldersgate St.)
Virgin Active Barbican
................................5F 9 (4E 63)
................................(off Aldersgate St.)
Virgin Active Broadgate
................................5D 11 (4A 64)
................................(off Exchange Pl.)
Virgin Active Chelsea...........2E 87
Virgin Active Chiswick..........4A 84
Virgin Active Cricklewood.....5A 30
Virgin Active Crouch End.....1A 34
................................(off Tottenham La.)
Virgin Active Fulham Pools...2A 86
Virgin Active Hammersmith...5F 71
................................(off Hammersmith Rd.)
Virgin Active Islington
................................1D 9 (1D 63)

Virgin Active Kensington.....3D 73
................................(off Old Court Pl.)
Virgin Active Mansion Ho.
................................4A 18 (1E 77)
................................(off Lit. Trinity La.)
Virgin Active Mayfair
................................3B 12 (5C 60)
Virgin Active Moorgate
................................4B 10 (3F 63)
Virgin Active Notting Hill..... 5A 58
Virgin Active Smugglers Way
................................2D 101
Virgin Active Strand
................................5E 15 (1A 76)
Virgin Active Streatham.......3A 118
Virgin Active Swiss Cottage
................................3E 45
................................(within O2 Centre)
Virgin Active Tower Bridge
................................4F 19 (1B 78)
................................(off Haydon St.)
Virgin Active Walbrook
................................4B 18 (1F 77)
Virgin Active West London...2A 70
Virginia Ct. SE16................. 3F 79
................................(off Eleanor Cl.)
Virginia Ct. WC1.....3C 6 (3F 61)
................................(off Burton St.)
Virginia Ho. E14.................. 1E 81
................................(off Newby Pl.)
Virginia Quay Pk................. 1F 81
................................(off Newport Avenue)
Virginia Rd. E2....... 2F 11 (2B 64)
Virginia St. E1..................... 1C 78
Virginia Wlk. SW2............... 4B 104
Viridian Apts. SW8.............. 3E 89
Visage Apts. NW3............... 4F 45
................................(off Winchester Rd.)
Viscount Ct. W2................... 5C 58
................................(off Pembridge Vs.)
Viscount St. EC1...... 4F 9 (3E 63)
Vista, The SE9.................... 4F 111
Vista Bldg. E3.................... 2B 66
................................(off Bow Rd.)
Vista Ct. E1........................ 4A 66
................................(off Ocean Est.)
Vista Dr. IG4: IIf................. 1F 41
Vista Ho. N4....................... 4C 34
Vitae Apts. W6..................... 4C 70
Vitali Cl. SW15................... 4C 98
Vittoria Ho. N1.................... 5B 48
................................(off High Rd.)
Vivian Av. NW4................... 1D 29
Vivian Comma Cl. N4...........5D 35
Vivian Ct. W9...................... 1D 59
Vivian Mans. NW4............... 1D 29
................................(off Vivian Av.)
Vivian Rd. E3...................... 1A 66
Vivian Sq. SE15.................. 1D 107
Vixen M. E8........................ 4B 50
................................(off Haggerston Rd.)
Vogans Mill SE1.................. 3B 78
Vogler Ho. E1..................... 1E 79
................................(off Cable St.)
Vollasky Ho. E1................... 4C 64
................................(off Daplyn St.)
Voltaire Rd. SW4................. 1F 103
Volt Av. NW10..................... 2A 56
Voluntary Pl. E11................ 1C 40
Vorley Rd. N19.................... 4E 33
Voss St. E2......................... 2C 64
Voyager Bus. Est. SE16.......4C 78
................................(off Spa Rd.)
Voyager Ct. E16.................. 4C 68
................................(off Hammersley Rd.)
Voysey Sq. E3.................... 3D 67

Vue Cinema Apollo....5B 14 (1F 75)
................(off Regent St.)
Vue Cinema Finchley Rd. ...3E 45
................(within O2 Centre)
Vue Cinema Fulham Broadway
................3C 86
Vue Cinema Islington 1C 62
Vue Cinema Leicester Square
................4C 14 (1F 75)
................(off Cranbourn St.)
Vue Cinema Shepherds Bush
................3F 71
Vue Cinema Stratford City ...3E 53
................(in Shopping Cen.)
Vue Cinema Westfield 2E 71
Vulcan Rd. SE4................5B 94
Vulcan Sq. E14................5D 81
Vulcan Ter. SE4................5B 94
Vulcan Way N7................3B 48
Vulcan Wharf E15............1D 67
................(off Cook's Rd.)
Vyner Rd. W3................1A 70
Vyner St. E2................5D 51

W

Wadding St. SE17............5F 77
Waddington Rd. E15........2F 53
Waddington St. E15........3F 53
Wade Ho. SE1................3C 78
................(off Parkers Row)
Wadeson St. E2................1D 65
Wade's Pl. E14................1D 81
Wadham Gdns. NW3........5A 46
Wadham Rd. SW15........2A 100
Wadhurst Rd. SW8..........4E 89
Wadley Rd. E11................2A 40
Wager St. E3................3B 66
Waghorn Rd. E13............5E 55
Waghorn St. SE15..........1C 106
Wagner St. SE15............3E 93
Wagtail Cl. SW15............4E 99
Wainford Cl. SW19........1F 113
Wainwright Ho. E1..........2E 79
................(off Garnet St.)
Waite Davies Rd. SE12 ...5B 110
Waite Ho. W3................2B 70
Waite St. SE15................2B 92
Waithman St. EC4 ...3D 17 (5D 63)
................(off Black Friars La.)
Wakefield Ct. SE26..........1E 121
Wakefield Gdns. IG1: Ilf 1F 41
Wakefield Ho. SE15..........4C 92
Wakefield M. WC1 ...2E 7 (2A 62)
Wakefield Rd. N15..........1B 36
Wakefield St. E6................5F 55
Wakefield St. WC1 ...2E 7 (2A 62)
Wakeford Cl. SW4..........3E 103
Wakeham St. N1..............3F 49
Wakehurst Rd. SW11......3A 102
Wakeling St. E14............5A 66
Wakelin Ho. N1................4D 49
................(off Sebbon St.)
Wakelin Ho. E15..............1A 68
Wakeman Ho. NW10........2F 57
................(off Wakeman Rd.)
Wakeman Rd. NW10........2E 57
Wakeup Docklands 1C 82
Wakley St. EC1....1D 9 (2D 63)
Walberswick St. SW8 ......3A 90
Walbrook EC4 ....4B 18 (1F 77)
................(not continuous)
Walbrook Bldg., The
EC4................4B 18 (1F 77)
................(off Walbrook)

Walbrook Ct. N1................1A 64
................(off Hemsworth St.)
Walbrook Wharf
EC4................5A 18 (1E 77)
................(off Cousin La.)
Walburgh St. E1..............5D 65
Walcorde Av. SE17..........5E 77
Walcot Gdns. SE11..........5C 76
................(off Kennington Rd.)
Walcot Sq. SE11..............5C 76
Walcott St. SW1..............5E 75
Waldeck Gro. SE27..........3D 119
Waldemar Av. SW6..........4A 86
Waldemar Rd. SW19........5C 114
Walden Ct. SW8..............4F 89
Walden Ho. SW1..............5C 74
................(off Pimlico Rd.)
Walden Ho. SW11............4C 88
................(off Dagnall St.)
Waldenshaw Rd. SE23......1E 121
Walden St. E1..................5D 65
................(not continuous)
Waldo Cl. SW4................3E 103
Waldo Ho. NW10..............2D 57
................(off Waldo Rd.)
Waldo Rd. NW10..............2C 56
Waldram Cres. SE23........1E 121
Waldram Pk. Rd. SE23......1F 121
Waldram Pl. SE23............1E 121
Waldron M. SW3..............2F 87
Waldron Rd. SW18..........3E 115
Waleorde Rd. SE17..........1E 91
Walerand Rd. SE13..........5E 95
Waleran Flats SE1............5A 78
Wales Cl. SE15................2D 93
Wales Office 2D 23 (2A 76)
................(off Whitehall)
Waley St. E1....................4A 66
Walford Ho. E1................5D 65
Walford Rd. N16..............1A 50
WALHAM GREEN 4C 86
................(off Waterford Rd.)
Walham Grn. Ct. SW6......3D 87
Walham Gro. SW6............3C 86
Walham Ri. SW19............5A 114
Walham Yd. SW6............3C 86
Walker Ho. NW1 ......1B 6 (1F 61)
Walker Ho. SE16..............4B 80
................(off Redriff Est.)
Walker M. SW2................3C 104
Walker's Ct. W1 ....4B 14 (1F 75)
................(off Brewer St.)
Walkerscroft Mead SE21....1E 119
Walkers Lodge E14..........3E 81
................(off Manchester Rd.)
Walkers Pl. SW15..........2A 100
Walkinshaw Ct. N1..........4E 49
................(off Rotherfield St.)
Walkynscroft SE15..........5D 93
................(off Caulfield Rd.)
Wallace Bldg. NW8..........3F 59
................(off Penfold St.)
Wallace Collection ...2B 12 (5C 60)
Wallace Ct. NW1..............4A 60
................(off Old Marylebone Rd.)
Wallace Ct. SE3..............2D 111
Wallace Ho. N7................3B 48
................(off Caledonian Rd.)
Wallace Rd. N1................3E 49
Wallace Way N13..............4F 33
................(off St John's Way)
Wallbutton Rd. SE4..........5A 94
Wallcote Av. NW2............3F 29
Wall Ct. N4....................3B 34
................(off Stroud Grn. Rd.)

Wallenberg Pl. W1 ...3A 12 (5B 60)
................(off Gt. Cumberland Pl.)
Waller Rd. SE14..............4F 93
Waller Way SE10..............3D 95
Wallflower St. W12..........1B 70
Wallgrave Rd. SW5..........5D 73
Wallingford Av. W10........4F 57
Wallis All. SE1........3A 26 (3E 77)
................(off Marshalsea Rd.)
Wallis Cl. SW11..............1F 101
Wallis Ho. SE14..............3B 94
Wallis Rd. E9..................3B 52
Wallis's Cotts. SW2..........5A 104
Wallorton Gdns. SW14......2A 98
Wallpaper Apts., The N1.....4C 48
................(off Offord Rd.)
Wallside EC2..................1A 18 (4E 63)
................(off Monkwell Sq.)
Wall St. N1....................3F 49
Wallwood Rd. E11............2F 39
Wallwood St. E14............4B 66
Walmer Ho. W10..............5F 57
................(off Bramley Rd.)
Walmer Pl. W1................4B 60
................(off Walmer St.)
Walmer Rd. W10..............5F 57
Walmer Rd. W11..............1A 72
Walmer St. W1................4B 60
Walmer Ter. SE18............2D 97
Walm La. NW2................3E 43
Walney Wlk. N1................3E 49
Walnut Cl. SE8................2B 94
Walnut Ct. W8................4D 73
................(off St Mary's Ga.)
Walnut Gdns. E15............2A 54
Walnut Ho. E3................5B 52
................(off Barge La.)
Walnut Rd. E10................4C 38
Walnut Tree Cl. SW13......4B 84
Walnut Tree Cotts. SW19...5A 114
Walnut Tree Ho. SW10......2D 87
................(off Tregunter Rd.)
Walnut Tree Rd. SE10......1A 96
................(not continuous)
Walnut Tree Wlk. SE11......5C 76
Walpole Ct. NW6..............4E 45
................(off Fairfax Rd.)
Walpole Ct. W14..............4F 71
................(off Blythe Rd.)
Walpole Ho. SE1......4B 24 (3C 76)
................(off Westminster Bri. Rd.)
Walpole Ho. SW15..........3A 100
................(off Plaza Gdns.)
Walpole M. NW8..............5F 45
Walpole Rd. E6................4E 55
Walpole Rd. SW19............5F 115
Walpole St. SW3..............1B 88
Walsham Cl. N16..............3C 36
Walsham Ho. SE14..........5F 93
Walsham Ho. SE17..........1F 91
................(off Blackwood St.)
Walsham Rd. SE14..........5F 93
Walsingham NW8..............5F 45
Walsingham Lodge SW13...4C 84
Walsingham Mans. SW6.....3D 87
................(off Fulham Rd.)
Walsingham Pl. SW4........4C 102
Walsingham Rd. E5..........5C 36
Walston Ho. SW1..............1F 89
................(off Aylesford St.)
Walter Besant Ho. E1........2F 65
................(off Bancroft Rd.)
Walter Grn. Ho. SE15........4E 93
................(off Lausanne Rd.)
Walter Ho. SW10..............3F 87
................(off Riley Rd.)

Walter Langley Ct. SE16 ....3E **79**
................................(off Brunel Rd.)
Walter Savil Twr. E17 ....1C **38**
................................(off Colchester Rd.)
Walters Cl. SE17 ....5F **77**
................................(off Brandon St.)
Walters Ho. N1 ....5D **49**
................................(off Essex Rd.)
Walters Rd. SE17 ....2D **91**
................................(off Otto St.)
Walter Sickert Hall
N1 ....1F **9** (1E **63**)
................................(off Graham St.)
Walter St. E2 ....2F **65**
Walters Way SE23 ....4F **107**
Walter Ter. E1 ....5F **65**
Walterton Rd. W9 ....3B **58**
Waltham Ho. N4 ....5E **45**
Walthamstow Leisure Cen. 1B **38**
Walthamstow Marsh Nature
Reserve 2D **37**
Walthamstow Pumphouse Mus.
....1A **38**
Walthamstow Queens Road
Station (Overground) 1C **38**
Walton Cl. E5 ....5F **37**
................................(off Orient Way)
Walton Cl. NW2 ....4D **29**
Walton Cl. SW8 ....3A **90**
Walton Ct. NW6 ....4E **45**
................................(off Fairfax Rd.)
Walton Dr. NW10 ....3A **42**
Walton Ho. E2 ....3F **11** (3B **64**)
................................(off Montclare St.)
Walton Ho. NW1 ....3E **5** (3D **61**)
................................(off Longford St.)
Walton Ho. SW3 ....4B **74**
................................(off Walton St.)
Walton Pl. SW3 ....5A **20** (4B **74**)
Walton Rd. E13 ....1E **69**
Walton St. SW3 ....5A **74**
Walton Vs. N1 ....4A **50**
................................(off Downham Rd.)
Walt Whitman Cl. SE24 ....2D **105**
WALWORTH 1E **91**
Walworth Pl. SE17 ....1E **91**
Walworth Rd. SE1 ....5E **77**
Walworth Rd. SE17 ....5E **77**
Walworth Sq. SE17 ....5E **77**
Wanborough Dr. SW15 ....1D **113**
Wandle Ho. BR1: Broml 5F **123**
Wandle Ho. NW8 ....4A **60**
................................(off Penfold St.)
Wandle Meadow Nature Pk.
....5E **115**
Wandle Recreation Cen. 4D **101**
Wandle Rd. SW17 ....2A **116**
Wandle Way SW18 ....1D **115**
Wandon Rd. SW6 ....3D **87**
WANDSWORTH 3D **101**
Wandsworth Bri. SW6 ....4D **87**
WANDSWORTH COMMON 1B **116**
Wandsworth Common Station
(Rail) 1B **116**
Wandsworth Comn. W. Side
SW18 ....3E **101**
WANDSWORTH GYRATORY 3D **101**
Wandsworth High St.
SW18 ....3C **100**
Wandsworth Mus. 3C **100**
Wandsworth Plain SW18 ....3C **100**
Wandsworth Riverside Quarter
Pier (River Bus) 2C **100**
Wandsworth Rd. SW8 ....1D **103**

Wandsworth Road Station
(Overground) 5E **89**
Wandsworth Town Station (Rail)
....2D **101**
Wangford Ho. SW9 ....2D **105**
................................(off Loughborough Pk.)
Wanless Rd. SE24 ....1E **105**
Wanley Rd. SE5 ....2F **105**
Wanlip Rd. E13 ....3D **69**
Wansbeck Rd. E9 ....4B **52**
Wansdown Pl. SW6 ....3D **87**
Wansey St. SE17 ....5E **77**
WANSTEAD 1D **41**
Wanstead Gdns. IG4: Ilf 1F **41**
Wanstead Golf Course 2E **41**
Wanstead La. IG1: Ilf 1F **41**
Wanstead Leisure Cen. 1E **41**
Wanstead Pk. Av. E12 ....3F **41**
Wanstead Pk. Rd. IG1: Ilf 1F **41**
Wanstead Park Station
(Overground) 1D **55**
Wanstead Pl. E11 ....1C **40**
Wanstead Station (Underground)
....1D **41**
Wantage Rd. SE12 ....3B **110**
WAPPING 2D **79**
Wapping Dock St. E1 ....2D **79**
Wapping High St. E1 ....2C **78**
Wapping La. E1 ....1D **79**
Wapping Station (Overground)
....2E **79**
Wapping Wall E1 ....2E **79**
Warbeck Rd. W12 ....3D **71**
Warburton Cl. N1 ....3A **50**
................................(off Culford Rd.)
Warburton Ho. E8 ....5D **51**
................................(off Warburton St.)
Warburton Rd. E8 ....5D **51**
Warburton St. E8 ....5D **51**
Wardalls Gro. SE14 ....3E **93**
Wardalls Ho. SE8 ....2B **94**
................................(off Staunton St.)
Wardell Ho. SE10 ....2E **95**
................................(off Welland St.)
Wardell M. SW4 ....1D **103**
Warden Rd. NW5 ....3C **46**
Wardens Gro. SE1 ......1F **25** (2E **77**)
Ward La. E9 ....2A **52**
Wardle St. E9 ....2F **51**
Wardley St. SW18 ....5D **101**
Wardour Av. SW6 ....4A **86**
Wardour M. W1 ....3A **14** (5E **61**)
................................(off D'Arblay St.)
Wardour St. W1 ....2A **14** (5E **61**)
Ward Point SE11 ....5C **76**
Ward Rd. E15 ....5F **53**
Ward Rd. N19 ....5E **33**
Wardrobe Pl. EC4 ....3E **17** (5D **63**)
................................(off Carter La.)
Wardrobe Ter. EC4 .....4E **17** (1D **77**)
................................(off Addle Hill)
Wardroper Ho. SE1 ....5D **25** (4D **77**)
................................(off St George's St.)
Wards Wharf App. E16 ....2F **83**
Wareham Ct. N1 ....4A **50**
................................(off Hertford Rd.)
Wareham Ho. SW8 ....3B **90**
Warehome M. E13 ....3C **68**
................................(off Jutland Rd.)
Warehouse, The 2C **24** (2C **76**)
................................(off Theed St.)
Warehouse Way E16 ....1D **83**
Warfield Rd. NW10 ....2F **57**
Warfield Yd. NW10 ....2F **57**
................................(off Warfield Rd.)

Wargrave Av. N15 ....1B **36**
Wargrave Ho. E2 ....2F **11** (2B **64**)
................................(off Navarre St.)
Warham Rd. N4 ....1C **34**
Warham St. SE5 ....3D **91**
Waring St. SE27 ....4E **119**
Warley Cl. E10 ....3B **38**
Warley St. E2 ....2F **65**
Warlingham Ct. SE13 ....4E **109**
Warlock Rd. W9 ....3B **58**
Warlters Cl. N7 ....1A **48**
Warlters Rd. N7 ....1A **48**
Warltersville Mans. N19 ....2A **34**
Warltersville Rd. N19 ....2A **34**
Warmington Cl. E5 ....5F **37**
Warmington Rd. SE24 ....4E **105**
Warmington St. E13 ....3C **68**
Warmsworth NW1 ....5E **47**
................................(off Pratt St.)
Warndon St. SE16 ....5F **79**
Warneford St. E9 ....5D **51**
Warner Cl. E15 ....2A **54**
Warner Ho. BR3: Beck 5D **123**
Warner Ho. NW8 ....2E **59**
Warner Ho. SE13 ....5D **95**
................................(off Russett Way)
Warner Pl. E2 ....1C **64**
Warner Rd. SE5 ....4E **91**
Warner St. EC1 ....4B **8** (3C **62**)
Warner Ter. E14 ....4D **67**
................................(off Broomfield St.)
Warner Yd. EC1 ....4B **8** (3C **62**)
Warnford Ct. EC2 ....2C **18** (5F **63**)
................................(off Throgmorton Av.)
Warnford Ho. SW15 ....4A **98**
................................(off Tunworth Cres.)
Warnham WC1 ....2F **7** (2B **62**)
................................(off Sidmouth St.)
Warnham Ho. SW2 ....5B **104**
................................(off Up. Tulse Hill)
Warple M. W3 ....3A **70**
Warple Way W3 ....3A **70**
Warren Av. E10 ....5E **39**
Warren Cl. SE21 ....5E **105**
Warren Ct. NW1 ....3A **6** (3E **61**)
................................(off Warren St.)
Warren Ct. SE7 ....2E **97**
Warrender Rd. N19 ....5E **33**
Warren Dr., The E11 ....2E **41**
Warren Gdns. E15 ....2E **53**
Warren Ho. E3 ....2D **67**
................................(off Bromley High St.)
Warren Ho. W14 ....5B **72**
Warren M. W1 ....4F **5** (3E **61**)
Warren Pl. E1 ....5F **65**
................................(off Pitsea St.)
Warren Rd. E10 ....5E **39**
Warren Rd. E11 ....1E **41**
Warren Rd. NW2 ....4B **28**
Warren St. W1 ....4F **5** (3E **61**)
Warren Street Station
(Underground) 3A **6** (3E **61**)
Warren Wlk. SE7 ....2E **97**
Warriner Gdns. SW11 ....4B **88**
Warrington Cres. W9 ....3E **59**
Warrington Gdns. W9 ....3E **59**
................................(not continuous)
Warrior Cl. SW9 ....1D **105**
................................(off Coldharbour Rd.)
Warspite Ho. E14 ....5D **81**
................................(off Cahir St.)
Warspite Rd. SE18 ....4F **83**
Warton Ct. E1 ....1F **79**
................................(off Cable St.)

Warton Ho. E15 ....5E 53
.... (off High St.)
Warton Rd. E15 ....5E 53
Warwick W14 ....5B 72
.... (off Kensington Village)
Warwick Av. W2 ....4E 59
Warwick Av. W9 ....3D 59
Warwick Avenue Station
(Underground) 3E 59
Warwick Bldg. SW11 ....2D 89
Warwick Chambers W8 ....4C 72
.... (off Pater St.)
Warwick Cl. W8 ....4B 72
.... (off Kensington High St.)
Warwick Ct. EC4 ....3E 17 (5D 63)
.... (off Warwick La.)
Warwick Ct. WC1 ....1A 16 (4B 62)
Warwick Cres. W2 ....4E 59
Warwick Dr. SW15 ....1D 99
Warwick Est. W2 ....4D 59
Warwick Gdns. N4 ....1E 35
Warwick Gdns. W14 ....4B 72
Warwick Gro. E5 ....3D 37
Warwick Ho. E16 ....2C 82
.... (off Wesley Av.)
Warwick Ho. W9 ....5C 90
Warwick Ho. St.
SW1 ....1C 22 (2F 75)
Warwick La. EC4 ....2E 17 (5D 63)
Warwick La. W14 ....5B 72
Warwick Mans. SW5 ....5C 72
.... (off Cromwell Cres.)
Warwick Pas. EC4 ...2E 17 (5D 63)
.... (off Old Bailey)
Warwick Pl. W9 ....4E 59
Warwick Pl. Nth. SW1 ....5E 75
Warwick Rd. E12 ....2F 55
Warwick Rd. E15 ....3B 54
Warwick Rd. SW5 ....5C 72
Warwick Rd. W14 ....5B 72
Warwick Row SW1 ....5E 21 (4E 75)
Warwickshire Path SE8 ......3B 94
Warwickshire Rd. N16 ....1A 50
Warwick Sq. EC4 ....2E 17 (5D 63)
Warwick Sq. SW1 ....1E 89
.... (not continuous)
Warwick Sq. M. SW1 ....5E 75
Warwick St. W1 ....4A 14 (1E 75)
Warwick Ter. E17 ....1F 39
.... (off Lea Bri. Rd.)
Warwick Way SW1 ....1D 89
Warwick Yd. EC1 ....4A 10 (3E 63)
Wasdale NW1 ....1E 5 (2D 61)
.... (off Cumberland Mkt.)
Washbourne Rd. NW10 ....5A 42
Washington Bldg. SE13 .....4D 95
.... (off Deal's Gateway)
Washington Cl. E3 ....2D 67
Washington Ho.
SW3 ....4A 20 (3B 74)
.... (off Basil St.)
Washington Rd. E6 ....4E 55
Washington Rd. SW13 ....3C 84
Wastdale Rd. SE23 ....1F 121
Waterbank Rd. SW18 ....1D 115
.... (off Knaresborough Dr.)
Waterbank Rd. SE6 ....3D 123
Water Brook La. NW4 ....1E 29
Watercress Pl. N1 ....4A 50
Waterden Ct. W11 ....2A 72
Waterden Rd. E20 ....2C 52
Waterer Ho. SE6 ....4E 123
Waterfall Cotts. SW19 .....5F 115
Waterfall Ho. SE2 ....3C 104
.... (off Brixton Water La.)

Waterfall Rd. SW19 ....5F 115
Waterfall Ter. SW17 ....5A 116
Waterford Ho. W11 ....1B 72
.... (off Kensington Pk. Rd.)
Waterford Point SW8 ....3A 90
Waterford Rd. SW6 ....3D 87
Waterford Way NW10 ....2D 43
Waterfront W6 ....2E 85
Waterfront Dr. SW10 ......4E 87
Waterfront Ho. E5 ....4E 37
.... (off Harry Zeital Way)
Waterfront M. N1 ....1E 63
Waterfront Studios Bus. Cen.
E16 ....2B 82
.... (off Dock Rd.)
Water Gdns., The W2 ......5A 60
Water Gdns. Sq. SE16 .....3F 79
Watergate EC4 ....4D 17 (1D 77)
Watergate St. SE8 ....2C 94
Watergate Wlk. E14 ....4D 81
Watergate Wlk.
WC2 ....1E 23 (2A 76)
Waterhead NW1 ......1F 5 (2E 61)
.... (off Varndell St.)
Waterhouse Cl. E16 ....4F 69
Waterhouse Cl. NW3 ....2F 45
Waterhouse Cl. W6 ....5F 71
Waterhouse Sq.
EC1 ....1B 16 (4C 62)
Wateridge Cl. E14 ....4C 80
Water La. E15 ....3A 54
Water La. EC3 .....5E 19 (1A 78)
Water La. NW1 ....4D 47
Water La. SE14 ....3E 93
Waterline Ho. W2 ....4A 60
.... (off Harbet Rd.)
Waterloo Bri. WC2 ...1A 24 (1B 76)
Waterloo Cl. E9 ....2E 51
Waterloo East Station (Rail)
..................2C 24 (2C 76)
Waterloo East Theatre
..................2C 24 (2C 76)
.... (off Brad St.)
Waterloo Gdns. E2 ....1E 65
Waterloo Gdns. N1 ....4D 49
Waterloo Pas. NW6 ....4B 44
Waterloo Pl. SW1 ...1B 22 (2F 75)
Waterloo Rd. E6 ....2C 38
Waterloo Rd. E10 ....2C 38
Waterloo Rd. E6 ....4E 55
Waterloo Rd. E7 ....2B 54
Waterloo Rd. NW2 ....3C 28
Waterloo Rd. SE1 ...1A 24 (2B 76)
Waterloo Station (Rail &
Underground) 3A 24 (3C 76)
Waterloo Ter. N1 ....4D 49
Waterloo Bldg., The E3 ....4B 66
.... (off Weatherley Cl.)
Waterlow Ct. NW11 ....2D 31
Waterlow Pk. Cen. 3D 33
Waterlow Rd. N19 ....3E 33
Waterman Bldg. E14 ....3B 80
Waterman Ho. E15 ....1F 53
.... (off Forrester Way)
Watermans Ho. E14 ....5F 67
.... (off New Village Av.)
Waterman's Quay SW6 ....5E 87
Waterman St. SW15 ....1F 99
Watermans Wlk. SE16 .....3A 80
Waterman Way E1 ....2D 79
Watermead Ho. E9 ....2A 52
Watermead Lodge SE16 ....2F 79
.... (off Princes Riverside Rd.)
Watermeadow La. SW6 ....5E 87
Watermead Rd. SE6 ....4E 123
Water M. SE15 ....2E 107

Watermint Quay N16 ....2C 36
Water's Edge SW6 ....4E 85
.... (off Palemead Cl.)
Waterside E17 ....1E 37
Waterside N1 ....1E 63
Waterside W2 ....4F 59
.... (off Nth. Wharf Rd.)
Waterside Apts. N4 ....3E 35
.... (off Goodchild Rd.)
Waterside Cl. E3 ....5B 52
Waterside Cl. SE16 ....3E 79
Waterside Hgts. E16 ....1E 83
.... (off Booth Rd.)
Waterside Pl. NW1 ....5C 46
Waterside Point SW11 .....3A 88
Waterside Twr. SW6 ....5E 87
.... (off The Boulevard)
Waterside Way SW17 ......4E 115
Watermeet Pl. N4 ....3E 35
Waterson St. E2 .....1E 11 (2A 64)
Waters Pl. SW15 ....5E 85
Watersreach Apts. N4 .....3E 35
.... (off Kayani Av.)
Waters Rd. SE6 ....3A 124
Water St. E14 ....2D 81
Water St. WC2 ....4A 16 (1C 76)
.... (off Maltravers St.)
Water Twr. Pl. N1 ....5C 48
Waterview Dr. SE10 ....2F 81
Waterview Ho. E14 ....4A 66
.... (off Carr St.)
Waterway Av. SE13 ....1D 109
Waterworks Cen. 4A 38
Waterworks La. E5 ....4F 37
Waterworks Nature Reserve
................................4A 38
Waterworks Rd. SW2 .....4B 104
Watford Cl. SW11 ....4A 88
Watford Rd. E16 ....4C 68
Watkins Ho. E14 ....3E 81
.... (off Manchester Rd.)
Watkinson Rd. N7 ....3B 48
Watling Ct. EC4 ....3A 18 (5E 63)
.... (off Watling St.)
Watling Ho. SE7 ....5E 77
.... (off New Kent Rd.)
Watling St. EC4 ....3A 18 (5E 63)
Watling St. SE15 ....2A 92
Watlington Gro. SE26 .....5A 122
Watney Mkt. E1 ....5D 65
Watney St. E1 ....5D 65
Watson Cl. N16 ....2F 49
Watson Ct. E3 ....2C 66
.... (off Campbell Rd.)
Watson Ho. SW11 ....3F 89
.... (off Ponton Rd.)
Watsons Ho. N1 ....5A 50
.... (off Nuttall St.)
Watson's M. W1 ....4A 60
Watsons St. SE8 ....3C 94
Watson St. E13 ....1D 69
Watt. Ct. W3 ....3A 70
Wattisfield Rd. E5 ....5E 37
Watts Apts. SW8 ....3A 90
.... (off Cellini St.)
Wattsdown Cl. E13 ....5C 54
Watts Gro. E3 ....4C 66
Watts Ho. W10 ....4A 58
.... (off Wornington Rd.)
Watts St. SW16 ....5F 117
Watts St. E1 ....2D 79
Watts St. SE15 ....4B 92
Wat Tyler Ho. SE10 ....5E 95
Wat Tyler Rd. SE3 ....5F 95

Wavel Ct. E1.................................2E 79
..................................(off Garnet St.)
Wavelengths Leisure Cen.... 3C 94
Wavell Ho. N6..............................1C 32
..................................(off Hillcrest)
Wavel M. NW6............................4D 45
Wavel Pl. SE26..................4B 120
Waveney Av. SE15.............2D 107
Waveney Cl. E1.........................2C 78
Waveney Ho. SE15.............2D 107
Waverley Cl. NW3.....................3B 46
Waverley Ct. NW6....................4A 44
Waverley Ct. SE26.............5E 121
Waverley Lodge E15..............3A 54
..................................(off Litchfield Av.)
Waverley Pl. N4........................4D 35
Waverley Pl. N4..........................1F 59
Waverley Rd. N8.......................1A 34
Waverton Ho. E3......................5B 52
Waverton Rd. SW18.............5E 101
Waverton St. W1... 1C 20 (2C 74)
Wavertree Ct. SW2.................1A 118
Wavertree Rd. SW2................1B 118
Waxham NW3...............................2B 46
Wayford St. SW11...................5A 88
Wayland Av. E8.........................2C 50
Wayland Ho. SW9....................5C 90
..................................(off Robsart St.)
Waylett Ho. SE11......................1B 90
..................................(off Loughborough St.)
Waylett Pl. SE27....................3D 119
Wayman Ct. E8.......................3D 51
Wayne Kirkum Way NW6.......2B 44
Waynflete Ho. SE1... 2F 25 (2E 77)
..................................(off Union St.)
Waynflete Sq. W10...................1F 71
..................................(not continuous)
Waynflete St. SW18............2E 115
Waypoint Way E16...................3D 83
Wayside NW11..........................3A 30
WC1 WC1...................4A 8 (3B 62)
Weald Cl. SE16.........................1D 93
Wealden Ho. E3........................2D 67
..................................(off Talwin St.)
Weald Sq. E5.............................4C 36
Weardale Rd. SE13.................2F 109
Wearmouth Ho. E3..................3B 66
..................................(off Joseph St.)
Wear Pl. E2................................2D 65
..................................(not continuous)
Wearside Rd. SE13................2D 109
Weatherbury W2.......................5C 58
..................................(off Talbot Rd.)
Weatherbury Ho. N19.............5F 33
..................................(off Wedmore St.)
Weatherley Cl. E3.....................4B 66
Weaver Ho. E1...........................3C 64
..................................(off Pedley St.)
Weavers Almshouses E11.. 1B 40
..................................(off Cambridge Rd.)
Weavers Ho. E11......................1C 40
..................................(off New Wanstead)
Weavers La. SE1... 2E 27 (2A 78)
Weavers Row E20..................2D 53
Weavers Ter. SW6..................2C 86
..................................(off Micklethwaite Rd.)
Weaver St. E1...........................3C 64
..................................(not continuous)
Weavers Way NW1...................5F 47
Weaver Wlk. SE27................4E 119
Webb Cl. W10............................3E 57
Webber Path E14......................1E 81
..................................(off Bullivant St.)
Webber Row SE1... 4C 24 (3D 77)
Webber St. SE1..........3C 24 (3C 76)

Webb Est. E5.............................2C 36
Webb Gdns. E13.......................3C 68
Webb Ho. E3.............................2C 66
..................................(off Trevithick Way)
Webb Ho. SW8..........................3F 89
Webb Ho. NW10.......................2B 56
Webb Rd. SE3...........................2B 96
Webb's Rd. SW11...................2B 102
Webb St. SE1..........5D 27 (4A 78)
Webheath NW6.........................4B 44
..................................(not continuous)
Webster Rd. E11.......................5E 39
Webster Rd. SE16....................4C 78
Weddell Ho. E1.........................3F 65
..................................(off Duckett St.)
Wedderburn Ho. SW1............1C 88
..................................(off Lwr. Sloane St.)
Wedderburn Rd. NW3............2F 45
Wedgewood Apts. SW8.........3A 90
Wedgewood Ho. SW1.............1D 89
..................................(off Churchill Gdns.)
Wedgewood M. SW6..............5A 86
Wedgewood M. W1...3C 14 (5F 61)
Wedgwood Ho. E2....................2F 65
..................................(off Warley St.)
Wedgwood Ho. SE11..............4C 76
..................................(off Lambeth Wlk.)
Wedgwood Wlk. NW6............2D 45
..................................(off Dresden Cl.)
Wedlake St. W10......................3A 58
Wedmore Gdns. N19...............4F 33
Wedmore M. N19......................5F 33
Wedmore St. N19.....................5F 33
Weech Rd. NW6........................1C 44
Weedington Rd. NW5..............2C 46
Weedon Ho. W12.....................5C 56
Weekley Sq. SW11..................1F 101
Weigall Rd. SE12....................3C 110
Weighhouse St. W1...3C 12 (5C 60)
Weightman Ho. SE16..............4C 78
Weimar St. SW15...................1A 100
Weir Rd. SW12........................5E 103
Weir Rd. SW19.......................3D 115
Weir's Pas. NW1......1C 6 (2F 61)
Weiss Rd. SW15.......................1F 99
Welbeck Av. BR1: Broml 4C 124
Welbeck Ct. W14......................5B 72
..................................(off Addison Br. Pl.)
Welbeck Ho. W1.....2D 13 (5D 60)
..................................(off Welbeck St.)
Welbeck Rd. E6........................2F 69
Welbeck St. W1.......1C 12 (4C 60)
Welbeck Way W1....2D 13 (5D 61)
Welbury Ct. E8..........................4A 50
..................................(off Kingsland Rd.)
Welby Ho. N19..........................2F 33
Welby St. SE5...........................4D 91
Welcome Ct. E17......................2C 38
..................................(off Saxon Cl.)
Weldin M. SW18.......................3C 100
..................................(off Lebanon Rd.)
Weld Works M. SW2...............4B 104
Welfare Rd. E15........................4A 54
Welford Cl. E5...........................5F 37
Welford Ct. NW1......................4D 47
..................................(off Castlehaven Rd.)
Welford Ct. SW8......................5E 89
Welford Ct. W9.........................4C 58
..................................(off Elmfield Way)
Welford Pl. SW19...................4A 114
Welham Rd. SW16..................5D 117
Welham Rd. SW17..................5C 116
Welland Cl. SE6.......................2B 122
..................................(off Oakham Cl.)

Welland Ho. SE15..................2E 107
Welland M. E1...........................2C 78
Welland St. SE10.....................2E 95
Wellby Ct. E13..........................5E 55
Well Cl. SW16..........................4B 118
Wellclose Sq. E1......................1C 78
..................................(not continuous)
Wellclose St. E1.......................1C 78
Wellcome Collection....3B 6 (3F 61)
..................................(off Euston Rd.)
Wellcome Mus., The2A 16 (5B 62)
..................................(within Royal College of Surgeons)
Well Cott. Cl. E11....................1E 41
Well Ct. EC4................3A 18 (5E 63)
..................................(off Bow La.)
Wellday Ho. E9..........................3A 52
..................................(off Hedger's Gro.)
Weller Ct. W11.........................2B 72
..................................(off Ladbroke Rd.)
Weller Ho. SE16.......................3C 78
..................................(off George Row)
Weller St. SE1..........3F 25 (3E 77)
Welles Ct. E14..........................1C 80
..................................(off Premiere Pl.)
Wellesley Av. W6......................4D 71
Wellesley Cl. SE7.....................1E 97
Wellesley Ct. NW2...................4C 28
Wellesley Ct. SE1.... 5F 25 (4E 77)
..................................(off Rockingham St.)
Wellesley Ct. W9......................2E 59
Wellesley Ho. NW1... 2B 6 (2F 61)
..................................(off Wellesley Pl.)
Wellesley Ho. SW1..................1D 89
..................................(off Ebury Bri. Rd.)
Wellesley Mans. W14.............1B 86
..................................(off Edith Vs.)
Wellesley Pl. NW1... 2B 6 (2F 61)
Wellesley Rd. NW5..................2C 46
Wellesley Rd. E11.....................1C 40
Wellesley Rd. E17.....................1C 38
Wellesley Rd. NW5..................2C 46
Wellesley St. E1........................4F 65
Wellesley Ter. N1......1A 10 (2E 63)
Wellfield Av. N10.....................4A 118
Wellfield Wlk. SW16..............4B 118
Wellfit St. SE24.......................1D 105
Wellgarth Rd. NW11...............3D 31
Wellington Arch....3C 20 (3C 74)
Wellington Av. N15..................1B 36
Wellington Bldgs. E3...............2C 66
..................................(off Wellington Way)
Wellington Bldgs. SW1...........1C 88
Wellington Cl. SE14.................4F 93
Wellington Cl. W11..................5C 58
Wellington Ct. NW8.................1F 59
..................................(off Wellington Rd.)
Wellington Ct. SW1.................3B 74
..................................(off Knightsbridge)
Wellington Ct. SW6.................4D 87
..................................(off Maltings Pl.)
Wellington Gdns. SE7............2E 97
Wellington Gro. SE10.............3F 95
WELLINGTON HOSPITAL, THE
....2F 59
Wellington Ho. E16.................2C 82
..................................(off Pepys Cres.)
Wellington Ho. NW3................3B 46
..................................(off Eton Rd.)
Wellington Ho. SE17...............2E 91
..................................(off Arnside St.)
Wellington Lodge
SE1...........................4C 24 (3C 76)
..................................(off Waterloo Rd.)
Wellington Mans. E10.............3C 38
Wellington Mans. SE7.............1E 97
..................................(off Wellington Gdns.)

Wellington Mans. W14.......... 2B 86
.... (off Queen's Club Gdns.)
Wellington M. N7 .... 3B 48
.... (off Roman Way)
Wellington M. SE22 .... 2C 106
Wellington M. SE7 .... 2E 97
Wellington M. SW16 .... 3F 117
Wellington Monument London
..............................3C 20 (3C 74)
Wellington Mus. London
..............................3C 20 (3C 74)
Wellington Pk. Est. NW2 ...... 4C 28
Wellington Pas. E11 .... 1C 40
Wellington Pl. NW8 .... 2F 59
Wellington Rd. E10 .... 3A 38
Wellington Rd. E11 .... 1C 40
Wellington Rd. E7 .... 1B 54
Wellington Rd. NW10 .... 2F 57
Wellington Rd. NW8 .... 1F 59
Wellington Rd. SW19 .... 2C 114
Wellington Row E2 .... 2B 64
Wellington Sq. N1 .... 5A 48
Wellington Sq. SW3 .... 1B 88
Wellington St. WC2 ..4E 15 (1B 76)
Wellington Ter. E1 .... 2D 79
Wellington Ter. N1 .... 1C 72
Wellington Way E3 .... 2C 66
Wellmeadow Rd. SE13...... 4A 110
..................................(not continuous)
Wellmeadow Rd. SE6...... 5A 110
Well Pl. NW3.......................... 5F 31
Well Rd. NW3 .... 5F 31
Wells Ct. NW6 .... 1C 58
.... (off Cambridge Av.)
Wells Gdns. IG1: Ilf................. 2F 41
Wells Ho. BR1: Broml 5D 125
.... (off Pike Cl.)
Wells Ho. EC1................ 1C 8 (2C 62)
.... (off Spa Grn. Est.)
Wells Ho. SE16...................... 4E 79
.... (off Howland Est.)
Wells Ho. W10 .... 3A 58
.... (off Wornington Rd.)
Wells Ho. Rd. NW10 .... 4A 56
Wells M. W1 .... 1A 14 (4E 61)
Wells Pk. Rd. SE26 .... 3C 120
Wells Pl. SW18 .... 5E 101
Wellspring Cl. E14 .... 4E 67
Wellspring M. SE26 .... 3D 121
Wells Ri. NW8 .... 5B 46
Wells Rd. W12 .... 3E 71
Wells Sq. WC1 .... 2F 7 (2B 62)
Wells St. W1 .... 1F 13 (4E 61)
Wells Ter. N4......................... 4C 34
Well St. E15........................... 3A 54
Well St. E9............................. 4E 51
Wells Way SE5 .... 2F 91
Wells Way SW7 .... 4F 73
Wells Yd. N7 .... 2C 48
Well Wlk. NW3 .... 1F 45
Welmar M. SW4 .... 3F 103
.... (off Clapham Pk. Rd.)
Welsford St. SE1 .... 5C 78
..................................(not continuous)
Welsh Cl. E13 .... 2C 68
Welsh Harp Reservoir 3B 28
Welsh Ho. E1 .... 2D 79
.................................(off Wapping La.)
Welshpool Ho. E8.................. 5C 50
.... (off Welshpool St.)
Welshpool St. E8................... 5C 50
..................................(not continuous)
Welshside NW9 .... 1A 28
.... (off Ruthin Cl.)
Welshside Wlk. NW9.............. 1A 28

Welstead Ho. E1 .... 5D 65
.... (off Cannon St. Rd.)
Welstead Way W4 .... 5B 70
Weltje Rd. W6........................ 5C 70
Welton Cl. SE5 .... 4A 92
Welton Ho. E1 .... 4F 65
.................................(off Stepney Way)
Welwyn St. E2........................ 2E 65
Wembley Sailing Club 4A 38
Wembury M. N6...................... 2C 33
Wemyss Rd. SE3.................... 5B 96
Wendell Ho. W12 .... 3B 70
Wendell Rd. W12................... 4B 70
Wendle Sq. SW11 .... 4A 88
Wendling NW5....................... 2C 46
Wendon St. E3 .... 5B 52
Wendover SE17 .... 1A 92
..................................(not continuous)
Wendover Ct. W1................... 5C 30
Wendover Ct. W1.......1B 12 (4C 60)
.... (off Chiltern St.)
Wendover Ho. W1 .....1B 12 (4C 60)
.... (off Chiltern St.)
Wendover Rd. NW10 .... 1B 56
Wendover Rd. SE9 ....1F 111
Wenham Ho. SW8 ....3E 89
Wenlake Ho. EC1............3F 9 (3E 63)
.... (off Old St.)
Wenlock Barn Est. N1.........1F 63
.... (off Wenlock St.)
Wenlock Ct. N1 ....1C 10 (1F 63)
Wenlock M. E10..................... 2C 38
Wenlock Rd. N1 ....1A 10 (1E 63)
Wenlock St. N1 ....1A 10 (1E 63)
Wennington Rd. E3 .... 1F 65
Wensdale Ho. E5.................... 4C 36
Wentland Cl. SE6 ....2F 123
Wentland Rd. SE6.................2F 123
Wentworth Ct. SW1.............. 1D 89
.... (off Garratt La.)
Wentworth Ct. SW18............ 4D 101
.... (off Garratt La.)
Wentworth Ct. W6 .... 2A 86
.... (off Paynes Wlk.)
Wentworth Cres. SE15......... 3C 92
Wentworth Dwellings
E1 ....2F 19 (5B 64)
.... (off Wentworth St.)
Wentworth M. E3 .... 3A 66
Wentworth M. W3 .... 5A 56
Wentworth Rd. E12............... 1F 55
Wentworth Rd. NW11 .... 1B 30
Wentworth St. E1 .....2F 19 (5B 64)
Werrington St. NW1 ..1B 6 (1E 61)
Werter Rd. SW15................. 2A 100
Wesleyan Pl. NW5................. 1D 47
Wesley Apts. SW8...............4F 89
Wesley Av. E16...................... 2C 82
Wesley Cl. N7........................ 4B 34
Wesley Cl. SE17 .... 5D 77
Wesley Cl. SE16 .... 4D 79
Wesley Rd. E10 .... 2E 39
Wesley's House & Mus. of
Methodism 3C 10 (3F 63)
Wesley Sq. W11 .... 5A 58
Wesley St. W1 ....1C 12 (4C 60)
Wessex Gdns. NW11........... 3A 30
Wessex Ho. SE1 .... 1B 92
Wessex St. E2 .... 2E 65
Wessex Way NW11 .... 3A 30
Wesson Mead SE5 .... 3E 91
.... (off Camberwell Rd.)
Westacott Cl. N19................. 3F 33
West Arbour St. E1 .... 5F 65
West Av. NW4 .... 1F 29

West Bank N16...................... 2A 36
WEST BECKTON 5F 69
Westbere Rd. NW2 .... 1A 44
West Block SE1.......4A 24 (3B 76)
.... (off York Rd.)
Westbourne Apts. SW6........ 1D 101
Westbourne Bri. W2............... 4E 59
Westbourne Ct. W2................ 5E 59
Westbourne Cres. W2............ 1F 73
Westbourne Cres. M. W2 ...... 1F 73
.... (off Westbourne Cres.)
Westbourne Dr. SE23............2F 121
Westbourne Gdns. W2........... 5D 59
WESTBOURNE GREEN 4C 58
Westbourne Gro. W11............ 1B 72
Westbourne Gro. W2.............. 5C 58
Westbourne Gro. M. W11...... 5C 58
Westbourne Gro. Ter. W2 ..... 5D 59
Westbourne Ho. SW1 .... 1D 89
.... (off Ebury Bri. Rd.)
Westbourne Pk. Pas. W2...... 4C 58
.... (off Harrow Rd.)
Westbourne Pk. Rd. W11..... 5A 58
Westbourne Pk. Rd. W2........ 4C 58
Westbourne Park Station
(Underground) 4B 58
Westbourne Pk. Vs. W2........ 4C 58
Westbourne Rd. N7................ 3B 48
Westbourne Rd. SE26...........5F 121
Westbourne St. W2................ 1F 73
Westbourne Ter. SE23 ....2F 121
.... (off Westbourne Dr.)
Westbourne Ter. W2.............. 5E 59
Westbourne Ter. M. W2 .... 5E 59
WESTBOURNE TER. RD. BRI....4E 59
.... (off Westbourne Ter. Rd.)
Westbridge Cl. W12............... 3C 70
Westbridge Ho. SW11 .... 4A 88
.... (off Westbridge Rd.)
Westbridge Rd. SW11 .... 4F 87
WEST BROMPTON 2E 87
West Brompton Station
(Underground & Overground)
.... 2E 86
Westbrook Ho. E2 .... 2E 65
.... (off Victoria Pk. Sq.)
Westbrook Rd. SE3................ 4D 97
Westbury Ho. W11 .... 4C 58
.... (off Aldridge Rd. Vs.)
Westbury Pde. SW12 .... 4D 103
.... (off Balham Hill)
Westbury Rd. E7.................... 3D 55
Westbury Ter. E7 .... 3D 55
Westbush Ct. W12 .... 3D 71
.... (off Goldhawk Rd.)
West Carriage Dr.
W2: Lon Nth. Ride............... 1A 74
West Carriage Dr.
W2: Lon Rotten Row 3F 73
West Central St.
WC1...........................2D 15 (5A 62)
Westcliffe Apts. W2................4F 59
Westcombe Cl. SE3 .... 3B 96
Westcombe Hill SE10............. 1C 96
Westcombe Hill SE3.............. 3C 96
Westcombe Pk. Rd. SE3 ...... 2A 96
Westcombe Park Station (Rail)
.... 1C 96
Westcote Rd. SW16 .... 5E 117
West Cotts. NW6 .... 2C 44
Westcott Cl. N15.................... 1B 36
Westcott Ho. E14................... 1C 80
Westcott Rd. SE17 .... 2D 91
Westcroft Cl. NW2................. 1A 44

Westcroft Est. NW2................1A 44
Westcroft Sq. W6.................5C 70
Westcroft Way NW2..............1A 44
West Cromwell Rd. SW5.........5C 72
West Cromwell Rd. W14....1B 86
West Cross Route W10.......1F 71
Westdean Av. SE12........1D 125
Westdean Cl. SW18.........4D 101
Westdown Rd. E15..............1E 53
Westdown Rd. SE6............5C 108
West Dr. SW16...................4E 117
WEST DULWICH...................2F 119
....2F 119
West Dulwich Station (Rail)

West Eaton Pl. SW1.............5C 74
West Eaton Pl. M. SW1....5C 74
.............................(off W. Eaton Pl.)
West Ella Rd. NW10...........4A 42
West Elms Studios SW8......4E 89
West End Av. E10................1F 39
West End Ct. NW6..............4D 45
West End Grn..................2C 44
.........................(off West End Lane)
West End La. NW6..............2C 44
....(not continuous)
West End Quay W2...............4F 59
.........................(off Harbet Rd.)

Westerdale Ct. N5...............1D 49
...........................(off Hamilton Pk. W.)
Westerdale Rd. SE10..........1C 96
Westerham NW1................5E 47
.............................(off Bayham St.)
Westerham Ho. SE1 .5C 26 (4F 77)
.............................(off Law St.)
Westerham Rd. E10............2D 39
Westerley Cres. SE26........5B 122
Western Av. NW11..............1F 29
Western Beach Apts. E16....2C 82
Western Ct. NW6...............1B 58
Western Ctyd. EC2 ...1E 19 (4A 64)
...........................(off Cutlers Gdns.)
WESTERN EYE HOSPITAL....4B 60
Western Gateway E16........1C 82
Western La. SW12..............5C 102
Western M. W9.................3B 58
Western Pl. SE16................3E 79
Western Rd. E13................1E 69
Western Rd. E17................1E 39
Western Rd. SW9...............1C 104
Western Ter. W6................1C 84
Western Transit Shed N1 ....5A 48
Westferry Cir. E14............2B 80
Westferry Rd. E14............1B 80
Westferry Station (DLR) 1C 80
Westfield Av. E20..............30 63
Westfield Cl. SW10...........3E 87
Westfield Ct. NW10..........2F 57
.........................(off Chamberlayne Rd.)
Westfield Ho. SE16.............5F 79
...........................(off Rotherhithe New Rd.)
Westfield Ho. SW10..........3E 87
.............................(off Worlds End Est.)
Westfield London Bus Station

....2E 71
Westfields SW13................1B 98
Westfields Av. SW13...........1A 98
Westfield St. SE18.............4F 83
Westfield Way SE18............2A 66
West Gdn. Pl. W2...............5A 60
West Gdns. E1...................1D 79
West Gdns. SW17............5A 116
Westgate Apts. E16...........1C 82
.........................(off Western Gateway)
Westgate St. SE12............1C 124
.............................(off Burnt Ash Hill)

Westgate Ct. SW9..............1C 104
.............................(off Canterbury Cres.)
Westgate M. W10.................3A 58
.................................(off West Row)
Westgate St. E8.................5D 51
Westgate Ter. SW10..........2D 87
West Gro. SE10................4E 95
West Gro. SE17................5E 77
Westgrove La. SE10..........4E 95
West Gro. Sq. SE17...........5E 95
West Halkin St. SW15B 20 (4C 74)
West Hallowes SE9.............1F 125
WEST HAM.........................5B 54
West Ham La. E15..............4F 53
West Ham Pk. E7................4C 54
WEST HAMPSTEAD...............3D 45
West Hampstead M. NW6....3D 45
West Hampstead Station
(Underground & Overground)
....3C 44
West Hampstead Thameslink
Station (Rail) 3C 44
West Ham Station (DLR)....2A 68
West Ham Station (Rail &
Underground)....................2A 68
West Ham Utd FC..............5D 53
West Handyside Canopy
N1..................................5A 48
West Harding St.
EC4...................2C 16 (5C 62)
West Heath Av. NW11..........3C 30
West Heath Cl. NW3............5C 30
West Heath Ct. NW11..........3C 30
West Heath Dr. NW11..........3C 30
West Heath Gdns. NW3........4C 30
West Heath Rd. NW3............4C 30
WEST HENDON....................2C 28
West Hendon B'way. NW9...1B 28
West Hill SW15..................5F 99
West Hill SW18..................3B 100
WEST HILL........................4B 100
West Hill Ct. N6..................5C 32
Westhill Ct. W11................1B 72
.............................(off Denbigh Rd.)
West Hill Pk. N6..................4B 32
....(not continuous)
West Hill Rd. SW18...........4B 100
Westhope Ho. E2................3C 64
.............................(off Derbyshire St.)
Westhorne Av. SE12..........5C 110
Westhorne Av. SE9............3F 111
Westhorpe Rd. SW15.........1E 99
West Ho. Cl. SW19............1A 114
West India Av. E14.............2C 80
West India Dock Rd. E14....1B 80
West India Ho. E14............1C 80
.............................(off W. India Dock Rd.)
West India Quay Station (DLR)

....1C 80
WEST KENSINGTON...........5A 72
West Kensington Ct. W14....1B 86
.................................(off Edith Vs.)
West Kensington Mans.
W14..............................1B 86
.............................(off Beaumont Cres.)
West Kensington Station
(Underground)...................1B 86
WEST KILBURN..................2B 58
Westking Pl. WC1 ....2F 7 (2B 62)
Westlake SE16...................5E 79
Westland Pl. N1 ....1B 10 (2F 63)
Westlands Ter. SW12.........4E 103
West La. SE16...................3D 79
Westleigh Av. SW15...........3D 99

Westleigh Ct. E11...............1C 40
.............................(off Nightingale La.)
West Lodge E16..................2C 82
.............................(off Britannia Ga.)
West London Crematorium...3D 57
West London Studios SW6....3D 87
.............................(off Fulham Rd.)
Westmacott Ho. NW8...........3F 59
.................................(off Hatton St.)
West Mall W8....................2C 72
.............................(off Kensington Mall)
Westmark Point SW15.......1D 113
.............................(off Norley Va.)
Westmead SW15...............4D 99
Westmead Ct. SE6.............4C 108
West Mersea Cl. E16..........2D 83
West M. SW1...................5D 75
.............................(off W. Warwick Pl.)
WESTMINSTER.........4D 23 (3A 76)
Westminster Abbey Chapter
House......................5D 23 (4A 76)
.............................(within Abbey)
Westminster Abbey Mus.
..........................5D 23 (4A 76)
Westminster Abbey Pyx Chamber
..........................5D 23 (4A 76)
.............................(within Westminster Abbey)
Westminster Boating Base & Pier
....2F 89
Westminster Bri.
SW1......................4E 23 (3A 76)
Westminster Bri. Ho.
SE1......................5D 25 (4D 77)
.............................(off Lambeth Rd.)
Westminster Bri. Rd. S
E1......................4B 24 (3B 76)
Westminster Bus. Sq. SE11...2B 90
.............................(off Durham St.)
Westminster Ct. E11...........1D 41
.............................(off Cambridge Pk.)
Westminster Ct. NW8..........3F 59
.............................(off Aberdeen Pl.)
Westminster Ct. SE16.........2F 79
.............................(off King & Queen Wharf)
Westminster Gdns. SW1.....5A 76
.............................(off Vincent St.)
Westminster Hall.....4D 23 (3A 76)
.............................(off St Margaret St.)
Westminster Ind. Est. SE18...4F 83
Westminster Mans.
SW1......................5C 22 (4F 75)
.............................(off Gt. Smith St.)
Westminster Millennium Pier
(River Bus & Tours)
..........................3E 23 (3A 76)
Westminster Pal. Gdns.
SW1......................5B 22 (4F 75)
.............................(off Artillery Row)
Westminster RC Cathedral...4E 75
Westminster Station
(Underground)........3D 23 (3A 76)
Westmoor St. SE7..............4E 83
Westmore Ct. SW15...........3A 100
Westmoreland Ho. E16.......2C 82
.............................(off Gatcombe Rd.)
Westmoreland Ho. NW10....2C 56
Westmoreland Pl. SW1.......1D 89
Westmoreland Rd. SE17.....2F 91
....(not continuous)
Westmoreland Rd. SW13....4B 84
Westmoreland St.
W1..................1C 12 (4C 60)
Westmoreland Ter. SW1.....1D 89
Westmoreland Wlk. SE17....2F 91
....(not continuous)

Westmorland Cl. E12.........4F 41
Westmorland Rd. E17.........1C 38
WEST NORWOOD...........4E 119
West Norwood Crematorium
....3E 119
West Norwood Station (Rail)
....4D 119
Westonbirt Ct. SE15...........2B 92
..................................(off Ebley Cl.)
Weston Ct. N4.......................5E 35
West One Ho. W1 .... 1F 13 (4E 61)
.................................(off Wells St.)
Weston Ho. E9......................5E 51
.........................(off King Edward's Rd.)
Weston Ho. NW6..................4A 44
Weston Pk. N8......................1A 34
Weston Ri. WC1 .... 1A 8 (2B 62)
Weston St. SE1 ..... 2C 26 (3A 78)
.................................(not continuous)
Weston Wlk. E8....................4D 51
Westover Hill NW3................4C 30
Westover Rd. SW18............5E 101
Westow Hill SE19................5A 120
Westow St. SE19................5A 120
West Pk. SE9.......................2F 125
West Parkside SE10.............3A 82
West Pk. Wlk. E20................3E 53
West Pl. SW19.....................5E 113
West Point E14....................1B 80
.............................(off Grenade St.)
West Point SE1....................1C 92
Westport Rd. E13.................3D 69
Westport St. E1...................5F 65
West Poultry Av.
EC1...................1D 17 (4D 63)
West Quarters W12.............5C 56
West Quay SW10..................4E 87
West Quay Wlk. E14.............4D 81
West Reservoir Cen..............3E 35
West Ri. W2...........................1A 74
.........................(off St George's Flds.)
West Rd. E15........................5B 54
West Rd. SE1............3A 24 (3B 76)
West Rd. SW3......................1B 88
West Rd. SW4.......................3F 103
Westrovia Ct. SW1................1F 89
.............................(off Moreton St.)
West Row W10......................3A 58
Westrow SW15......................4E 99
West Side Comn. SW19........5E 113
Westside Ct. W9....................3C 58
.................................(off Elgin Av.)
West Silvertown Station (DLR)
....2C 82
West Smithfield EC1 ... 1D 17 (4D 63)
West Sq. SE11...........5D 25 (4D 77)
West Stand N5.......................1D 49
West St. E11..........................5A 40
West St. E17...........................1D 39
West St. E2...........................1D 65
West St. WC2 ....3C 14 (5F 61)
West Tenter St. E1...3F 19 (5B 64)
West Twr. E14......................3D 81
.........................(off Pan Peninsula Sq.)
West Twr. SW10.....................4F 87
Westvale M. W3.....................3A 70
West View Apts. N7..............4A 48
.................................(off York Way)
Westview Cl. NW10...............2B 42
Westview Cl. W10.................5E 57
Westville Rd. W12.................3C 70
Westward Pde. E14...............4D 81
.................................(off Pepper St.)
West Warwick Pl. SW1..........5E 75
West Way NW10....................5A 28

Westway W10........................4B 58
Westway W12........................1B 70
Westway Est. W3...................4A 56
Westway Lodge W9................4C 58
.............................(off Amberley Rd.)
Westway Sports Cen..............5F 57
Westway Travellers Site
W12......................................1F 71
.................................(off Stable Way)
Westwell M. SW16................5A 118
Westwell Rd. App. SW16.....5A 118
Westwick Gdns. W14.............3F 71
West Wintergarden.................2D 81
.................................(off Bank St.)
Westwood Bus. Cen. NW10...3A 56
Westwood Gdns. SW13.........1B 98
Westwood Hill SE26.............5C 120
Westwood Ho. W12................2E 71
.................................(off Wood La.)
Westwood M. E3....................2C 66
.........................(off Addington Rd.)
Westwood Pk. SE23.............5D 107
Westwood Pl. SE26...............4C 120
Westwood Rd. E16.................2D 83
Westwood Rd. SW13.............1B 98
Wetherby Gdns. SW5.............5E 73
Wetherby Mans. SW5.............1D 87
.................................(off Earls Ct. Sq.)
Wetherby M. SW5..................1D 87
Wetherby Pl. SW7..................5E 73
Wetherden St. E17.................2B 38
Wetherell Rd. E9...................5E 51
Wevco Wharf SE15.................2D 93
Wexford Ho. E1.....................4E 65
.................................(off Sidney St.)
Wexford Rd. SW12................5B 102
Wexner Bldg. E1 ..... 1F 19 (4B 64)
.................................(off Strype St.)
Weybourne St. SW18............2E 115
Weybridge Ct. SE16...............1D 93
Weybridge Point SW11..........5B 88
Weydown Cl. SW19..............1A 114
Weyhill Rd. E1......................5C 64
Wey Ho. NW8.........................3F 59
.................................(off Church St. Est.)
Weyman Rd. SE3....................4E 97
Weymouth Ct. E2...................1B 64
Weymouth Ho. SW8................3B 90
.................................(off Bolney St.)
Weymouth M. W1............5D 5 (4D 61)
Weymouth St. W1 .... 1C 12 (4C 60)
WEYMOUTH STREET HOSPITAL
..........................5C 4 (4C 60)
Weymouth Ter. E2 .... 1F 11 (1B 64)
Weymouth Vs. N4...................4B 34
.................................(off Moray Rd.)
Whadcoat St. N4....................4C 34
Whaddon Ho. SE22...............1A 106
Whalebone Ct. EC2... 2B 18 (5F 63)
.........................(off Telegraph St.)
Whalebone La. E15.................4A 54
Whales Yd. E15......................4A 54
.........................(off West Ham La.)
Wharf, The EC3 ..... 1E 27 (2B 78)
Wharfdale Rd. N1...................1A 62
Wharfedale Ct. E5...................1F 51
Wharfedale Ho. NW6..............5D 45
.........................(off Kilburn Vale)
Wharfedale St. SW10.............1D 87
Wharfedale Yd. N1.................1A 62
.........................(off Wharfedale Rd.)
Wharf La. E14........................5B 66
Wharf Mill Apts. E2................5B 50
.........................(off Laburnum St.)

Wharf Pl. E2..........................5D 51
Wharf Rd. N1: Lon City Rd.
....1F 9 (1E 63)
Wharf Rd. N1: Lon York Way 5A 48
Wharf Rd. E15.......................2E 83
Wharfside Point Nth. E14......1E 81
.........................(off Poplar High St.)
Wharfside Point Sth. E14.......1E 81
Wharfside Rd. E16.................4A 68
Wharf St. E16........................4A 68
Wharf St. SE8.......................1C 94
Wharf Vw. Ct. E14..................5E 67
.................................(off Blair St.)
Wharncliffe M. SW4...............4F 103
Wharton Cl. NW10.................3A 42
Wharton Cotts. WC1..2B 8 (2C 62)
Wharton Ho. E2......................2F 65
Wharton Ho. SE1 .... 5F 27 (4B 78)
.........................(off St Saviour's Est.)
Wharton St. WC1.....2A 8 (2B 62)
Whatcott's Yd. N16................1A 50
Whateley Rd. SE22...............3B 106
Whatman Ho. E14..................5B 66
.........................(off Wallwood St.)
Whatman Rd. SE23...............5F 107
Wheatfield Ho. NW6...............2C 58
.........................(off Kilburn Pk. Rd.)
Wheathill Ho. SE22...............1A 106
Wheatlands Rd. SW17...........3C 116
Wheatley Ct. E3......................2D 67
.................................(off Bruce Rd.)
Wheatley Ho. SW15...............5C 98
.........................(off Ellisfield Dr)
Wheatley St. W1.......1C 12 (4C 60)
Wheat Sheaf Cl. E14.............5D 81
Wheatsheaf La. SW6..............3E 85
Wheatsheaf La. SW8..............3A 90
Wheatsheaf Ter. SW6.............3B 86
Wheatstone Ho. SE1...............4E 77
.................................(off County St.)
Wheeler Gdns. N1..................5A 48
.................................(off Outram Pl.)
Wheel Ho. E14.......................1D 95
.........................(off Burrells Wharf Sq.)
Wheelwright St. N7.................4B 48
Wheler Ho. E1 ....4F 11 (3B 64)
.................................(off Quaker St.)
Wheler St. E1 ....4F 11 (3B 64)
Whellock Rd. W4....................4A 70
Whetstone Pk. WC2 .2F 15 (5B 62)
Whetstone Rd. SE3.................5E 97
Whewell Rd. N19....................4A 34
Whidborne Bldgs.
WC1............................2E 7 (2A 62)
.........................(off Whidborne St.)
Whidborne Cl. SE8.................5C 94
Whidborne St. WC1 .. 2E 7 (2A 62)
.................................(not continuous)
Whidbourne M. SW8..............4F 89
Whinfell Cl. SW16.................5F 117
Whinyates Rd. SE9................1F 111
Whippingham Ho. E3.............2B 66
.........................(off Merchant St.)
Whipps Cross Rd. E11..........1F 39
.................................(not continuous)
WHIPPS CROSS UNIVERSITY
HOSPITAL............................1F 39
Whiskin St. EC1 ......2D 9 (2D 63)
Whistler M. SE15...................3B 92
Whistlers Av. SW11................3F 87
Whistler St. N5.......................2D 49
Whistler Twr. SW10...............3E 87
.........................(off Worlds End Est.)
Whistler Wlk. SW10................3F 87
Whiston Ho. N1......................4D 49
.........................(off Richmond Gro.)

Whiston Rd. E2 ....1B 64
Whitacre M. SE11 ....1C 90
Whitbread Ho. SW11 ....3F 89
..........(off Charles Clowes Wlk.)
Whitbread Rd. SE4 ....2A 106
Whitburn Rd. SE13 ....2D 109
Whitby Cl. N7 ....1A 48
Whitby Ho. NW8 ....5E 45
.....................(off Boundary Rd.)
Whitby St. E1 ....3F 11 (3B 64)
..............................(not continuous)
Whitcher Cl. SE14 ....2A 94
Whitcher Pl. NW1 ....3E 47
Whitchurch Ho. W10 ....5F 57
...................(off Kingsdown Cl.)
Whitchurch Rd. W11 ....1F 71
Whitcomb Ct. WC2 ....5C 14 (1F 75)
.........................(off Whitcomb St.)
Whitcomb St. WC2 ...5C 14 (1F 75)
Whiteadder Way E14 ....5D 81
Whitear Wlk. E15 ....3F 53
Whitebeam Cl. SW9 ....3B 90
Whitebeam Ho. E15 ....2A 68
...........................(off Teasel Way)
White Bear Pl. NW3 ....1F 45
White Bear Yd. EC1 ....4B 8 (5C 62)
.......................(off Clerkenwell Rd.)
WHITECHAPEL 4C 65
Whitechapel Art Gallery 5B 64
Whitechapel High St.
E1 ....2F 19 (5B 64)
Whitechapel Rd. E1 ....4C 64
Whitechapel Sports Cen. 4D 65
Whitechapel Station
(Underground, Overground &
Crossrail) 4D 65
White Church La. E1 ....5C 64
White Church Pas. E1 ....5C 64
........................(off White Church La.)
WHITE CITY 1D 71
WHITE CITY 5E 57
White City Cl. W12 ....1E 71
White City Est. W12 ....1D 71
White City Rd. W12 ....1D 71
White City Station (Underground)
....1E 71
White Collar Factory
EC1 ....3B 10 (3F 63)
....(off City Rd.)
Whitecross Pl. EC2 ...5C 10 (4F 63)
Whitecross St. EC1 ...3A 10 (3E 63)
Whitefield Av. NW2 ....3E 29
Whitefield Cl. SW15 ....4A 100
Whitefoot La. BR1: Brom! ...4E 123
Whitefoot La. SE6 ....4E 123
Whitefoot Ter. BR1: Brom! ..3B 124
Whitefriars St. EC4 ...3C 16 (5C 62)
Whitehall SW1 ....1D 23 (2A 76)
.............................(not continuous)
Whitehall Ct. SW1 ....2D 23 (2A 76)
Whitehall Gdns.
SW1 ....2D 23 (2A 76)
..................(off Horseguards Av.)
Whitehall Pk. N19 ....3E 33
Whitehall Pl. E7 ....2C 54
Whitehall Pl. SW1 ....2D 23 (2A 76)
White Hart Ct. EC2 ...1D 19 (4A 64)
.........................(off Liverpool St.)
White Hart La. NW10 ....3B 42
White Hart La. SW13 ....5A 84
White Hart La. EC4 ...2E 17 (5D 63)
White Hart St. SE11 ....1C 90
White Hart Yd. SE1 ...2B 26 (2F 77)
Whitehaven St. NW8 ....3A 60

Whitehead Cl. SW18 ....5E 101
Whiteheads Gro. SW3 ....5A 74
White Heather Ho.
WC1 ....2E 7 (2A 62)
.................................(off Cromer St.)
White Horse All. EC1 ..5D 9 (4D 63)
.............................(off Cowcross St.)
White Horse Apts. N1 ....5C 48
...........................(off Liverpool Rd.)
White Horse La. E1 ....5F 65
Whitehorse M. SE1 ....5C 24 (4C 76)
White Horse Rd. E1 ....5A 66
..............................(not continuous)
White Horse St. W1 ...2E 21 (2D 75)
White Horse Yd. EC2 2B 18 (5F 63)
White Ho., The NW1 ...3E 5 (3D 61)
...................................(off Albany St.)
White Ho. SW11 ....4F 87
White Ho. SW4 ....5F 103
.......................(off Clapham Pk. Est.)
Whitehouse E10 ....1E 39
.....................(off Leyton Grn. Rd.)
Whitehouse Apts.
SE1 ....2A 24 (2B 76)
White Ho. M. E10 ....1E 39
White Kennett St. E1 ..2E 19 (5B 64)
Whitelands Cres. SW18 ......5A 100
Whitelands Ho. SW3 ....1B 88
....................(off Cheltenham Ter.)
Whitelegg Rd. E13 ....1B 68
Whiteley Rd. SE19 ....5F 119
White Lion Cen. 1C 62
........................(off White Lion St.)
White Lion Ct. EC3 ...3D 19 (5A 64)
....(off Cornhill)
White Lion Hill EC4 ...4E 17 (1D 77)
White Lion St. N1 ....1C 62
White Lodge Cl. N2 ....1F 31
White Lyon Ct. EC2 ....4F 9 (3E 63)
..................................(off Fann St.)
White Post La. E9 ....4B 52
White Post St. SE15 ....3E 93
White Rd. E15 ....5A 54
White Rose Ct. E1 ....1E 19 (4A 64)
..............................(off Widegate St.)
Whites Grounds Est.
SE1 ....3E 27 (3A 78)
...................(off White's Grounds)
White's Row E1 ....1F 19 (4B 64)
Whitestone La. NW3 ....5E 31
Whitestone Wlk. NW3 ....5E 31
White Swan M. W4 ....1A 84
Whitethorn Ho. E1 ....2E 79
.................................(off Prusom St.)
Whitethorn Pas. E3 ....3C 66
.............................(off Whitethorn St.)
Whitethorn St. E3 ....4C 66
White Tower, The ...5F 19 (1B 78)
White Twr. Way E1 ....4A 66
Whitfield Ho. NW8 ....3A 60
..................................(off Salisbury St.)
Whitfield Pl. W1 ....4F 5 (3E 61)
............................(off Whitfield St.)
Whitfield Rd. E6 ....4E 55
Whitfield St. W1 ....4A 6 (3E 61)
Whitgift Ho. SE11 ....5B 76
Whitgift Ho. SW11 ....4A 88
Whitgift St. SE11 ....5B 76
Whiting Way SE16 ....5A 80
Whitley Ho. SW1 ....2E 89
.............................(off Churchill Gdns.)
Whitlock Dr. SW19 ....5A 100

Whitman Ho. E2 ....2E 65
...............................(off Cornwall Av.)
Whitman Rd. E3 ....3A 66
Whitmore Bldg.
SE16 ....5F 27 (4B 78)
.................................(off Arts La.)
Whitmore Est. N1 ....1A 50
Whitmore Gdns. NW10 ....1E 57
Whitmore Ho. N1 ....5A 50
.............................(off Whitmore Est.)
Whitmore Rd. N1 ....5A 90
Whitnell Way SW15 ....1E 99
..............................(not continuous)
Whitney Rd. E10 ....2D 39
Whitstable Ho. W10 ....5F 57
.............................(off Silchester Rd.)
Whittaker Rd. E6 ....4E 55
Whittaker St. SW1 ....5C 74
Whittaker Way SE1 ....5C 78
Whitta Rd. E12 ....1F 55
Whittell Gdns. SE26 ....3E 121
Whittingham Ct. W4 ....3A 84
Whittingstall Rd. SW6 ....4B 86
Whittington Apts. E1 ....5F 65
.............................(off E. Arbour St.)
Whittington Av. EC3 .3D 19 (5A 64)
Whittington Ct. N2 ....1B 32
WHITTINGTON HOSPITAL 4F 33
Whittington Ho. N19 ....4F 33
.................................(off Holloway Rd.)
Whittlebury M. E. NW1 ....4C 46
Whittlebury M. W. NW1 ....4C 46
Whittle Cl. E17 ....1A 38
Whittlesey St. SE1 ...2B 24 (2C 76)
Whitton NW3 ....4B 46
Whitton Wlk. E3 ....2C 66
..............................(not continuous)
Whitwell Rd. E13 ....2C 68
Whitworth Ho. SE1 ...5A 26 (4E 77)
Whitworth St. SE10 ....1A 96
Whorlton Rd. SE15 ....1D 107
Whychcote Point NW2 ....3E 29
.............................(off Whitefield Av.)
Whyteville Rd. E7 ....3D 55
Whytlaw Ho. E3 ....4B 66
.................................(off Baythorne St.)
Wiblin M. NW5 ....1D 47
Wickersley Rd. SW11 ....5C 88
Wickers Oake SE19 ....4B 120
Wicker St. E1 ....5D 65
Wickfield Apts. E15 ....3F 53
.............................(off Grove Cres. Rd.)
Wickfield Ho. SE16 ....3D 79
.................................(off Wilson Gro.)
Wickford Ho. E1 ....3E 65
.............................(off Wickford St.)
Wickford St. E1 ....4E 65
Wickham Cl. E1 ....4E 65
Wickham Gdns. SE4 ....1B 108
Wickham Ho. N1 ....5A 50
.............................(off Halcomb St.)
Wickham M. SE4 ....5B 94
Wickham Rd. SE4 ....2B 108
Wickham St. SE11 ....1B 90
Wick La. E3 ....5C 52
Wicklow Ho. N16 ....3B 36
Wicklow St. WC1 ......1F 7 (2B 62)
Wick Rd. E9 ....3F 51
Wicks Cl. SE9 ....4F 125
Wicksteed Ho. SE1 ....4E 77
Wicks Way SE19 ....:.......5F 119
Wickway Ct. SE15 ....2B 92
.....................................(off Cator St.)
Wickwood St. SE5 ....5D 91
Widdenham Rd. N7 ....1B 48

Widdin St. E15 ....4A **54**
Widegate St. E1 ....1E **19** (4A **64**)
Widford NW1 ....3D **47**
.............................(off Lewis St.)
Widford Ho. N1. ....1D **63**
...........................(off Colebrooke Rd.)
Widgeon Cl. E16. ....5D **69**
Widley Rd. W9. ....2C **58**
Wigan Ho. E5. ....3D **37**
Wightman M. N4. ....1C **34**
Wigmore Hall 2D **13** (5D **61**)
...........................(off Wigmore St.)
Wigmore Pl. W1. ....2D **13** (5D **61**)
Wigmore St. W1 ....2B **12** (5D **60**)
Wigram Ho. E14. ....1D **81**
...............................(off Wade's Pl.)
Wigram Rd. E11. ....1E **41**
Wigston Rd. E13. ....3D **69**
Wigton Pl. SE11. ....1C **90**
Wilberforce M. SW4. ....2F **103**
Wilberforce Rd. N4. ....4D **35**
Wilberforce Rd. NW9 ....1C **28**
Wilberforce Wlk. E15. ....2A **54**
Wilberforce Way SW19. ....5F **113**
Wilbraham Ho. SW8. ....3A **90**
..........................(off Wandsworth Rd.)
Wilbraham Mans. SW1. ....5C **74**
...........................(off Wilbraham Pl.)
Wilbraham Pl. SW1. ....5B **74**
Wilbrooke Pl. SE3 ....4D **97**
Wilby M. W11. ....2B **72**
Wilcox Cl. SW8. ....3A **90**
...........................(not continuous)
Wilcox Ho. E3. ....4B **66**
...........................(off Ackroyd Dr.)
Wilcox Pl. SW1. ....5A **22** (4E **75**)
Wilcox Rd. SW8. ....3A **90**
Wildbore Ho. N1. ....4C **48**
...........................(off Liverpool Rd.)
Wild Ct. WC2 ....3F **15** (5B **62**)
Wildcroft Mnr. SW15. ....5E **99**
Wildcroft Rd. SW15. ....5E **99**
Wilde Cl. E8. ....5C **50**
Wilde Ho. W2. ....1F **73**
...........................(off Gloucester Ter.)
Wilde Pl. SW18. ....5F **101**
Wilderness Local Nature Reserve,
The. 3D **89**
...........................(off Queenstown Rd.)
Wilderness M. SW4. ....2D **103**
Wilderton Rd. N16. ....2A **36**
Wilder Wlk. W1 ....5A **14** (1E **75**)
...........................(off Glasshouse St.)
Wildfell Rd. SE6. ....5D **109**
Wild Goose Dr. SE14. ....4E **93**
Wild Hatch NW11. ....1C **30**
Wild's Rents SE1. ....5D **27** (4A **78**)
Wild St. WC2 ....3E **15** (5A **62**)
Wildwood Cl. SE12. ....5B **110**
Wildwood Gro. NW3. ....3E **31**
Wildwood Ri. NW11 ....3E **31**
Wildwood Rd. NW11 ....1D **31**
Wildwood Ter. NW3 ....3E **31**
Wilfred St. N15. ....1F **35**
...........................(off South Gro.)
Wilfred Owen Cl. SW19. ....5E **115**
Wilfred St. SW1. .....5F **21** (4E **75**)
Wilfred Wood Ct. NW6. ....5E **71**
...........................(off Samuel's Cl.)
Wilkes St. E1 ....5F **11** (4B **64**)
Wilkie Ho. SW1. ....1F **89**
...........................(off Cureton St.)
Wilkins Ho. SW1. ....2D **89**
...........................(off Churchill Gdns.)
Wilkinson Cl. NW2 ....4E **29**

Wilkinson Cl. SW17 ....4F **115**
Wilkinson Ho. N1 ....1F **63**
...........................(off Cranston St.)
Wilkinson Rd. E16. ....5E **69**
Wilkinson St. SW8 ....3B **90**
Wilkin St. NW5 ....3C **46**
Wilkin St. M. NW5. ....3C **47**
Wilks Pl. N1. ....1A **64**
Willard St. SW8. ....1D **103**
Will Crooks Gdns. SE9 ....2E **111**
WILLESDEN 3C **42**
WILLESDEN CENTRE FOR HEALTH
& CARE 4C **42**
WILLESDEN GREEN 3E **43**
Willesden Green Station
(Underground) 3E **43**
Willesden Junction Station
(Underground & Overground)
.................................2B **56**
Willesden La. NW2. ....3E **43**
Willesden La. NW6. ....4F **43**
Willesden Section Ho. NW6 ....4F **43**
...........................(off Willesden La.)
Willesden Sports Cen. 5D **43**
Willesden Sports Stadium. 5D **43**
Willett Ho. NW5. ....3D **47**
Willett Ho. E13 ....1D **69**
...........................(off Queens Rd. W.)
William IV St. WC2. ...5D **15** (1A **76**)
William Banfield Ho. SW6. ....5B **86**
...........................(off Munster Rd.)
William Blake Ho. SW11 ....4A **88**
William Bonney Est. SW4 ....2F **103**
William Booth Ho. E14. ....5C **66**
...........................(off Hind Gro.)
William Caslon Ho. E2 ....1D **65**
...........................(off Patriot Sq.)
William Channing Ho. E2 ....2D **65**
...........................(off Canrobert St.)
William Cl. SE13. ....1E **109**
William Cl. SE7. ....1F **97**
William Cobbett Ho. W8. ....4D **73**
...........................(off Scarsdale Pl.)
William Congreve M. N1. ....5E **49**
William Cotton Ct. E14. ....4C **66**
...........................(off Selsey St.)
William Ct. NW8. ....2E **59**
William Ct. SE10 ....4D **95**
...........................(off Greenwich High Rd.)
William Dromey Ct. NW6. ....4B **44**
William Dunbar Ho. NW6 ....1B **58**
...........................(off Albert Rd.)
William Dyce M. SW16 ....4F **117**
William Ellis Way SE16. ....4C **78**
...........................(off St James's Rd.)
William Evans Ho. SE8. ....5F **79**
...........................(off Haddonfield)
William Farm La. SW15 ....1D **99**
William Fenn Ho. E2 ....2C **64**
...........................(off Shipton St.)
William Fry Ho. E1 ....5F **65**
...........................(off W. Arbour St.)
William Gdns. SW15. ....3D **99**
William Gibbs Ct.
SW1. ....5B **22** (4F **75**)
...........................(off Old Pye St.)
William Gunn Ho. NW3. ....2A **46**
William Guy Gdns. E3 ....2D **67**
William Harvey Ho. SW19 ....1A **114**
...........................(off Whitlock Dr.)
William Henry Wlk. SW11. ....2F **89**
William Hunt Mans. SW13. ....2E **85**
William Margrie Cl. SE15. ....5C **92**
William Marshall Cl. E17 ....1A **38**
William M. N1 ....4A **50**

William M. SW1. ....4A **20** (3B **74**)
William Morley Cl. E6. ....5F **55**
William Morris Ho. W6. ....2F **85**
William Morris Way SW6. ....1E **101**
William Murdoch Ct. E14. ....4F **67**
...........................(off Connaught Rd.)
William Owston Ct. E16. ....2F **83**
...........................(off Shipyard Street)
William Parry Ho. E16. ....3D **83**
...........................(off Shipyard Street)
William Pl. E3. ....1B **66**
William Rathbone Ho. E2. ....2D **65**
...........................(off Florida St.)
William Rd. NW1 .....2F **5** (2E **61**)
William Rushbrooke Ho.
SE16. ....5C **78**
...........................(off Rouel Rd.)
William Saville Ho. NW6 ....1B **58**
...........................(off Denmark Rd.)
William's Bldgs. E2. ....3E **65**
Williamsburg Plaza E14 ....1E **81**
Williams Cl. N8 ....1F **33**
Williams Cl. SW6. ....3A **86**
Williams Ho. E3. ....2C **66**
...........................(off Alfred St.)
Williams Ho. E9. ....5D **51**
...........................(off King Edward's Rd.)
Williams Ho. NW2 ....5E **29**
...........................(off Stoll Cl.)
Williams Ho. SW1. ....5F **75**
...........................(off Montaigne Cl.)
Williams M. SE4. ....4B **108**
William Smith Ho. E3. ....2C **66**
...........................(off Ireton St.)
Williamson Cl. SE10. ....1B **96**
Williamson Ct. SE17 ....1E **91**
Williamson Rd. N4 ....1D **35**
Williamson St. N7. ....1A **48**
William Sq. SE16. ....1A **80**
...........................(off Sovereign Cres.)
William St. E10. ....1D **39**
William St. SW1 ....4A **20** (3B **74**)
William Whiffin Sq. E3. ....3B **66**
William Wood Ho. SE26. ....3E **121**
...........................(off Shrublands Cl.)
Willingham Cl. NW5. ....2E **47**
Willingham Ter. NW5. ....2E **47**
Willington Ct. E5. ....5A **38**
Willington Rd. SW9. ....1A **104**
Willis Ho. E14. ....1D **81**
...........................(off Hale St.)
Willis Rd. E15. ....1B **68**
Willis St. E14. ....5D **67**
Willoughby Highwalk
EC2. ....1B **18** (4F **63**)
...........................(off Moor La.)
Willoughby Ho. E1. ....2D **79**
...........................(off Reardon Path)
Willoughby Ho. EC2. ....1B **18** (4F **63**)
...........................(off Moor La.)
Willoughby Ho. SW4. ....2D **103**
...........................(off Cedars M.)
Willoughby M. SW4. ....2D **103**
...........................(off Cedars M.)
Willoughby Pas. E14. ....2C **80**
...........................(off W. India Av.)
Willoughby Rd. NW3. ....1F **45**
Willoughbys, The SW14 ....1A **98**
Willoughby St. WC1. ...1D **15** (4A **62**)
...........................(off Gt. Russell St.)
Willoughby Way SE7. ....5D **83**
Willow Av. SW13. ....5B **84**
Willow Bank SW6 ....1A **100**
Willow Bri. Rd. N1. ....3E **49**
...........................(not continuous)
Willowbrook Est. SE15. ....3C **92**
Willow Brook Rd. SE15. ....3B **92**
Willow Bus. Pk. SE26 ....3E **121**

Willow Cl. SE6.................... 1B 124
Willow Ct. E11.................... 4A 40
........................(off Trinity Pl.)
Willow Ct. EC2........3D 11 (3A 64)
Willow Ct. NW6.................. 4A 44
Willow Ct. W4...................... 3A 84
........................(off Corney Reach Way)
Willow Ct. W9...................... 4C 58
........................(off Admiral Wlk.)
Willowdene N6.................... 2B 32
Willowdene SE15................ 3D 93
Willow Gro. E13.................. 1C 68
Willow Ho. SE1.................... 5B 78
........................(off Curtis St.)
Willow Ho. SE4.................... 1A 108
........................(off Dragonfly Pl.)
Willow Ho. W10.................. 3F 57
........................(off Maple Wlk.)
Willow Lodge SW6.............. 4F 85
Willow Pl. SW1.................... 5E 75
Willow Rd. NW3.................. 1F 45
Willows, The SE1................ 5A 78
Willows Ter. NW10.............. 1B 56
........................(off Rucklidge Av.)
Willow St. EC2........3D 11 (3A 64)
Willow Tree Cl. E3.............. 5B 52
Willow Tree Cl. SW18........ 1D 115
Willow Va. W12.................... 2C 70
Willow Wlk. N1.................... 1D 63
Willow Wlk. SE1.................. 4A 78
Willow Way SE26................ 3E 121
Willow Way W11.................. 1F 71
Willsbridge Ct. SE15.......... 2B 92
Will Wyatt Ct. N1................ 1A 64
........................(off Pitfield St.)
Wilman Gro. E8.................... 4C 50
Wilmcote Ho. W2................ 4D 59
........................(off Woodchester Sq.)
Wilment Ct. NW2.................. 5E 29
Wilmer Gdns. N1................ 5A 50
Wilmer Ho. E3.................... 1A 66
........................(off Daling Way)
Wilmer Lea Cl. E15.............. 4F 53
Wilmer Pl. N16.................... 4B 36
Wilmington Sq. WC1..2B 8 (2C 62)
Wilmington St. WC1..2B 8 (2C 62)
........................(off Camilla Rd.)
Wilmington Ter. SE16.......... 5D 79
Wilmot Cl. SE15.................. 3C 92
Wilmot Ho. SE11................ 5D 77
........................(off George Mathers Rd.)
Wilmot Pl. NW1.................. 4E 47
........................(not continuous)
Wilmot Rd. E10.................... 4D 39
Wilmot St. E2...................... 3D 65
Wilna Rd. SW18.................. 5E 101
Wilsham St. W11................ 2F 71
Wilshaw Ho. SE8................ 3C 94
Wilshaw St. SE14................ 4C 94
Wilson Gro. SE16................ 3D 79
Wilson Ho. NW6.................. 4E 45
........................(off Goldhurst Ter.)
Wilson Rd. E6...................... 2F 69
Wilson Rd. SE5.................... 4A 92
Wilson's Rd. W6.................. 1F 85
Wilson St. EC2........5C 10 (4F 63)
Wilson Wlk. W4.................... 5B 70
........................(off Prebend Gdns.)
Wiltern Ct. NW2.................. 3A 44
Wilton Av. W4...................... 1A 84
Wilton Ct. E1...................... 5D 65
........................(off Cavell St.)
Wilton Cres. SW1......4B 20 (3C 74)

Wilton Est. E8...................... 3C 50
Wilton M. E8........................ 3D 51
Wilton M. SW1.........5C 20 (4C 74)
Wilton Pl. SW1.........4B 20 (3C 74)
Wilton Plaza SW1................ 5E 75
........................(off Wilton Rd.)
Wilton Rd. SW1.......5E 21 (4D 75)
Wilton Row SW1.......4B 20 (3C 74)
Wilton's Music Hall............ 1C 78
........................(off Graces Ali.)
Wilton Sq. N1...................... 5F 49
Wilton St. SW1.......5D 21 (4D 75)
Wilton Ter. SW1.......5C 20 (4C 74)
Wilton Vs. N1...................... 5F 49
........................(off Wilton Sq.)
Wilton Way E8...................... 3C 50
Wiltshire Cl. SW3................ 5B 74
Wiltshire Ct. N4.................. 3B 34
........................(off Marquis Rd.)
Wiltshire Gdns. N4.............. 1E 35
Wiltshire Rd. SW9.............. 1C 104
Wiltshire Row N1................ 5F 49
Wimbart Rd. SW2................ 5B 104
WIMBLEDON........................ 5A 114
Wimbledon All England Lawn
Tennis & Croquet Club....4A 114
Wimbledon Common........ 4C 112
Wimbledon Common Golf Course
.... 5D 113
Wimbledon Hill Rd. SW19..5A 114
Wimbledon Lawn Tennis Mus.
.... 3A 114
Wimbledon Pk. Athletics Track
.... 2B 114
Wimbledon Pk. Ct. SW19..1B 114
Wimbledon Pk. Golf Course
.... 3B 114
Wimbledon Pk. Rd. SW18...1B 114
Wimbledon Pk. Rd. SW19...2A 114
Wimbledon Pk. Side SW19...3F 113
Wimbledon Park Station
(Underground).................. 3C 114
Wimbledon Pk. Watersports Cen.
.... 2B 114
Wimbledon Rd. SW17.......... 4E 115
Wimbledon Stadium Bus. Cen.
SW17.................................... 3D 115
Wimbledon Windmill Mus...3D 113
Wimbolt St. E2.................... 2C 64
Wimborne Cl. SE12............ 3B 110
Wimborne Ct. SW12............ 3E 117
Wimborne Ho. E16.............. 1B 82
........................(off Victoria Dock Rd.)
Wimborne Ho. NW1............ 3A 60
........................(off Harewood Av.)
Wimborne Ho. SW12.......... 3E 117
Wimborne Ho. SW8............ 3B 90
........................(off Dorset Rd.)
Wimbourne Ct. N1.............. 1F 63
Wimbourne St. N1.............. 1F 63
Wimpole M. W1.........5D 5 (4D 61)
Wimpole St. W1........1D 13 (4D 61)
Winans Wlk. SW9................ 5C 90
Winant Ho. E14.................. 1D 81
........................(off Simpson's Rd.)
Wincanton Rd. SW18.......... 5B 100
Winchcomb Gdns. SE9...... 1F 111
Winchelsea Cl. SW15........ 3F 99
Winchelsea Ho. SE16........ 3E 79
........................(off Swan Rd.)
Winchelsea Rd. E7.............. 5C 40
Winchelsea Rd. NW10........ 5A 42
Winchendon Rd. SW6.......... 4B 86

Winchester Av. NW6............ 5A 44
Winchester Bldgs.
SE1..............................3F 25 (3E 77)
........................(off Copperfield St.)
Winchester Cl. SE17.......... 5D 77
Winchester Cl. W8.............. 3C 72
........................(off Vicarage Ga.)
Winchester Ho. E14............ 5C 66
........................(off New Festival Av.)
Winchester Ho. E3.............. 2B 66
........................(off Hamlets Way)
Winchester Ho. SE18.......... 3F 97
........................(off Portway Gdns.)
Winchester Ho. SW3.......... 2F 87
........................(off Beaufort St.)
Winchester Ho. SW9.......... 3C 90
Winchester Ho. W2............ 5E 59
........................(off Hallfield Est.)
Winchester Palace..1A 26 (2F 77)
........................(off Stoney St.)
Winchester Pl. E8................ 2B 50
Winchester Pl. N6................ 3D 33
Winchester Rd. N6.............. 2D 33
Winchester Rd. NW3.......... 4F 45
Winchester Sq. SE1...1B 26 (2F 77)
........................(off Winchester Wlk.)
Winchester Sq. SE8............ 5B 80
Winchester St. SW1............ 1D 89
Winchester Wlk. SE11..1B 26 (2F 77)
Winchester Wlk. SW15...... 3B 100
........................(off Up. Richmond Rd.)
Winchester Wharf
SE1..............................1B 26 (2F 77)
........................(off Clink St.)
Winchfield Ho. SW15.......... 4B 98
Winchfield Rd. SE26.......... 5A 122
Winch Ho. E14.................... 4D 81
........................(off Tiller Rd.)
Winch Ho. SW10................ 3E 87
........................(off King's Rd.)
Winchilsea Ho. NW8.......... 2F 59
........................(off St John's Wood Rd.)
Winckworth Ct. N1.....2C 10 (2F 63)
........................(off Charles Sq. Est.)
Wincott Pde. SE11.............. 5C 76
........................(off Wincott St.)
Wincott St. SE11................ 5C 76
Windermere NW1........2E 5 (2D 61)
........................(off Albany St.)
Windermere Av. NW6........ 5A 44
Windermere Ct. SW13........ 2B 84
Windermere Ho. E3............ 3B 66
Windermere Point SE15.... 3E 93
........................(off Old Kent Rd.)
Windermere Rd. N19.......... 4E 33
Windermere Rd. SW15...... 4A 112
Winders Rd. SW11.............. 5A 88
........................(not continuous)
Windfield Cl. SE26.............. 4F 121
Windlass Ho. E16................ 3D 83
........................(off Schooner Rd.)
Windlass Pl. SE8................ 5A 80
Windlesham Gro. SW19...... 1F 113
Windlesham Ho. SE12E 27 (2B 78)
........................(off Duchess Wlk.)
Windley Cl. SE23................ 2E 121
Windmill WC1..........5F 7 (4B 62)
........................(off New North St.)
Windmill Cl. SE1................ 5C 78
........................(off Beatrice Rd.)
Windmill Cl. SE13.............. 5E 95
Windmill Ct. NW2................ 3A 44
Windmill Dr. NW2................ 5A 30

Windmill Dr. SW4..............3D 103
Windmill Hill NW3..............5E 31
Windmill Ho. E14..............5C 80
Windmill Ho. SE1 ...2C 24 (3C 76)
............................(off Windmill Wlk.)
Windmill La. E15..............3F 53
Windmill M. W4..............5A 70
Windmill Pas. W4..............5A 70
Windmill Rd. SW18..............4F 101
Windmill Rd. SW19..............2D 113
Windmill Rd. W4..............5A 70
Windmill Row SE11..............1C 90
Windmill St. W1 .....1B 14 (4F 61)
............................(not continuous)
Windmill Wlk. SE1 ...2C 24 (2C 76)
Windrose Cl. SE16..............3F 79
Windrush Cl. E8..............4C 50
Windrush Cl. SW11..............2F 101
Windrush Ho. NW8..............3F 59
............................(off Church St. Est.)
Windrush La. SE23..............3F 121
Windrush Sq. SW2..............2C 104
Windsock Cl. SE16..............5B 80
Windsor Cen., The N1..............5D 49
............................(off Windsor St.)
Windsor Cl. SE27..............4E 119
Windsor Cotts. SE14..............3B 94
............................(off Amersham Gro.)
Windsor Ct. E3..............1C 66
............................(off Mostyn Gro.)
Windsor Ct. NW11..............1A 30
............................(off Golders Grn. Rd.)
Windsor Ct. NW3..............1C 44
Windsor Ct. SE16..............1F 79
............................(off King & Queen Wharf)
Windsor Ct. SW11..............5F 87
Windsor Ct. SW3..............1A 88
............................(off Jubilee Pl.)
Windsor Ct. W10..............5F 57
............................(off Bramley Rd.)
Windsor Ct. W2..............1D 73
............................(off Moscow Rd.)
Windsor Gdns. W9..............4C 58
Windsor Gro. SE27..............4E 119
Windsor Hall E16..............2D 83
............................(off Wesley Av.)
Windsor Ho. E2..............2F 65
............................(off Knottisford St.)
Windsor Ho. E20..............2D 53
............................(off Peloton Av.)
Windsor Ho. N1..............1E 63
Windsor Ho. NW1 ...1E 5 (2D 61)
............................(off Cumberland Mkt.)
Windsor Ho. NW2..............3A 44
............................(off Chatsworth Rd.)
Windsor M. SE23..............1A 122
Windsor M. SE6..............1E 123
Windsor Pl. SW1..............4E 75
Windsor Rd. E10..............4D 39
Windsor Rd. E11..............3C 40
Windsor Rd. E7..............2D 55
Windsor Rd. N7..............5A 34
Windsor Rd. NW2..............3D 43
Windsor St. N1..............5D 49
Windsor Ter. N1 ...1A 10 (2E 63)
Windsor Wlk. SE5..............5F 91
Windsor Way W14..............5F 71
Windsor Wharf E9..............2B 52
Windspoint Dr. SE15..............2D 93
Windus M. N16..............3B 36
Windus Rd. N16..............3B 36
Windus Wlk. N16..............3B 36
Windy Ridge Cl. SW19..............5F 113
Wine Cl. E1..............2E 79
............................(not continuous)

Wine Office Ct. EC4: Lon
Peterborough Ct.....2C 16 (5C 62)
Winford Ct. SE15..............4D 93
Winford Ho. E3..............4B 52
Winforton St. SE10..............4E 95
Winfrith Rd. SW18..............5E 101
Wingate Ho. E3..............2D 67
............................(off Bruce Rd.)
Wingate Rd. W6..............4D 71
Wingate Sq. SW4..............1E 103
Wingfield Ct. E14..............1F 81
............................(off Newport Av.)
Wingfield Ho. E2 .....2F 11 (2B 64)
............................(off Virginia Rd.)
Wingfield M. SE15..............1C 106
Wingfield Rd. E15..............1A 54
Wingfield St. SE15..............1C 106
Wingford Rd. SW2..............4A 104
Wingmore Rd. SE24..............1E 105
Wingrad Ho. E1..............4E 65
............................(off Jubilee St.)
Wingrave Rd. W6..............2E 85
Wingreen NW8..............5D 45
............................(off Abbey Rd.)
Wingrove Rd. SE6..............2A 124
Wing Yip Bus. Cen. NW2..............4D 29
Winicotte Ho. W2..............4F 59
............................(off Paddington Grn.)
Winkfield Rd. E13..............1D 69
Winkley St. E2..............1D 65
Winkworth Cotts. E1..............3E 65
............................(off Cephas St.)
Winlaton Rd. BR1: Broml...4F 123
Winnepeg Ho. SE16..............3E 79
............................(off Province Dr.)
Winnett St. W1 .....4B 14 (1F 75)
Winnington Cl. N2..............1F 31
Winnington Ho. SE5..............3E 91
............................(off Wyndham Est.)
Winnington Ho. W10..............3A 58
............................(off Southern Row)
Winnington Rd. N2..............1F 31
Winn Ho. SE12..............1C 124
Winscombe St. N19..............4D 33
Winsford Rd. SE6..............3B 122
Winsham Gro. SW11..............3C 102
Winsham Ho. NW1 ...1C 6 (2F 61)
............................(off Churchway)
Winslade Rd. SW2..............3A 104
Winslade Way SE6..............5D 109
Winsland M. W2..............5F 59
Winsland St. W2..............5F 59
Winsley St. W1 .....2A 14 (5E 61)
Winslow SE17..............1A 92
Winslow Cl. NW10..............5A 28
Winslow Ho. W6..............2E 85
Winstanley Est. SW11..............1F 101
Winstanley Rd. SW11..............1F 101
............................(not continuous)
Winston Av. NW9..............2A 28
Winston Ho. WC1 .....3C 6 (3F 61)
............................(off Endsleigh St.)
Winston Rd. N16..............1F 49
Winterbourne Ho. W11 .....1A 72
............................(off Portland Rd.)
Winterbrook Rd. SE24..............4E 105
Winterfold Cl. SW19..............2A 114
Wintergreen Cl. E6..............4F 69
Winterleys NW6..............1B 58
............................(off Denmark Rd.)
Winter Lodge SE16..............1C 92
............................(off Fern Wlk.)
Winterslow Ho. SE5..............5E 91
............................(off Flaxman Rd.)

Winterslow Rd. SW9..............4D 91
Winterstoke Rd. SE6..............1B 122
Winterton Ho. E1..............5E 65
............................(off Deancross St.)
Winterton Pl. SW10..............2E 87
Winterwell Rd. SW2..............3A 104
Winthorpe Rd. SW15..............2A 100
Winthrop Ho. W12..............1D 71
............................(off White City Est.)
Winthrop St. E1..............4D 65
Winton Cl. N1..............1B 62
............................(off Calshot St.)
Winton Way SW16..............5C 118
Wireworks Ct. SE1 ...4E 25 (3E 77)
............................(off Gt. Suffolk St.)
Wirrall Ho. SE26..............3C 120
Wisbech N4..............3B 34
............................(off Lorne Rd.)
Wisden Ho. SW8..............2B 90
Wiseman Rd. E10..............4C 38
Wise Rd. E15..............5F 53
Wiseton Rd. SW17..............1A 116
Wishart Rd. SE3..............5F 97
Wisley Ho. SW1..............1F 89
............................(off Rampayne St.)
Wisley Rd. SW11..............3C 102
Wisteria Apts. E9..............3E 51
............................(off Chatham Pl.)
Wisteria Rd. SE13..............2F 109
Wistow Ho. E2..............5C 50
............................(off Whiston Rd.)
Witanhurst La. N6..............3C 32
Witan St. E2..............2D 65
Witchwood Ho. SW9..............1C 104
............................(off Gresham Rd.)
Witham Ct. E10..............5D 39
Witham Ct. SW17..............3B 116
Witherington Rd. N5..............2C 48
Withers Pl. EC1 ...3A 10 (3E 63)
Withycombe Rd. SW19..............5F 99
Withy Ho. E1..............3F 65
............................(off Globe Rd.)
Witley Ct. WC1 ...3D 7 (3A 62)
............................(off Coram St.)
Witley Ho. SW2..............5A 104
Witley Point SW15..............1D 113
............................(off Wanborough Dr.)
Witley Rd. N19..............4E 33
Witney Path SE23..............3F 121
Wittersham Rd. BR1: Broml5B 124
Wivenhoe Cl. SE15..............1D 107
Wiverton Rd. SE26..............5E 121
Wiverton Twr. E1..............5B 64
............................(off Aldgate Pl.)
Wix's La. SW4..............1D 103
Woburn Ct. SE16..............1D 92
............................(off Masters Dr.)
Woburn Ct. WC1 ...4D 7 (3A 62)
............................(off Bernard St.)
Woburn Mans. WC1 ...5B 6 (4F 61)
............................(off Torrington Pl.)
Woburn M. WC1 ...3C 6 (3F 61)
Woburn Pl. WC1 ...3C 6 (3A 62)
Woburn Sq. WC1 ...4C 6 (3F 61)
............................(not continuous)
Woburn Wlk. WC1 ...2C 6 (2F 61)
Wodeham Gdns. E1..............4C 64
Wodehouse Av. SE5..............4B 92
Wogan Ho. W1 ...1E 13 (4D 61)
............................(off Portland Pl.)
Woking Cl. SW15..............2B 98
Wolcot Ho. NW1 ...1A 6 (1E 61)
............................(off Aldenham St.)
Wolfe Cres. SE16..............3F 79
Wolfe Cres. SE7..............1F 97

Wolfe Ho. W12.................1D 71
.................(off White City Est.)
Wolfe Ho. W14.................5B 72
Wolffe Gdns. E15.................3B 54
Wolfington Rd. SE27.................4D 119
Wolfram Cl. SE13.................3A 110
Wolftencroft Cl. SW11.................1A 102
Wollaston Cl. SE1.................5E 77
Wollaton Ho. N1.................1C 62
.................(off Batchelor St.)
Wollett Ct. NW1.................4E 47
.................(off St Pancras Way)
Wollstonecraft St. N1.................5F 47
Wolseley Av. SW19.................2C 114
Wolseley Rd. E7.................4D 55
Wolseley Rd. N8.................1F 33
Wolseley St. SE1.................3C 78
Wolsey Cl. SW11.................4A 88
.................(off Westbridge Rd.)
Wolsey M. NW5.................3E 47
Wolsey Rd. N1.................2F 49
Wolsey St. E1.................4E 65
Wolverley St. E2.................2D 65
Wolverton SE17.................1A 92
.................(not continuous)
Wolverton Gdns. W6.................5F 71
Womersley Rd. N8.................1B 34
Wontner Cl. N1.................4E 49
Wontner Rd. SW17.................2B 116
Woodall Cl. E14.................1D 81
Woodbank Rd.
BR1: Broml.................3B 124
Woodbastwick Rd. SE26.................5F 121
Woodberry Down N4.................2E 35
Woodberry Down Est. N4....2E 35
.................(not continuous)
Woodberry Gro. N4.................2E 35
Woodbine Pl. E11.................1C 40
Woodbine Ter. E9.................3E 51
Woodborough Rd. SW15...2D 99
Woodbourne Av. SW16.................3F 117
Woodbourne Cl. SW16.................3A 118
Woodbridge Cl. N7.................4B 34
Woodbridge Cl. NW2.................5C 28
Woodbridge Ho. E11.................3B 40
Woodbridge St. EC1...3D 9 (3D 63)
.................(not continuous)
Woodburn Cl. NW4.................1F 29
Woodbury Gdns. SE12...3D 125
Woodbury Ho. SE26.................3C 120
Woodbury St. SW17.................5A 116
WOODBURY UNIT.................1A 40
Woodchester Ho. E14.................4D 81
.................(off Selsdon Way)
Woodchester Sq. W2.................4D 59
Woodchurch Rd. NW6.................4C 44
Wood Cl. E2.................3C 64
Wood Cl. NW9.................2A 28
Woodcock Ho. E14.................4C 66
.................(off Burgess St.)
Woodcocks E16.................4E 69
Woodcombe Cres. SE23...1E 121
Woodcote Ho. SE8.................2B 94
.................(off Prince St.)
Woodcote Pl. SE27.................5D 119
Woodcote Rd. E11.................2C 40
Woodcote's. SE27.................5E 119
.................(off Woodcote Pl.)
Wood Cres. W12.................1E 71
Woodcroft M. SE8.................5A 80
Wood Dr. BR7: Chst.................5F 125
Woodend SE19.................5E 119
Wooder Gdns. E7.................1C 54
Woodfall Rd. N4.................4C 34

Woodfall St. SW3.................1B 88
Woodfarrs SE5.................2F 105
Wood Fld. NW3.................2B 46
Woodfield Av. SW16.................3F 117
Woodfield Gro. SW16.................3F 117
Woodfield Ho. SE23.................3F 121
.................(off Dacres Rd.)
Woodfield La. SW16.................3F 117
Woodfield Pl. W9.................3B 58
Woodfield Rd. W9.................4B 58
Woodford Ct. W12.................3F 71
.................(off Shepherd's Bush Grn.)
Woodger Rd. W12.................3E 71
Woodgrange Park Station
(Overground).................2F 55
Woodgrange Rd. E7.................2D 55
Woodhall NW1.....2F 5 (2E 61)
.................(off Robert St.)
Woodhall Av. SE21.................3B 120
Woodhall Dr. SE21.................3B 120
Woodhall Ho. SW18.................4F 101
Woodham Rd. SE6.................3E 123
Woodhatch Cl. E6.................4F 69
Woodheyes Rd. NW10.................2A 42
Wood Ho. NW6.................1B 58
.................(off Albert Rd.)
Woodhouse Cl. SE22.................2C 106
Woodhouse Gro. E12.................3F 55
Woodhouse Rd. E11.................5B 40
Woodland Cl. SE19.................5A 120
Woodland Cl. E11.................1C 40
.................(off New Wanstead)
Woodland Ct. N7.................3A 48
Woodland Cres. SE10.................2A 96
Woodland Cres. SE16.................3F 79
Woodland Gro. SE10.................1A 96
Woodland Hill SE19.................5A 120
Woodland M. SE13.................1D 109
.................(off Loampit Hill)
Woodland M. SW16.................3A 118
Woodland Rd. SE19.................5A 120
Woodlands, The N5.................1E 49
Woodlands, The SE13...5F 109
Woodlands, The SW9.................3D 91
.................(off Langton Rd.)
Woodlands NW11.................1A 30
Woodlands Av. E11.................3D 41
WOODLANDS BRIDGE.................3B 100
.................(off Woodlands Way)
Woodlands Cl. NW11.................1A 30
Woodlands Cl. NW10.................5F 43
.................(off Wrentham Av.)
Woodlands Ct. SE23.................5D 107
Woodlands Ga. SW15.................3B 100
.................(off Woodlands Way)
Woodlands Hgts. SE3.................2B 96
.................(off Vanburgh Hill)
Woodlands Pk. Rd. N15....1D 35
Woodlands Pk. Rd. SE10...2A 96
.................(not continuous)
Woodlands Rd. E11.................4A 40
Woodlands Rd. SW13.................1B 98
Woodlands St. SE13.................5F 109
Woodland St. E8.................3B 50
Woodlands Way SW15.....3B 100
Woodland Ter. SE7.................5F 83
Woodland Wlk. SE10: Lon Maze
Hill.................1A 96
Woodland Wlk. BR1: Broml
Southend.................4F 123
.................(not continuous)
Woodland Wlk. NW3.................2A 46
Wood La. N6.................1D 33
Wood La. W12.................5E 57

Wood Lane Station
(Underground).................1E 71
Wood La. Studios W12.....5E 57
Woodlawn Cl. SW15.................3B 100
Woodlawn Rd. SW6.................3F 85
Woodlea Rd. N16.................5A 36
Woodleigh Gdns. SW16...3A 118
Woodmans Gro. NW10.....2B 42
Woodman's M. W12.................4D 57
Woodmere Cl. SW11.................1C 102
Woodmill Cl. SW15.................4C 98
Woodmill Rd. E5.................4E 37
Woodmill St. SE16...5B 27 (4B 78)
Woodpecker M. SE13.................2F 109
.................(off Freshfield Cl.)
Woodpecker Rd. SE14.....2A 94
Woodquest Av. SE24.................3E 105
Woodriffe Rd. E11.................2F 39
Woodrow Ct. SE13.................4E 91
.................(off Camberwell Sta. Rd.)
Woodrush Cl. SE14.................3A 94
Wood's Bldgs. E1.................4D 65
.................(off Winthrop St.)
Woodseer St. E1.................4B 64
Woodsford SE17.................1F 91
.................(off Portland St.)
Woodsford Sq. W14.................3A 72
Woods Ho. SW1.................1D 89
Woods Ho. SW8.................4E 89
.................(off Wadhurst Rd.)
Woodside SW19.................5B 114
Woodside Av. N6.................1B 32
Woodside Cl. E12.................3E 41
Woodside Ho. SW19.................5B 114
Woodside M. SE22.................3B 106
Woodside Rd. E13.................3E 69
Woods M. W1......4A 12 (1C 74)
Woodsome Rd. NW5.................5C 32
Woods St. E1......5E 27 (4A 78)
Woodspring Rd. SW19.....2A 114
Wood St. SE15.................4D 93
Woodstar Ho. SE15.................3C 92
.................(off Reddins Rd.)
Woodstock Av. NW11.................2A 30
Woodstock Cl. SE11.................1B 90
Woodstock Ct. SE12.................4D 110
Woodstock Ct. SE22.................2C 106
Woodstock Gro. W12.................3F 71
Woodstock M. W1....1D 13 (5D 61)
.................(off Westmoreland St.)
Woodstock Rd. E7.................4E 55
Woodstock Rd. N4.................3C 34
Woodstock Rd. NW11.................2B 30
Woodstock Rd. W4.................5A 70
Woodstock St. W1...3D 13 (5D 61)
Woodstock Studios W12...3F 71
.................(off Woodstock Gro.)
Woodstock Ter. E14.................1D 81
Wood St. EC2.....2A 18 (5E 63)
.................(not continuous)
Wood St. W4.................1A 84
Woodsyre SE26.................4B 120
Wood Ter. NW2.................5D 29
Woodthorpe Rd. SW15....2D 99
Wood Va. N10.................1E 33
Wood Va. SE23.................1D 121
Wood Va. Est. SE23.................5E 107
Woodvale Wlk. SE27.................5E 119
Woodvale Way NW11.................5F 29
Woodview Cl. N4.................2D 35
Woodville Cl. SE12.................3C 110
Woodville Cl. SE3.................4D 97
Woodville Ct. SE14.................4E 95
.................(off Blissett St.)
Woodville Gdns. NW11....2F 29

Woodville Ho. SE1....5F **27** (4B **78**)
..............(off St Saviour's Est.)
Woodville Rd. E11............3B **40**
Woodville Rd. N16............2A **50**
Woodville Rd. NW11............2F **29**
Woodville Rd. NW6............1B **58**
Woodward Av. NW4............1C **28**
Woodwarde Rd. SE22....4A **106**
Woodwell St. SW18............3E **101**
Wood Wharf SE10............2D **95**
Woodyard Cl. NW5............2C **46**
Woodyard La. SE21....5A **106**
Woodyates Rd. SE12............4C **110**
Woolacombe Rd. SE3............4E **97**
Woolcombes Cl. SE16............2F **79**
..............(off Princes Riverside Rd.)
Wooler St. SE17............1F **91**
Woolf M. WC1............3C **6** (3F **61**)
..............(off Burton Pl.)
Woolford Cl. SE5............5E **91**
..............(off Coldharbour La.)
Woolgar M. N16............2A **50**
..............(off Gillett St.)
Woollaston Rd. N4............1D **35**
Woolley Ho. SW9............1D **105**
..............(off Loughborough Rd.)
Woollon Ho. E1............5E **65**
..............(off Clark St.)
Woolmead Av. NW9............2C **28**
Woolmore St. E14............1E **81**
Woolneigh St. SW6............1D **101**
Woolridge Way E9............4E **51**
Woolstaplers Way SE16....4C **78**
Woolstone Ho. E2............5C **50**
..............(off Whiston Rd.)
Woolstone Rd. SE23............2A **122**
Woolwich Chu. St. SE18............4F **83**
Woolwich Rd. SE10............1B **96**
Woolwich Rd. SE7............1C **96**
Wooster Gdns. E14............5F **67**
Wooster Pl. SE1............5F **77**
..............(off Searles Rd.)
Wootton St. SE1....2C **24** (2C **76**)
Worcester Cl. NW2............5D **29**
Worcester Ct. W9............4C **58**
..............(off Elmfield Way)
Worcester Dr. W4............3A **70**
Worcester Gdns. SW11....3B **102**
..............(off Grandison Rd.)
Worcester Ho. SE11....5B **24** (4C **76**)
..............(off Kennington Rd.)
Worcester Ho. SW9............3C **90**
..............(off Cranmer Rd.)
Worcester Ho. W2............5E **59**
..............(off Hallfield Est.)
Worcester M. NW6............3D **45**
Worcester Point EC1....2F **9** (2E **63**)
Worcester Rd. SW19............5B **114**
Wordsworth Av. E12............4F **55**
Wordsworth Ho. NW6............2C **58**
..............(off Stafford Rd.)
Wordsworth Mans. W14....2B **86**
..............(off Queens Club Gdns.)
Wordsworth Pl. NW5............2B **46**
Wordsworth Rd. N16............1A **50**
Wordsworth Rd. SE1............5B **78**
Worfield St. SW11............3A **88**
Worgan St. SE11............1B **90**
Worgan St. SE16............5F **79**
Worland Rd. E15............4A **54**
Worlds End St. SW10............3F **87**
World's End Pas. SW10............3F **87**
..............(off Worlds End Est.)
World's End Pl. SW10............3F **87**
..............(off Worlds End Est.)
Worlidge St. W6............1E **85**

Worlingham Rd. SE22............2B **106**
Wormholt Rd. W12............1C **70**
Wormwood Scrubs Pk.............4B **56**
Wormwood St. EC2..2D **19** (5A **64**)
Wornington Rd. W10............3A **58**
..............(not continuous)
Woronzow Rd. NW8............5F **45**
Worple Ho. SW19............5B **114**
Worple St. SW14............1A **98**
Worship St. EC2....4C **10** (3F **63**)
..............(not continuous)
Worslade Rd. SW17............4F **115**
Worsley Bri. Rd. SE26............4B **122**
Worsley Gro. E5............1C **50**
Worsley Ho. SE23............2E **121**
Worsley Rd. E11............1A **54**
Worsopp Dr. SW4............3E **103**
Worth Gro. SE17............1F **91**
Worthing Cl. E15............5A **54**
Worthington Ho. EC1..1C **8** (2C **62**)
..............(off Myddelton Pas.)
Wortley Rd. E6............4F **55**
Wotton Ct. E14............2F **81**
..............(off Jamestown Way)
Wotton Rd. NW2............5E **29**
Wotton Rd. SE8............2B **94**
Wouldham Rd. E16............5B **68**
Wragby Rd. E11............5A **40**
Wraxall Rd. E3............3B **66**
..............(off Hamlets Way)
Wrayburn Ho. SE16............3C **78**
..............(off Llewellyn St.)
Wray Cres. N4............4A **34**
Wren Av. NW2............1E **43**
Wren Cl. E16............5B **68**
Wren Ho. E3............1A **66**
..............(off Gernon Rd.)
Wren Ho. SW1............1F **89**
..............(off Aylesford St.)
Wren Landing E14............2C **80**
Wren M. SE11............5B **76**
Wren M. SE13............2A **110**
Wrenn Ho. SW13............2E **85**
Wren Rd. SE5............4F **91**
Wren's Pk. Ho. E5............4D **37**
Wren St. WC1............3A **8** (3B **62**)
Wrentham Av. NW10............1F **57**
Wrenthorpe Rd. BR1: Broml..4A **124**
Wren Vw. N6............2E **33**
Wrexham Rd. E3............1C **66**
Wricklemarsh Rd. SE3............5D **97**
..............(not continuous)
Wrigglesworth St. SE14............3F **93**
Wright Cl. SE13............2F **109**
Wrights Grn. SW4............2F **103**
Wright's La. W8............4D **73**
Wright's Rd. E3............1B **66**
..............(not continuous)
Wrotham Ho. SE1....5C **26** (4F **77**)
..............(off Law St.)
Wrotham Rd. NW1............4E **47**
Wrottesley Rd. NW10............1C **56**
Wroughton Rd. SW11............3B **102**
Wroxton Rd. SE15............5E **93**
Wulfstan St. W12............4B **56**
Wyatt Cl. SE16............3B **80**
Wyatt Dr. SW13............2D **85**
Wyatt Ho. NW8............3F **59**
..............(off Frampton St.)
Wyatt Ho. SE3............5B **96**
Wyatt Pk. Rd. SW2............2A **118**
Wyatt Rd. E7............3C **54**
Wyatt Rd. N5............5E **35**
Wybert St. NW1............3F **5** (3E **61**)
Wychcombe Studios NW3 ..3B **46**

Wycherley Cl. SE3............3B **96**
Wychwood End N6............2E **33**
Wychwood Way SW19............5F **119**
Wyclif Ct. EC1............2D **9** (2D **63**)
..............(off Wyclif St.)
Wycliffe Rd. SW11............5C **88**
Wyclif St. EC1............2D **9** (2D **63**)
Wycombe Gdns. NW11............4C **30**
Wycombe Ho. NW8............3A **60**
..............(off Grendon St.)
Wycombe Pl. SW18............4E **101**
Wycombe Sq. W8............2B **72**
Wydeville Mnr. Rd. SE12 ..4D **125**
Wye St. SW11............5F **87**
Wyfold Rd. SW6............3A **86**
Wykeham Ct. NW4............1E **29**
..............(off Wykeham Rd.)
Wykeham Ho. SE1...2F **25** (2E **77**)
..............(off Union St.)
Wyke Rd. E3............4C **52**
Wyldes Cl. NW11............3E **31**
Wyleu St. SE23............5A **108**
Wyllen Cl. E1............3E **65**
Wymering Mans. W9............2C **58**
..............(off Wymering Rd.)
Wymering Rd. W9............2C **58**
Wymondham Ct. NW8............5F **45**
..............(off Queensmead)
Wymond St. SW15............1E **99**
Wynan Rd. E14............1D **95**
Wyndcliff Rd. SE7............2D **97**
Wyndham Apts. SE10............1A **96**
Wyndham Cres. N19............5E **33**
Wyndham Deedes Ho. E2 ..1C **64**
..............(off Hackney Rd.)
Wyndham Est. SE5............3E **91**
Wyndham Ho. E14............3D **81**
..............(off Marsh Wall)
Wyndham Ho. SW1............5C **74**
..............(off Sloane Sq.)
Wyndham M. W1....1A **12** (4B **60**)
Wyndham Pl. W1....1A **12** (4B **60**)
Wyndham Rd. SE5............4F **55**
Wyndham St. W1............4B **60**
Wyndhams Ct. E8............4B **50**
..............(off Celandine Dr.)
Wyndham's Theatre
..............4D **15** (1A **76**)
..............(off Charing Cross Rd.)
Wyndham St. W1............4B **60**
Wyndham Yd. W1............4B **60**
Wyneham Rd. SE24............3F **105**
Wynell Rd. SE23............3F **121**
Wynford Rd. N1............1B **62**
Wynne Rd. SW9............5C **90**
Wynnstay Gdns. W8............4C **72**
Wynter St. SW11............2E **101**
Wynyard Ho. SE11............1B **90**
..............(off Newburn St.)
Wynyard Ter. SE11............1B **90**
Wynyatt St. EC1....2D **9** (2D **63**)
Wytham Ho. NW8............3F **59**
..............(off Church St. Est.)
Wythburn Ct. W1.....2A **12** (5B **60**)
..............(off Wythburn Pl.)
Wythburn Pl. W1...3A **12** (5B **60**)
Wythes Rd. E16............2F **83**
Wyvil Rd. SW8............3A **90**
Wyvis St. E14............4D **67**

Y

Yabsley St. E14............2E **81**
Yaldham Ho. SE1............5A **78**
..............(off Old Kent Rd.)

Yalding Rd. SE16 ....4C 78
Yale Ct. NW6 ....2D 45
.............(off Caledonia Rd.)
Yard, The N1 ....1E 7 (1A 62)
Yardley St. WC1 ......2B 8 (2C 62)
..........................(not continuous)
Yarmouth Pl. W1 ......2D 21 (2D 75)
Yarnfield Sq. SE15 ....4C 92
Yarrell Mans. W14 ....2B 86
.............(off Queen's Club Gdns.)
Yarrow Cres. E6 ....4F 69
Yarrow Ho. E14 ....4E 81
.........................(off Stewart St.)
Yarrow Ho. W10 ....4E 57
.........................(off Sutton Way)
Yateley St. SE18 ....4F 83
Yatesbury Ct. E5 ....2A 52
.........................(off Studley Cl.)
Yates Ct. NW2 ....3F 43
.........................(off Willesden La.)
Yates Ct. SE1 ....3B 78
.........................(off Abbey St.)
Yates Ho. E2 ....2C 64
.........................(off Roberta St.)
Yatton Ho. W10 ....4E 57
.........................(off Sutton Way)
Yeadon Ho. W10 ....4E 57
.........................(off Sutton Way)
Yearby Ho. W10 ....3E 57
.........................(off Sutton Way)
Yeate St. N1 ....4F 49
Yeatman Rd. N6 ....1B 32
Yeats Cl. NW10 ....2A 42
Yeats Cl. SE13 ....5F 95
Yeldham Ho. W6 ....1F 85
.........................(off Yeldham Rd.)
Yeldham Rd. W6 ....1F 85
Yeldham Vs. W6 ....1F 85
.........................(off Yeldham Rd.)
Yelverton Rd. SW11 ....5F 87
Yeoman Ct. SE27 ....3D 119
Yeoman Ct. E14 ....3E 67
.........................(off Tweed Wlk.)
Yeoman's Row SW3 ....4A 74
Yeoman St. SE8 ....5A 80
Yeoman's Yd. E1 ....1B 78
.........................(off Chamber St.)
Yeo St. E3 ....4D 67
Yeovil Ho. W10 ....3E 57
.........................(off Sutton Way)
Yerbury Rd. N19 ....5F 33
.........................(not continuous)
Yetev Lev Ct. E5 ....3C 36
Yewfield Rd. NW10 ....3B 42
Yew Gro. NW2 ....1F 43
Yew Ho. SE16 ....3F 79
.........................(off Woodland Cres.)
Yew Tree Cl. SE13 ....1E 109
Yew Tree Cl. NW11 ....1B 30
.........................(off Bridge La.)
Yew Tree Lodge SW16 ......4E 117
Yew Tree Rd. W12 ....1B 70
YMCA E16: Lon George Williams
   College 4D 69
YMCA W2: Lon German...1E 73
.........................(off Craven Ter.)

Yoakley Rd. N16 ....4A 36
Yoke Cl. N7 ....3A 48
Yolande Gdns. SE9 ....3F 111
Yonge Pk. N4 ....5C 34
York Bri. NW1 ....3B 4 (3C 60)
York Bldgs. WC2 ...5E 15 (1A 76)
York Cl. SE5 ....5E 91
.........................(off Lilford Rd.)
York Ga. NW1 ....4B 4 (3C 60)
York Gro. SE15 ....4E 93
York Hall Leisure Cen. 1D 65
York Hill SE27 ....3D 119
York Ho. E16 ....2C 82
.........................(off De Quincey M.)
York Ho. SE1 ....5A 24 (4B 76)
York Ho. SW3 ....1B 88
.........................(off Turks Row)
York Ho. W1 ....5A 4 (4B 60)
.........................(off York St.)
York Ho. W8 ....3D 73
.........................(off York Ho. Pl.)
York Ho. Pl. W8 ....3D 73
Yorkley Ho. W10 ....3E 57
.........................(off Sutton Way)
York Mans. SE17 ....1E 91
.........................(off Browning St.)
York Mans. SW11 ....4C 88
.........................(off Prince of Wales Dr.)
York Mans. SW5 ....1C 87
.........................(off Earls Ct. Rd.)
York Mans. W1 ....5B 4 (4C 60)
.........................(off Chiltern St.)
York M. NW5 ....2D 47
York Pde. NW9 ....1C 28
York Pl. SW11 ....1F 101
York Pl. WC2 ....5E 15 (1A 76)
.........................(off Villiers St.)
York Pl. Mans. W1 ...5A 4 (4B 60)
.........................(off Baker St.)
York Ri. NW5 ....5D 33
York Rd. E10 ....5E 39
York Rd. E17 ....1F 37
York Rd. E7 ....3C 54
York Rd. SE1 ....3A 24 (3B 76)
York Rd. SW11 ....2E 101
York Rd. SW18 ....2E 101
York Rd. SW19 ....5E 115
York Rd. Bus. Cen. SW11 ...5F 87
Yorkshire Cl. N16 ....5A 36
YORKSHIRE GREY 3F 111
Yorkshire Grey Pl. NW3 ......1E 45
Yorkshire Grey Yd.
   WC1 ....1F 15 (4B 62)
.........................(off Eagle St.)
Yorkshire Rd. E14 ....5A 66
York Sq. E14 ....5A 66
York St. W1 ....5A 4 (4B 60)
York St. Chambers W1 ....4B 60
.........................(off York St.)
York Ter. SE7 ....5E 83
York Ter. E. NW1 ......4C 4 (3C 60)
York Ter. W. NW1 .....4B 4 (3C 60)
Yorkton St. E2 ....1C 64
York Way N1 ....1E 7 (1A 62)

York Way N7 ....3F 47
York Way Ct. N1 ....5A 48
.........................(not continuous)
York Way Est. N7 ....3A 48
Young Ct. NW6 ....4A 44
Young Rd. E16 ....5D 69
Youngs Bldgs. EC1 ...3A 10 (3E 63)
.........................(off Old St.)
Youngs Ct. SW11 ....4C 88
Young St. W8 ....3D 73
Young Vic Theatre, The
   ....3C 24 (3C 76)
.........................(off The Cut)
Yoxall Ho. W10 ....3E 57
.........................(off Sutton Way)
Yukon Rd. SW12 ....5D 103
Yunus Khan Cl. E17 ....1C 38
Yvon Ho. SW11 ....4C 88
.........................(off Alexandra Av.)

Z

Zachary Ct. SW1 ....5F 75
.........................(off Montaigne Cl.)
Zachary Ho. SW9 ....4B 90
.........................(off Lett Rd.)
Zachary M. E3 ....2B 66
.........................(off Tredegar Sq.)
Zahra Ho. NW10 ....2E 57
.........................(off Harrow Rd.)
Zampa Rd. SE16 ....1E 93
Zanara Ct. SE26 ....5E 121
Zander Ct. E2 ....2C 64
Zangwill Ho. NW6 ....1B 58
.........................(off Carlton Va.)
Zangwill Rd. SE3 ....4F 97
Zapotec Ho. SE8 ....5F 79
.........................(off Chilton Gro.)
Zealand Ho. SE18 ....5F 83
Zealand Rd. E3 ....5A 52
.........................(off Denmark Rd.)
Zealand Rd. SE5 ....5E 91
Zealand Rd. E3 ....1A 66
Zeller Ho. E20 ....2D 53
.........................(off Scarlet Cl.)
Zennor Rd. SW12 ....1E 117
Zennor Rd. Ind. Est.
   SW12 ....1E 117
Zenobia Mans. W14 ....2B 86
.........................(off Queen's Club Gdns.)
Zenoria St. SE22 ....2B 106
Zetland Ho. W8 ....4D 73
.........................(off Marloes Rd.)
Zetland St. E14 ....4D 67
Zinc Bldg., The SE13 ....2A 110
Zinnia Mans. E20 ....3D 53
.........................(off Olympic Pk. Av.)
Zion Ho. E1 ....5E 65
.........................(off Jubilee St.)
Zoar St. SE1 ....1F 25 (2E 77)
Zodiac Ho. E3 ....3C 66
.........................(off Wellington Way)
Zoffany St. N19 ....4F 33
Zona Ct. SE1 ....5F 27 (4B 78)
.........................(off Grange Wlk.)
Zulu M. SW11 ....5A 88